高橋和希

YES! THE YU-GI-OH! GRAPHIC NOVEL'S BEEN RELEASED! FOR ALL OF YOU WHO'VE PURCHASED THIS, THANK YOU SO MUCH! AND FOR THOSE OF YOU WHO ARE BORROWING IT FROM YOUR FRIENDS...PLEASE BUY ONE! IT MUST SOUND WEIRD FOR THE ARTIST TO BE SAYING THIS, BUT I THINK THAT YU-GI-OH! IS KIND OF A STRANGE STORY. ALTHOUGH AT FIRST I WANTED TO CREATE A STORY THAT CENTERED AROUND "THE MYSTERIOUS" IN EVERYDAY LIFE, BEFORE I REALIZED IT, I ENDED UP INCORPORATING THIS AND THAT—SO MANY DIFFERENT THINGS. I HOPE YOU ALL BECOME GOOD FRIENDS OF YUGI, JÔNOUCHI, AND ANZU!

—KAZUKI TAKAHASHI, 1997

Artist/author Kazuki Takahashi first tried to break into the manga business in 1982, but success eluded him until **Yu-Gi-Oh!** debuted in the Japanese **Weekly Shonen Jump** magazine in 1996. **Yu-Gi-Oh!**'s themes of friendship and competition, together with Takahashi's weird and wonderful art, soon became enormously successful, spawning a real-world card game, video games, and two anime series. A lifelong gamer, Takahashi enjoys Shogi (Japanese chess), Mahjong (the traditional Chinese tile game), card games, and tabletop RPGs, among other games.

YU-GI-OH!

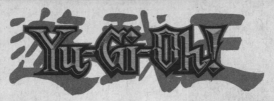

Yu-Gi-Oh!
3-in-1 Edition
Volume 1

SHONEN JUMP Manga Omnibus Edition
A compilation of the graphic novel volumes 1-2-3

STORY AND ART BY Kazuki Takahashi

Translation & English Adaptation/Anita Sengupta
Touch-up Art & Lettering/Kelle Han
Design/Sean Lee (Manga Edition)
Design/Sam Elzway (Omnibus Edition)
Editor/Jason Thompson (Manga Edition)
Managing Editor/Erica Yee (Omnibus Edition)

Printed in the U.S.A.

Published by VIZ Media, LLC
P.O. Box 77010
San Francisco, CA 94107

10 9 8 7 6 5 4 3 2 1
Omnibus edition first printing, February 2015

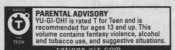

viz media
www.viz.com

RATED T FOR TEEN

PARENTAL ADVISORY
YU-GI-OH! is rated T for Teen and is recommended for ages 13 and up. This volume contains fantasy violence, alcohol and tobacco use, and suggestive situations.
ratings.viz.com

THE WORLD'S MOST POPULAR MANGA
SHONEN JUMP
www.shonenjump.com

SHONEN JUMP MANGA

Yu-Gi-Oh!

Vol. 1
THE MILLENNIUM PUZZLE

STORY AND ART BY
KAZUKI TAKAHASHI

Yu-Gi-Oh!

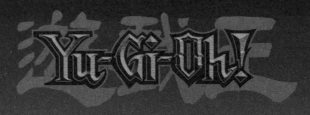

Vol. 1

CONTENTS

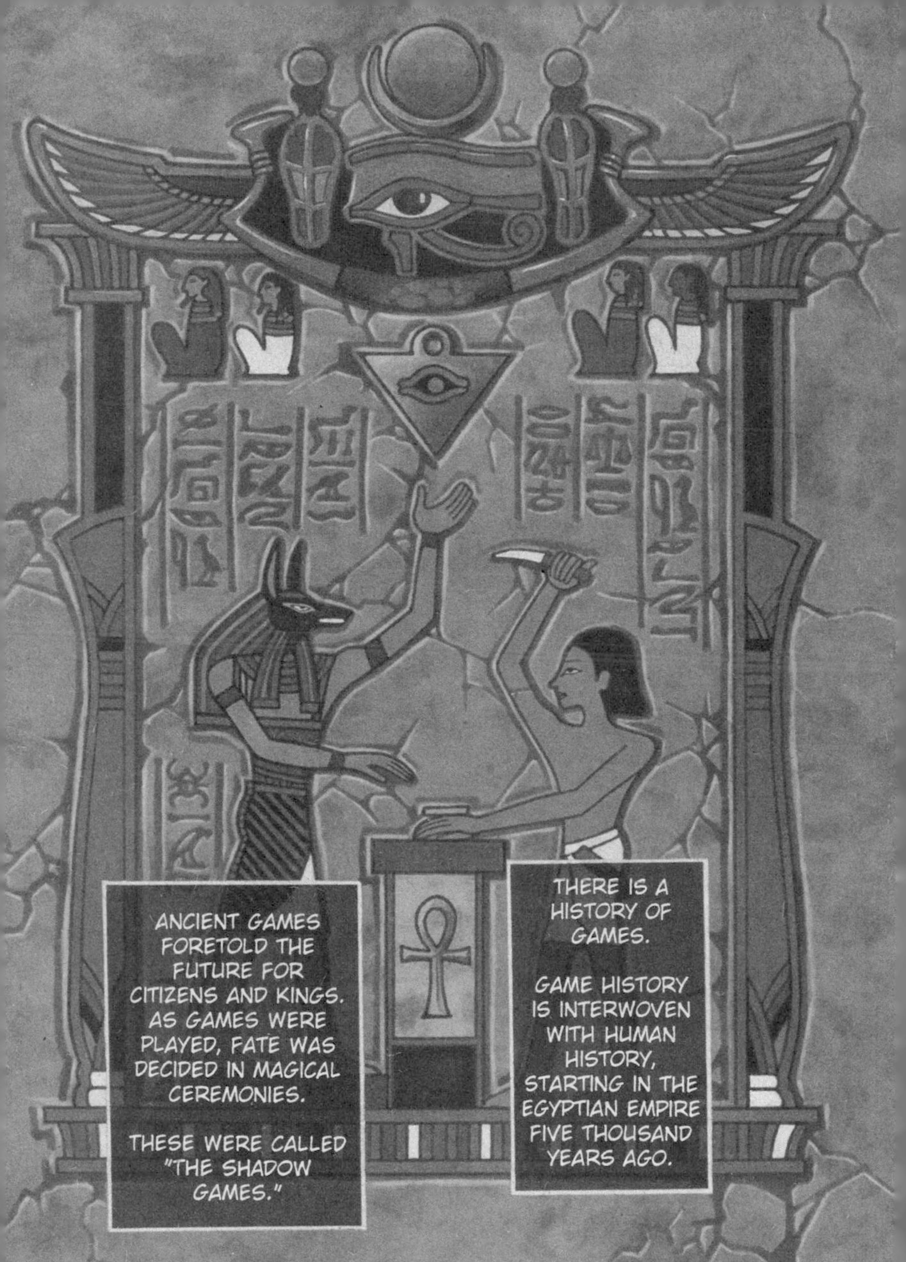
THERE IS A HISTORY OF GAMES.
GAME HISTORY IS INTERWOVEN WITH HUMAN HISTORY, STARTING IN THE EGYPTIAN EMPIRE FIVE THOUSAND YEARS AGO.
ANCIENT GAMES FORETOLD THE FUTURE FOR CITIZENS AND KINGS. AS GAMES WERE PLAYED, FATE WAS DECIDED IN MAGICAL CEREMONIES.
THESE WERE CALLED "THE SHADOW GAMES."

DUEL 1: THE PUZZLE OF THE GODS

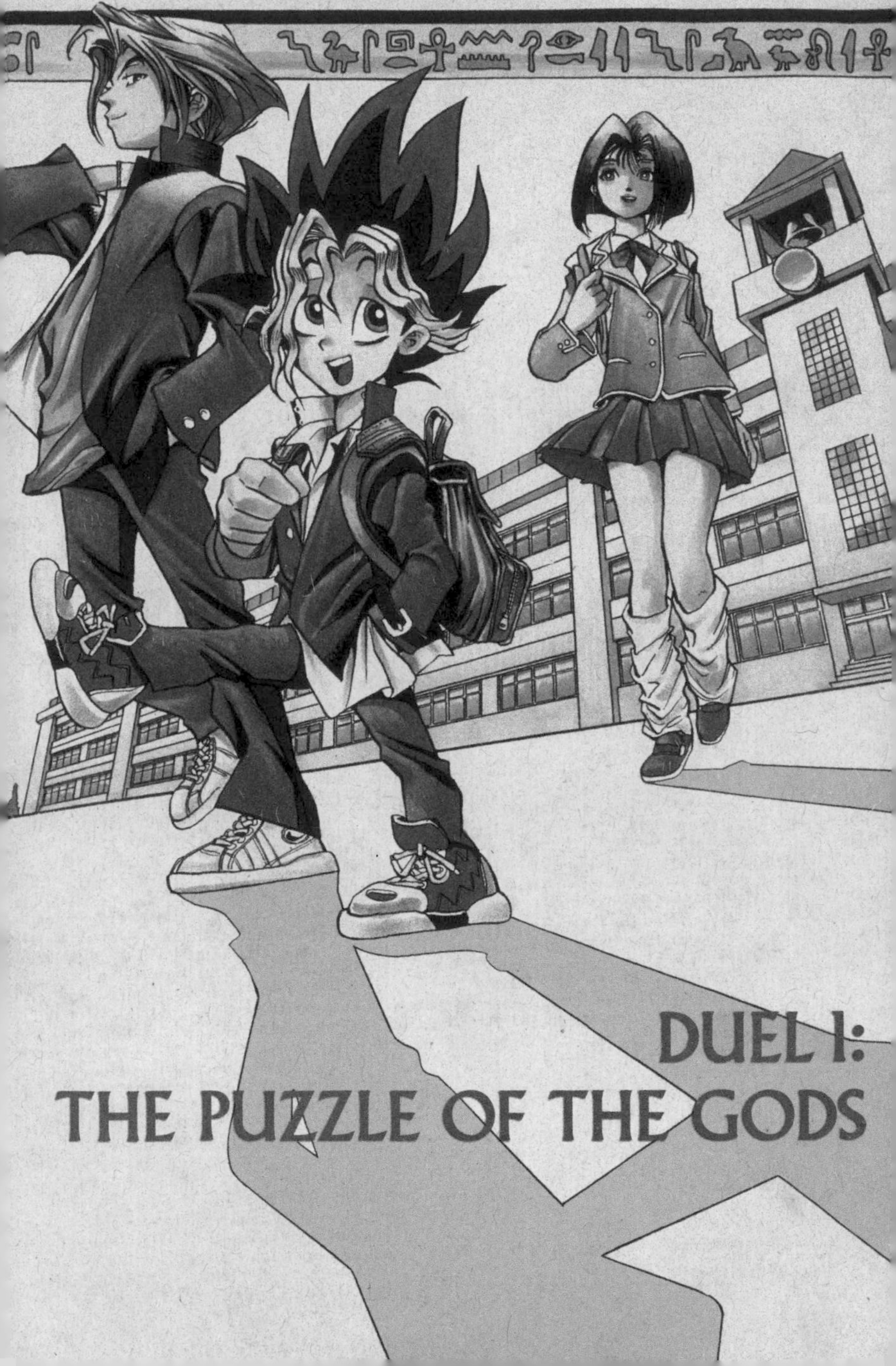
DUEL 1:
THE PUZZLE OF THE GODS

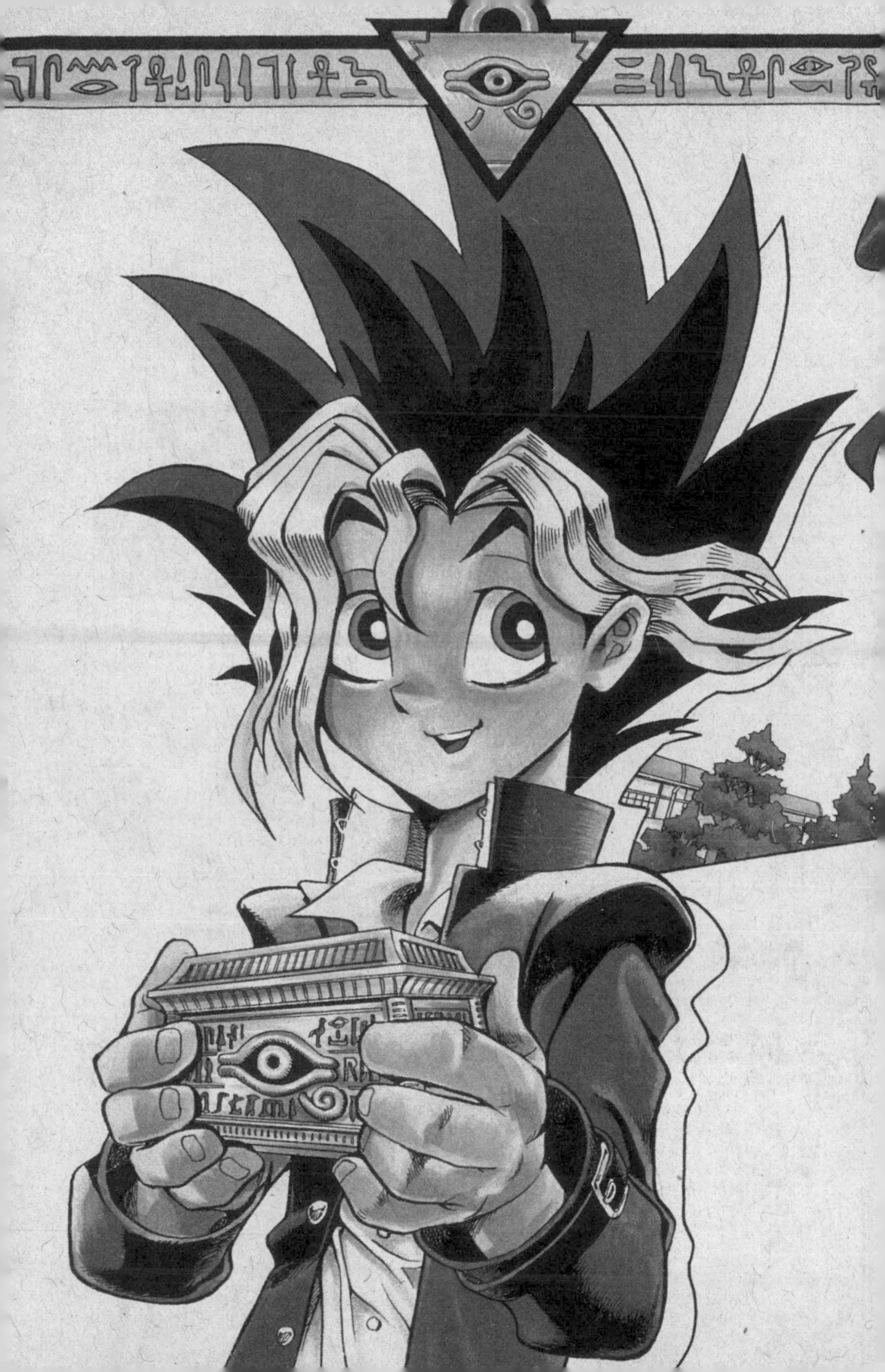

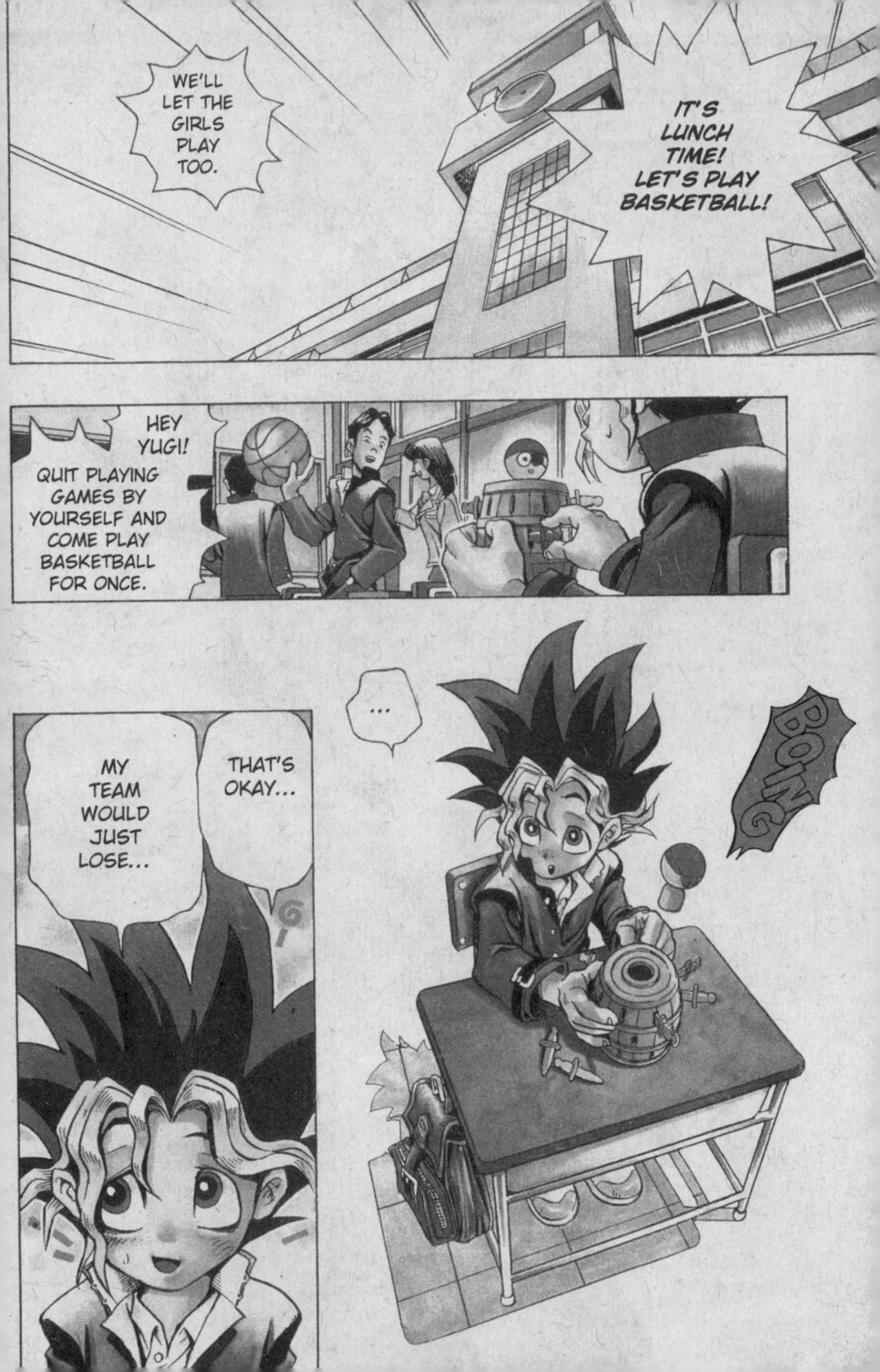
IT'S LUNCH TIME! LET'S PLAY BASKETBALL!
WE'LL LET THE GIRLS PLAY TOO.
HEY YUGI!
QUIT PLAYING GAMES BY YOURSELF AND COME PLAY BASKETBALL FOR ONCE.
BOING
...
THAT'S OKAY...
MY TEAM WOULD JUST LOSE...

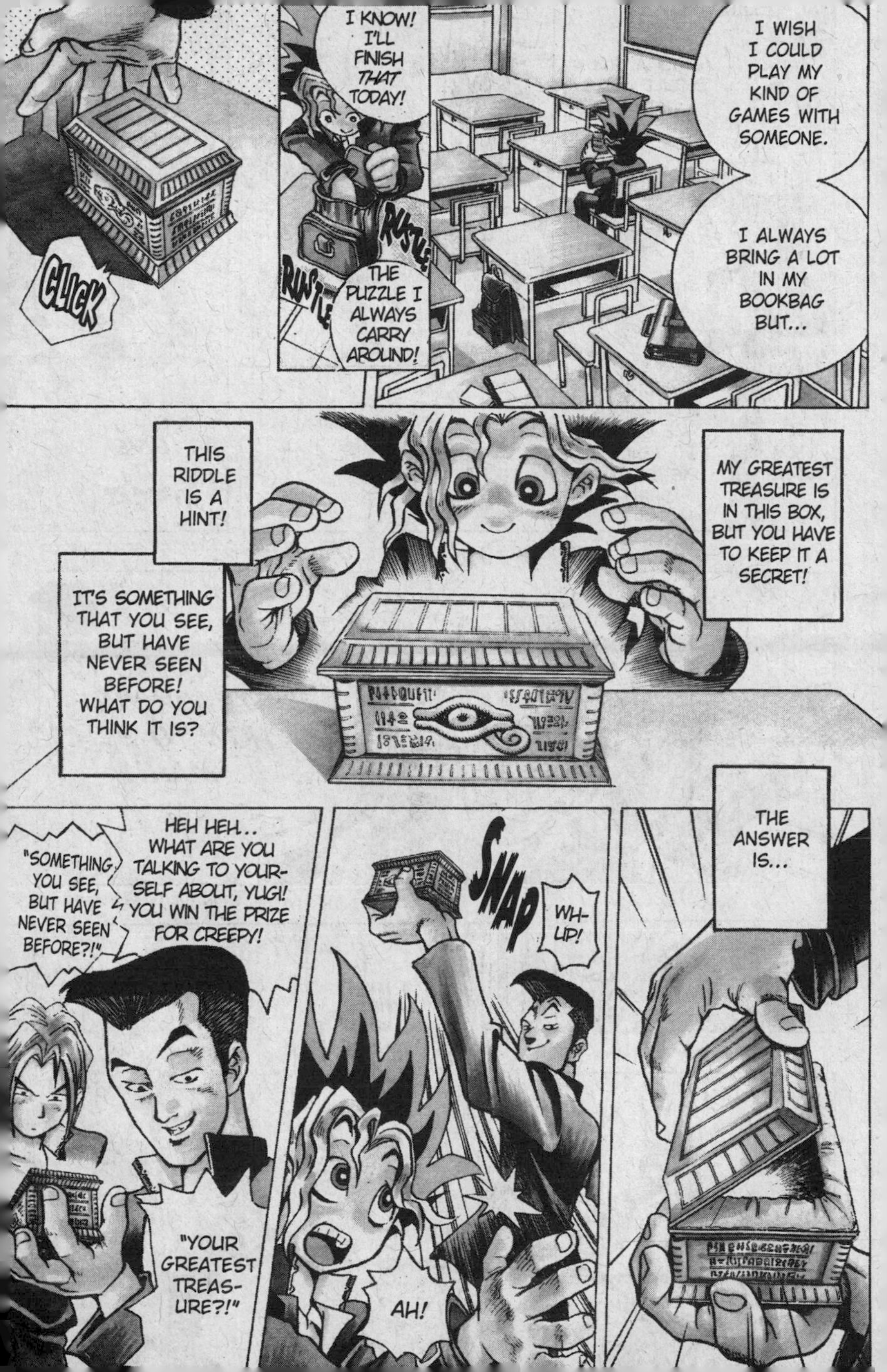
I WISH I COULD PLAY MY KIND OF GAMES WITH SOMEONE.
I ALWAYS BRING A LOT IN MY BOOKBAG BUT...
I KNOW! I'LL FINISH THAT TODAY!
RUSTLE
RUSTLE
THE PUZZLE I ALWAYS CARRY AROUND!
CLICK
MY GREATEST TREASURE IS IN THIS BOX, BUT YOU HAVE TO KEEP IT A SECRET!
THIS RIDDLE IS A HINT!
IT'S SOMETHING THAT YOU SEE, BUT HAVE NEVER SEEN BEFORE! WHAT DO YOU THINK IT IS?
THE ANSWER IS...
SNAP
WH-UP!
AH!
HEH HEH... WHAT ARE YOU TALKING TO YOUR-SELF ABOUT, YUGI! YOU WIN THE PRIZE FOR CREEPY!
"SOMETHING YOU SEE, BUT HAVE NEVER SEEN BEFORE?!"
"YOUR GREATEST TREAS-URE?!"

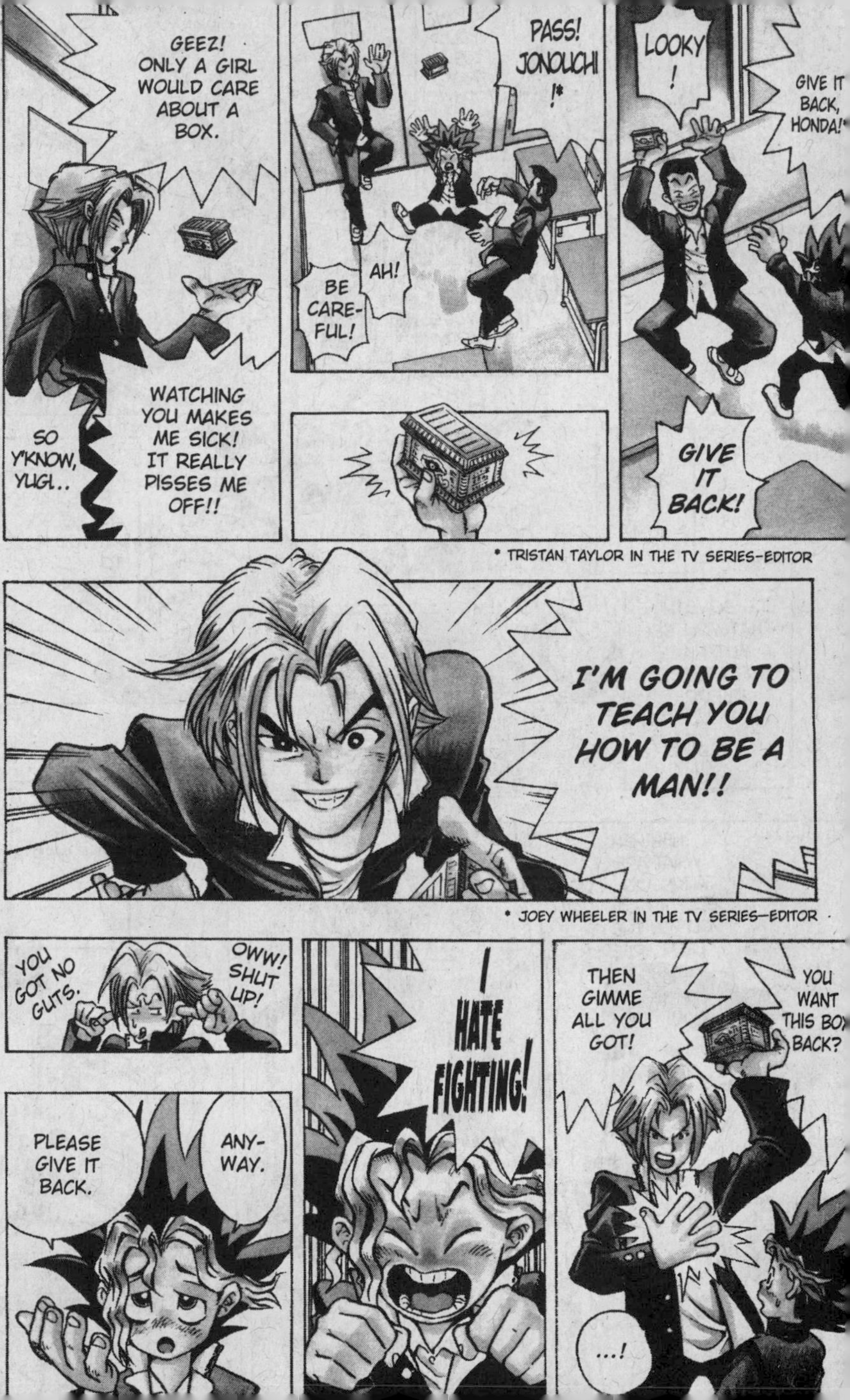
LOOKY!
GIVE IT BACK, HONDA!
GIVE IT BACK!
PASS! JONOUCHI!*
AH!
BE CAREFUL!
GEEZ! ONLY A GIRL WOULD CARE ABOUT A BOX.
WATCHING YOU MAKES ME SICK! IT REALLY PISSES ME OFF!!
SO Y'KNOW, YUGI..
I'M GOING TO TEACH YOU HOW TO BE A MAN!!
YOU WANT THIS BOX BACK?
THEN GIMME ALL YOU GOT!
...!
I HATE FIGHTING!
OWW! SHUT UP!
YOU GOT NO GUTS.
ANY-WAY.
PLEASE GIVE IT BACK.

* TRISTAN TAYLOR IN THE TV SERIES—EDITOR

* JOEY WHEELER IN THE TV SERIES—EDITOR

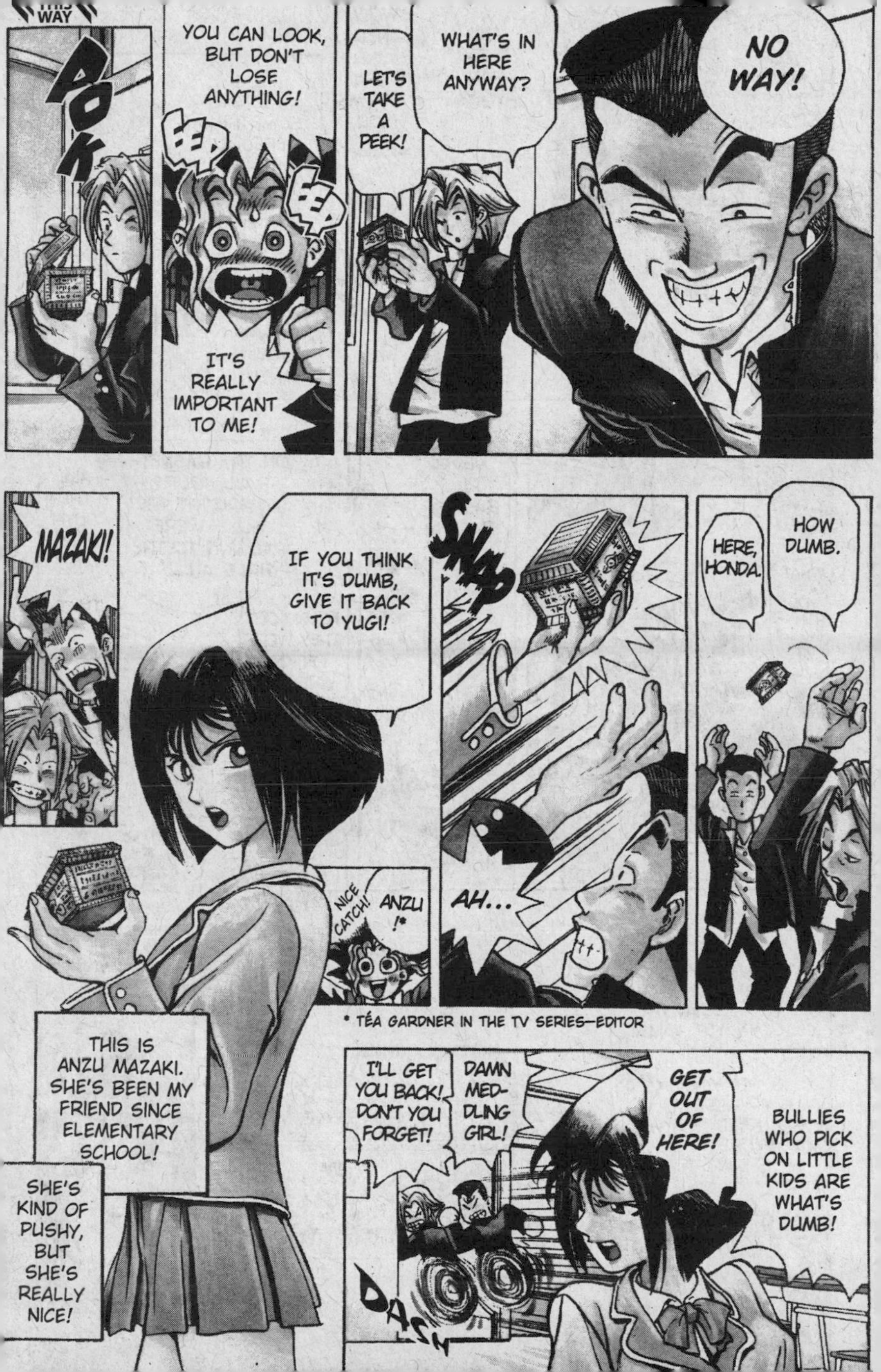
NO WAY!
WHAT'S IN HERE ANYWAY?
LET'S TAKE A PEEK!
YOU CAN LOOK, BUT DON'T LOSE ANYTHING!
EEP
EEP
IT'S REALLY IMPORTANT TO ME!
POK
HOW DUMB.
HERE, HONDA.
SNAP
AH...
ANZU!*
NICE CATCH!
IF YOU THINK IT'S DUMB, GIVE IT BACK TO YUGI!
MAZAKI!
* TÉA GARDNER IN THE TV SERIES—EDITOR
BULLIES WHO PICK ON LITTLE KIDS ARE WHAT'S DUMB!
GET OUT OF HERE!
DAMN MED-DLING GIRL!
I'LL GET YOU BACK! DON'T YOU FORGET!
DASH
THIS IS ANZU MAZAKI. SHE'S BEEN MY FRIEND SINCE ELEMENTARY SCHOOL!
SHE'S KIND OF PUSHY, BUT SHE'S REALLY NICE!

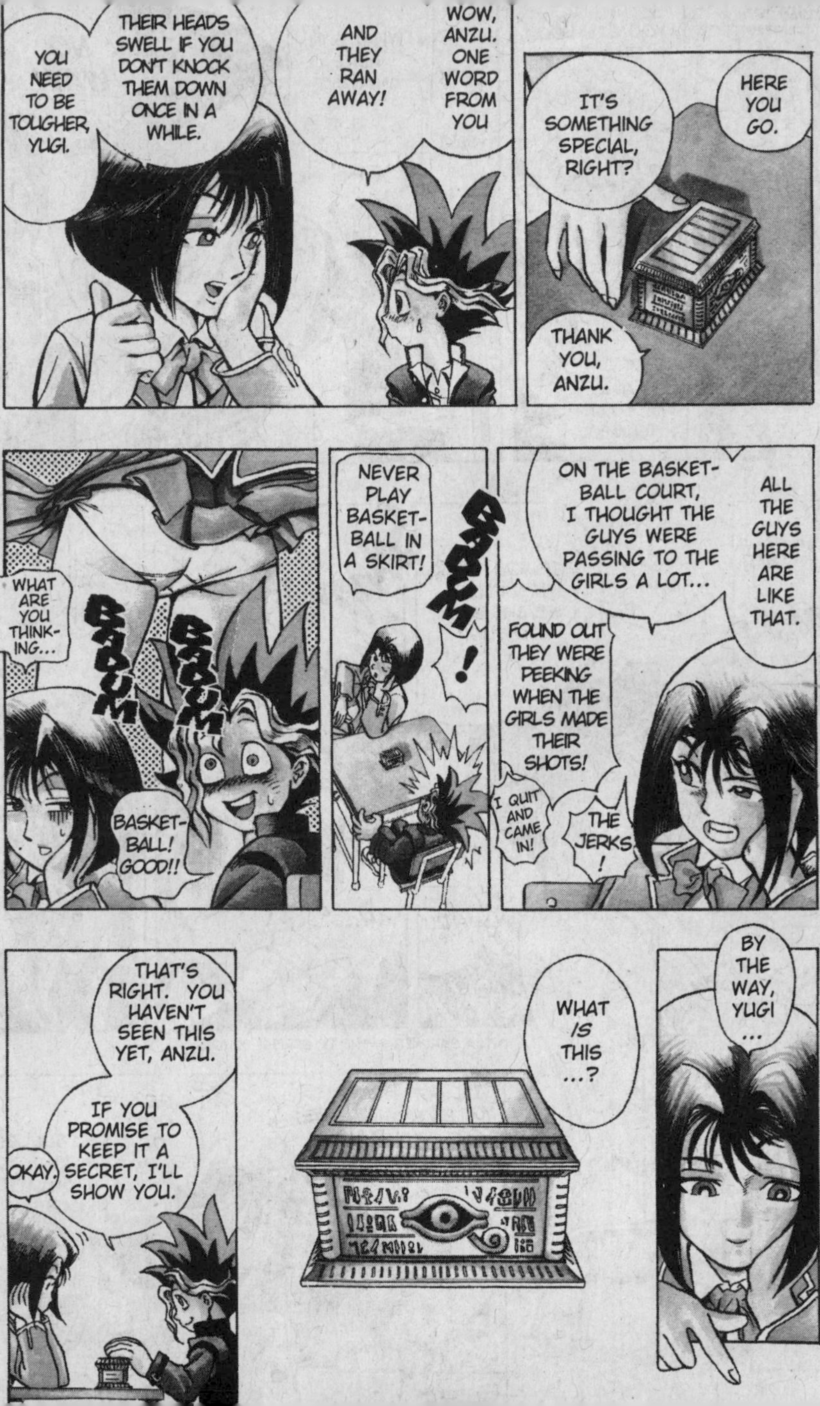
HERE YOU GO.
IT'S SOMETHING SPECIAL, RIGHT?
THANK YOU, ANZU.
WOW, ANZU. ONE WORD FROM YOU
AND THEY RAN AWAY!
THEIR HEADS SWELL IF YOU DON'T KNOCK THEM DOWN ONCE IN A WHILE.
YOU NEED TO BE TOUGHER, YUGI.
ON THE BASKET-BALL COURT, I THOUGHT THE GUYS WERE PASSING TO THE GIRLS A LOT...
FOUND OUT THEY WERE PEEKING WHEN THE GIRLS MADE THEIR SHOTS!
THE JERKS!
I QUIT AND CAME IN!
ALL THE GUYS HERE ARE LIKE THAT.
BADUM
!
NEVER PLAY BASKET-BALL IN A SKIRT!
BADUM
BADUM
WHAT ARE YOU THINK-ING...
BASKET-BALL! GOOD!!
BY THE WAY, YUGI ...
WHAT IS THIS ...?
THAT'S RIGHT. YOU HAVEN'T SEEN THIS YET, ANZU.
IF YOU PROMISE TO KEEP IT A SECRET, I'LL SHOW YOU.
OKAY.

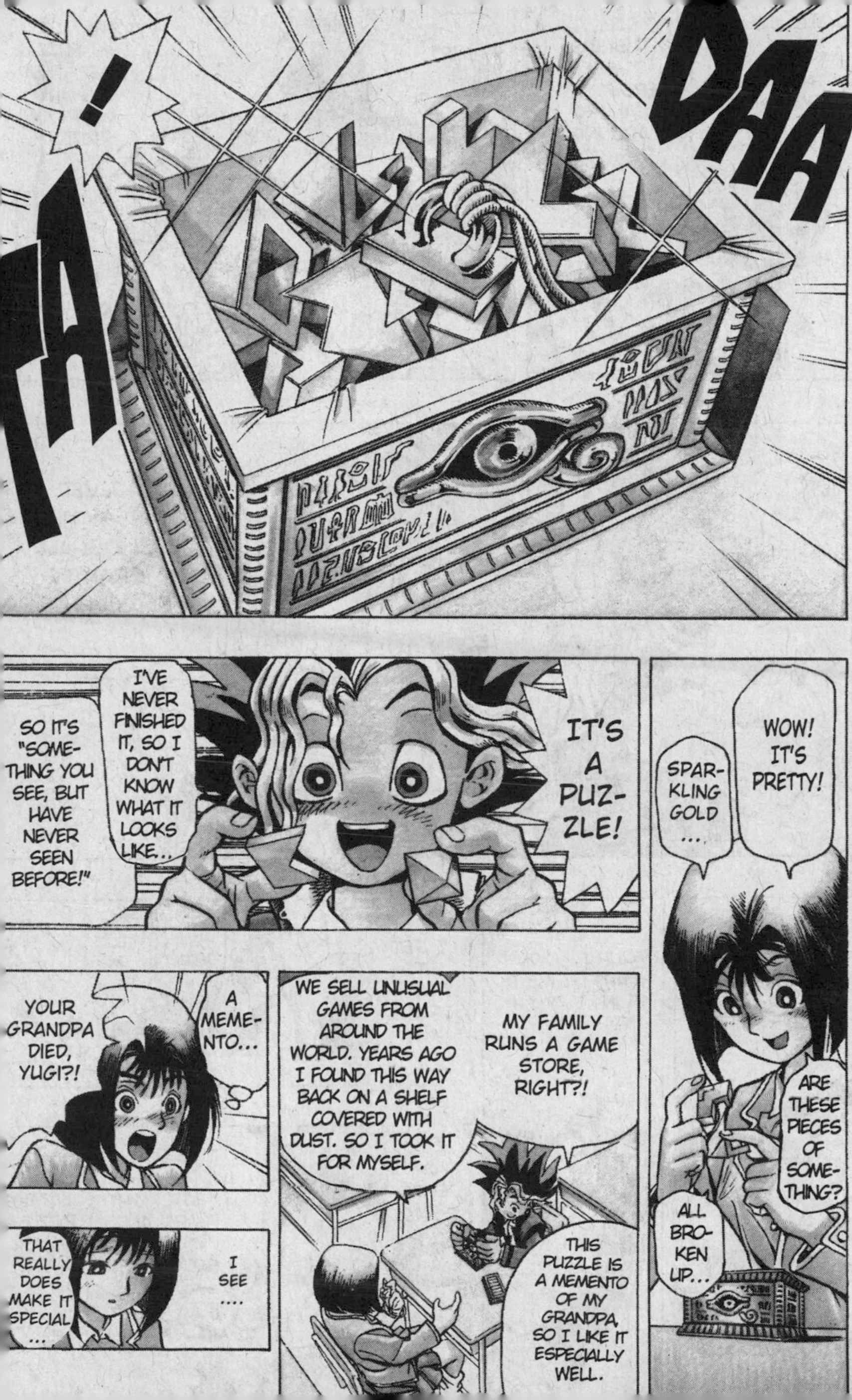
!
TA
DAA
WOW! IT'S PRETTY!
SPARKLING GOLD...
ARE THESE PIECES OF SOMETHING?
ALL BROKEN UP...
IT'S A PUZZLE!
I'VE NEVER FINISHED IT, SO I DON'T KNOW WHAT IT LOOKS LIKE...
SO IT'S "SOMETHING YOU SEE, BUT HAVE NEVER SEEN BEFORE!"
MY FAMILY RUNS A GAME STORE, RIGHT?!
WE SELL UNUSUAL GAMES FROM AROUND THE WORLD. YEARS AGO I FOUND THIS WAY BACK ON A SHELF COVERED WITH DUST. SO I TOOK IT FOR MYSELF.
THIS PUZZLE IS A MEMENTO OF MY GRANDPA, SO I LIKE IT ESPECIALLY WELL.
A MEMENTO...
YOUR GRANDPA DIED, YUGI?!
I SEE....
THAT REALLY DOES MAKE IT SPECIAL...

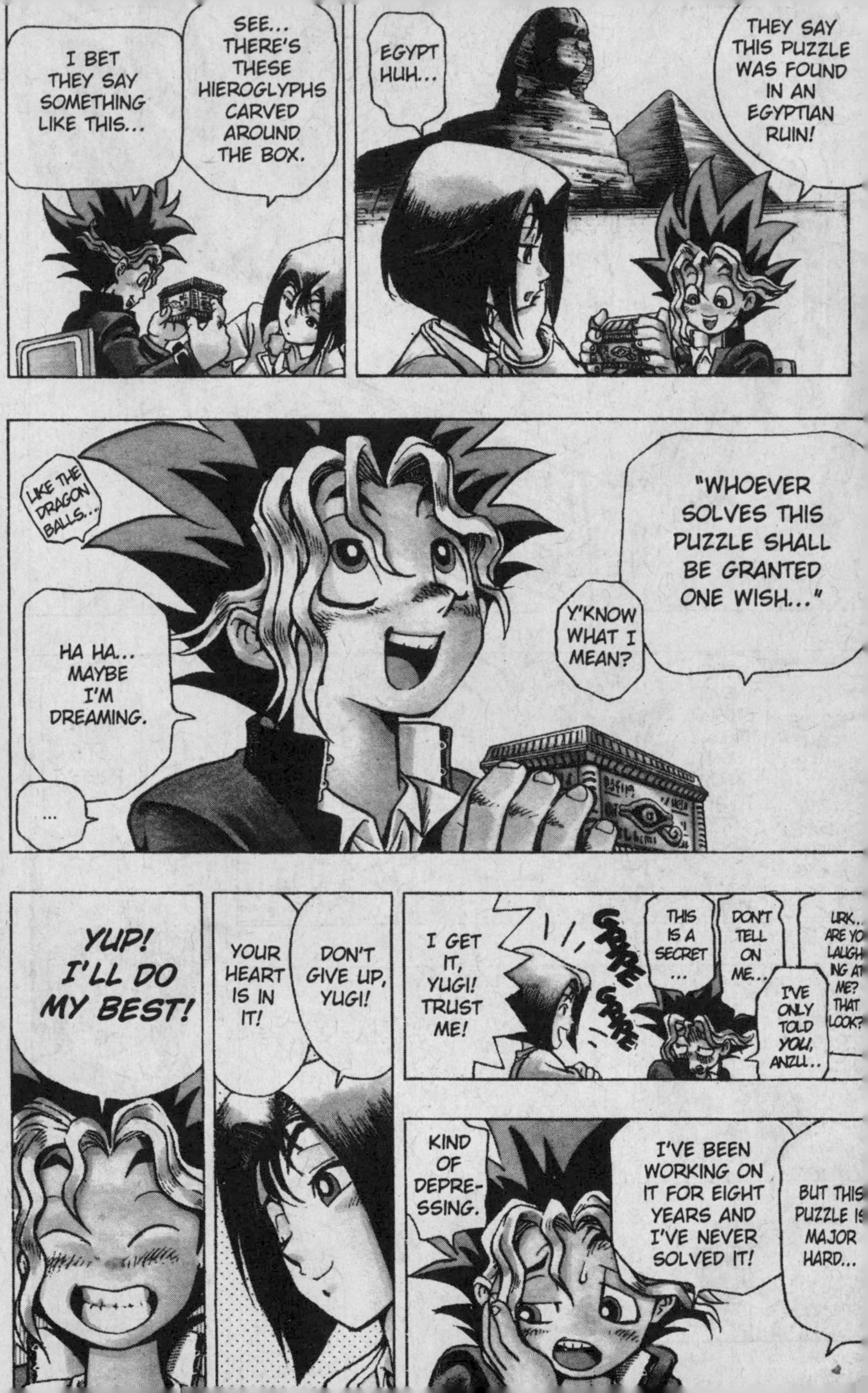
THEY SAY THIS PUZZLE WAS FOUND IN AN EGYPTIAN RUIN!
EGYPT HUH...
SEE... THERE'S THESE HIEROGLYPHS CARVED AROUND THE BOX.
I BET THEY SAY SOMETHING LIKE THIS...
"WHOEVER SOLVES THIS PUZZLE SHALL BE GRANTED ONE WISH..."
Y'KNOW WHAT I MEAN?
LIKE THE DRAGON BALLS...
HA HA... MAYBE I'M DREAMING.
...
URK... ARE YO LAUGHING AT ME? THAT LOOK?
DON'T TELL ON ME...
THIS IS A SECRET...
I'VE ONLY TOLD YOU, ANZU...
I GET IT, YUGI! TRUST ME!
BUT THIS PUZZLE IS MAJOR HARD...
I'VE BEEN WORKING ON IT FOR EIGHT YEARS AND I'VE NEVER SOLVED IT!
KIND OF DEPRESSING.
DON'T GIVE UP, YUGI!
YOUR HEART IS IN IT!
YUP! I'LL DO MY BEST!

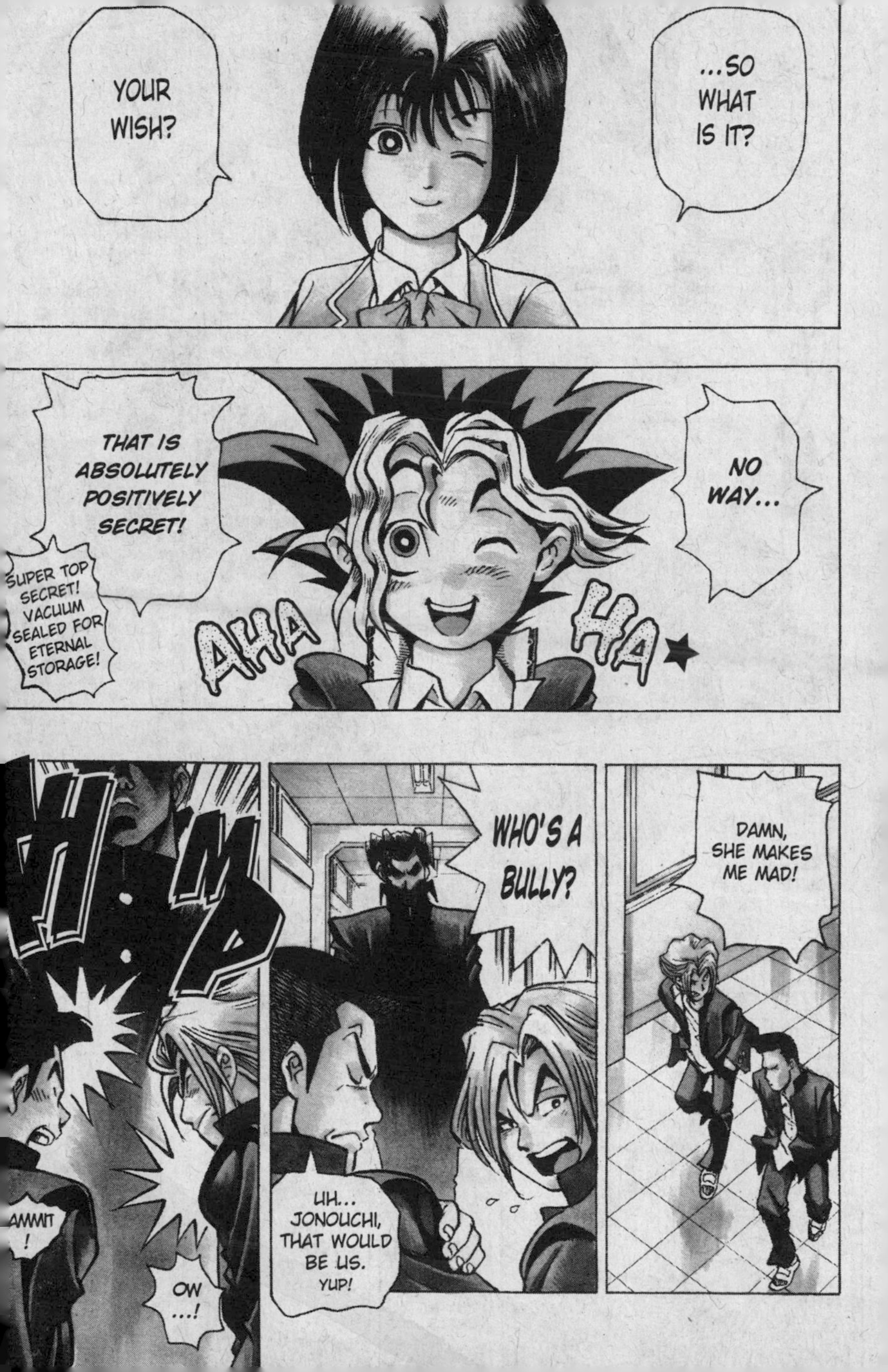
...SO WHAT IS IT?
YOUR WISH?
NO WAY...
THAT IS ABSOLUTELY POSITIVELY SECRET!
SUPER TOP SECRET! VACUUM SEALED FOR ETERNAL STORAGE!
AHA HA★
DAMN, SHE MAKES ME MAD!
WHO'S A BULLY?
UH... JONOUCHI, THAT WOULD BE US. YUP!
AMMIT !
OW ...!

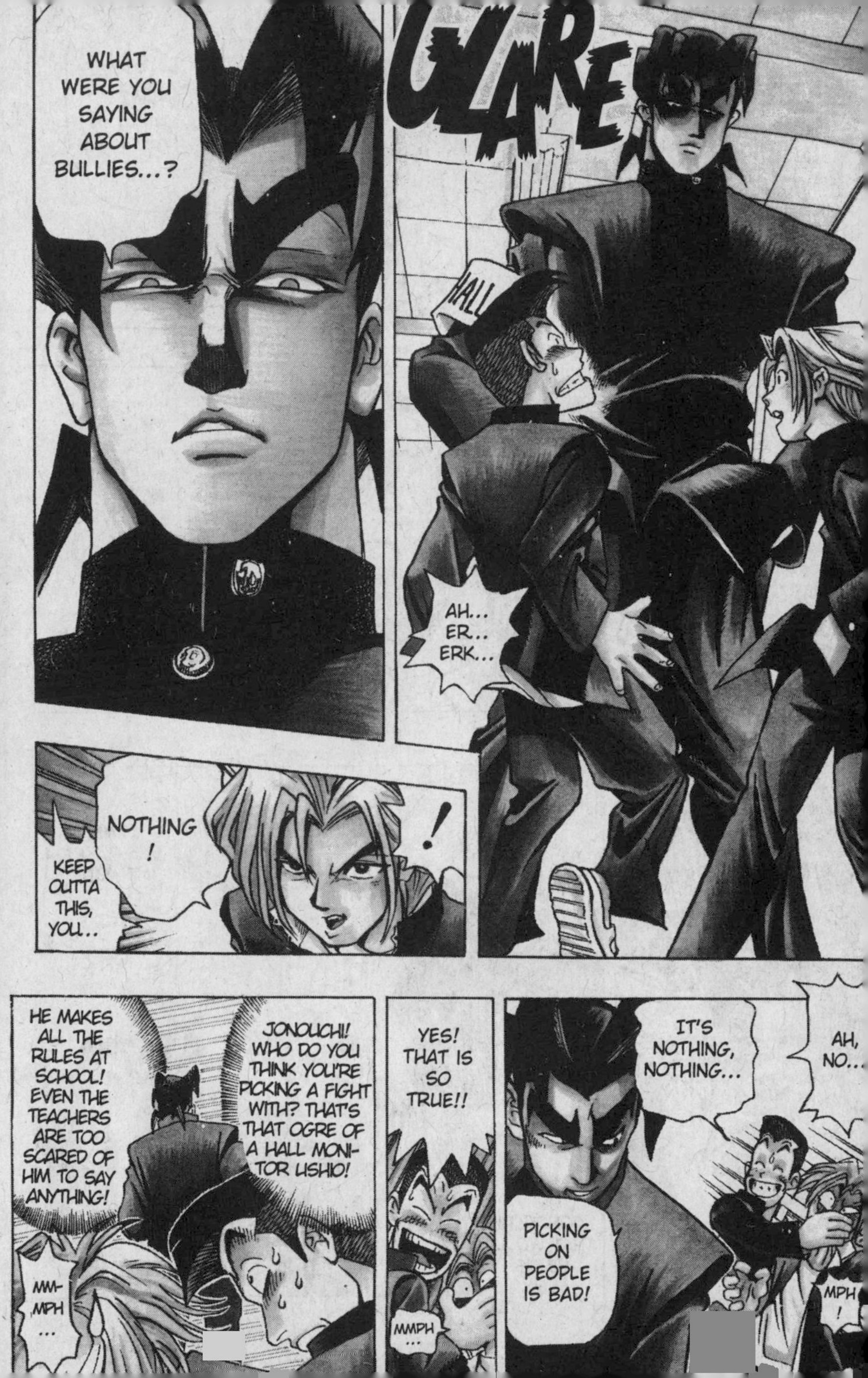
GLARE
HALL
AH... ER.. ERK...
WHAT WERE YOU SAYING ABOUT BULLIES...?
NOTHING!
KEEP OUTTA THIS, YOU..
!
AH, NO...
IT'S NOTHING, NOTHING...
PICKING ON PEOPLE IS BAD!
MPH!
YES! THAT IS SO TRUE!!
MMPH...
JONOUCHI! WHO DO YOU THINK YOU'RE PICKING A FIGHT WITH? THAT'S THAT OGRE OF A HALL MONI-TOR USHIO!
HE MAKES ALL THE RULES AT SCHOOL! EVEN THE TEACHERS ARE TOO SCARED OF HIM TO SAY ANYTHING!
MM-MPH...

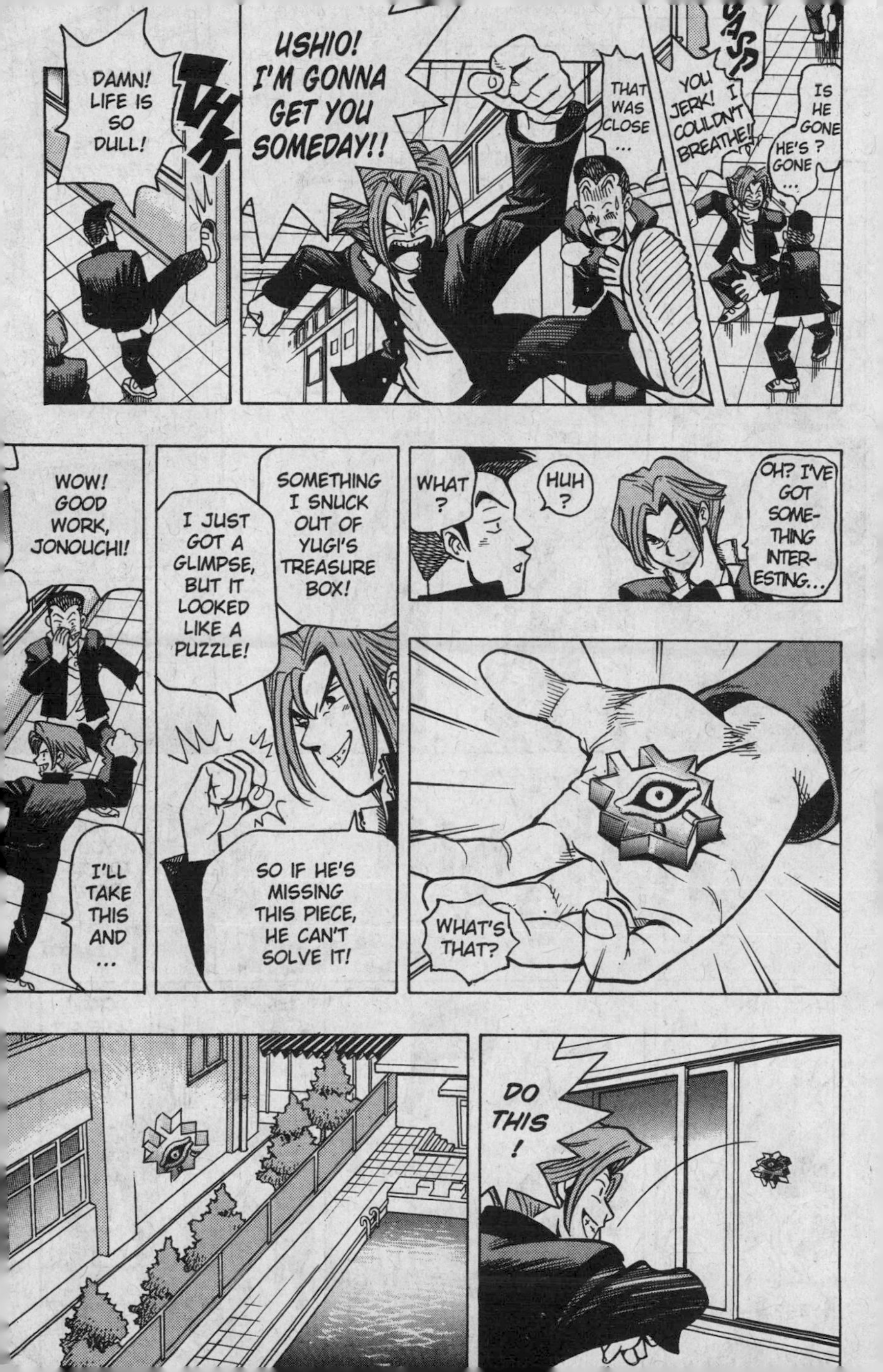
GASP
YOU JERK! I COULDN'T BREATHE!!
IS HE GONE?
HE'S GONE...
THAT WAS CLOSE...
USHIO! I'M GONNA GET YOU SOMEDAY!!
DAMN! LIFE IS SO DULL!
OH? I'VE GOT SOME-THING INTER-ESTING...
HUH?
WHAT?
WHAT'S THAT?
SOMETHING I SNUCK OUT OF YUGI'S TREASURE BOX!
I JUST GOT A GLIMPSE, BUT IT LOOKED LIKE A PUZZLE!
SO IF HE'S MISSING THIS PIECE, HE CAN'T SOLVE IT!
WOW! GOOD WORK, JONOUCHI!
I'LL TAKE THIS AND ...
DO THIS!

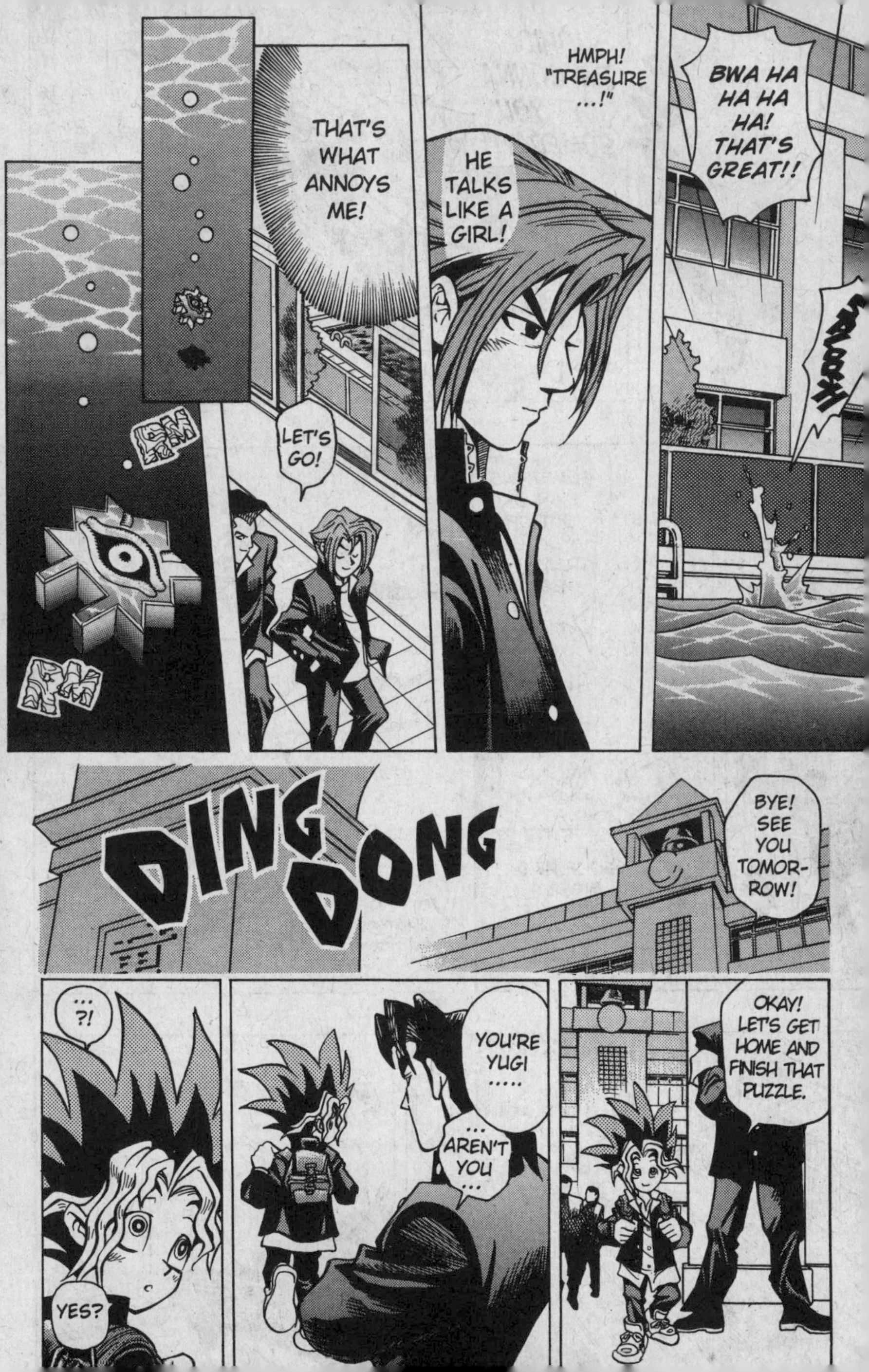
BWA HA HA HA HA! THAT'S GREAT!!
HMPH! "TREASURE ...!"
HE TALKS LIKE A GIRL!
THAT'S WHAT ANNOYS ME!
LET'S GO!
BYE! SEE YOU TOMOR-ROW!
DING DONG
OKAY! LET'S GET HOME AND FINISH THAT PUZZLE.
YOU'RE YUGI .....
... AREN'T YOU ...
... ?!
YES?

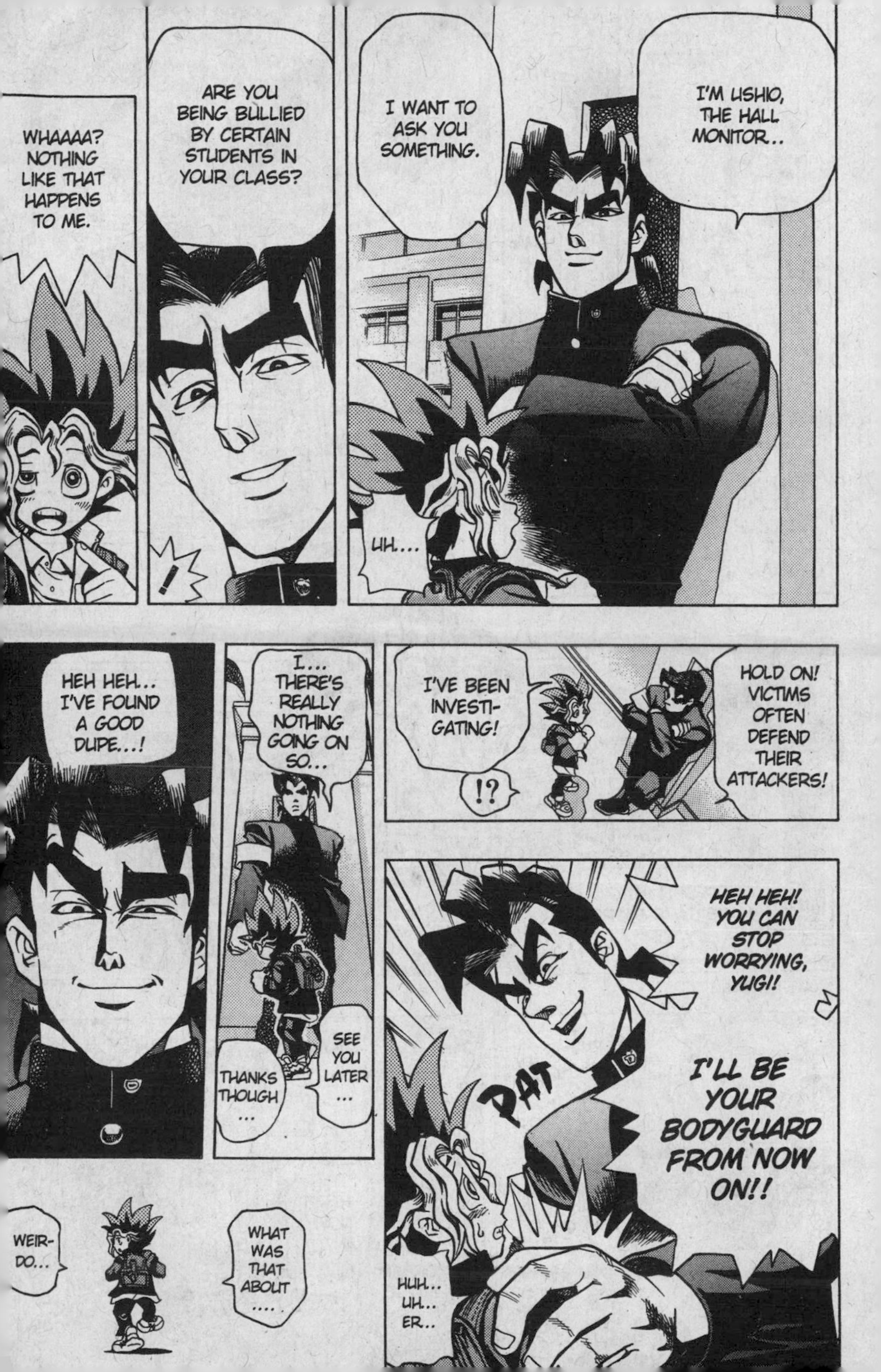
I'M USHIO, THE HALL MONITOR...
I WANT TO ASK YOU SOMETHING.
UH....
ARE YOU BEING BULLIED BY CERTAIN STUDENTS IN YOUR CLASS?
!
WHAAAA? NOTHING LIKE THAT HAPPENS TO ME.
HOLD ON! VICTIMS OFTEN DEFEND THEIR ATTACKERS!
I'VE BEEN INVESTI-GATING!
!?
HEH HEH! YOU CAN STOP WORRYING, YUGI!
I'LL BE YOUR BODYGUARD FROM NOW ON!!
PAT
HUH... UH... ER...
I... THERE'S REALLY NOTHING GOING ON SO...
SEE YOU LATER ...
THANKS THOUGH ...
HEH HEH... I'VE FOUND A GOOD DUPE...!
WHAT WAS THAT ABOUT ....
WEIR-DO...

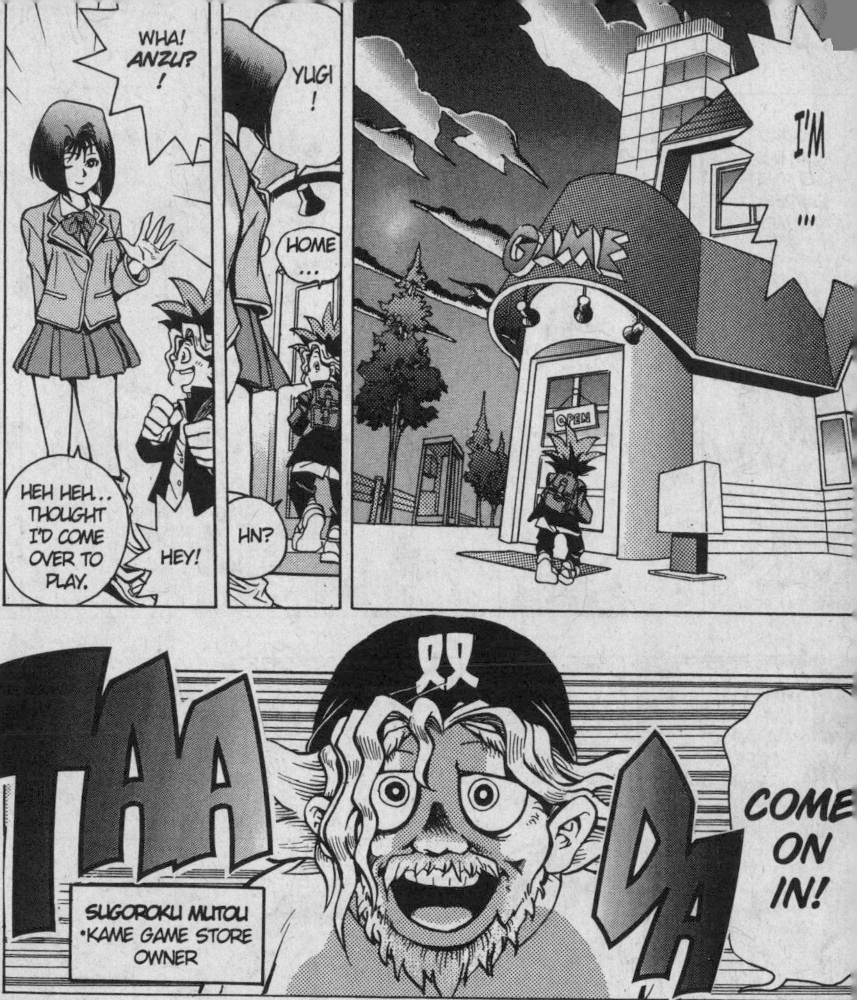
I'M '''
YUGI !
HOME ...
HN?
WHA! ANZU?!
HEY!
HEH HEH.. THOUGHT I'D COME OVER TO PLAY.
COME ON IN!
TAA DA
SUGOROKU MUTOU *KAME GAME STORE OWNER

* KAME = TURTLE

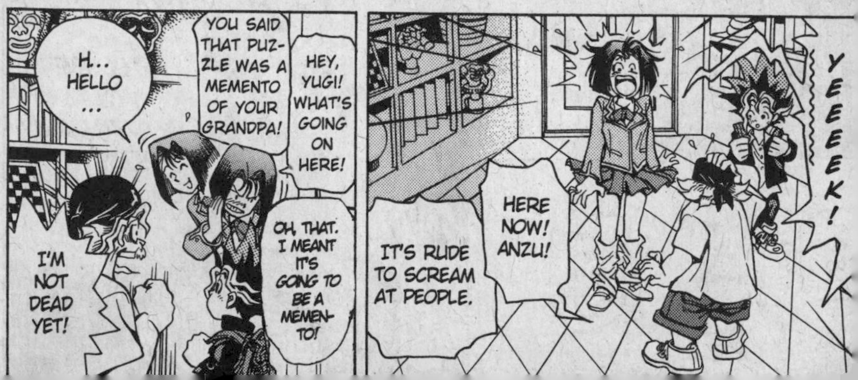
YEEEEK!
HERE NOW! ANZU!
IT'S RUDE TO SCREAM AT PEOPLE.
HEY, YUGI! WHAT'S GOING ON HERE!
YOU SAID THAT PUZ-ZLE WAS A MEMENTO OF YOUR GRANDPA!
H... HELLO ...
OH, THAT. I MEANT IT'S GOING TO BE A MEMEN-TO!
I'M NOT DEAD YET!

READ THIS WAY

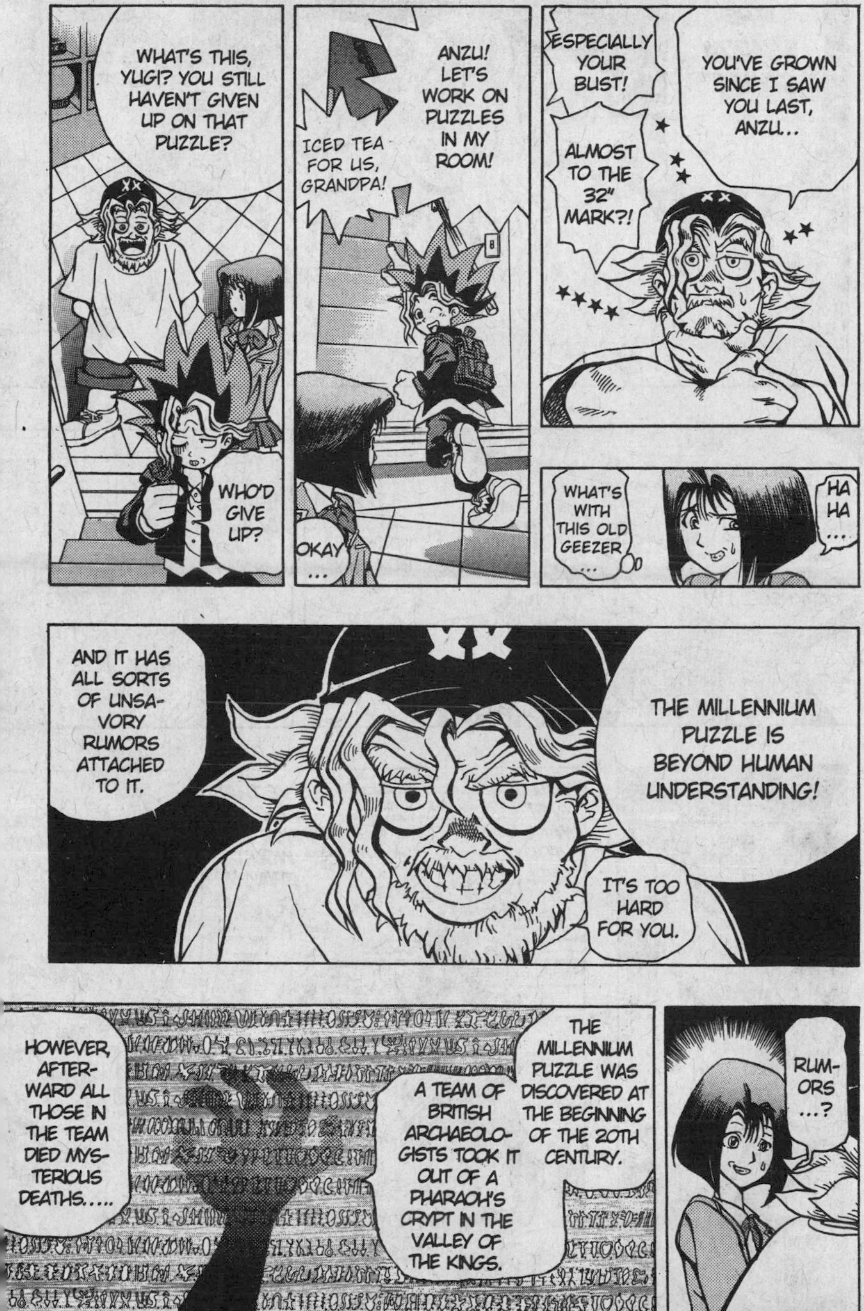
YOU'VE GROWN SINCE I SAW YOU LAST, ANZU...
ESPECIALLY YOUR BUST!
ALMOST TO THE 32" MARK?!
HA HA ...
WHAT'S WITH THIS OLD GEEZER ...
ANZU! LET'S WORK ON PUZZLES IN MY ROOM!
ICED TEA FOR US, GRANDPA!
OKAY ...
WHAT'S THIS, YUGI? YOU STILL HAVEN'T GIVEN UP ON THAT PUZZLE?
WHO'D GIVE UP?
THE MILLENNIUM PUZZLE IS BEYOND HUMAN UNDERSTANDING!
IT'S TOO HARD FOR YOU.
AND IT HAS ALL SORTS OF UNSAVORY RUMORS ATTACHED TO IT.
RUMORS ...?
THE MILLENNIUM PUZZLE WAS DISCOVERED AT THE BEGINNING OF THE 20TH CENTURY.
A TEAM OF BRITISH ARCHAEOLOGISTS TOOK IT OUT OF A PHARAOH'S CRYPT IN THE VALLEY OF THE KINGS.
HOWEVER, AFTERWARD ALL THOSE IN THE TEAM DIED MYSTERIOUS DEATHS.....

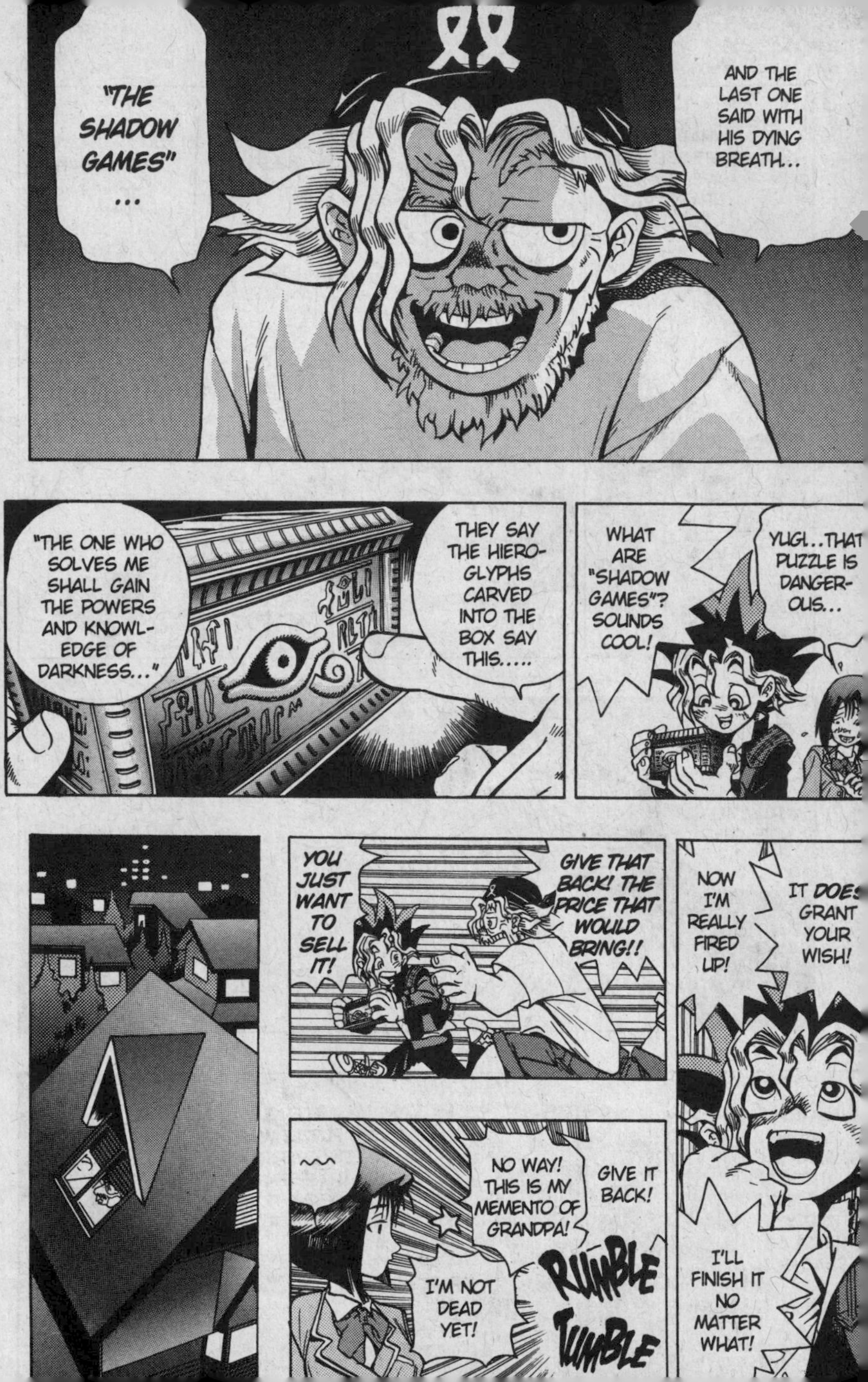
双
AND THE LAST ONE SAID WITH HIS DYING BREATH...
"THE SHADOW GAMES" ...
THEY SAY THE HIEROGLYPHS CARVED INTO THE BOX SAY THIS.....
"THE ONE WHO SOLVES ME SHALL GAIN THE POWERS AND KNOWLEDGE OF DARKNESS..."
WHAT ARE "SHADOW GAMES"? SOUNDS COOL!
YUGI...THAT PUZZLE IS DANGEROUS...
GIVE THAT BACK! THE PRICE THAT WOULD BRING!!
YOU JUST WANT TO SELL IT!
GIVE IT BACK!
NO WAY! THIS IS MY MEMENTO OF GRANDPA!
I'M NOT DEAD YET!
RUMBLE
TUMBLE
IT DOES GRANT YOUR WISH!
NOW I'M REALLY FIRED UP!
I'LL FINISH IT NO MATTER WHAT!

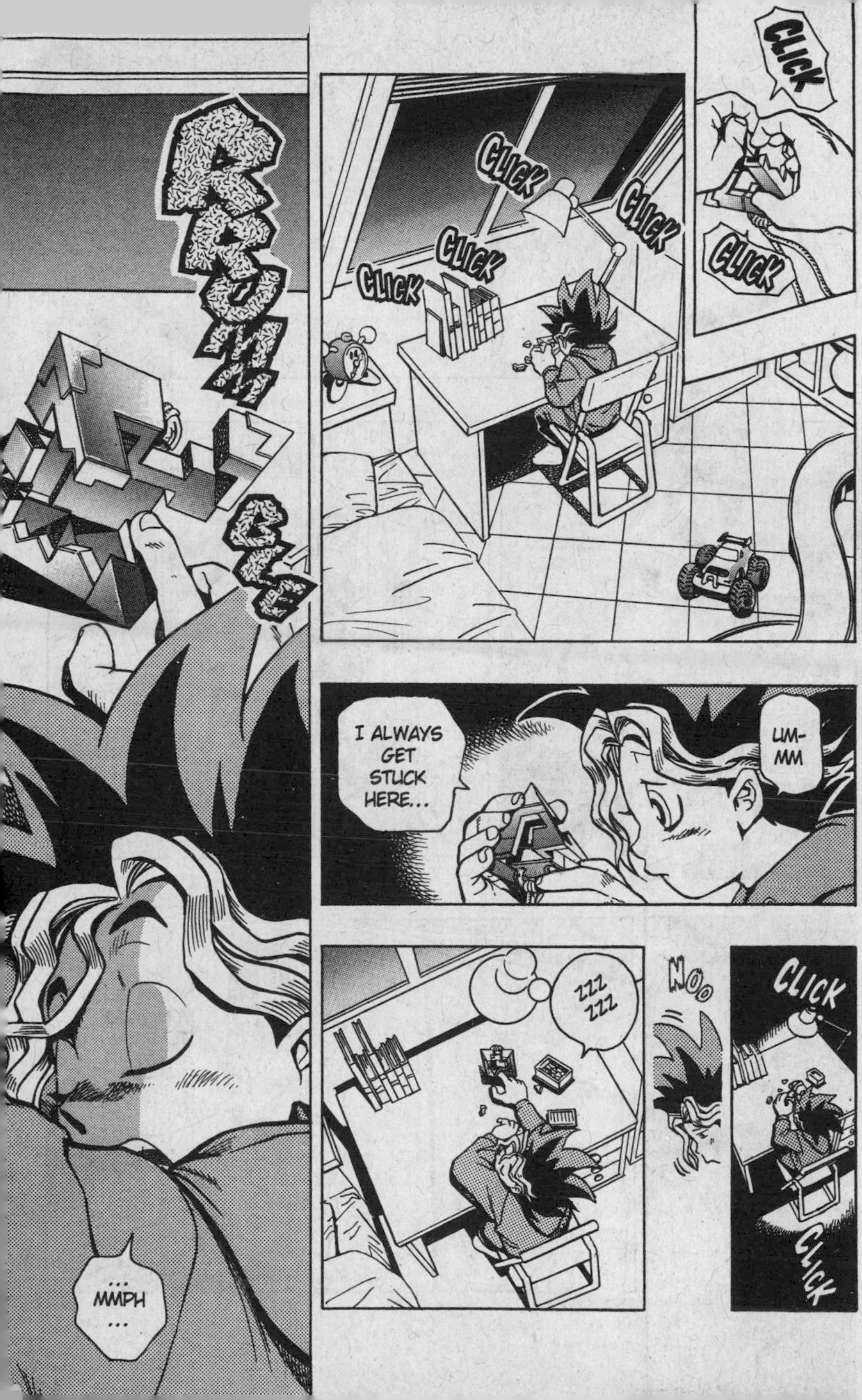
CLICK
CLICK
CLICK
CLICK
CLICK
CLICK
UM-MM
I ALWAYS GET STUCK HERE...
CLICK
CLICK
NOo
ZZZ ZZZ
...MMPH...

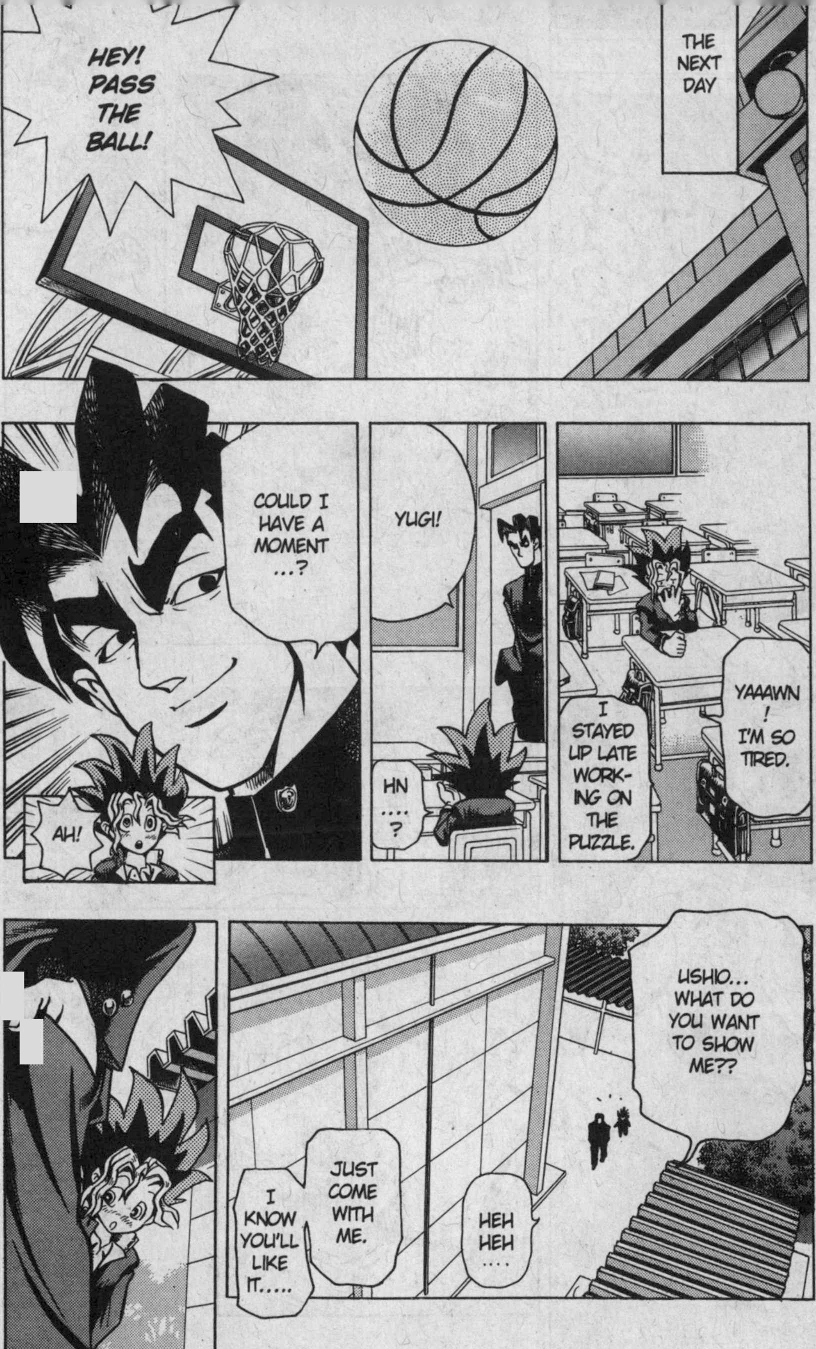
THE NEXT DAY
HEY! PASS THE BALL!
YAAAWN! I'M SO TIRED.
I STAYED UP LATE WORKING ON THE PUZZLE.
YUGI!
HN....?
COULD I HAVE A MOMENT...?
AH!
USHIO... WHAT DO YOU WANT TO SHOW ME??
HEH HEH....
JUST COME WITH ME.
I KNOW YOU'LL LIKE IT.....

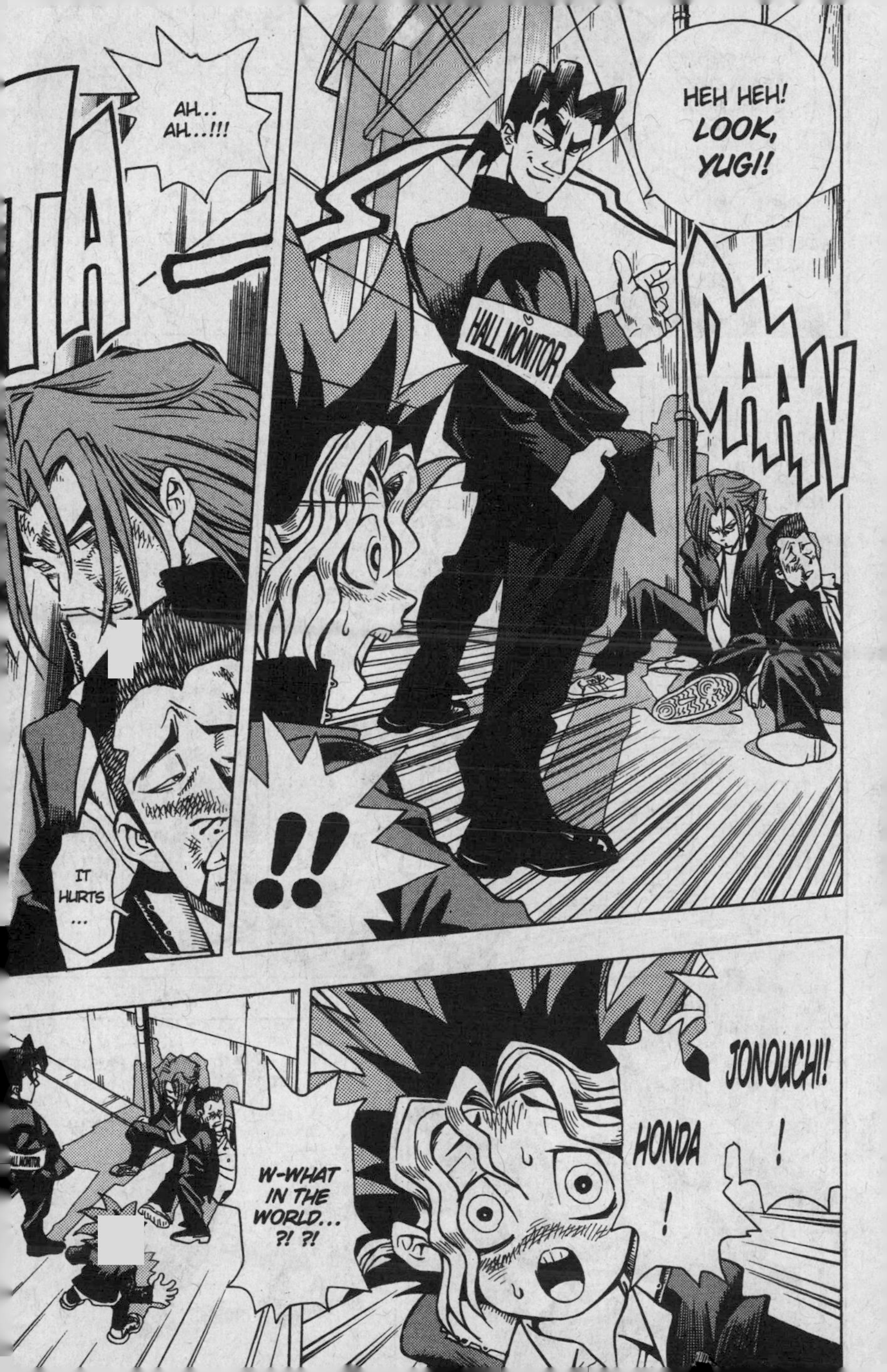
HEH HEH! LOOK, YUGI!
HALL MONITOR
!!
TA-
AH... AH...!!!
IT HURTS ...
JONOUCHI!
HONDA!
W-WHAT IN THE WORLD... ?! ?!
HALL MONITOR

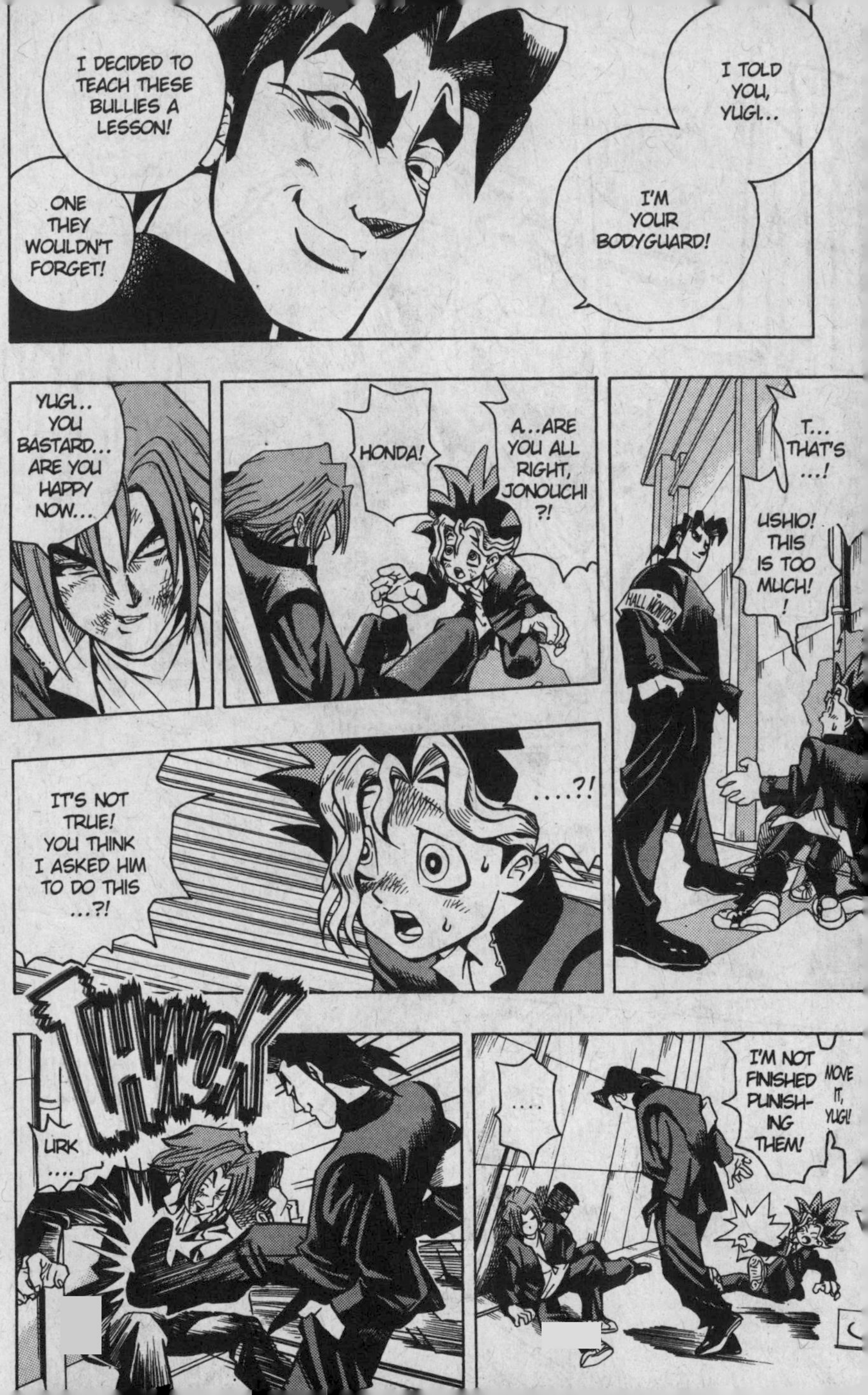
I TOLD YOU, YUGI...
I'M YOUR BODYGUARD!
I DECIDED TO TEACH THESE BULLIES A LESSON!
ONE THEY WOULDN'T FORGET!
T... THAT'S ...!
USHIO! THIS IS TOO MUCH!!
A...ARE YOU ALL RIGHT, JONOUCHI ?!
HONDA!
YUGI.. YOU BASTARD... ARE YOU HAPPY NOW...
....?!
IT'S NOT TRUE! YOU THINK I ASKED HIM TO DO THIS ...?!
MOVE IT, YUGI!
I'M NOT FINISHED PUNISH-ING THEM!
....
THWOCK
URK ....

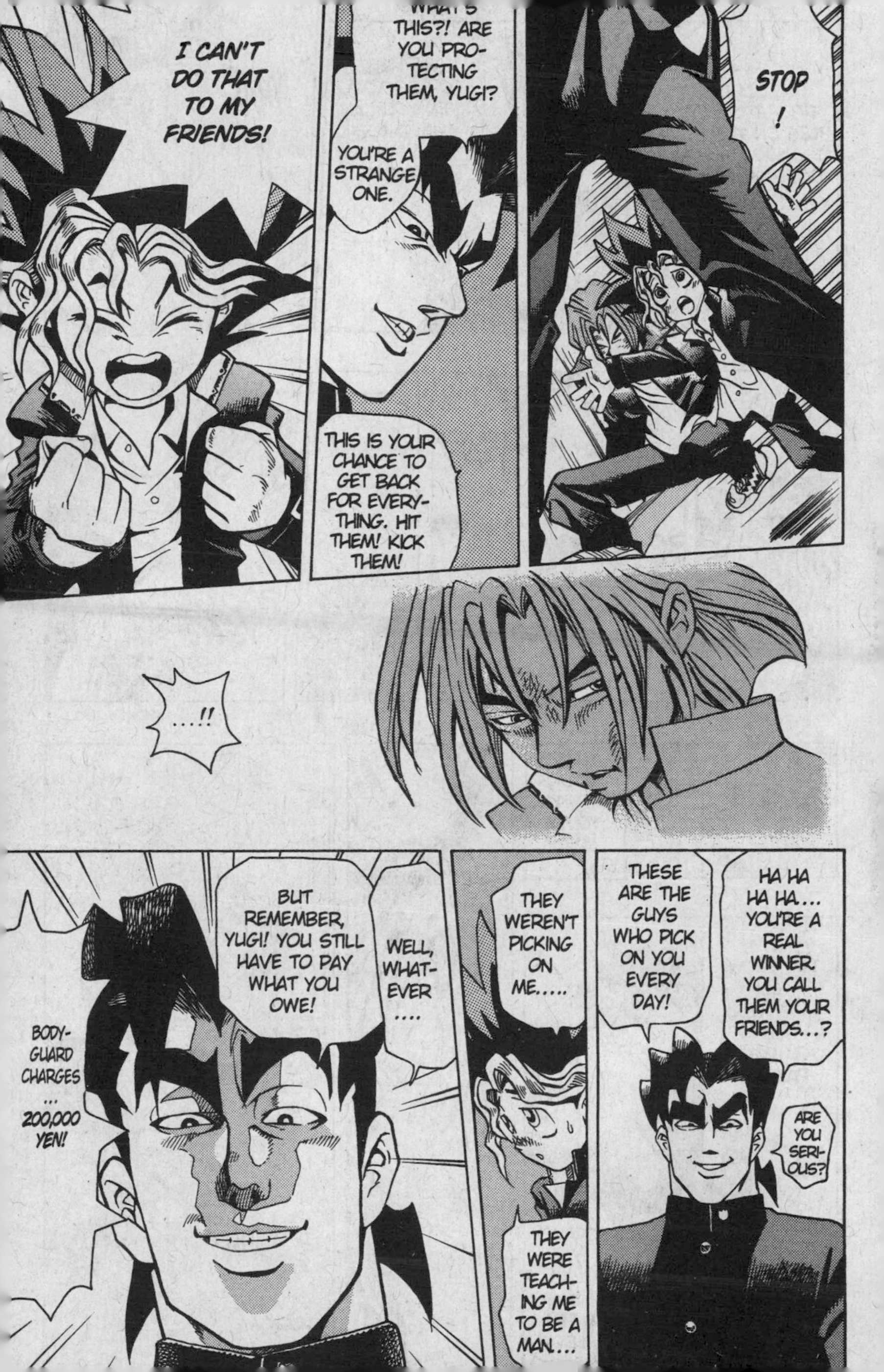
STOP!
WHAT'S THIS?! ARE YOU PROTECTING THEM, YUGI?
YOU'RE A STRANGE ONE.
THIS IS YOUR CHANCE TO GET BACK FOR EVERYTHING. HIT THEM! KICK THEM!
I CAN'T DO THAT TO MY FRIENDS!
....!!
HA HA HA HA.... YOU'RE A REAL WINNER. YOU CALL THEM YOUR FRIENDS...?
ARE YOU SERIOUS?
THESE ARE THE GUYS WHO PICK ON YOU EVERY DAY!
THEY WEREN'T PICKING ON ME.....
THEY WERE TEACHING ME TO BE A MAN...
WELL, WHATEVER....
BUT REMEMBER, YUGI! YOU STILL HAVE TO PAY WHAT YOU OWE!
BODYGUARD CHARGES... 200,000 YEN!

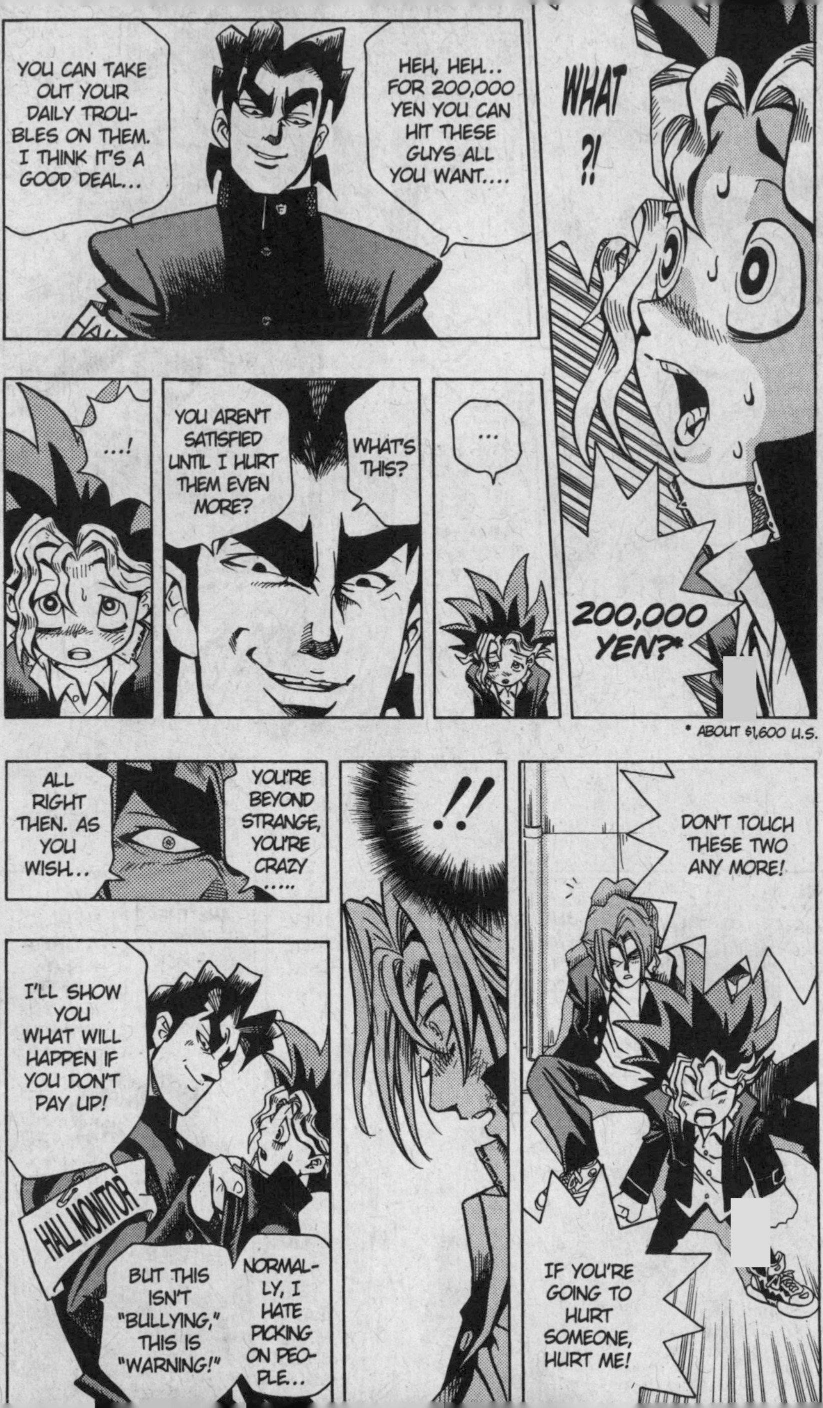
HEH, HEH.. FOR 200,000 YEN YOU CAN HIT THESE GUYS ALL YOU WANT....
YOU CAN TAKE OUT YOUR DAILY TROUBLES ON THEM. I THINK IT'S A GOOD DEAL...
WHAT ?!
200,000 YEN?*
...
WHAT'S THIS?
YOU AREN'T SATISFIED UNTIL I HURT THEM EVEN MORE?
...!
* ABOUT $1,600 U.S.
DON'T TOUCH THESE TWO ANY MORE!
IF YOU'RE GOING TO HURT SOMEONE, HURT ME!
!!
YOU'RE BEYOND STRANGE, YOU'RE CRAZY .....
ALL RIGHT THEN. AS YOU WISH...
I'LL SHOW YOU WHAT WILL HAPPEN IF YOU DON'T PAY UP!
HALL MONITOR
NORMALLY, I HATE PICKING ON PEOPLE...
BUT THIS ISN'T "BULLYING," THIS IS "WARNING!"

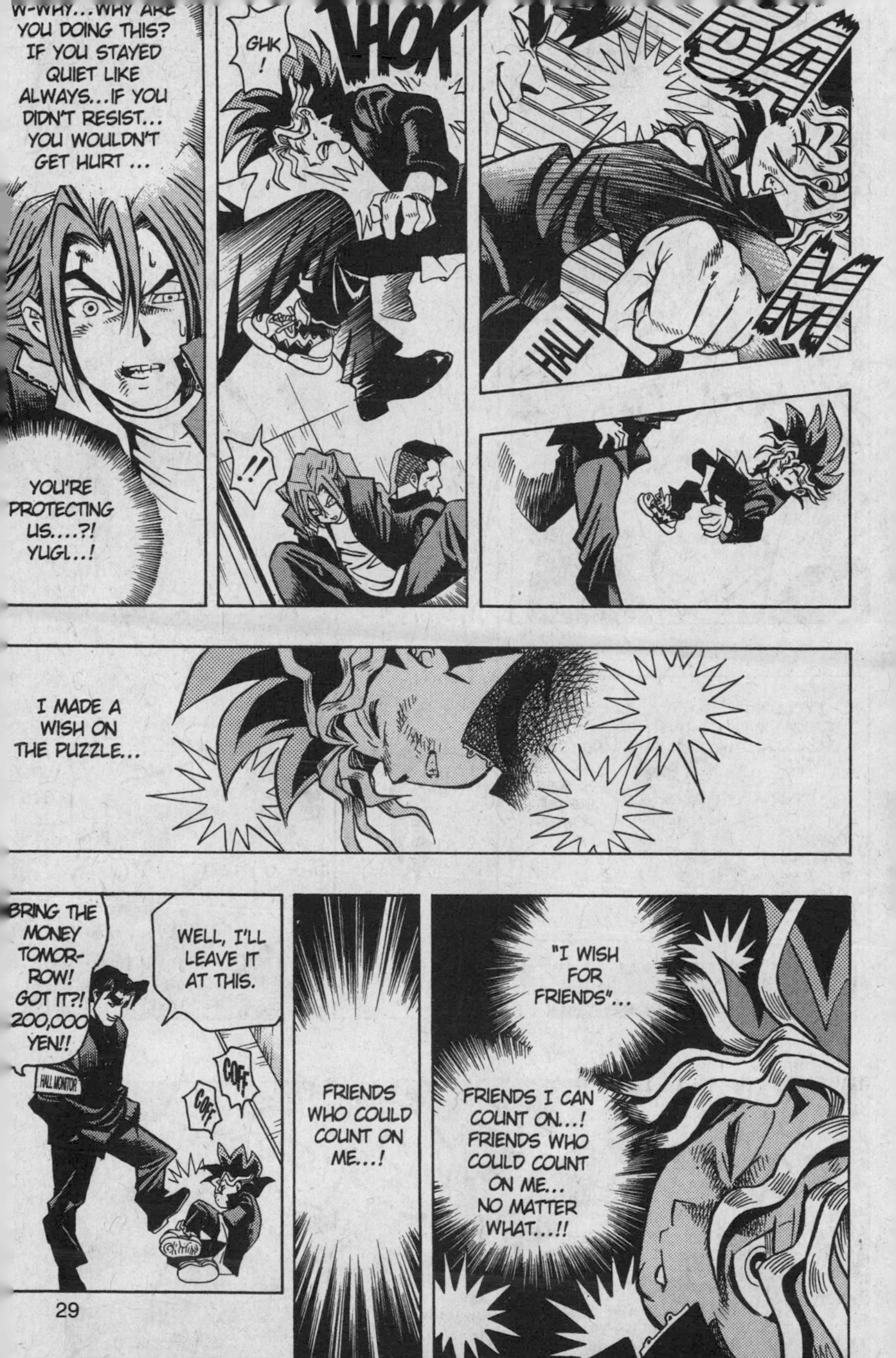
DAM
HALL M
HOK
GHK!
!!
W-WHY... WHY ARE YOU DOING THIS? IF YOU STAYED QUIET LIKE ALWAYS... IF YOU DIDN'T RESIST... YOU WOULDN'T GET HURT ...
YOU'RE PROTECTING US....?! YUGI...!
I MADE A WISH ON THE PUZZLE...
"I WISH FOR FRIENDS"...
FRIENDS I CAN COUNT ON...! FRIENDS WHO COULD COUNT ON ME... NO MATTER WHAT...!!
FRIENDS WHO COULD COUNT ON ME...!
WELL, I'LL LEAVE IT AT THIS.
BRING THE MONEY TOMOR-ROW! GOT IT?! 200,000 YEN!!
HALL MONITOR
COFF
COFF

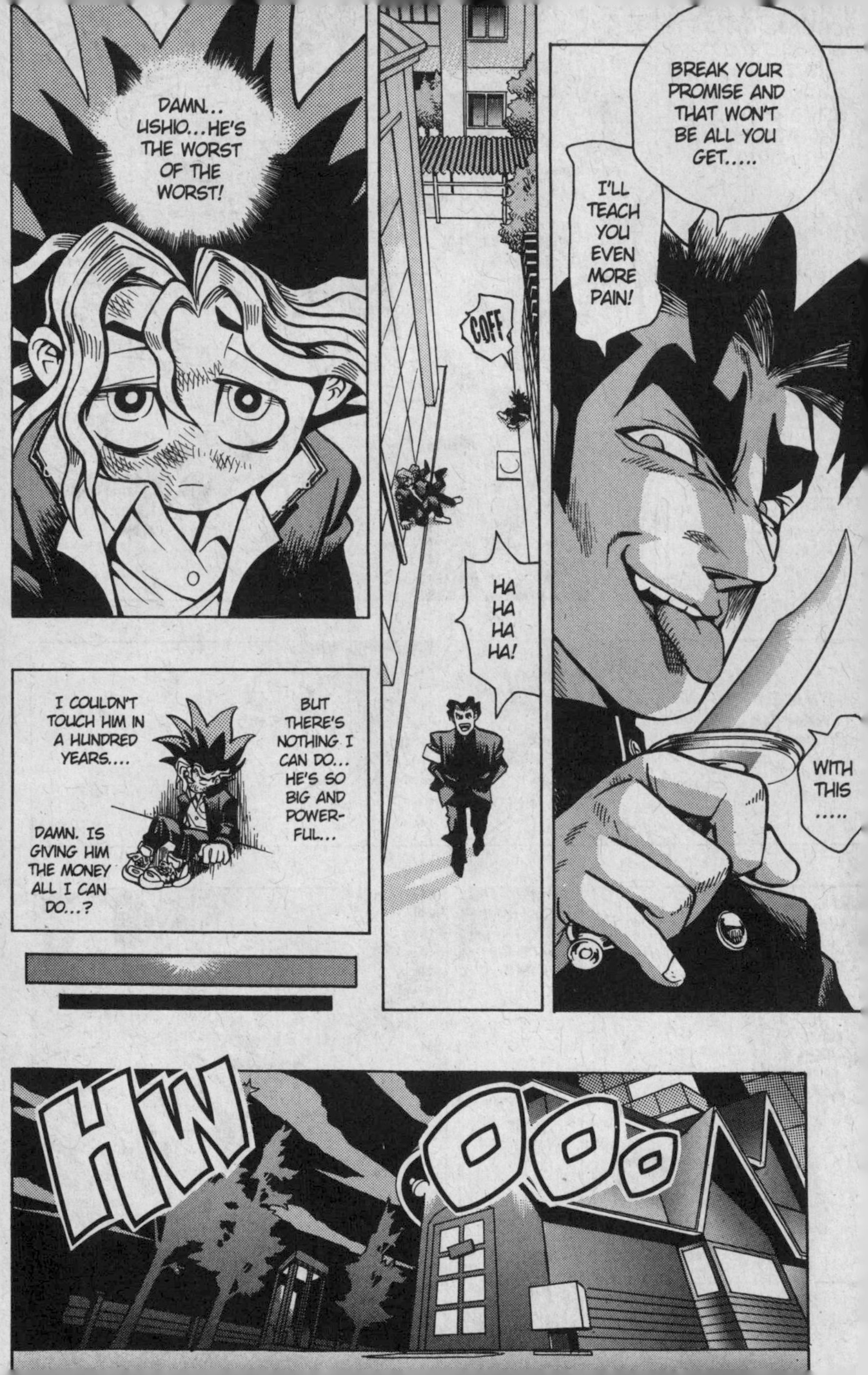
BREAK YOUR PROMISE AND THAT WON'T BE ALL YOU GET.....
I'LL TEACH YOU EVEN MORE PAIN!
WITH THIS .....
COFF
HA HA HA HA!
DAMN... USHIO...HE'S THE WORST OF THE WORST!
BUT THERE'S NOTHING I CAN DO... HE'S SO BIG AND POWERFUL...
I COULDN'T TOUCH HIM IN A HUNDRED YEARS....
DAMN. IS GIVING HIM THE MONEY ALL I CAN DO...?
HWOOO

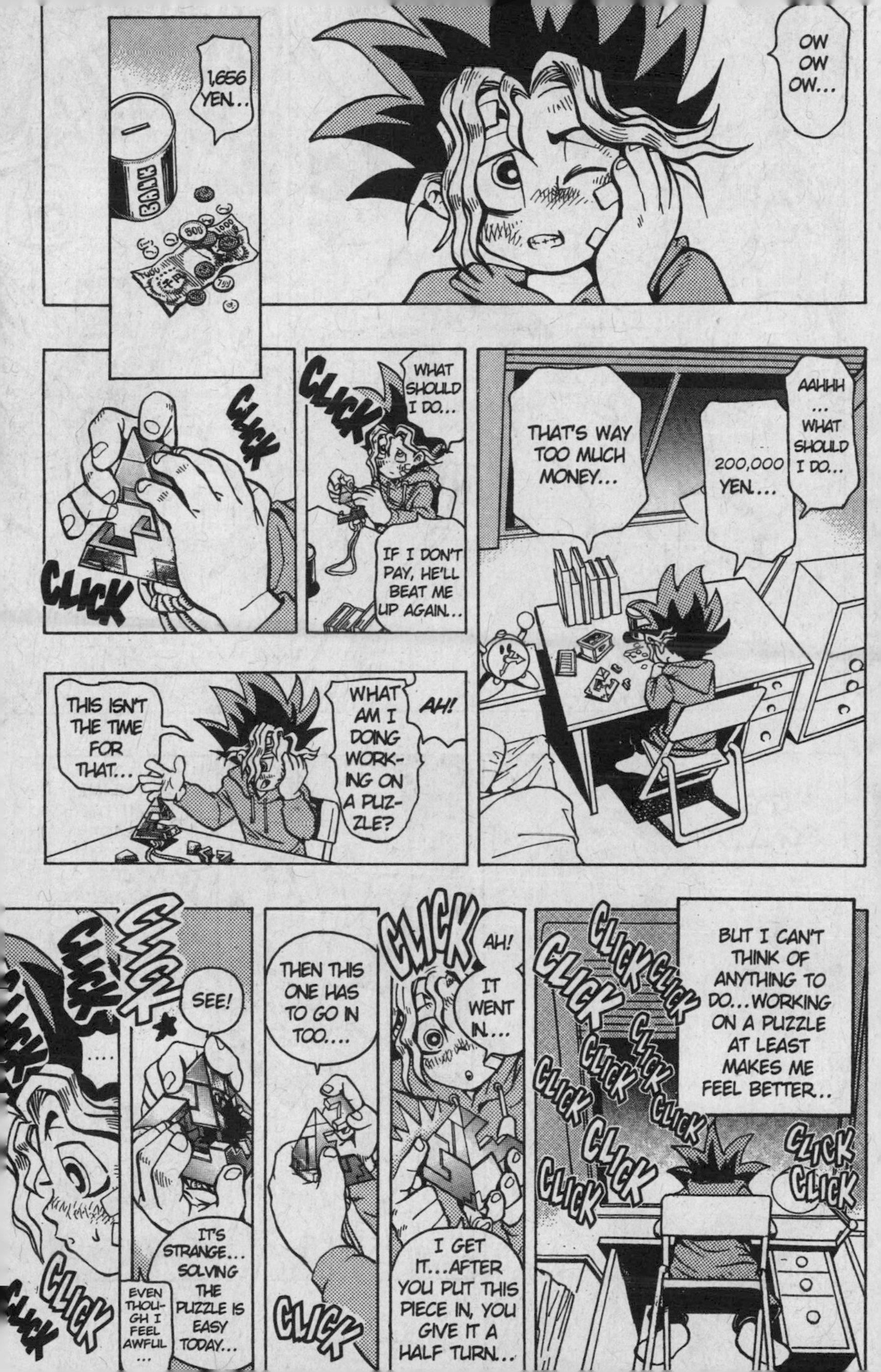
OW OW OW...
1,656 YEN...
BANK
AAHHH... WHAT SHOULD I DO...
200,000 YEN....
THAT'S WAY TOO MUCH MONEY...
WHAT SHOULD I DO...
CLICK
IF I DON'T PAY, HE'LL BEAT ME UP AGAIN...
CLICK
CLICK
AH!
WHAT AM I DOING WORK-ING ON A PUZ-ZLE?
THIS ISN'T THE TIME FOR THAT...
BUT I CAN'T THINK OF ANYTHING TO DO...WORKING ON A PUZZLE AT LEAST MAKES ME FEEL BETTER...
CLICK CLICK CLICK CLICK CLICK CLICK CLICK CLICK CLICK
CLICK CLICK
AH!
IT WENT IN....
CLICK
THEN THIS ONE HAS TO GO IN TOO....
I GET IT...AFTER YOU PUT THIS PIECE IN, YOU GIVE IT A HALF TURN...
CLICK
CLICK
SEE!
IT'S STRANGE... SOLVING THE PUZZLE IS EASY TODAY...
EVEN THOUGH I FEEL AWFUL...
CLICK
....
CLICK
CLICK

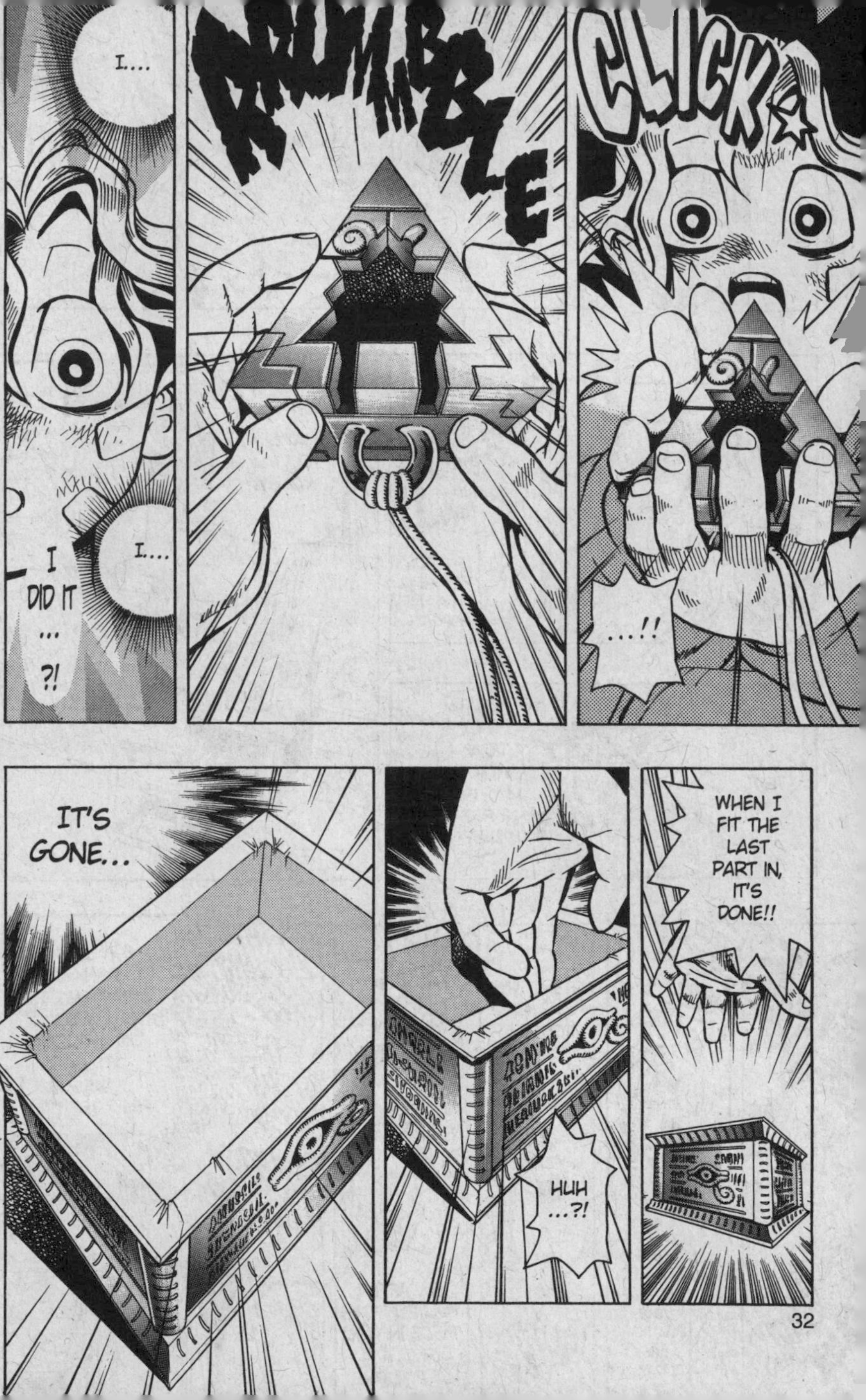
CLICK
...!!
RUMBLE
I...
I...
I DID IT...?!
WHEN I FIT THE LAST PART IN, IT'S DONE!!
HUH...?!
IT'S GONE...

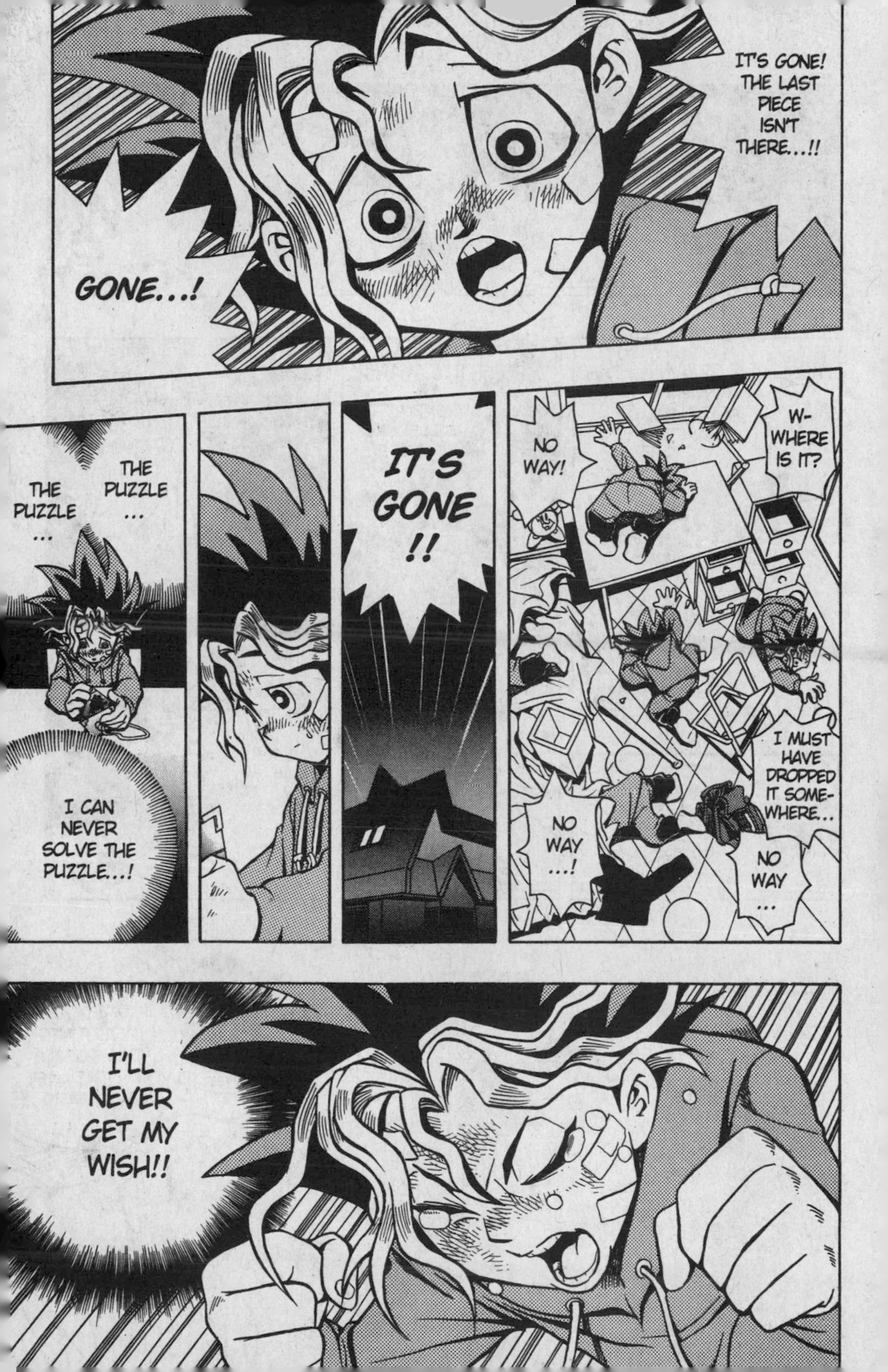
IT'S GONE! THE LAST PIECE ISN'T THERE...!!
GONE...!
W-WHERE IS IT?
NO WAY!
I MUST HAVE DROPPED IT SOMEWHERE...
NO WAY...
NO WAY...!
IT'S GONE!!
THE PUZZLE...
THE PUZZLE...
I CAN NEVER SOLVE THE PUZZLE...!
I'LL NEVER GET MY WISH!!

READ THIS WAY

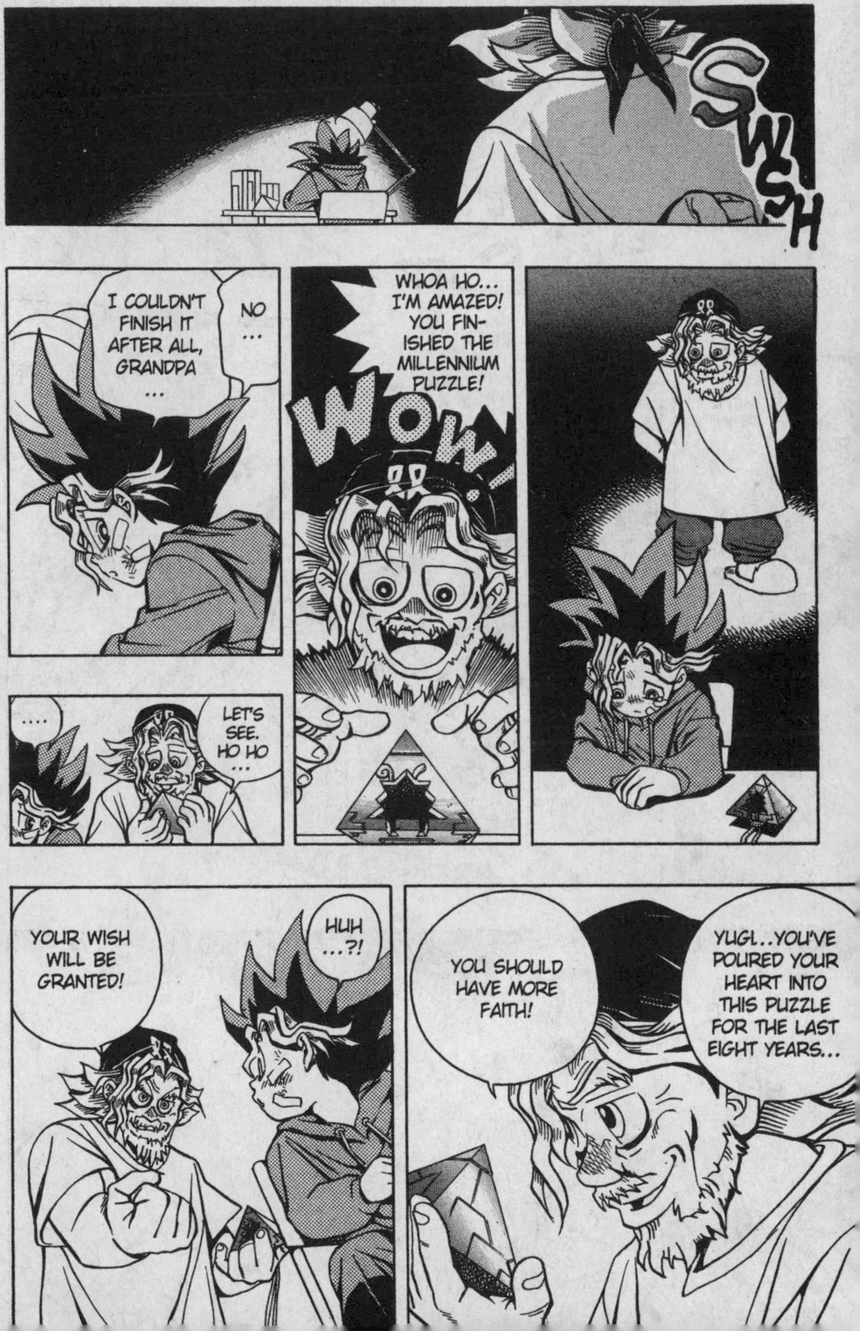
SWSH
I COULDN'T FINISH IT AFTER ALL, GRANDPA ...
NO ...
....
LET'S SEE. HO HO ...
WHOA HO... I'M AMAZED! YOU FIN-ISHED THE MILLENNIUM PUZZLE!
WOW!
YUGI...YOU'VE POURED YOUR HEART INTO THIS PUZZLE FOR THE LAST EIGHT YEARS...
YOU SHOULD HAVE MORE FAITH!
HUH ...?!
YOUR WISH WILL BE GRANTED!

READ THIS WAY

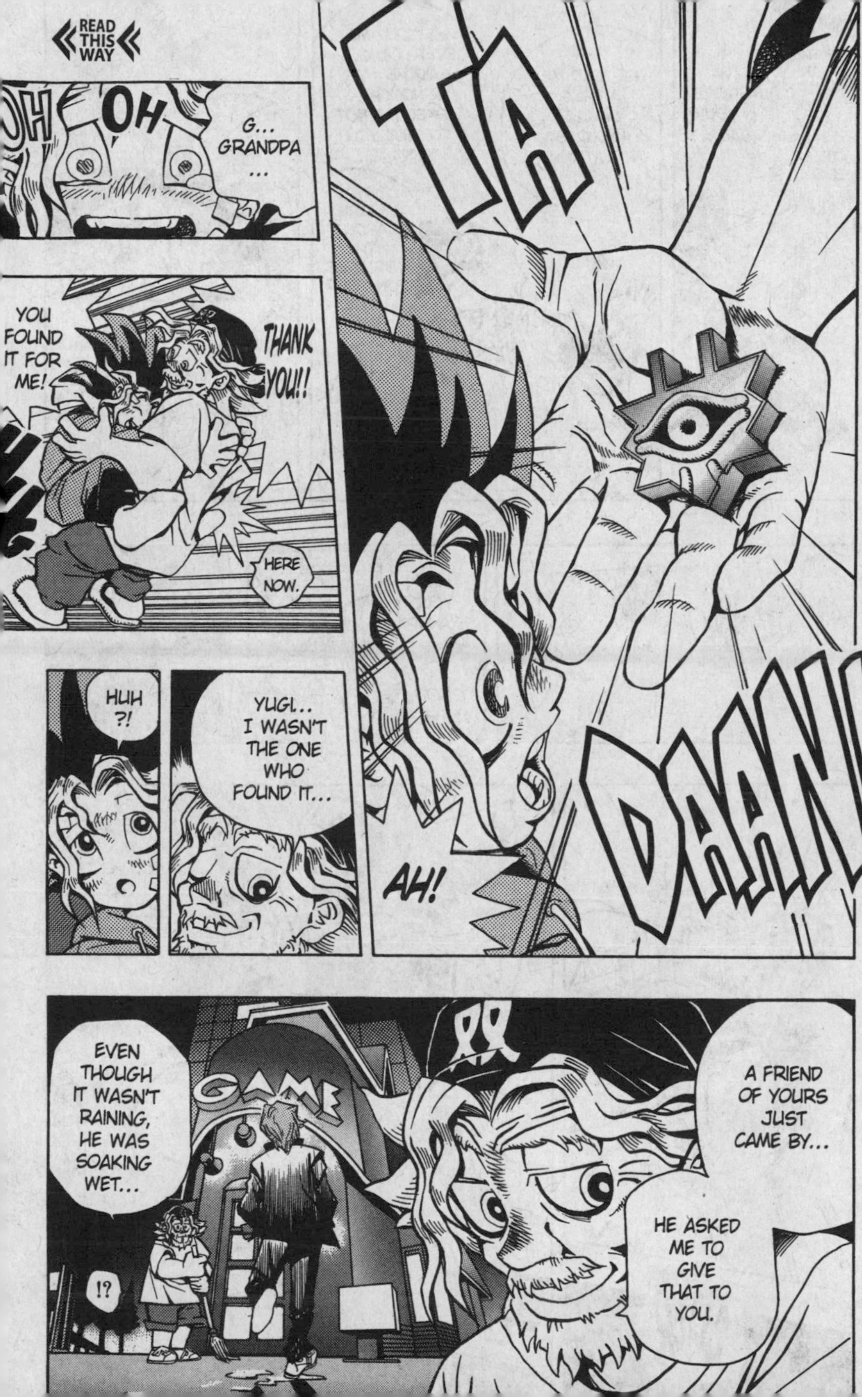
TA
DAAN!
AH!
OH OH
G... GRANDPA ...
YOU FOUND IT FOR ME!
THANK YOU!!
HERE NOW.
YUGI... I WASN'T THE ONE WHO FOUND IT...
HUH ?!
A FRIEND OF YOURS JUST CAME BY...
HE ASKED ME TO GIVE THAT TO YOU.
EVEN THOUGH IT WASN'T RAINING, HE WAS SOAKING WET...
GAME
!?

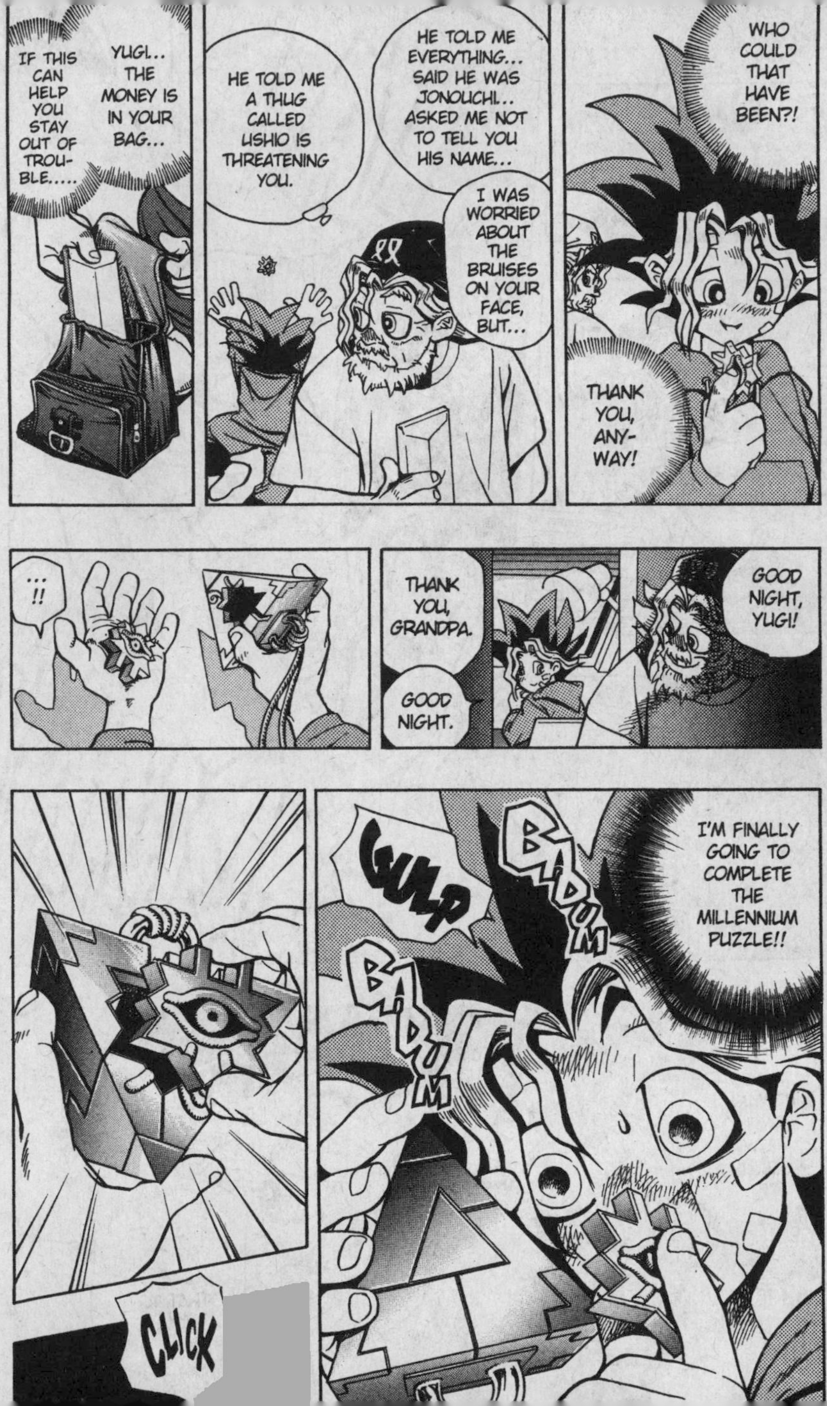
WHO COULD THAT HAVE BEEN?!
THANK YOU, ANY-WAY!
HE TOLD ME EVERYTHING... SAID HE WAS JONOUCHI.. ASKED ME NOT TO TELL YOU HIS NAME...
HE TOLD ME A THUG CALLED USHIO IS THREATENING YOU.
I WAS WORRIED ABOUT THE BRUISES ON YOUR FACE, BUT...
YUGI... THE MONEY IS IN YOUR BAG...
IF THIS CAN HELP YOU STAY OUT OF TROU-BLE.....
GOOD NIGHT, YUGI!
THANK YOU, GRANDPA.
GOOD NIGHT.
... !!
I'M FINALLY GOING TO COMPLETE THE MILLENNIUM PUZZLE!!
BADUM
GULP
BADUM
CLICK

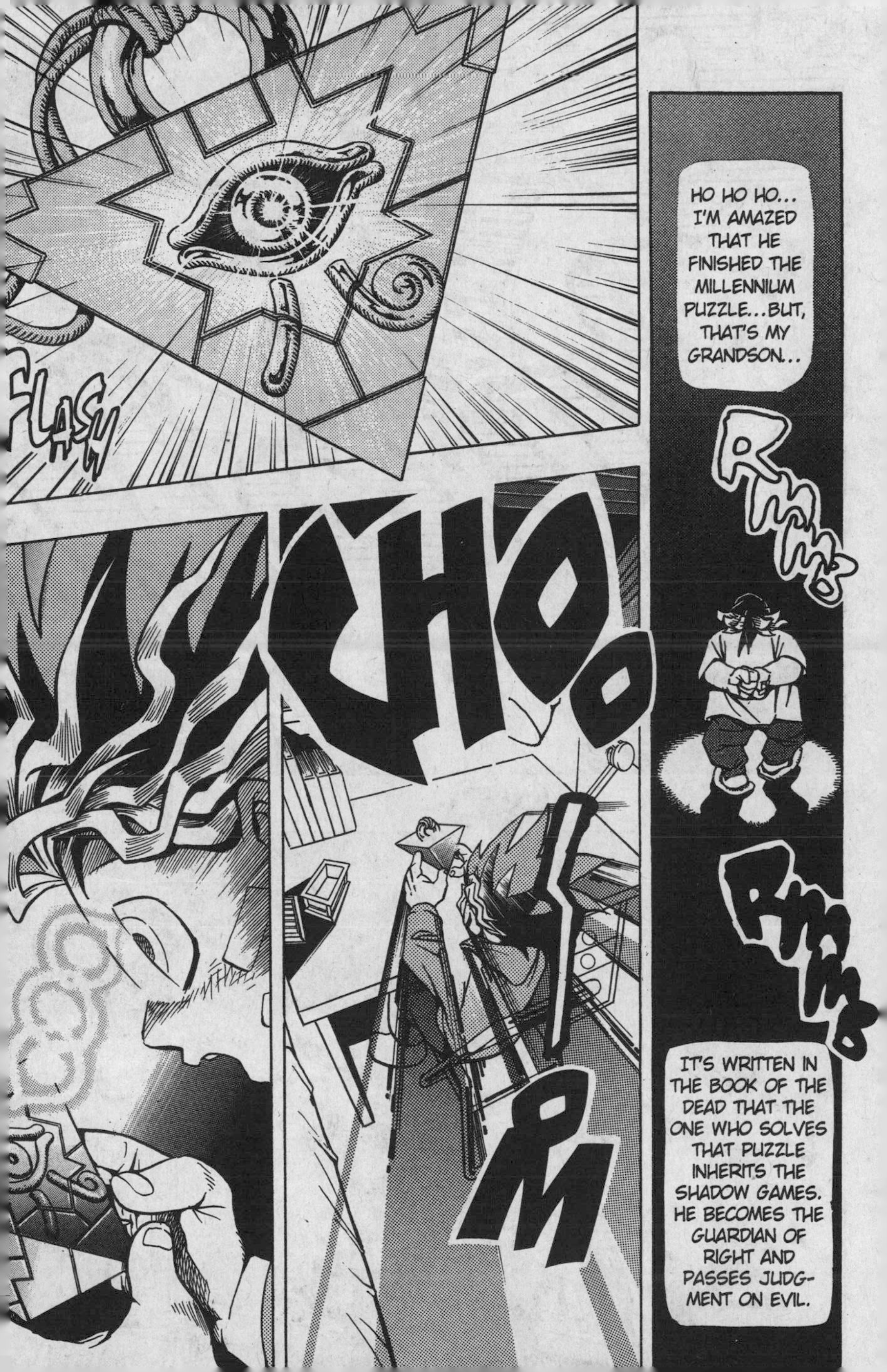
HO HO HO... I'M AMAZED THAT HE FINISHED THE MILLENNIUM PUZZLE...BUT, THAT'S MY GRANDSON...
IT'S WRITTEN IN THE BOOK OF THE DEAD THAT THE ONE WHO SOLVES THAT PUZZLE INHERITS THE SHADOW GAMES. HE BECOMES THE GUARDIAN OF RIGHT AND PASSES JUDG-MENT ON EVIL.
FLASH

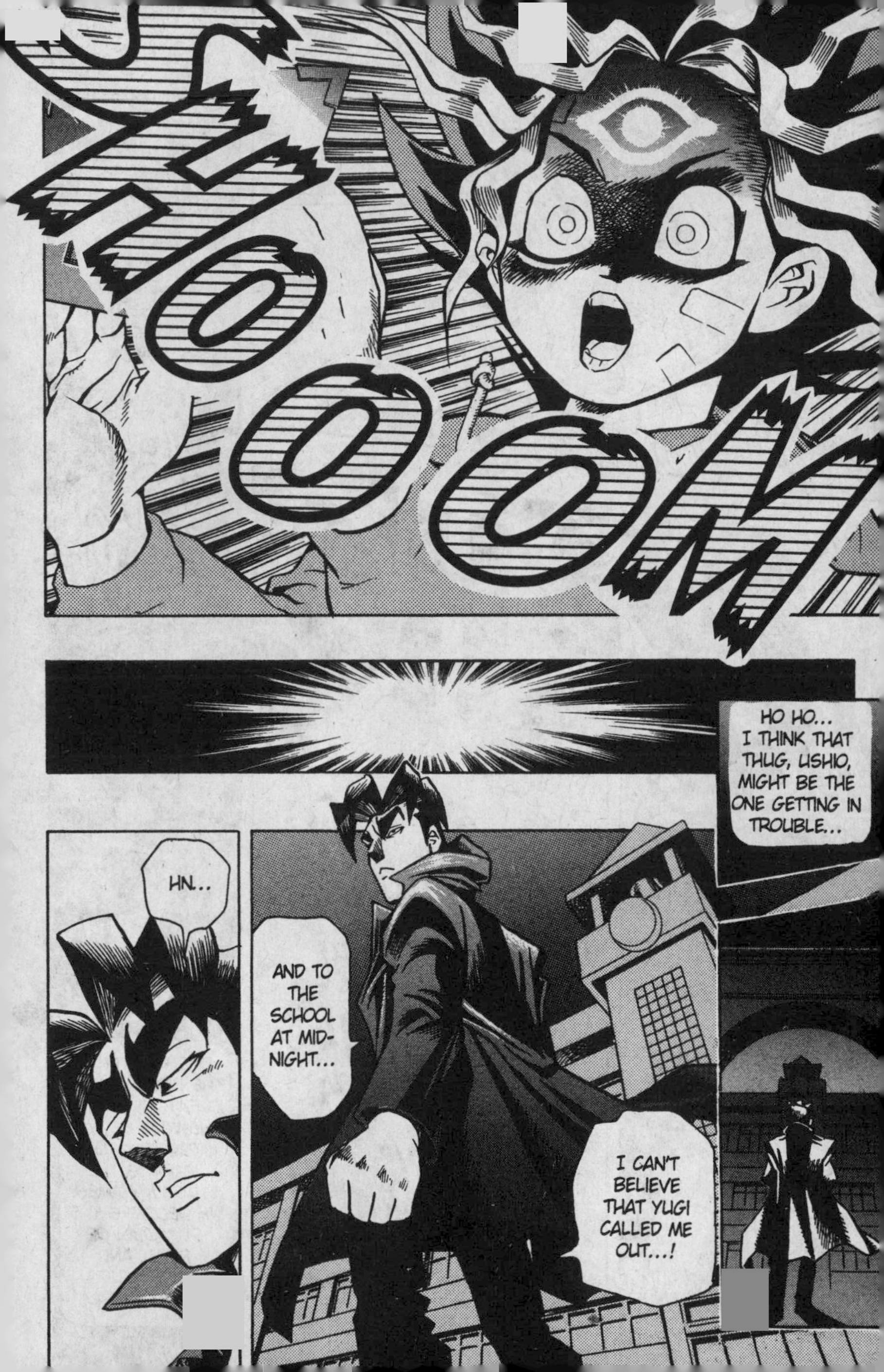

HO HO... I THINK THAT THUG, USHIO, MIGHT BE THE ONE GETTING IN TROUBLE...
I CAN'T BELIEVE THAT YUGI CALLED ME OUT...!
AND TO THE SCHOOL AT MID-NIGHT...
HN...

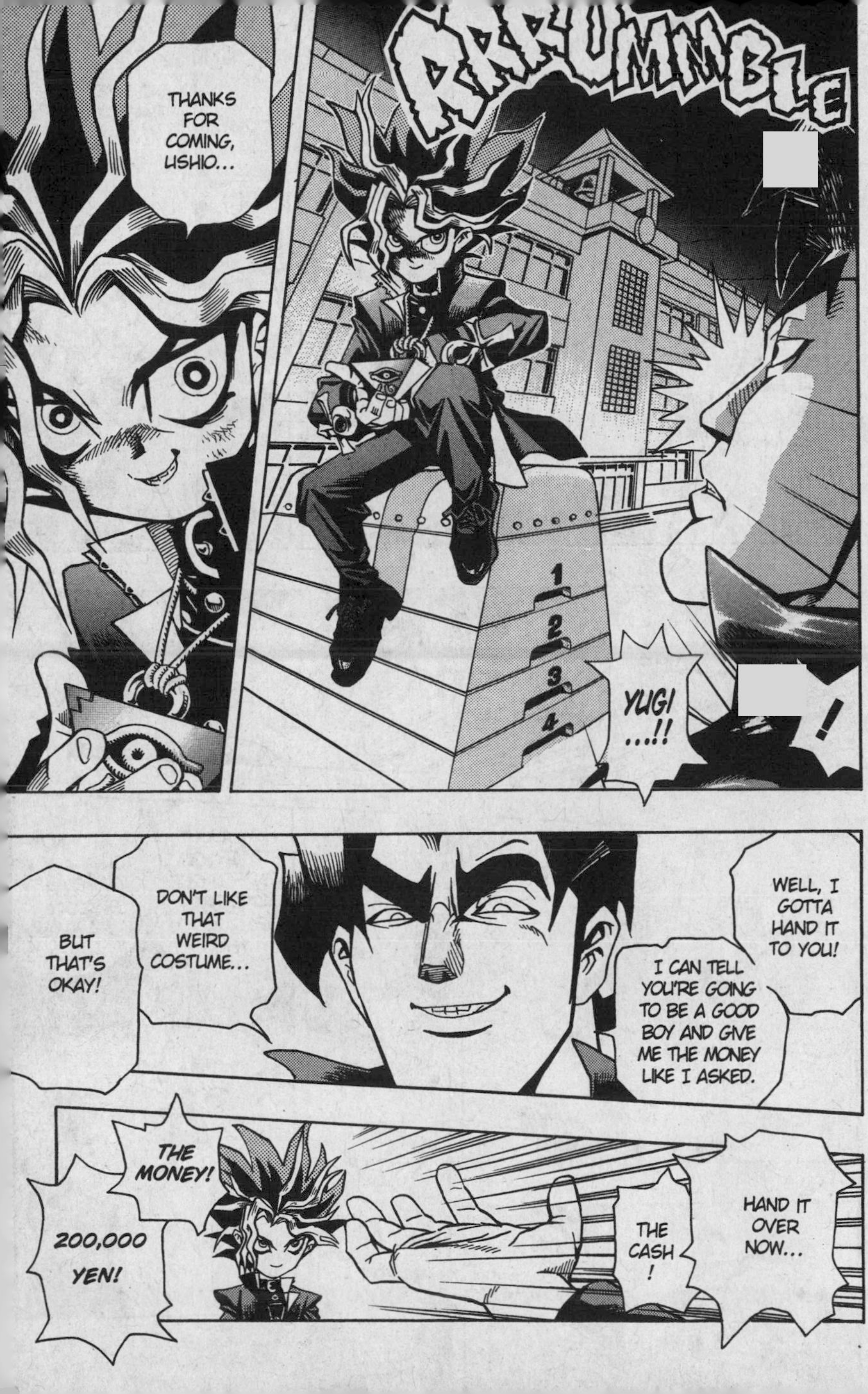
RRRUMMBLE
YUGI ...!!
THANKS FOR COMING, USHIO...
WELL, I GOTTA HAND IT TO YOU!
I CAN TELL YOU'RE GOING TO BE A GOOD BOY AND GIVE ME THE MONEY LIKE I ASKED.
DON'T LIKE THAT WEIRD COSTUME...
BUT THAT'S OKAY!
HAND IT OVER NOW...
THE CASH!
THE MONEY!
200,000 YEN!

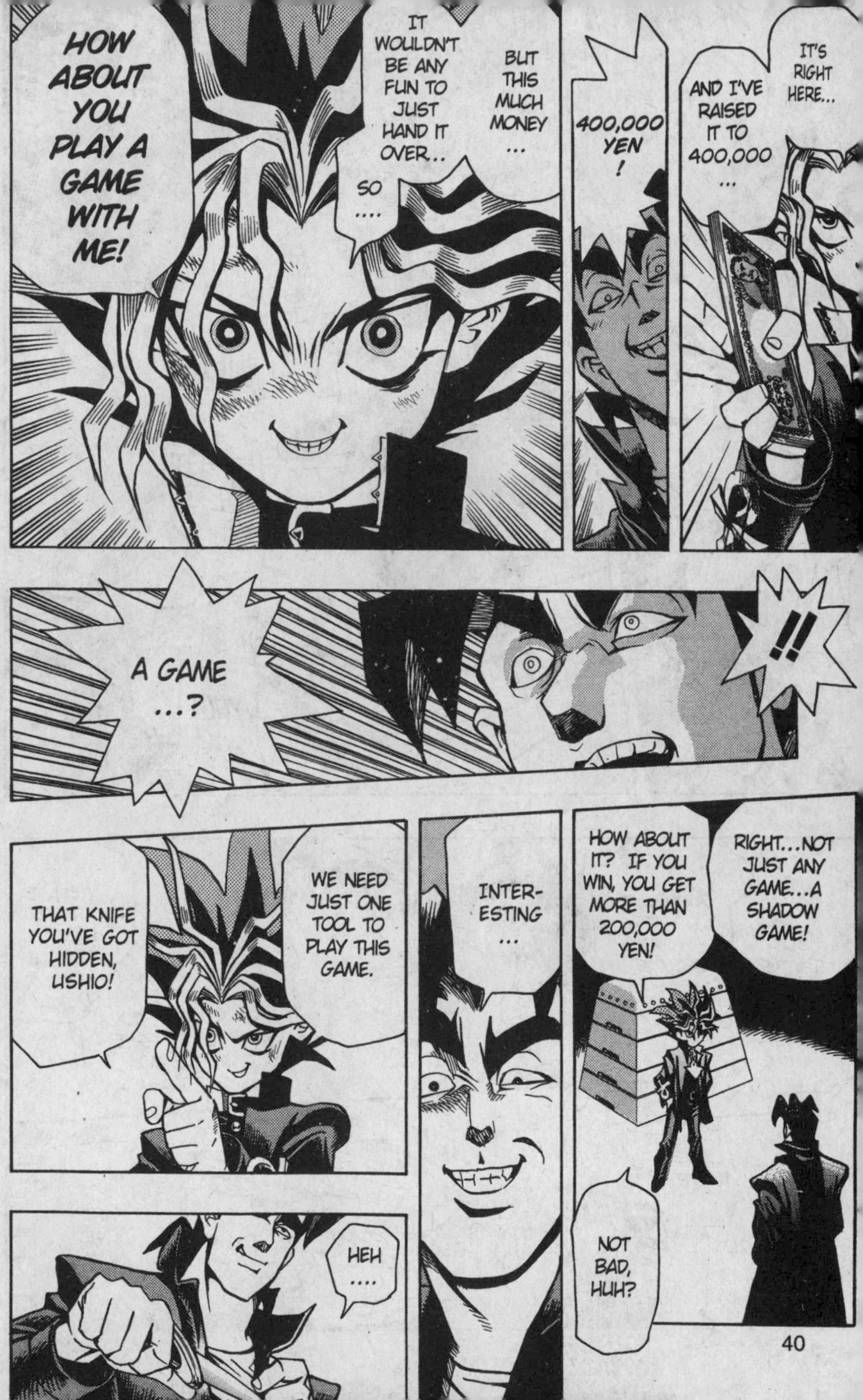
IT'S RIGHT HERE...
AND I'VE RAISED IT TO 400,000 ...
400,000 YEN !
BUT THIS MUCH MONEY ...
IT WOULDN'T BE ANY FUN TO JUST HAND IT OVER...
SO ....
HOW ABOUT YOU PLAY A GAME WITH ME!
!!
A GAME ...?
RIGHT...NOT JUST ANY GAME...A SHADOW GAME!
HOW ABOUT IT? IF YOU WIN, YOU GET MORE THAN 200,000 YEN!
NOT BAD, HUH?
INTER-ESTING ...
WE NEED JUST ONE TOOL TO PLAY THIS GAME.
THAT KNIFE YOU'VE GOT HIDDEN, USHIO!
HEH ....

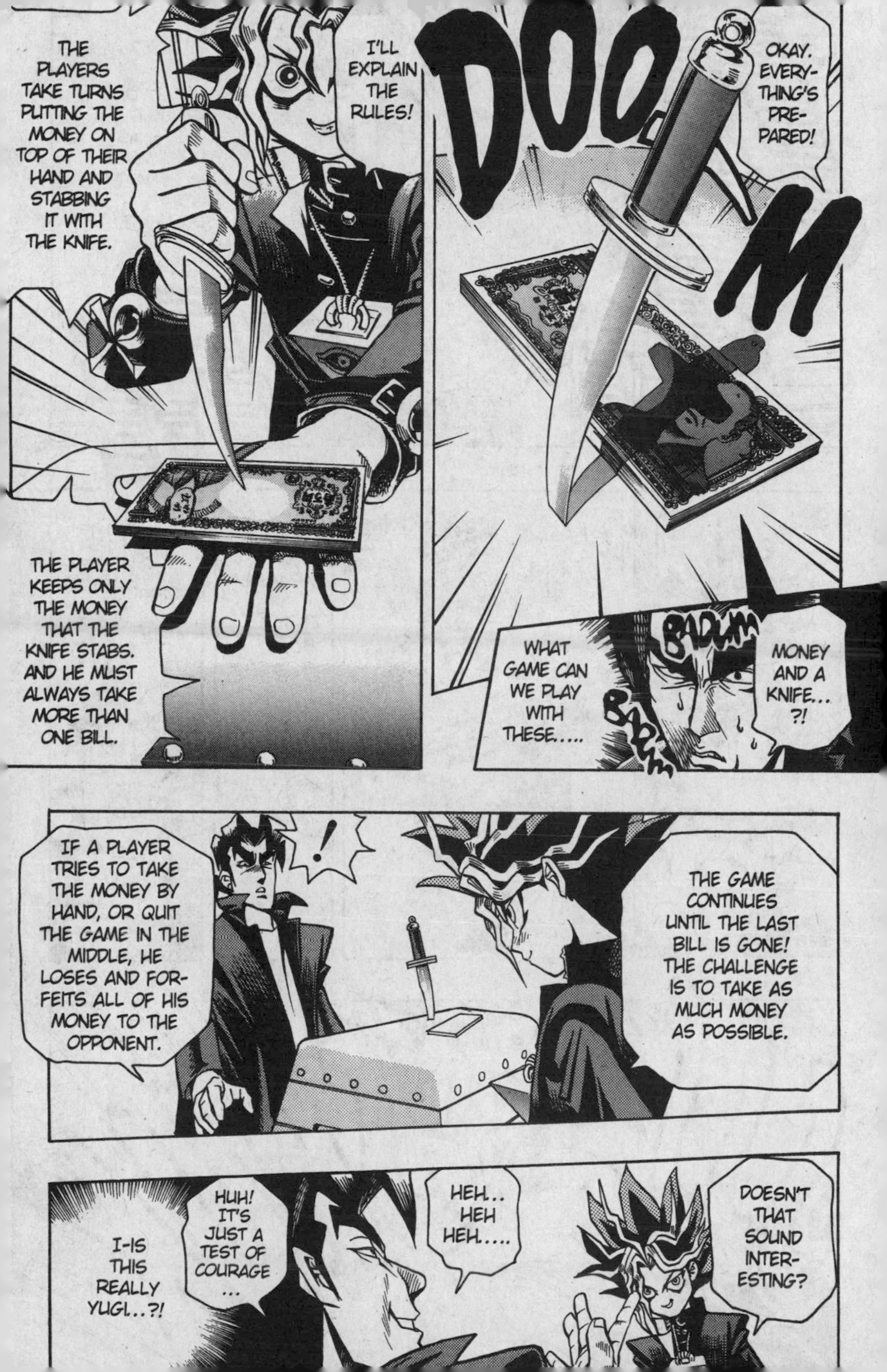
OKAY. EVERYTHING'S PREPARED!
DOOM
MONEY AND A KNIFE...?!
BADUM
BADUM
WHAT GAME CAN WE PLAY WITH THESE.....
I'LL EXPLAIN THE RULES!
THE PLAYERS TAKE TURNS PUTTING THE MONEY ON TOP OF THEIR HAND AND STABBING IT WITH THE KNIFE.
THE PLAYER KEEPS ONLY THE MONEY THAT THE KNIFE STABS. AND HE MUST ALWAYS TAKE MORE THAN ONE BILL.
THE GAME CONTINUES UNTIL THE LAST BILL IS GONE! THE CHALLENGE IS TO TAKE AS MUCH MONEY AS POSSIBLE.
!
IF A PLAYER TRIES TO TAKE THE MONEY BY HAND, OR QUIT THE GAME IN THE MIDDLE, HE LOSES AND FORFEITS ALL OF HIS MONEY TO THE OPPONENT.
DOESN'T THAT SOUND INTERESTING?
HEH.. HEH HEH.....
HUH! IT'S JUST A TEST OF COURAGE ...
I-IS THIS REALLY YUGI...?!

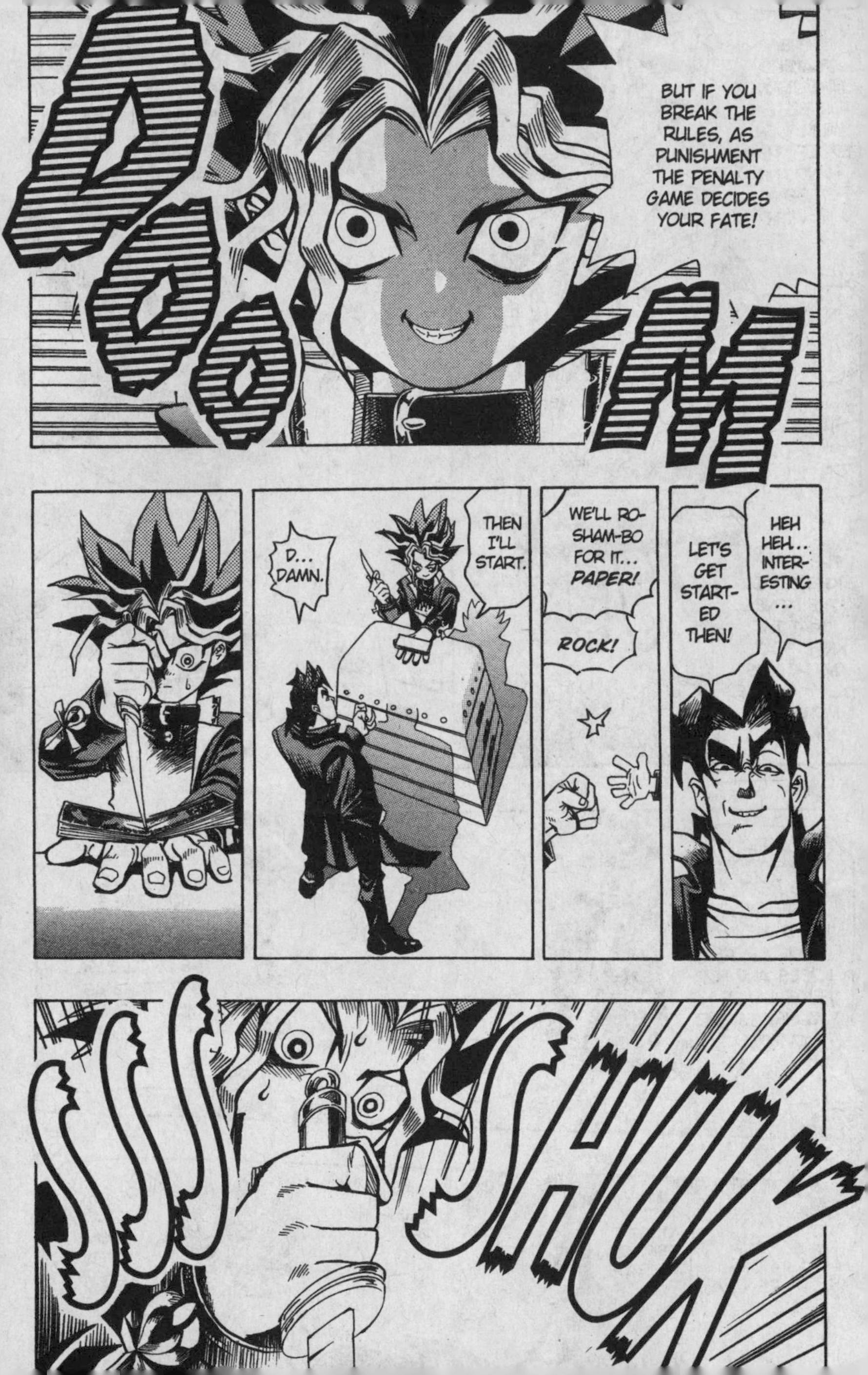
BUT IF YOU BREAK THE RULES, AS PUNISHMENT THE PENALTY GAME DECIDES YOUR FATE!
DOOOM
HEH HEH... INTER-ESTING...
LET'S GET START-ED THEN!
WE'LL RO-SHAM-BO FOR IT... PAPER!
ROCK!
THEN I'LL START.
D... DAMN.
SSSHUK

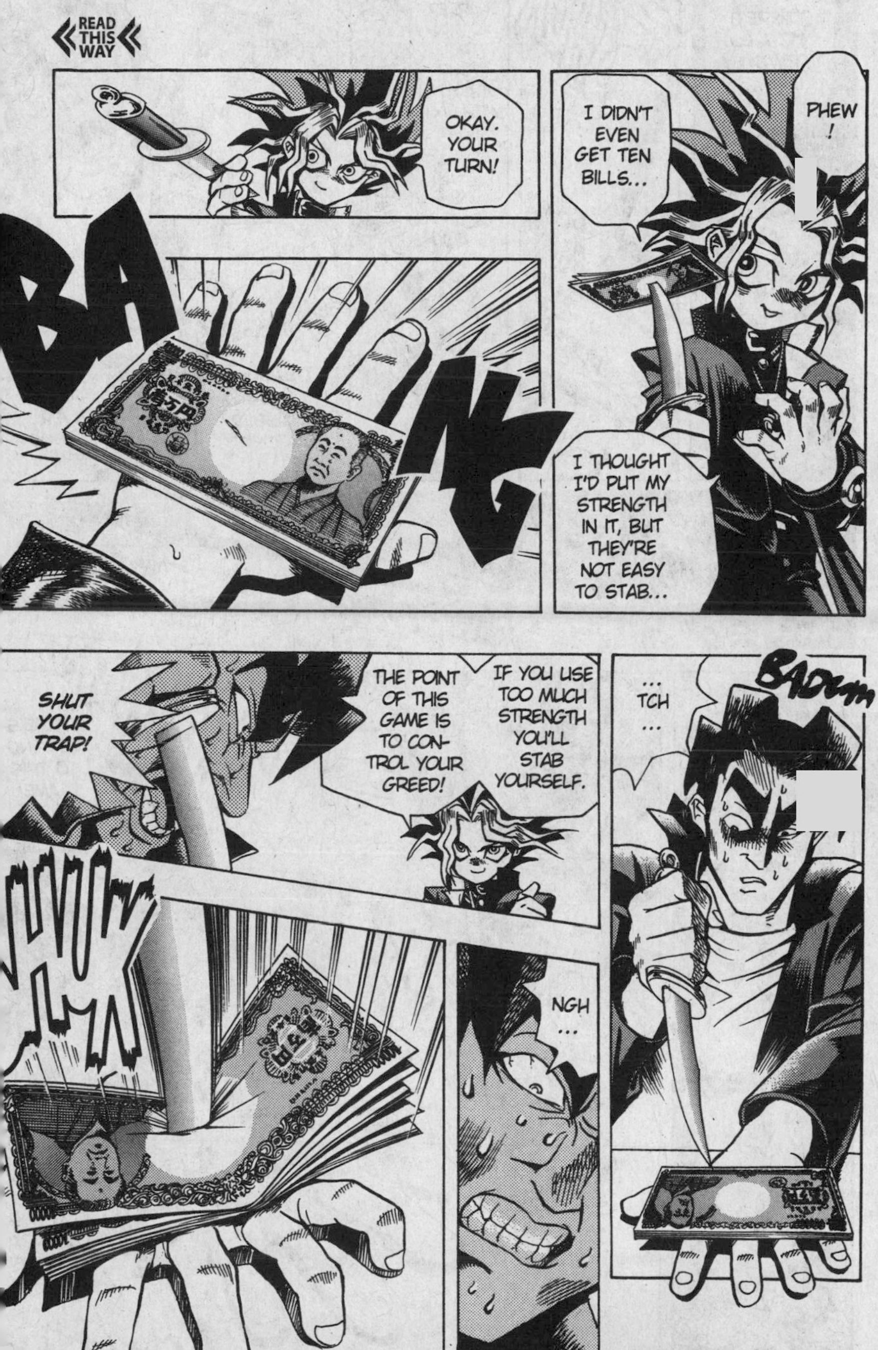
READ THIS WAY
PHEW!
I DIDN'T EVEN GET TEN BILLS...
I THOUGHT I'D PUT MY STRENGTH IN IT, BUT THEY'RE NOT EASY TO STAB...
OKAY. YOUR TURN!
... TCH ...
IF YOU USE TOO MUCH STRENGTH YOU'LL STAB YOURSELF.
THE POINT OF THIS GAME IS TO CONTROL YOUR GREED!
SHUT YOUR TRAP!
NGH ...

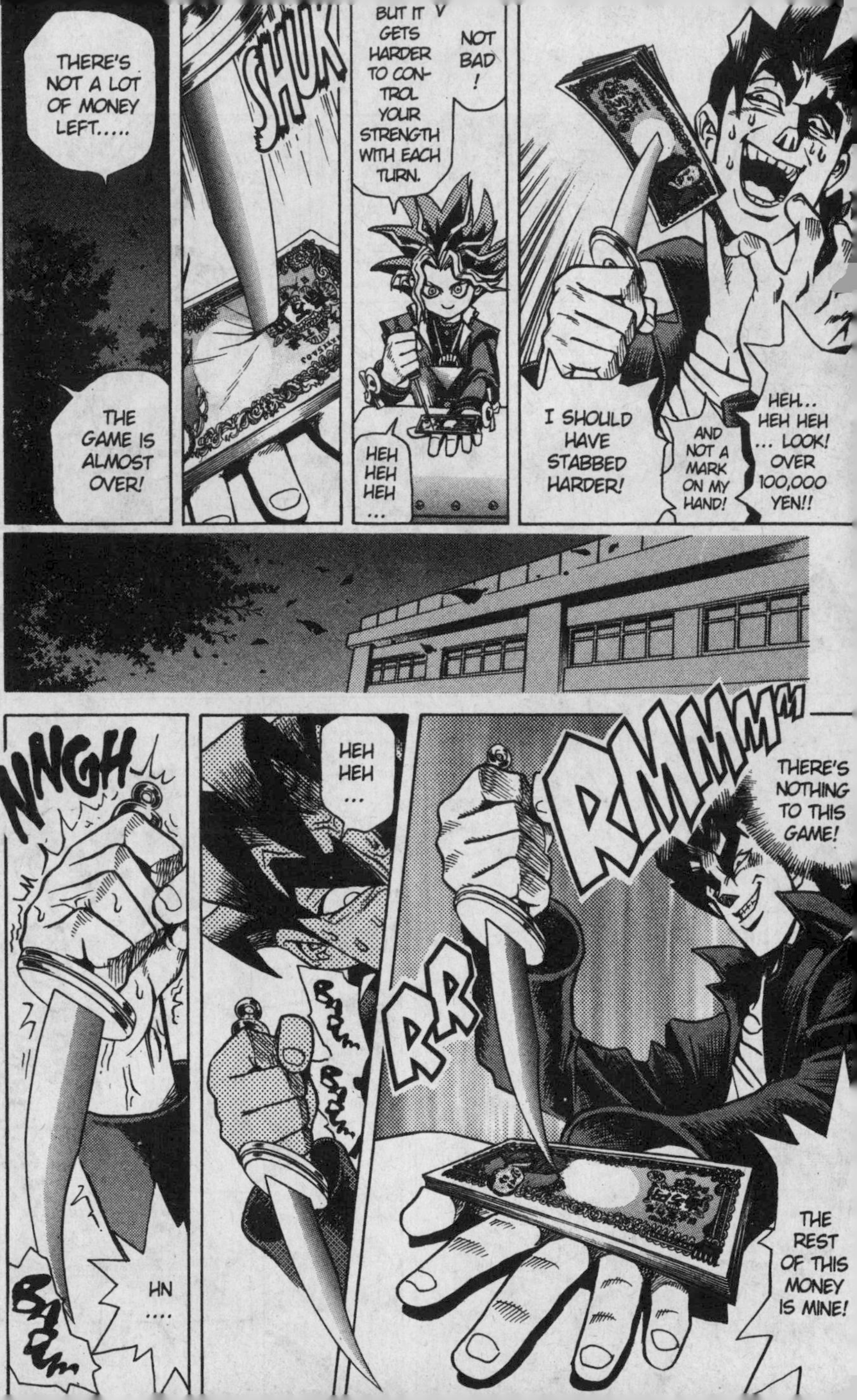
HEH... HEH HEH ... LOOK! OVER 100,000 YEN!!
AND NOT A MARK ON MY HAND!
I SHOULD HAVE STABBED HARDER!
NOT BAD!
BUT IT GETS HARDER TO CONTROL YOUR STRENGTH WITH EACH TURN.
HEH HEH HEH ...
SHUK
THERE'S NOT A LOT OF MONEY LEFT.....
THE GAME IS ALMOST OVER!
RMMMM
THERE'S NOTHING TO THIS GAME!
RR
THE REST OF THIS MONEY IS MINE!
HEH HEH ...
HN ....
NNGH

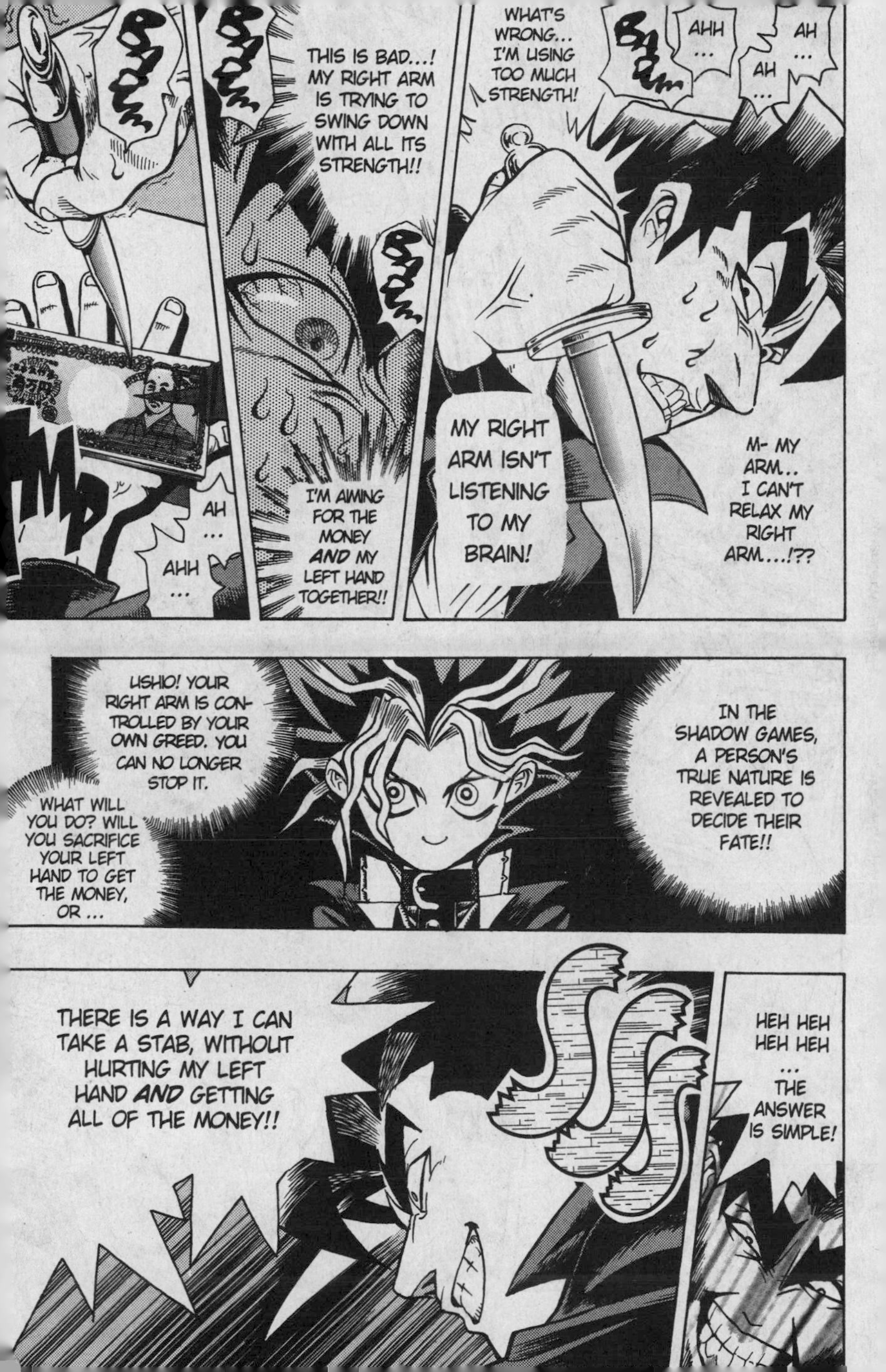
AH ... AH ...
AHH ...
WHAT'S WRONG... I'M USING TOO MUCH STRENGTH!
M- MY ARM.. I CAN'T RELAX MY RIGHT ARM...!??
MY RIGHT ARM ISN'T LISTENING TO MY BRAIN!
THIS IS BAD...! MY RIGHT ARM IS TRYING TO SWING DOWN WITH ALL ITS STRENGTH!!
I'M AIMING FOR THE MONEY *AND* MY LEFT HAND TOGETHER!!
AH ... AHH ...
IN THE SHADOW GAMES, A PERSON'S TRUE NATURE IS REVEALED TO DECIDE THEIR FATE!!
USHIO! YOUR RIGHT ARM IS CONTROLLED BY YOUR OWN GREED. YOU CAN NO LONGER STOP IT.
WHAT WILL YOU DO? WILL YOU SACRIFICE YOUR LEFT HAND TO GET THE MONEY, OR ...
HEH HEH HEH HEH ... THE ANSWER IS SIMPLE!
THERE IS A WAY I CAN TAKE A STAB, WITHOUT HURTING MY LEFT HAND *AND* GETTING ALL OF THE MONEY!!

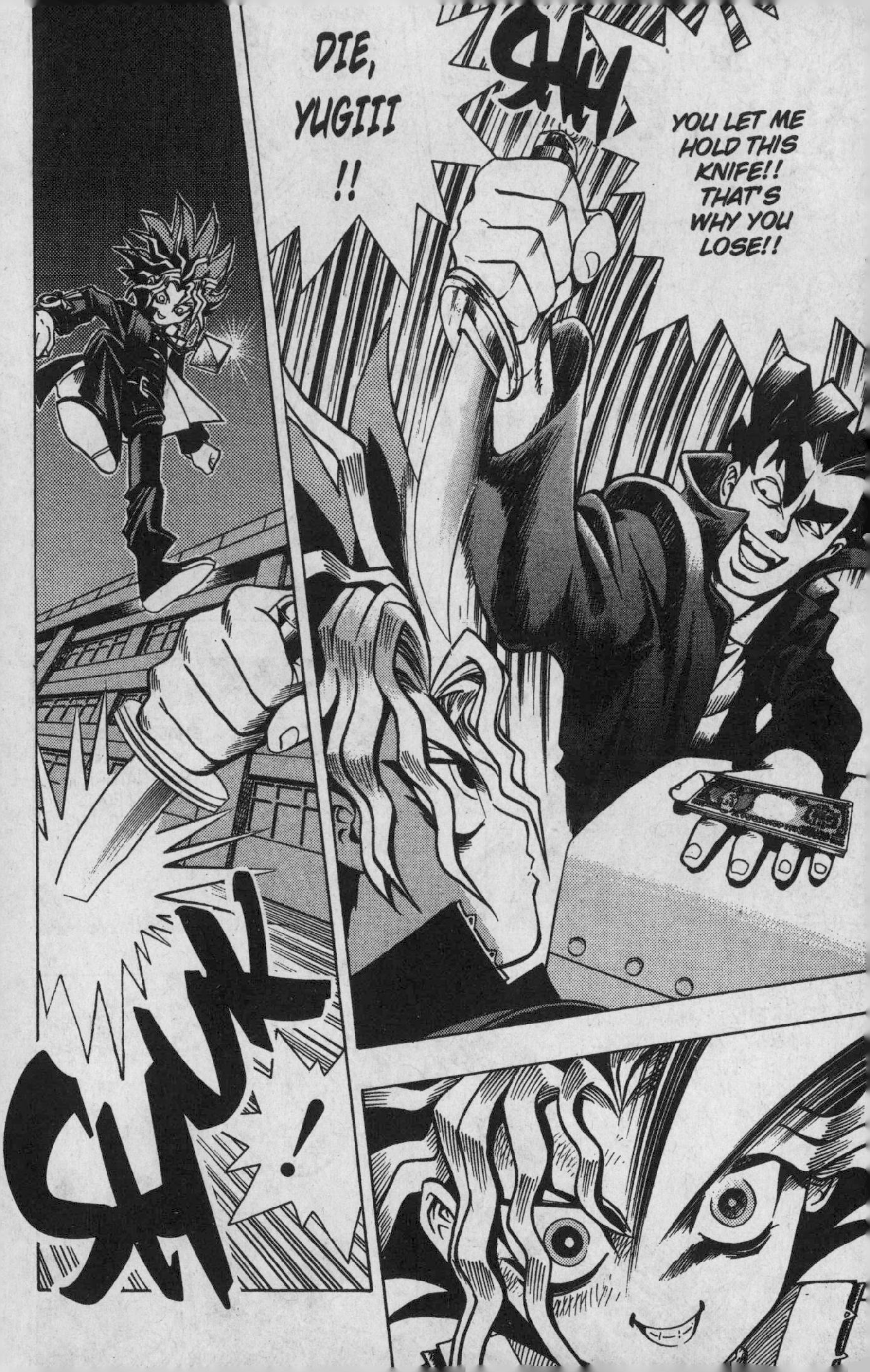
SHH
YOU LET ME HOLD THIS KNIFE!! THAT'S WHY YOU LOSE!!
DIE, YUGIII !!
SHK!

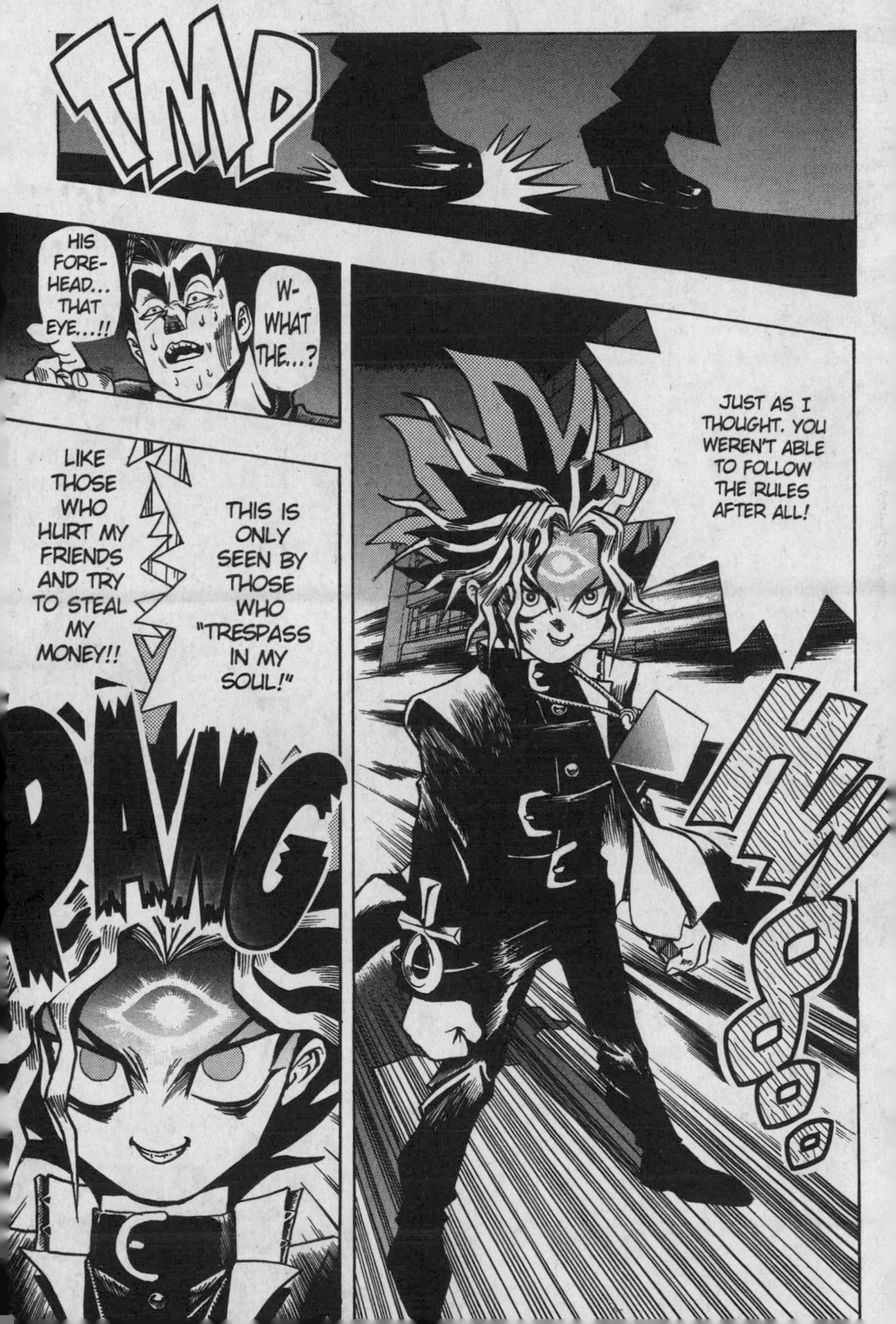
TMP
JUST AS I THOUGHT. YOU WEREN'T ABLE TO FOLLOW THE RULES AFTER ALL!
W-WHAT THE...?
HIS FOREHEAD... THAT EYE...!!
THIS IS ONLY SEEN BY THOSE WHO "TRESPASS IN MY SOUL!"
LIKE THOSE WHO HURT MY FRIENDS AND TRY TO STEAL MY MONEY!!
PAWG

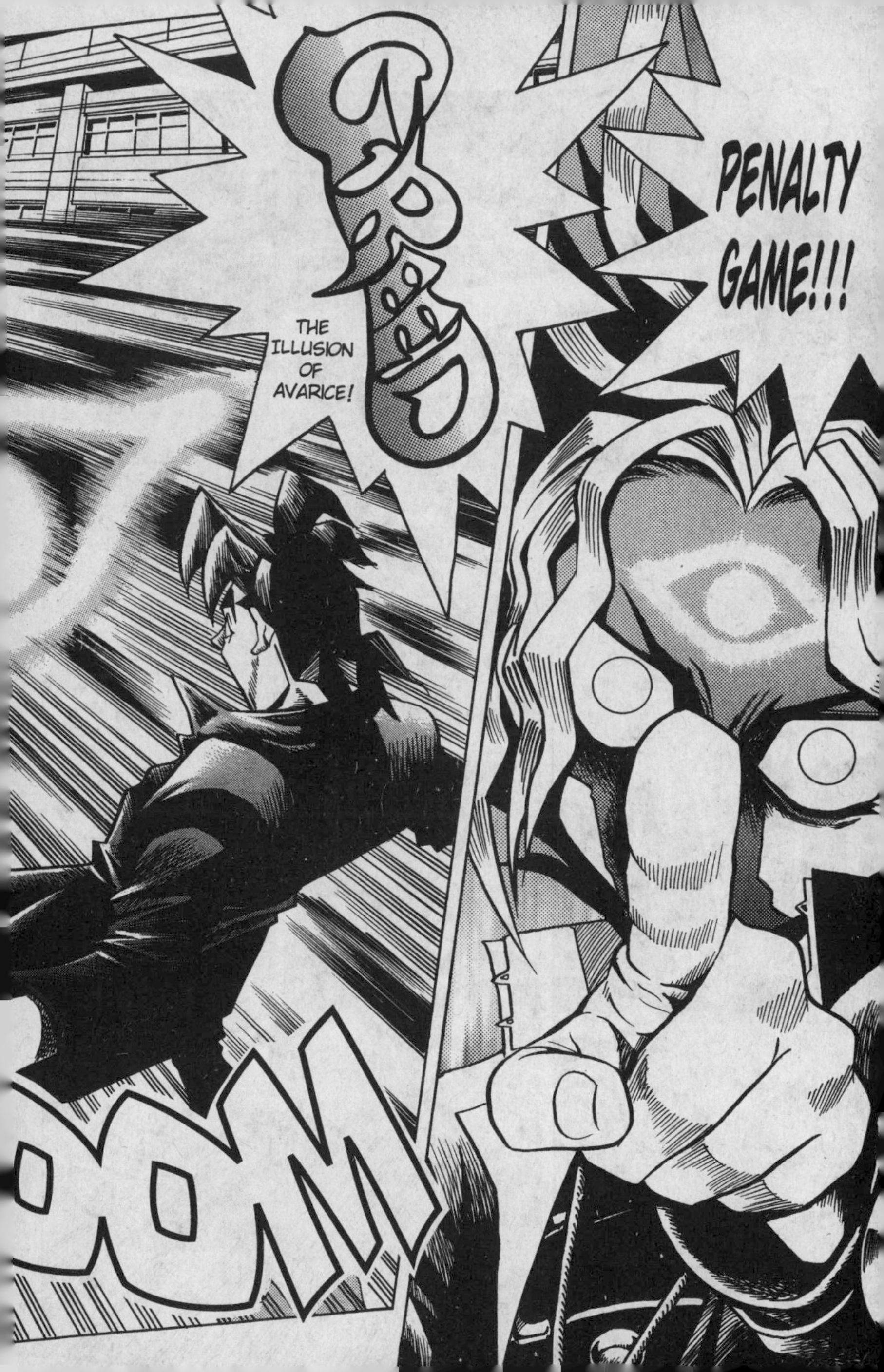
PENALTY GAME!!!
THE ILLUSION OF AVARICE!

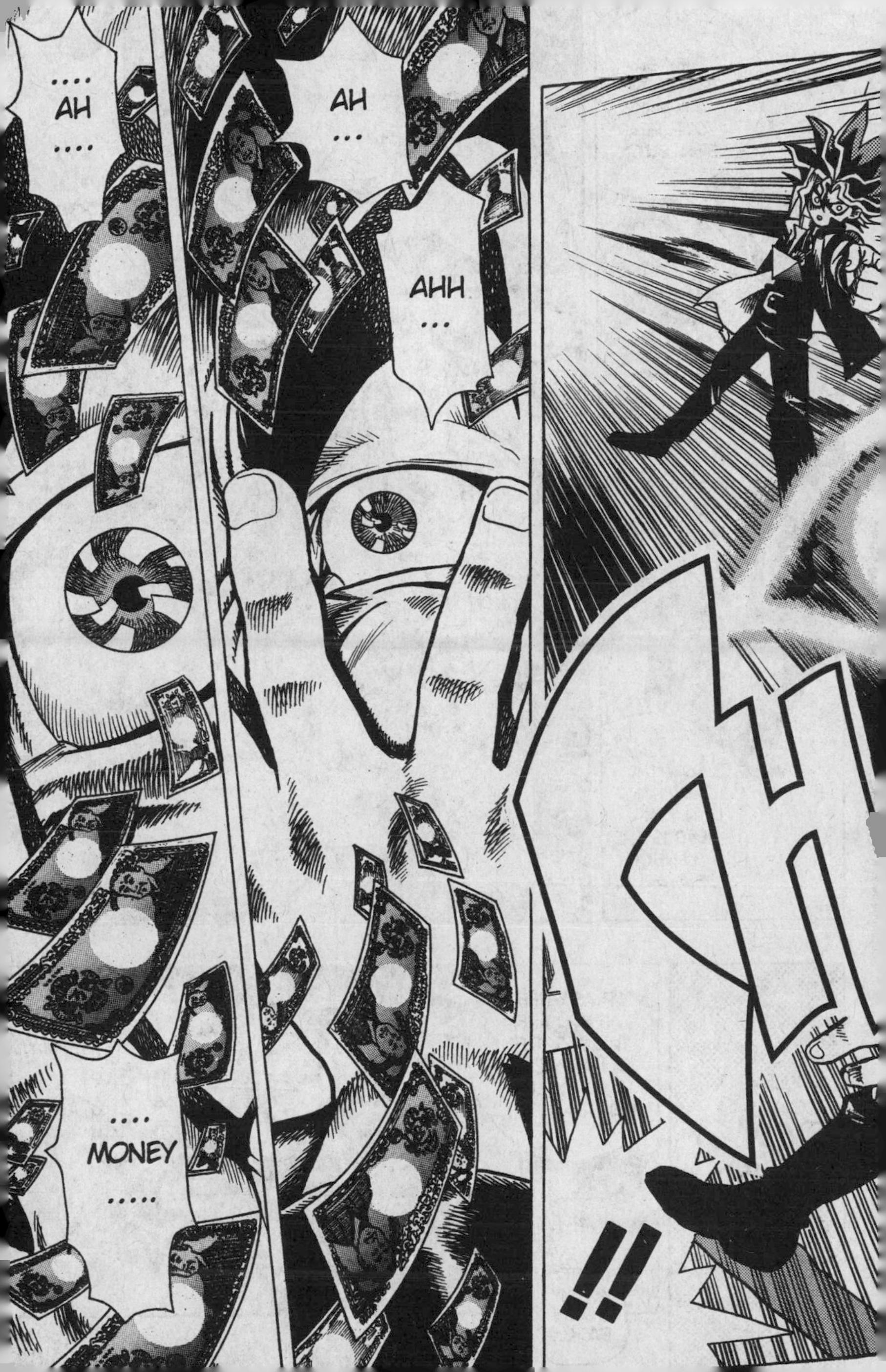
CH
!!
AH ...
AHH ...
.... AH ....
.... MONEY .....

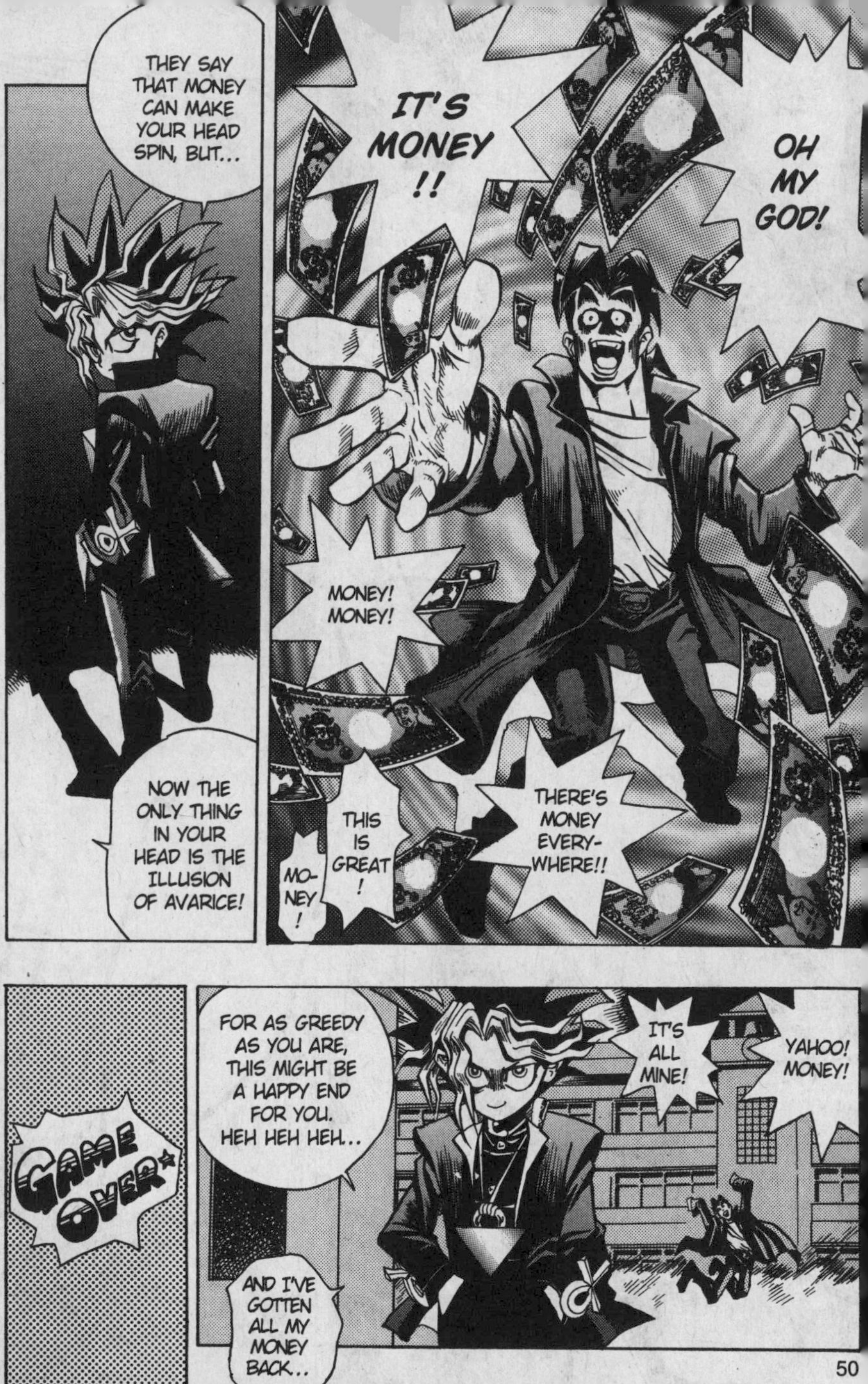
OH MY GOD!
IT'S MONEY!!
MONEY! MONEY!
THERE'S MONEY EVERY-WHERE!!
THIS IS GREAT!
MO-NEY!
THEY SAY THAT MONEY CAN MAKE YOUR HEAD SPIN, BUT...
NOW THE ONLY THING IN YOUR HEAD IS THE ILLUSION OF AVARICE!
YAHOO! MONEY!
IT'S ALL MINE!
FOR AS GREEDY AS YOU ARE, THIS MIGHT BE A HAPPY END FOR YOU. HEH HEH HEH...
AND I'VE GOTTEN ALL MY MONEY BACK..
GAME OVER

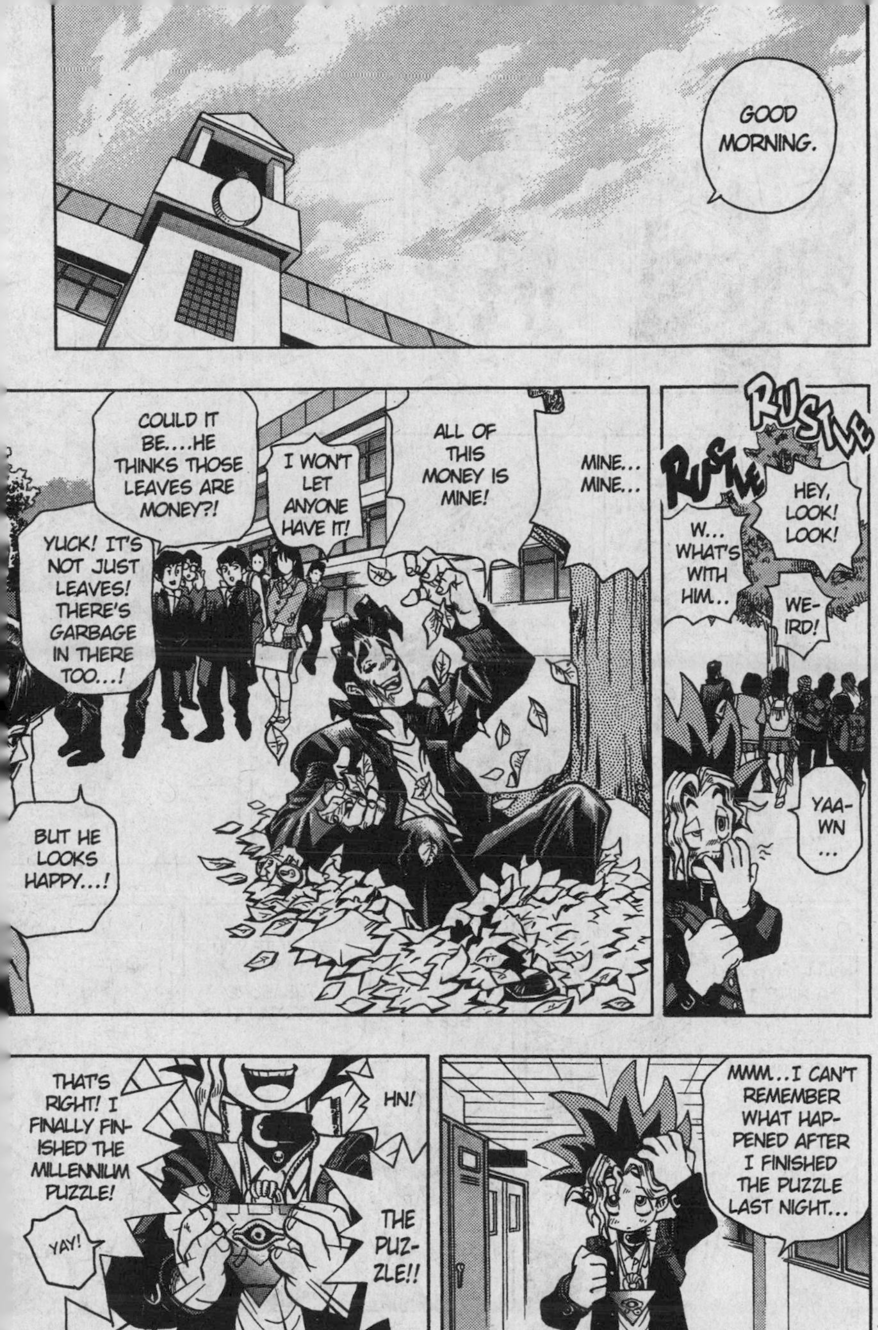
GOOD MORNING.
RUSTLE
RUSTLE
HEY, LOOK! LOOK!
W... WHAT'S WITH HIM...
WE-IRD!
YAA-WN...
MINE... MINE...
ALL OF THIS MONEY IS MINE!
I WON'T LET ANYONE HAVE IT!
COULD IT BE....HE THINKS THOSE LEAVES ARE MONEY?!
YUCK! IT'S NOT JUST LEAVES! THERE'S GARBAGE IN THERE TOO...!
BUT HE LOOKS HAPPY...!
MMM...I CAN'T REMEMBER WHAT HAPPENED AFTER I FINISHED THE PUZZLE LAST NIGHT...
HN!
THE PUZZLE!!
THAT'S RIGHT! I FINALLY FINISHED THE MILLENNIUM PUZZLE!
YAY!

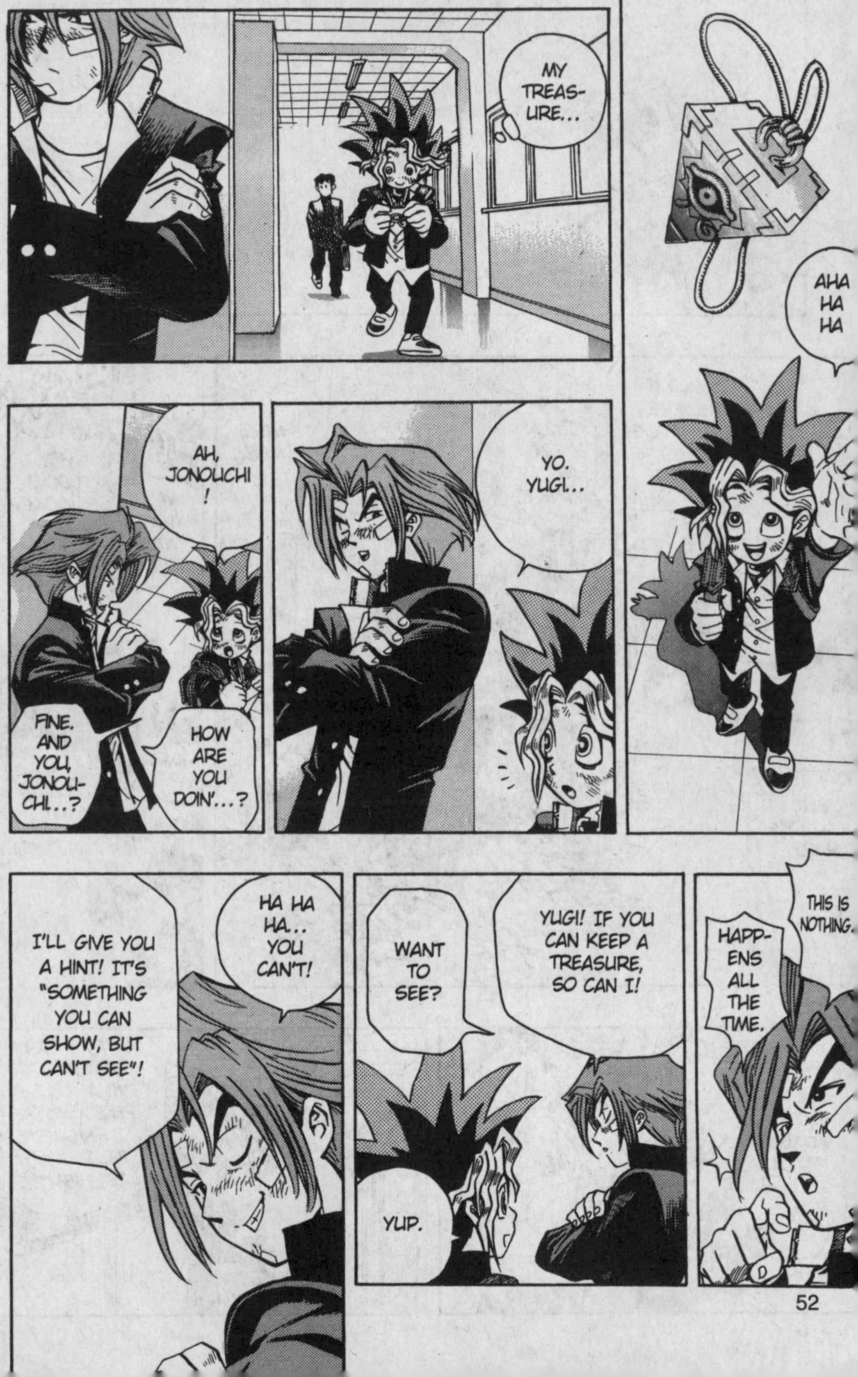
AHA HA HA
MY TREAS-URE...
YO. YUGI...
AH, JONOUCHI!
HOW ARE YOU DOIN'...?
FINE. AND YOU, JONOU-CHI...?
THIS IS NOTHING.
HAPP-ENS ALL THE TIME.
YUGI! IF YOU CAN KEEP A TREASURE, SO CAN I!
WANT TO SEE?
YUP.
HA HA HA... YOU CAN'T!
I'LL GIVE YOU A HINT! IT'S "SOMETHING YOU CAN SHOW, BUT CAN'T SEE"!

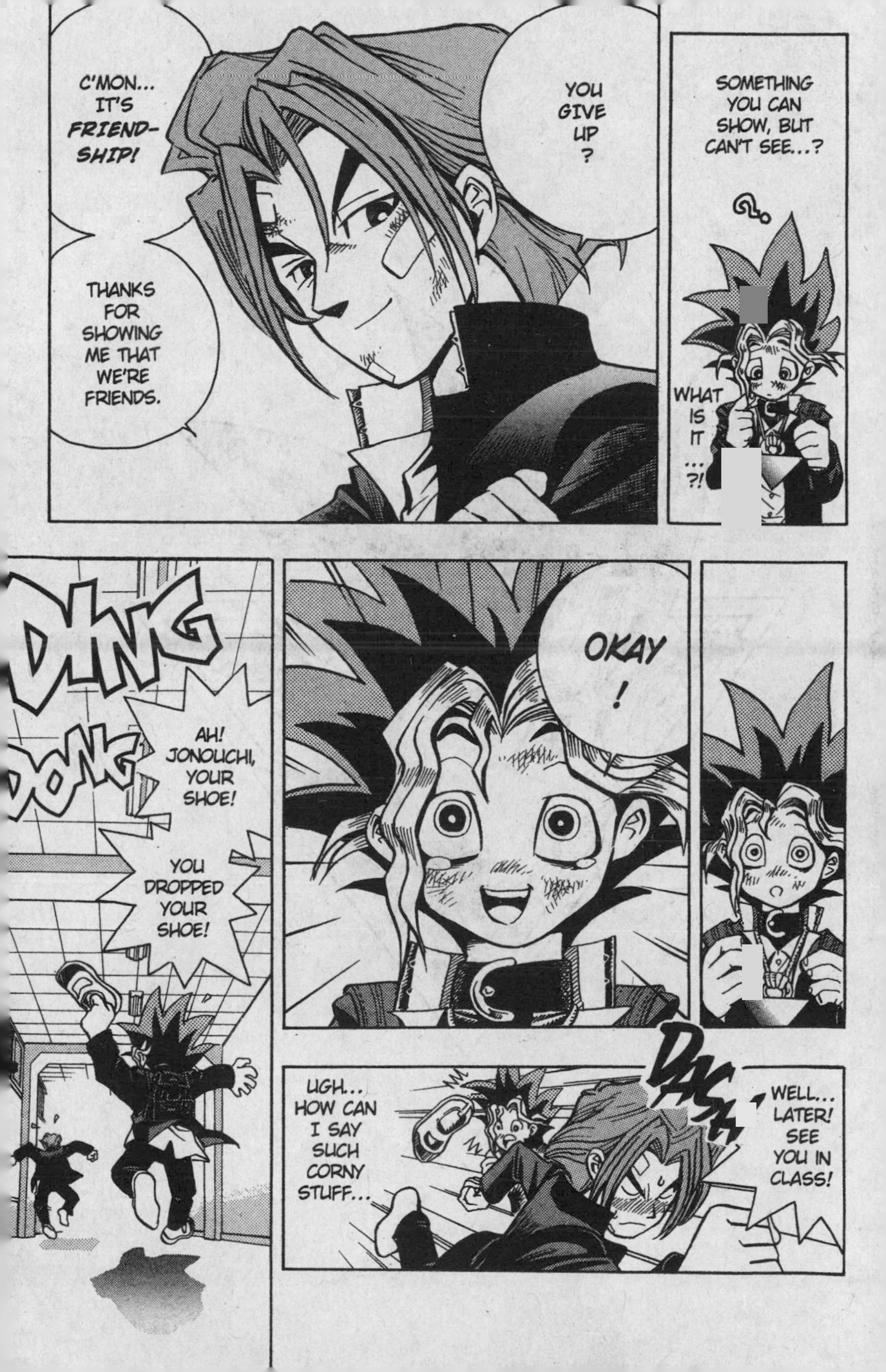
SOMETHING YOU CAN SHOW, BUT CAN'T SEE...?
WHAT IS IT ...?!
YOU GIVE UP ?
C'MON... IT'S *FRIENDSHIP!*
THANKS FOR SHOWING ME THAT WE'RE FRIENDS.
OKAY !
WELL... LATER! SEE YOU IN CLASS!
DASH
UGH... HOW CAN I SAY SUCH CORNY STUFF...
DING
DONG
AH! JONOUCHI, YOUR SHOE!
YOU DROPPED YOUR SHOE!

Duel 2: Lying Eyes

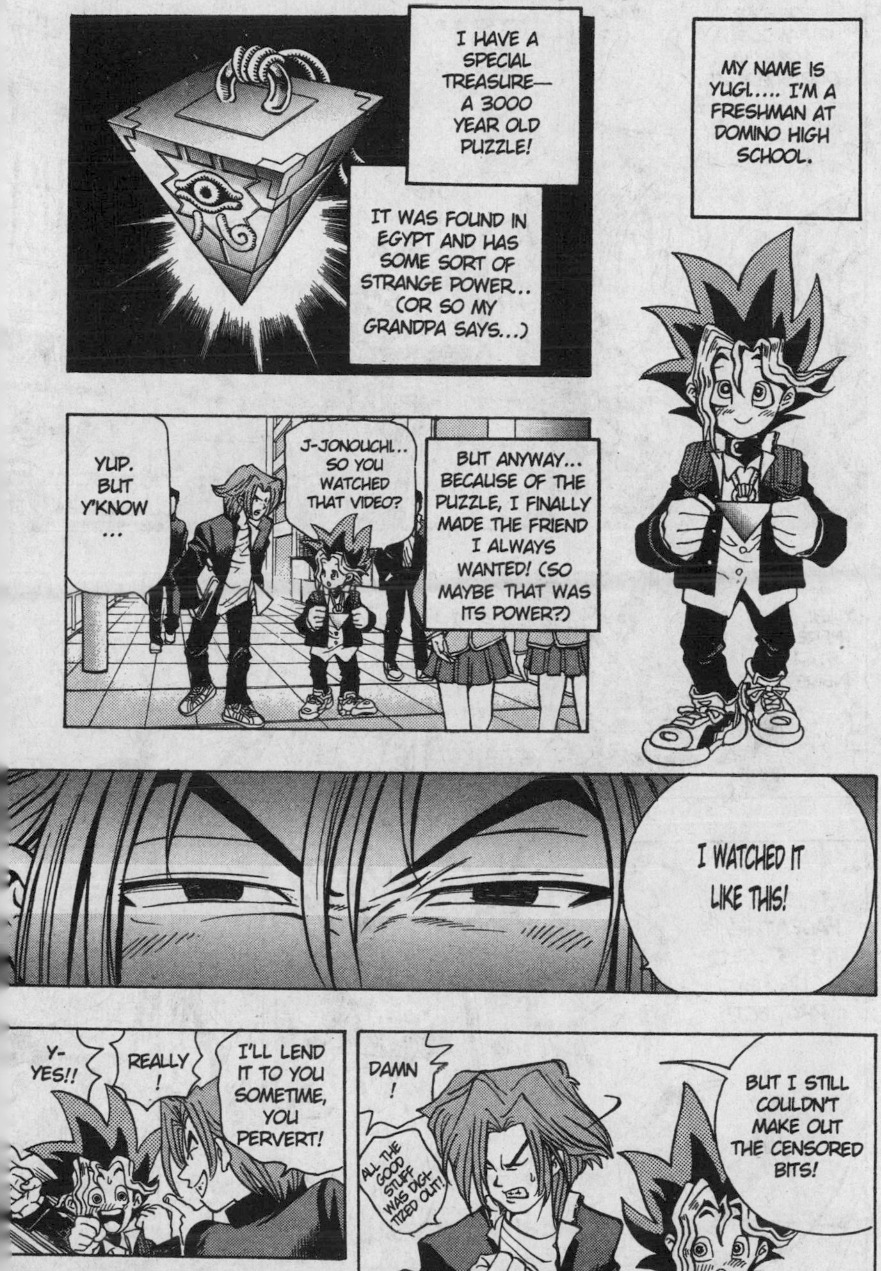
MY NAME IS YUGI.... I'M A FRESHMAN AT DOMINO HIGH SCHOOL.
I HAVE A SPECIAL TREASURE— A 3000 YEAR OLD PUZZLE!
IT WAS FOUND IN EGYPT AND HAS SOME SORT OF STRANGE POWER.. (OR SO MY GRANDPA SAYS...)
BUT ANYWAY... BECAUSE OF THE PUZZLE, I FINALLY MADE THE FRIEND I ALWAYS WANTED! (SO MAYBE THAT WAS ITS POWER?)
J-JONOUCHI.. SO YOU WATCHED THAT VIDEO?
YUP. BUT Y'KNOW ...
I WATCHED IT LIKE THIS!
BUT I STILL COULDN'T MAKE OUT THE CENSORED BITS!
DAMN !
ALL THE GOOD STUFF WAS DIGI-TIZED OUT!
I'LL LEND IT TO YOU SOMETIME, YOU PERVERT!
REALLY !
Y- YES!!

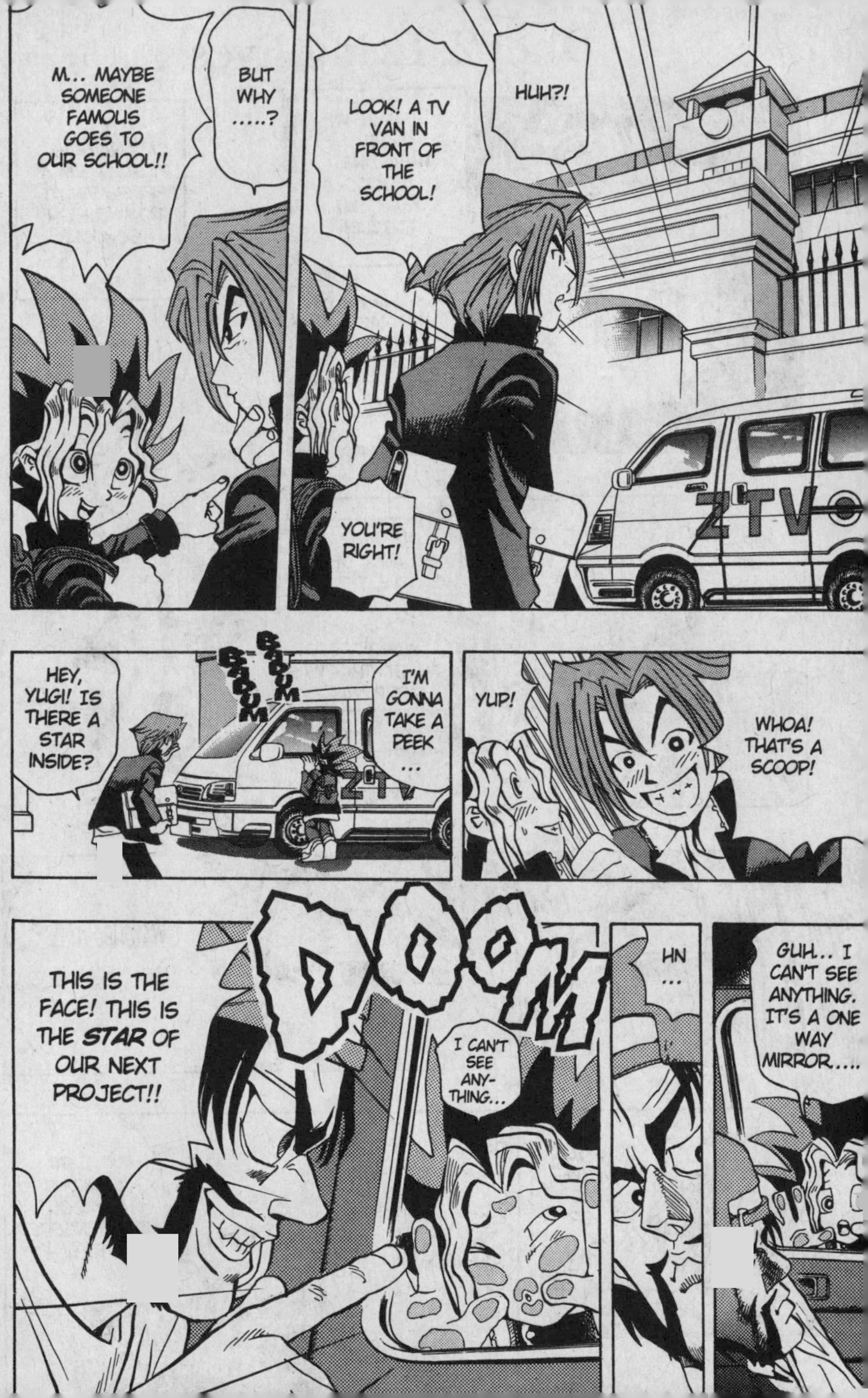
HUH?!
LOOK! A TV VAN IN FRONT OF THE SCHOOL!
YOU'RE RIGHT!
BUT WHY .....?
M... MAYBE SOMEONE FAMOUS GOES TO OUR SCHOOL!!
WHOA! THAT'S A SCOOP!
YUP!
I'M GONNA TAKE A PEEK ...
BADUM
BADUM
HEY, YUGI! IS THERE A STAR INSIDE?
GUH... I CAN'T SEE ANYTHING. IT'S A ONE WAY MIRROR....
HN ...
DOOM
I CAN'T SEE ANY-THING...
THIS IS THE FACE! THIS IS THE *STAR* OF OUR NEXT PROJECT!!

Duel 2: Lying Eyes

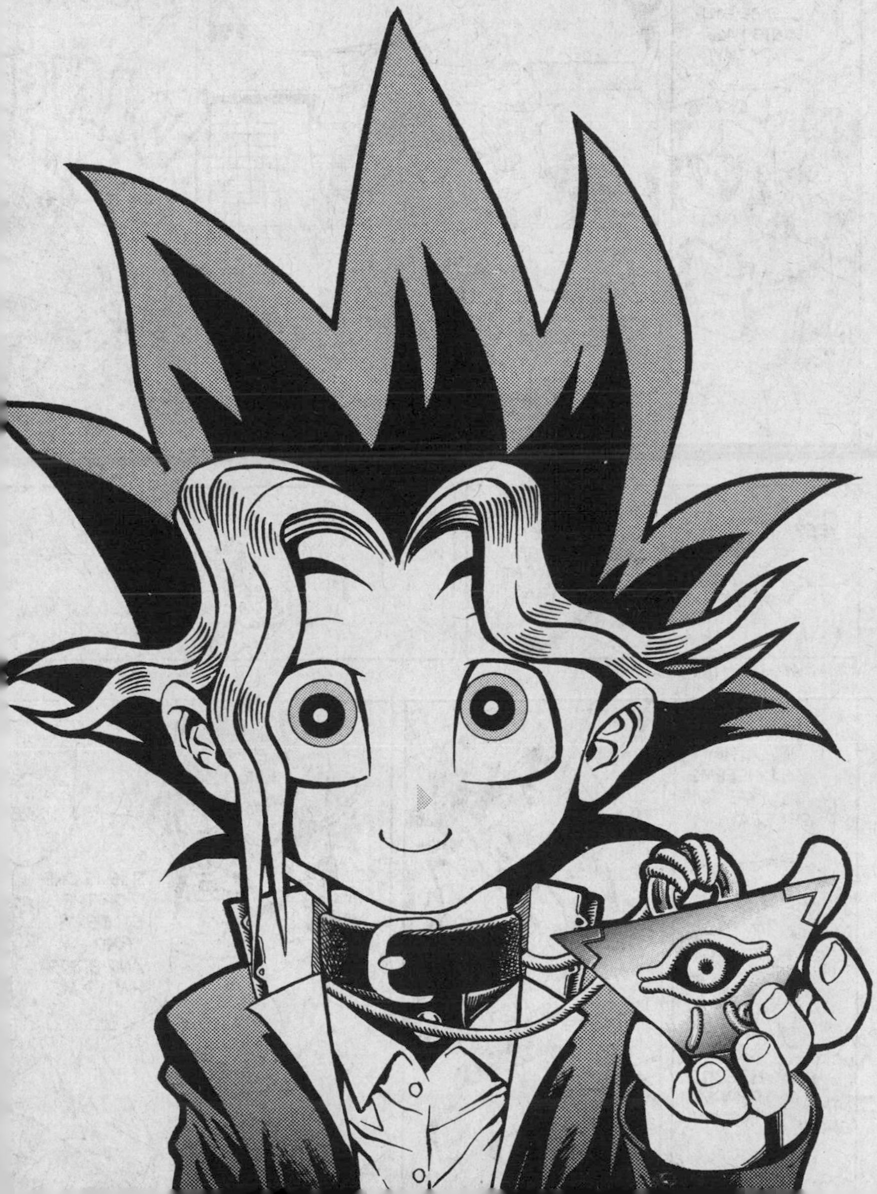

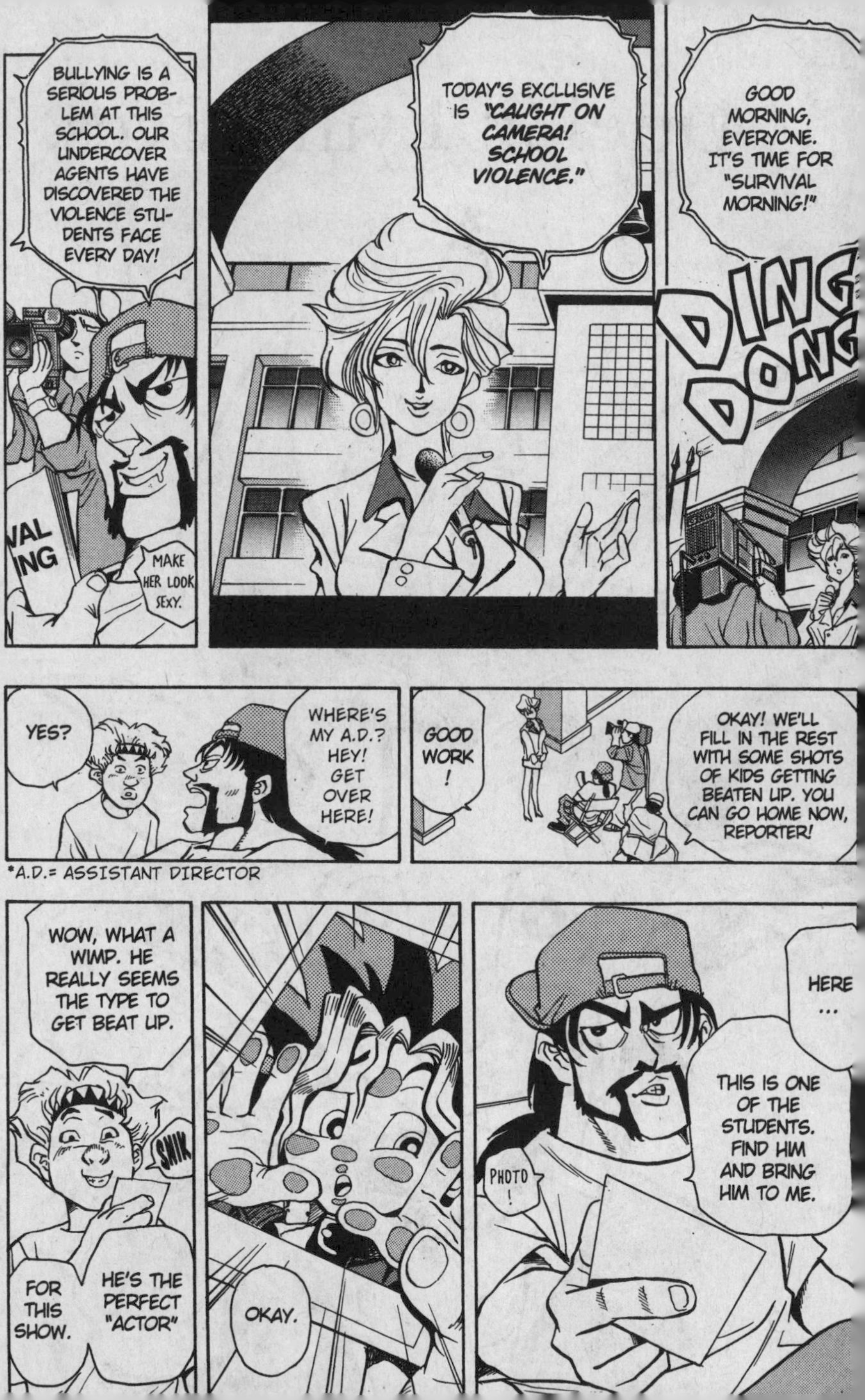
DING DONG
GOOD MORNING, EVERYONE. IT'S TIME FOR "SURVIVAL MORNING!"
TODAY'S EXCLUSIVE IS "CAUGHT ON CAMERA! SCHOOL VIOLENCE."
BULLYING IS A SERIOUS PROBLEM AT THIS SCHOOL. OUR UNDERCOVER AGENTS HAVE DISCOVERED THE VIOLENCE STUDENTS FACE EVERY DAY!
MAKE HER LOOK SEXY.
OKAY! WE'LL FILL IN THE REST WITH SOME SHOTS OF KIDS GETTING BEATEN UP. YOU CAN GO HOME NOW, REPORTER!
GOOD WORK!
WHERE'S MY A.D.? HEY! GET OVER HERE!
YES?
*A.D.= ASSISTANT DIRECTOR
HERE...
THIS IS ONE OF THE STUDENTS. FIND HIM AND BRING HIM TO ME.
PHOTO!
OKAY.
WOW, WHAT A WIMP. HE REALLY SEEMS THE TYPE TO GET BEAT UP.
SNIK
HE'S THE PERFECT "ACTOR"
FOR THIS SHOW.

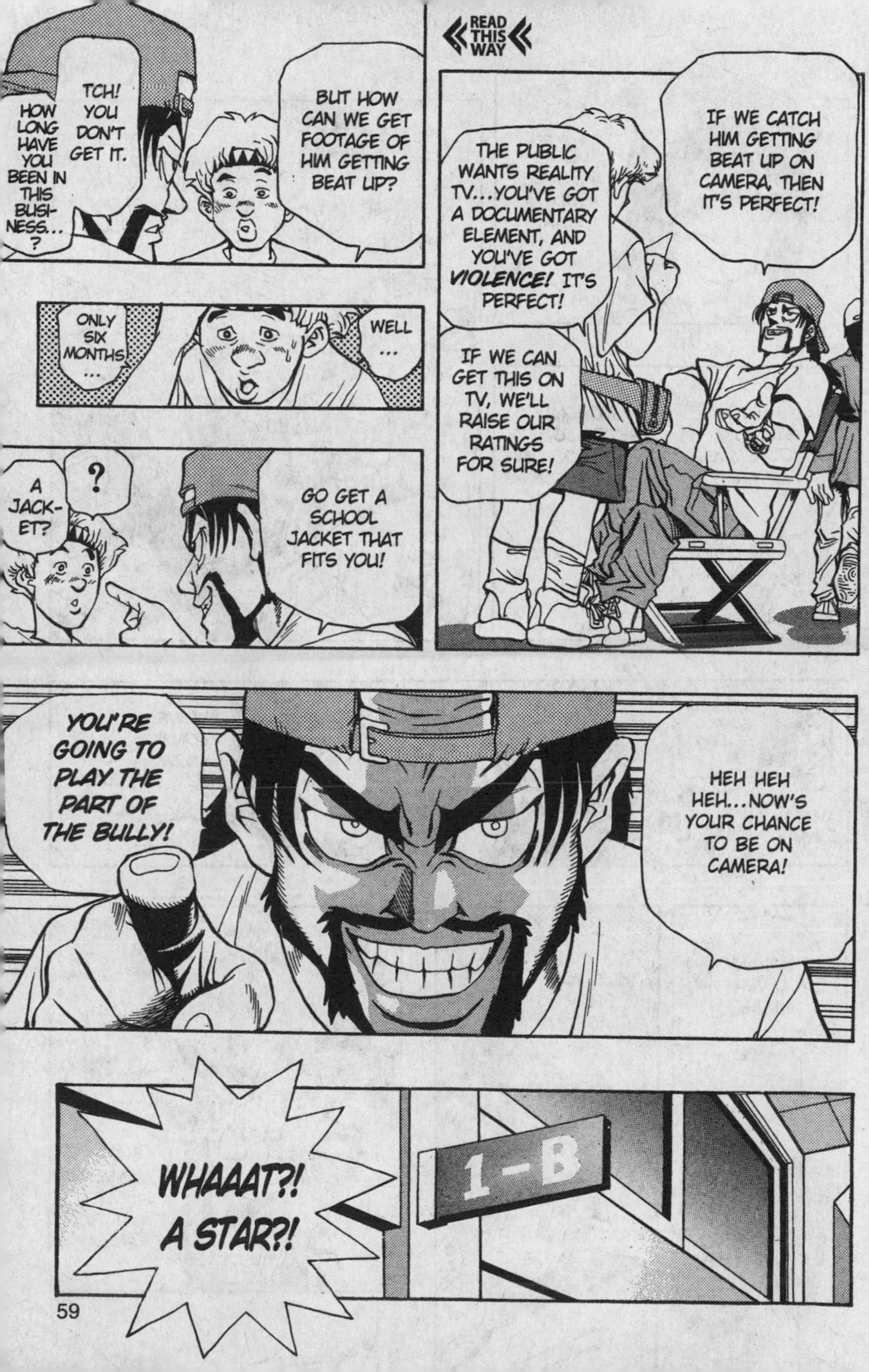
READ THIS WAY
IF WE CATCH HIM GETTING BEAT UP ON CAMERA, THEN IT'S PERFECT!
THE PUBLIC WANTS REALITY TV...YOU'VE GOT A DOCUMENTARY ELEMENT, AND YOU'VE GOT *VIOLENCE!* IT'S PERFECT!
IF WE CAN GET THIS ON TV, WE'LL RAISE OUR RATINGS FOR SURE!
BUT HOW CAN WE GET FOOTAGE OF HIM GETTING BEAT UP?
TCH! YOU DON'T GET IT.
HOW LONG HAVE YOU BEEN IN THIS BUSINESS...?
WELL ...
ONLY SIX MONTHS ...
GO GET A SCHOOL JACKET THAT FITS YOU!
?
A JACKET?
HEH HEH HEH...NOW'S YOUR CHANCE TO BE ON CAMERA!
YOU'RE GOING TO PLAY THE PART OF THE BULLY!
1-B
WHAAAT?! A STAR?!

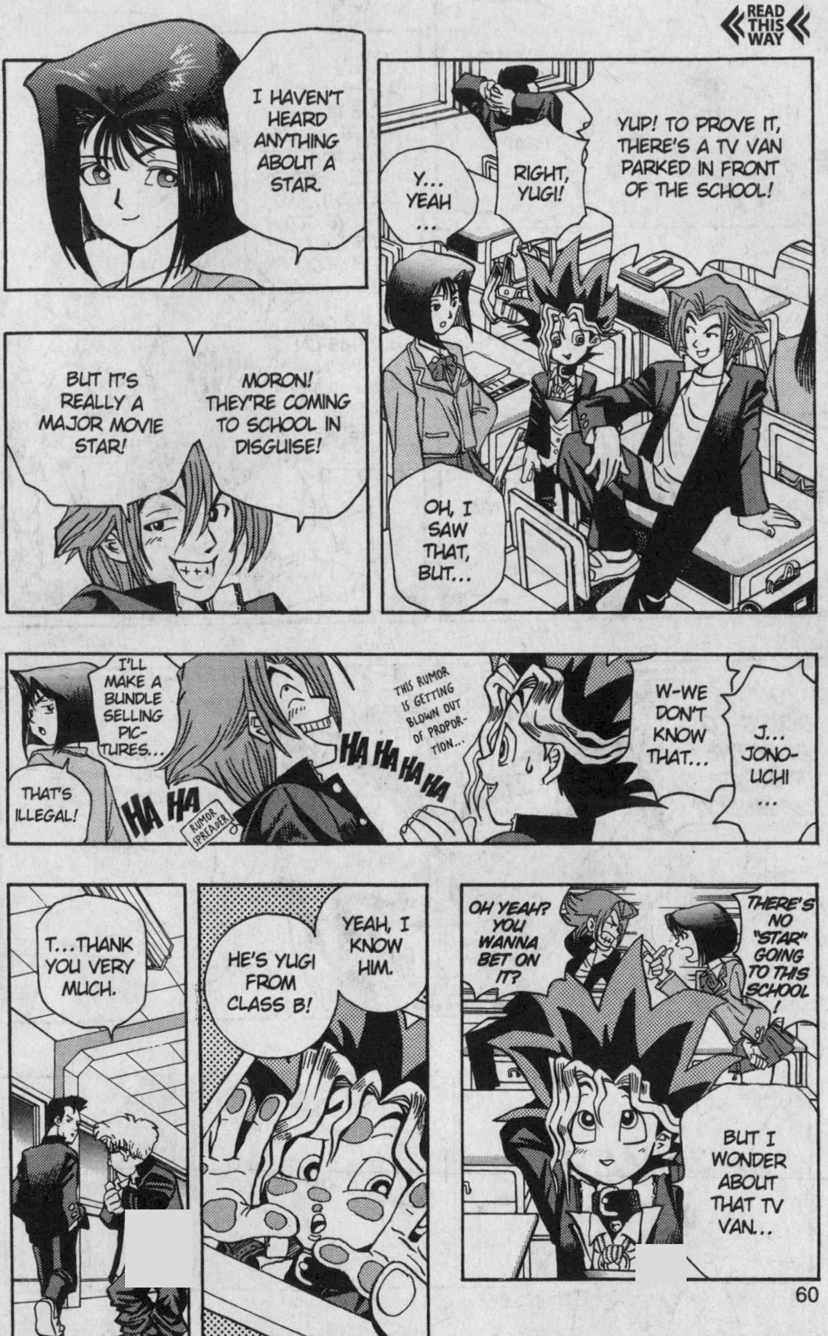
READ THIS WAY
YUP! TO PROVE IT, THERE'S A TV VAN PARKED IN FRONT OF THE SCHOOL!
RIGHT, YUGI!
Y... YEAH ...
OH, I SAW THAT, BUT...
I HAVEN'T HEARD ANYTHING ABOUT A STAR.
MORON! THEY'RE COMING TO SCHOOL IN DISGUISE!
BUT IT'S REALLY A MAJOR MOVIE STAR!
J... JONO-UCHI ...
W-WE DON'T KNOW THAT...
THIS RUMOR IS GETTING BLOWN OUT OF PROPOR-TION...
HA HA HA HA
I'LL MAKE A BUNDLE SELLING PIC-TURES...
HA HA
RUMOR SPREADER
THAT'S ILLEGAL!
THERE'S NO "STAR" GOING TO THIS SCHOOL!
OH YEAH? YOU WANNA BET ON IT?
BUT I WONDER ABOUT THAT TV VAN...
YEAH, I KNOW HIM.
HE'S YUGI FROM CLASS B!
T...THANK YOU VERY MUCH.

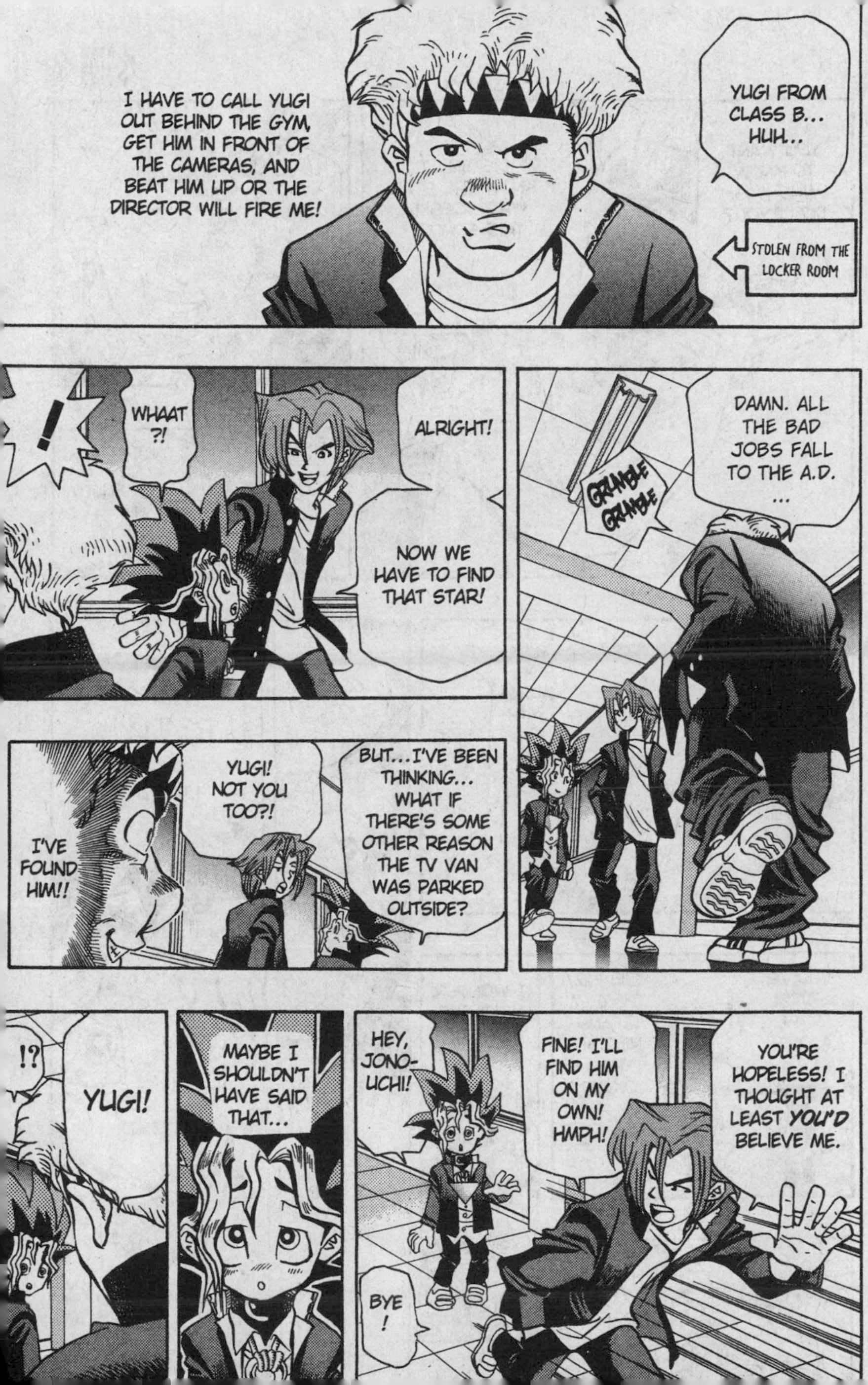
YUGI FROM CLASS B... HUH...
STOLEN FROM THE LOCKER ROOM
I HAVE TO CALL YUGI OUT BEHIND THE GYM, GET HIM IN FRONT OF THE CAMERAS, AND BEAT HIM UP OR THE DIRECTOR WILL FIRE ME!
DAMN. ALL THE BAD JOBS FALL TO THE A.D. ...
GRUMBLE GRUMBLE
ALRIGHT!
NOW WE HAVE TO FIND THAT STAR!
WHAAT ?!
!
BUT...I'VE BEEN THINKING... WHAT IF THERE'S SOME OTHER REASON THE TV VAN WAS PARKED OUTSIDE?
YUGI! NOT YOU TOO?!
I'VE FOUND HIM!!
YOU'RE HOPELESS! I THOUGHT AT LEAST *YOU'D* BELIEVE ME.
FINE! I'LL FIND HIM ON MY OWN! HMPH!
HEY, JONO-UCHI!
BYE!
MAYBE I SHOULDN'T HAVE SAID THAT...
YUGI!
!?

READ THIS WAY

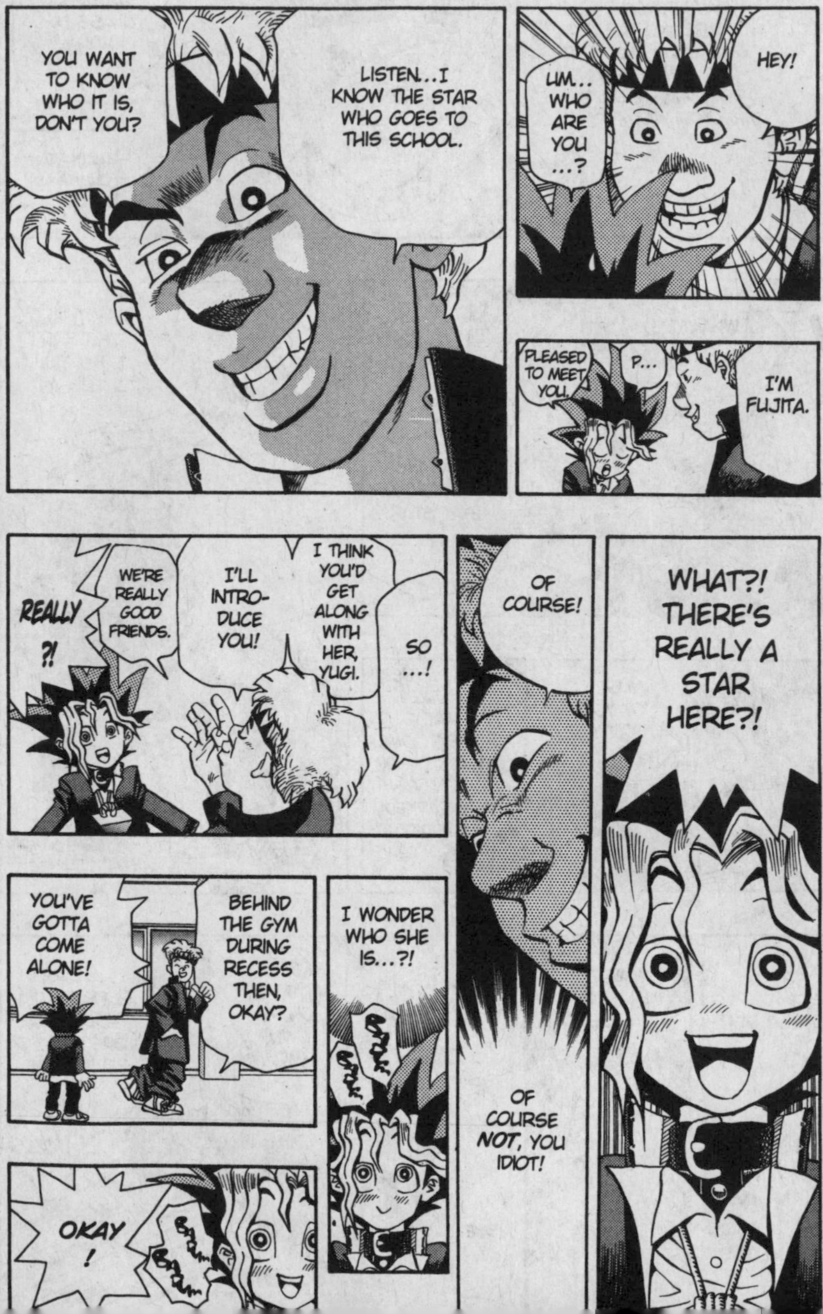
HEY!
UM... WHO ARE YOU ...?
I'M FUJITA.
P...
PLEASED TO MEET YOU.
LISTEN...I KNOW THE STAR WHO GOES TO THIS SCHOOL.
YOU WANT TO KNOW WHO IT IS, DON'T YOU?
WHAT?! THERE'S REALLY A STAR HERE?!
OF COURSE!
OF COURSE NOT, YOU IDIOT!
SO...!
I THINK YOU'D GET ALONG WITH HER, YUGI.
I'LL INTRO-DUCE YOU!
WE'RE REALLY GOOD FRIENDS.
REALLY ?!
I WONDER WHO SHE IS...?!
BEHIND THE GYM DURING RECESS THEN, OKAY?
YOU'VE GOTTA COME ALONE!
OKAY !

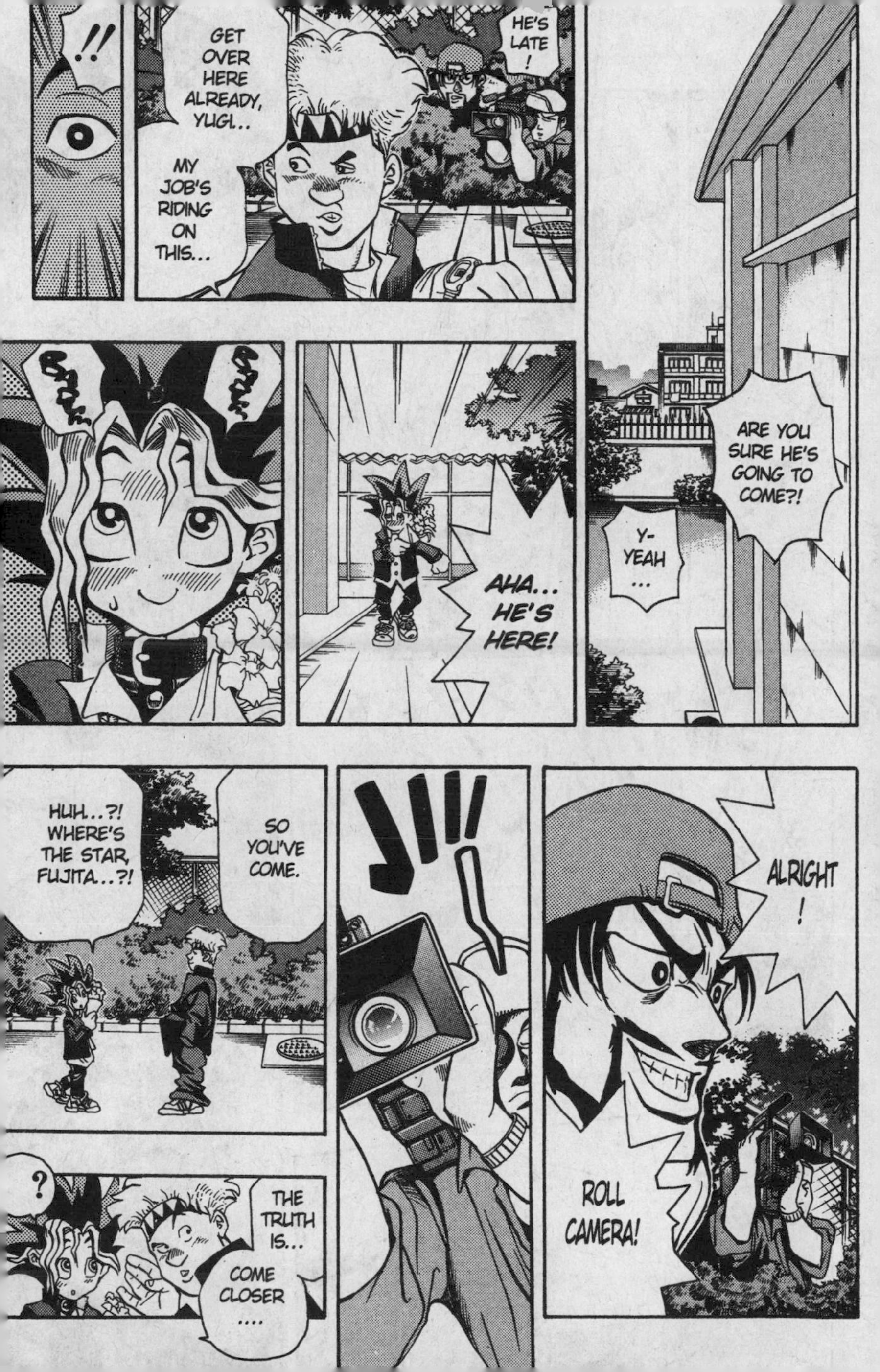

ARE YOU SURE HE'S GOING TO COME?!
Y-YEAH ...
HE'S LATE !
GET OVER HERE ALREADY, YUGI...
MY JOB'S RIDING ON THIS...
!!
AHA... HE'S HERE!
ALRIGHT !
ROLL CAMERA!
SO YOU'VE COME.
HUH...?! WHERE'S THE STAR, FUJITA...?!
THE TRUTH IS...
COME CLOSER ....
?

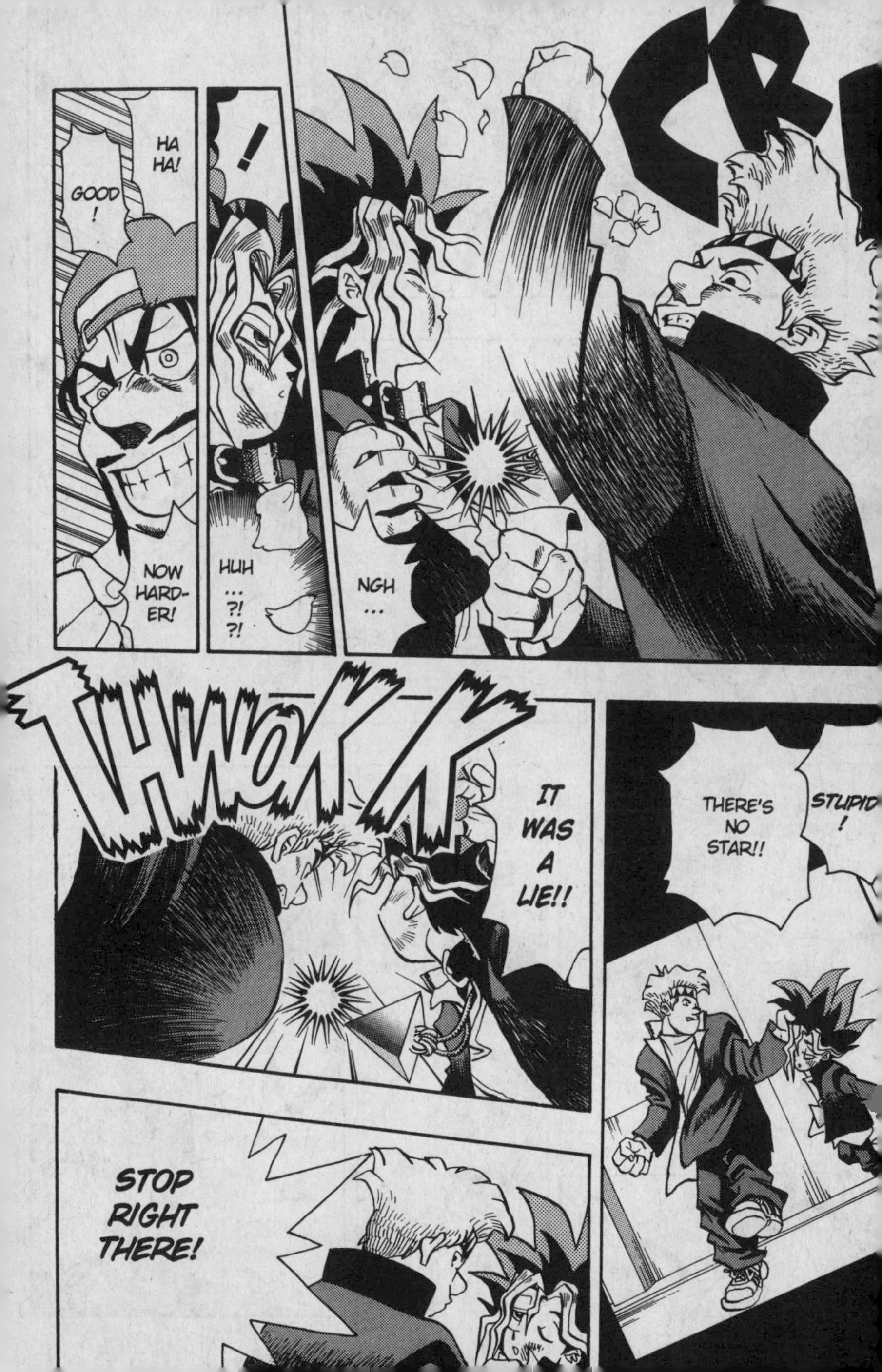
CR
NGH ...
!
HUH ...?! ?!
HA HA! GOOD!
NOW HARDER!
STUPID!
THERE'S NO STAR!!
THWOK
IT WAS A LIE!!
STOP RIGHT THERE!

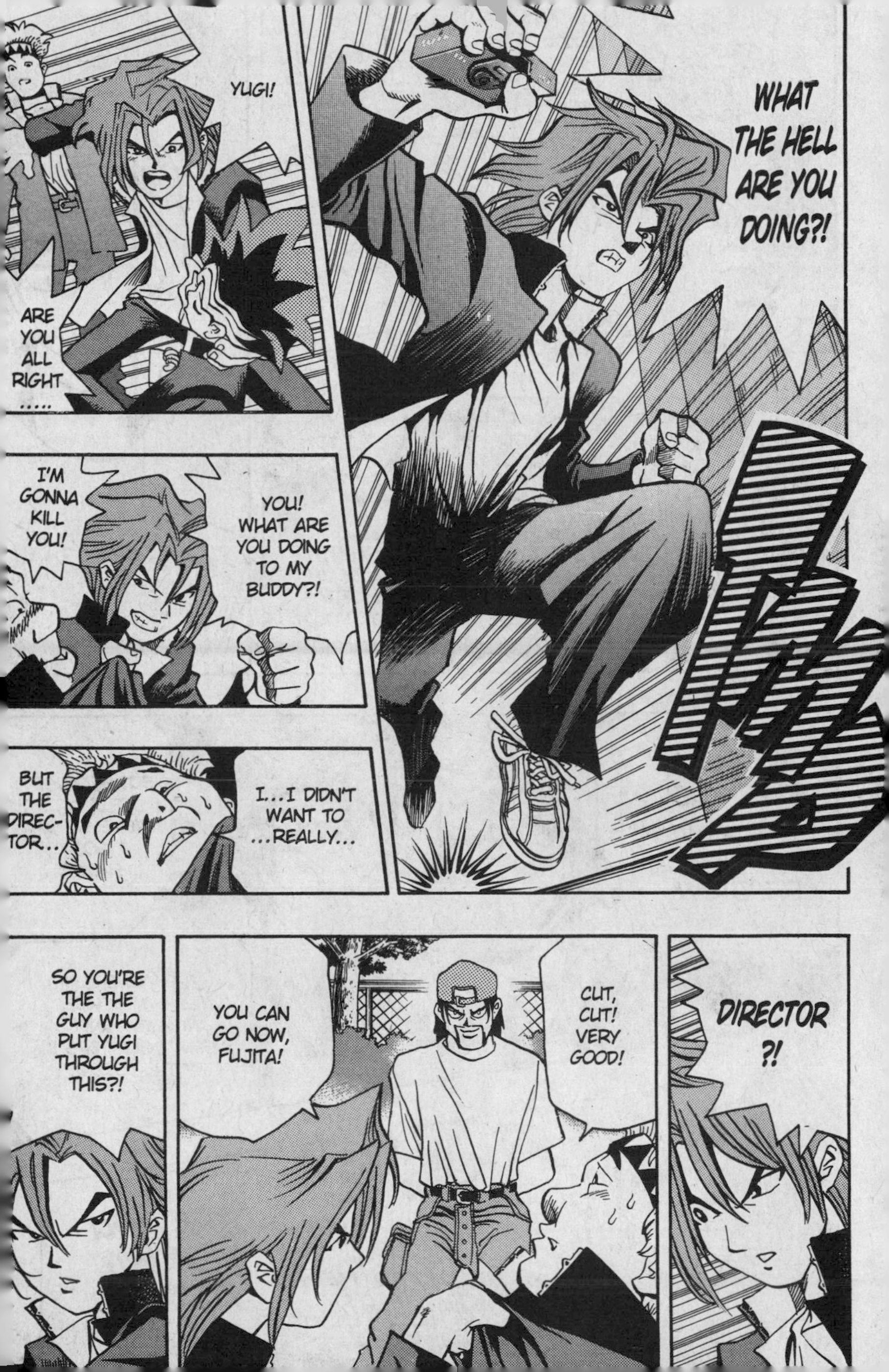
WHAT THE HELL ARE YOU DOING?!
YUGI!
ARE YOU ALL RIGHT .....
YOU! WHAT ARE YOU DOING TO MY BUDDY?!
I'M GONNA KILL YOU!
I...I DIDN'T WANT TO ...REALLY...
BUT THE DIREC-TOR...
DIRECTOR ?!
CUT, CUT! VERY GOOD!
YOU CAN GO NOW, FUJITA!
SO YOU'RE THE THE GUY WHO PUT YUGI THROUGH THIS?!

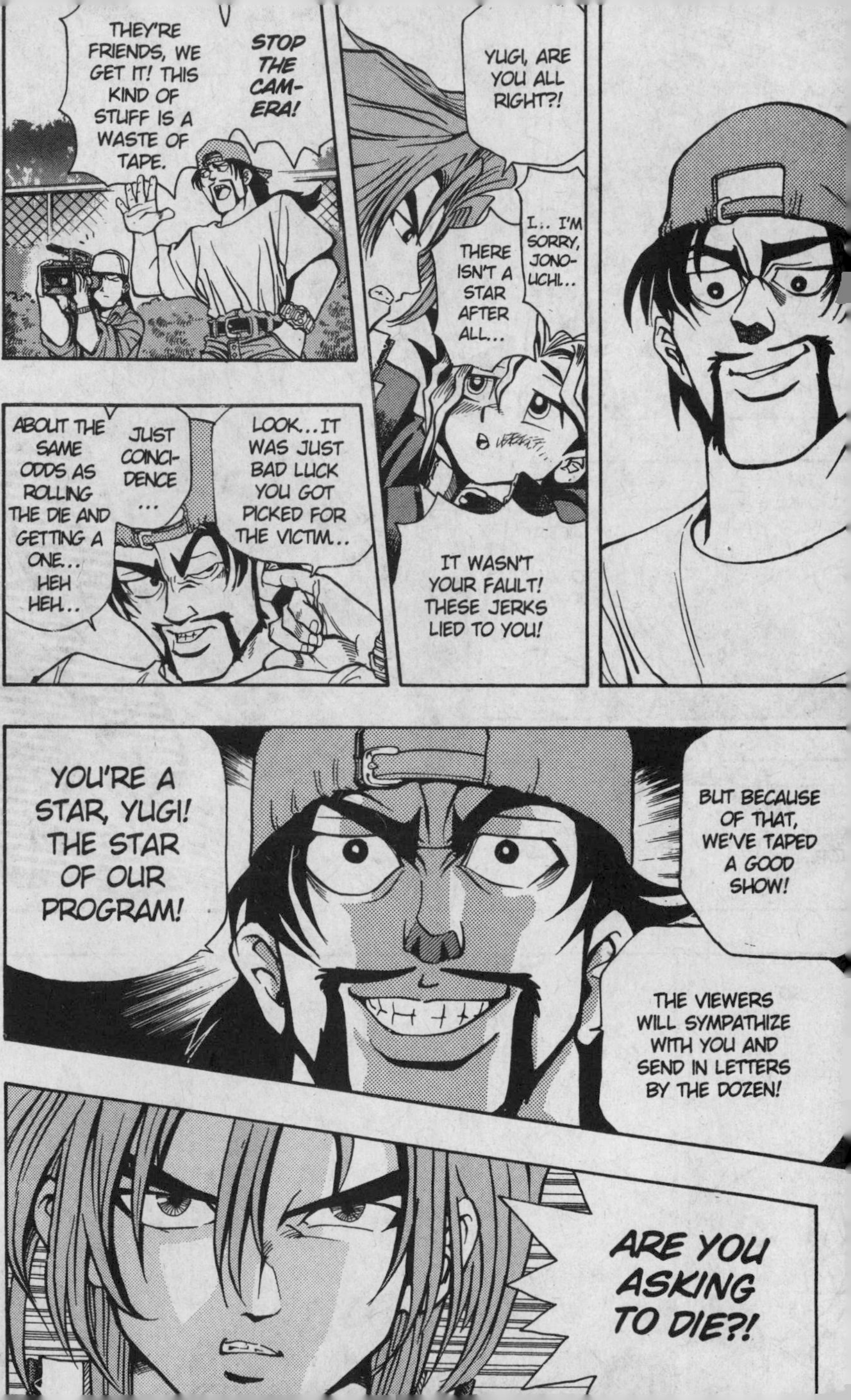
YUGI, ARE YOU ALL RIGHT?!
I... I'M SORRY, JONOUCHI...
THERE ISN'T A STAR AFTER ALL...
IT WASN'T YOUR FAULT! THESE JERKS LIED TO YOU!
STOP THE CAMERA!
THEY'RE FRIENDS, WE GET IT! THIS KIND OF STUFF IS A WASTE OF TAPE.
LOOK...IT WAS JUST BAD LUCK YOU GOT PICKED FOR THE VICTIM...
JUST COINCIDENCE...
ABOUT THE SAME ODDS AS ROLLING THE DIE AND GETTING A ONE... HEH HEH...
BUT BECAUSE OF THAT, WE'VE TAPED A GOOD SHOW!
YOU'RE A STAR, YUGI! THE STAR OF OUR PROGRAM!
THE VIEWERS WILL SYMPATHIZE WITH YOU AND SEND IN LETTERS BY THE DOZEN!
ARE YOU ASKING TO DIE?!

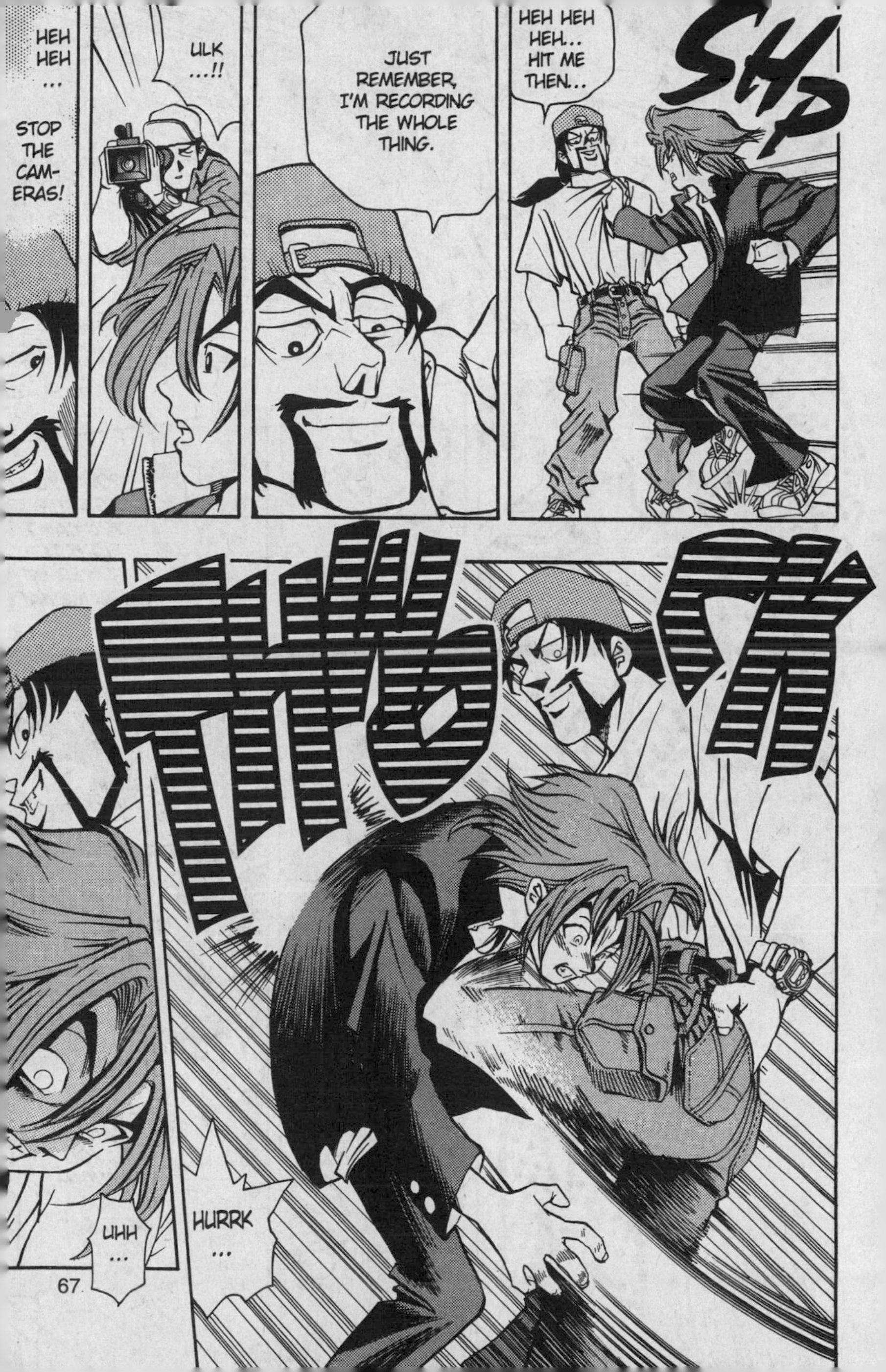
SHP
HEH HEH HEH... HIT ME THEN...
JUST REMEMBER, I'M RECORDING THE WHOLE THING.
ULK ...!!
HEH HEH ...
STOP THE CAM-ERAS!
HURRK ...
UHH ...

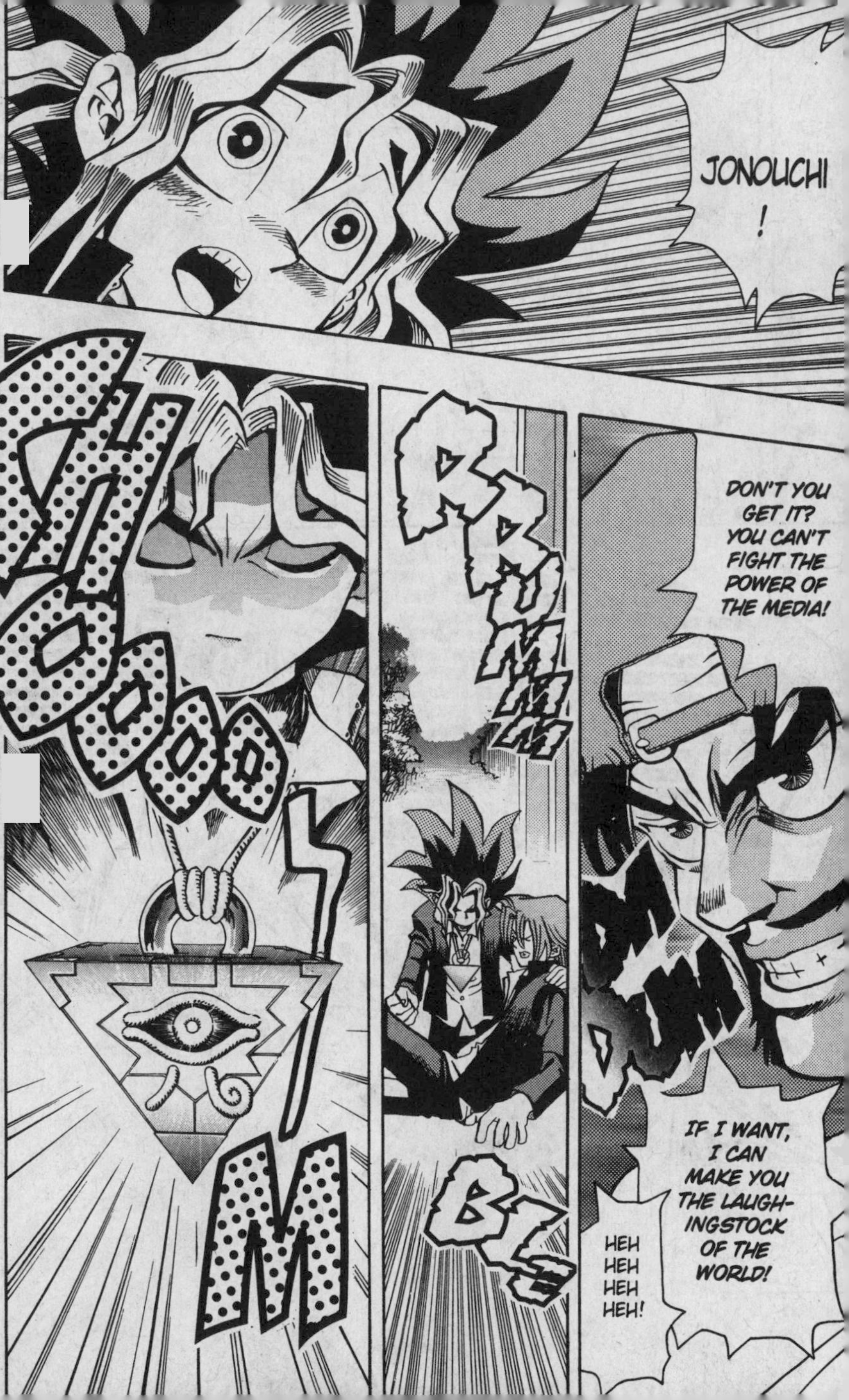
JONOUCHI !
DON'T YOU GET IT? YOU CAN'T FIGHT THE POWER OF THE MEDIA!
IF I WANT, I CAN MAKE YOU THE LAUGHINGSTOCK OF THE WORLD!
HEH HEH HEH HEH!

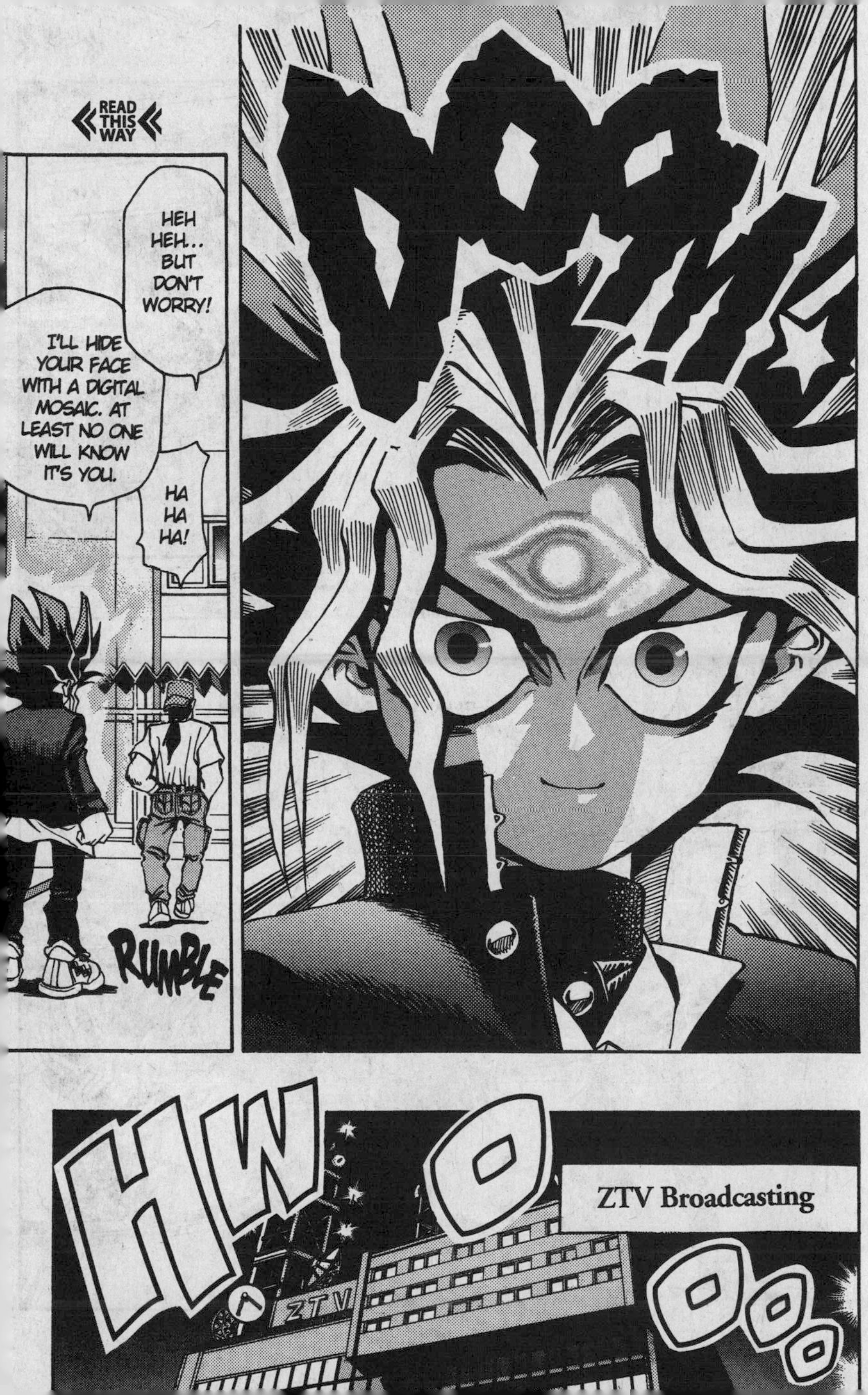
READ THIS WAY
HEH HEH... BUT DON'T WORRY!
I'LL HIDE YOUR FACE WITH A DIGITAL MOSAIC. AT LEAST NO ONE WILL KNOW IT'S YOU.
HA HA HA!
RUMBLE
ZTV Broadcasting
ZTV
HWOOOO

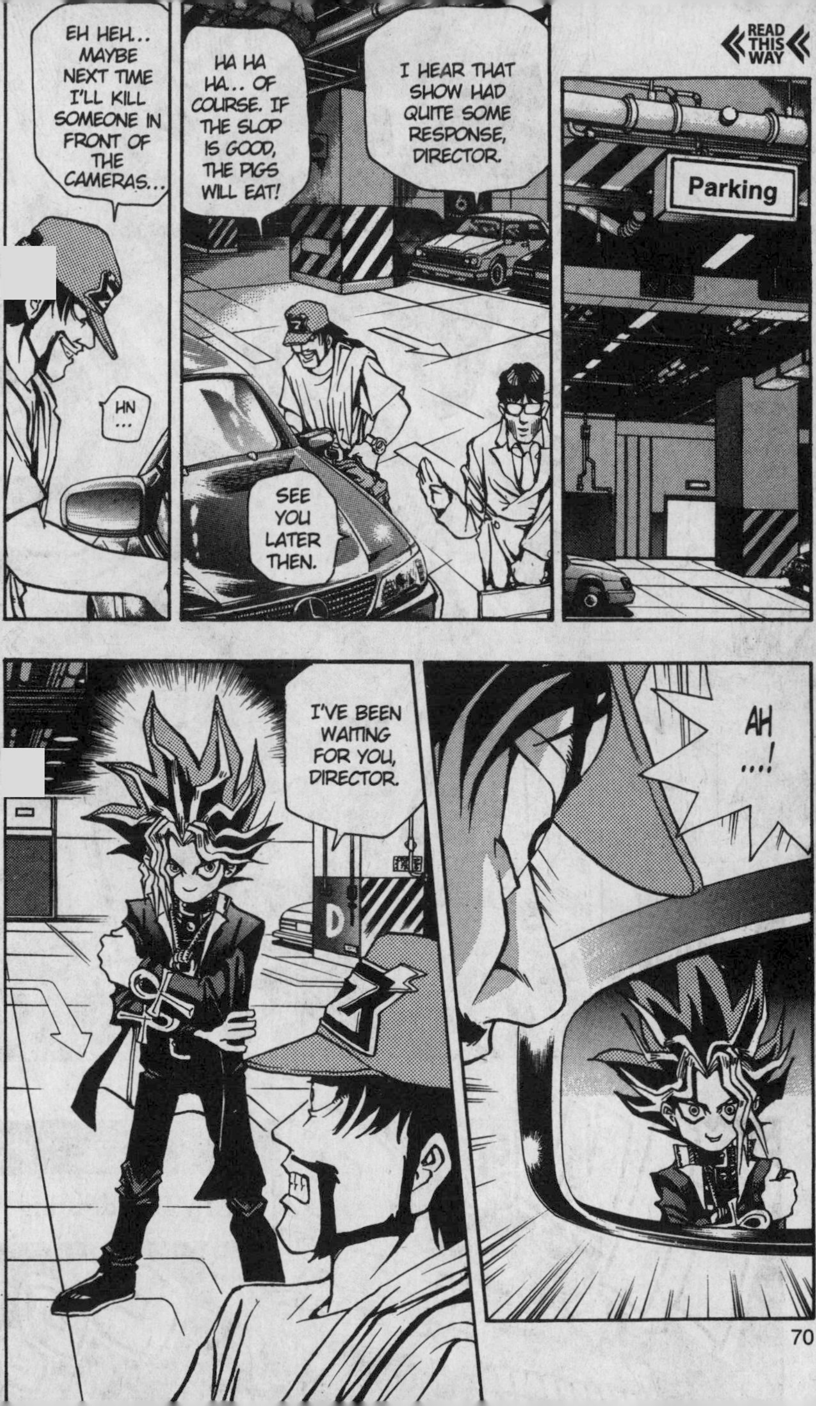
READ THIS WAY
Parking
I HEAR THAT SHOW HAD QUITE SOME RESPONSE, DIRECTOR.
HA HA HA... OF COURSE. IF THE SLOP IS GOOD, THE PIGS WILL EAT!
SEE YOU LATER THEN.
EH HEH... MAYBE NEXT TIME I'LL KILL SOMEONE IN FRONT OF THE CAMERAS...
HN ...
AH ...!
I'VE BEEN WAITING FOR YOU, DIRECTOR.

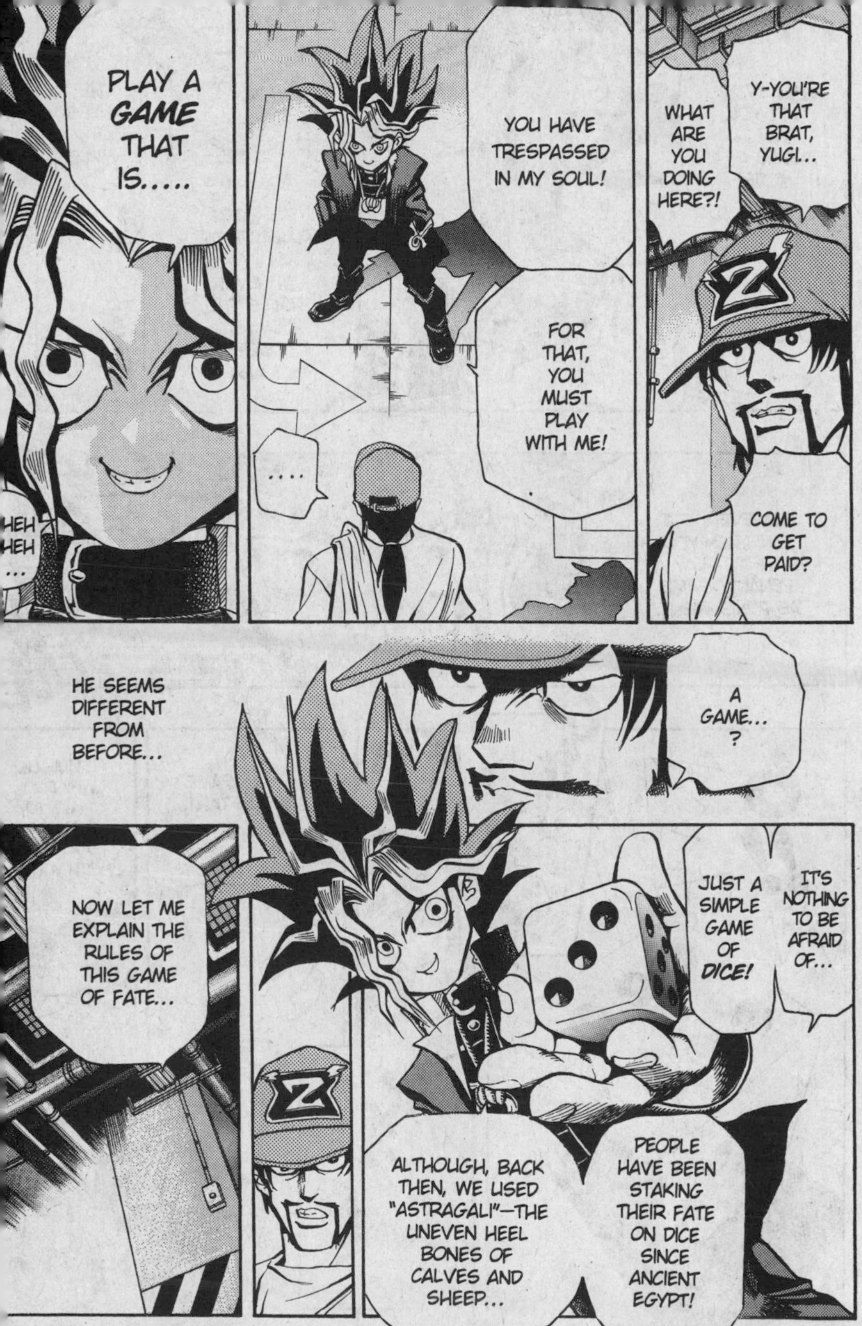
Y-YOU'RE THAT BRAT, YUGI...
WHAT ARE YOU DOING HERE?!
COME TO GET PAID?
YOU HAVE TRESPASSED IN MY SOUL!
FOR THAT, YOU MUST PLAY WITH ME!
....
PLAY A *GAME* THAT IS.....
HEH HEH ...
A GAME...?
HE SEEMS DIFFERENT FROM BEFORE...
IT'S NOTHING TO BE AFRAID OF...
JUST A SIMPLE GAME OF *DICE!*
PEOPLE HAVE BEEN STAKING THEIR FATE ON DICE SINCE ANCIENT EGYPT!
ALTHOUGH, BACK THEN, WE USED "ASTRAGALI"—THE UNEVEN HEEL BONES OF CALVES AND SHEEP...
NOW LET ME EXPLAIN THE RULES OF THIS GAME OF FATE...

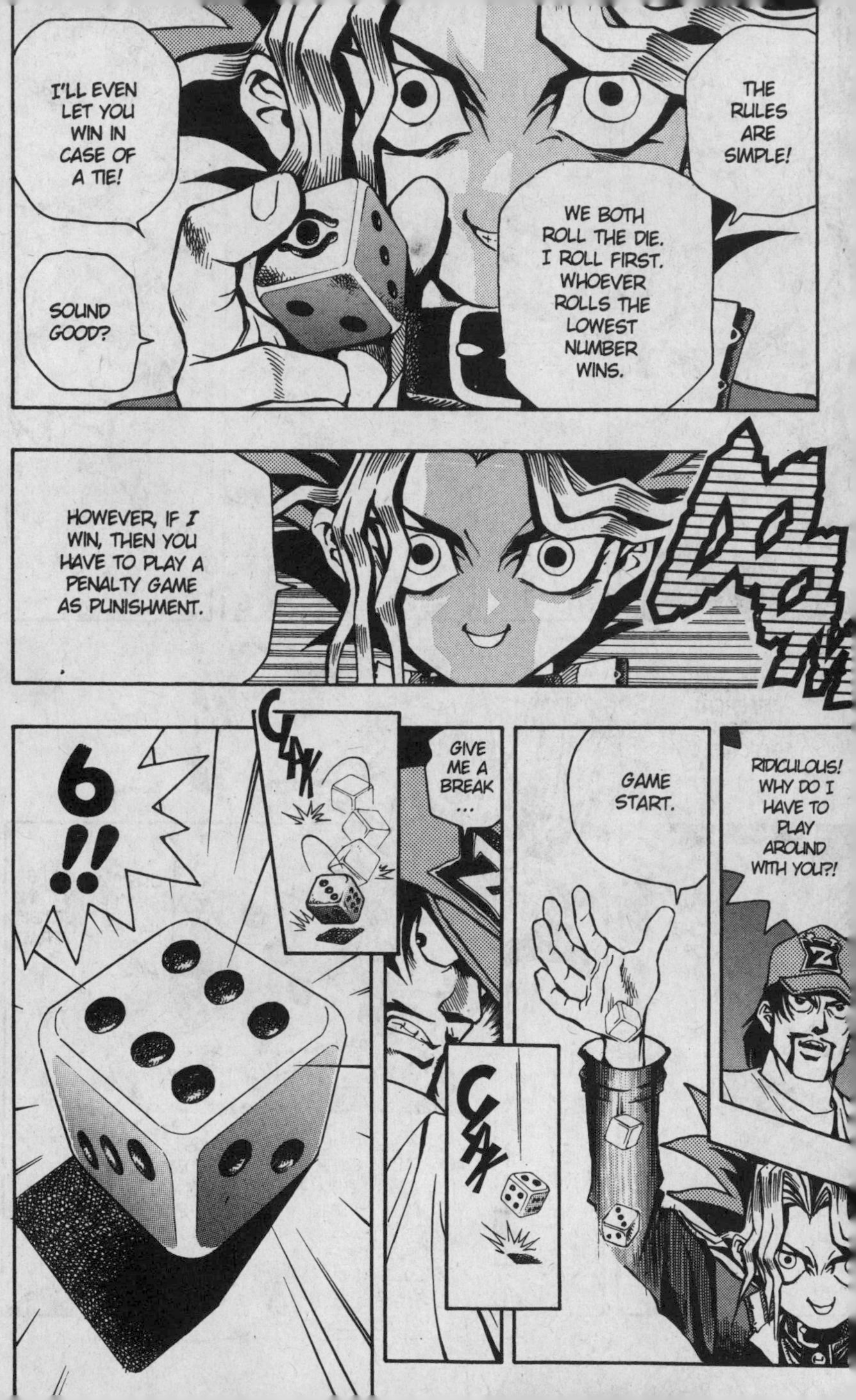
THE RULES ARE SIMPLE!
WE BOTH ROLL THE DIE. I ROLL FIRST. WHOEVER ROLLS THE LOWEST NUMBER WINS.
I'LL EVEN LET YOU WIN IN CASE OF A TIE!
SOUND GOOD?
HOWEVER, IF I WIN, THEN YOU HAVE TO PLAY A PENALTY GAME AS PUNISHMENT.
RIDICULOUS! WHY DO I HAVE TO PLAY AROUND WITH YOU?!
GAME START.
CLAK
GIVE ME A BREAK...
CLAK
6!!

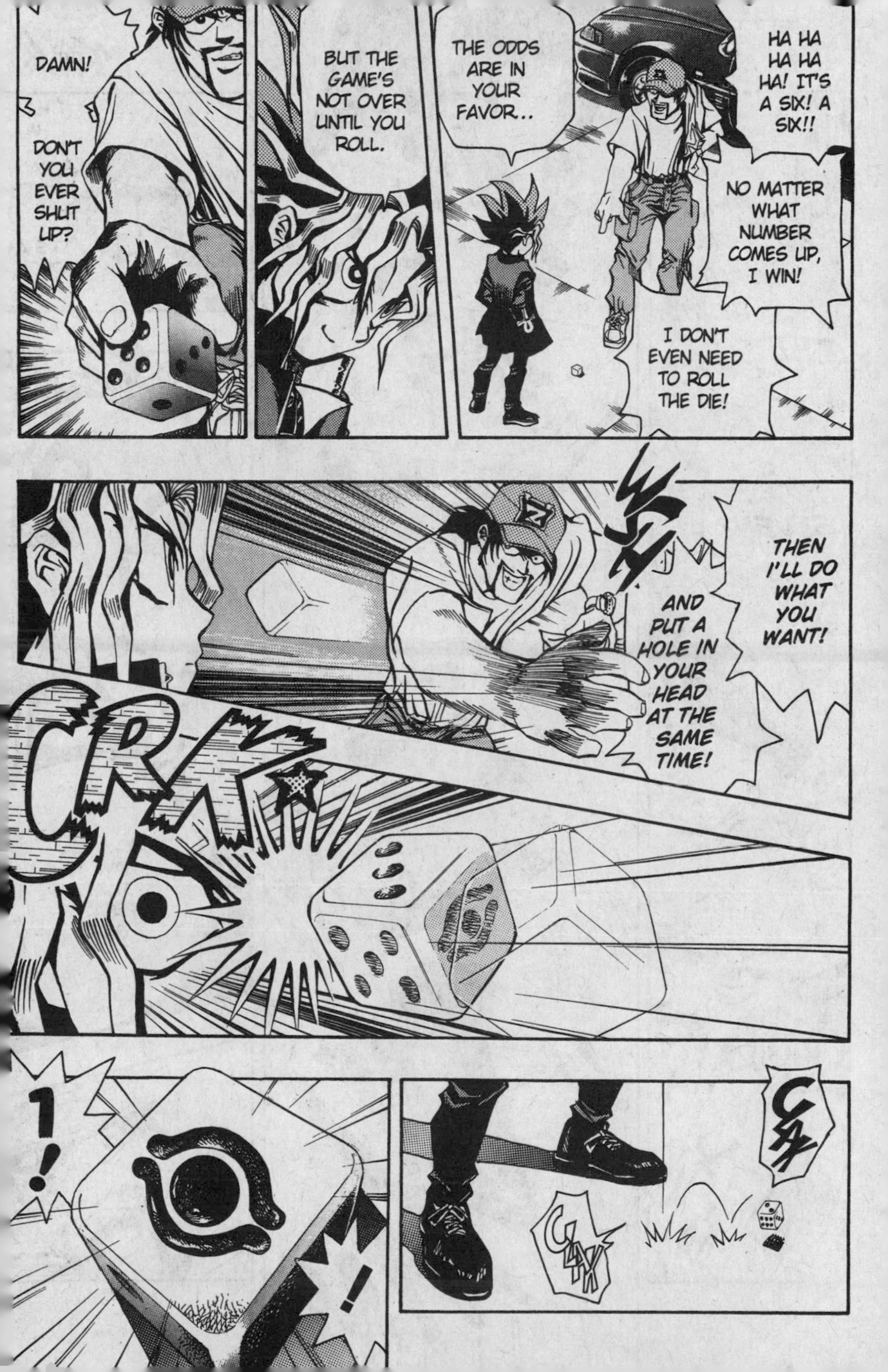
HA HA HA HA HA! IT'S A SIX! A SIX!!
NO MATTER WHAT NUMBER COMES UP, I WIN!
I DON'T EVEN NEED TO ROLL THE DIE!
THE ODDS ARE IN YOUR FAVOR..
BUT THE GAME'S NOT OVER UNTIL YOU ROLL.
DAMN!
DON'T YOU EVER SHUT UP?
WSSH
THEN I'LL DO WHAT YOU WANT!
AND PUT A HOLE IN YOUR HEAD AT THE SAME TIME!
CRAK
CLAK
CLAK
!
!

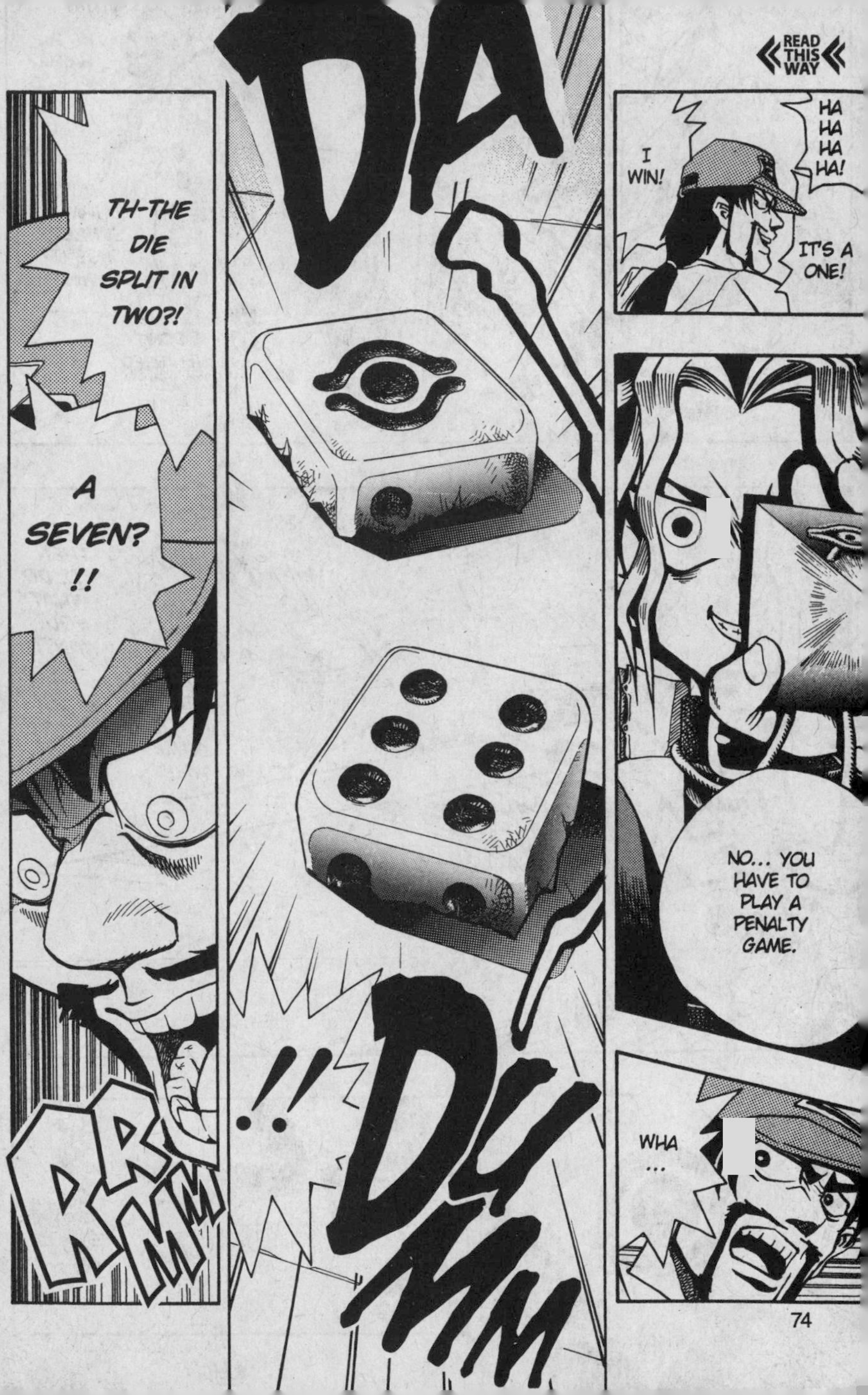
READ THIS WAY
HA HA HA HA!
I WIN!
IT'S A ONE!
NO... YOU HAVE TO PLAY A PENALTY GAME.
WHA...
DA
!!
DUMMM
TH-THE DIE SPLIT IN TWO?!
A SEVEN?!!
RRMMM

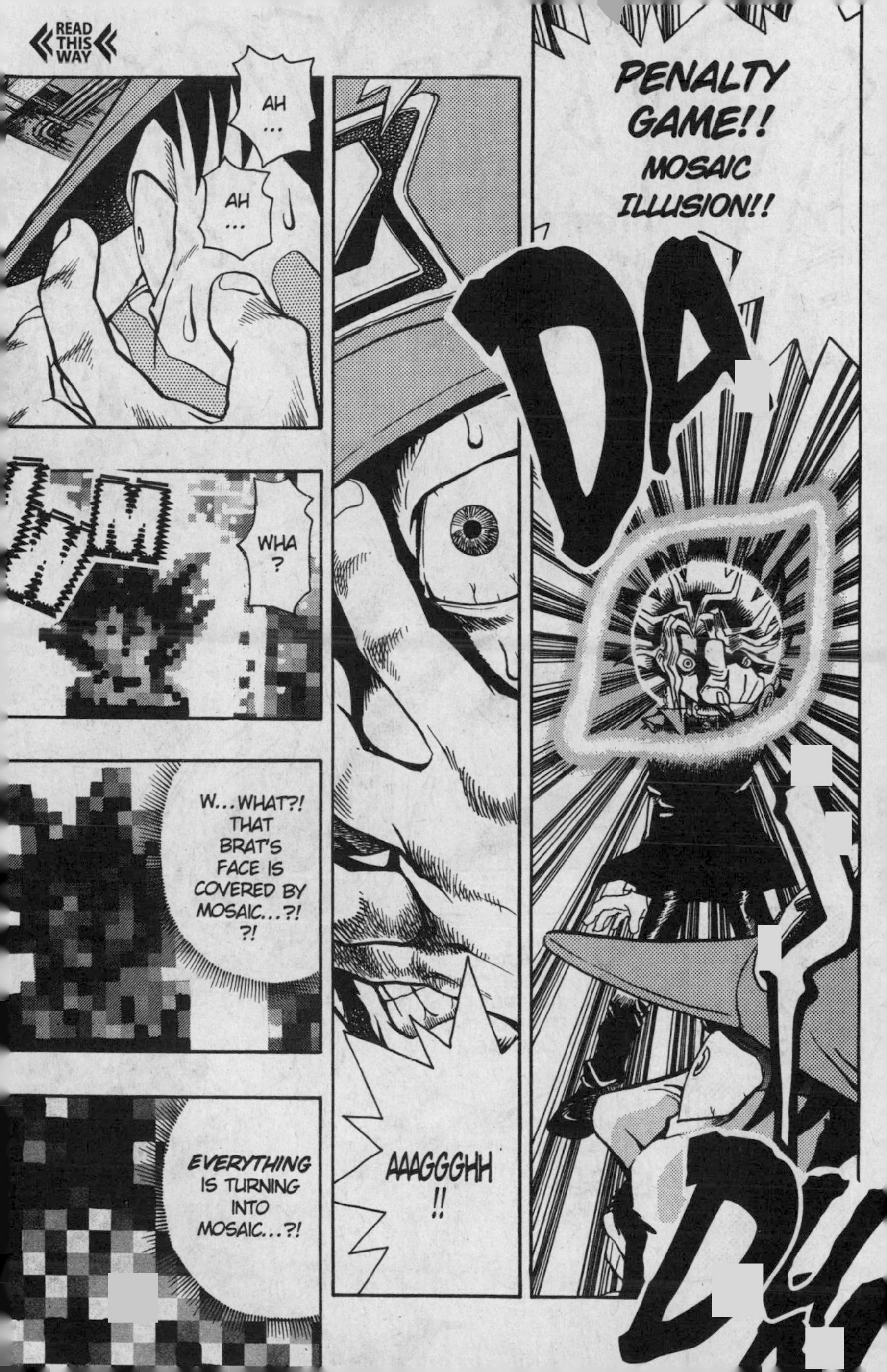
READ THIS WAY
PENALTY GAME!! MOSAIC ILLUSION!!
AAAGGGHH !!
AH ...
AH ...
WHA ?
W...WHAT?! THAT BRAT'S FACE IS COVERED BY MOSAIC...?! ?!
EVERYTHING IS TURNING INTO MOSAIC...?!

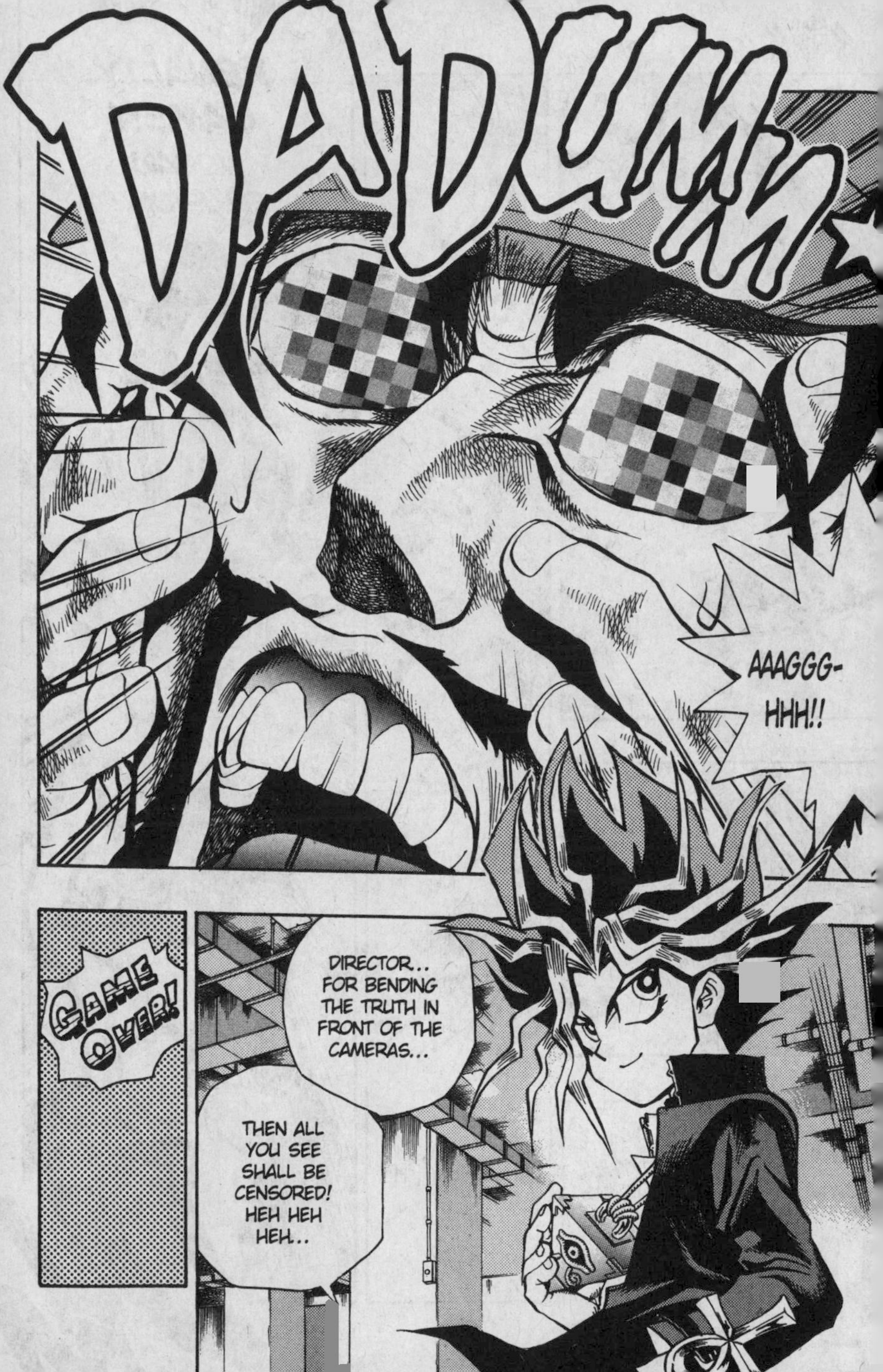
DADUMM
AAAGGG-HHH!!
DIRECTOR... FOR BENDING THE TRUTH IN FRONT OF THE CAMERAS...
THEN ALL YOU SEE SHALL BE CENSORED! HEH HEH HEH...
GAME OVER!

READ THIS WAY

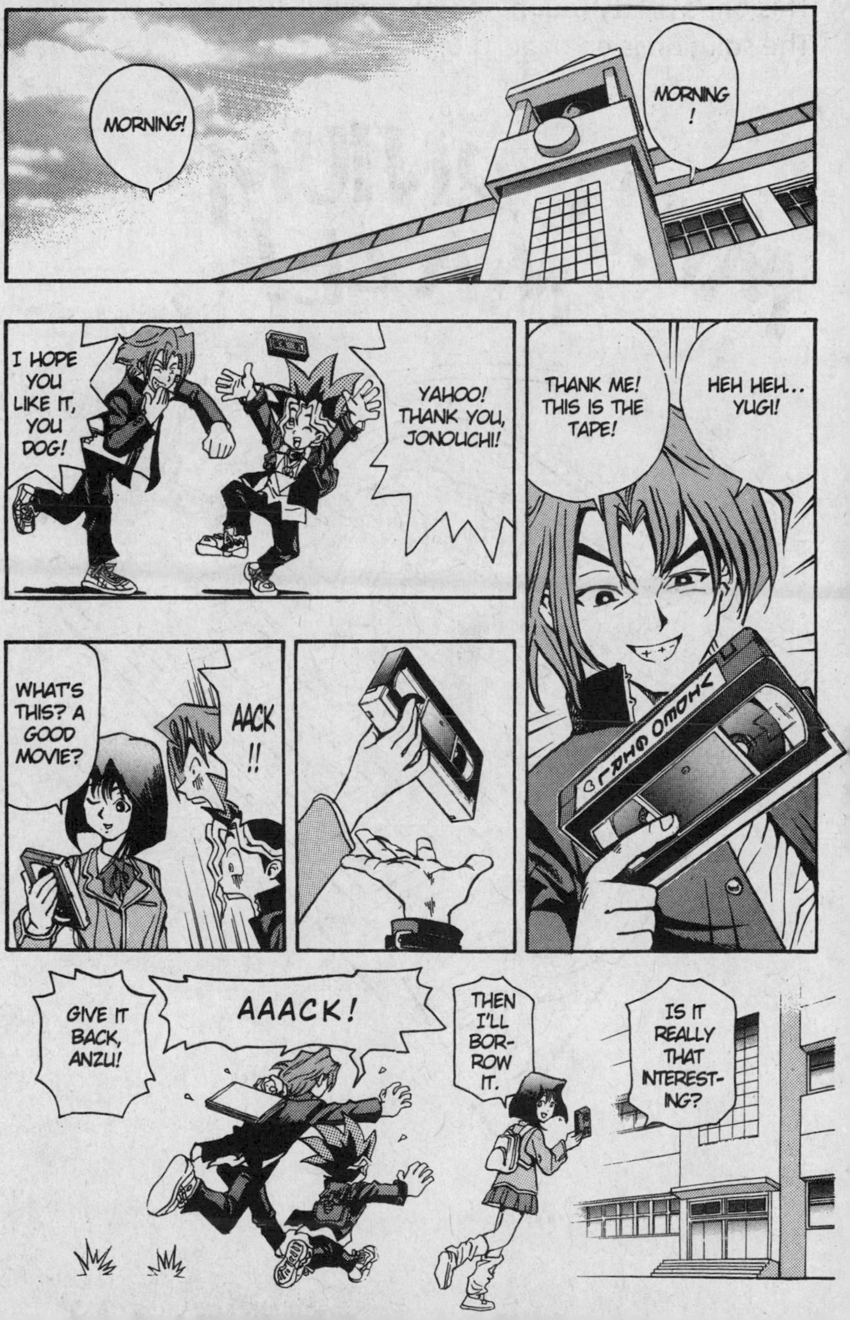
MORNING!
MORNING!
HEH HEH... YUGI!
THANK ME! THIS IS THE TAPE!
YAHOO! THANK YOU, JONOUCHI!
I HOPE YOU LIKE IT, YOU DOG!
AACK!!
WHAT'S THIS? A GOOD MOVIE?
IS IT REALLY THAT INTEREST-ING?
THEN I'LL BOR-ROW IT.
AAACK!
GIVE IT BACK, ANZU!

This one's pretty tough—think carefully!
The solution is on page 196.

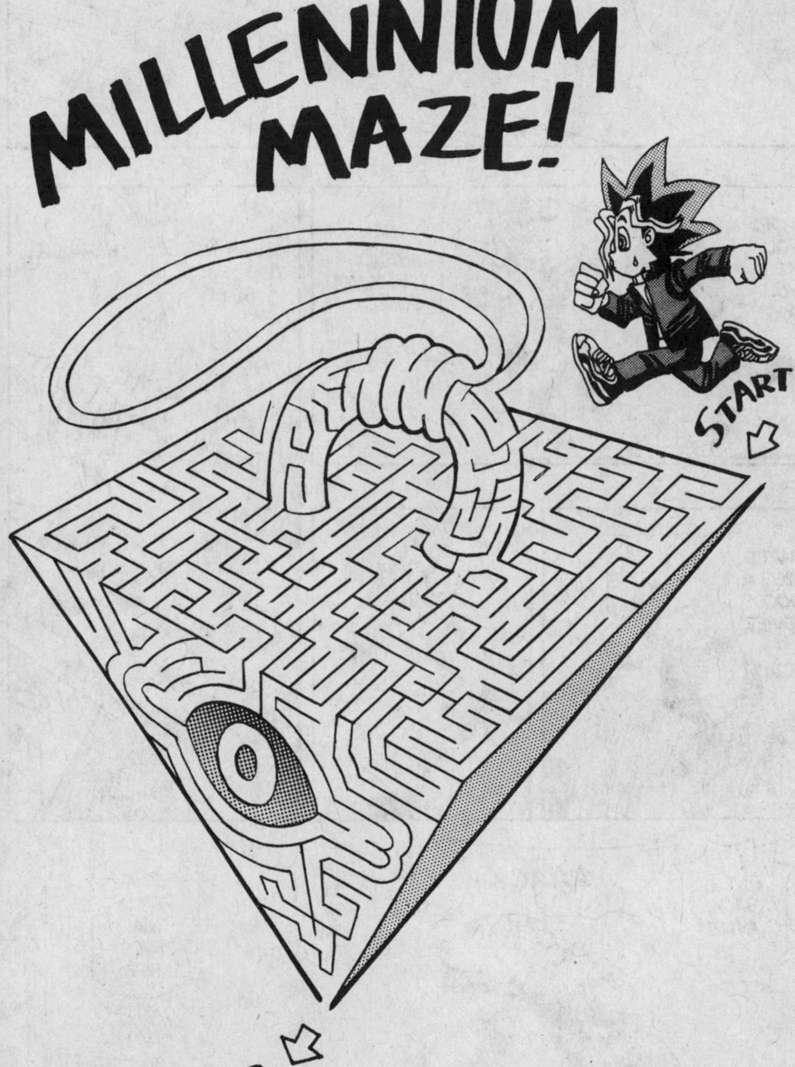
MILLENNIUM MAZE!
START
GOAL

Duel 3: Hard Beat!

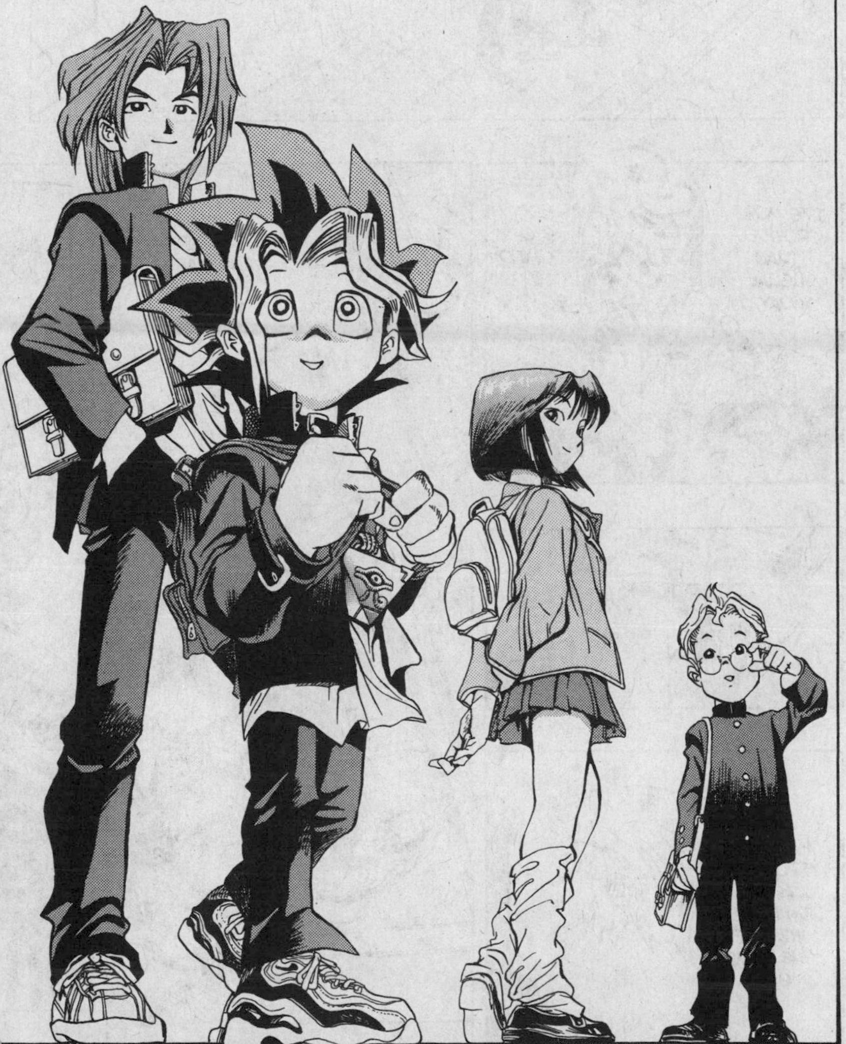

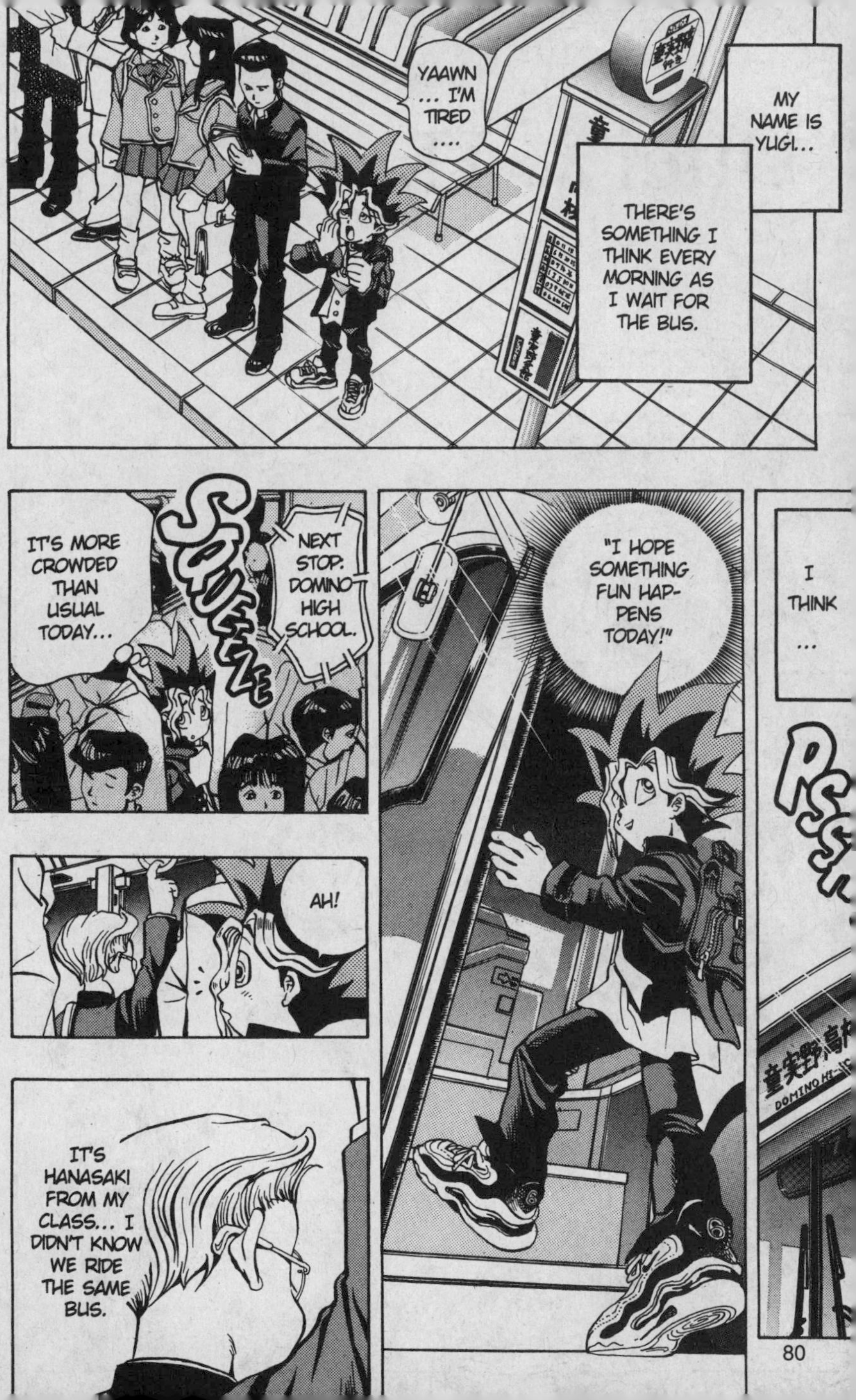
MY NAME IS YUGI...
THERE'S SOMETHING I THINK EVERY MORNING AS I WAIT FOR THE BUS.
YAAWN ... I'M TIRED ....
I THINK ...
"I HOPE SOMETHING FUN HAP-PENS TODAY!"
NEXT STOP: DOMINO HIGH SCHOOL.
SQUEEZE
IT'S MORE CROWDED THAN USUAL TODAY...
AH!
IT'S HANASAKI FROM MY CLASS... I DIDN'T KNOW WE RIDE THE SAME BUS.

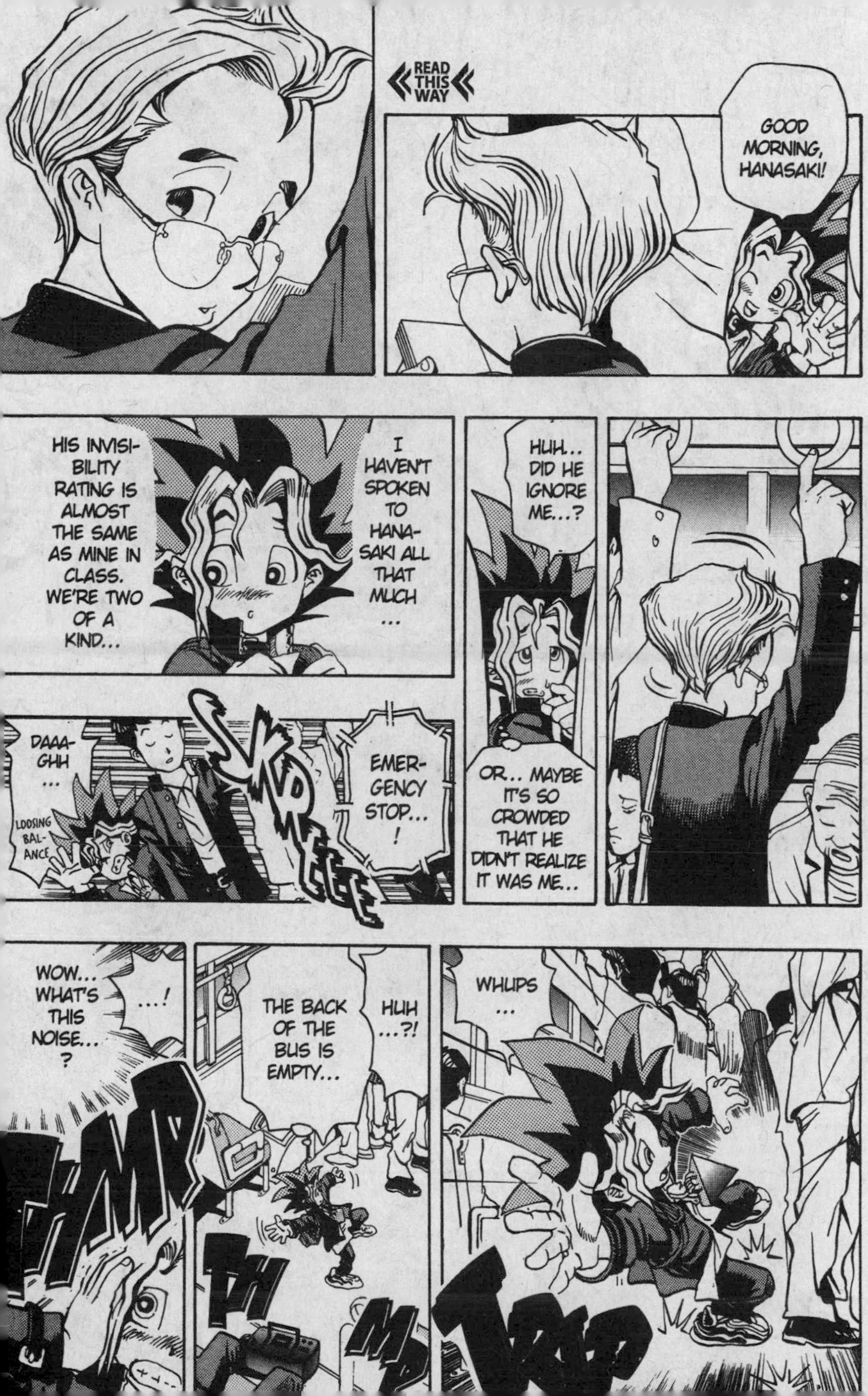
READ THIS WAY
GOOD MORNING, HANASAKI!
HUH... DID HE IGNORE ME...?
OR... MAYBE IT'S SO CROWDED THAT HE DIDN'T REALIZE IT WAS ME...
I HAVEN'T SPOKEN TO HANA-SAKI ALL THAT MUCH ...
HIS INVISI-BILITY RATING IS ALMOST THE SAME AS MINE IN CLASS. WE'RE TWO OF A KIND...
EMER-GENCY STOP... !
DAAA-GHH ...
LOOSING BAL-ANCE
WHUPS ...
HUH ...?!
THE BACK OF THE BUS IS EMPTY...
...!
WOW... WHAT'S THIS NOISE... ?

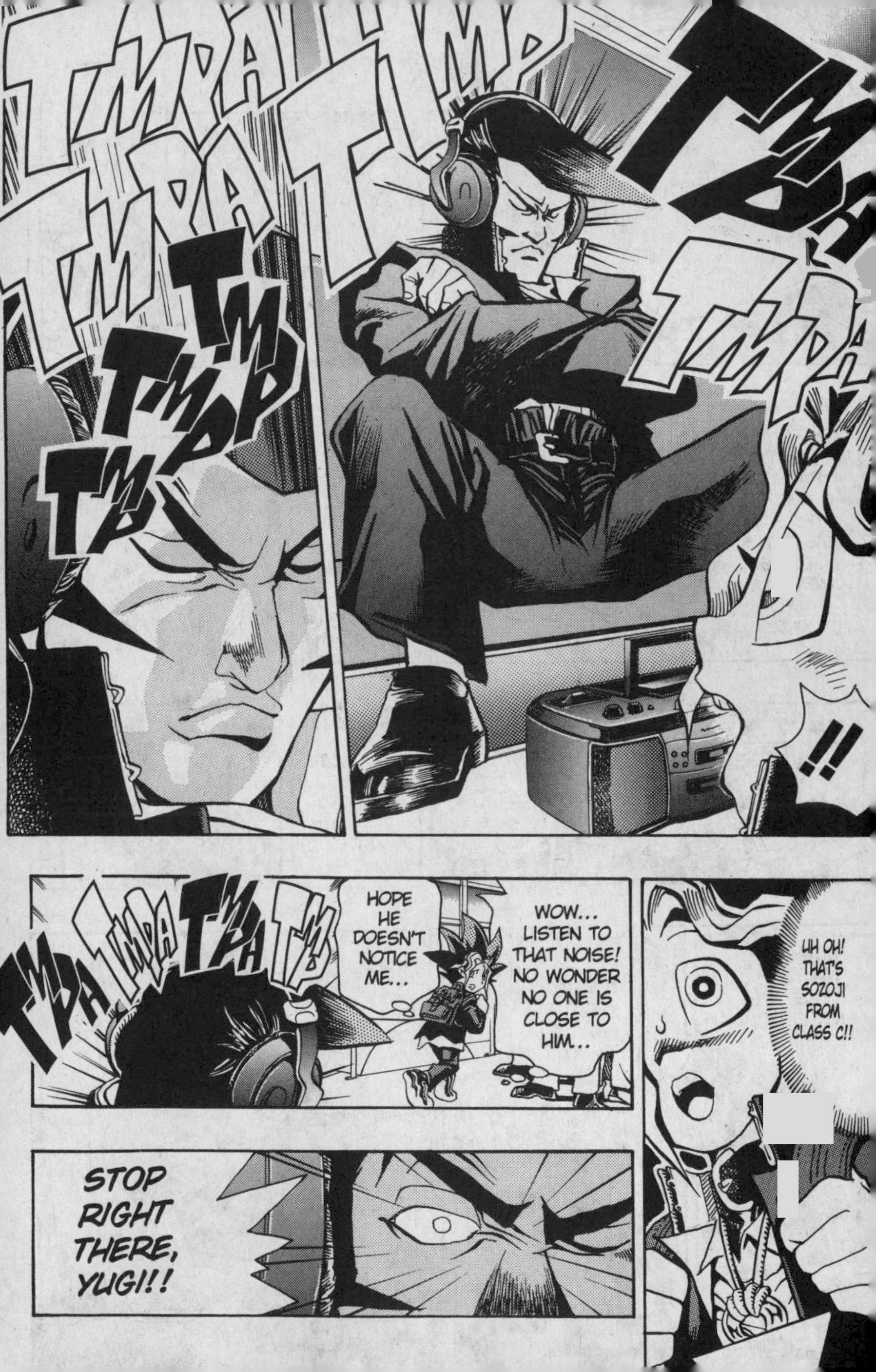
!!
WOW... LISTEN TO THAT NOISE! NO WONDER NO ONE IS CLOSE TO HIM...
HOPE HE DOESN'T NOTICE ME...
UH OH! THAT'S SOZOJI FROM CLASS C!!
STOP RIGHT THERE, YUGI!!

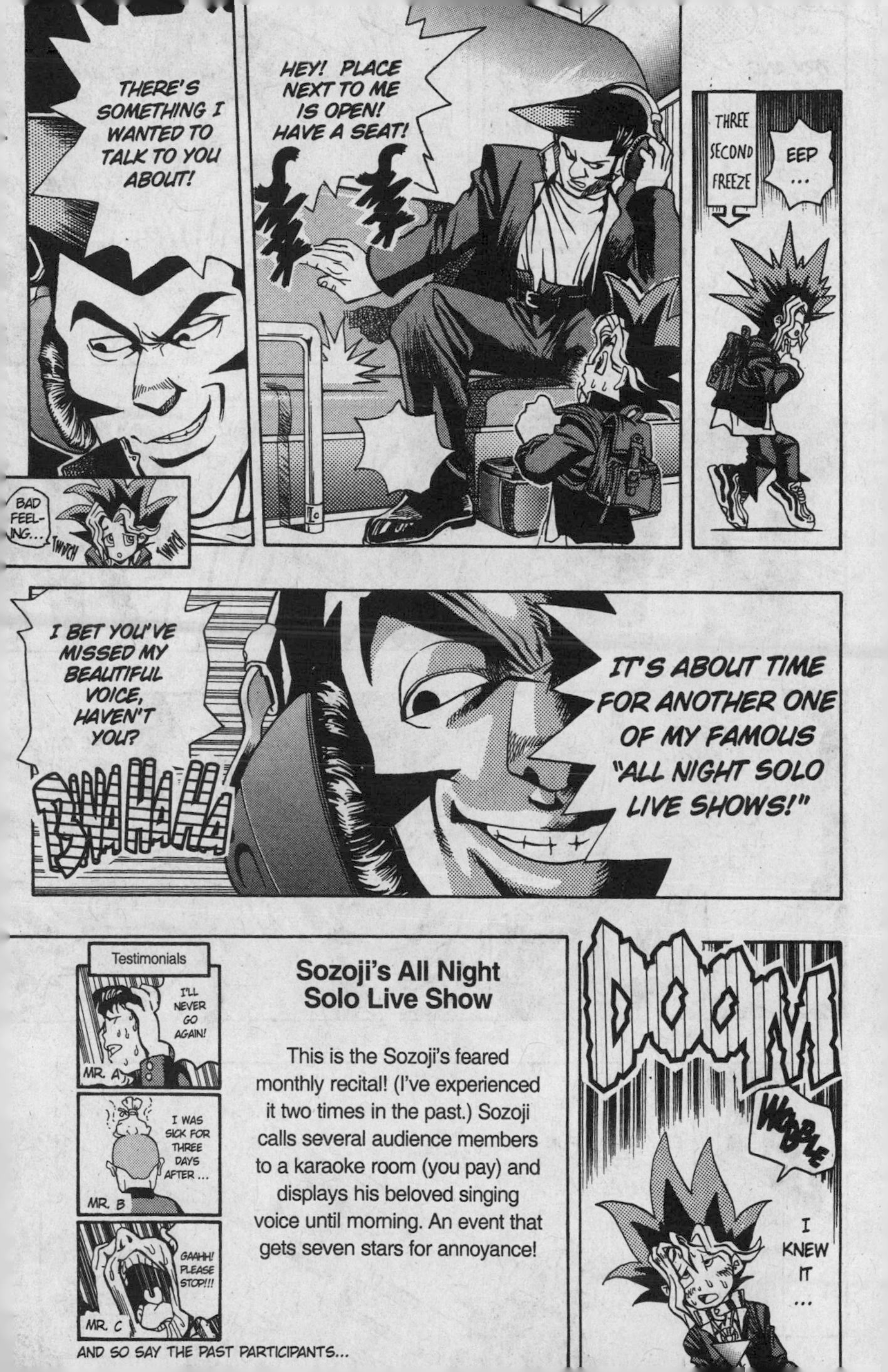
THERE'S SOMETHING I WANTED TO TALK TO YOU ABOUT!
BAD FEEL-ING...
TWITCH
TWITCH
HEY! PLACE NEXT TO ME IS OPEN! HAVE A SEAT!
THREE SECOND FREEZE
EEP ...
I BET YOU'VE MISSED MY BEAUTIFUL VOICE, HAVEN'T YOU?
IT'S ABOUT TIME FOR ANOTHER ONE OF MY FAMOUS "ALL NIGHT SOLO LIVE SHOWS!"
Testimonials
I'LL NEVER GO AGAIN!
MR. A
I WAS SICK FOR THREE DAYS AFTER ...
MR. B
GAAHH! PLEASE STOP!!!
MR. C
AND SO SAY THE PAST PARTICIPANTS...
Sozoji's All Night Solo Live Show
This is the Sozoji's feared monthly recital! (I've experienced it two times in the past.) Sozoji calls several audience members to a karaoke room (you pay) and displays his beloved singing voice until morning. An event that gets seven stars for annoyance!
DOOM
WOBBLE
I KNEW IT ...

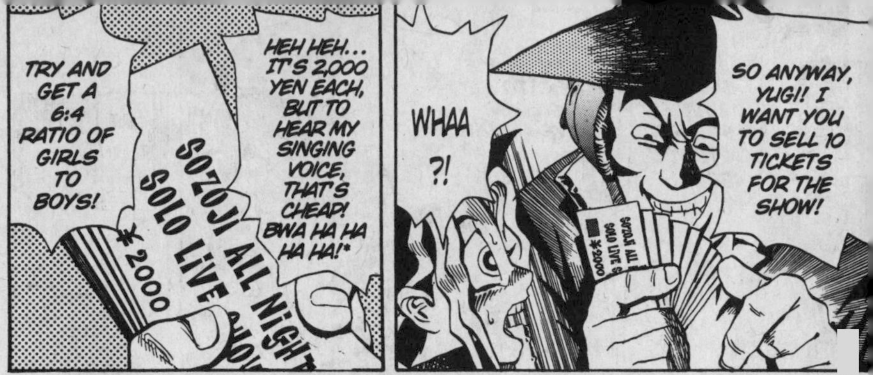
SO ANYWAY, YUGI! I WANT YOU TO SELL 10 TICKETS FOR THE SHOW!
WHAA ?!
HEH HEH... IT'S 2,000 YEN EACH, BUT TO HEAR MY SINGING VOICE, THAT'S CHEAP! BWA HA HA HA HA!*
TRY AND GET A 6:4 RATIO OF GIRLS TO BOYS!
SOZOJI ALL NIGHT
SOLO LIVE
¥2000

*ABOUT $17 U.S.

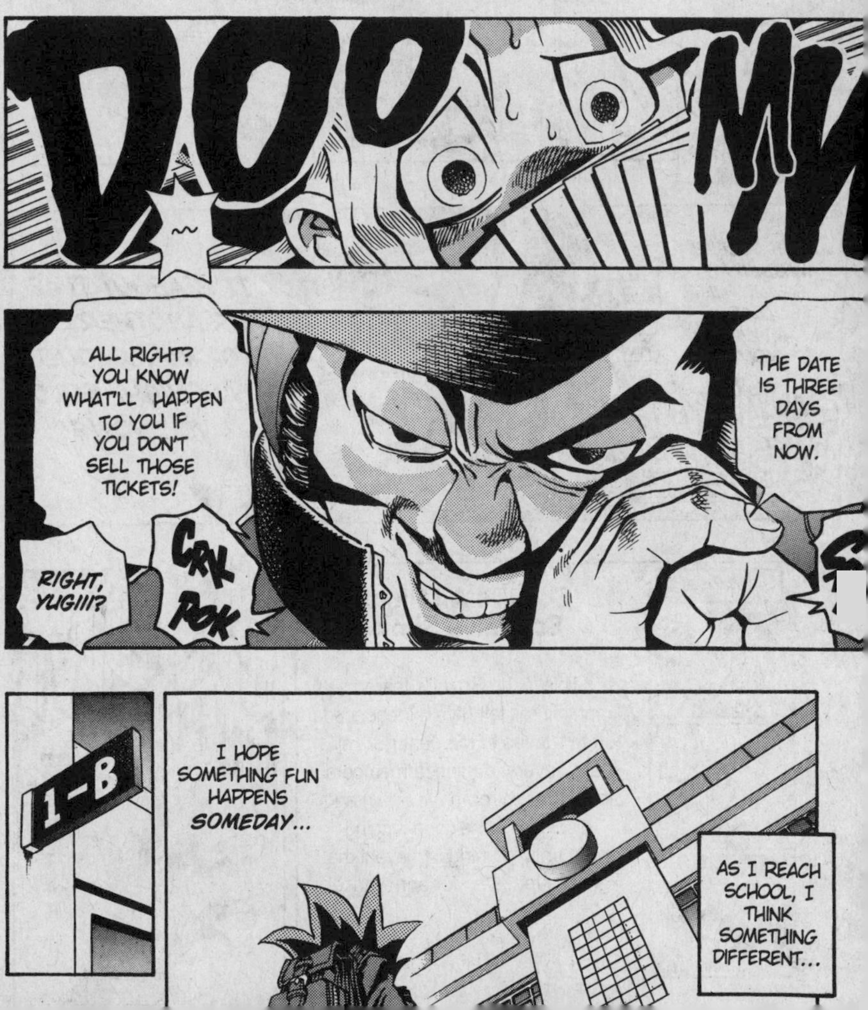
DOOM
THE DATE IS THREE DAYS FROM NOW.
ALL RIGHT? YOU KNOW WHAT'LL HAPPEN TO YOU IF YOU DON'T SELL THOSE TICKETS!
RIGHT, YUGIII?
CRAK ROK
AS I REACH SCHOOL, I THINK SOMETHING DIFFERENT...
I HOPE SOMETHING FUN HAPPENS SOMEDAY...
1-B

READ THIS WAY

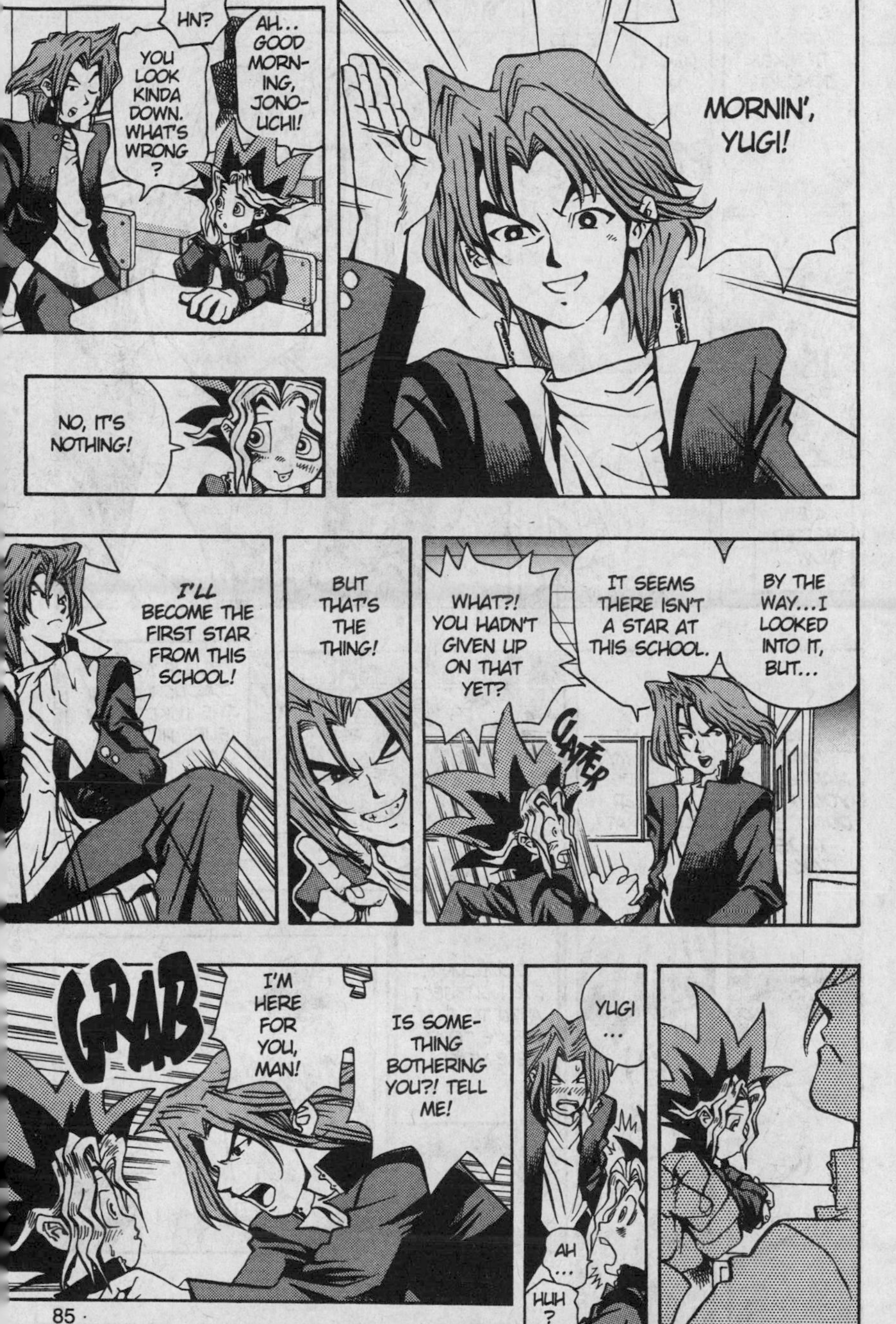

MORNIN', YUGI!
AH... GOOD MORN-ING, JONO-UCHI!
HN?
YOU LOOK KINDA DOWN. WHAT'S WRONG ?
NO, IT'S NOTHING!
BY THE WAY...I LOOKED INTO IT, BUT...
IT SEEMS THERE ISN'T A STAR AT THIS SCHOOL.
CLATTER
WHAT?! YOU HADN'T GIVEN UP ON THAT YET?
BUT THAT'S THE THING!
I'LL BECOME THE FIRST STAR FROM THIS SCHOOL!
YUGI ...
AH ...
HUH ?
IS SOME-THING BOTHERING YOU?! TELL ME!
I'M HERE FOR YOU, MAN!
GRAB

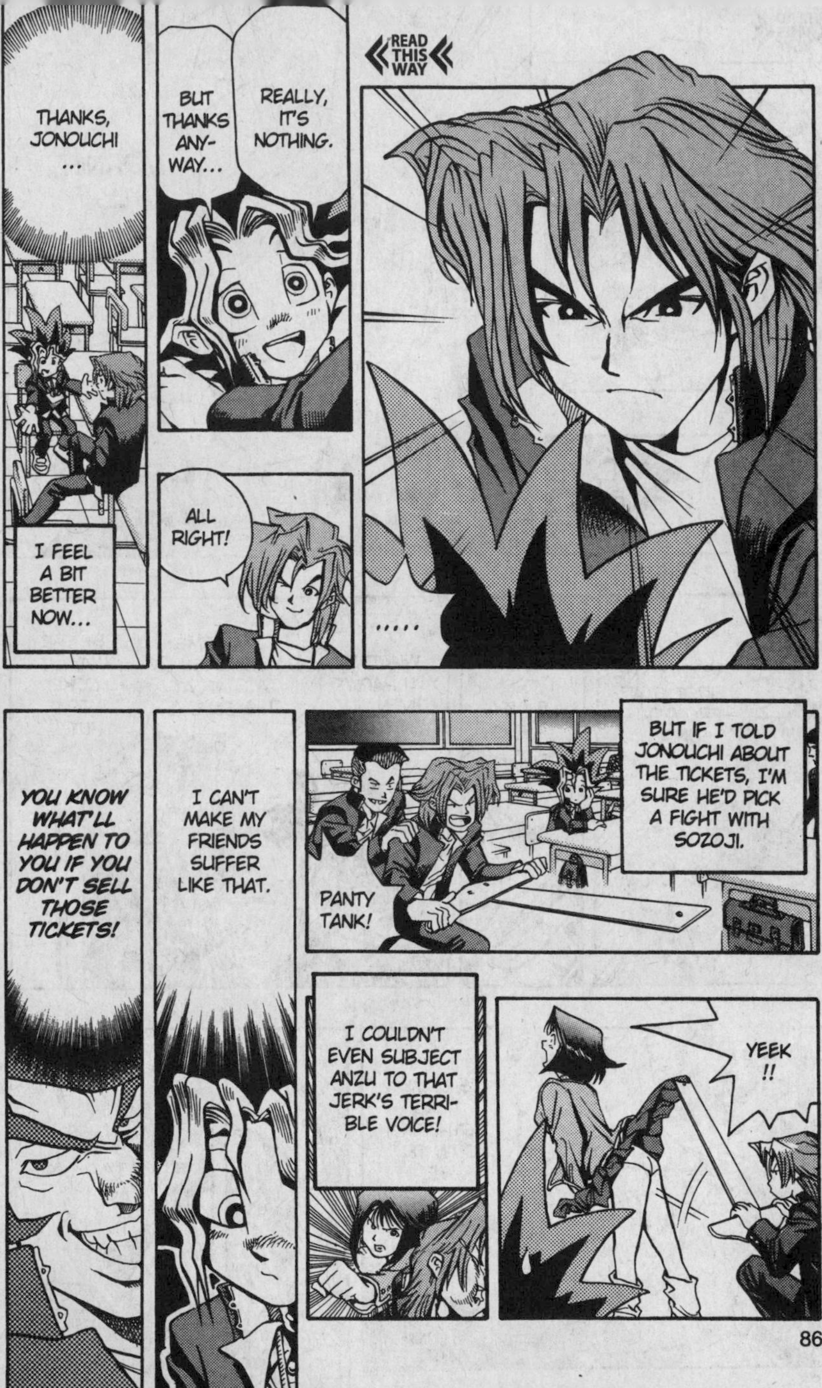
READ THIS WAY
.....
REALLY, IT'S NOTHING.
BUT THANKS ANY-WAY...
ALL RIGHT!
THANKS, JONOUCHI ...
I FEEL A BIT BETTER NOW...
BUT IF I TOLD JONOUCHI ABOUT THE TICKETS, I'M SURE HE'D PICK A FIGHT WITH SOZOJI.
PANTY TANK!
YEEK !!
I COULDN'T EVEN SUBJECT ANZU TO THAT JERK'S TERRI-BLE VOICE!
I CAN'T MAKE MY FRIENDS SUFFER LIKE THAT.
YOU KNOW WHAT'LL HAPPEN TO YOU IF YOU DON'T SELL THOSE TICKETS!

READ THIS WAY

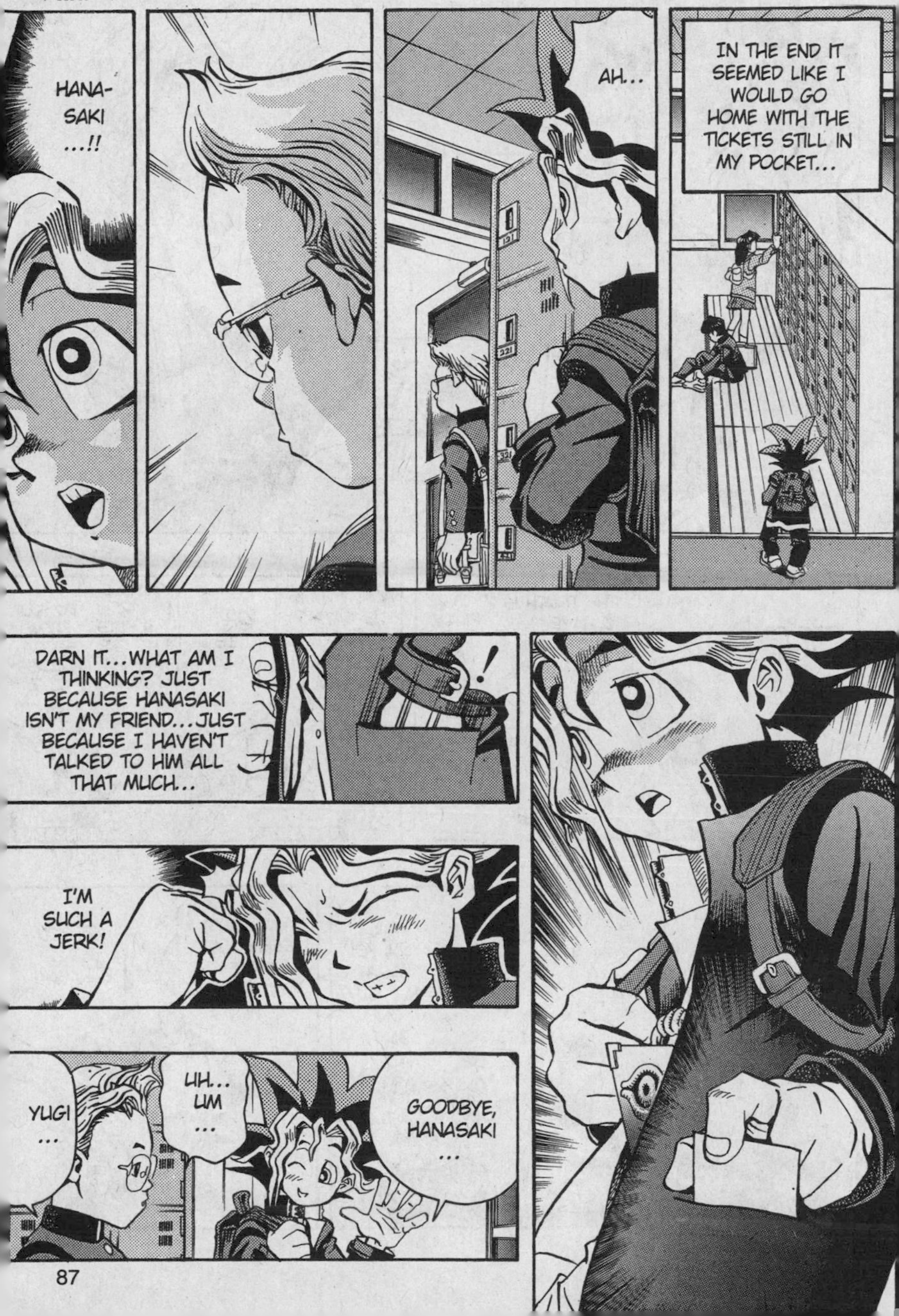

IN THE END IT SEEMED LIKE I WOULD GO HOME WITH THE TICKETS STILL IN MY POCKET...
AH...
HANA-SAKI ...!!
DARN IT...WHAT AM I THINKING? JUST BECAUSE HANASAKI ISN'T MY FRIEND...JUST BECAUSE I HAVEN'T TALKED TO HIM ALL THAT MUCH...
!
I'M SUCH A JERK!
GOODBYE, HANASAKI ...
UH... UM ...
YUGI ...

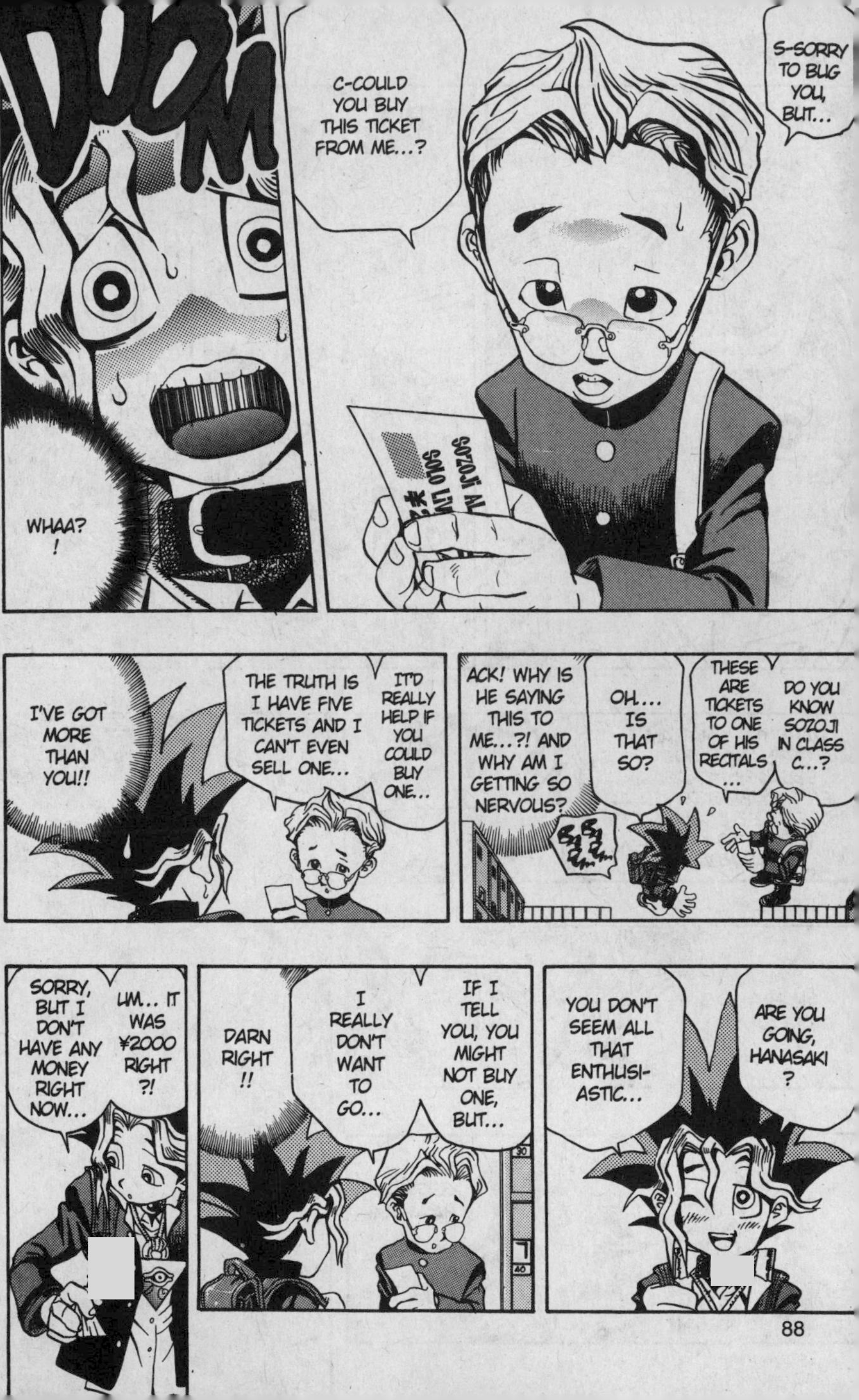
S-SORRY TO BUG YOU, BUT...
C-COULD YOU BUY THIS TICKET FROM ME...?
DOOM
WHAA?
!
DO YOU KNOW SOZOJI IN CLASS C...?
THESE ARE TICKETS TO ONE OF HIS RECITALS...
OH... IS THAT SO?
ACK! WHY IS HE SAYING THIS TO ME...?! AND WHY AM I GETTING SO NERVOUS?
IT'D REALLY HELP IF YOU COULD BUY ONE...
THE TRUTH IS I HAVE FIVE TICKETS AND I CAN'T EVEN SELL ONE...
I'VE GOT MORE THAN YOU!!
ARE YOU GOING, HANASAKI?
YOU DON'T SEEM ALL THAT ENTHUSI-ASTIC...
IF I TELL YOU, YOU MIGHT NOT BUY ONE, BUT...
I REALLY DON'T WANT TO GO...
DARN RIGHT!!
UM... IT WAS ¥2000 RIGHT?!
SORRY, BUT I DON'T HAVE ANY MONEY RIGHT NOW...

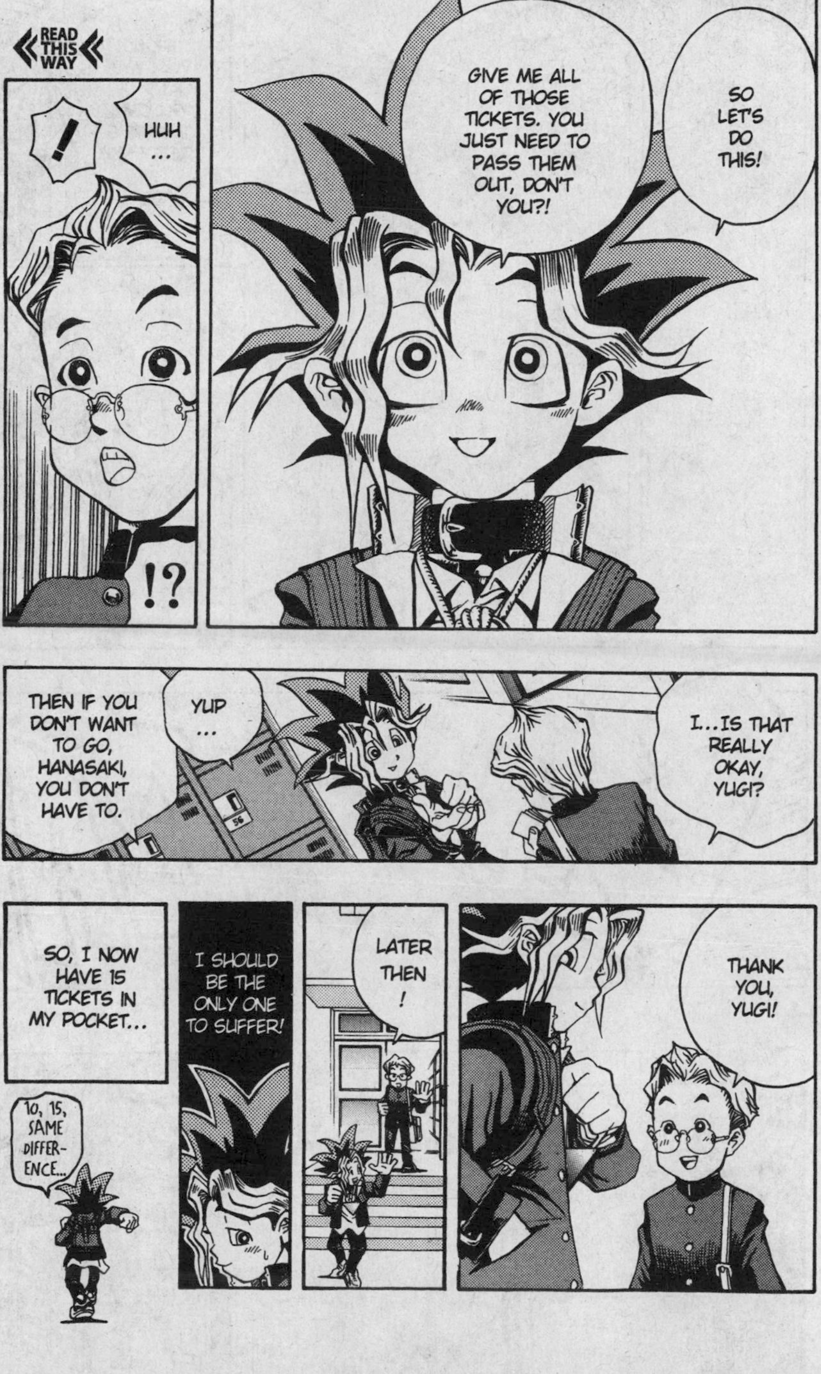
READ THIS WAY
SO LET'S DO THIS!
GIVE ME ALL OF THOSE TICKETS. YOU JUST NEED TO PASS THEM OUT, DON'T YOU?!
HUH ...
!
!?
I...IS THAT REALLY OKAY, YUGI?
YUP ...
THEN IF YOU DON'T WANT TO GO, HANASAKI, YOU DON'T HAVE TO.
THANK YOU, YUGI!
LATER THEN !
I SHOULD BE THE ONLY ONE TO SUFFER!
SO, I NOW HAVE 15 TICKETS IN MY POCKET...
10, 15, SAME DIFFER-ENCE...

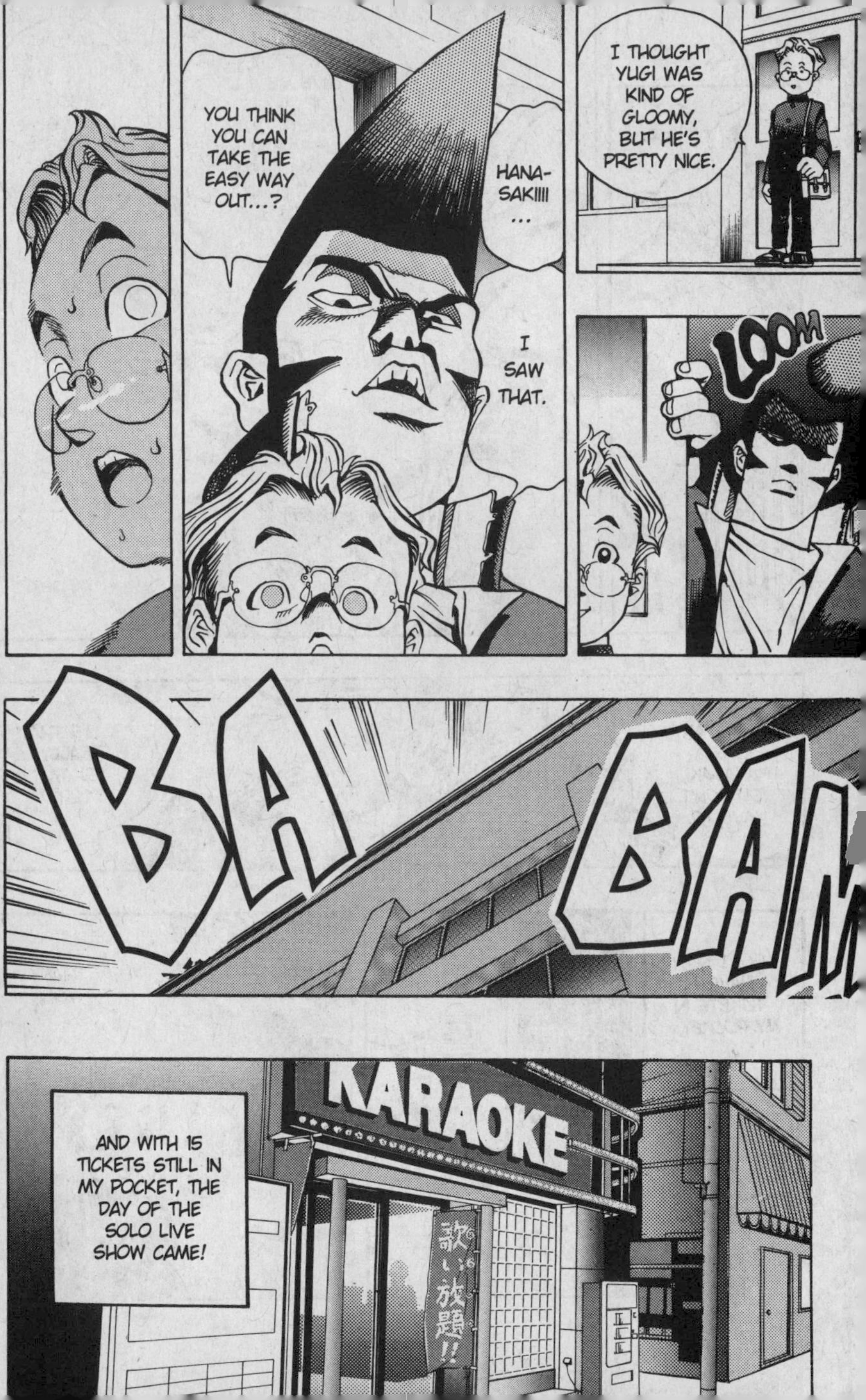
I THOUGHT YUGI WAS KIND OF GLOOMY, BUT HE'S PRETTY NICE.
LOOM
HANA-SAKIIII ...
I SAW THAT.
YOU THINK YOU CAN TAKE THE EASY WAY OUT...?
BA BAM
KARAOKE
歌い放題!!
AND WITH 15 TICKETS STILL IN MY POCKET, THE DAY OF THE SOLO LIVE SHOW CAME!

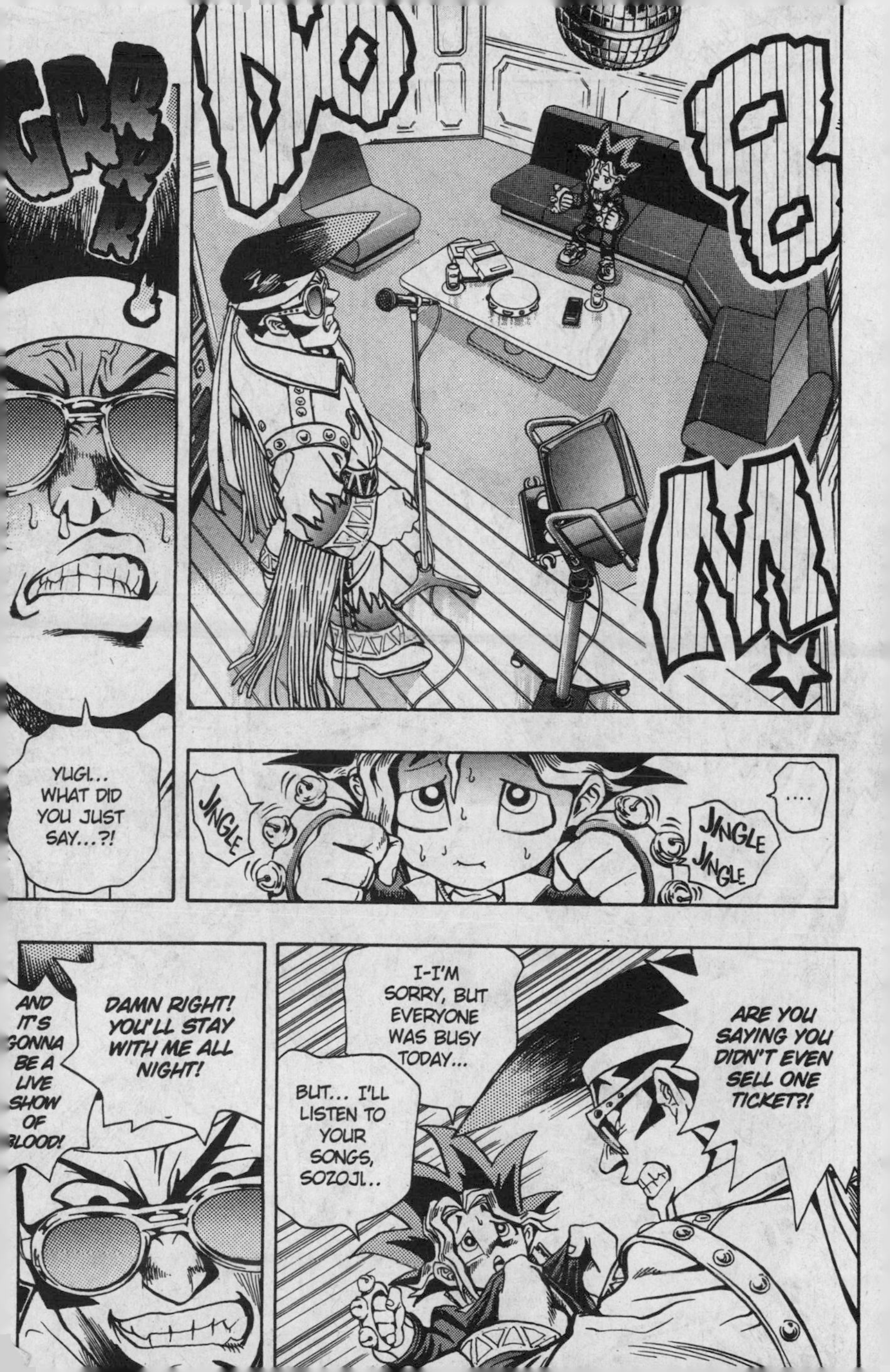

JINGLE JINGLE
....
JINGLE
YUGI... WHAT DID YOU JUST SAY...?!
ARE YOU SAYING YOU DIDN'T EVEN SELL ONE TICKET?!
I-I'M SORRY, BUT EVERYONE WAS BUSY TODAY...
BUT... I'LL LISTEN TO YOUR SONGS, SOZOJI...
DAMN RIGHT! YOU'LL STAY WITH ME ALL NIGHT!
AND IT'S GONNA BE A LIVE SHOW OF BLOOD!

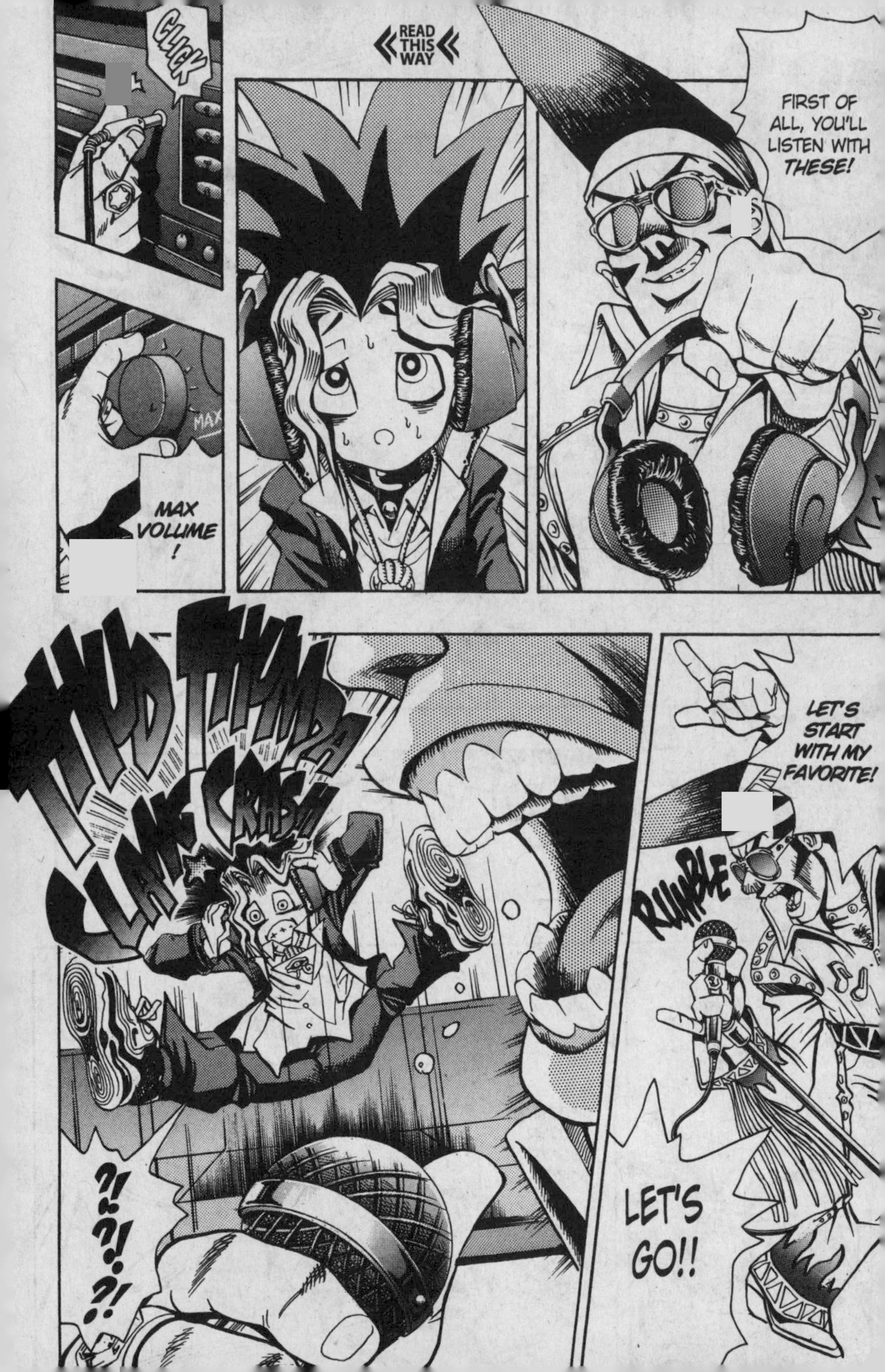
READ THIS WAY
FIRST OF ALL, YOU'LL LISTEN WITH THESE!
CLICK
MAX VOLUME!
LET'S START WITH MY FAVORITE!
RUMBLE
LET'S GO!!
THUD
CLANK
CRASH
?!?!?!

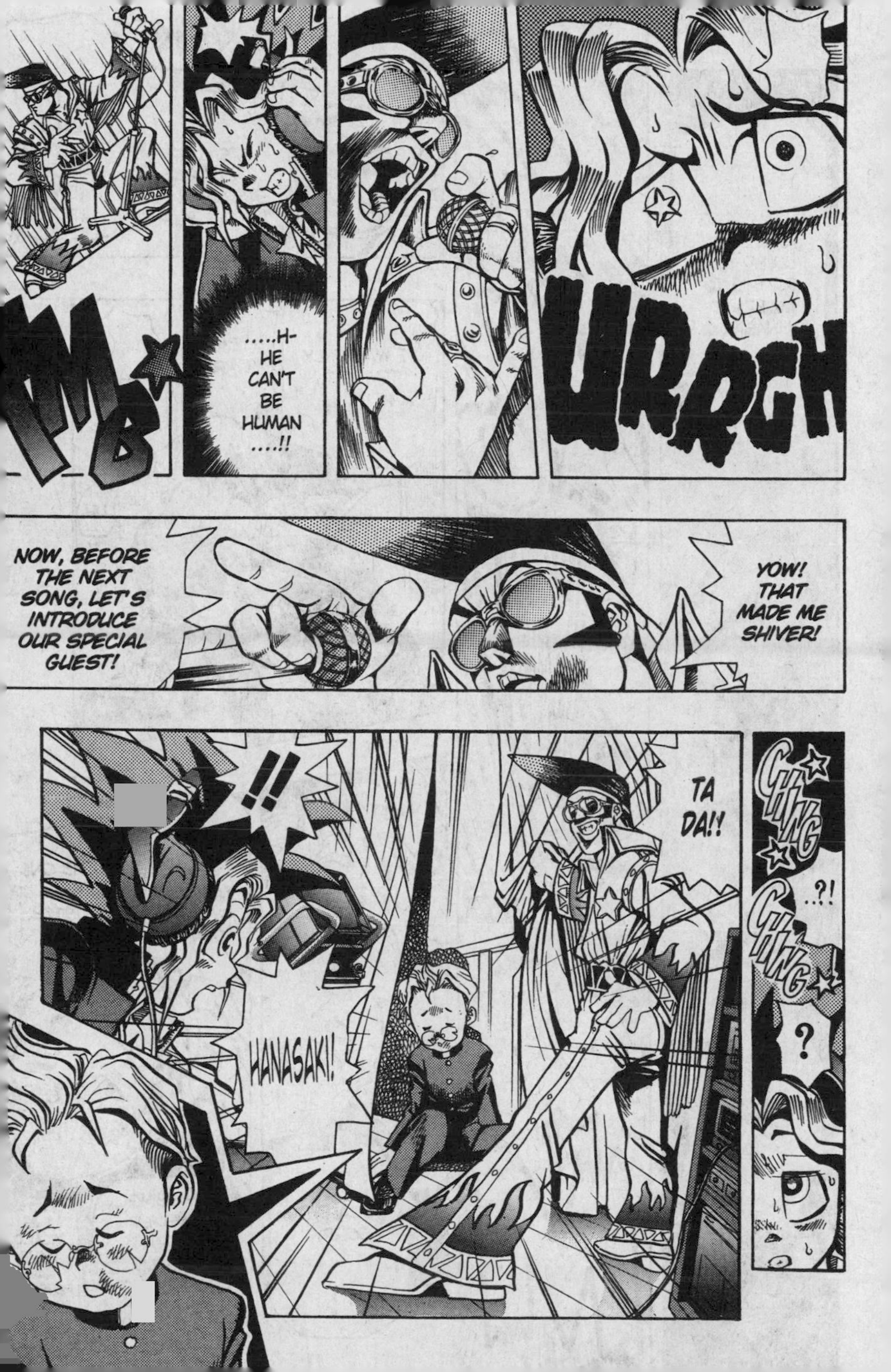
URRGH
....H- HE CAN'T BE HUMAN ....!!
YOW! THAT MADE ME SHIVER!
NOW, BEFORE THE NEXT SONG, LET'S INTRODUCE OUR SPECIAL GUEST!
CHING
CHING
..?!
?
TA DA!!
!!
HANASAKI!

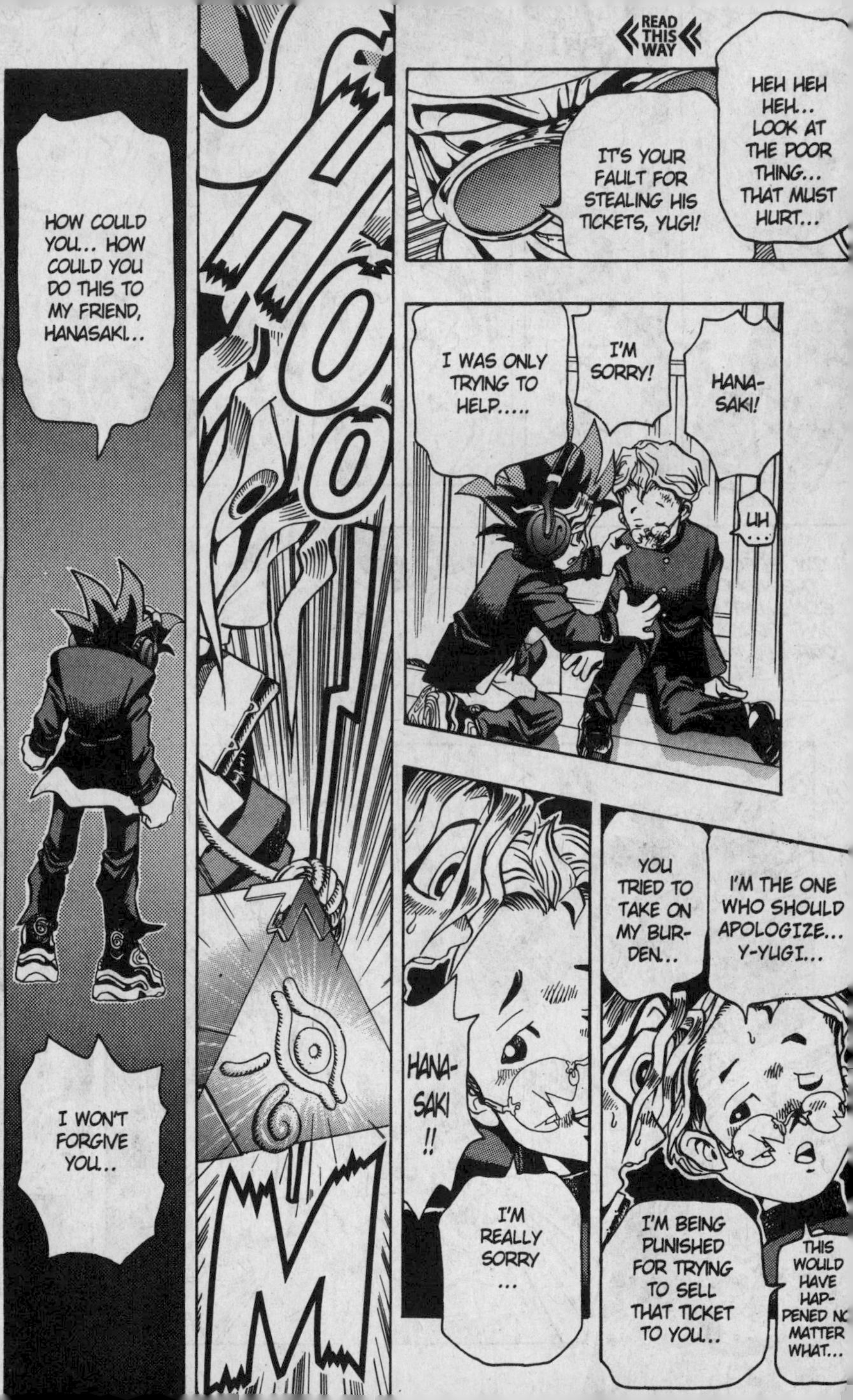
READ THIS WAY
HEH HEH HEH... LOOK AT THE POOR THING... THAT MUST HURT...
IT'S YOUR FAULT FOR STEALING HIS TICKETS, YUGI!
HANA-SAKI!
UH...
I'M SORRY!
I WAS ONLY TRYING TO HELP.....
I'M THE ONE WHO SHOULD APOLOGIZE... Y-YUGI...
YOU TRIED TO TAKE ON MY BUR-DEN...
THIS WOULD HAVE HAP-PENED NO MATTER WHAT...
I'M BEING PUNISHED FOR TRYING TO SELL THAT TICKET TO YOU...
HANA-SAKI !!
I'M REALLY SORRY ...
HOOM
HOW COULD YOU... HOW COULD YOU DO THIS TO MY FRIEND, HANASAKI...
I WON'T FORGIVE YOU...

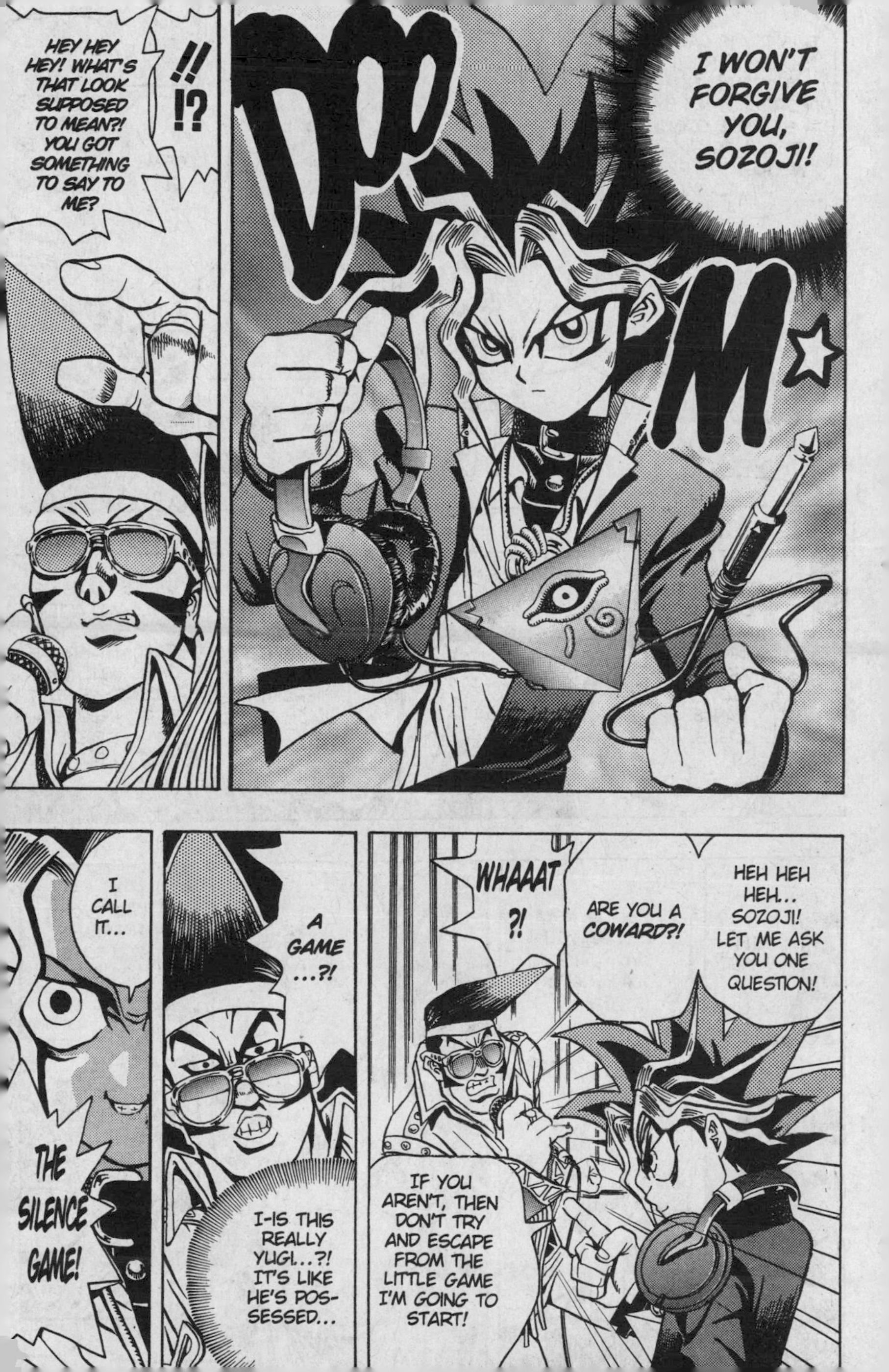
DOOM
I WON'T FORGIVE YOU, SOZOJI!
!!
!?
HEY HEY HEY! WHAT'S THAT LOOK SUPPOSED TO MEAN?! YOU GOT SOMETHING TO SAY TO ME?
HEH HEH HEH... SOZOJI! LET ME ASK YOU ONE QUESTION!
ARE YOU A COWARD?!
WHAAAT ?!
IF YOU AREN'T, THEN DON'T TRY AND ESCAPE FROM THE LITTLE GAME I'M GOING TO START!
A GAME ...?!
I-IS THIS REALLY YUGI...?! IT'S LIKE HE'S POS-SESSED...
I CALL IT...
THE SILENCE GAME!

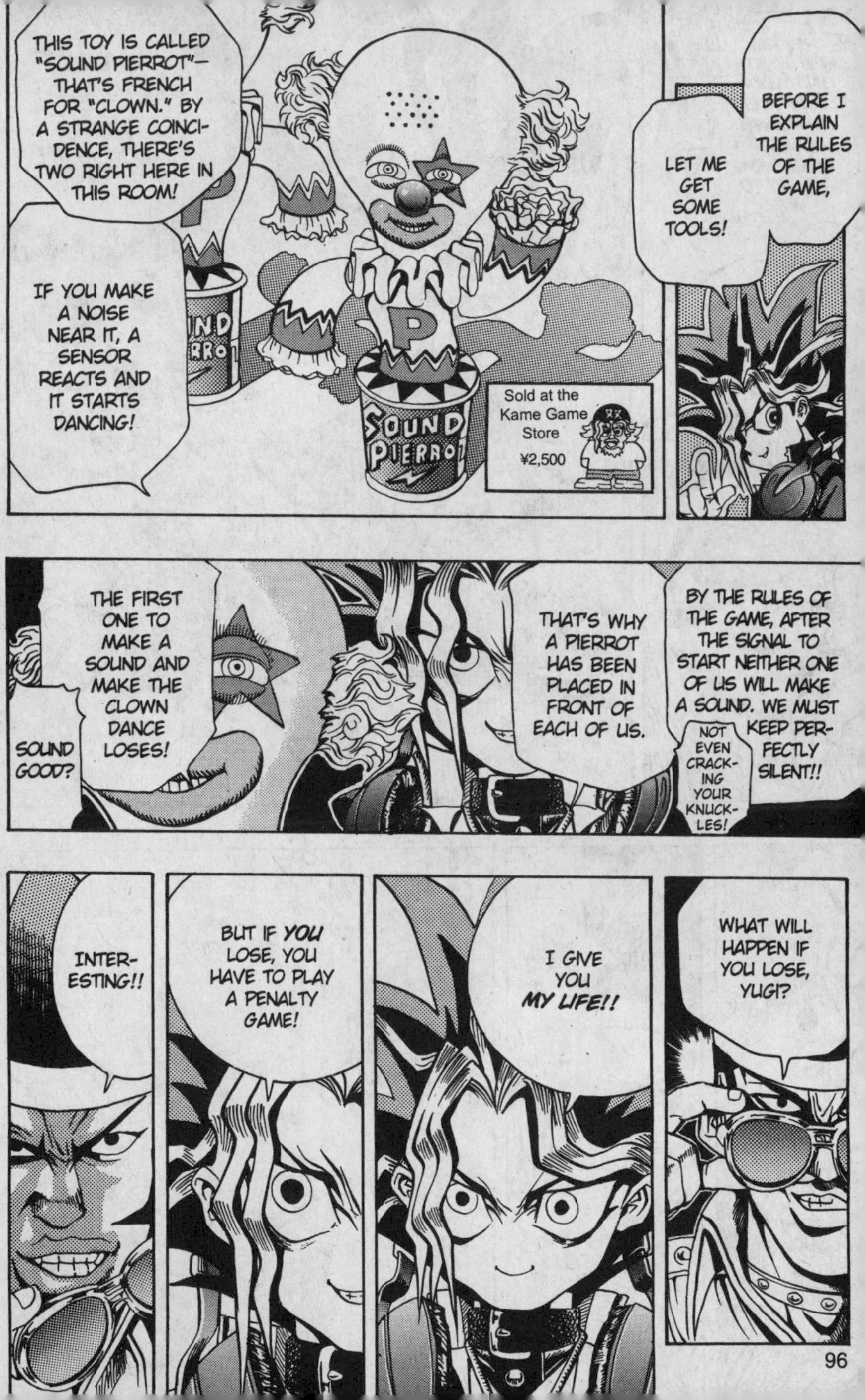
BEFORE I EXPLAIN THE RULES OF THE GAME,
LET ME GET SOME TOOLS!
THIS TOY IS CALLED "SOUND PIERROT"—THAT'S FRENCH FOR "CLOWN." BY A STRANGE COINCIDENCE, THERE'S TWO RIGHT HERE IN THIS ROOM!
IF YOU MAKE A NOISE NEAR IT, A SENSOR REACTS AND IT STARTS DANCING!
SOUND PIERROT
Sold at the Kame Game Store ¥2,500
BY THE RULES OF THE GAME, AFTER THE SIGNAL TO START NEITHER ONE OF US WILL MAKE A SOUND. WE MUST KEEP PERFECTLY SILENT!!
NOT EVEN CRACKING YOUR KNUCKLES!
THAT'S WHY A PIERROT HAS BEEN PLACED IN FRONT OF EACH OF US.
THE FIRST ONE TO MAKE A SOUND AND MAKE THE CLOWN DANCE LOSES!
SOUND GOOD?
WHAT WILL HAPPEN IF YOU LOSE, YUGI?
I GIVE YOU *MY LIFE!!*
BUT IF *YOU* LOSE, YOU HAVE TO PLAY A PENALTY GAME!
INTERESTING!!

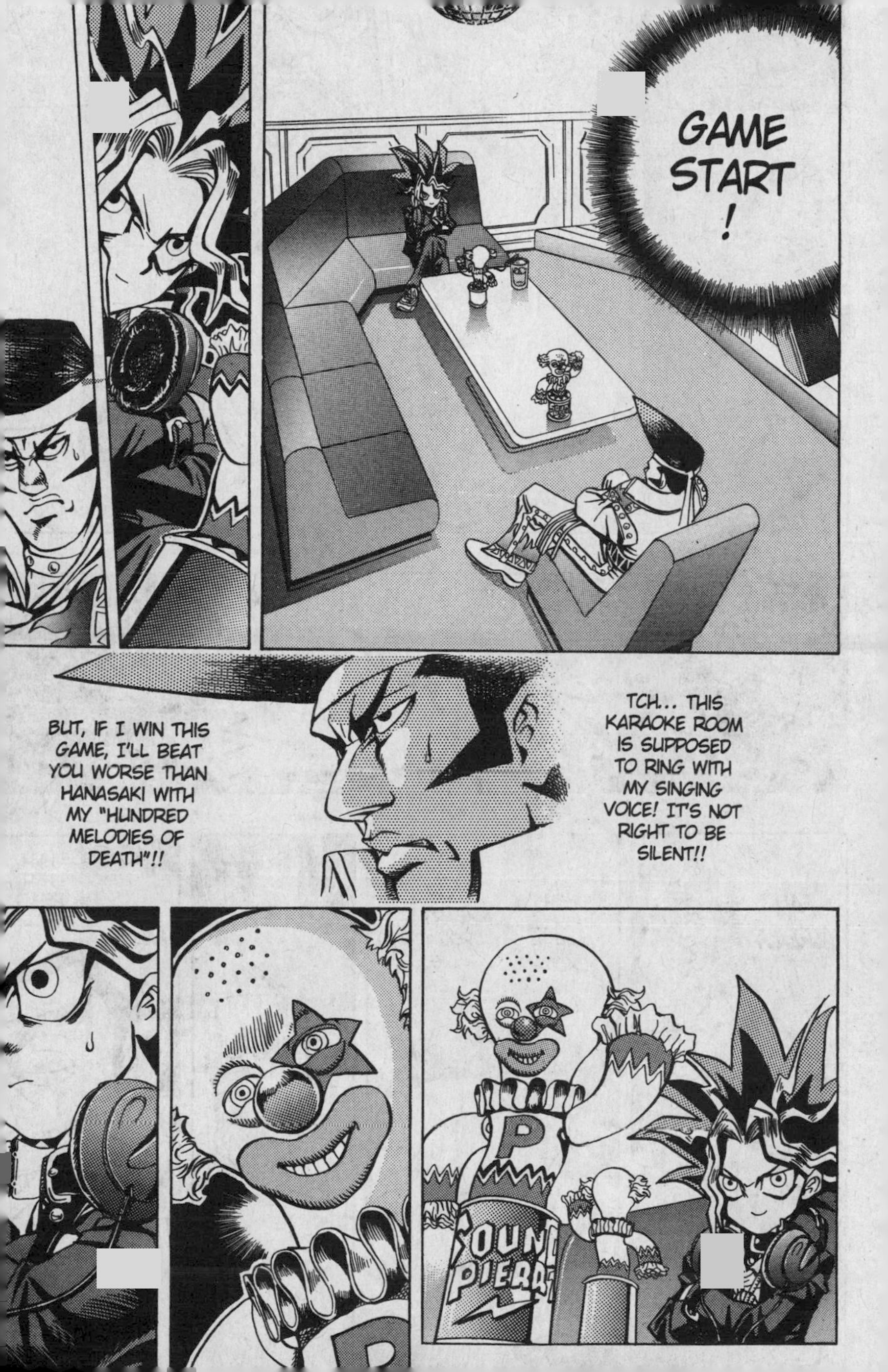
GAME START!
TCH... THIS KARAOKE ROOM IS SUPPOSED TO RING WITH MY SINGING VOICE! IT'S NOT RIGHT TO BE SILENT!!
BUT, IF I WIN THIS GAME, I'LL BEAT YOU WORSE THAN HANASAKI WITH MY "HUNDRED MELODIES OF DEATH"!!

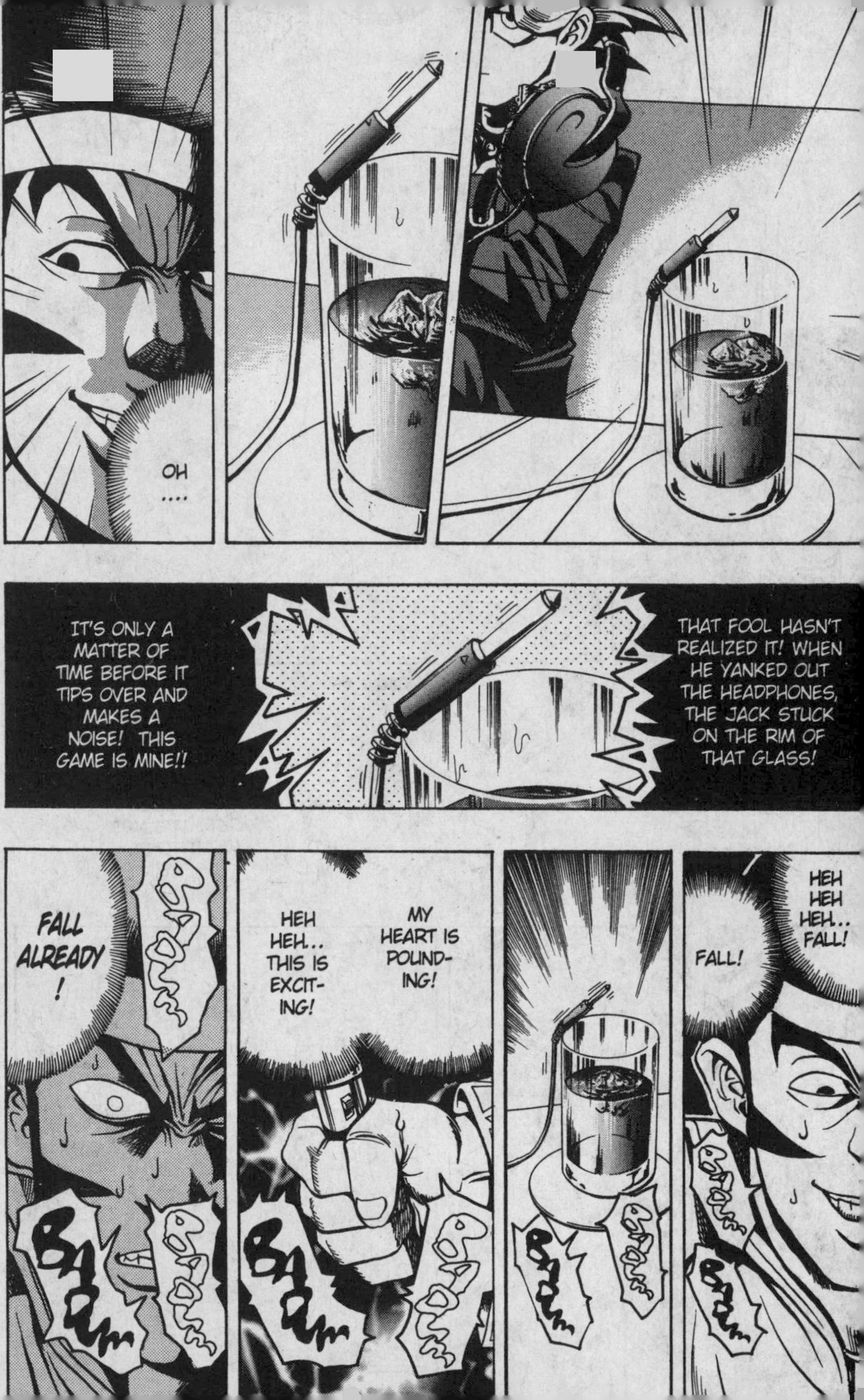
OH ....
THAT FOOL HASN'T REALIZED IT! WHEN HE YANKED OUT THE HEADPHONES, THE JACK STUCK ON THE RIM OF THAT GLASS!
IT'S ONLY A MATTER OF TIME BEFORE IT TIPS OVER AND MAKES A NOISE! THIS GAME IS MINE!!
HEH HEH HEH... FALL!
FALL!
BADUM
BADUM
BADUM
BADUM
MY HEART IS POUND-ING!
HEH HEH... THIS IS EXCIT-ING!
BADUM
BADUM
FALL ALREADY!
BADUM
BADUM
BADUM

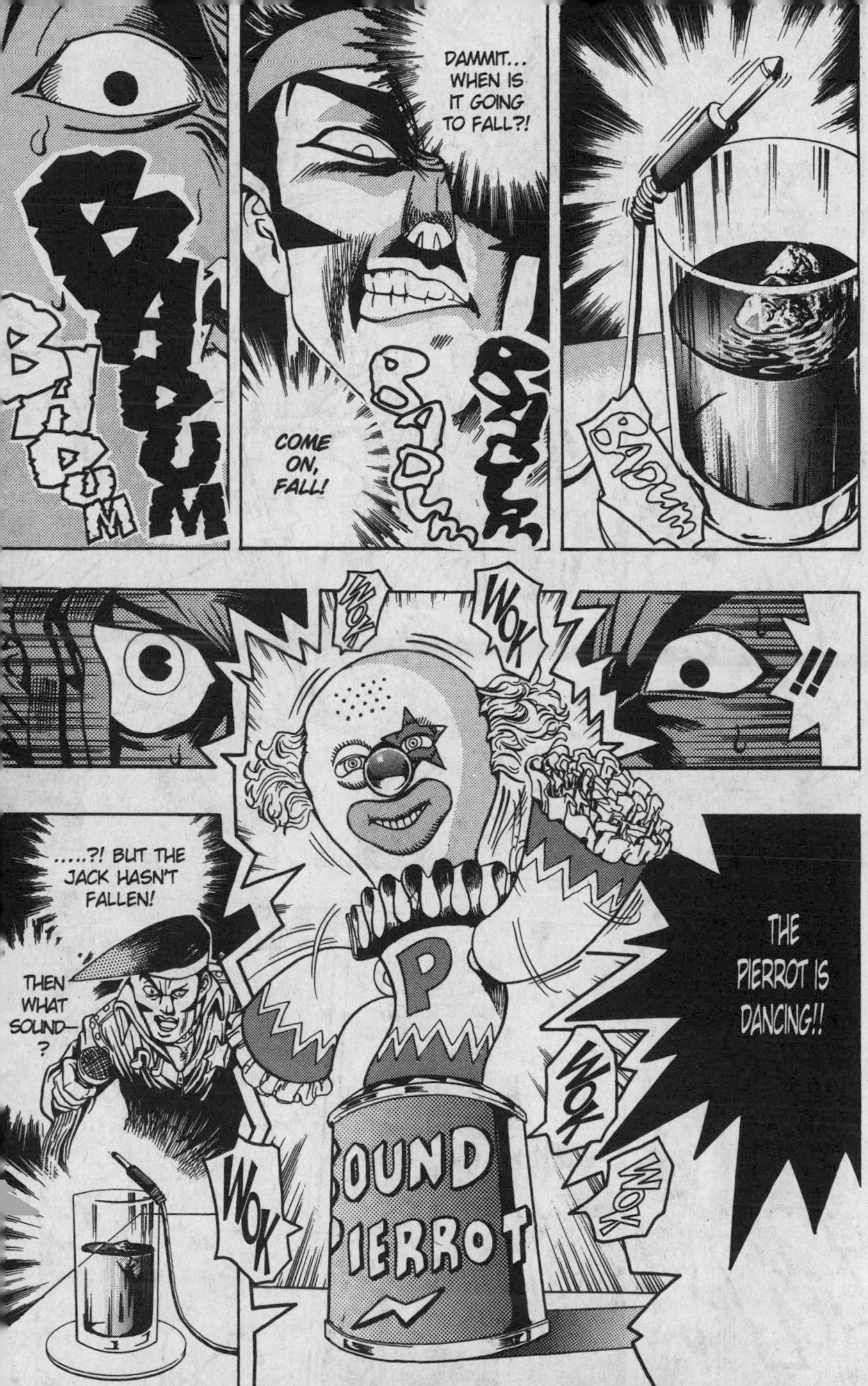
BADUM
DAMMIT... WHEN IS IT GOING TO FALL?!
BADUM
COME ON, FALL!
BADUM
BADUM
!!
WOK
WOK
THE PIERROT IS DANCING!!
WOK
WOK
.....?! BUT THE JACK HASN'T FALLEN!
THEN WHAT SOUND—?
SOUND PIERROT
WOK

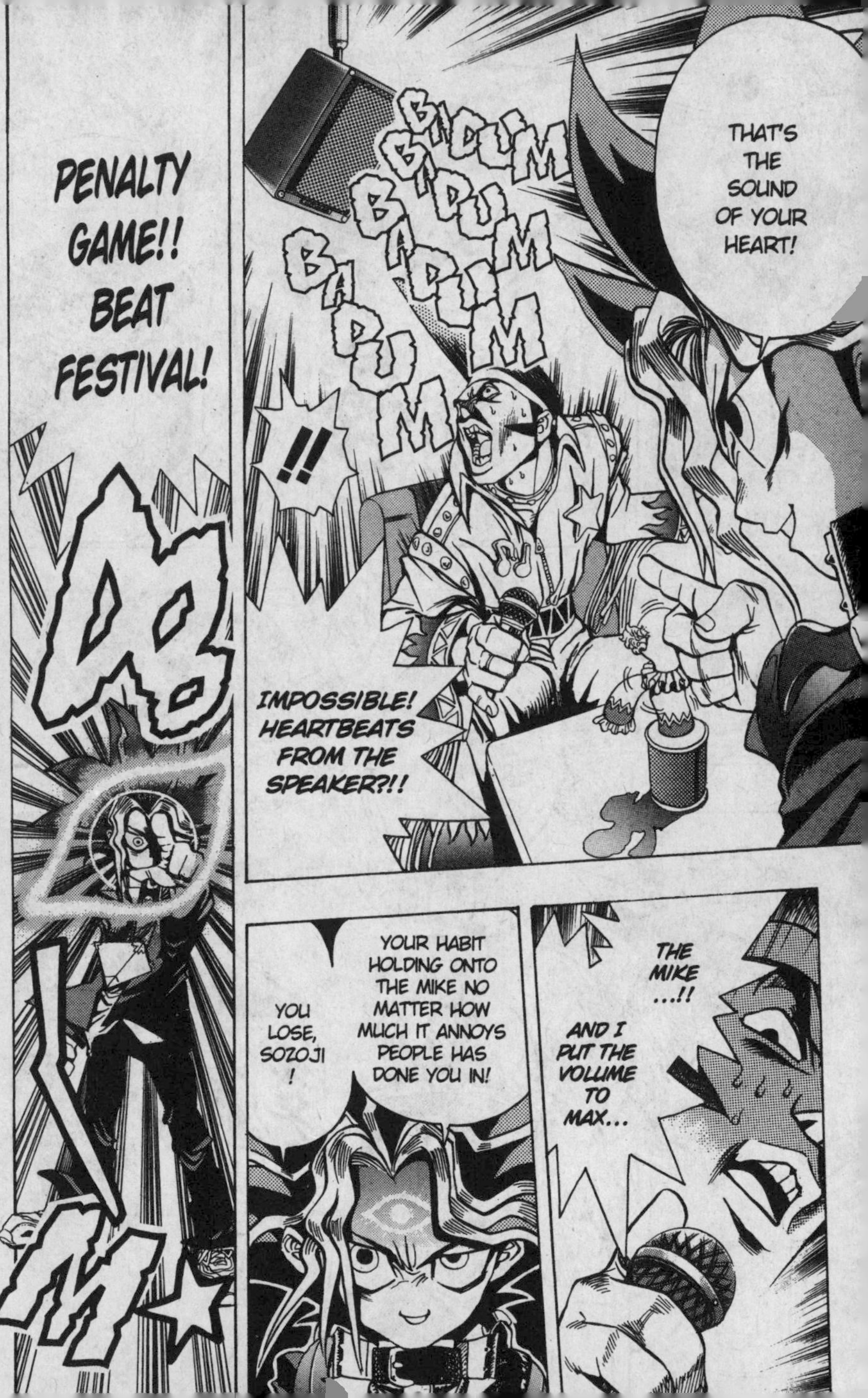
THAT'S THE SOUND OF YOUR HEART!
BA-DUM BA-DUM BA-DUM BA-DUM
!!
IMPOSSIBLE! HEARTBEATS FROM THE SPEAKER?!!
THE MIKE ...!!
AND I PUT THE VOLUME TO MAX...
YOUR HABIT HOLDING ONTO THE MIKE NO MATTER HOW MUCH IT ANNOYS PEOPLE HAS DONE YOU IN!
YOU LOSE, SOZOJI!
PENALTY GAME!! BEAT FESTIVAL!

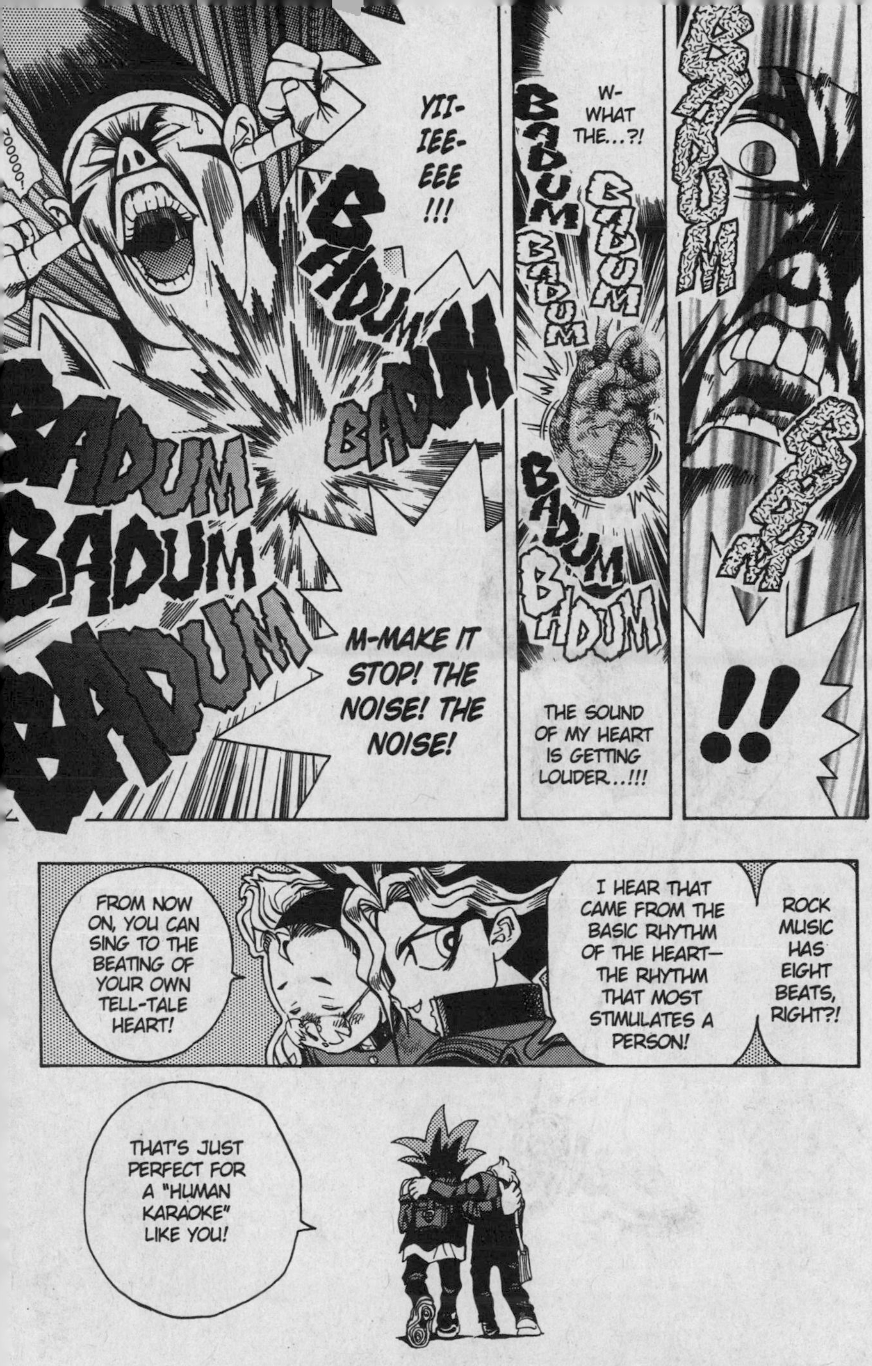

BADUM
BADUM
!!
W-WHAT THE...?!
BADUM BADUM BADUM
BADUM
BADUM
BADUM BADUM
THE SOUND OF MY HEART IS GETTING LOUDER...!!!
YIII-IEEE-EEE!!!
BADUM
BADUM
BADUM
BADUM
BADUM
M-MAKE IT STOP! THE NOISE! THE NOISE!
ROCK MUSIC HAS EIGHT BEATS, RIGHT?!
I HEAR THAT CAME FROM THE BASIC RHYTHM OF THE HEART—THE RHYTHM THAT MOST STIMULATES A PERSON!
FROM NOW ON, YOU CAN SING TO THE BEATING OF YOUR OWN TELL-TALE HEART!
THAT'S JUST PERFECT FOR A "HUMAN KARAOKE" LIKE YOU!

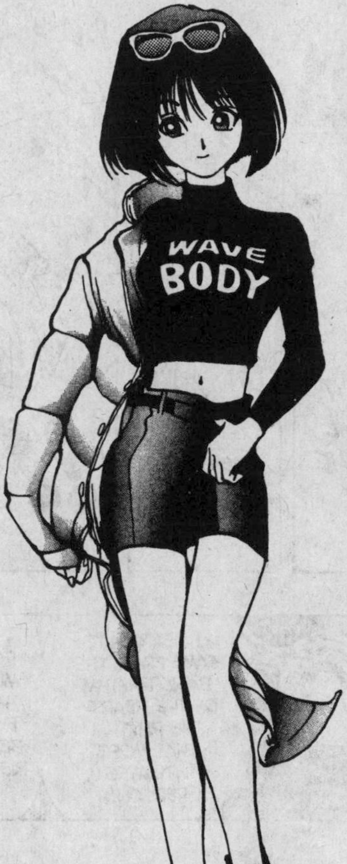
WAVE
BODY

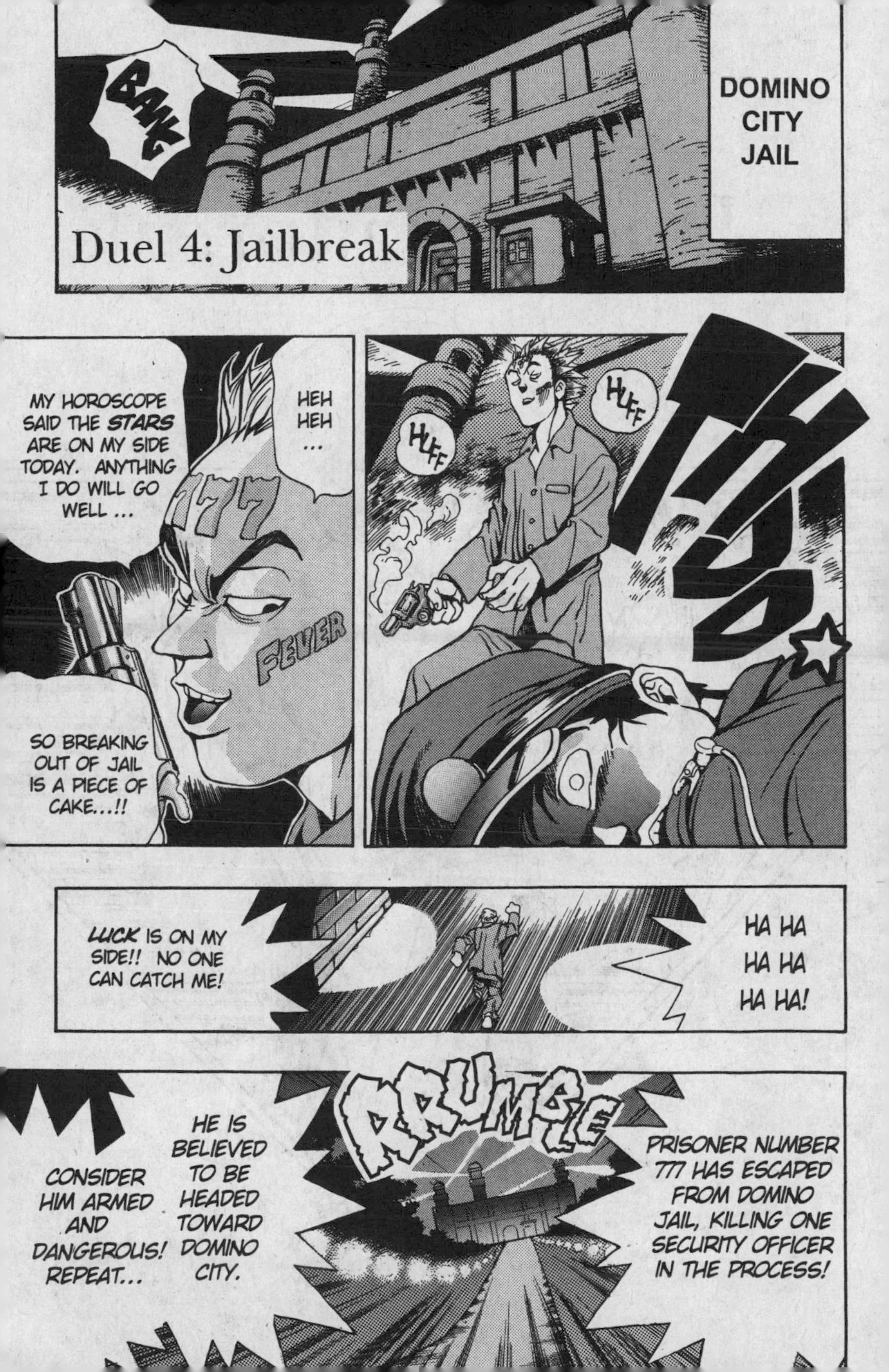
DOMINO CITY JAIL
BANG
Duel 4: Jailbreak
HUFF
HUFF
HEH HEH ...
MY HOROSCOPE SAID THE STARS ARE ON MY SIDE TODAY. ANYTHING I DO WILL GO WELL ...
SO BREAKING OUT OF JAIL IS A PIECE OF CAKE...!!
HA HA HA HA HA HA!
LUCK IS ON MY SIDE!! NO ONE CAN CATCH ME!
RRUMBLE
PRISONER NUMBER 777 HAS ESCAPED FROM DOMINO JAIL, KILLING ONE SECURITY OFFICER IN THE PROCESS!
HE IS BELIEVED TO BE HEADED TOWARD DOMINO CITY.
CONSIDER HIM ARMED AND DANGEROUS! REPEAT...

Duel 4: Jailbreak

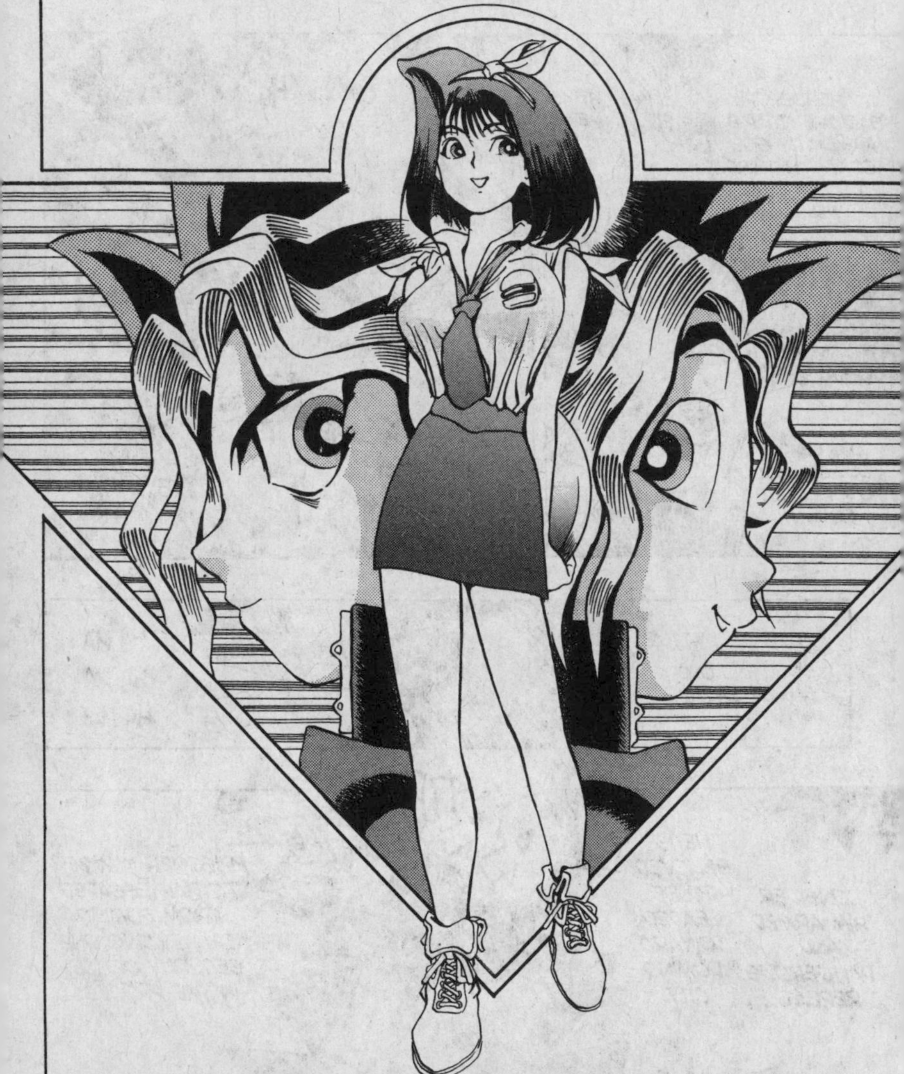

READ THIS WAY

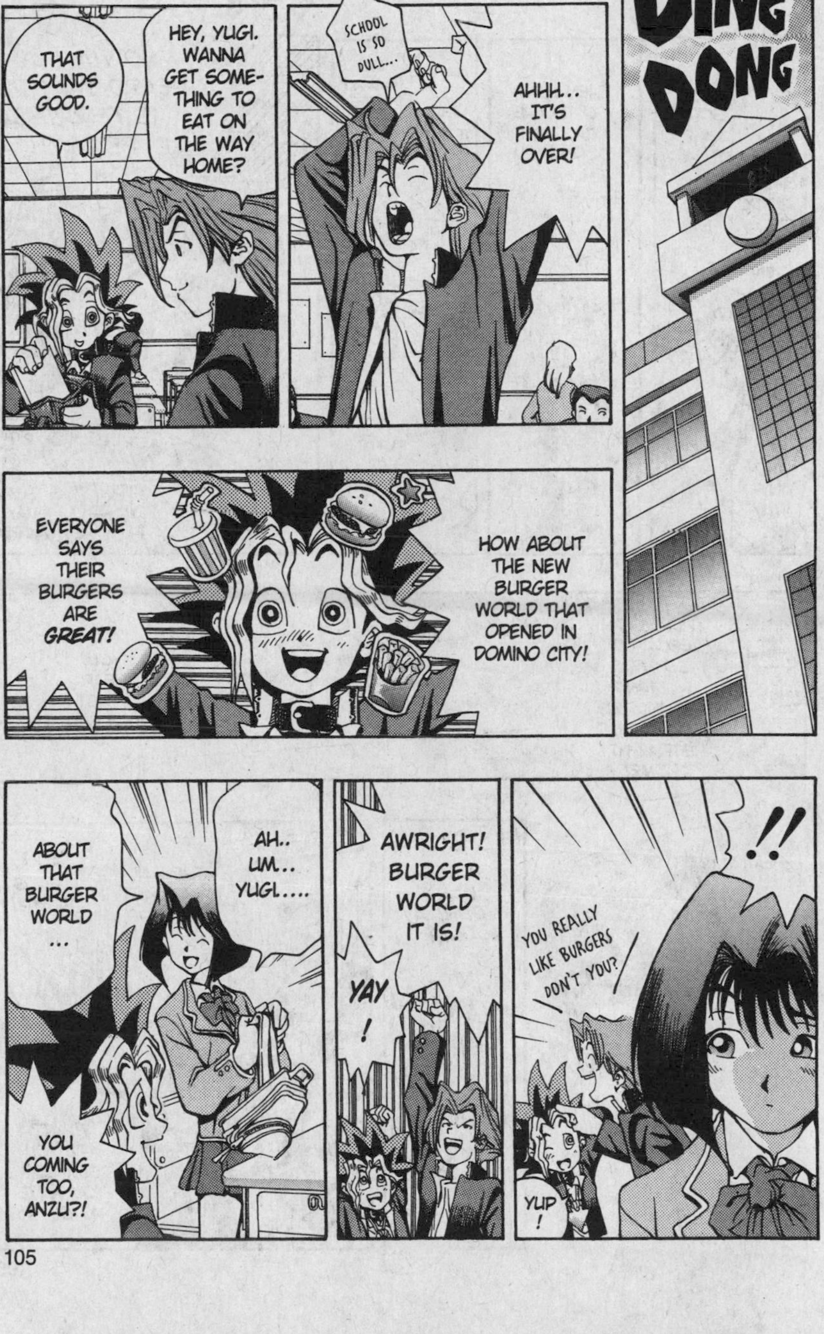

DING DONG
AHHH.. IT'S FINALLY OVER!
SCHOOL IS SO DULL...
HEY, YUGI. WANNA GET SOME-THING TO EAT ON THE WAY HOME?
THAT SOUNDS GOOD.
HOW ABOUT THE NEW BURGER WORLD THAT OPENED IN DOMINO CITY!
EVERYONE SAYS THEIR BURGERS ARE GREAT!
!!
YOU REALLY LIKE BURGERS DON'T YOU?
YUP!
AWRIGHT! BURGER WORLD IT IS!
YAY!
AH.. UM.. YUGI....
ABOUT THAT BURGER WORLD ...
YOU COMING TOO, ANZU?!

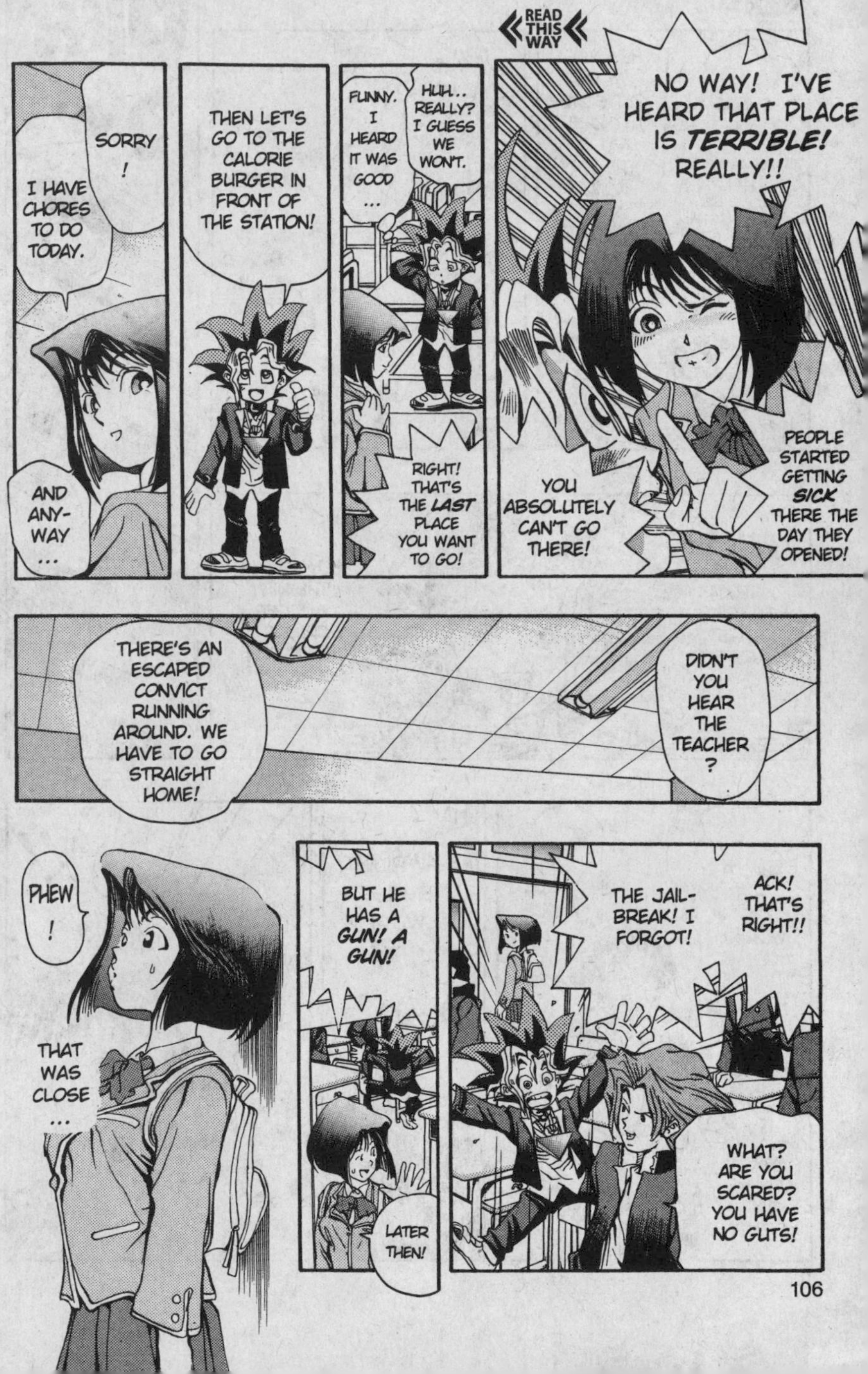
READ THIS WAY
NO WAY! I'VE HEARD THAT PLACE IS *TERRIBLE!* REALLY!!
PEOPLE STARTED GETTING *SICK* THERE THE DAY THEY OPENED!
YOU ABSOLUTELY CAN'T GO THERE!
HUH.. REALLY? I GUESS WE WON'T.
FUNNY. I HEARD IT WAS GOOD ...
RIGHT! THAT'S THE *LAST* PLACE YOU WANT TO GO!
THEN LET'S GO TO THE CALORIE BURGER IN FRONT OF THE STATION!
SORRY!
I HAVE CHORES TO DO TODAY.
AND ANY-WAY ...
DIDN'T YOU HEAR THE TEACHER?
THERE'S AN ESCAPED CONVICT RUNNING AROUND. WE HAVE TO GO STRAIGHT HOME!
ACK! THAT'S RIGHT!!
THE JAIL-BREAK! I FORGOT!
WHAT? ARE YOU SCARED? YOU HAVE NO GUTS!
BUT HE HAS A *GUN! A GUN!*
LATER THEN!
PHEW!
THAT WAS CLOSE ...

READ THIS WAY

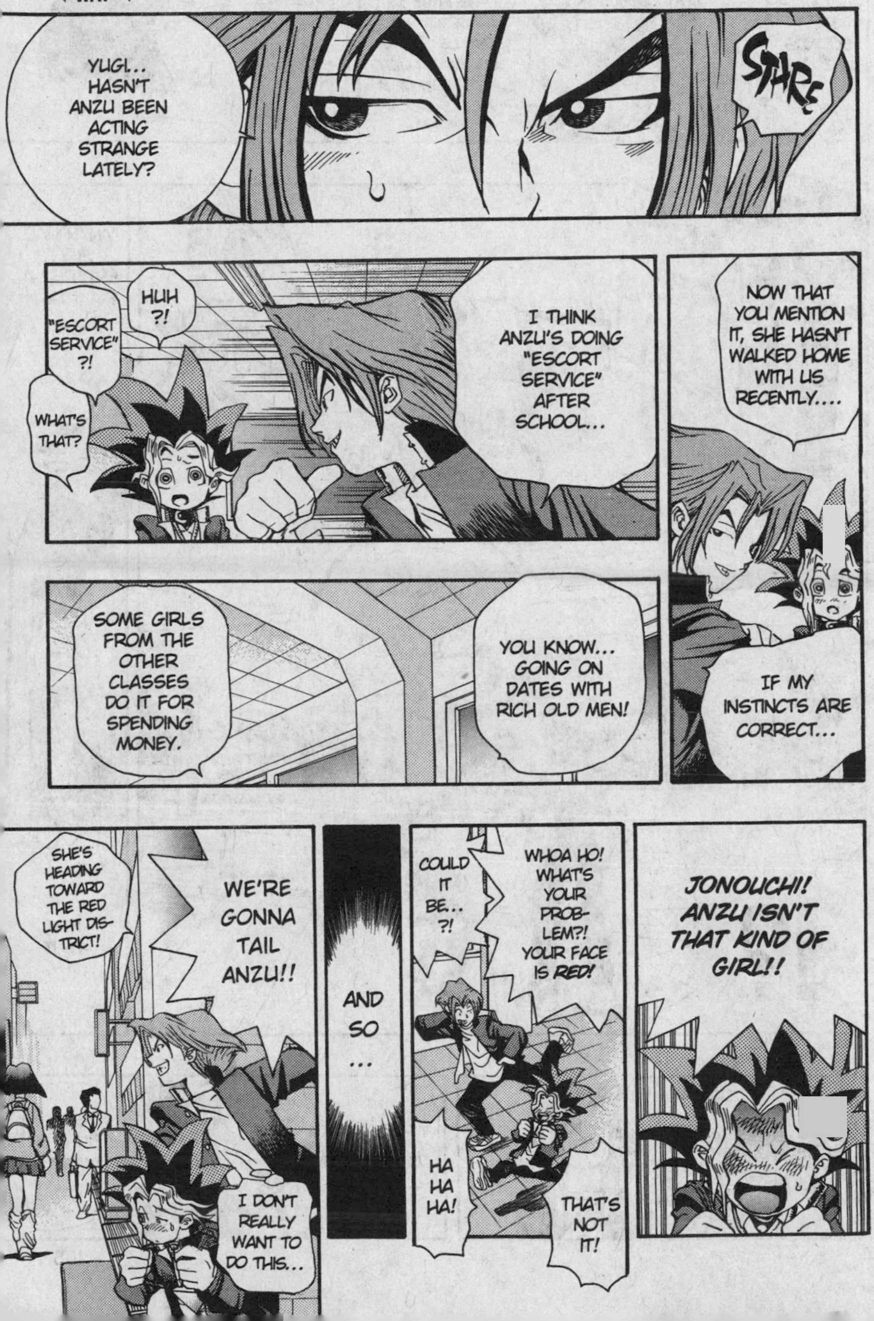
STARE
YUGI... HASN'T ANZU BEEN ACTING STRANGE LATELY?
NOW THAT YOU MENTION IT, SHE HASN'T WALKED HOME WITH US RECENTLY....
IF MY INSTINCTS ARE CORRECT...
I THINK ANZU'S DOING "ESCORT SERVICE" AFTER SCHOOL...
HUH ?!
"ESCORT SERVICE" ?!
WHAT'S THAT?
YOU KNOW... GOING ON DATES WITH RICH OLD MEN!
SOME GIRLS FROM THE OTHER CLASSES DO IT FOR SPENDING MONEY.
JONOUCHI! ANZU ISN'T THAT KIND OF GIRL!!
WHOA HO! WHAT'S YOUR PROB-LEM?! YOUR FACE IS RED!
COULD IT BE... ?!
HA HA HA!
THAT'S NOT IT!
AND SO...
WE'RE GONNA TAIL ANZU!!
SHE'S HEADING TOWARD THE RED LIGHT DIS-TRICT!
I DON'T REALLY WANT TO DO THIS...

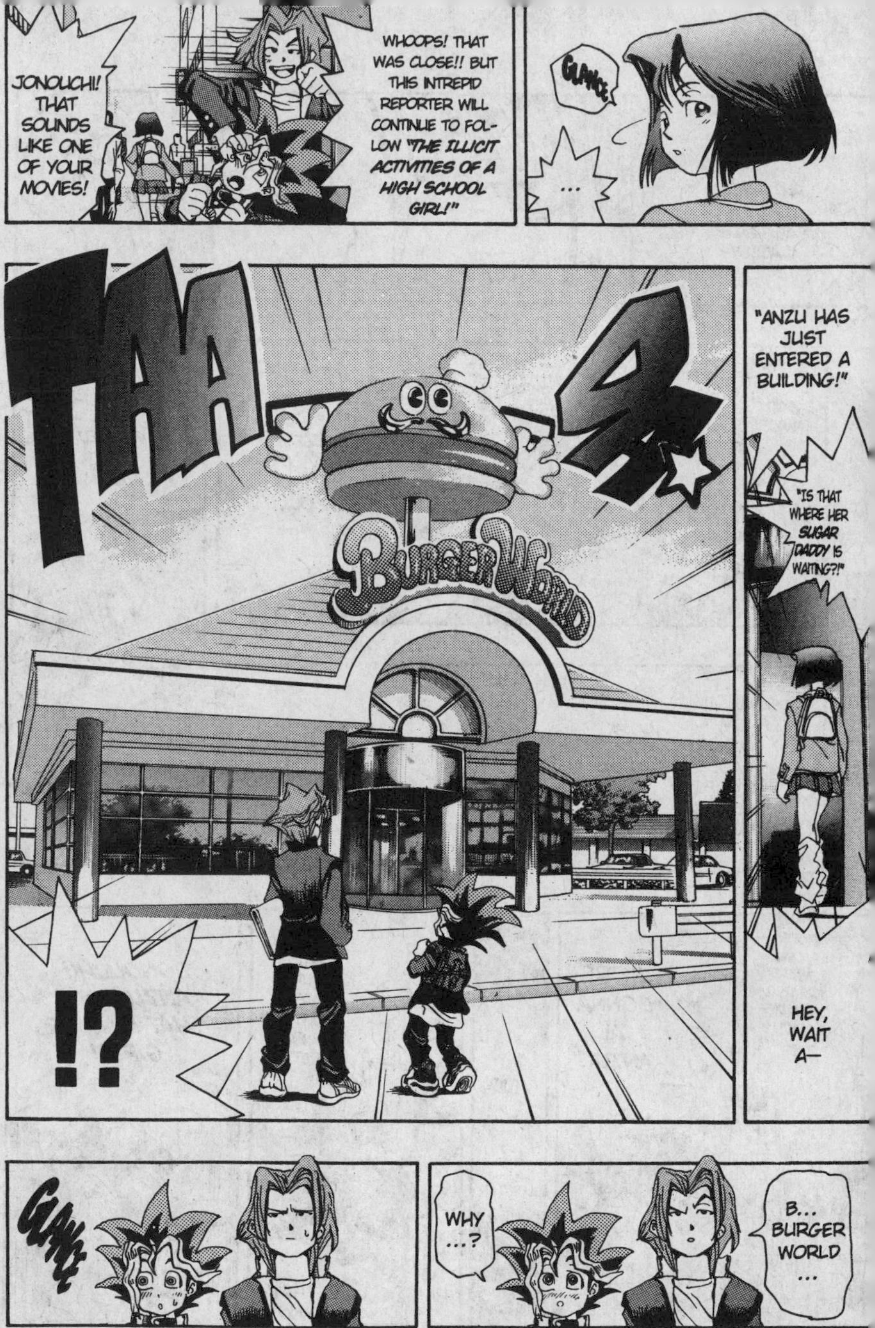
GLANCE
...
WHOOPS! THAT WAS CLOSE!! BUT THIS INTREPID REPORTER WILL CONTINUE TO FOL-LOW "THE ILLICIT ACTIVITIES OF A HIGH SCHOOL GIRL!"
JONOUCHI! THAT SOUNDS LIKE ONE OF YOUR MOVIES!
"ANZU HAS JUST ENTERED A BUILDING!"
"IS THAT WHERE HER SUGAR DADDY IS WAITING?!"
HEY, WAIT A—
TAA-DA
BURGER WORLD
!?
B... BURGER WORLD ...
WHY ...?
GLANCE

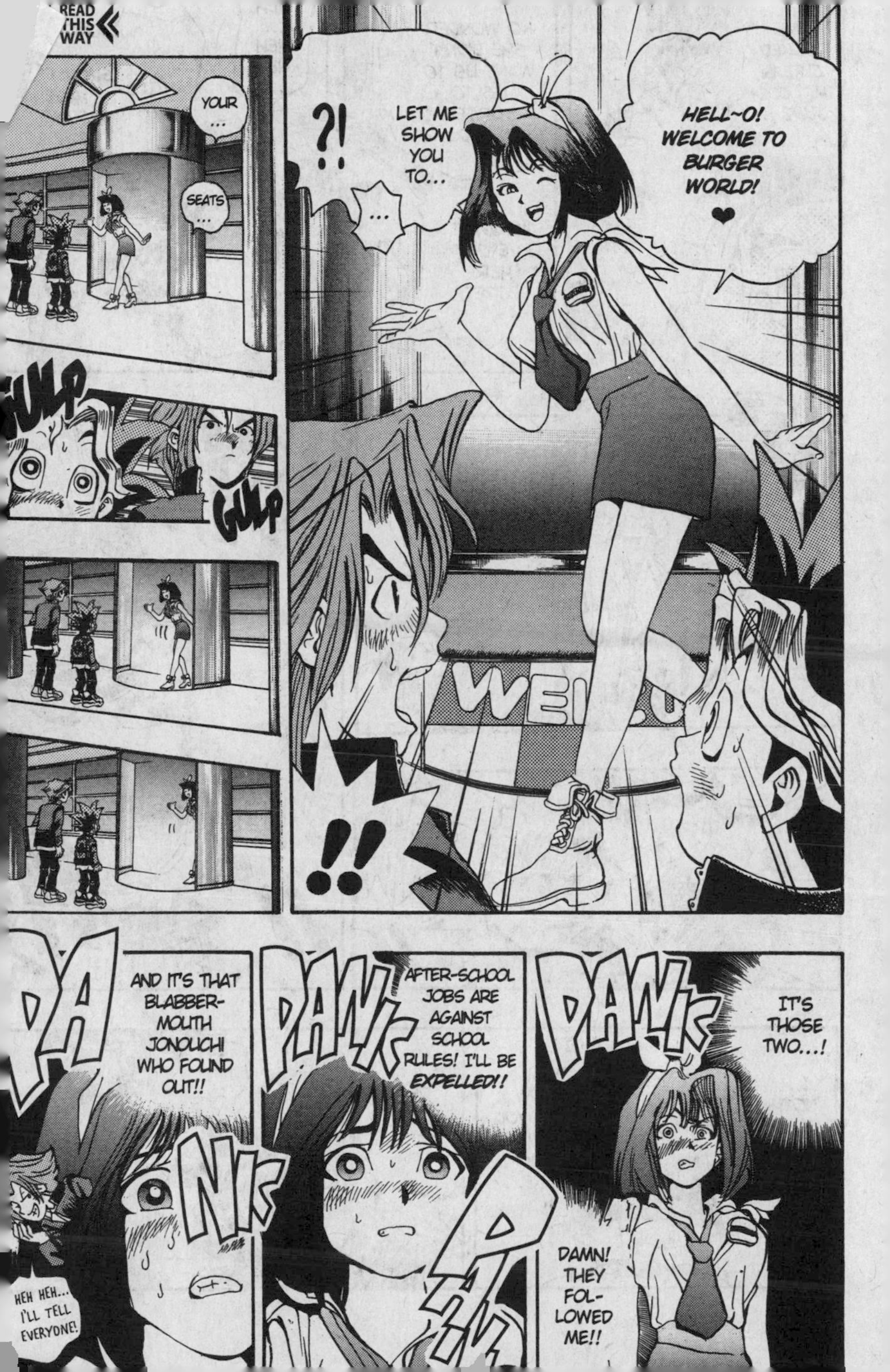
READ THIS WAY
HELL~O! WELCOME TO BURGER WORLD! ❤
LET ME SHOW YOU TO...
?!
...
!!
YOUR ...
SEATS ...
GULP
GULP
PANIC
IT'S THOSE TWO...!
DAMN! THEY FOL-LOWED ME!!
PANIC
AFTER-SCHOOL JOBS ARE AGAINST SCHOOL RULES! I'LL BE EXPELLED!!
PANIC
AND IT'S THAT BLABBER-MOUTH JONOUCHI WHO FOUND OUT!!
HEH HEH... I'LL TELL EVERYONE!

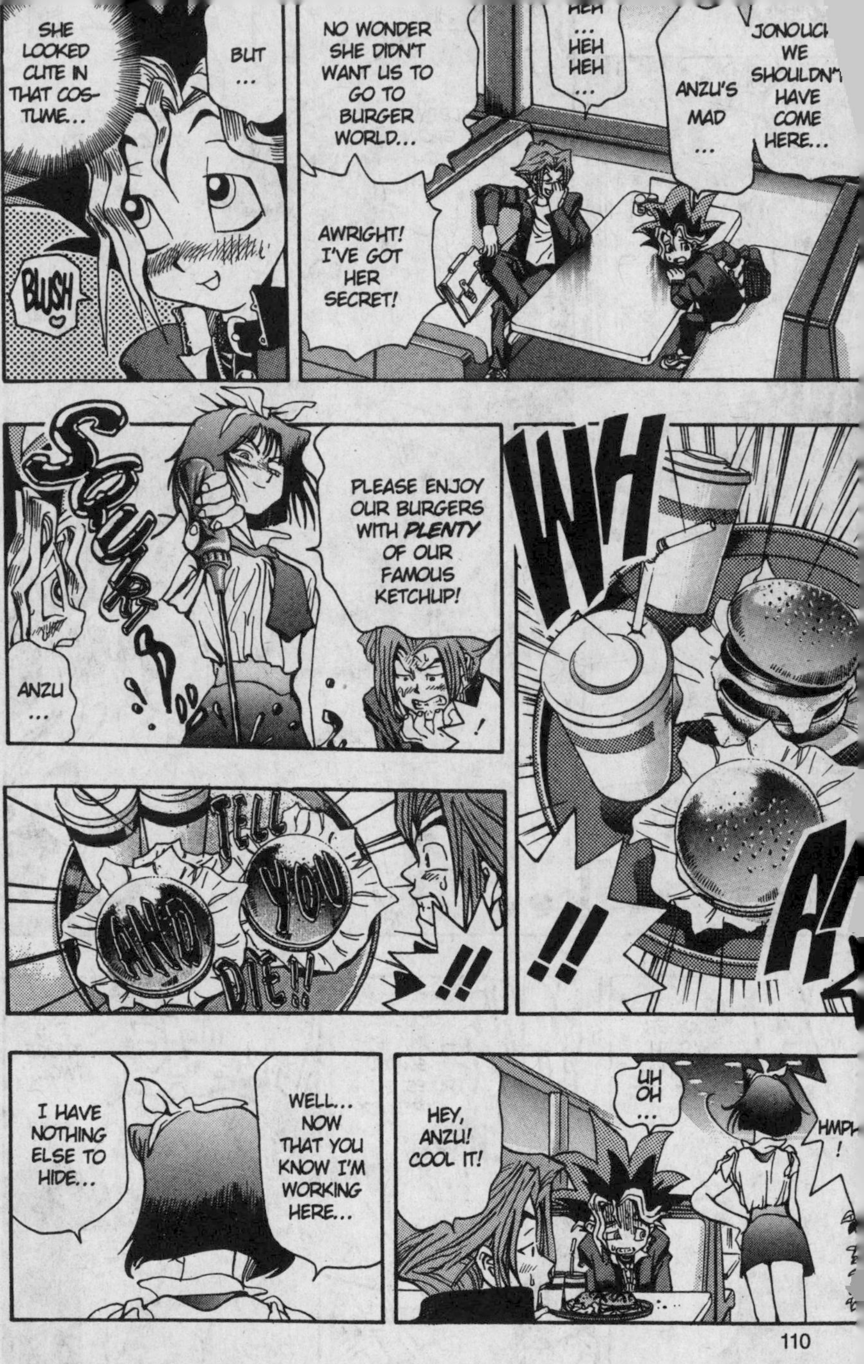
JONOUCHI WE SHOULDN'T HAVE COME HERE...
ANZU'S MAD...
HEH... HEH HEH...
NO WONDER SHE DIDN'T WANT US TO GO TO BURGER WORLD...
AWRIGHT! I'VE GOT HER SECRET!
BUT...
SHE LOOKED CUTE IN THAT COSTUME...
BLUSH
WH
A
!!
PLEASE ENJOY OUR BURGERS WITH *PLENTY* OF OUR FAMOUS KETCHUP!
!
SQUIRT
ANZU...
TELL
YOU
AND
DIE!!
!!
HMPH!
UH OH...
HEY, ANZU! COOL IT!
WELL... NOW THAT YOU KNOW I'M WORKING HERE...
I HAVE NOTHING ELSE TO HIDE...

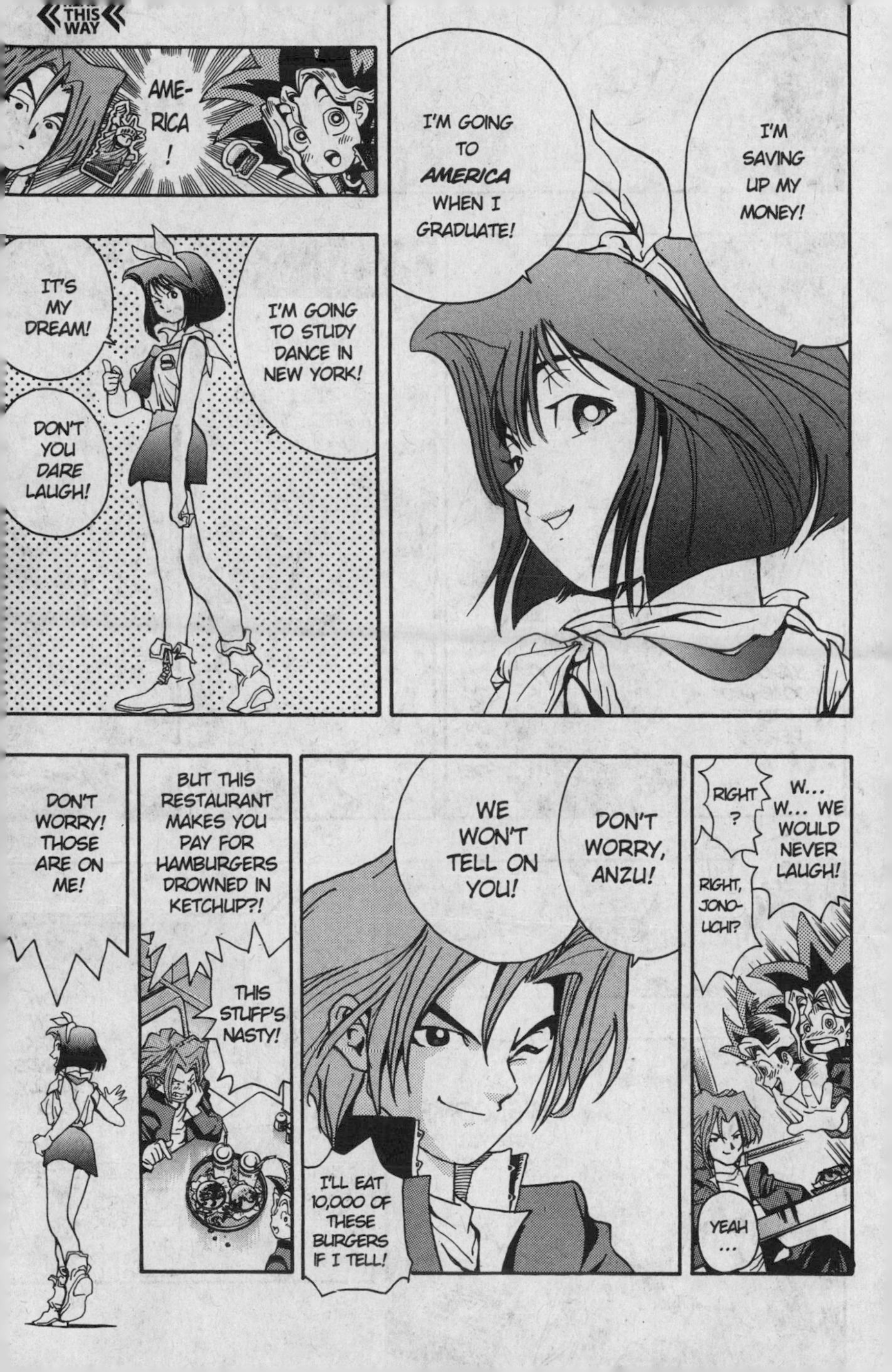
THIS WAY
I'M GOING TO AMERICA WHEN I GRADUATE!
I'M SAVING UP MY MONEY!
AME-RICA !
I'M GOING TO STUDY DANCE IN NEW YORK!
IT'S MY DREAM!
DON'T YOU DARE LAUGH!
W... W... WE WOULD NEVER LAUGH!
RIGHT ?
RIGHT, JONO-UCHI?
YEAH ...
DON'T WORRY, ANZU!
WE WON'T TELL ON YOU!
I'LL EAT 10,000 OF THESE BURGERS IF I TELL!
BUT THIS RESTAURANT MAKES YOU PAY FOR HAMBURGERS DROWNED IN KETCHUP?!
THIS STUFF'S NASTY!
DON'T WORRY! THOSE ARE ON ME!

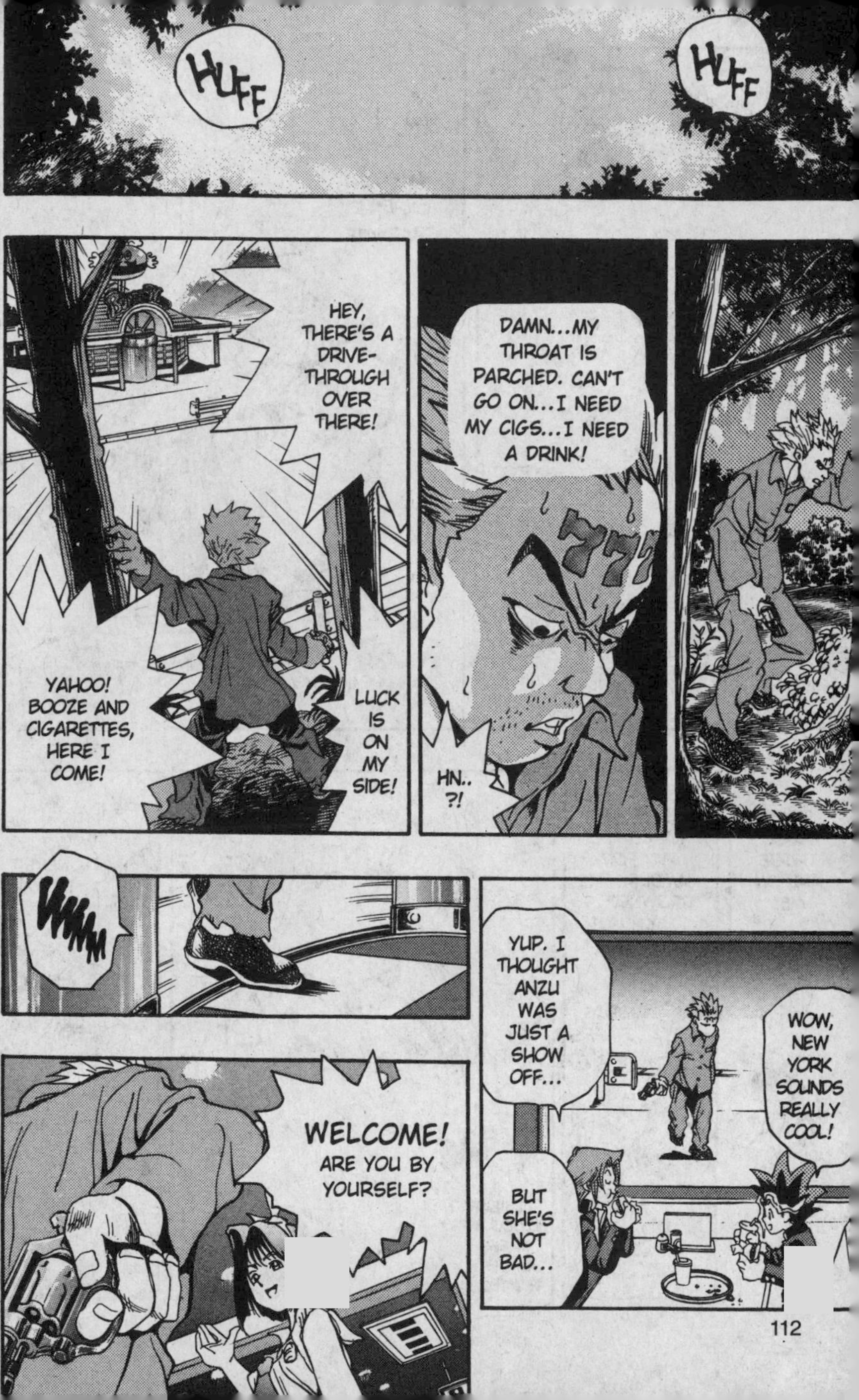
HUFF
HUFF
DAMN...MY THROAT IS PARCHED. CAN'T GO ON...I NEED MY CIGS...I NEED A DRINK!
HN.. ?!
HEY, THERE'S A DRIVE-THROUGH OVER THERE!
LUCK IS ON MY SIDE!
YAHOO! BOOZE AND CIGARETTES, HERE I COME!
WOW, NEW YORK SOUNDS REALLY COOL!
YUP. I THOUGHT ANZU WAS JUST A SHOW OFF...
BUT SHE'S NOT BAD...
VWMM
WELCOME! ARE YOU BY YOURSELF?

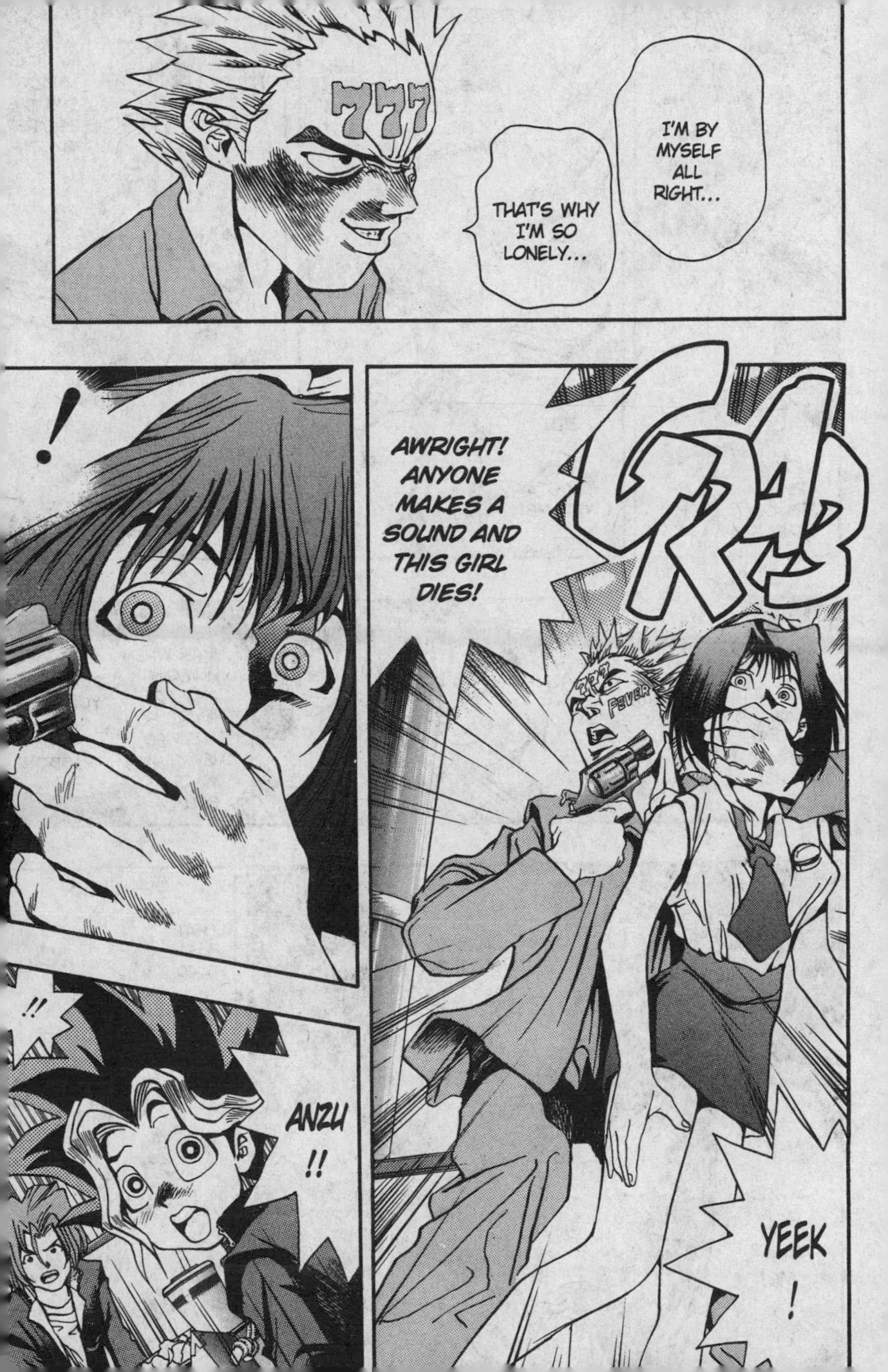
777
I'M BY MYSELF ALL RIGHT...
THAT'S WHY I'M SO LONELY...
GRAB
AWRIGHT! ANYONE MAKES A SOUND AND THIS GIRL DIES!
FEVER
YEEK !
!
!!
ANZU !!

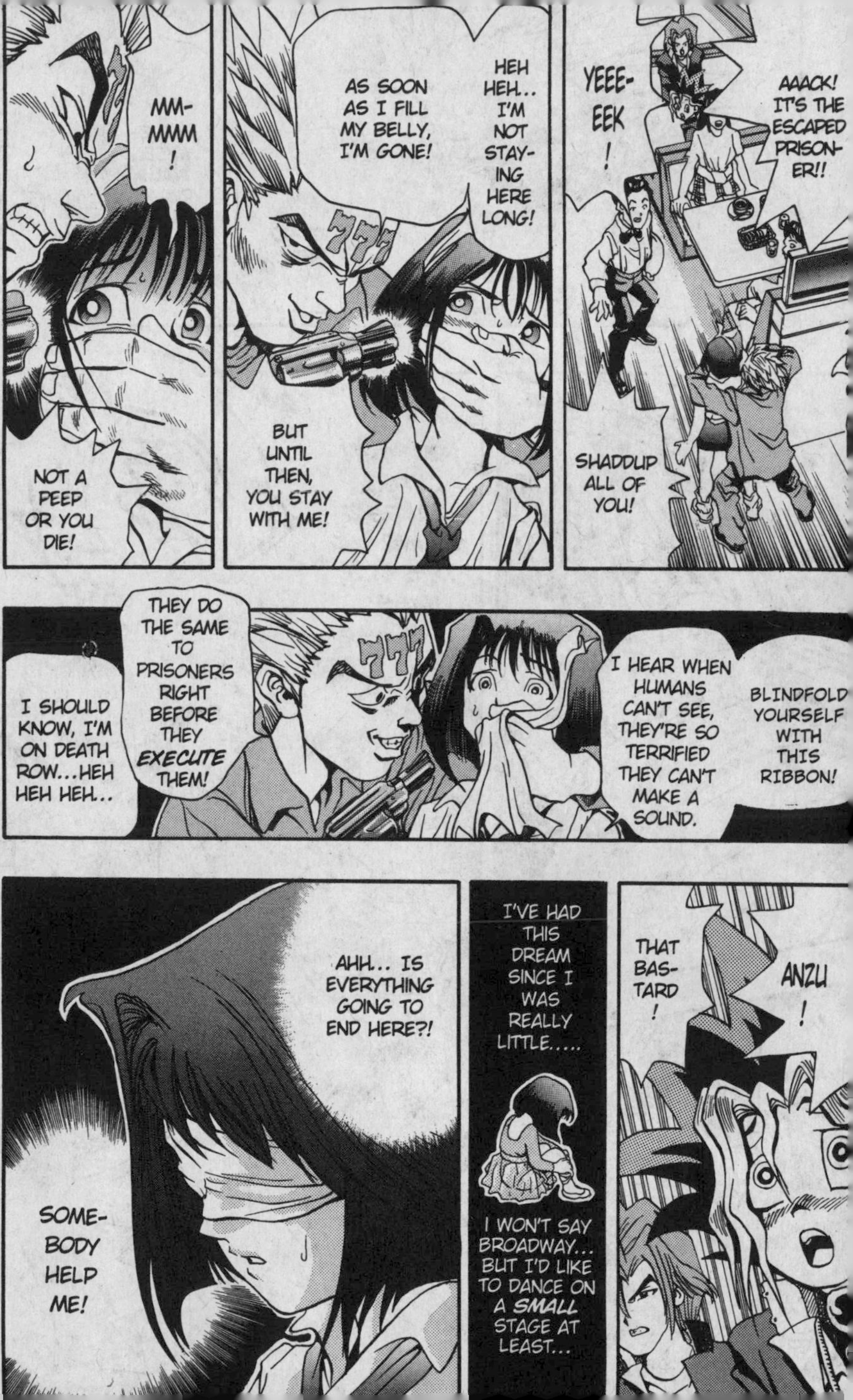
AAACK! IT'S THE ESCAPED PRISONER!!
YEEE-EEK!
SHADDUP ALL OF YOU!
HEH HEH... I'M NOT STAYING HERE LONG!
AS SOON AS I FILL MY BELLY, I'M GONE!
BUT UNTIL THEN, YOU STAY WITH ME!
MM-MMM!
NOT A PEEP OR YOU DIE!
BLINDFOLD YOURSELF WITH THIS RIBBON!
I HEAR WHEN HUMANS CAN'T SEE, THEY'RE SO TERRIFIED THEY CAN'T MAKE A SOUND.
THEY DO THE SAME TO PRISONERS RIGHT BEFORE THEY *EXECUTE* THEM!
I SHOULD KNOW, I'M ON DEATH ROW...HEH HEH HEH...
ANZU!
THAT BASTARD!
I'VE HAD THIS DREAM SINCE I WAS REALLY LITTLE.....
I WON'T SAY BROADWAY... BUT I'D LIKE TO DANCE ON A *SMALL* STAGE AT LEAST...
AHH... IS EVERYTHING GOING TO END HERE?!
SOMEBODY HELP ME!

READ THIS WAY

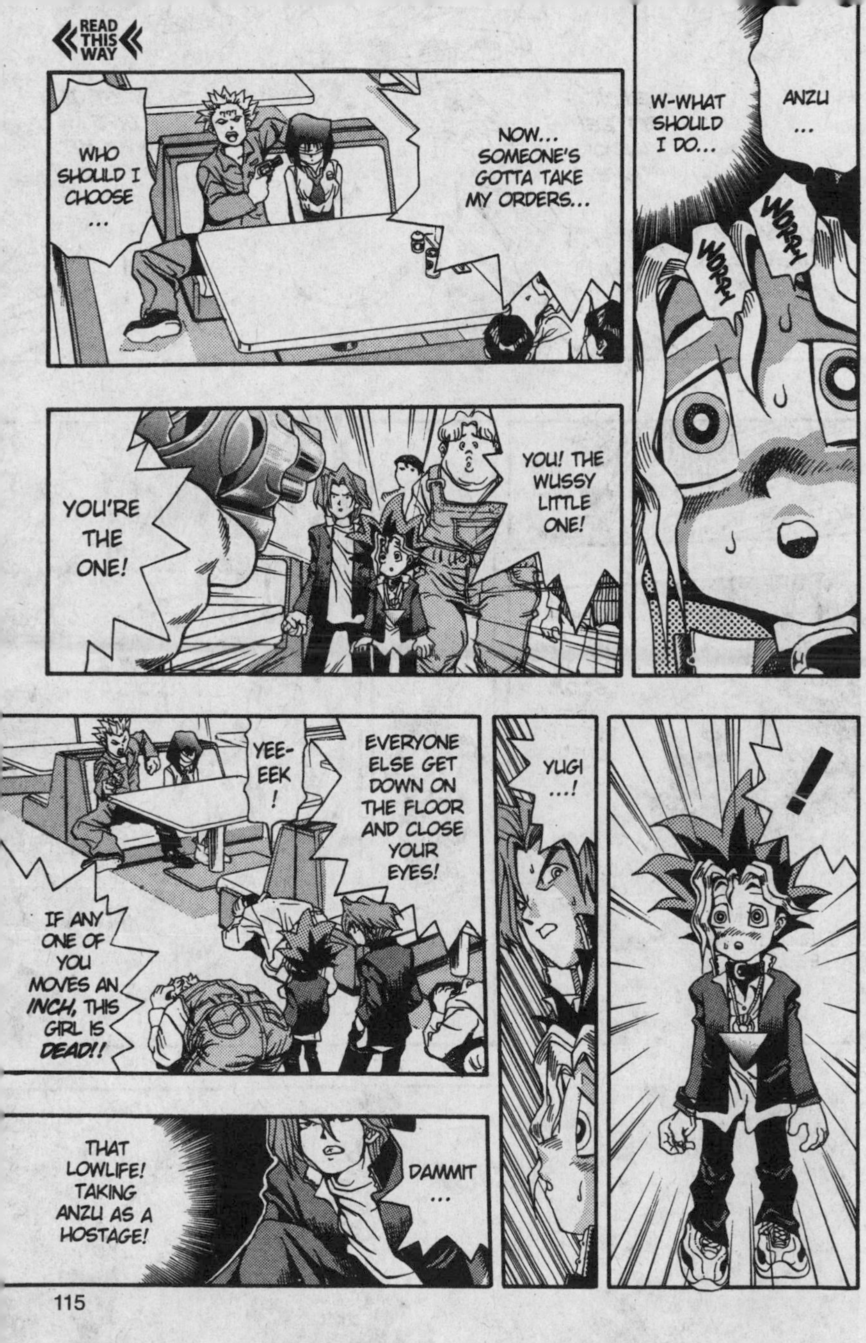
ANZU ...
W-WHAT SHOULD I DO...
WORRY
WORRY
NOW... SOMEONE'S GOTTA TAKE MY ORDERS...
WHO SHOULD I CHOOSE ...
YOU! THE WUSSY LITTLE ONE!
YOU'RE THE ONE!
!
YUGI ...!
EVERYONE ELSE GET DOWN ON THE FLOOR AND CLOSE YOUR EYES!
YEE-EEK!
IF ANY ONE OF YOU MOVES AN *INCH*, THIS GIRL IS *DEAD!!*
DAMMIT ...
THAT LOWLIFE! TAKING ANZU AS A HOSTAGE!

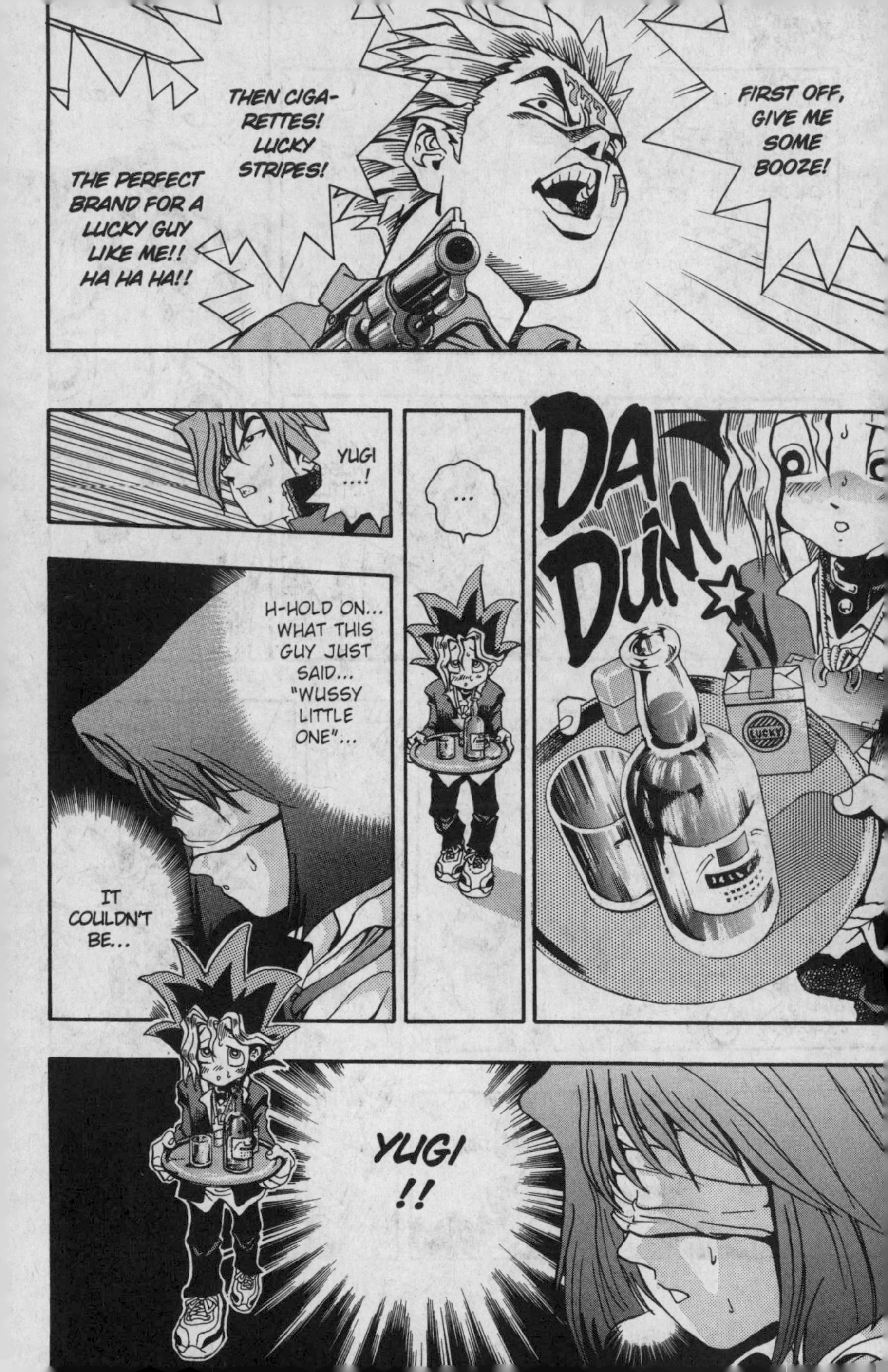
FIRST OFF, GIVE ME SOME BOOZE!
THEN CIGA-RETTES! LUCKY STRIPES!
THE PERFECT BRAND FOR A LUCKY GUY LIKE ME!! HA HA HA!!
DA DUM
LUCKY
...
YUGI ...!
H-HOLD ON... WHAT THIS GUY JUST SAID... "WUSSY LITTLE ONE"...
IT COULDN'T BE...
YUGI !!

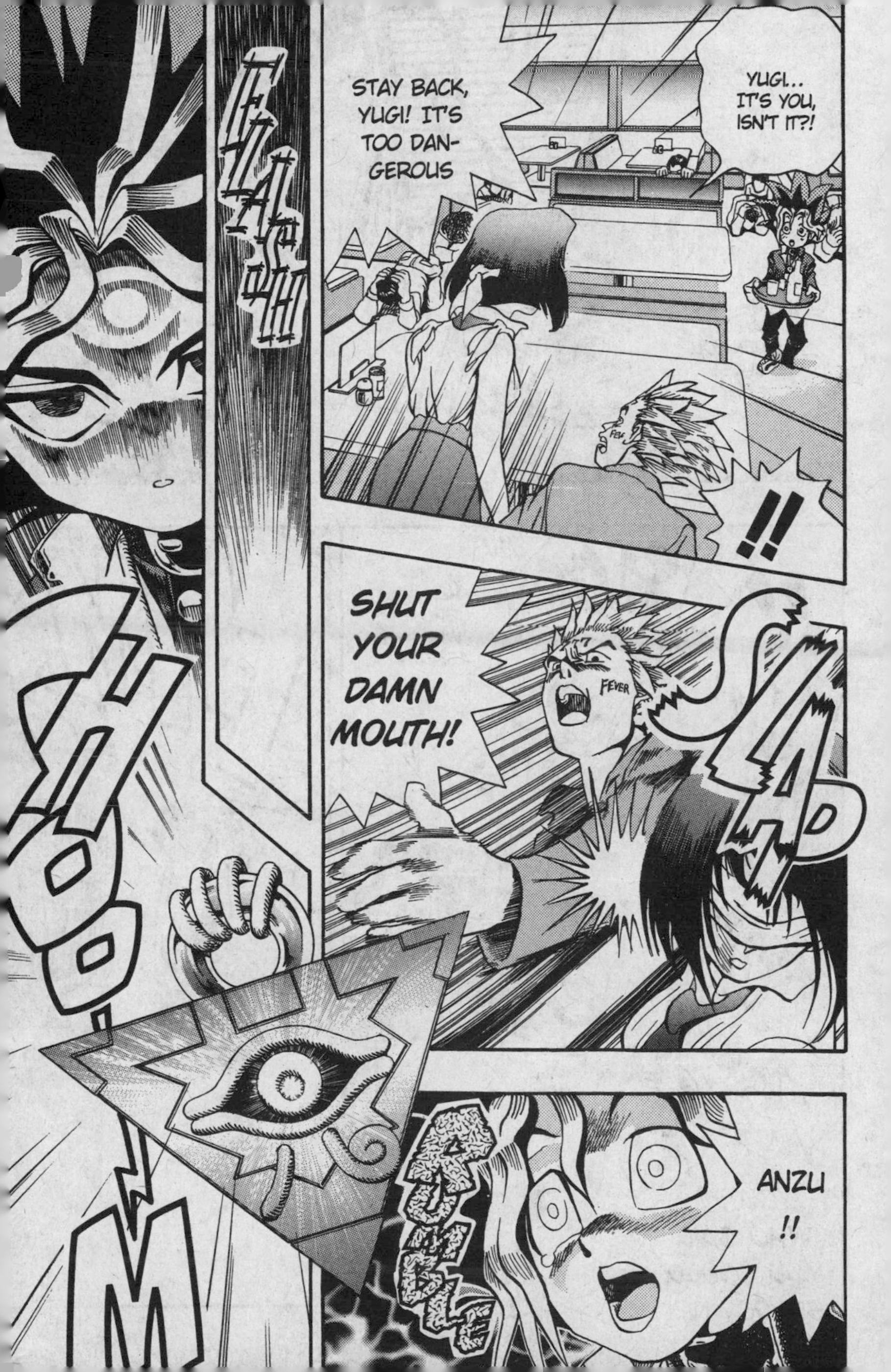
YUGI... IT'S YOU, ISN'T IT?!
STAY BACK, YUGI! IT'S TOO DAN-GEROUS
!!
SHUT YOUR DAMN MOUTH!
ANZU !!

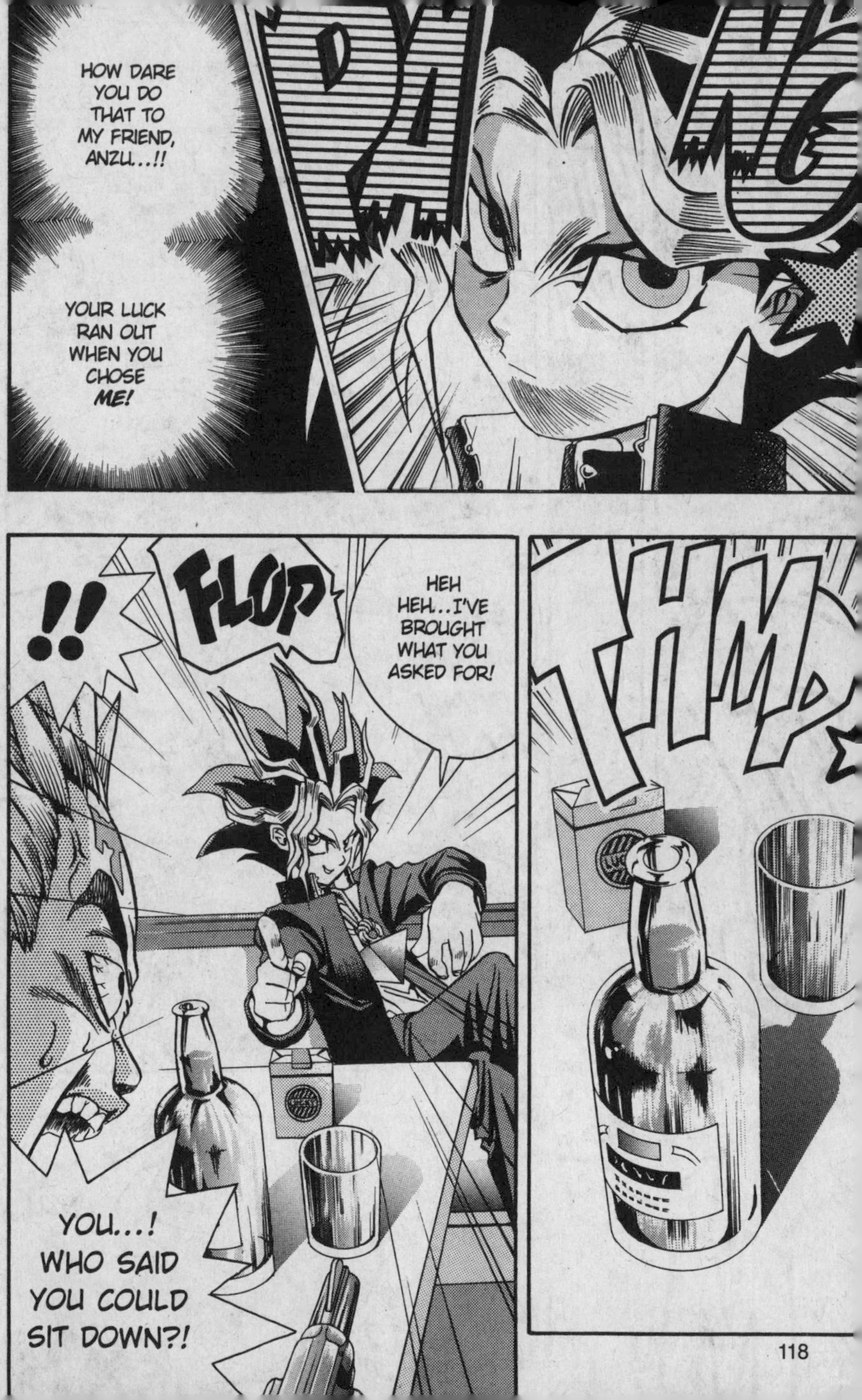
PAWNG
HOW DARE YOU DO THAT TO MY FRIEND, ANZU...!!
YOUR LUCK RAN OUT WHEN YOU CHOSE *ME!*
THMP
HEH HEH...I'VE BROUGHT WHAT YOU ASKED FOR!
FLOP
!!
YOU...! WHO SAID YOU COULD SIT DOWN?!

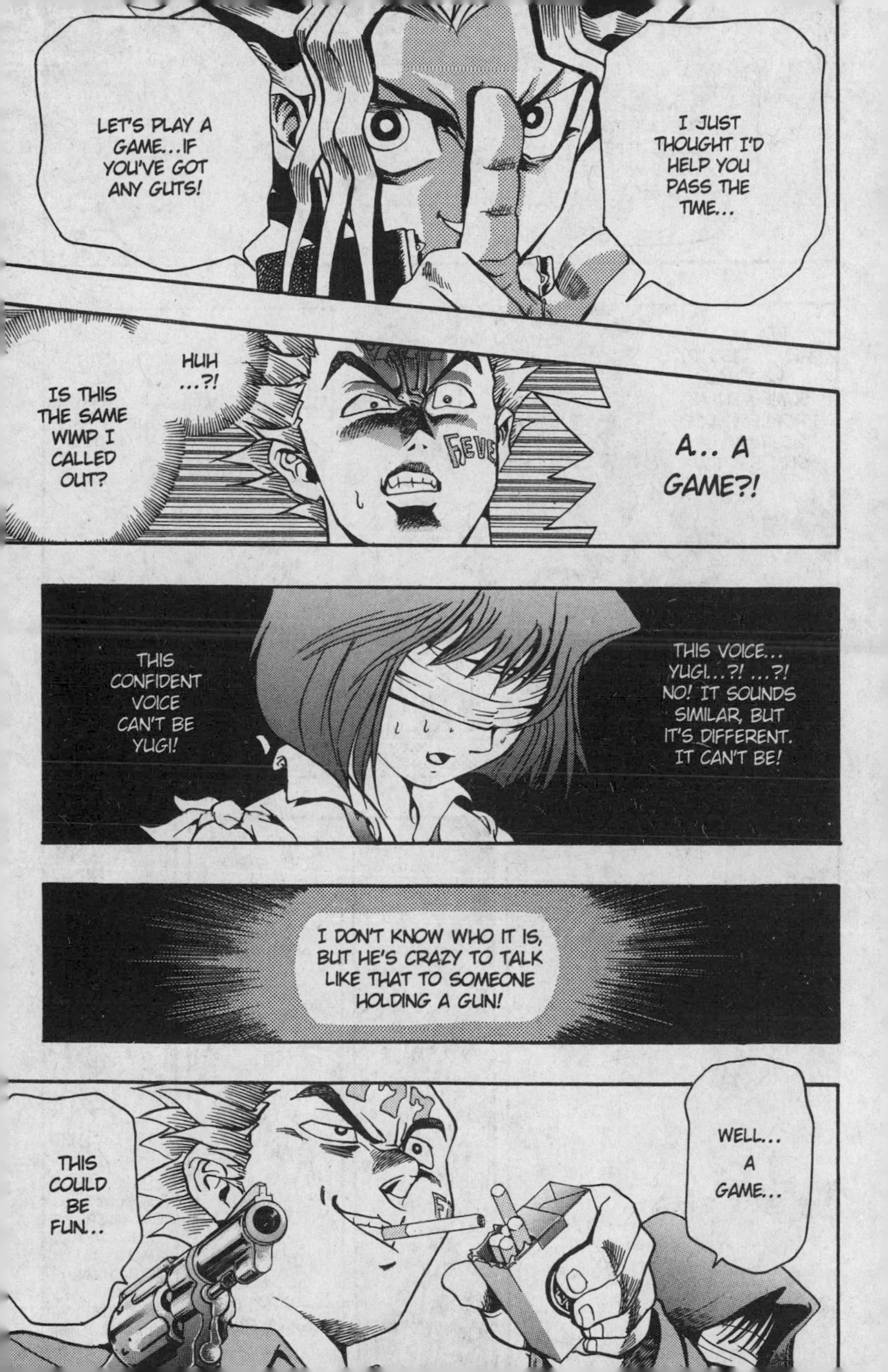
I JUST THOUGHT I'D HELP YOU PASS THE TIME...
LET'S PLAY A GAME...IF YOU'VE GOT ANY GUTS!
A... A GAME?!
HUH ...?!
IS THIS THE SAME WIMP I CALLED OUT?
THIS VOICE... YUGI...?! ...?! NO! IT SOUNDS SIMILAR, BUT IT'S DIFFERENT. IT CAN'T BE!
THIS CONFIDENT VOICE CAN'T BE YUGI!
I DON'T KNOW WHO IT IS, BUT HE'S CRAZY TO TALK LIKE THAT TO SOMEONE HOLDING A GUN!
WELL... A GAME...
THIS COULD BE FUN...

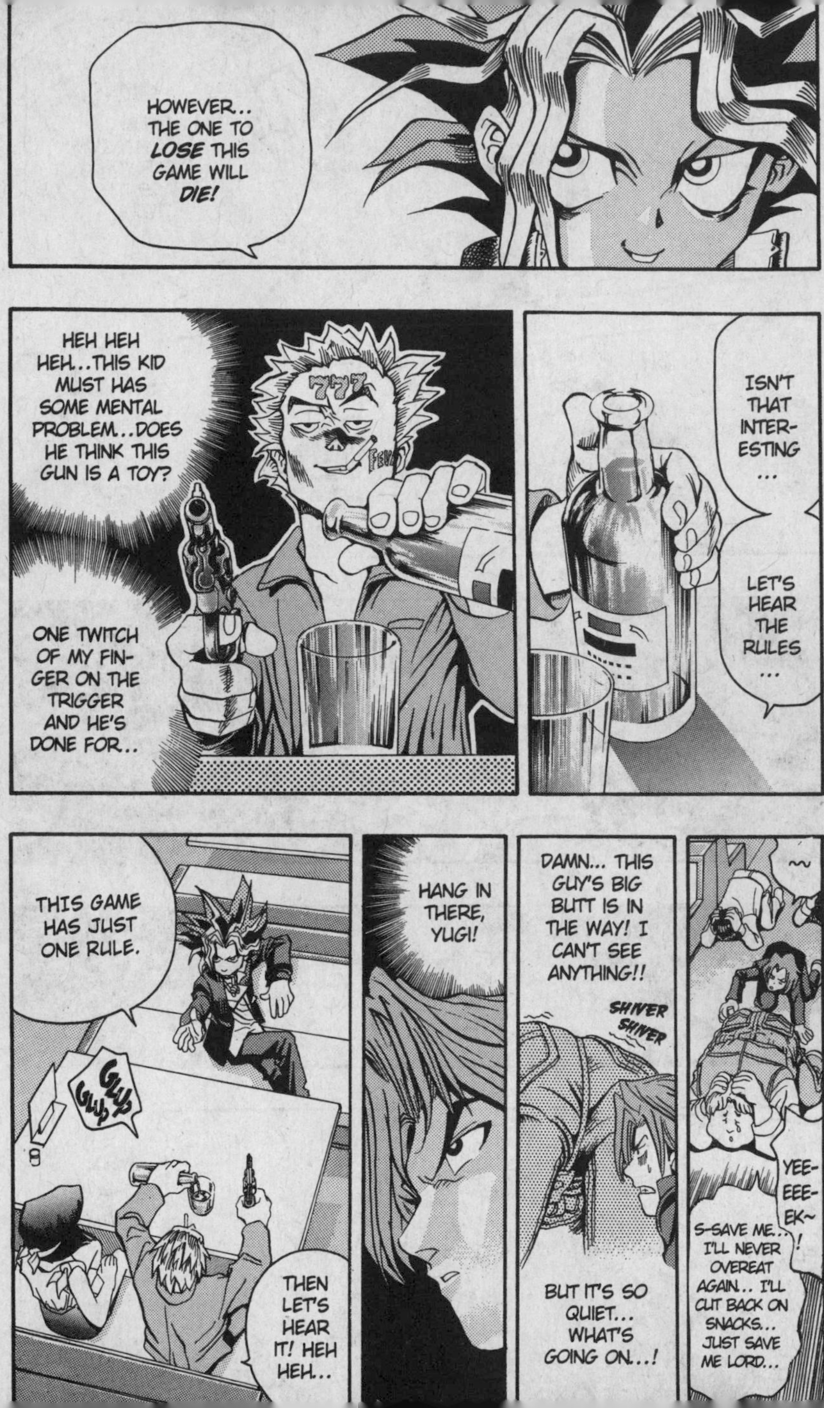
HOWEVER... THE ONE TO LOSE THIS GAME WILL DIE!
ISN'T THAT INTERESTING...
LET'S HEAR THE RULES...
HEH HEH HEH...THIS KID MUST HAS SOME MENTAL PROBLEM...DOES HE THINK THIS GUN IS A TOY?
ONE TWITCH OF MY FINGER ON THE TRIGGER AND HE'S DONE FOR...
~
YEEEEEEK~!
S-SAVE ME... I'LL NEVER OVEREAT AGAIN... I'LL CUT BACK ON SNACKS... JUST SAVE ME LORD...
DAMN... THIS GUY'S BIG BUTT IS IN THE WAY! I CAN'T SEE ANYTHING!!
SHIVER SHIVER
BUT IT'S SO QUIET... WHAT'S GOING ON...!
HANG IN THERE, YUGI!
THIS GAME HAS JUST ONE RULE.
GLUP GLUP
THEN LET'S HEAR IT! HEH HEH...

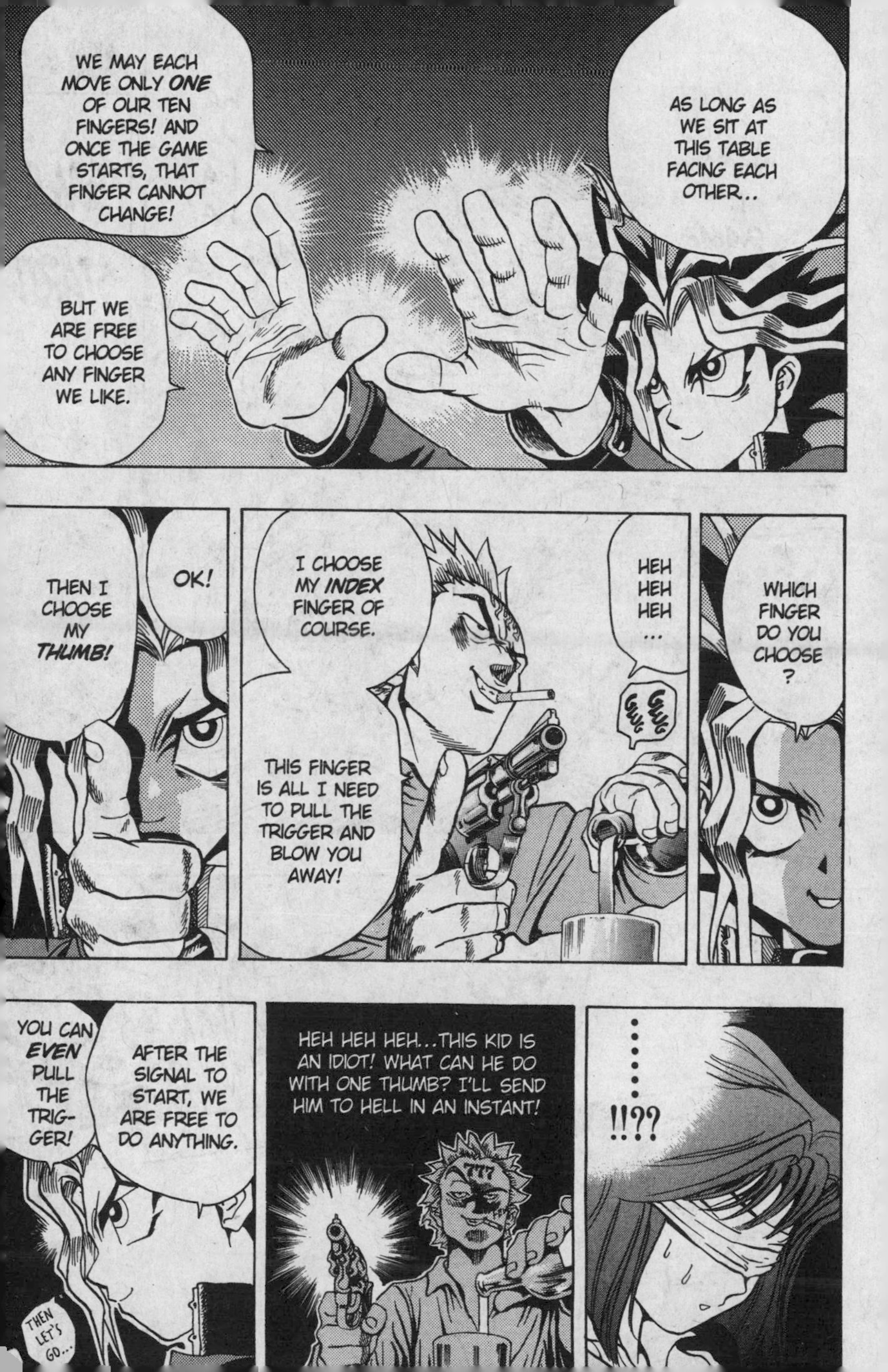
AS LONG AS WE SIT AT THIS TABLE FACING EACH OTHER...
WE MAY EACH MOVE ONLY ONE OF OUR TEN FINGERS! AND ONCE THE GAME STARTS, THAT FINGER CANNOT CHANGE!
BUT WE ARE FREE TO CHOOSE ANY FINGER WE LIKE.
WHICH FINGER DO YOU CHOOSE?
HEH HEH HEH...
I CHOOSE MY INDEX FINGER OF COURSE.
THIS FINGER IS ALL I NEED TO PULL THE TRIGGER AND BLOW YOU AWAY!
OK!
THEN I CHOOSE MY THUMB!
......
!!??
HEH HEH HEH...THIS KID IS AN IDIOT! WHAT CAN HE DO WITH ONE THUMB? I'LL SEND HIM TO HELL IN AN INSTANT!
AFTER THE SIGNAL TO START, WE ARE FREE TO DO ANYTHING.
YOU CAN EVEN PULL THE TRIGGER!
THEN LET'S GO...

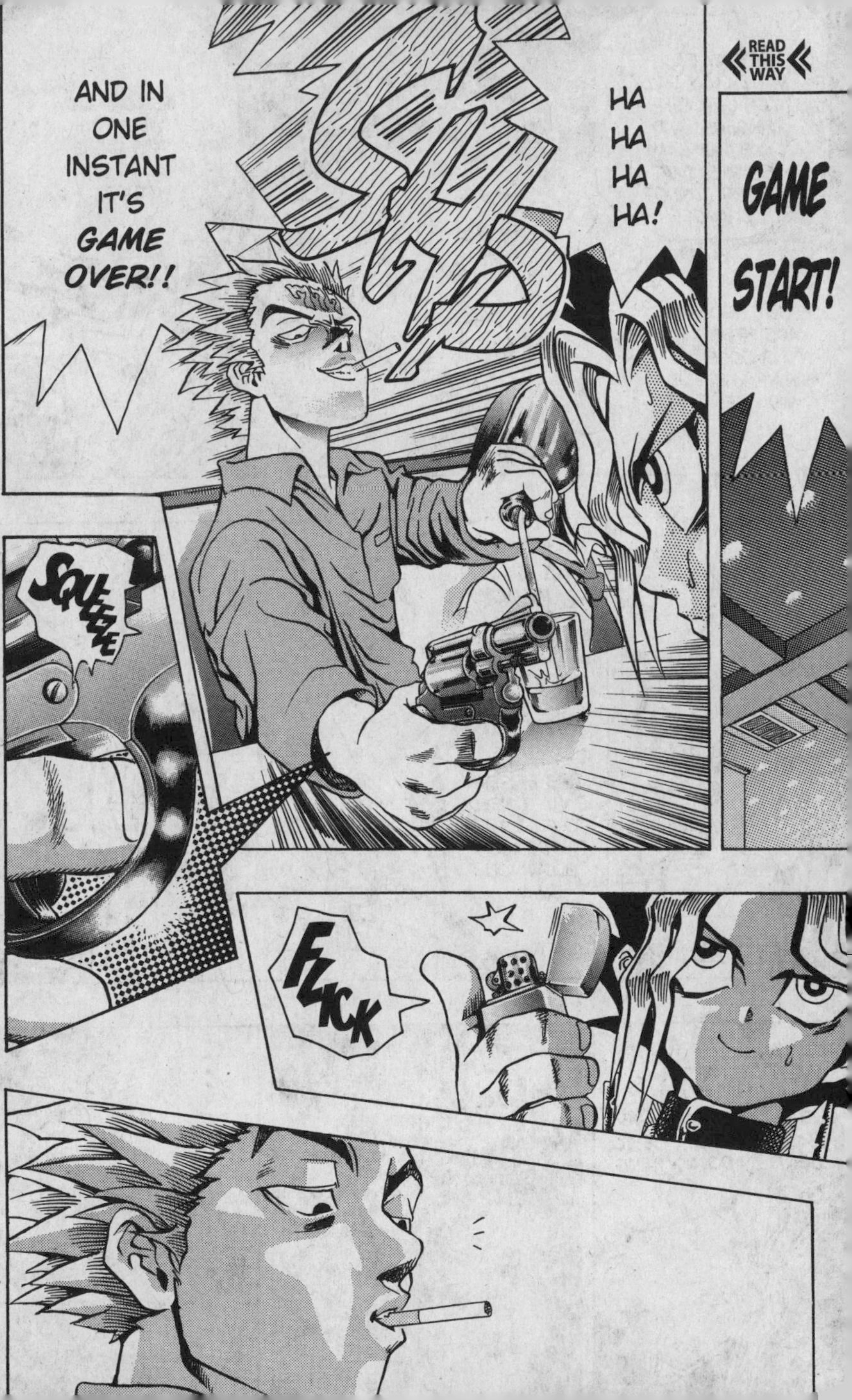
READ THIS WAY
GAME START!
HA HA HA HA!
AND IN ONE INSTANT IT'S GAME OVER!!
SQUEEZE
FLICK

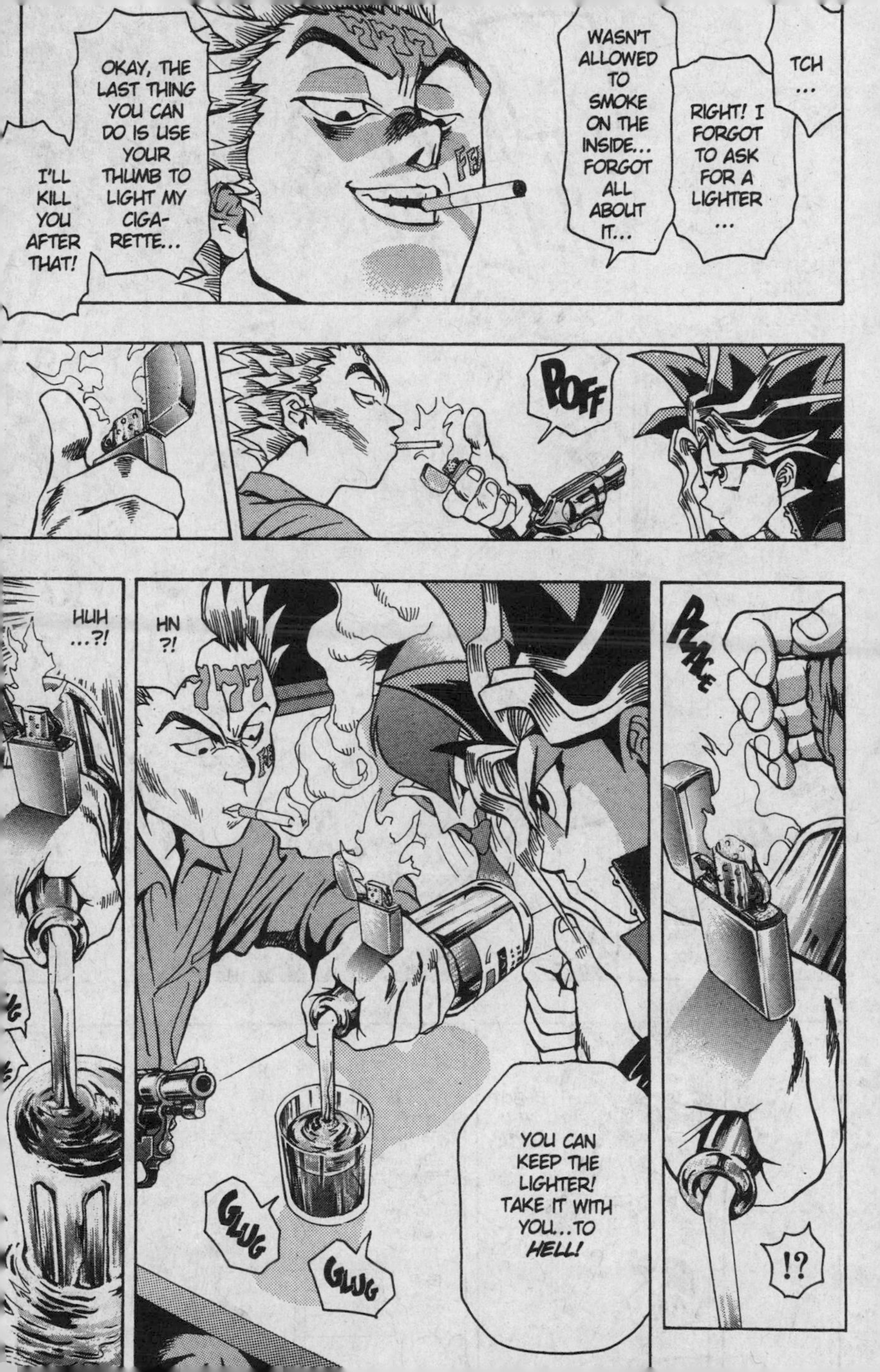
TCH ...
RIGHT! I FORGOT TO ASK FOR A LIGHTER ...
WASN'T ALLOWED TO SMOKE ON THE INSIDE... FORGOT ALL ABOUT IT...
OKAY, THE LAST THING YOU CAN DO IS USE YOUR THUMB TO LIGHT MY CIGA-RETTE...
I'LL KILL YOU AFTER THAT!
BOFF
!?
HN ?!
YOU CAN KEEP THE LIGHTER! TAKE IT WITH YOU...TO *HELL!*
GLUG
GLUG
HUH ...?!

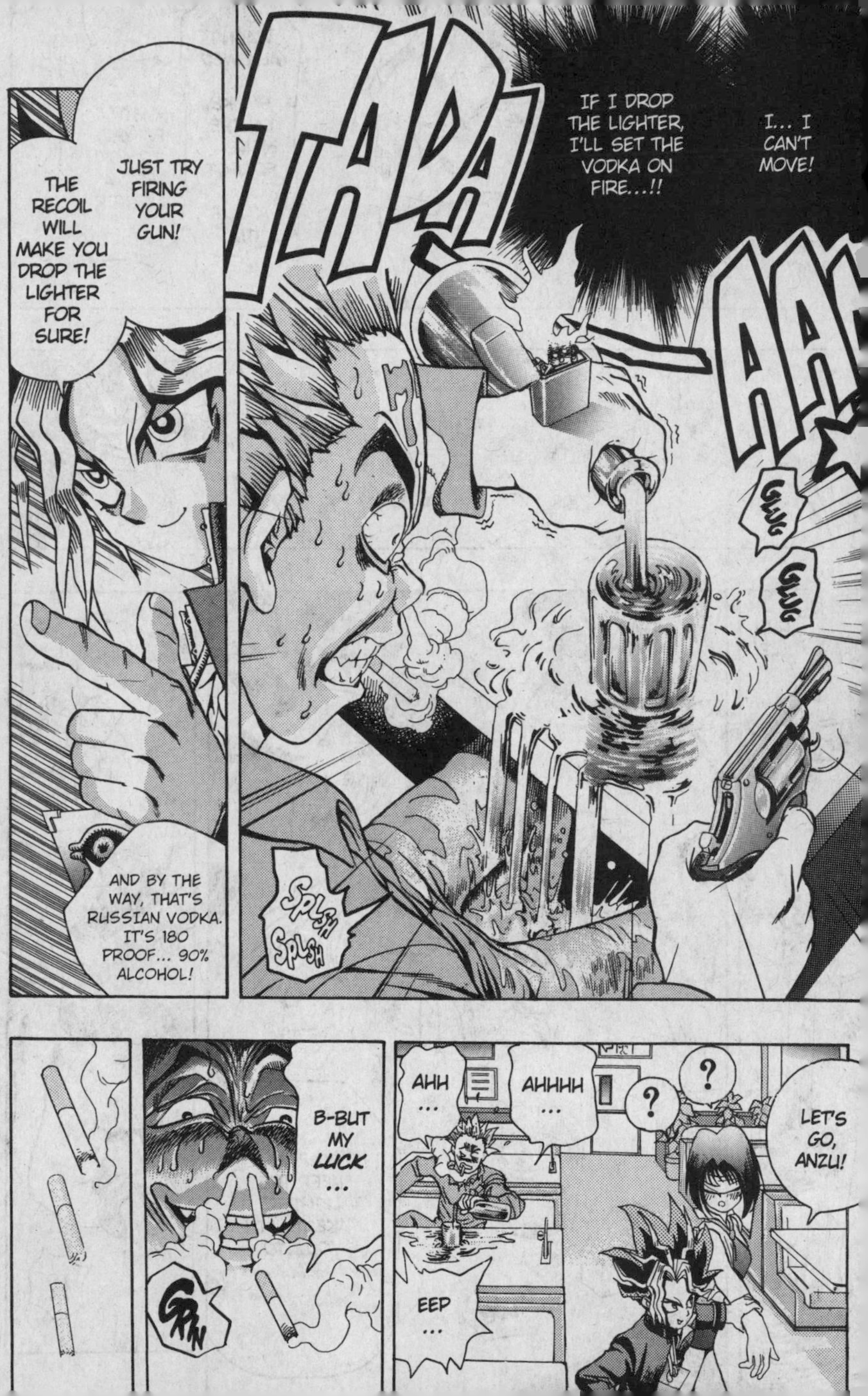
I... I CAN'T MOVE!
IF I DROP THE LIGHTER, I'LL SET THE VODKA ON FIRE...!!
TAPA
AA
GLUG
GLUG
SPLSH
SPLSH
JUST TRY FIRING YOUR GUN!
THE RECOIL WILL MAKE YOU DROP THE LIGHTER FOR SURE!
AND BY THE WAY, THAT'S RUSSIAN VODKA. IT'S 180 PROOF... 90% ALCOHOL!
LET'S GO, ANZU!
?
?
AHHHH ...
AHH ...
EEP ...
B-BUT MY *LUCK* ...
GRIN

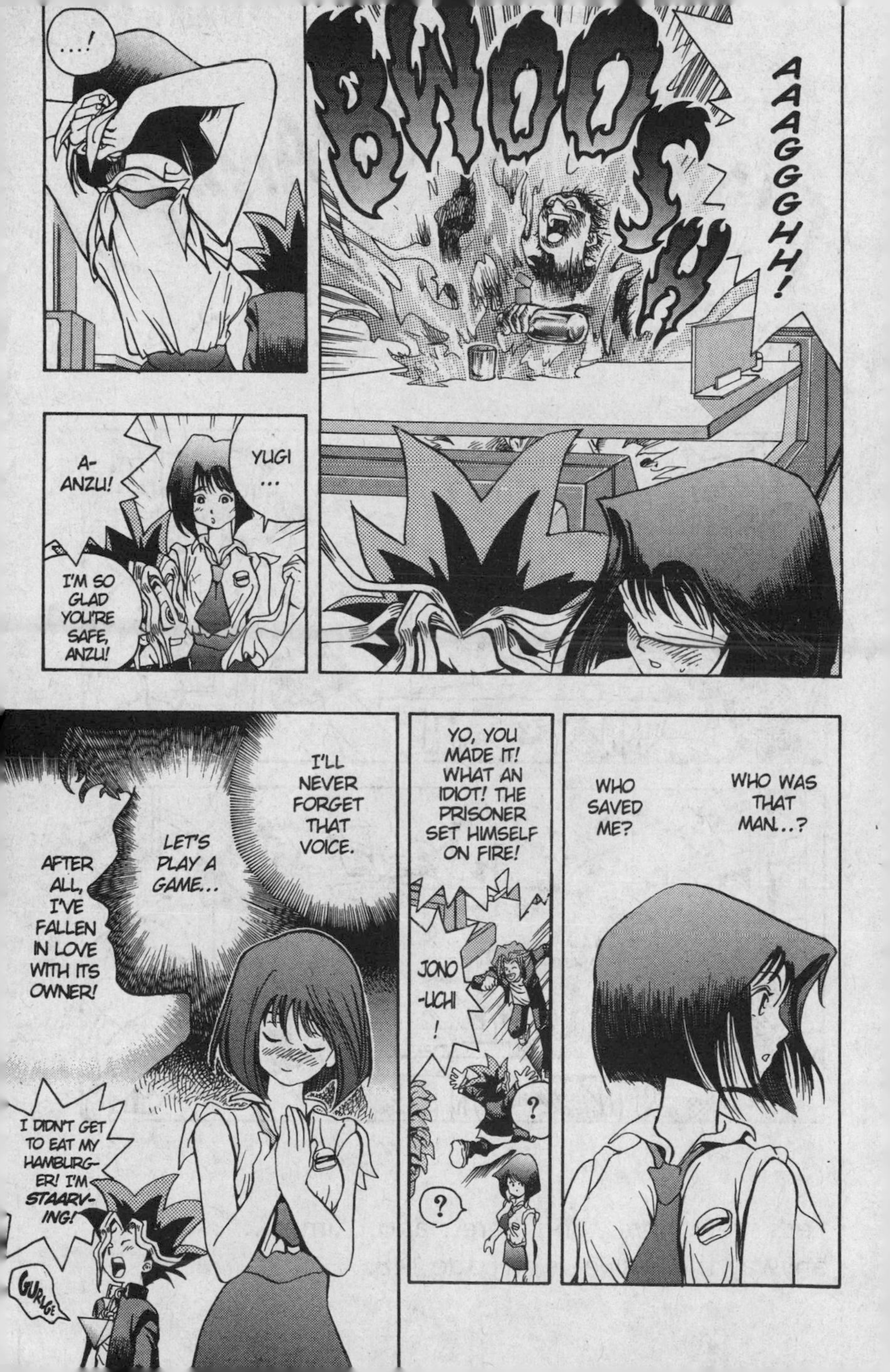
BWOOSH
AAAAGGGHH!
....!
YUGI ...
A-ANZU!
I'M SO GLAD YOU'RE SAFE, ANZU!
WHO WAS THAT MAN...?
WHO SAVED ME?
YO, YOU MADE IT! WHAT AN IDIOT! THE PRISONER SET HIMSELF ON FIRE!
JONO-UCHI!
?
?
I'LL NEVER FORGET THAT VOICE.
LET'S PLAY A GAME...
AFTER ALL, I'VE FALLEN IN LOVE WITH ITS OWNER!
I DIDN'T GET TO EAT MY HAMBURGER! I'M STAARVING!

FIND THE CHANGES!

There are five mistakes in the bottom panel
Can you find them all?

Let's see…there…and there…and…umm…
anyway, the answer is on page 148.

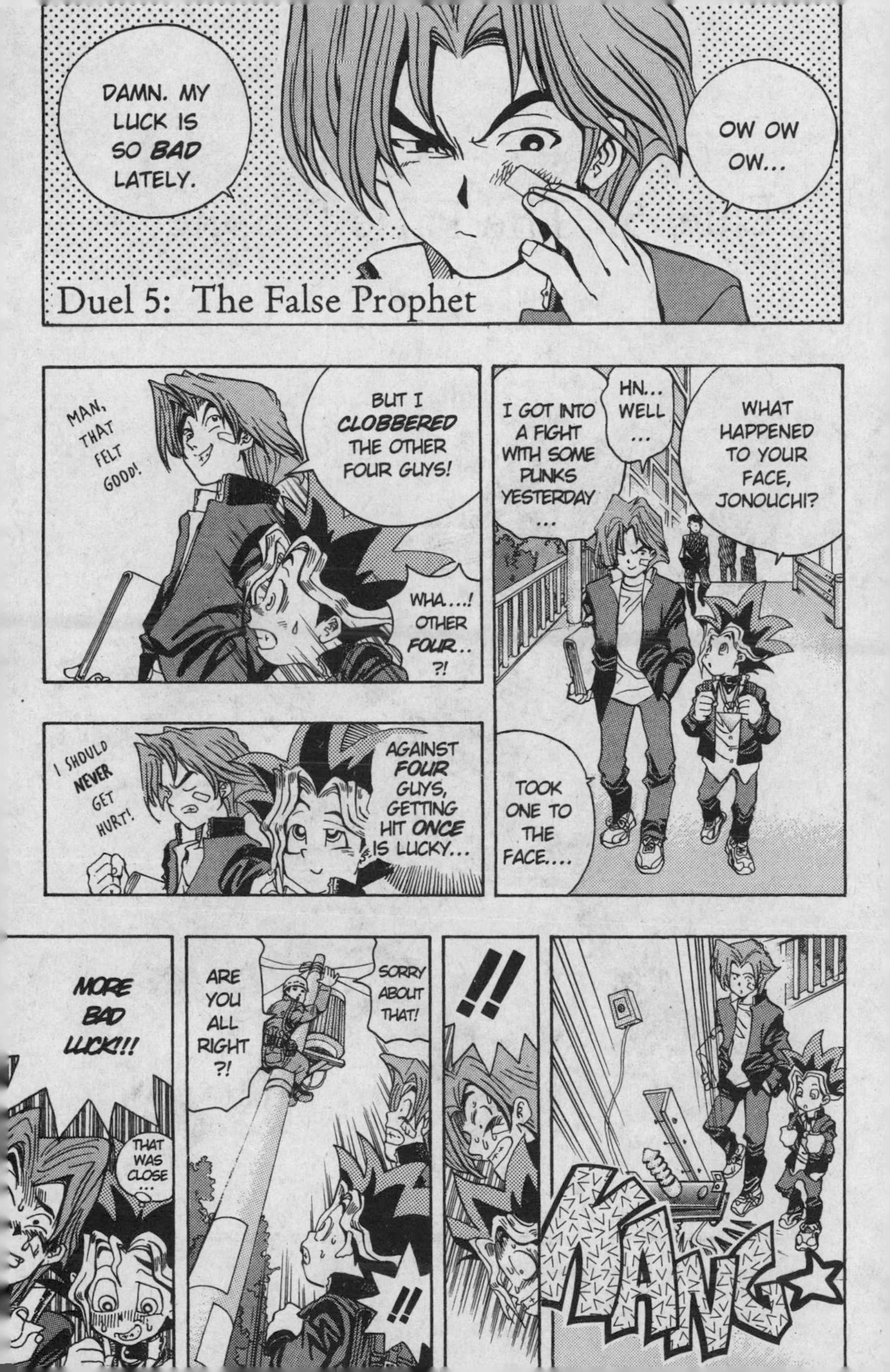
OW OW OW...
DAMN. MY LUCK IS SO BAD LATELY.
Duel 5: The False Prophet
WHAT HAPPENED TO YOUR FACE, JONOUCHI?
HN... WELL ...
I GOT INTO A FIGHT WITH SOME PUNKS YESTERDAY ...
TOOK ONE TO THE FACE....
BUT I CLOBBERED THE OTHER FOUR GUYS!
MAN, THAT FELT GOOD!
WHA....! OTHER FOUR.. ?!
AGAINST FOUR GUYS, GETTING HIT ONCE IS LUCKY...
I SHOULD NEVER GET HURT!
!!
!!
SORRY ABOUT THAT!
ARE YOU ALL RIGHT ?!
MORE BAD LUCK!!!
THAT WAS CLOSE ...

Duel 5: The False Prophet

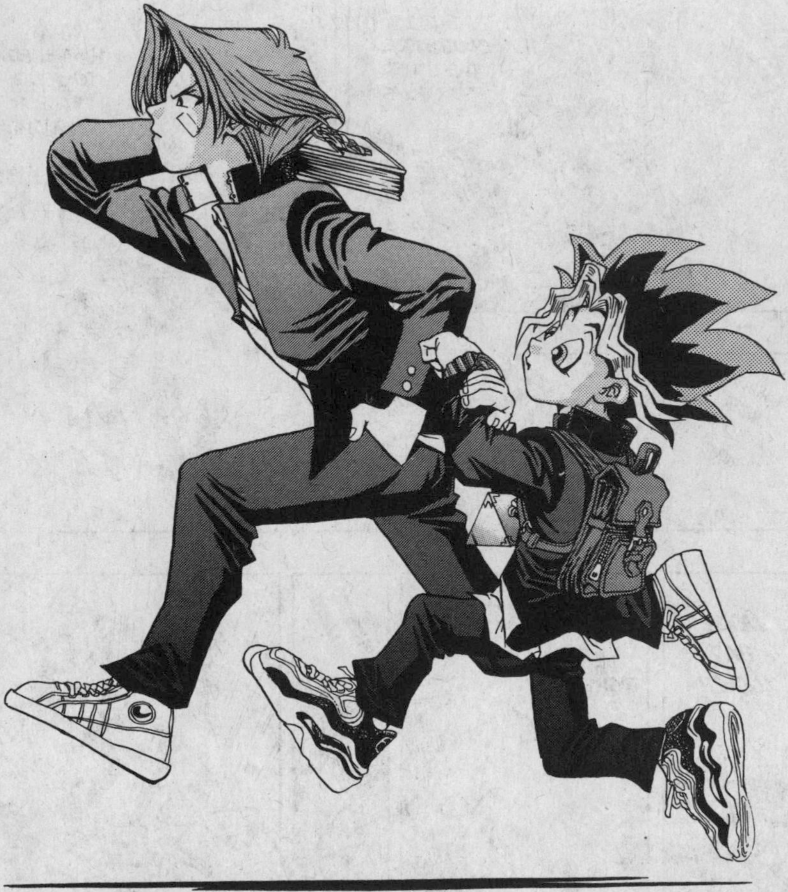

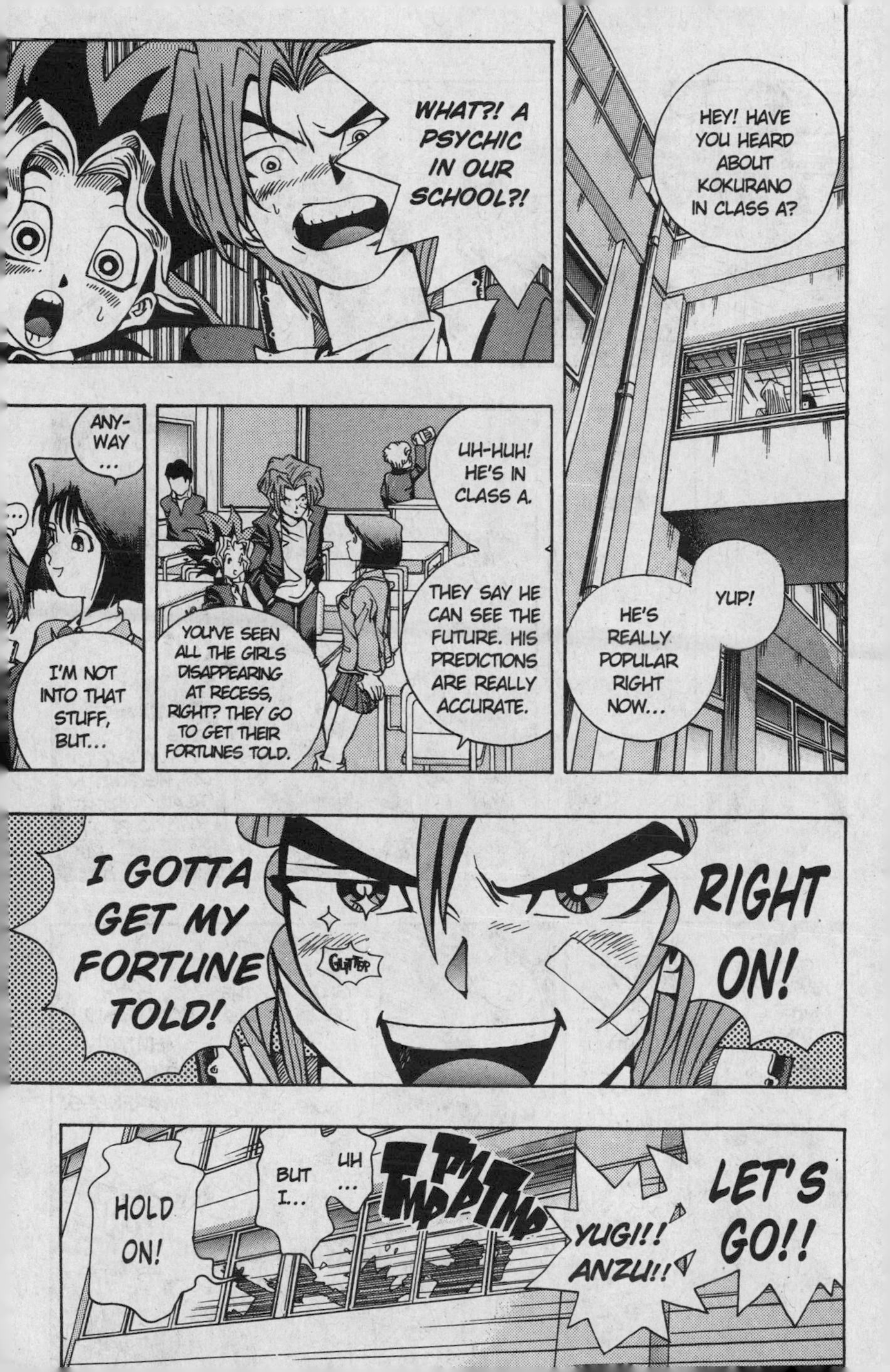
HEY! HAVE YOU HEARD ABOUT KOKURANO IN CLASS A?
HE'S REALLY POPULAR RIGHT NOW...
YUP!
WHAT?! A PSYCHIC IN OUR SCHOOL?!
UH-HUH! HE'S IN CLASS A.
THEY SAY HE CAN SEE THE FUTURE. HIS PREDICTIONS ARE REALLY ACCURATE.
YOU'VE SEEN ALL THE GIRLS DISAPPEARING AT RECESS, RIGHT? THEY GO TO GET THEIR FORTUNES TOLD.
ANY-WAY...
...
I'M NOT INTO THAT STUFF, BUT...
RIGHT ON!
I GOTTA GET MY FORTUNE TOLD!
GLITTER
LET'S GO!!
YUGI!! ANZU!!
TMP TMP TMP TMP
UH...
BUT I...
HOLD ON!

READ THIS WAY

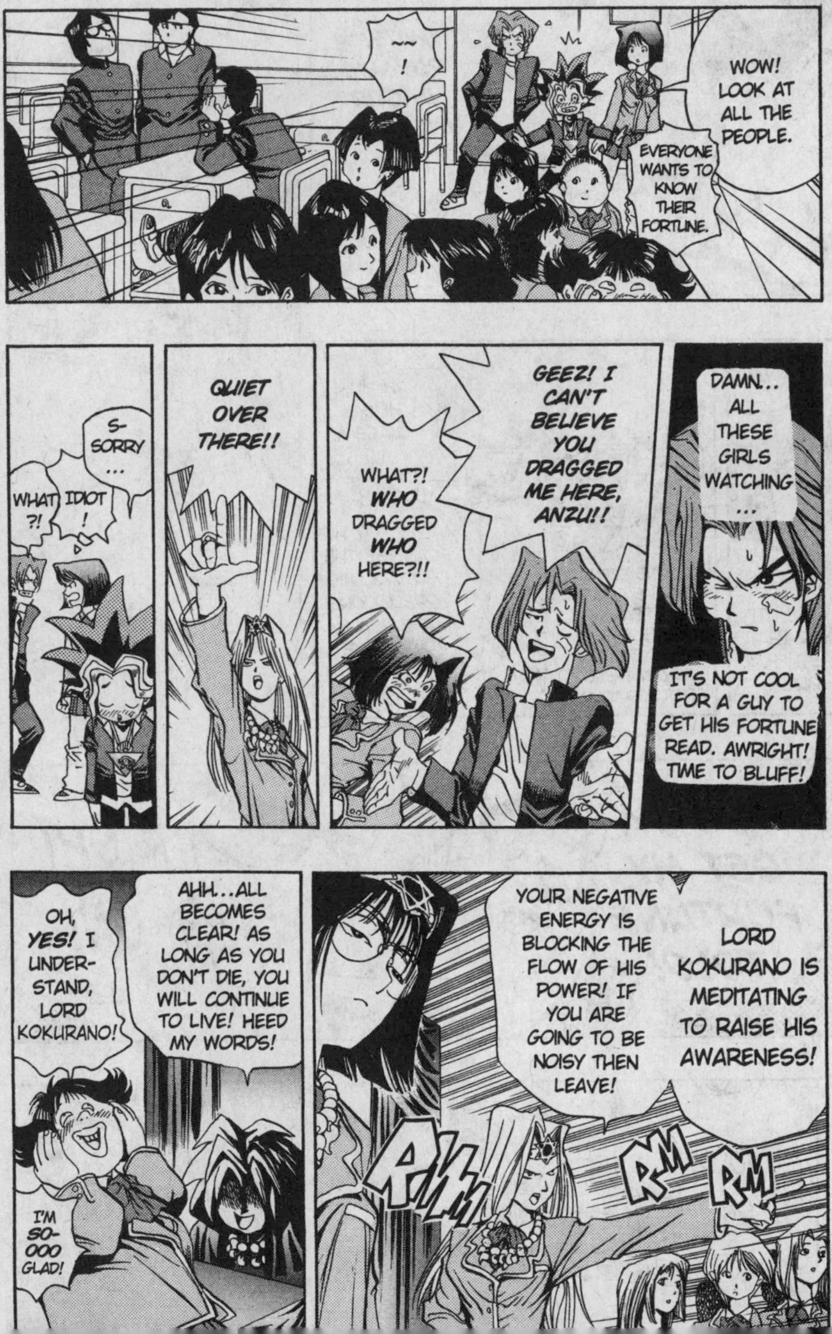
WOW! LOOK AT ALL THE PEOPLE.
EVERYONE WANTS TO KNOW THEIR FORTUNE.
~~ !
DAMN... ALL THESE GIRLS WATCHING...
IT'S NOT COOL FOR A GUY TO GET HIS FORTUNE READ. AWRIGHT! TIME TO BLUFF!
GEEZ! I CAN'T BELIEVE YOU DRAGGED ME HERE, ANZU!!
WHAT?! WHO DRAGGED WHO HERE?!!
QUIET OVER THERE!!
S-SORRY...
IDIOT!
WHAT?!
LORD KOKURANO IS MEDITATING TO RAISE HIS AWARENESS!
YOUR NEGATIVE ENERGY IS BLOCKING THE FLOW OF HIS POWER! IF YOU ARE GOING TO BE NOISY THEN LEAVE!
RM
RM
RM
AHH...ALL BECOMES CLEAR! AS LONG AS YOU DON'T DIE, YOU WILL CONTINUE TO LIVE! HEED MY WORDS!
OH, YES! I UNDERSTAND, LORD KOKURANO!
I'M SO-OOO GLAD!

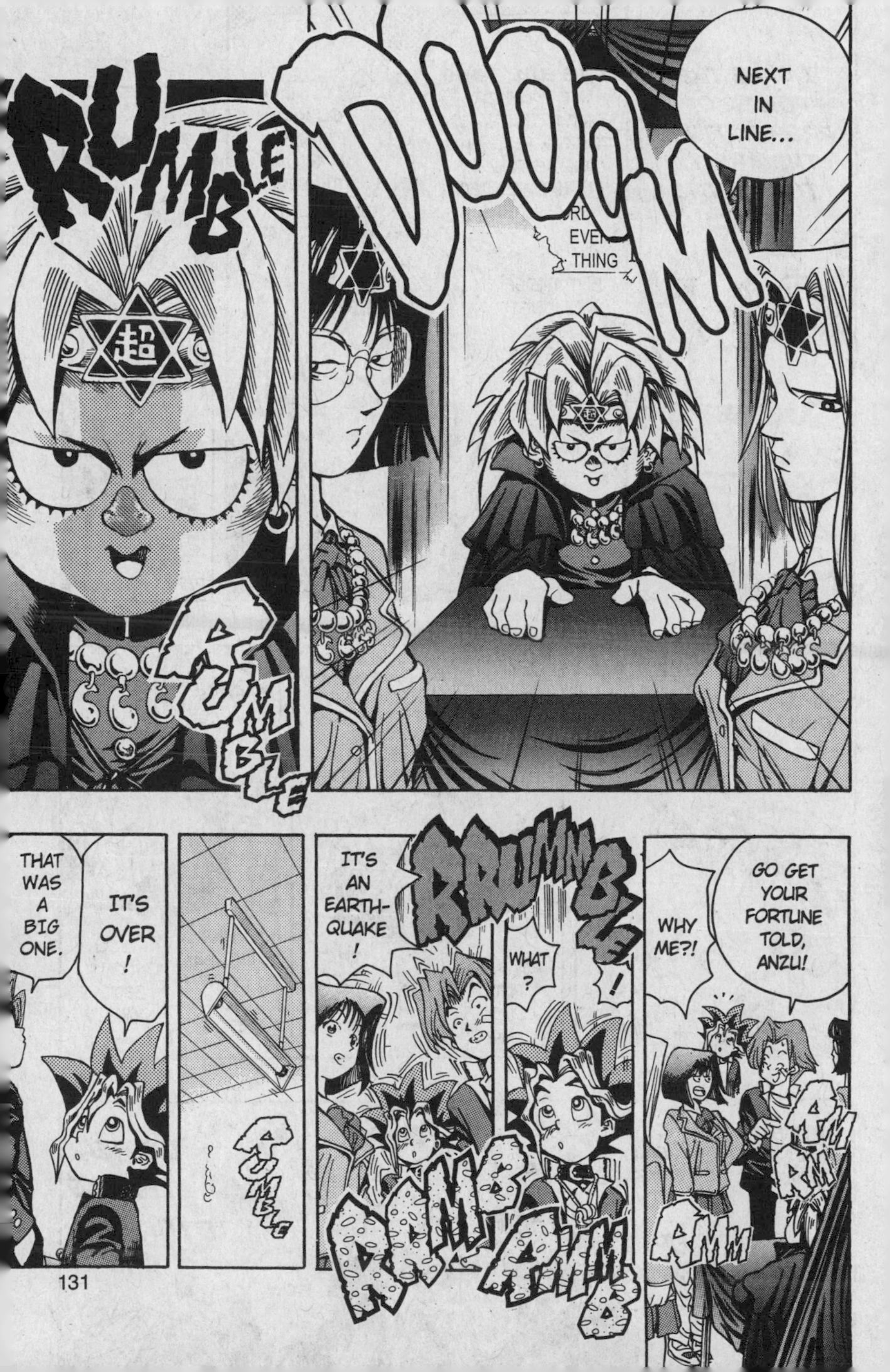
NEXT IN LINE...
DOOOM
EVERY THING
RUMBLE
RUMBLE
GO GET YOUR FORTUNE TOLD, ANZU!
WHY ME?!
RMM
RMM
RMM
RRUMMBLE
!
WHAT?
IT'S AN EARTH-QUAKE!
RMMB
RMMB
RUMBLE
IT'S OVER!
THAT WAS A BIG ONE.

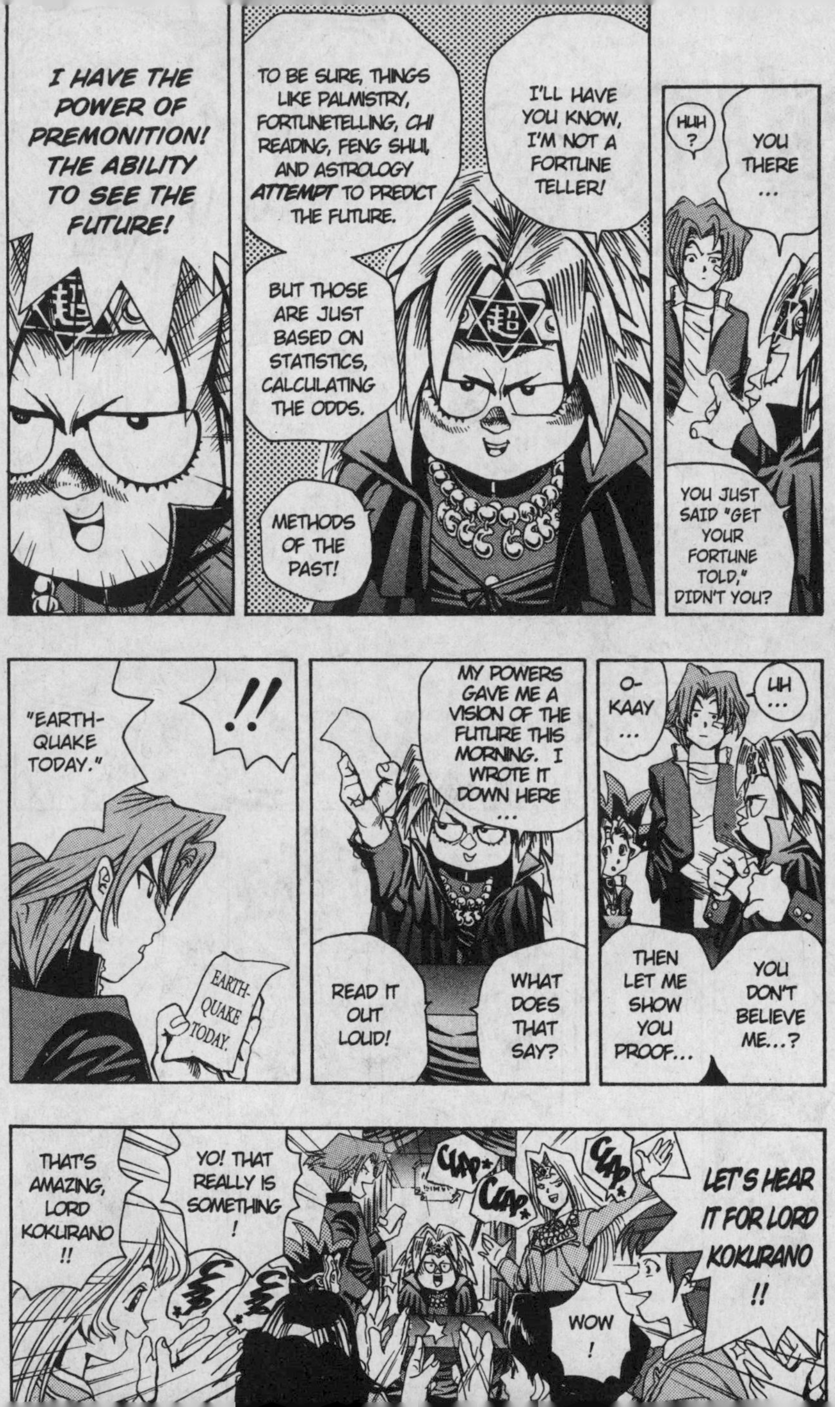
YOU THERE ...
HUH ?
YOU JUST SAID "GET YOUR FORTUNE TOLD," DIDN'T YOU?
I'LL HAVE YOU KNOW, I'M NOT A FORTUNE TELLER!
TO BE SURE, THINGS LIKE PALMISTRY, FORTUNETELLING, *CHI* READING, FENG SHUI, AND ASTROLOGY ***ATTEMPT*** TO PREDICT THE FUTURE.
BUT THOSE ARE JUST BASED ON STATISTICS, CALCULATING THE ODDS.
METHODS OF THE PAST!
I HAVE THE POWER OF PREMONITION! THE ABILITY TO SEE THE FUTURE!
UH ...
O-KAAY ...
YOU DON'T BELIEVE ME...?
THEN LET ME SHOW YOU PROOF...
MY POWERS GAVE ME A VISION OF THE FUTURE THIS MORNING. I WROTE IT DOWN HERE ...
WHAT DOES THAT SAY?
READ IT OUT LOUD!
!!
"EARTH-QUAKE TODAY."
EARTH-QUAKE TODAY.
LET'S HEAR IT FOR LORD KOKURANO !!
CLAP
CLAP
CLAP
YO! THAT REALLY IS SOMETHING !
THAT'S AMAZING, LORD KOKURANO !!
WOW !

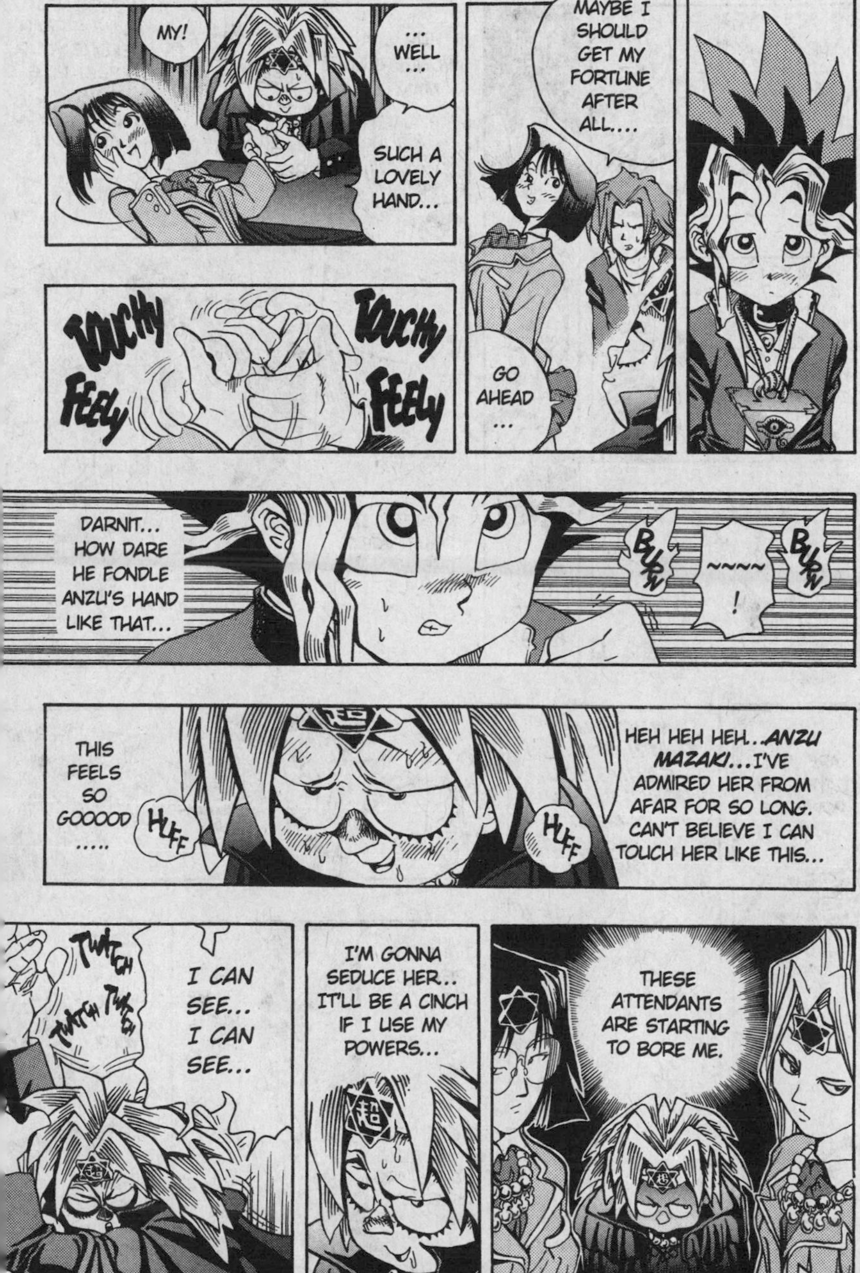
MAYBE I SHOULD GET MY FORTUNE AFTER ALL....
GO AHEAD ...
... WELL ...
MY!
SUCH A LOVELY HAND...
TOUCHY FEELY
TOUCHY FEELY
BURN
~~~~ !
BURN
DARNIT... HOW DARE HE FONDLE ANZU'S HAND LIKE THAT...
HEH HEH HEH...*ANZU MAZAKI*...I'VE ADMIRED HER FROM AFAR FOR SO LONG. CAN'T BELIEVE I CAN TOUCH HER LIKE THIS...
HUFF
HUFF
THIS FEELS SO GOOOOD .....
THESE ATTENDANTS ARE STARTING TO BORE ME.
I'M GONNA SEDUCE HER... IT'LL BE A CINCH IF I USE MY POWERS...
I CAN SEE... I CAN SEE...
TWITCH TWITCH TWITCH
~~~~

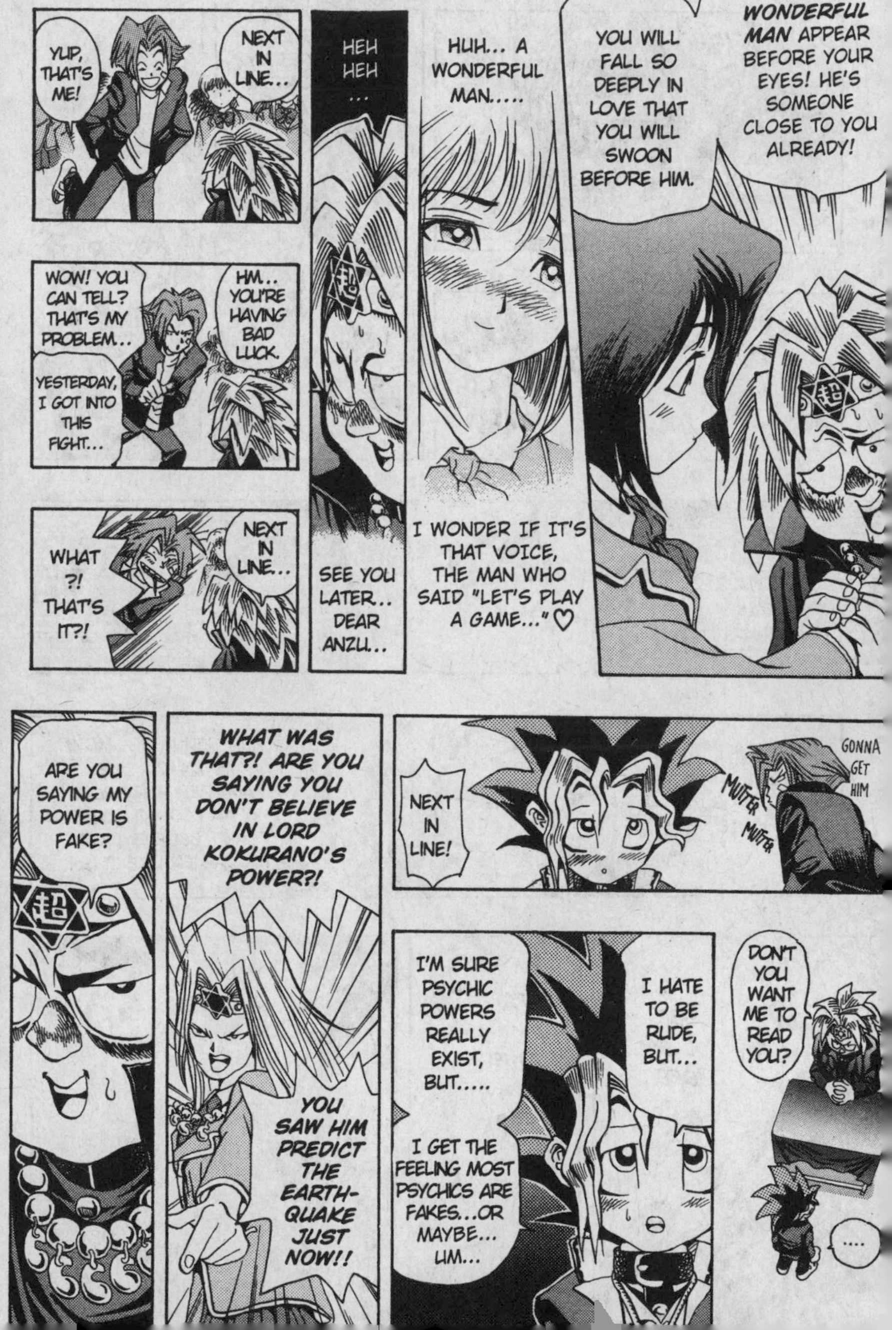
I SEE A ***WONDERFUL MAN*** APPEAR BEFORE YOUR EYES! HE'S SOMEONE CLOSE TO YOU ALREADY!
YOU WILL FALL SO DEEPLY IN LOVE THAT YOU WILL SWOON BEFORE HIM.
HUH... A WONDERFUL MAN.....
I WONDER IF IT'S THAT VOICE, THE MAN WHO SAID "LET'S PLAY A GAME..."♡
HEH HEH ...
SEE YOU LATER... DEAR ANZU...
NEXT IN LINE...
YUP, THAT'S ME!
HM... YOU'RE HAVING BAD LUCK.
WOW! YOU CAN TELL? THAT'S MY PROBLEM...
YESTERDAY, I GOT INTO THIS FIGHT...
NEXT IN LINE...
WHAT ?! THAT'S IT?!
GONNA GET HIM
MUTTER MUTTER
NEXT IN LINE!
DON'T YOU WANT ME TO READ YOU?
....
I HATE TO BE RUDE, BUT...
I'M SURE PSYCHIC POWERS REALLY EXIST, BUT.....
I GET THE FEELING MOST PSYCHICS ARE FAKES...OR MAYBE... UM...
WHAT WAS THAT?! ARE YOU SAYING YOU DON'T BELIEVE IN LORD KOKURANO'S POWER?!
YOU SAW HIM PREDICT THE EARTH-QUAKE JUST NOW!!
ARE YOU SAYING MY POWER IS FAKE?

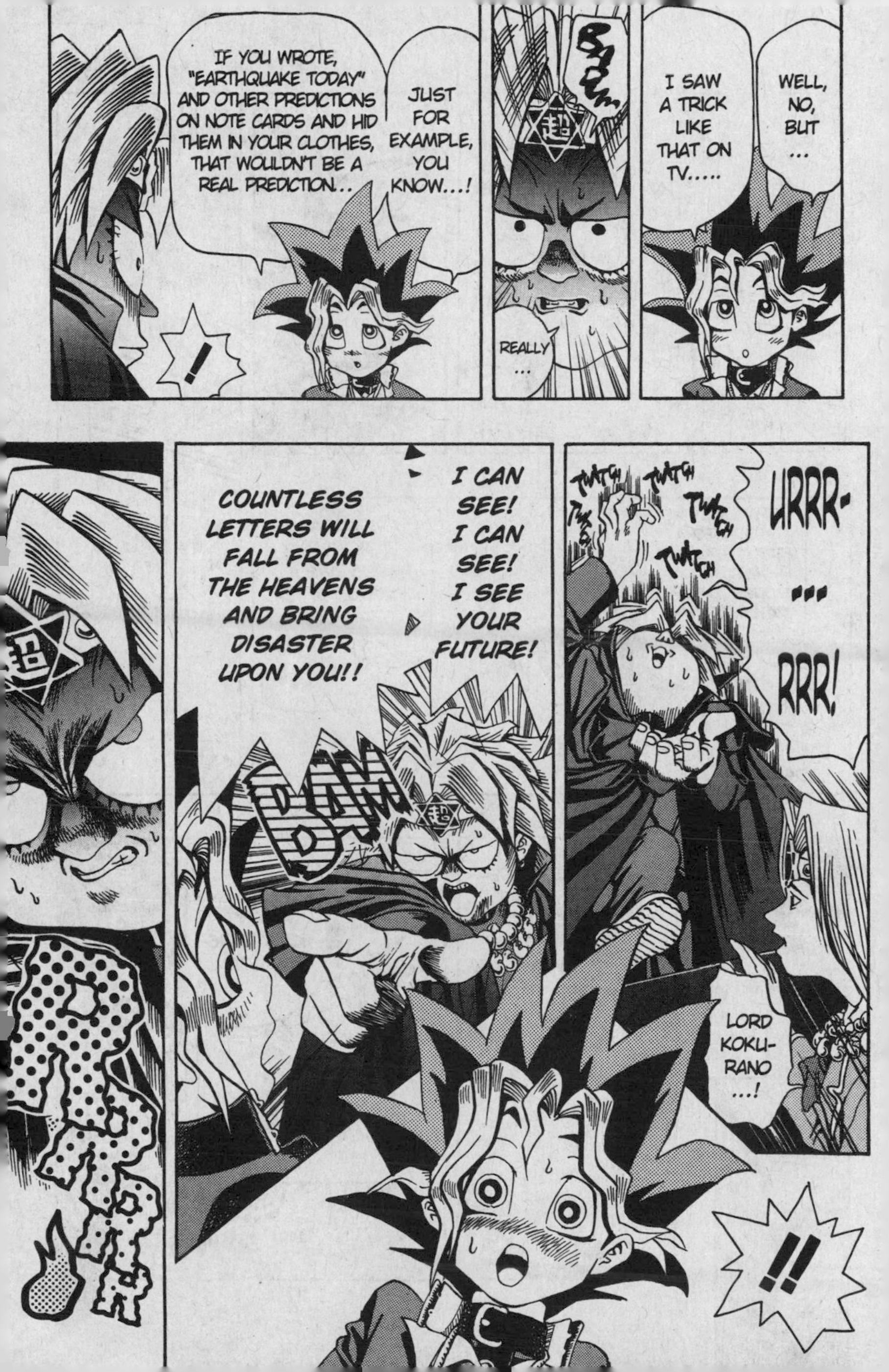
WELL, NO, BUT ...
I SAW A TRICK LIKE THAT ON TV.....
REALLY ...
JUST FOR EXAMPLE, YOU KNOW...!
IF YOU WROTE, "EARTHQUAKE TODAY" AND OTHER PREDICTIONS ON NOTE CARDS AND HID THEM IN YOUR CLOTHES, THAT WOULDN'T BE A REAL PREDICTION...
!
URRR-...RRR!
TWITCH TWITCH TWITCH TWITCH TWITCH
LORD KOKU-RANO ...!
I CAN SEE! I CAN SEE! I SEE YOUR FUTURE!
COUNTLESS LETTERS WILL FALL FROM THE HEAVENS AND BRING DISASTER UPON YOU!!
BAM
!!

READ THIS WAY

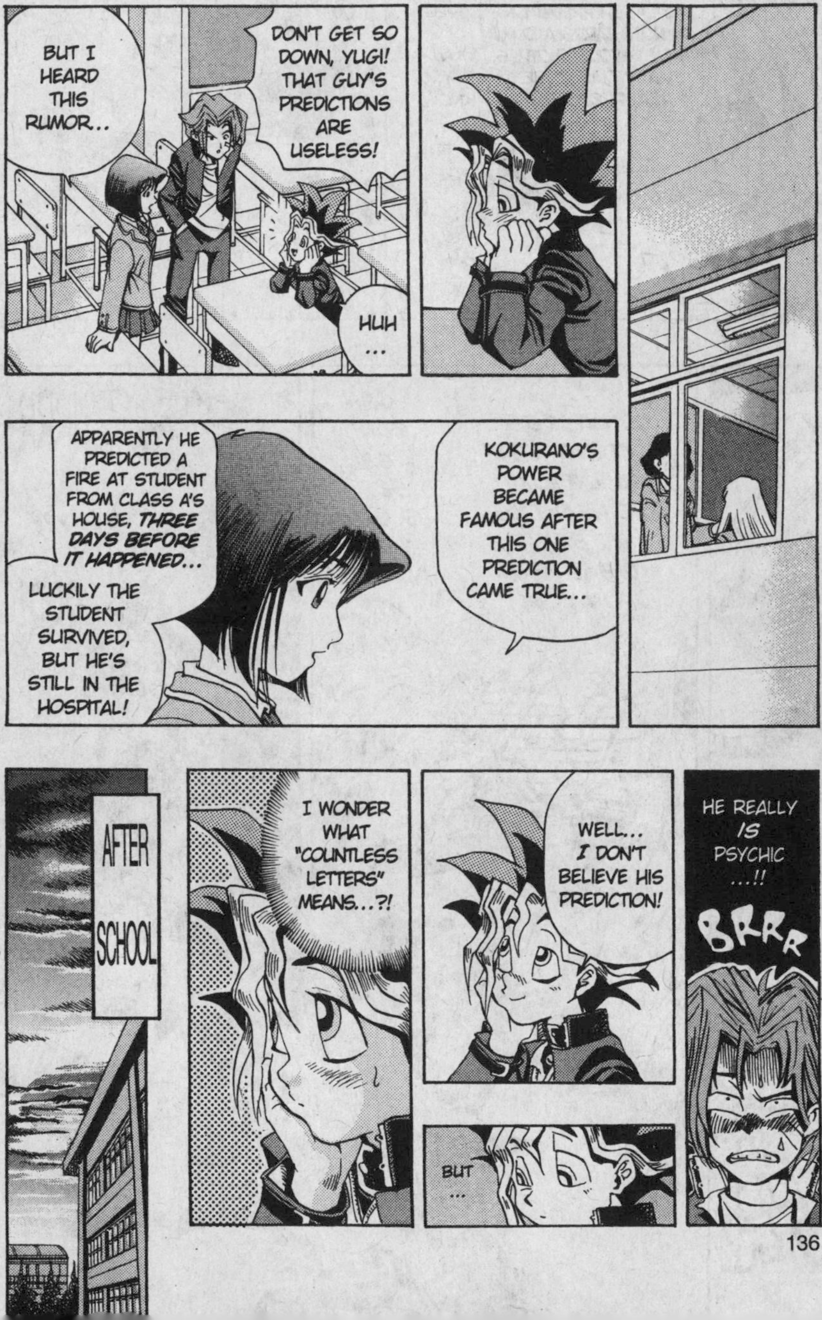

DON'T GET SO DOWN, YUGI! THAT GUY'S PREDICTIONS ARE USELESS!
BUT I HEARD THIS RUMOR...
HUH ...
KOKURANO'S POWER BECAME FAMOUS AFTER THIS ONE PREDICTION CAME TRUE...
APPARENTLY HE PREDICTED A FIRE AT STUDENT FROM CLASS A'S HOUSE, *THREE DAYS BEFORE IT HAPPENED...*
LUCKILY THE STUDENT SURVIVED, BUT HE'S STILL IN THE HOSPITAL!
HE REALLY *IS* PSYCHIC ...!!
BRRR
WELL... *I* DON'T BELIEVE HIS PREDICTION!
BUT ...
I WONDER WHAT "COUNTLESS LETTERS" MEANS...?!
AFTER SCHOOL

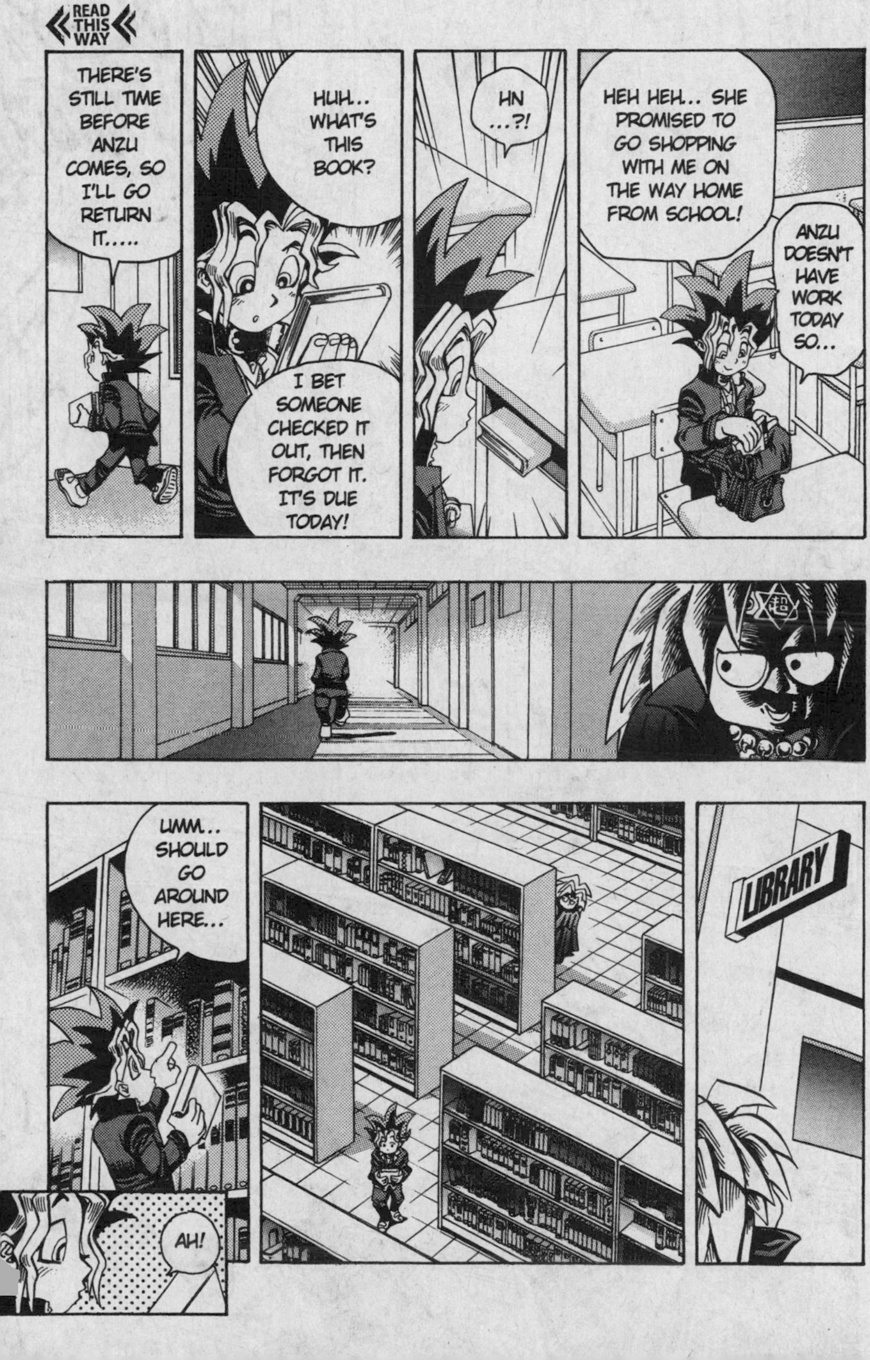
READ THIS WAY
HEH HEH... SHE PROMISED TO GO SHOPPING WITH ME ON THE WAY HOME FROM SCHOOL!
ANZU DOESN'T HAVE WORK TODAY SO...
HN ...?!
HUH... WHAT'S THIS BOOK?
I BET SOMEONE CHECKED IT OUT, THEN FORGOT IT. IT'S DUE TODAY!
THERE'S STILL TIME BEFORE ANZU COMES, SO I'LL GO RETURN IT.....
LIBRARY
UMM.. SHOULD GO AROUND HERE...
AH!

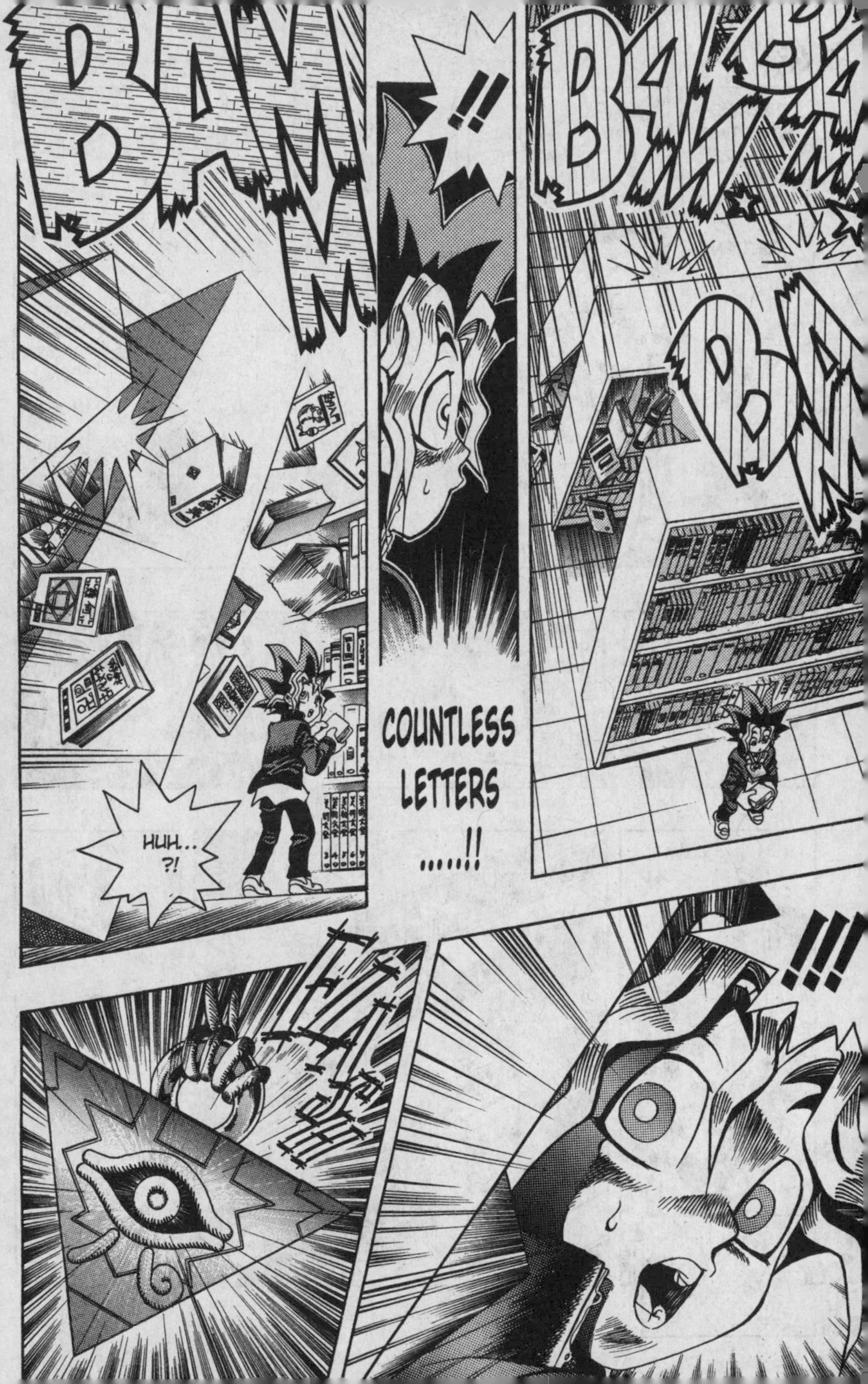
BAM
BA
!!
COUNTLESS LETTERS ......!!
HUH... ?!
!!!

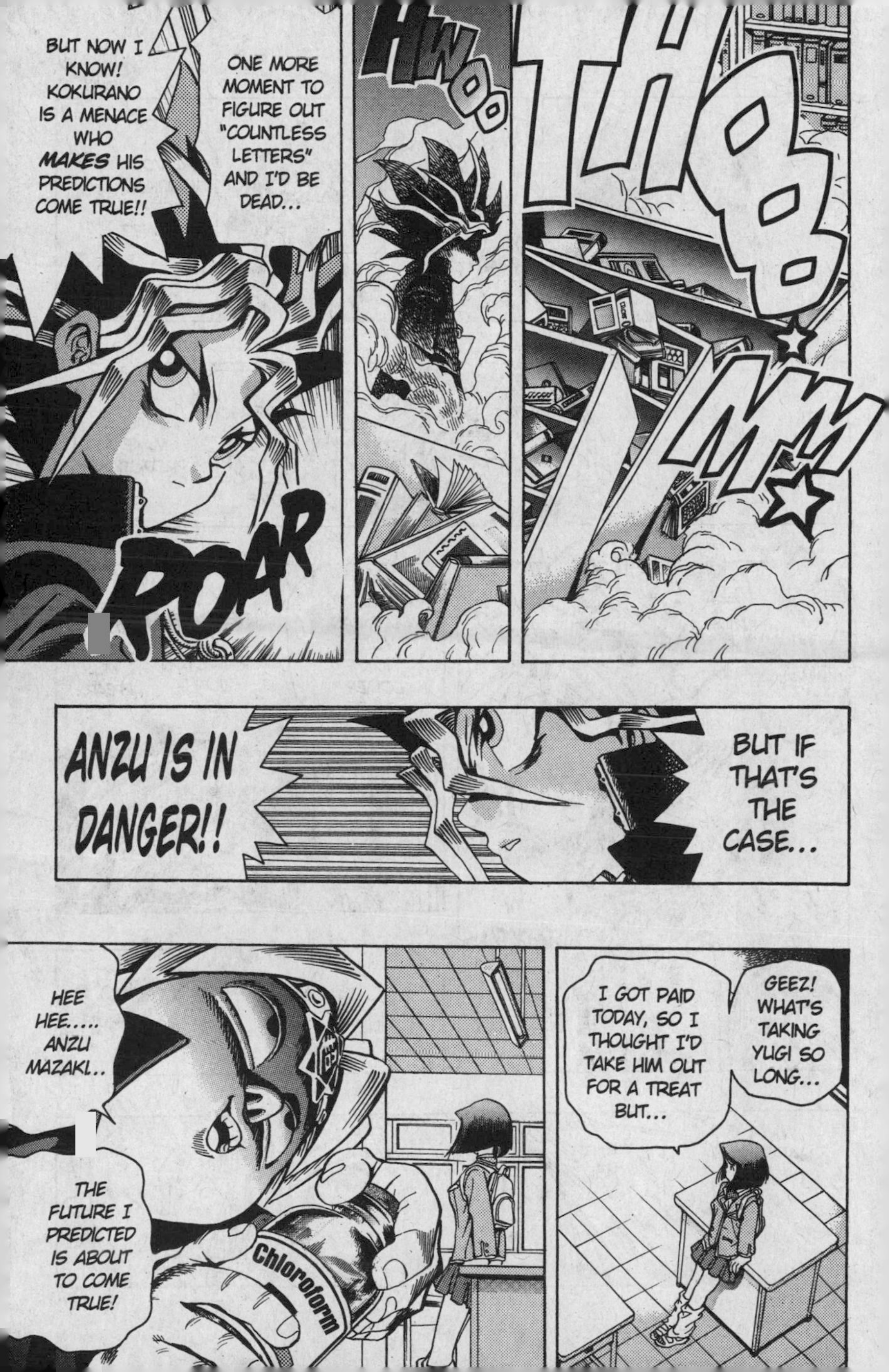
ONE MORE MOMENT TO FIGURE OUT "COUNTLESS LETTERS" AND I'D BE DEAD...
BUT NOW I KNOW! KOKURANO IS A MENACE WHO *MAKES* HIS PREDICTIONS COME TRUE!!
ROAR
BUT IF THAT'S THE CASE...
ANZU IS IN DANGER!!
GEEZ! WHAT'S TAKING YUGI SO LONG...
I GOT PAID TODAY, SO I THOUGHT I'D TAKE HIM OUT FOR A TREAT BUT...
HEE HEE..... ANZU MAZAKI..
THE FUTURE I PREDICTED IS ABOUT TO COME TRUE!
Chloroform

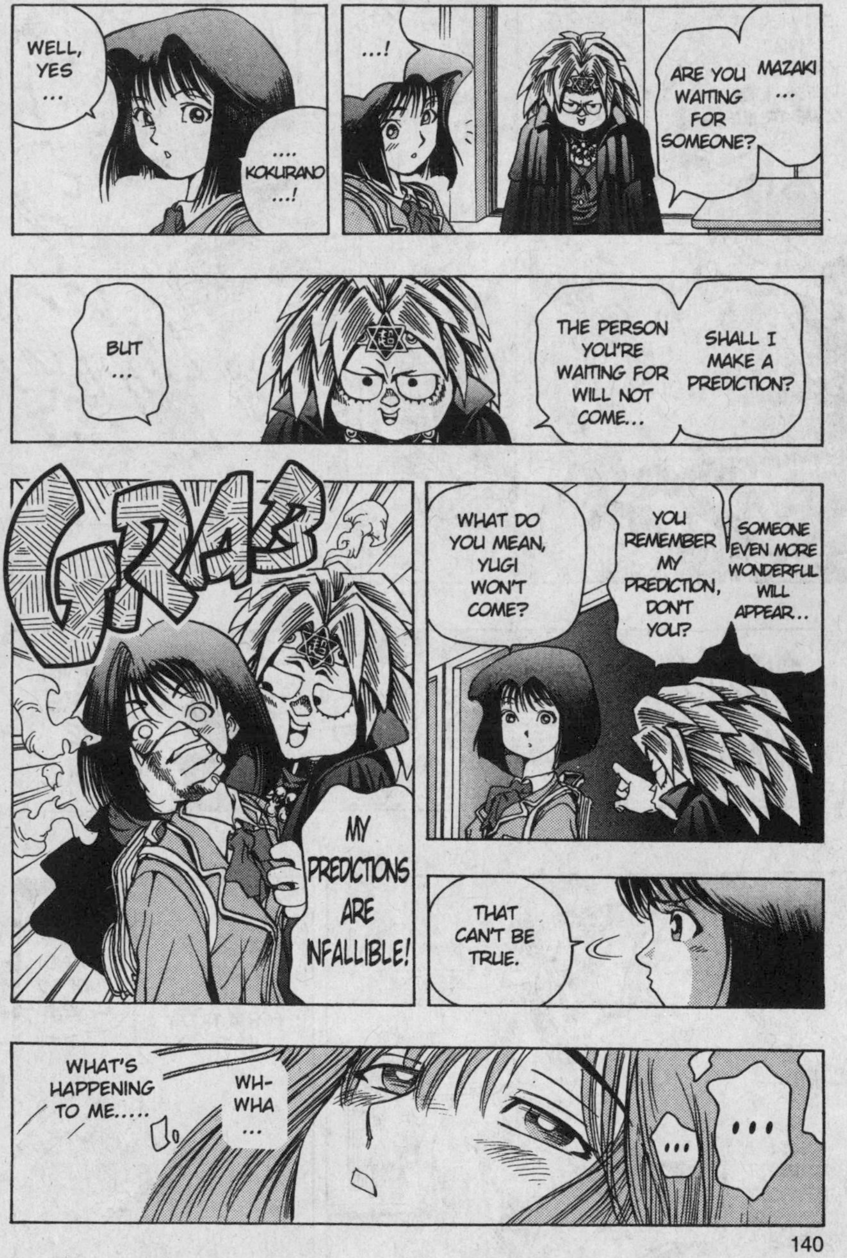
MAZAKI ...
ARE YOU WAITING FOR SOMEONE?
...!
.... KOKURANO ....!
WELL, YES ...
SHALL I MAKE A PREDICTION?
THE PERSON YOU'RE WAITING FOR WILL NOT COME...
BUT ...
SOMEONE EVEN MORE WONDERFUL WILL APPEAR...
YOU REMEMBER MY PREDICTION, DON'T YOU?
WHAT DO YOU MEAN, YUGI WON'T COME?
THAT CAN'T BE TRUE.
GRAB
MY PREDICTIONS ARE INFALLIBLE!
...
...
WH- WHA ...
WHAT'S HAPPENING TO ME.....

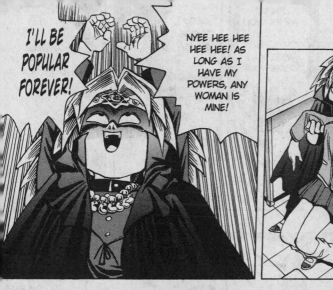

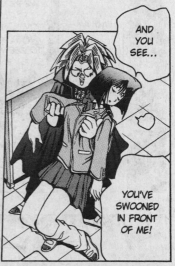

AND YOU SEE...
YOU'VE SWOONED IN FRONT OF ME!
NYEE HEE HEE HEE HEE! AS LONG AS I HAVE MY POWERS, ANY WOMAN IS MINE!
I'LL BE POPULAR FOREVER!
YOU THINK SO?
BAM
ACK!!
YUGI ...!!
...IT'S YOU...?!
TOO BAD, KOKU-RANO!
YOUR PREDICTION FAILED!

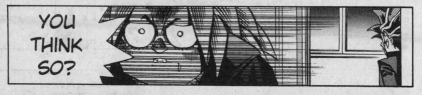

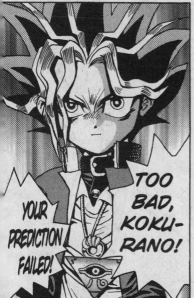

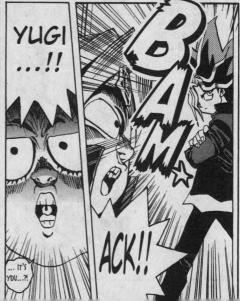

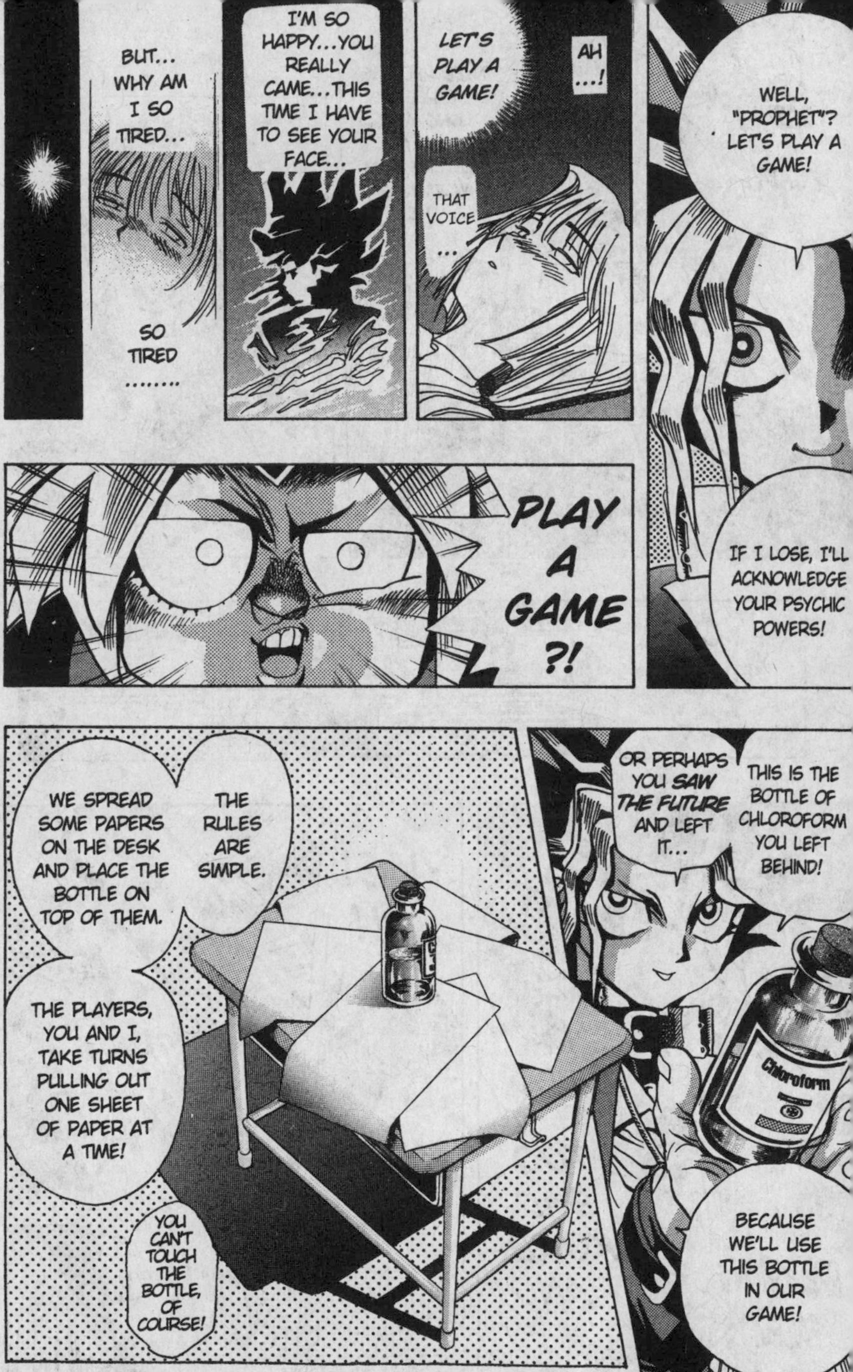
WELL, "PROPHET"? LET'S PLAY A GAME!
IF I LOSE, I'LL ACKNOWLEDGE YOUR PSYCHIC POWERS!
AH ...!
LET'S PLAY A GAME!
THAT VOICE ...
I'M SO HAPPY...YOU REALLY CAME...THIS TIME I HAVE TO SEE YOUR FACE...
BUT... WHY AM I SO TIRED...
SO TIRED ....
PLAY A GAME ?!
THIS IS THE BOTTLE OF CHLOROFORM YOU LEFT BEHIND!
OR PERHAPS YOU *SAW THE FUTURE* AND LEFT IT...
Chloroform
BECAUSE WE'LL USE THIS BOTTLE IN OUR GAME!
THE RULES ARE SIMPLE.
WE SPREAD SOME PAPERS ON THE DESK AND PLACE THE BOTTLE ON TOP OF THEM.
THE PLAYERS, YOU AND I, TAKE TURNS PULLING OUT ONE SHEET OF PAPER AT A TIME!
YOU CAN'T TOUCH THE BOTTLE, OF COURSE!

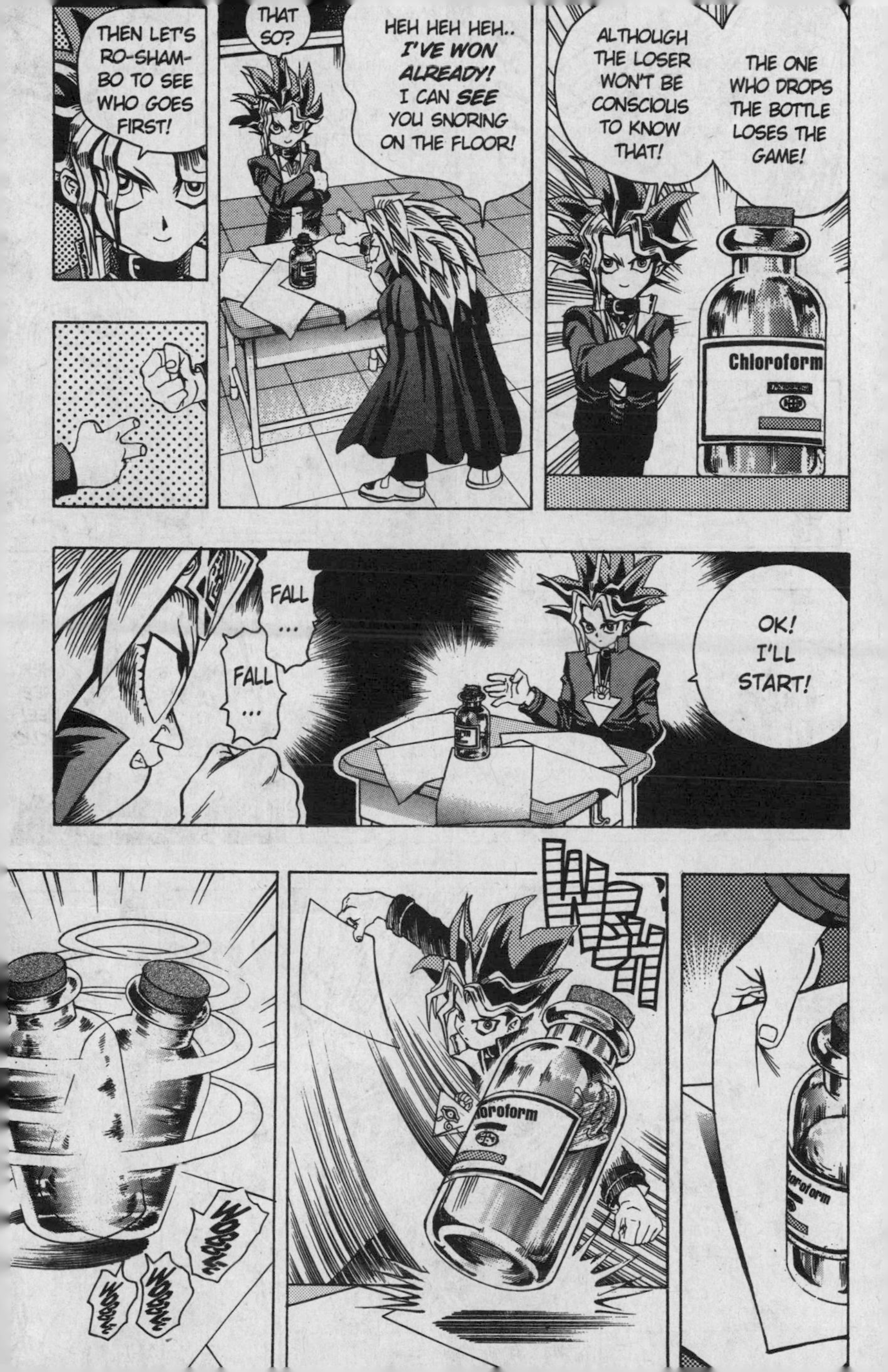
THE ONE WHO DROPS THE BOTTLE LOSES THE GAME!
ALTHOUGH THE LOSER WON'T BE CONSCIOUS TO KNOW THAT!
Chloroform
HEH HEH HEH.. *I'VE WON ALREADY!* I CAN *SEE* YOU SNORING ON THE FLOOR!
THAT SO?
THEN LET'S RO-SHAMBO TO SEE WHO GOES FIRST!
OK! I'LL START!
FALL ...
FALL ...
WSSH
Chloroform
Chloroform
WOBBLE
WOBBLE
WOBBLE

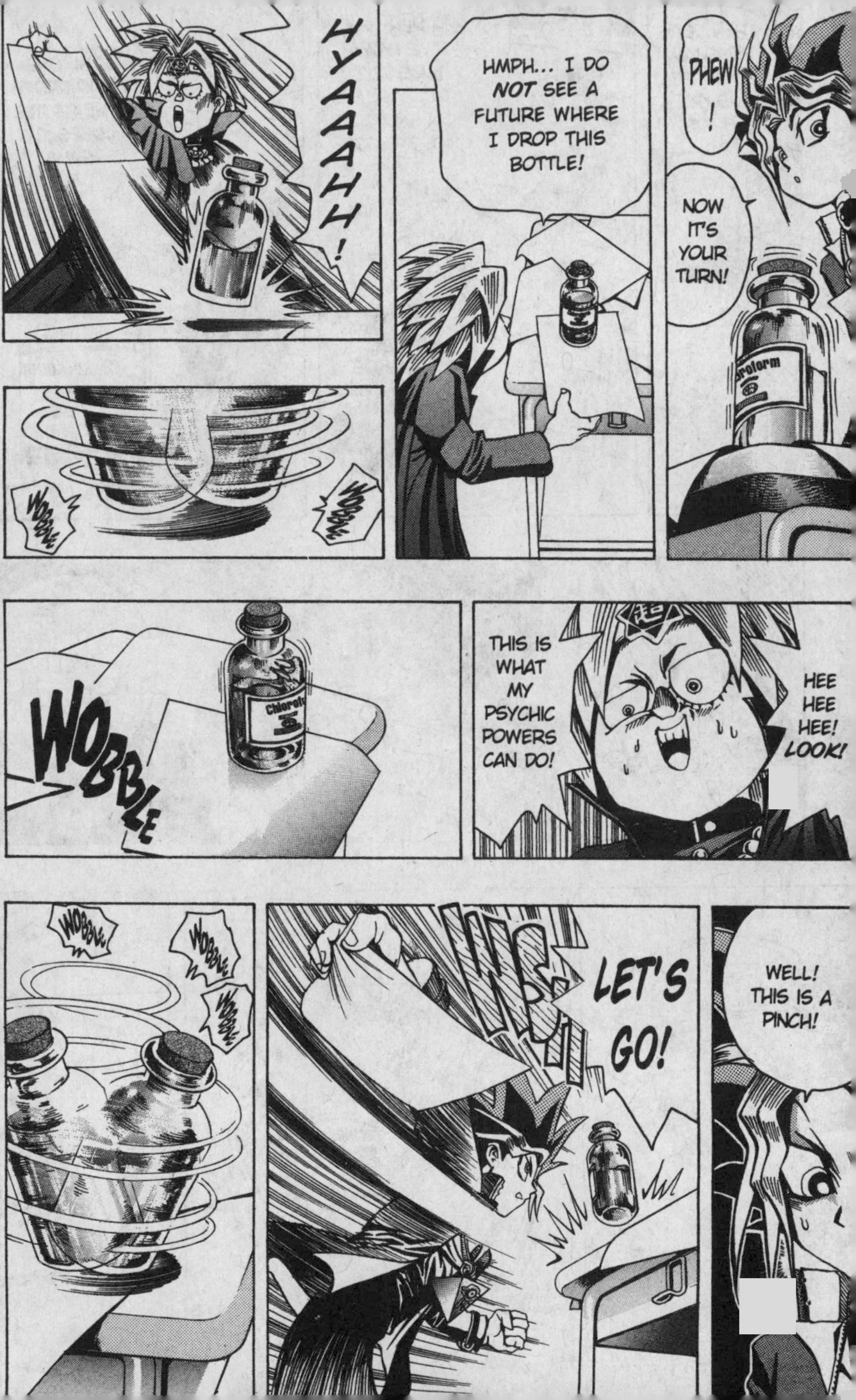
PHEW!
NOW IT'S YOUR TURN!
HMPH... I DO *NOT* SEE A FUTURE WHERE I DROP THIS BOTTLE!
HYAAAAHH!
WOBBLE
WOBBLE
HEE HEE HEE! *LOOK!*
THIS IS WHAT MY PSYCHIC POWERS CAN DO!
WOBBLE
WELL! THIS IS A PINCH!
LET'S GO!
WOBBLE
WOBBLE
WOBBLE

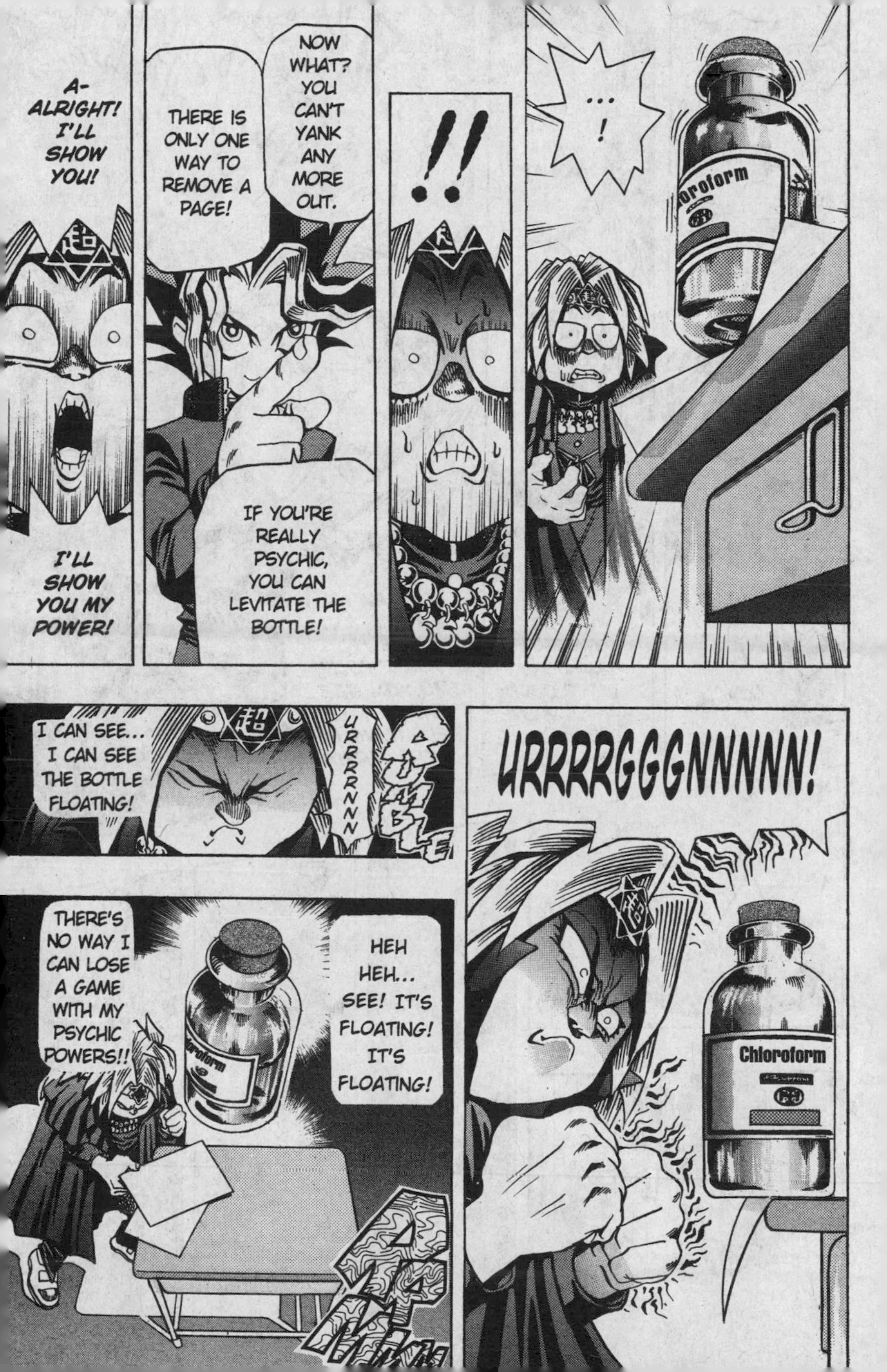
...!
!!
NOW WHAT? YOU CAN'T YANK ANY MORE OUT.
THERE IS ONLY ONE WAY TO REMOVE A PAGE!
IF YOU'RE REALLY PSYCHIC, YOU CAN LEVITATE THE BOTTLE!
A-ALRIGHT! I'LL SHOW YOU!
I'LL SHOW YOU MY POWER!
URRRRGGGNNNNN!
Chloroform
RUMBLE
URRRRNNNN
I CAN SEE... I CAN SEE THE BOTTLE FLOATING!
HEH HEH... SEE! IT'S FLOATING! IT'S FLOATING!
THERE'S NO WAY I CAN LOSE A GAME WITH MY PSYCHIC POWERS!!

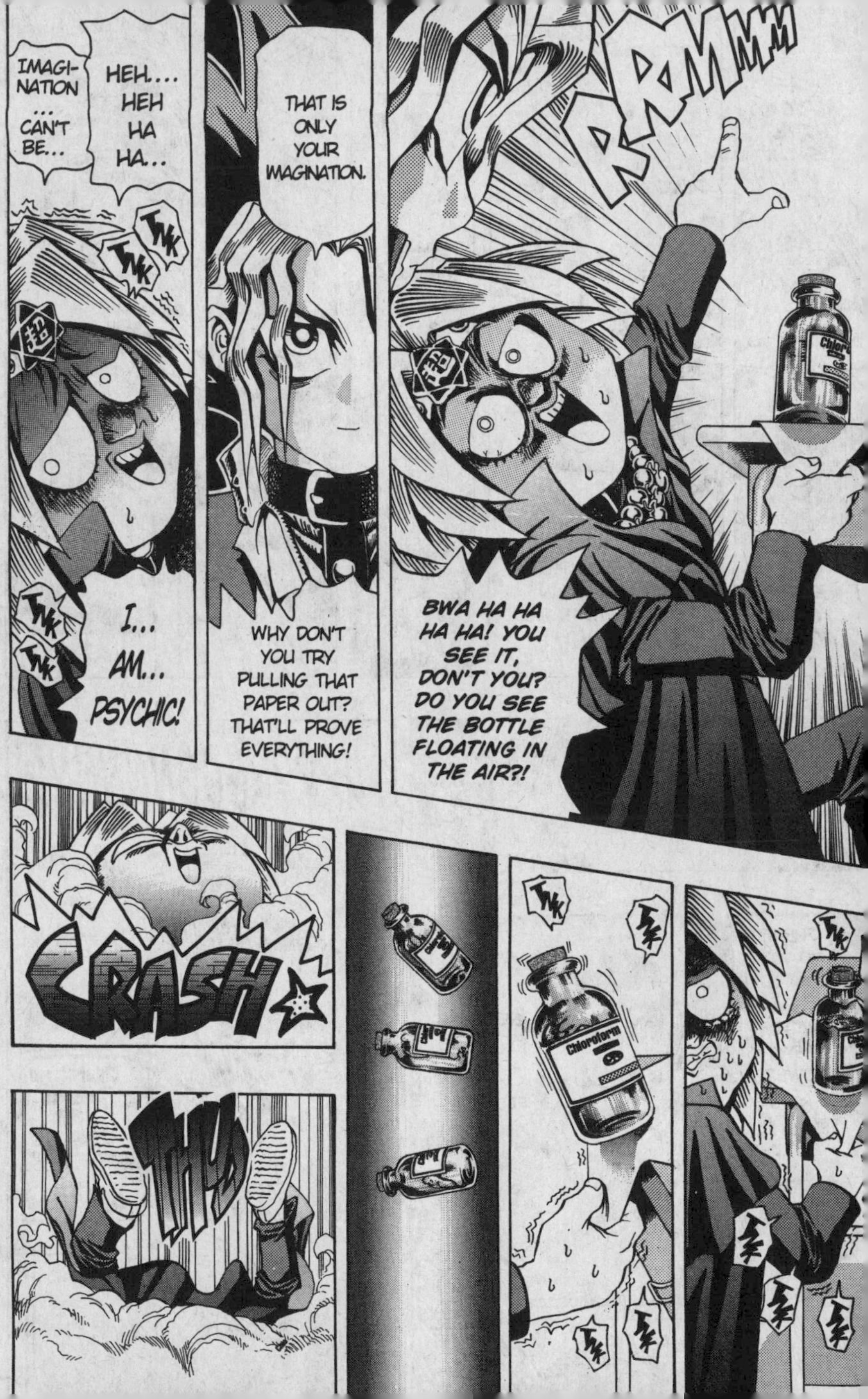
BRAMMM
BWA HA HA HA HA! YOU SEE IT, DON'T YOU? DO YOU SEE THE BOTTLE FLOATING IN THE AIR?!
THAT IS ONLY YOUR IMAGINATION.
WHY DON'T YOU TRY PULLING THAT PAPER OUT? THAT'LL PROVE EVERYTHING!
HEH.... HEH HA HA...
IMAGINATION ... CAN'T BE...
TNK
TNK
I... AM... PSYCHIC!
TNK
TNK
TNK
TNK
TNK
TNK
Chloroform
TNK
TNK
TNK
CRASH
THUD

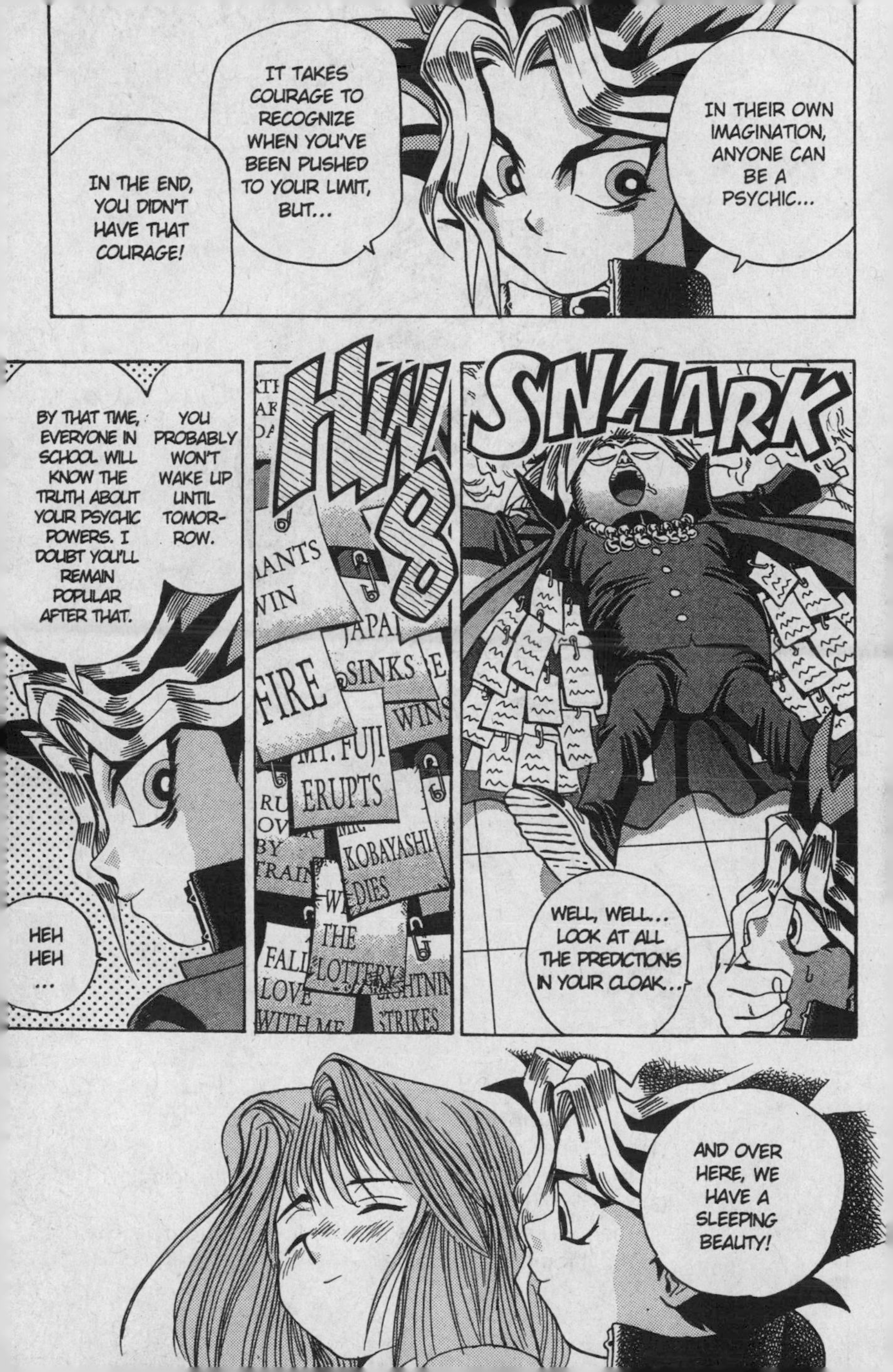
IN THEIR OWN IMAGINATION, ANYONE CAN BE A PSYCHIC...
IT TAKES COURAGE TO RECOGNIZE WHEN YOU'VE BEEN PUSHED TO YOUR LIMIT, BUT...
IN THE END, YOU DIDN'T HAVE THAT COURAGE!
SNAARK
WELL, WELL... LOOK AT ALL THE PREDICTIONS IN YOUR CLOAK...
SINKS
FIRE
MT. FUJI ERUPTS
KOBAYASHI DIES
THE LOTTERY
STRIKES
YOU PROBABLY WON'T WAKE UP UNTIL TOMORROW.
BY THAT TIME, EVERYONE IN SCHOOL WILL KNOW THE TRUTH ABOUT YOUR PSYCHIC POWERS. I DOUBT YOU'LL REMAIN POPULAR AFTER THAT.
HEH HEH ...
AND OVER HERE, WE HAVE A SLEEPING BEAUTY!

"FIND THE CHANGES" ANSWERS (From Page 126)
(1) Anzu's necktie
(2) The straw in the drink on the plate Anzu is holding
(3) Yugi's pendant
(4) There's a heart in the plant leaves in the bottom panel!
(5) The thickness of the table

Duel 6: Into the Fire

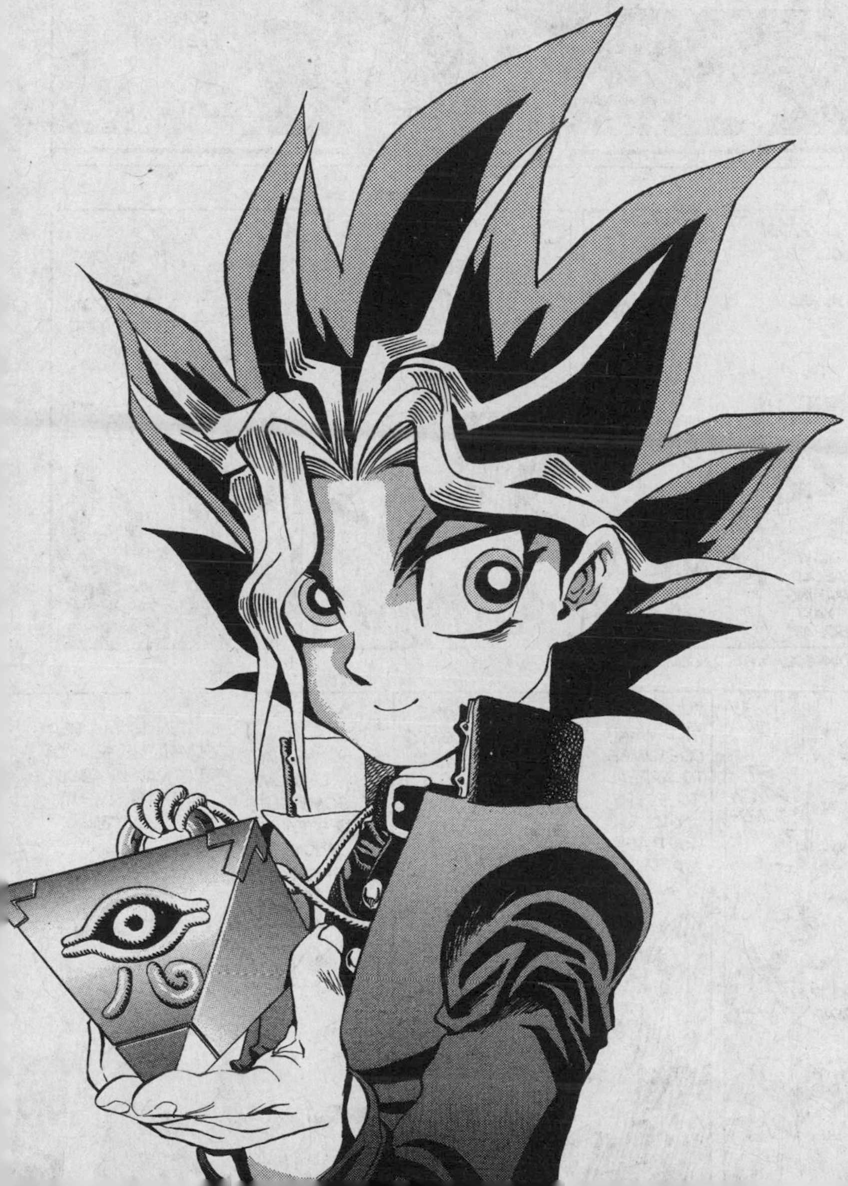

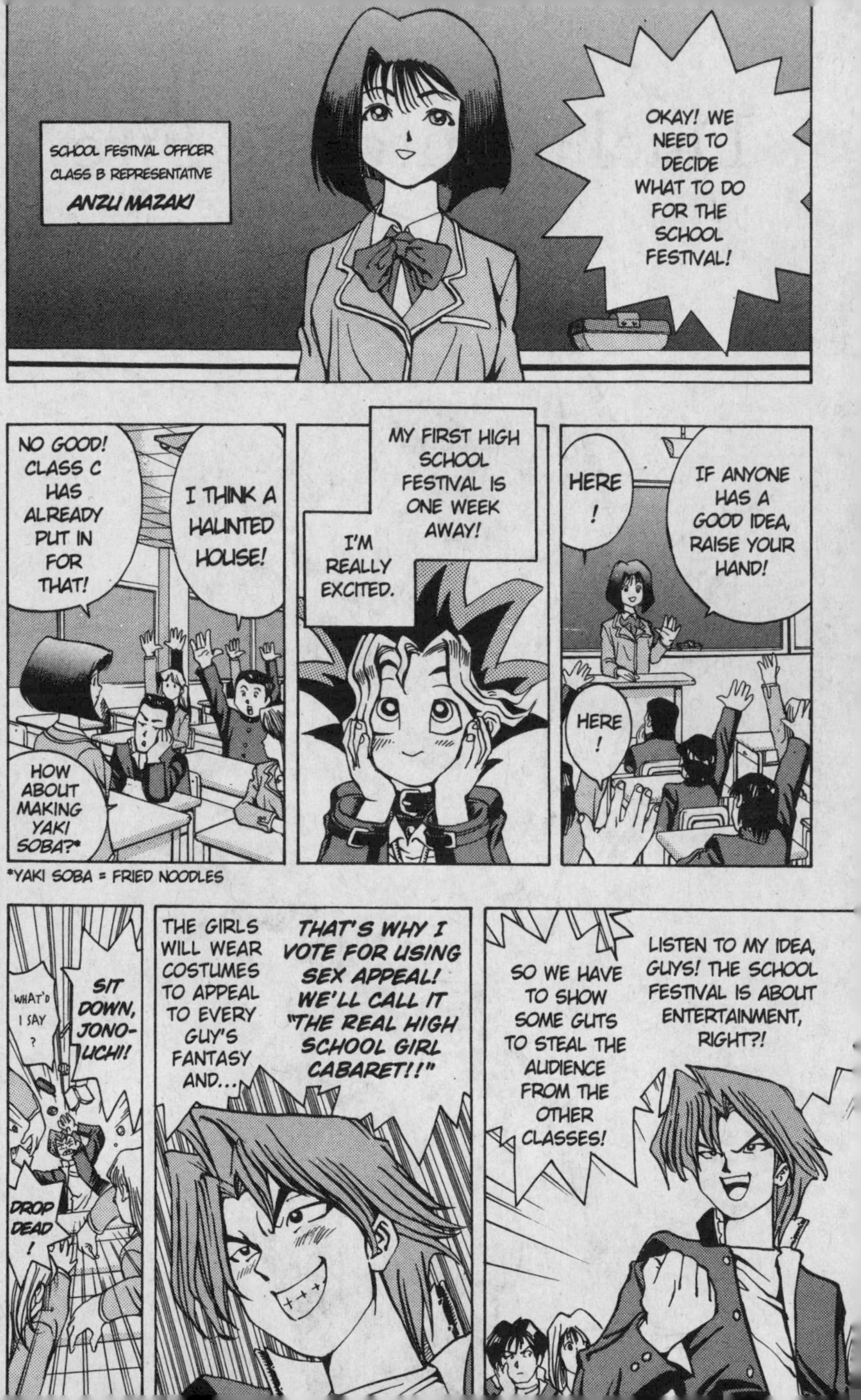
OKAY! WE NEED TO DECIDE WHAT TO DO FOR THE SCHOOL FESTIVAL!
SCHOOL FESTIVAL OFFICER
CLASS B REPRESENTATIVE
ANZU MAZAKI
IF ANYONE HAS A GOOD IDEA, RAISE YOUR HAND!
HERE!
HERE!
MY FIRST HIGH SCHOOL FESTIVAL IS ONE WEEK AWAY!
I'M REALLY EXCITED.
I THINK A HAUNTED HOUSE!
NO GOOD! CLASS C HAS ALREADY PUT IN FOR THAT!
HOW ABOUT MAKING YAKI SOBA?*
LISTEN TO MY IDEA, GUYS! THE SCHOOL FESTIVAL IS ABOUT ENTERTAINMENT, RIGHT?!
SO WE HAVE TO SHOW SOME GUTS TO STEAL THE AUDIENCE FROM THE OTHER CLASSES!
THE GIRLS WILL WEAR COSTUMES TO APPEAL TO EVERY GUY'S FANTASY AND...
THAT'S WHY I VOTE FOR USING SEX APPEAL! WE'LL CALL IT "THE REAL HIGH SCHOOL GIRL CABARET!!"
SIT DOWN, JONOUCHI!
WHAT'D I SAY?
DROP DEAD!

*YAKI SOBA = FRIED NOODLES

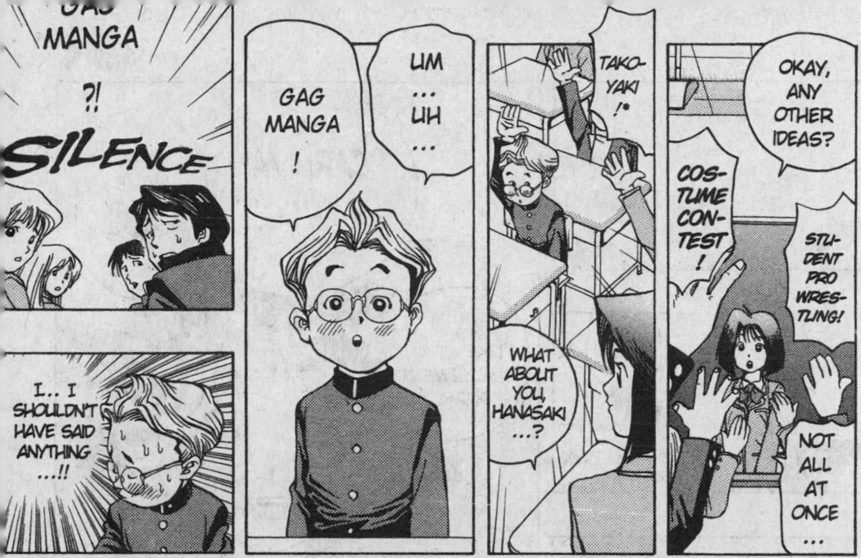
OKAY, ANY OTHER IDEAS?
COSTUME CONTEST!
STUDENT PRO WRESTLING!
NOT ALL AT ONCE...
TAKOYAKI!*
WHAT ABOUT YOU, HANASAKI...?
UM... UH...
GAG MANGA!
GAG MANGA ?!
SILENCE
I.. I SHOULDN'T HAVE SAID ANYTHING...!!

* TAKOYAKI = OCTOPUS DUMPLINGS

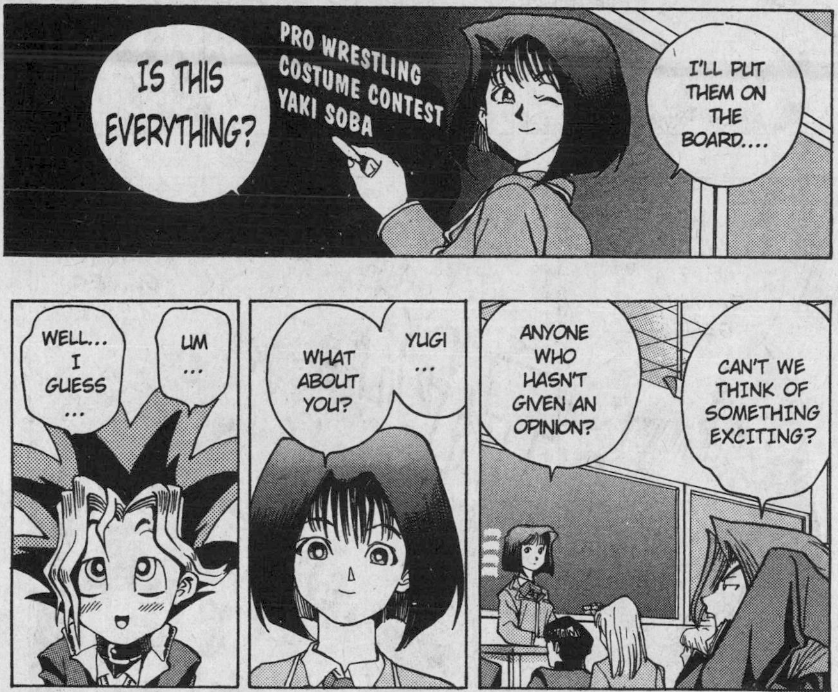
I'LL PUT THEM ON THE BOARD....
PRO WRESTLING
COSTUME CONTEST
YAKI SOBA
IS THIS EVERYTHING?
CAN'T WE THINK OF SOMETHING EXCITING?
ANYONE WHO HASN'T GIVEN AN OPINION?
YUGI...
WHAT ABOUT YOU?
UM...
WELL... I GUESS...

READ THIS WAY

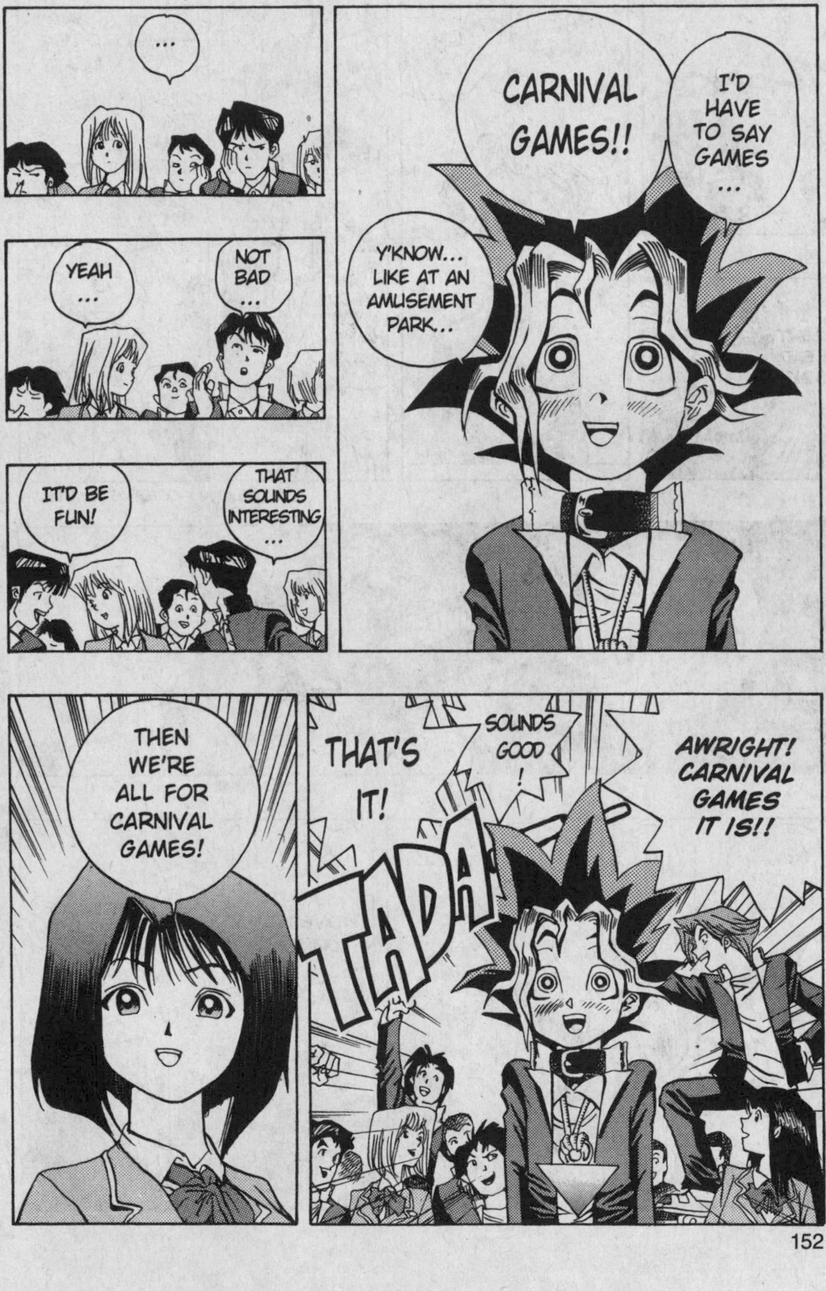
I'D HAVE TO SAY GAMES ...
CARNIVAL GAMES!!
Y'KNOW... LIKE AT AN AMUSEMENT PARK...
...
NOT BAD ...
YEAH ...
THAT SOUNDS INTERESTING ...
IT'D BE FUN!
AWRIGHT! CARNIVAL GAMES IT IS!!
SOUNDS GOOD !
THAT'S IT!
TADA
THEN WE'RE ALL FOR CARNIVAL GAMES!

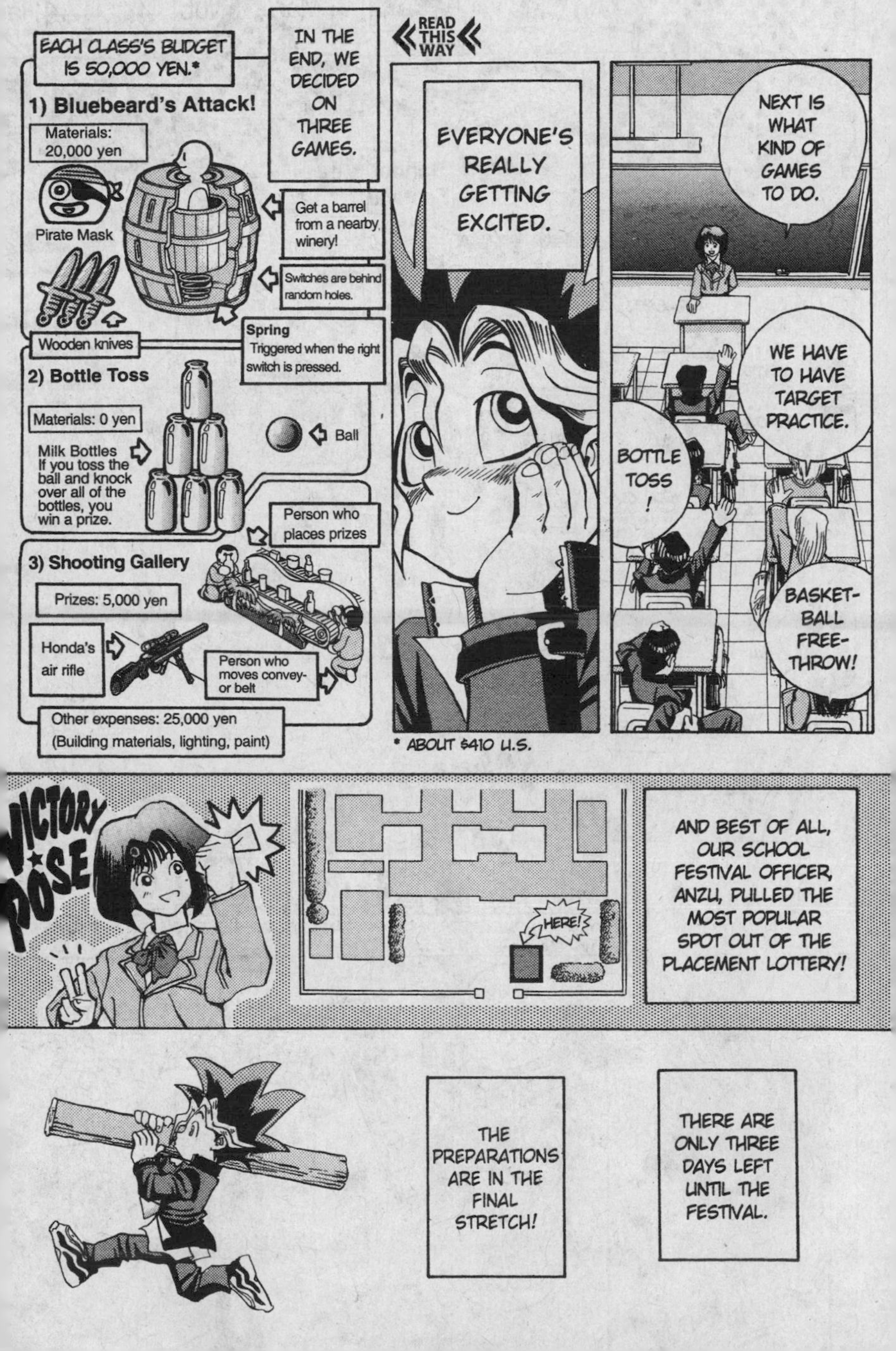
READ THIS WAY
NEXT IS WHAT KIND OF GAMES TO DO.
WE HAVE TO HAVE TARGET PRACTICE.
BOTTLE TOSS!
BASKET-BALL FREE-THROW!
EVERYONE'S REALLY GETTING EXCITED.
IN THE END, WE DECIDED ON THREE GAMES.
EACH CLASS'S BUDGET IS 50,000 YEN.*
1) Bluebeard's Attack!
Materials: 20,000 yen
Pirate Mask
Get a barrel from a nearby winery!
Switches are behind random holes.
Wooden knives
Spring
Triggered when the right switch is pressed.
2) Bottle Toss
Materials: 0 yen
Milk Bottles
If you toss the ball and knock over all of the bottles, you win a prize.
Ball
Person who places prizes
3) Shooting Gallery
Prizes: 5,000 yen
Honda's air rifle
Person who moves convey-or belt
Other expenses: 25,000 yen
(Building materials, lighting, paint)
* ABOUT $410 U.S.
AND BEST OF ALL, OUR SCHOOL FESTIVAL OFFICER, ANZU, PULLED THE MOST POPULAR SPOT OUT OF THE PLACEMENT LOTTERY!
HERE!
VICTORY POSE
THERE ARE ONLY THREE DAYS LEFT UNTIL THE FESTIVAL.
THE PREPARATIONS ARE IN THE FINAL STRETCH!

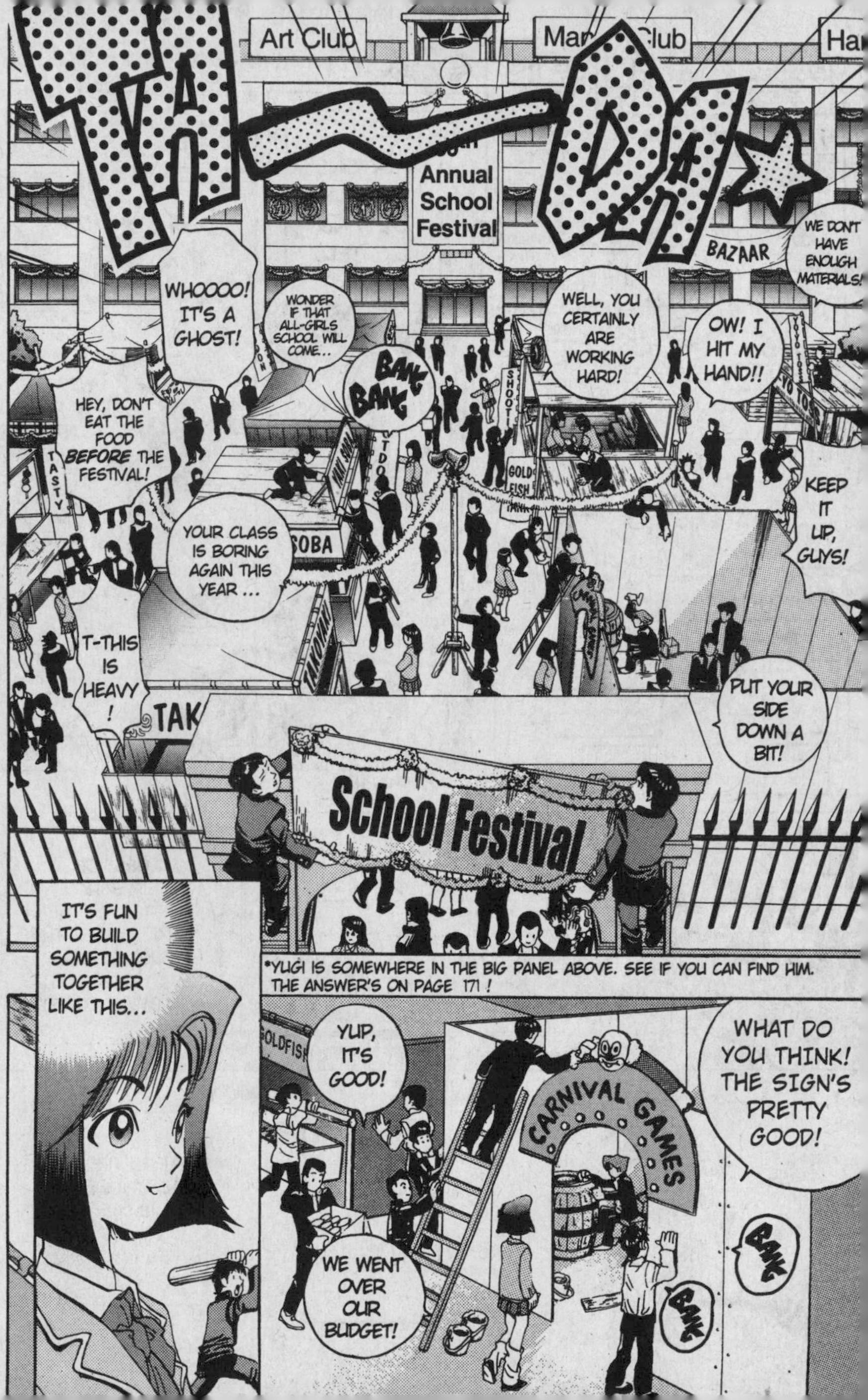
YA—DA☆
Art Club
Annual School Festival
BAZAAR
WE DON'T HAVE ENOUGH MATERIALS!
OW! I HIT MY HAND!!
WELL, YOU CERTAINLY ARE WORKING HARD!
BANG BANG
WONDER IF THAT ALL-GIRLS SCHOOL WILL COME...
WHOOOO! IT'S A GHOST!
KEEP IT UP, GUYS!
GOLD FISH TANK
HEY, DON'T EAT THE FOOD *BEFORE* THE FESTIVAL!
TASTY
SOBA
YOUR CLASS IS BORING AGAIN THIS YEAR...
TAKOYAKI
PUT YOUR SIDE DOWN A BIT!
T-THIS IS HEAVY!
School Festival
*YUGI IS SOMEWHERE IN THE BIG PANEL ABOVE. SEE IF YOU CAN FIND HIM. THE ANSWER'S ON PAGE 171!
WHAT DO YOU THINK! THE SIGN'S PRETTY GOOD!
YUP, IT'S GOOD!
GOLDFISH
CARNIVAL GAMES
BANG
BANG
WE WENT OVER OUR BUDGET!
IT'S FUN TO BUILD SOMETHING TOGETHER LIKE THIS...

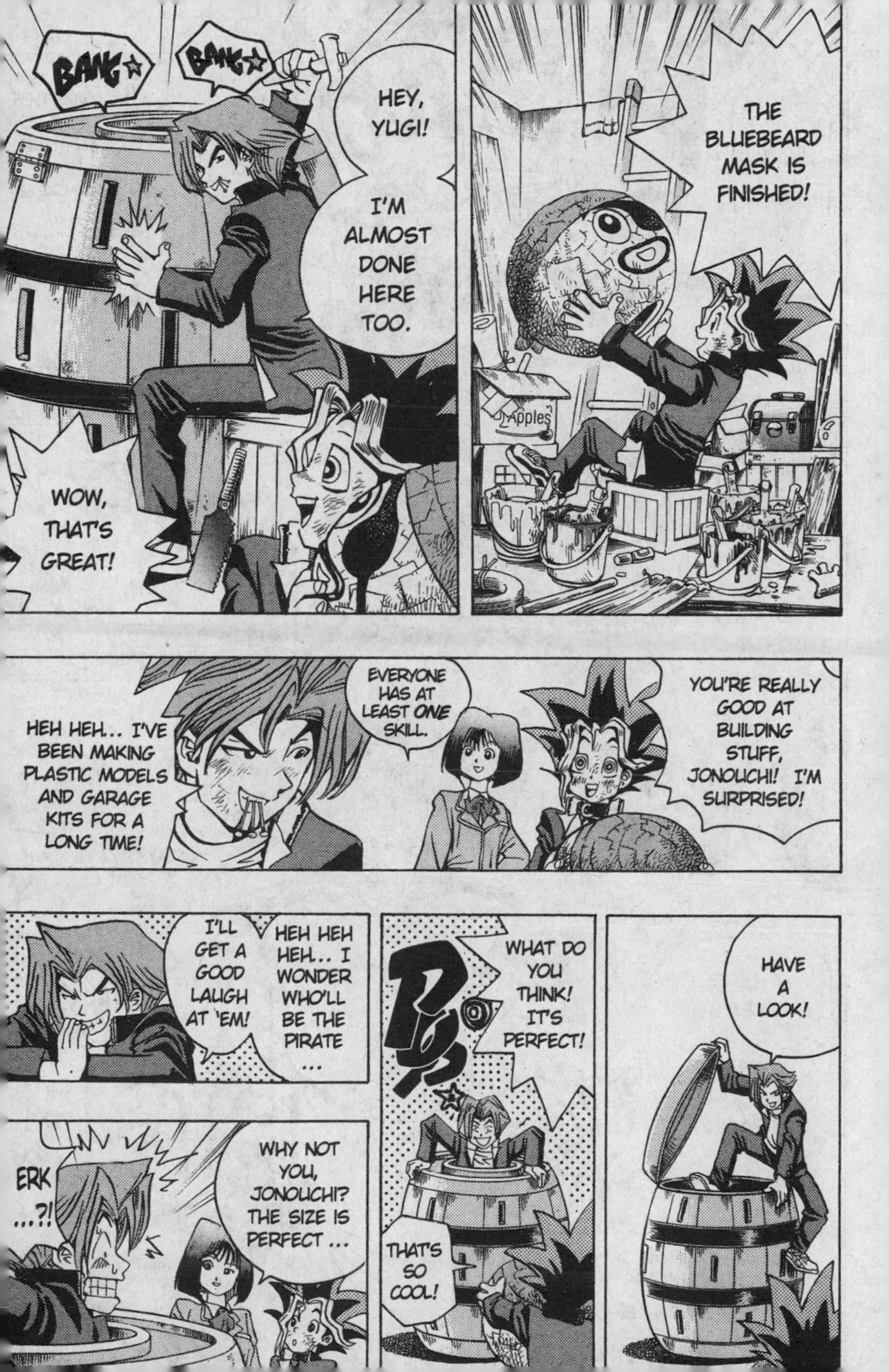
THE BLUEBEARD MASK IS FINISHED!
Apples
BANG☆
BANG☆
HEY, YUGI!
I'M ALMOST DONE HERE TOO.
WOW, THAT'S GREAT!
YOU'RE REALLY GOOD AT BUILDING STUFF, JONOUCHI! I'M SURPRISED!
EVERYONE HAS AT LEAST ONE SKILL.
HEH HEH... I'VE BEEN MAKING PLASTIC MODELS AND GARAGE KITS FOR A LONG TIME!
HAVE A LOOK!
WHAT DO YOU THINK! IT'S PERFECT!
THAT'S SO COOL!
HEH HEH HEH... I WONDER WHO'LL BE THE PIRATE ...
I'LL GET A GOOD LAUGH AT 'EM!
WHY NOT YOU, JONOUCHI? THE SIZE IS PERFECT ...
ERK ...?!

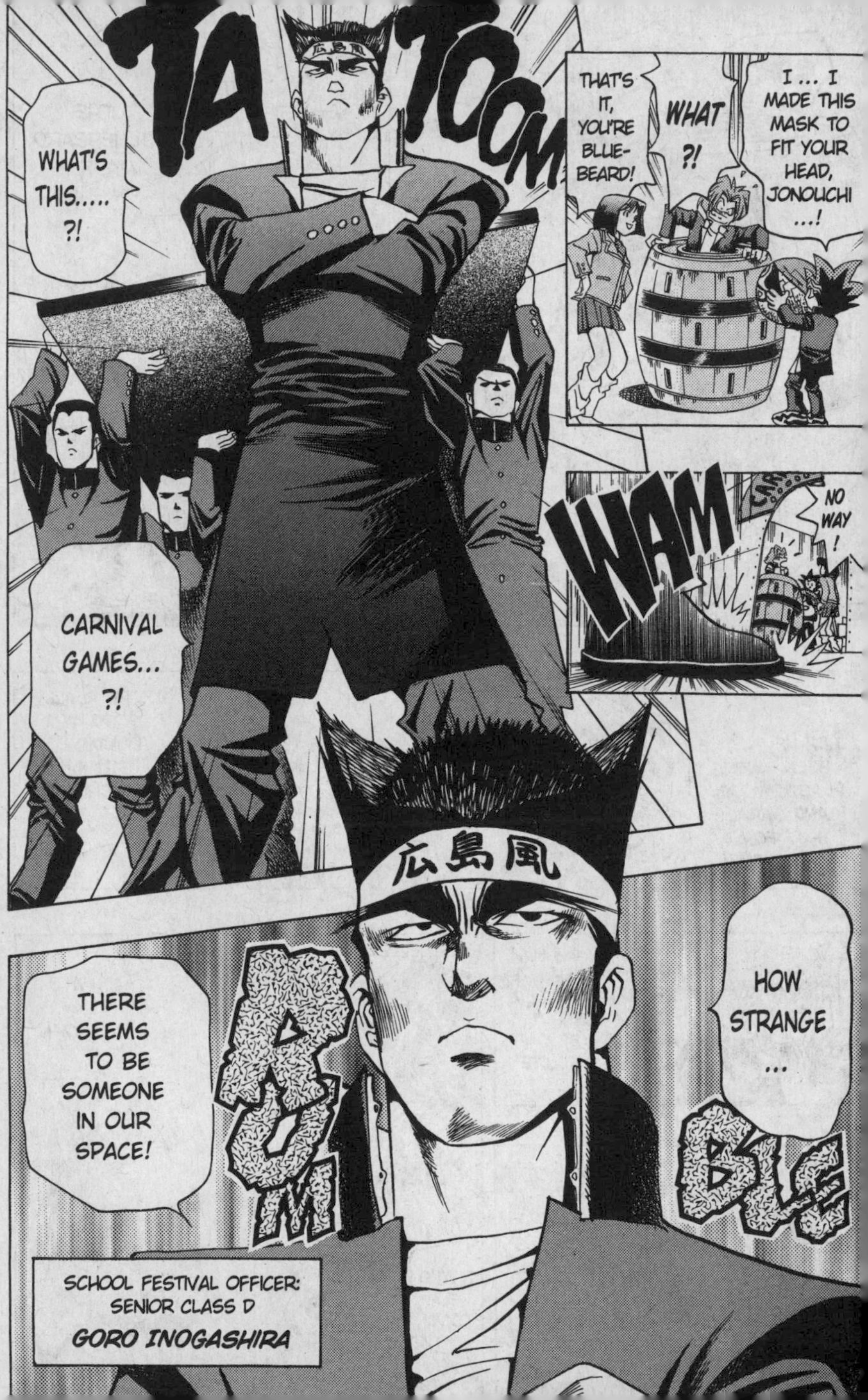
I ... I MADE THIS MASK TO FIT YOUR HEAD, JONOUCHI ...!
WHAT ?!
THAT'S IT, YOU'RE BLUE-BEARD!
NO WAY !
WAM
TA TOOM
広島風
WHAT'S THIS..... ?!
CARNIVAL GAMES... ?!
広島風
HOW STRANGE ...
THERE SEEMS TO BE SOMEONE IN OUR SPACE!
SCHOOL FESTIVAL OFFICER: SENIOR CLASS D
GORO INOGASHIRA

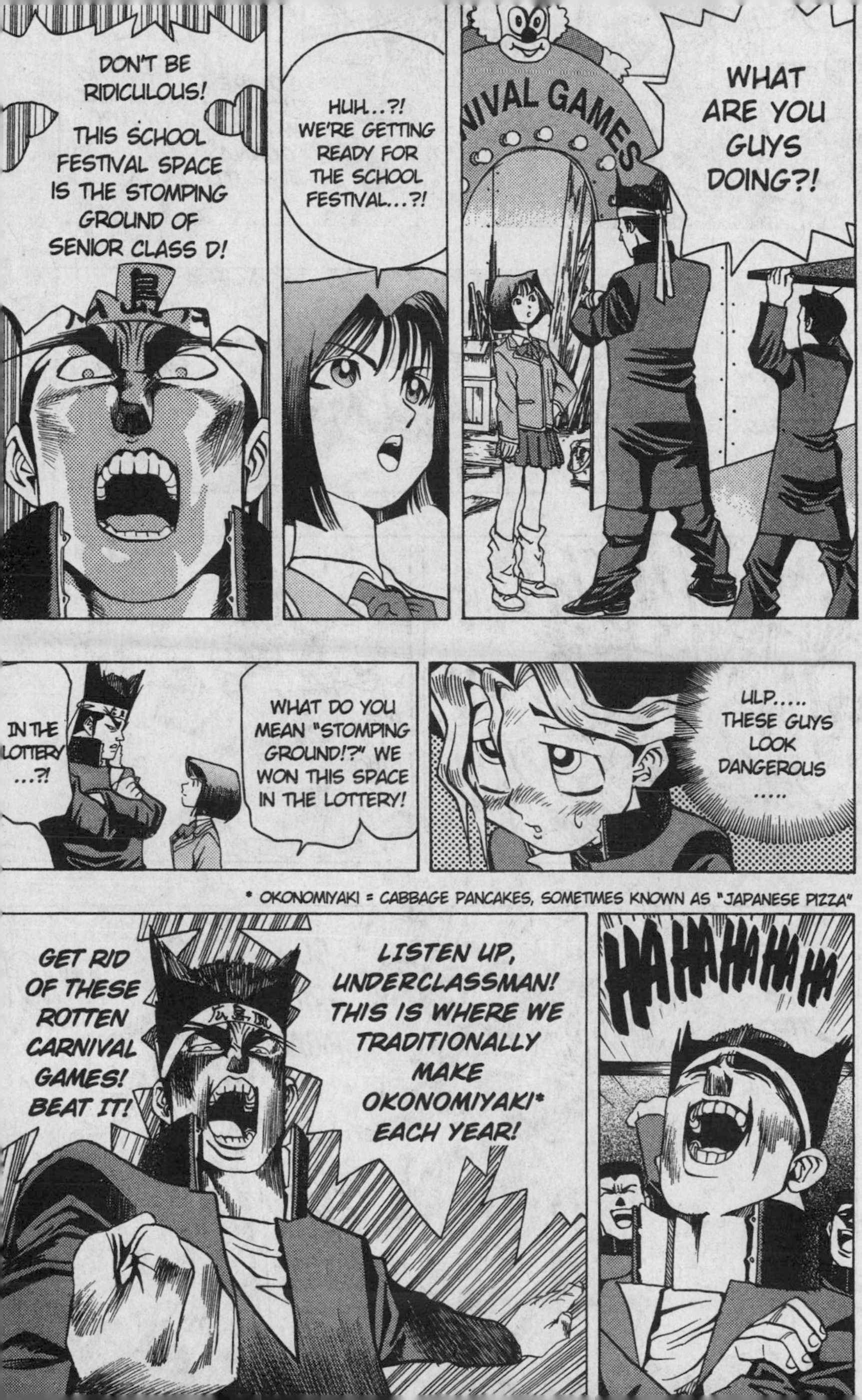
NIVAL GAMES
WHAT ARE YOU GUYS DOING?!
HUH..?! WE'RE GETTING READY FOR THE SCHOOL FESTIVAL...?!
DON'T BE RIDICULOUS!
THIS SCHOOL FESTIVAL SPACE IS THE STOMPING GROUND OF SENIOR CLASS D!
ULP..... THESE GUYS LOOK DANGEROUS .....
WHAT DO YOU MEAN "STOMPING GROUND!?" WE WON THIS SPACE IN THE LOTTERY!
IN THE LOTTERY ...?!
HA HA HA HA HA HA
LISTEN UP, UNDERCLASSMAN! THIS IS WHERE WE TRADITIONALLY MAKE OKONOMIYAKI* EACH YEAR!
GET RID OF THESE ROTTEN CARNIVAL GAMES! BEAT IT!

* OKONOMIYAKI = CABBAGE PANCAKES, SOMETIMES KNOWN AS "JAPANESE PIZZA"

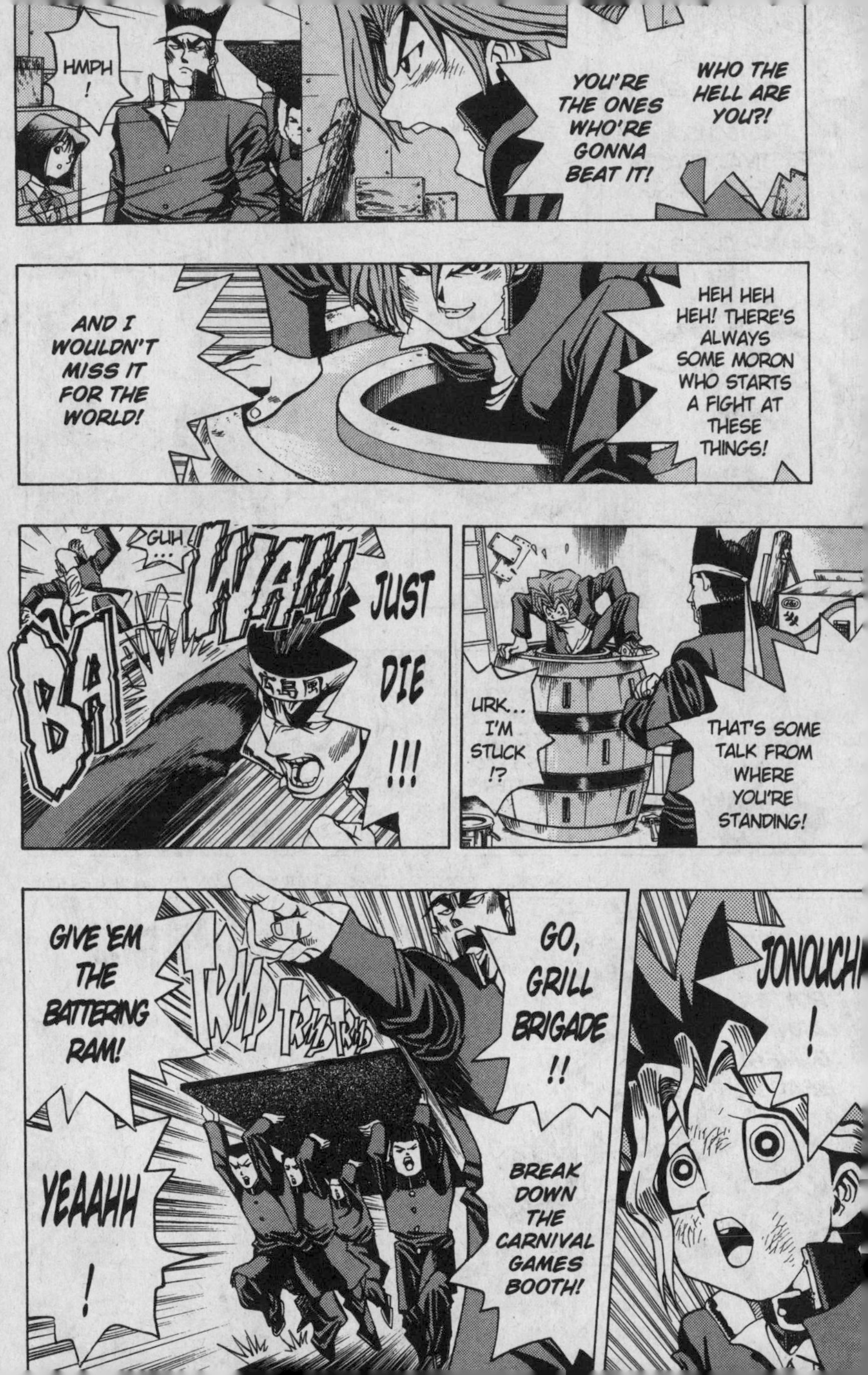
WHO THE HELL ARE YOU?!
YOU'RE THE ONES WHO'RE GONNA BEAT IT!
HMPH!
HEH HEH HEH! THERE'S ALWAYS SOME MORON WHO STARTS A FIGHT AT THESE THINGS!
AND I WOULDN'T MISS IT FOR THE WORLD!
URK... I'M STUCK!?
THAT'S SOME TALK FROM WHERE YOU'RE STANDING!
JUST DIE!!!
WHAM
GUH...
JONOUCHI
!
GO, GRILL BRIGADE!!
GIVE 'EM THE BATTERING RAM!
BREAK DOWN THE CARNIVAL GAMES BOOTH!
YEAAHH!

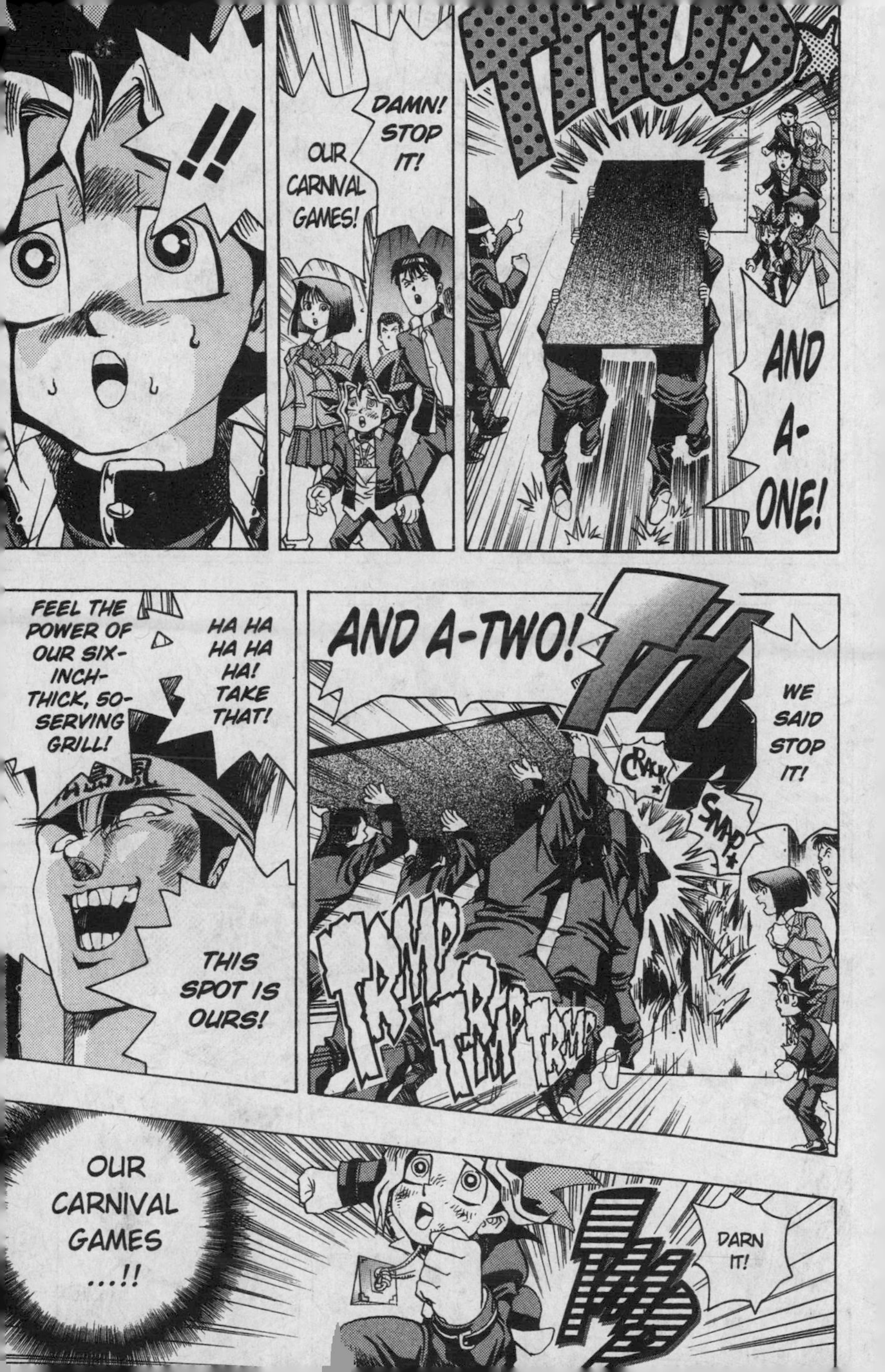
THUD
AND A-ONE!
DAMN! STOP IT!
OUR CARNIVAL GAMES!
!!
AND A-TWO!
CRACK
SNAP
WE SAID STOP IT!
HA HA HA HA HA! TAKE THAT!
FEEL THE POWER OF OUR SIX-INCH-THICK, SO-SERVING GRILL!
THIS SPOT IS OURS!
DARN IT!
OUR CARNIVAL GAMES ...!!

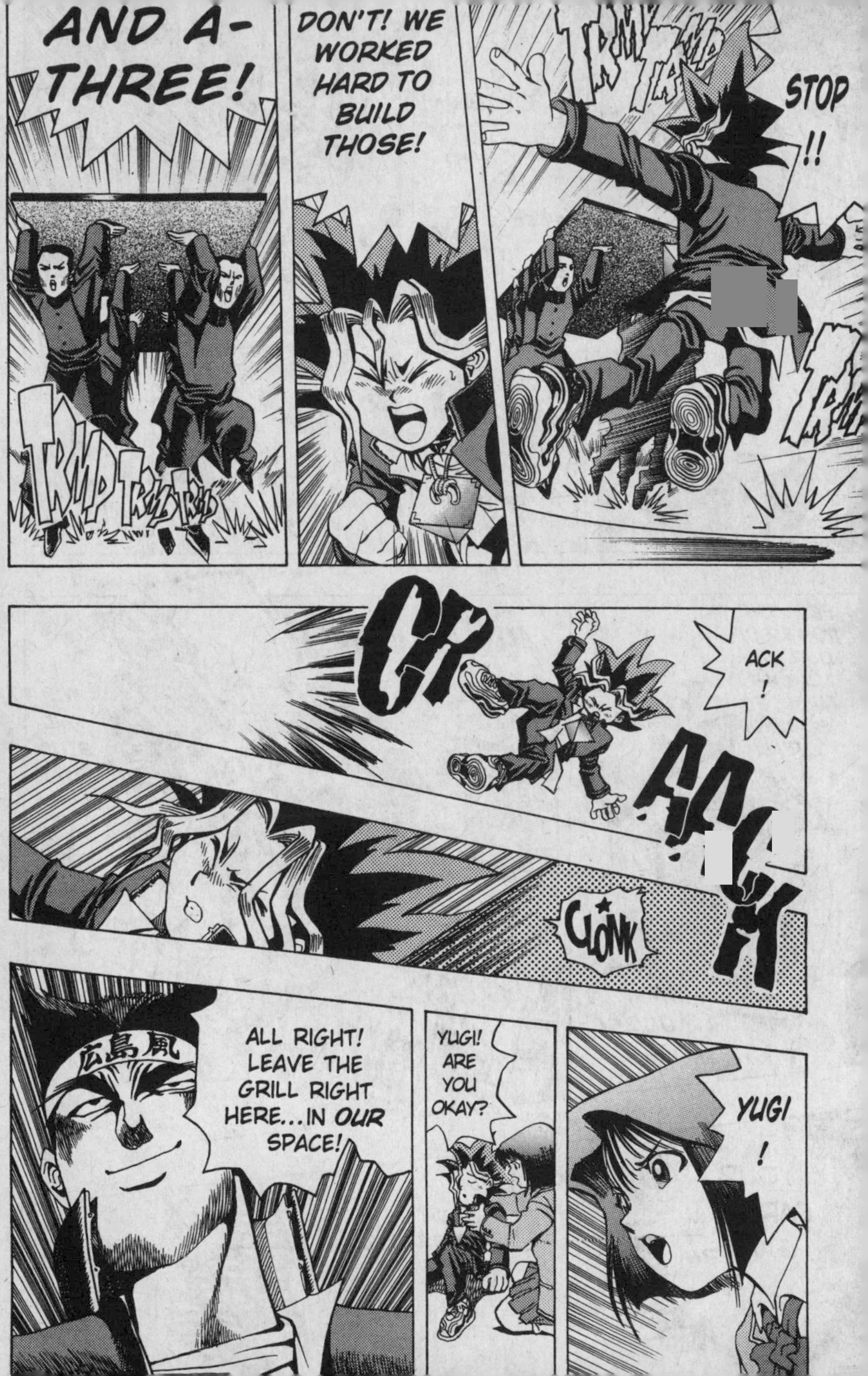
AND A-THREE!
DON'T! WE WORKED HARD TO BUILD THOSE!
STOP!!
ACK!
CLONK
ALL RIGHT! LEAVE THE GRILL RIGHT HERE...IN OUR SPACE!
YUGI! ARE YOU OKAY?
YUGI!

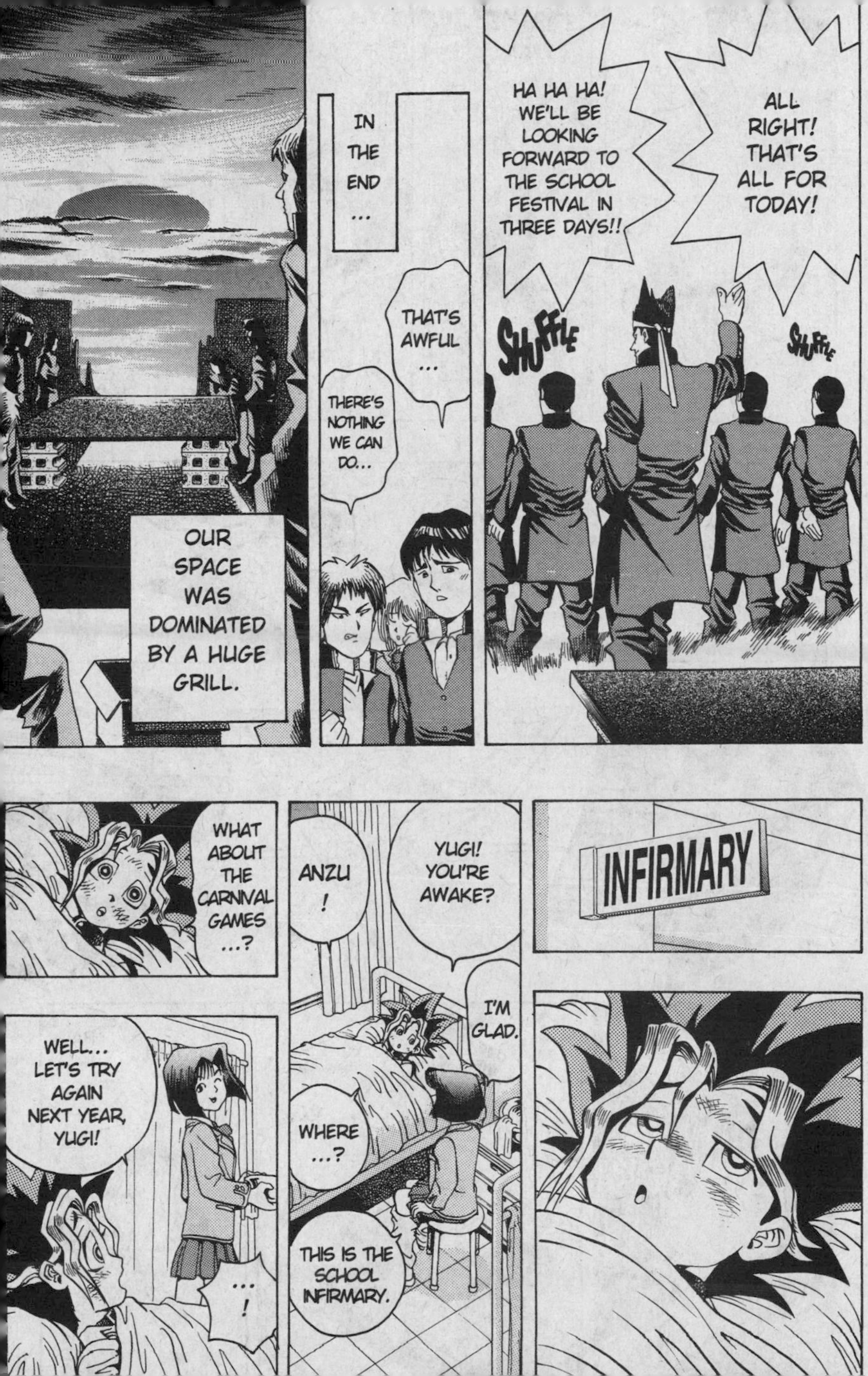
ALL RIGHT! THAT'S ALL FOR TODAY!
HA HA HA! WE'LL BE LOOKING FORWARD TO THE SCHOOL FESTIVAL IN THREE DAYS!!
SHUFFLE
SHUFFLE
IN THE END...
THAT'S AWFUL...
THERE'S NOTHING WE CAN DO...
OUR SPACE WAS DOMINATED BY A HUGE GRILL.
INFIRMARY
YUGI! YOU'RE AWAKE?
ANZU!
I'M GLAD.
WHERE...?
THIS IS THE SCHOOL INFIRMARY.
WHAT ABOUT THE CARNIVAL GAMES...?
WELL... LET'S TRY AGAIN NEXT YEAR, YUGI!
...!

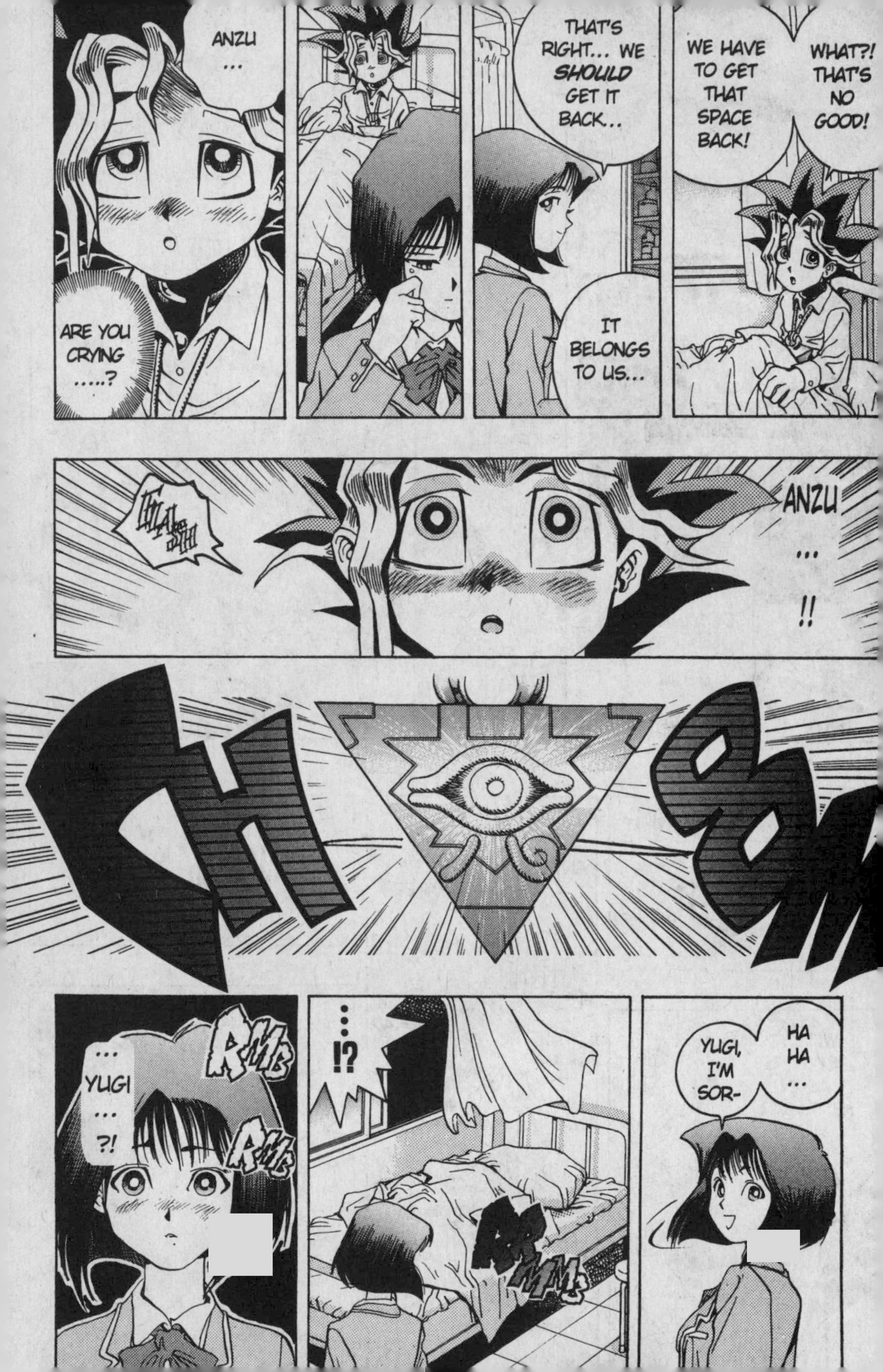
WHAT?! THAT'S NO GOOD!
WE HAVE TO GET THAT SPACE BACK!
THAT'S RIGHT... WE SHOULD GET IT BACK...
IT BELONGS TO US...
ANZU ...
ARE YOU CRYING .....?
ANZU ... !!
HA HA ...
YUGI, I'M SOR-
...!?
... YUGI ... ?!

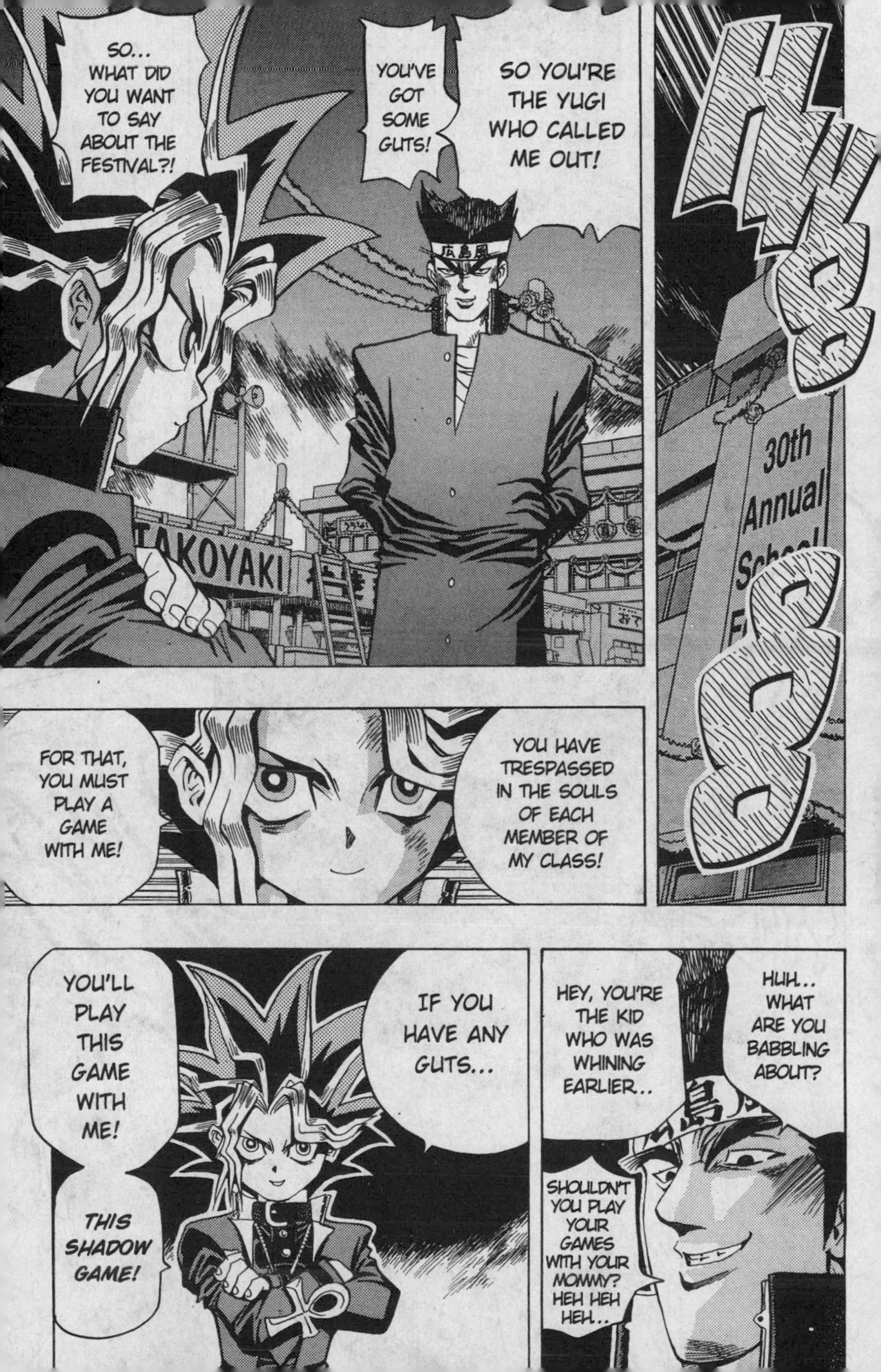
30th
Annual
SO YOU'RE THE YUGI WHO CALLED ME OUT!
YOU'VE GOT SOME GUTS!
SO... WHAT DID YOU WANT TO SAY ABOUT THE FESTIVAL?!
TAKOYAKI
YOU HAVE TRESPASSED IN THE SOULS OF EACH MEMBER OF MY CLASS!
FOR THAT, YOU MUST PLAY A GAME WITH ME!
HUH... WHAT ARE YOU BABBLING ABOUT?
HEY, YOU'RE THE KID WHO WAS WHINING EARLIER..
SHOULDN'T YOU PLAY YOUR GAMES WITH YOUR MOMMY? HEH HEH HEH..
IF YOU HAVE ANY GUTS...
YOU'LL PLAY THIS GAME WITH ME!
THIS SHADOW GAME!

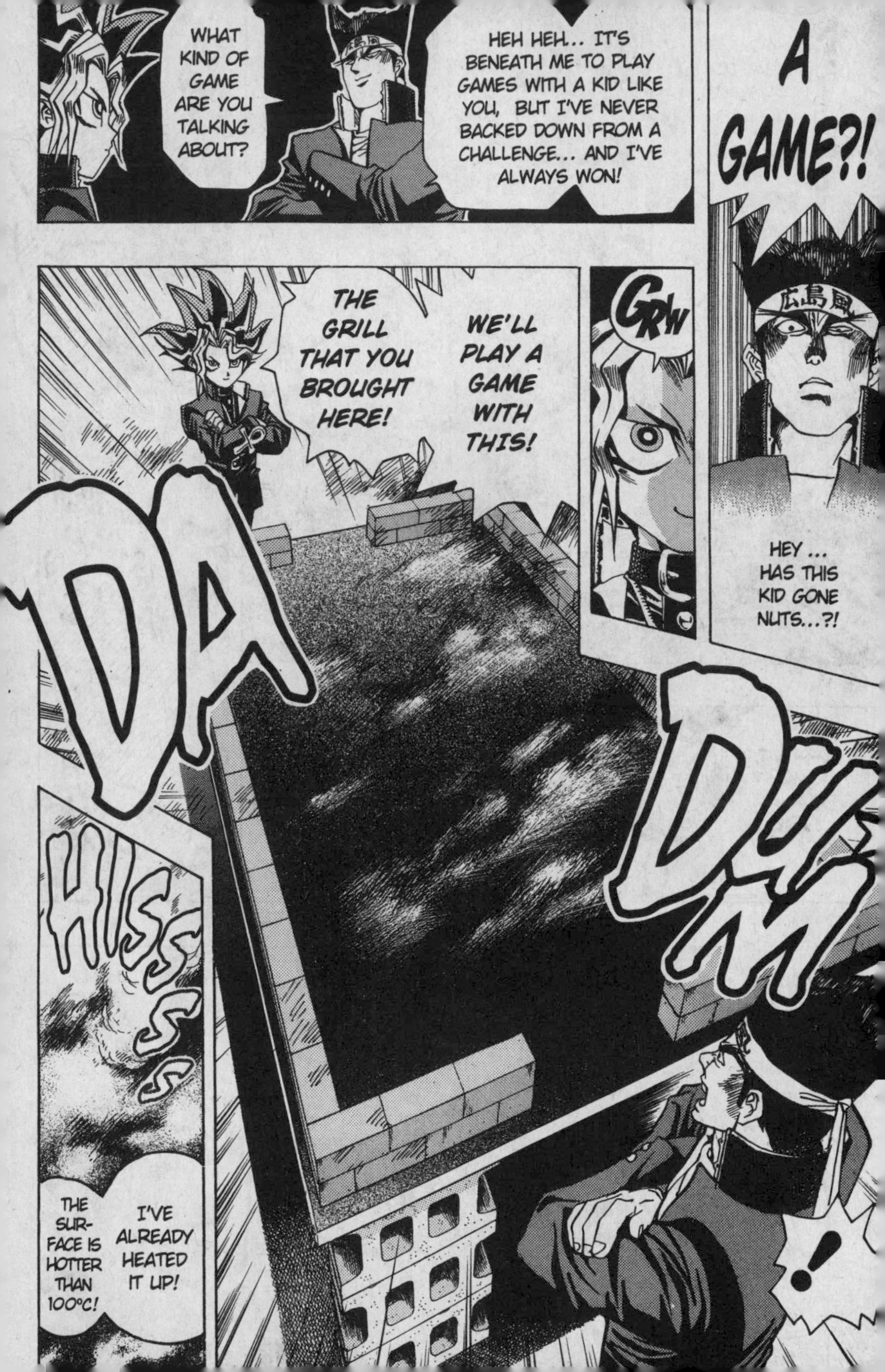

A GAME?!
HEH HEH... IT'S BENEATH ME TO PLAY GAMES WITH A KID LIKE YOU, BUT I'VE NEVER BACKED DOWN FROM A CHALLENGE... AND I'VE ALWAYS WON!
WHAT KIND OF GAME ARE YOU TALKING ABOUT?
HEY ... HAS THIS KID GONE NUTS...?!
GRW
WE'LL PLAY A GAME WITH THIS!
THE GRILL THAT YOU BROUGHT HERE!
DA
DUM
HISSSS
I'VE ALREADY HEATED IT UP!
THE SURFACE IS HOTTER THAN 100°C!
!

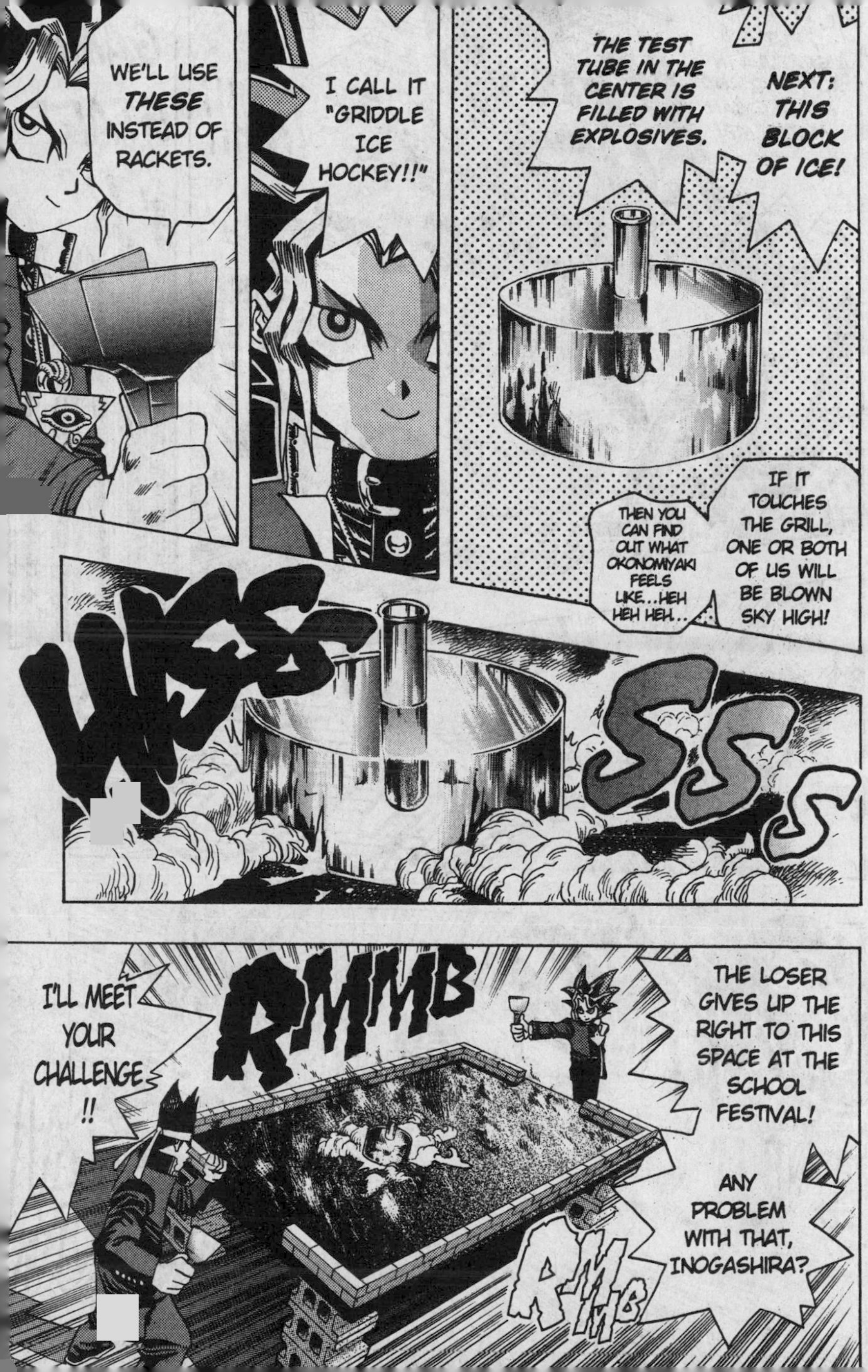
NEXT: THIS BLOCK OF ICE!
THE TEST TUBE IN THE CENTER IS FILLED WITH EXPLOSIVES.
IF IT TOUCHES THE GRILL, ONE OR BOTH OF US WILL BE BLOWN SKY HIGH!
THEN YOU CAN FIND OUT WHAT OKONOMIYAKI FEELS LIKE...HEH HEH HEH...
I CALL IT "GRIDDLE ICE HOCKEY!!"
WE'LL USE THESE INSTEAD OF RACKETS.
WHSSS
SSS
THE LOSER GIVES UP THE RIGHT TO THIS SPACE AT THE SCHOOL FESTIVAL!
ANY PROBLEM WITH THAT, INOGASHIRA?
RMMB
I'LL MEET YOUR CHALLENGE!!
RMMB

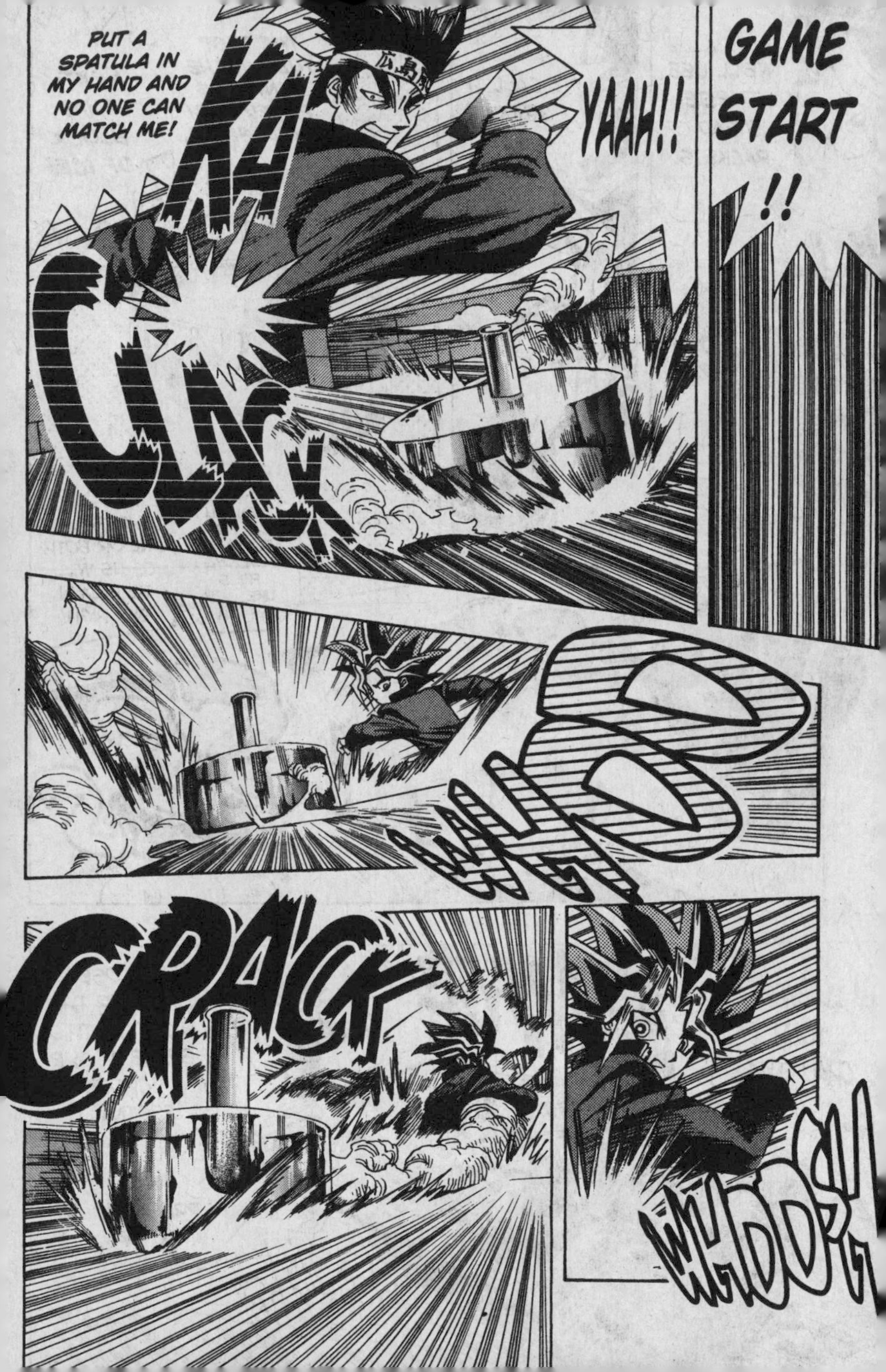
GAME START!!
YAAH!!
PUT A SPATULA IN MY HAND AND NO ONE CAN MATCH ME!
KA
CLACK
WHOOSH!
CRACK

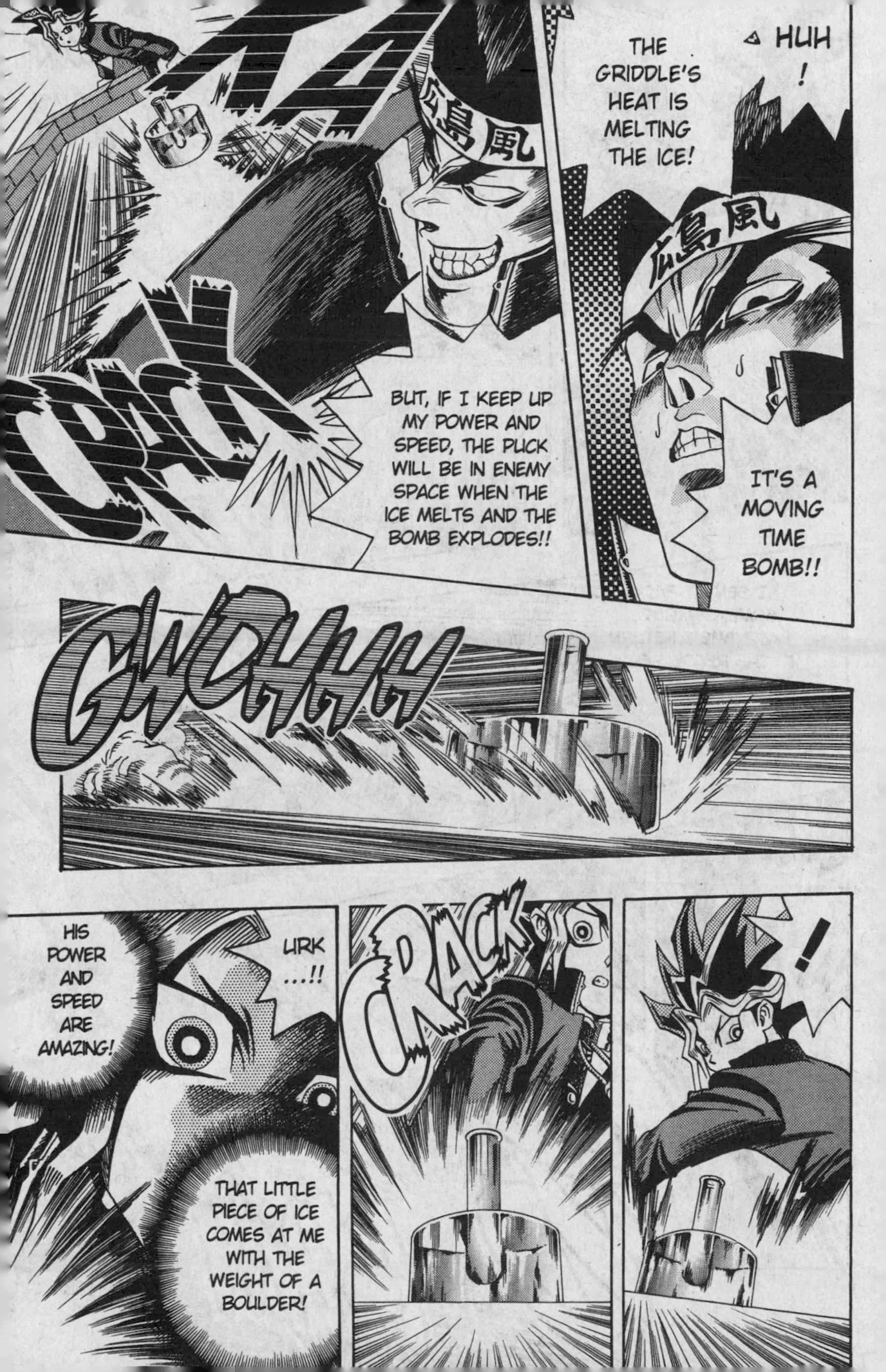
HUH
!
THE GRIDDLE'S HEAT IS MELTING THE ICE!
IT'S A MOVING TIME BOMB!!
CRACK
BUT, IF I KEEP UP MY POWER AND SPEED, THE PUCK WILL BE IN ENEMY SPACE WHEN THE ICE MELTS AND THE BOMB EXPLODES!!
!
CRACK
URK ...!!
HIS POWER AND SPEED ARE AMAZING!
THAT LITTLE PIECE OF ICE COMES AT ME WITH THE WEIGHT OF A BOULDER!

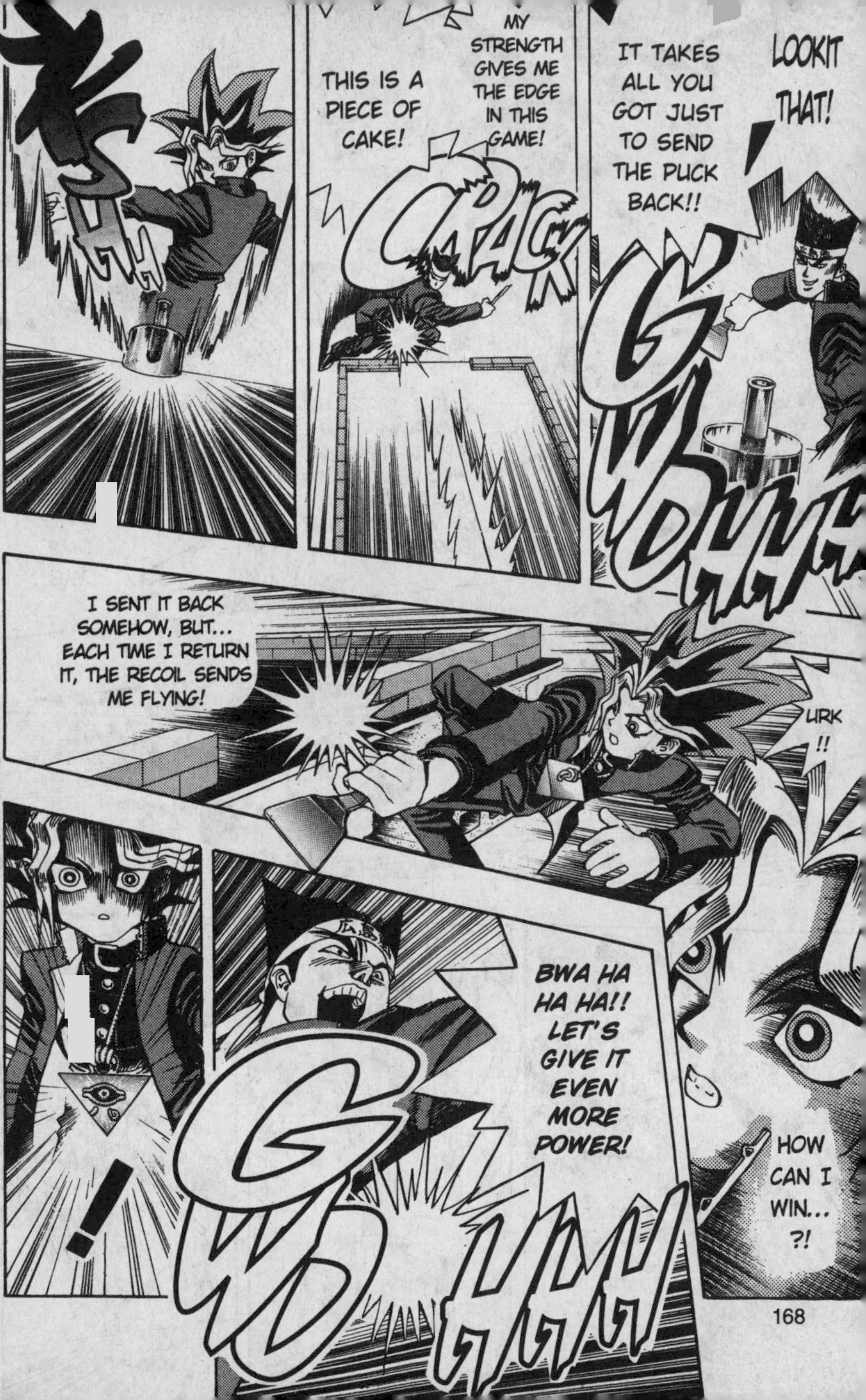
LOOKIT THAT!
IT TAKES ALL YOU GOT JUST TO SEND THE PUCK BACK!!
GWOHHH
MY STRENGTH GIVES ME THE EDGE IN THIS GAME!
THIS IS A PIECE OF CAKE!
CRACK
SHH
URK!!
I SENT IT BACK SOMEHOW, BUT... EACH TIME I RETURN IT, THE RECOIL SENDS ME FLYING!
HOW CAN I WIN...?!
BWA HA HA HA!! LET'S GIVE IT EVEN MORE POWER!
GWOHHH
!

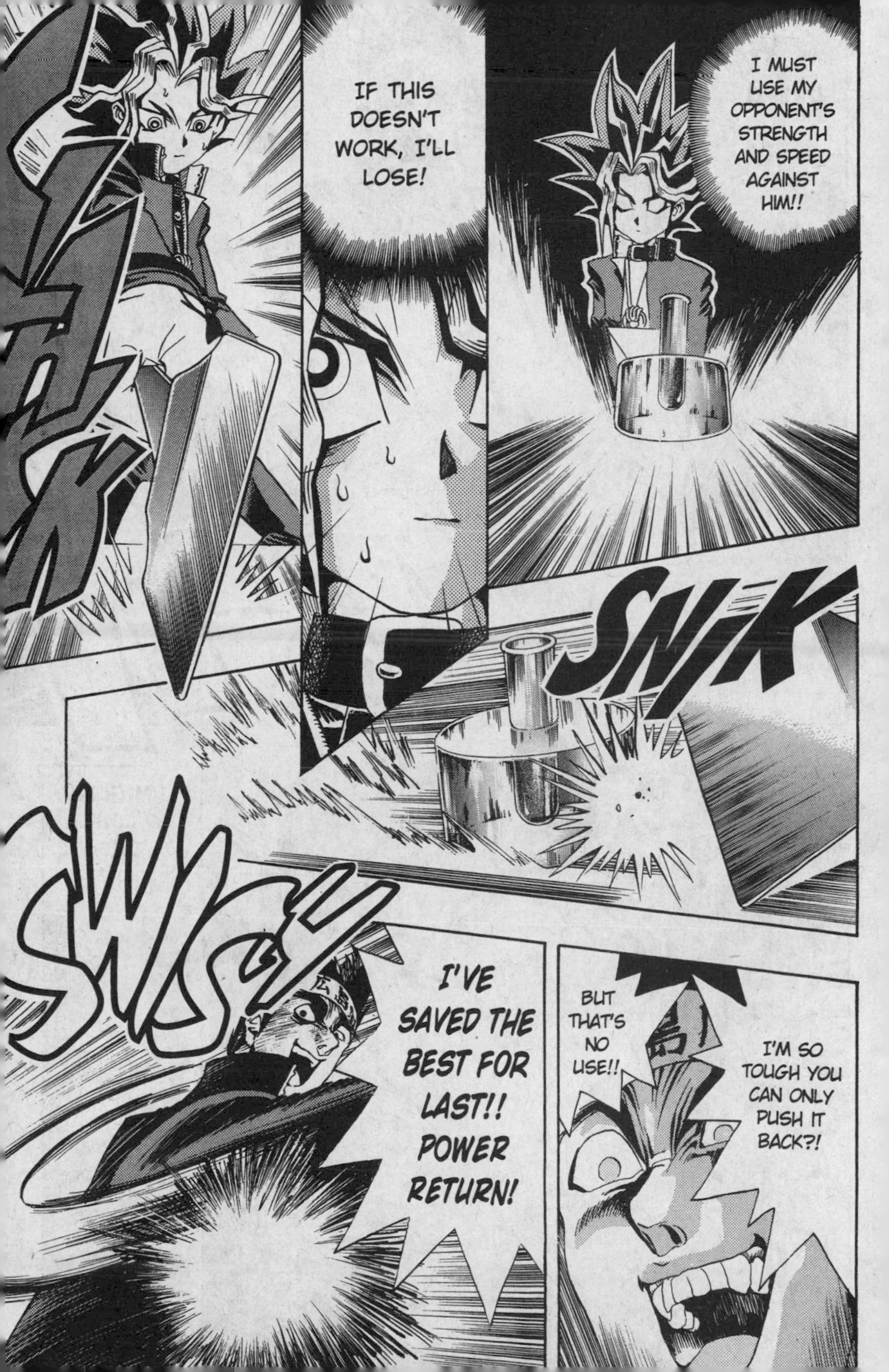
I MUST USE MY OPPONENT'S STRENGTH AND SPEED AGAINST HIM!!
IF THIS DOESN'T WORK, I'LL LOSE!
SNIK
BUT THAT'S NO USE!!
I'M SO TOUGH YOU CAN ONLY PUSH IT BACK?!
I'VE SAVED THE BEST FOR LAST!! POWER RETURN!

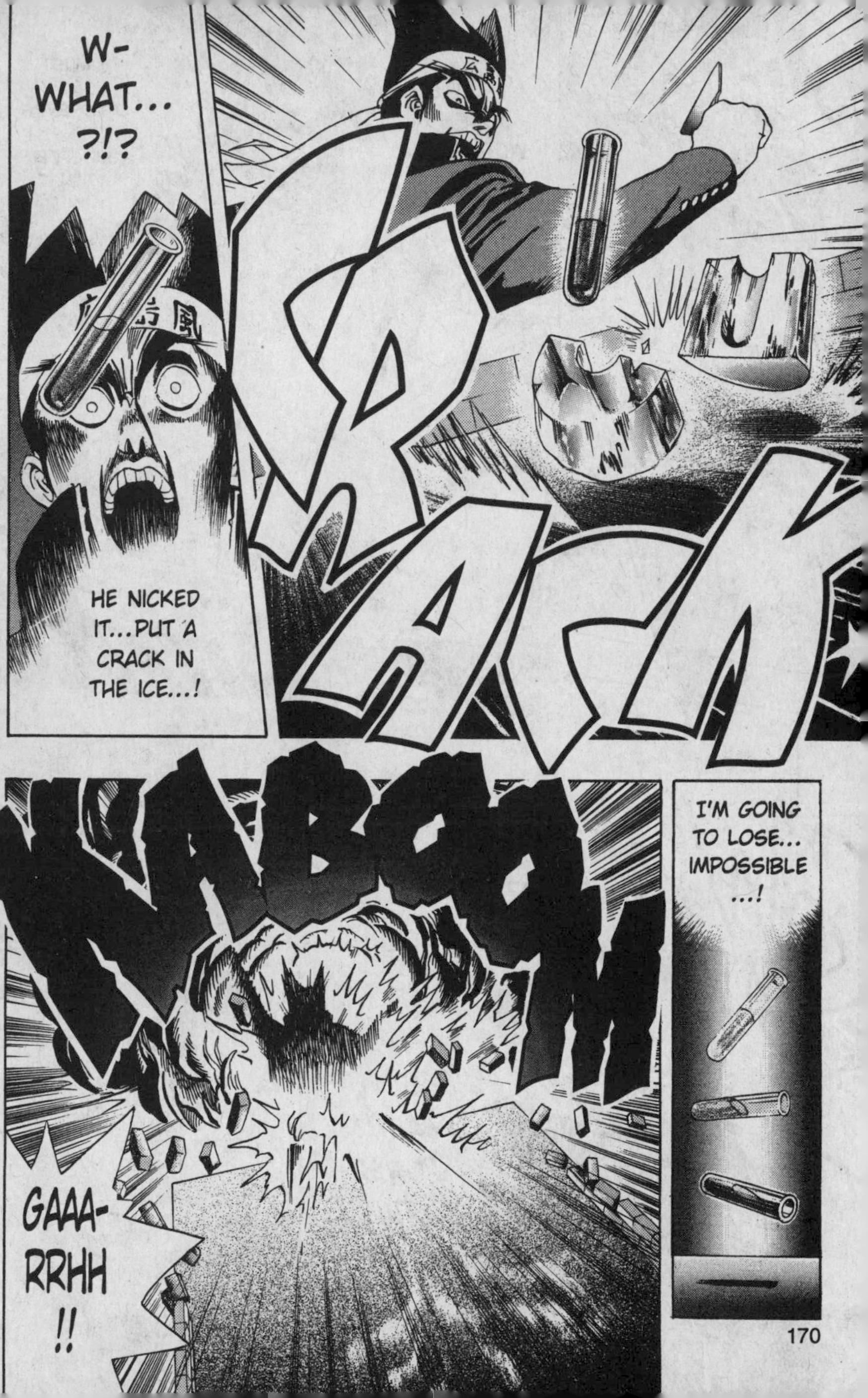
W-WHAT...?!?
HE NICKED IT...PUT A CRACK IN THE ICE...!
I'M GOING TO LOSE... IMPOSSIBLE...!
KABOOM
GAAA-RRHH!!

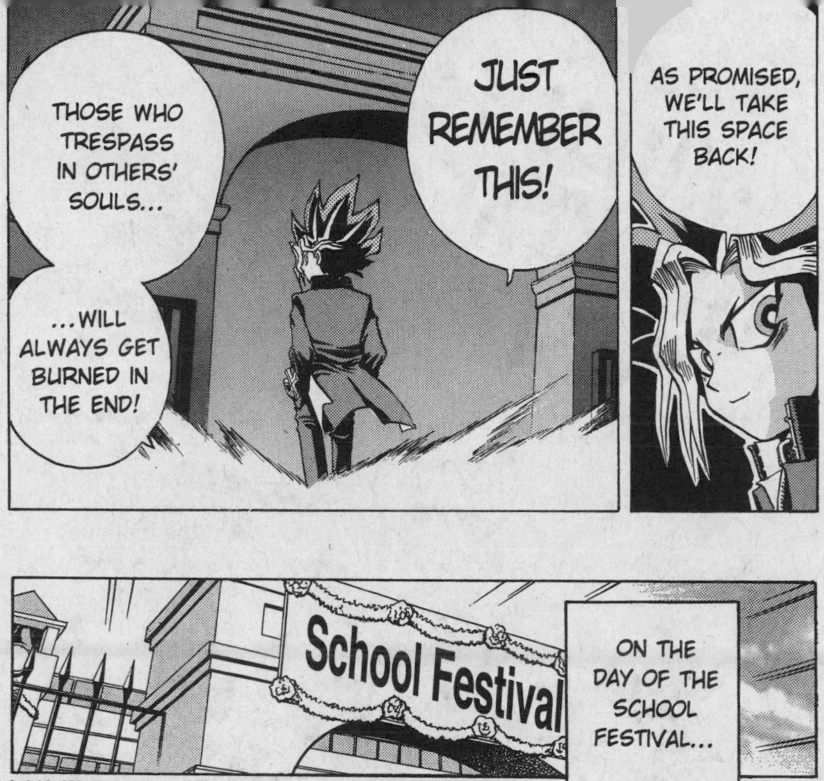
AS PROMISED, WE'LL TAKE THIS SPACE BACK!
JUST REMEMBER THIS!
THOSE WHO TRESPASS IN OTHERS' SOULS...
...WILL ALWAYS GET BURNED IN THE END!
ON THE DAY OF THE SCHOOL FESTIVAL...
School Festival

* ANSWER TO PAGE 154: HE'S UNDER THE "SCHOOL FESTIVAL" SIGN THEY'RE TRYING TO HANG.

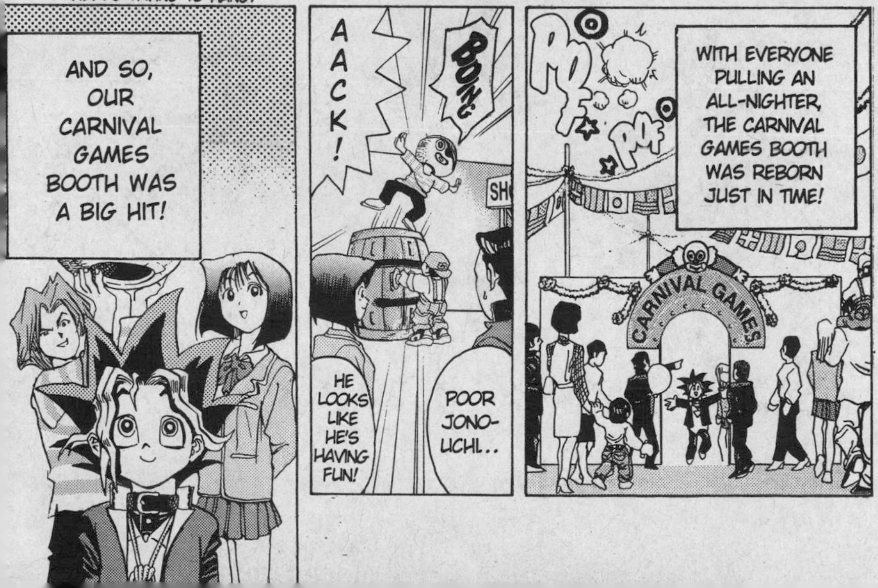
WITH EVERYONE PULLING AN ALL-NIGHTER, THE CARNIVAL GAMES BOOTH WAS REBORN JUST IN TIME!
POF
POF
CARNIVAL GAMES
BOING
AACK!
POOR JONO-UCHI...
HE LOOKS LIKE HE'S HAVING FUN!
AND SO, OUR CARNIVAL GAMES BOOTH WAS A BIG HIT!

WHICH IS THE REAL YUGI?

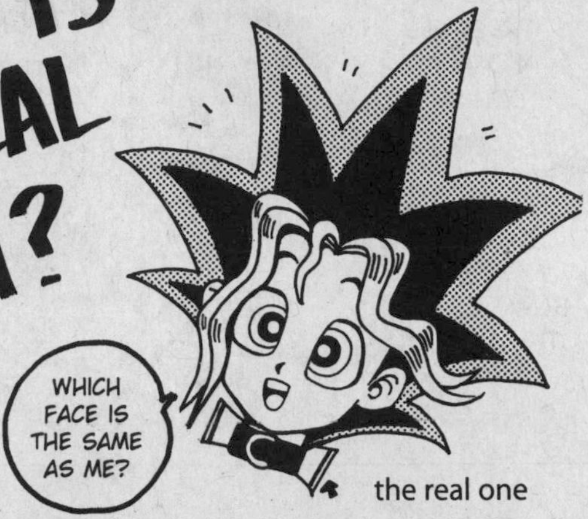
WHICH FACE IS THE SAME AS ME?

the real one

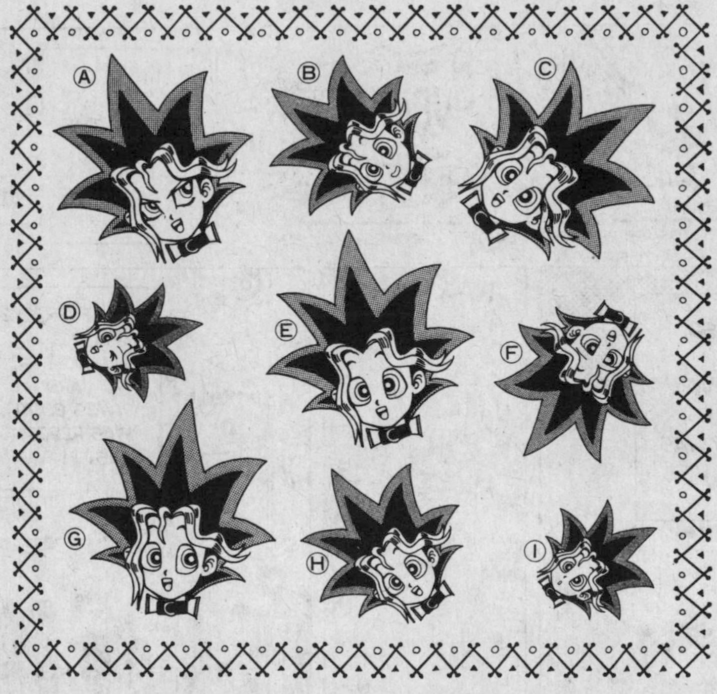
A
B
C
D
E
F
G
H
I

The answer is on page 196!

Duel 7: The Face of Truth

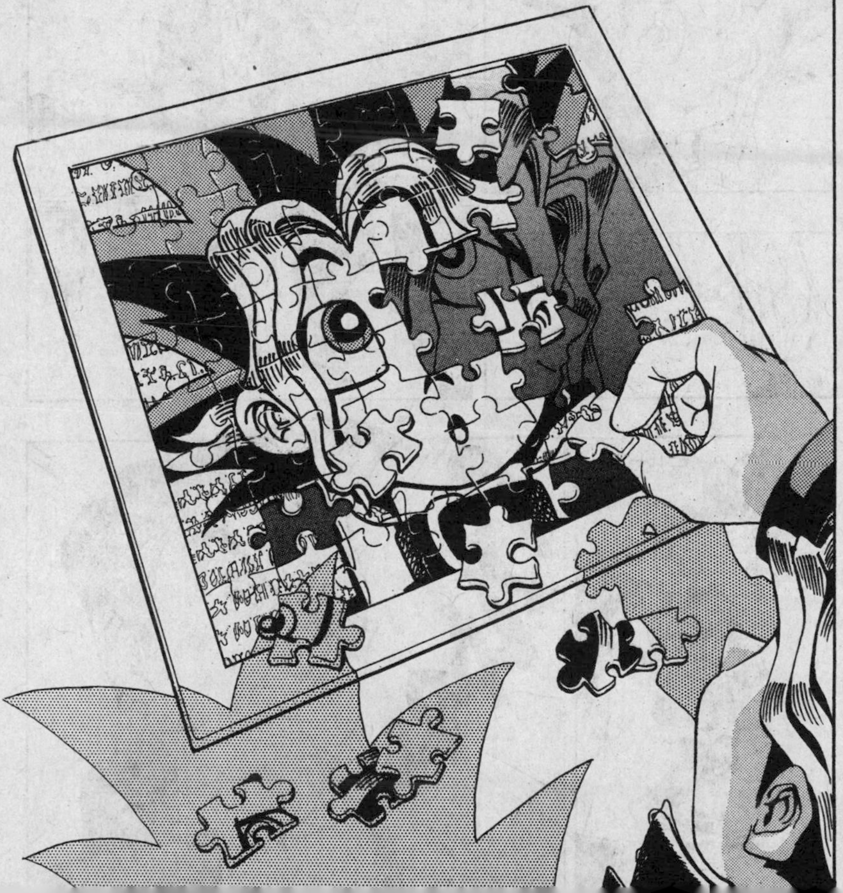

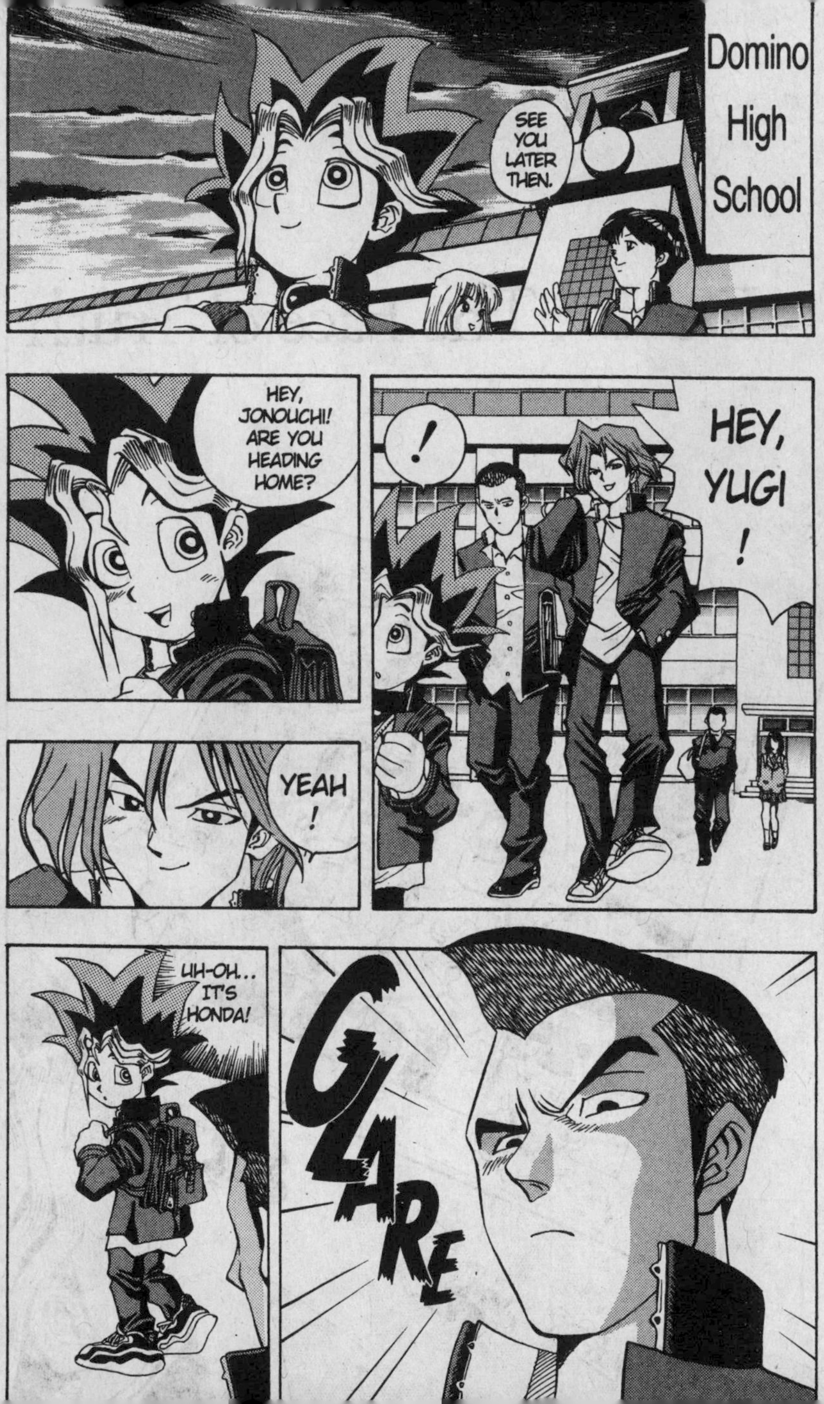
Domino High School
SEE YOU LATER THEN.
HEY, YUGI!
!
HEY, JONOUCHI! ARE YOU HEADING HOME?
YEAH!
GLARE
UH-OH... IT'S HONDA!

READ THIS WAY

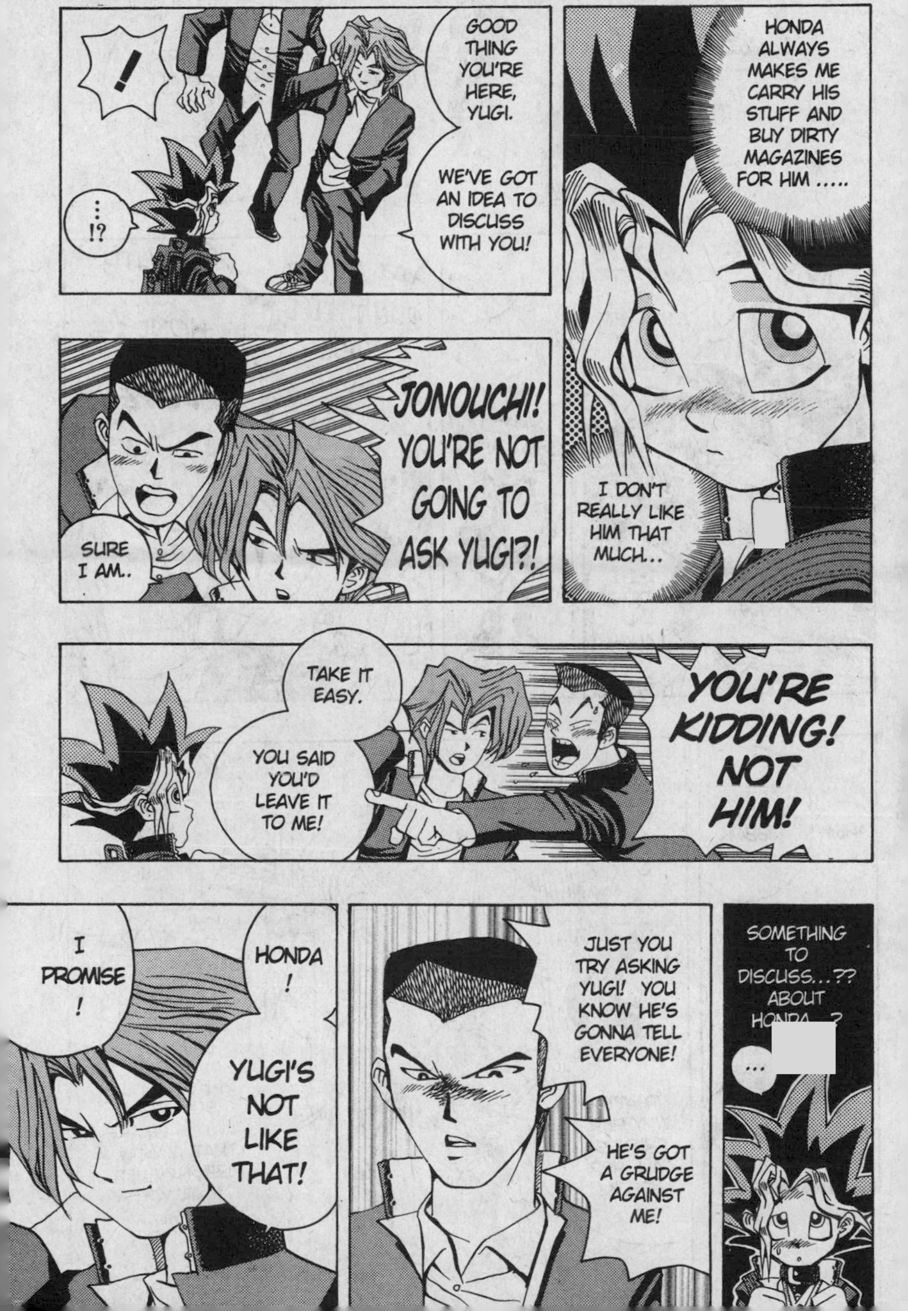
HONDA ALWAYS MAKES ME CARRY HIS STUFF AND BUY DIRTY MAGAZINES FOR HIM .....
I DON'T REALLY LIKE HIM THAT MUCH...
GOOD THING YOU'RE HERE, YUGI.
WE'VE GOT AN IDEA TO DISCUSS WITH YOU!
!
...!?
JONOUCHI! YOU'RE NOT GOING TO ASK YUGI?!
SURE I AM..
YOU'RE KIDDING! NOT HIM!
TAKE IT EASY.
YOU SAID YOU'D LEAVE IT TO ME!
SOMETHING TO DISCUSS...?? ABOUT HO ?
...
JUST YOU TRY ASKING YUGI! YOU KNOW HE'S GONNA TELL EVERYONE!
HE'S GOT A GRUDGE AGAINST ME!
HONDA !
I PROMISE !
YUGI'S NOT LIKE THAT!

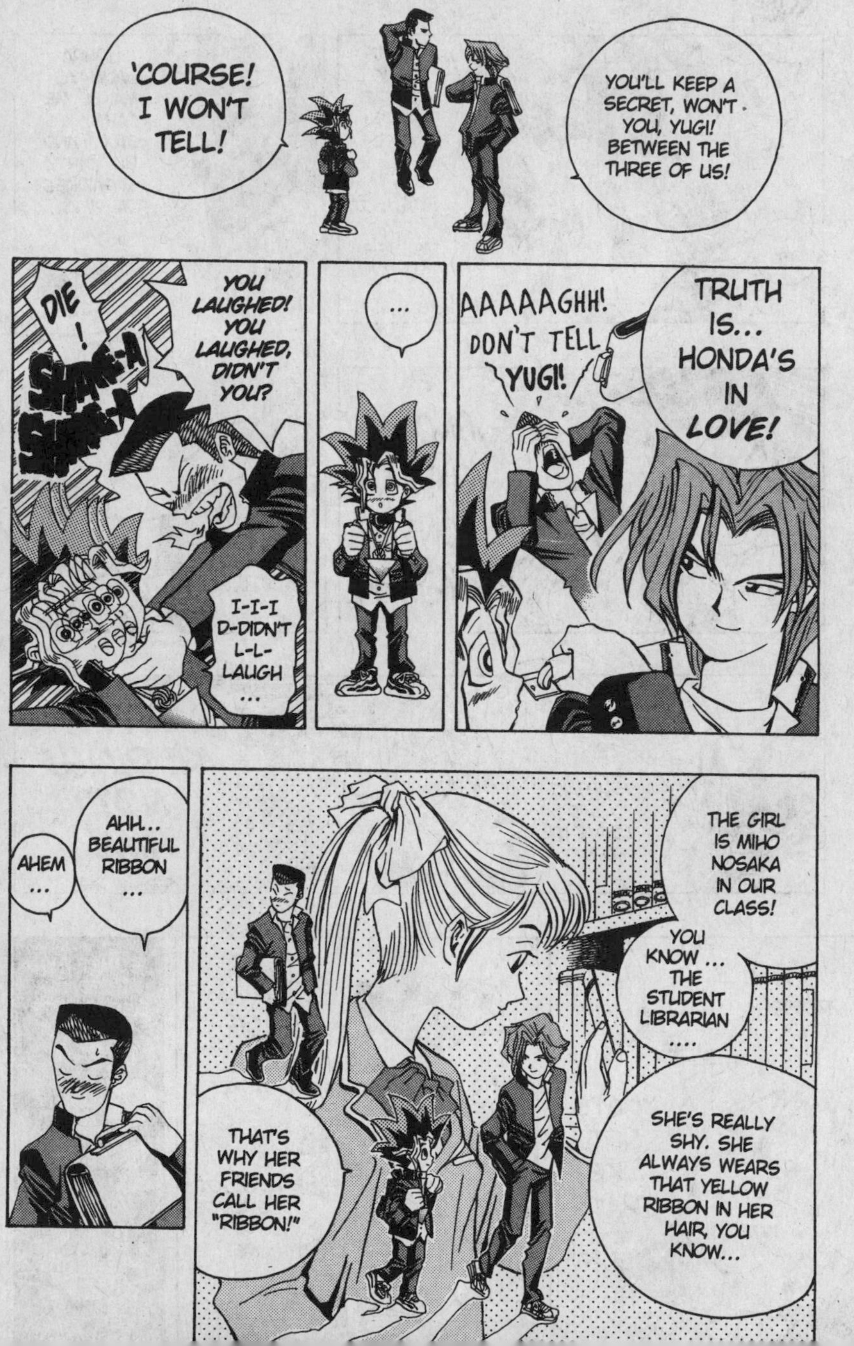
YOU'LL KEEP A SECRET, WON'T YOU, YUGI! BETWEEN THE THREE OF US!
'COURSE! I WON'T TELL!
TRUTH IS... HONDA'S IN LOVE!
AAAAAGHH! DON'T TELL YUGI!
...
DIE!
YOU LAUGHED! YOU LAUGHED, DIDN'T YOU?
I-I-I D-DIDN'T L-L-LAUGH ...
THE GIRL IS MIHO NOSAKA IN OUR CLASS!
YOU KNOW ... THE STUDENT LIBRARIAN ....
SHE'S REALLY SHY. SHE ALWAYS WEARS THAT YELLOW RIBBON IN HER HAIR, YOU KNOW...
THAT'S WHY HER FRIENDS CALL HER "RIBBON!"
AHH... BEAUTIFUL RIBBON ...
AHEM ...

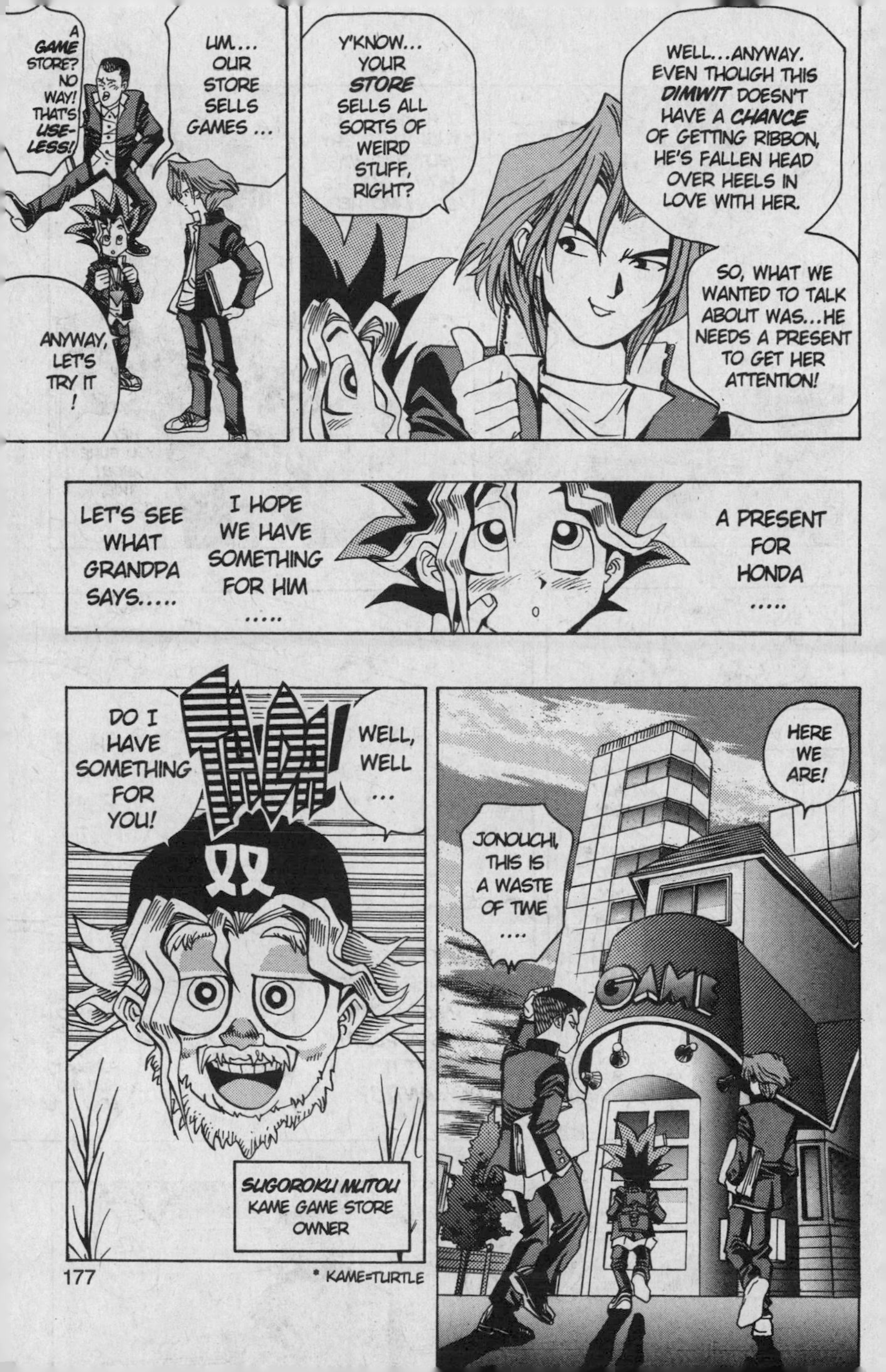
WELL...ANYWAY. EVEN THOUGH THIS DIMWIT DOESN'T HAVE A CHANCE OF GETTING RIBBON, HE'S FALLEN HEAD OVER HEELS IN LOVE WITH HER.
SO, WHAT WE WANTED TO TALK ABOUT WAS...HE NEEDS A PRESENT TO GET HER ATTENTION!
Y'KNOW... YOUR STORE SELLS ALL SORTS OF WEIRD STUFF, RIGHT?
UM... OUR STORE SELLS GAMES ...
A GAME STORE? NO WAY! THAT'S USE-LESS!
ANYWAY, LET'S TRY IT!
A PRESENT FOR HONDA .....
I HOPE WE HAVE SOMETHING FOR HIM .....
LET'S SEE WHAT GRANDPA SAYS.....
HERE WE ARE!
JONOUCHI, THIS IS A WASTE OF TIME ....
GAME
WELL, WELL ...
DO I HAVE SOMETHING FOR YOU!
SUGOROKU MUTOU
KAME GAME STORE OWNER

* KAME=TURTLE

READ THIS WAY

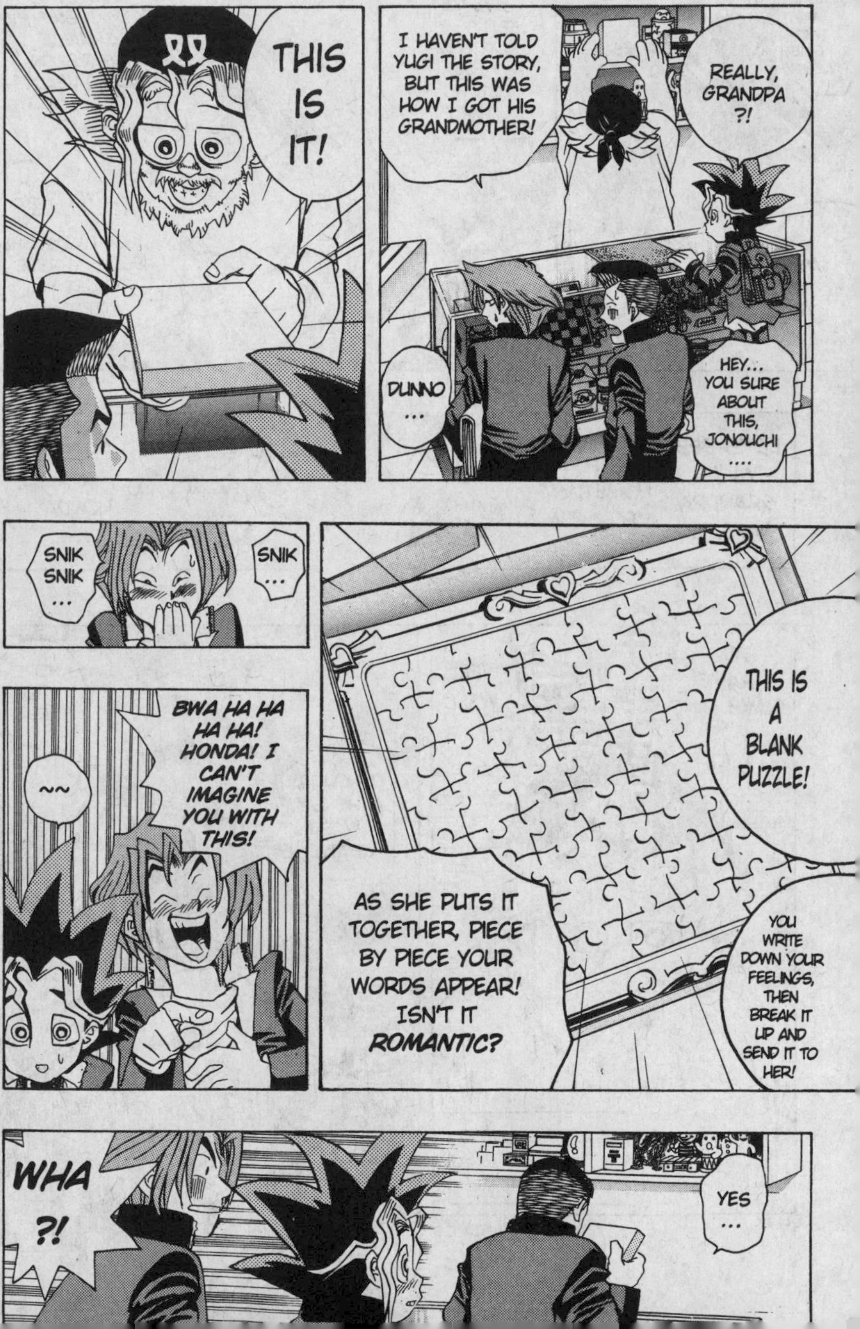
REALLY, GRANDPA?!
I HAVEN'T TOLD YUGI THE STORY, BUT THIS WAS HOW I GOT HIS GRANDMOTHER!
HEY... YOU SURE ABOUT THIS, JONOUCHI....
DUNNO...
THIS IS IT!
THIS IS A BLANK PUZZLE!
YOU WRITE DOWN YOUR FEELINGS, THEN BREAK IT UP AND SEND IT TO HER!
AS SHE PUTS IT TOGETHER, PIECE BY PIECE YOUR WORDS APPEAR! ISN'T IT *ROMANTIC?*
SNIK...
SNIK SNIK...
BWA HA HA HA HA HA! HONDA! I CAN'T IMAGINE YOU WITH THIS!
~~
YES...
WHA?!

READ THIS WAY

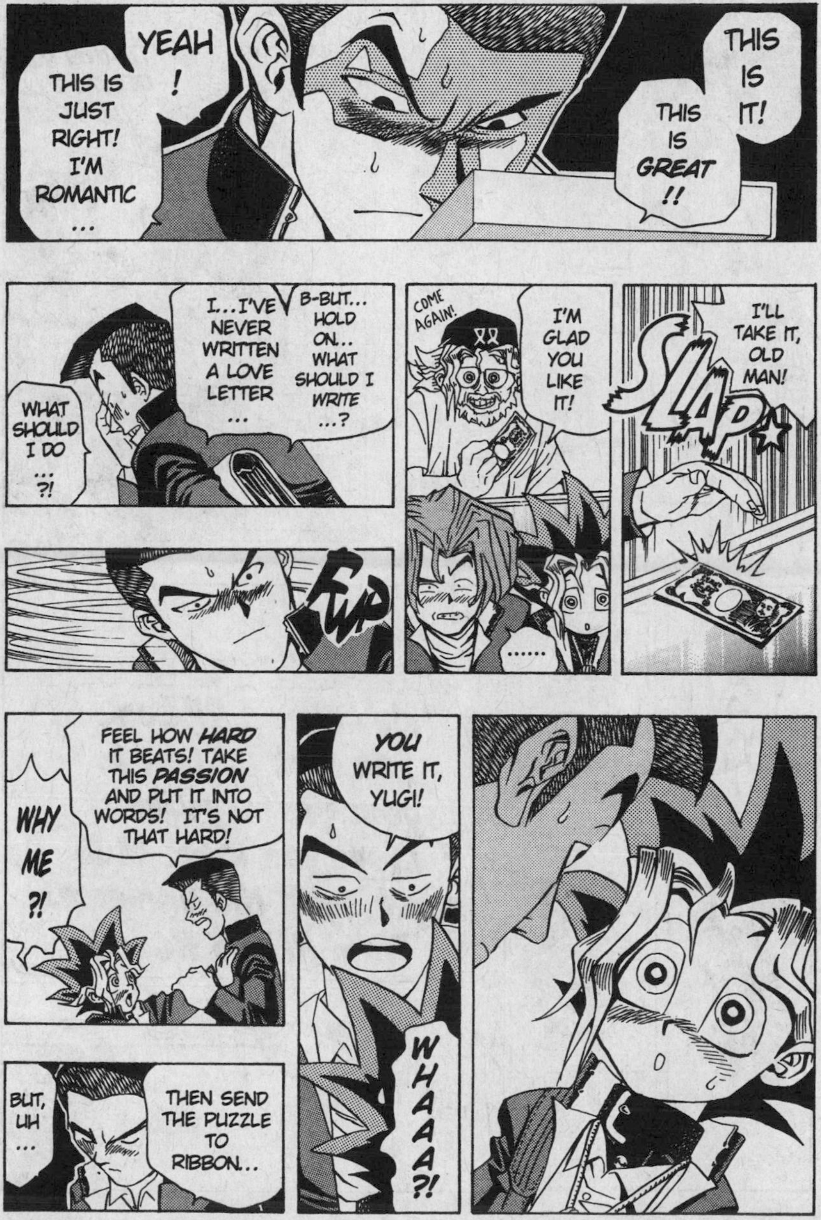
THIS IS IT!
THIS IS *GREAT* !!
YEAH!
THIS IS JUST RIGHT! I'M ROMANTIC ...
I'LL TAKE IT, OLD MAN!
SLAP
COME AGAIN!
I'M GLAD YOU LIKE IT!
......
B-BUT... HOLD ON... WHAT SHOULD I *WRITE* ...?
I...I'VE NEVER WRITTEN A LOVE LETTER ...
WHAT SHOULD I DO ...?!
FWP
YOU WRITE IT, YUGI!
WHAAAA?!
FEEL HOW *HARD* IT BEATS! TAKE THIS *PASSION* AND PUT IT INTO WORDS! IT'S NOT THAT HARD!
WHY ME?!
THEN SEND THE PUZZLE TO RIBBON...
BUT, UH ...

READ THIS WAY

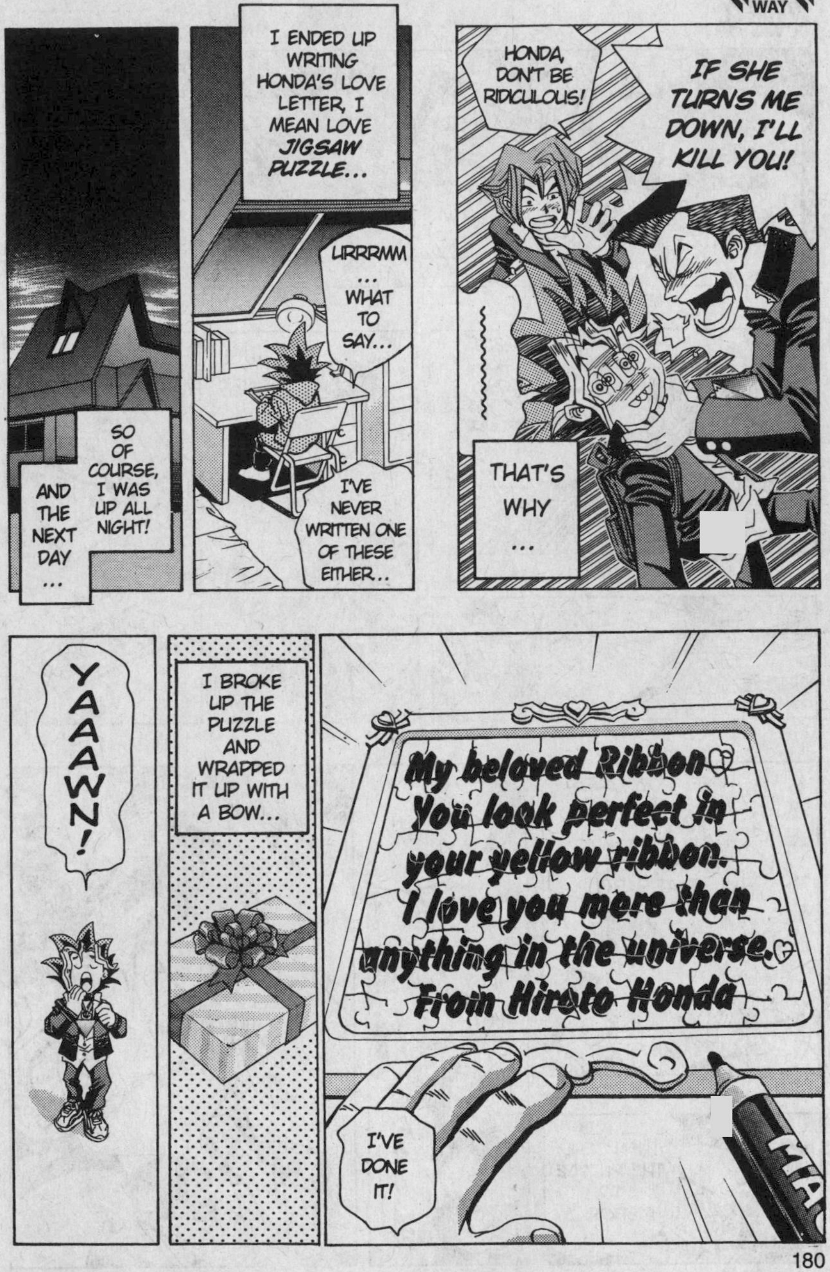

IF SHE TURNS ME DOWN, I'LL KILL YOU!
HONDA, DON'T BE RIDICULOUS!
THAT'S WHY ...
I ENDED UP WRITING HONDA'S LOVE LETTER, I MEAN LOVE JIGSAW PUZZLE...
URRRMM ... WHAT TO SAY...
I'VE NEVER WRITTEN ONE OF THESE EITHER..
SO OF COURSE, I WAS UP ALL NIGHT!
AND THE NEXT DAY ...
My beloved Ribbon
You look perfect in your yellow ribbon.
I love you more than anything in the universe.
From Hiroto Honda
I'VE DONE IT!
I BROKE UP THE PUZZLE AND WRAPPED IT UP WITH A BOW...
YAAAWN!

READ THIS WAY

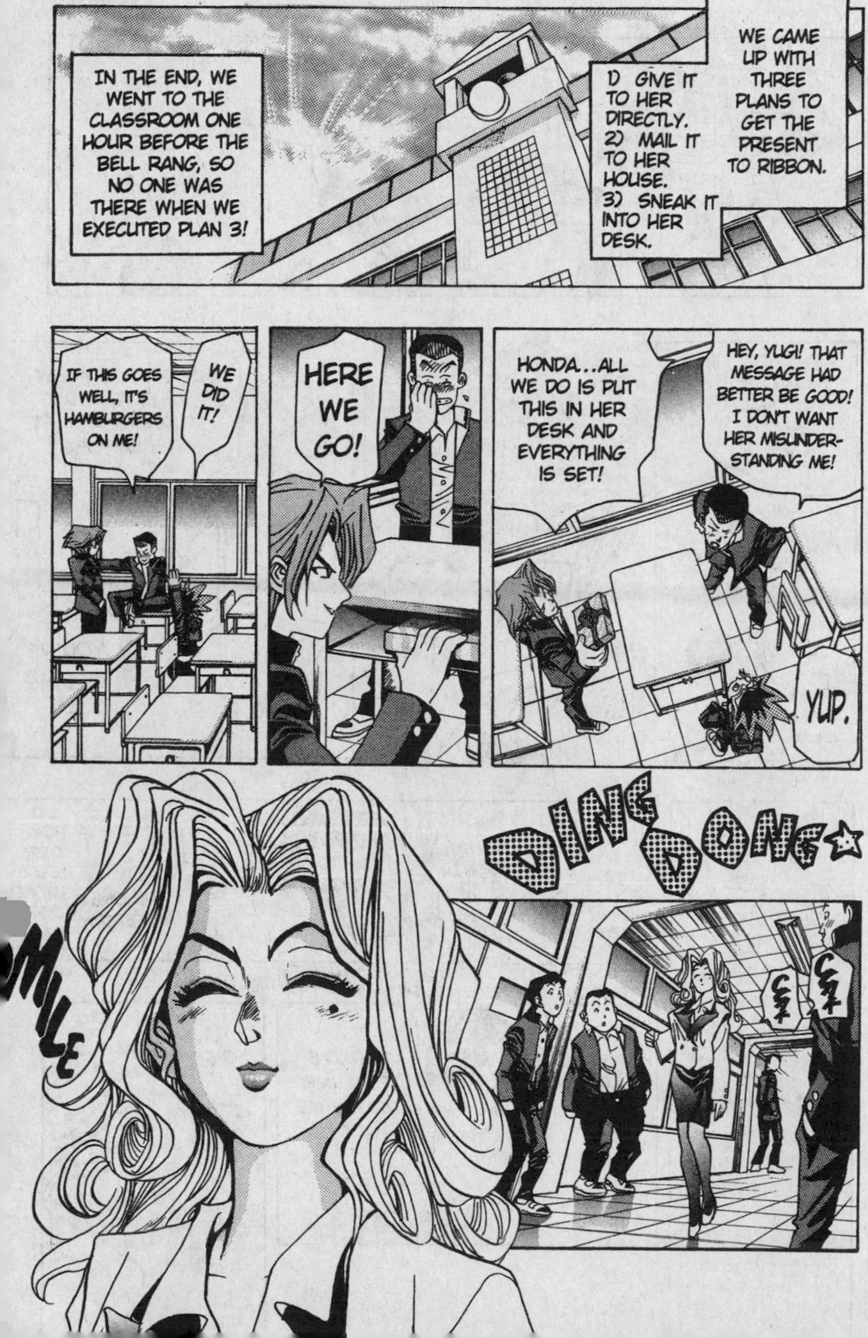
WE CAME UP WITH THREE PLANS TO GET THE PRESENT TO RIBBON.
1) GIVE IT TO HER DIRECTLY. 2) MAIL IT TO HER HOUSE. 3) SNEAK IT INTO HER DESK.
IN THE END, WE WENT TO THE CLASSROOM ONE HOUR BEFORE THE BELL RANG, SO NO ONE WAS THERE WHEN WE EXECUTED PLAN 3!
HEY, YUGI! THAT MESSAGE HAD BETTER BE GOOD! I DON'T WANT HER MISUNDERSTANDING ME!
HONDA...ALL WE DO IS PUT THIS IN HER DESK AND EVERYTHING IS SET!
YUP.
HERE WE GO!
WE DID IT!
IF THIS GOES WELL, IT'S HAMBURGERS ON ME!
DING DONG
MILE

READ THIS WAY

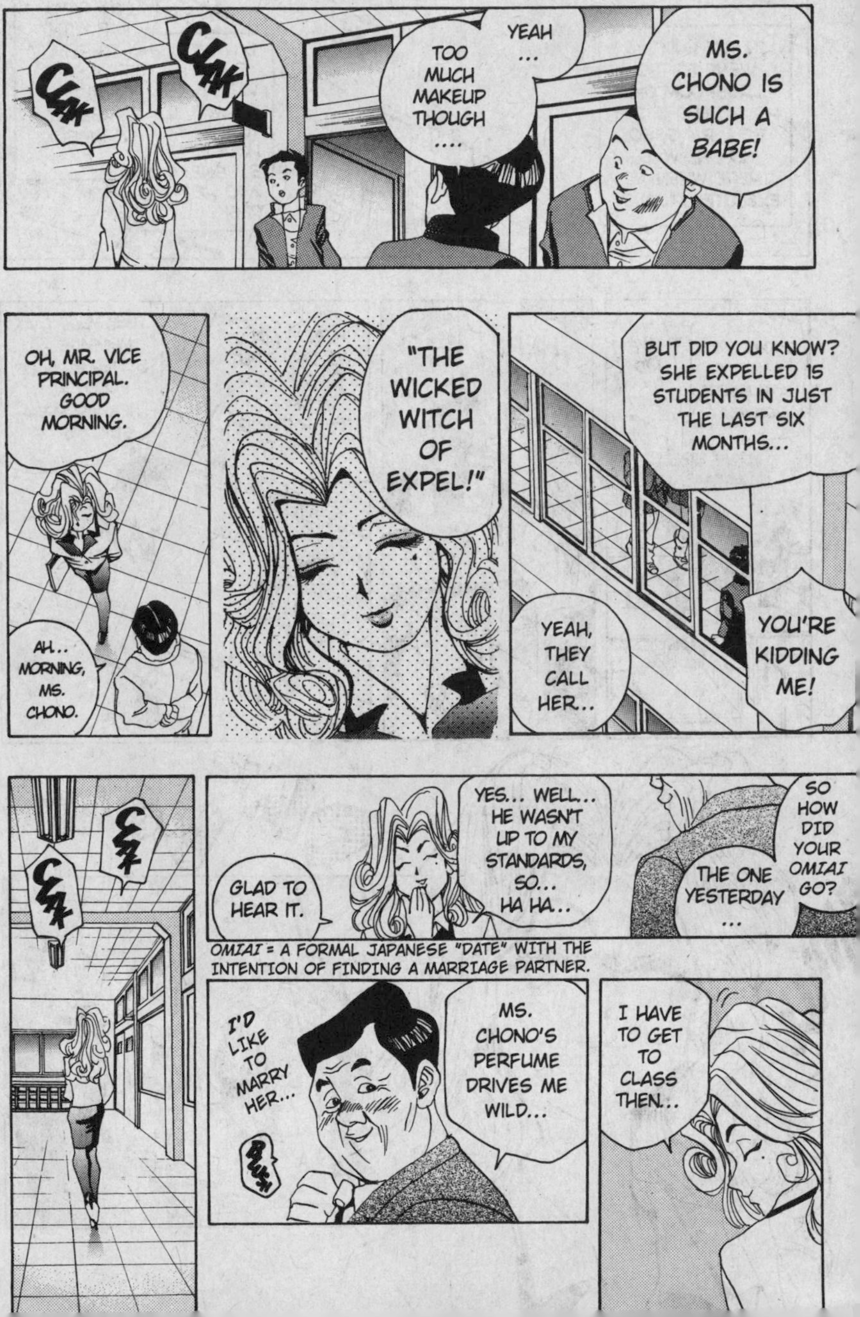
MS. CHONO IS SUCH A BABE!
YEAH ...
TOO MUCH MAKEUP THOUGH ....
CLAK
CLAK
BUT DID YOU KNOW? SHE EXPELLED 15 STUDENTS IN JUST THE LAST SIX MONTHS...
YOU'RE KIDDING ME!
YEAH, THEY CALL HER..
"THE WICKED WITCH OF EXPEL!"
OH, MR. VICE PRINCIPAL. GOOD MORNING.
AH... MORNING, MS. CHONO.
SO HOW DID YOUR OMIAI GO?
THE ONE YESTERDAY ...
YES... WELL... HE WASN'T UP TO MY STANDARDS, SO... HA HA...
GLAD TO HEAR IT.
OMIAI = A FORMAL JAPANESE "DATE" WITH THE INTENTION OF FINDING A MARRIAGE PARTNER.
I HAVE TO GET TO CLASS THEN...
MS. CHONO'S PERFUME DRIVES ME WILD...
I'D LIKE TO MARRY HER...
BLUSH
CLAK
CLAK

READ THIS WAY

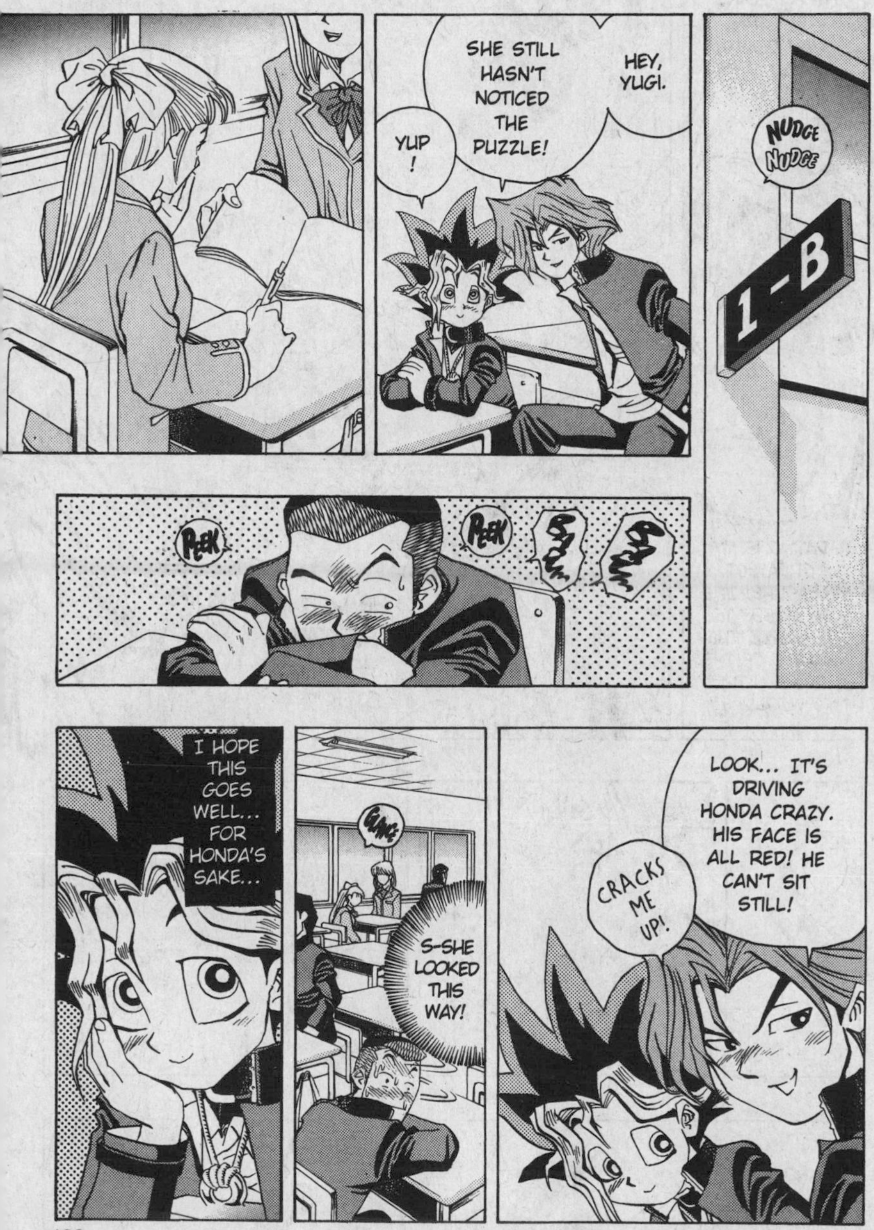
NUDGE NUDGE
HEY, YUGI.
SHE STILL HASN'T NOTICED THE PUZZLE!
YUP!
PEEK
PEEK
LOOK... IT'S DRIVING HONDA CRAZY. HIS FACE IS ALL RED! HE CAN'T SIT STILL!
CRACKS ME UP!
GLANCE
S-SHE LOOKED THIS WAY!
I HOPE THIS GOES WELL... FOR HONDA'S SAKE...

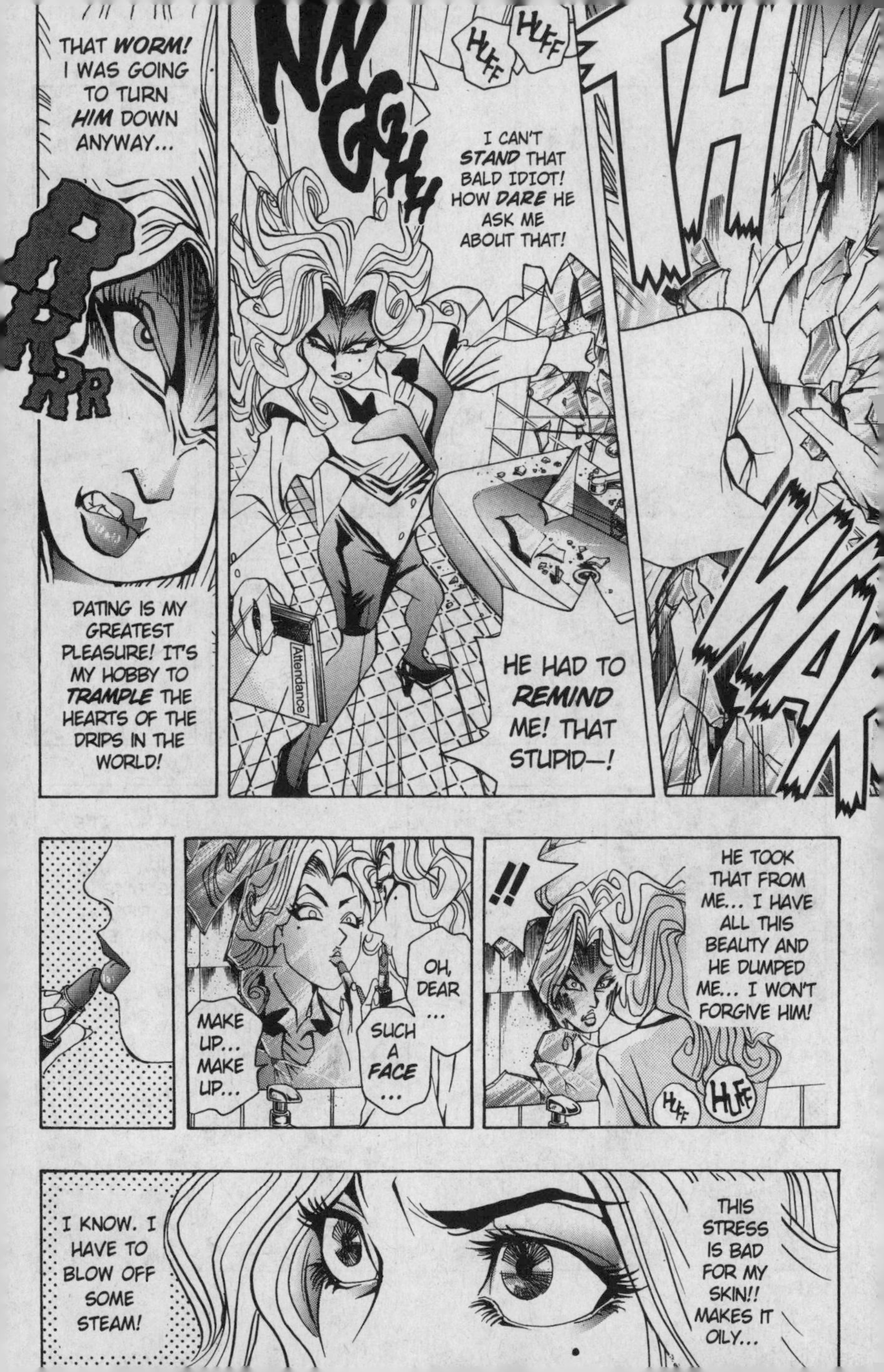
THWA
HUFF
HUFF
NNGGHH
I CAN'T STAND THAT BALD IDIOT! HOW DARE HE ASK ME ABOUT THAT!
HE HAD TO REMIND ME! THAT STUPID—!
Attendance
THAT WORM! I WAS GOING TO TURN HIM DOWN ANYWAY...
PRRR
DATING IS MY GREATEST PLEASURE! IT'S MY HOBBY TO TRAMPLE THE HEARTS OF THE DRIPS IN THE WORLD!
HE TOOK THAT FROM ME... I HAVE ALL THIS BEAUTY AND HE DUMPED ME... I WON'T FORGIVE HIM!
!!
HUFF
HUFF
OH, DEAR...
SUCH A FACE...
MAKE UP... MAKE UP...
THIS STRESS IS BAD FOR MY SKIN!! MAKES IT OILY...
I KNOW. I HAVE TO BLOW OFF SOME STEAM!

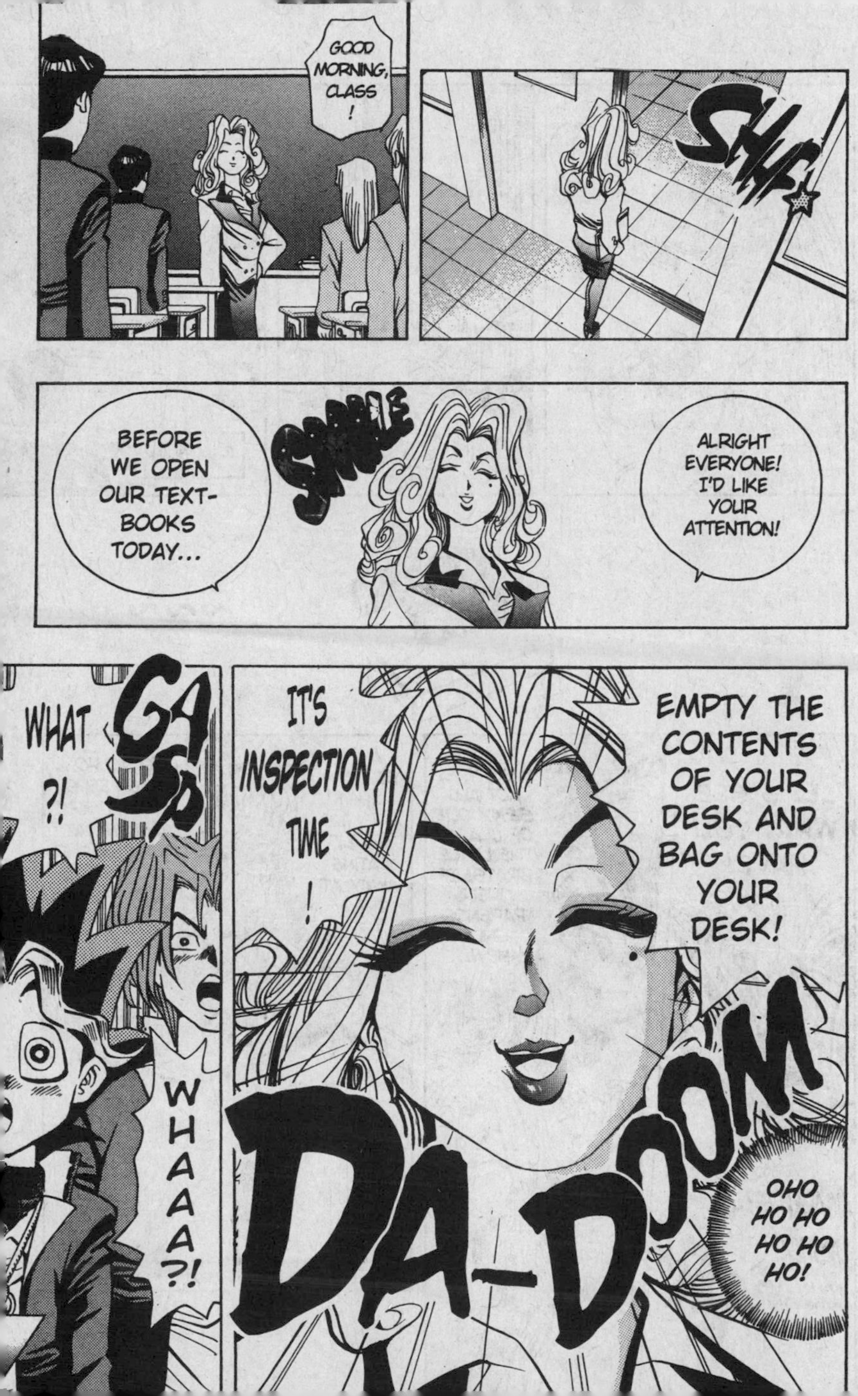
SHUF
GOOD MORNING, CLASS!
ALRIGHT EVERYONE! I'D LIKE YOUR ATTENTION!
SMILE
BEFORE WE OPEN OUR TEXT-BOOKS TODAY...
EMPTY THE CONTENTS OF YOUR DESK AND BAG ONTO YOUR DESK!
IT'S INSPECTION TIME!
DA-DOOM
OHO HO HO HO HO HO!
GASP
WHAT?!
WHAAAA?!

READ THIS WAY

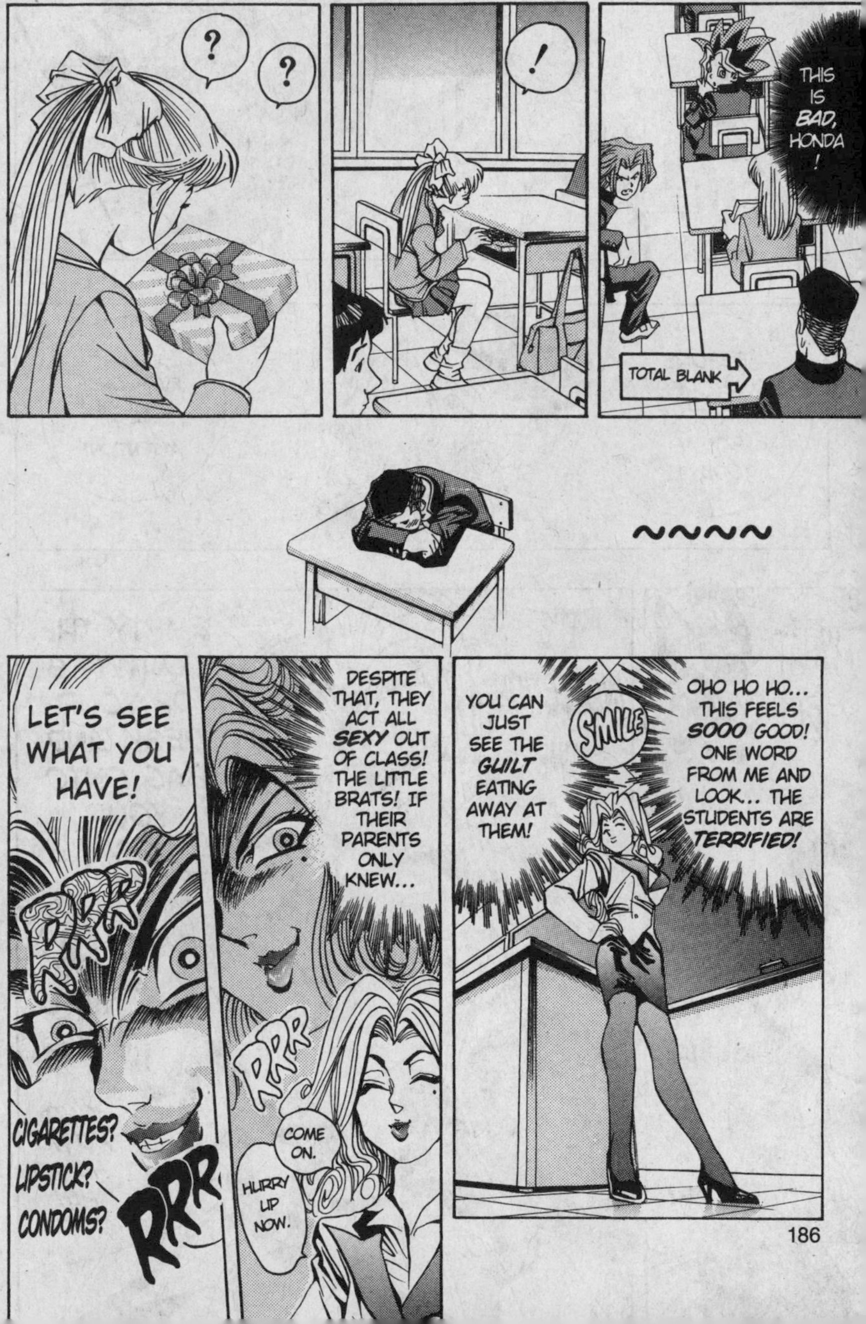
THIS IS BAD, HONDA!
TOTAL BLANK
!
?
?
~~~~
OHO HO HO... THIS FEELS SOOO GOOD! ONE WORD FROM ME AND LOOK... THE STUDENTS ARE TERRIFIED!
SMILE
YOU CAN JUST SEE THE GUILT EATING AWAY AT THEM!
DESPITE THAT, THEY ACT ALL SEXY OUT OF CLASS! THE LITTLE BRATS! IF THEIR PARENTS ONLY KNEW...
RRR
COME ON.
HURRY UP NOW.
LET'S SEE WHAT YOU HAVE!
RRR
CIGARETTES? LIPSTICK? CONDOMS?
RRR
~~~~

READ THIS WAY

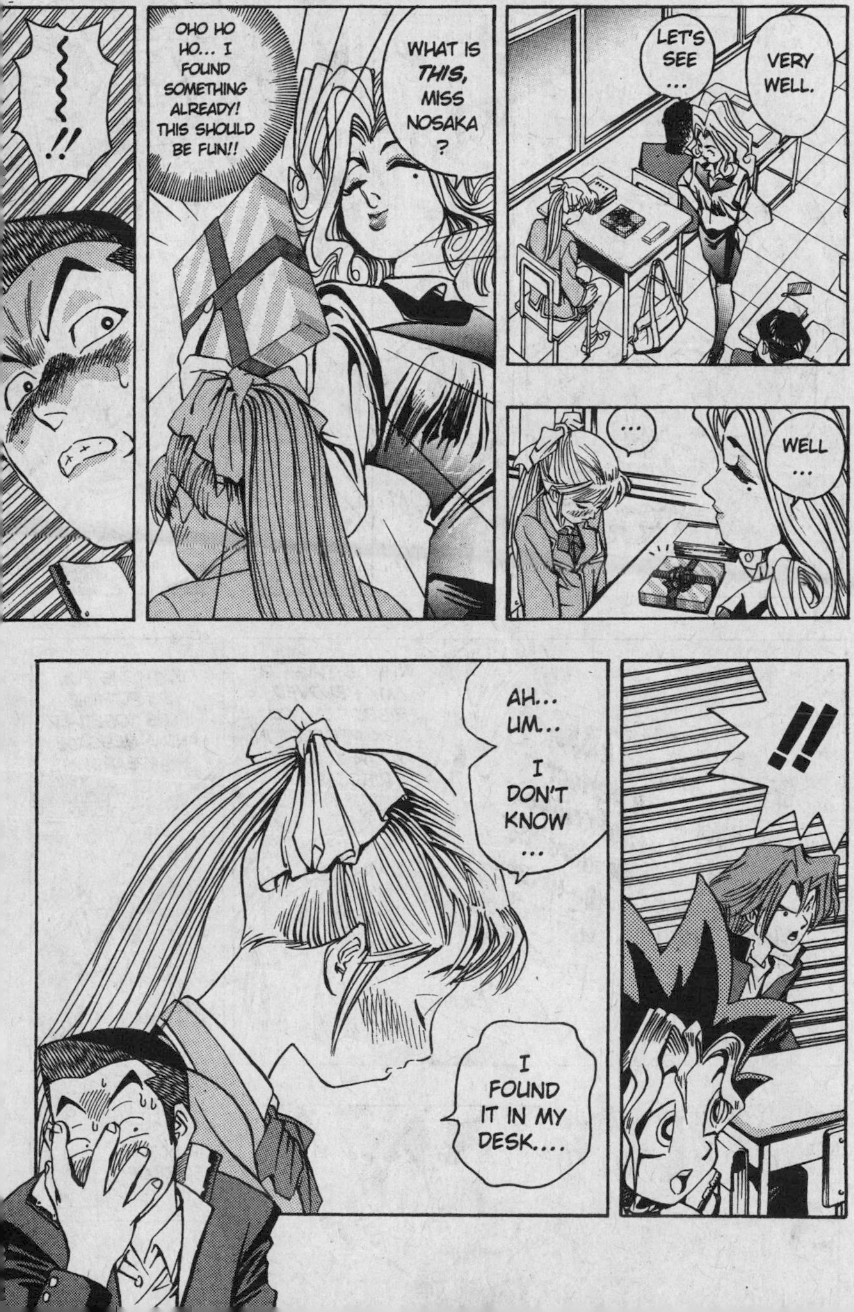
VERY WELL.
LET'S SEE ...
WELL ...
...
WHAT IS THIS, MISS NOSAKA?
OHO HO HO... I FOUND SOMETHING ALREADY! THIS SHOULD BE FUN!!
~~~~!!
!!
AH... UM... I DON'T KNOW ...
I FOUND IT IN MY DESK....
~~~~

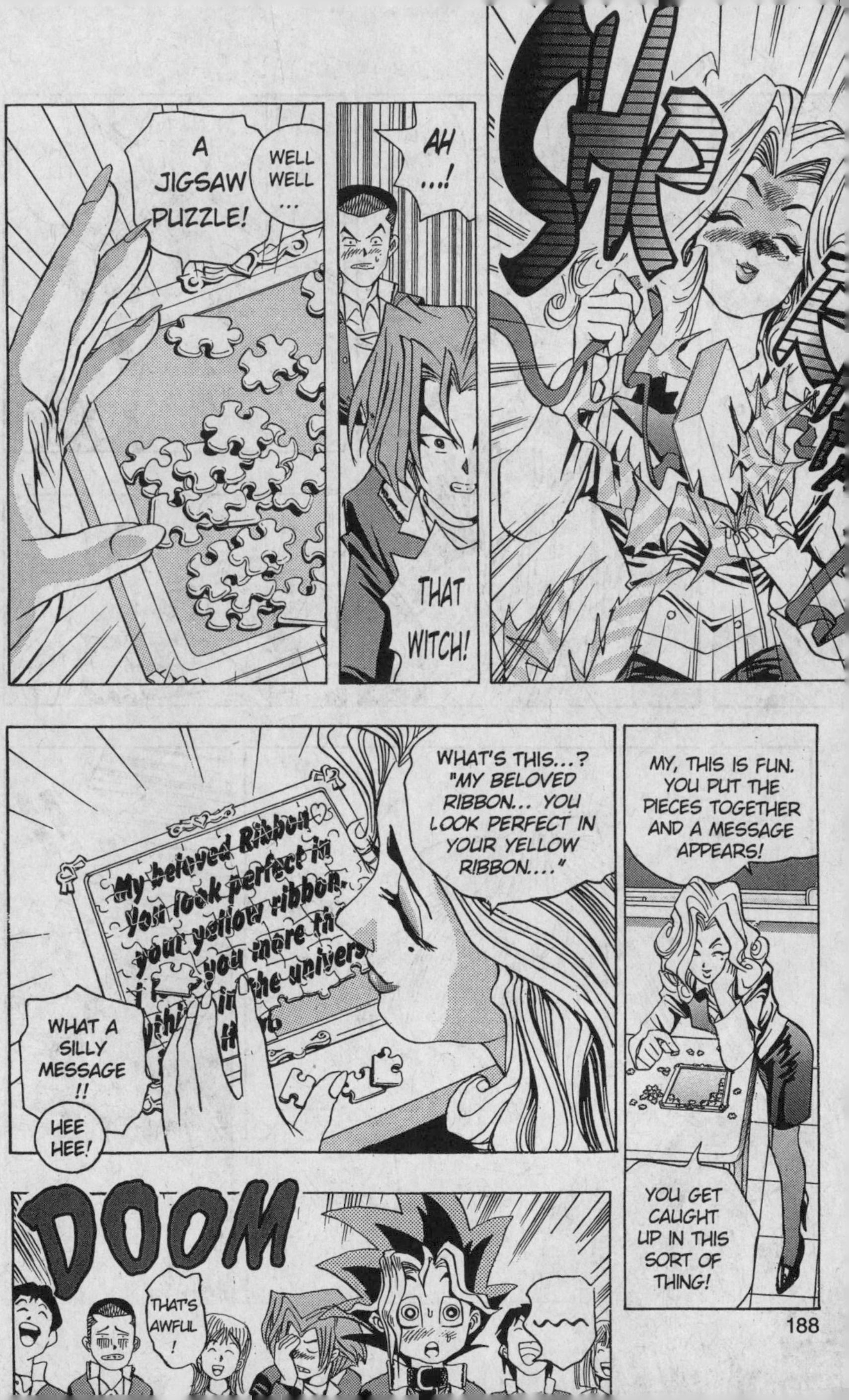
AH ...!
THAT WITCH!
WELL WELL ...
A JIGSAW PUZZLE!
MY, THIS IS FUN. YOU PUT THE PIECES TOGETHER AND A MESSAGE APPEARS!
YOU GET CAUGHT UP IN THIS SORT OF THING!
WHAT'S THIS...? "MY BELOVED RIBBON... YOU LOOK PERFECT IN YOUR YELLOW RIBBON...."
My beloved Ribbon
You look perfect in
your yellow ribbon.
WHAT A SILLY MESSAGE !!
HEE HEE!
DOOM
THAT'S AWFUL !

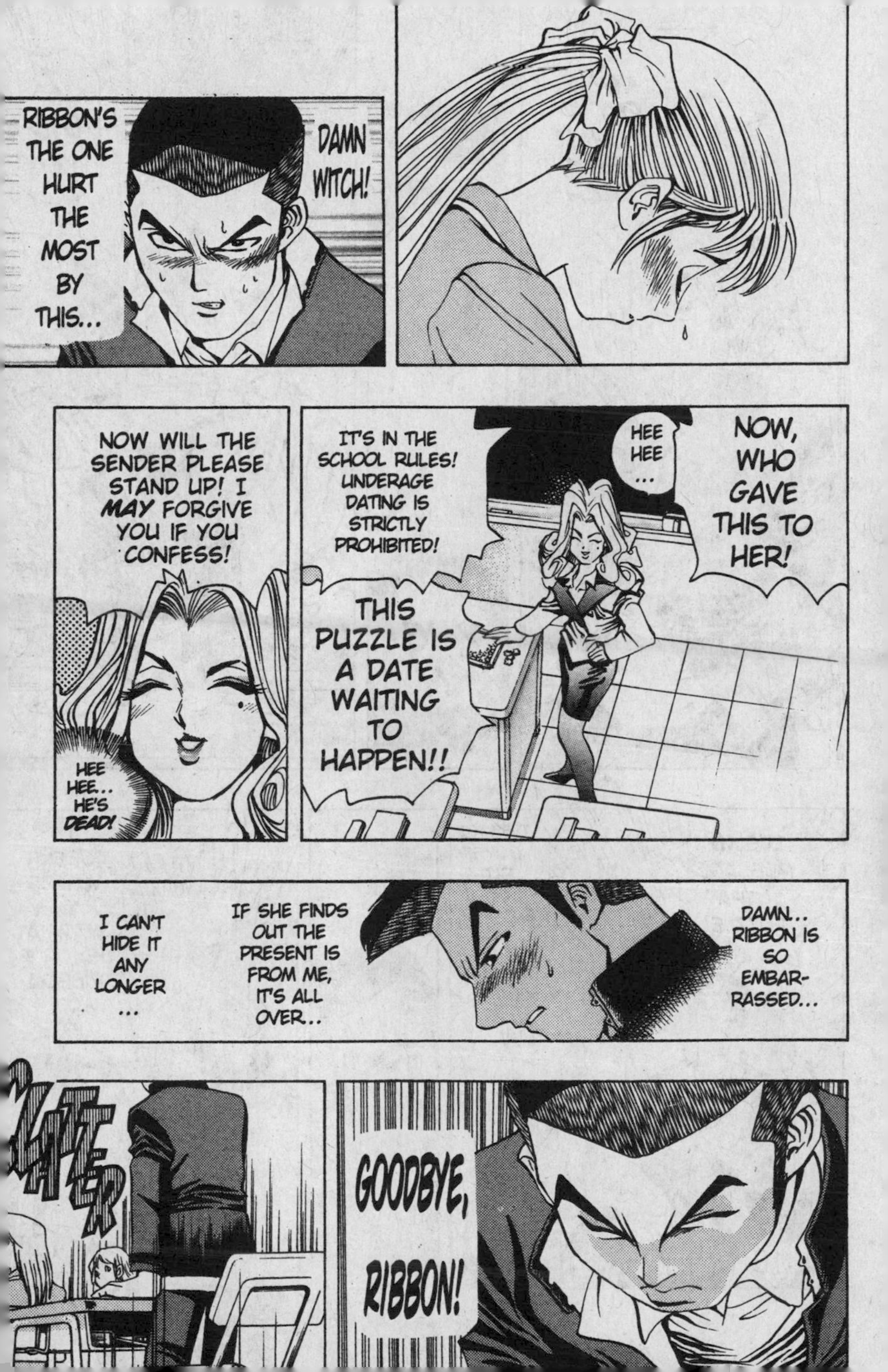
DAMN WITCH!
RIBBON'S THE ONE HURT THE MOST BY THIS...
NOW, WHO GAVE THIS TO HER!
HEE HEE ...
IT'S IN THE SCHOOL RULES! UNDERAGE DATING IS STRICTLY PROHIBITED!
THIS PUZZLE IS A DATE WAITING TO HAPPEN!!
NOW WILL THE SENDER PLEASE STAND UP! I *MAY* FORGIVE YOU IF YOU CONFESS!
HEE HEE... HE'S *DEAD!*
DAMN... RIBBON IS SO EMBAR-RASSED...
IF SHE FINDS OUT THE PRESENT IS FROM ME, IT'S ALL OVER...
I CAN'T HIDE IT ANY LONGER ...
GOODBYE, RIBBON!

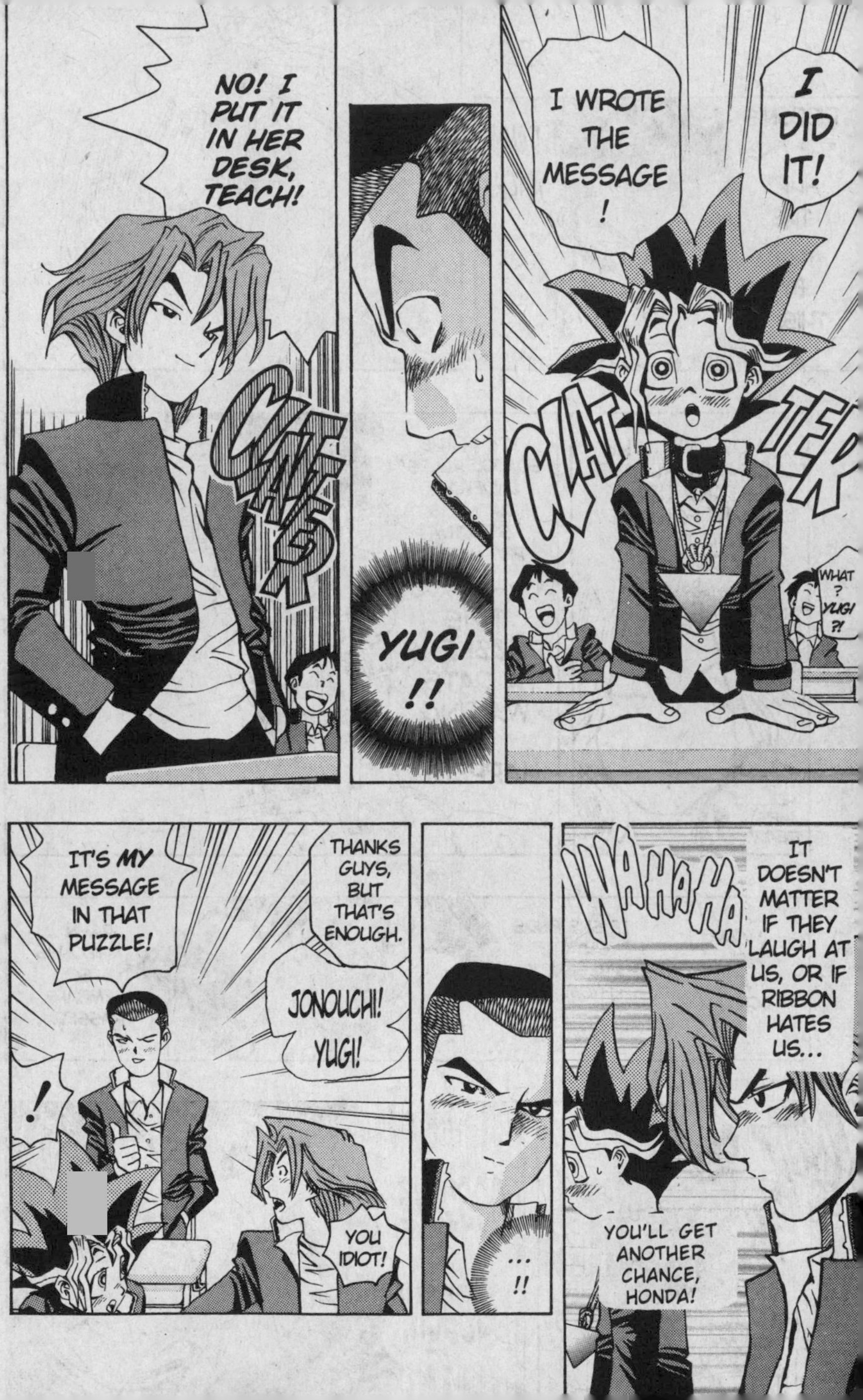
I DID IT!
I WROTE THE MESSAGE!
CLATTER
WHAT? YUGI?!
YUGI!!
NO! I PUT IT IN HER DESK, TEACH!
CLATTER
WAHAHAHA
IT DOESN'T MATTER IF THEY LAUGH AT US, OR IF RIBBON HATES US...
YOU'LL GET ANOTHER CHANCE, HONDA!
...!!
THANKS GUYS, BUT THAT'S ENOUGH.
IT'S MY MESSAGE IN THAT PUZZLE!
JONOUCHI! YUGI!
!
YOU IDIOT!

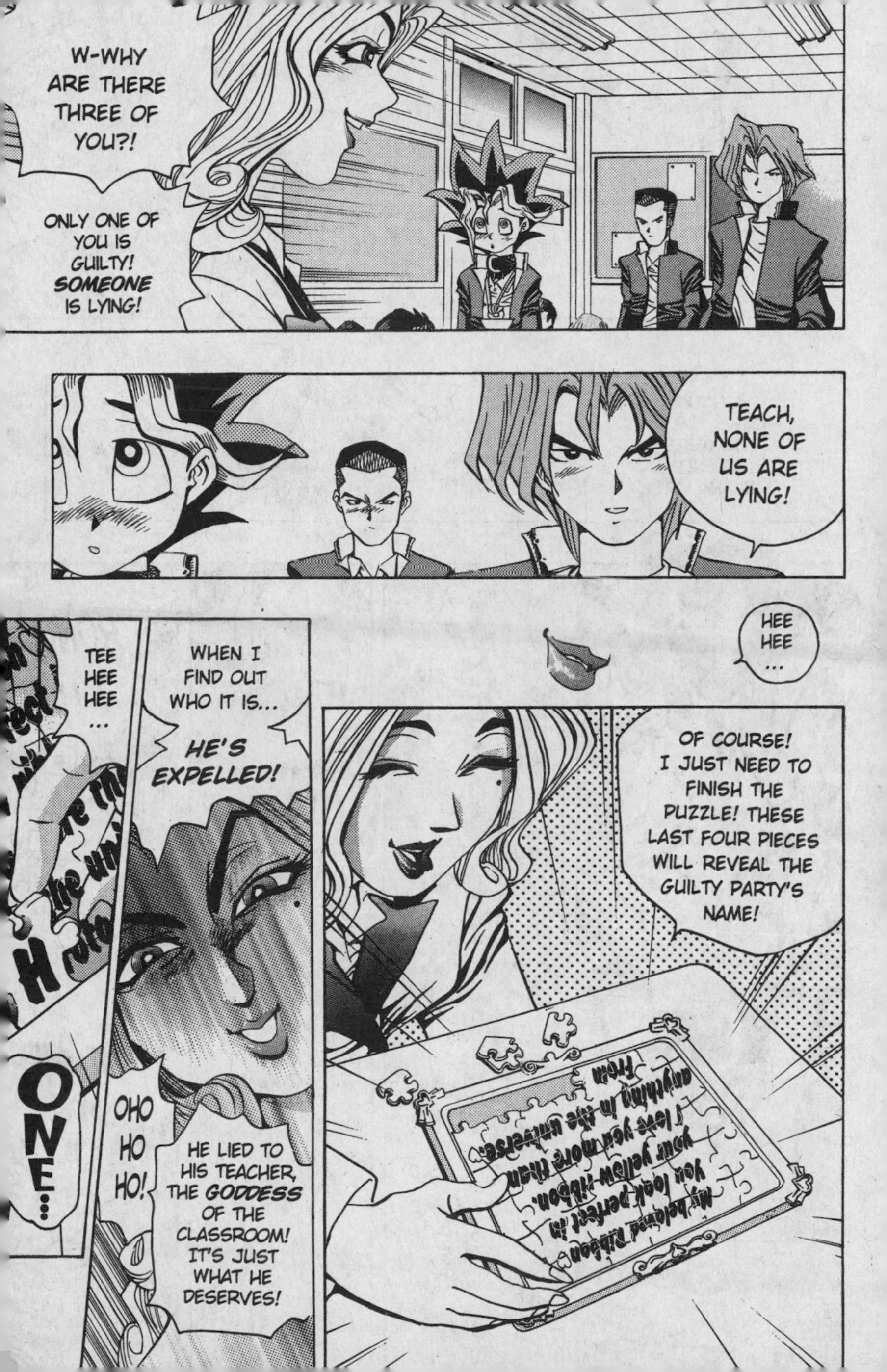
W-WHY ARE THERE THREE OF YOU?!
ONLY ONE OF YOU IS GUILTY! SOMEONE IS LYING!
TEACH, NONE OF US ARE LYING!
HEE HEE ...
OF COURSE! I JUST NEED TO FINISH THE PUZZLE! THESE LAST FOUR PIECES WILL REVEAL THE GUILTY PARTY'S NAME!
My beloved Ribbon
You look perfect in
your yellow ribbon.
I love you more than
anything in the universe.
From
WHEN I FIND OUT WHO IT IS... HE'S EXPELLED!
OHO HO HO!
HE LIED TO HIS TEACHER, THE GODDESS OF THE CLASSROOM! IT'S JUST WHAT HE DESERVES!
TEE HEE HEE ...
ONE...

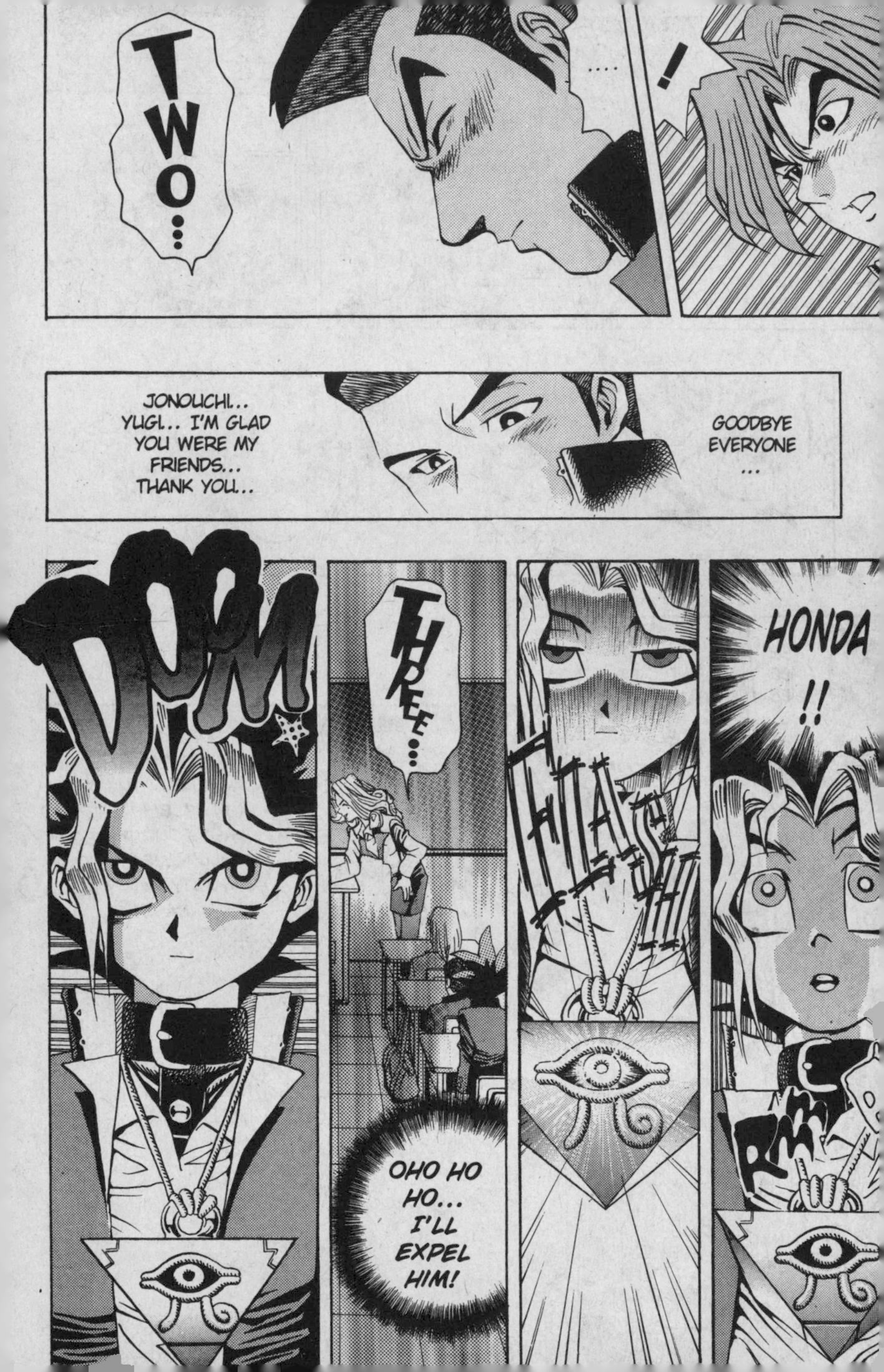
!
....
TWO...
GOODBYE EVERYONE ...
JONOUCHI... YUGI... I'M GLAD YOU WERE MY FRIENDS... THANK YOU...
HONDA !!
THREE...
OHO HO HO... I'LL EXPEL HIM!
DOOM

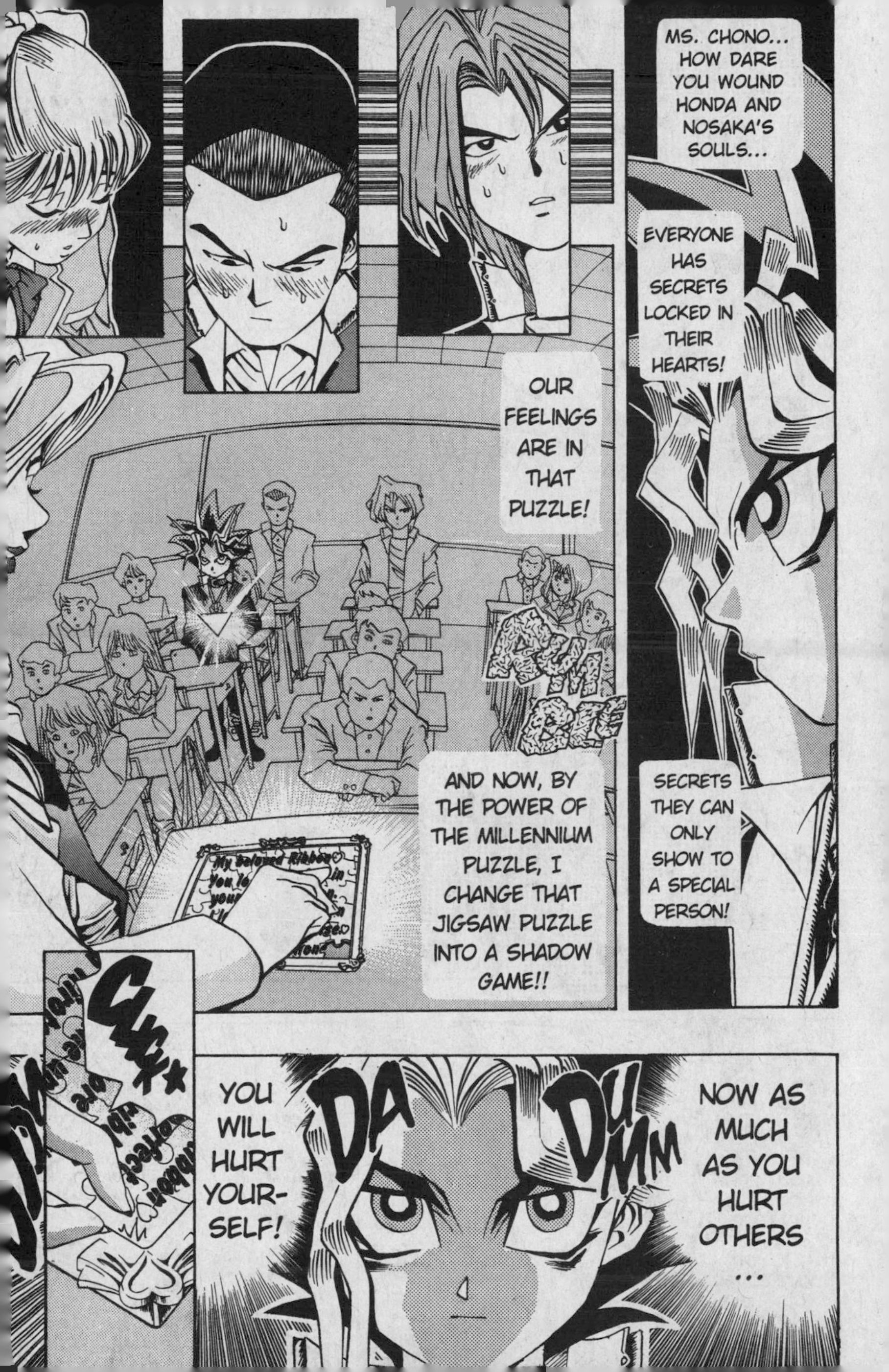
MS. CHONO... HOW DARE YOU WOUND HONDA AND NOSAKA'S SOULS...
EVERYONE HAS SECRETS LOCKED IN THEIR HEARTS!
SECRETS THEY CAN ONLY SHOW TO A SPECIAL PERSON!
OUR FEELINGS ARE IN THAT PUZZLE!
AND NOW, BY THE POWER OF THE MILLENNIUM PUZZLE, I CHANGE THAT JIGSAW PUZZLE INTO A SHADOW GAME!!
NOW AS MUCH AS YOU HURT OTHERS...
DA DUMM
YOU WILL HURT YOURSELF!
CLICK

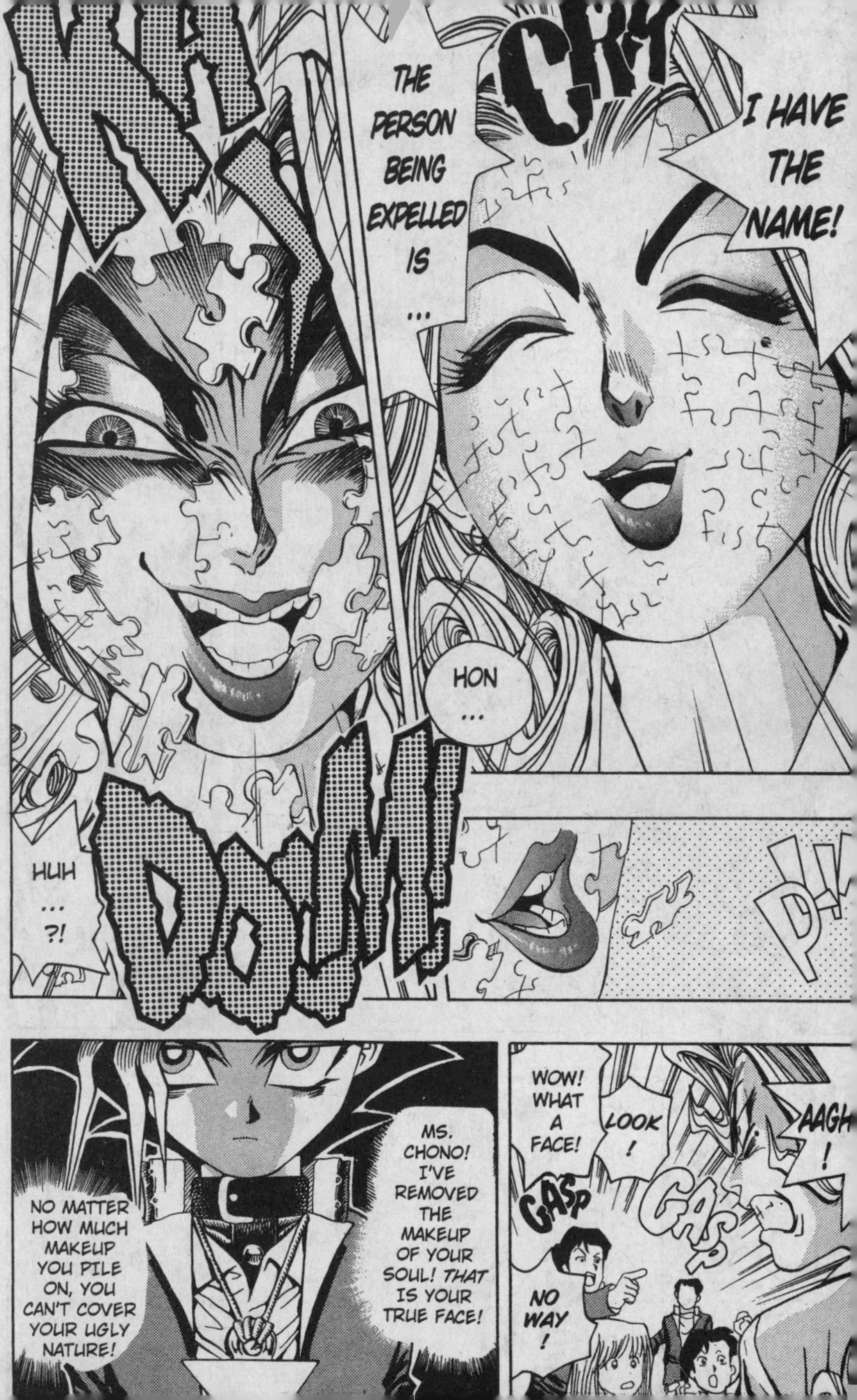
I HAVE THE NAME!
THE PERSON BEING EXPELLED IS ...
HON ...
DOOM!
HUH ... ?!
AAGH !
LOOK !
WOW! WHAT A FACE!
GASP
GASP
NO WAY !
MS. CHONO! I'VE REMOVED THE MAKEUP OF YOUR SOUL! THAT IS YOUR TRUE FACE!
NO MATTER HOW MUCH MAKEUP YOU PILE ON, YOU CAN'T COVER YOUR UGLY NATURE!

READ THIS WAY

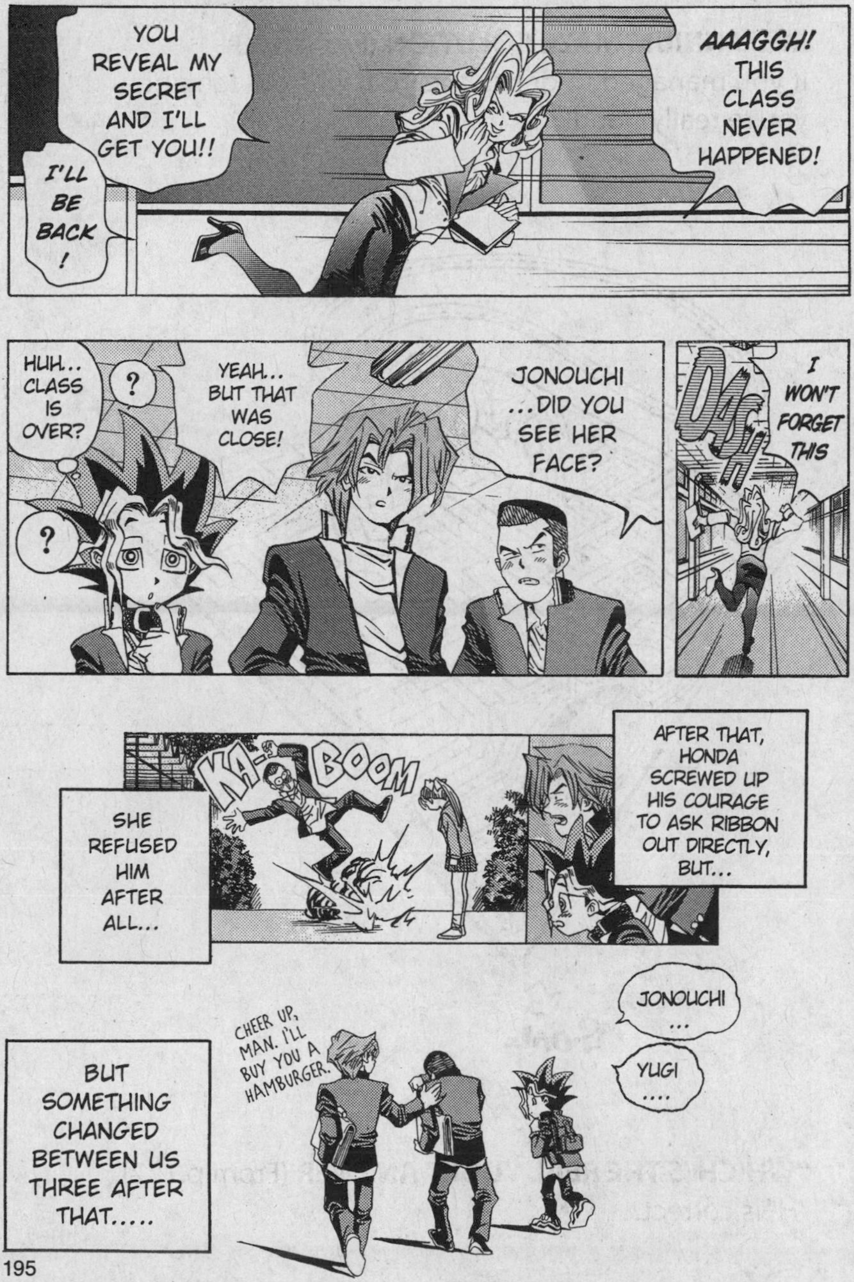
AAAGGH! THIS CLASS NEVER HAPPENED!
YOU REVEAL MY SECRET AND I'LL GET YOU!!
I'LL BE BACK!
DASH
I WON'T FORGET THIS
JONOUCHI ...DID YOU SEE HER FACE?
YEAH... BUT THAT WAS CLOSE!
?
HUH.. CLASS IS OVER?
?
AFTER THAT, HONDA SCREWED UP HIS COURAGE TO ASK RIBBON OUT DIRECTLY, BUT...
KA-BOOM
SHE REFUSED HIM AFTER ALL...
JONOUCHI ...
YUGI ....
CHEER UP, MAN. I'LL BUY YOU A HAMBURGER.
BUT SOMETHING CHANGED BETWEEN US THREE AFTER THAT.....

MILLENNIUM MAZE SOLUTION (From p.78)
If you managed to get to the goal without looking, you're really good!

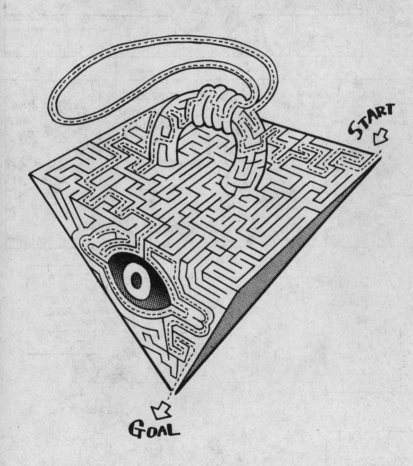

START

GOAL

"WHICH IS THE REAL YUGI?" ANSWER (From p.172)
"H" is correct.

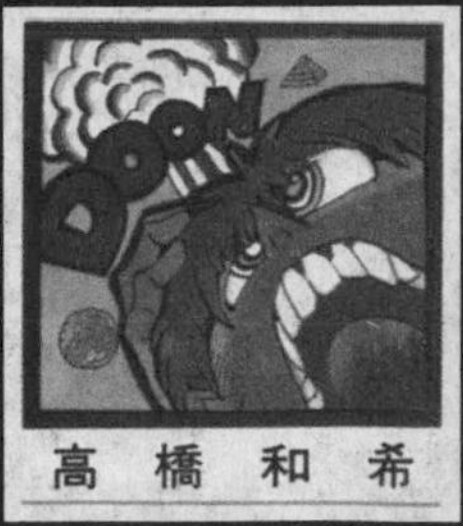
DOOM
高橋和希

BEFORE I WROTE THIS SERIES, I WENT TO EGYPT FOR BACKGROUND RESEARCH. I WAS PARTICULARLY STRUCK BY HOW OPEN-HEARTED AND FRIENDLY THE EGYPTIAN PEOPLE WERE. WHEN THEIR SMILING FACES GREETED ME, I ENDED UP BUYING STONES THAT I WASN'T INTERESTED IN BUYING, RIDING DONKEYS THAT I HAD NO INTEREST IN RIDING, AND BUYING PHOTOGRAPHS THAT WERE FORCED ON ME. BUT ONE LOOK AT THOSE FACES, AND YOU JUST HAD TO FORGIVE THEM!

–KAZUKI TAKAHASHI, 1997

SHONEN JUMP MANGA

Vol. 2
THE CARDS WITH TEETH

STORY AND ART BY
KAZUKI TAKAHASHI

THE STORY SO FAR...

Shy and easily picked on, 10th-grader Yugi spent most of his time alone playing games...until he solved the Millennium Puzzle, a mysterious Egyptian artifact passed down from his grandfather. Possessed by the puzzle, Yugi became a different person, and challenged bullies and criminals to weird games where the loser *loses their mind!* Now, Yugi has become *Yu-Gi-Oh!*, the King of Games...and the Shadow Games have begun!

DARK YUGI

武藤遊戯

YUGI MUTOU

The main character. Normally he's a nice guy—even a pushover—until his *other* personality takes over. Afterwards, he doesn't remember what happened.

城之内克也
KATSUYA JONOUCHI

Yugi's classmate, a tough guy who gets in lots of fights. He used to think Yugi was a wimp, but now they are good friends. In the English anime he's known as "Joey Wheeler."

真崎杏子
ANZU MAZAKI

Yugi's classmate and childhood friend. She fell in love with the charismatic voice of Yugi's alter ego, but doesn't know that they're the same person. Her first name means "Peach." In the English anime she's known as "Téa Gardner."

本田ヒロト
HIROTO HONDA

Yugi's classmate, a friend of Jonouchi. In the English anime he's known as "Tristan Taylor."

武藤双六
SUGOROKU MUTOU

Yugi's grandfather, the owner of the Kame ("Turtle") game store, which sells rare and interesting games.

Yu-Gi-Oh!

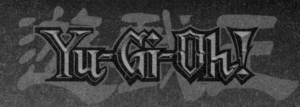

Vol. 2

CONTENTS

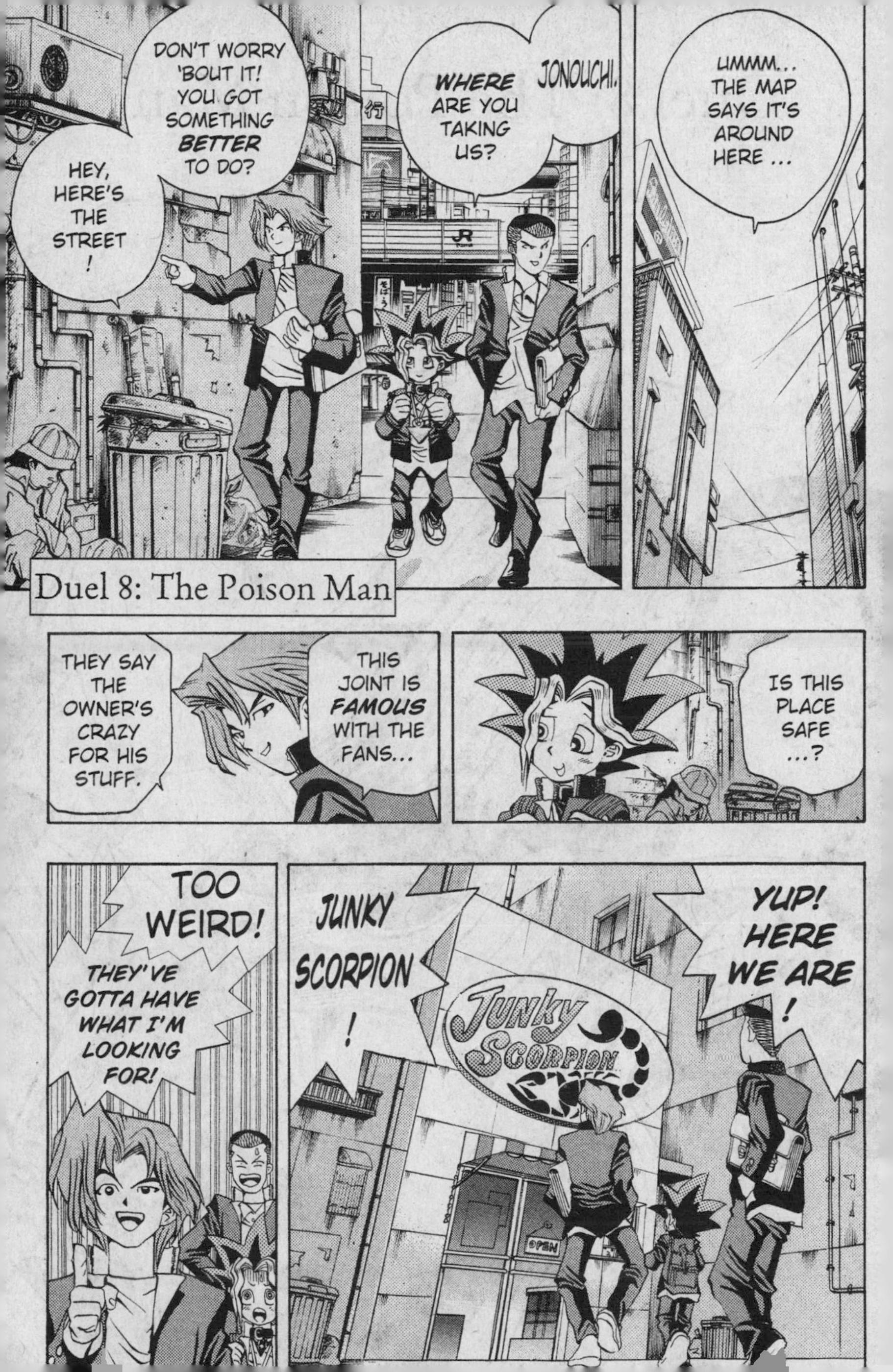
UMMM... THE MAP SAYS IT'S AROUND HERE ...
JONOUCHI.
WHERE ARE YOU TAKING US?
DON'T WORRY 'BOUT IT! YOU GOT SOMETHING BETTER TO DO?
HEY, HERE'S THE STREET !
Duel 8: The Poison Man
IS THIS PLACE SAFE ...?
THIS JOINT IS FAMOUS WITH THE FANS...
THEY SAY THE OWNER'S CRAZY FOR HIS STUFF.
YUP! HERE WE ARE !
JUNKY SCORPION !
Junky Scorpion
OPEN
TOO WEIRD!
THEY'VE GOTTA HAVE WHAT I'M LOOKING FOR!

Duel 8: The Poison Man

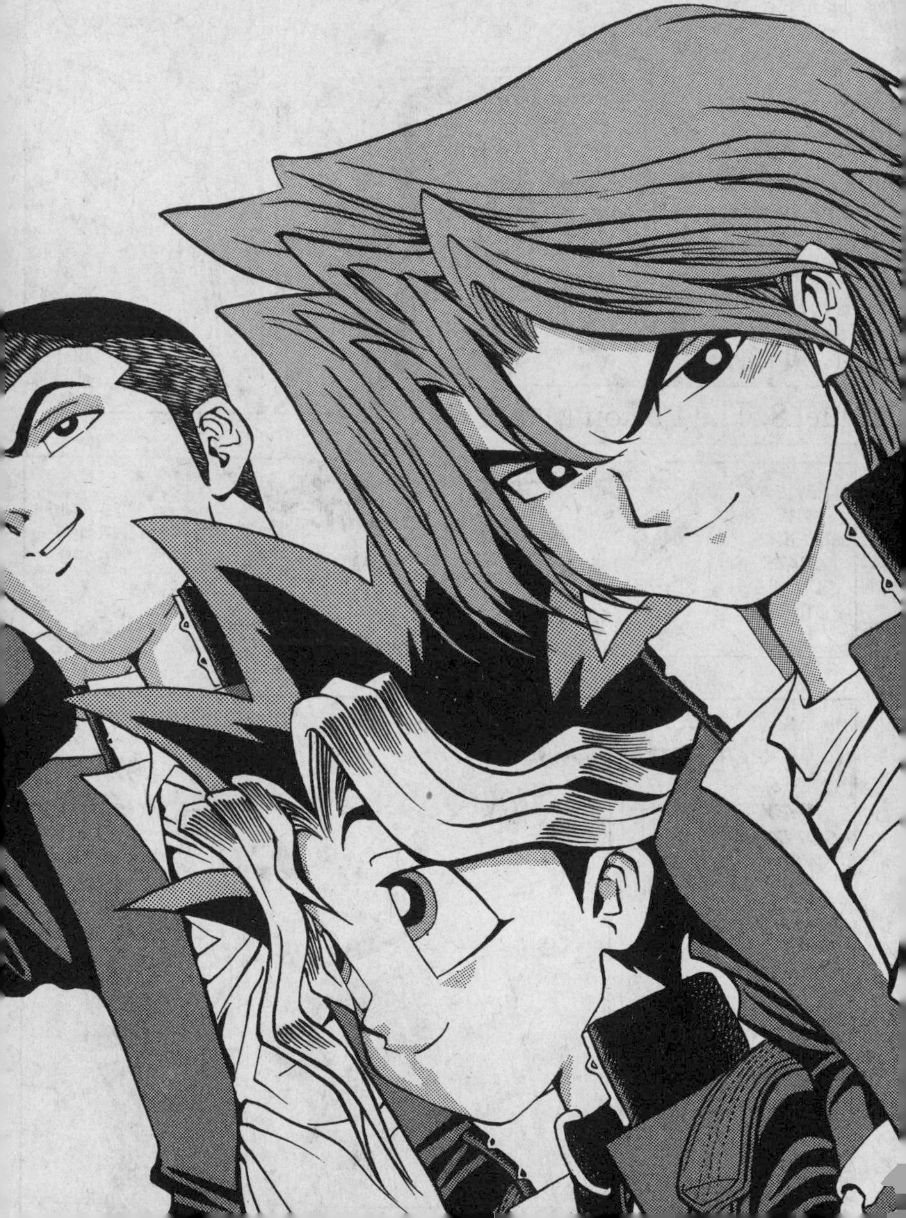

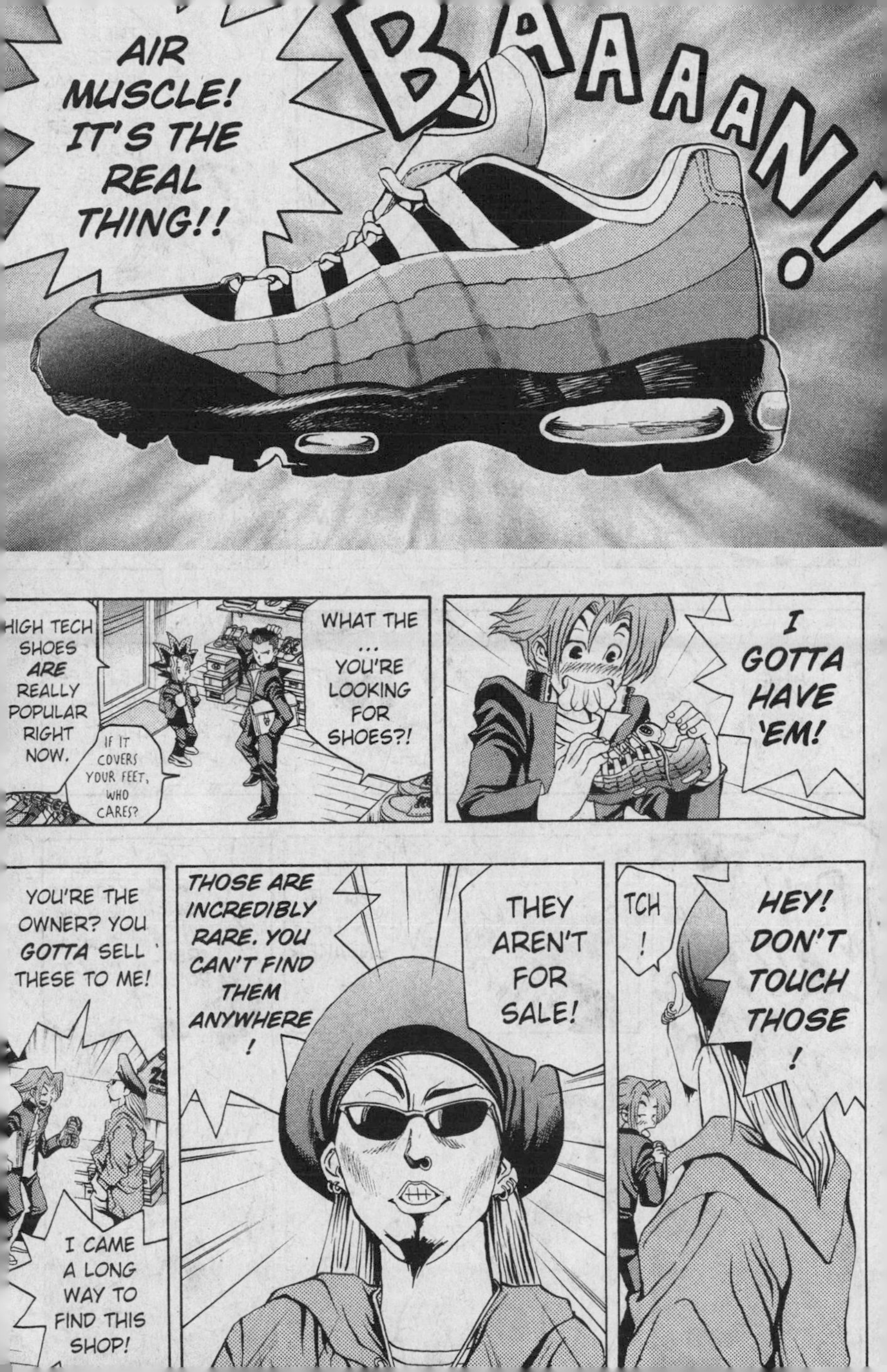
BAAAAN!!
AIR MUSCLE! IT'S THE REAL THING!!
I GOTTA HAVE 'EM!
WHAT THE ... YOU'RE LOOKING FOR SHOES?!
HIGH TECH SHOES ARE REALLY POPULAR RIGHT NOW.
IF IT COVERS YOUR FEET, WHO CARES?
HEY! DON'T TOUCH THOSE!
TCH!
THEY AREN'T FOR SALE!
THOSE ARE INCREDIBLY RARE. YOU CAN'T FIND THEM ANYWHERE!
YOU'RE THE OWNER? YOU GOTTA SELL THESE TO ME!
I CAME A LONG WAY TO FIND THIS SHOP!

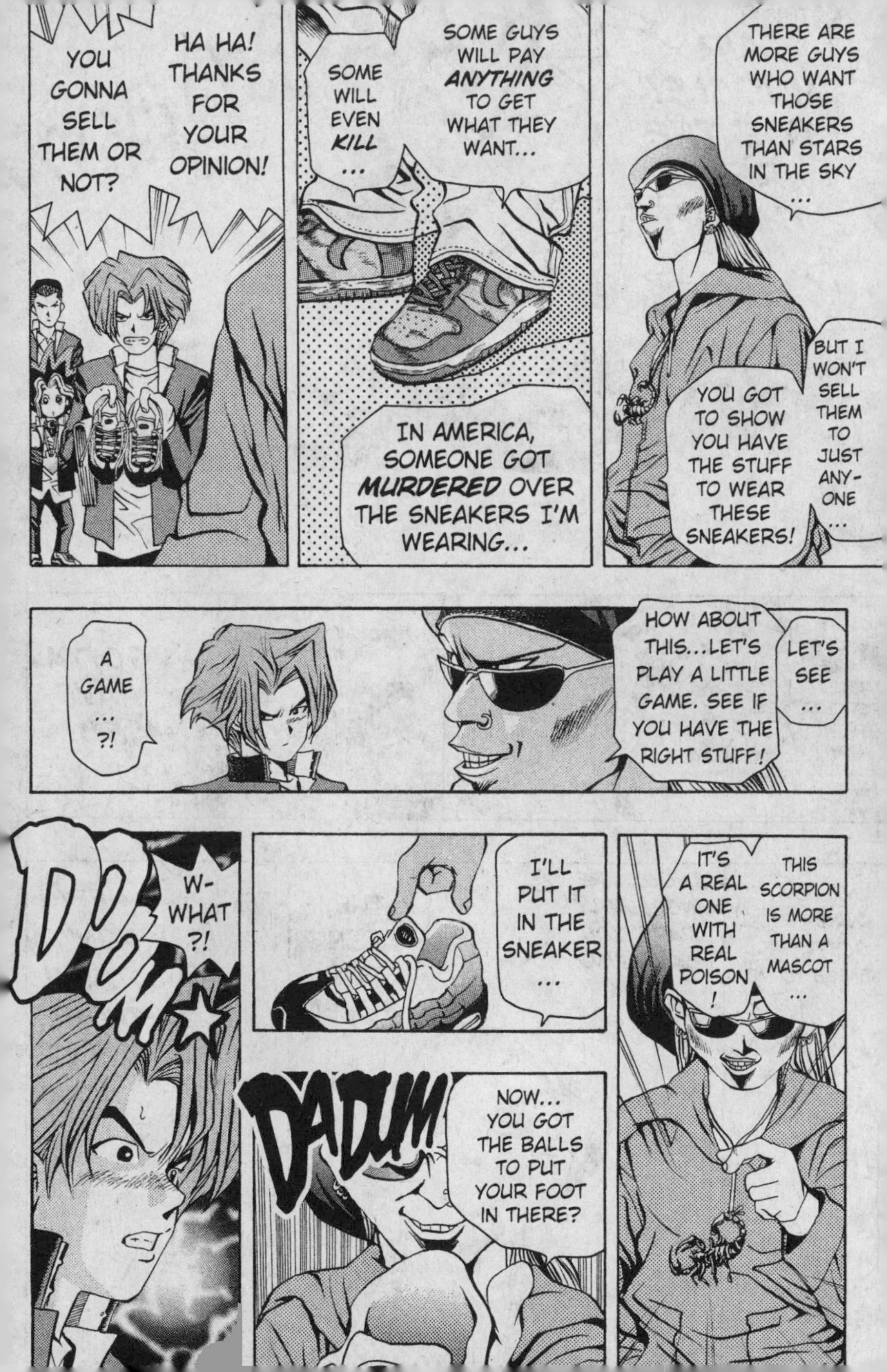
THERE ARE MORE GUYS WHO WANT THOSE SNEAKERS THAN STARS IN THE SKY ...
BUT I WON'T SELL THEM TO JUST ANY-ONE ...
YOU GOT TO SHOW YOU HAVE THE STUFF TO WEAR THESE SNEAKERS!
SOME GUYS WILL PAY ANYTHING TO GET WHAT THEY WANT...
SOME WILL EVEN KILL ...
IN AMERICA, SOMEONE GOT MURDERED OVER THE SNEAKERS I'M WEARING...
HA HA! THANKS FOR YOUR OPINION!
YOU GONNA SELL THEM OR NOT?
LET'S SEE ...
HOW ABOUT THIS...LET'S PLAY A LITTLE GAME. SEE IF YOU HAVE THE RIGHT STUFF!
A GAME ... ?!
THIS SCORPION IS MORE THAN A MASCOT ...
IT'S A REAL ONE WITH REAL POISON!
I'LL PUT IT IN THE SNEAKER ...
NOW... YOU GOT THE BALLS TO PUT YOUR FOOT IN THERE?
DADUM
DOOM
W-WHAT?!

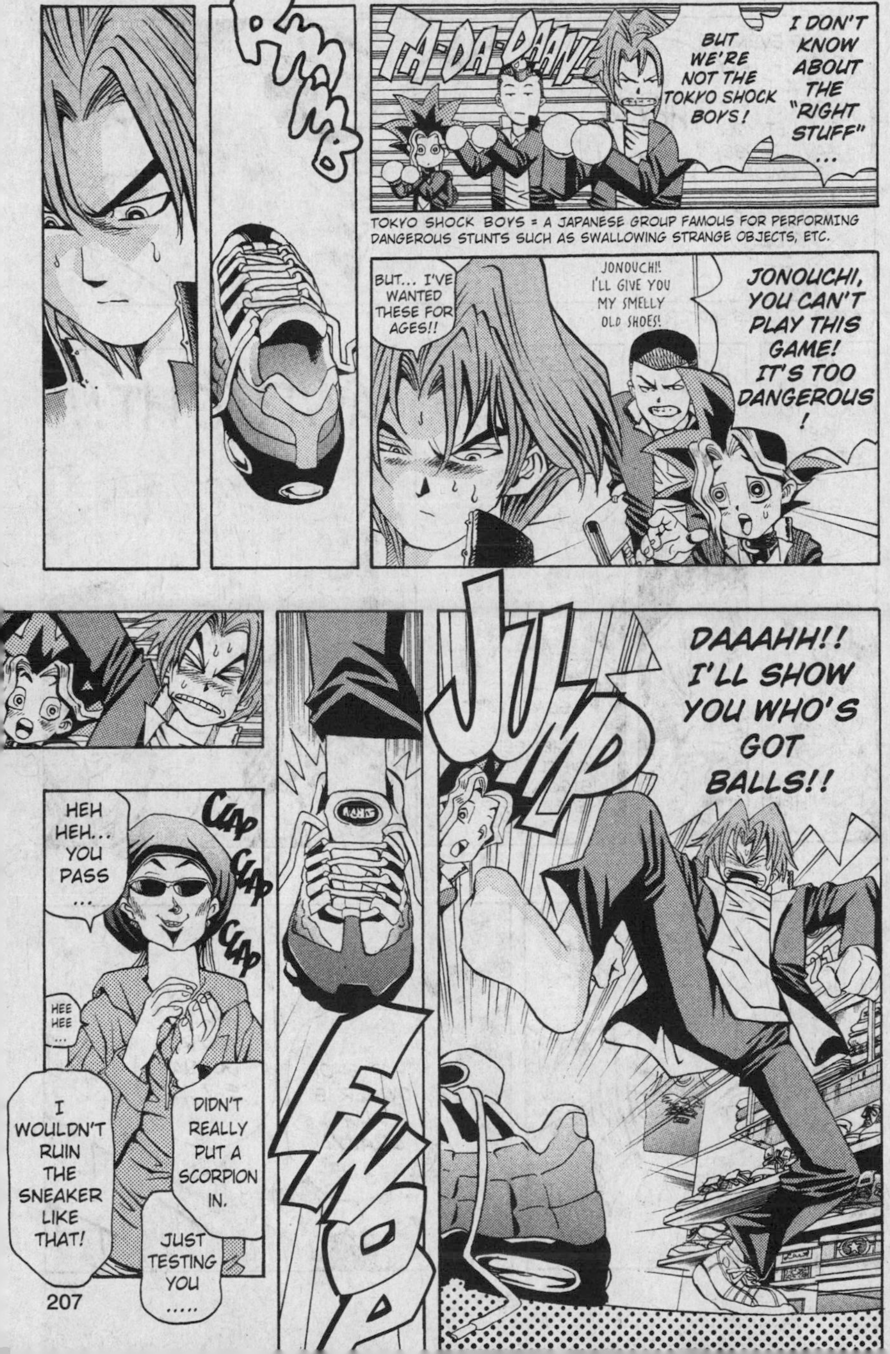
I DON'T KNOW ABOUT THE "RIGHT STUFF" ...
BUT WE'RE NOT THE TOKYO SHOCK BOYS!
TA-DA-DAAN!
TOKYO SHOCK BOYS = A JAPANESE GROUP FAMOUS FOR PERFORMING DANGEROUS STUNTS SUCH AS SWALLOWING STRANGE OBJECTS, ETC.
JONOUCHI, YOU CAN'T PLAY THIS GAME! IT'S TOO DANGEROUS!
JONOUCHI!! I'LL GIVE YOU MY SMELLY OLD SHOES!
BUT... I'VE WANTED THESE FOR AGES!!
DAAAHH!! I'LL SHOW YOU WHO'S GOT BALLS!!
JUMP
CLAP CLAP CLAP
HEH HEH... YOU PASS ...
HEE HEE ...
DIDN'T REALLY PUT A SCORPION IN.
I WOULDN'T RUIN THE SNEAKER LIKE THAT!
JUST TESTING YOU .....

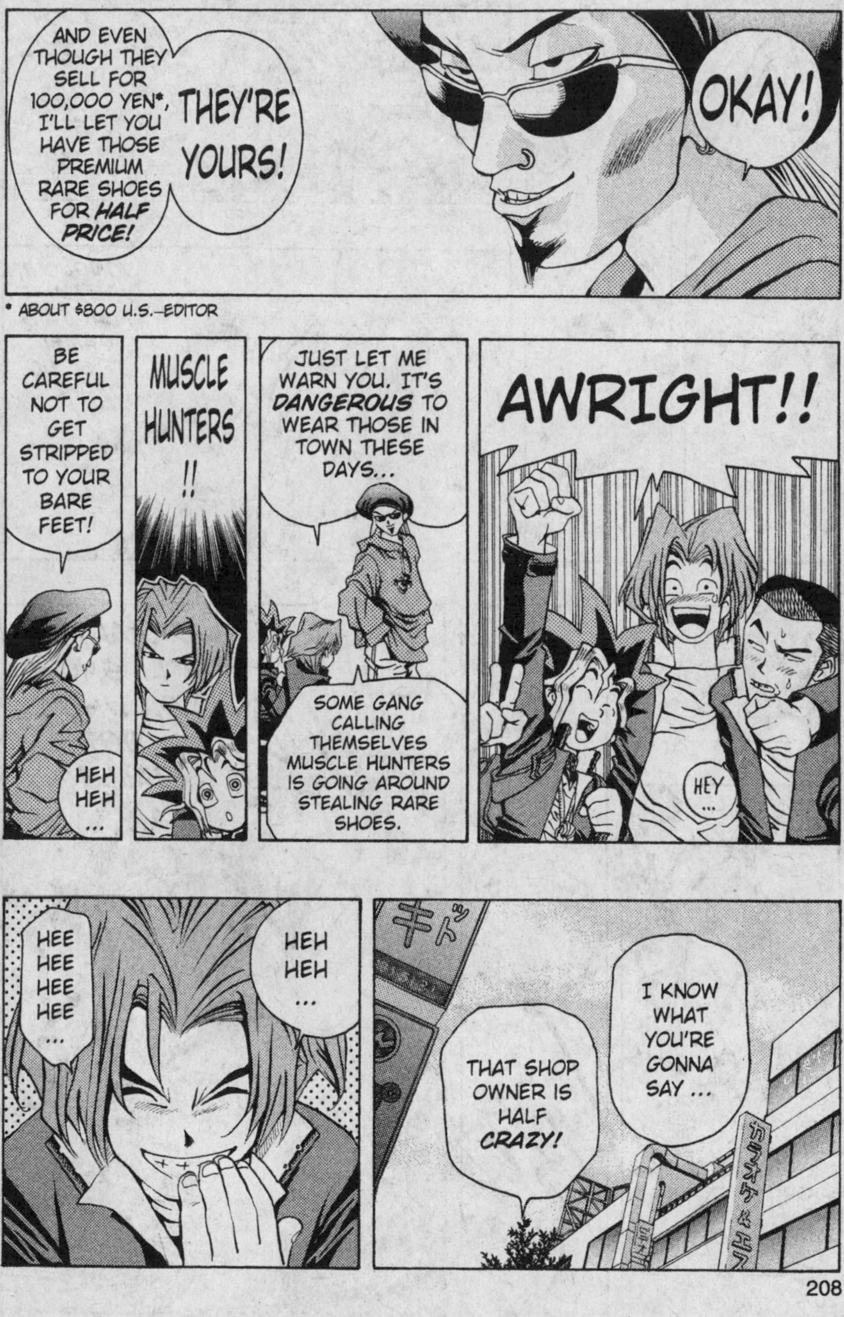
OKAY!
AND EVEN THOUGH THEY SELL FOR 100,000 YEN*, I'LL LET YOU HAVE THOSE PREMIUM RARE SHOES FOR HALF PRICE!
THEY'RE YOURS!
AWRIGHT!!
HEY ...
JUST LET ME WARN YOU. IT'S DANGEROUS TO WEAR THOSE IN TOWN THESE DAYS...
SOME GANG CALLING THEMSELVES MUSCLE HUNTERS IS GOING AROUND STEALING RARE SHOES.
MUSCLE HUNTERS !!
BE CAREFUL NOT TO GET STRIPPED TO YOUR BARE FEET!
HEH HEH ...
I KNOW WHAT YOU'RE GONNA SAY ...
THAT SHOP OWNER IS HALF CRAZY!
HEH HEH ...
HEE HEE HEE HEE ...

* ABOUT $800 U.S.—EDITOR

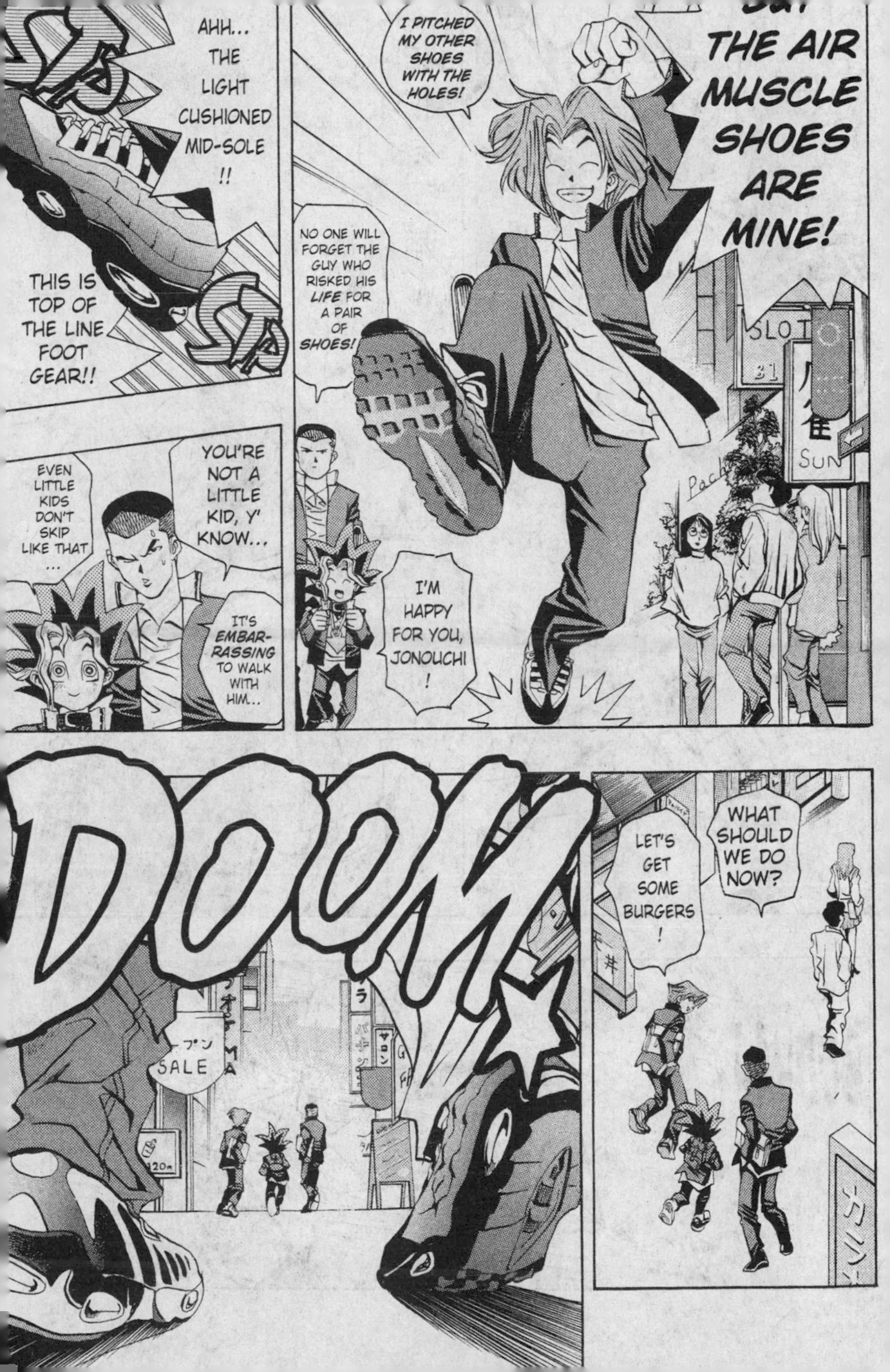
THE AIR MUSCLE SHOES ARE MINE!
I PITCHED MY OTHER SHOES WITH THE HOLES!
NO ONE WILL FORGET THE GUY WHO RISKED HIS LIFE FOR A PAIR OF SHOES!
I'M HAPPY FOR YOU, JONOUCHI!
AHH... THE LIGHT CUSHIONED MID-SOLE !!
THIS IS TOP OF THE LINE FOOT GEAR!!
YOU'RE NOT A LITTLE KID, Y' KNOW...
EVEN LITTLE KIDS DON'T SKIP LIKE THAT ...
IT'S EMBARRASSING TO WALK WITH HIM...
WHAT SHOULD WE DO NOW?
LET'S GET SOME BURGERS!
DOOM
SALE

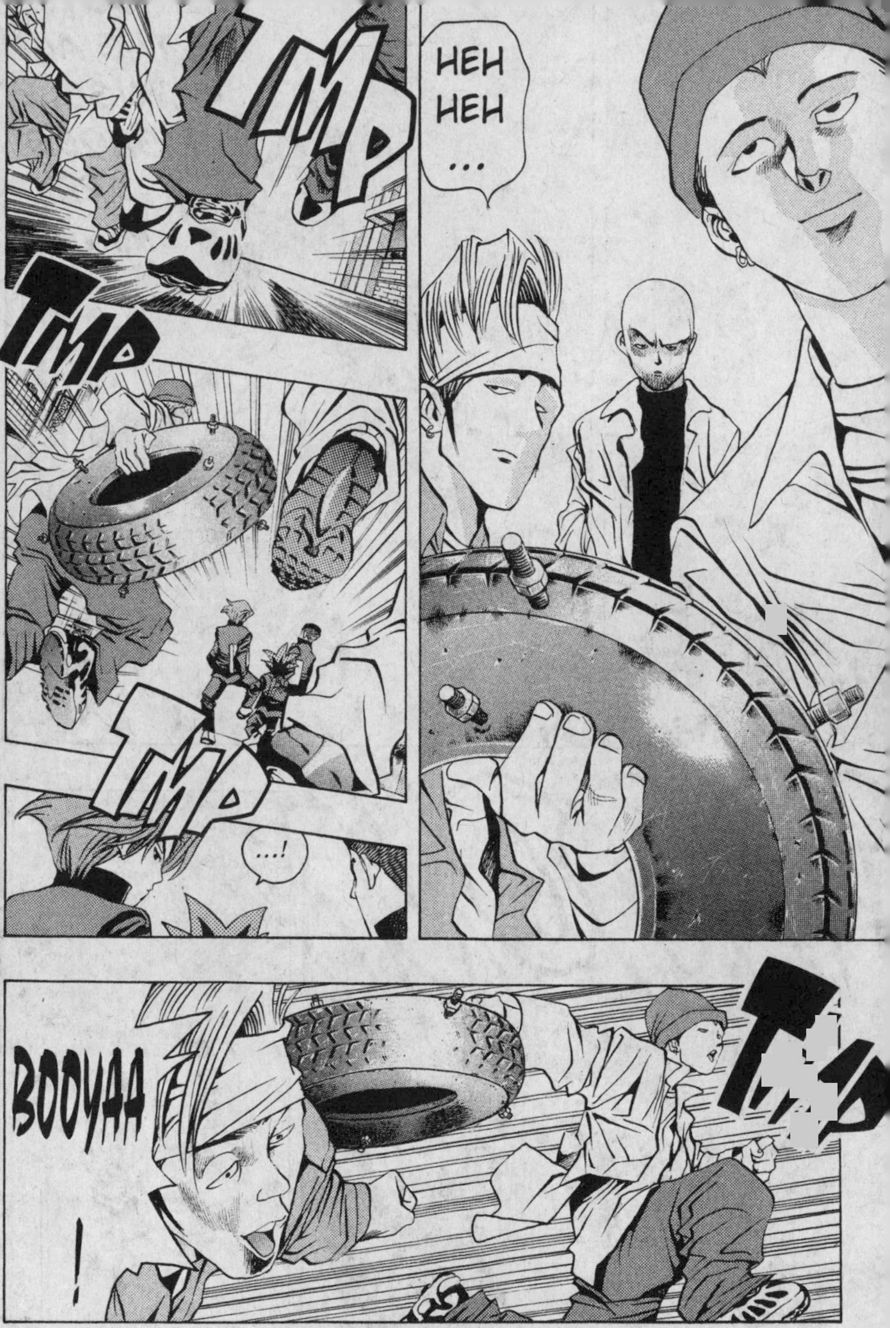
HEH HEH ...
LMP
TMP
TMP
...!
TMP
BOOYAA !

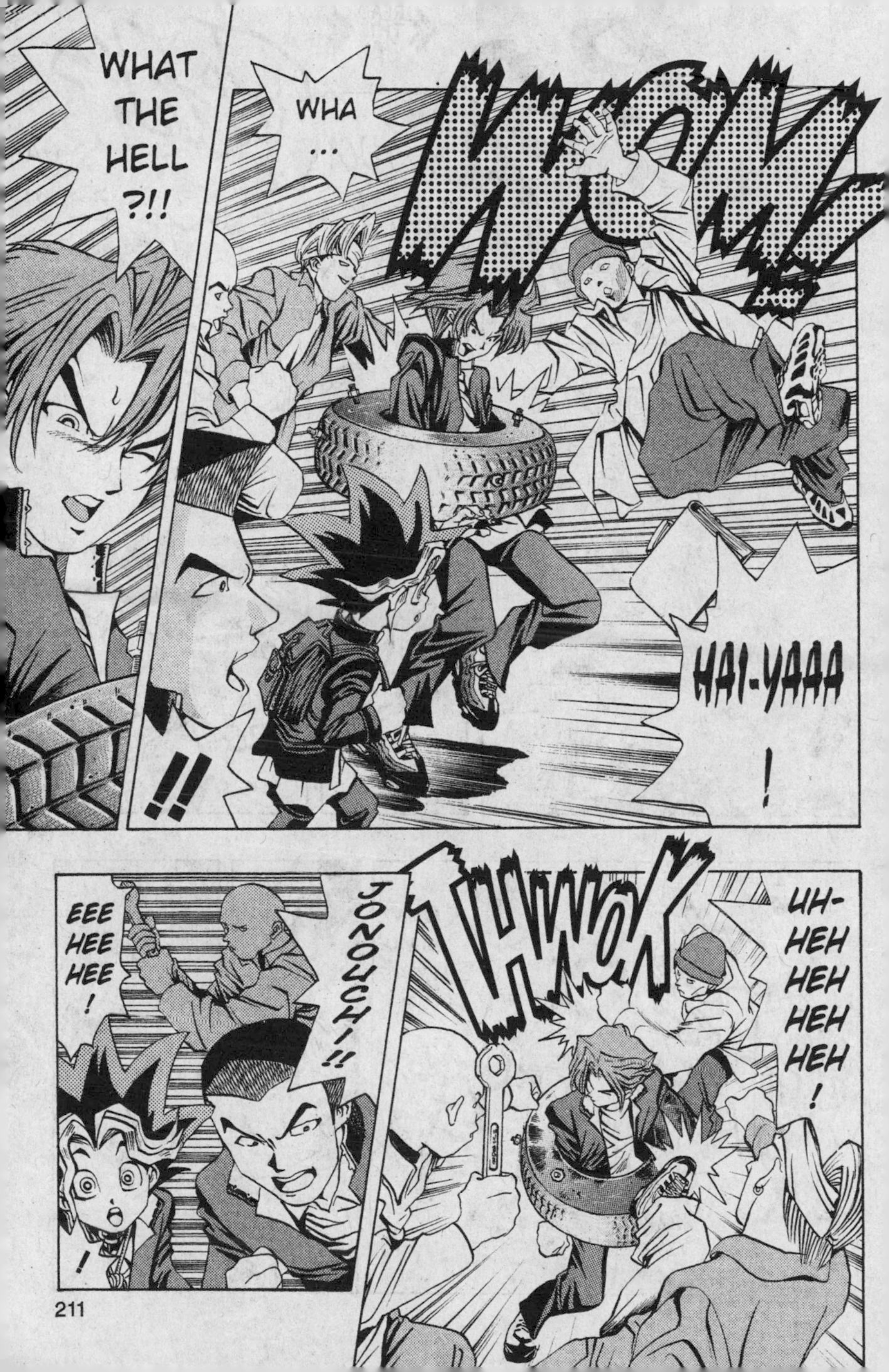
WHOMP
WHA ...
HAI-YAAA !
!!
WHAT THE HELL ?!!
THWOK
UH-HEH HEH HEH HEH !
JONOUCHI !!
EEE HEE HEE !
!

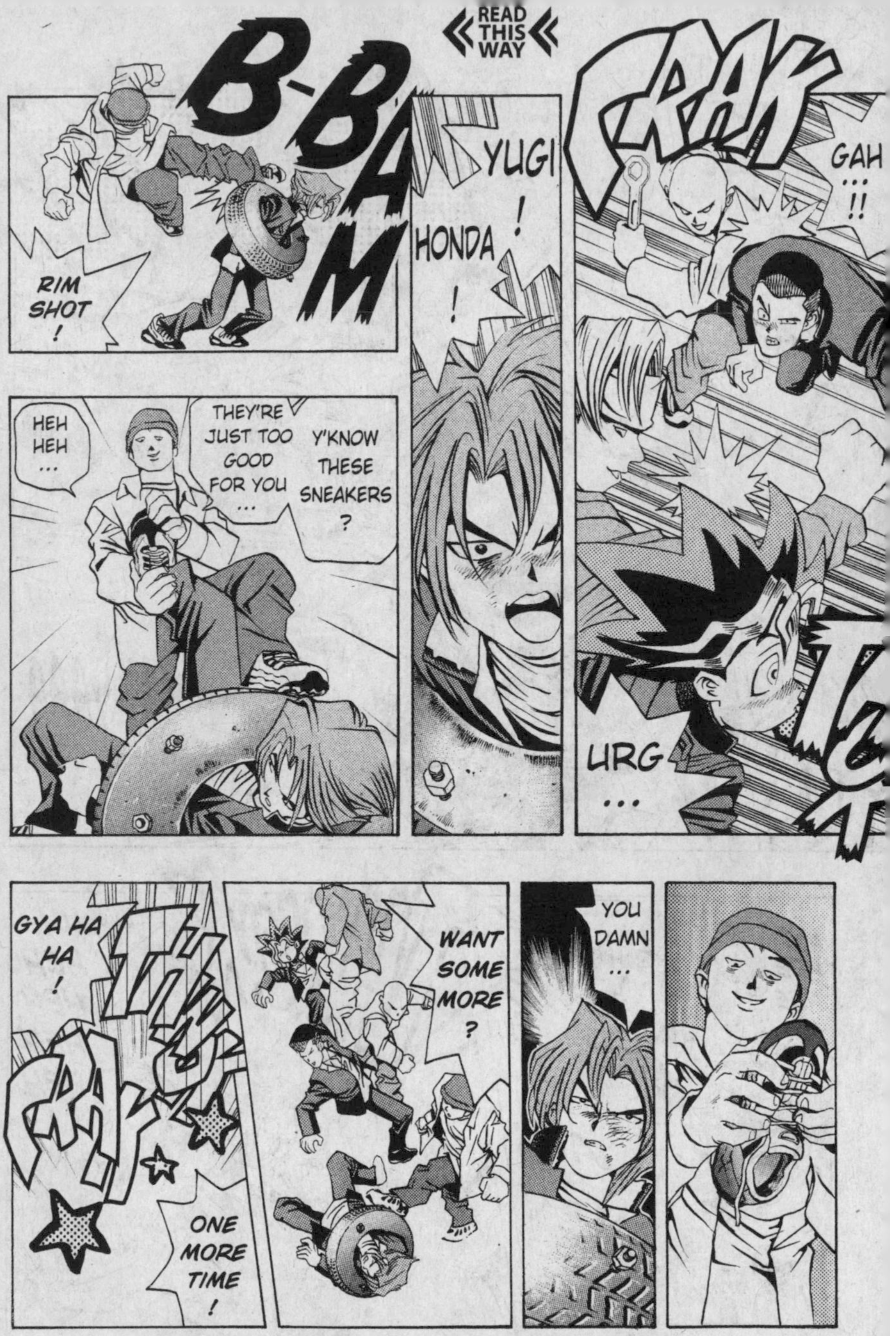
READ THIS WAY
CRAK
GAH...!!
URG...
YUGI!
HONDA!
B-BAM
RIM SHOT!
Y'KNOW THESE SNEAKERS?
THEY'RE JUST TOO GOOD FOR YOU...
HEH HEH...
YOU DAMN...
WANT SOME MORE?
ONE MORE TIME!
GYA HA HA!

READ THIS WAY

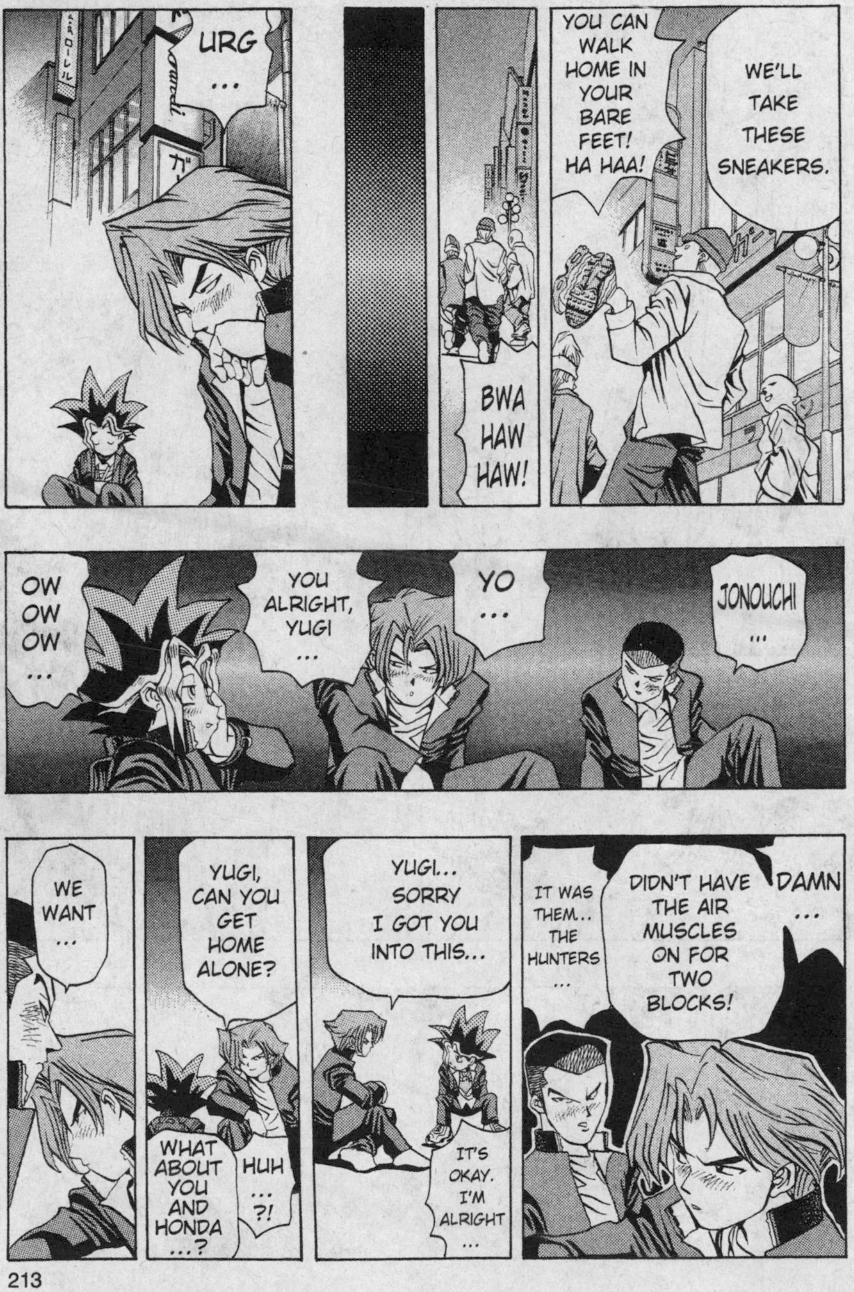
WE'LL TAKE THESE SNEAKERS.
YOU CAN WALK HOME IN YOUR BARE FEET! HA HAA!
BWA HAW HAW!
URG ...
JONOUCHI ...
YO ...
YOU ALRIGHT, YUGI ...
OW OW OW ...
DAMN ...
DIDN'T HAVE THE AIR MUSCLES ON FOR TWO BLOCKS!
IT WAS THEM.. THE HUNTERS ...
YUGI... SORRY I GOT YOU INTO THIS...
IT'S OKAY. I'M ALRIGHT ...
YUGI, CAN YOU GET HOME ALONE?
HUH ...?!
WHAT ABOUT YOU AND HONDA ...?
WE WANT ...

READ THIS WAY

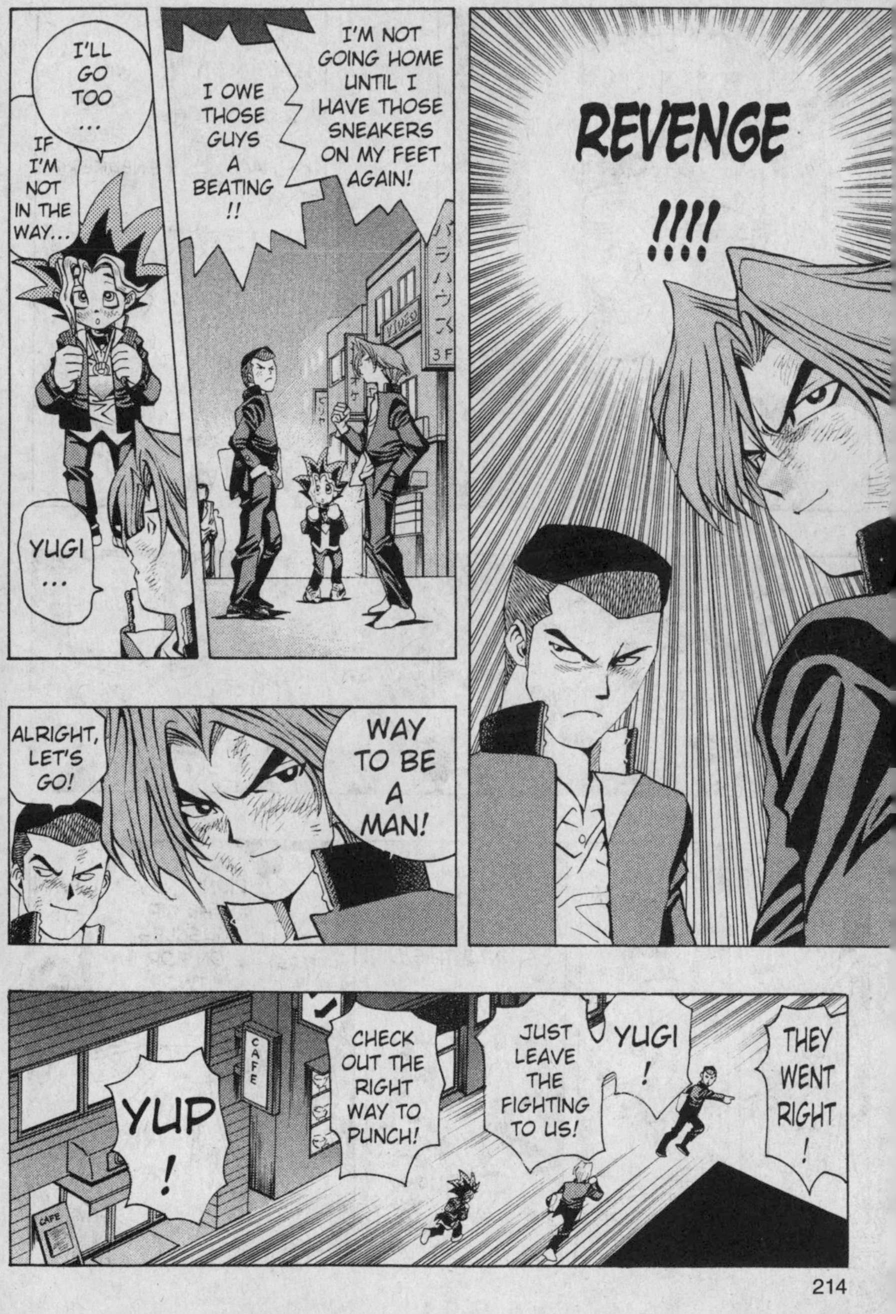
REVENGE !!!!
I'M NOT GOING HOME UNTIL I HAVE THOSE SNEAKERS ON MY FEET AGAIN!
I OWE THOSE GUYS A BEATING !!
I'LL GO TOO ...
IF I'M NOT IN THE WAY...
YUGI ...
WAY TO BE A MAN!
ALRIGHT, LET'S GO!
THEY WENT RIGHT !
YUGI !
JUST LEAVE THE FIGHTING TO US!
CHECK OUT THE RIGHT WAY TO PUNCH!
YUP !

READ THIS WAY

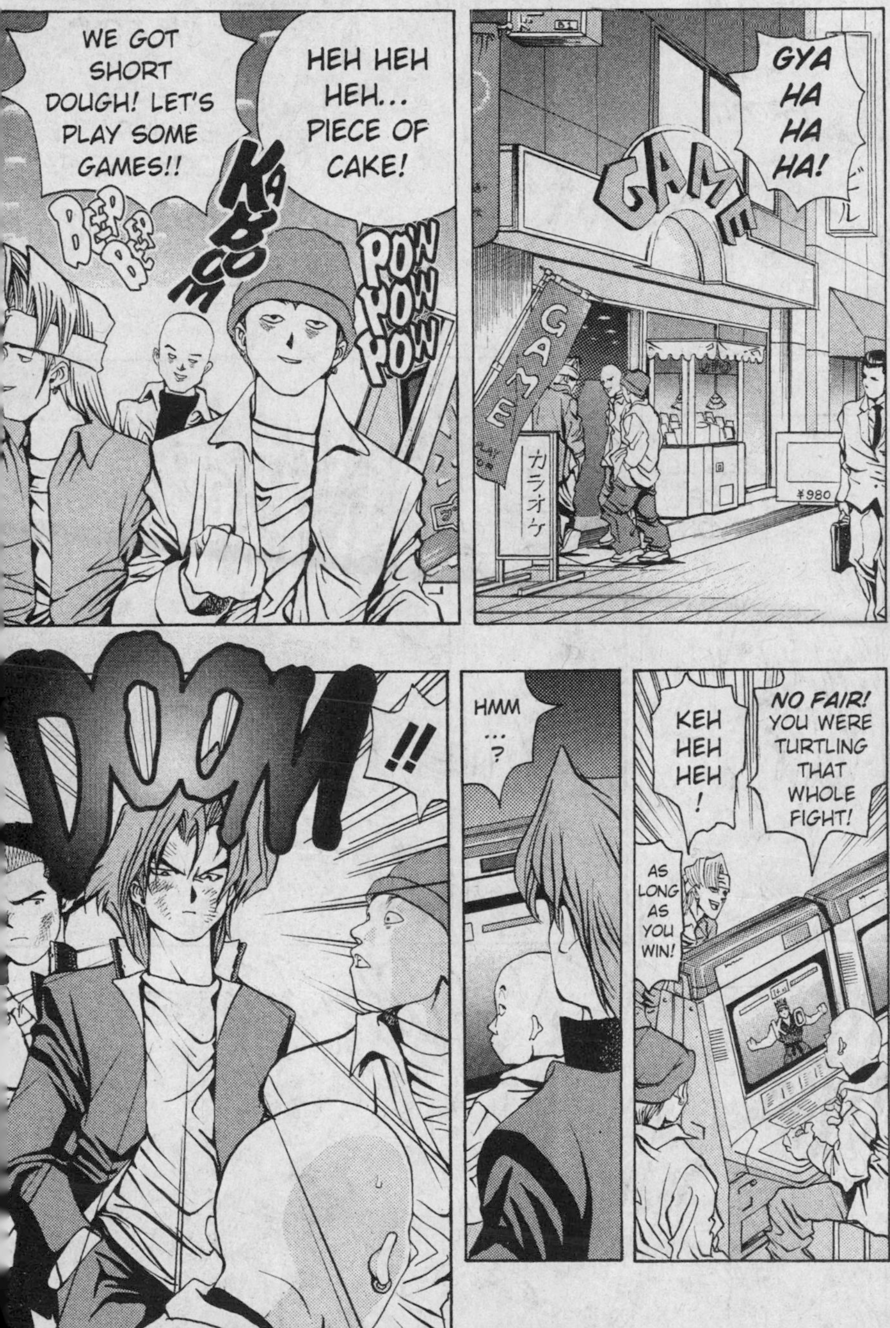
GYA HA HA HA!
GAME
GAME
カラオケ
¥980
HEH HEH HEH... PIECE OF CAKE!
WE GOT SHORT DOUGH! LET'S PLAY SOME GAMES!!
POW POW POW
KABOOM
BEEP BEEP
NO FAIR! YOU WERE TURTLING THAT WHOLE FIGHT!
KEH HEH HEH!
AS LONG AS YOU WIN!
HMM ...?
DOOM!!

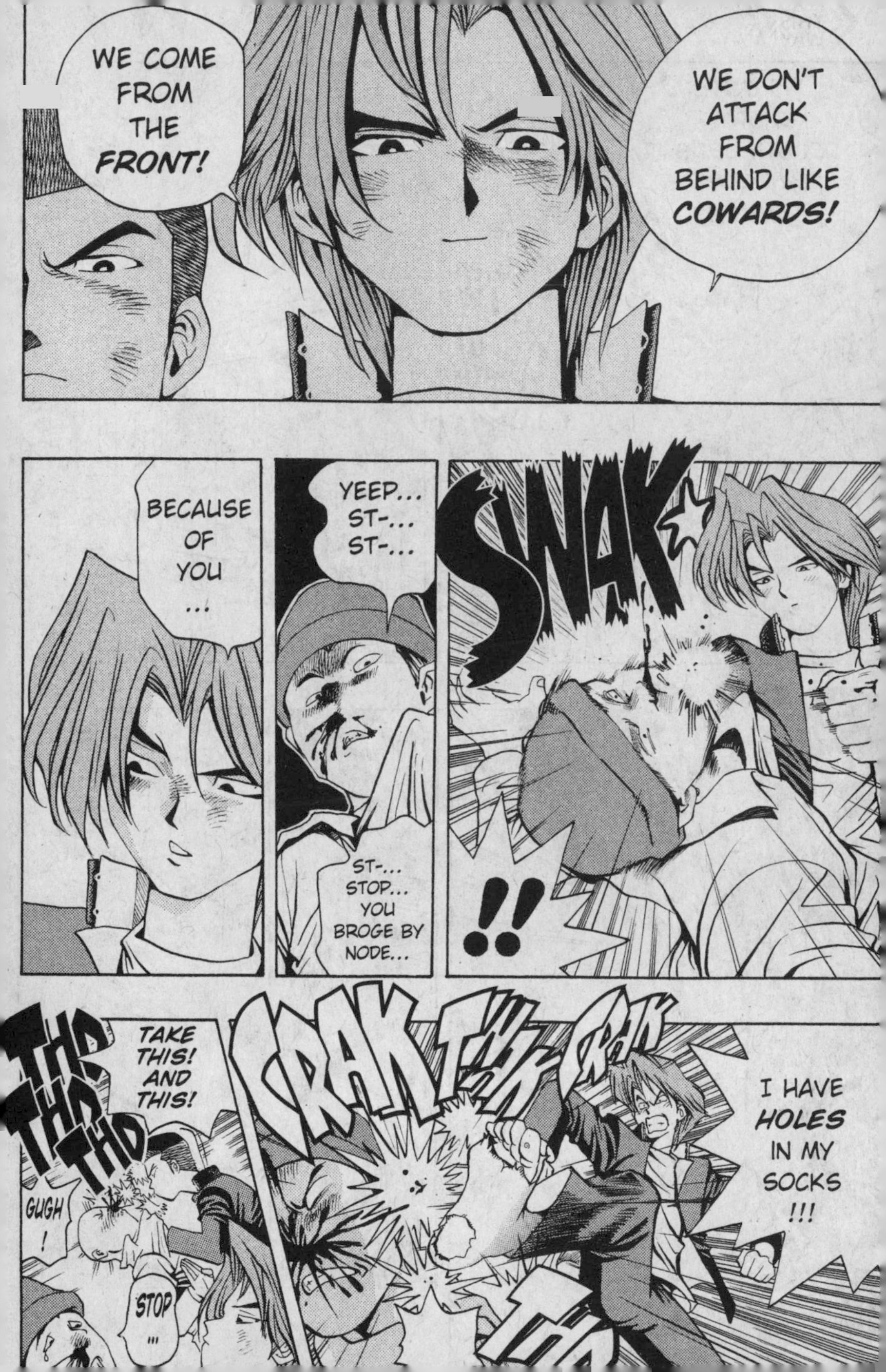
WE DON'T ATTACK FROM BEHIND LIKE *COWARDS!*
WE COME FROM THE *FRONT!*
SWAK
!!
YEEP... ST-... ST-...
ST-... STOP... YOU BROGE BY NODE...
BECAUSE OF YOU ...
I HAVE *HOLES* IN MY SOCKS !!!
CRAK THK CRAK
TAKE THIS! AND THIS!
THD THD THD
GUGH !
STOP ...

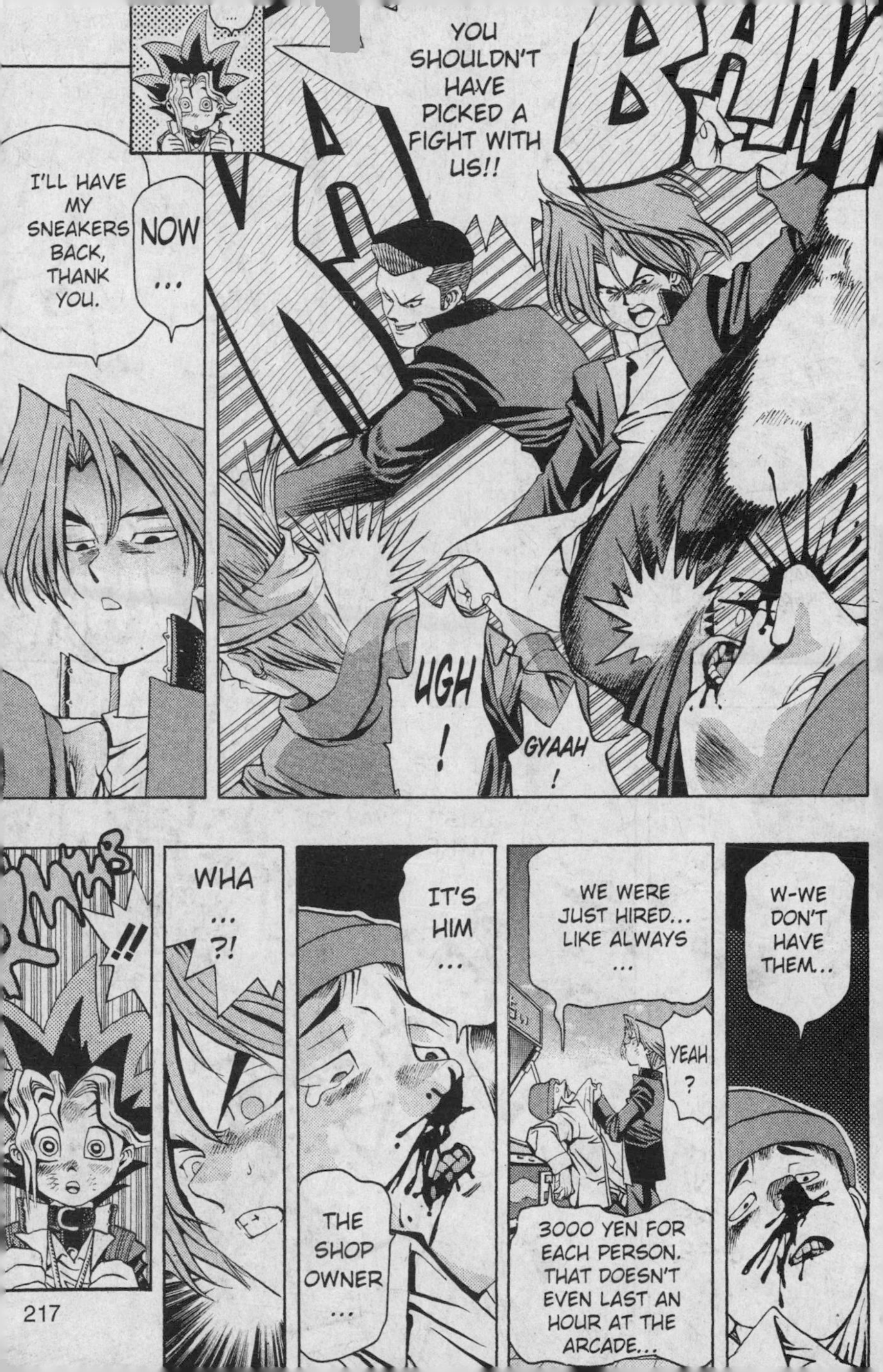
BAM
YOU SHOULDN'T HAVE PICKED A FIGHT WITH US!!
UGH!
GYAAH!
...
NOW...
I'LL HAVE MY SNEAKERS BACK, THANK YOU.
W-WE DON'T HAVE THEM...
WE WERE JUST HIRED... LIKE ALWAYS...
YEAH?
3000 YEN FOR EACH PERSON. THAT DOESN'T EVEN LAST AN HOUR AT THE ARCADE...
IT'S HIM...
THE SHOP OWNER...
WHA...?!
!!

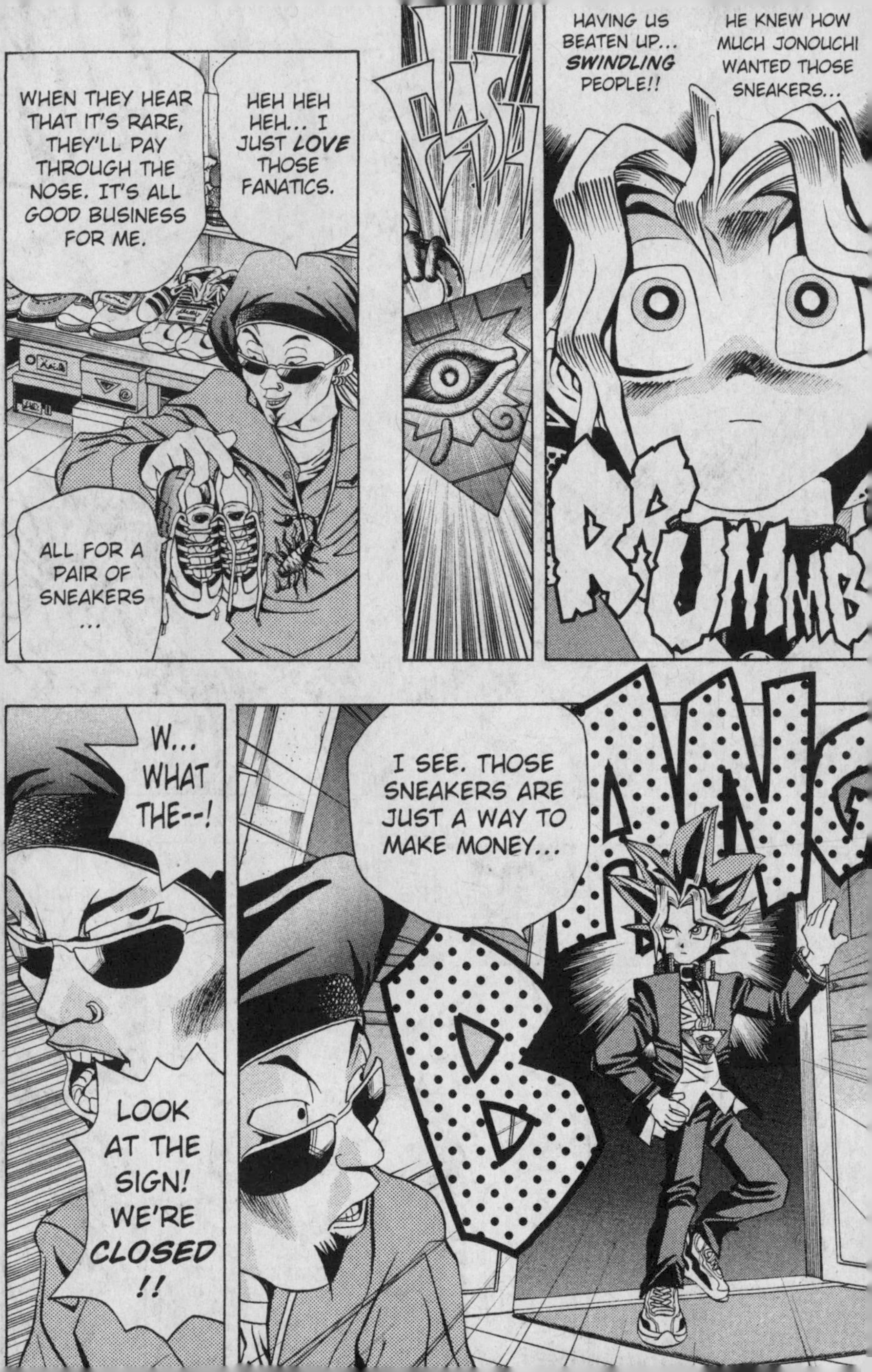
HE KNEW HOW MUCH JONOUCHI WANTED THOSE SNEAKERS...
HAVING US BEATEN UP... SWINDLING PEOPLE!!
HEH HEH HEH... I JUST LOVE THOSE FANATICS.
WHEN THEY HEAR THAT IT'S RARE, THEY'LL PAY THROUGH THE NOSE. IT'S ALL GOOD BUSINESS FOR ME.
ALL FOR A PAIR OF SNEAKERS ...
I SEE. THOSE SNEAKERS ARE JUST A WAY TO MAKE MONEY...
W... WHAT THE--!
LOOK AT THE SIGN! WE'RE CLOSED !!

THIS WAY

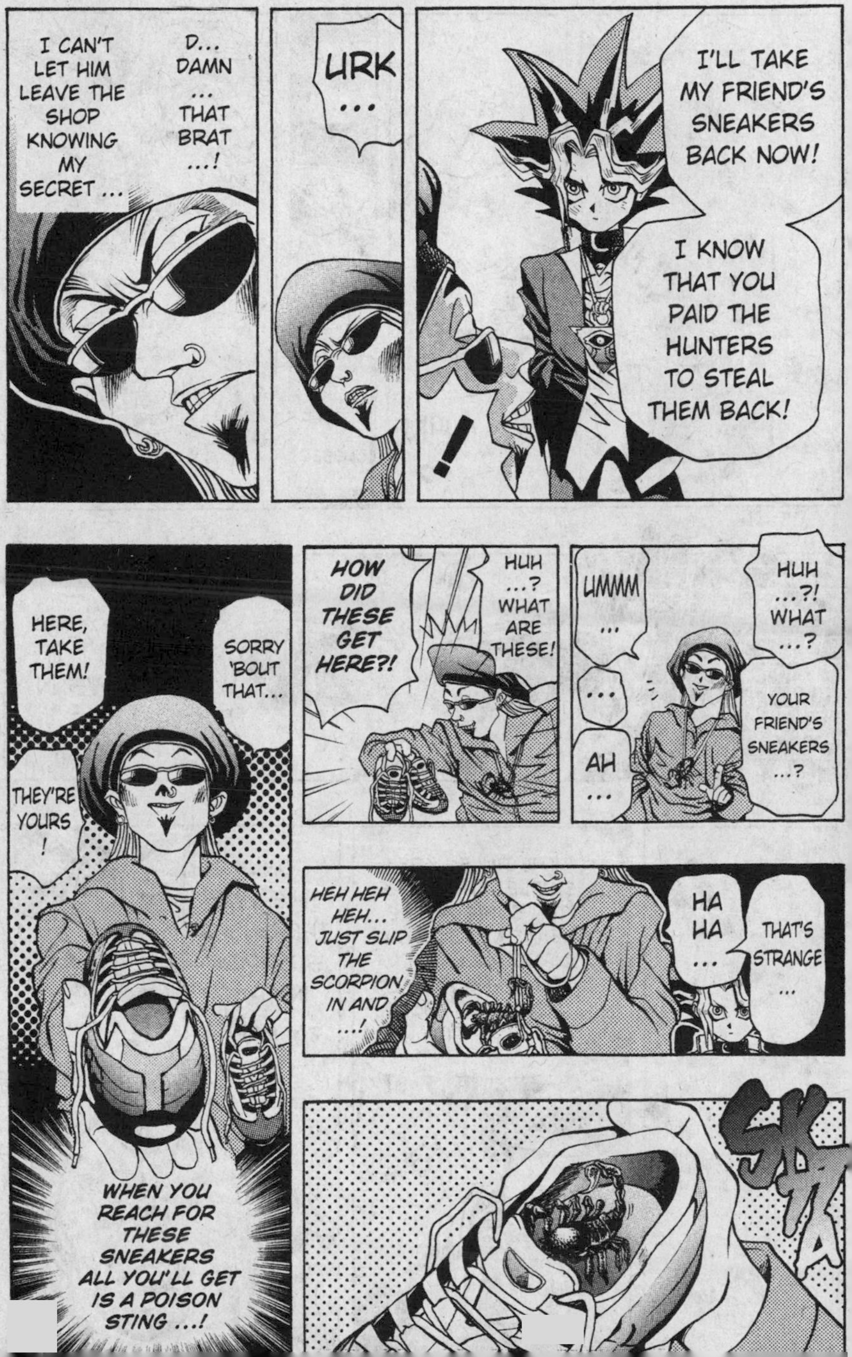
I'LL TAKE MY FRIEND'S SNEAKERS BACK NOW!
I KNOW THAT YOU PAID THE HUNTERS TO STEAL THEM BACK!
!
URK ...
D... DAMN ... THAT BRAT ...!
I CAN'T LET HIM LEAVE THE SHOP KNOWING MY SECRET ...
HUH ...?! WHAT ...?
UMMM ...
YOUR FRIEND'S SNEAKERS ...?
...
AH ...
HUH ...? WHAT ARE THESE!
HOW DID THESE GET HERE?!
THAT'S STRANGE ...
HA HA ...
HEH HEH HEH... JUST SLIP THE SCORPION IN AND ...!
SORRY 'BOUT THAT...
HERE, TAKE THEM!
THEY'RE YOURS!
WHEN YOU REACH FOR THESE SNEAKERS ALL YOU'LL GET IS A POISON STING ...!

THIS WAY

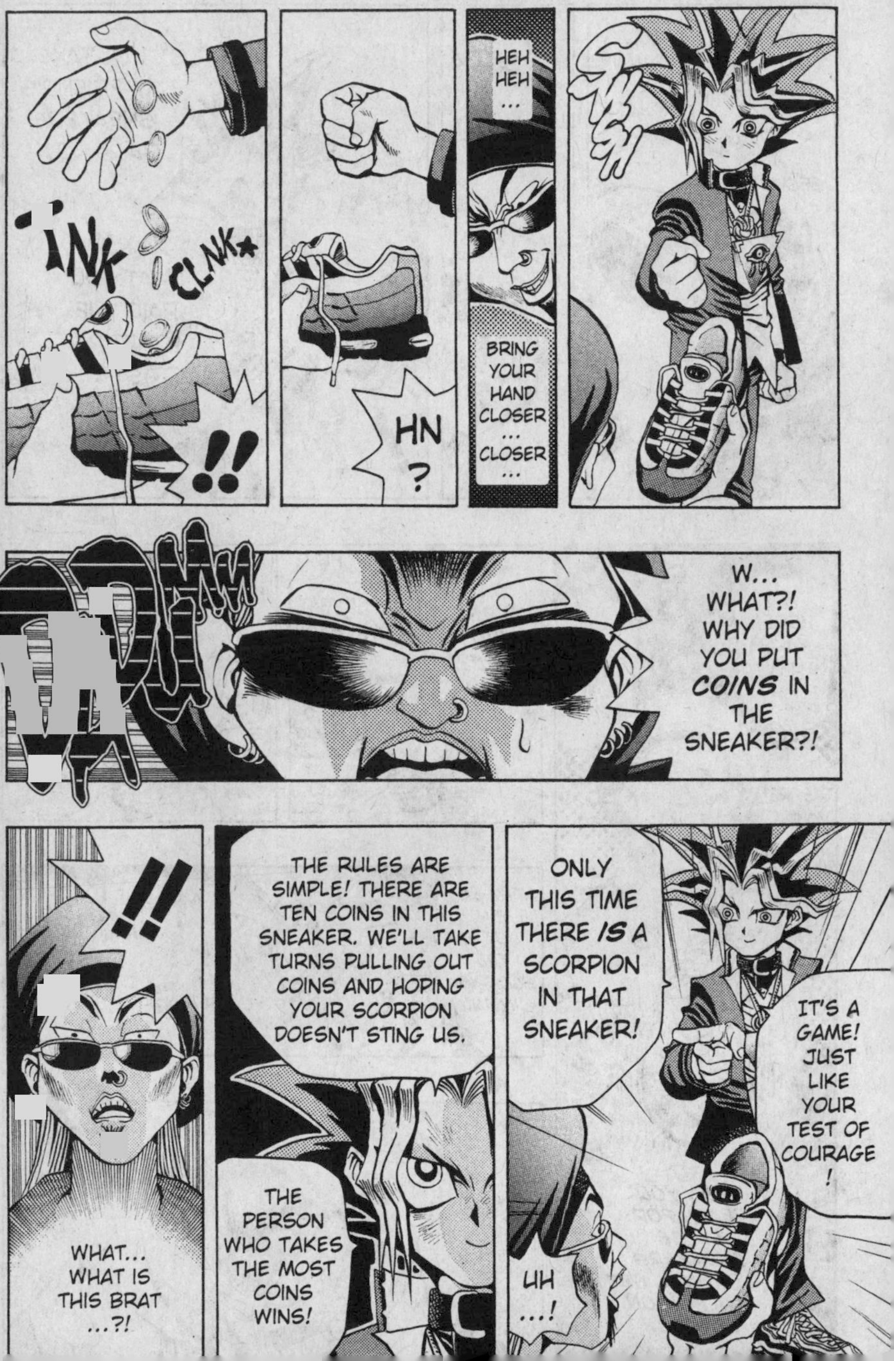
HEH HEH ...
BRING YOUR HAND CLOSER ... CLOSER ...
HN ?
INK
CLNK
!!
W... WHAT?! WHY DID YOU PUT *COINS* IN THE SNEAKER?!
ONLY THIS TIME THERE *IS* A SCORPION IN THAT SNEAKER!
IT'S A GAME! JUST LIKE YOUR TEST OF COURAGE!
UH ...!
THE RULES ARE SIMPLE! THERE ARE TEN COINS IN THIS SNEAKER. WE'LL TAKE TURNS PULLING OUT COINS AND HOPING YOUR SCORPION DOESN'T STING US.
THE PERSON WHO TAKES THE MOST COINS WINS!
!!
WHAT... WHAT IS THIS BRAT ...?!

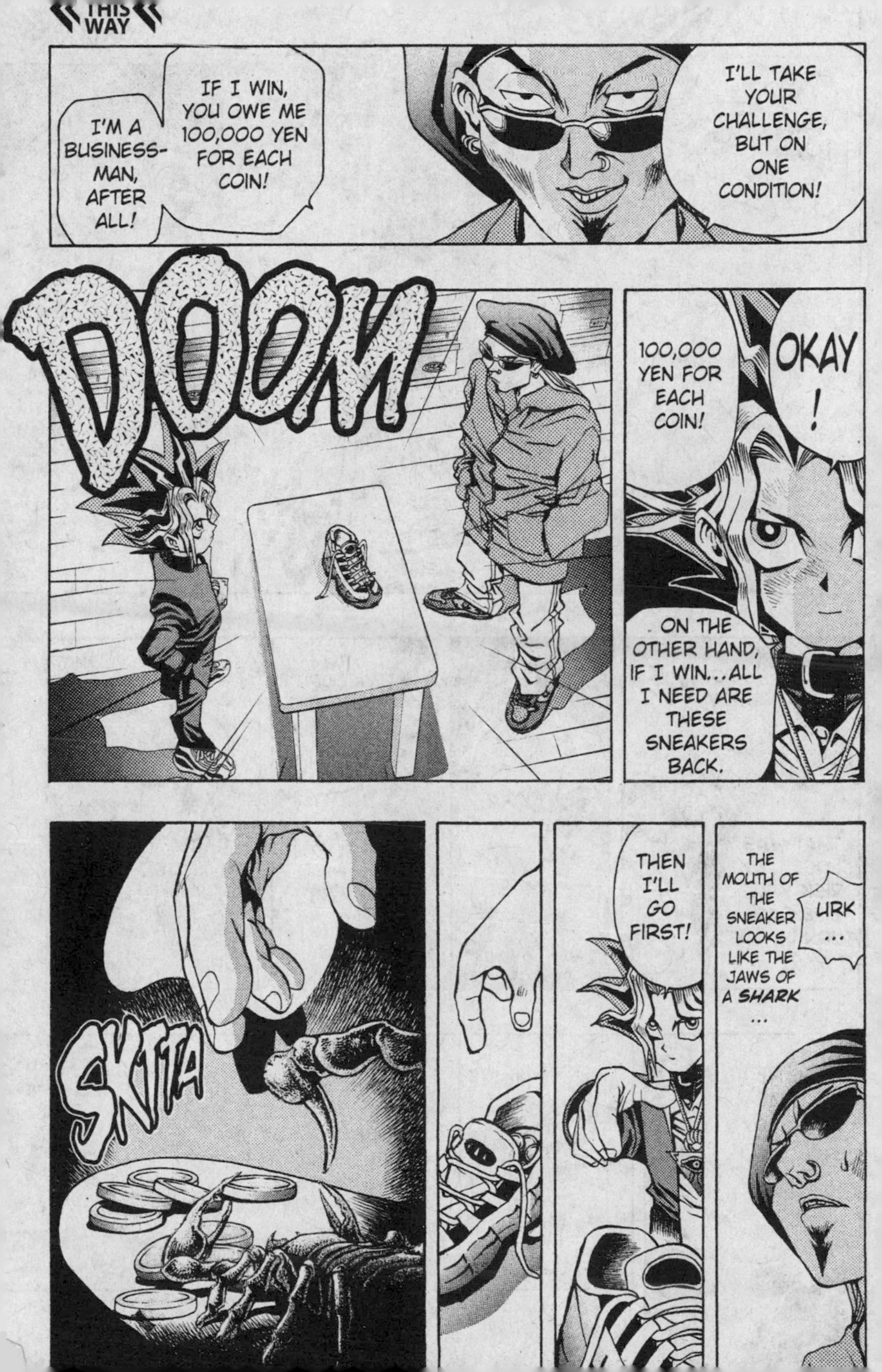
THIS WAY
I'LL TAKE YOUR CHALLENGE, BUT ON ONE CONDITION!
IF I WIN, YOU OWE ME 100,000 YEN FOR EACH COIN!
I'M A BUSINESS-MAN, AFTER ALL!
OKAY!
100,000 YEN FOR EACH COIN!
...ON THE OTHER HAND, IF I WIN...ALL I NEED ARE THESE SNEAKERS BACK.
DOOM
URK...
THE MOUTH OF THE SNEAKER LOOKS LIKE THE JAWS OF A ***SHARK***...
THEN I'LL GO FIRST!
SKITTA

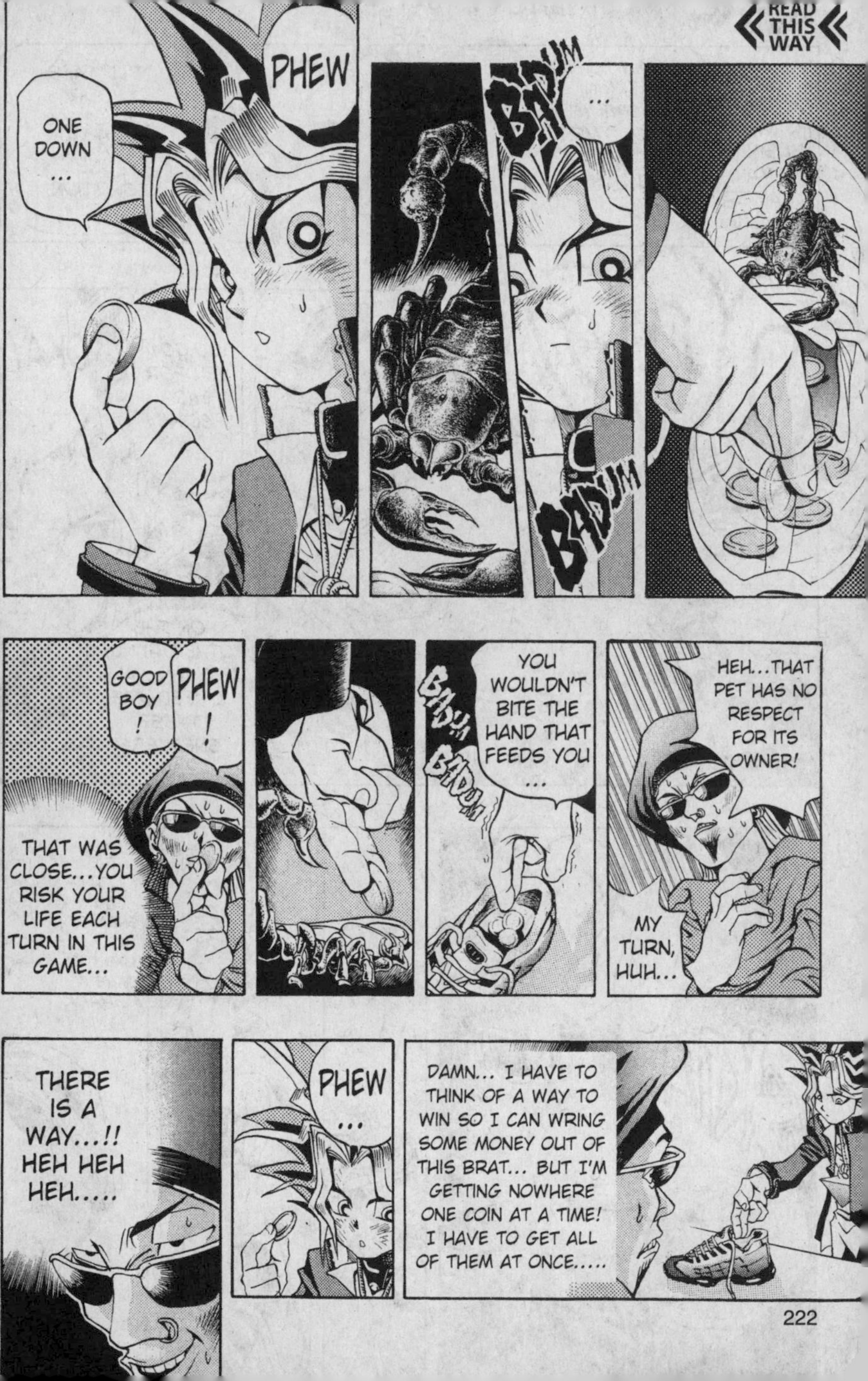
BADUM
...
BADUM
BADUM
PHEW
ONE DOWN ...
HEH...THAT PET HAS NO RESPECT FOR ITS OWNER!
MY TURN, HUH...
YOU WOULDN'T BITE THE HAND THAT FEEDS YOU ...
BADUM
BADUM
PHEW !
GOOD BOY !
THAT WAS CLOSE...YOU RISK YOUR LIFE EACH TURN IN THIS GAME...
DAMN... I HAVE TO THINK OF A WAY TO WIN SO I CAN WRING SOME MONEY OUT OF THIS BRAT... BUT I'M GETTING NOWHERE ONE COIN AT A TIME! I HAVE TO GET ALL OF THEM AT ONCE.....
PHEW ...
THERE IS A WAY...!! HEH HEH HEH.....

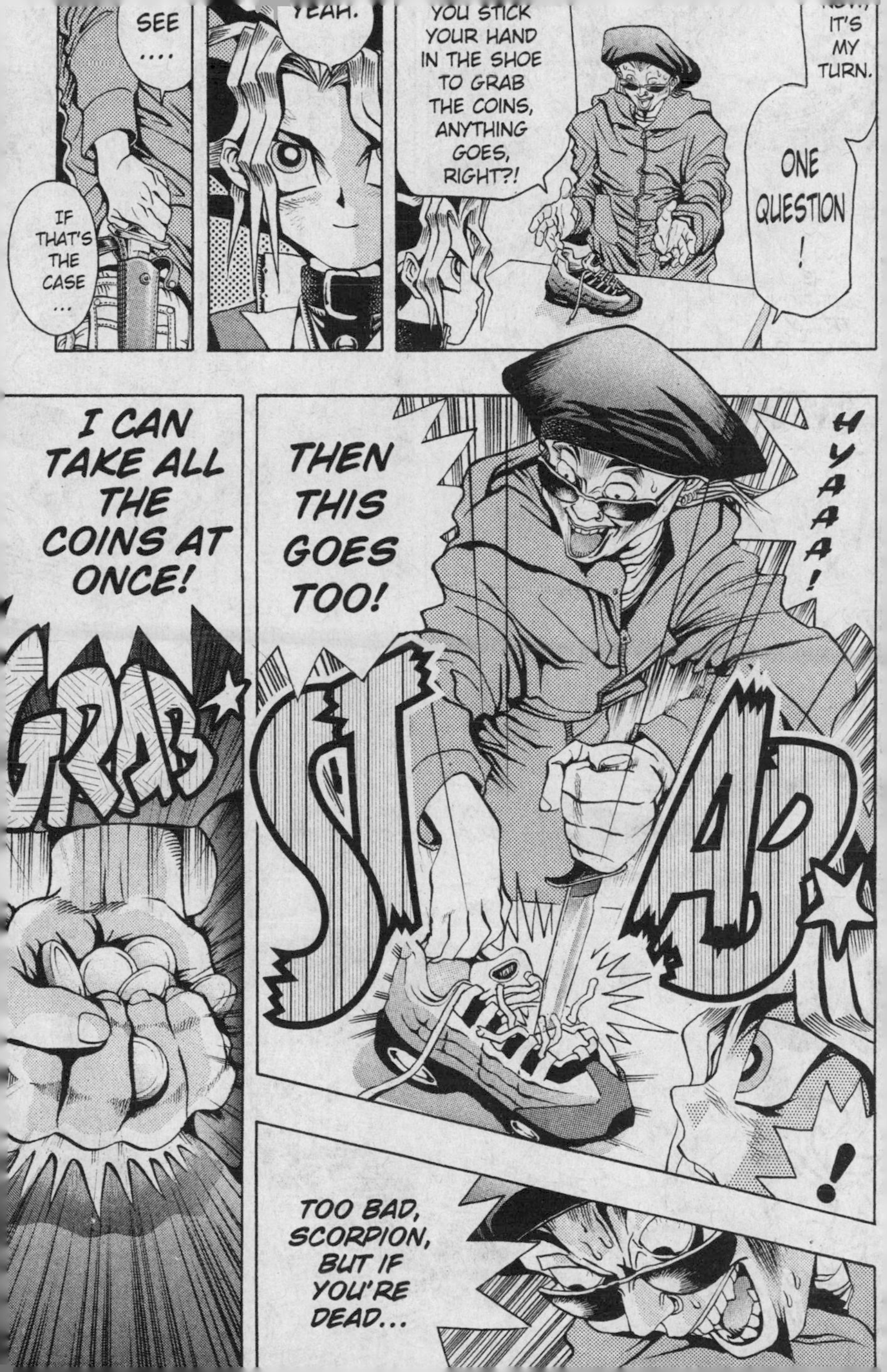
IT'S MY TURN.
ONE QUESTION!
YOU STICK YOUR HAND IN THE SHOE TO GRAB THE COINS, ANYTHING GOES, RIGHT?!
YEAH.
SEE ....
IF THAT'S THE CASE ...
HYAAAA!
THEN THIS GOES TOO!
STAB
!
TOO BAD, SCORPION, BUT IF YOU'RE DEAD...
I CAN TAKE ALL THE COINS AT ONCE!
GRAB

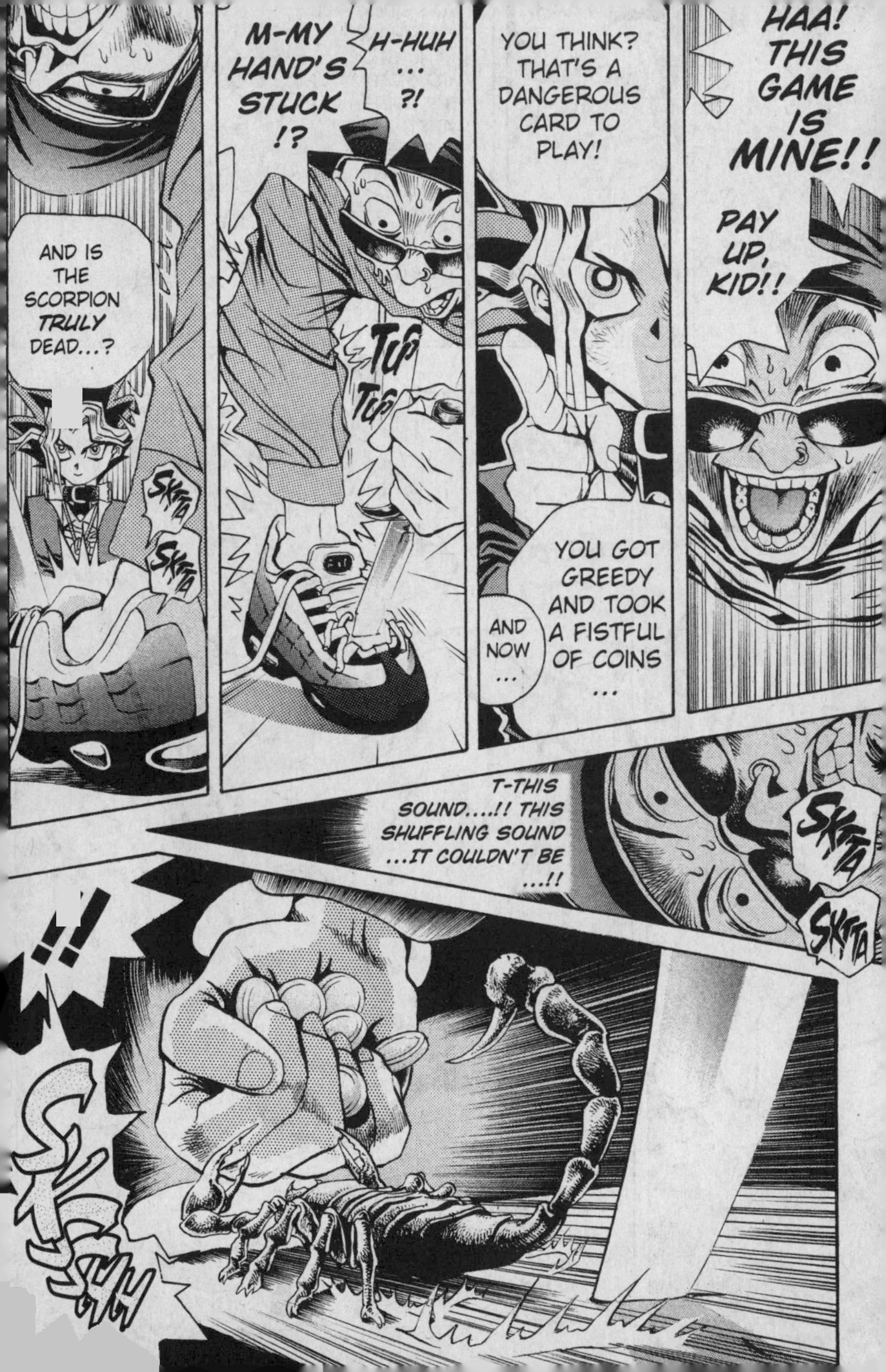
HAA! THIS GAME IS MINE!!
PAY UP, KID!!
YOU THINK? THAT'S A DANGEROUS CARD TO PLAY!
YOU GOT GREEDY AND TOOK A FISTFUL OF COINS ...
AND NOW ...
H-HUH ... ?!
M-MY HAND'S STUCK !?
TUP
TUP
AND IS THE SCORPION TRULY DEAD...?
SKTTA
SKTTA
T-THIS SOUND....!! THIS SHUFFLING SOUND ...IT COULDN'T BE ...!!
SKTTA
SKTTA
!!

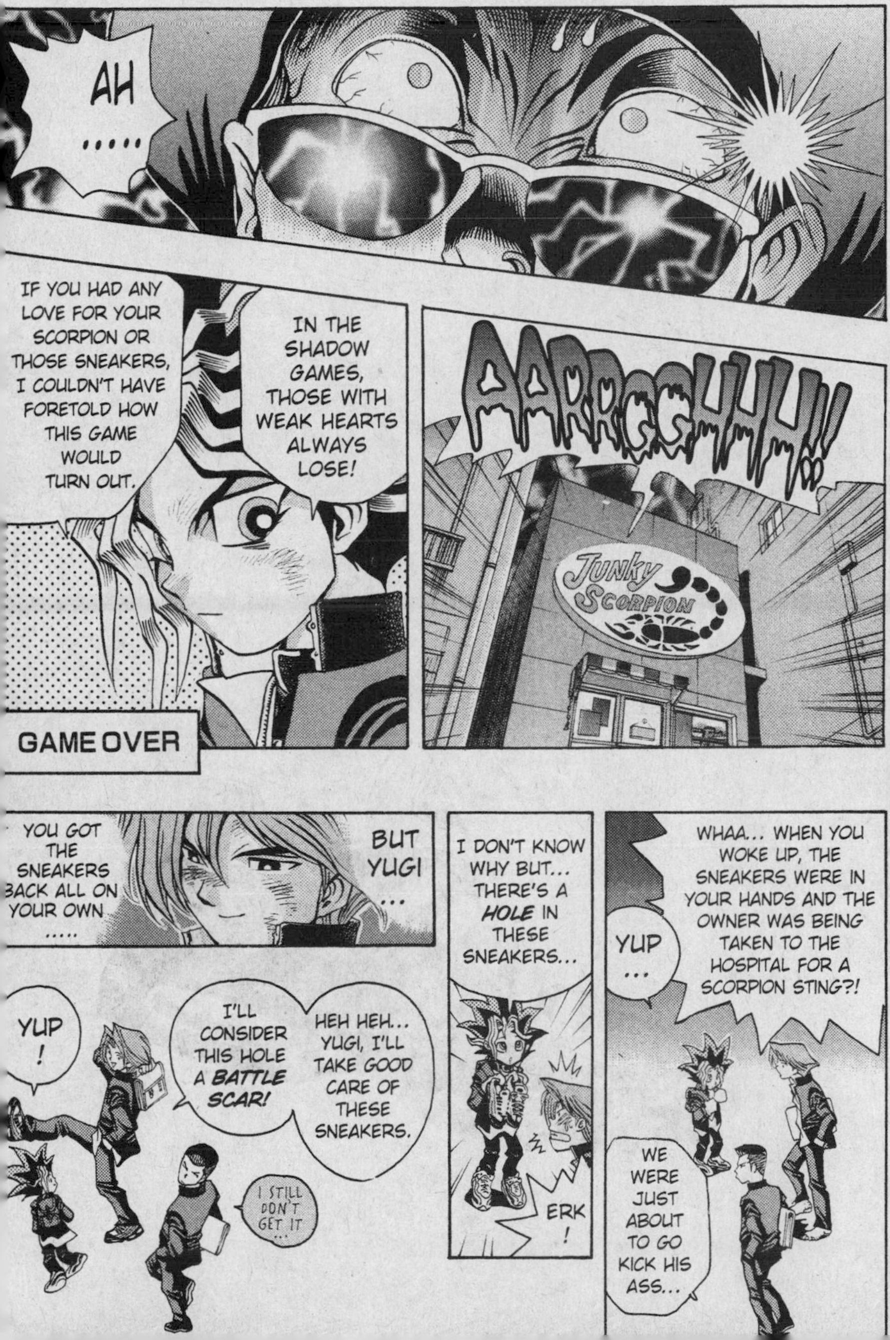
AH ......
AARRGHHH!!
IN THE SHADOW GAMES, THOSE WITH WEAK HEARTS ALWAYS LOSE!
IF YOU HAD ANY LOVE FOR YOUR SCORPION OR THOSE SNEAKERS, I COULDN'T HAVE FORETOLD HOW THIS GAME WOULD TURN OUT.
JUNKY SCORPION
GAME OVER
WHAA... WHEN YOU WOKE UP, THE SNEAKERS WERE IN YOUR HANDS AND THE OWNER WAS BEING TAKEN TO THE HOSPITAL FOR A SCORPION STING?!
YUP ...
WE WERE JUST ABOUT TO GO KICK HIS ASS...
I DON'T KNOW WHY BUT... THERE'S A HOLE IN THESE SNEAKERS...
ERK !
BUT YUGI ...
YOU GOT THE SNEAKERS BACK ALL ON YOUR OWN .....
HEH HEH... YUGI, I'LL TAKE GOOD CARE OF THESE SNEAKERS.
I'LL CONSIDER THIS HOLE A BATTLE SCAR!
YUP !
I STILL DON'T GET IT ...

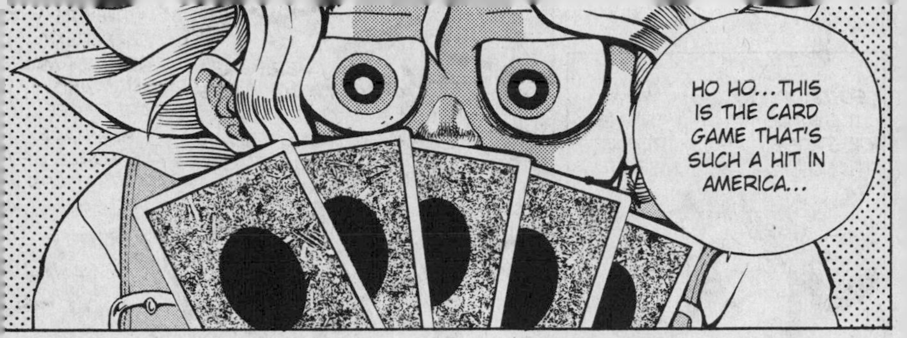
HO HO...THIS IS THE CARD GAME THAT'S SUCH A HIT IN AMERICA...

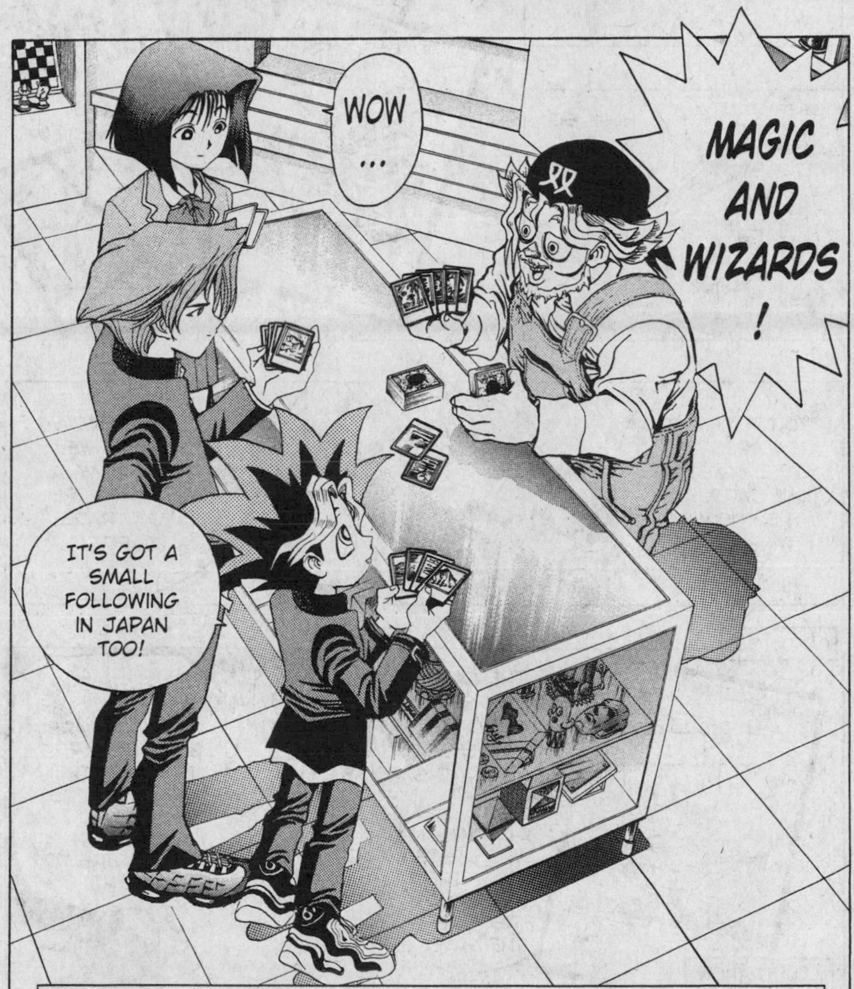
MAGIC AND WIZARDS!
WOW...
IT'S GOT A SMALL FOLLOWING IN JAPAN TOO!

Duel 9: The Cards with Teeth (Part 1)

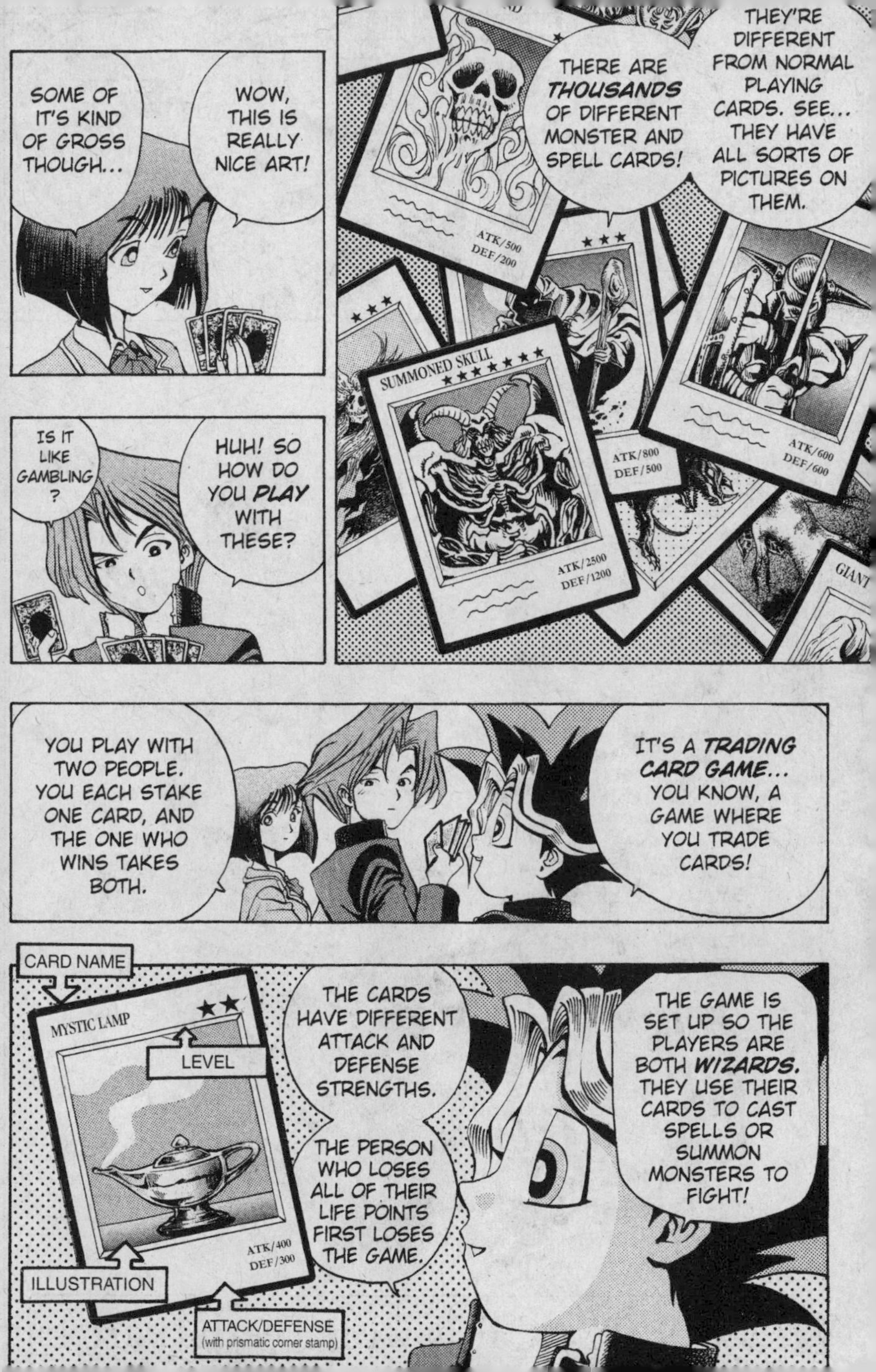
THEY'RE DIFFERENT FROM NORMAL PLAYING CARDS. SEE... THEY HAVE ALL SORTS OF PICTURES ON THEM.
THERE ARE **THOUSANDS** OF DIFFERENT MONSTER AND SPELL CARDS!
ATK/500
DEF/200
ATK/600
DEF/600
ATK/800
DEF/500
SUMMONED SKULL
ATK/2500
DEF/1200
GIANT
WOW, THIS IS REALLY NICE ART!
SOME OF IT'S KIND OF GROSS THOUGH...
HUH! SO HOW DO YOU *PLAY* WITH THESE?
IS IT LIKE GAMBLING?
IT'S A ***TRADING CARD GAME...*** YOU KNOW, A GAME WHERE YOU TRADE CARDS!
YOU PLAY WITH TWO PEOPLE. YOU EACH STAKE ONE CARD, AND THE ONE WHO WINS TAKES BOTH.
THE GAME IS SET UP SO THE PLAYERS ARE BOTH ***WIZARDS.*** THEY USE THEIR CARDS TO CAST SPELLS OR SUMMON MONSTERS TO FIGHT!
THE CARDS HAVE DIFFERENT ATTACK AND DEFENSE STRENGTHS.
THE PERSON WHO LOSES ALL OF THEIR LIFE POINTS FIRST LOSES THE GAME.
CARD NAME
MYSTIC LAMP
LEVEL
ILLUSTRATION
ATK/400
DEF/300
ATTACK/DEFENSE
(with prismatic corner stamp)

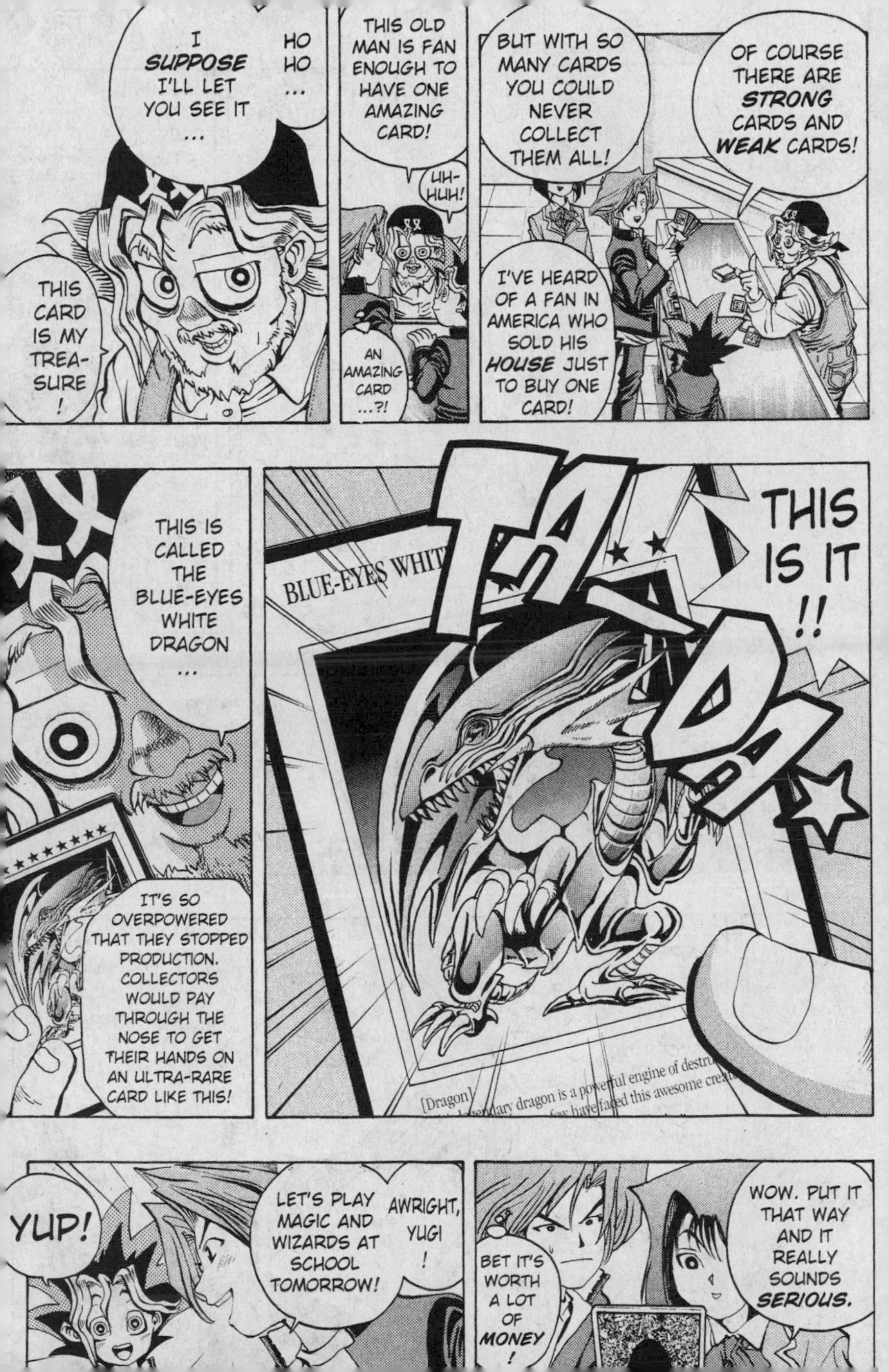
OF COURSE THERE ARE STRONG CARDS AND WEAK CARDS!
BUT WITH SO MANY CARDS YOU COULD NEVER COLLECT THEM ALL!
I'VE HEARD OF A FAN IN AMERICA WHO SOLD HIS HOUSE JUST TO BUY ONE CARD!
THIS OLD MAN IS FAN ENOUGH TO HAVE ONE AMAZING CARD!
UH-HUH!
AN AMAZING CARD ...?!
HO HO ...
I SUPPOSE I'LL LET YOU SEE IT ...
THIS CARD IS MY TREA-SURE!
THIS IS IT!!
TA-DA
BLUE-EYES WHIT
[Dragon]
THIS IS CALLED THE BLUE-EYES WHITE DRAGON ...
IT'S SO OVERPOWERED THAT THEY STOPPED PRODUCTION. COLLECTORS WOULD PAY THROUGH THE NOSE TO GET THEIR HANDS ON AN ULTRA-RARE CARD LIKE THIS!
WOW. PUT IT THAT WAY AND IT REALLY SOUNDS SERIOUS.
BET IT'S WORTH A LOT OF MONEY!
AWRIGHT, YUGI!
LET'S PLAY MAGIC AND WIZARDS AT SCHOOL TOMORROW!
YUP!

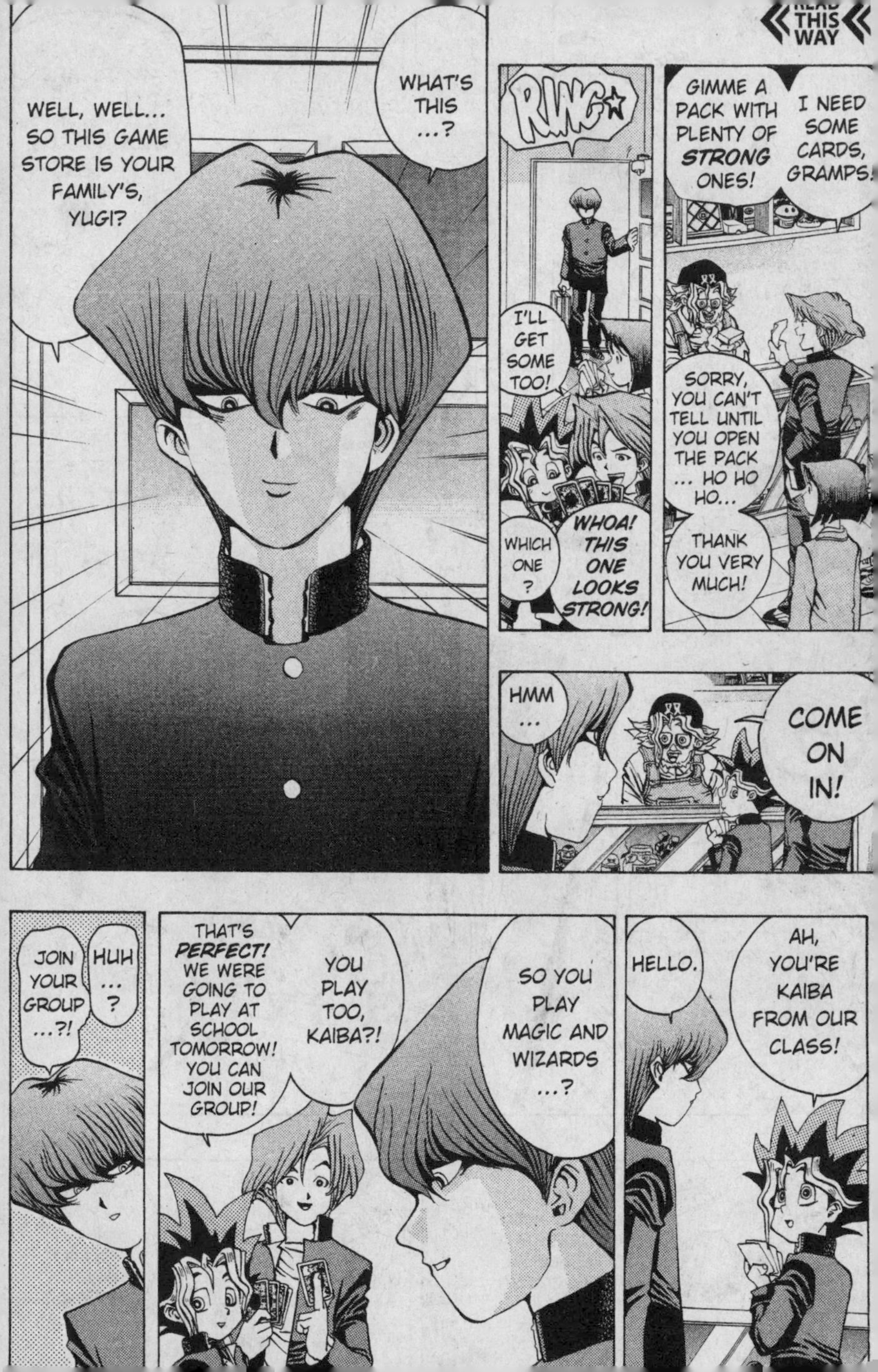

READ THIS WAY
I NEED SOME CARDS, GRAMPS!
GIMME A PACK WITH PLENTY OF STRONG ONES!
SORRY, YOU CAN'T TELL UNTIL YOU OPEN THE PACK ... HO HO HO...
THANK YOU VERY MUCH!
RING☆
I'LL GET SOME TOO!
WHOA! THIS ONE LOOKS STRONG!
WHICH ONE ?
COME ON IN!
HMM ...
WHAT'S THIS ...?
WELL, WELL... SO THIS GAME STORE IS YOUR FAMILY'S, YUGI?
AH, YOU'RE KAIBA FROM OUR CLASS!
HELLO.
SO YOU PLAY MAGIC AND WIZARDS ...?
YOU PLAY TOO, KAIBA?!
THAT'S PERFECT! WE WERE GOING TO PLAY AT SCHOOL TOMORROW! YOU CAN JOIN OUR GROUP!
HUH ... ?
JOIN YOUR GROUP ...?!

READ THIS WAY

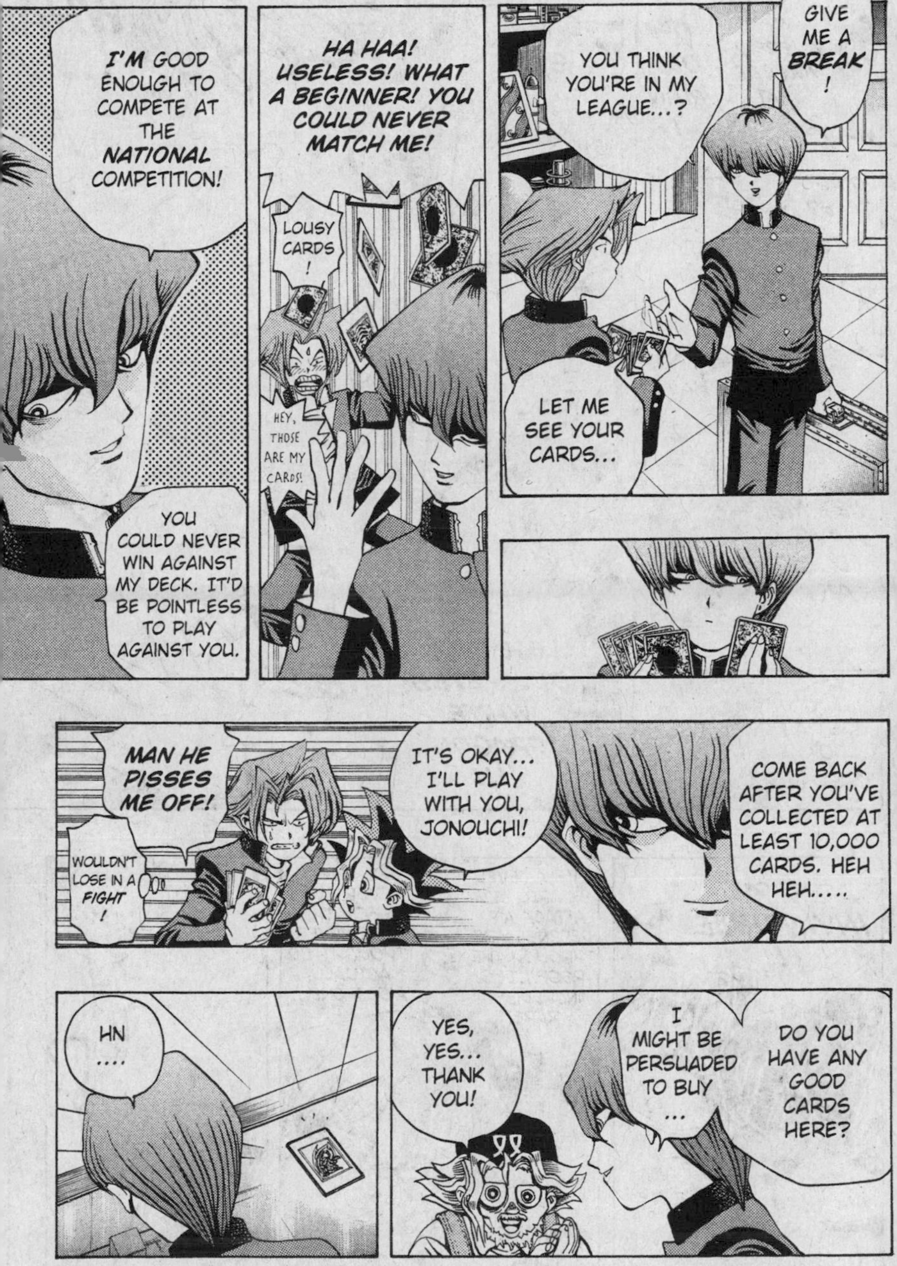
GIVE ME A BREAK!
YOU THINK YOU'RE IN MY LEAGUE...?
LET ME SEE YOUR CARDS...
HA HAA! USELESS! WHAT A BEGINNER! YOU COULD NEVER MATCH ME!
LOUSY CARDS!
HEY, THOSE ARE MY CARDS!
I'M GOOD ENOUGH TO COMPETE AT THE NATIONAL COMPETITION!
YOU COULD NEVER WIN AGAINST MY DECK. IT'D BE POINTLESS TO PLAY AGAINST YOU.
COME BACK AFTER YOU'VE COLLECTED AT LEAST 10,000 CARDS. HEH HEH.....
MAN HE PISSES ME OFF!
WOULDN'T LOSE IN A FIGHT!
IT'S OKAY... I'LL PLAY WITH YOU, JONOUCHI!
DO YOU HAVE ANY GOOD CARDS HERE?
I MIGHT BE PERSUADED TO BUY...
YES, YES... THANK YOU!
HN....

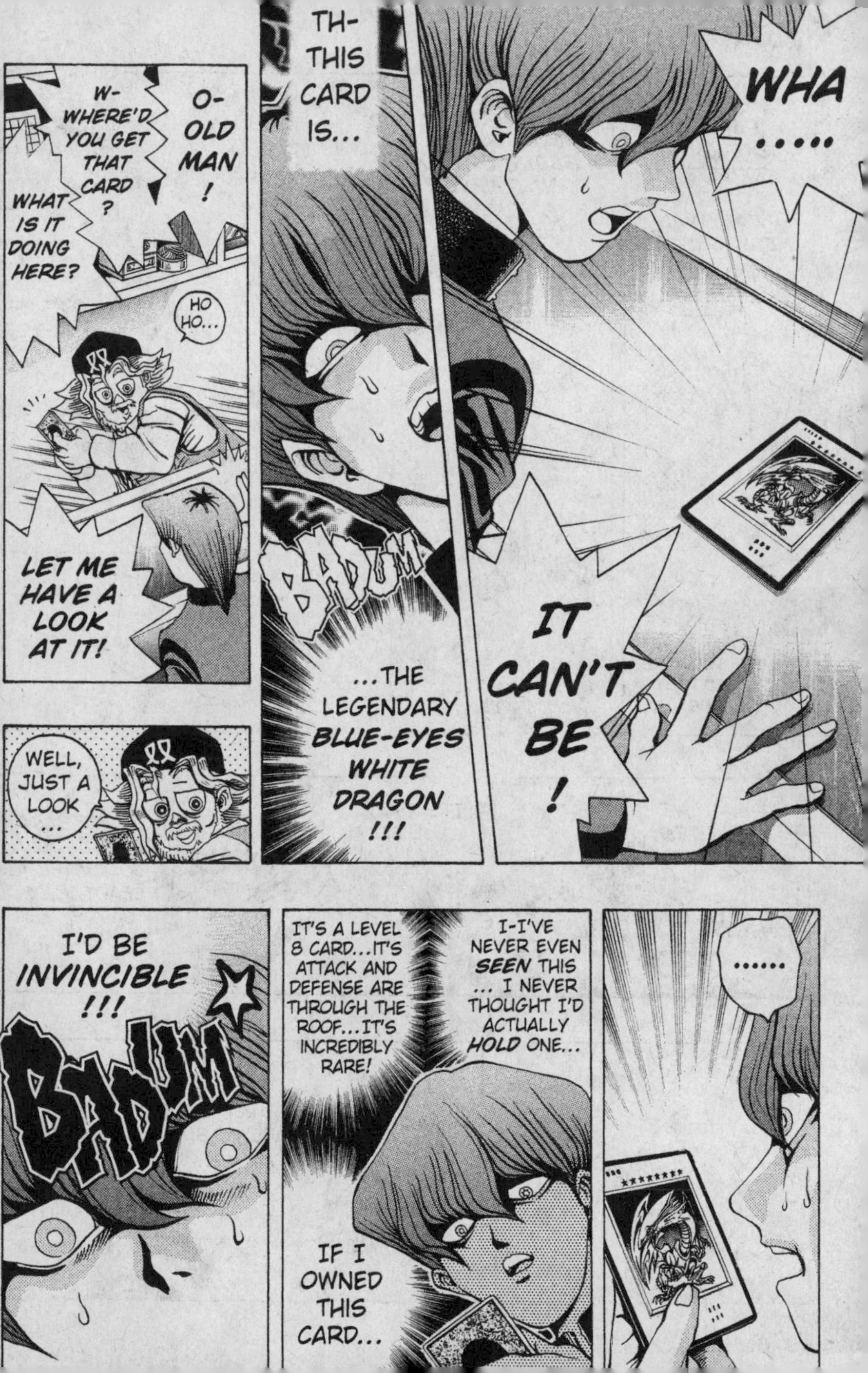
WHA .....
IT CAN'T BE!
TH-THIS CARD IS...
BADUM
...THE LEGENDARY BLUE-EYES WHITE DRAGON!!!
O-OLD MAN!
W-WHERE'D YOU GET THAT CARD?
WHAT IS IT DOING HERE?
HO HO...
LET ME HAVE A LOOK AT IT!
WELL, JUST A LOOK...
......
I-I'VE NEVER EVEN SEEN THIS ... I NEVER THOUGHT I'D ACTUALLY HOLD ONE...
IT'S A LEVEL 8 CARD...IT'S ATTACK AND DEFENSE ARE THROUGH THE ROOF...IT'S INCREDIBLY RARE!
IF I OWNED THIS CARD...
I'D BE INVINCIBLE!!!
BADUM

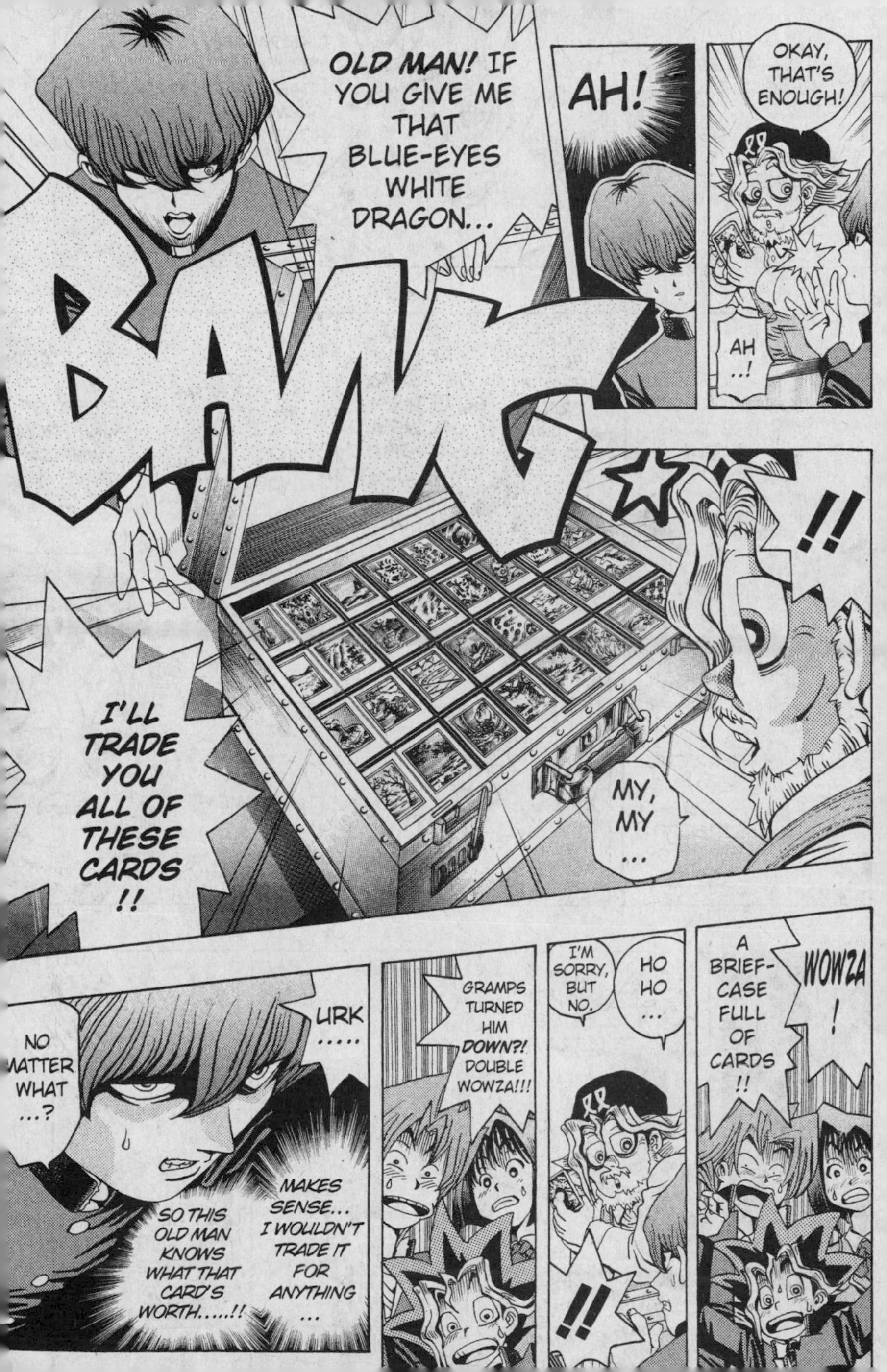
OKAY, THAT'S ENOUGH!
AH ..!
AH!
OLD MAN! IF YOU GIVE ME THAT BLUE-EYES WHITE DRAGON...
BANG
I'LL TRADE YOU ALL OF THESE CARDS !!
!!
MY, MY ...
WOWZA !
A BRIEF-CASE FULL OF CARDS !!
HO HO ...
I'M SORRY, BUT NO.
!!
GRAMPS TURNED HIM DOWN?! DOUBLE WOWZA!!!
URK .....
NO MATTER WHAT ...?
MAKES SENSE... I WOULDN'T TRADE IT FOR ANYTHING ...
SO THIS OLD MAN KNOWS WHAT THAT CARD'S WORTH.....!!

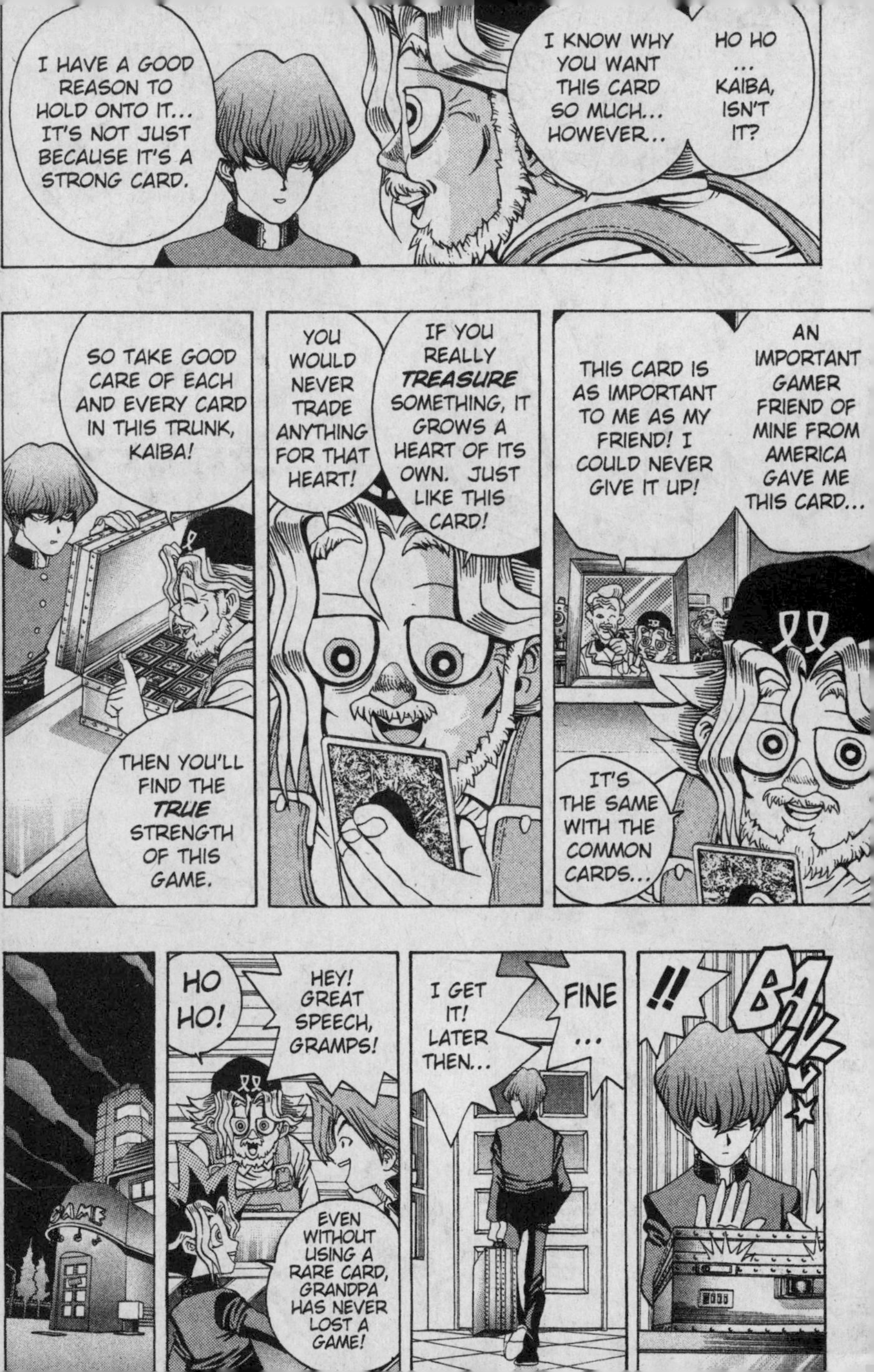
HO HO ... KAIBA, ISN'T IT?
I KNOW WHY YOU WANT THIS CARD SO MUCH... HOWEVER...
I HAVE A GOOD REASON TO HOLD ONTO IT... IT'S NOT JUST BECAUSE IT'S A STRONG CARD.
AN IMPORTANT GAMER FRIEND OF MINE FROM AMERICA GAVE ME THIS CARD...
THIS CARD IS AS IMPORTANT TO ME AS MY FRIEND! I COULD NEVER GIVE IT UP!
IT'S THE SAME WITH THE COMMON CARDS...
IF YOU REALLY *TREASURE* SOMETHING, IT GROWS A HEART OF ITS OWN. JUST LIKE THIS CARD!
YOU WOULD NEVER TRADE ANYTHING FOR THAT HEART!
SO TAKE GOOD CARE OF EACH AND EVERY CARD IN THIS TRUNK, KAIBA!
THEN YOU'LL FIND THE *TRUE* STRENGTH OF THIS GAME.
!!
BANG
FINE ...
I GET IT! LATER THEN...
HEY! GREAT SPEECH, GRAMPS!
HO HO!
EVEN WITHOUT USING A RARE CARD, GRANDPA HAS NEVER LOST A GAME!
GAME

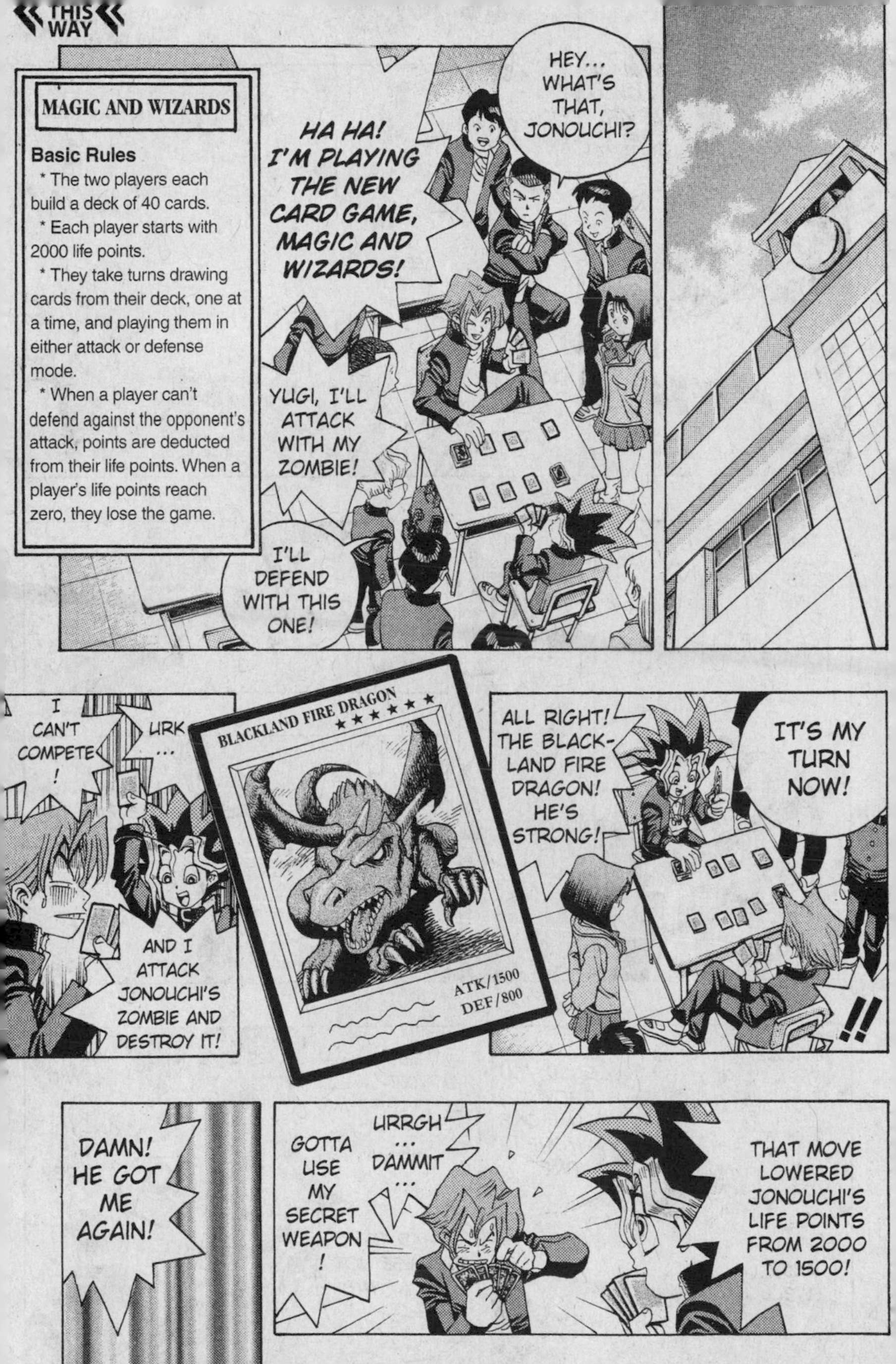
THIS WAY
HEY... WHAT'S THAT, JONOUCHI?
HA HA! I'M PLAYING THE NEW CARD GAME, MAGIC AND WIZARDS!
MAGIC AND WIZARDS
Basic Rules
* The two players each build a deck of 40 cards.
* Each player starts with 2000 life points.
* They take turns drawing cards from their deck, one at a time, and playing them in either attack or defense mode.
* When a player can't defend against the opponent's attack, points are deducted from their life points. When a player's life points reach zero, they lose the game.
YUGI, I'LL ATTACK WITH MY ZOMBIE!
I'LL DEFEND WITH THIS ONE!
IT'S MY TURN NOW!
ALL RIGHT! THE BLACKLAND FIRE DRAGON! HE'S STRONG!
!!
BLACKLAND FIRE DRAGON
ATK/1500
DEF/800
URK...
I CAN'T COMPETE!
AND I ATTACK JONOUCHI'S ZOMBIE AND DESTROY IT!
THAT MOVE LOWERED JONOUCHI'S LIFE POINTS FROM 2000 TO 1500!
URRGH... DAMMIT...
GOTTA USE MY SECRET WEAPON!
DAMN! HE GOT ME AGAIN!

READ THIS WAY

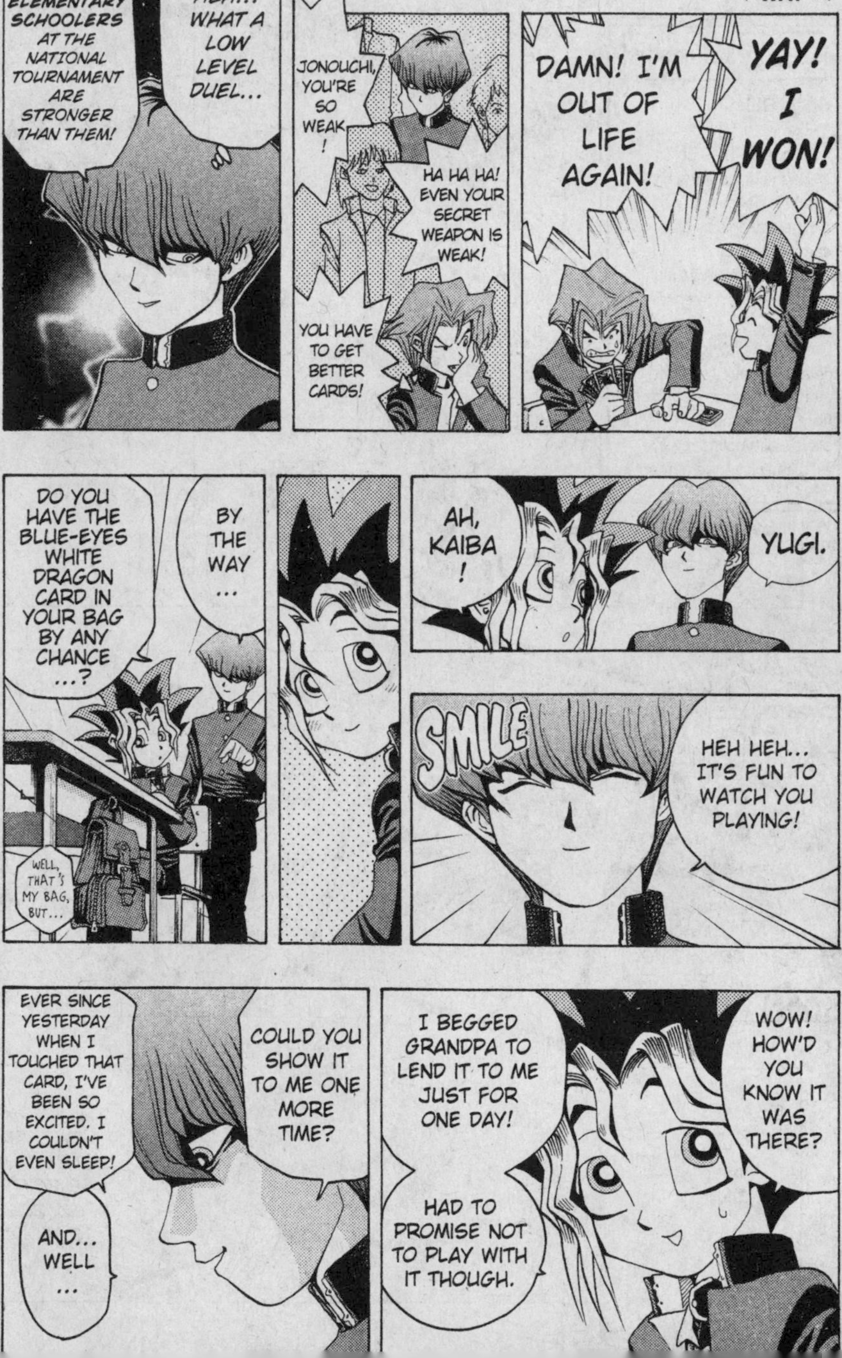
YAY! I WON!
DAMN! I'M OUT OF LIFE AGAIN!
JONOUCHI, YOU'RE SO WEAK!
HA HA HA! EVEN YOUR SECRET WEAPON IS WEAK!
YOU HAVE TO GET BETTER CARDS!
HEH... WHAT A LOW LEVEL DUEL...
THE ELEMENTARY SCHOOLERS AT THE NATIONAL TOURNAMENT ARE STRONGER THAN THEM!
YUGI.
AH, KAIBA!
SMILE
HEH HEH... IT'S FUN TO WATCH YOU PLAYING!
BY THE WAY ...
DO YOU HAVE THE BLUE-EYES WHITE DRAGON CARD IN YOUR BAG BY ANY CHANCE ...?
WELL, THAT'S MY BAG, BUT...
WOW! HOW'D YOU KNOW IT WAS THERE?
I BEGGED GRANDPA TO LEND IT TO ME JUST FOR ONE DAY!
HAD TO PROMISE NOT TO PLAY WITH IT THOUGH.
COULD YOU SHOW IT TO ME ONE MORE TIME?
EVER SINCE YESTERDAY WHEN I TOUCHED THAT CARD, I'VE BEEN SO EXCITED. I COULDN'T EVEN SLEEP!
AND... WELL ...

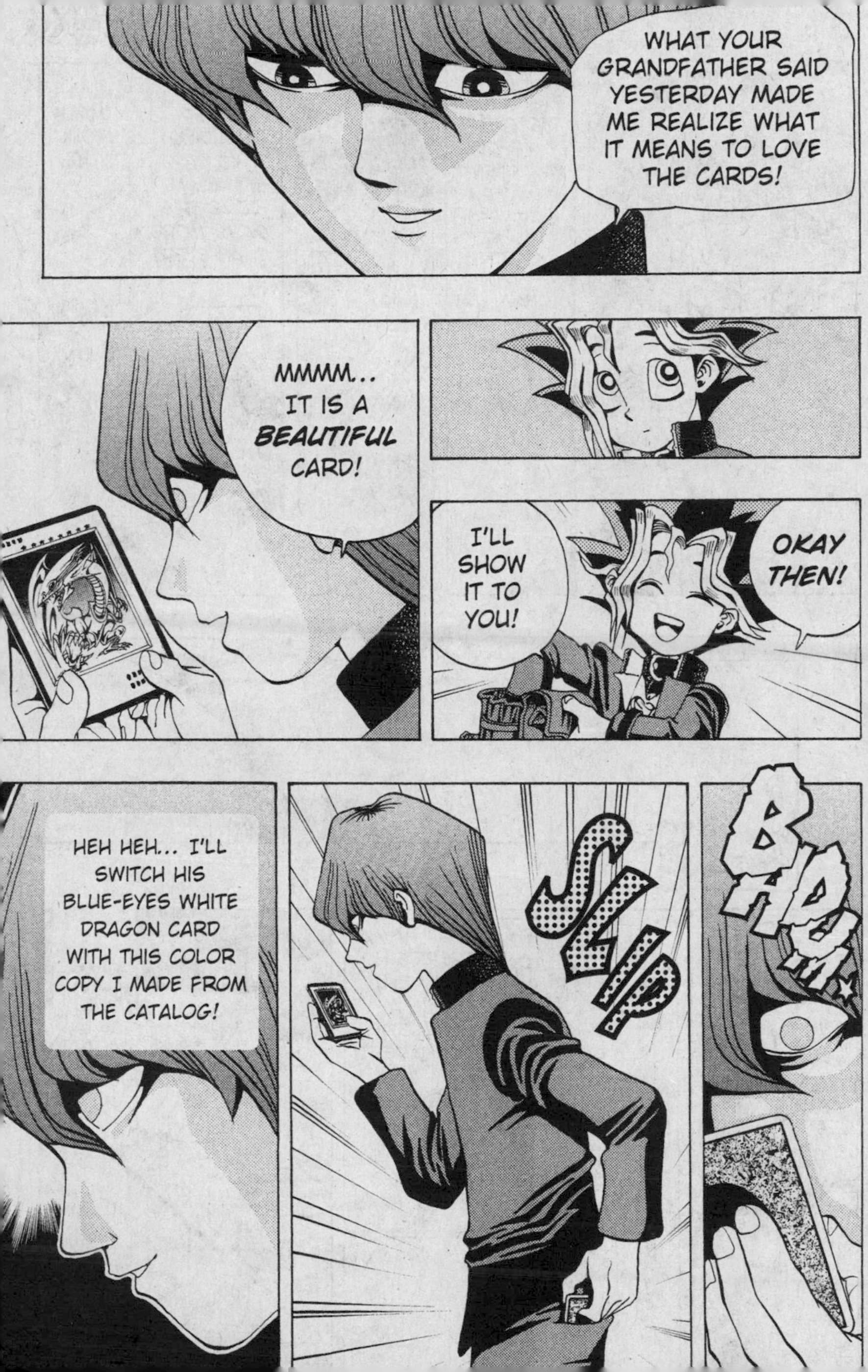
WHAT YOUR GRANDFATHER SAID YESTERDAY MADE ME REALIZE WHAT IT MEANS TO LOVE THE CARDS!
OKAY THEN!
I'LL SHOW IT TO YOU!
MMMM... IT IS A *BEAUTIFUL* CARD!
BADUM★
SLIP
HEH HEH... I'LL SWITCH HIS BLUE-EYES WHITE DRAGON CARD WITH THIS COLOR COPY I MADE FROM THE CATALOG!

READ THIS WAY

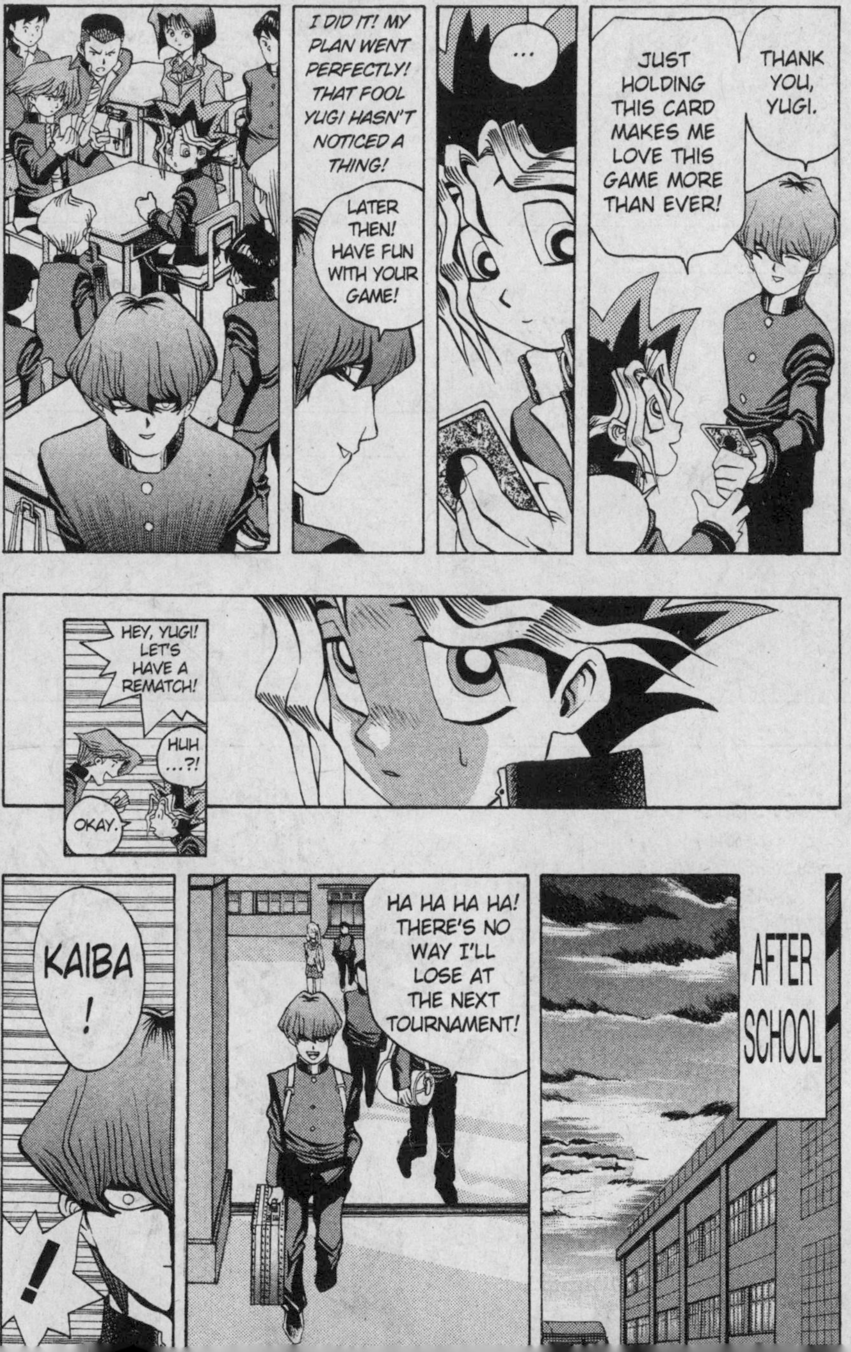
THANK YOU, YUGI.
JUST HOLDING THIS CARD MAKES ME LOVE THIS GAME MORE THAN EVER!
...
I DID IT! MY PLAN WENT PERFECTLY! THAT FOOL YUGI HASN'T NOTICED A THING!
LATER THEN! HAVE FUN WITH YOUR GAME!
HEY, YUGI! LET'S HAVE A REMATCH!
HUH ...?!
OKAY.
AFTER SCHOOL
HA HA HA HA! THERE'S NO WAY I'LL LOSE AT THE NEXT TOURNAMENT!
KAIBA !
!

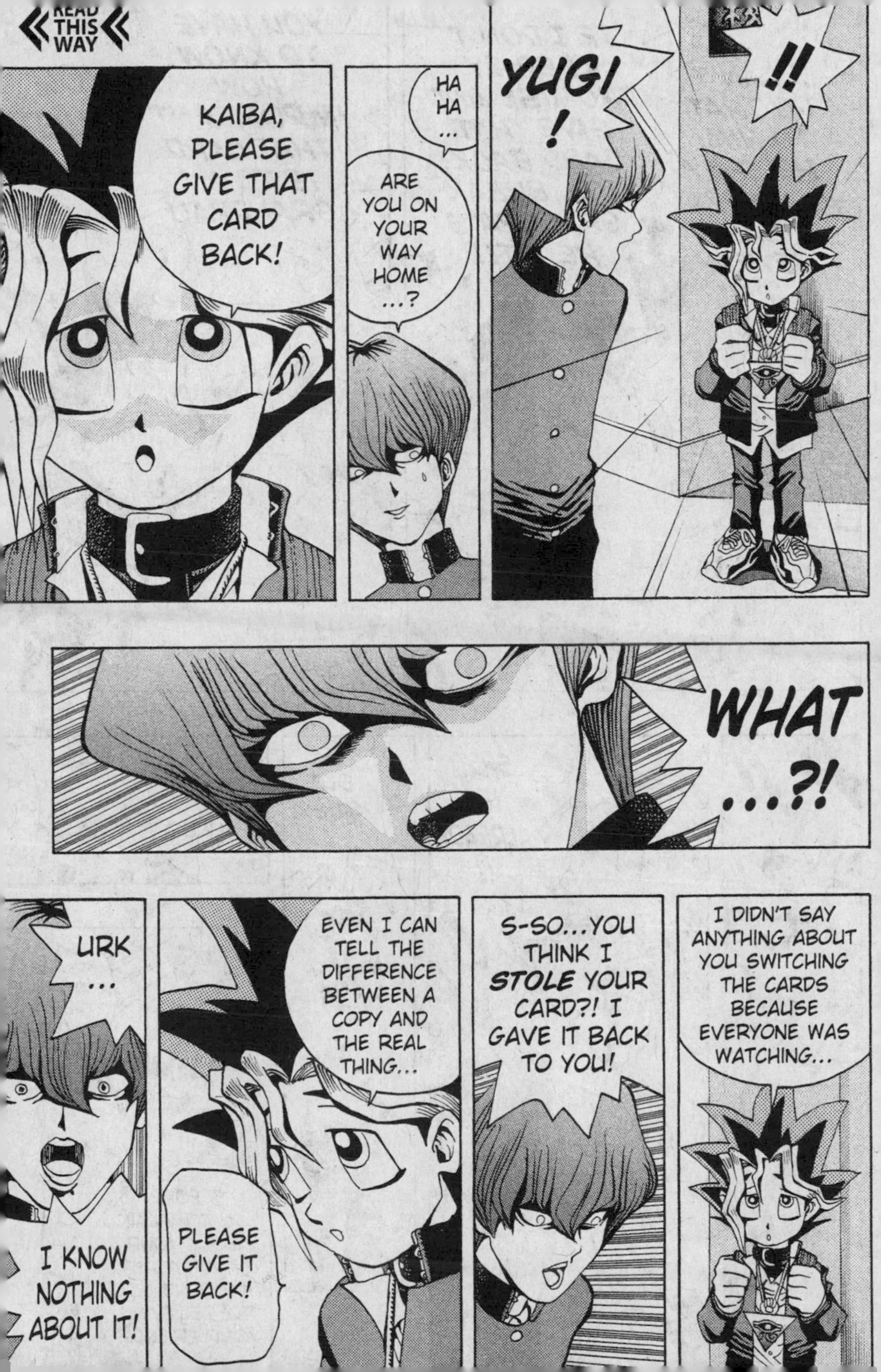
READ THIS WAY
!!
YUGI!
HA HA...
ARE YOU ON YOUR WAY HOME...?
KAIBA, PLEASE GIVE THAT CARD BACK!
WHAT...?!
I DIDN'T SAY ANYTHING ABOUT YOU SWITCHING THE CARDS BECAUSE EVERYONE WAS WATCHING...
S-SO...YOU THINK I ***STOLE*** YOUR CARD?! I GAVE IT BACK TO YOU!
EVEN I CAN TELL THE DIFFERENCE BETWEEN A COPY AND THE REAL THING...
PLEASE GIVE IT BACK!
URK...
I KNOW NOTHING ABOUT IT!

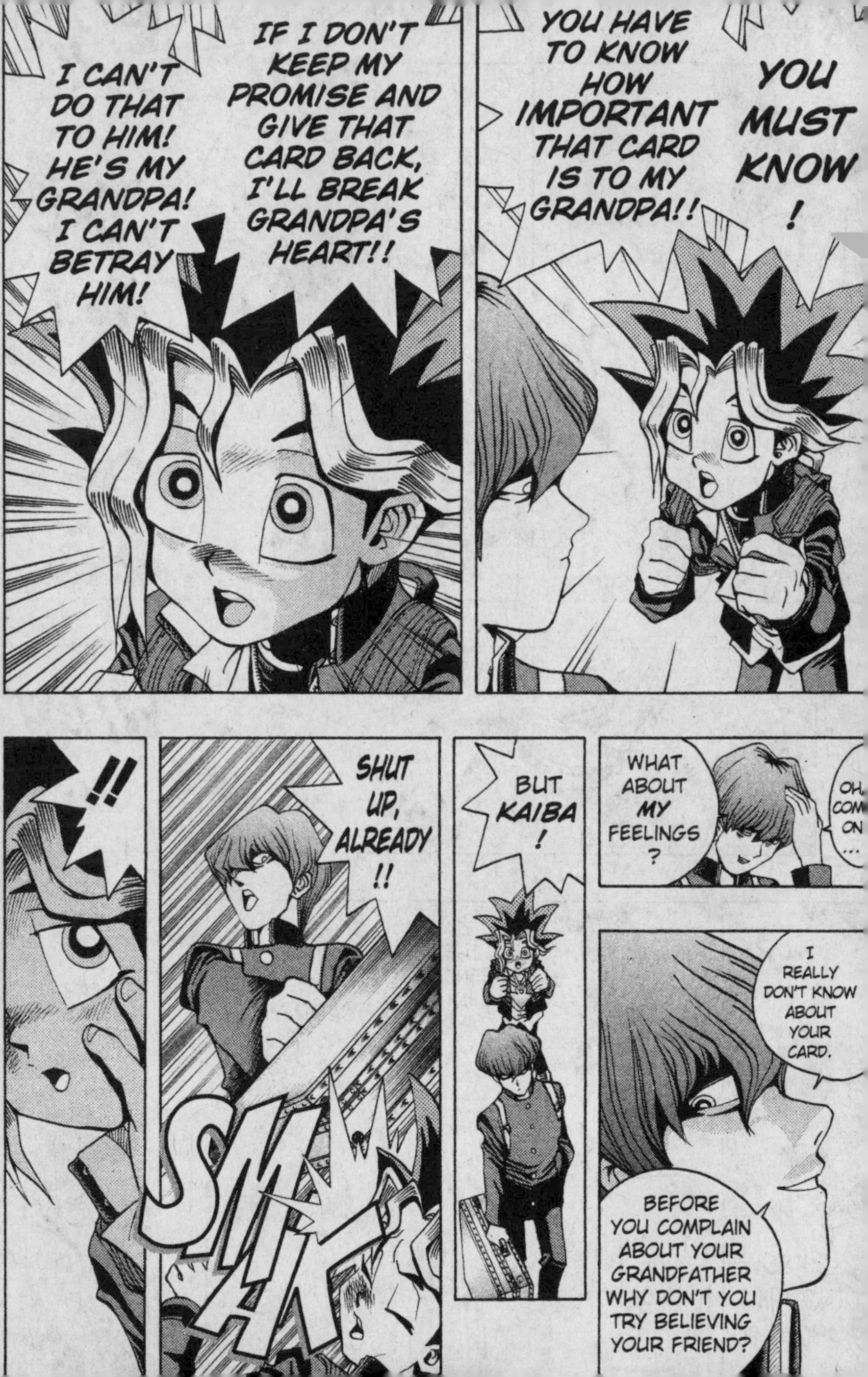
YOU MUST KNOW!
YOU HAVE TO KNOW HOW IMPORTANT THAT CARD IS TO MY GRANDPA!!
IF I DON'T KEEP MY PROMISE AND GIVE THAT CARD BACK, I'LL BREAK GRANDPA'S HEART!!
I CAN'T DO THAT TO HIM! HE'S MY GRANDPA! I CAN'T BETRAY HIM!
OH, COM ON ...
WHAT ABOUT MY FEELINGS?
I REALLY DON'T KNOW ABOUT YOUR CARD.
BEFORE YOU COMPLAIN ABOUT YOUR GRANDFATHER WHY DON'T YOU TRY BELIEVING YOUR FRIEND?
BUT KAIBA!
SHUT UP, ALREADY!!
!!

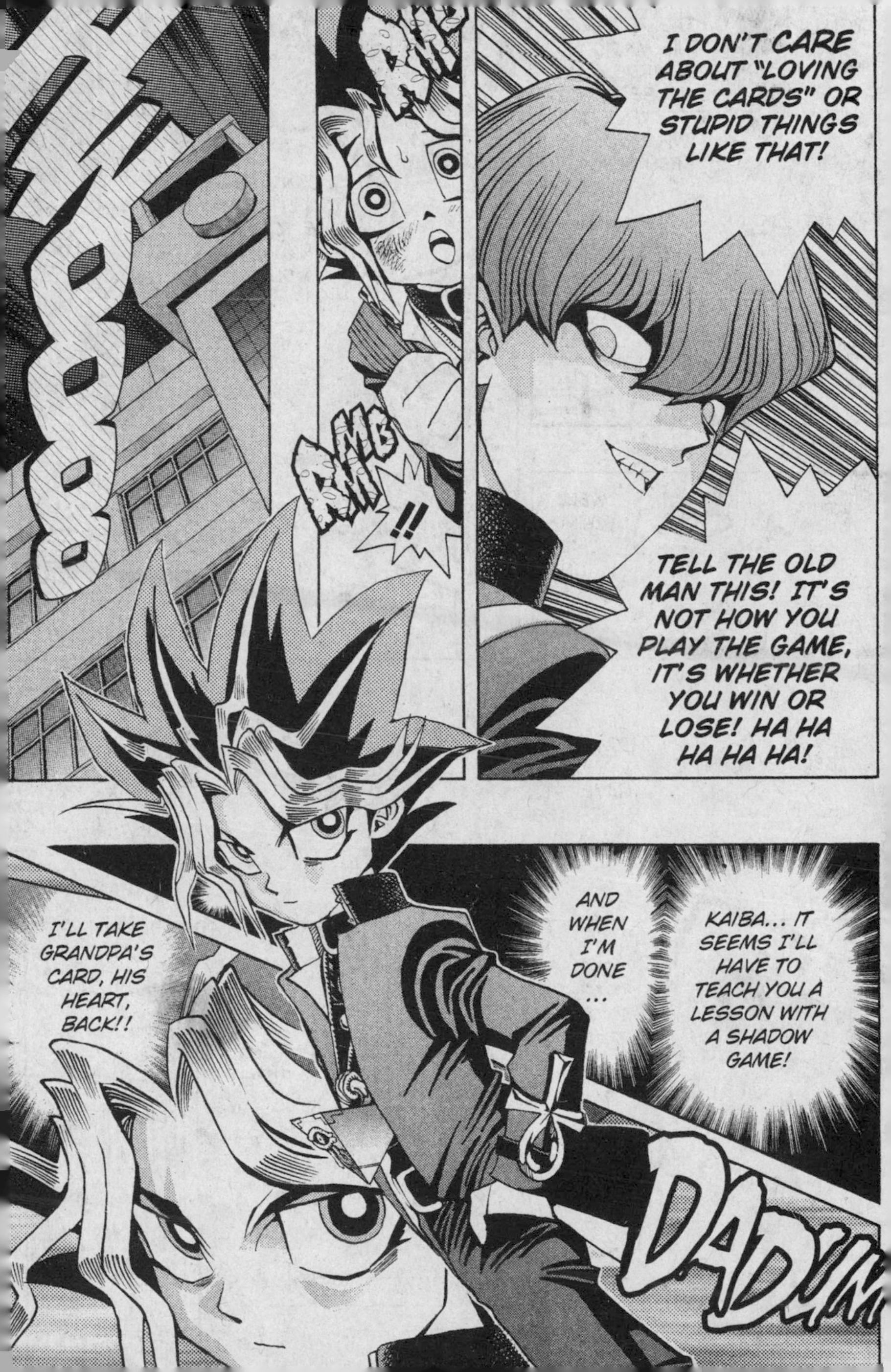
I DON'T CARE ABOUT "LOVING THE CARDS" OR STUPID THINGS LIKE THAT!
TELL THE OLD MAN THIS! IT'S NOT HOW YOU PLAY THE GAME, IT'S WHETHER YOU WIN OR LOSE! HA HA HA HA HA!
!!
KAIBA... IT SEEMS I'LL HAVE TO TEACH YOU A LESSON WITH A SHADOW GAME!
AND WHEN I'M DONE ...
I'LL TAKE GRANDPA'S CARD, HIS HEART, BACK!!

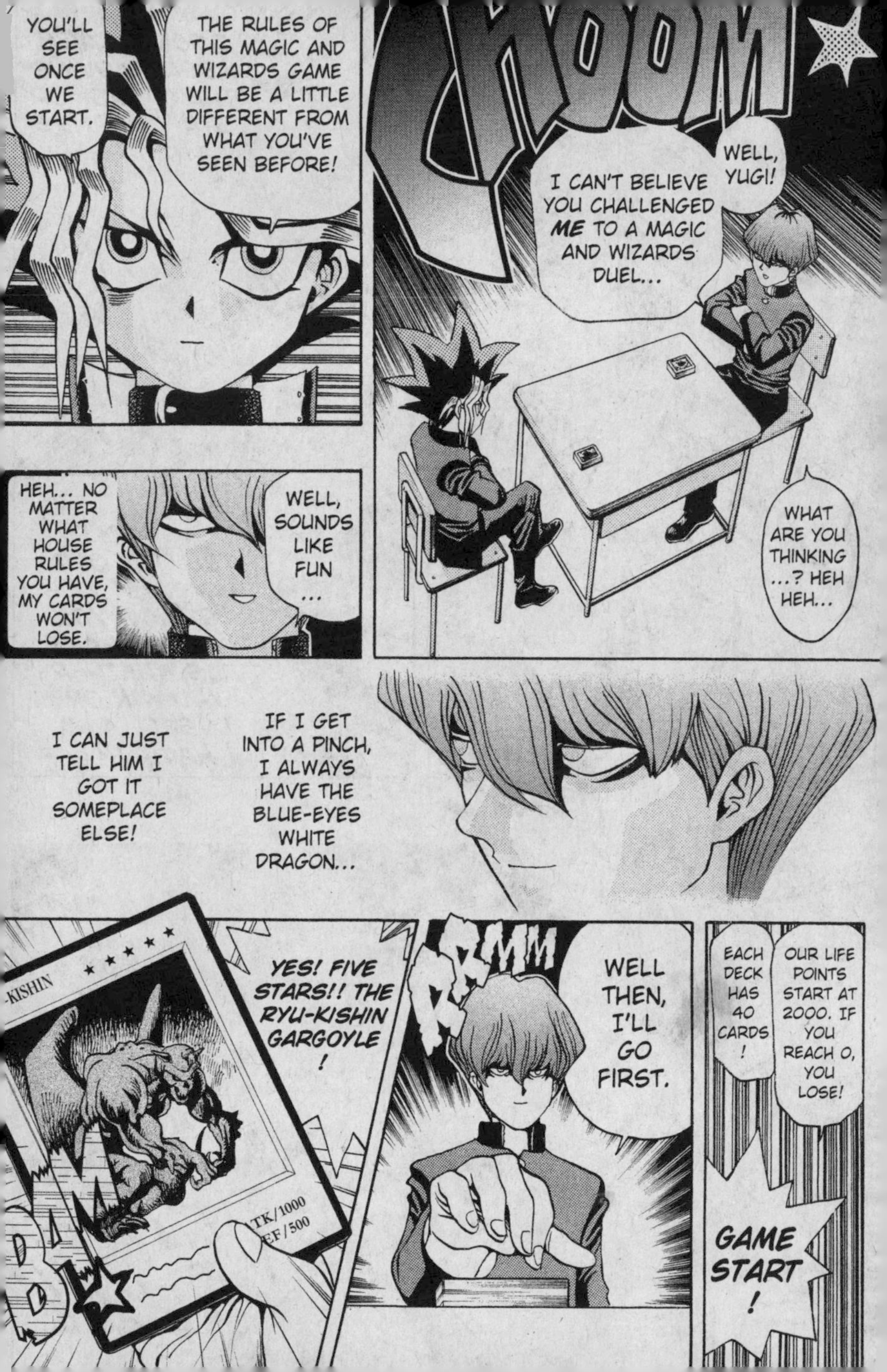
WELL, YUGI!
I CAN'T BELIEVE YOU CHALLENGED *ME* TO A MAGIC AND WIZARDS DUEL...
WHAT ARE YOU THINKING...? HEH HEH...
THE RULES OF THIS MAGIC AND WIZARDS GAME WILL BE A LITTLE DIFFERENT FROM WHAT YOU'VE SEEN BEFORE!
YOU'LL SEE ONCE WE START.
WELL, SOUNDS LIKE FUN...
HEH... NO MATTER WHAT HOUSE RULES YOU HAVE, MY CARDS WON'T LOSE.
IF I GET INTO A PINCH, I ALWAYS HAVE THE BLUE-EYES WHITE DRAGON...
I CAN JUST TELL HIM I GOT IT SOMEPLACE ELSE!
OUR LIFE POINTS START AT 2000. IF YOU REACH 0, YOU LOSE!
EACH DECK HAS 40 CARDS!
GAME START!
WELL THEN, I'LL GO FIRST.
YES! FIVE STARS!! THE RYU-KISHIN GARGOYLE!
-KISHIN
TK/1000
EF/500

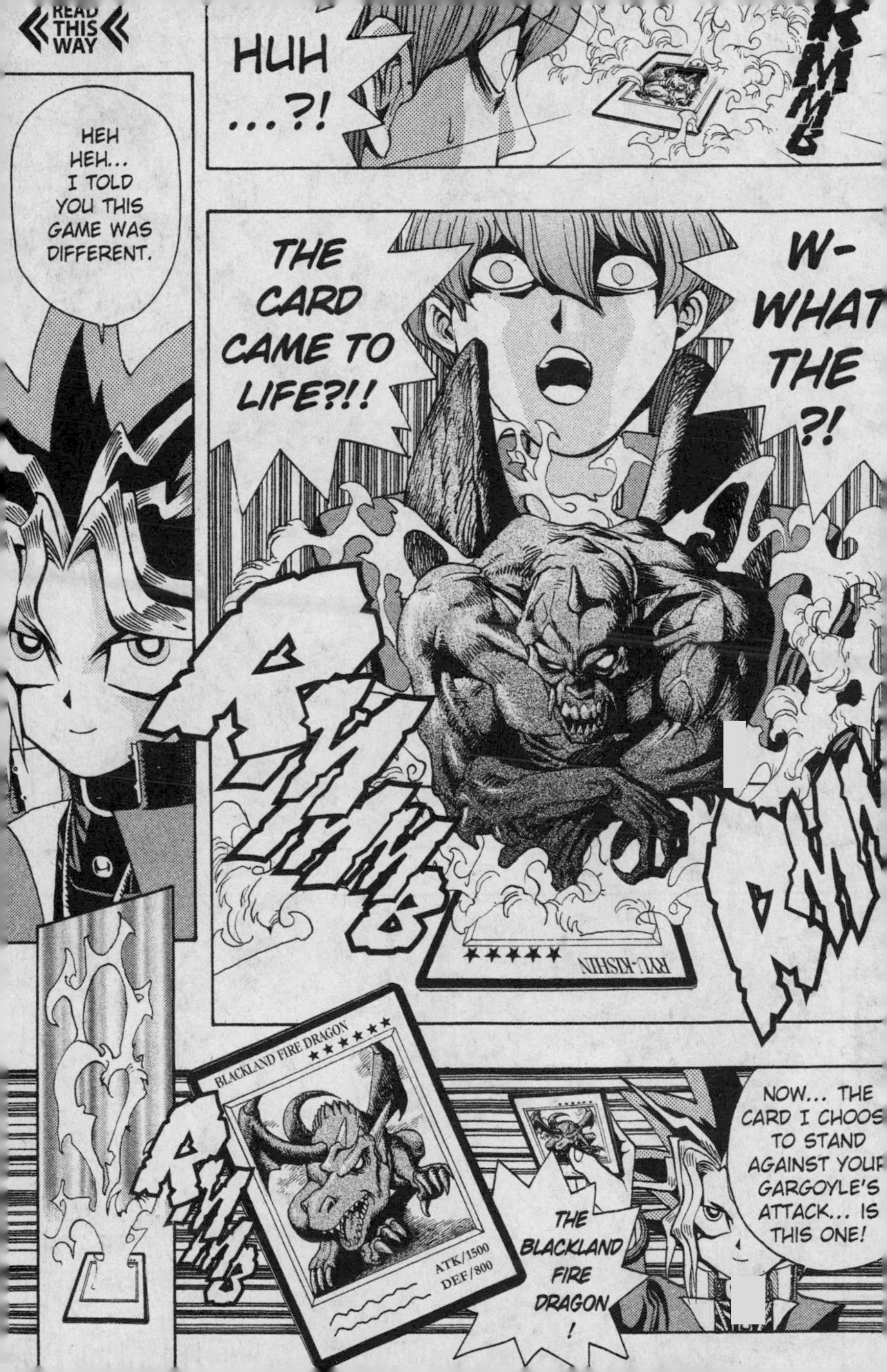

READ THIS WAY
KMMB
HUH ...?!
W-WHAT THE ?!
THE CARD CAME TO LIFE?!!
RYU-KISHIN
HEH HEH... I TOLD YOU THIS GAME WAS DIFFERENT.
NOW... THE CARD I CHOOS TO STAND AGAINST YOUR GARGOYLE'S ATTACK... IS THIS ONE!
THE BLACKLAND FIRE DRAGON !
BLACKLAND FIRE DRAGON
ATK/1500
DEF/800

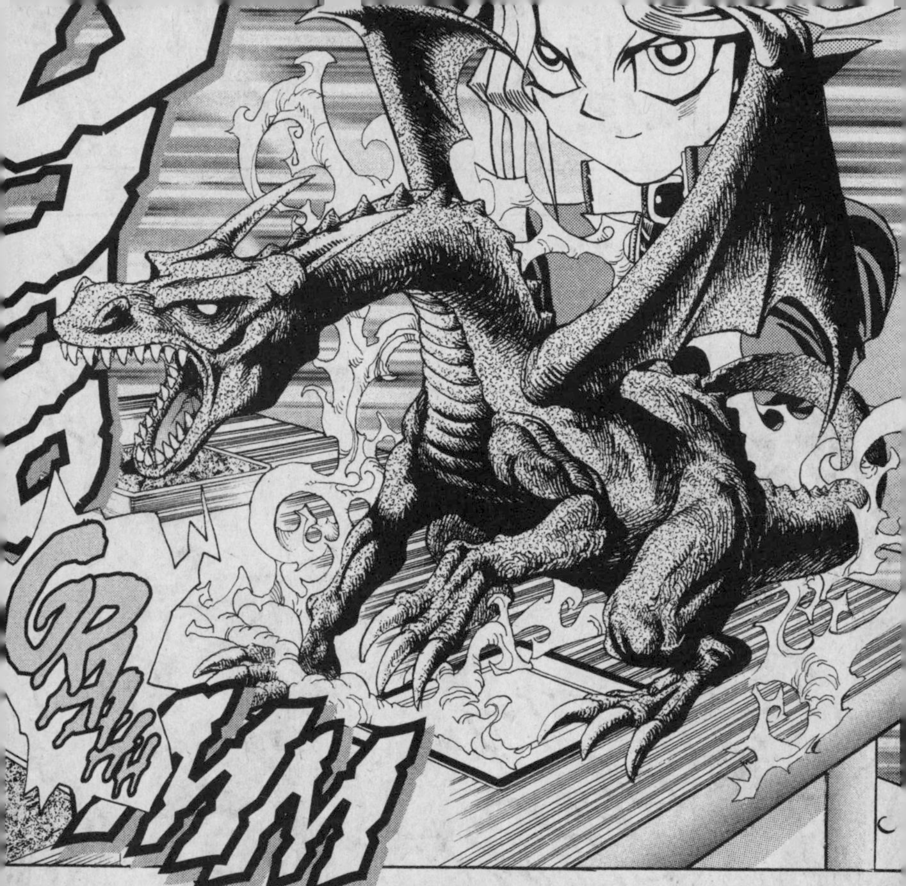

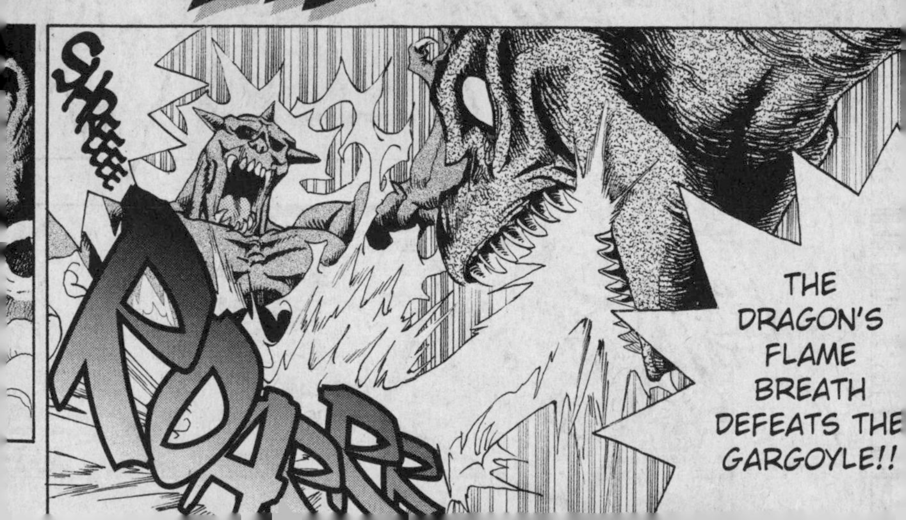
SHREEE
ROARRR
THE DRAGON'S FLAME BREATH DEFEATS THE GARGOYLE!!

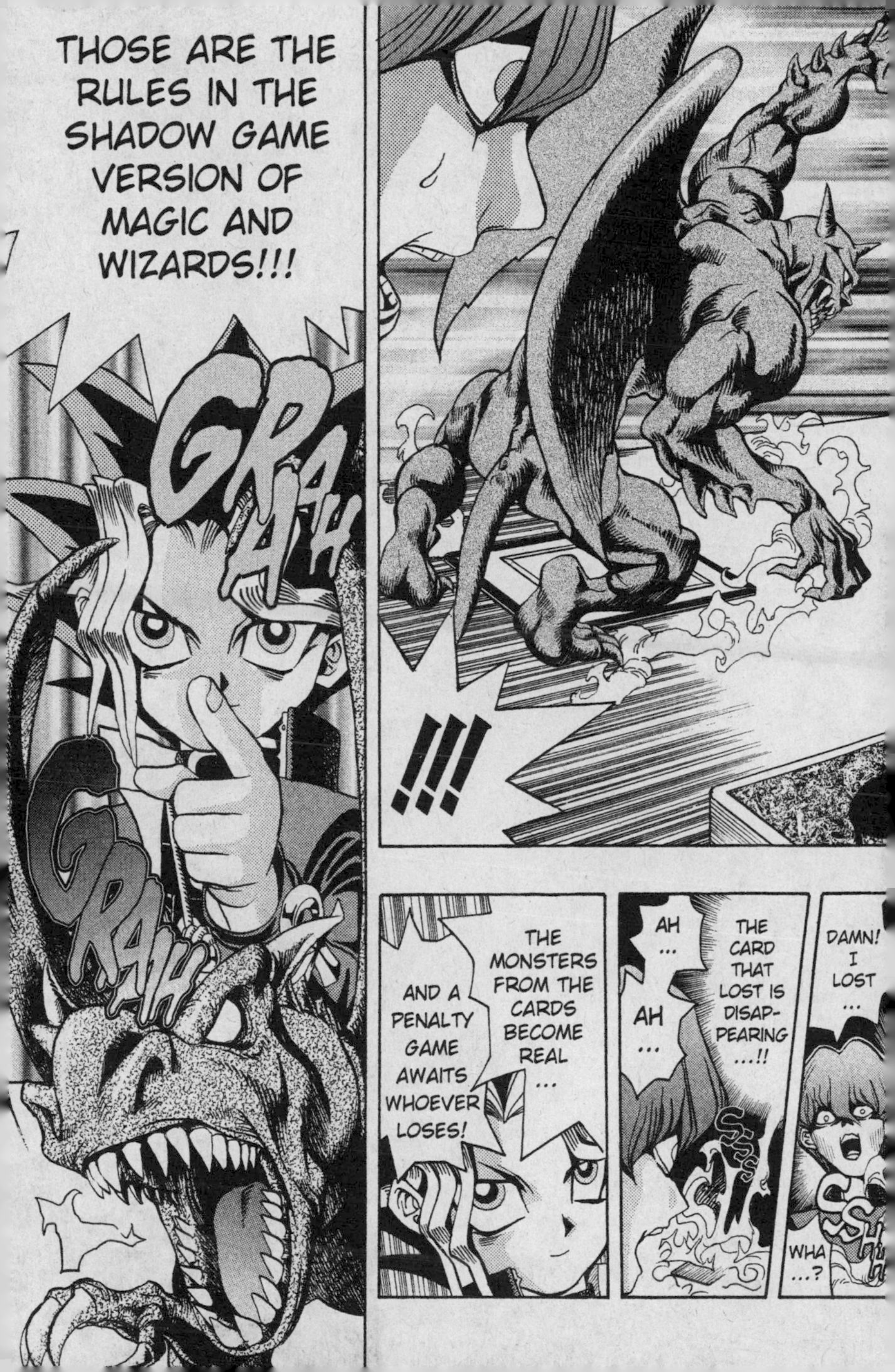

!!!
DAMN! I LOST ...
WHA ...?
THE CARD THAT LOST IS DISAP-PEARING ...!!
AH ...
AH ...
SSS
THE MONSTERS FROM THE CARDS BECOME REAL ...
AND A PENALTY GAME AWAITS WHOEVER LOSES!
THOSE ARE THE RULES IN THE SHADOW GAME VERSION OF MAGIC AND WIZARDS!!!
GRAH
GRAH

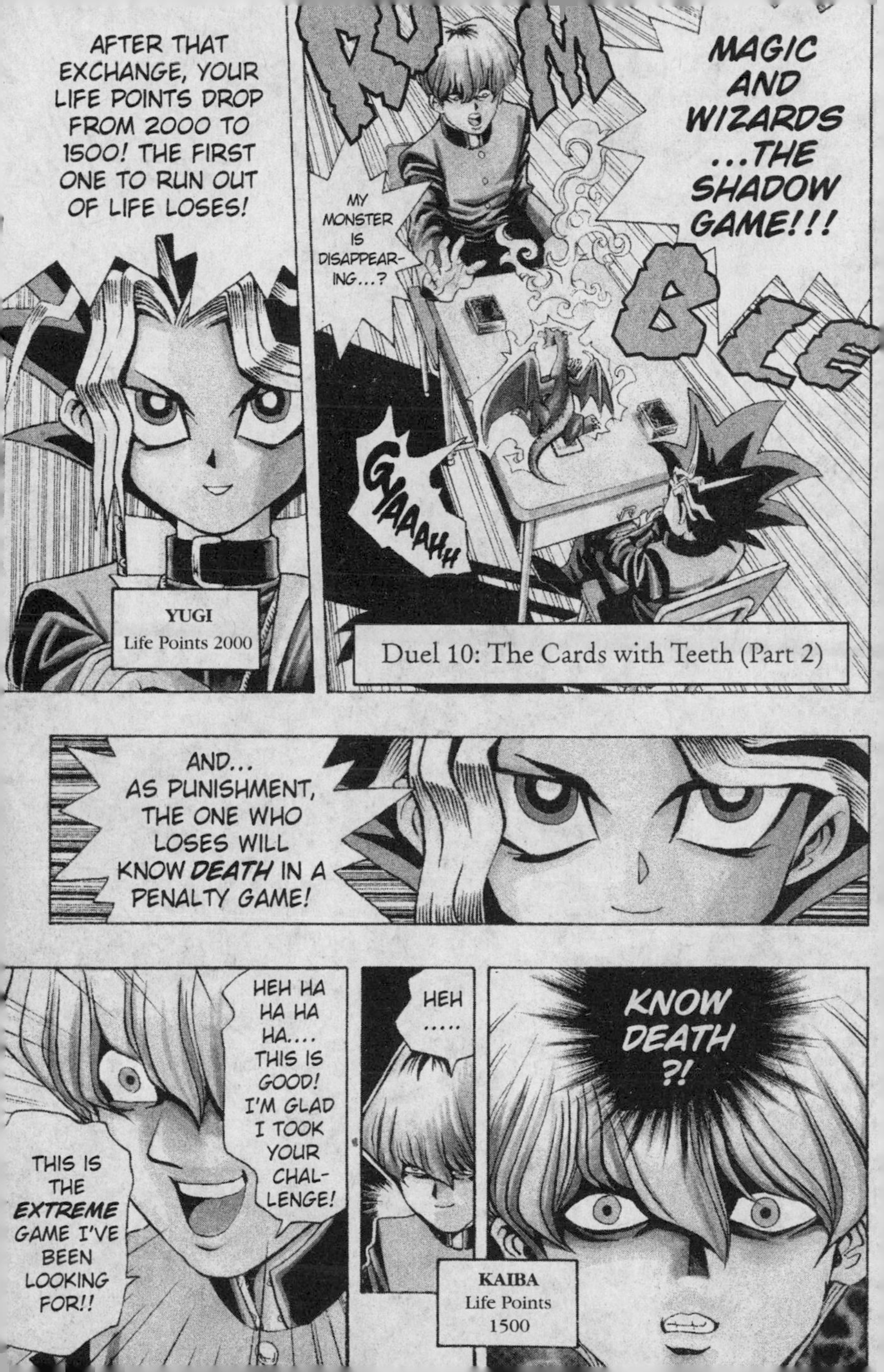
MAGIC AND WIZARDS ...THE SHADOW GAME!!!
RUMBLE
MY MONSTER IS DISAPPEARING...?
GYAAAAHH
Duel 10: The Cards with Teeth (Part 2)
AFTER THAT EXCHANGE, YOUR LIFE POINTS DROP FROM 2000 TO 1500! THE FIRST ONE TO RUN OUT OF LIFE LOSES!
YUGI
Life Points 2000
AND... AS PUNISHMENT, THE ONE WHO LOSES WILL KNOW DEATH IN A PENALTY GAME!
KNOW DEATH ?!
KAIBA
Life Points 1500
HEH .....
HEH HA HA HA HA.... THIS IS GOOD! I'M GLAD I TOOK YOUR CHALLENGE!
THIS IS THE EXTREME GAME I'VE BEEN LOOKING FOR!!

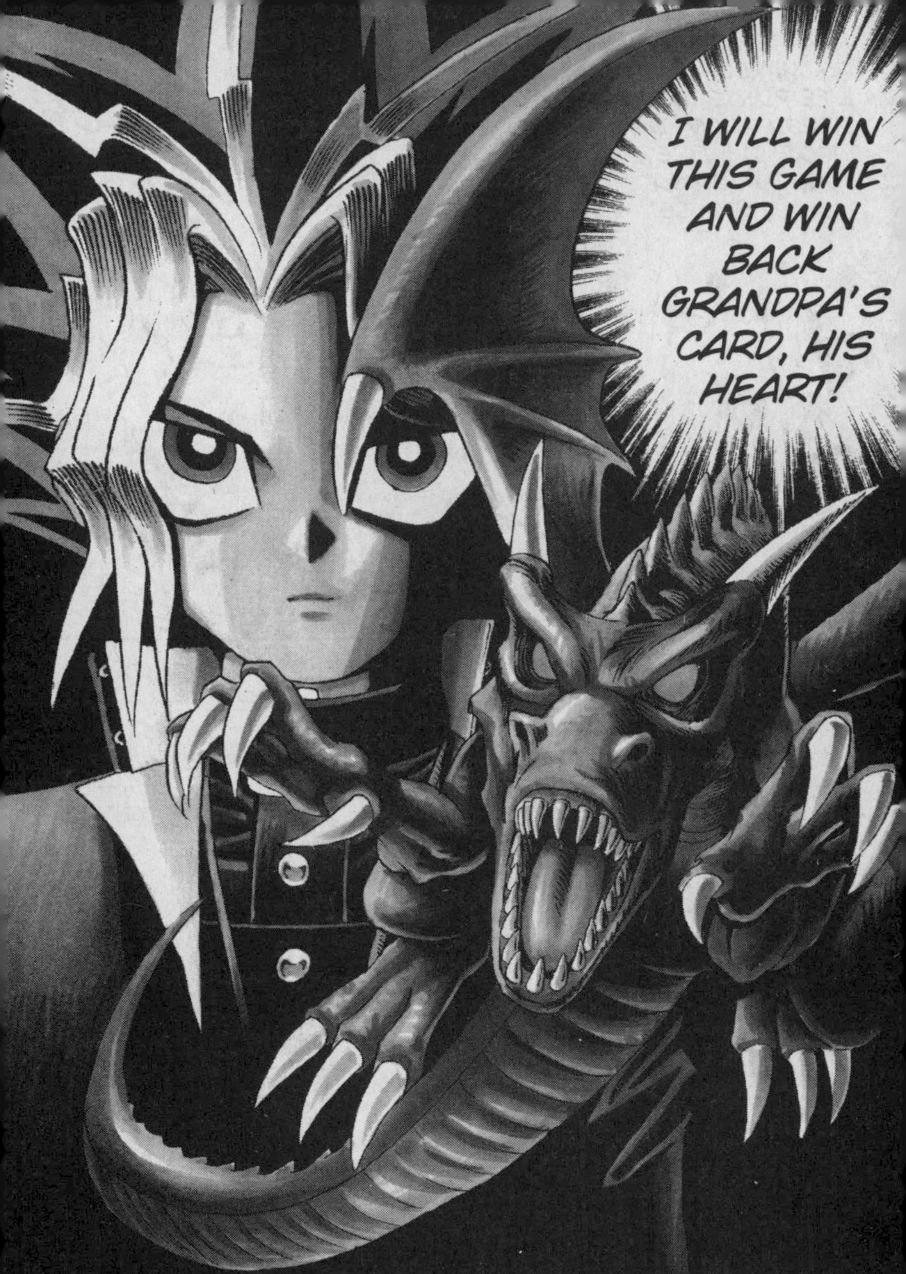
I WILL WIN THIS GAME AND WIN BACK GRANDPA'S CARD, HIS HEART!

Duel 10: The Cards with Teeth (Part 2)

READ THIS WAY

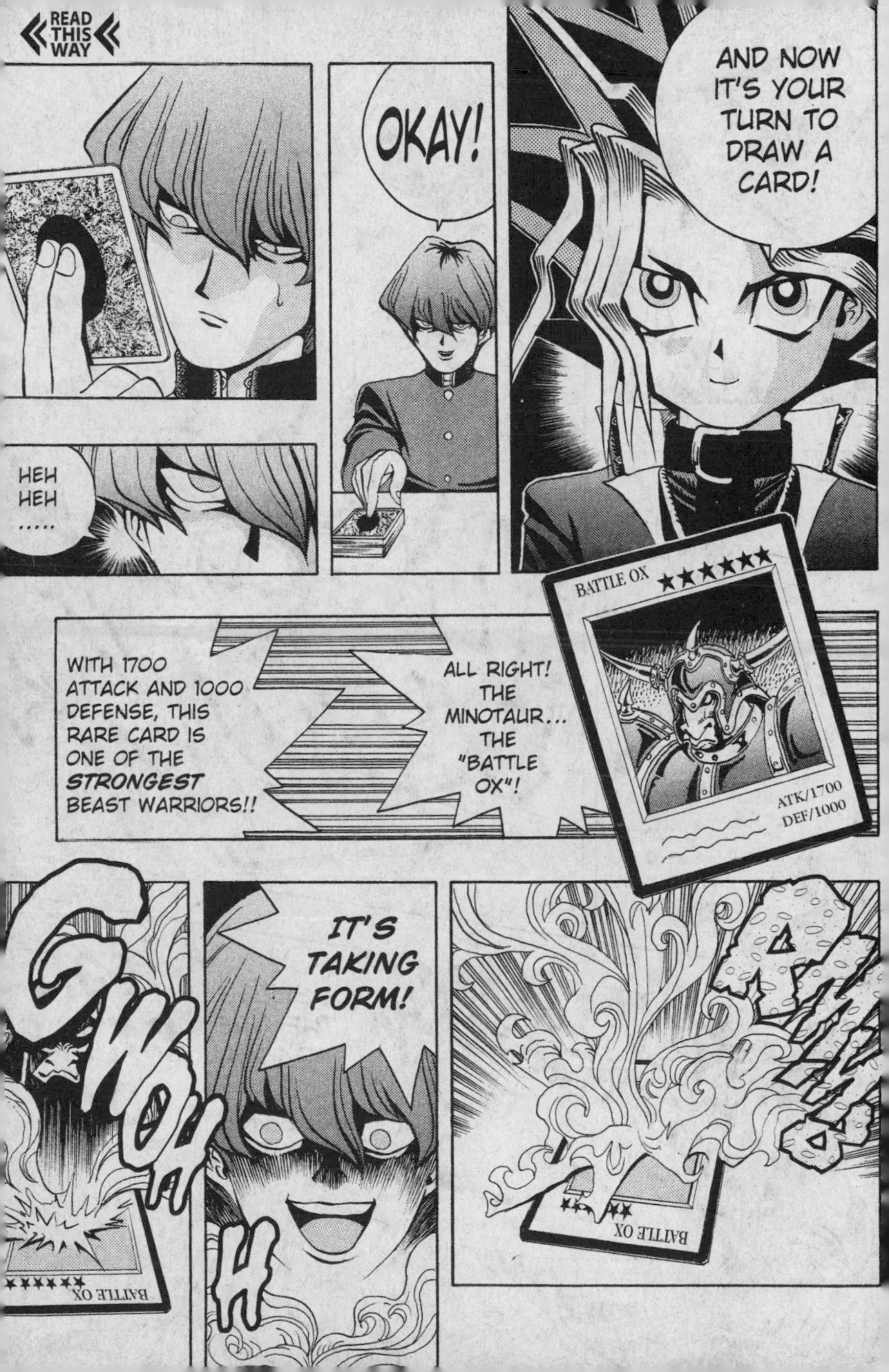
AND NOW IT'S YOUR TURN TO DRAW A CARD!
OKAY!
HEH HEH .....
BATTLE OX
ATK/1700
DEF/1000
ALL RIGHT! THE MINOTAUR... THE "BATTLE OX"!
WITH 1700 ATTACK AND 1000 DEFENSE, THIS RARE CARD IS ONE OF THE *STRONGEST* BEAST WARRIORS!!
BATTLE OX
IT'S TAKING FORM!
GWOH
BATTLE OX

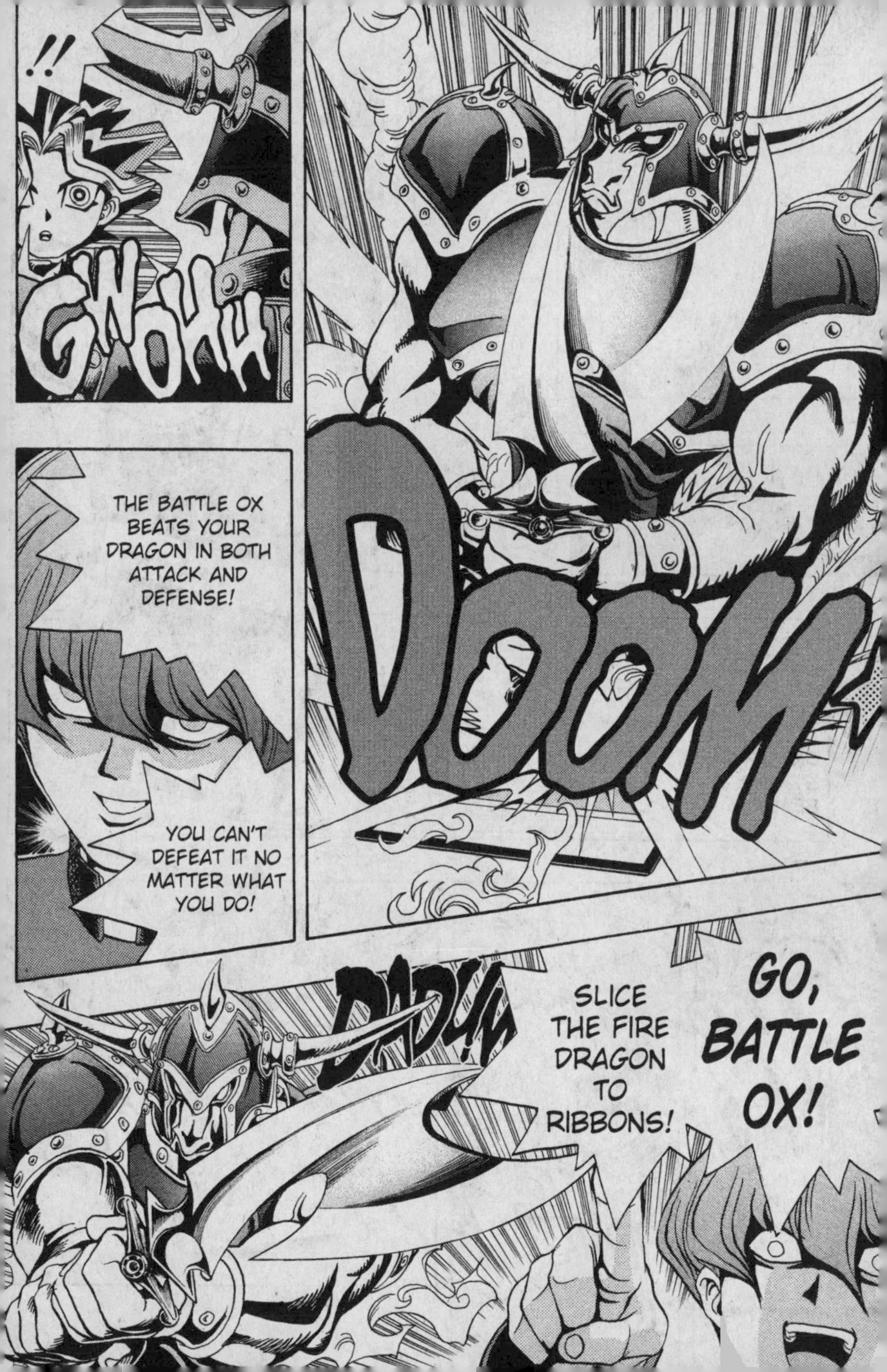
DOOM
!!
GWOHH
THE BATTLE OX BEATS YOUR DRAGON IN BOTH ATTACK AND DEFENSE!
YOU CAN'T DEFEAT IT NO MATTER WHAT YOU DO!
GO, BATTLE OX!
SLICE THE FIRE DRAGON TO RIBBONS!
DADUN

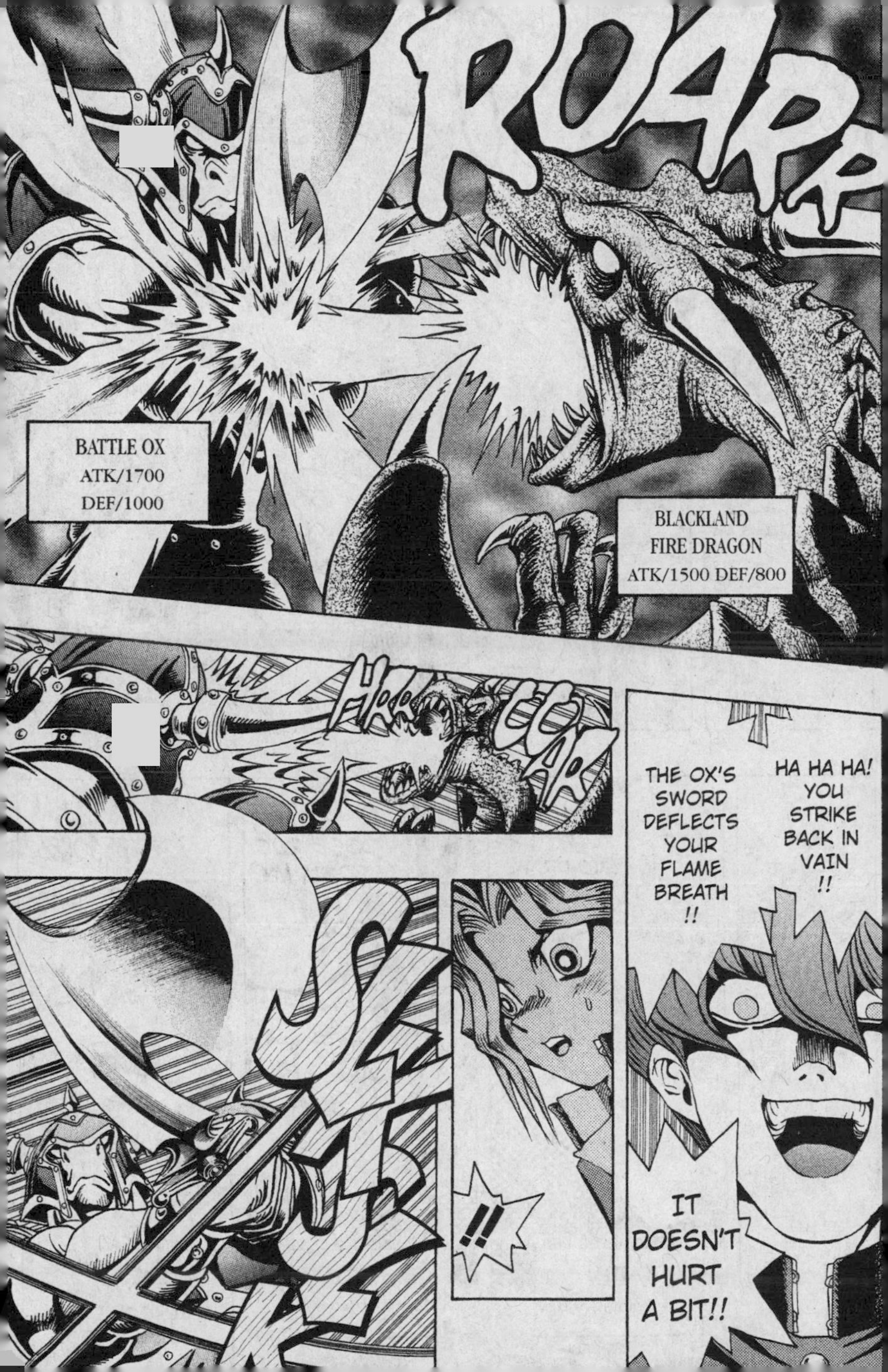
ROARR
BLACKLAND FIRE DRAGON ATK/1500 DEF/800
BATTLE OX ATK/1700 DEF/1000
HA HA HA! YOU STRIKE BACK IN VAIN!!
THE OX'S SWORD DEFLECTS YOUR FLAME BREATH!!
IT DOESN'T HURT A BIT!!
!!

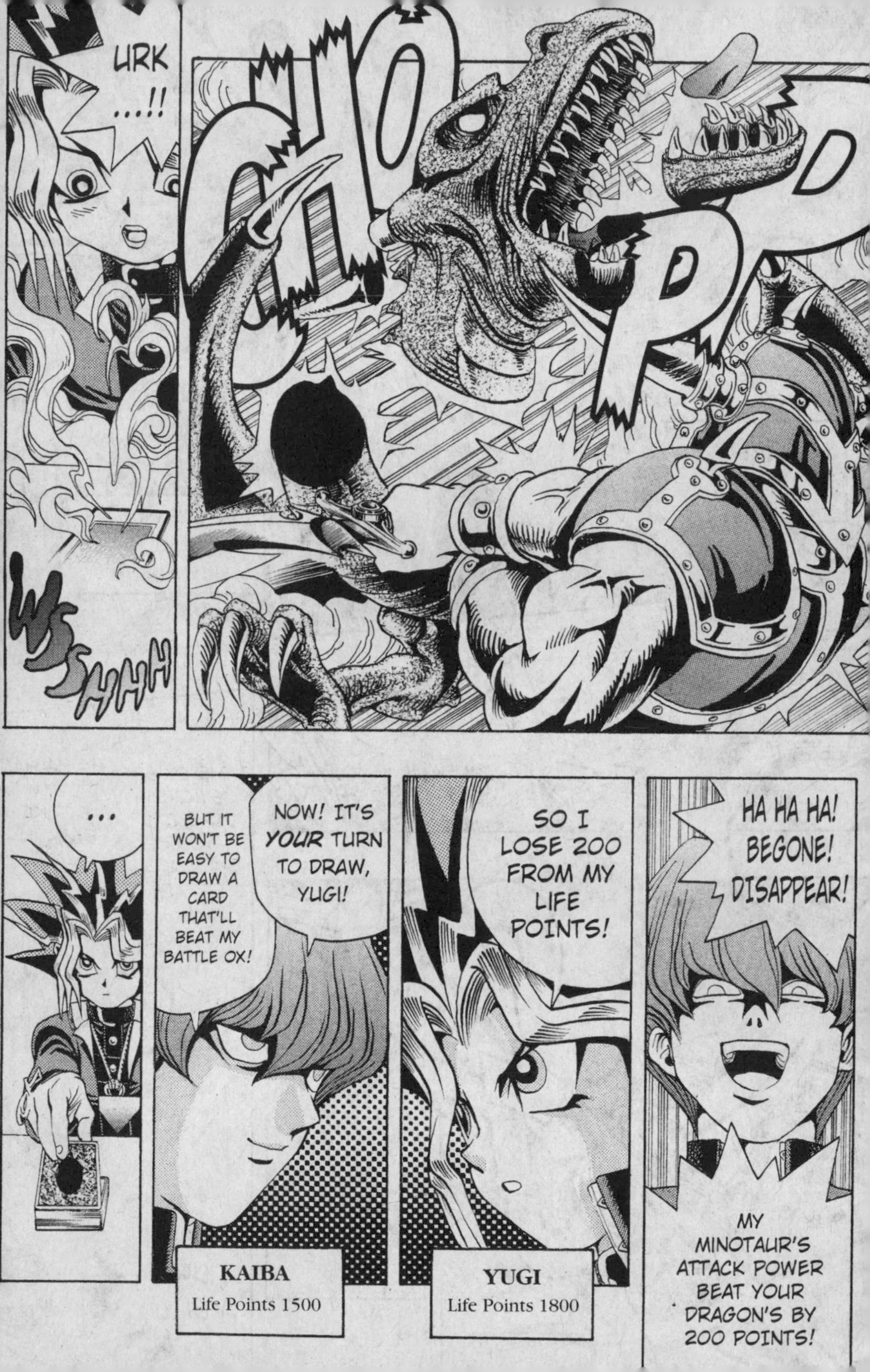
URK ...!!
HA HA HA! BEGONE! DISAPPEAR!
MY MINOTAUR'S ATTACK POWER BEAT YOUR DRAGON'S BY 200 POINTS!
SO I LOSE 200 FROM MY LIFE POINTS!
YUGI
Life Points 1800
NOW! IT'S *YOUR* TURN TO DRAW, YUGI!
BUT IT WON'T BE EASY TO DRAW A CARD THAT'LL BEAT MY BATTLE OX!
KAIBA
Life Points 1500
...

READ THIS WAY

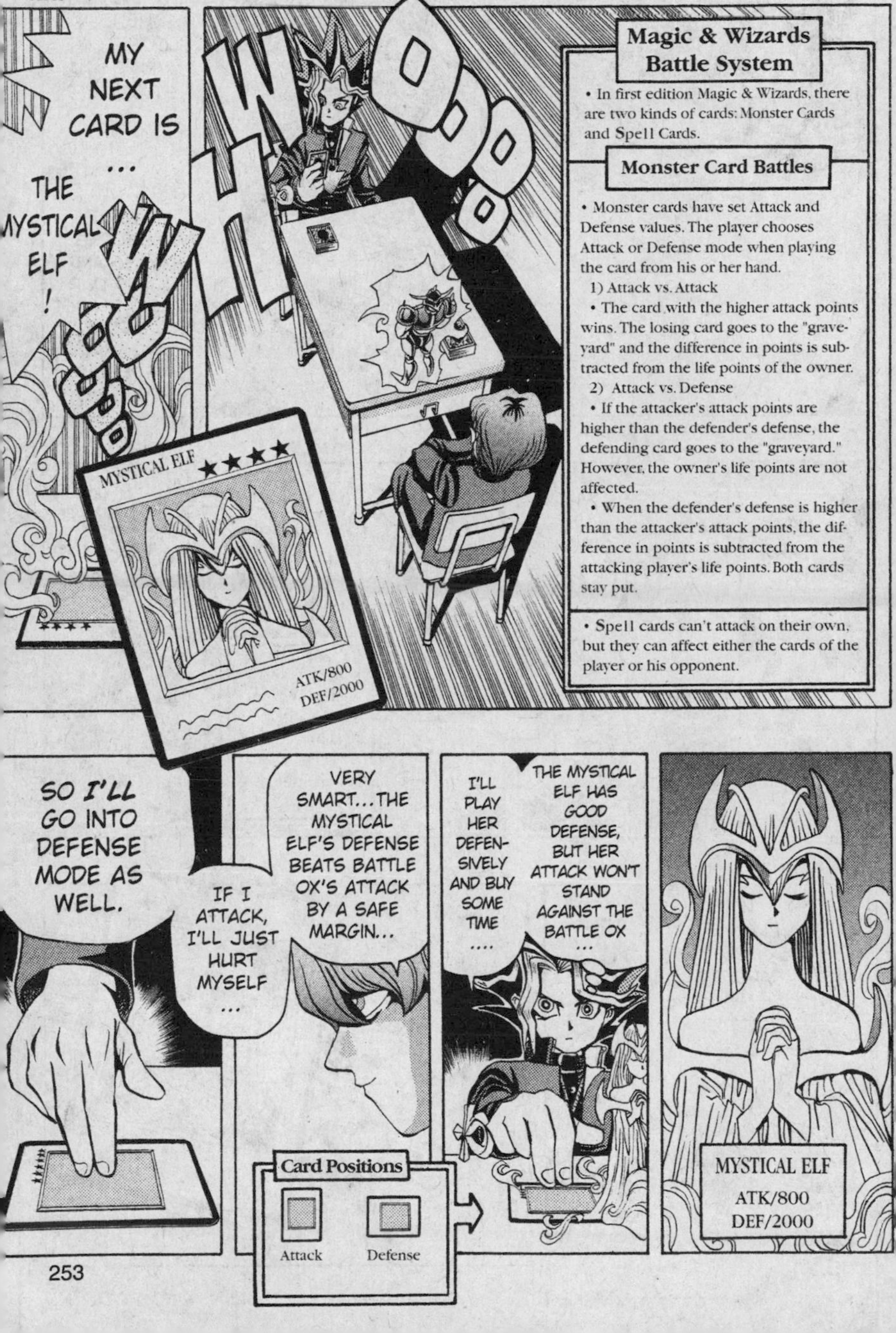
WOOOOO
WOOOOO
Magic & Wizards Battle System
• In first edition Magic & Wizards, there are two kinds of cards: Monster Cards and Spell Cards.
Monster Card Battles
• Monster cards have set Attack and Defense values. The player chooses Attack or Defense mode when playing the card from his or her hand.
1) Attack vs. Attack
• The card with the higher attack points wins. The losing card goes to the "graveyard" and the difference in points is subtracted from the life points of the owner.
2) Attack vs. Defense
• If the attacker's attack points are higher than the defender's defense, the defending card goes to the "graveyard." However, the owner's life points are not affected.
• When the defender's defense is higher than the attacker's attack points, the difference in points is subtracted from the attacking player's life points. Both cards stay put.
• Spell cards can't attack on their own, but they can affect either the cards of the player or his opponent.
MY NEXT CARD IS ...
THE MYSTICAL ELF !
MYSTICAL ELF
ATK/800
DEF/2000
MYSTICAL ELF
ATK/800
DEF/2000
THE MYSTICAL ELF HAS GOOD DEFENSE, BUT HER ATTACK WON'T STAND AGAINST THE BATTLE OX ...
I'LL PLAY HER DEFENSIVELY AND BUY SOME TIME ....
VERY SMART... THE MYSTICAL ELF'S DEFENSE BEATS BATTLE OX'S ATTACK BY A SAFE MARGIN...
IF I ATTACK, I'LL JUST HURT MYSELF ...
Card Positions
Attack
Defense
SO I'LL GO INTO DEFENSE MODE AS WELL.

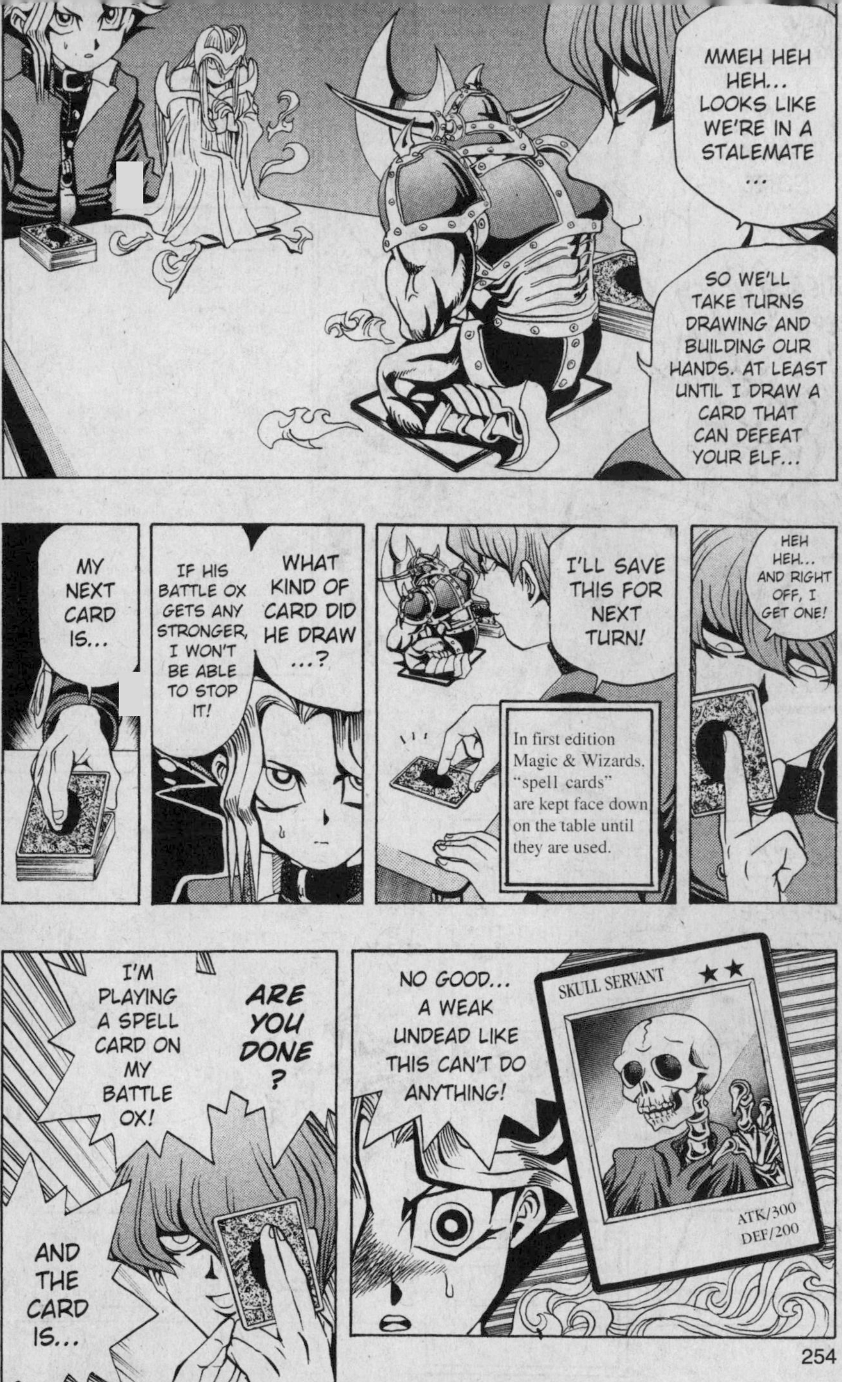
MMEH HEH HEH... LOOKS LIKE WE'RE IN A STALEMATE ...
SO WE'LL TAKE TURNS DRAWING AND BUILDING OUR HANDS. AT LEAST UNTIL I DRAW A CARD THAT CAN DEFEAT YOUR ELF...
HEH HEH... AND RIGHT OFF, I GET ONE!
I'LL SAVE THIS FOR NEXT TURN!
In first edition Magic & Wizards, "spell cards" are kept face down on the table until they are used.
WHAT KIND OF CARD DID HE DRAW ...?
IF HIS BATTLE OX GETS ANY STRONGER, I WON'T BE ABLE TO STOP IT!
MY NEXT CARD IS...
NO GOOD... A WEAK UNDEAD LIKE THIS CAN'T DO ANYTHING!
SKULL SERVANT
ATK/300
DEF/200
ARE YOU DONE ?
I'M PLAYING A SPELL CARD ON MY BATTLE OX!
AND THE CARD IS...

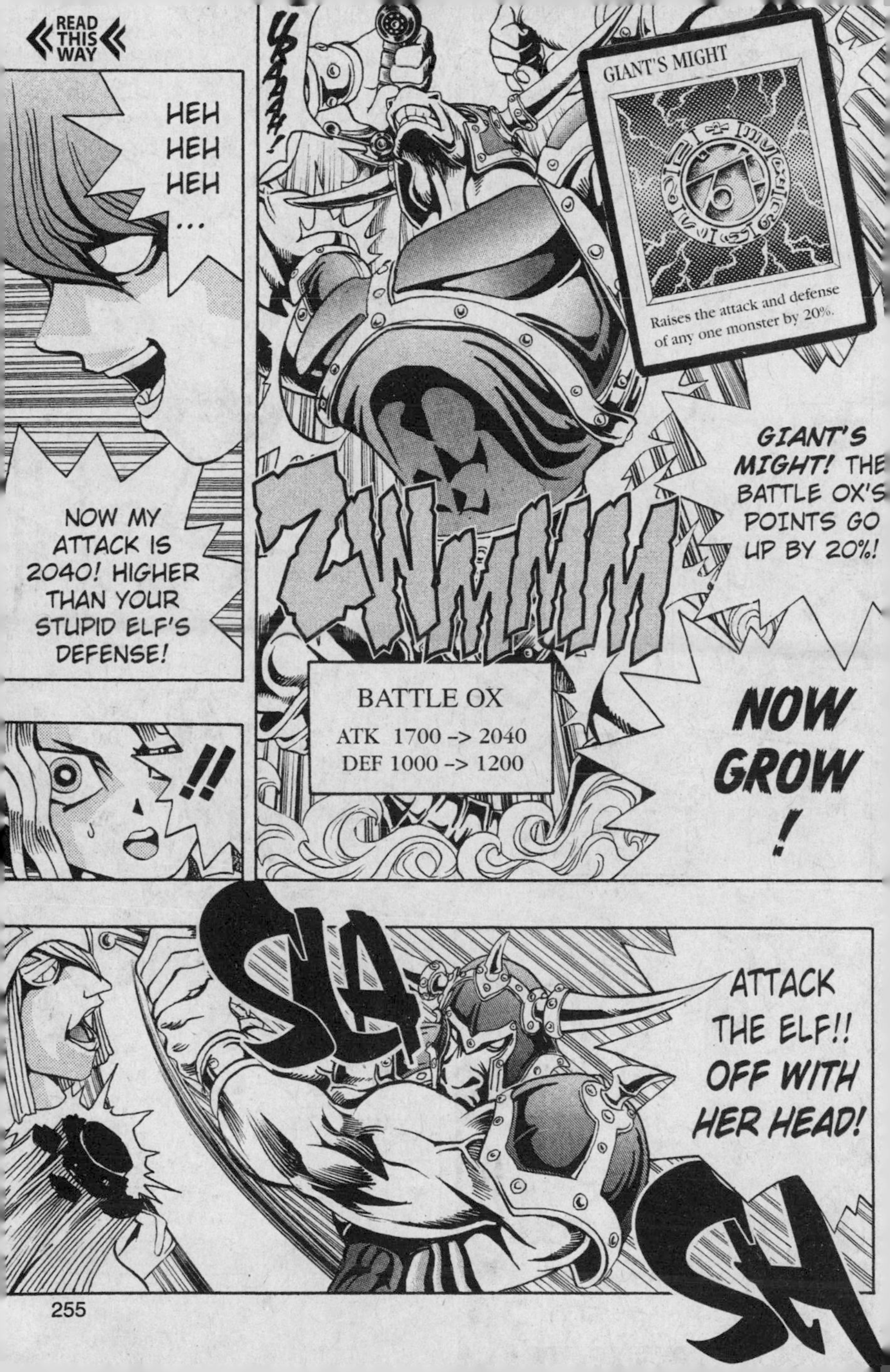
READ THIS WAY
URAAAH!
GIANT'S MIGHT
Raises the attack and defense of any one monster by 20%.
GIANT'S MIGHT! THE BATTLE OX'S POINTS GO UP BY 20%!
ZWMMM
BATTLE OX
ATK 1700 -> 2040
DEF 1000 -> 1200
NOW GROW!
HEH HEH HEH...
NOW MY ATTACK IS 2040! HIGHER THAN YOUR STUPID ELF'S DEFENSE!
!!
ATTACK THE ELF!! OFF WITH HER HEAD!
SA
SA

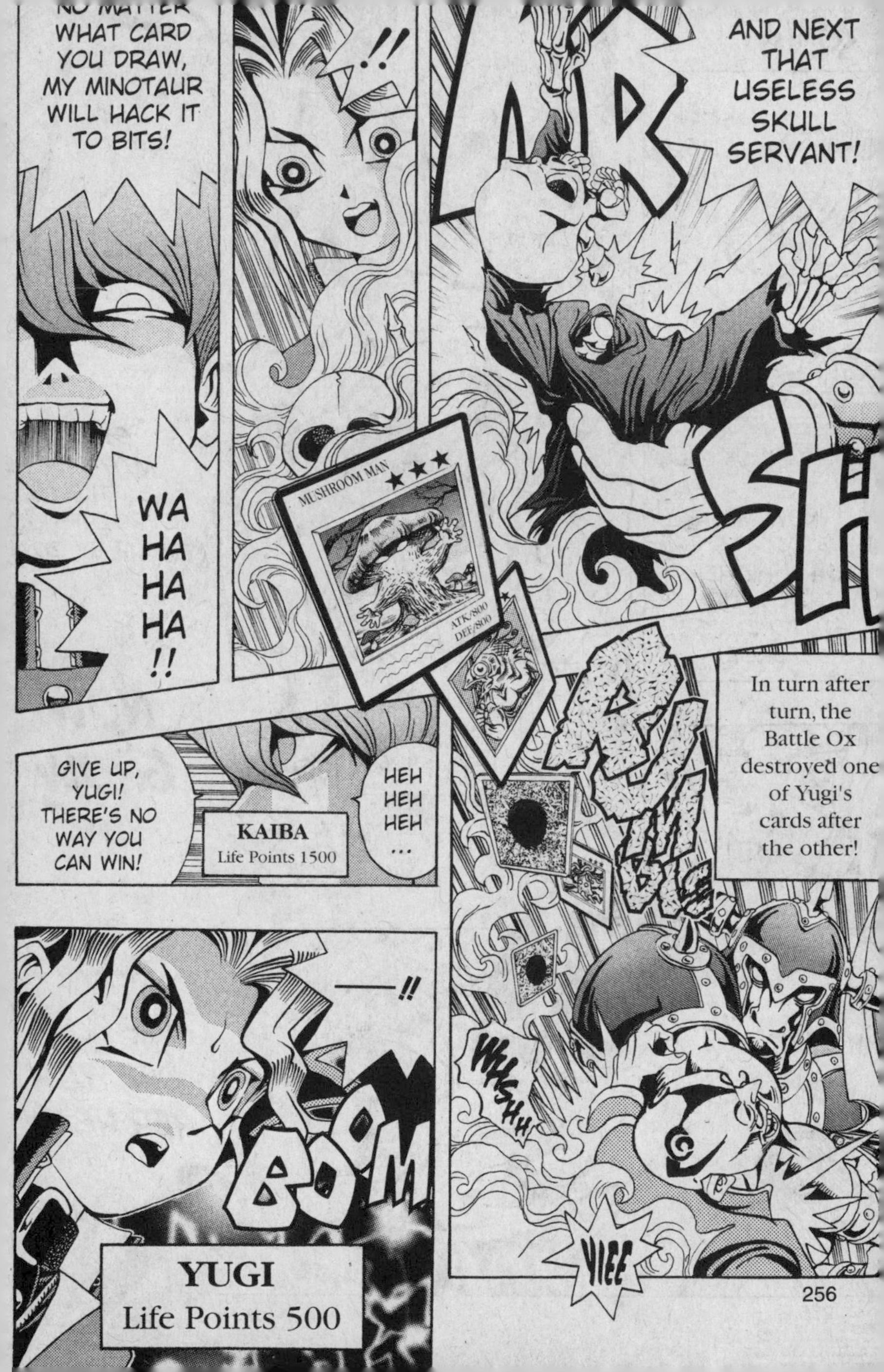
AND NEXT THAT USELESS SKULL SERVANT!
!!
NO MATTER WHAT CARD YOU DRAW, MY MINOTAUR WILL HACK IT TO BITS!
WA HA HA HA !!
MUSHROOM MAN
ATK/800 DEF/800
In turn after turn, the Battle Ox destroyed one of Yugi's cards after the other!
WHSHH
YIEE
HEH HEH HEH ...
GIVE UP, YUGI! THERE'S NO WAY YOU CAN WIN!
KAIBA
Life Points 1500
——!!
BOOM
YUGI
Life Points 500

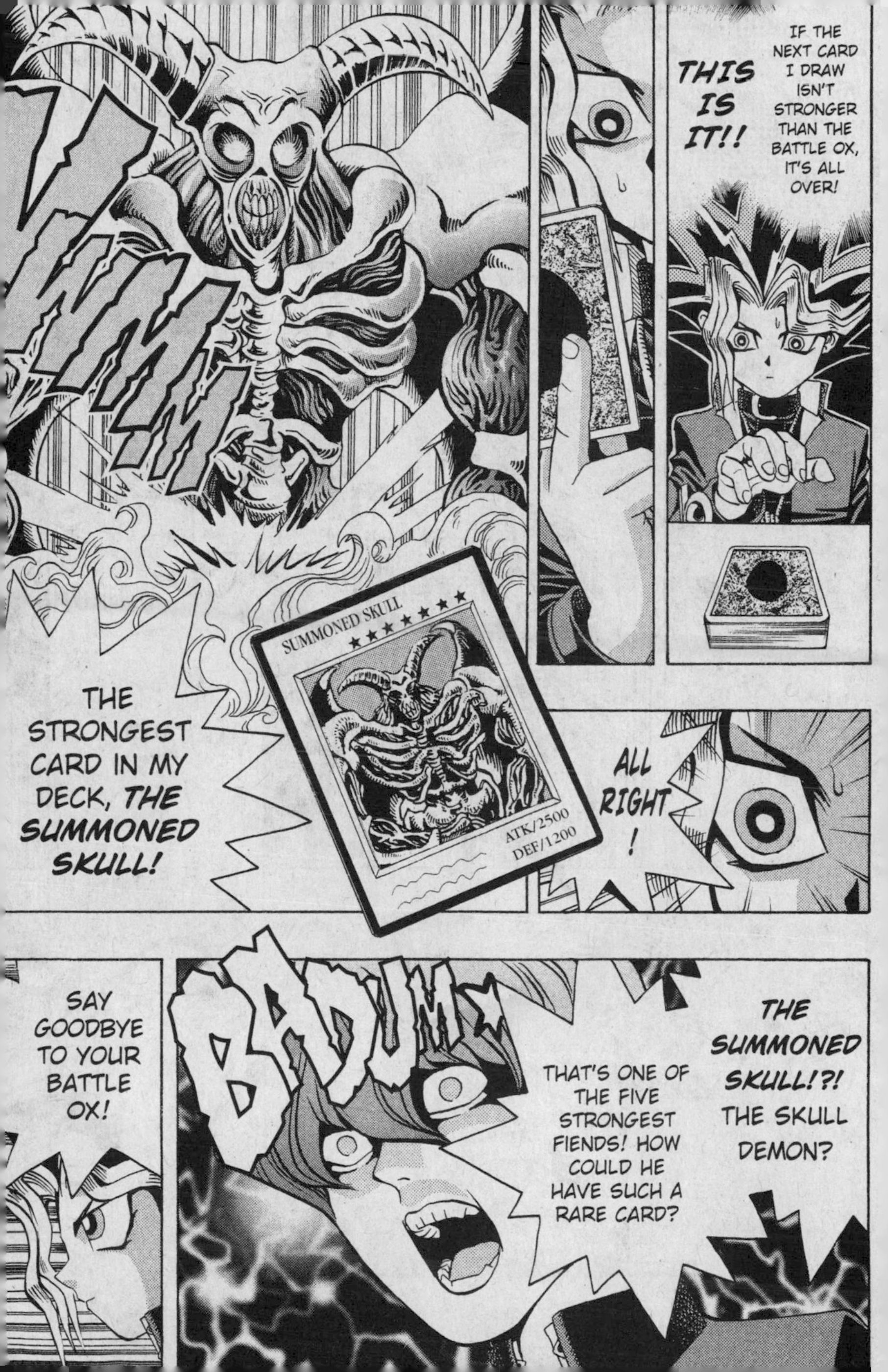
IF THE NEXT CARD I DRAW ISN'T STRONGER THAN THE BATTLE OX, IT'S ALL OVER!
THIS IS IT!!
ALL RIGHT!
THE STRONGEST CARD IN MY DECK, THE SUMMONED SKULL!
SUMMONED SKULL
ATK/2500
DEF/1200
THE SUMMONED SKULL!?! THE SKULL DEMON?
THAT'S ONE OF THE FIVE STRONGEST FIENDS! HOW COULD HE HAVE SUCH A RARE CARD?
BADUM
SAY GOODBYE TO YOUR BATTLE OX!

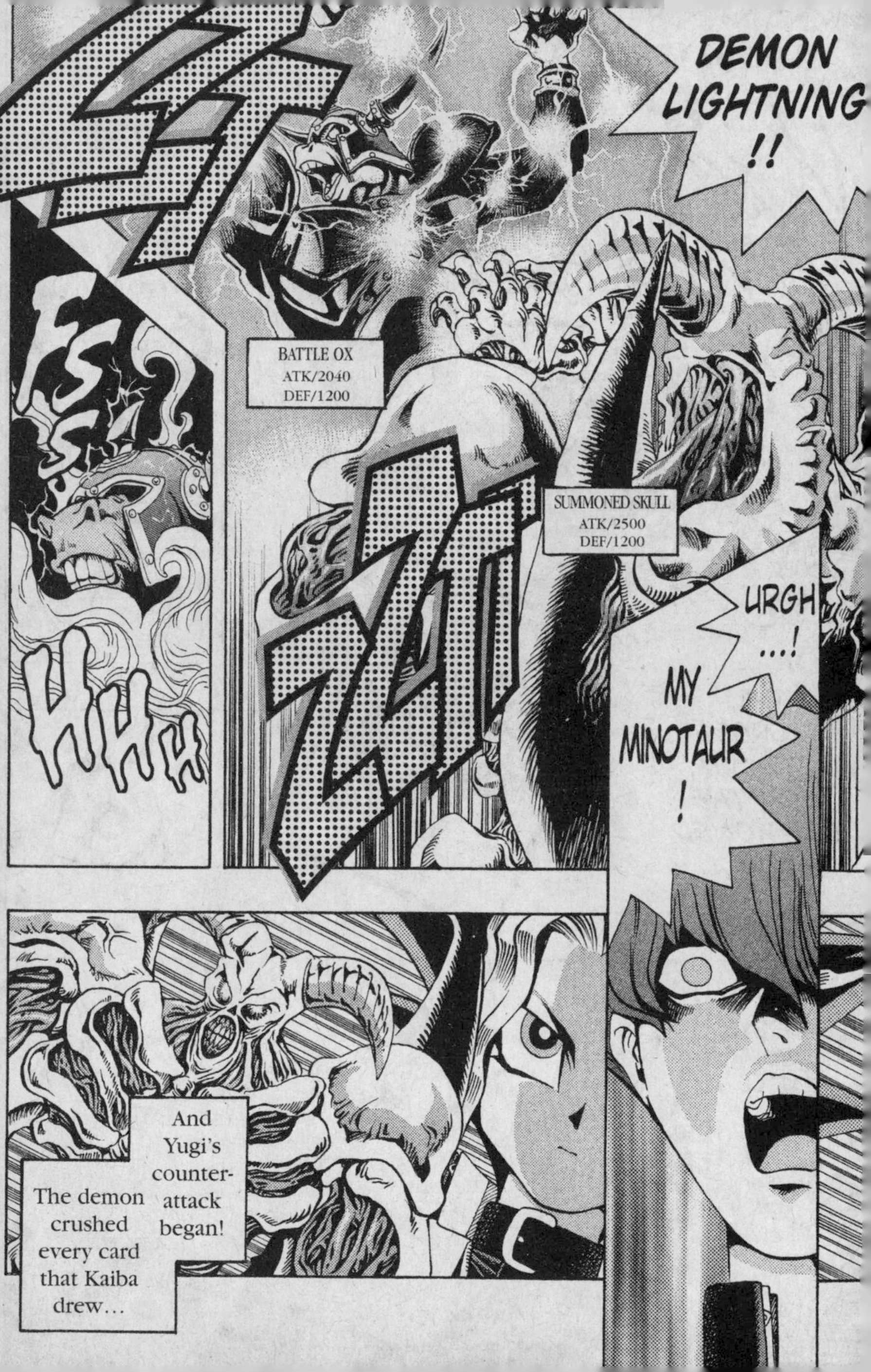
DEMON LIGHTNING!!
SUMMONED SKULL
ATK/2500
DEF/1200
BATTLE OX
ATK/2040
DEF/1200
ZAT
FSS
HUH
URGH...!
MY MINOTAUR!
The demon crushed every card that Kaiba drew...
And Yugi's counter-attack began!

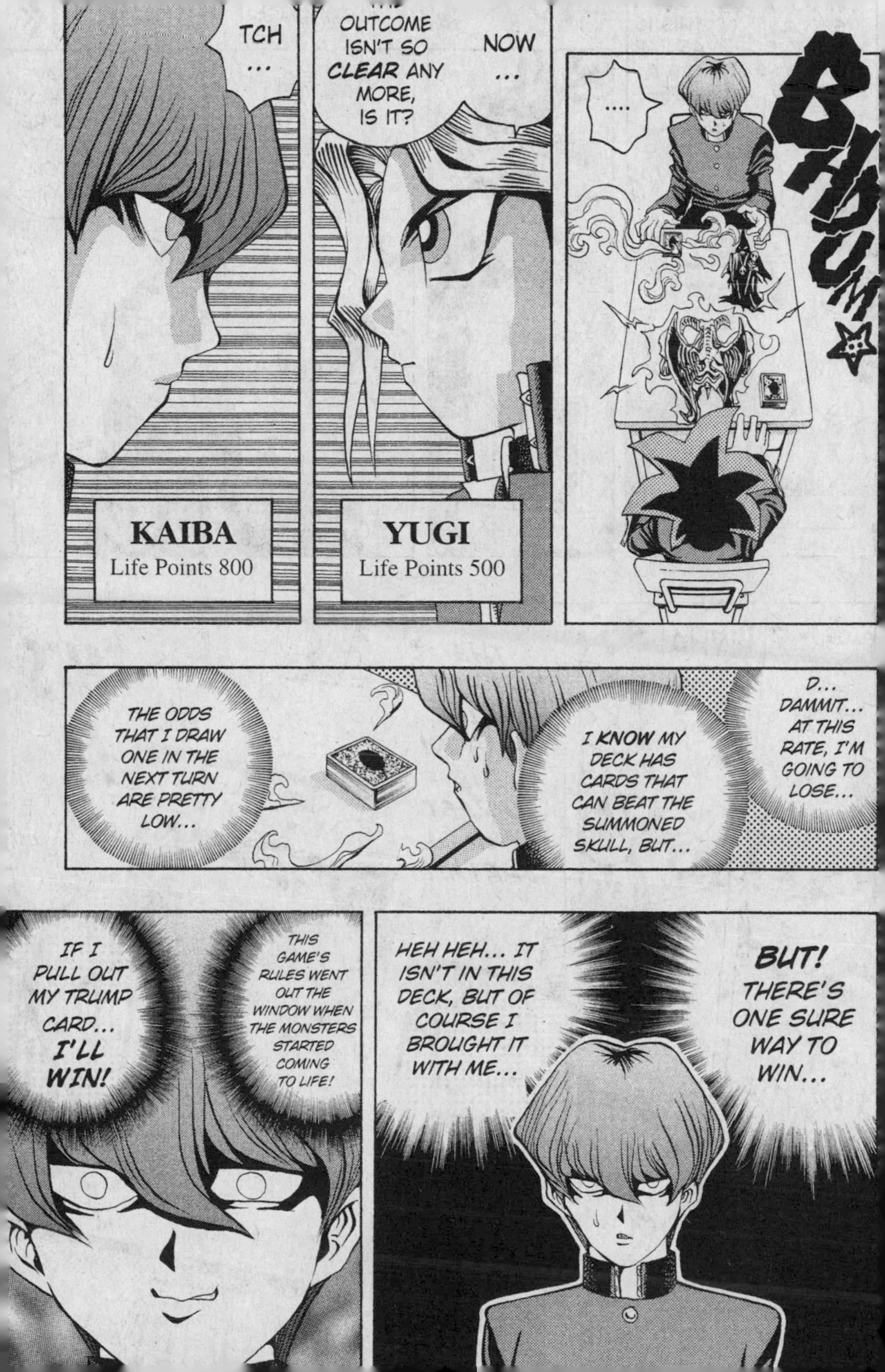
....
BADUM☆
NOW ...
OUTCOME ISN'T SO CLEAR ANY MORE, IS IT?
YUGI
Life Points 500
TCH ...
KAIBA
Life Points 800
D... DAMMIT... AT THIS RATE, I'M GOING TO LOSE...
I KNOW MY DECK HAS CARDS THAT CAN BEAT THE SUMMONED SKULL, BUT...
THE ODDS THAT I DRAW ONE IN THE NEXT TURN ARE PRETTY LOW...
BUT! THERE'S ONE SURE WAY TO WIN...
HEH HEH... IT ISN'T IN THIS DECK, BUT OF COURSE I BROUGHT IT WITH ME...
THIS GAME'S RULES WENT OUT THE WINDOW WHEN THE MONSTERS STARTED COMING TO LIFE!
IF I PULL OUT MY TRUMP CARD... I'LL WIN!

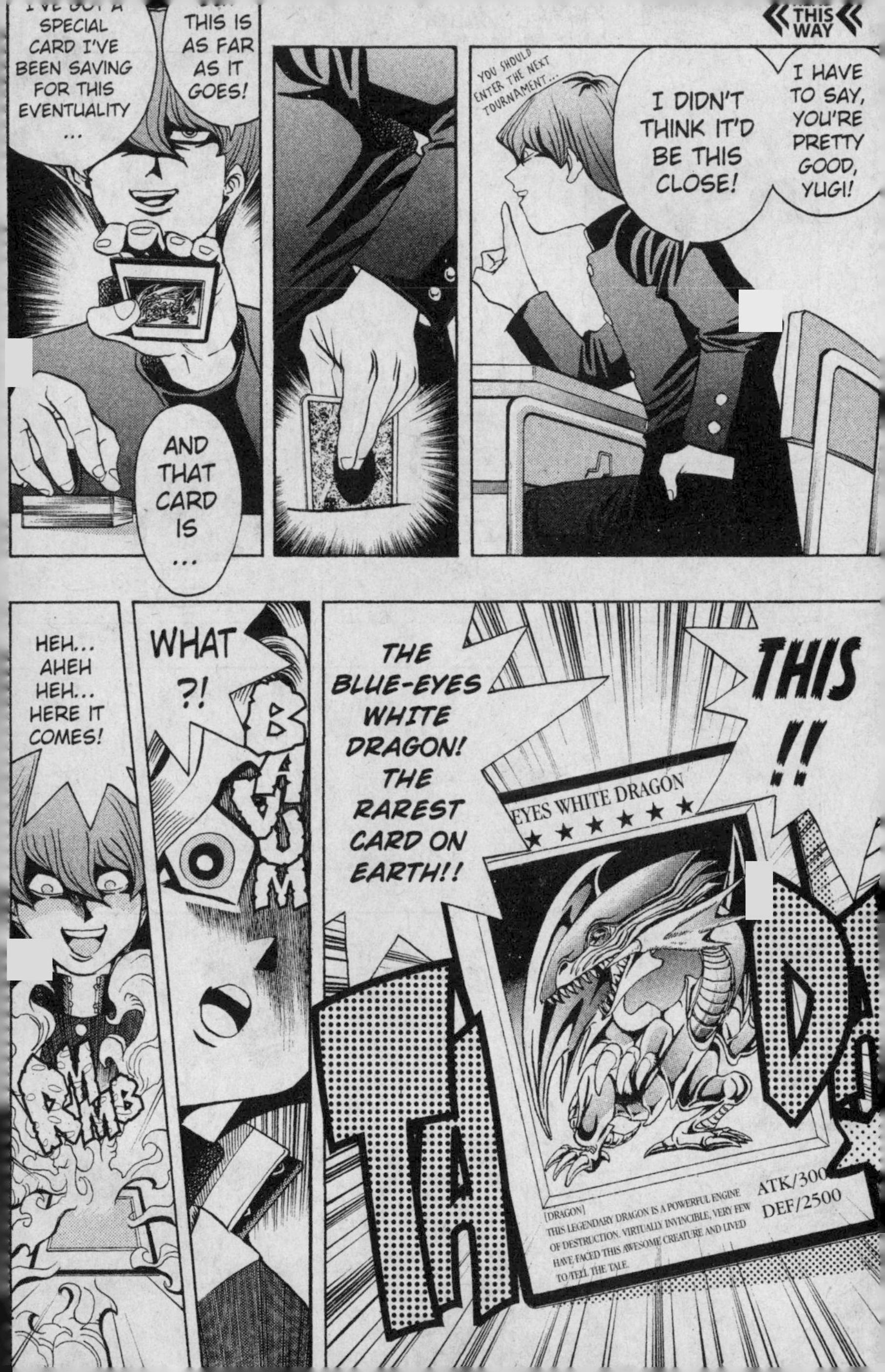
THIS WAY
I HAVE TO SAY, YOU'RE PRETTY GOOD, YUGI!
I DIDN'T THINK IT'D BE THIS CLOSE!
YOU SHOULD ENTER THE NEXT TOURNAMENT...
THIS IS AS FAR AS IT GOES!
SPECIAL CARD I'VE BEEN SAVING FOR THIS EVENTUALITY ...
AND THAT CARD IS ...
THIS !!
THE BLUE-EYES WHITE DRAGON! THE RAREST CARD ON EARTH!!
EYES WHITE DRAGON
[DRAGON]
THIS LEGENDARY DRAGON IS A POWERFUL ENGINE OF DESTRUCTION. VIRTUALLY INVINCIBLE, VERY FEW HAVE FACED THIS AWESOME CREATURE AND LIVED TO TELL THE TALE.
ATK/300
DEF/2500
WHAT ?!
HEH... AHEH HEH... HERE IT COMES!

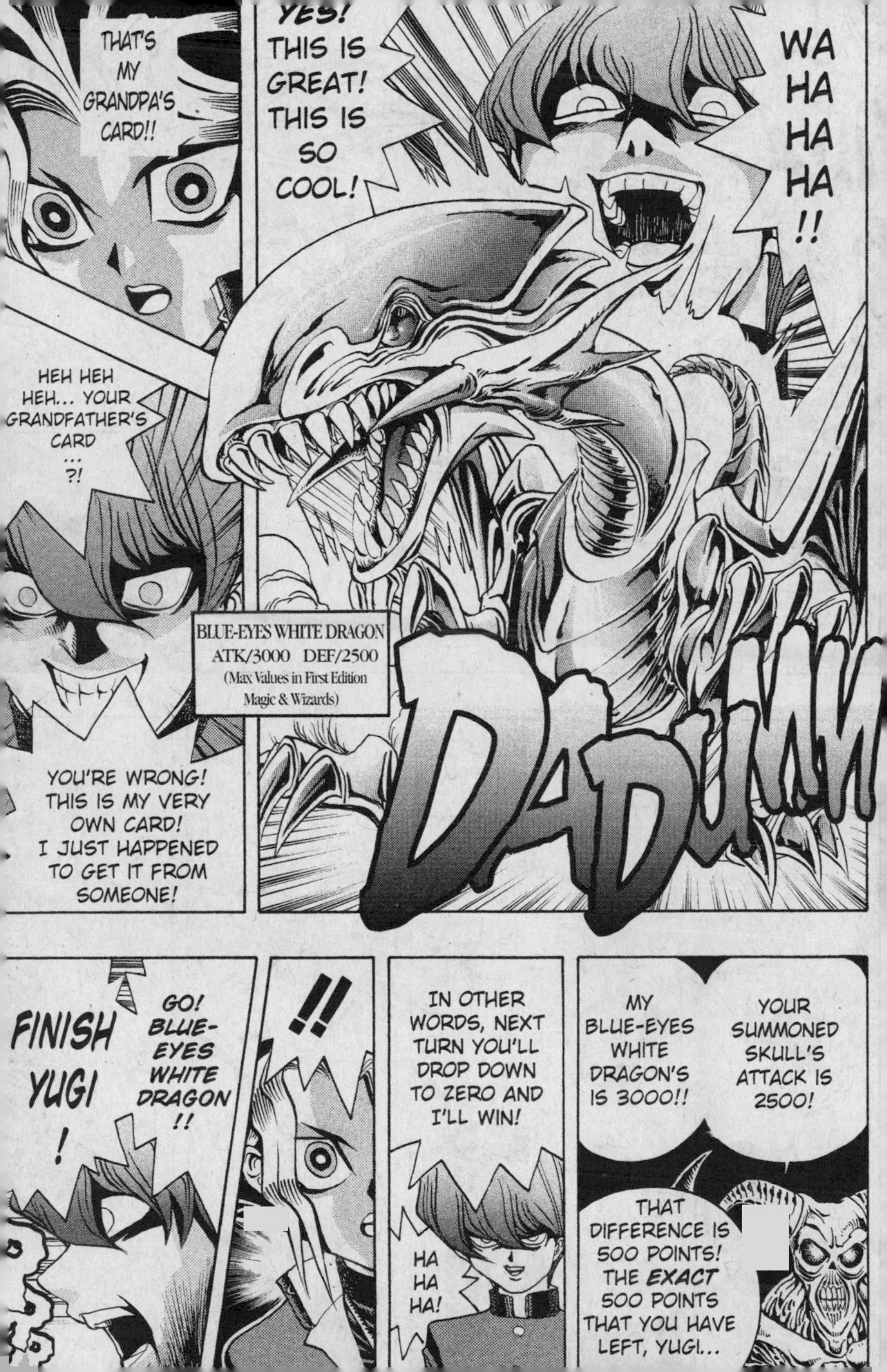
WA HA HA HA!!
YES! THIS IS GREAT! THIS IS SO COOL!
BLUE-EYES WHITE DRAGON
ATK/3000 DEF/2500
(Max Values in First Edition Magic & Wizards)
DADUMM
THAT'S MY GRANDPA'S CARD!!
HEH HEH HEH... YOUR GRANDFATHER'S CARD...?!
YOU'RE WRONG! THIS IS MY VERY OWN CARD! I JUST HAPPENED TO GET IT FROM SOMEONE!
YOUR SUMMONED SKULL'S ATTACK IS 2500!
MY BLUE-EYES WHITE DRAGON'S IS 3000!!
THAT DIFFERENCE IS 500 POINTS! THE *EXACT* 500 POINTS THAT YOU HAVE LEFT, YUGI...
IN OTHER WORDS, NEXT TURN YOU'LL DROP DOWN TO ZERO AND I'LL WIN!
HA HA HA!
!!
GO! BLUE-EYES WHITE DRAGON!!
FINISH YUGI!

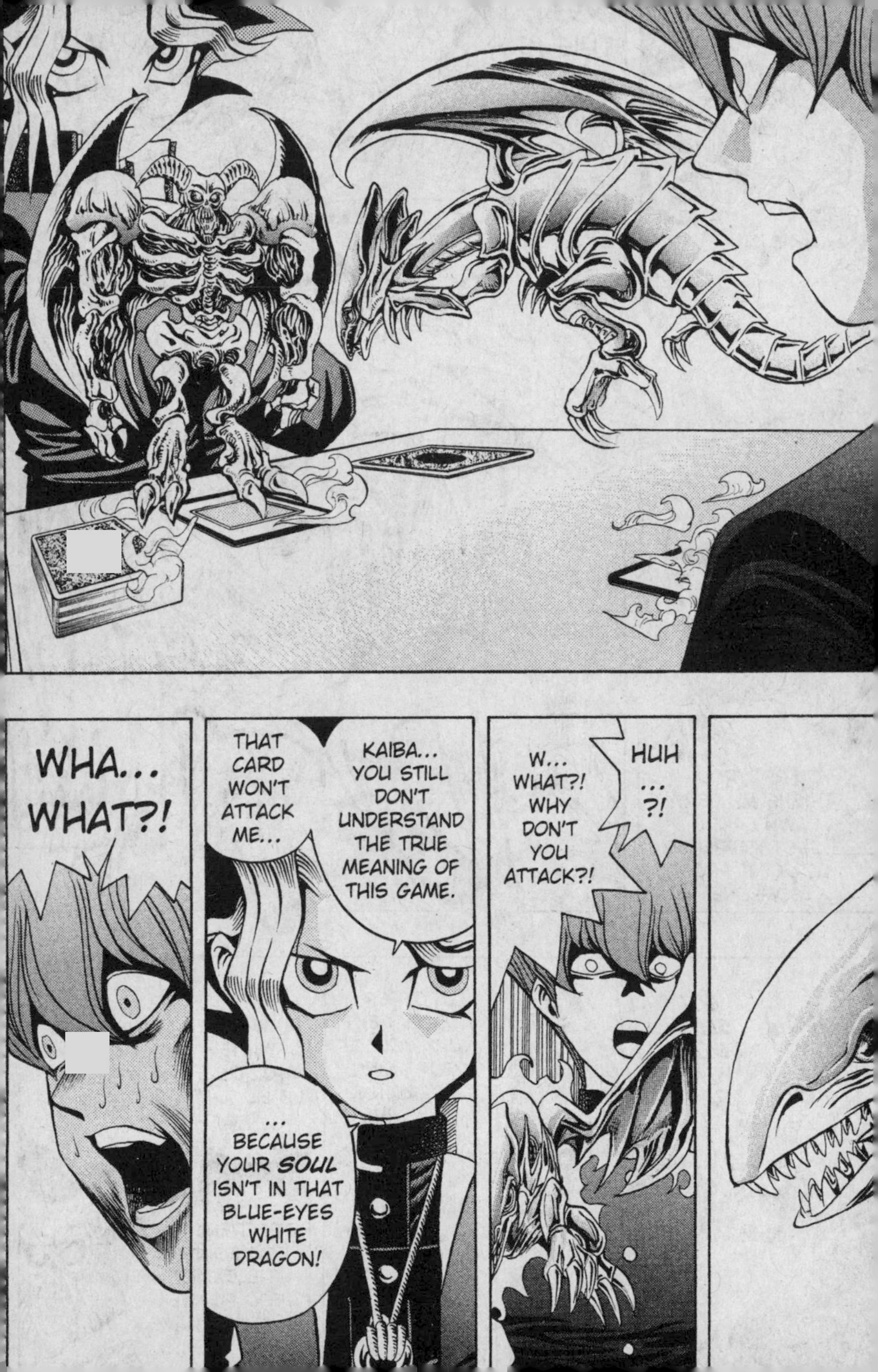
HUH ...?!
W... WHAT?! WHY DON'T YOU ATTACK?!
KAIBA... YOU STILL DON'T UNDERSTAND THE TRUE MEANING OF THIS GAME.
THAT CARD WON'T ATTACK ME...
... BECAUSE YOUR SOUL ISN'T IN THAT BLUE-EYES WHITE DRAGON!
WHA... WHAT?!

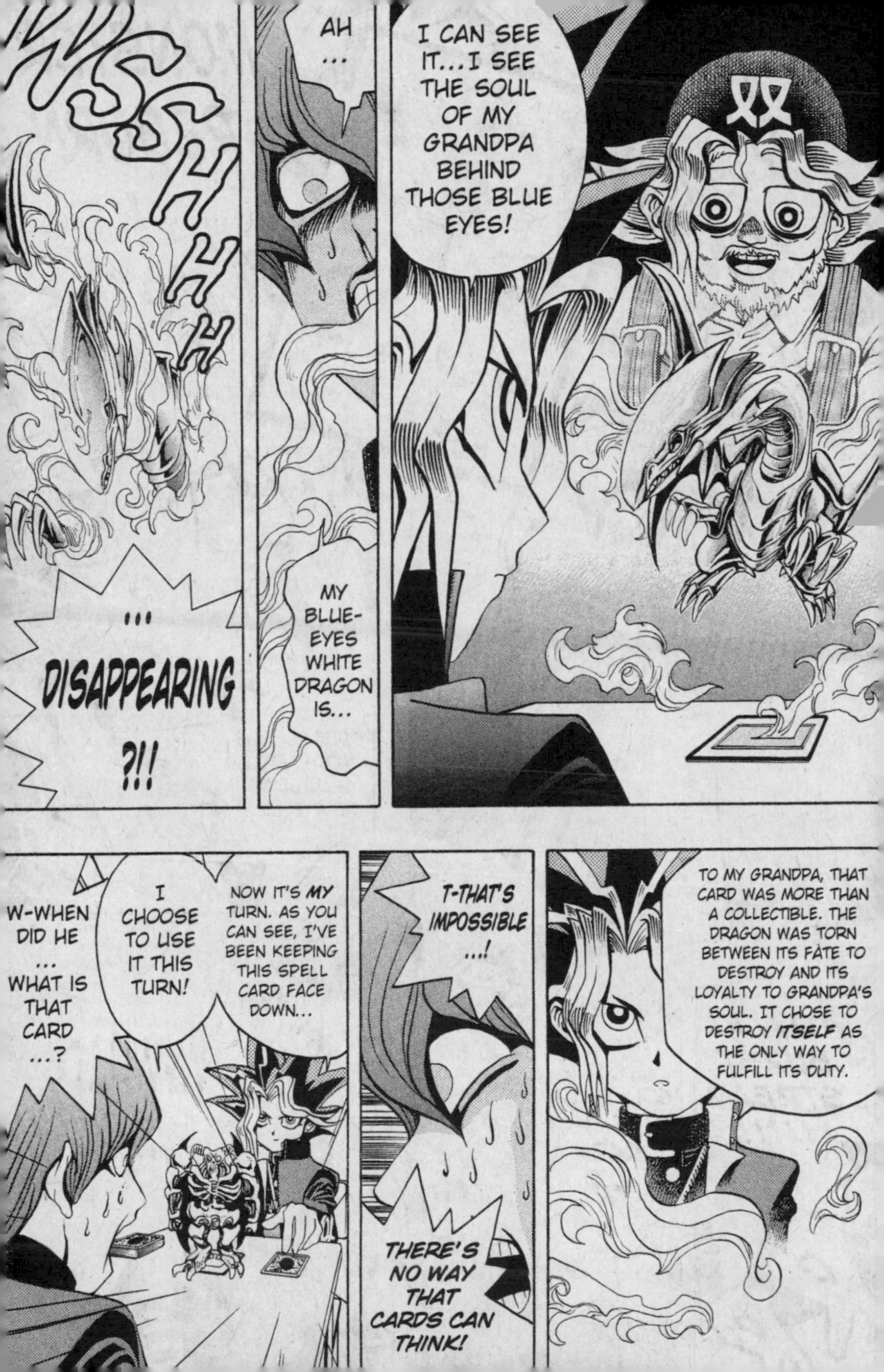
I CAN SEE IT...I SEE THE SOUL OF MY GRANDPA BEHIND THOSE BLUE EYES!
AH ...
MY BLUE-EYES WHITE DRAGON IS...
WSSHHH
... DISAPPEARING ?!!
TO MY GRANDPA, THAT CARD WAS MORE THAN A COLLECTIBLE. THE DRAGON WAS TORN BETWEEN ITS FATE TO DESTROY AND ITS LOYALTY TO GRANDPA'S SOUL. IT CHOSE TO DESTROY *ITSELF* AS THE ONLY WAY TO FULFILL ITS DUTY.
T-THAT'S IMPOSSIBLE ...!
THERE'S NO WAY THAT CARDS CAN THINK!
NOW IT'S *MY* TURN. AS YOU CAN SEE, I'VE BEEN KEEPING THIS SPELL CARD FACE DOWN...
I CHOOSE TO USE IT THIS TURN!
W-WHEN DID HE ... WHAT IS THAT CARD ...?

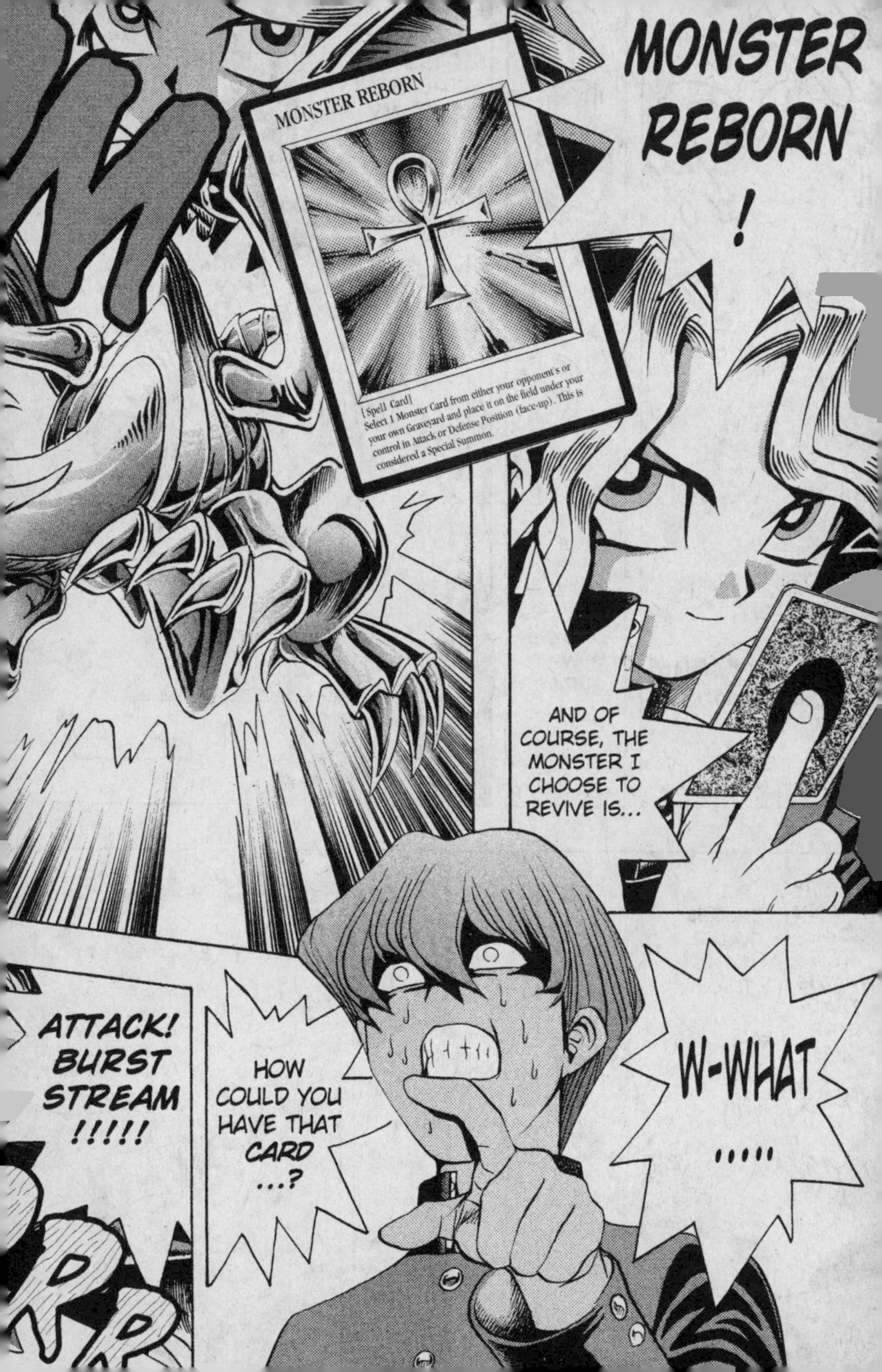
MONSTER REBORN !
MONSTER REBORN
[Spell Card] Select 1 Monster Card from either your opponent's or your own Graveyard and place it on the field under your control in Attack or Defense Position (face-up). This is considered a Special Summon.
AND OF COURSE, THE MONSTER I CHOOSE TO REVIVE IS...
W-WHAT .....
HOW COULD YOU HAVE THAT CARD ...?
ATTACK! BURST STREAM !!!!!

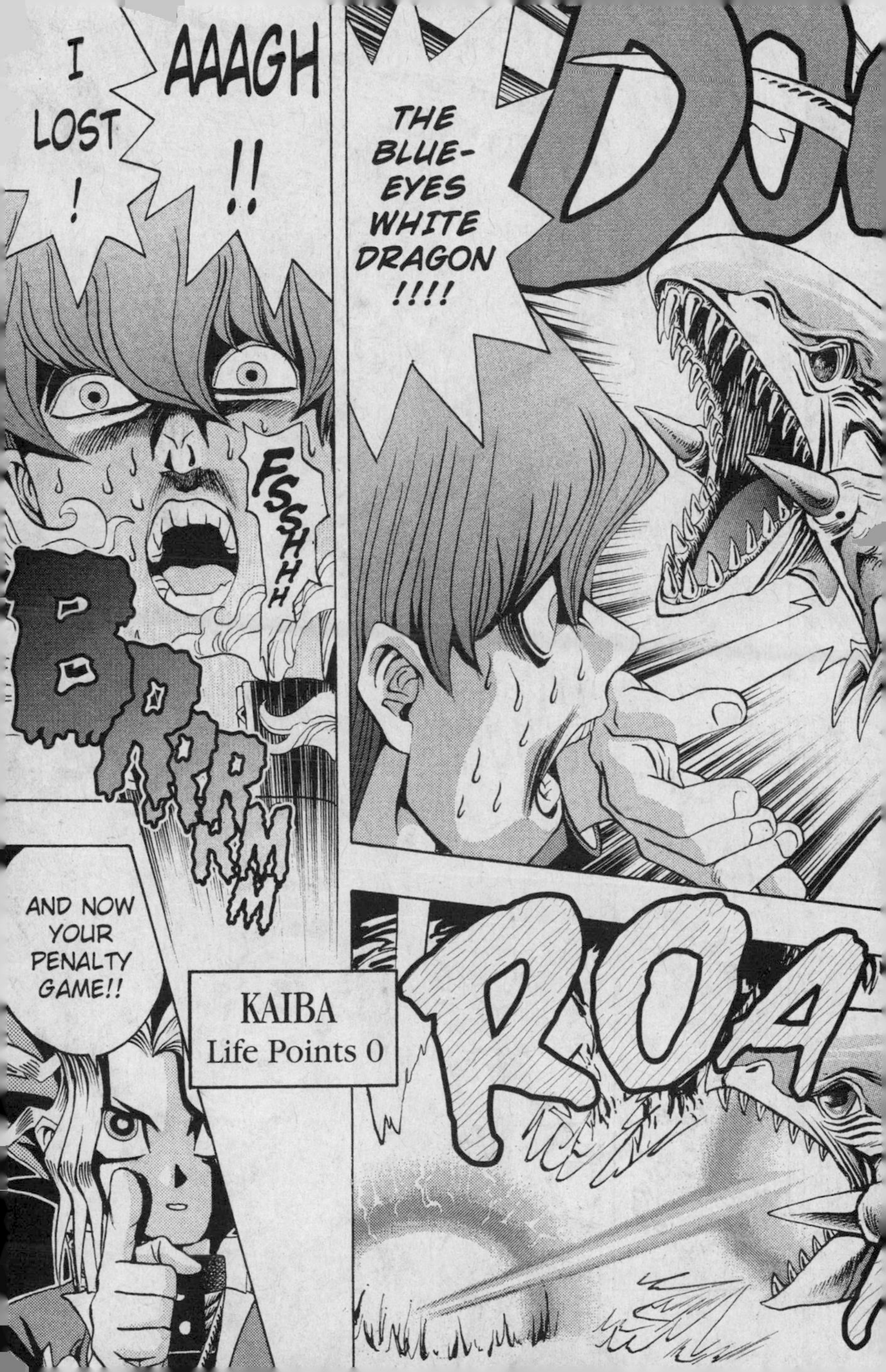
DO
THE BLUE-EYES WHITE DRAGON!!!!
AAAGH!!
I LOST!
FSSHHH
ROA
KAIBA
Life Points 0
AND NOW YOUR PENALTY GAME!!

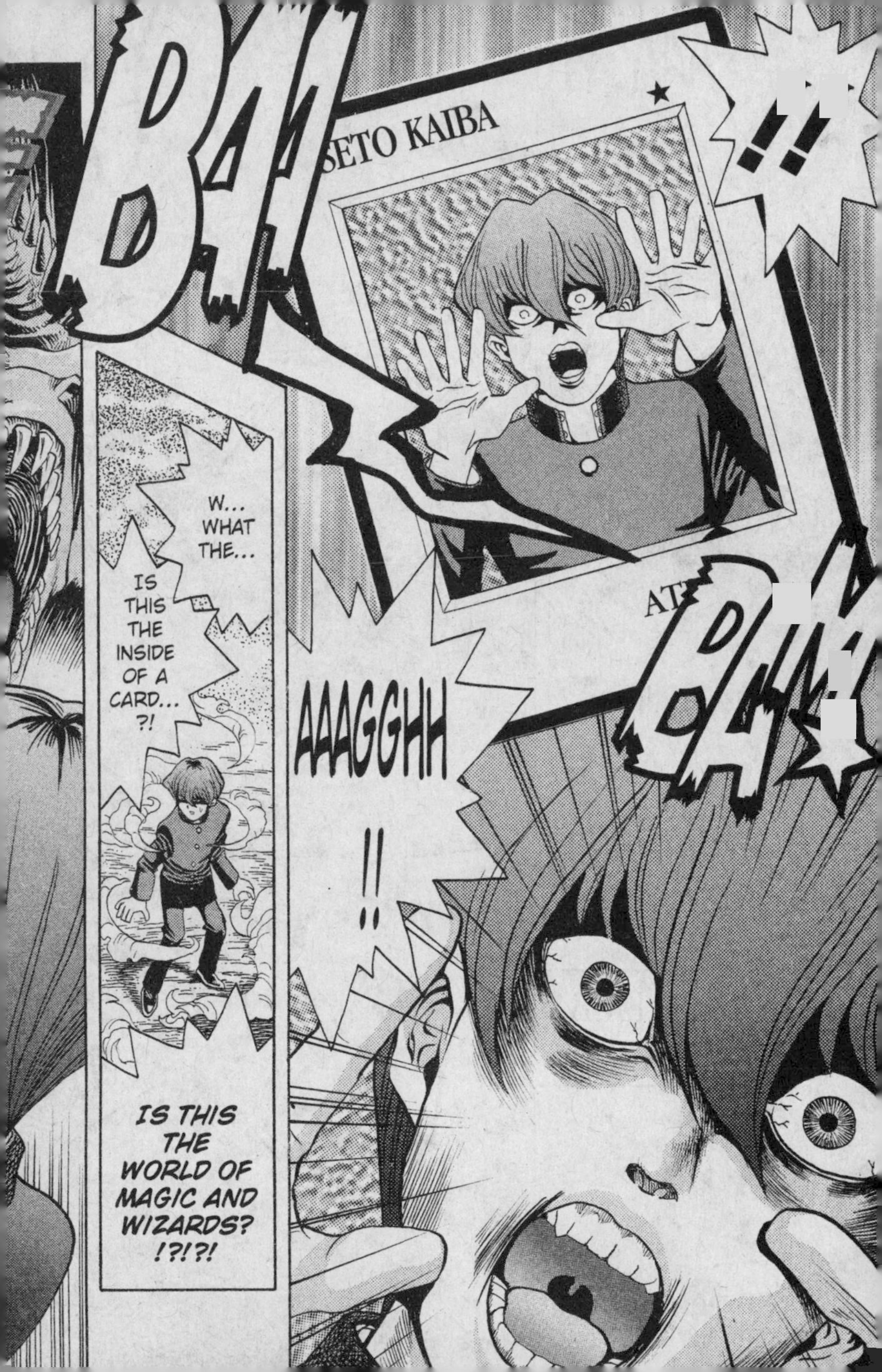
SETO KAIBA
!!
BA
AAAGGHH!!
W... WHAT THE...
IS THIS THE INSIDE OF A CARD...?!
IS THIS THE WORLD OF MAGIC AND WIZARDS?!?!?!

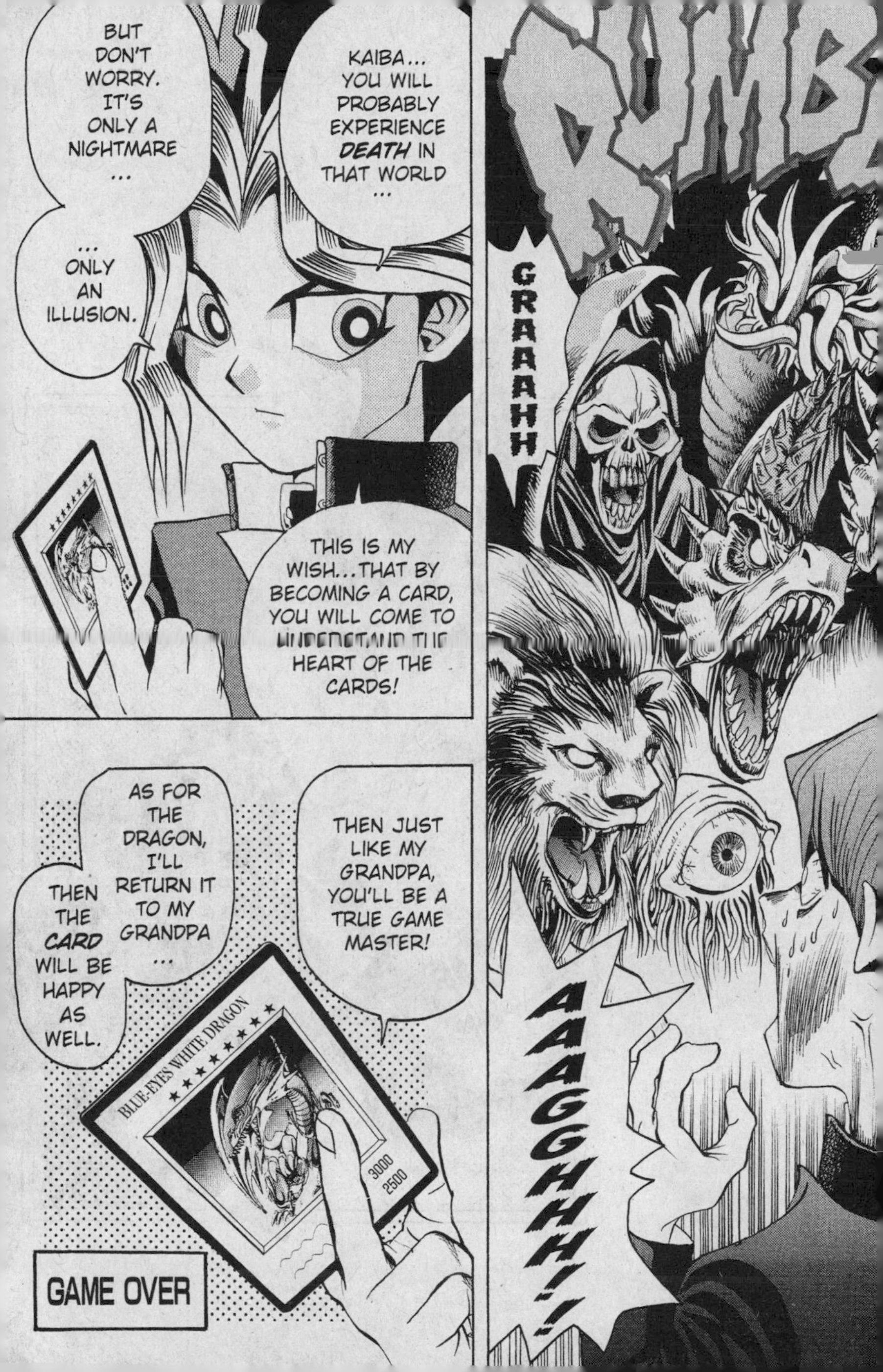
RUMB
GRAAAAHH
AAAAGGHHH!!!
KAIBA... YOU WILL PROBABLY EXPERIENCE DEATH IN THAT WORLD ...
BUT DON'T WORRY. IT'S ONLY A NIGHTMARE ...
... ONLY AN ILLUSION.
THIS IS MY WISH...THAT BY BECOMING A CARD, YOU WILL COME TO UNDERSTAND THE HEART OF THE CARDS!
THEN JUST LIKE MY GRANDPA, YOU'LL BE A TRUE GAME MASTER!
AS FOR THE DRAGON, I'LL RETURN IT TO MY GRANDPA ...
THEN THE CARD WILL BE HAPPY AS WELL.
BLUE-EYES WHITE DRAGON
3000
2500
GAME OVER

Duel 11: The Wild Gang (Part 1)

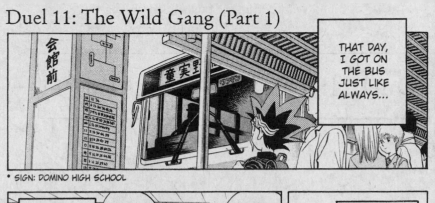

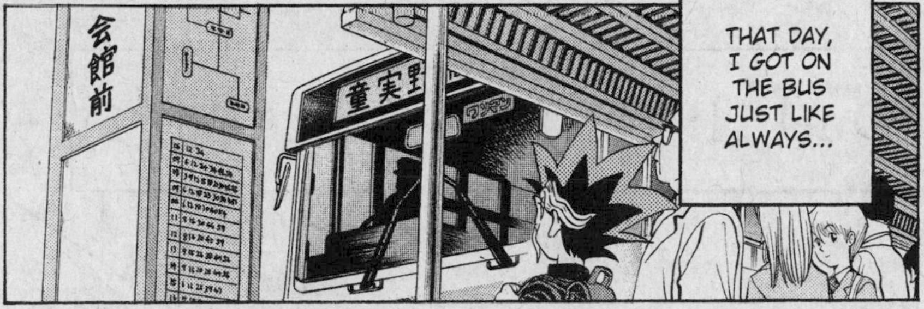
THAT DAY, I GOT ON THE BUS JUST LIKE ALWAYS...
会館前
童実野

* SIGN: DOMINO HIGH SCHOOL

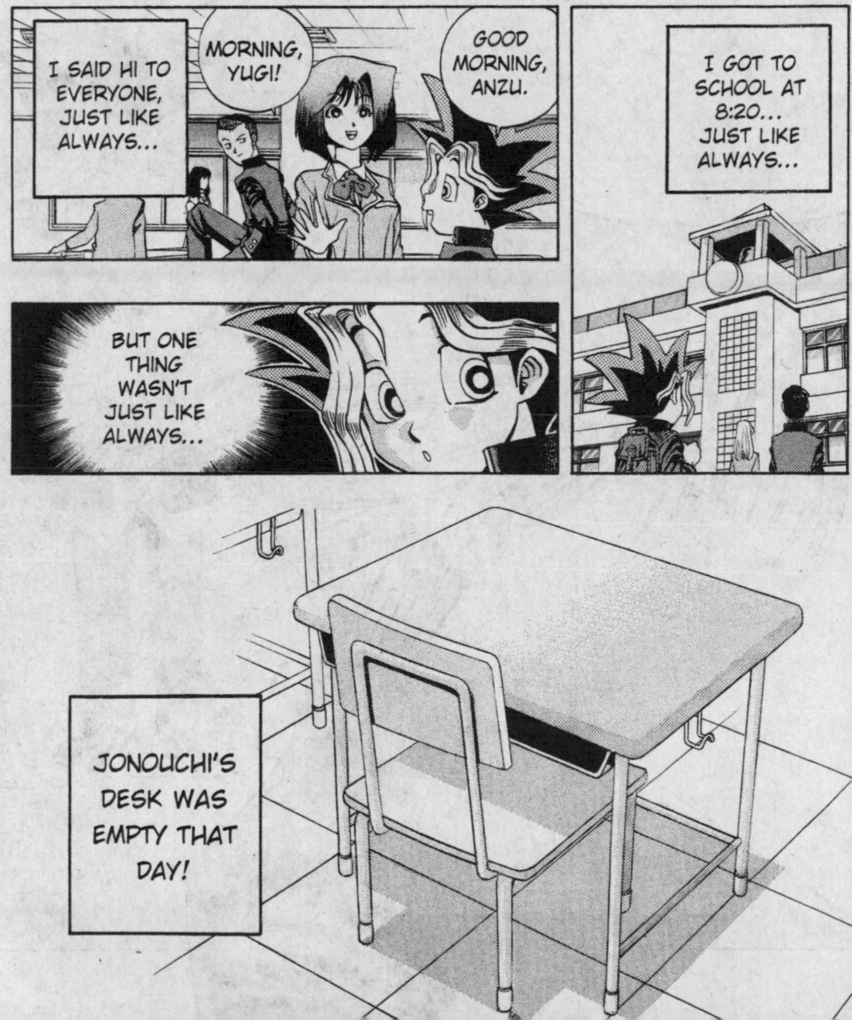
I GOT TO SCHOOL AT 8:20... JUST LIKE ALWAYS...
I SAID HI TO EVERYONE, JUST LIKE ALWAYS...
MORNING, YUGI!
GOOD MORNING, ANZU.
BUT ONE THING WASN'T JUST LIKE ALWAYS...
JONOUCHI'S DESK WAS EMPTY THAT DAY!

Duel 11: The Wild Gang (Part 1)

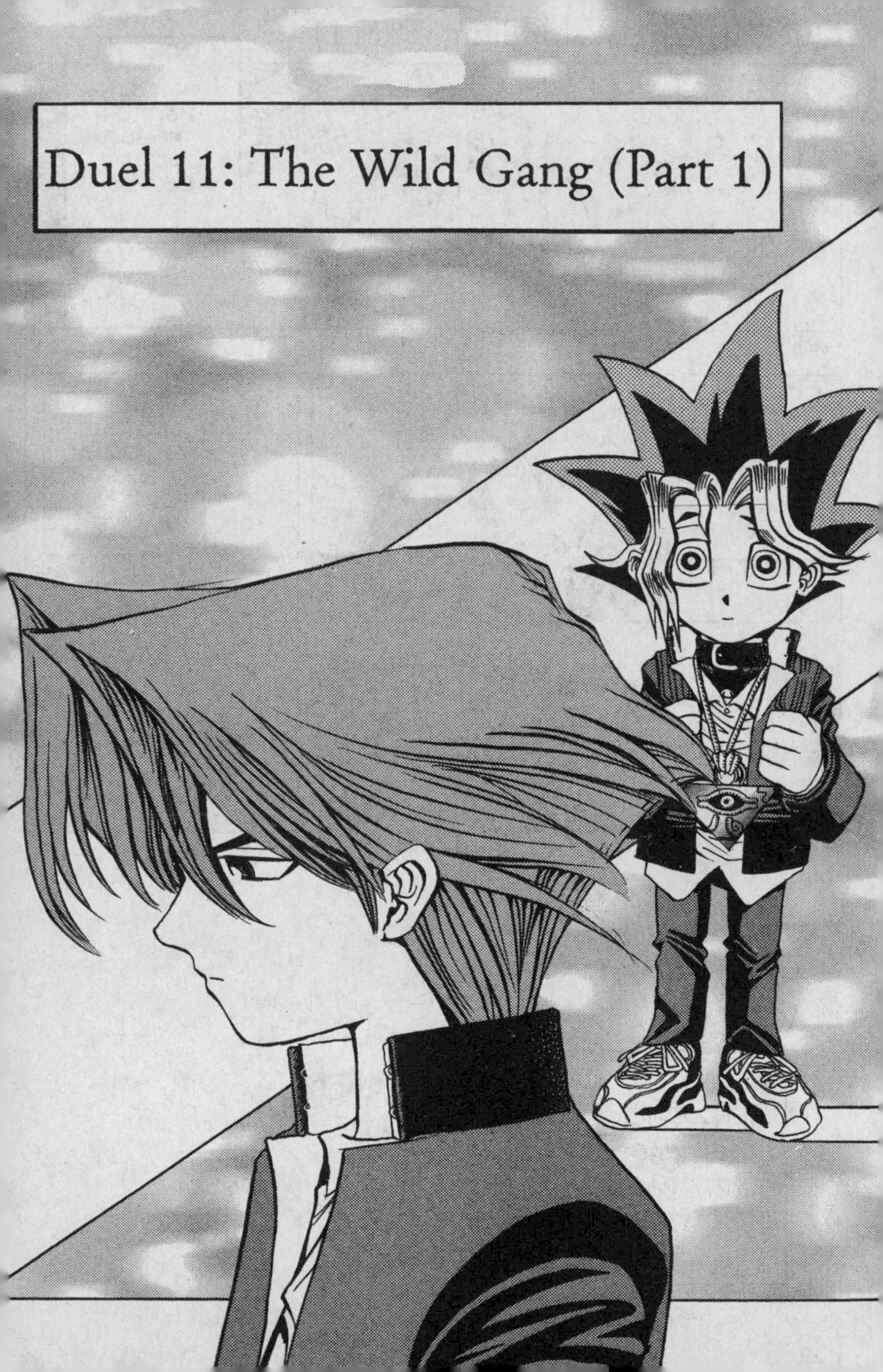

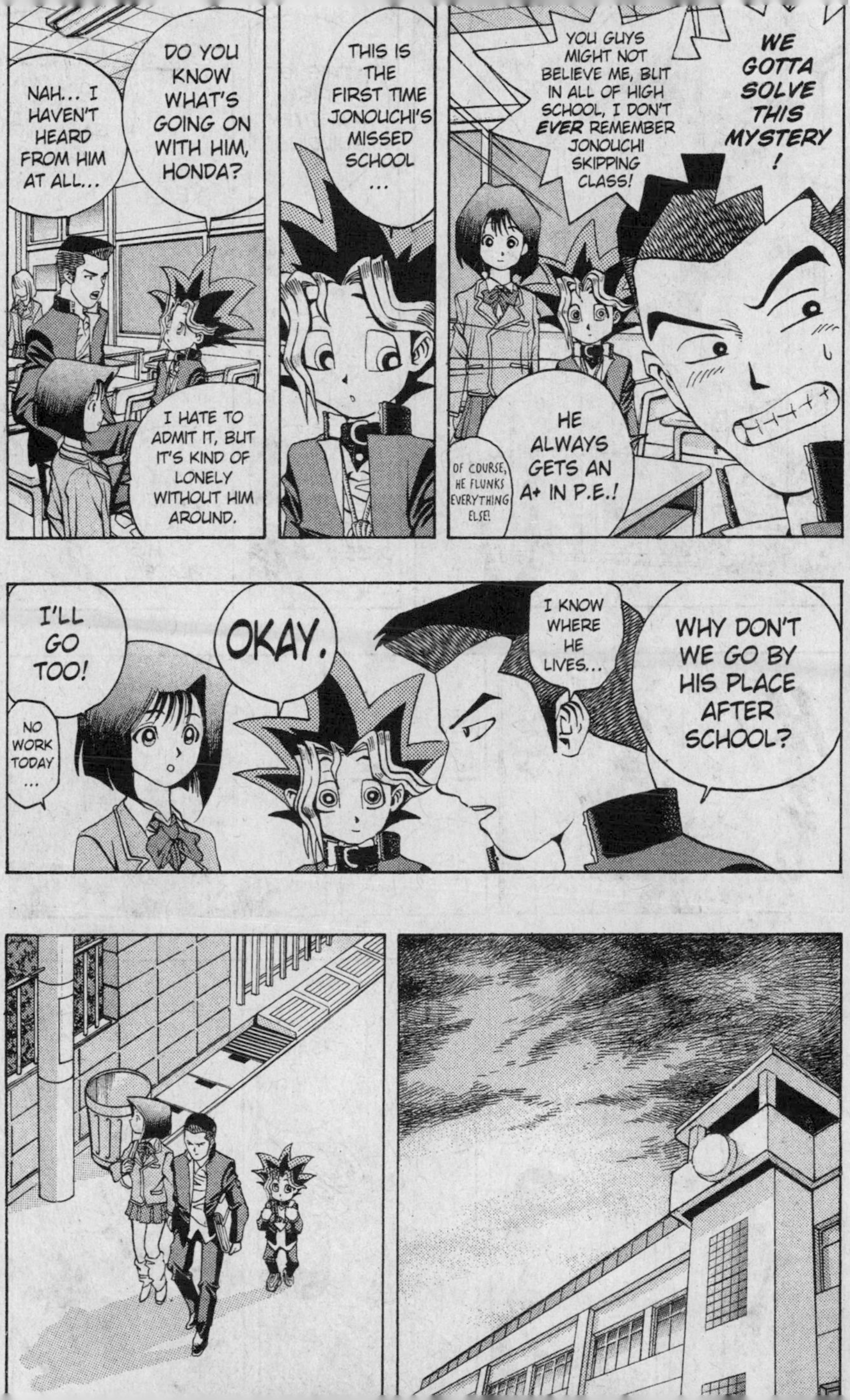
YOU GUYS MIGHT NOT BELIEVE ME, BUT IN ALL OF HIGH SCHOOL, I DON'T *EVER* REMEMBER JONOUCHI SKIPPING CLASS!
HE ALWAYS GETS AN A+ IN P.E.!
OF COURSE, HE FLUNKS EVERYTHING ELSE!
WE GOTTA SOLVE THIS MYSTERY!
THIS IS THE FIRST TIME JONOUCHI'S MISSED SCHOOL...
DO YOU KNOW WHAT'S GOING ON WITH HIM, HONDA?
NAH... I HAVEN'T HEARD FROM HIM AT ALL...
I HATE TO ADMIT IT, BUT IT'S KIND OF LONELY WITHOUT HIM AROUND.
WHY DON'T WE GO BY HIS PLACE AFTER SCHOOL?
I KNOW WHERE HE LIVES...
OKAY.
I'LL GO TOO!
NO WORK TODAY...

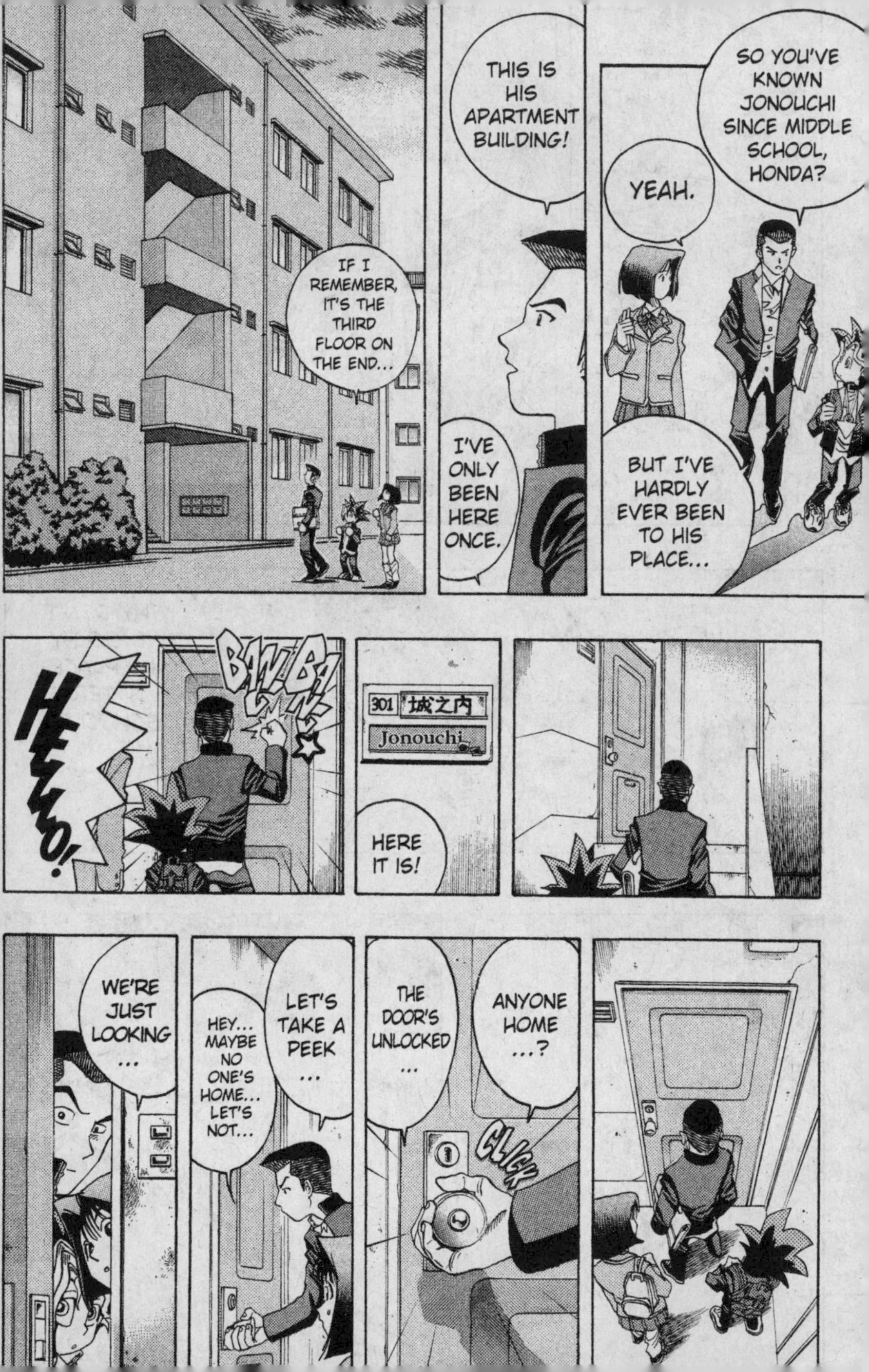
SO YOU'VE KNOWN JONOUCHI SINCE MIDDLE SCHOOL, HONDA?
YEAH.
BUT I'VE HARDLY EVER BEEN TO HIS PLACE...
THIS IS HIS APARTMENT BUILDING!
I'VE ONLY BEEN HERE ONCE.
IF I REMEMBER, IT'S THE THIRD FLOOR ON THE END...
301 城之内
Jonouchi
HERE IT IS!
BAN BAN
HELLO!
ANYONE HOME ...?
THE DOOR'S UNLOCKED ...
CLICK
LET'S TAKE A PEEK ...
HEY... MAYBE NO ONE'S HOME... LET'S NOT...
WE'RE JUST LOOKING ...

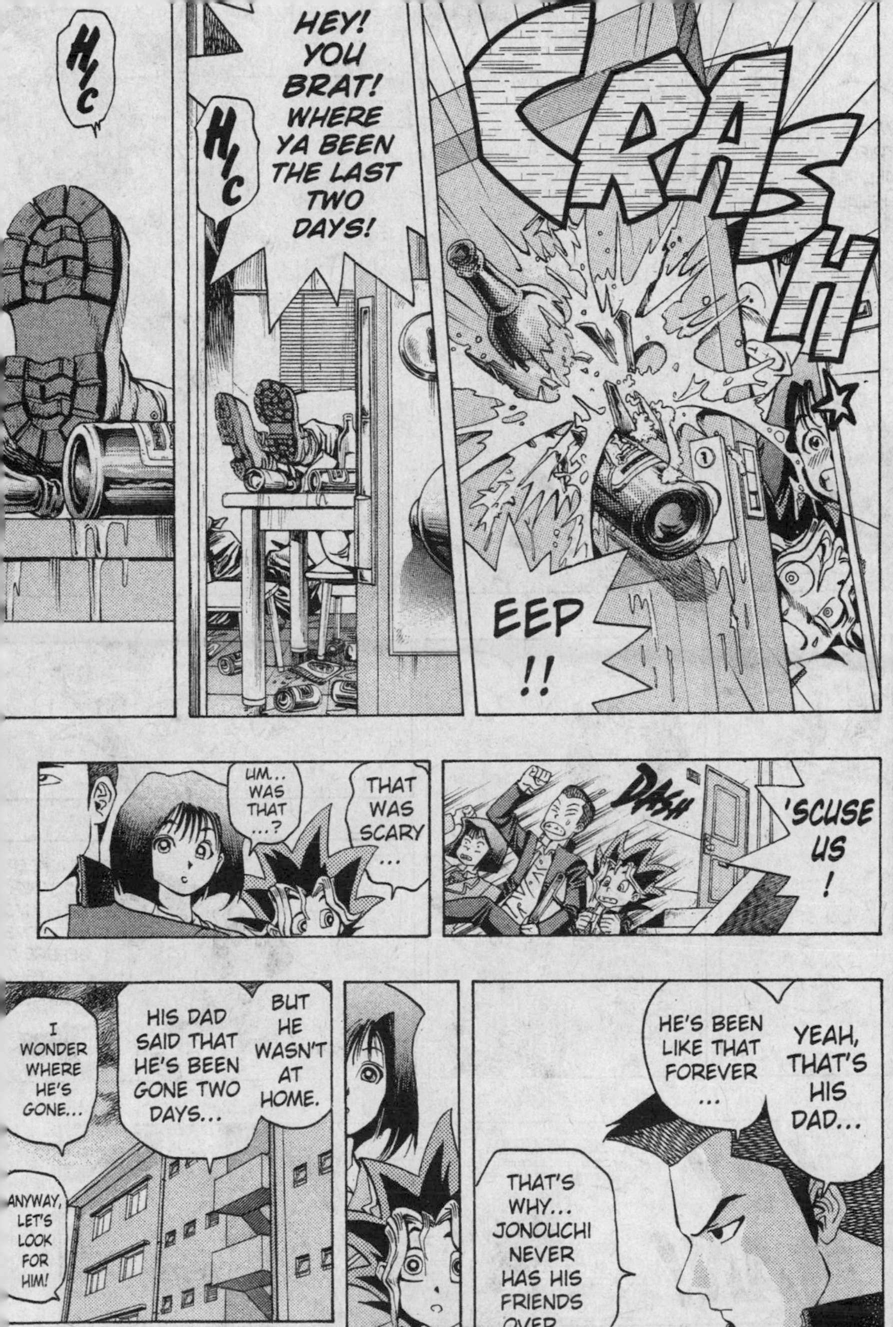
CRASH
EEP !!
HEY! YOU BRAT! WHERE YA BEEN THE LAST TWO DAYS!
HIC
HIC
DASH
'SCUSE US !
THAT WAS SCARY ...
UM... WAS THAT ...?
YEAH, THAT'S HIS DAD...
HE'S BEEN LIKE THAT FOREVER ...
THAT'S WHY... JONOUCHI NEVER HAS HIS FRIENDS OVER...
BUT HE WASN'T AT HOME.
HIS DAD SAID THAT HE'S BEEN GONE TWO DAYS...
I WONDER WHERE HE'S GONE...
ANYWAY, LET'S LOOK FOR HIM!

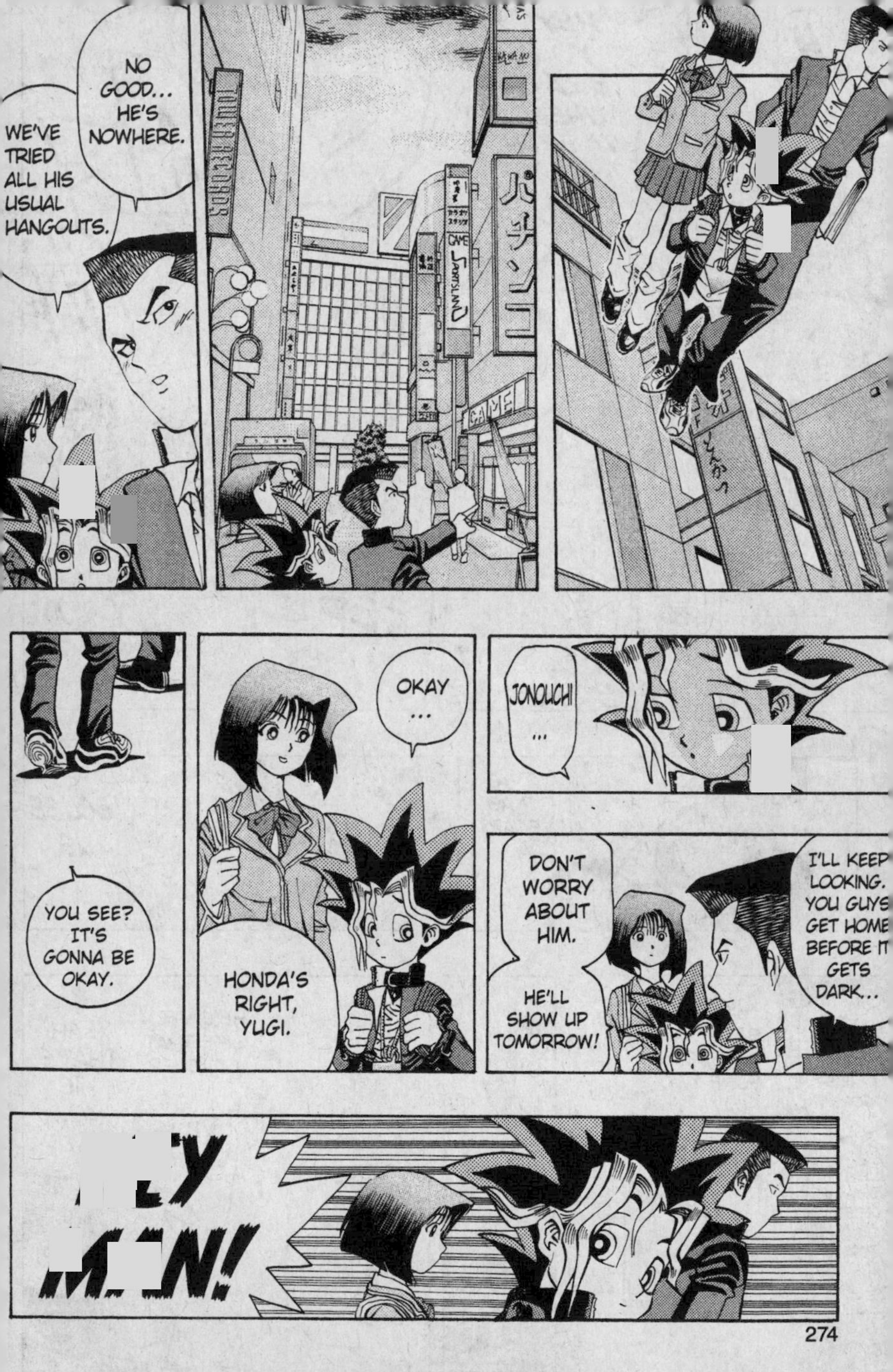
TOWER RECORDS
GAME SPORTSLAND
GAME
NO GOOD... HE'S NOWHERE.
WE'VE TRIED ALL HIS USUAL HANGOUTS.
JONOUCHI ...
I'LL KEEP LOOKING. YOU GUYS GET HOME BEFORE IT GETS DARK...
DON'T WORRY ABOUT HIM.
HE'LL SHOW UP TOMORROW!
OKAY ...
HONDA'S RIGHT, YUGI.
YOU SEE? IT'S GONNA BE OKAY.

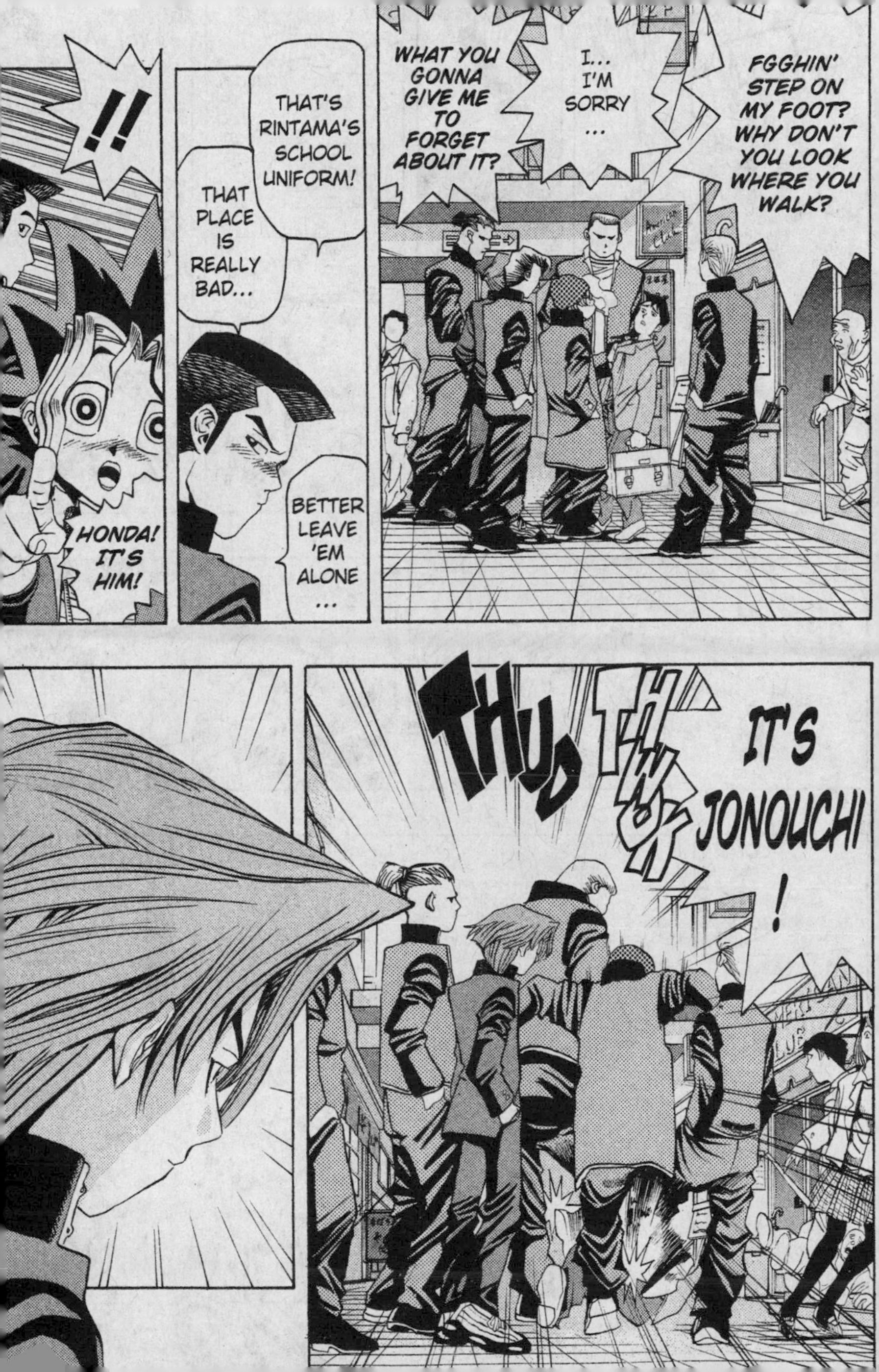
FGGHIN' STEP ON MY FOOT? WHY DON'T YOU LOOK WHERE YOU WALK?
I... I'M SORRY ...
WHAT YOU GONNA GIVE ME TO FORGET ABOUT IT?
THAT'S RINTAMA'S SCHOOL UNIFORM!
THAT PLACE IS REALLY BAD...
BETTER LEAVE 'EM ALONE ...
!!
HONDA! IT'S HIM!
IT'S JONOUCHI !
THUD

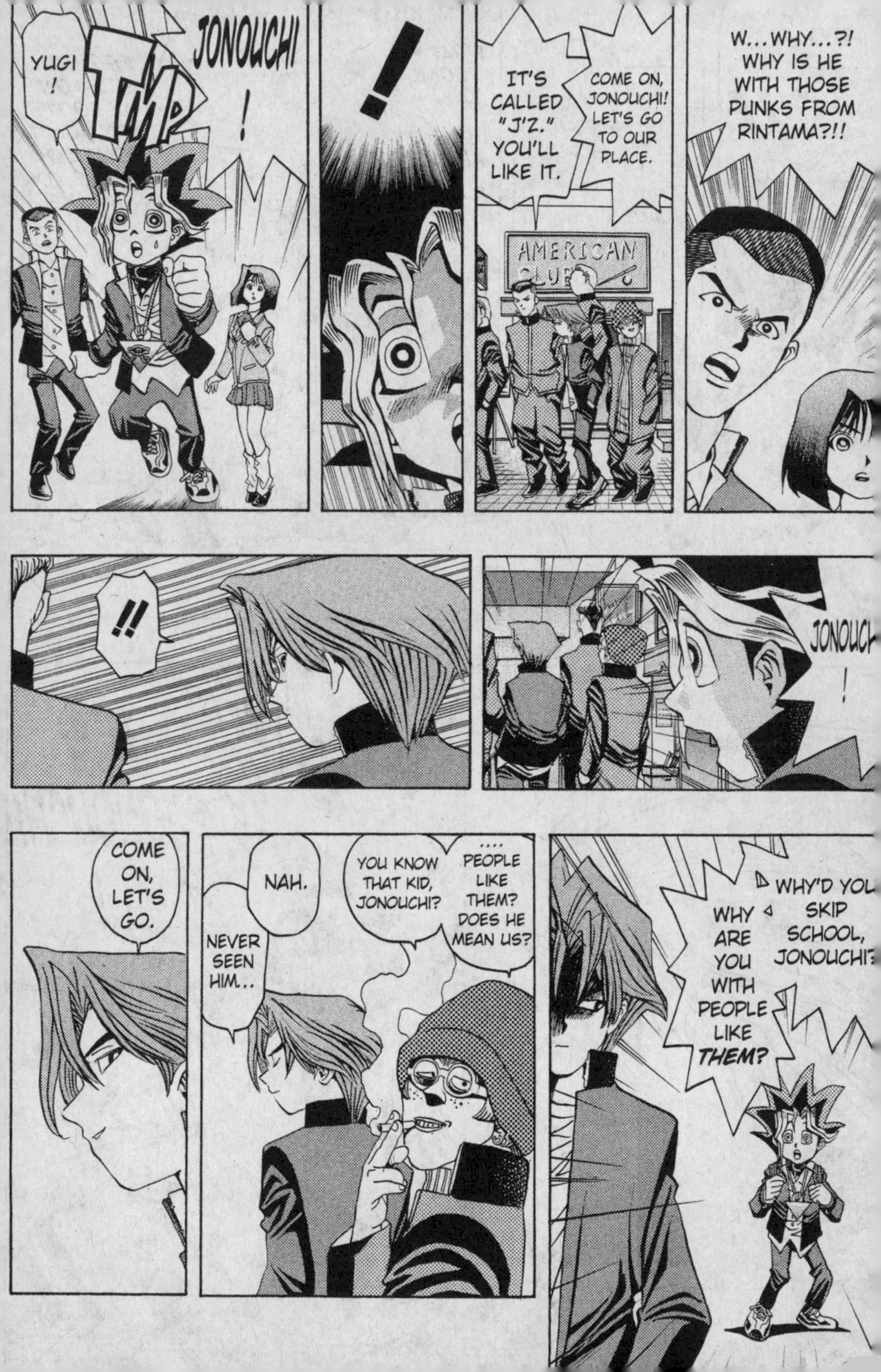
W...WHY...?! WHY IS HE WITH THOSE PUNKS FROM RINTAMA?!!
COME ON, JONOUCHI! LET'S GO TO OUR PLACE.
IT'S CALLED "J'Z." YOU'LL LIKE IT.
!
JONOUCHI !
YUGI !
JONOUCH !
!!
WHY'D YOU SKIP SCHOOL, JONOUCHI?
WHY ARE YOU WITH PEOPLE LIKE *THEM*?
.... PEOPLE LIKE THEM? DOES HE MEAN US?
YOU KNOW THAT KID, JONOUCHI?
NAH.
NEVER SEEN HIM..
COME ON, LET'S GO.

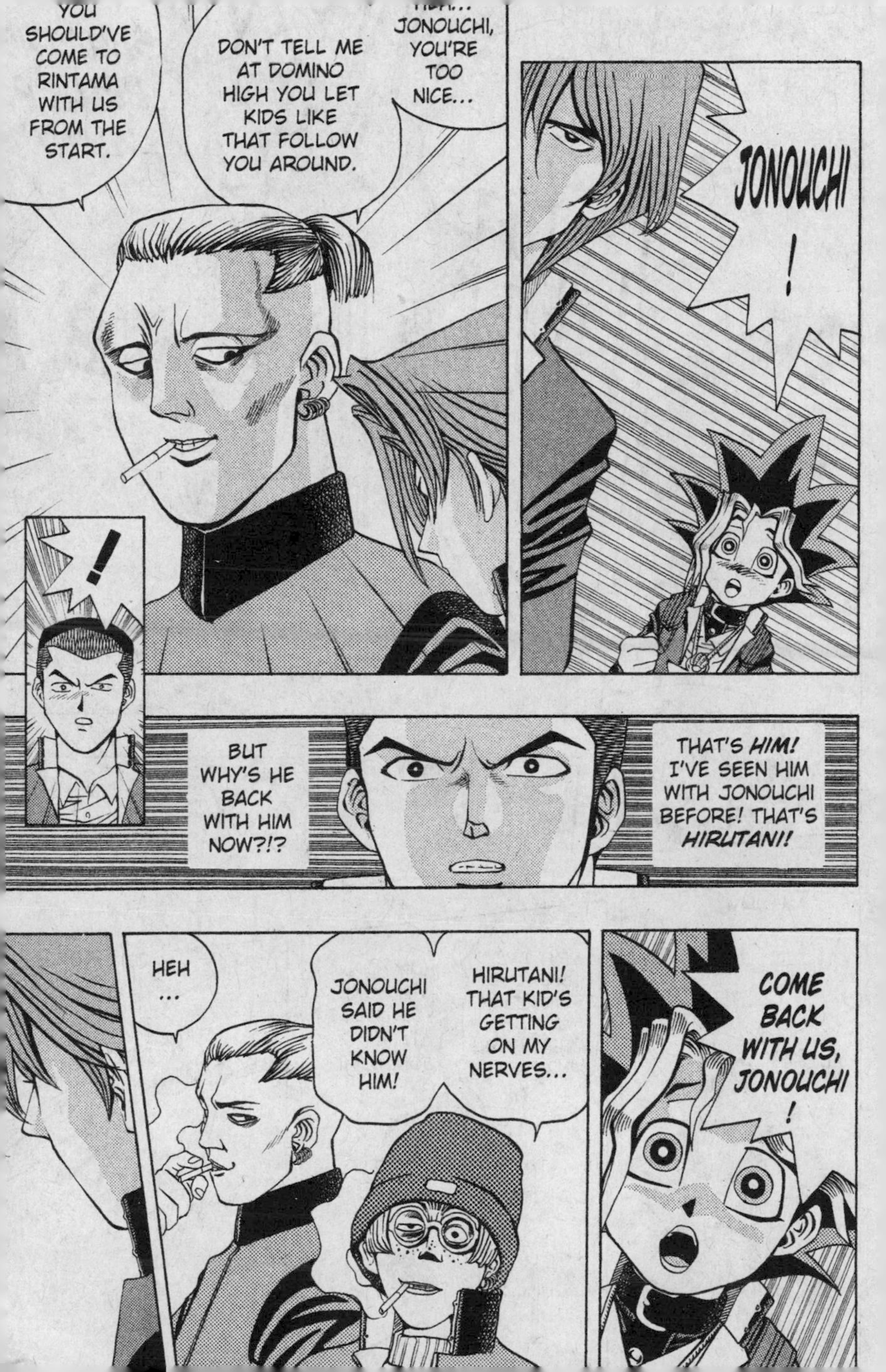
JONOUCHI!
JONOUCHI, YOU'RE TOO NICE...
DON'T TELL ME AT DOMINO HIGH YOU LET KIDS LIKE THAT FOLLOW YOU AROUND.
YOU SHOULD'VE COME TO RINTAMA WITH US FROM THE START.
!
THAT'S HIM! I'VE SEEN HIM WITH JONOUCHI BEFORE! THAT'S HIRUTANI!
BUT WHY'S HE BACK WITH HIM NOW?!?
COME BACK WITH US, JONOUCHI!
HIRUTANI! THAT KID'S GETTING ON MY NERVES...
JONOUCHI SAID HE DIDN'T KNOW HIM!
HEH ...

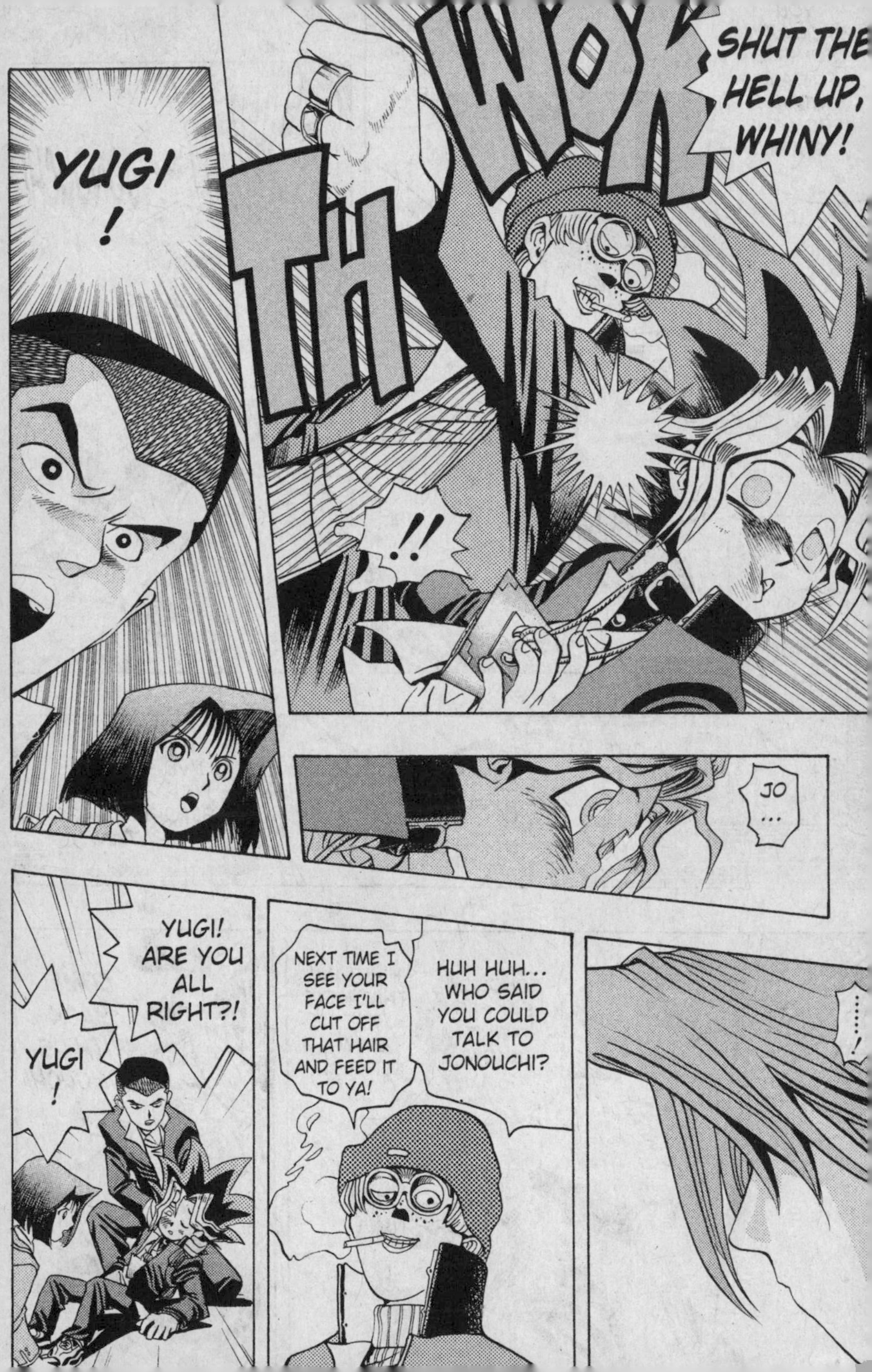

SHUT THE HELL UP, WHINY!
THWOK
!!
YUGI!
JO...
......!
HUH HUH... WHO SAID YOU COULD TALK TO JONOUCHI?
NEXT TIME I SEE YOUR FACE I'LL CUT OFF THAT HAIR AND FEED IT TO YA!
YUGI! ARE YOU ALL RIGHT?!
YUGI!

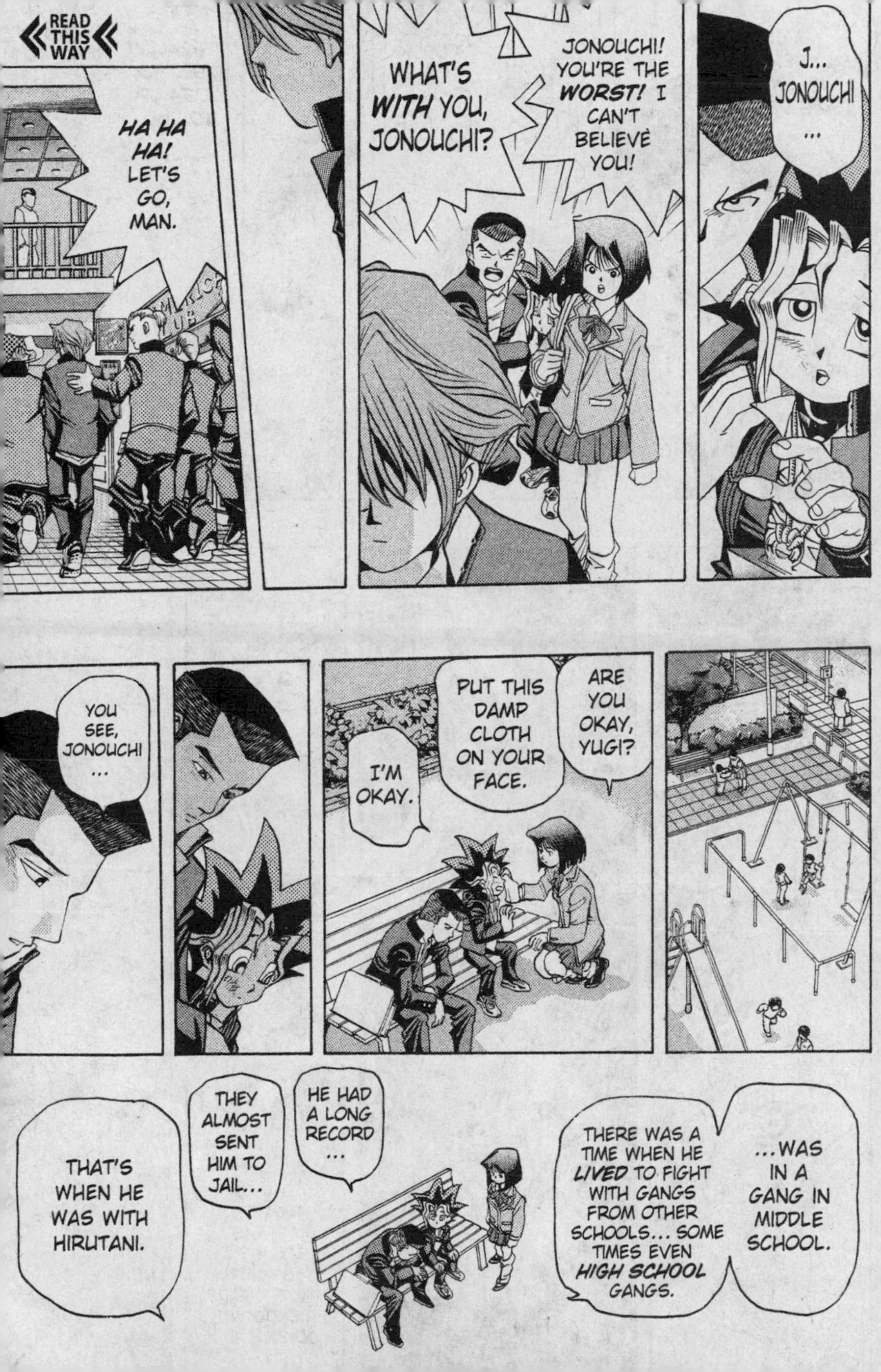
READ THIS WAY
J... JONOUCHI ...
JONOUCHI! YOU'RE THE WORST! I CAN'T BELIEVE YOU!
WHAT'S WITH YOU, JONOUCHI?
HA HA HA! LET'S GO, MAN.
ARE YOU OKAY, YUGI?
PUT THIS DAMP CLOTH ON YOUR FACE.
I'M OKAY.
YOU SEE, JONOUCHI ...
...WAS IN A GANG IN MIDDLE SCHOOL.
THERE WAS A TIME WHEN HE LIVED TO FIGHT WITH GANGS FROM OTHER SCHOOLS... SOME TIMES EVEN HIGH SCHOOL GANGS.
HE HAD A LONG RECORD ...
THEY ALMOST SENT HIM TO JAIL...
THAT'S WHEN HE WAS WITH HIRUTANI.

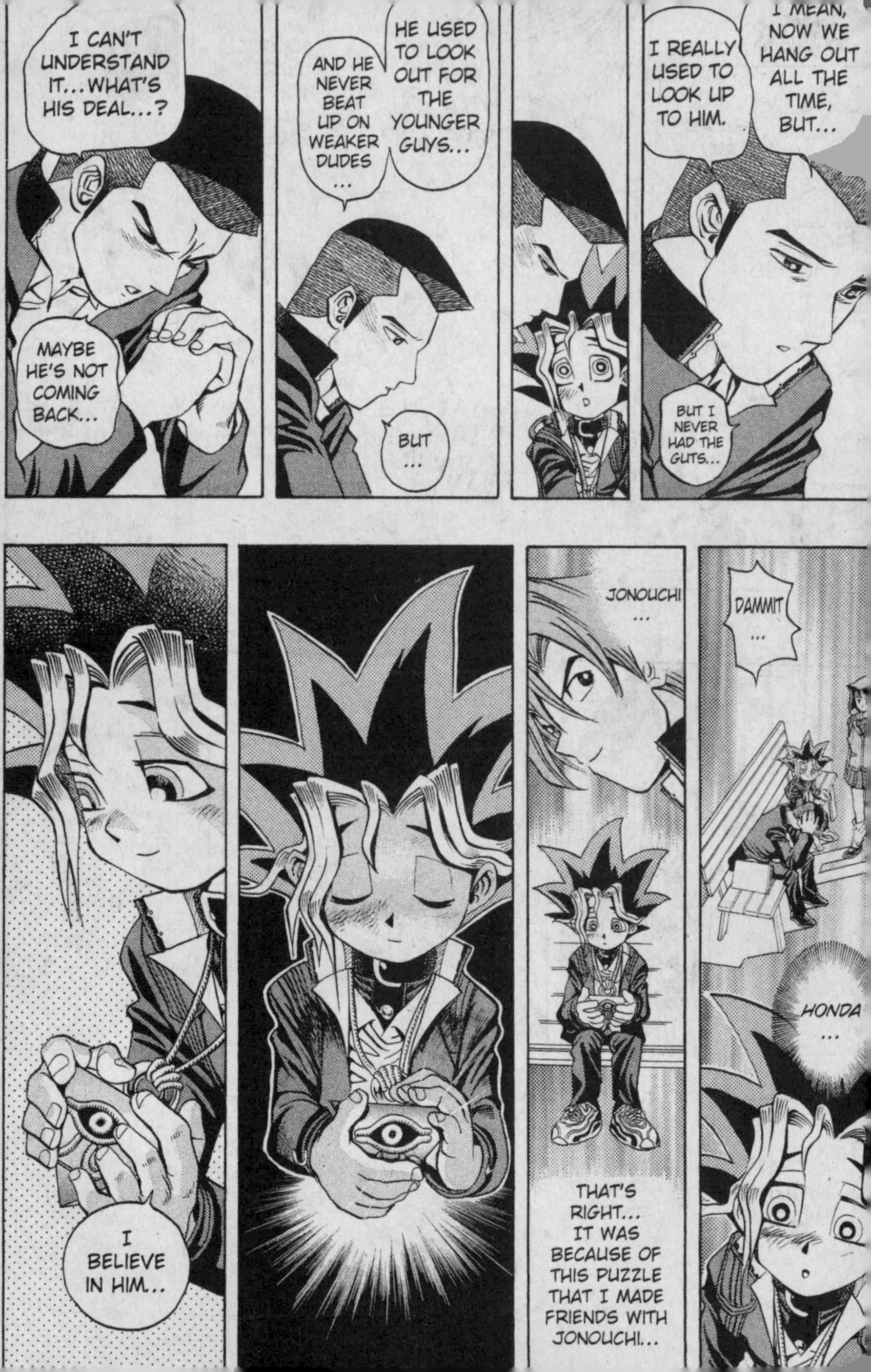
I CAN'T UNDERSTAND IT...WHAT'S HIS DEAL...?
MAYBE HE'S NOT COMING BACK...
HE USED TO LOOK OUT FOR THE YOUNGER GUYS...
AND HE NEVER BEAT UP ON WEAKER DUDES ...
BUT ...
I REALLY USED TO LOOK UP TO HIM.
I MEAN, NOW WE HANG OUT ALL THE TIME, BUT...
BUT I NEVER HAD THE GUTS...
I BELIEVE IN HIM..
JONOUCHI ...
THAT'S RIGHT... IT WAS BECAUSE OF THIS PUZZLE THAT I MADE FRIENDS WITH JONOUCHI...
DAMMIT ...
HONDA ...

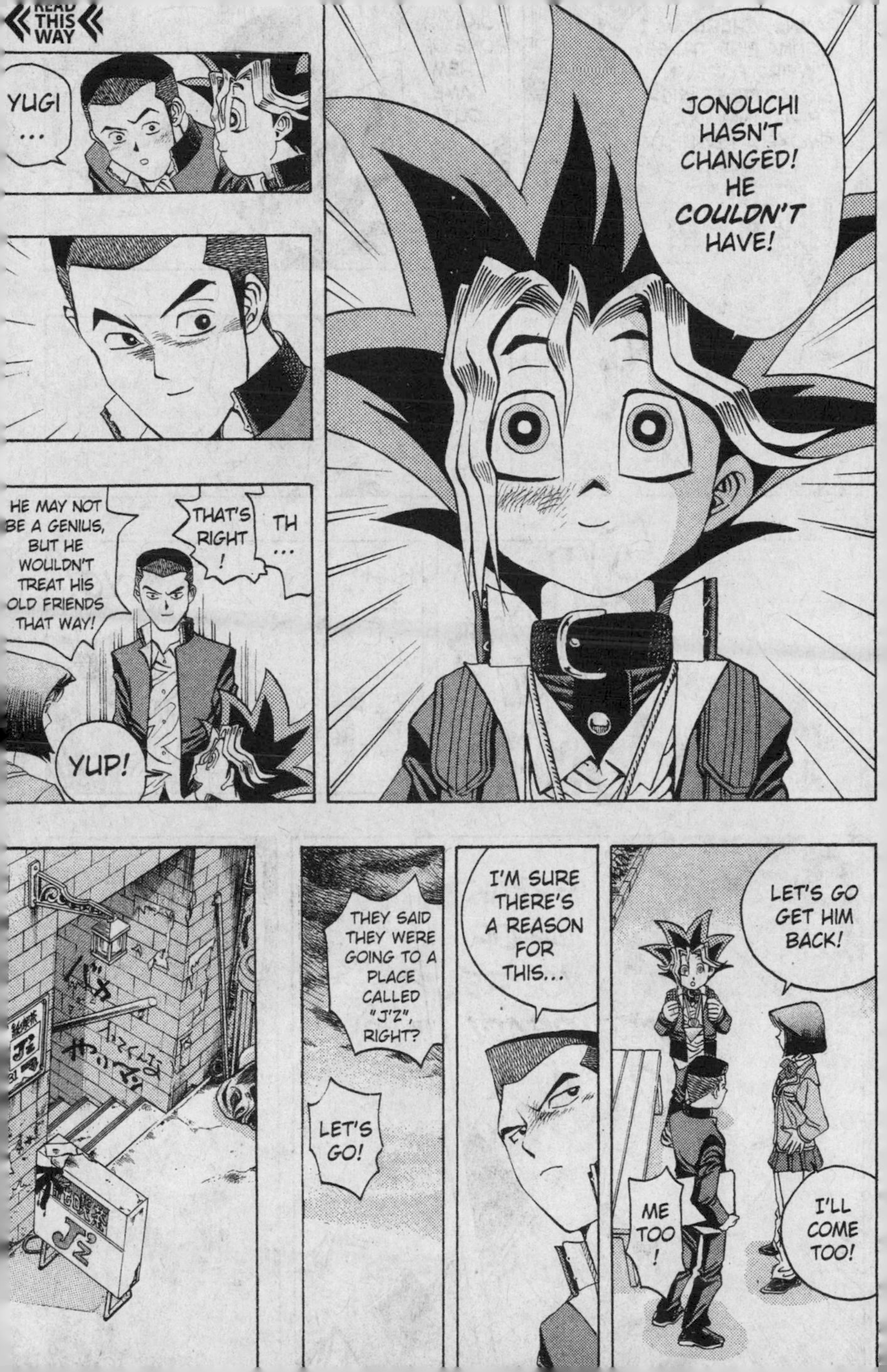
READ THIS WAY
JONOUCHI HASN'T CHANGED! HE COULDN'T HAVE!
YUGI ...
TH ...
THAT'S RIGHT!
HE MAY NOT BE A GENIUS, BUT HE WOULDN'T TREAT HIS OLD FRIENDS THAT WAY!
YUP!
LET'S GO GET HIM BACK!
I'LL COME TOO!
ME TOO!
I'M SURE THERE'S A REASON FOR THIS...
THEY SAID THEY WERE GOING TO A PLACE CALLED "J'Z", RIGHT?
LET'S GO!

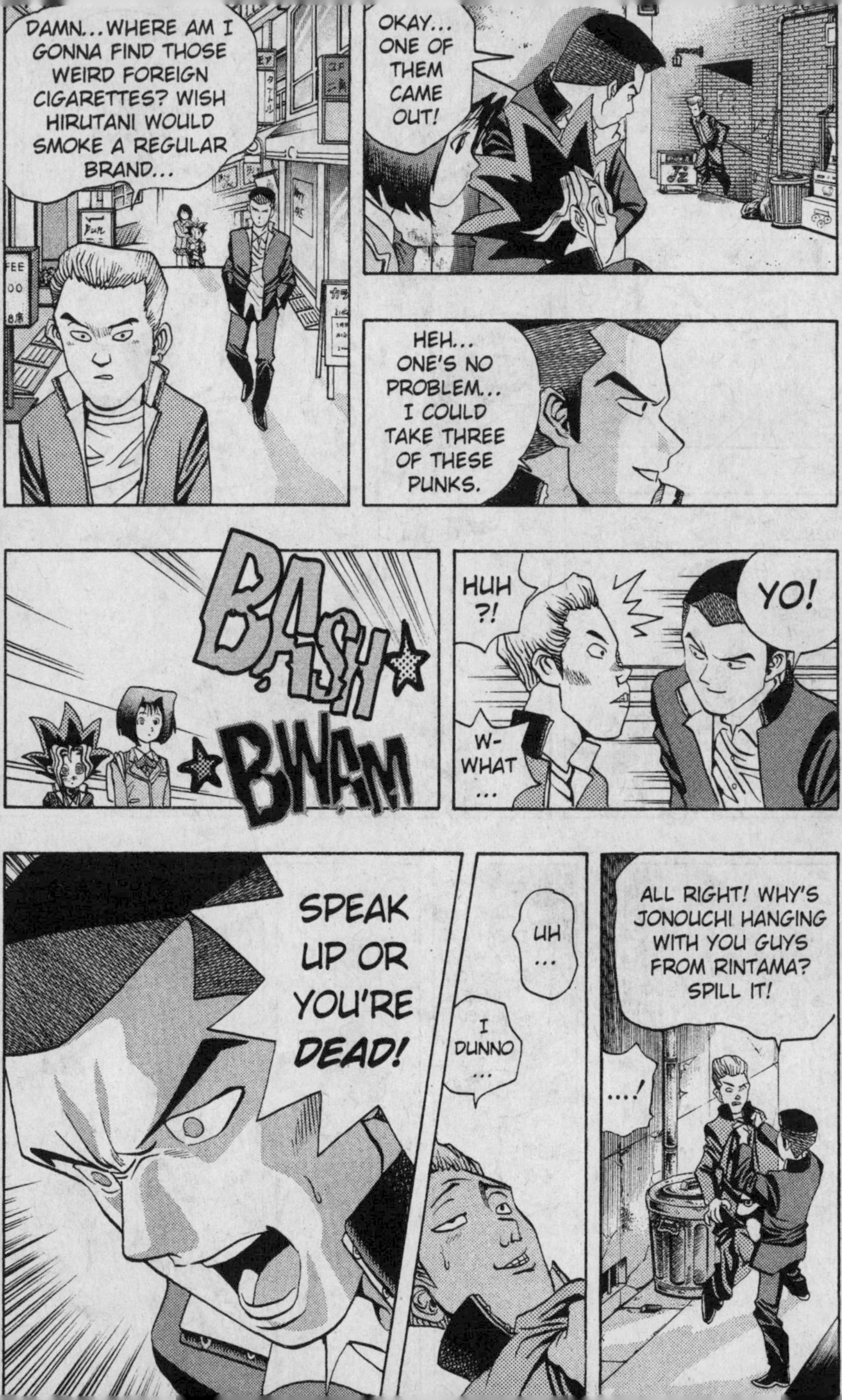
OKAY... ONE OF THEM CAME OUT!
HEH... ONE'S NO PROBLEM... I COULD TAKE THREE OF THESE PUNKS.
DAMN...WHERE AM I GONNA FIND THOSE WEIRD FOREIGN CIGARETTES? WISH HIRUTANI WOULD SMOKE A REGULAR BRAND...
YO!
HUH ?!
W-WHAT ...
BASH
BWAM
ALL RIGHT! WHY'S JONOUCHI HANGING WITH YOU GUYS FROM RINTAMA? SPILL IT!
...!
UH ...
I DUNNO ...
SPEAK UP OR YOU'RE DEAD!

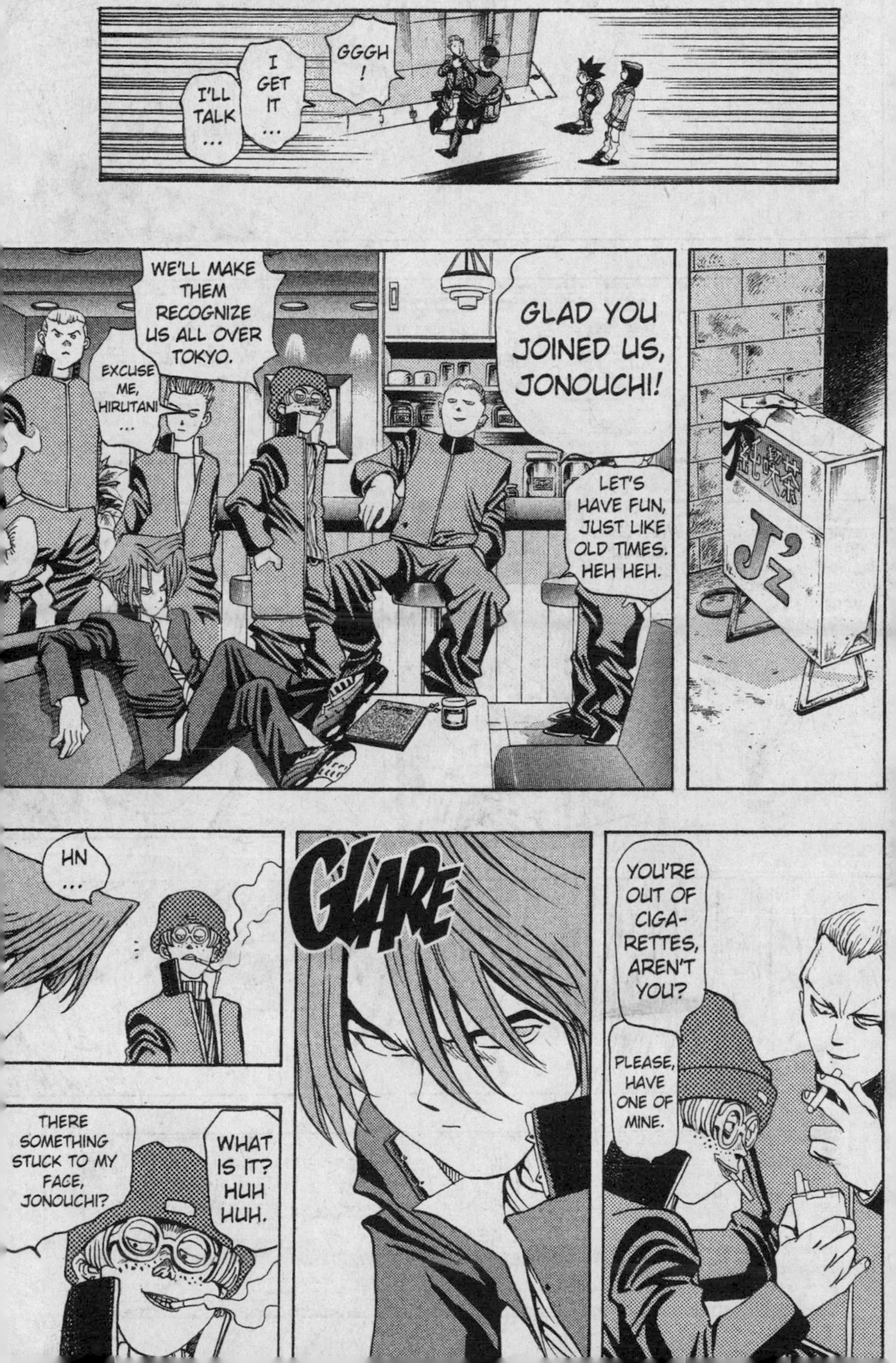
GGGH!
I GET IT...
I'LL TALK...
J'z
GLAD YOU JOINED US, JONOUCHI!
LET'S HAVE FUN, JUST LIKE OLD TIMES. HEH HEH.
WE'LL MAKE THEM RECOGNIZE US ALL OVER TOKYO.
EXCUSE ME, HIRUTANI...
YOU'RE OUT OF CIGARETTES, AREN'T YOU?
PLEASE, HAVE ONE OF MINE.
GLARE
HN...
WHAT IS IT? HUH HUH.
THERE SOMETHING STUCK TO MY FACE, JONOUCHI?

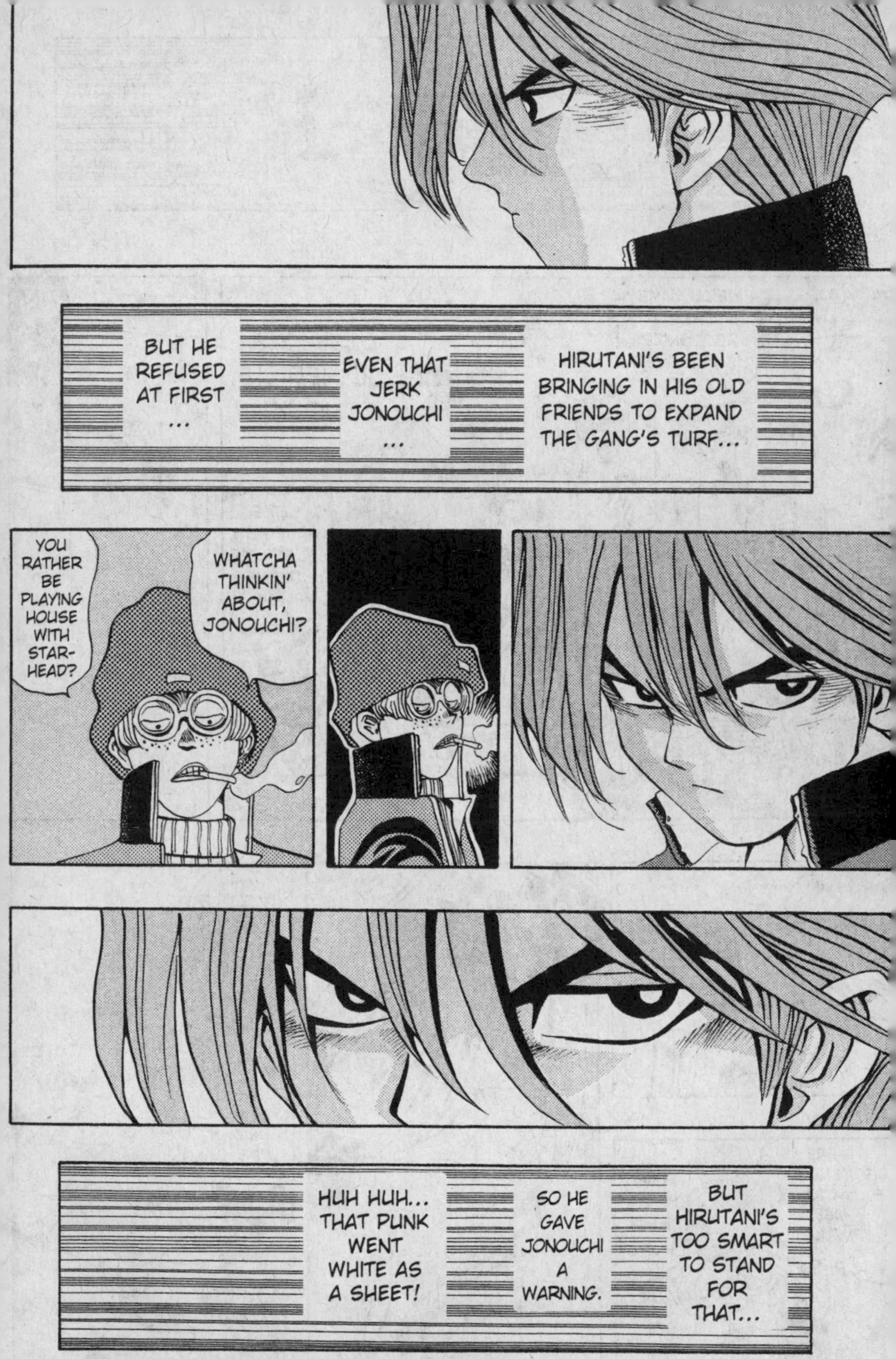
HIRUTANI'S BEEN BRINGING IN HIS OLD FRIENDS TO EXPAND THE GANG'S TURF...
EVEN THAT JERK JONOUCHI ...
BUT HE REFUSED AT FIRST ...
WHATCHA THINKIN' ABOUT, JONOUCHI?
YOU RATHER BE PLAYING HOUSE WITH STAR-HEAD?
BUT HIRUTANI'S TOO SMART TO STAND FOR THAT...
SO HE GAVE JONOUCHI A WARNING.
HUH HUH... THAT PUNK WENT WHITE AS A SHEET!

READ THIS WAY

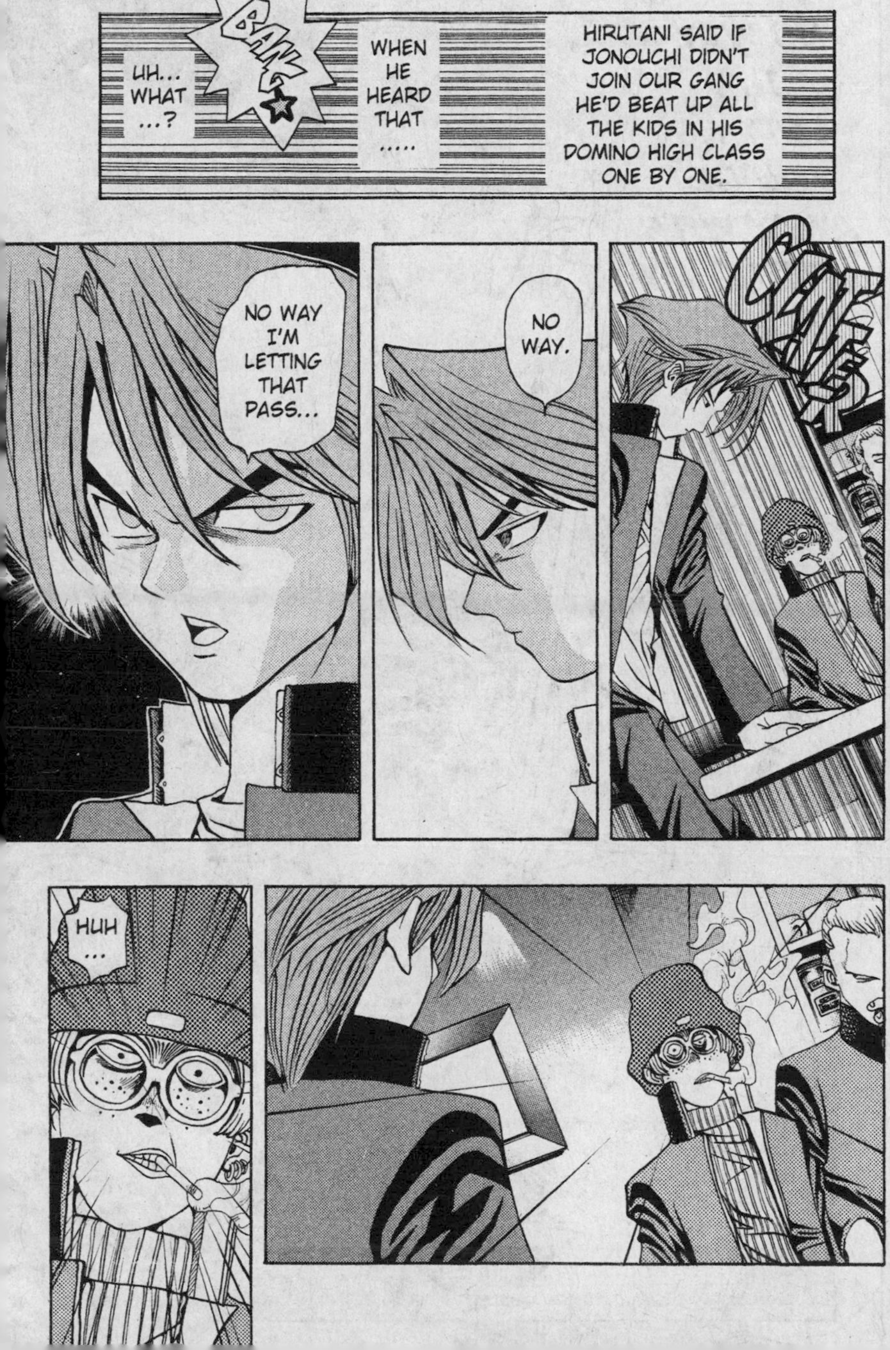
HIRUTANI SAID IF JONOUCHI DIDN'T JOIN OUR GANG HE'D BEAT UP ALL THE KIDS IN HIS DOMINO HIGH CLASS ONE BY ONE.
WHEN HE HEARD THAT .....
BANG
UH... WHAT ...?
NO WAY.
NO WAY I'M LETTING THAT PASS...
HUH ...

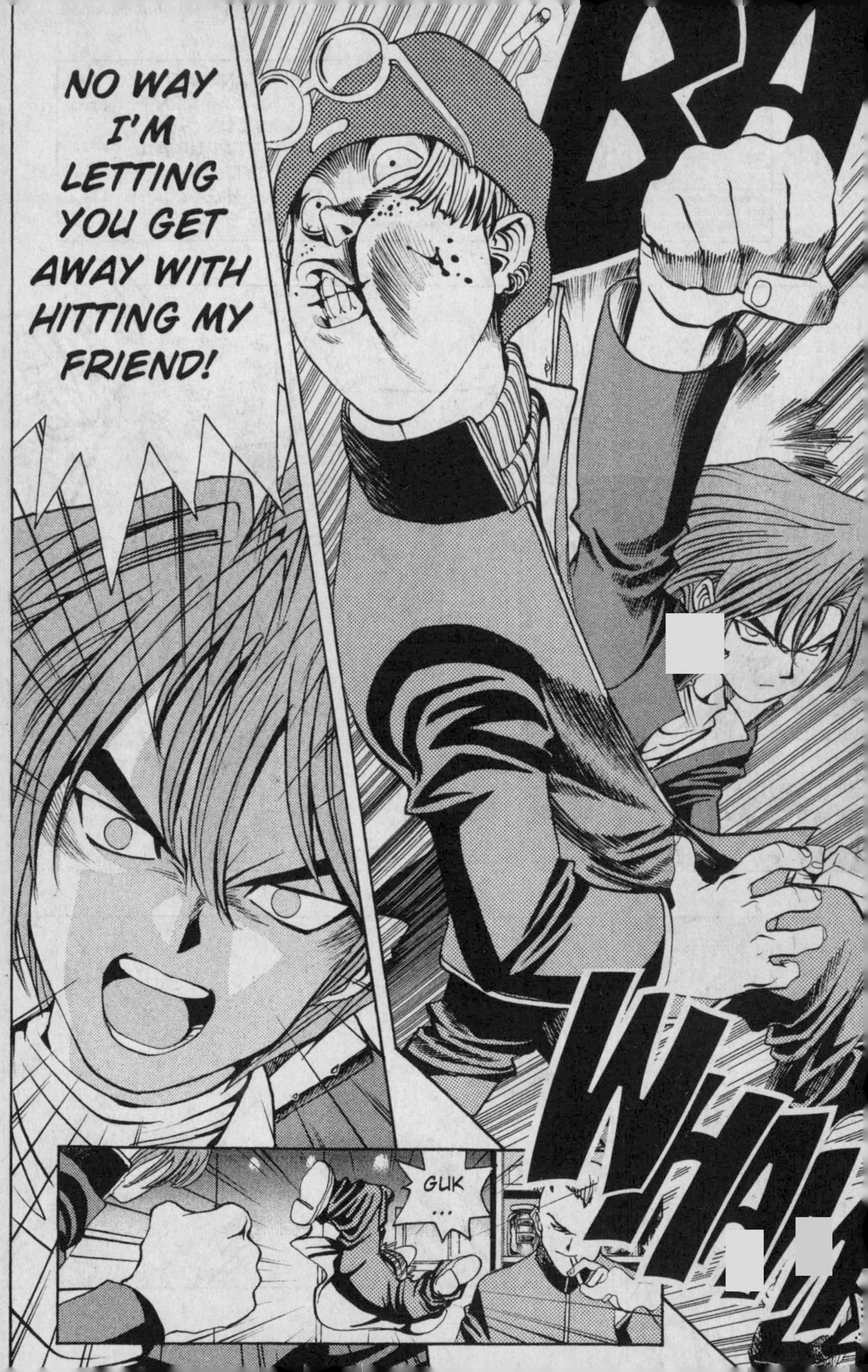
NO WAY I'M LETTING YOU GET AWAY WITH HITTING MY FRIEND!
GUK ...

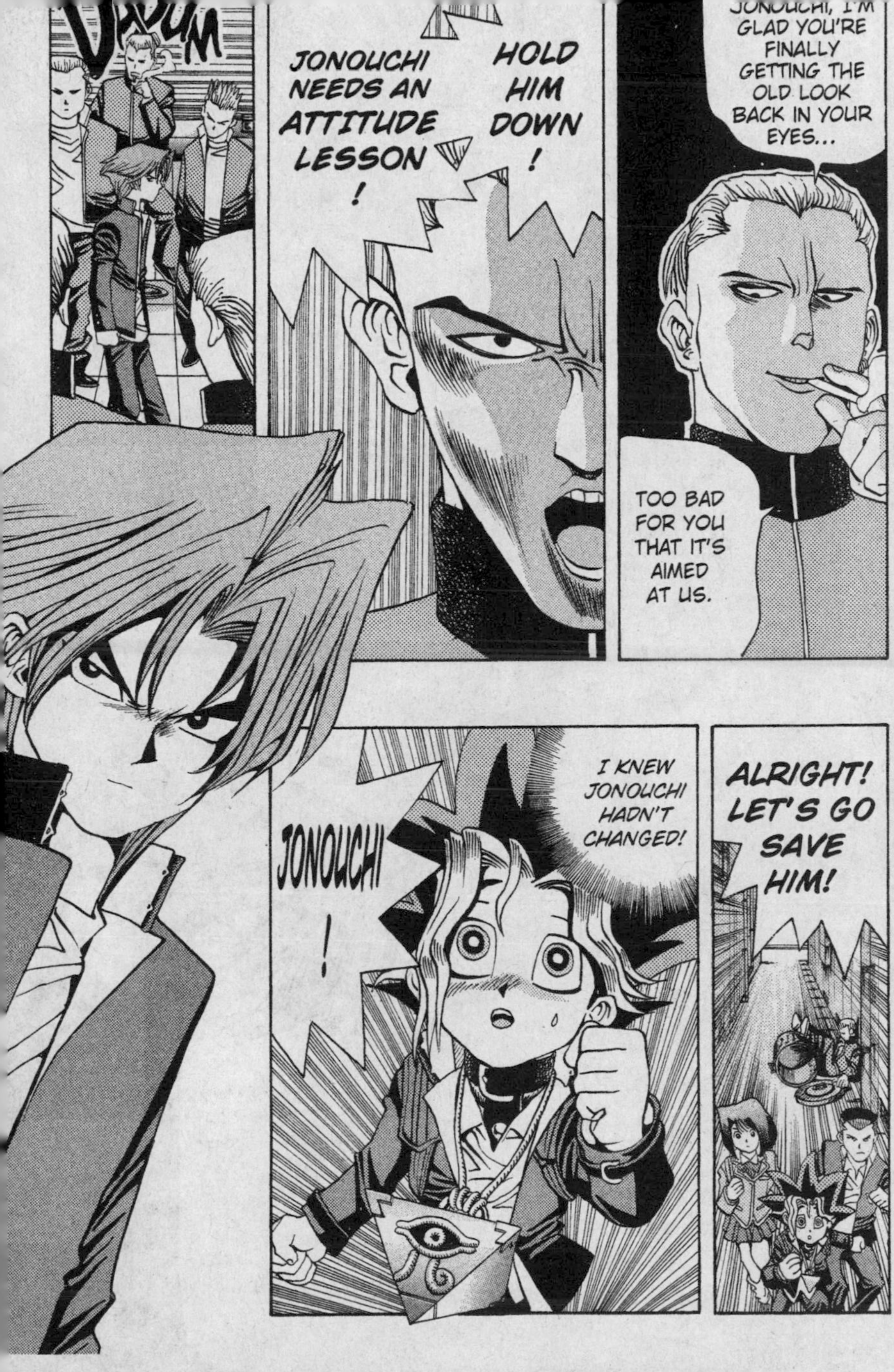
JONOUCHI, I'M GLAD YOU'RE FINALLY GETTING THE OLD LOOK BACK IN YOUR EYES...
TOO BAD FOR YOU THAT IT'S AIMED AT US.
HOLD HIM DOWN!
JONOUCHI NEEDS AN ATTITUDE LESSON!
ALRIGHT! LET'S GO SAVE HIM!
I KNEW JONOUCHI HADN'T CHANGED!
JONOUCHI!

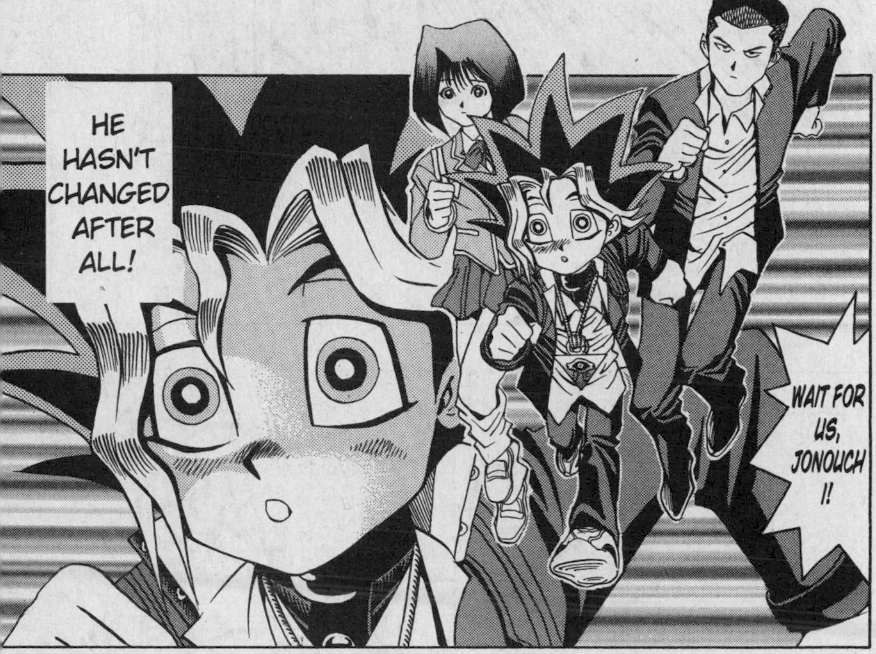
WAIT FOR US, JONOUCHI!
HE HASN'T CHANGED AFTER ALL!

Duel 12: The Wild Gang (Part 2)

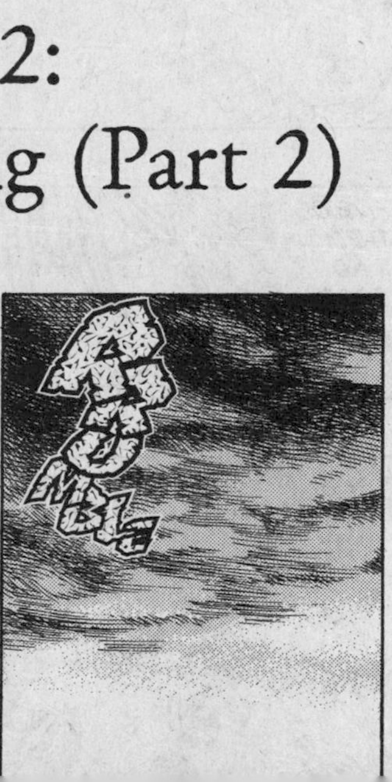
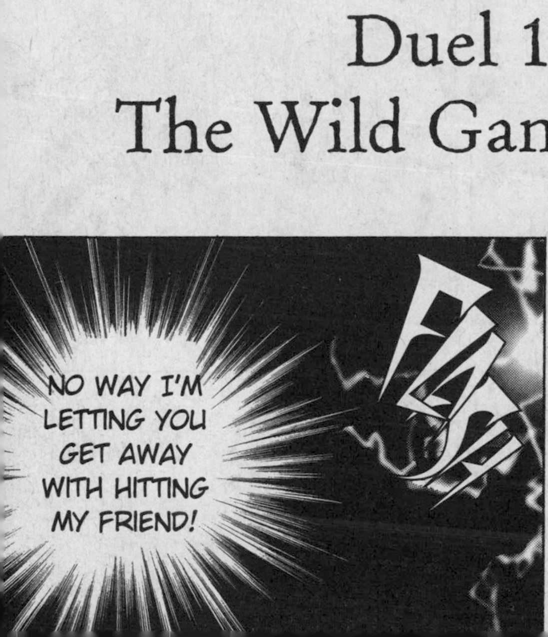
NO WAY I'M LETTING YOU GET AWAY WITH HITTING MY FRIEND!

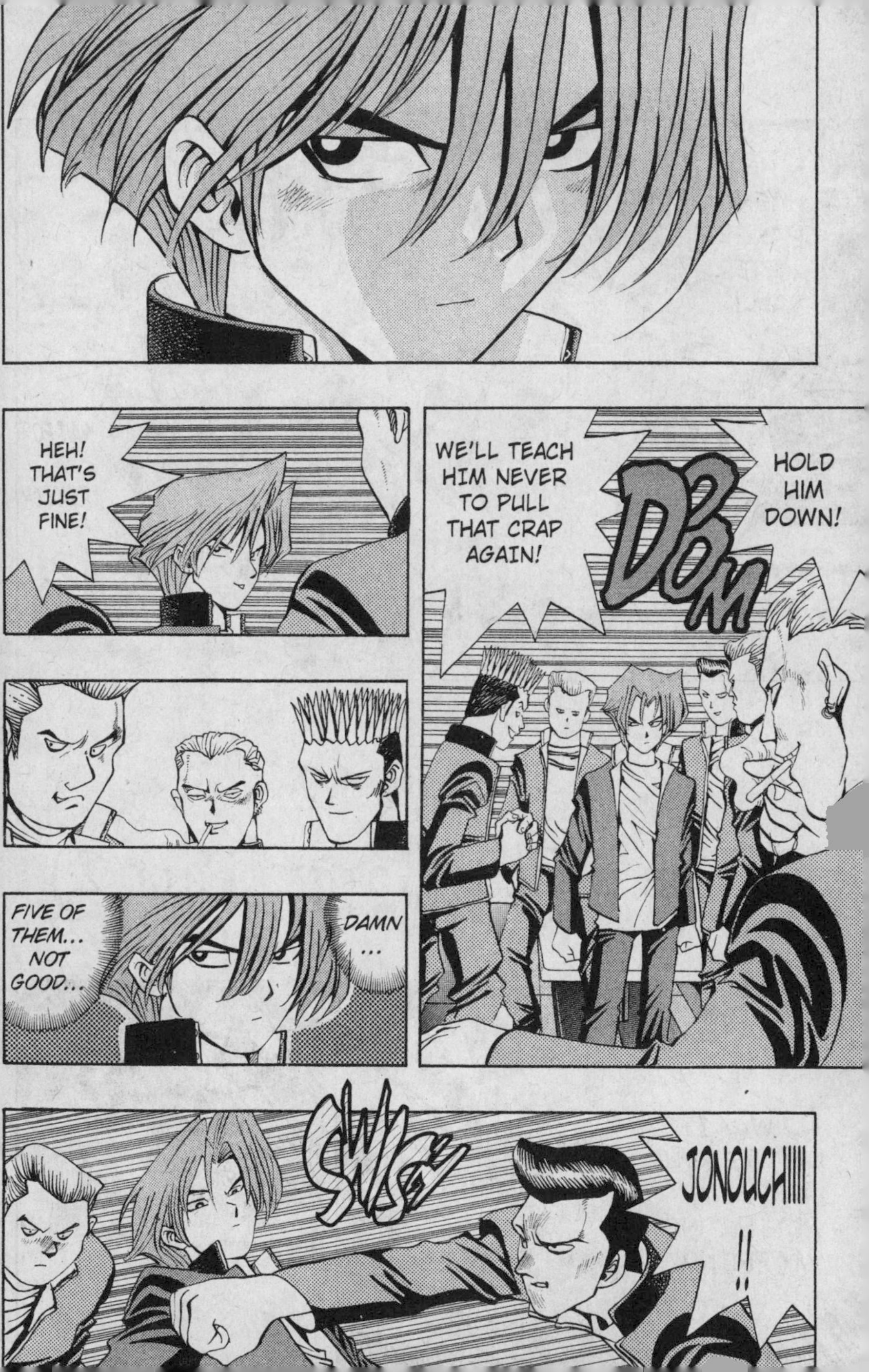
HOLD HIM DOWN!
DOM
WE'LL TEACH HIM NEVER TO PULL THAT CRAP AGAIN!
HEH! THAT'S JUST FINE!
DAMN ...
FIVE OF THEM... NOT GOOD...
JONOUCHIIIII !!
SWISH

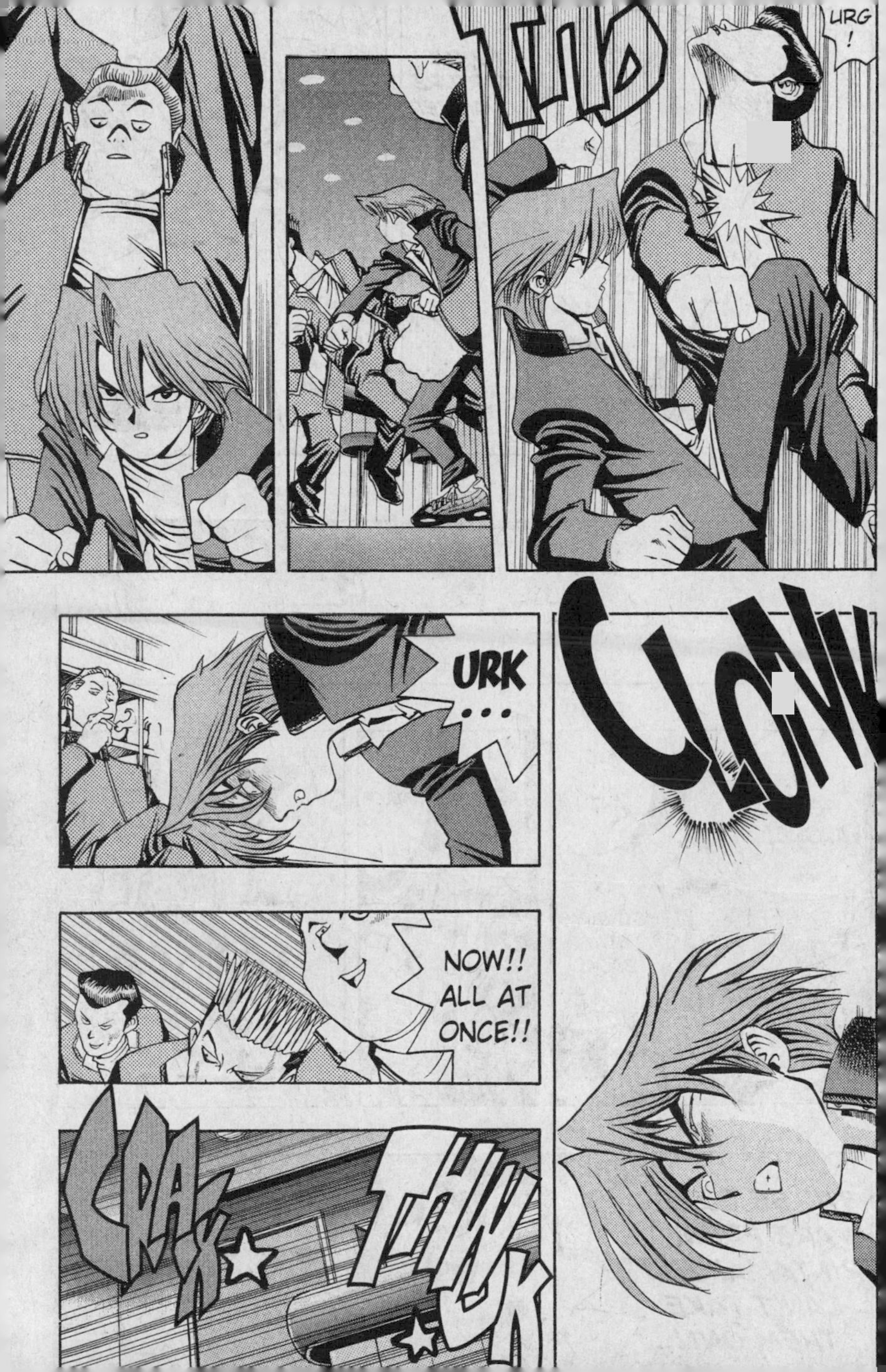
URG !
THUD
CLONK
URK ...
NOW!! ALL AT ONCE!!
CRAK
THUK

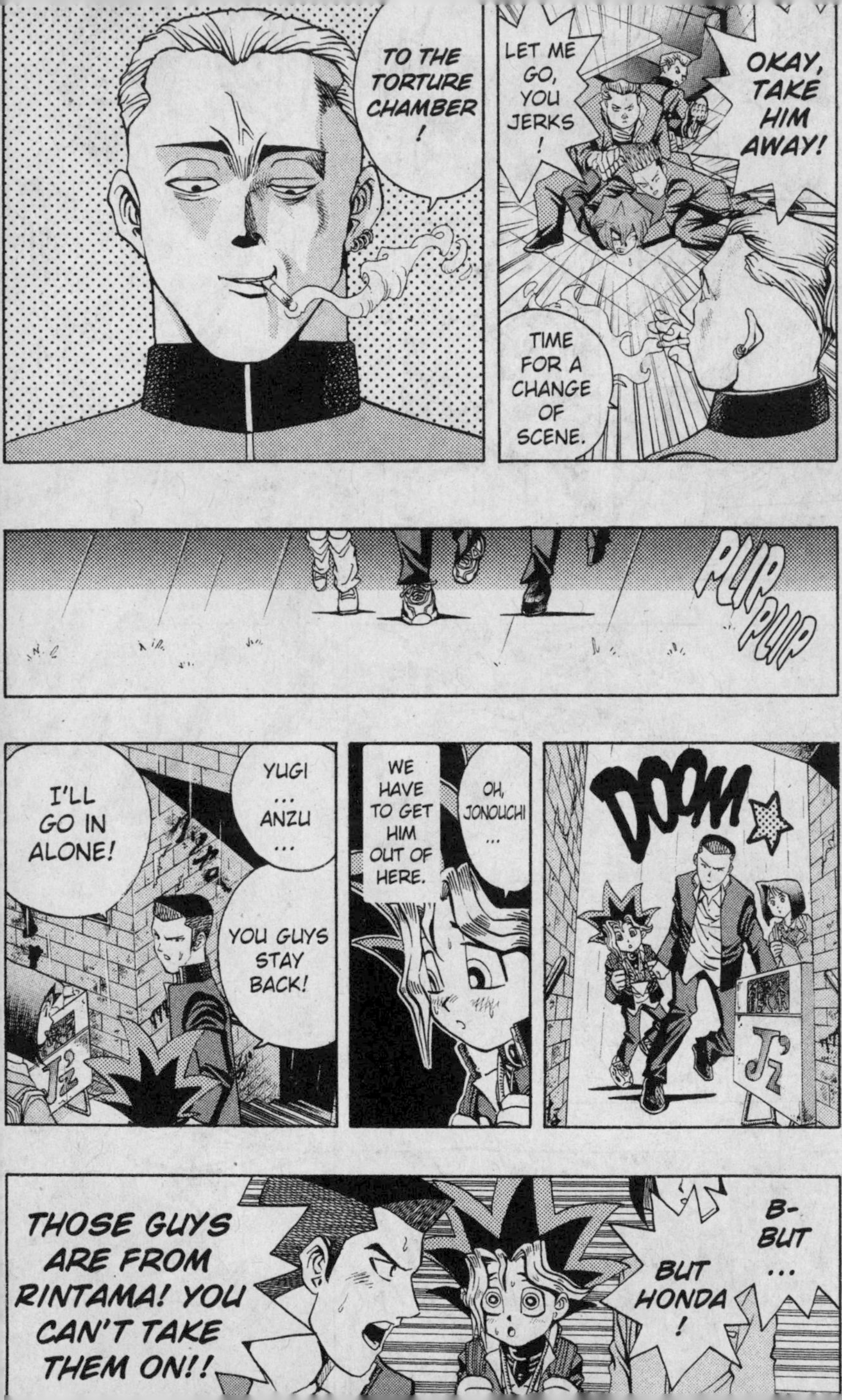
OKAY, TAKE HIM AWAY!
LET ME GO, YOU JERKS!
TIME FOR A CHANGE OF SCENE.
TO THE TORTURE CHAMBER!
PLIP PLIP
DOOM
OH, JONOUCHI...
WE HAVE TO GET HIM OUT OF HERE.
YUGI... ANZU...
I'LL GO IN ALONE!
YOU GUYS STAY BACK!
B-BUT...
BUT HONDA!
THOSE GUYS ARE FROM RINTAMA! YOU CAN'T TAKE THEM ON!!

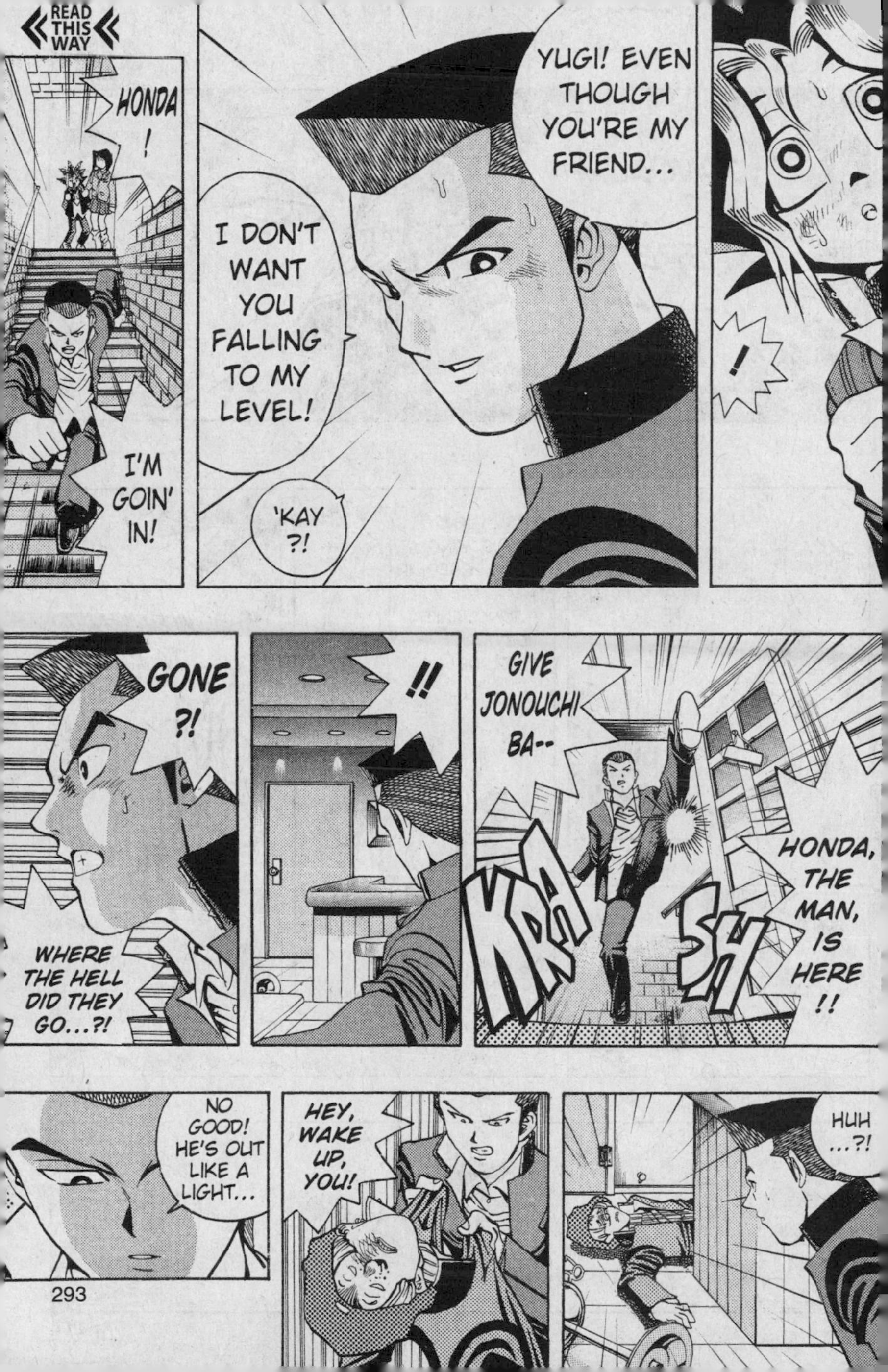
READ THIS WAY
!
YUGI! EVEN THOUGH YOU'RE MY FRIEND...
I DON'T WANT YOU FALLING TO MY LEVEL!
'KAY ?!
HONDA !
I'M GOIN' IN!
GIVE JONOUCHI BA--
KRASH
HONDA, THE MAN, IS HERE !!
!!
GONE ?!
WHERE THE HELL DID THEY GO...?!
HUH ...?!
HEY, WAKE UP, YOU!
NO GOOD! HE'S OUT LIKE A LIGHT...

READ THIS WAY

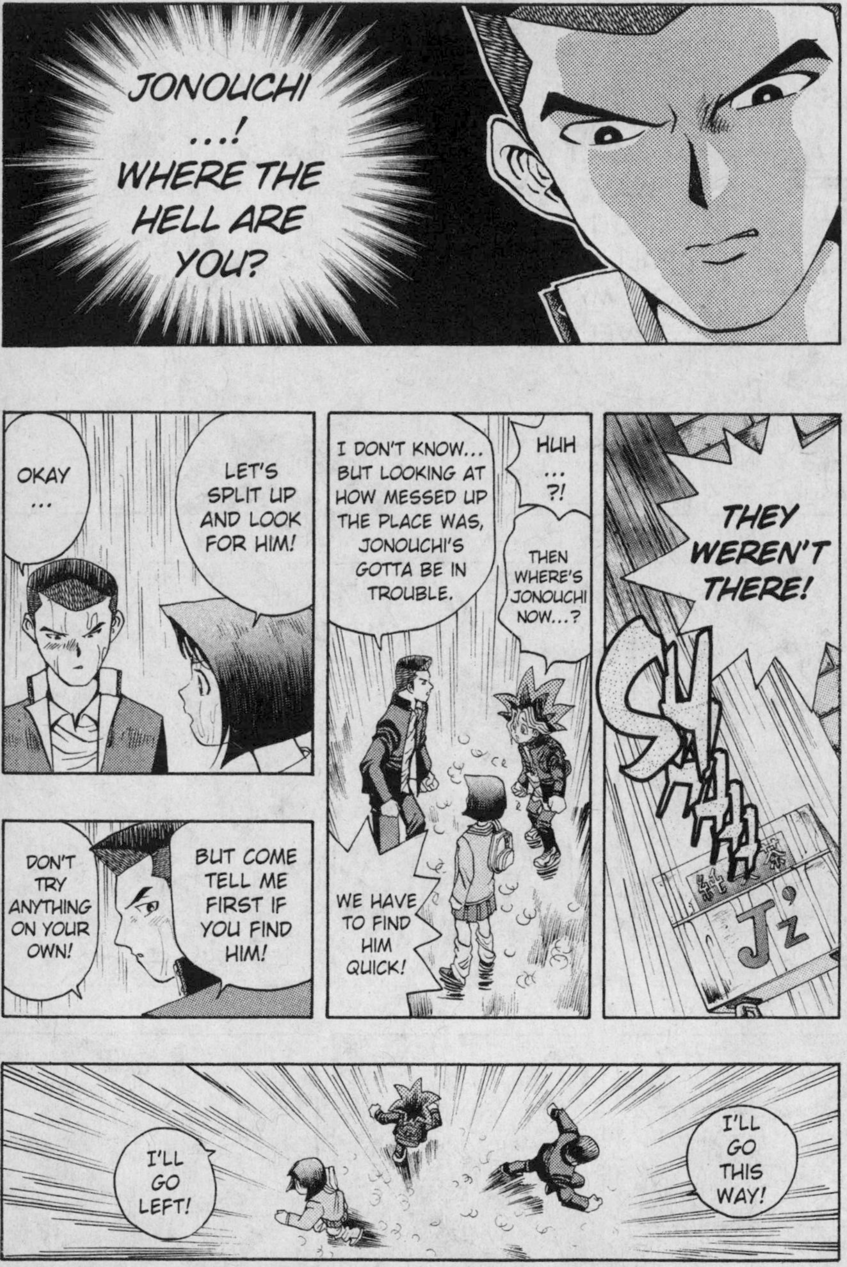

JONOUCHI ...! WHERE THE HELL ARE YOU?
THEY WEREN'T THERE!
J'z
HUH ...?!
THEN WHERE'S JONOUCHI NOW...?
I DON'T KNOW... BUT LOOKING AT HOW MESSED UP THE PLACE WAS, JONOUCHI'S GOTTA BE IN TROUBLE.
WE HAVE TO FIND HIM QUICK!
LET'S SPLIT UP AND LOOK FOR HIM!
OKAY ...
BUT COME TELL ME FIRST IF YOU FIND HIM!
DON'T TRY ANYTHING ON YOUR OWN!
I'LL GO THIS WAY!
I'LL GO LEFT!

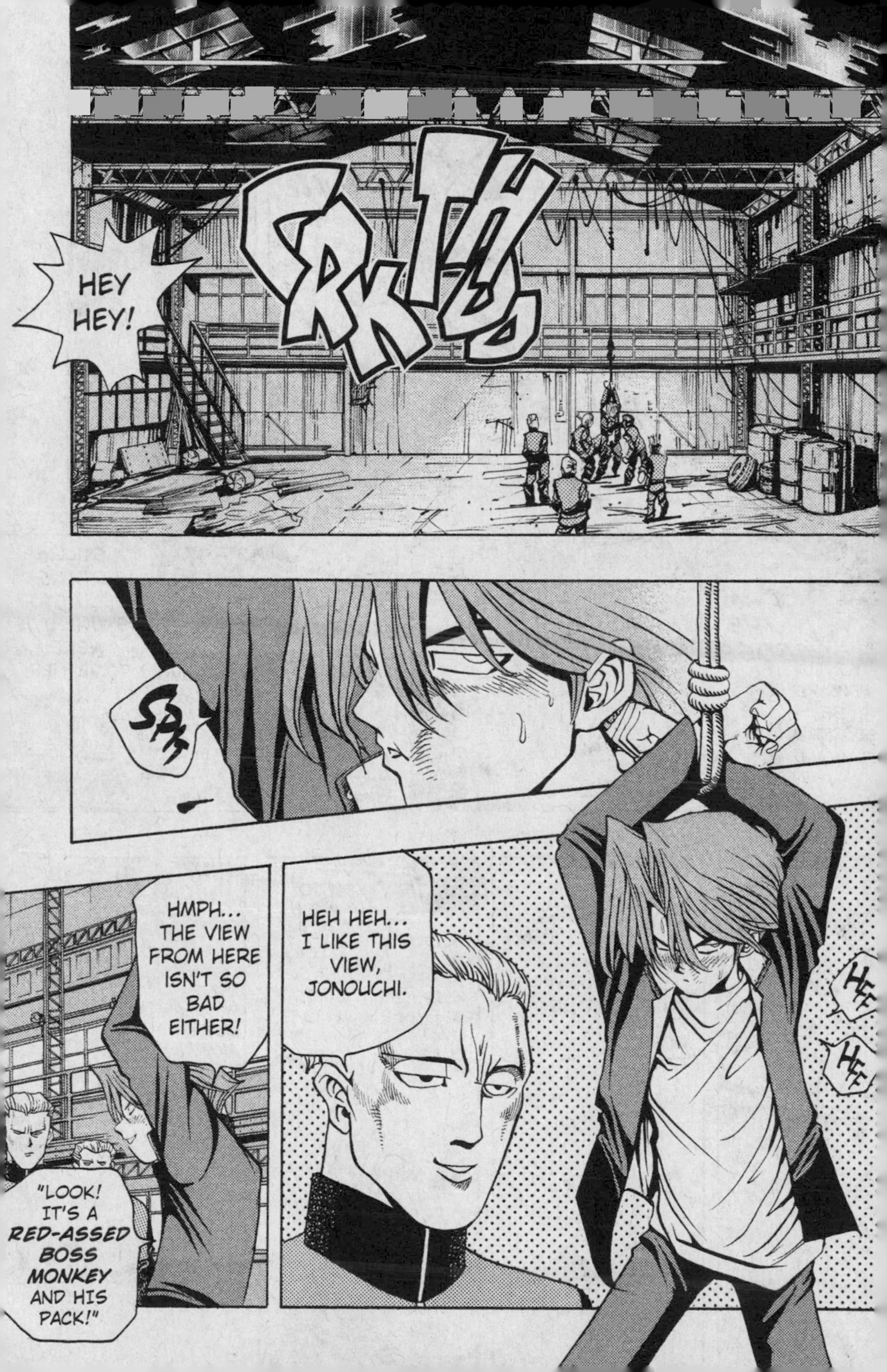
CRK
THUD
HEY HEY!
SPAT
HEH HEH... I LIKE THIS VIEW, JONOUCHI.
HFF
HFF
HMPH... THE VIEW FROM HERE ISN'T SO BAD EITHER!
"LOOK! IT'S A *RED-ASSED* **BOSS MONKEY** AND HIS PACK!"

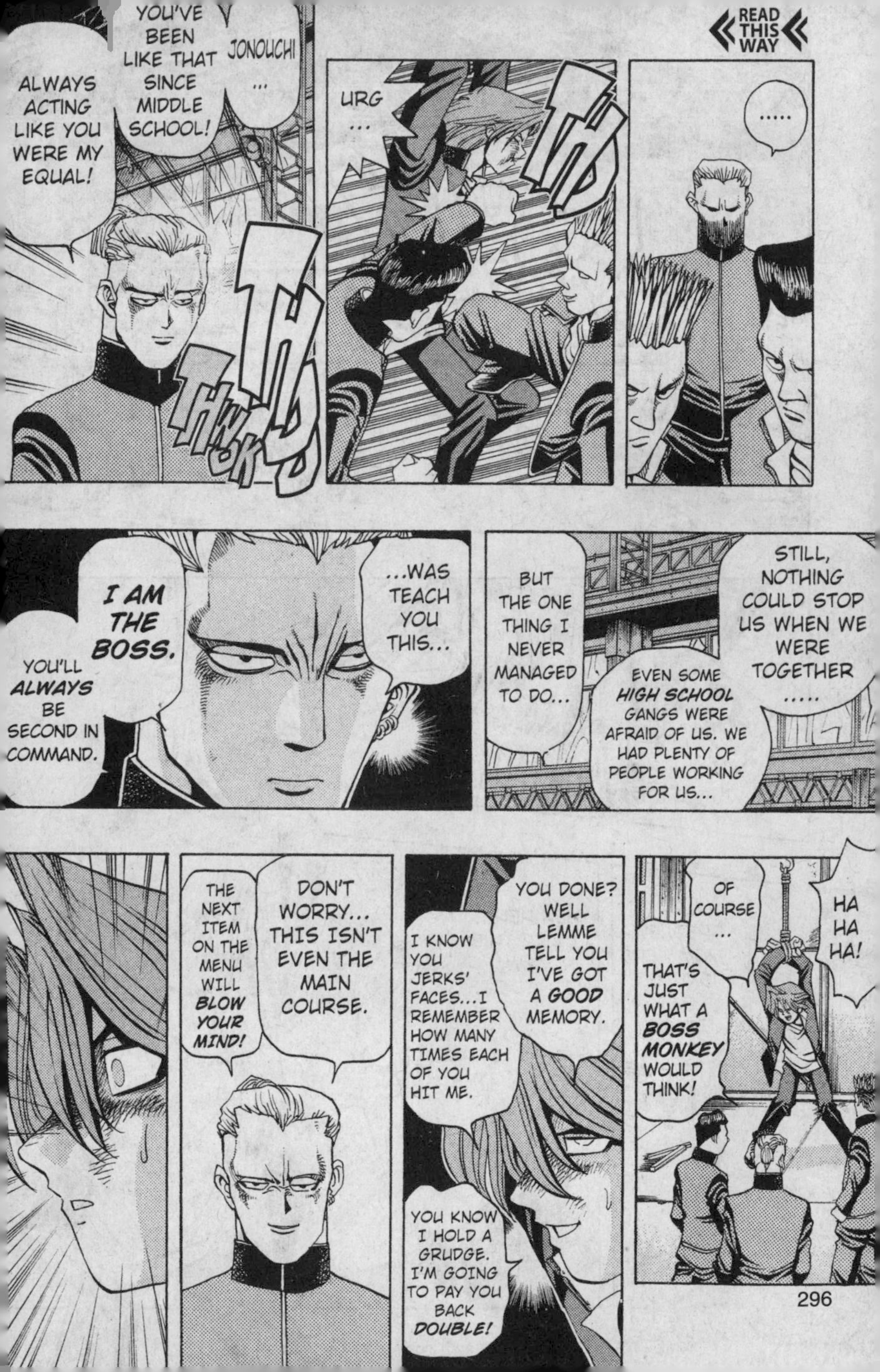
READ THIS WAY
.....
URG ...
JONOUCHI ...
YOU'VE BEEN LIKE THAT SINCE MIDDLE SCHOOL!
ALWAYS ACTING LIKE YOU WERE MY EQUAL!
THWOK
STILL, NOTHING COULD STOP US WHEN WE WERE TOGETHER .....
EVEN SOME **HIGH SCHOOL** GANGS WERE AFRAID OF US. WE HAD PLENTY OF PEOPLE WORKING FOR US...
BUT THE ONE THING I NEVER MANAGED TO DO...
...WAS TEACH YOU THIS...
I AM THE BOSS.
YOU'LL **ALWAYS** BE SECOND IN COMMAND.
HA HA HA!
OF COURSE ...
THAT'S JUST WHAT A **BOSS MONKEY** WOULD THINK!
YOU DONE? WELL LEMME TELL YOU I'VE GOT A **GOOD** MEMORY.
I KNOW YOU JERKS' FACES...I REMEMBER HOW MANY TIMES EACH OF YOU HIT ME.
YOU KNOW I HOLD A GRUDGE. I'M GOING TO PAY YOU BACK **DOUBLE!**
DON'T WORRY... THIS ISN'T EVEN THE MAIN COURSE.
THE NEXT ITEM ON THE MENU WILL **BLOW YOUR MIND!**

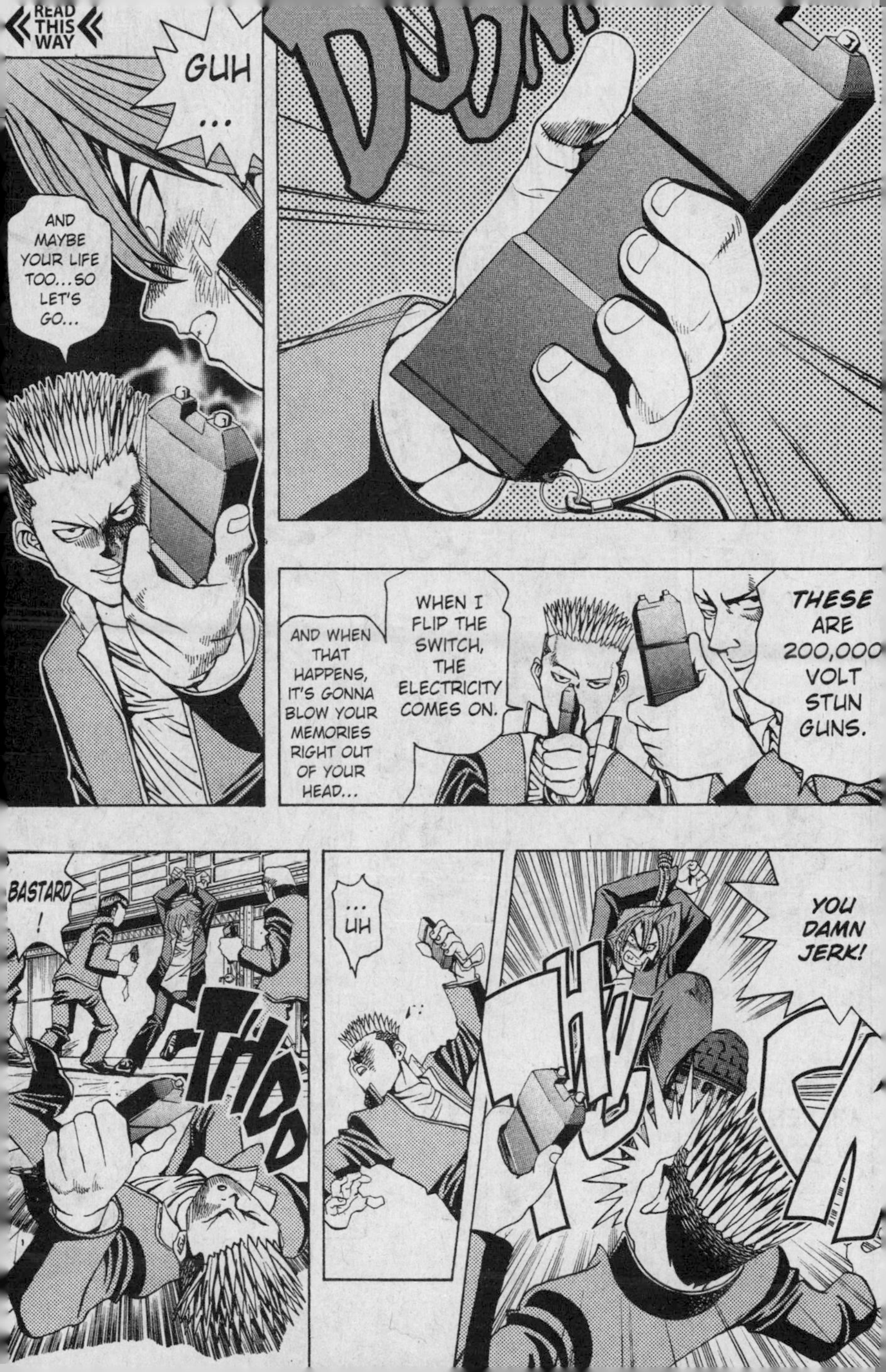
READ THIS WAY
THESE ARE 200,000 VOLT STUN GUNS.
WHEN I FLIP THE SWITCH, THE ELECTRICITY COMES ON.
AND WHEN THAT HAPPENS, IT'S GONNA BLOW YOUR MEMORIES RIGHT OUT OF YOUR HEAD...
GUH ...
AND MAYBE YOUR LIFE TOO...SO LET'S GO...
YOU DAMN JERK!
... UH
BASTARD!

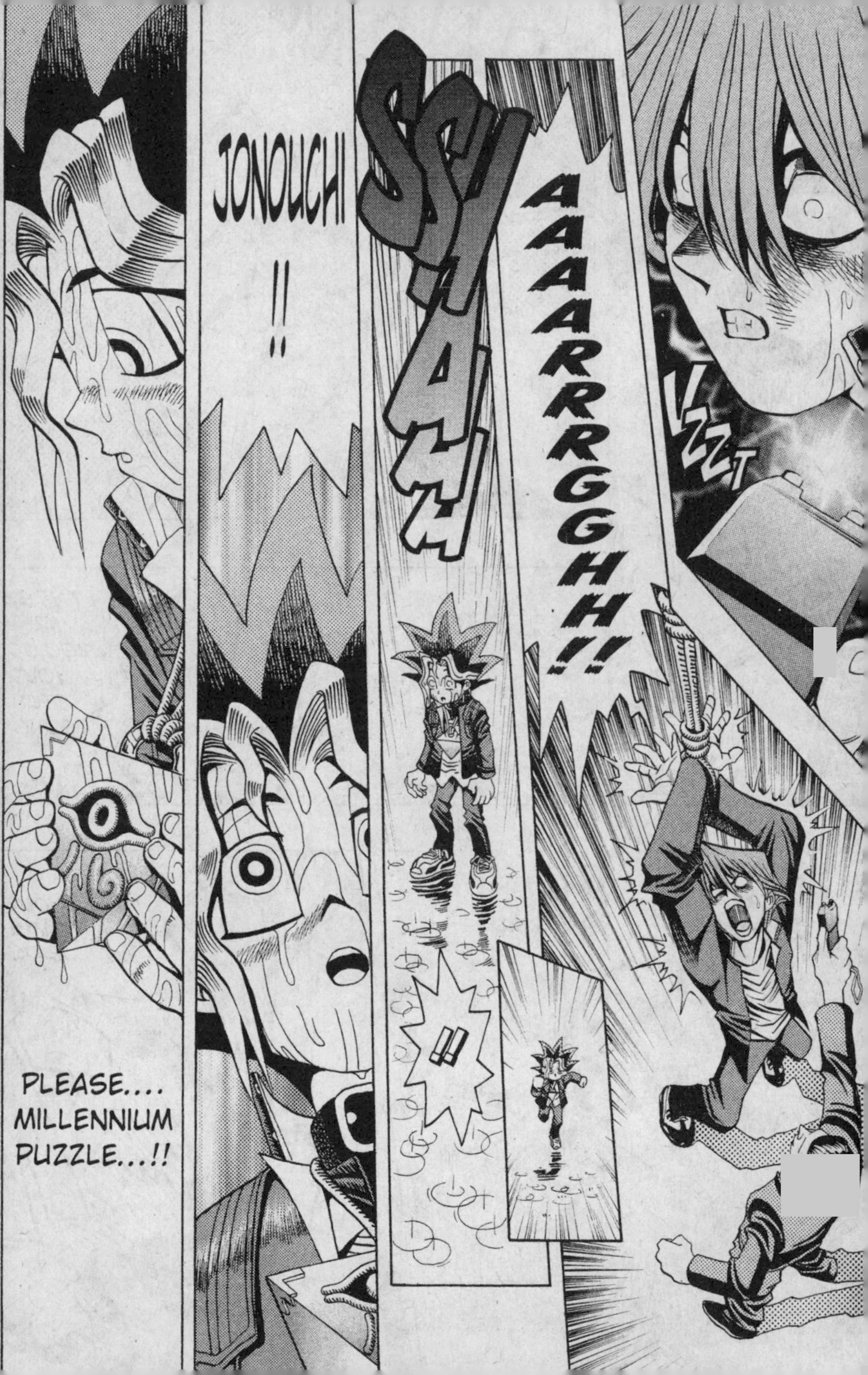

ZZZT
AAAARRRGGHH!!
SSHAH
!!
JONOUCHI !!
PLEASE.... MILLENNIUM PUZZLE...!!

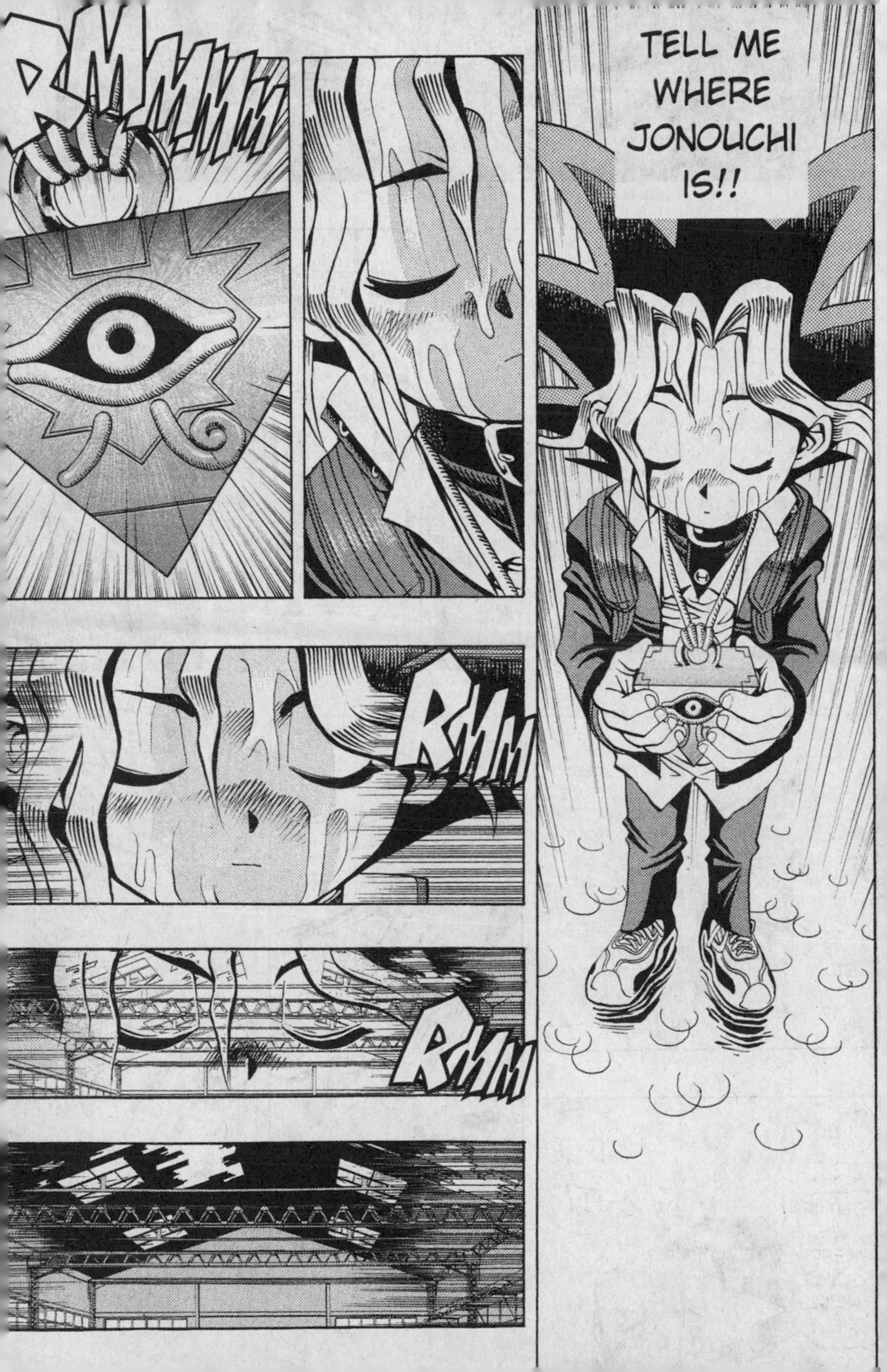
TELL ME WHERE JONOUCHI IS!!
RMMMMM
RMM
RMM

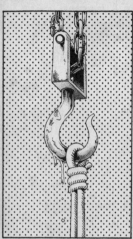

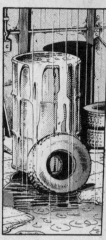

HEY, HIRUTANI... HE CAN'T EVEN TALK ANYMORE!

HE'S JUST TWITCHING NOW!

SHOULD WE STOP NOW ...?

TWITCH TWITCH

VZZT

SSH

UH ...

BUT IF WE KEEP GOING HE'LL DIE...

DO IT!

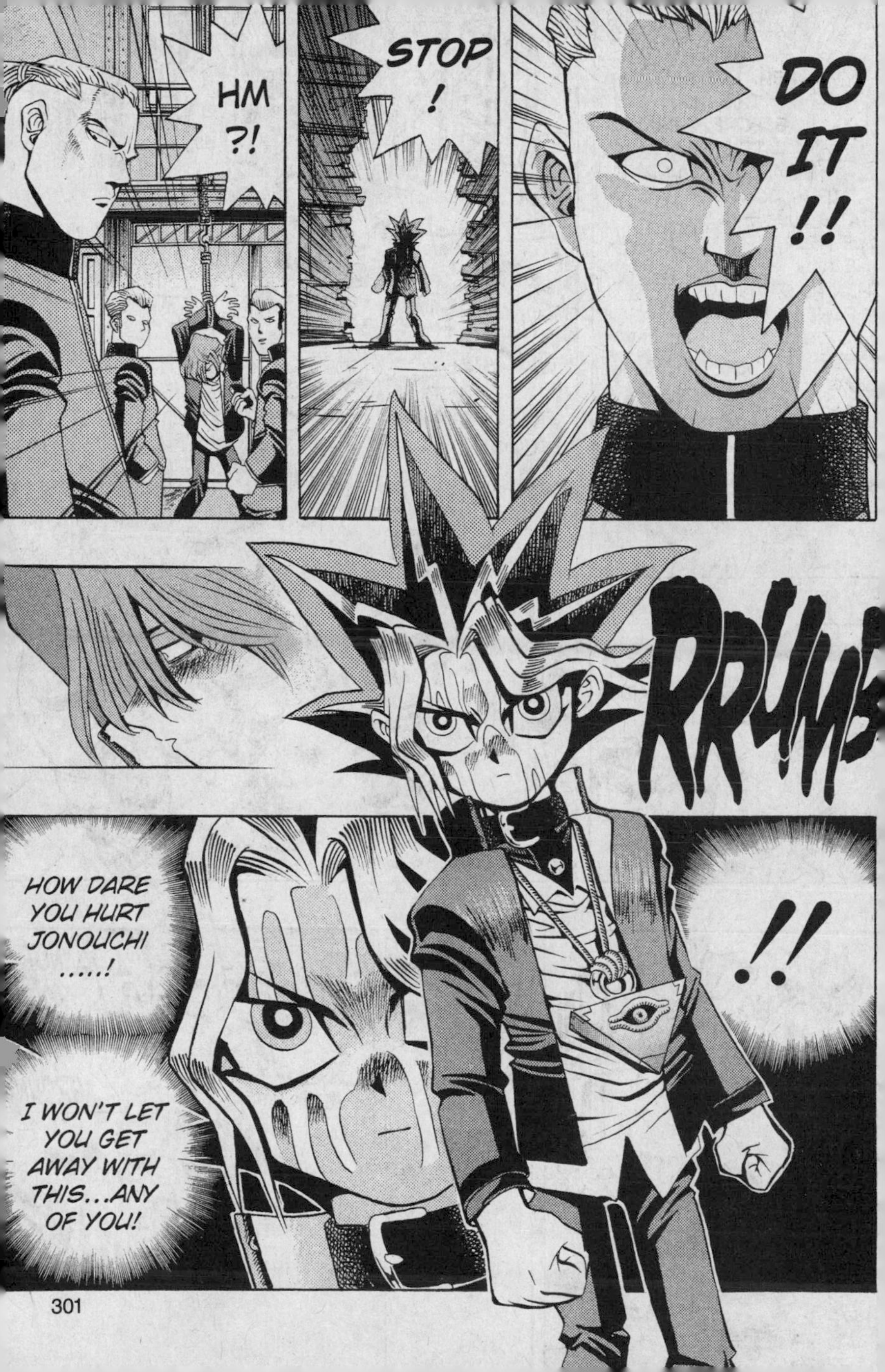
DO IT !!
STOP !
HM ?!
RRUMB
!!
HOW DARE YOU HURT JONOUCHI .....!
I WON'T LET YOU GET AWAY WITH THIS...ANY OF YOU!

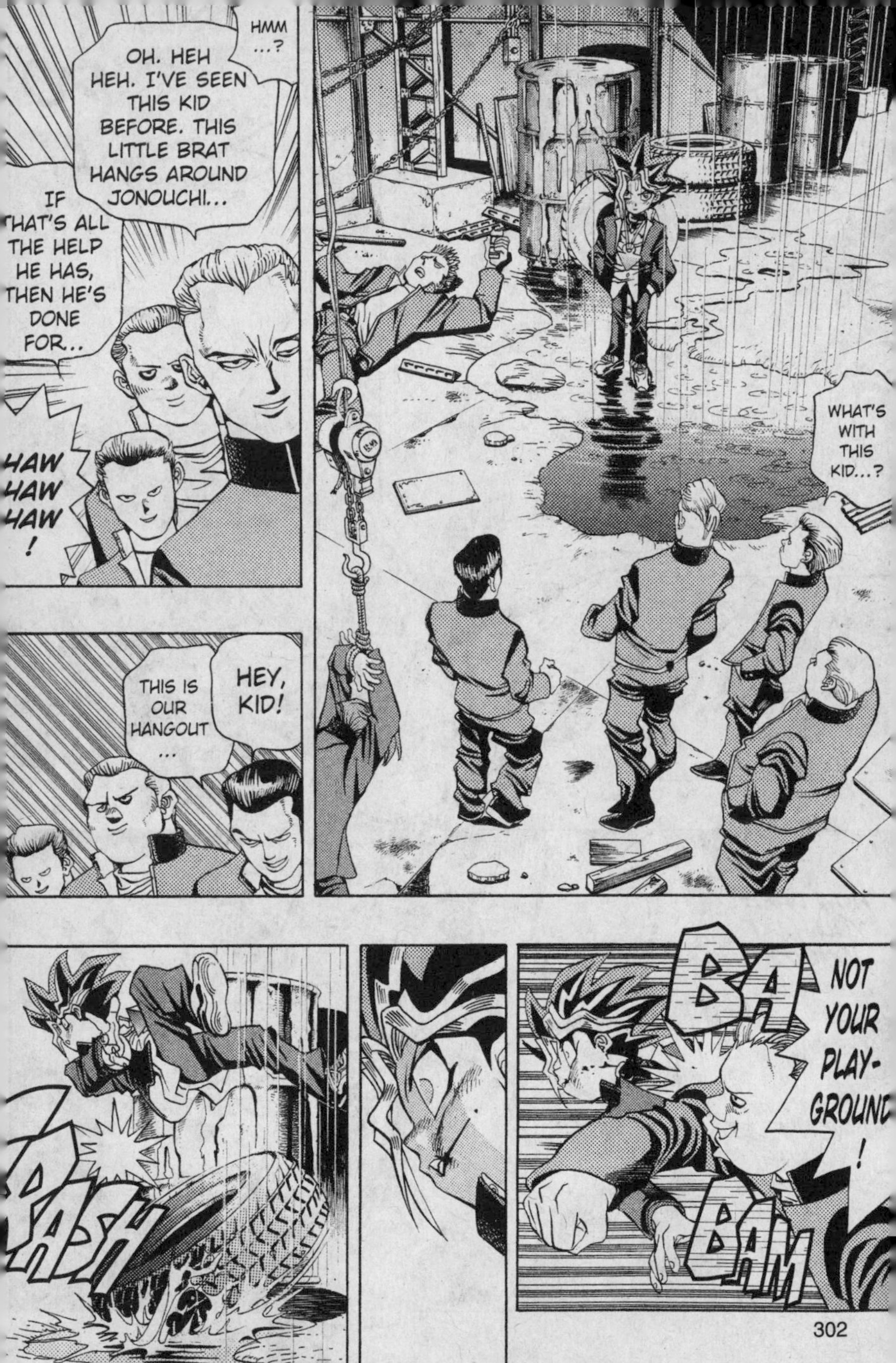
HMM ...?
OH. HEH HEH. I'VE SEEN THIS KID BEFORE. THIS LITTLE BRAT HANGS AROUND JONOUCHI...
IF THAT'S ALL THE HELP HE HAS, THEN HE'S DONE FOR...
HAW HAW HAW!
HEY, KID!
THIS IS OUR HANGOUT ...
WHAT'S WITH THIS KID...?
BASH
BA
NOT YOUR PLAY-GROUND!
BAM

« THIS WAY «

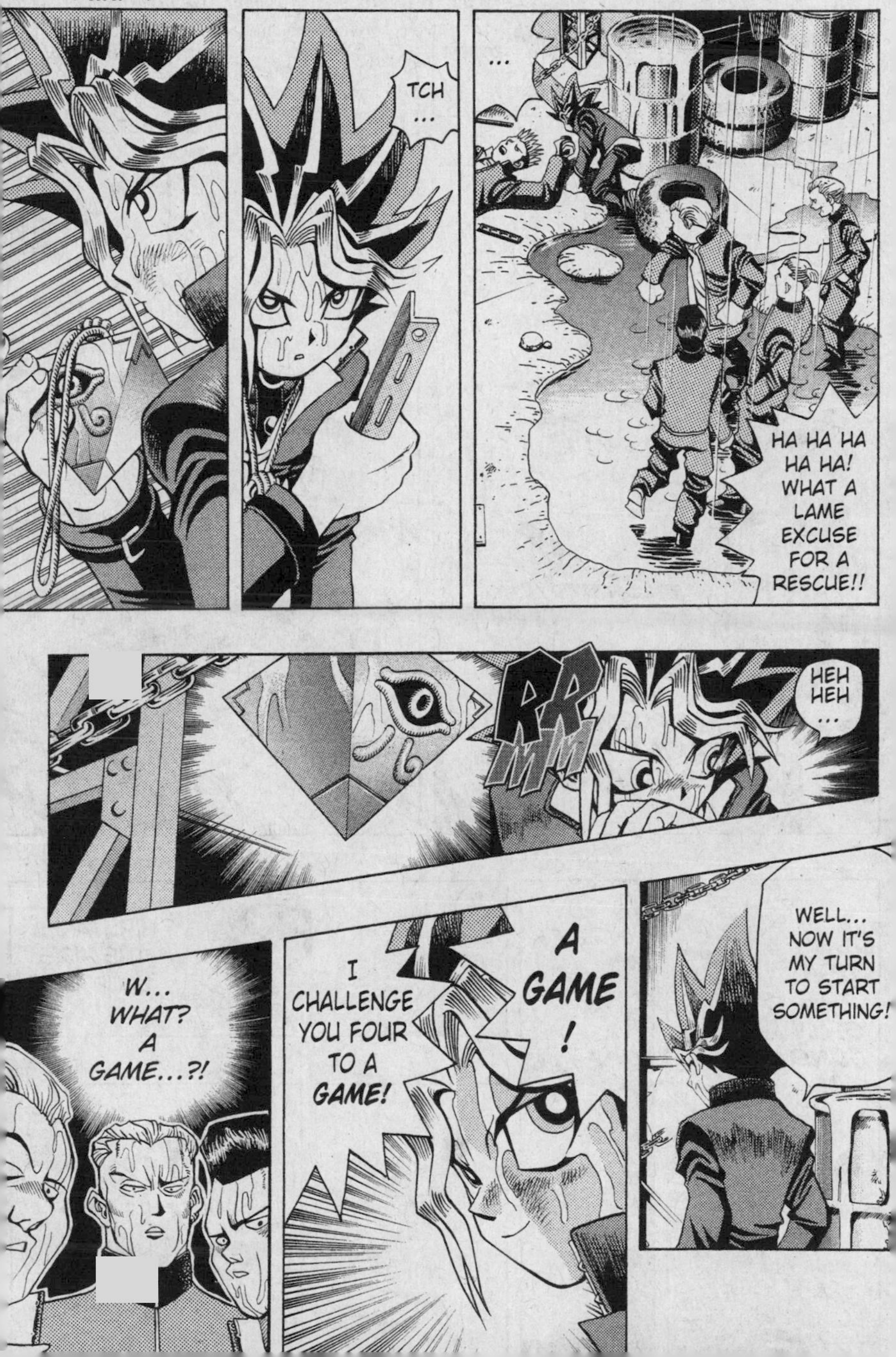
...
HA HA HA HA HA! WHAT A LAME EXCUSE FOR A RESCUE!!
TCH ...
HEH HEH ...
RRMM
WELL... NOW IT'S MY TURN TO START SOMETHING!
A GAME !
I CHALLENGE YOU FOUR TO A GAME!
W... WHAT? A GAME...?!

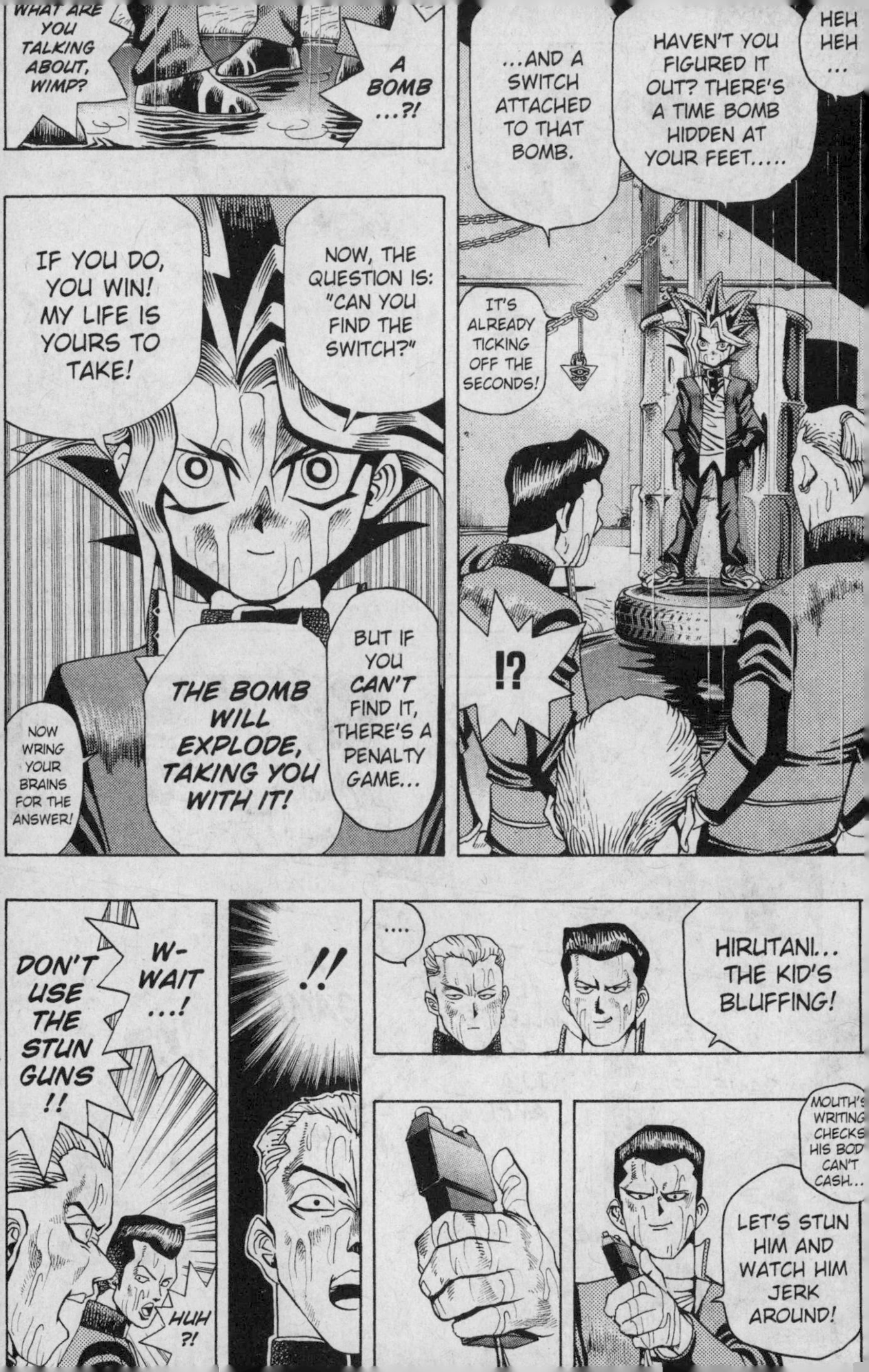
WHAT ARE YOU TALKING ABOUT, WIMP?
A BOMB ...?!
HEH HEH ...
HAVEN'T YOU FIGURED IT OUT? THERE'S A TIME BOMB HIDDEN AT YOUR FEET.....
...AND A SWITCH ATTACHED TO THAT BOMB.
IT'S ALREADY TICKING OFF THE SECONDS!
!?
NOW, THE QUESTION IS: "CAN YOU FIND THE SWITCH?"
IF YOU DO, YOU WIN! MY LIFE IS YOURS TO TAKE!
BUT IF YOU CAN'T FIND IT, THERE'S A PENALTY GAME...
THE BOMB WILL EXPLODE, TAKING YOU WITH IT!
NOW WRING YOUR BRAINS FOR THE ANSWER!
HIRUTANI... THE KID'S BLUFFING!
....
MOUTH'S WRITING CHECKS HIS BOD CAN'T CASH...
LET'S STUN HIM AND WATCH HIM JERK AROUND!
!!
W-WAIT ...!
DON'T USE THE STUN GUNS !!
HUH ?!

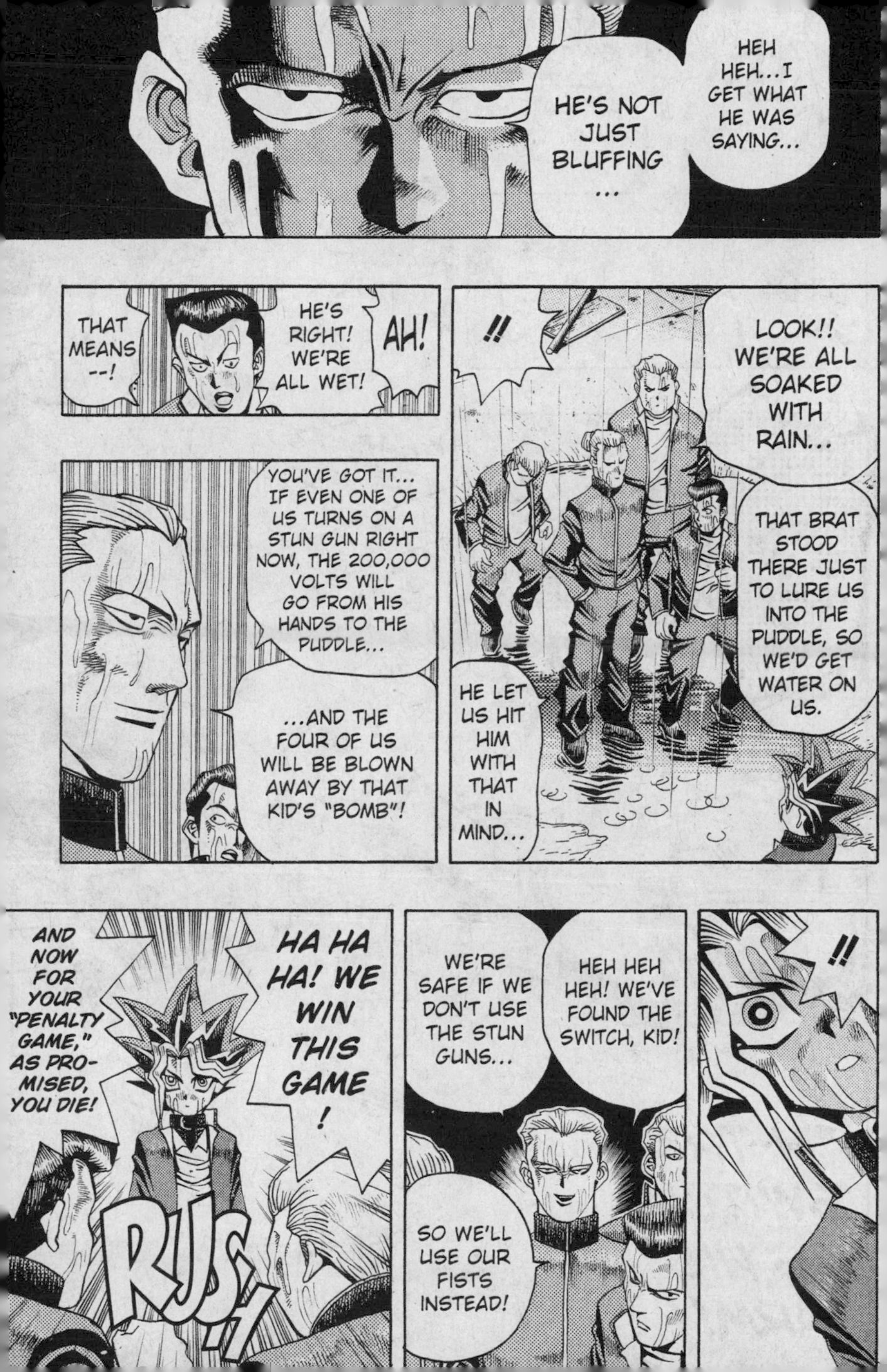
HEH HEH...I GET WHAT HE WAS SAYING...
HE'S NOT JUST BLUFFING ...
!!
LOOK!! WE'RE ALL SOAKED WITH RAIN...
THAT BRAT STOOD THERE JUST TO LURE US INTO THE PUDDLE, SO WE'D GET WATER ON US.
HE LET US HIT HIM WITH THAT IN MIND...
AH!
HE'S RIGHT! WE'RE ALL WET!
THAT MEANS --!
YOU'VE GOT IT... IF EVEN ONE OF US TURNS ON A STUN GUN RIGHT NOW, THE 200,000 VOLTS WILL GO FROM HIS HANDS TO THE PUDDLE...
...AND THE FOUR OF US WILL BE BLOWN AWAY BY THAT KID'S "BOMB"!
!!
HEH HEH HEH! WE'VE FOUND THE SWITCH, KID!
WE'RE SAFE IF WE DON'T USE THE STUN GUNS...
SO WE'LL USE OUR FISTS INSTEAD!
HA HA HA! WE WIN THIS GAME!
AND NOW FOR YOUR "PENALTY GAME," AS PRO-MISED, YOU DIE!
RUSH

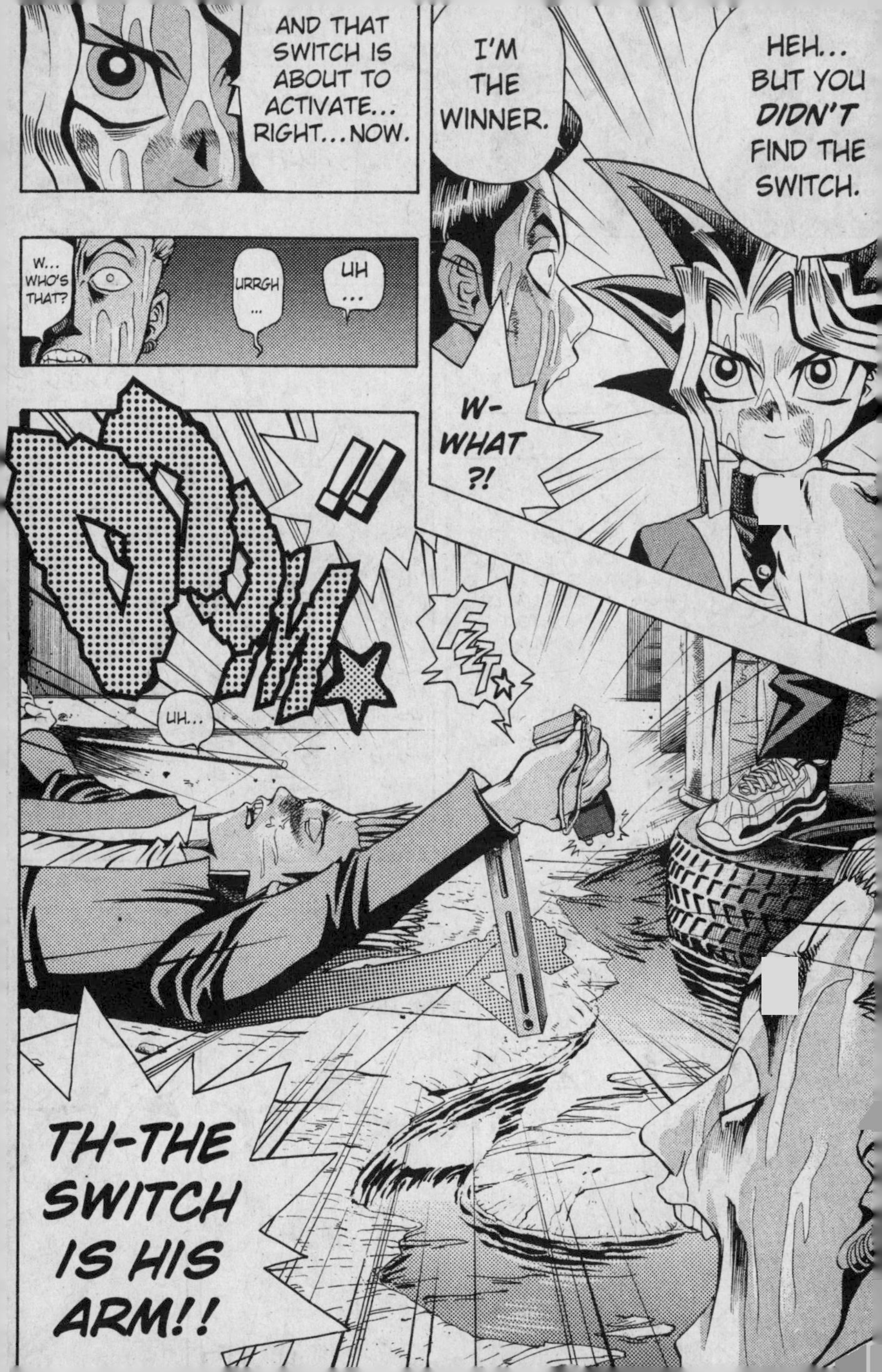
HEH... BUT YOU DIDN'T FIND THE SWITCH.
I'M THE WINNER.
W-WHAT?!
AND THAT SWITCH IS ABOUT TO ACTIVATE... RIGHT...NOW.
UH ...
URRGH ...
W... WHO'S THAT?
FZZT☆
UH...
TH-THE SWITCH IS HIS ARM!!

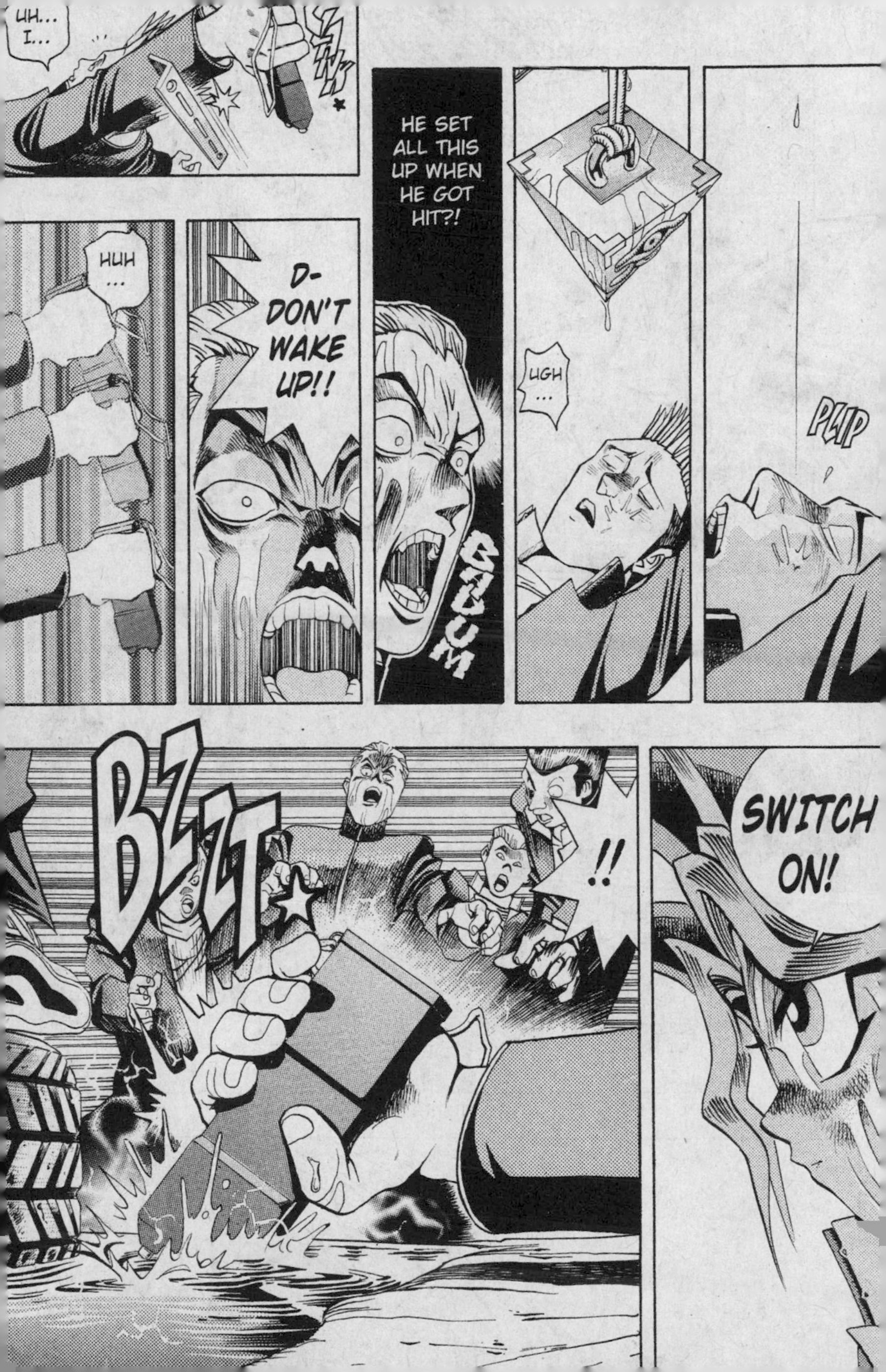
PLIP
UGH ...
HE SET ALL THIS UP WHEN HE GOT HIT?!
BADUM
D- DON'T WAKE UP!!
HUH ...
UH... I...
...
SWITCH ON!
!!
BZZT

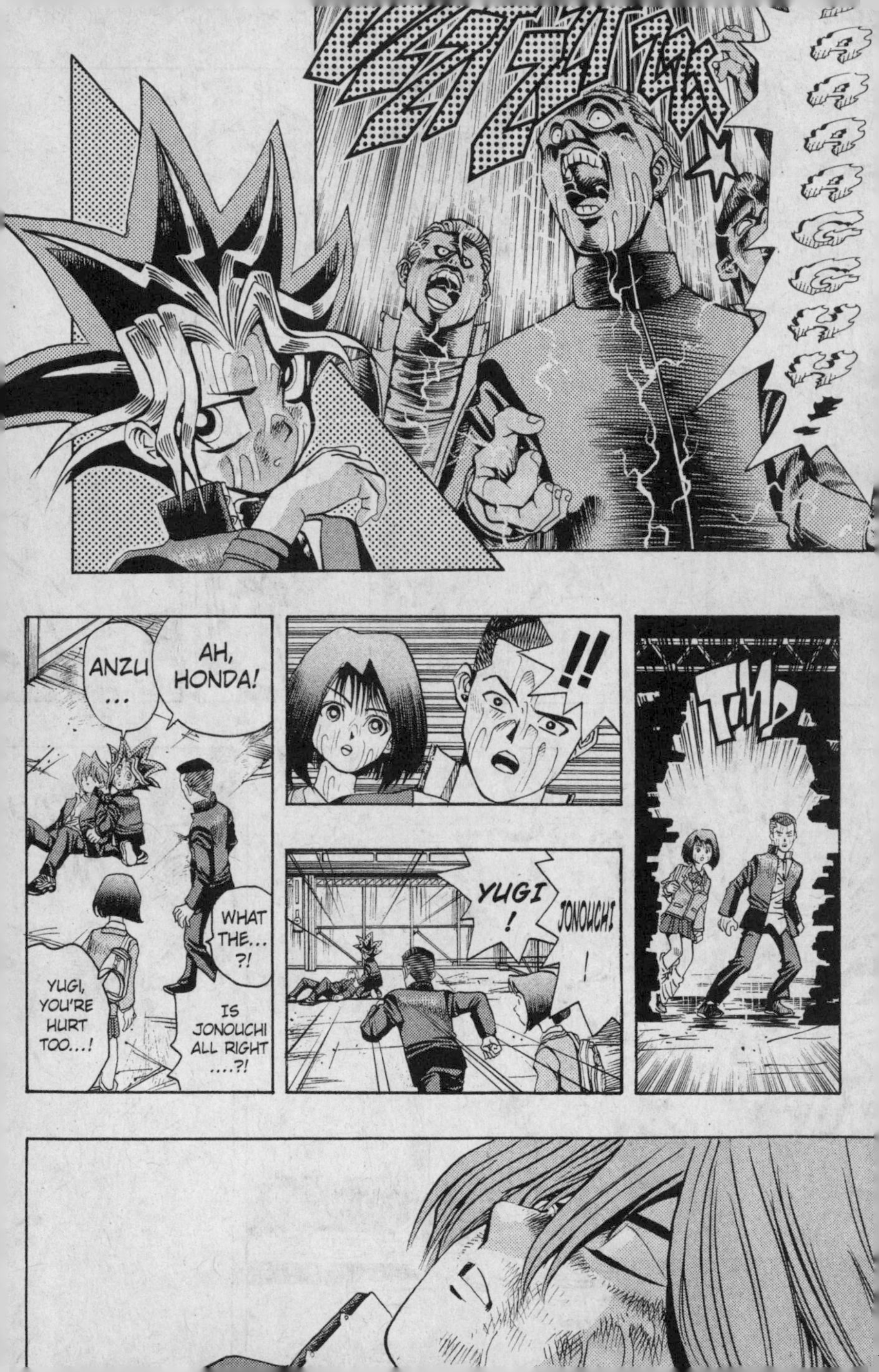
AAAAGGHH!
!!
JONOUCHI!
YUGI!
AH, HONDA!
ANZU...
WHAT THE...?!
IS JONOUCHI ALL RIGHT....?!
YUGI, YOU'RE HURT TOO...!

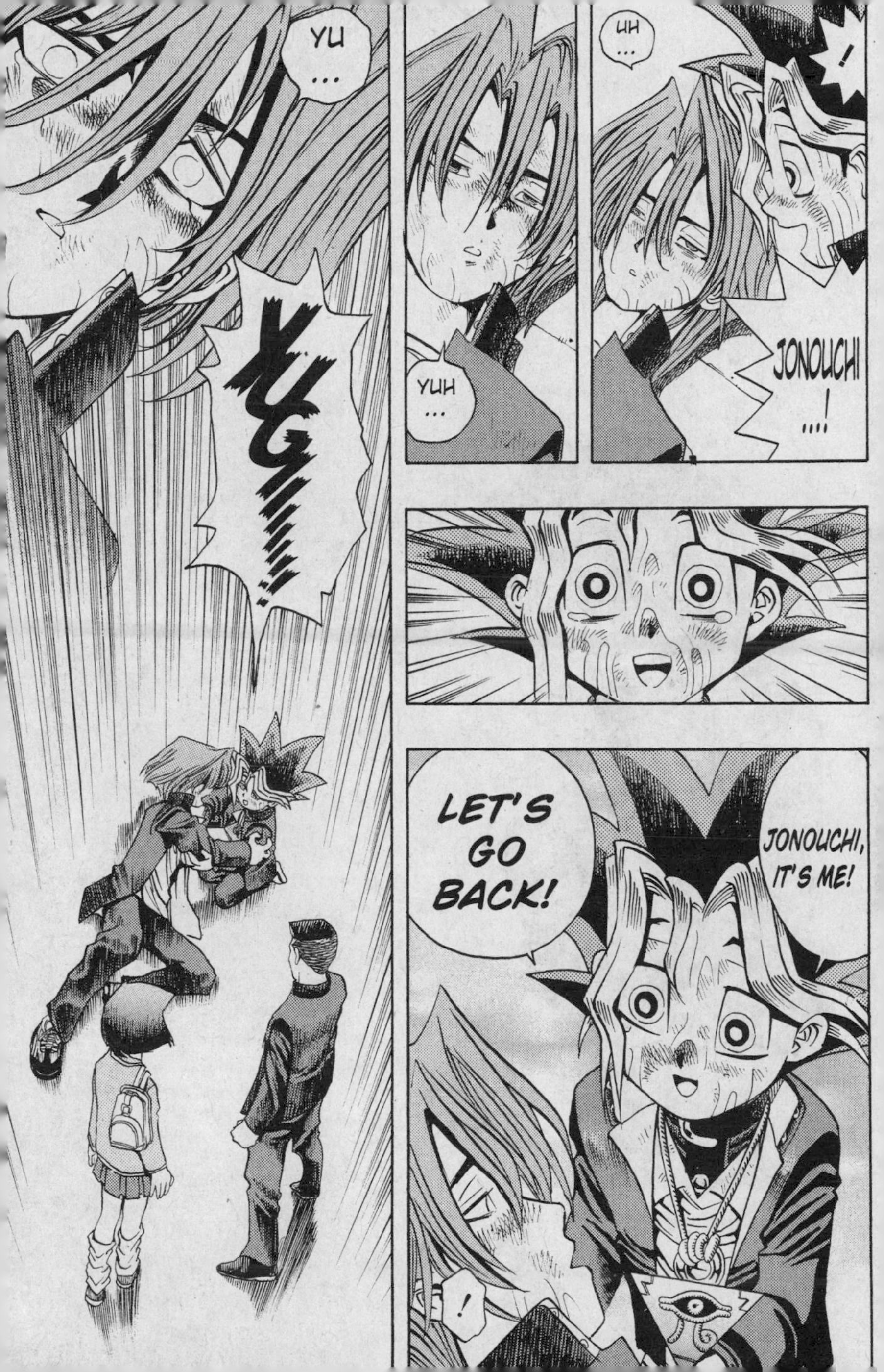
UH ...
!
JONOUCHI ...!
YUH ...
JONOUCHI, IT'S ME!
LET'S GO BACK!
!
YU ...
YUGI!!!!!

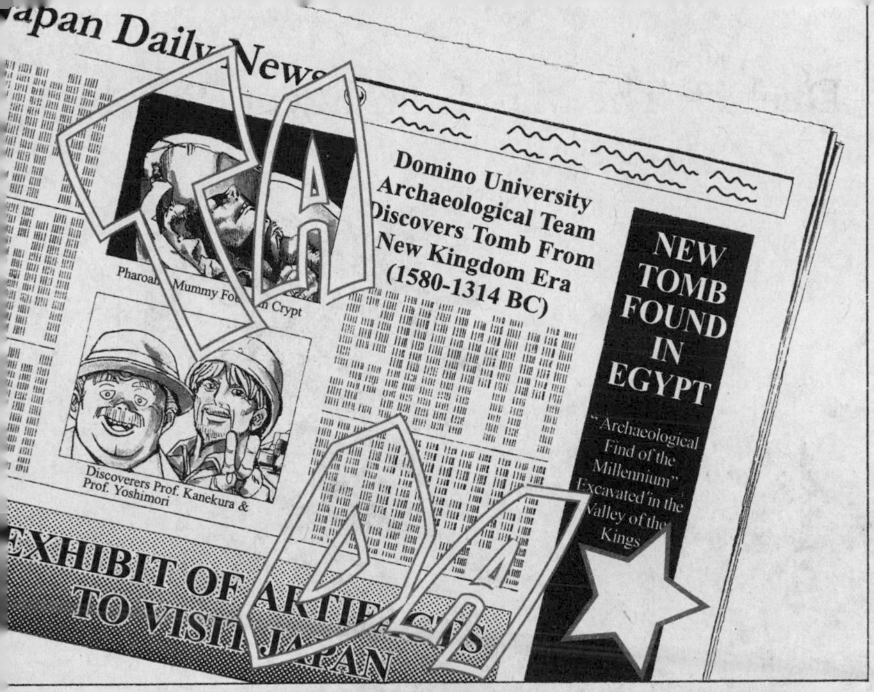
Japan Daily News
Domino University Archaeological Team Discovers Tomb From New Kingdom Era (1580-1314 BC)
NEW TOMB FOUND IN EGYPT
"Archaeological Find of the Millennium" Excavated in the Valley of the Kings
Discoverers Prof. Kanekura & Prof. Yoshimori
EXHIBIT OF ARTIFACTS TO VISIT JAPAN

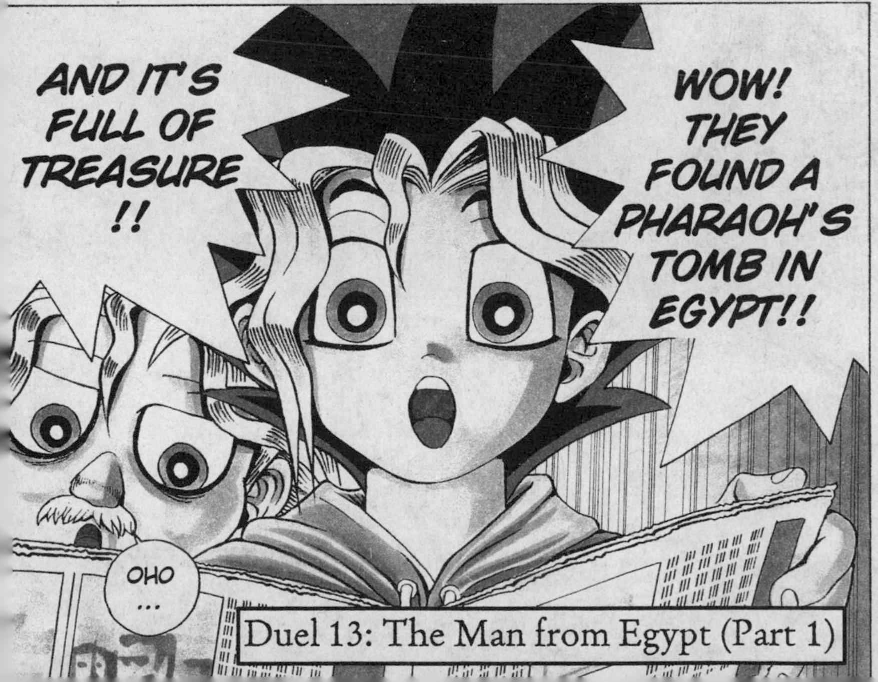
WOW! THEY FOUND A PHARAOH'S TOMB IN EGYPT!!
AND IT'S FULL OF TREASURE!!
OHO...

Duel 13: The Man from Egypt (Part 1)

Duel 13: The Man from Egypt (Part 1)

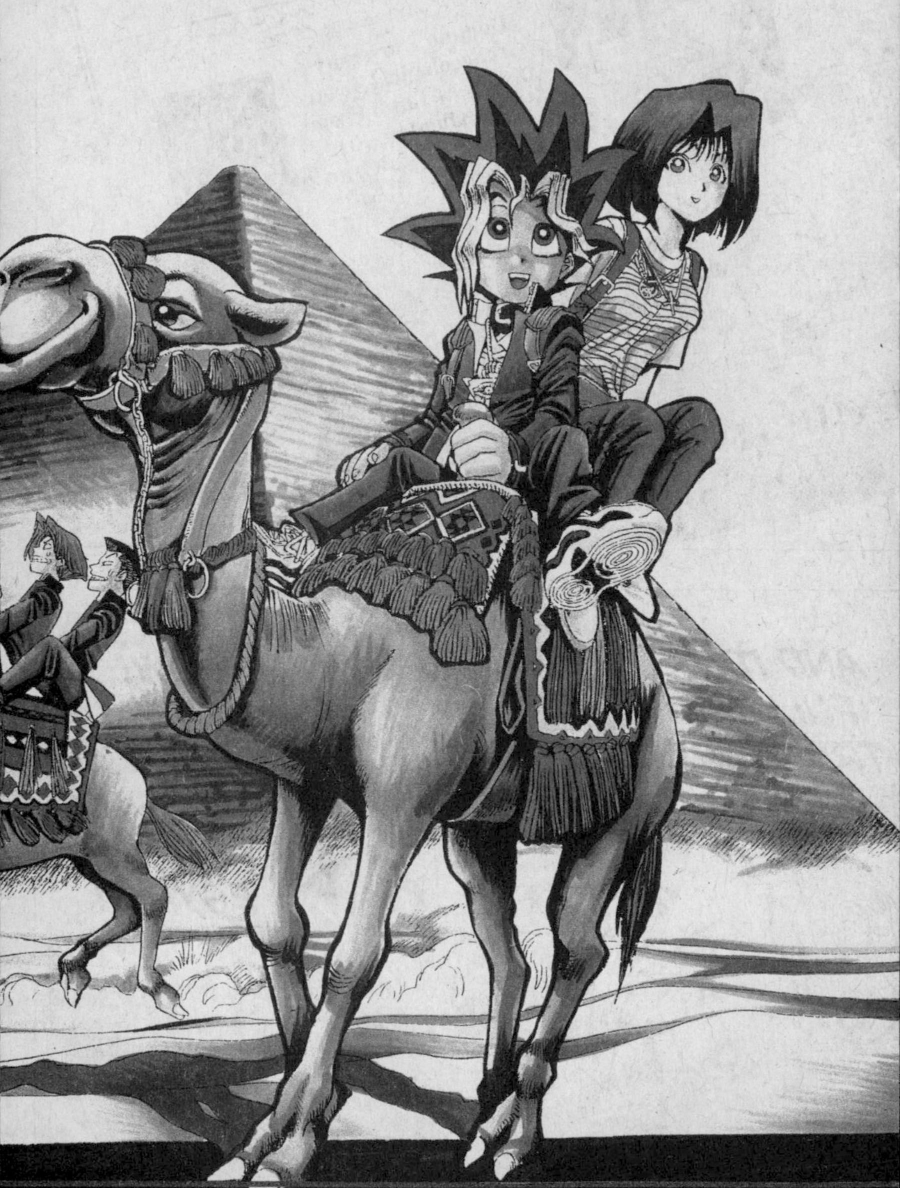

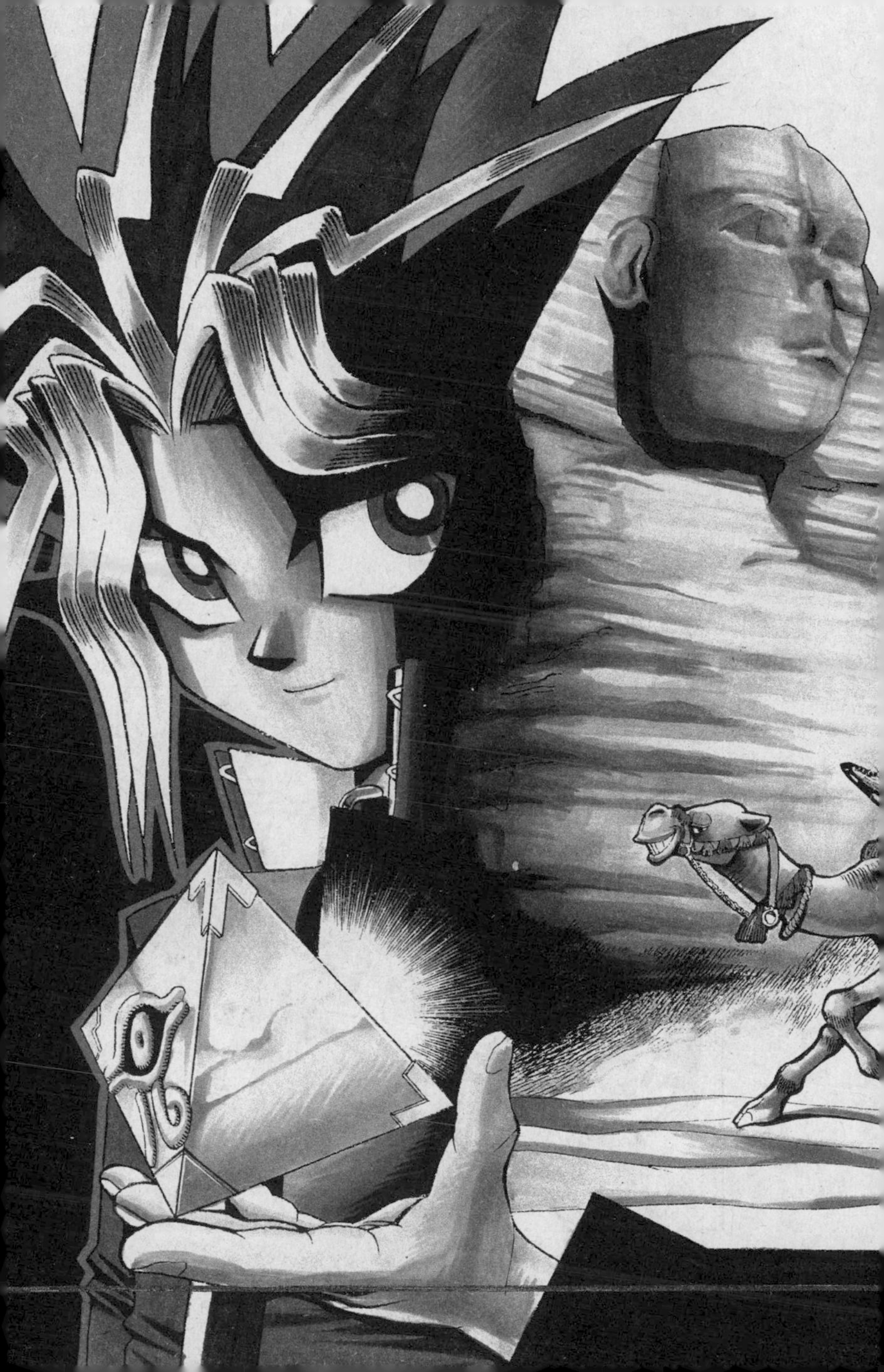

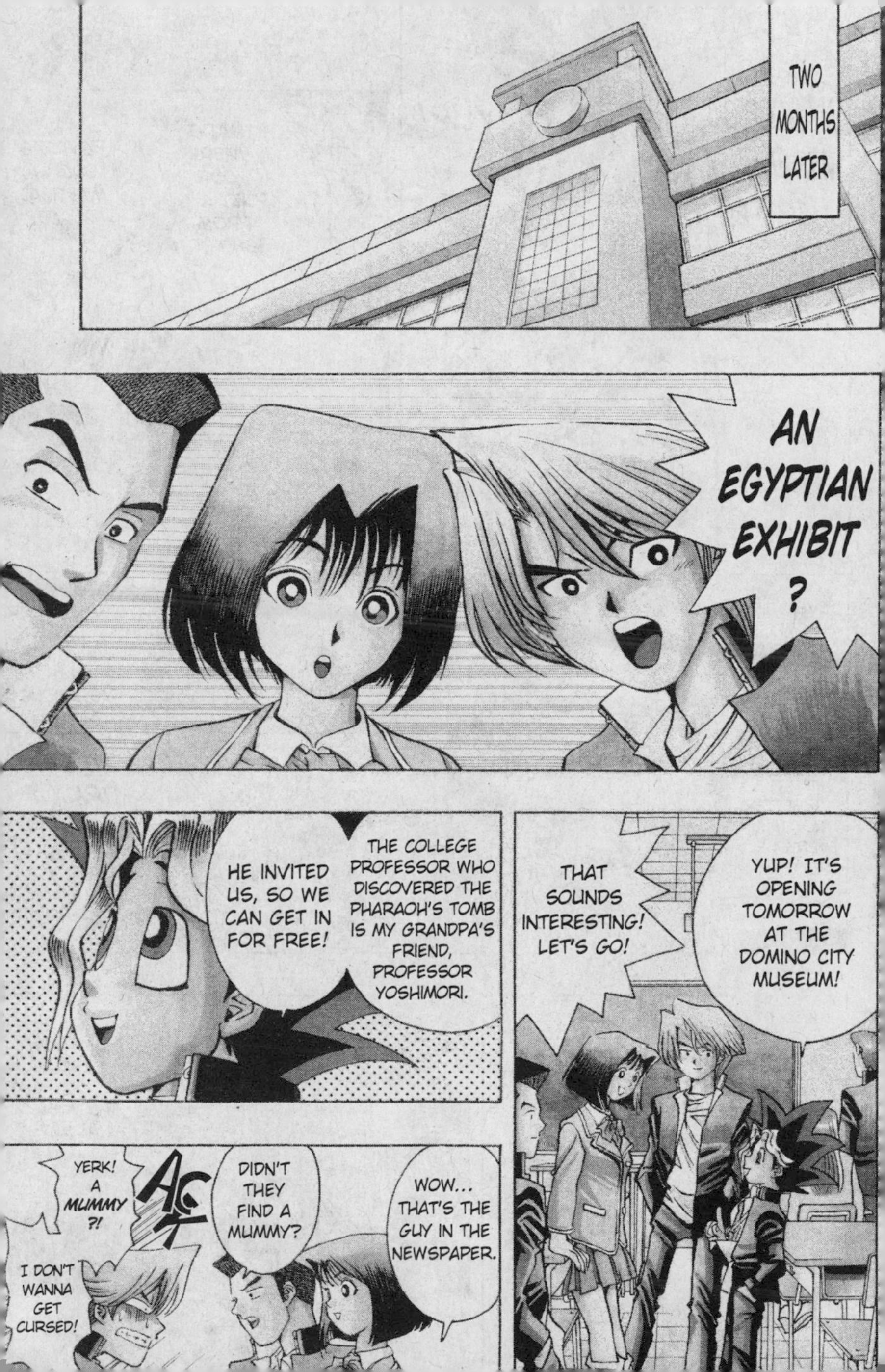
TWO MONTHS LATER
AN EGYPTIAN EXHIBIT ?
YUP! IT'S OPENING TOMORROW AT THE DOMINO CITY MUSEUM!
THAT SOUNDS INTERESTING! LET'S GO!
THE COLLEGE PROFESSOR WHO DISCOVERED THE PHARAOH'S TOMB IS MY GRANDPA'S FRIEND, PROFESSOR YOSHIMORI.
HE INVITED US, SO WE CAN GET IN FOR FREE!
WOW... THAT'S THE GUY IN THE NEWSPAPER.
DIDN'T THEY FIND A MUMMY?
ACK
YERK! A MUMMY ?!
I DON'T WANNA GET CURSED!

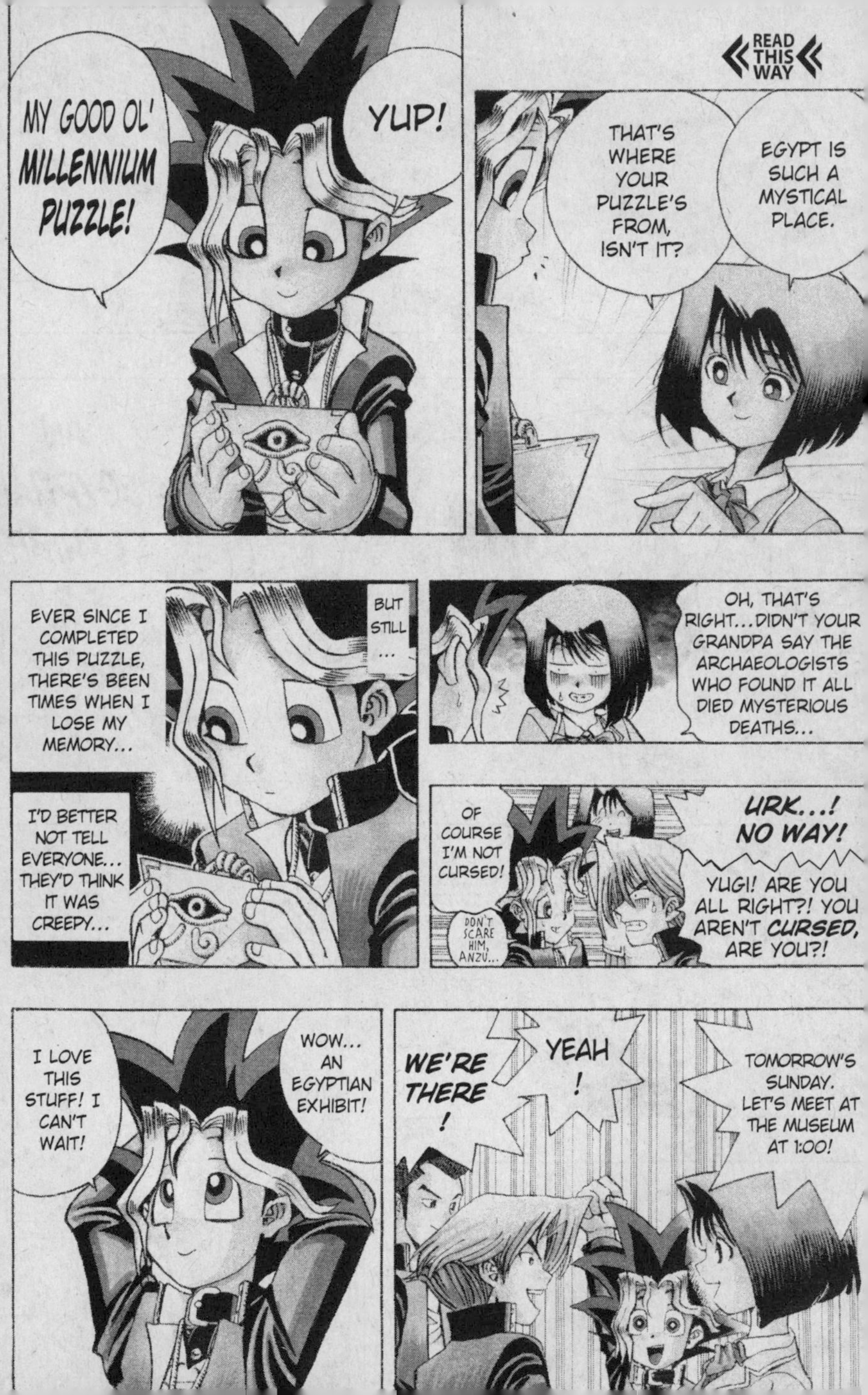
READ THIS WAY
EGYPT IS SUCH A MYSTICAL PLACE.
THAT'S WHERE YOUR PUZZLE'S FROM, ISN'T IT?
YUP!
MY GOOD OL' MILLENNIUM PUZZLE!
OH, THAT'S RIGHT...DIDN'T YOUR GRANDPA SAY THE ARCHAEOLOGISTS WHO FOUND IT ALL DIED MYSTERIOUS DEATHS...
URK...! NO WAY!
YUGI! ARE YOU ALL RIGHT?! YOU AREN'T CURSED, ARE YOU?!
OF COURSE I'M NOT CURSED!
DON'T SCARE HIM, ANZU...
BUT STILL...
EVER SINCE I COMPLETED THIS PUZZLE, THERE'S BEEN TIMES WHEN I LOSE MY MEMORY...
I'D BETTER NOT TELL EVERYONE... THEY'D THINK IT WAS CREEPY...
TOMORROW'S SUNDAY. LET'S MEET AT THE MUSEUM AT 1:00!
YEAH!
WE'RE THERE!
WOW... AN EGYPTIAN EXHIBIT!
I LOVE THIS STUFF! I CAN'T WAIT!

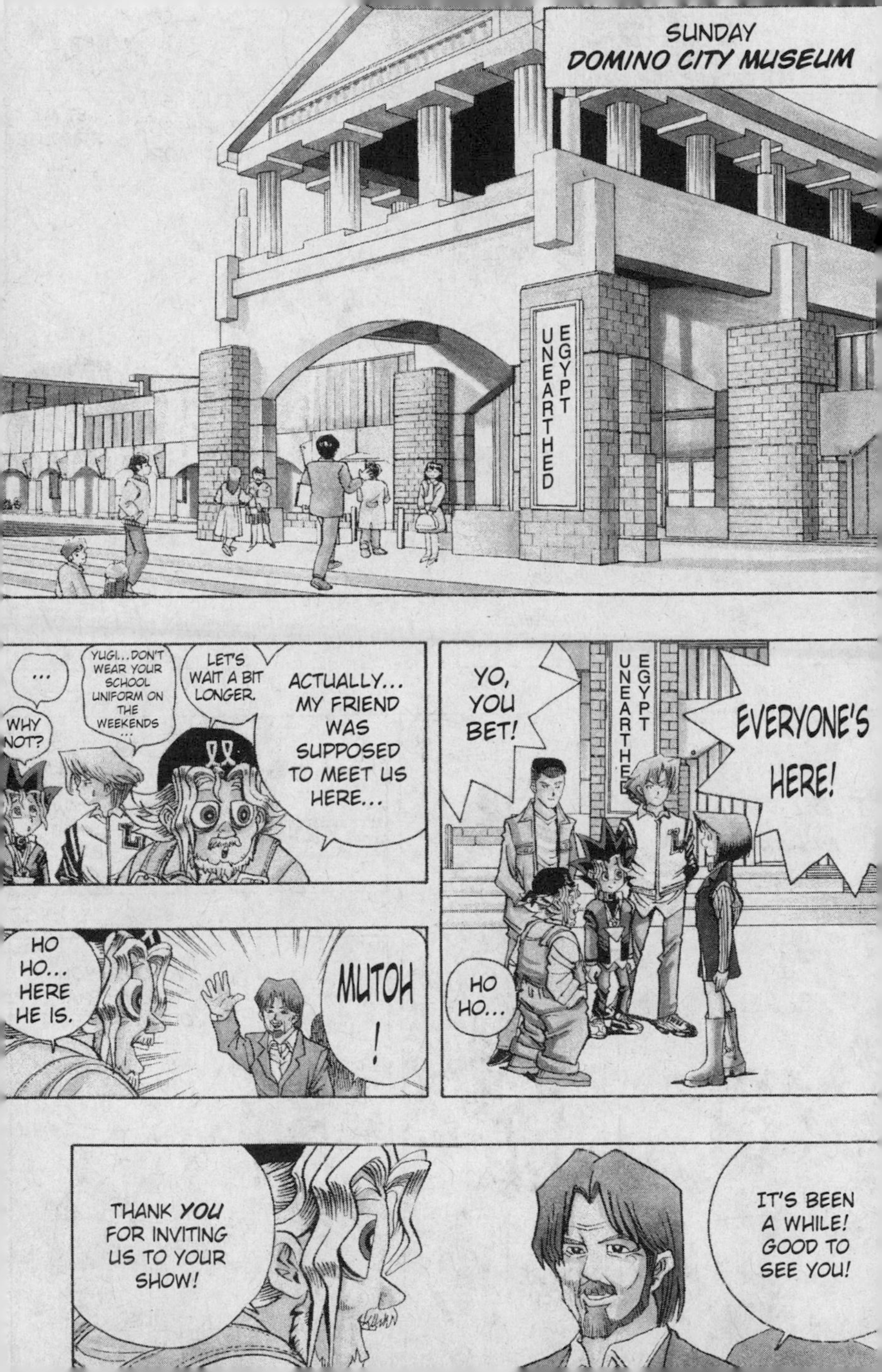
SUNDAY
DOMINO CITY MUSEUM
EGYPT UNEARTHED
EVERYONE'S HERE!
YO, YOU BET!
EGYPT UNEARTHED
HO HO...
ACTUALLY... MY FRIEND WAS SUPPOSED TO MEET US HERE...
LET'S WAIT A BIT LONGER.
YUGI...DON'T WEAR YOUR SCHOOL UNIFORM ON THE WEEKENDS...
WHY NOT?
...
MUTOH!
HO HO... HERE HE IS.
IT'S BEEN A WHILE! GOOD TO SEE YOU!
THANK *YOU* FOR INVITING US TO YOUR SHOW!

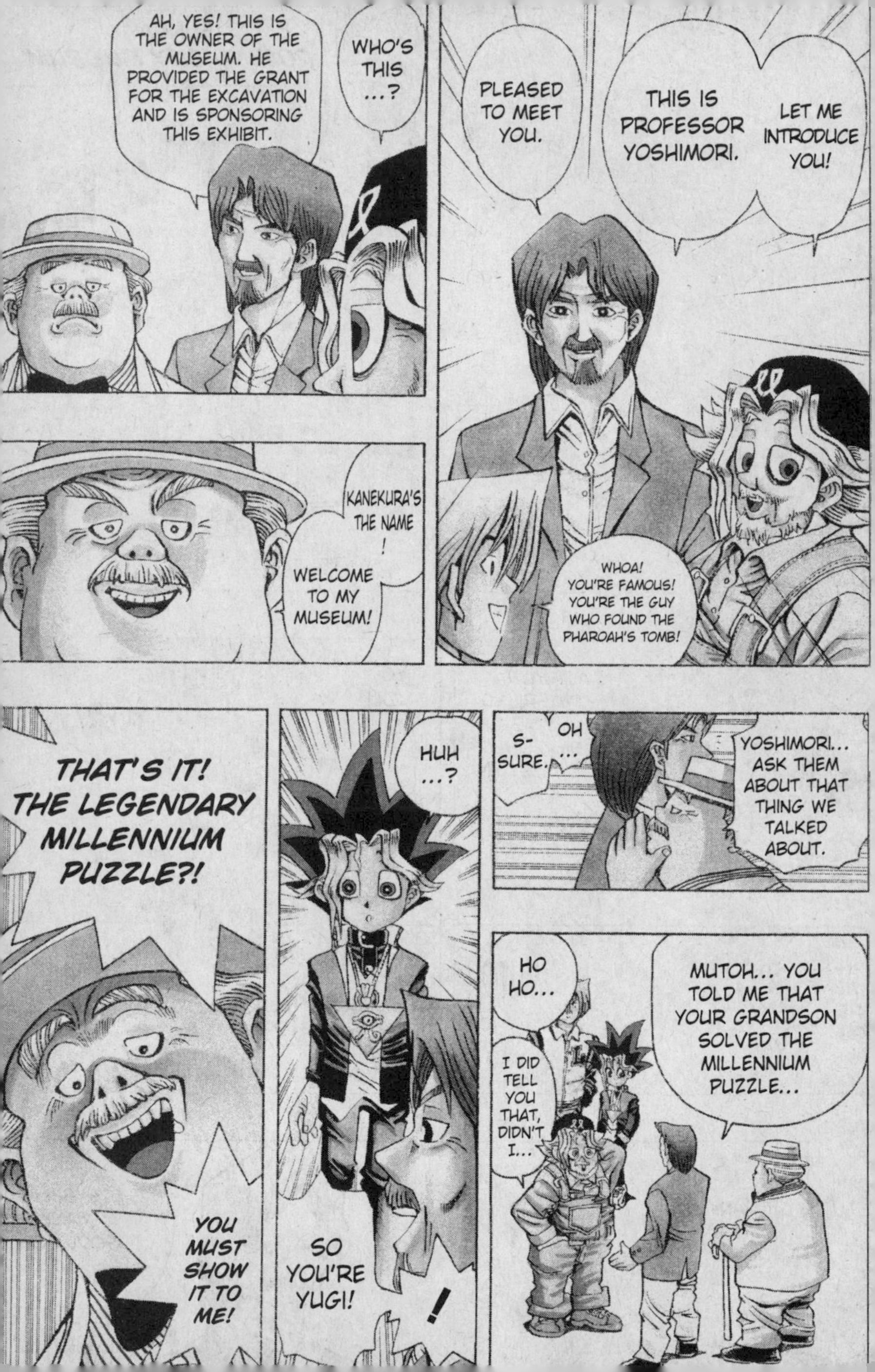
LET ME INTRODUCE YOU!
THIS IS PROFESSOR YOSHIMORI.
PLEASED TO MEET YOU.
WHOA! YOU'RE FAMOUS! YOU'RE THE GUY WHO FOUND THE PHAROAH'S TOMB!
WHO'S THIS ...?
AH, YES! THIS IS THE OWNER OF THE MUSEUM. HE PROVIDED THE GRANT FOR THE EXCAVATION AND IS SPONSORING THIS EXHIBIT.
KANEKURA'S THE NAME!
WELCOME TO MY MUSEUM!
YOSHIMORI... ASK THEM ABOUT THAT THING WE TALKED ABOUT.
OH ...
S-SURE.
MUTOH... YOU TOLD ME THAT YOUR GRANDSON SOLVED THE MILLENNIUM PUZZLE...
HO HO...
I DID TELL YOU THAT, DIDN'T I...
HUH ...?
SO YOU'RE YUGI!
!
THAT'S IT! THE LEGENDARY MILLENNIUM PUZZLE?!
YOU MUST SHOW IT TO ME!

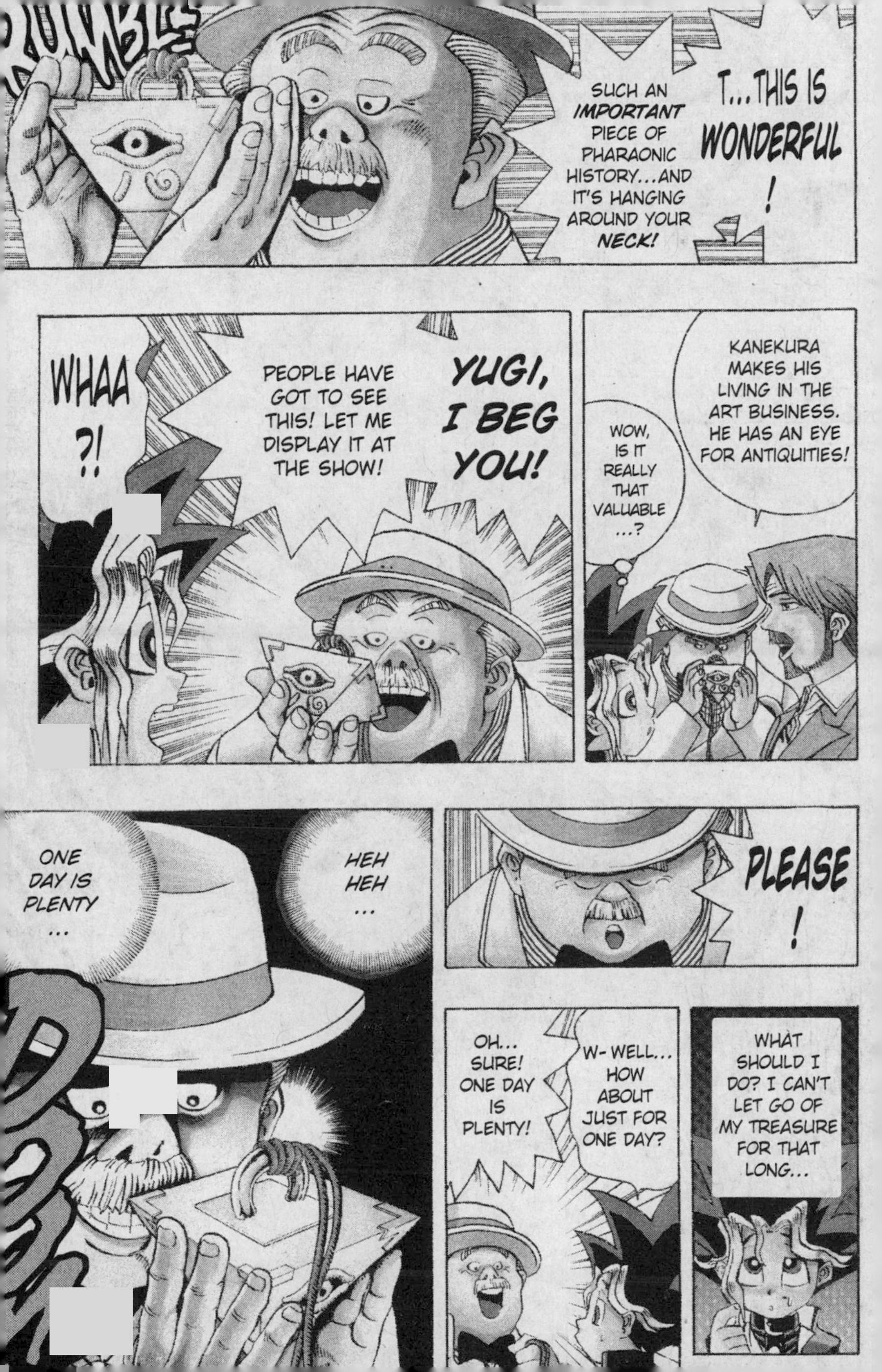
T...THIS IS WONDERFUL!
SUCH AN IMPORTANT PIECE OF PHARAONIC HISTORY...AND IT'S HANGING AROUND YOUR NECK!
KANEKURA MAKES HIS LIVING IN THE ART BUSINESS. HE HAS AN EYE FOR ANTIQUITIES!
WOW, IS IT REALLY THAT VALUABLE ...?
YUGI, I BEG YOU!
PEOPLE HAVE GOT TO SEE THIS! LET ME DISPLAY IT AT THE SHOW!
WHAA ?!
PLEASE!
WHAT SHOULD I DO? I CAN'T LET GO OF MY TREASURE FOR THAT LONG...
W-WELL... HOW ABOUT JUST FOR ONE DAY?
OH... SURE! ONE DAY IS PLENTY!
HEH HEH ...
ONE DAY IS PLENTY ...

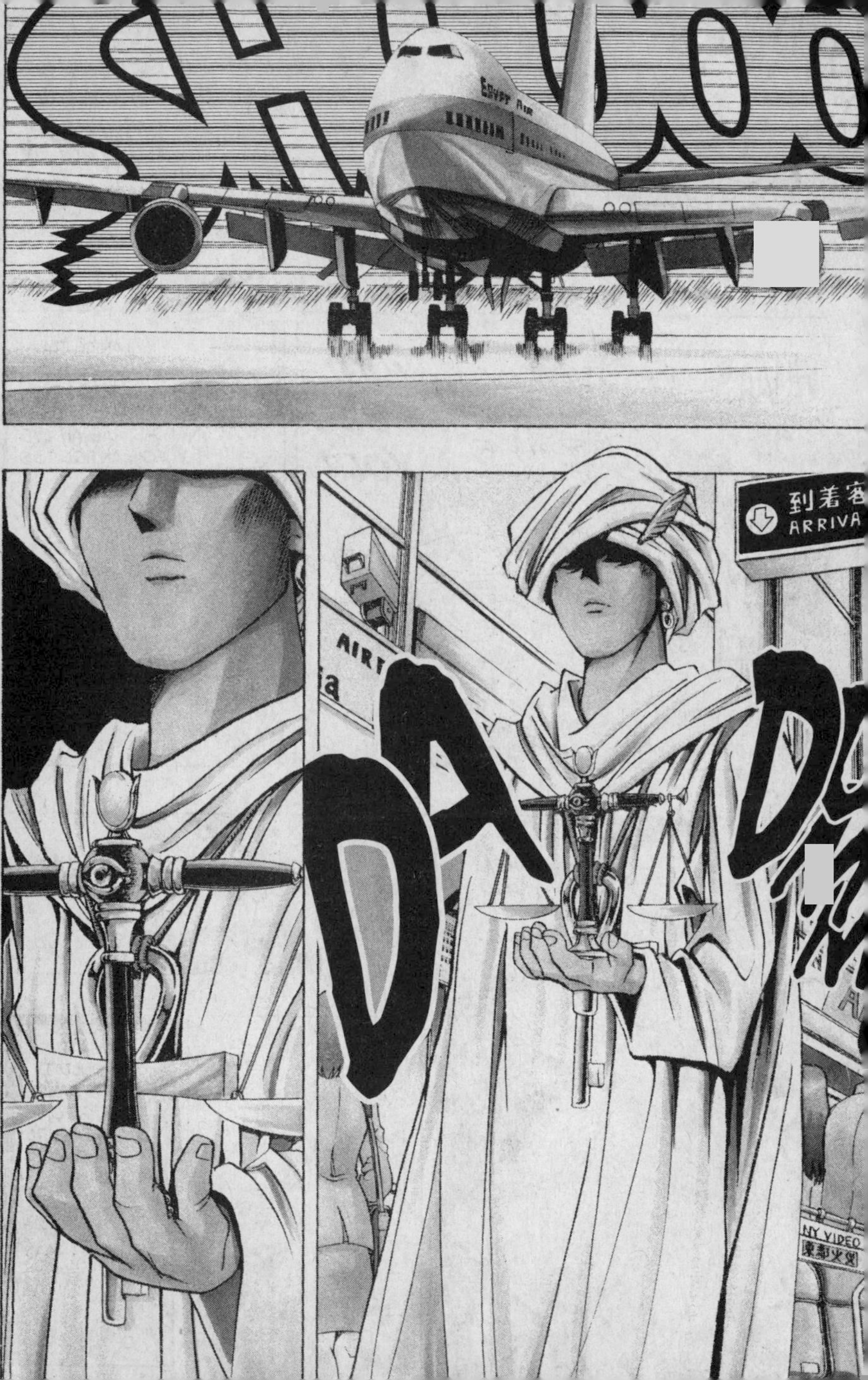

到着客
ARRIVA
DA

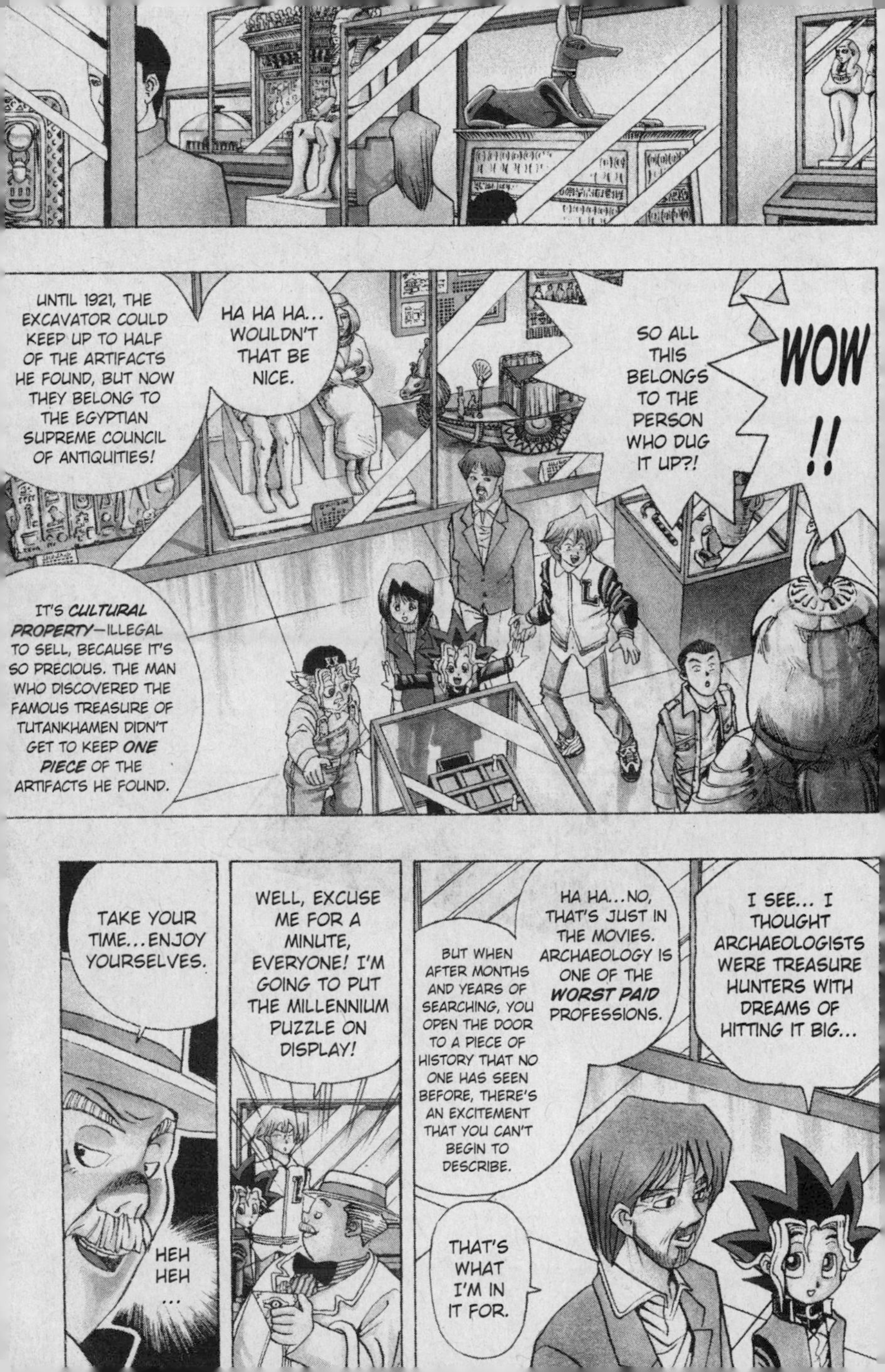
WOW!!
SO ALL THIS BELONGS TO THE PERSON WHO DUG IT UP?!
HA HA HA... WOULDN'T THAT BE NICE.
UNTIL 1921, THE EXCAVATOR COULD KEEP UP TO HALF OF THE ARTIFACTS HE FOUND, BUT NOW THEY BELONG TO THE EGYPTIAN SUPREME COUNCIL OF ANTIQUITIES!
IT'S CULTURAL PROPERTY—ILLEGAL TO SELL, BECAUSE IT'S SO PRECIOUS. THE MAN WHO DISCOVERED THE FAMOUS TREASURE OF TUTANKHAMEN DIDN'T GET TO KEEP ONE PIECE OF THE ARTIFACTS HE FOUND.
I SEE... I THOUGHT ARCHAEOLOGISTS WERE TREASURE HUNTERS WITH DREAMS OF HITTING IT BIG...
HA HA...NO, THAT'S JUST IN THE MOVIES. ARCHAEOLOGY IS ONE OF THE WORST PAID PROFESSIONS.
BUT WHEN AFTER MONTHS AND YEARS OF SEARCHING, YOU OPEN THE DOOR TO A PIECE OF HISTORY THAT NO ONE HAS SEEN BEFORE, THERE'S AN EXCITEMENT THAT YOU CAN'T BEGIN TO DESCRIBE.
THAT'S WHAT I'M IN IT FOR.
WELL, EXCUSE ME FOR A MINUTE, EVERYONE! I'M GOING TO PUT THE MILLENNIUM PUZZLE ON DISPLAY!
TAKE YOUR TIME...ENJOY YOURSELVES.
HEH HEH...

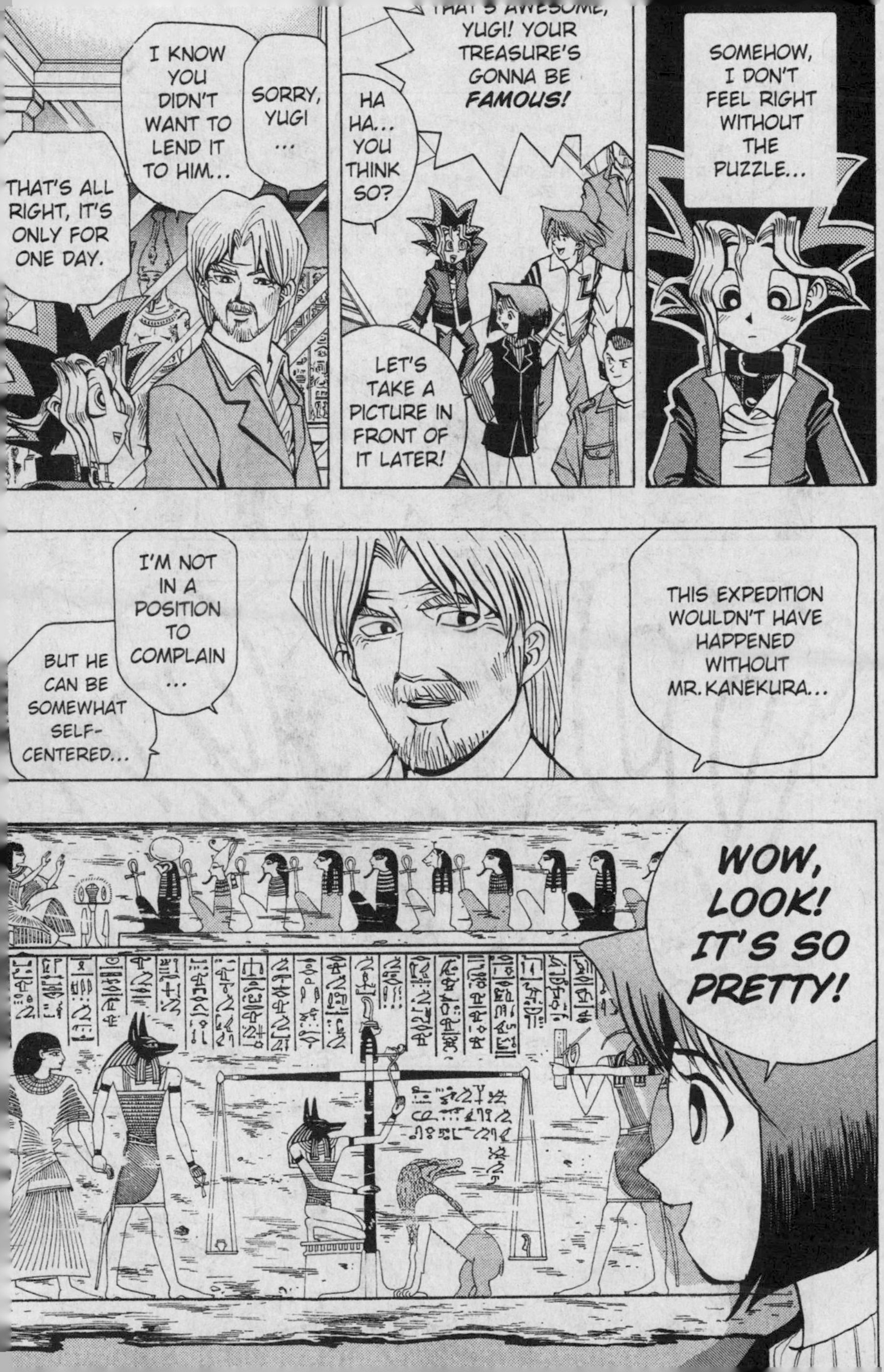
SOMEHOW, I DON'T FEEL RIGHT WITHOUT THE PUZZLE...
THAT'S AWESOME, YUGI! YOUR TREASURE'S GONNA BE *FAMOUS!*
HA HA... YOU THINK SO?
LET'S TAKE A PICTURE IN FRONT OF IT LATER!
SORRY, YUGI...
I KNOW YOU DIDN'T WANT TO LEND IT TO HIM...
THAT'S ALL RIGHT, IT'S ONLY FOR ONE DAY.
THIS EXPEDITION WOULDN'T HAVE HAPPENED WITHOUT MR. KANEKURA...
I'M NOT IN A POSITION TO COMPLAIN...
BUT HE CAN BE SOMEWHAT SELF-CENTERED...
WOW, LOOK! IT'S SO PRETTY!

READ THIS WAY

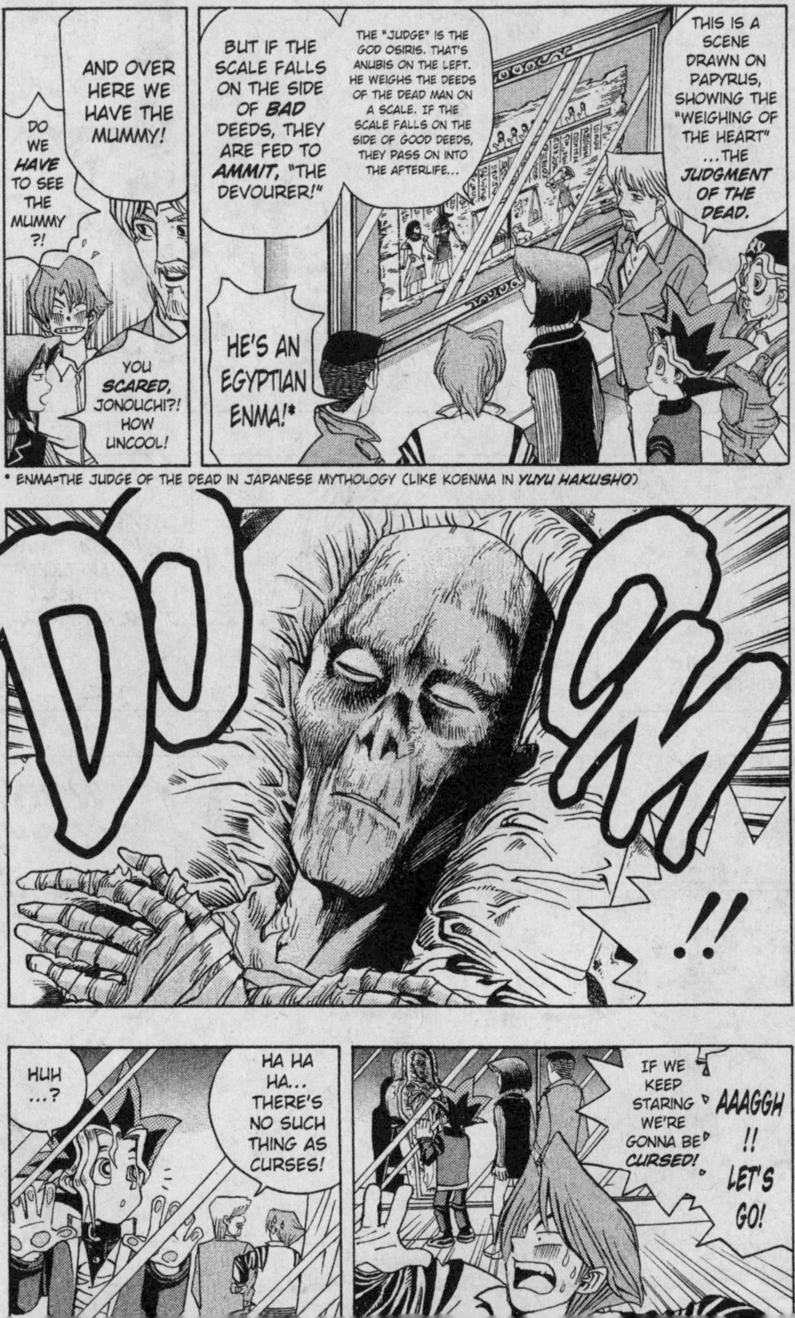

THIS IS A SCENE DRAWN ON PAPYRUS, SHOWING THE "WEIGHING OF THE HEART" ...THE *JUDGMENT OF THE DEAD.*
THE "JUDGE" IS THE GOD OSIRIS. THAT'S ANUBIS ON THE LEFT. HE WEIGHS THE DEEDS OF THE DEAD MAN ON A SCALE. IF THE SCALE FALLS ON THE SIDE OF GOOD DEEDS, THEY PASS ON INTO THE AFTERLIFE...
BUT IF THE SCALE FALLS ON THE SIDE OF *BAD* DEEDS, THEY ARE FED TO *AMMIT*, "THE DEVOURER!"
HE'S AN EGYPTIAN ENMA!*
AND OVER HERE WE HAVE THE MUMMY!
DO WE *HAVE* TO SEE THE MUMMY?!
YOU *SCARED*, JONOUCHI?! HOW UNCOOL!
* ENMA=THE JUDGE OF THE DEAD IN JAPANESE MYTHOLOGY (LIKE KOENMA IN *YUYU HAKUSHO*)
!!
IF WE KEEP STARING WE'RE GONNA BE *CURSED!*
AAAGGH!! LET'S GO!
HA HA HA... THERE'S NO SUCH THING AS CURSES!
HUH ...?

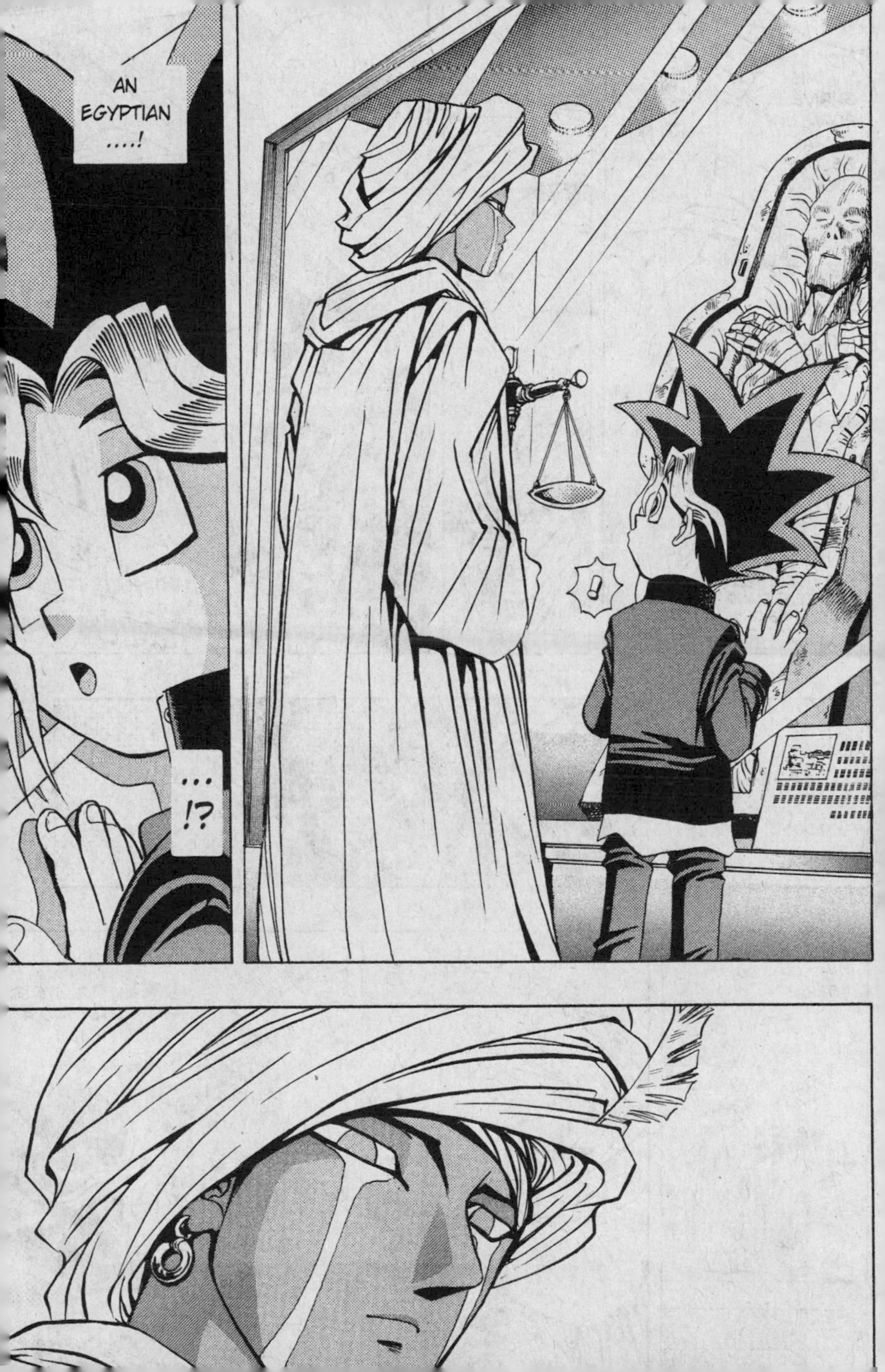
!
AN EGYPTIAN .....!
... !?

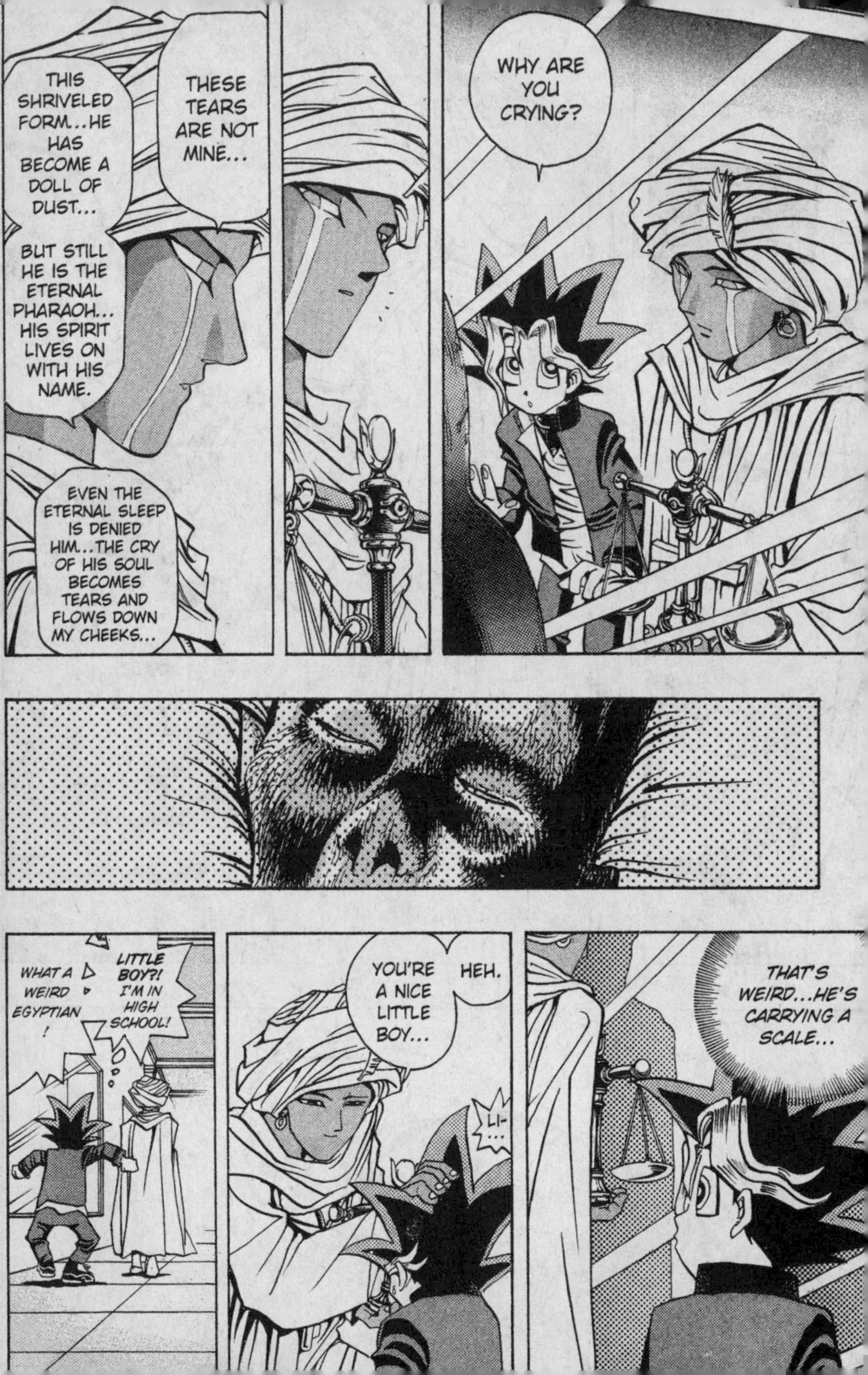
WHY ARE YOU CRYING?
THESE TEARS ARE NOT MINE...
THIS SHRIVELED FORM...HE HAS BECOME A DOLL OF DUST...
BUT STILL HE IS THE ETERNAL PHARAOH... HIS SPIRIT LIVES ON WITH HIS NAME.
EVEN THE ETERNAL SLEEP IS DENIED HIM...THE CRY OF HIS SOUL BECOMES TEARS AND FLOWS DOWN MY CHEEKS...
THAT'S WEIRD...HE'S CARRYING A SCALE...
HEH.
YOU'RE A NICE LITTLE BOY...
LI-...
LITTLE BOY?! I'M IN HIGH SCHOOL!
WHAT A WEIRD EGYPTIAN!

READ THIS WAY

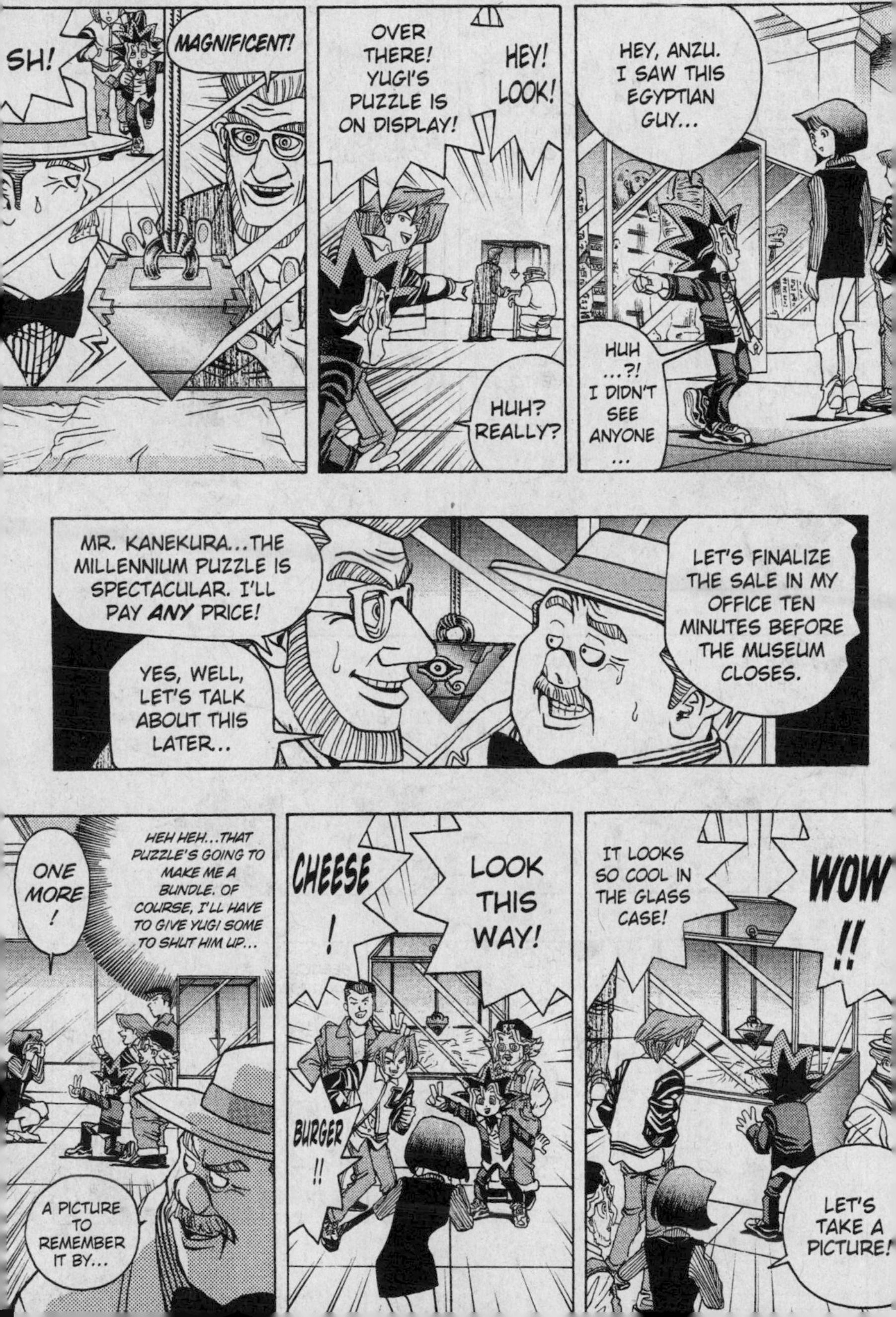
HEY, ANZU. I SAW THIS EGYPTIAN GUY...
HUH ...?! I DIDN'T SEE ANYONE ...
HEY! LOOK!
OVER THERE! YUGI'S PUZZLE IS ON DISPLAY!
HUH? REALLY?
MAGNIFICENT!
SH!
MR. KANEKURA...THE MILLENNIUM PUZZLE IS SPECTACULAR. I'LL PAY ANY PRICE!
YES, WELL, LET'S TALK ABOUT THIS LATER...
LET'S FINALIZE THE SALE IN MY OFFICE TEN MINUTES BEFORE THE MUSEUM CLOSES.
WOW!!
IT LOOKS SO COOL IN THE GLASS CASE!
LET'S TAKE A PICTURE!
LOOK THIS WAY!
CHEESE!
BURGER!!
ONE MORE!
A PICTURE TO REMEMBER IT BY...
HEH HEH...THAT PUZZLE'S GOING TO MAKE ME A BUNDLE. OF COURSE, I'LL HAVE TO GIVE YUGI SOME TO SHUT HIM UP...

READ THIS WAY

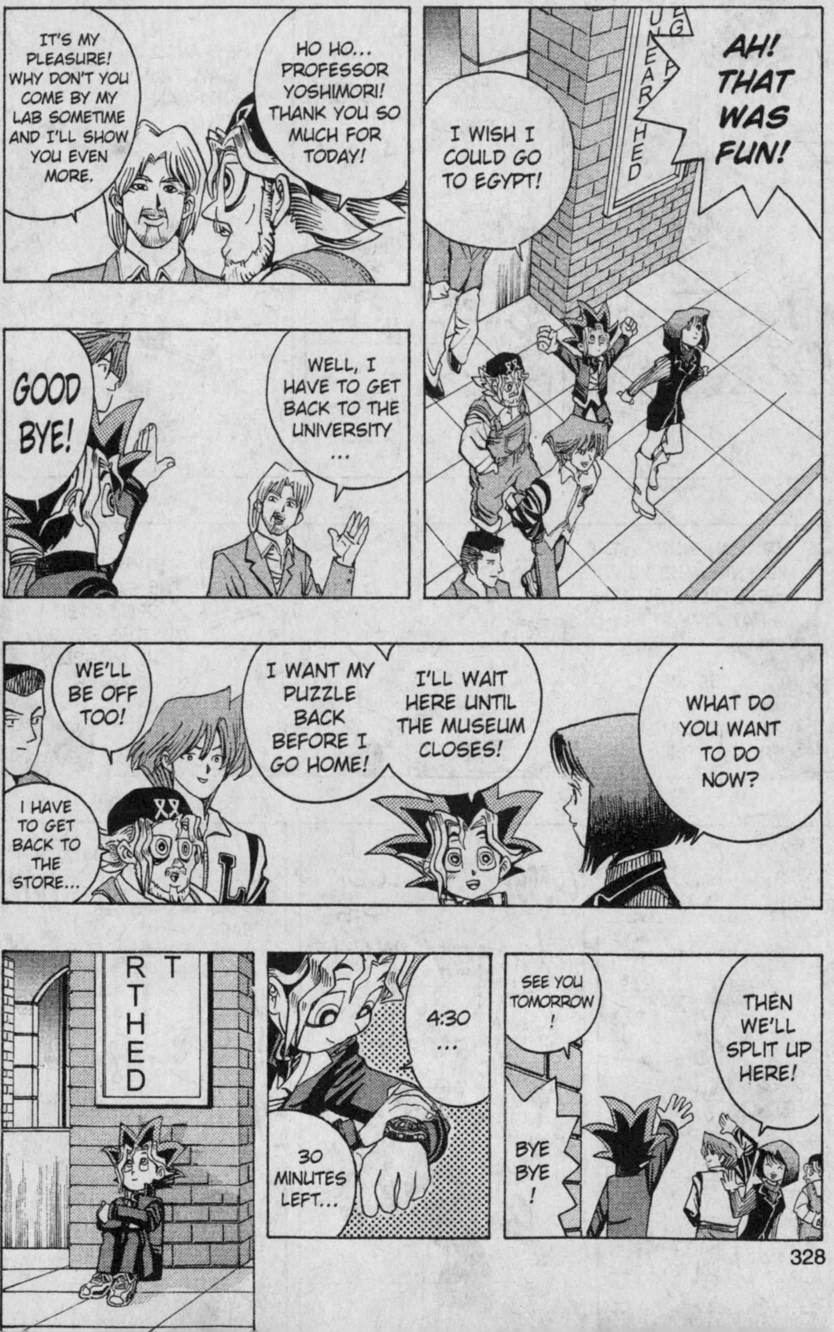

AH! THAT WAS FUN!
I WISH I COULD GO TO EGYPT!
HO HO... PROFESSOR YOSHIMORI! THANK YOU SO MUCH FOR TODAY!
IT'S MY PLEASURE! WHY DON'T YOU COME BY MY LAB SOMETIME AND I'LL SHOW YOU EVEN MORE.
WELL, I HAVE TO GET BACK TO THE UNIVERSITY ...
GOOD BYE!
WHAT DO YOU WANT TO DO NOW?
I'LL WAIT HERE UNTIL THE MUSEUM CLOSES!
I WANT MY PUZZLE BACK BEFORE I GO HOME!
WE'LL BE OFF TOO!
I HAVE TO GET BACK TO THE STORE...
THEN WE'LL SPLIT UP HERE!
SEE YOU TOMORROW !
BYE BYE !
4:30 ...
30 MINUTES LEFT...

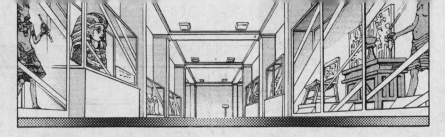

HEH HEH HEH ...

MY INVESTMENT FUNDED THE DISCOVERY OF THE PHARAOH'S TOMB...

AND NOW I CAN MAKE SOME MONEY ON THE MILLENNIUM PUZZLE. LUCK IS WITH ME!

CLICK

OH, HE'S HERE!

COME IN!

NOK NOK

MR. KANEKURA ...

OFFICE

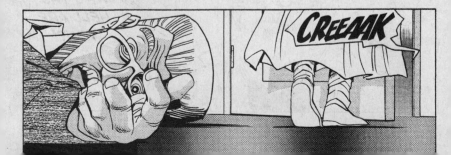

CREEAAK

READ THIS WAY

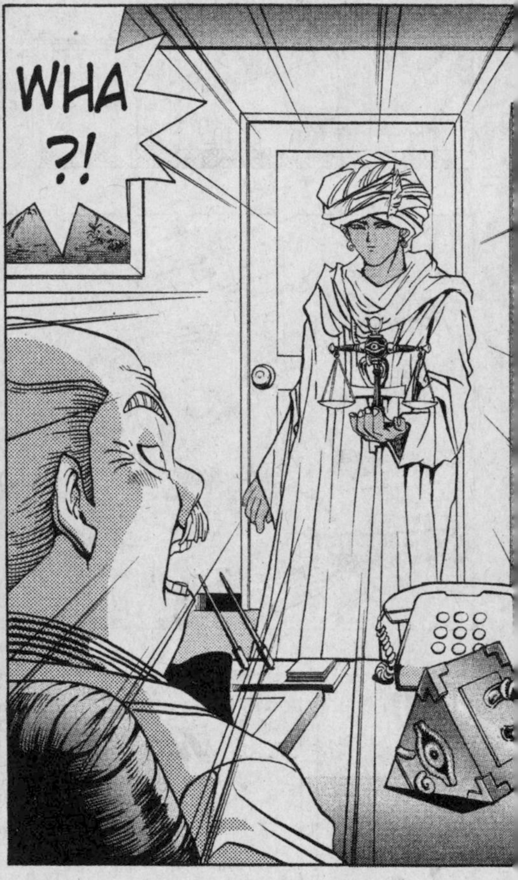
WHA ?!

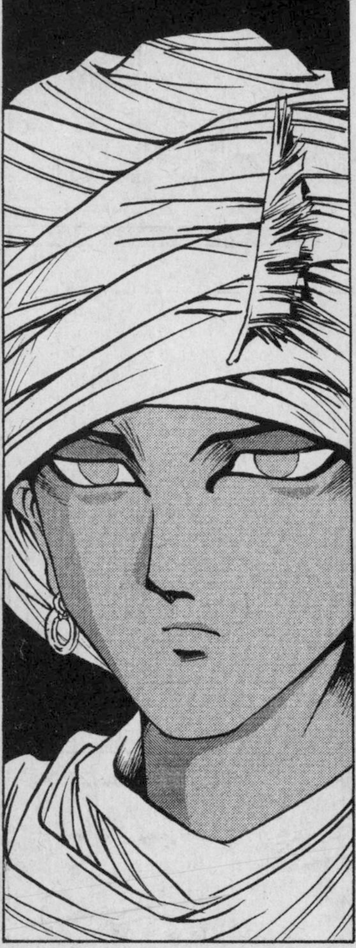

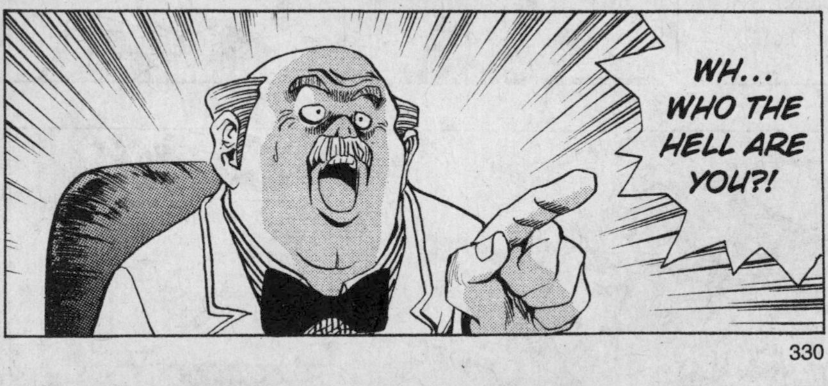
WH... WHO THE HELL ARE YOU?!

READ THIS WAY

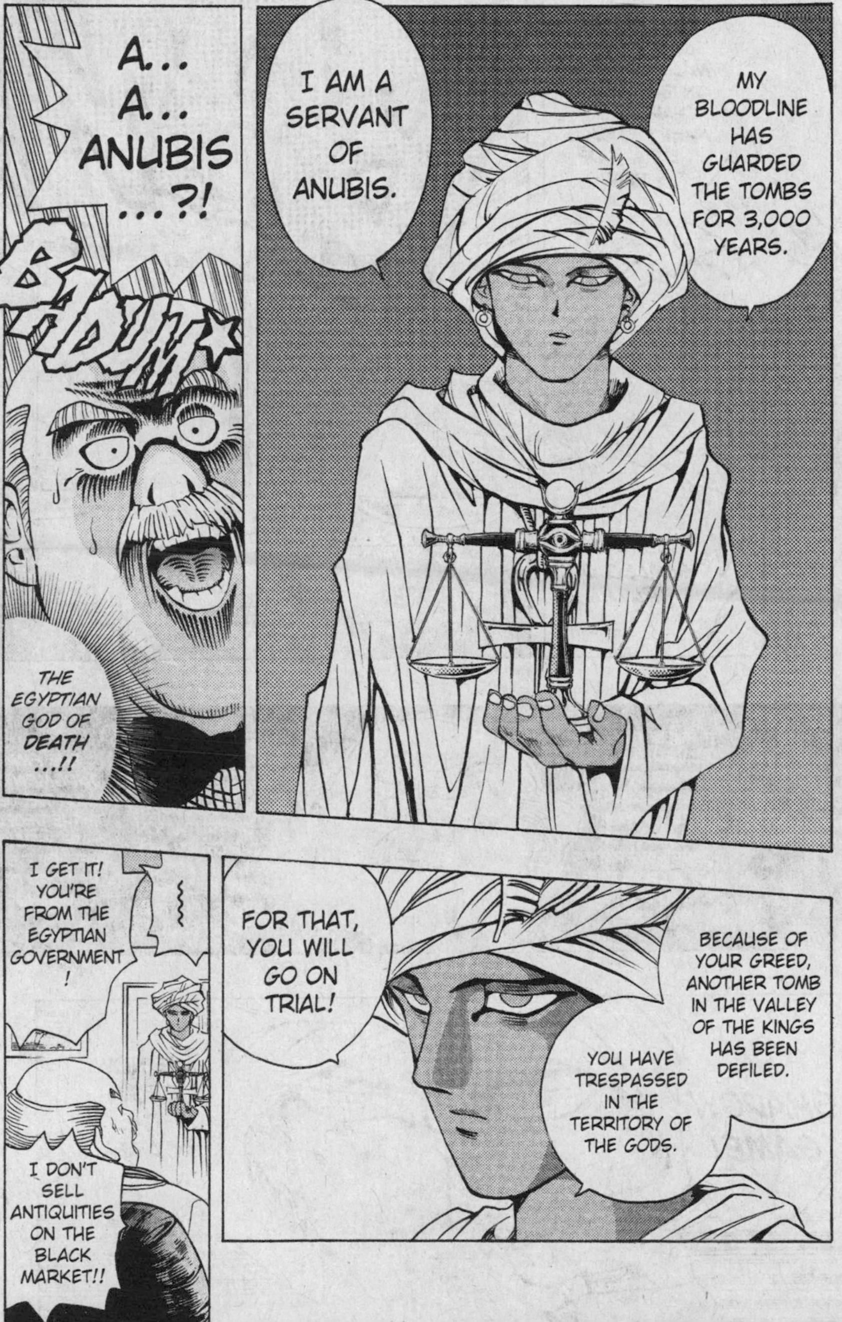
MY BLOODLINE HAS GUARDED THE TOMBS FOR 3,000 YEARS.
I AM A SERVANT OF ANUBIS.
A... A... ANUBIS ...?!
BADUM☆
THE EGYPTIAN GOD OF DEATH ...!!
BECAUSE OF YOUR GREED, ANOTHER TOMB IN THE VALLEY OF THE KINGS HAS BEEN DEFILED.
YOU HAVE TRESPASSED IN THE TERRITORY OF THE GODS.
FOR THAT, YOU WILL GO ON TRIAL!
I GET IT! YOU'RE FROM THE EGYPTIAN GOVERNMENT!
I DON'T SELL ANTIQUITIES ON THE BLACK MARKET!!

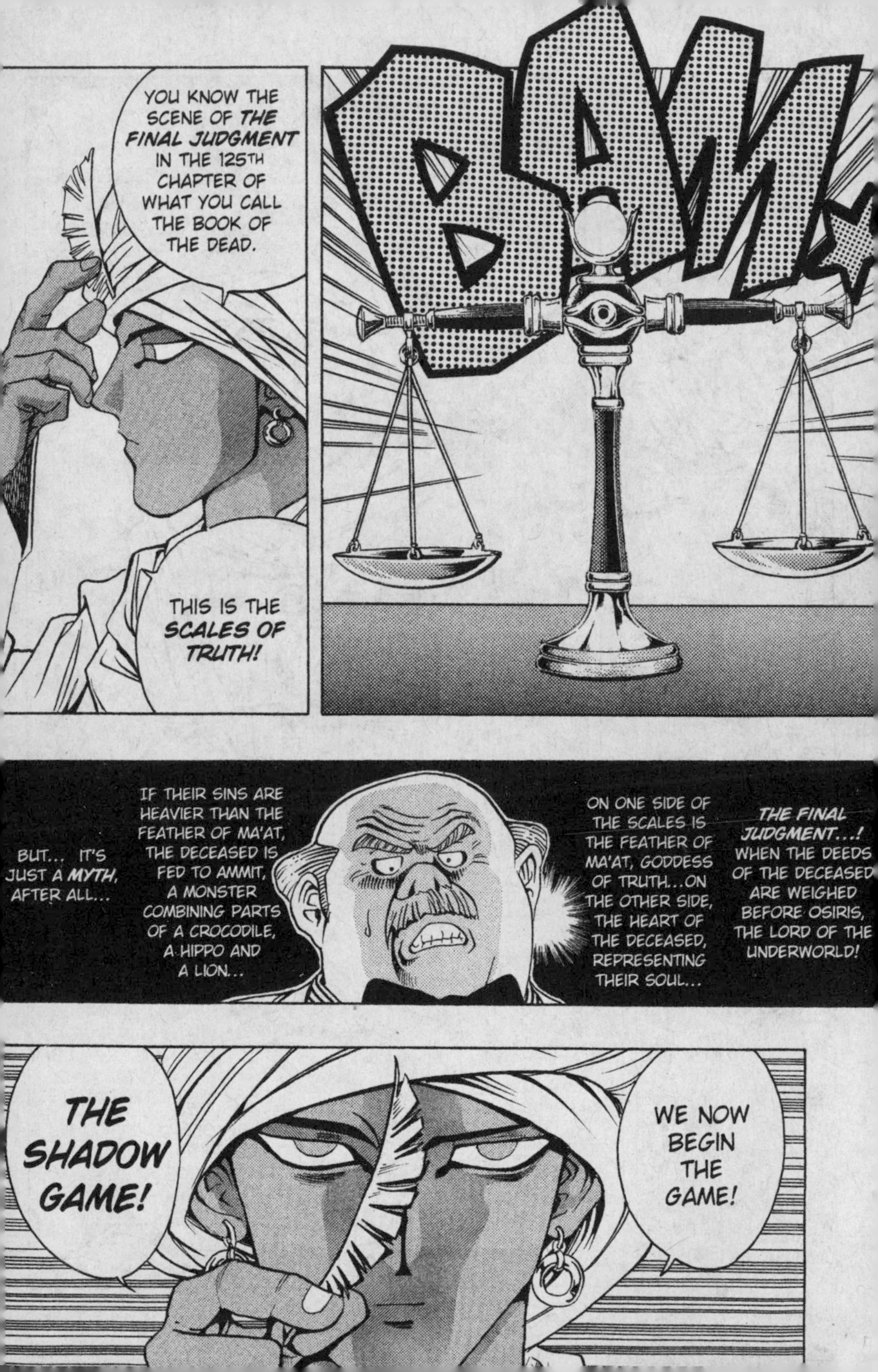
BAM!
YOU KNOW THE SCENE OF THE FINAL JUDGMENT IN THE 125TH CHAPTER OF WHAT YOU CALL THE BOOK OF THE DEAD.
THIS IS THE SCALES OF TRUTH!
THE FINAL JUDGMENT...! WHEN THE DEEDS OF THE DECEASED ARE WEIGHED BEFORE OSIRIS, THE LORD OF THE UNDERWORLD!
ON ONE SIDE OF THE SCALES IS THE FEATHER OF MA'AT, GODDESS OF TRUTH...ON THE OTHER SIDE, THE HEART OF THE DECEASED, REPRESENTING THEIR SOUL...
IF THEIR SINS ARE HEAVIER THAN THE FEATHER OF MA'AT, THE DECEASED IS FED TO AMMIT, A MONSTER COMBINING PARTS OF A CROCODILE, A HIPPO AND A LION...
BUT... IT'S JUST A MYTH, AFTER ALL...
WE NOW BEGIN THE GAME!
THE SHADOW GAME!

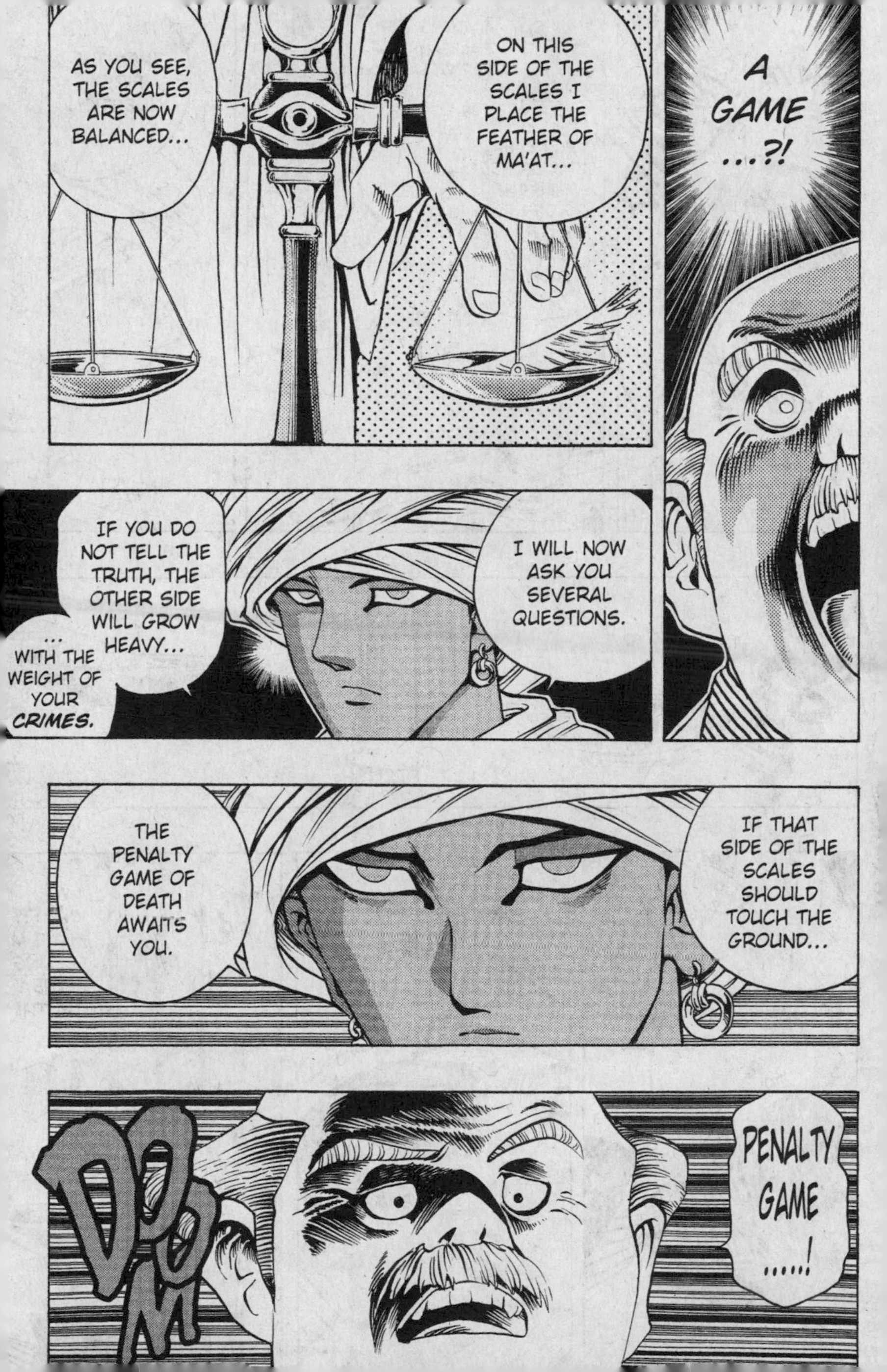
A GAME ...?!
ON THIS SIDE OF THE SCALES I PLACE THE FEATHER OF MA'AT...
AS YOU SEE, THE SCALES ARE NOW BALANCED...
I WILL NOW ASK YOU SEVERAL QUESTIONS.
IF YOU DO NOT TELL THE TRUTH, THE OTHER SIDE WILL GROW HEAVY...
... WITH THE WEIGHT OF YOUR CRIMES.
IF THAT SIDE OF THE SCALES SHOULD TOUCH THE GROUND...
THE PENALTY GAME OF DEATH AWAITS YOU.
PENALTY GAME .....!
DOOM

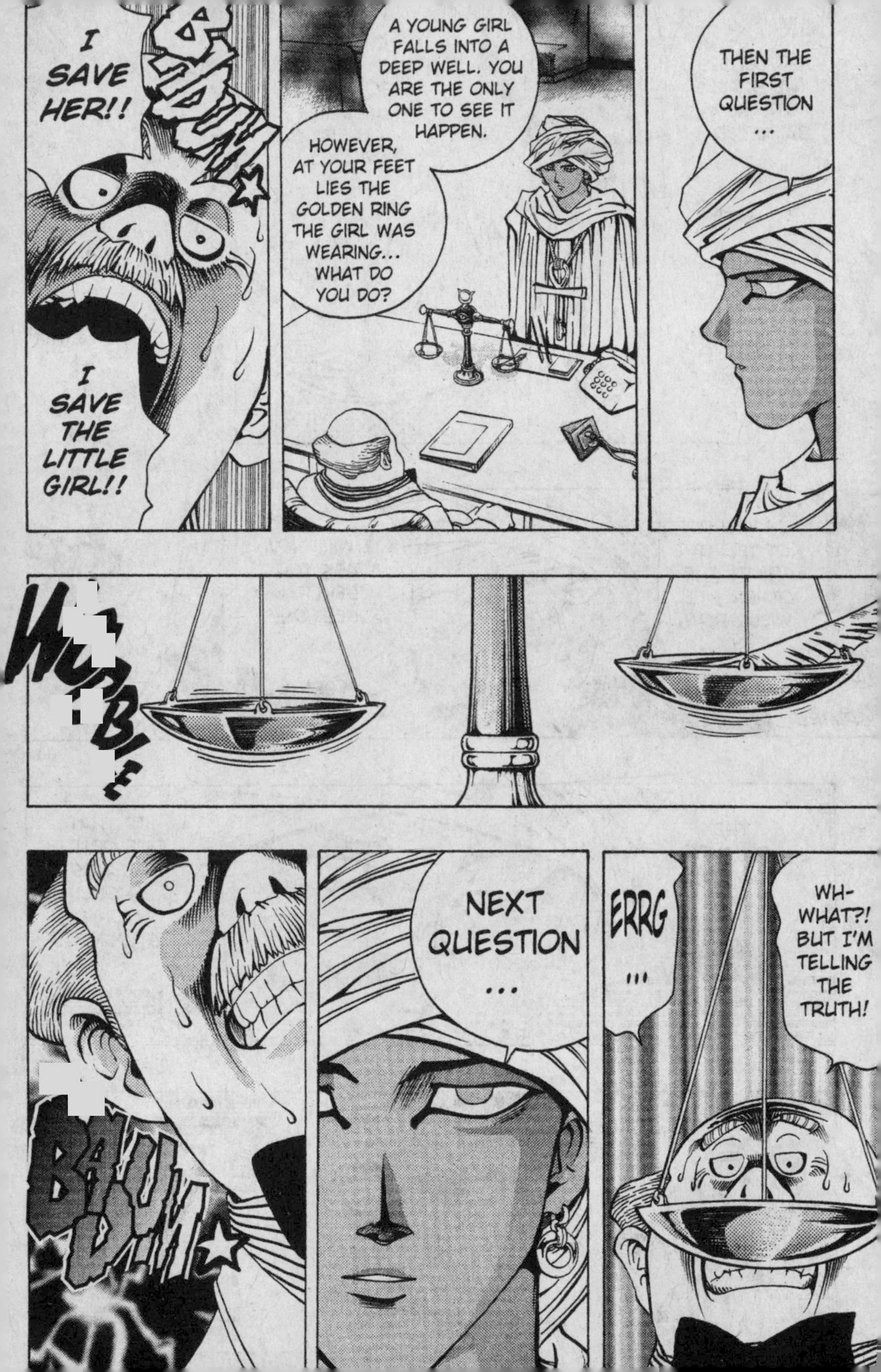
THEN THE FIRST QUESTION ...
A YOUNG GIRL FALLS INTO A DEEP WELL. YOU ARE THE ONLY ONE TO SEE IT HAPPEN.
HOWEVER, AT YOUR FEET LIES THE GOLDEN RING THE GIRL WAS WEARING... WHAT DO YOU DO?
I SAVE HER!!
I SAVE THE LITTLE GIRL!!
WH-WHAT?! BUT I'M TELLING THE TRUTH!
ERRG ...
NEXT QUESTION ...

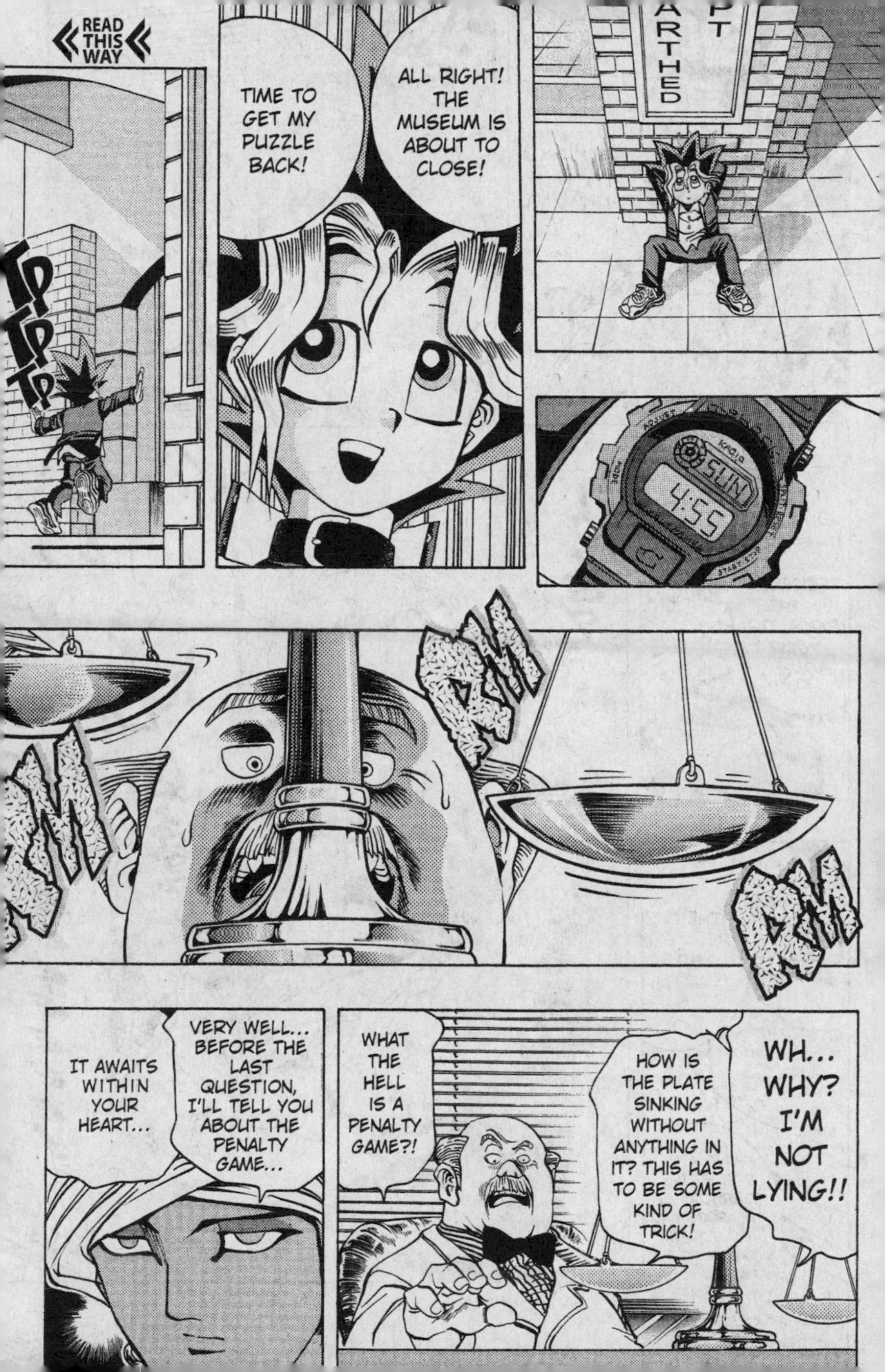
READ THIS WAY
SUN
4:55
ALL RIGHT! THE MUSEUM IS ABOUT TO CLOSE!
TIME TO GET MY PUZZLE BACK!
TP TP TP
WH... WHY? I'M NOT LYING!!
HOW IS THE PLATE SINKING WITHOUT ANYTHING IN IT? THIS HAS TO BE SOME KIND OF TRICK!
WHAT THE HELL IS A PENALTY GAME?!
VERY WELL... BEFORE THE LAST QUESTION, I'LL TELL YOU ABOUT THE PENALTY GAME...
IT AWAITS WITHIN YOUR HEART...

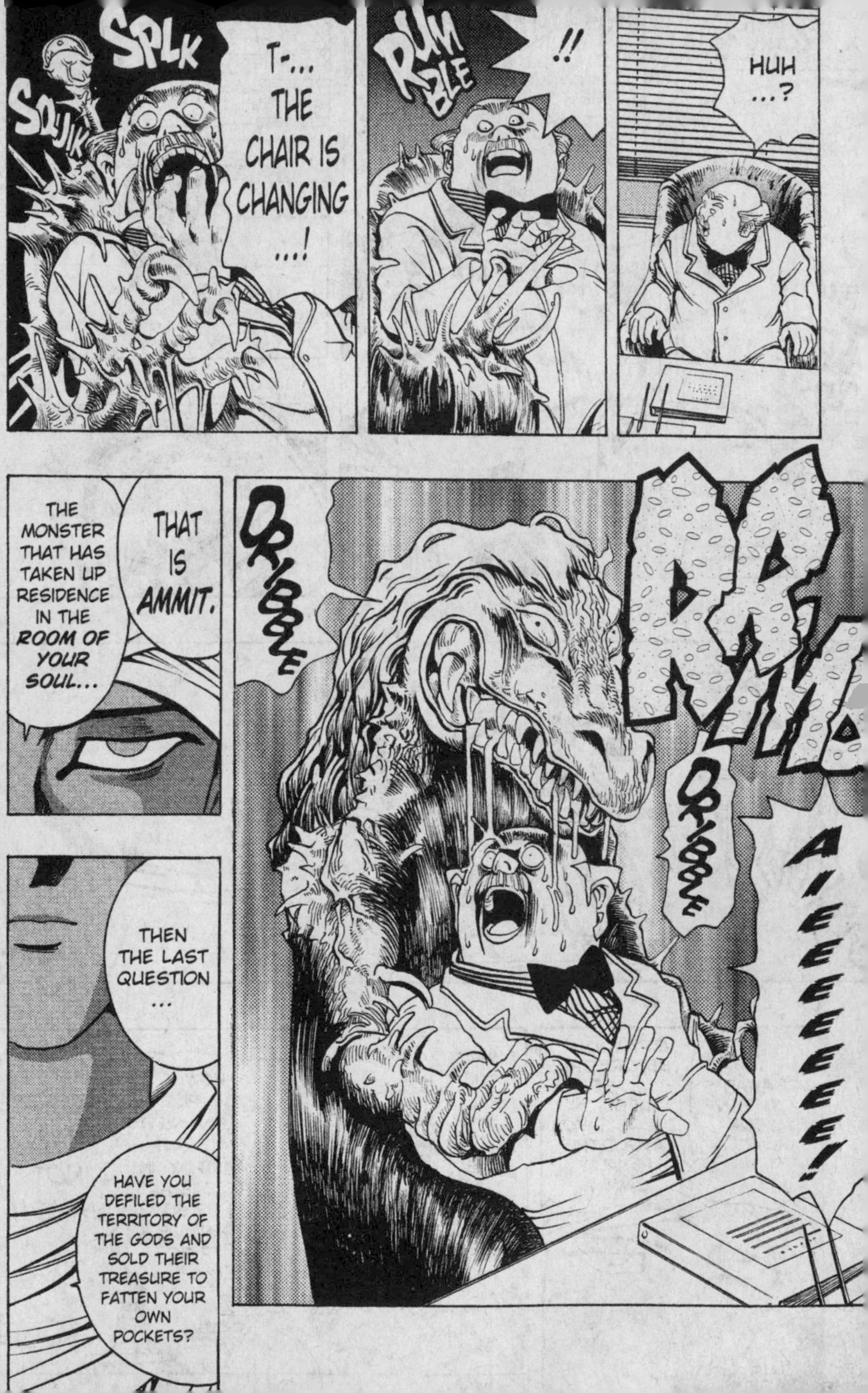
HUH ...?
RUMBLE
!!
T-... THE CHAIR IS CHANGING ...!
SPLK
SQUJIK
RRM
DRIBBLE
AIEEEEEEEEE!
DRIBBLE
THAT IS AMMIT.
THE MONSTER THAT HAS TAKEN UP RESIDENCE IN THE ROOM OF YOUR SOUL...
THEN THE LAST QUESTION ...
HAVE YOU DEFILED THE TERRITORY OF THE GODS AND SOLD THEIR TREASURE TO FATTEN YOUR OWN POCKETS?

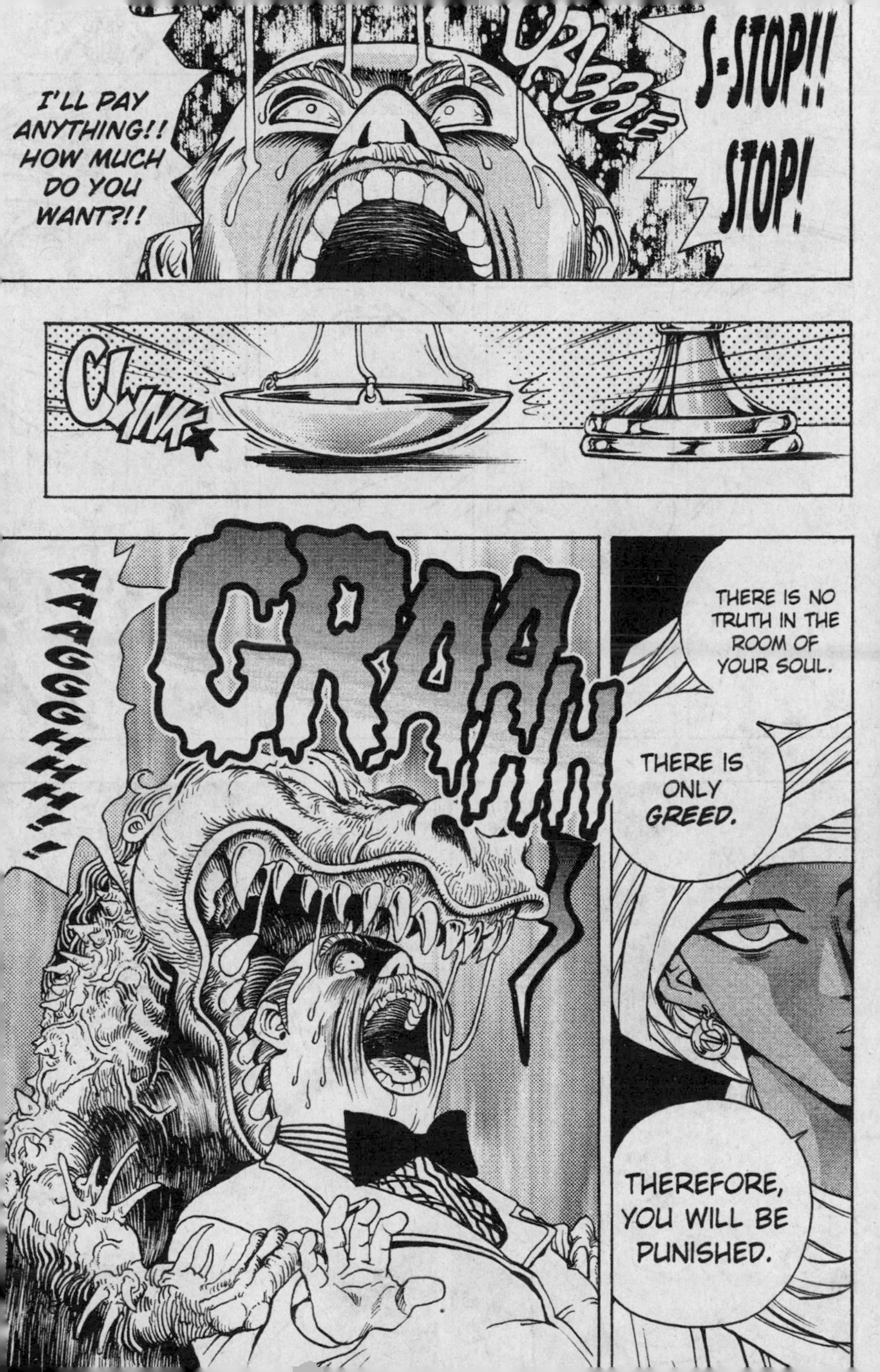
S-STOP!! STOP!
I'LL PAY ANYTHING!! HOW MUCH DO YOU WANT?!!
CLINK
THERE IS NO TRUTH IN THE ROOM OF YOUR SOUL.
THERE IS ONLY GREED.
THEREFORE, YOU WILL BE PUNISHED.
GRAAH
AAAGGGHHH!!

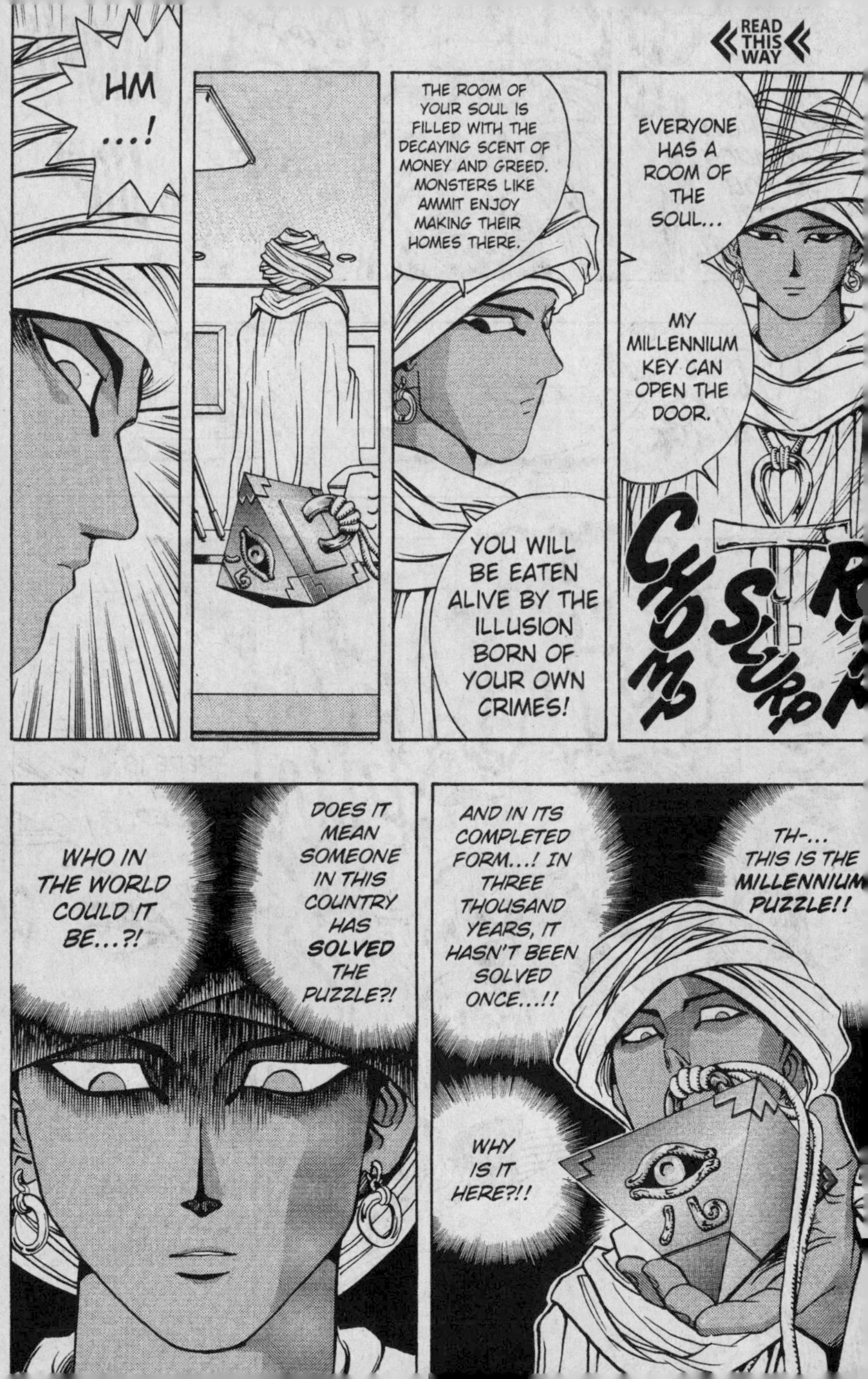
READ THIS WAY
EVERYONE HAS A ROOM OF THE SOUL...
MY MILLENNIUM KEY CAN OPEN THE DOOR.
CHOMP
SLURP
THE ROOM OF YOUR SOUL IS FILLED WITH THE DECAYING SCENT OF MONEY AND GREED. MONSTERS LIKE AMMIT ENJOY MAKING THEIR HOMES THERE.
YOU WILL BE EATEN ALIVE BY THE ILLUSION BORN OF YOUR OWN CRIMES!
HM ...!
TH-... THIS IS THE MILLENNIUM PUZZLE!!
AND IN ITS COMPLETED FORM...! IN THREE THOUSAND YEARS, IT HASN'T BEEN SOLVED ONCE...!!
WHY IS IT HERE?!!
DOES IT MEAN SOMEONE IN THIS COUNTRY HAS SOLVED THE PUZZLE?!
WHO IN THE WORLD COULD IT BE...?!

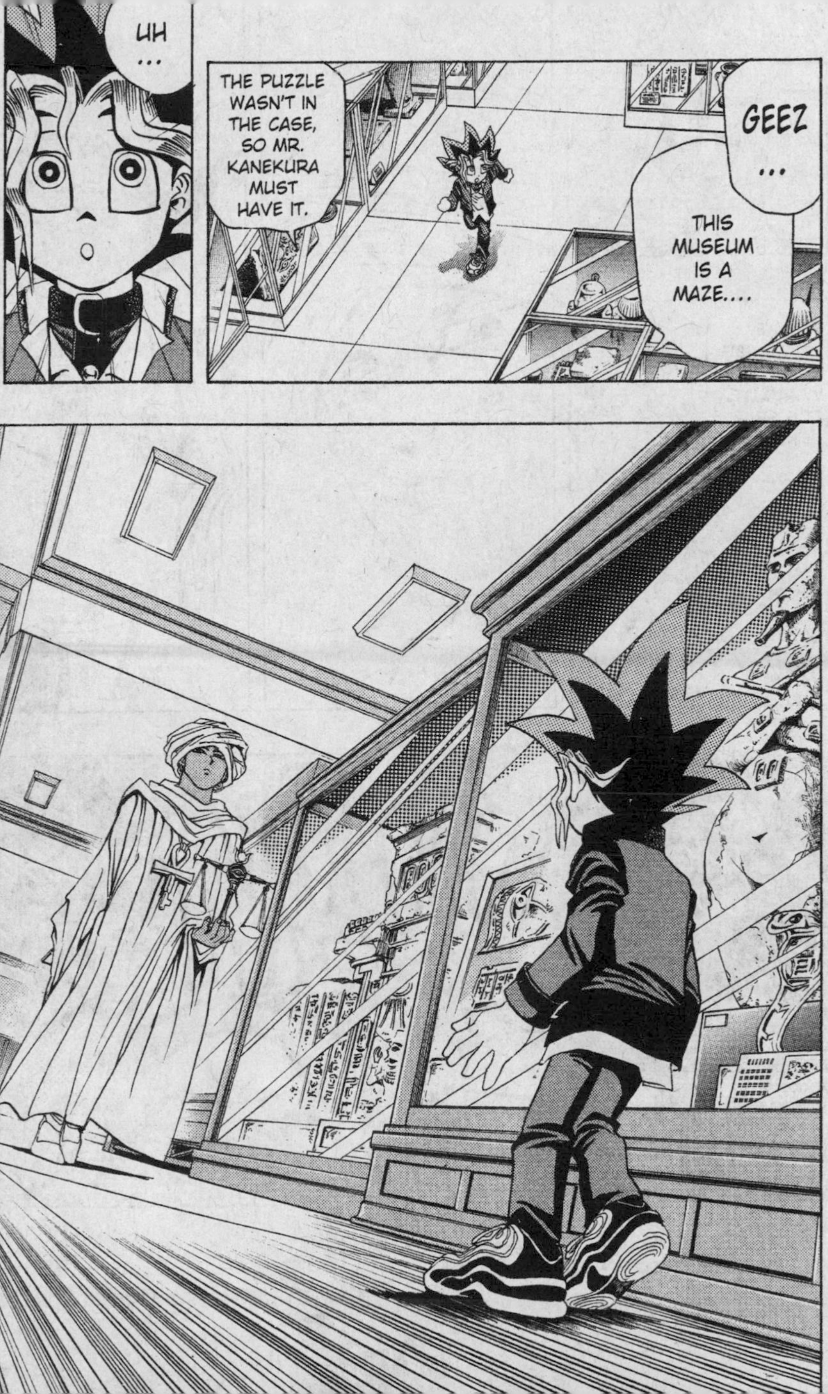
GEEZ ...
THIS MUSEUM IS A MAZE....
THE PUZZLE WASN'T IN THE CASE, SO MR. KANEKURA MUST HAVE IT.
UH ...

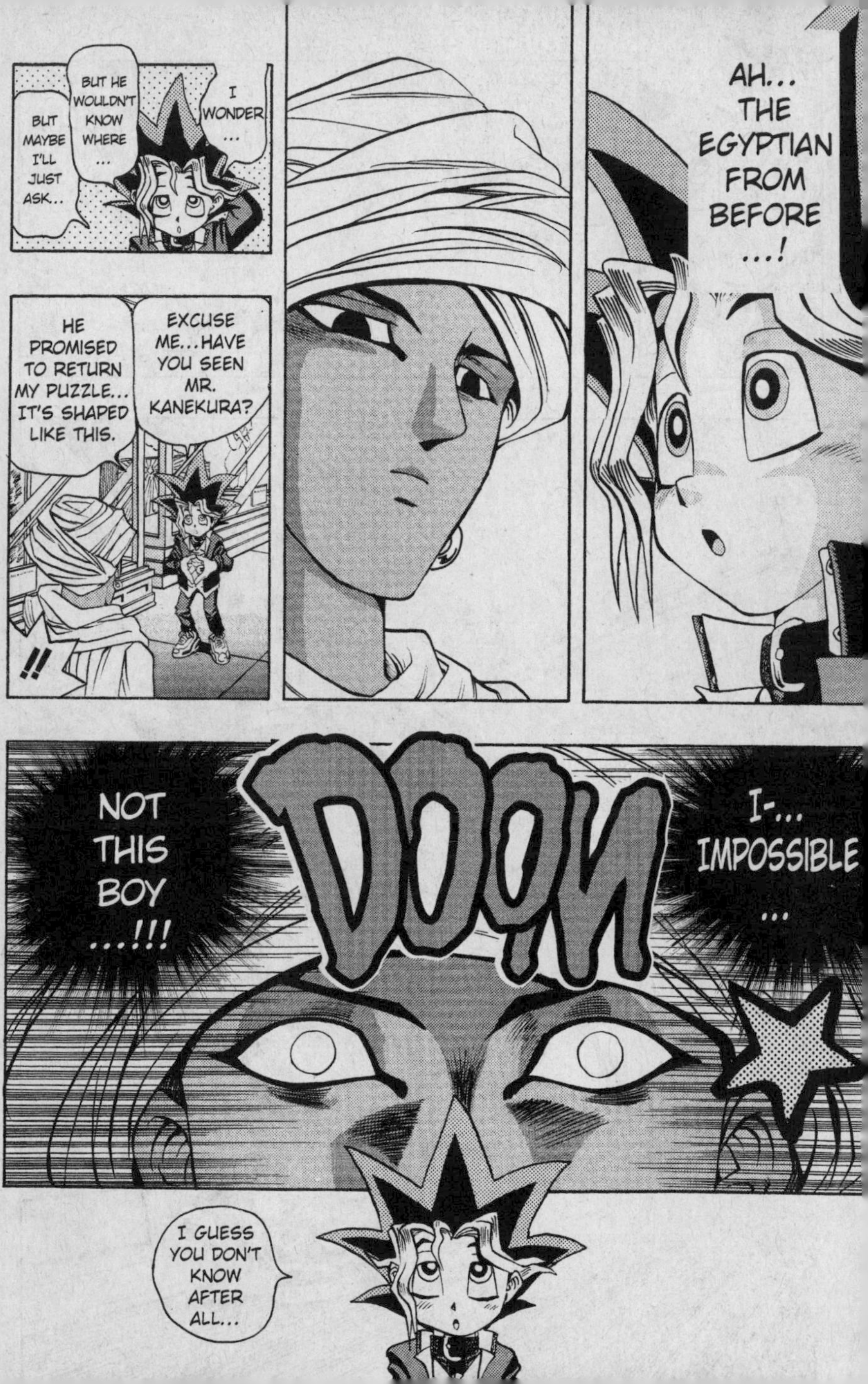
AH... THE EGYPTIAN FROM BEFORE ...!
I WONDER ...
BUT HE WOULDN'T KNOW WHERE ...
BUT MAYBE I'LL JUST ASK...
EXCUSE ME...HAVE YOU SEEN MR. KANEKURA?
HE PROMISED TO RETURN MY PUZZLE... IT'S SHAPED LIKE THIS.
!!
I-... IMPOSSIBLE ...
DOOM
NOT THIS BOY ...!!!
I GUESS YOU DON'T KNOW AFTER ALL...

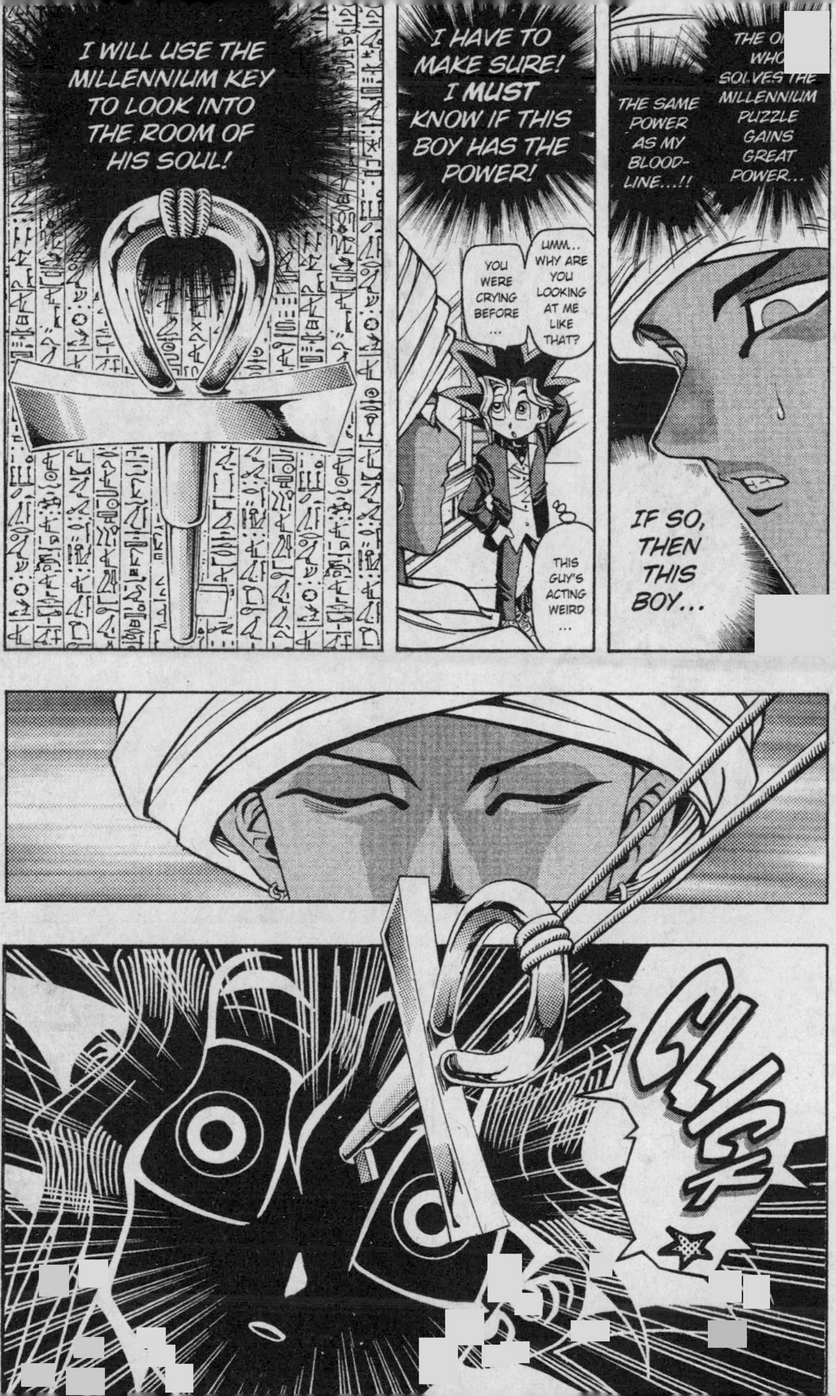
THE O WHO SOLVES THE MILLENNIUM PUZZLE GAINS GREAT POWER...
THE SAME POWER AS MY BLOOD-LINE...!!
IF SO, THEN THIS BOY...
I HAVE TO MAKE SURE! I MUST KNOW IF THIS BOY HAS THE POWER!
UMM... WHY ARE YOU LOOKING AT ME LIKE THAT?
YOU WERE CRYING BEFORE...
THIS GUY'S ACTING WEIRD...
I WILL USE THE MILLENNIUM KEY TO LOOK INTO THE ROOM OF HIS SOUL!
CLICK

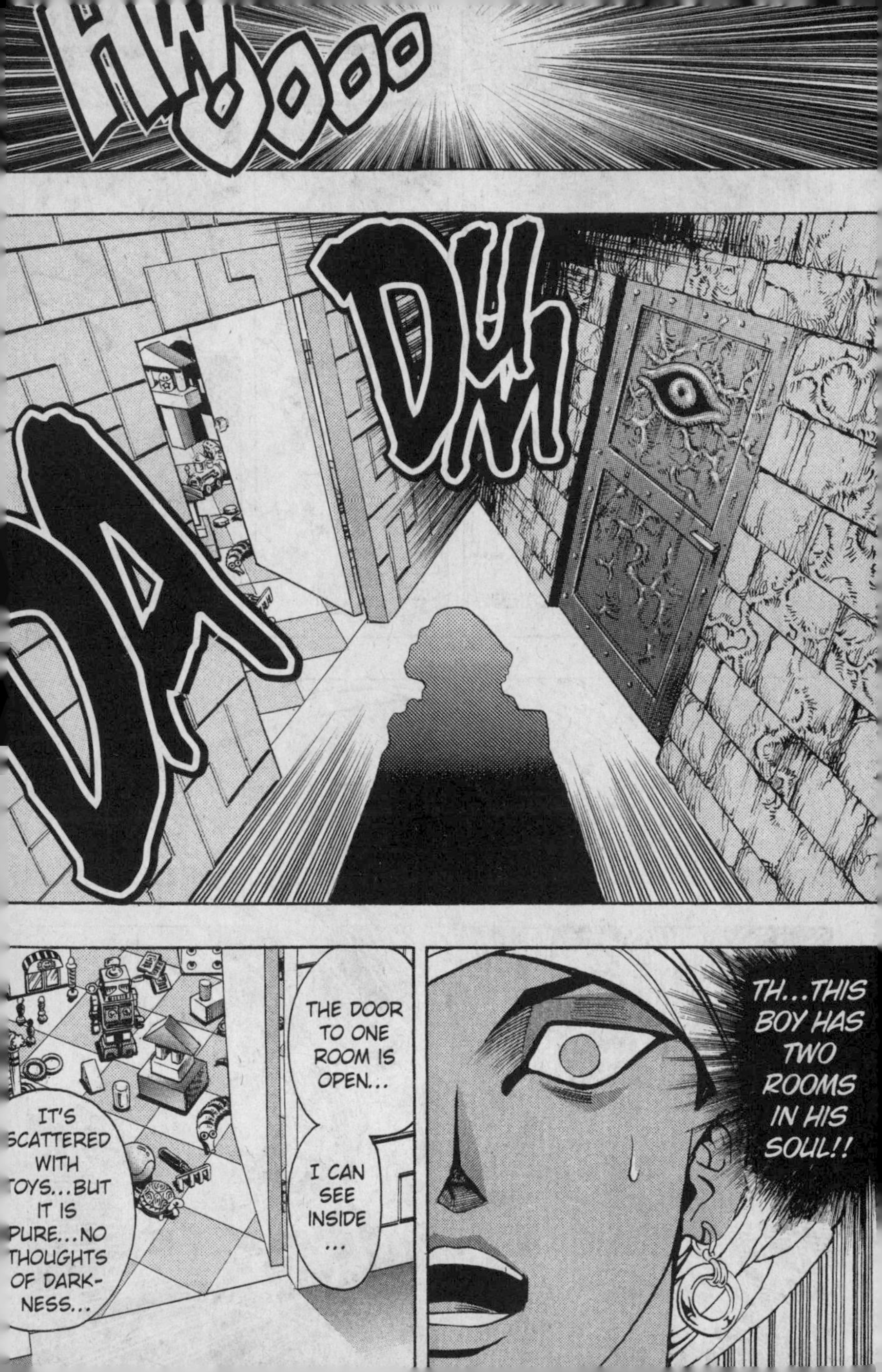
HWOOO
DUN
DA
TH...THIS BOY HAS TWO ROOMS IN HIS SOUL!!
THE DOOR TO ONE ROOM IS OPEN...
I CAN SEE INSIDE...
IT'S SCATTERED WITH TOYS...BUT IT IS PURE...NO THOUGHTS OF DARKNESS...

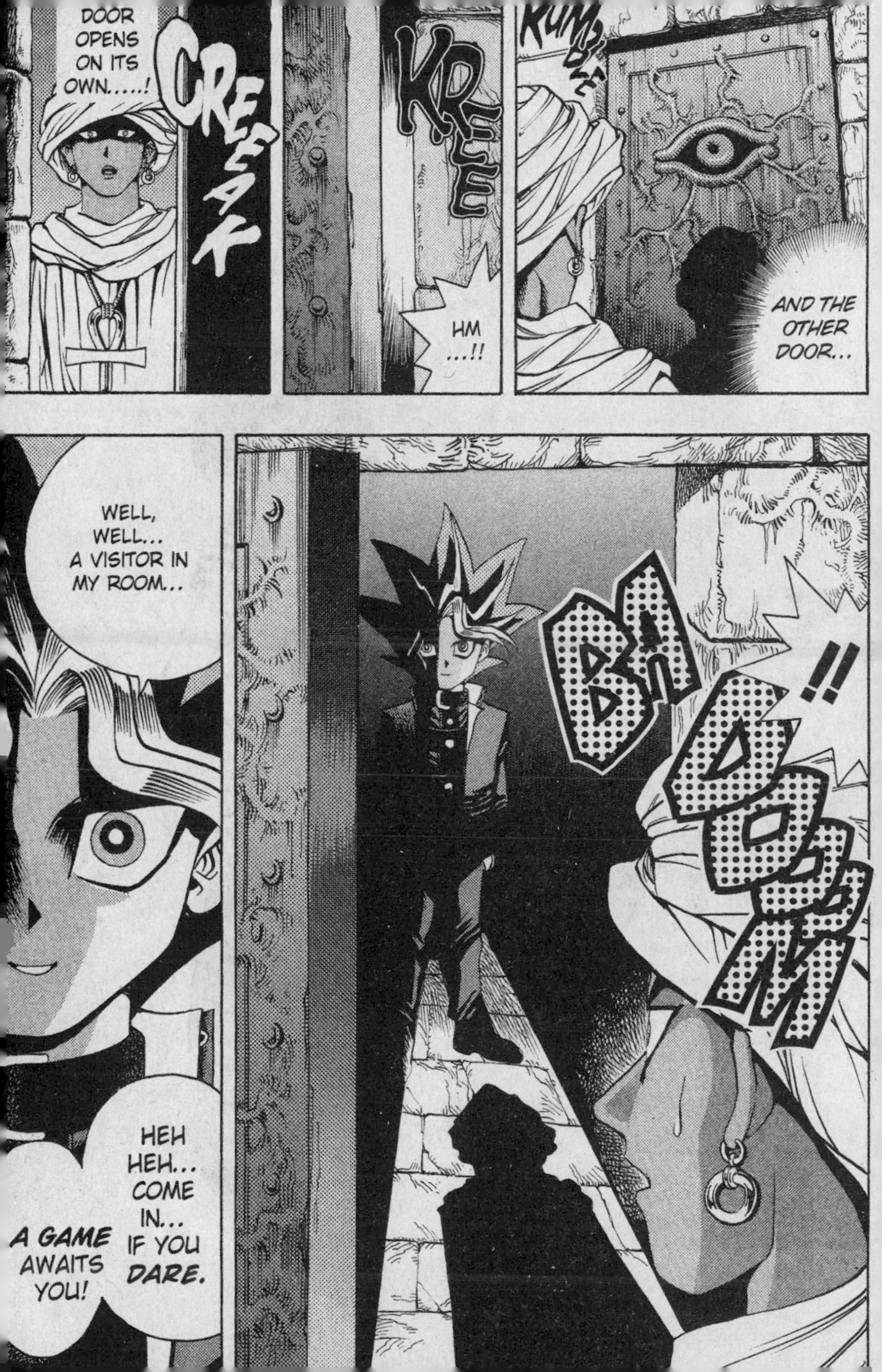
RUMBLE
AND THE OTHER DOOR...
KREEE
HM ...!!
CREEAK
DOOR OPENS ON ITS OWN.....!
BADOOM!!
WELL, WELL... A VISITOR IN MY ROOM...
HEH HEH... COME IN... IF YOU DARE.
A GAME AWAITS YOU!

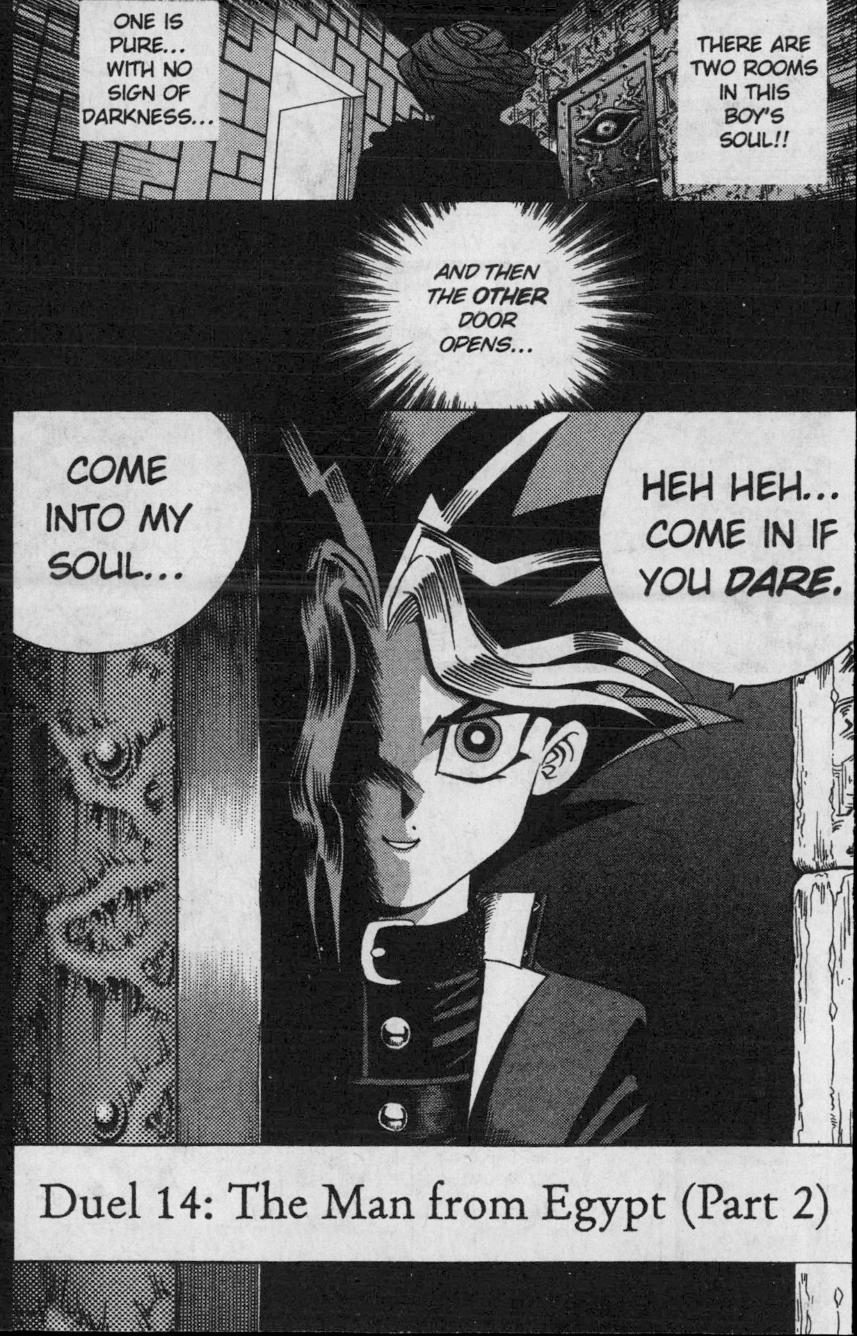
THERE ARE TWO ROOMS IN THIS BOY'S SOUL!!
ONE IS PURE... WITH NO SIGN OF DARKNESS...
AND THEN THE OTHER DOOR OPENS...
HEH HEH... COME IN IF YOU *DARE.*
COME INTO MY SOUL...

Duel 14: The Man from Egypt (Part 2)

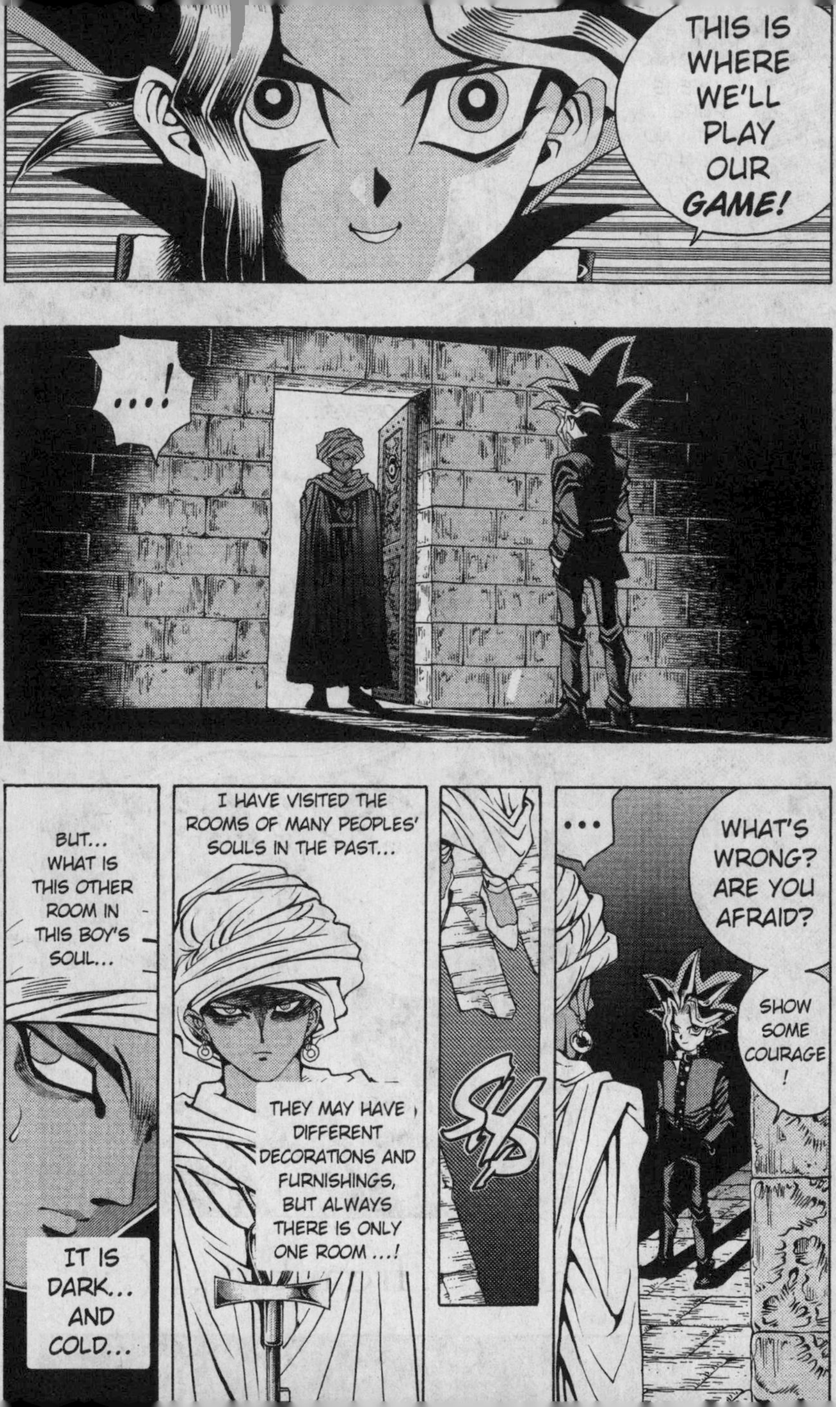

THIS IS WHERE WE'LL PLAY OUR GAME!
...!
WHAT'S WRONG? ARE YOU AFRAID?
...
SHOW SOME COURAGE!
I HAVE VISITED THE ROOMS OF MANY PEOPLES' SOULS IN THE PAST...
THEY MAY HAVE DIFFERENT DECORATIONS AND FURNISHINGS, BUT ALWAYS THERE IS ONLY ONE ROOM ...!
BUT... WHAT IS THIS OTHER ROOM IN THIS BOY'S SOUL...
IT IS DARK... AND COLD...

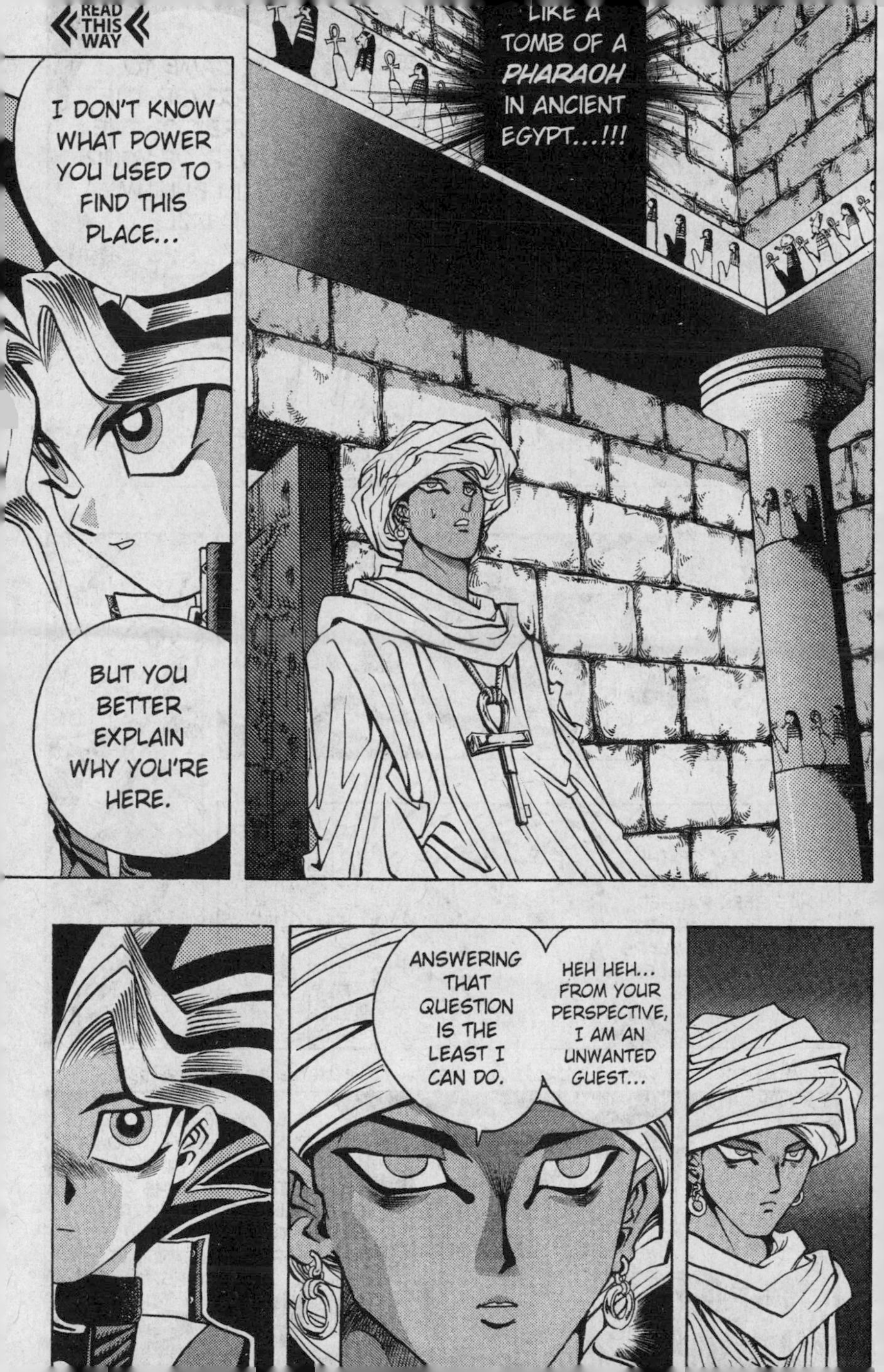
READ THIS WAY
LIKE A TOMB OF A PHARAOH IN ANCIENT EGYPT...!!!
I DON'T KNOW WHAT POWER YOU USED TO FIND THIS PLACE...
BUT YOU BETTER EXPLAIN WHY YOU'RE HERE.
HEH HEH... FROM YOUR PERSPECTIVE, I AM AN UNWANTED GUEST...
ANSWERING THAT QUESTION IS THE LEAST I CAN DO.

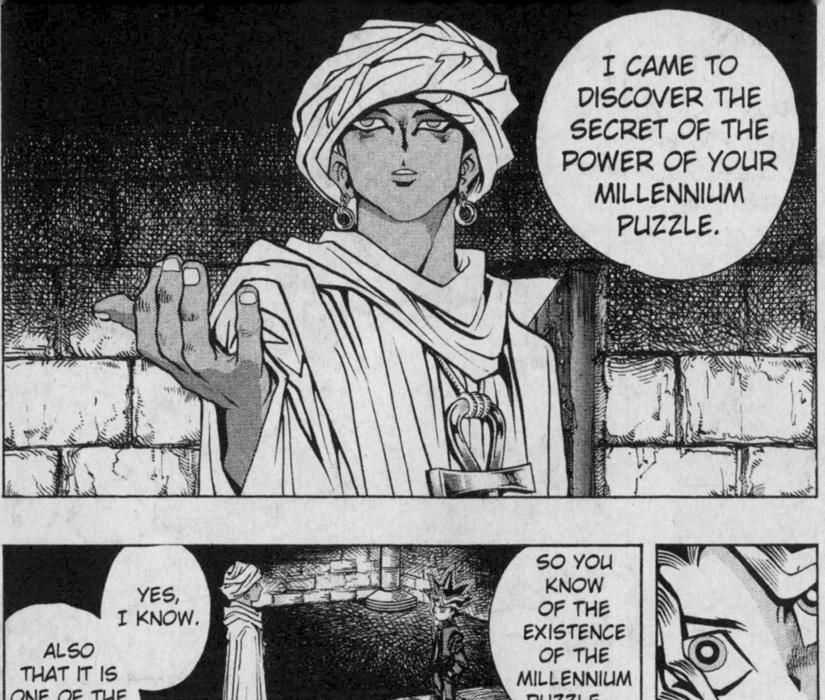
I CAME TO DISCOVER THE SECRET OF THE POWER OF YOUR MILLENNIUM PUZZLE.
SO YOU KNOW OF THE EXISTENCE OF THE MILLENNIUM PUZZLE...
YES, I KNOW.
ALSO THAT IT IS ONE OF THE MILLENNIUM ITEMS...
THE STORY OF THE MILLENNIUM ITEMS HAS BEEN PASSED DOWN FROM ANCIENT EGYPT...3,000 YEARS AGO IN THE VALLEY OF THE KINGS.

*"COMING FORTH BY DAY"--THE ORIGINAL EGYPTIAN TITLE OF THE BOOK OF THE DEAD

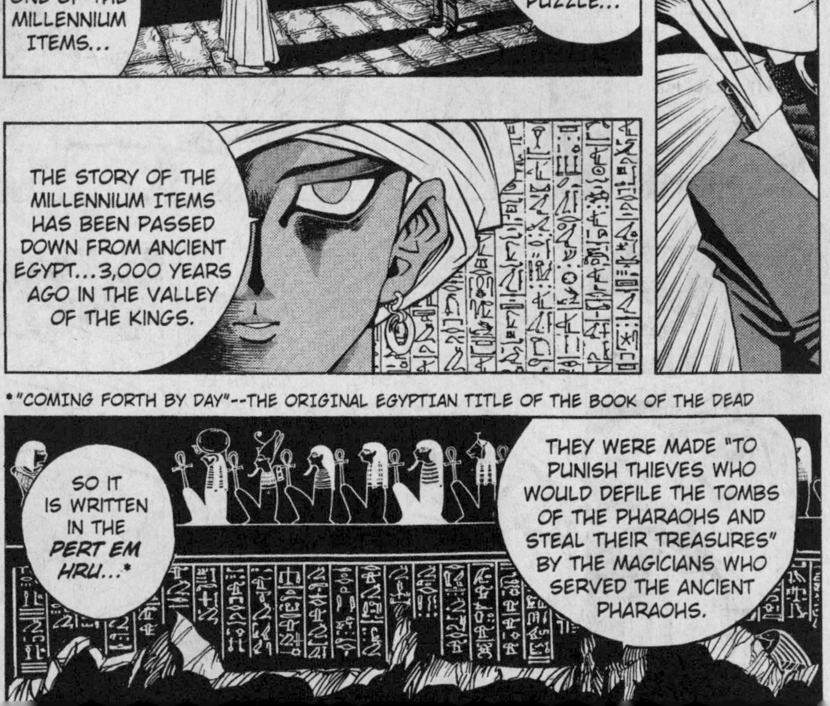
THEY WERE MADE "TO PUNISH THIEVES WHO WOULD DEFILE THE TOMBS OF THE PHARAOHS AND STEAL THEIR TREASURES" BY THE MAGICIANS WHO SERVED THE ANCIENT PHARAOHS.
SO IT IS WRITTEN IN THE *PERT EM HRU*...*

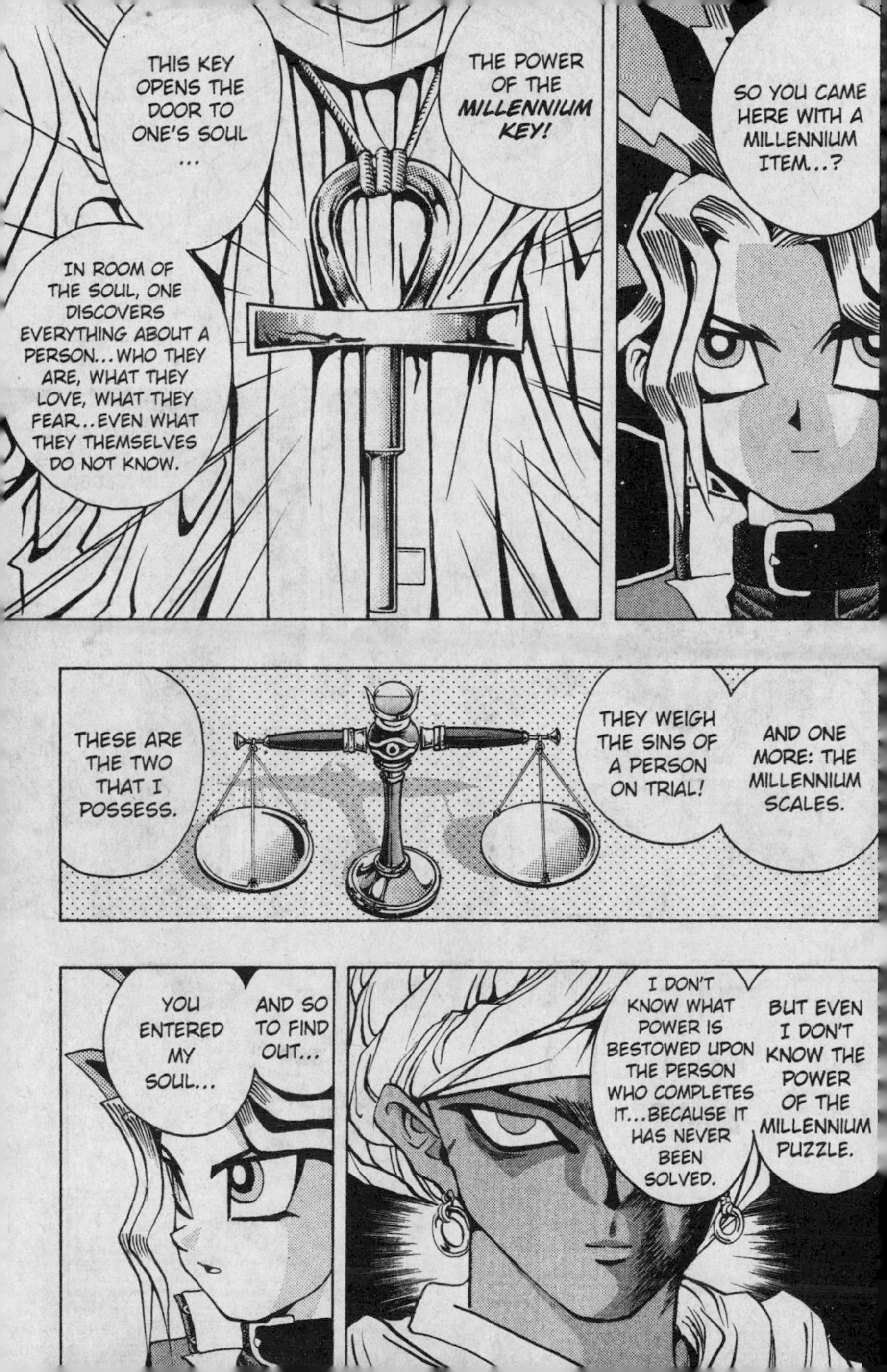
SO YOU CAME HERE WITH A MILLENNIUM ITEM..?
THE POWER OF THE MILLENNIUM KEY!
THIS KEY OPENS THE DOOR TO ONE'S SOUL ...
IN ROOM OF THE SOUL, ONE DISCOVERS EVERYTHING ABOUT A PERSON...WHO THEY ARE, WHAT THEY LOVE, WHAT THEY FEAR...EVEN WHAT THEY THEMSELVES DO NOT KNOW.
AND ONE MORE: THE MILLENNIUM SCALES.
THEY WEIGH THE SINS OF A PERSON ON TRIAL!
THESE ARE THE TWO THAT I POSSESS.
BUT EVEN I DON'T KNOW THE POWER OF THE MILLENNIUM PUZZLE.
I DON'T KNOW WHAT POWER IS BESTOWED UPON THE PERSON WHO COMPLETES IT...BECAUSE IT HAS NEVER BEEN SOLVED.
AND SO TO FIND OUT...
YOU ENTERED MY SOUL...

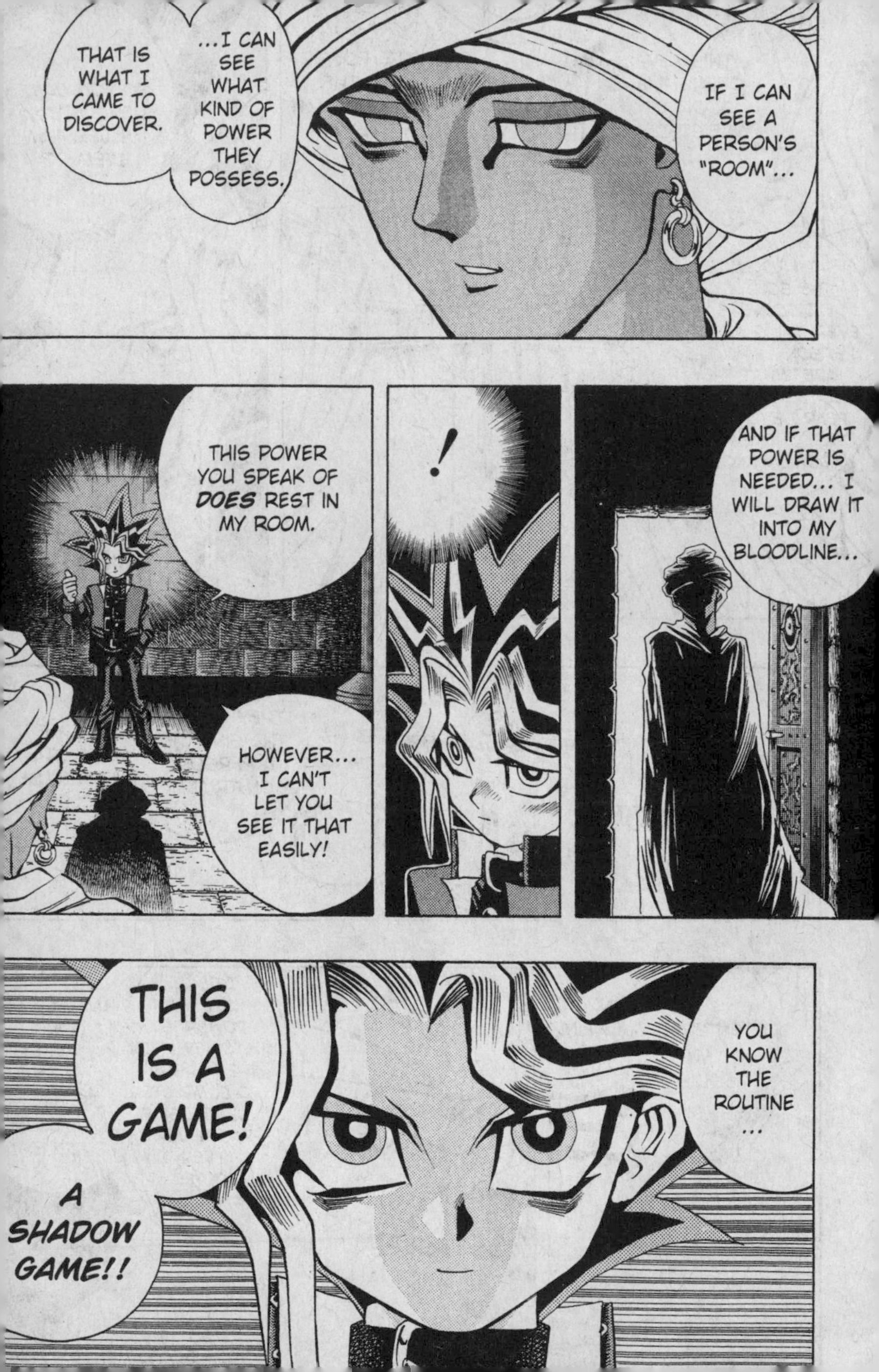
IF I CAN SEE A PERSON'S "ROOM"...
...I CAN SEE WHAT KIND OF POWER THEY POSSESS.
THAT IS WHAT I CAME TO DISCOVER.
AND IF THAT POWER IS NEEDED... I WILL DRAW IT INTO MY BLOODLINE...
!
THIS POWER YOU SPEAK OF DOES REST IN MY ROOM.
HOWEVER... I CAN'T LET YOU SEE IT THAT EASILY!
YOU KNOW THE ROUTINE...
THIS IS A GAME!
A SHADOW GAME!!

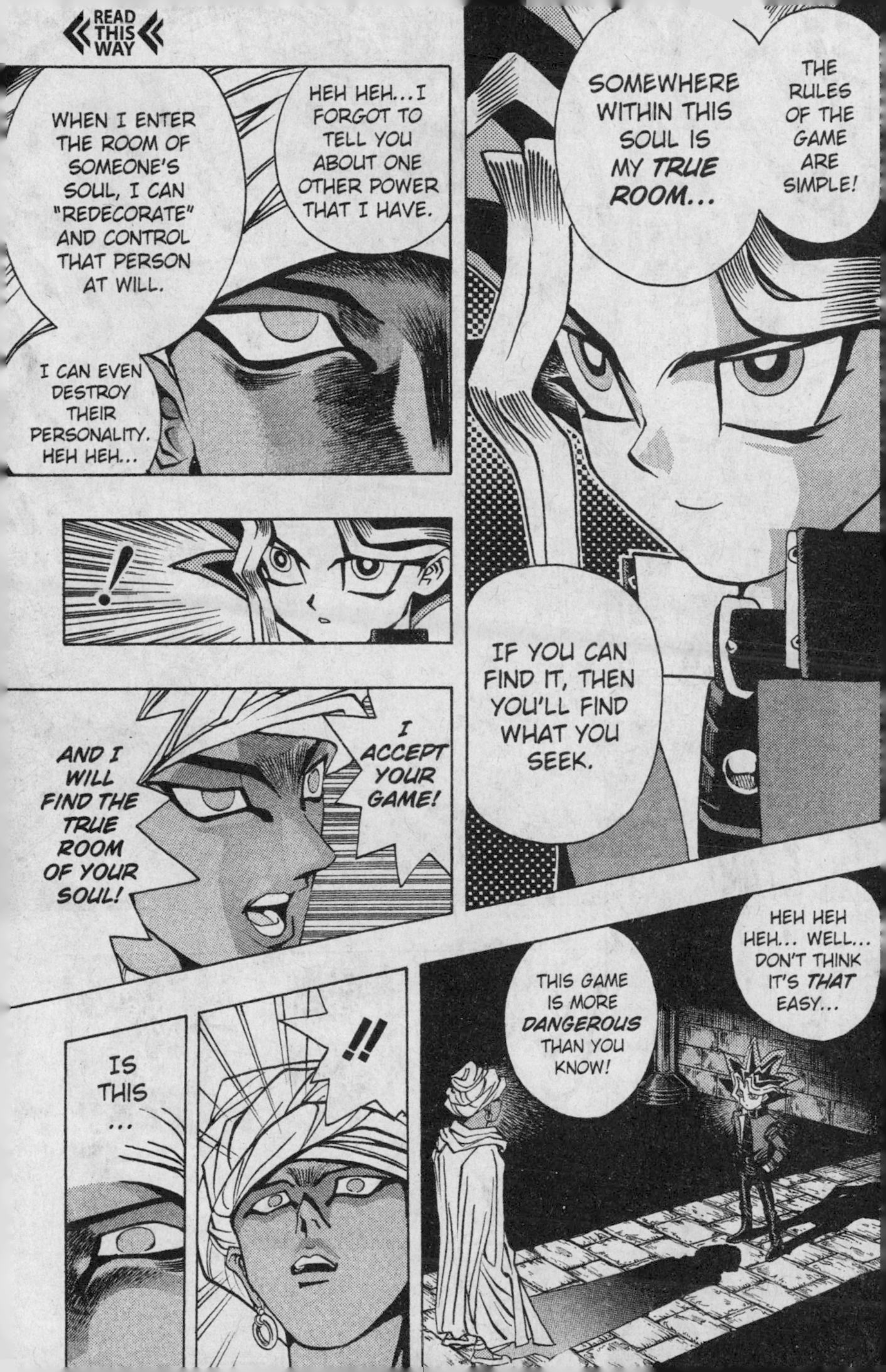
READ THIS WAY
THE RULES OF THE GAME ARE SIMPLE!
SOMEWHERE WITHIN THIS SOUL IS MY *TRUE ROOM...*
IF YOU CAN FIND IT, THEN YOU'LL FIND WHAT YOU SEEK.
HEH HEH...I FORGOT TO TELL YOU ABOUT ONE OTHER POWER THAT I HAVE.
WHEN I ENTER THE ROOM OF SOMEONE'S SOUL, I CAN "REDECORATE" AND CONTROL THAT PERSON AT WILL.
I CAN EVEN DESTROY THEIR PERSONALITY. HEH HEH...
!
I ACCEPT YOUR GAME!
AND I WILL FIND THE TRUE ROOM OF YOUR SOUL!
HEH HEH HEH... WELL... DON'T THINK IT'S *THAT* EASY...
THIS GAME IS MORE *DANGEROUS* THAN YOU KNOW!
!!
IS THIS ...

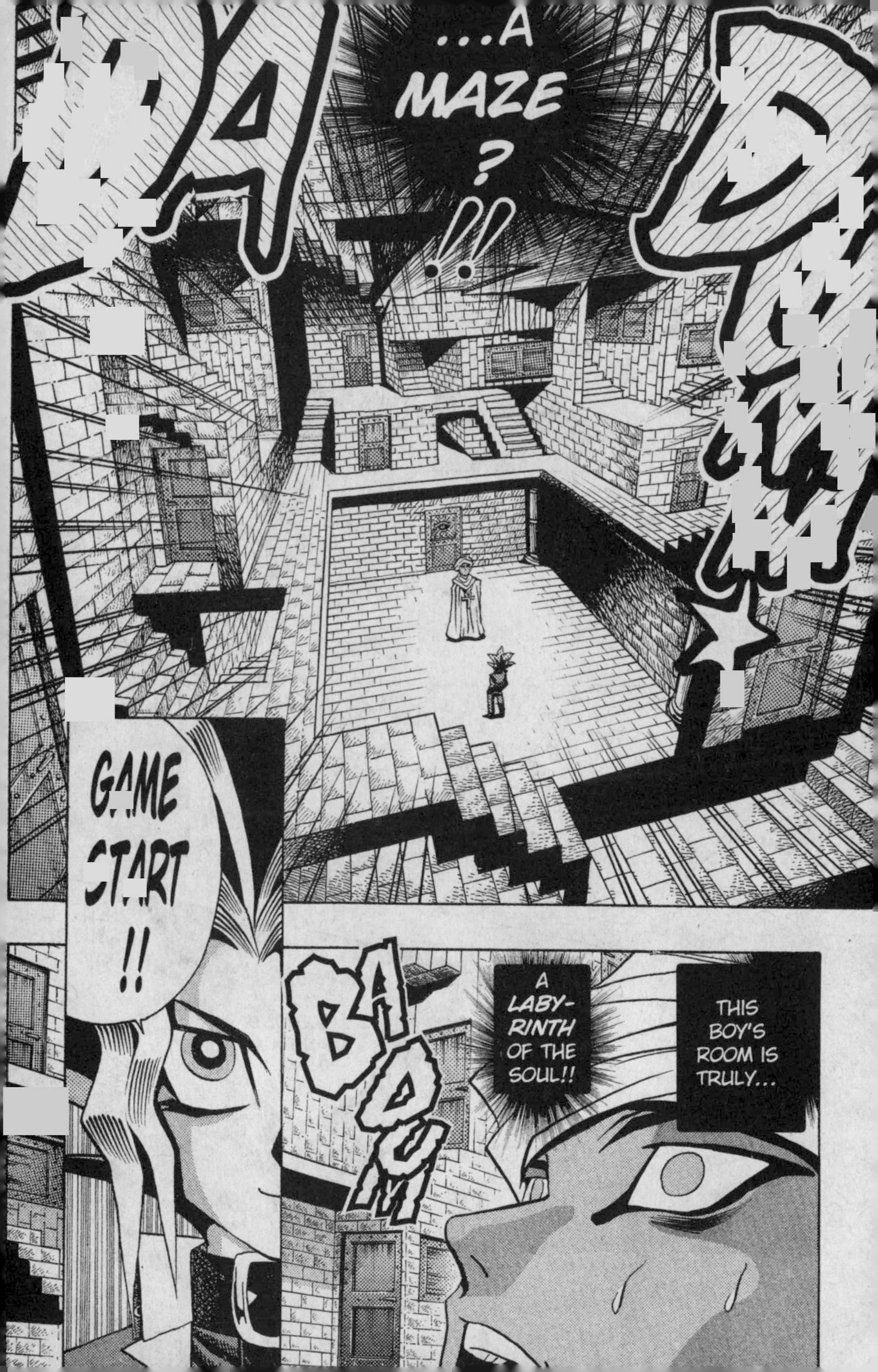
...A MAZE?!!
THIS BOY'S ROOM IS TRULY...
A LABYRINTH OF THE SOUL!!
GAME START!!

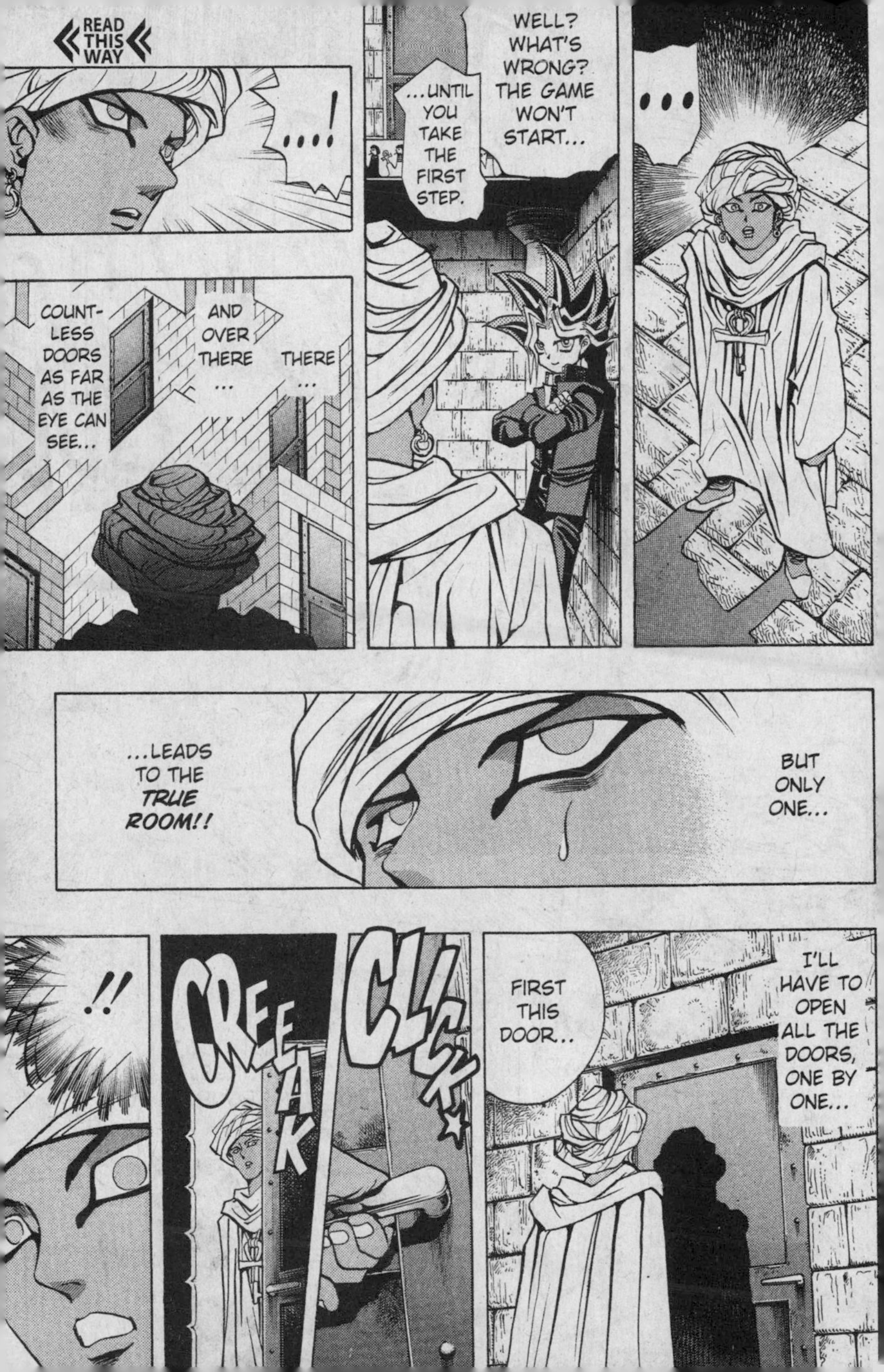
READ THIS WAY
...
WELL? WHAT'S WRONG? THE GAME WON'T START...
...UNTIL YOU TAKE THE FIRST STEP.
...!
THERE...
AND OVER THERE...
COUNT-LESS DOORS AS FAR AS THE EYE CAN SEE...
BUT ONLY ONE...
...LEADS TO THE *TRUE ROOM!!*
I'LL HAVE TO OPEN ALL THE DOORS, ONE BY ONE...
FIRST THIS DOOR...
CLICK
CREEAK
!!

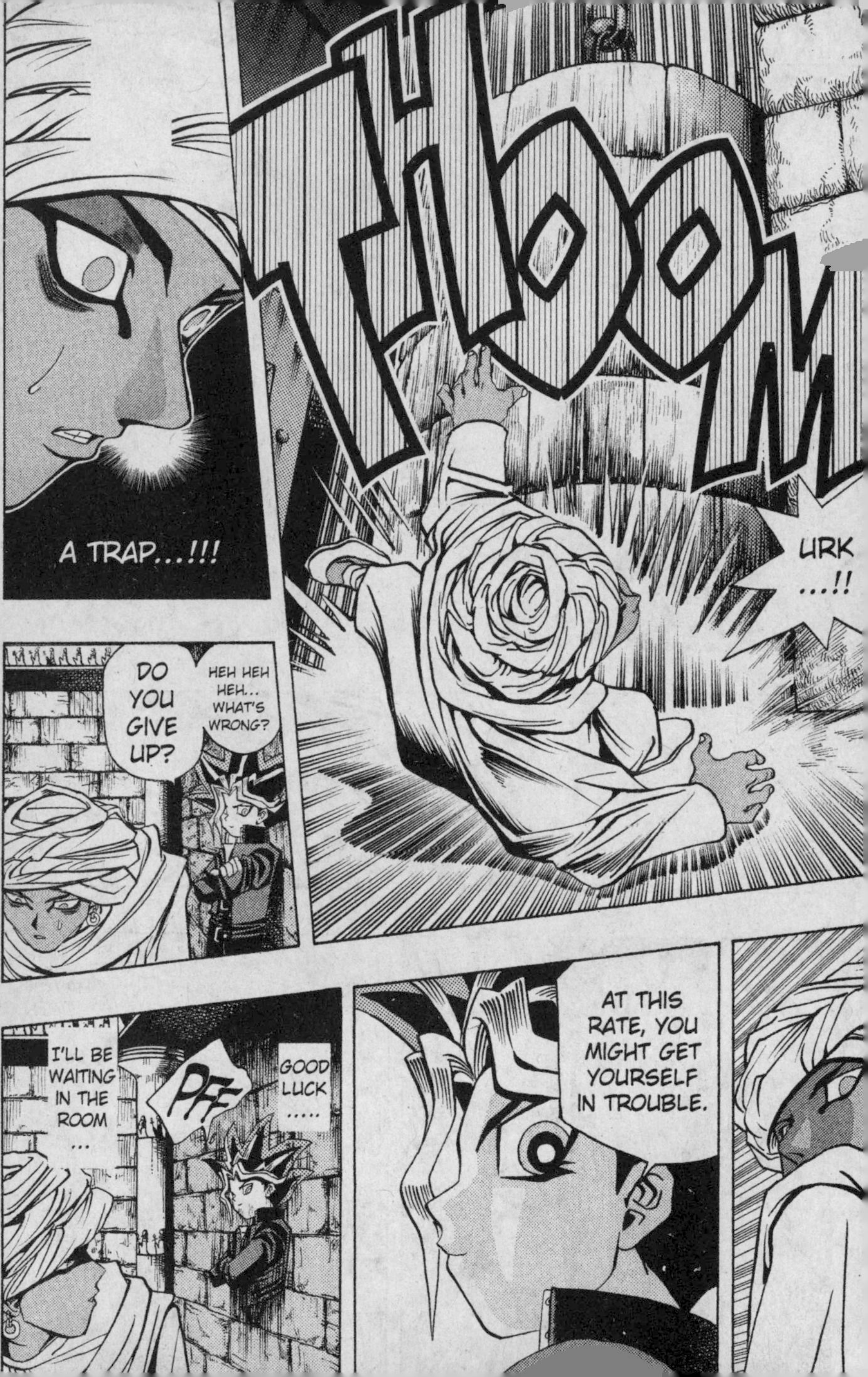
THOOM
URK ...!!
A TRAP...!!!
HEH HEH HEH... WHAT'S WRONG?
DO YOU GIVE UP?
AT THIS RATE, YOU MIGHT GET YOURSELF IN TROUBLE.
GOOD LUCK .....
PFF
I'LL BE WAITING IN THE ROOM ...

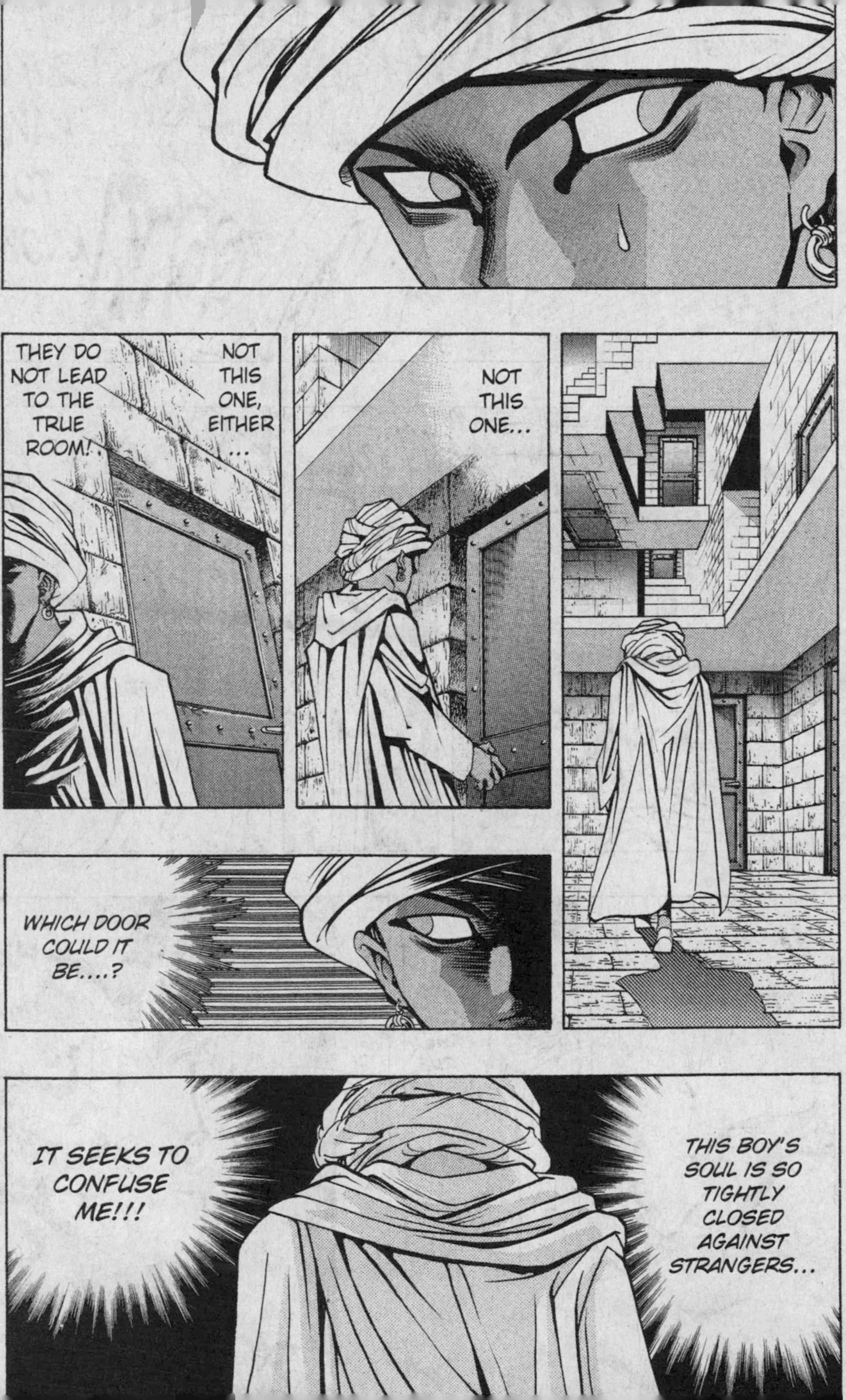
NOT THIS ONE...
NOT THIS ONE, EITHER...
THEY DO NOT LEAD TO THE TRUE ROOM!
WHICH DOOR COULD IT BE....?
THIS BOY'S SOUL IS SO TIGHTLY CLOSED AGAINST STRANGERS...
IT SEEKS TO CONFUSE ME!!!

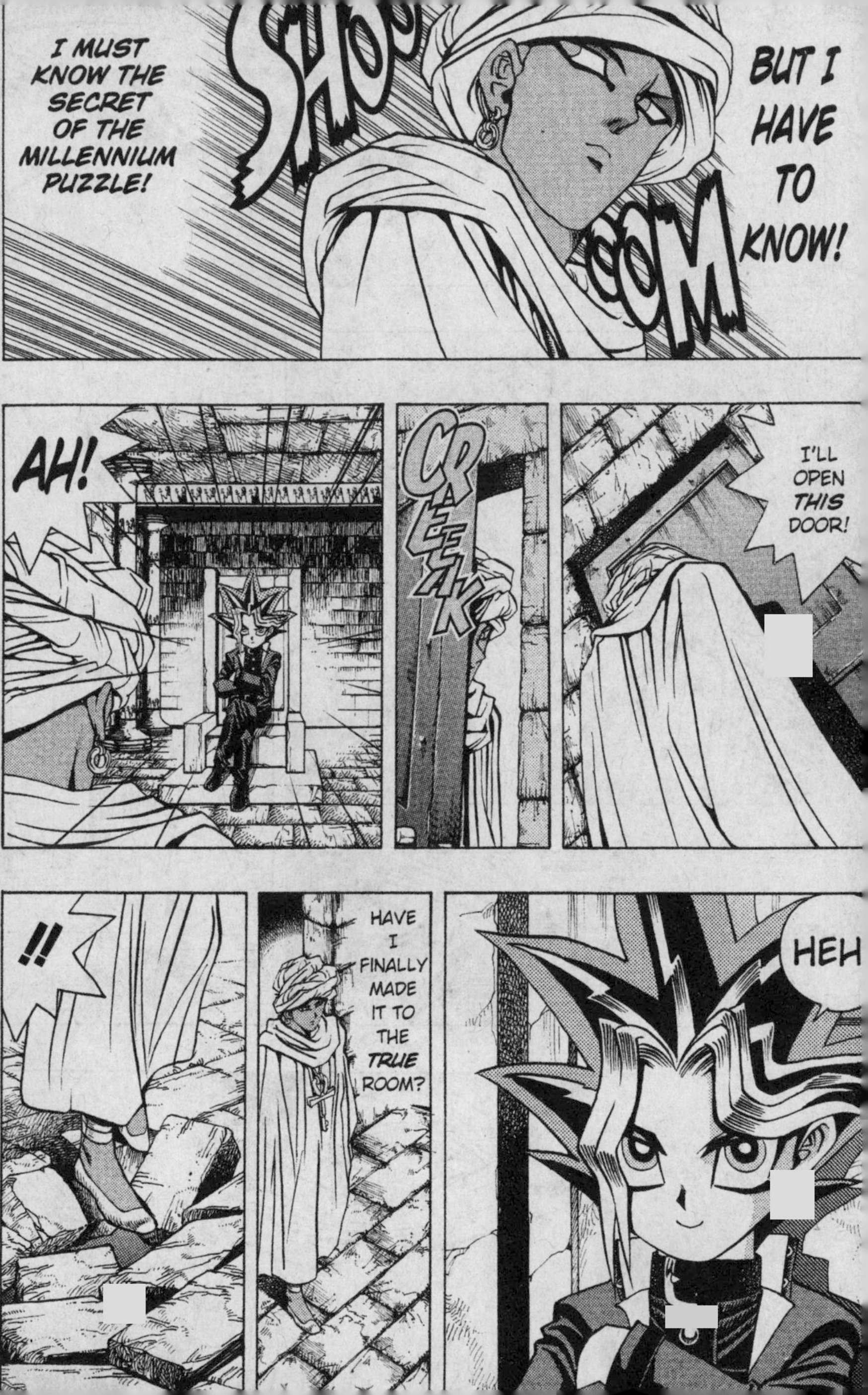
BUT I HAVE TO KNOW!
SHOOOM
I MUST KNOW THE SECRET OF THE MILLENNIUM PUZZLE!
I'LL OPEN THIS DOOR!
CREEEAK
AH!
HEH
HAVE I FINALLY MADE IT TO THE TRUE ROOM?
!!

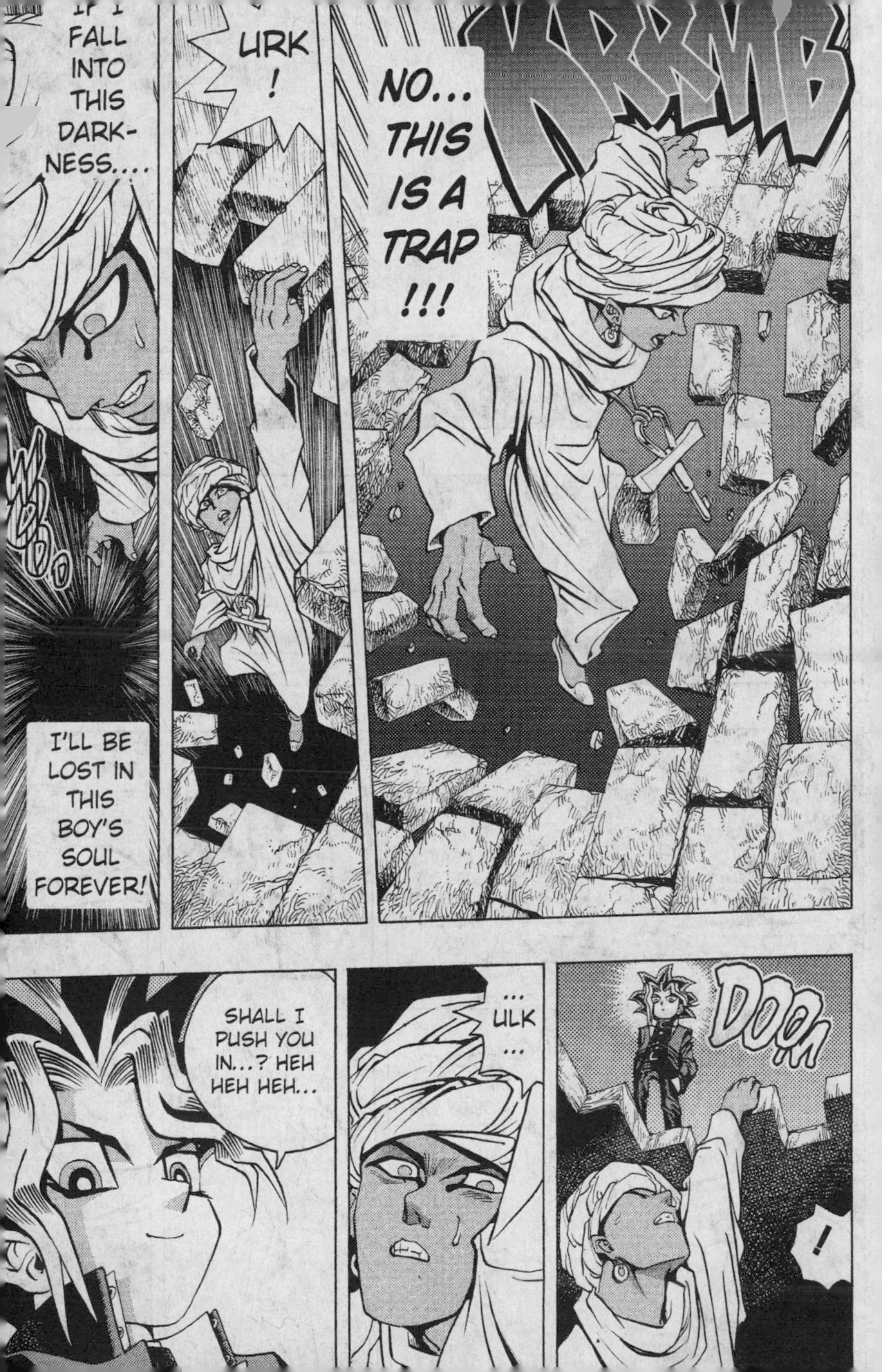
NO... THIS IS A TRAP!!!
URK!
IF I FALL INTO THIS DARKNESS....
I'LL BE LOST IN THIS BOY'S SOUL FOREVER!
!
...ULK...
SHALL I PUSH YOU IN...? HEH HEH HEH...

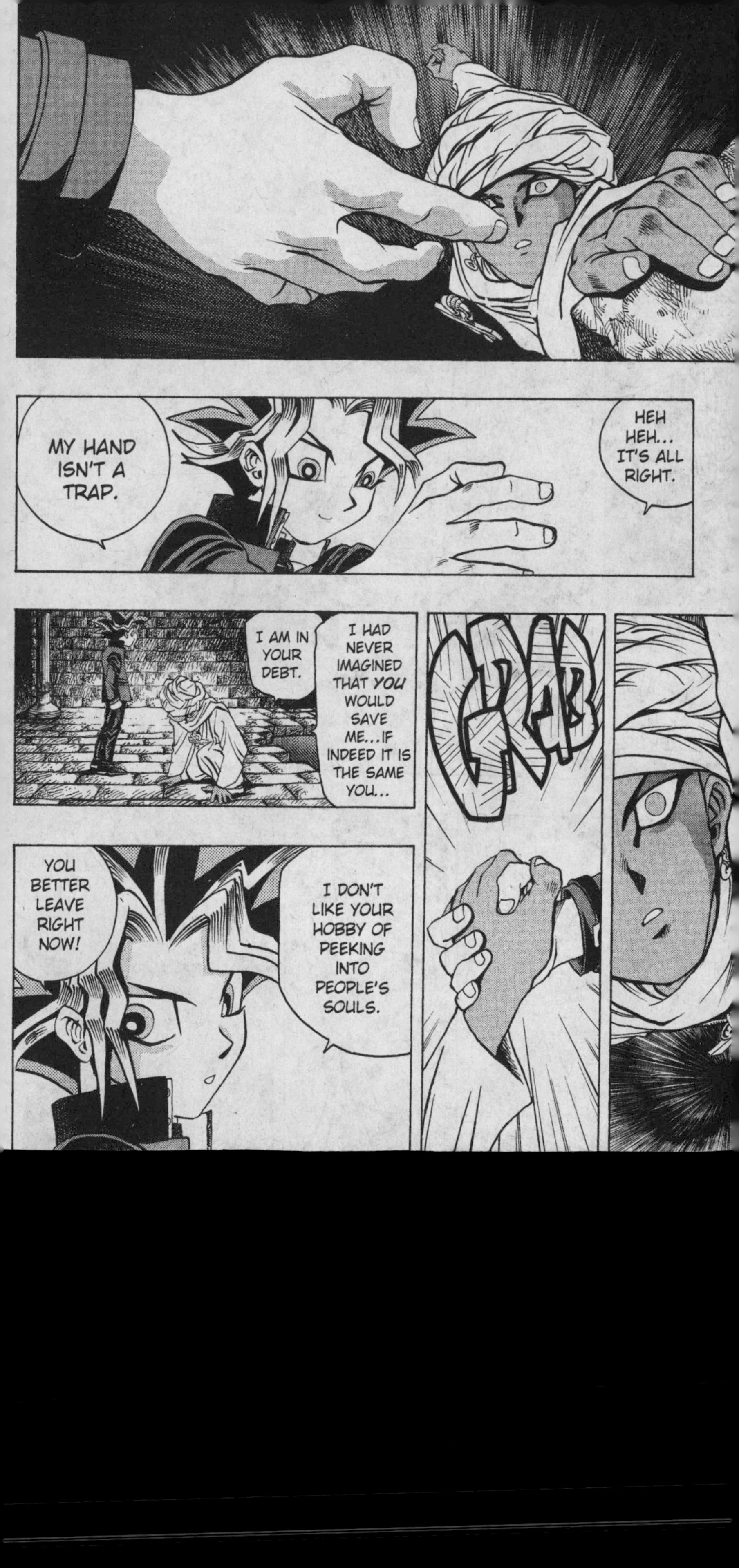
HEH HEH... IT'S ALL RIGHT.
MY HAND ISN'T A TRAP.
GRAB
I HAD NEVER IMAGINED THAT *YOU* WOULD SAVE ME...IF INDEED IT IS THE SAME YOU...
I AM IN YOUR DEBT.
I DON'T LIKE YOUR HOBBY OF PEEKING INTO PEOPLE'S SOULS.
YOU BETTER LEAVE RIGHT NOW!

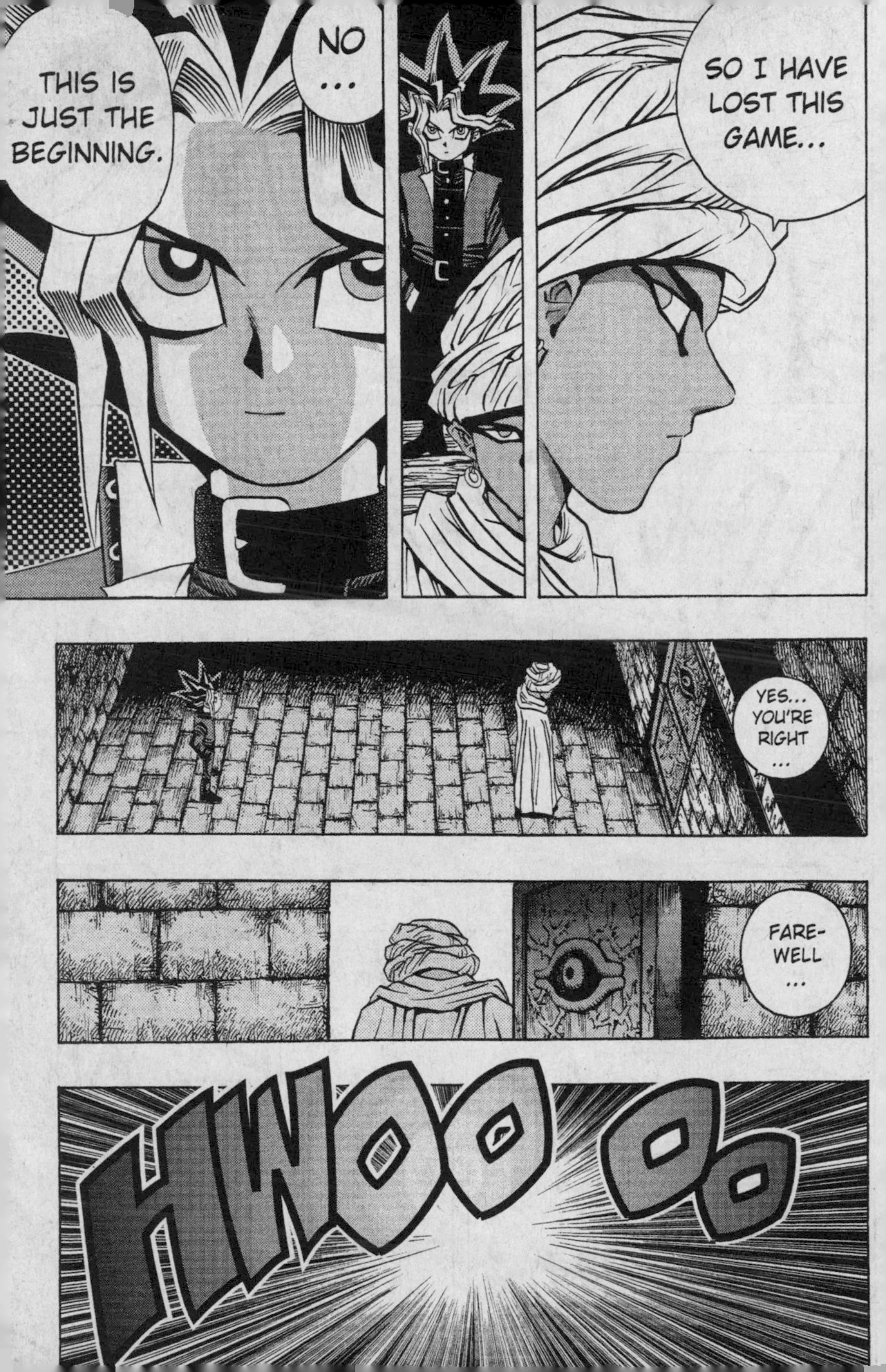
SO I HAVE LOST THIS GAME...
NO ...
THIS IS JUST THE BEGINNING.
YES... YOU'RE RIGHT ...
FARE-WELL ...
HWOOOO

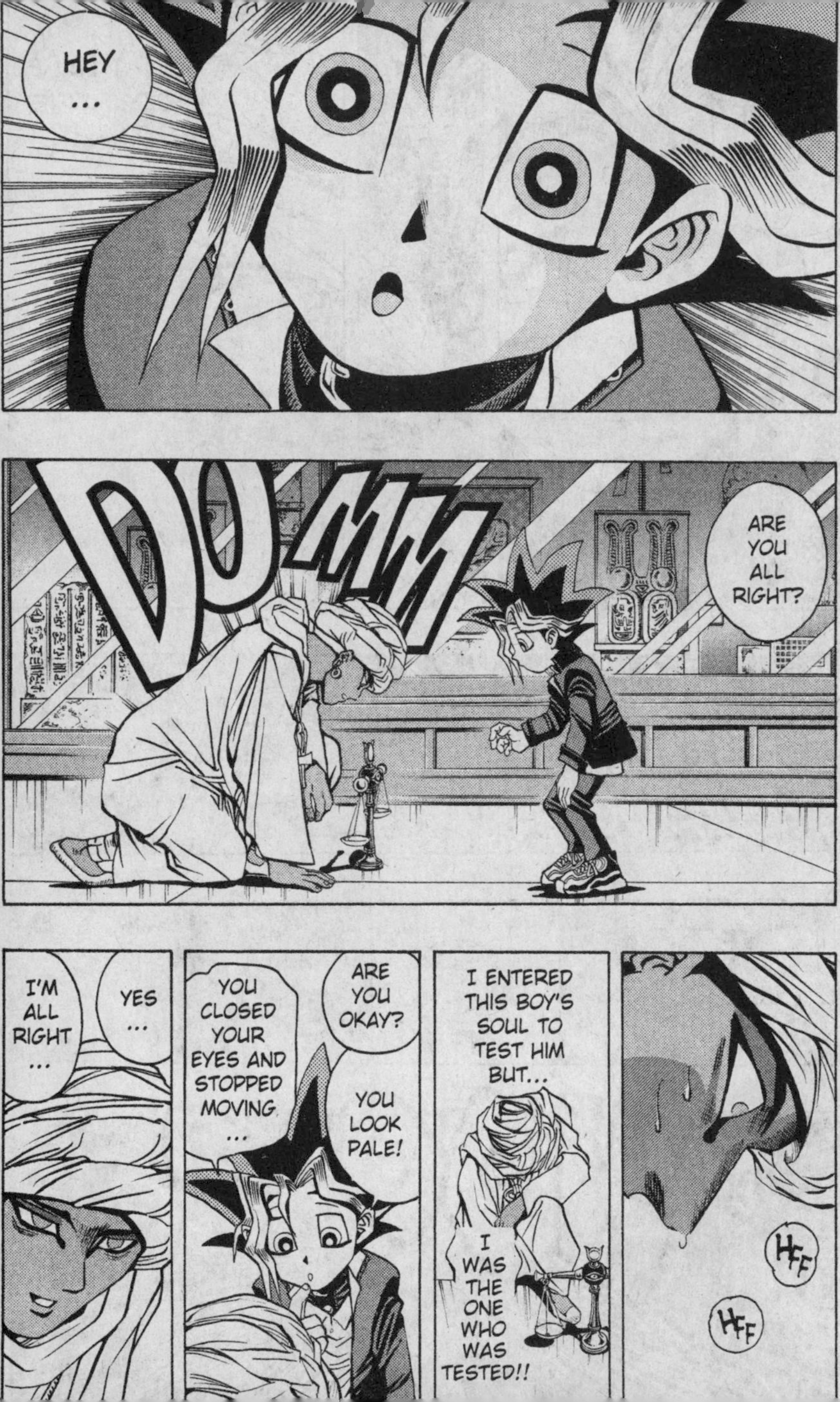
HEY ...
DOMM
ARE YOU ALL RIGHT?
HFF
HFF
I ENTERED THIS BOY'S SOUL TO TEST HIM BUT...
I WAS THE ONE WHO WAS TESTED!!
ARE YOU OKAY?
YOU CLOSED YOUR EYES AND STOPPED MOVING ...
YOU LOOK PALE!
YES ...
I'M ALL RIGHT ...

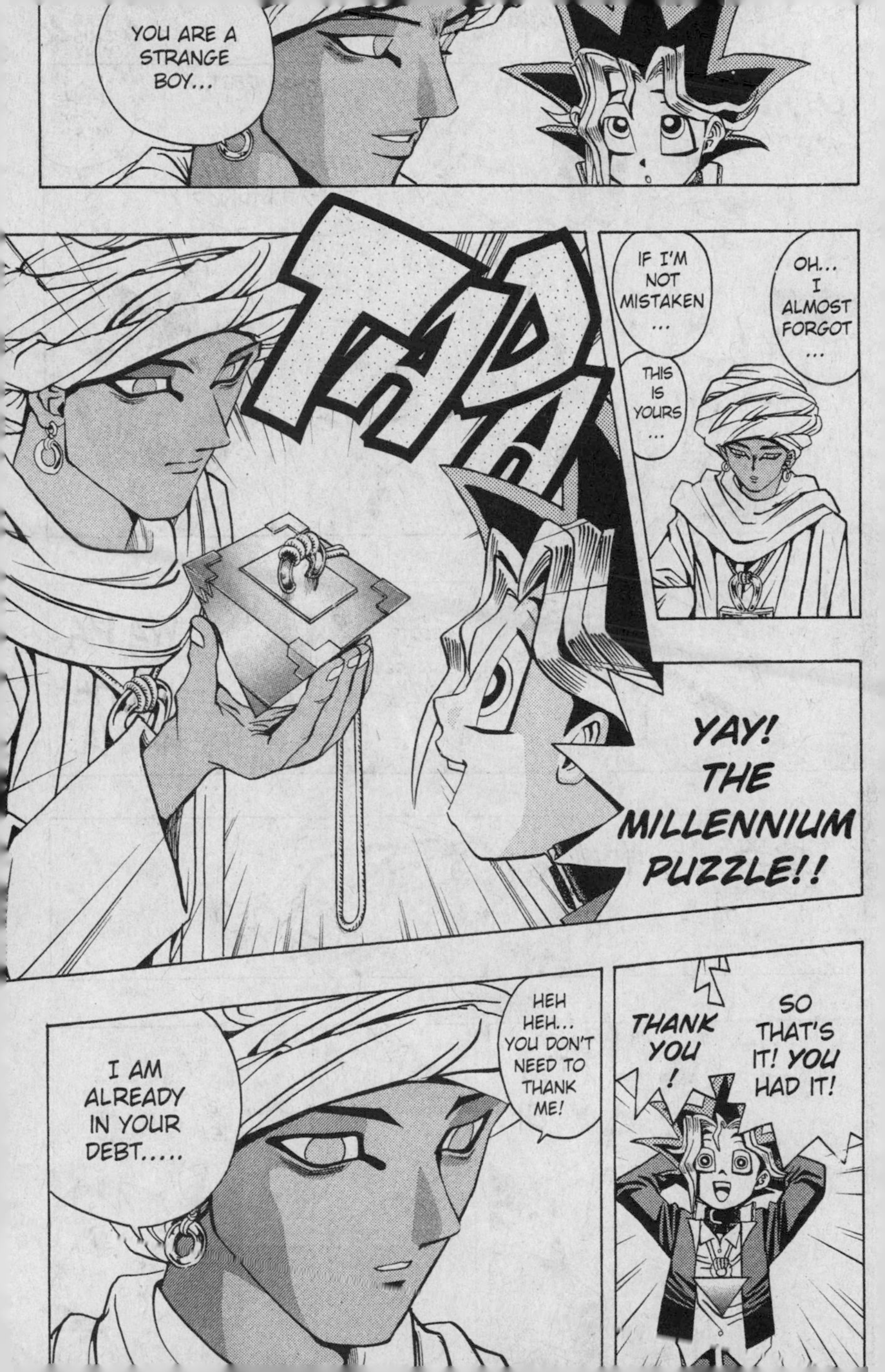
YOU ARE A STRANGE BOY...
OH... I ALMOST FORGOT...
IF I'M NOT MISTAKEN...
THIS IS YOURS...
TADA
YAY! THE MILLENNIUM PUZZLE!!
SO THAT'S IT! YOU HAD IT!
THANK YOU!
HEH HEH... YOU DON'T NEED TO THANK ME!
I AM ALREADY IN YOUR DEBT.....

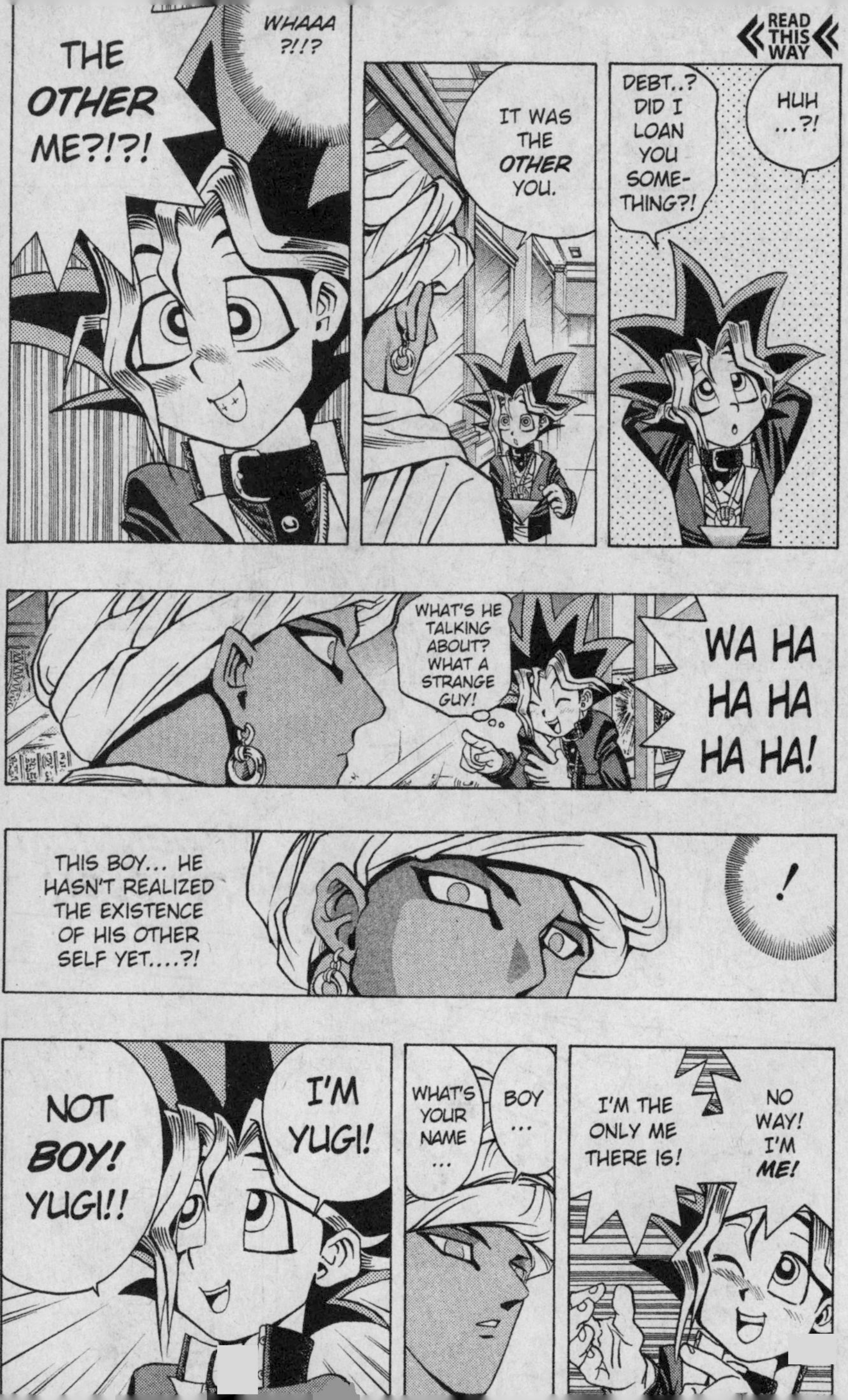
READ THIS WAY
HUH ...?!
DEBT..? DID I LOAN YOU SOME-THING?!
IT WAS THE OTHER YOU.
WHAAA ?!!?
THE OTHER ME?!?!
WA HA HA HA HA HA!
WHAT'S HE TALKING ABOUT? WHAT A STRANGE GUY!
!
THIS BOY... HE HASN'T REALIZED THE EXISTENCE OF HIS OTHER SELF YET....?!
NO WAY! I'M ME!
I'M THE ONLY ME THERE IS!
BOY ...
WHAT'S YOUR NAME ...
I'M YUGI!
NOT BOY! YUGI!!

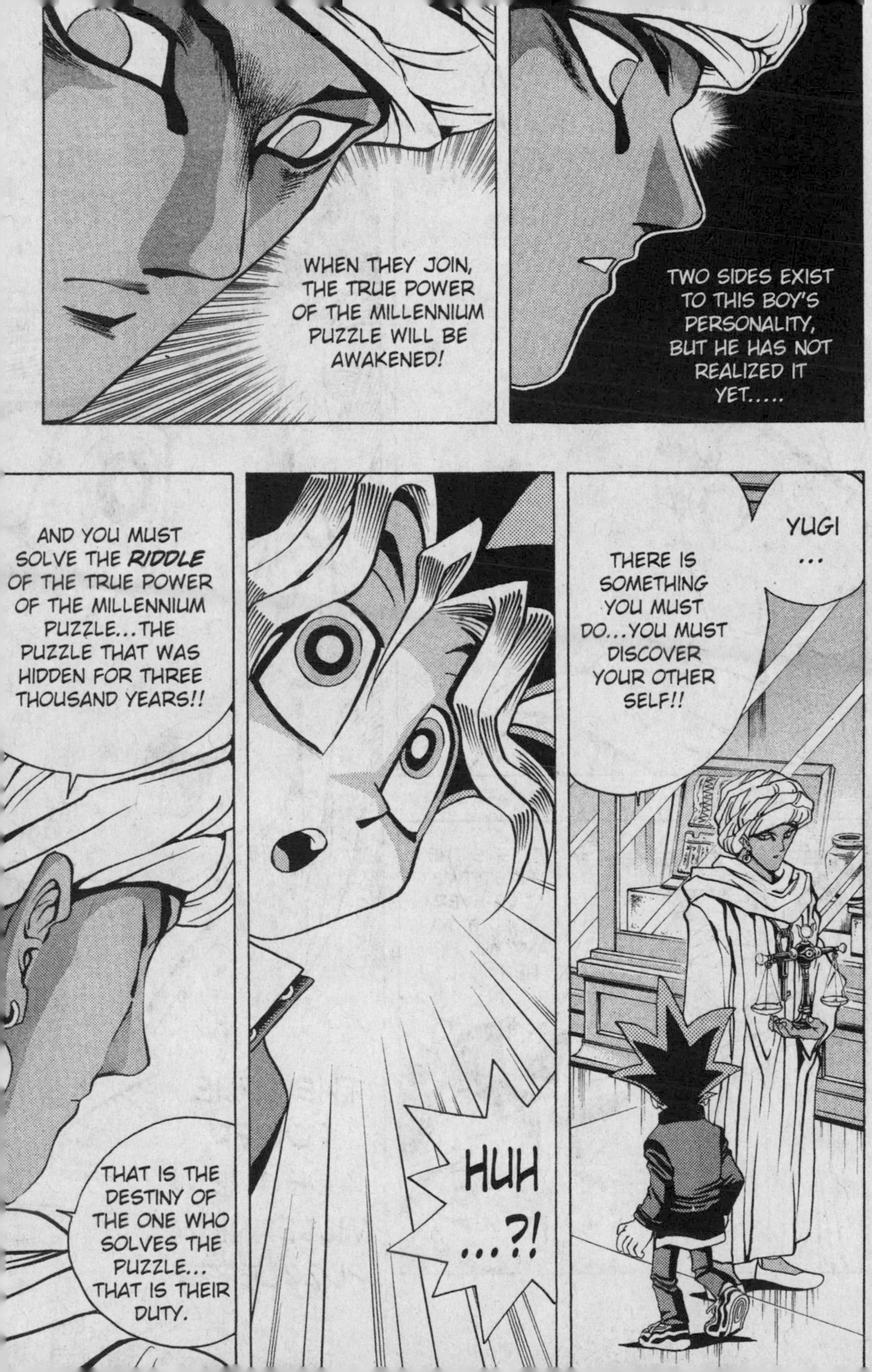
TWO SIDES EXIST TO THIS BOY'S PERSONALITY, BUT HE HAS NOT REALIZED IT YET.....
WHEN THEY JOIN, THE TRUE POWER OF THE MILLENNIUM PUZZLE WILL BE AWAKENED!
YUGI ...
THERE IS SOMETHING YOU MUST DO...YOU MUST DISCOVER YOUR OTHER SELF!!
HUH ...?!
AND YOU MUST SOLVE THE *RIDDLE* OF THE TRUE POWER OF THE MILLENNIUM PUZZLE...THE PUZZLE THAT WAS HIDDEN FOR THREE THOUSAND YEARS!!
THAT IS THE DESTINY OF THE ONE WHO SOLVES THE PUZZLE... THAT IS THEIR DUTY.

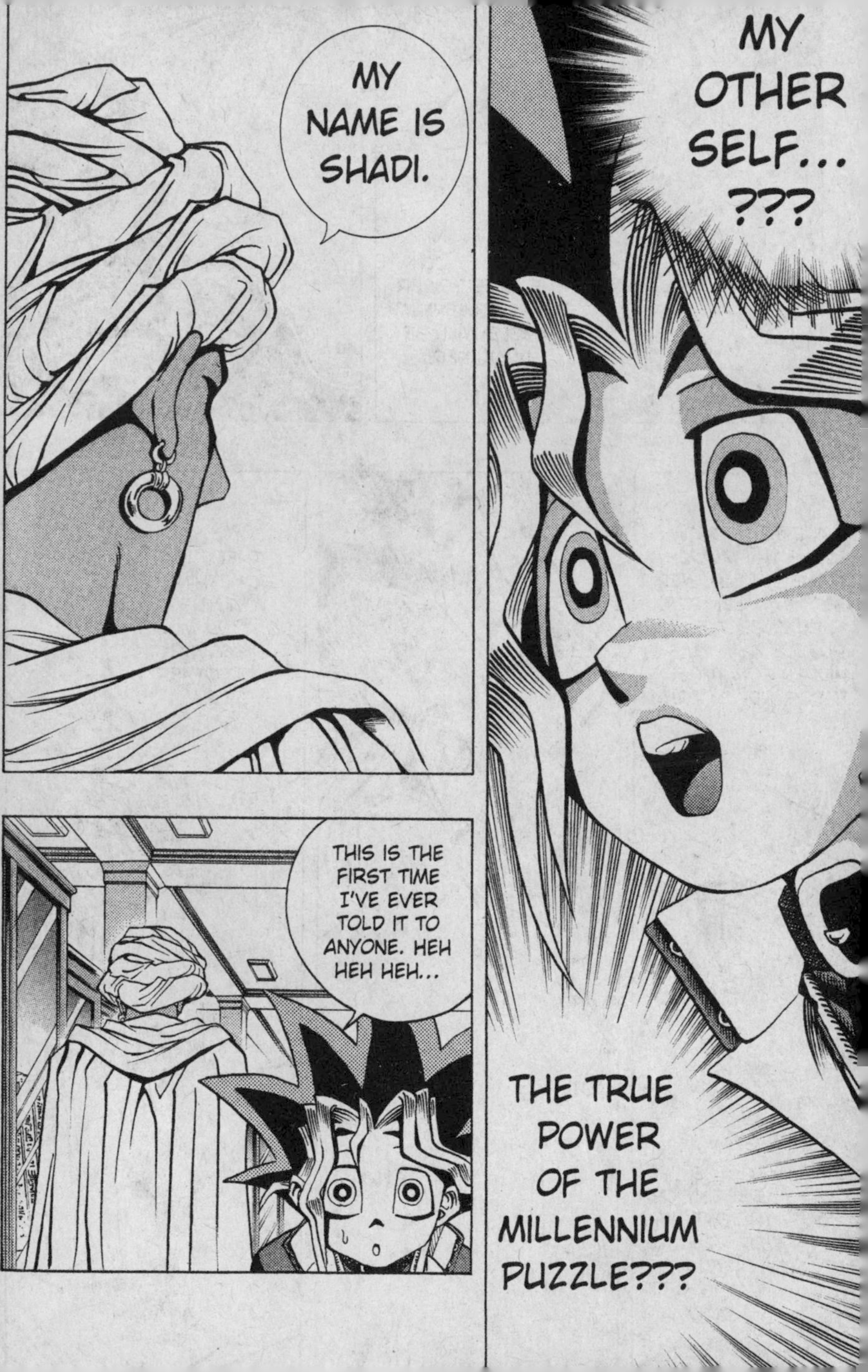
MY OTHER SELF... ???
THE TRUE POWER OF THE MILLENNIUM PUZZLE???
MY NAME IS SHADI.
THIS IS THE FIRST TIME I'VE EVER TOLD IT TO ANYONE. HEH HEH HEH...

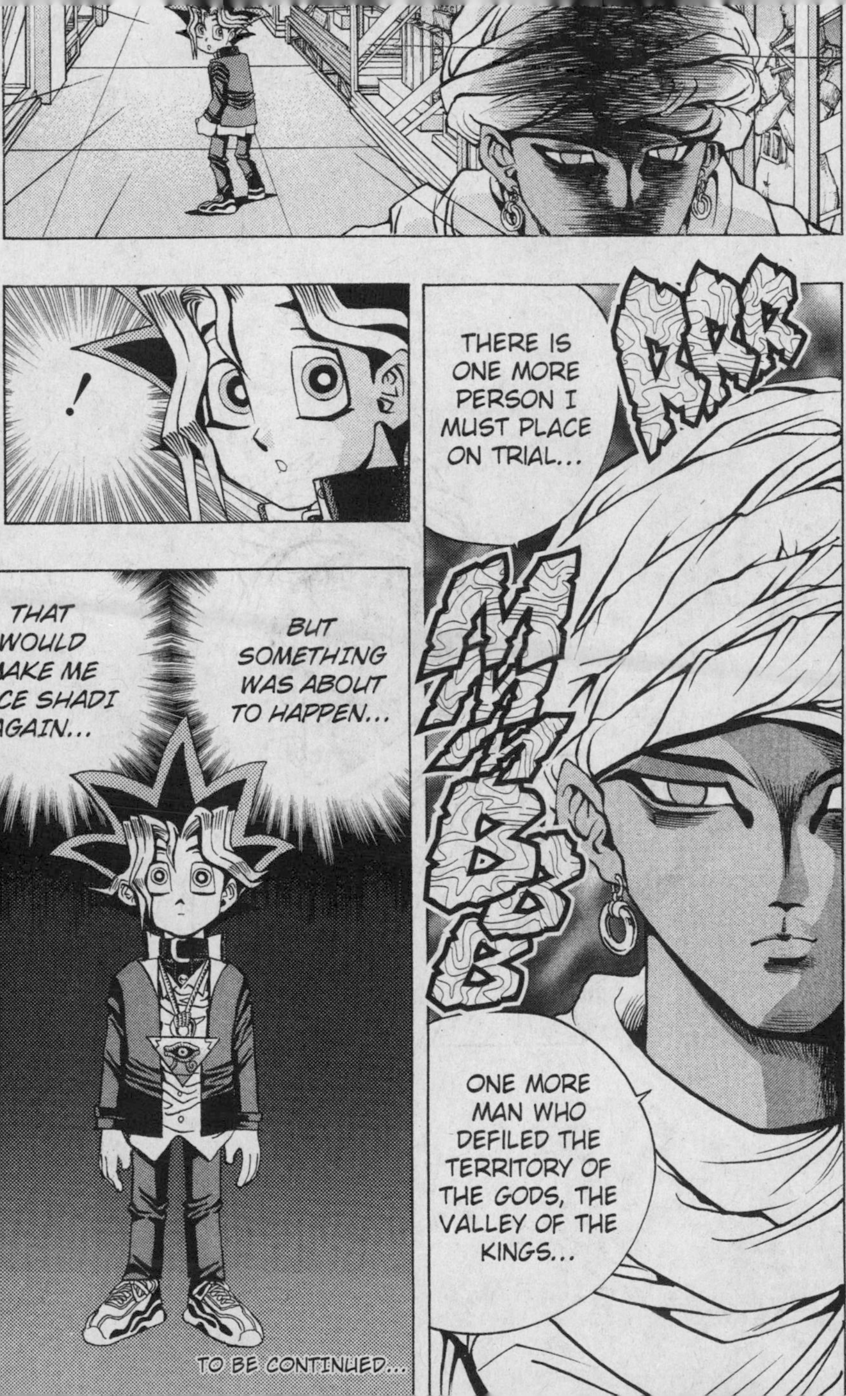
THERE IS ONE MORE PERSON I MUST PLACE ON TRIAL...
ONE MORE MAN WHO DEFILED THE TERRITORY OF THE GODS, THE VALLEY OF THE KINGS...
!
BUT SOMETHING WAS ABOUT TO HAPPEN...
THAT WOULD MAKE ME FACE SHADI AGAIN...
TO BE CONTINUED...

Duel 15: The Other Criminal

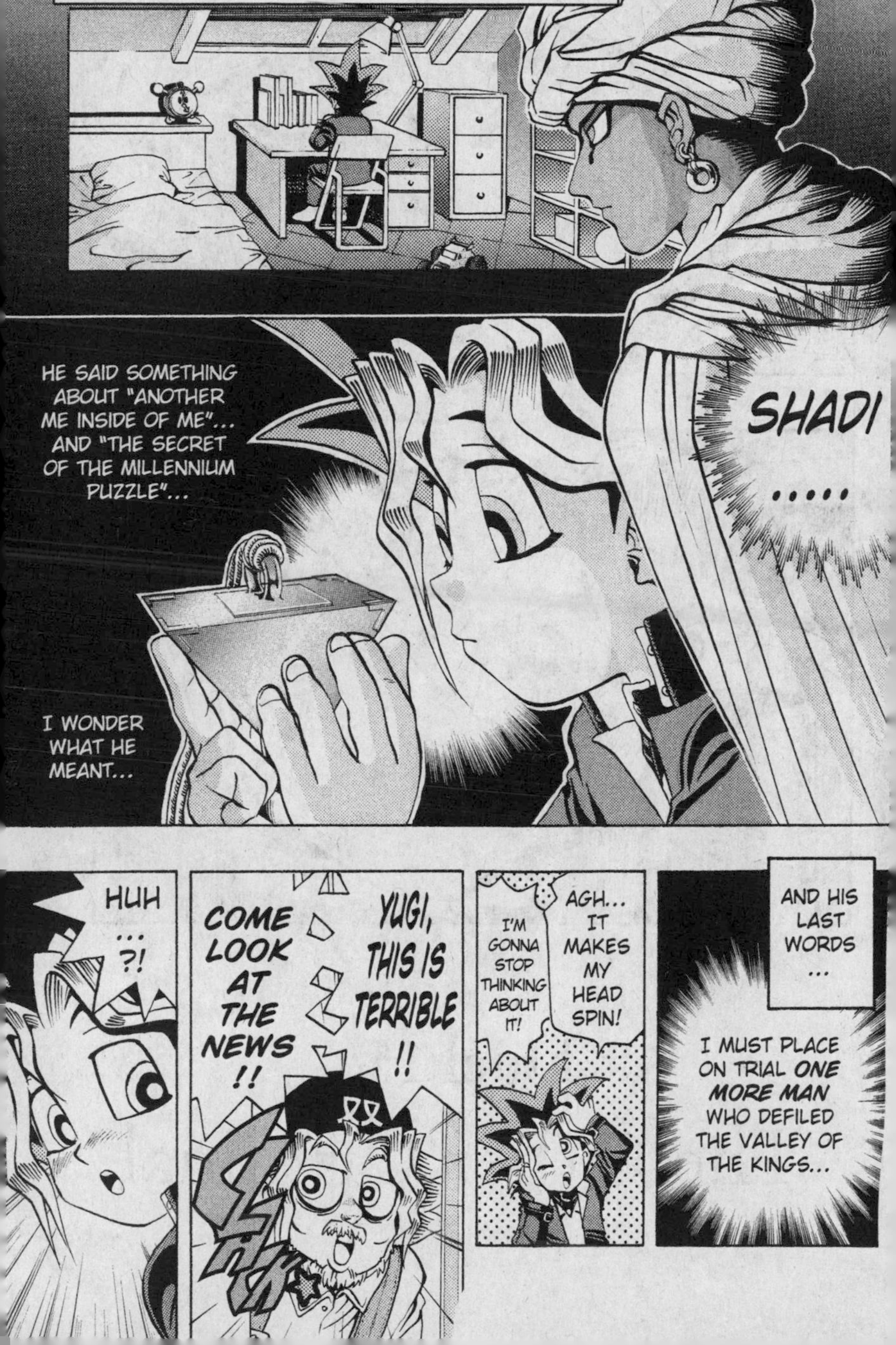
SHADI .....
HE SAID SOMETHING ABOUT "ANOTHER ME INSIDE OF ME"... AND "THE SECRET OF THE MILLENNIUM PUZZLE"...
I WONDER WHAT HE MEANT...
AND HIS LAST WORDS...
I MUST PLACE ON TRIAL ONE MORE MAN WHO DEFILED THE VALLEY OF THE KINGS...
AGH... IT MAKES MY HEAD SPIN!
I'M GONNA STOP THINKING ABOUT IT!
YUGI, THIS IS TERRIBLE!!
COME LOOK AT THE NEWS!!
HUH...?!

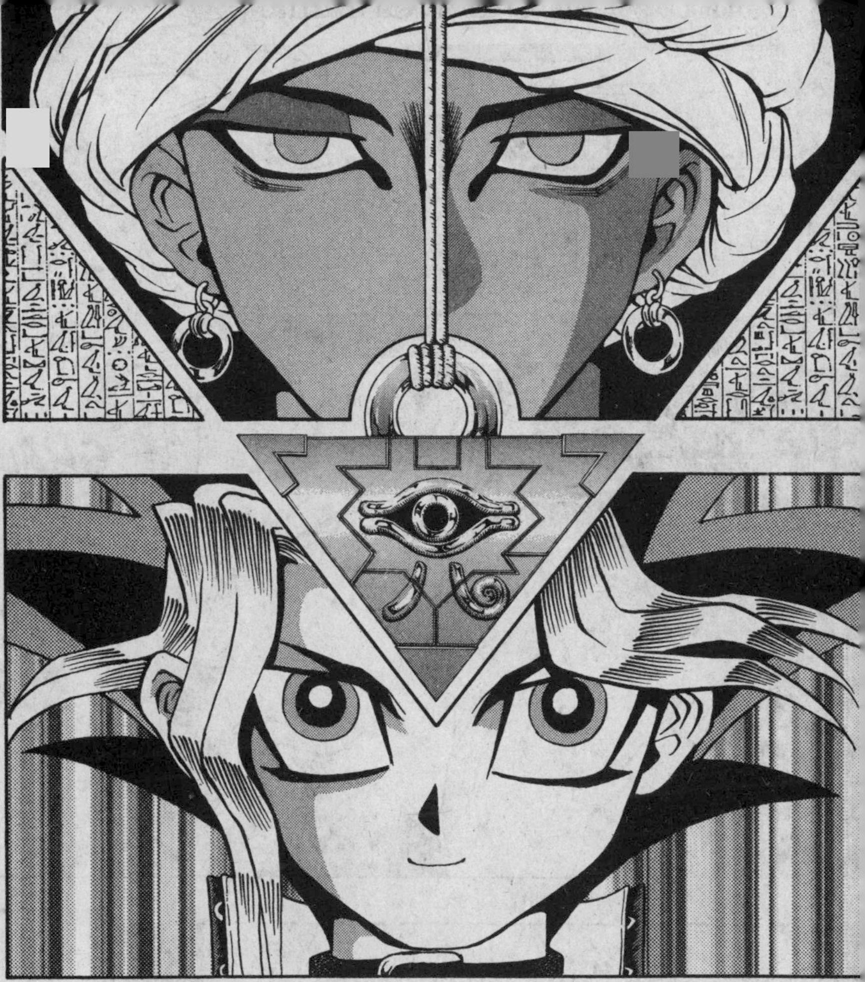

Duel 15:
The Other Criminal

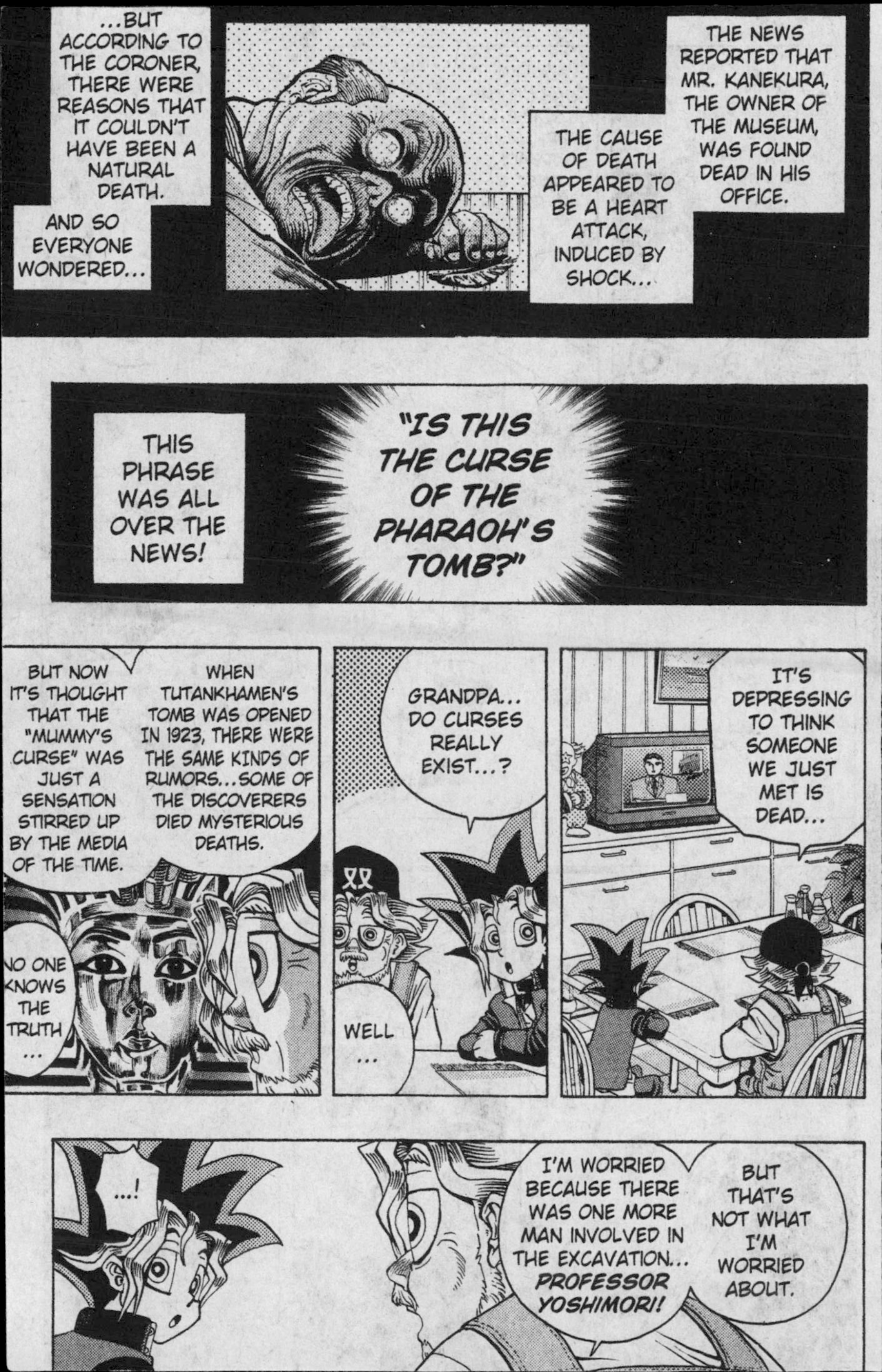
THE NEWS REPORTED THAT MR. KANEKURA, THE OWNER OF THE MUSEUM, WAS FOUND DEAD IN HIS OFFICE.
THE CAUSE OF DEATH APPEARED TO BE A HEART ATTACK, INDUCED BY SHOCK...
...BUT ACCORDING TO THE CORONER, THERE WERE REASONS THAT IT COULDN'T HAVE BEEN A NATURAL DEATH.
AND SO EVERYONE WONDERED...
"IS THIS THE CURSE OF THE PHARAOH'S TOMB?"
THIS PHRASE WAS ALL OVER THE NEWS!
IT'S DEPRESSING TO THINK SOMEONE WE JUST MET IS DEAD...
GRANDPA... DO CURSES REALLY EXIST...?
WELL...
WHEN TUTANKHAMEN'S TOMB WAS OPENED IN 1923, THERE WERE THE SAME KINDS OF RUMORS...SOME OF THE DISCOVERERS DIED MYSTERIOUS DEATHS.
BUT NOW IT'S THOUGHT THAT THE "MUMMY'S CURSE" WAS JUST A SENSATION STIRRED UP BY THE MEDIA OF THE TIME.
NO ONE KNOWS THE TRUTH...
BUT THAT'S NOT WHAT I'M WORRIED ABOUT.
I'M WORRIED BECAUSE THERE WAS ONE MORE MAN INVOLVED IN THE EXCAVATION... PROFESSOR YOSHIMORI!
...!

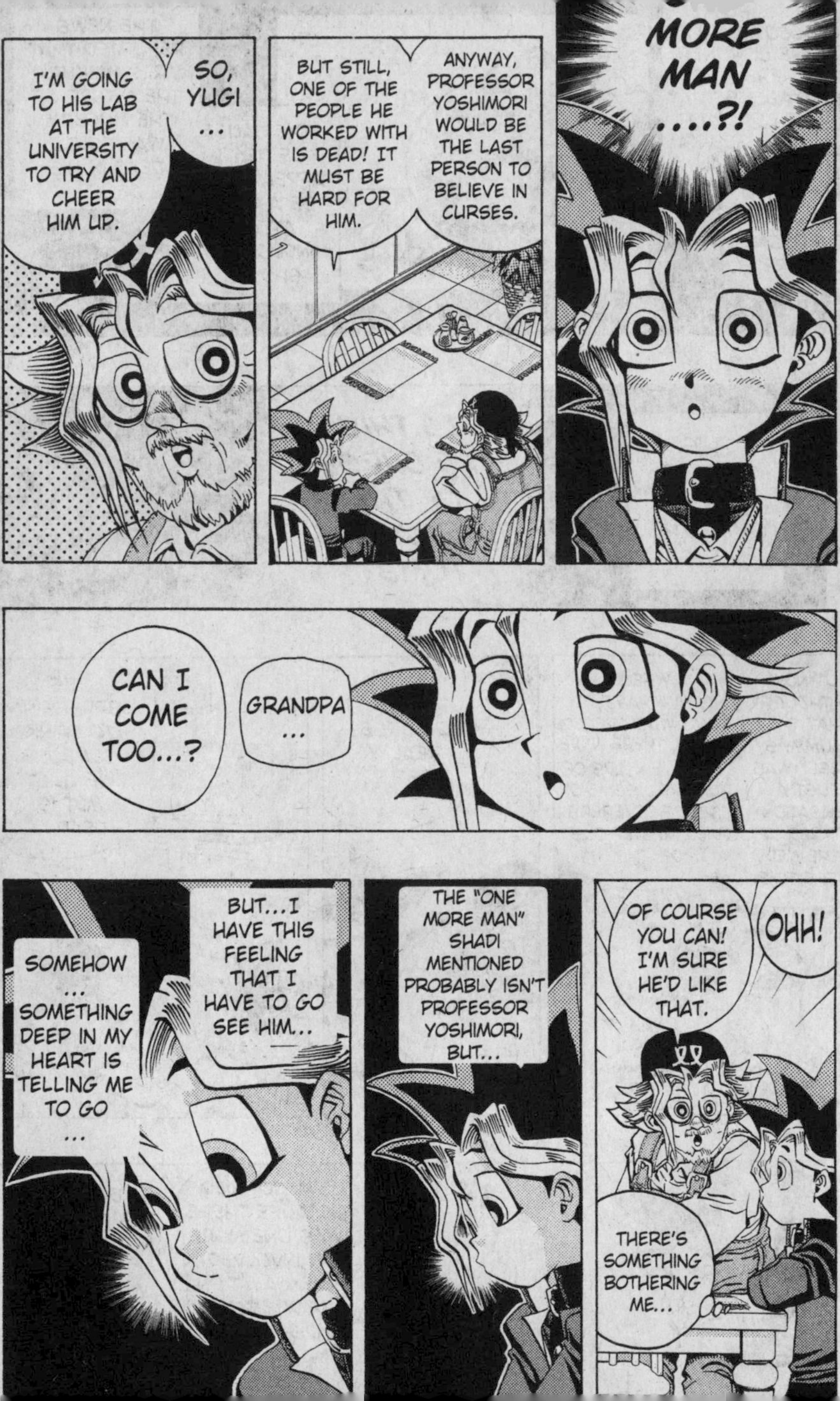
MORE MAN ....?!
ANYWAY, PROFESSOR YOSHIMORI WOULD BE THE LAST PERSON TO BELIEVE IN CURSES.
BUT STILL, ONE OF THE PEOPLE HE WORKED WITH IS DEAD! IT MUST BE HARD FOR HIM.
SO, YUGI ...
I'M GOING TO HIS LAB AT THE UNIVERSITY TO TRY AND CHEER HIM UP.
GRANDPA ...
CAN I COME TOO...?
OHH!
OF COURSE YOU CAN! I'M SURE HE'D LIKE THAT.
THERE'S SOMETHING BOTHERING ME...
THE "ONE MORE MAN" SHADI MENTIONED PROBABLY ISN'T PROFESSOR YOSHIMORI, BUT...
BUT...I HAVE THIS FEELING THAT I HAVE TO GO SEE HIM...
SOMEHOW ... SOMETHING DEEP IN MY HEART IS TELLING ME TO GO ...

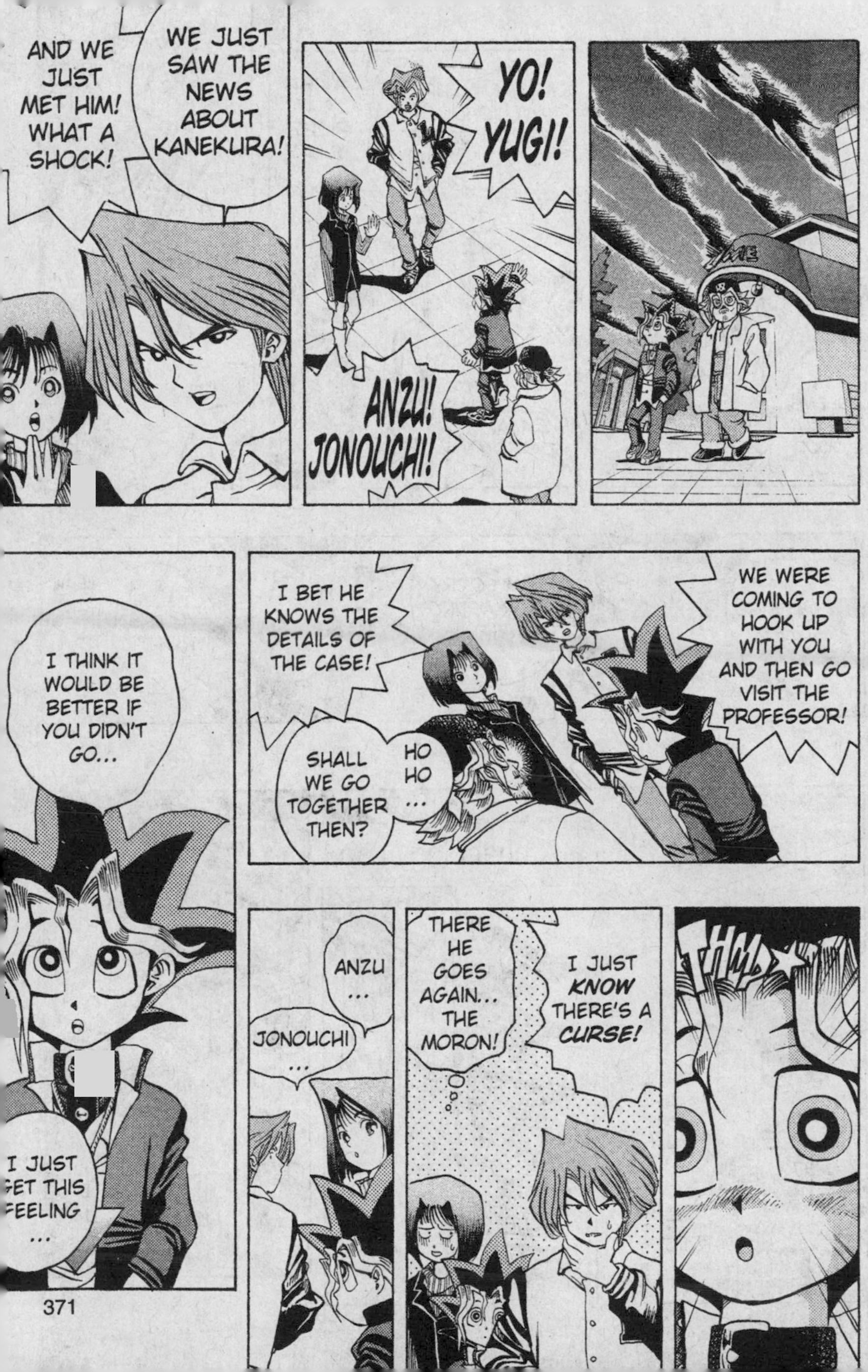
YO! YUGI!
ANZU! JONOUCHI!
WE JUST SAW THE NEWS ABOUT KANEKURA!
AND WE JUST MET HIM! WHAT A SHOCK!
WE WERE COMING TO HOOK UP WITH YOU AND THEN GO VISIT THE PROFESSOR!
I BET HE KNOWS THE DETAILS OF THE CASE!
HO HO ...
SHALL WE GO TOGETHER THEN?
THM★
I JUST KNOW THERE'S A CURSE!
THERE HE GOES AGAIN... THE MORON!
ANZU ...
JONOUCHI ...
I THINK IT WOULD BE BETTER IF YOU DIDN'T GO...
I JUST GET THIS FEELING ...

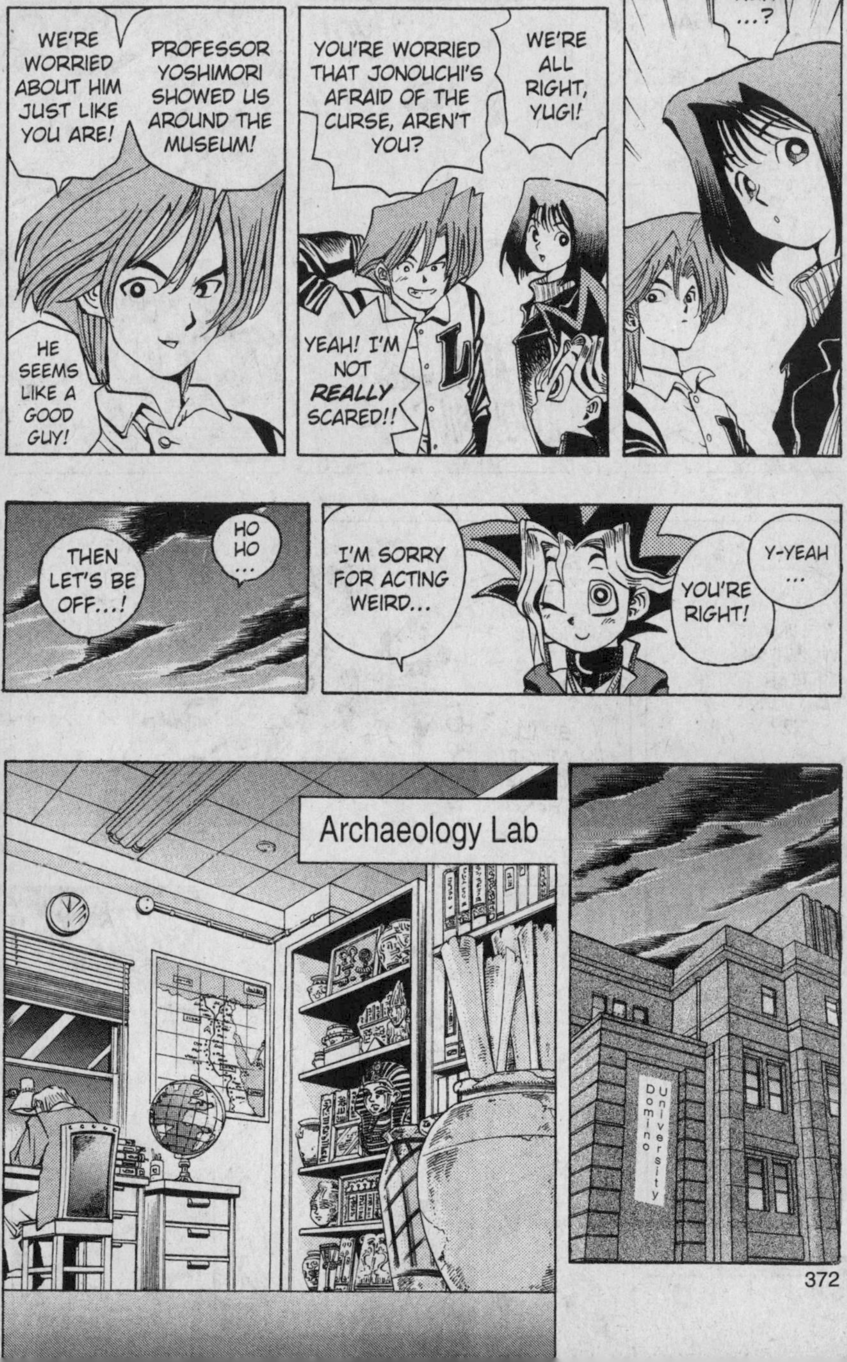
HUH ...?
WE'RE ALL RIGHT, YUGI!
YOU'RE WORRIED THAT JONOUCHI'S AFRAID OF THE CURSE, AREN'T YOU?
YEAH! I'M NOT *REALLY* SCARED!!
PROFESSOR YOSHIMORI SHOWED US AROUND THE MUSEUM!
WE'RE WORRIED ABOUT HIM JUST LIKE YOU ARE!
HE SEEMS LIKE A GOOD GUY!
Y-YEAH ...
YOU'RE RIGHT!
I'M SORRY FOR ACTING WEIRD...
HO HO ...
THEN LET'S BE OFF...!
Domino University
Archaeology Lab

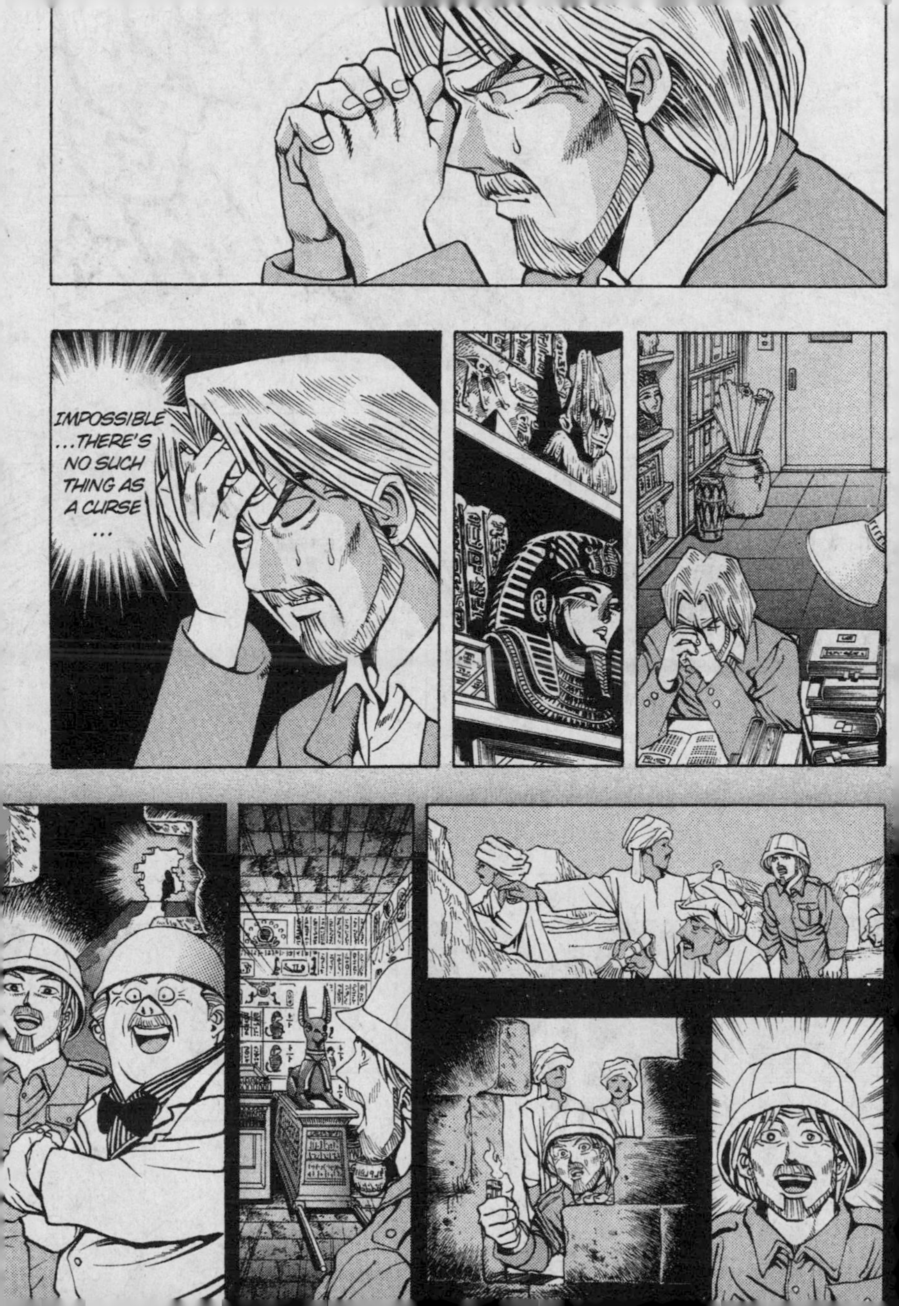
IMPOSSIBLE ...THERE'S NO SUCH THING AS A CURSE ...

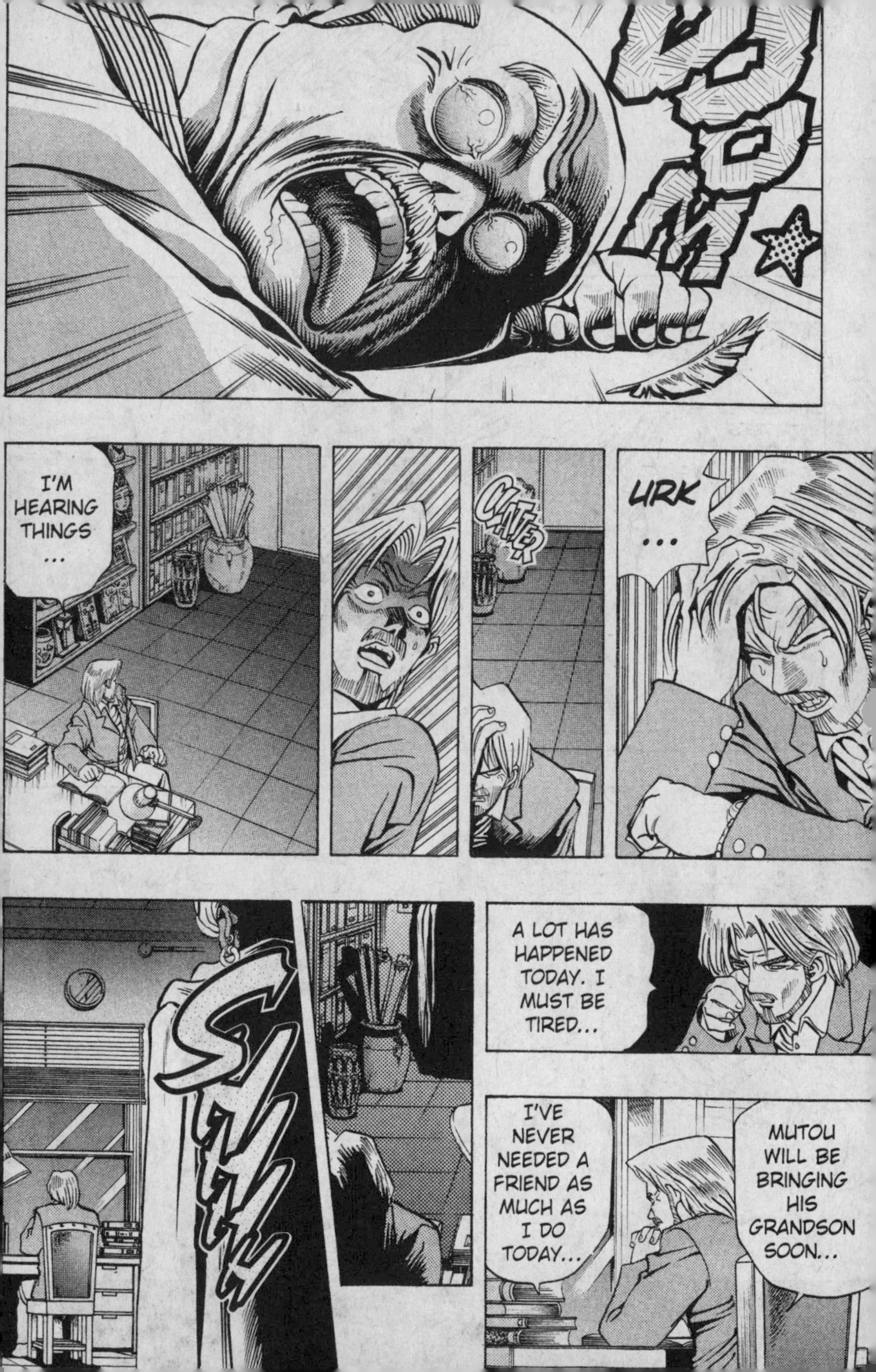
URK ...
I'M HEARING THINGS ...
A LOT HAS HAPPENED TODAY. I MUST BE TIRED...
MUTOU WILL BE BRINGING HIS GRANDSON SOON...
I'VE NEVER NEEDED A FRIEND AS MUCH AS I DO TODAY...

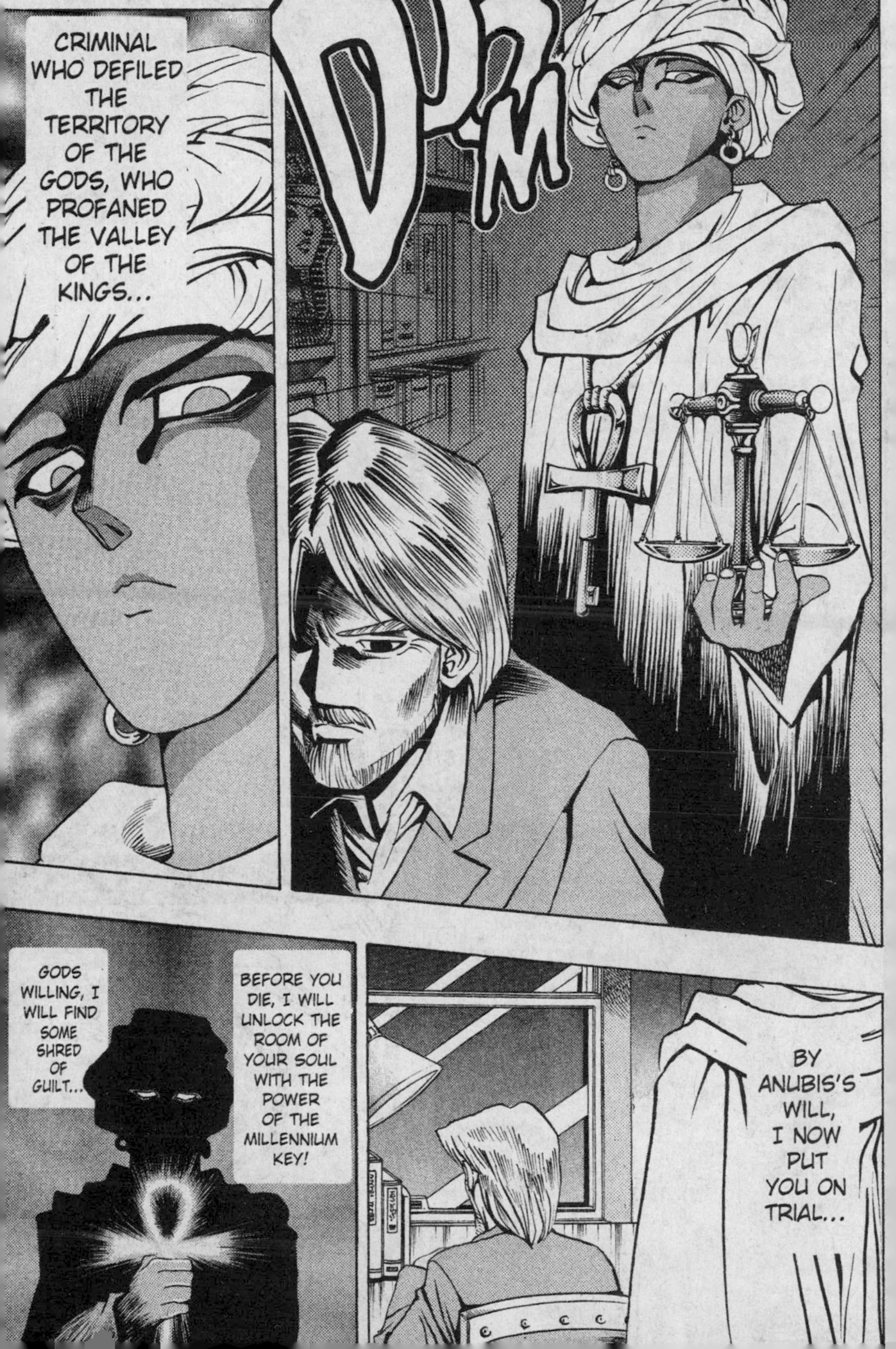
READ THIS WAY
DOOM
CRIMINAL WHO DEFILED THE TERRITORY OF THE GODS, WHO PROFANED THE VALLEY OF THE KINGS...
BY ANUBIS'S WILL, I NOW PUT YOU ON TRIAL...
BEFORE YOU DIE, I WILL UNLOCK THE ROOM OF YOUR SOUL WITH THE POWER OF THE MILLENNIUM KEY!
GODS WILLING, I WILL FIND SOME SHRED OF GUILT...

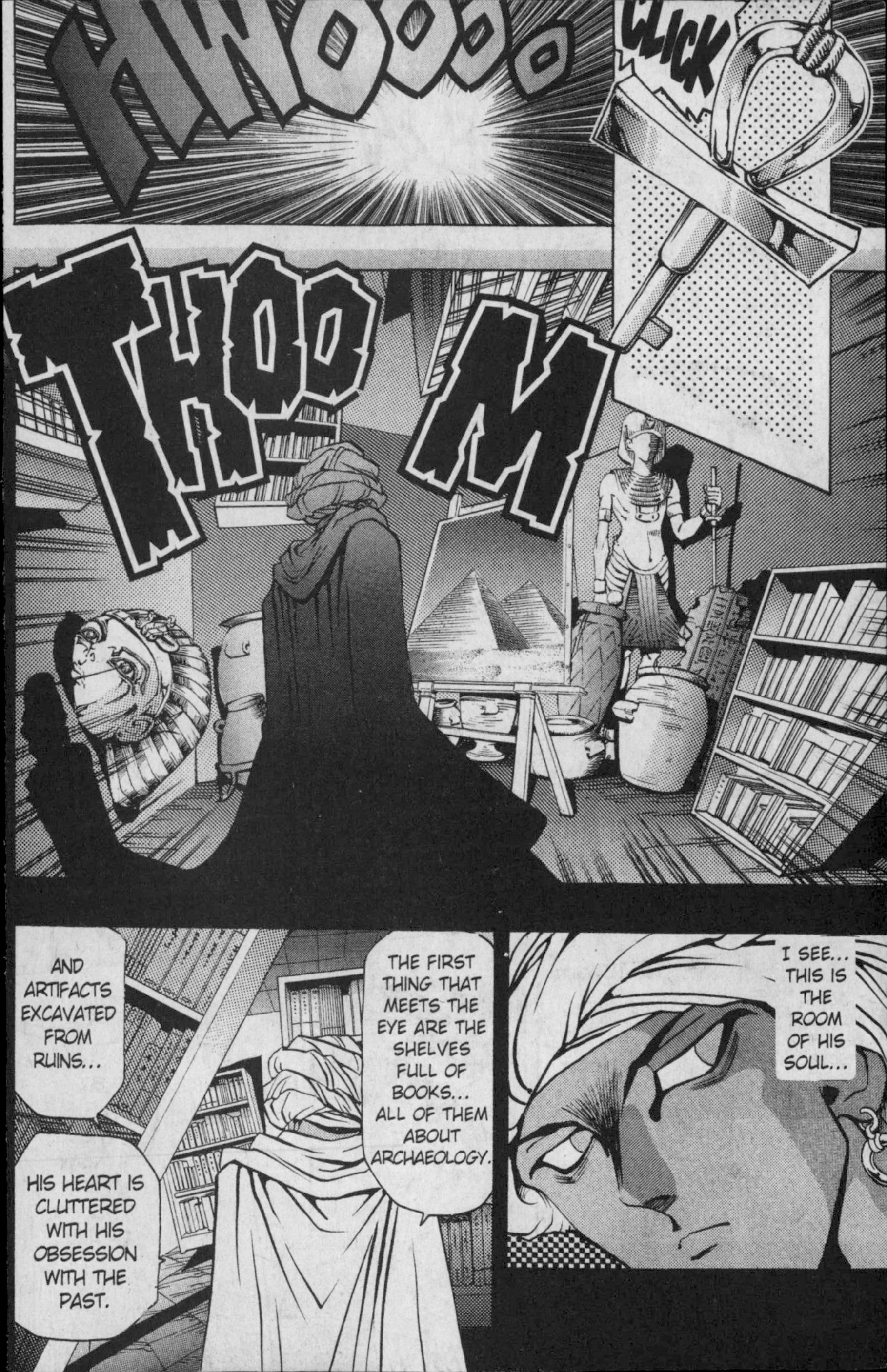
CLICK
HWOOOO
THOOM
I SEE... THIS IS THE ROOM OF HIS SOUL...
THE FIRST THING THAT MEETS THE EYE ARE THE SHELVES FULL OF BOOKS... ALL OF THEM ABOUT ARCHAEOLOGY.
AND ARTIFACTS EXCAVATED FROM RUINS...
HIS HEART IS CLUTTERED WITH HIS OBSESSION WITH THE PAST.

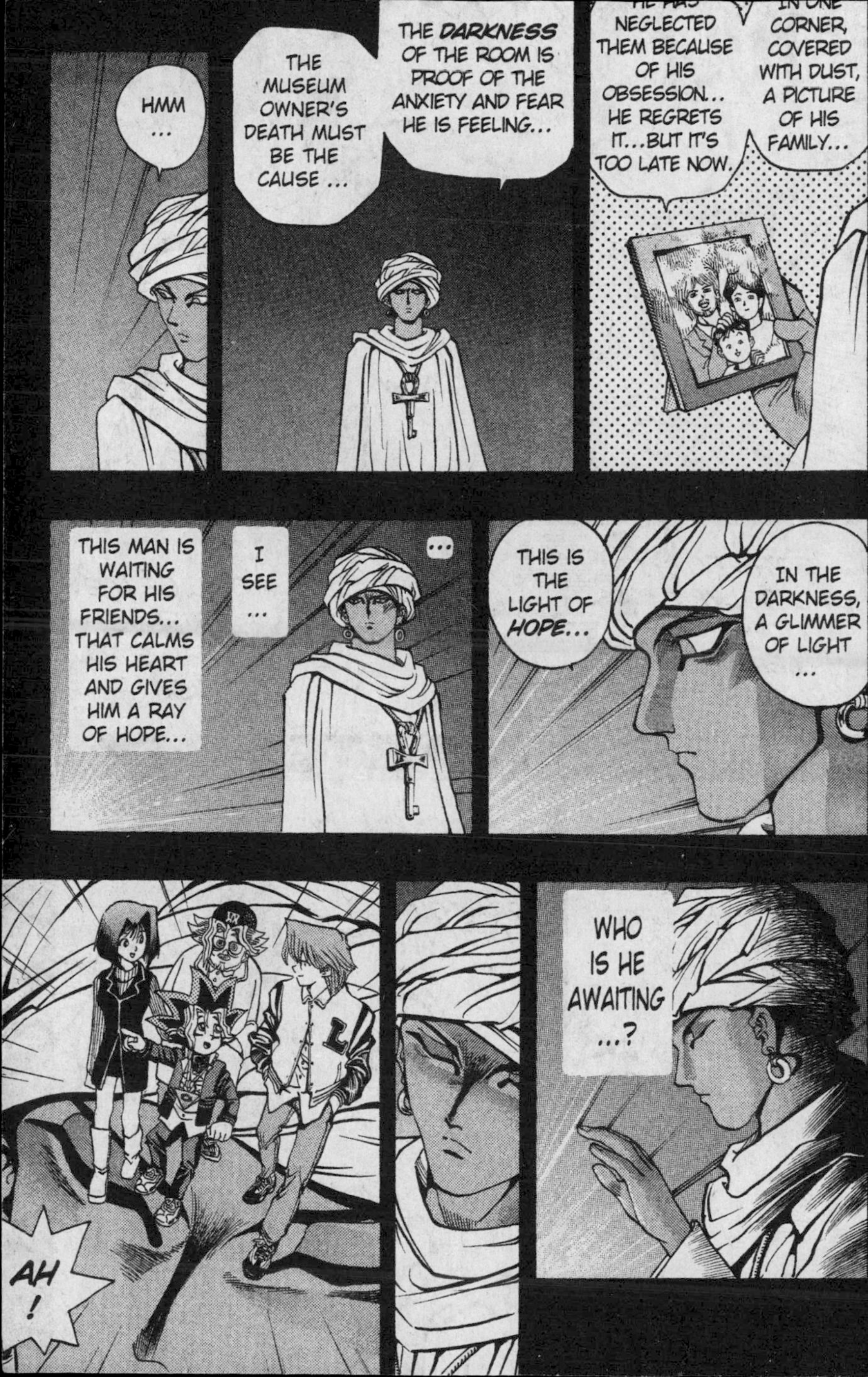

NEGLECTED THEM BECAUSE OF HIS OBSESSION... HE REGRETS IT...BUT IT'S TOO LATE NOW.
CORNER, COVERED WITH DUST, A PICTURE OF HIS FAMILY...
THE *DARKNESS* OF THE ROOM IS PROOF OF THE ANXIETY AND FEAR HE IS FEELING...
THE MUSEUM OWNER'S DEATH MUST BE THE CAUSE ...
HMM ...
IN THE DARKNESS, A GLIMMER OF LIGHT ...
THIS IS THE LIGHT OF *HOPE*...
...
I SEE ...
THIS MAN IS WAITING FOR HIS FRIENDS... THAT CALMS HIS HEART AND GIVES HIM A RAY OF HOPE...
WHO IS HE AWAITING ...?
AH!

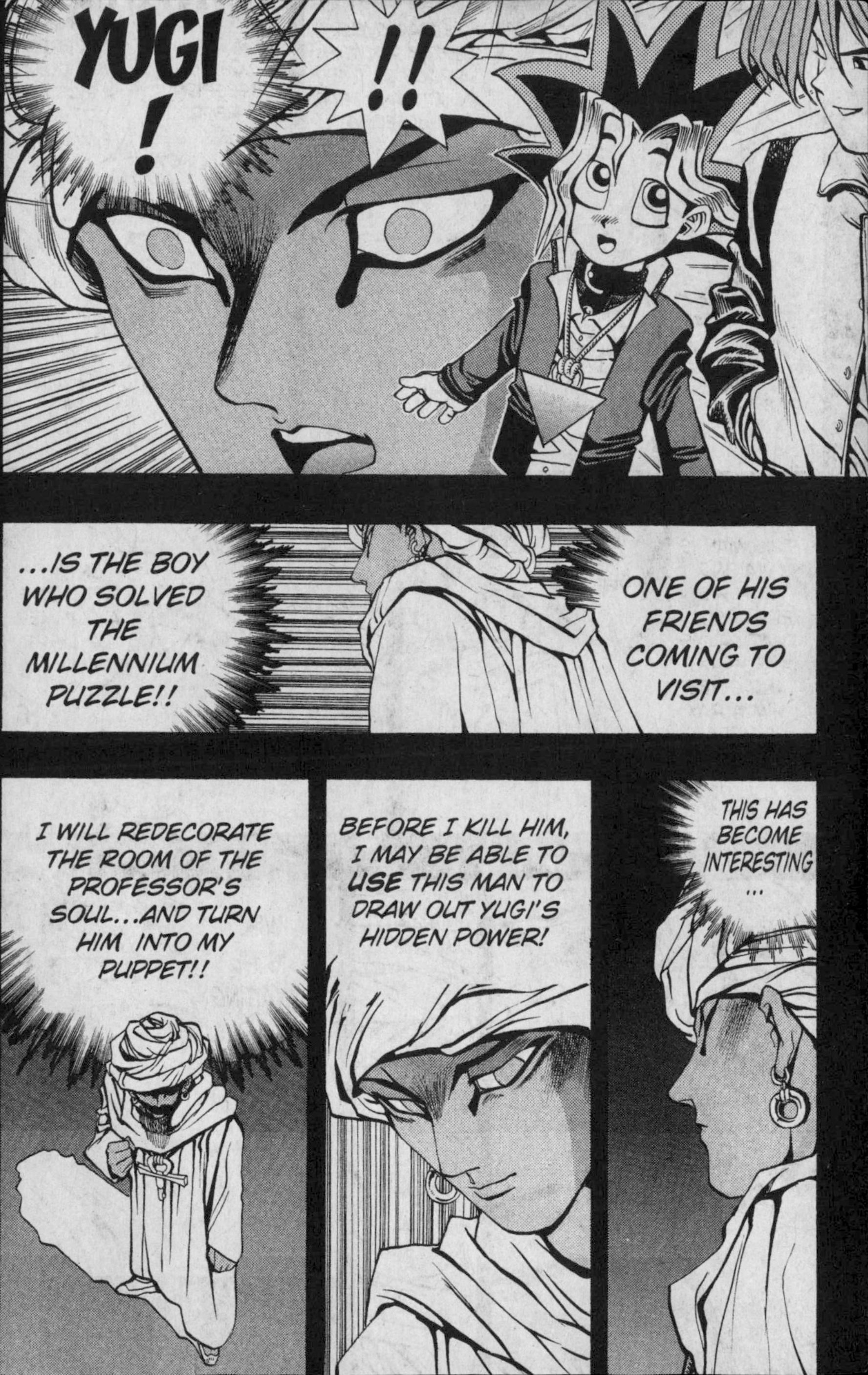
!!
YUGI!
ONE OF HIS FRIENDS COMING TO VISIT...
...IS THE BOY WHO SOLVED THE MILLENNIUM PUZZLE!!
THIS HAS BECOME INTERESTING...
BEFORE I KILL HIM, I MAY BE ABLE TO USE THIS MAN TO DRAW OUT YUGI'S HIDDEN POWER!
I WILL REDECORATE THE ROOM OF THE PROFESSOR'S SOUL...AND TURN HIM INTO MY PUPPET!!

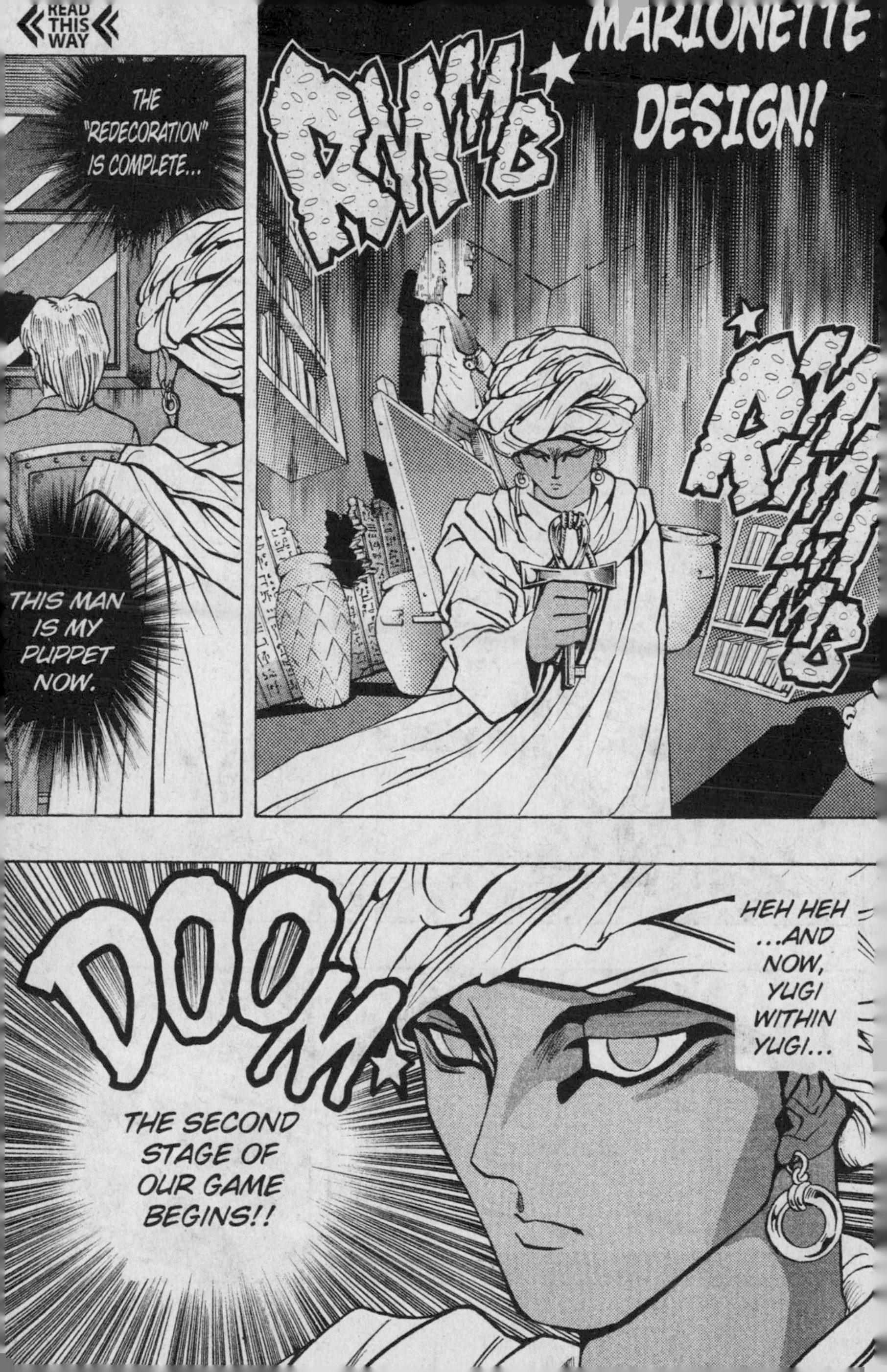
READ THIS WAY
MARIONETTE DESIGN!
RMMB
THE "REDECORATION" IS COMPLETE...
THIS MAN IS MY PUPPET NOW.
HEH HEH ...AND NOW, YUGI WITHIN YUGI...
DOOM
THE SECOND STAGE OF OUR GAME BEGINS!!

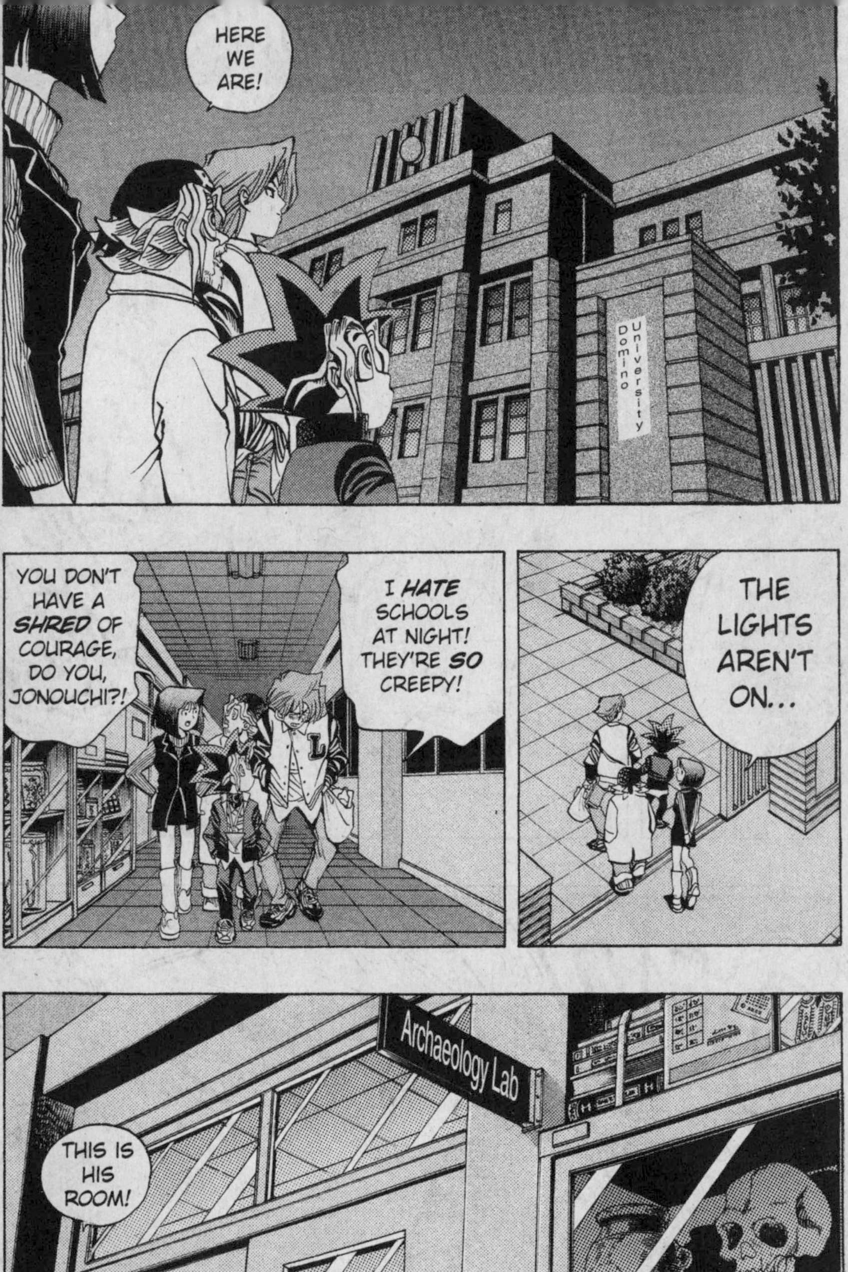
HERE WE ARE!
Domino University
THE LIGHTS AREN'T ON...
I HATE SCHOOLS AT NIGHT! THEY'RE SO CREEPY!
YOU DON'T HAVE A SHRED OF COURAGE, DO YOU, JONOUCHI?!
Archaeology Lab
THIS IS HIS ROOM!

READ THIS WAY

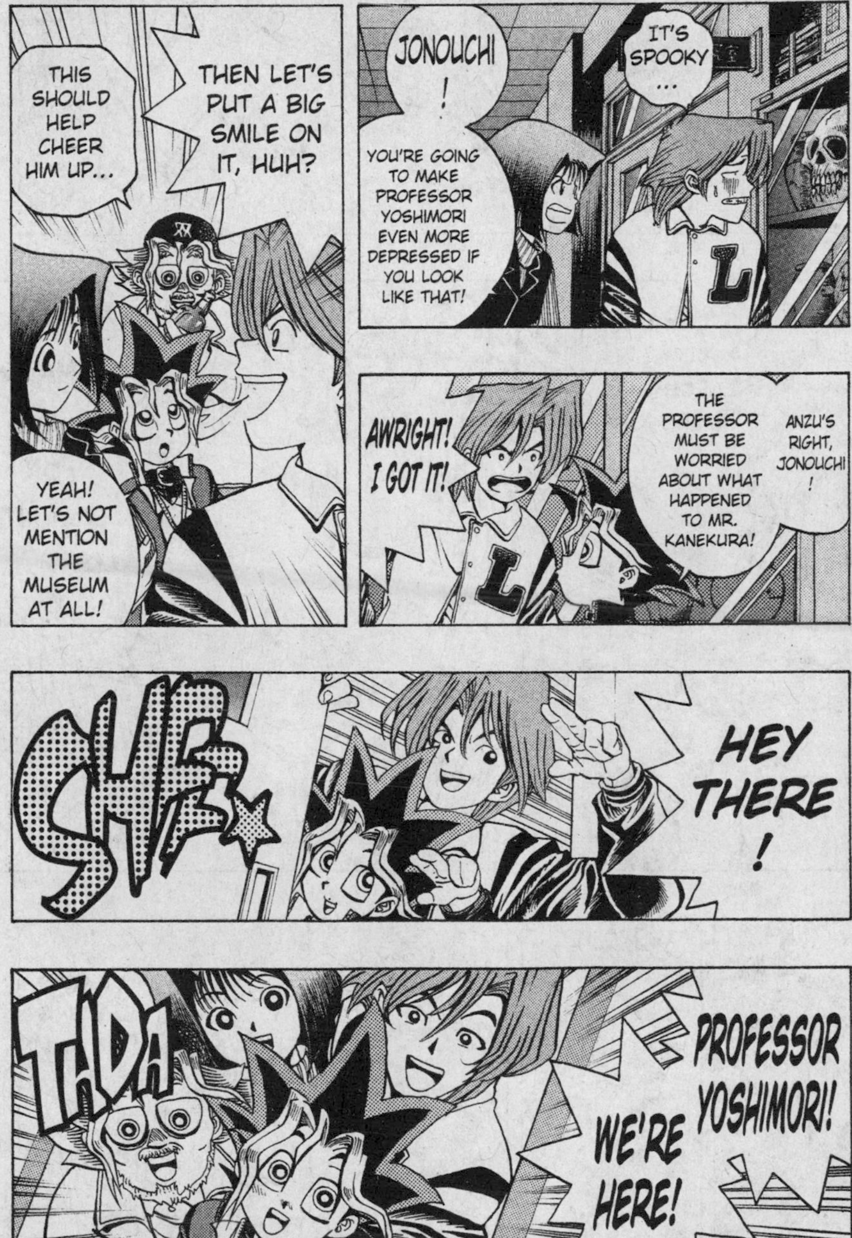
IT'S SPOOKY...
JONOUCHI!
YOU'RE GOING TO MAKE PROFESSOR YOSHIMORI EVEN MORE DEPRESSED IF YOU LOOK LIKE THAT!
ANZU'S RIGHT, JONOUCHI!
THE PROFESSOR MUST BE WORRIED ABOUT WHAT HAPPENED TO MR. KANEKURA!
AWRIGHT! I GOT IT!
THEN LET'S PUT A BIG SMILE ON IT, HUH?
THIS SHOULD HELP CHEER HIM UP...
YEAH! LET'S NOT MENTION THE MUSEUM AT ALL!
HEY THERE!
SHF
PROFESSOR YOSHIMORI!
WE'RE HERE!
TADA

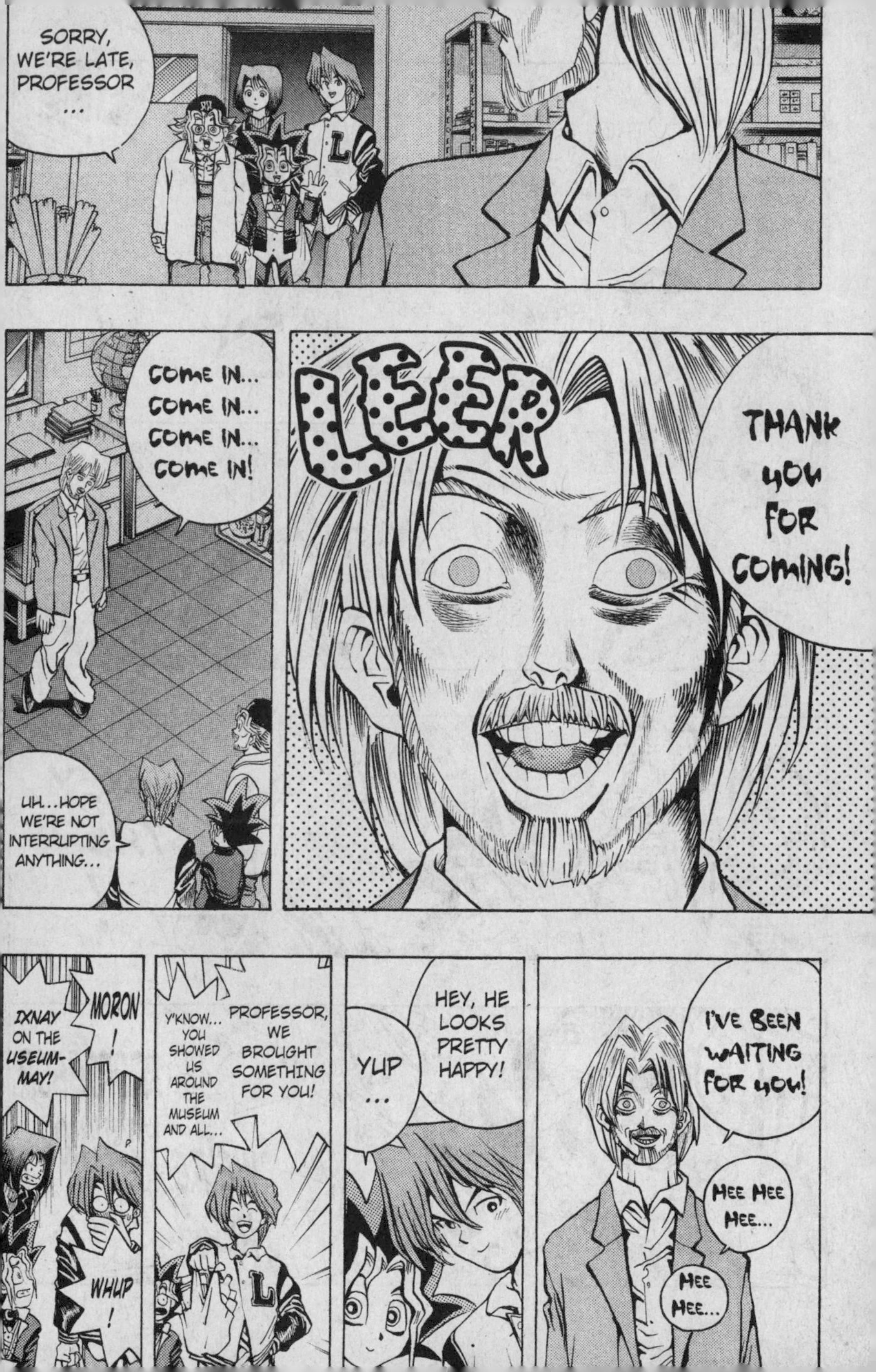
SORRY, WE'RE LATE, PROFESSOR ...
LEER
THANK YOU FOR COMING!
COME IN... COME IN... COME IN... COME IN!
UH...HOPE WE'RE NOT INTERRUPTING ANYTHING...
I'VE BEEN WAITING FOR YOU!
HEE HEE HEE...
HEE HEE...
HEY, HE LOOKS PRETTY HAPPY!
YUP ...
PROFESSOR, WE BROUGHT SOMETHING FOR YOU!
Y'KNOW... YOU SHOWED US AROUND THE MUSEUM AND ALL...
MORON!
IXNAY ON THE USEUM-MAY!
WHUP!

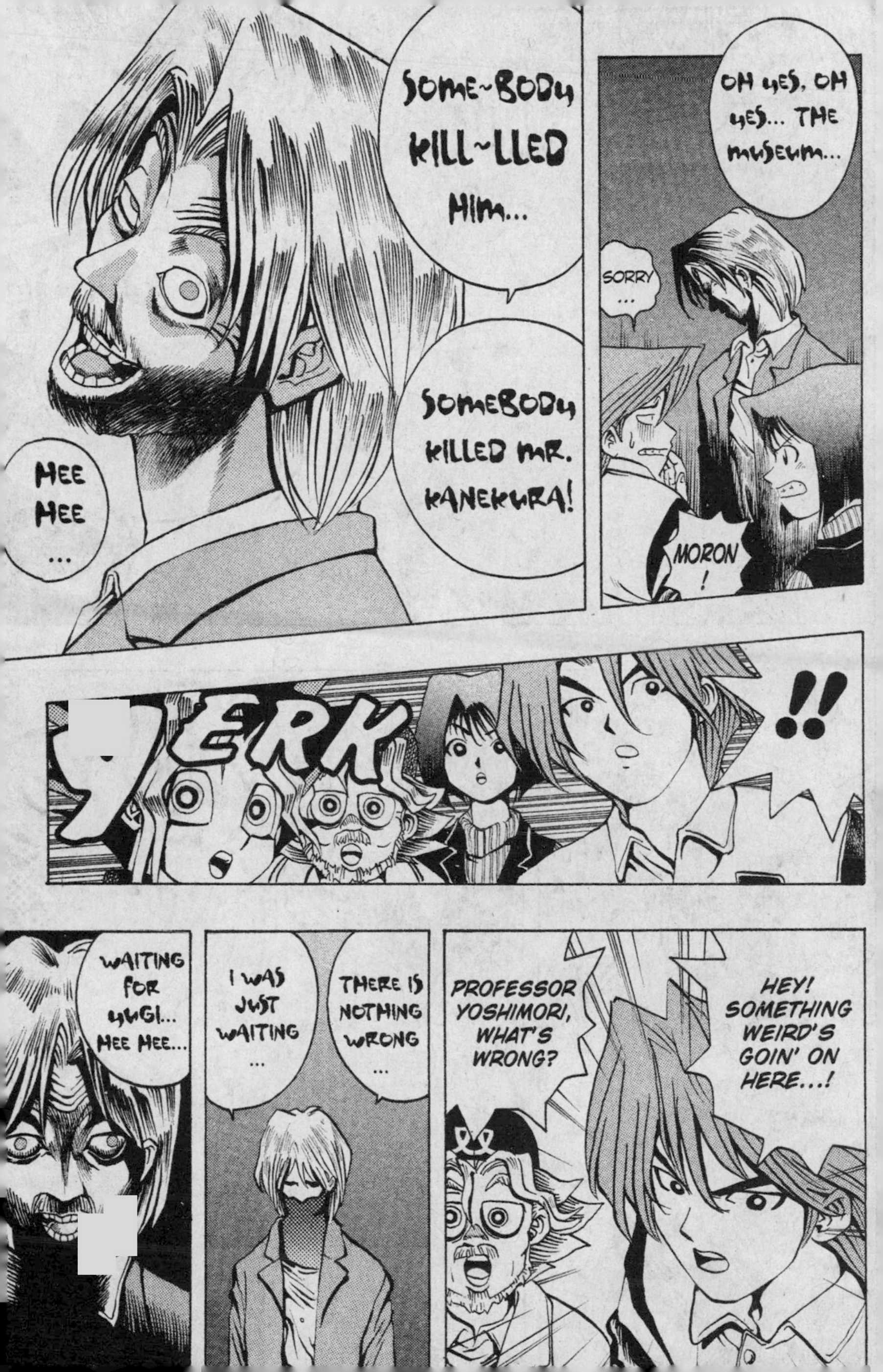
OH YES, OH YES... THE MUSEUM...
SORRY...
MORON!
SOME~BODY KILL~LLED HIM...
SOMEBODY KILLED MR. KANEKURA!
HEE HEE...
!!
ERK
HEY! SOMETHING WEIRD'S GOIN' ON HERE...!
PROFESSOR YOSHIMORI, WHAT'S WRONG?
THERE IS NOTHING WRONG...
I WAS JUST WAITING...
WAITING FOR YUGI... HEE HEE...

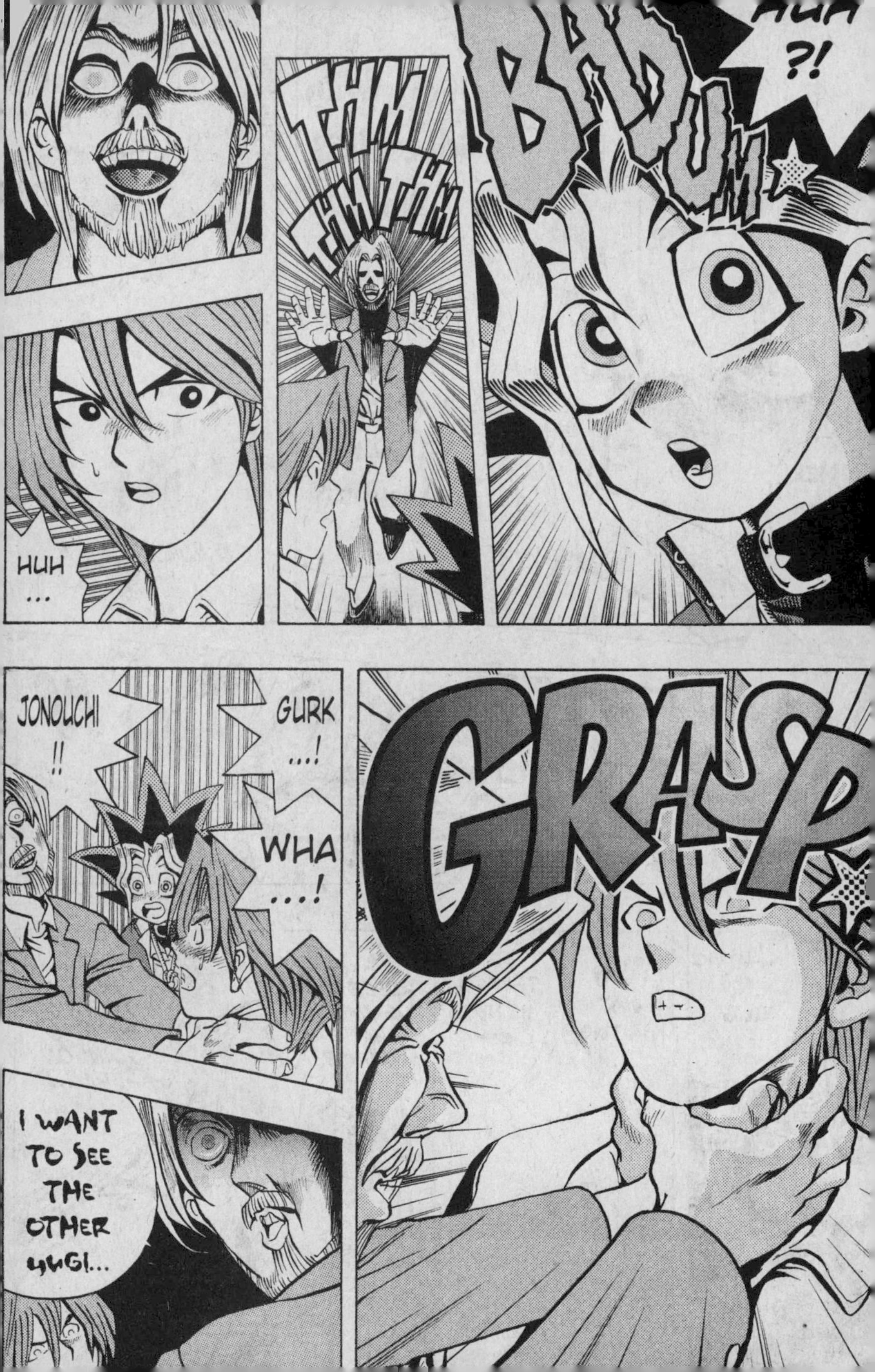
BADUM
HUH ?!
THM THM THM
HUH ...
GRASP
GURK ...!
WHA ...!
JONOUCHI !!
I WANT TO SEE THE OTHER YUGI...

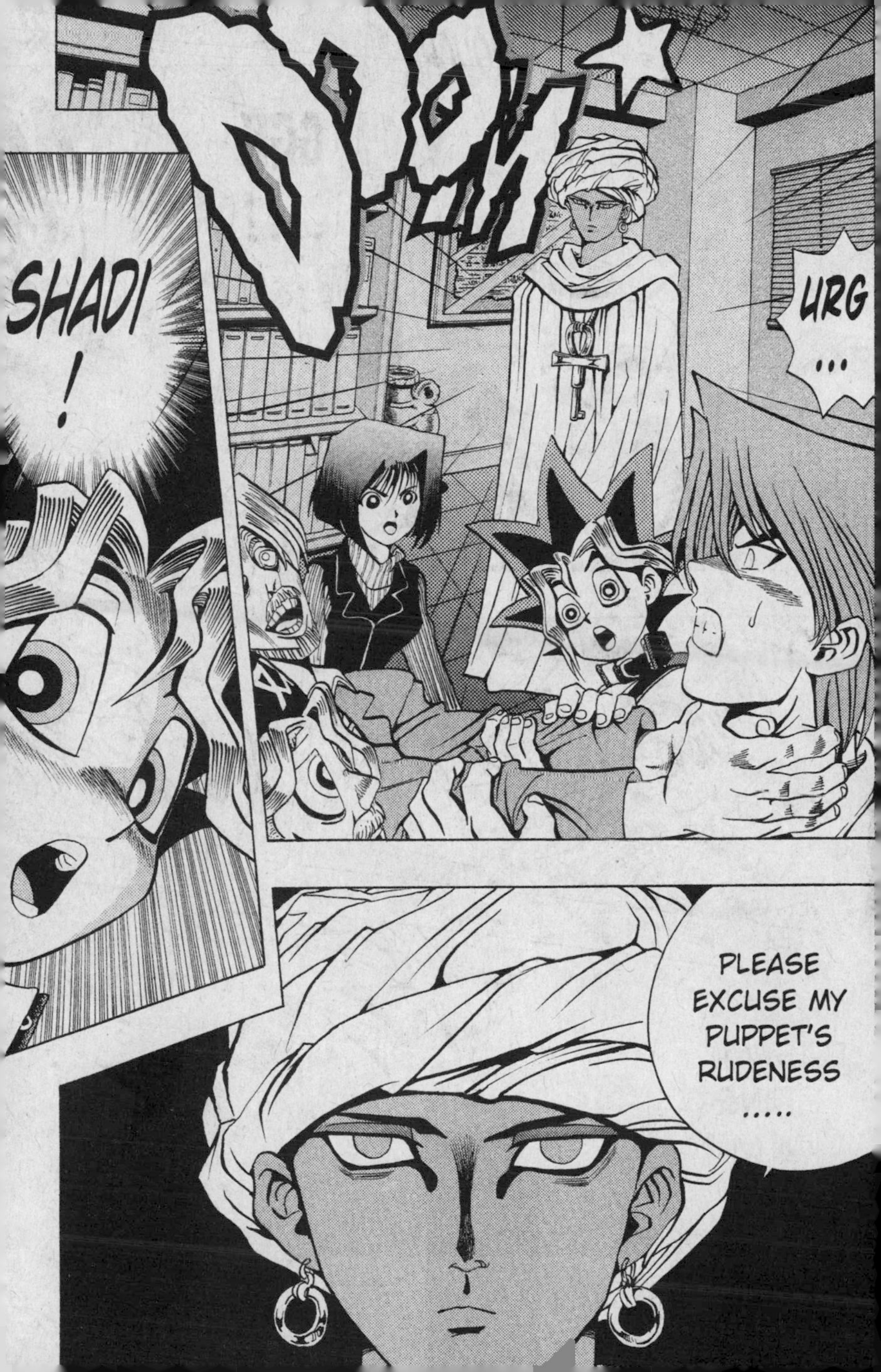
URG ...
SHADI !
PLEASE EXCUSE MY PUPPET'S RUDENESS .....

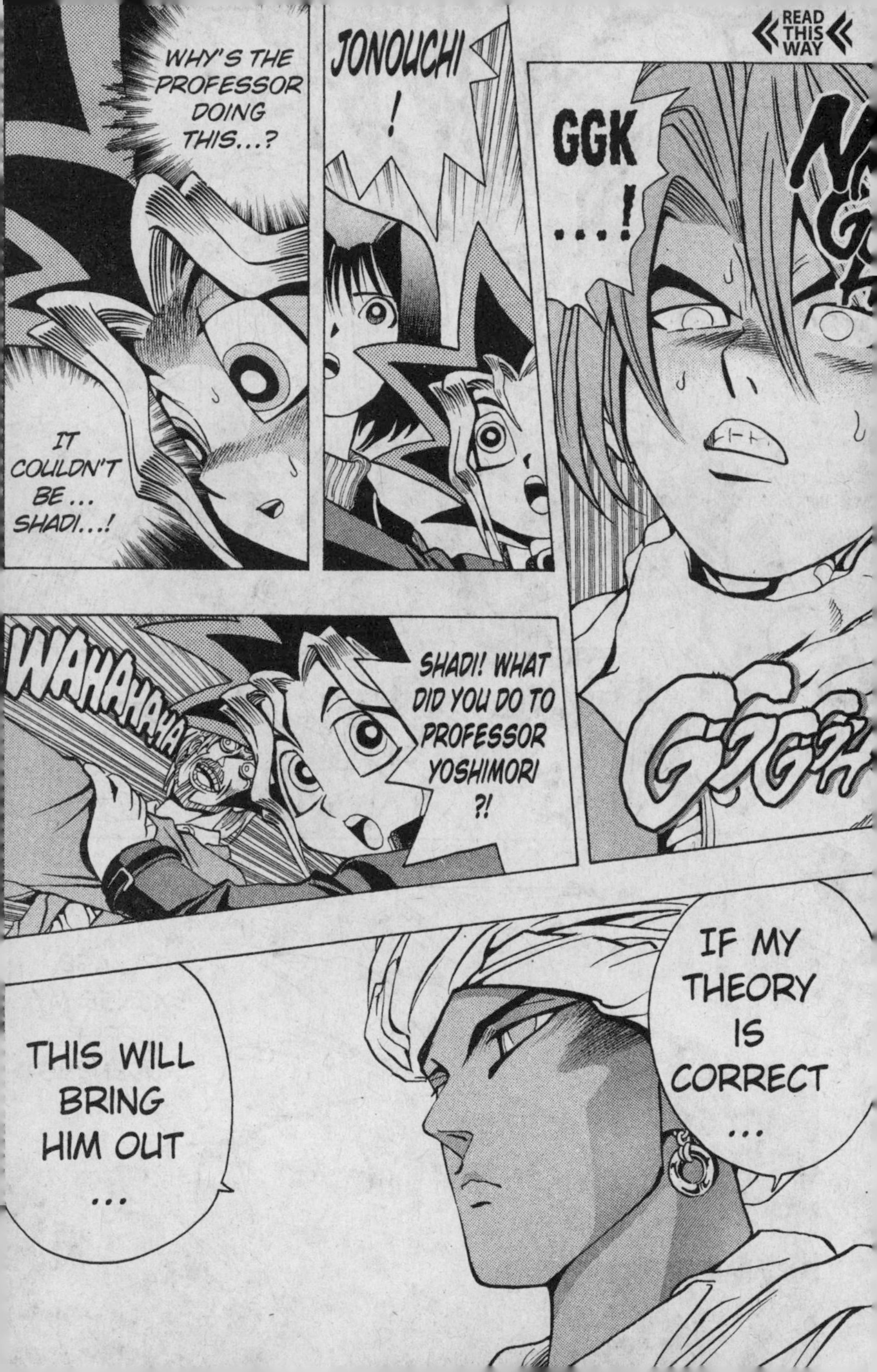
READ THIS WAY
GGK ...!
JONOUCHI !
WHY'S THE PROFESSOR DOING THIS...?
IT COULDN'T BE... SHADI...!
GGGGH
SHADI! WHAT DID YOU DO TO PROFESSOR YOSHIMORI ?!
WAHAHAHAHA
IF MY THEORY IS CORRECT ...
THIS WILL BRING HIM OUT ...

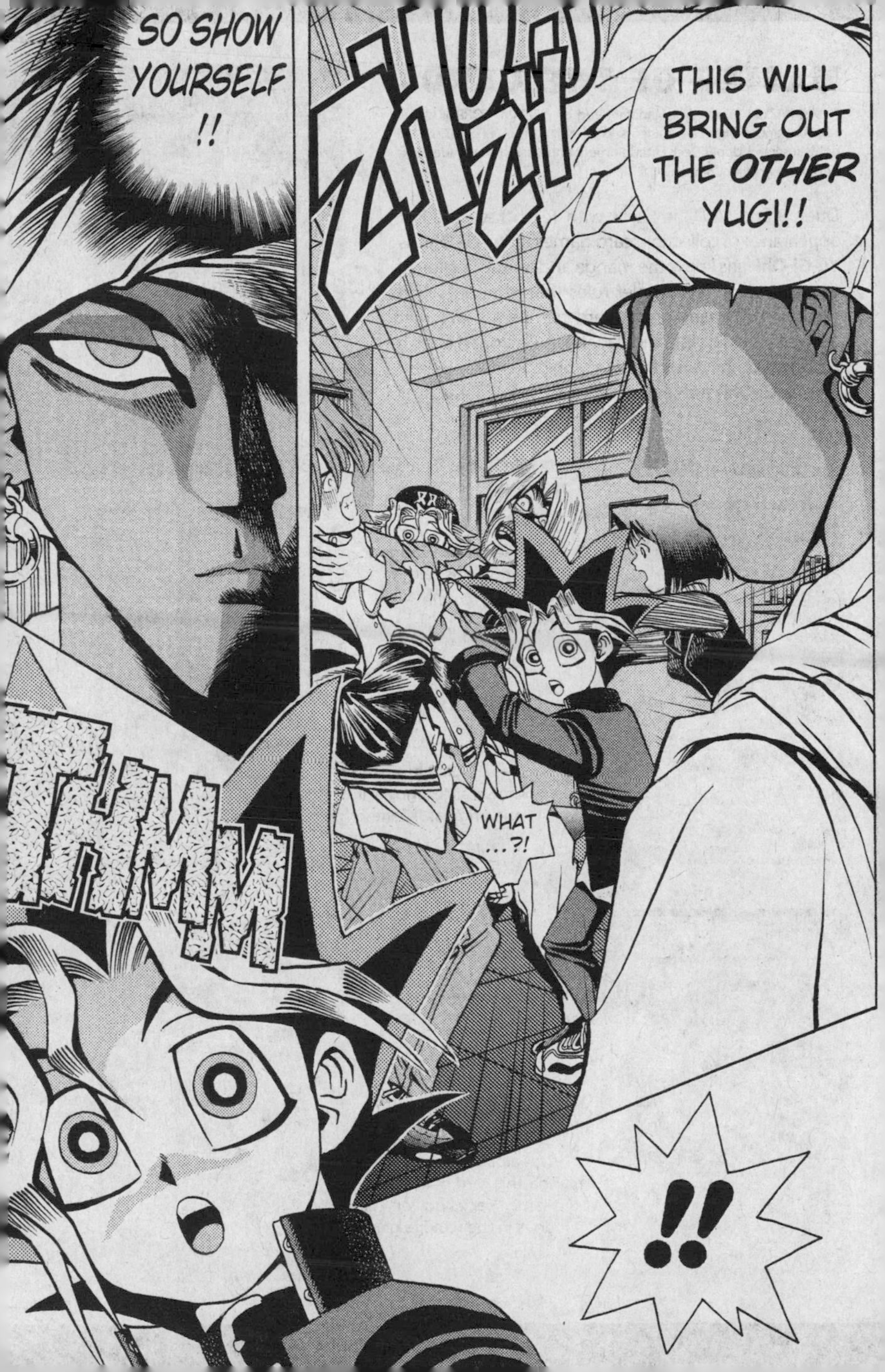
THIS WILL BRING OUT THE OTHER YUGI!!
WHAT ...?!
SO SHOW YOURSELF !!
THMM
!!

MASTER OF THE CARDS

Duels 9 and 10 ("The Cards with Teeth") are the first appearance of collectible card games in **Yu-Gi-Oh!**. As **Yu-Gi-Oh!** fans know, the manga and anime version of the card game has simpler rules than the real-world version. Also, many of the card names are different between the English and Japanese versions. Here's a rundown of the cards in this graphic novel—the very first **Yu-Gi-Oh!** cards ever created by Kazuki Takahashi!

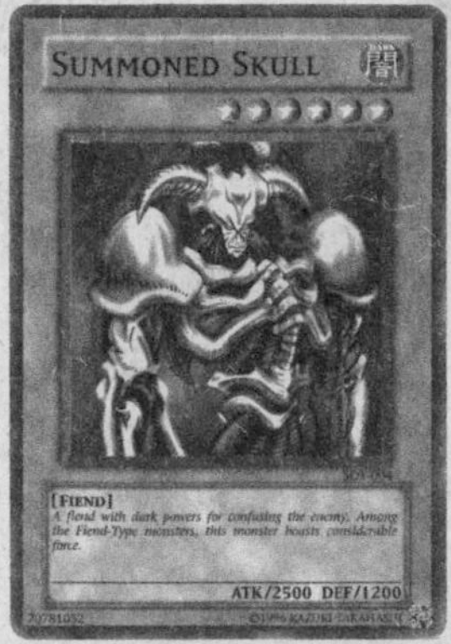
SUMMONED SKULL
[FIEND]
A fiend with dark powers for confusing the enemy. Among the Fiend-Type monsters, this monster boasts considerable force.
ATK/2500 DEF/1200

1. Summoned Skull
Known as "Summoned Demon" in the original Japanese.

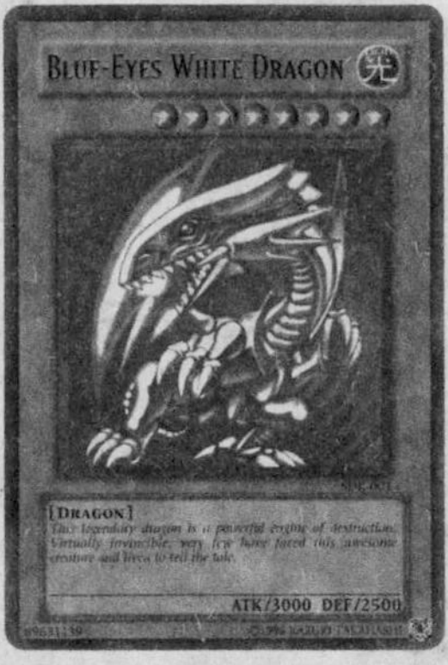
BLUE-EYES WHITE DRAGON
[DRAGON]
ATK/3000 DEF/2500

2. Blue-Eyes White Dragon
In the manga, this card is extremely rare—only a few are supposed to exist.

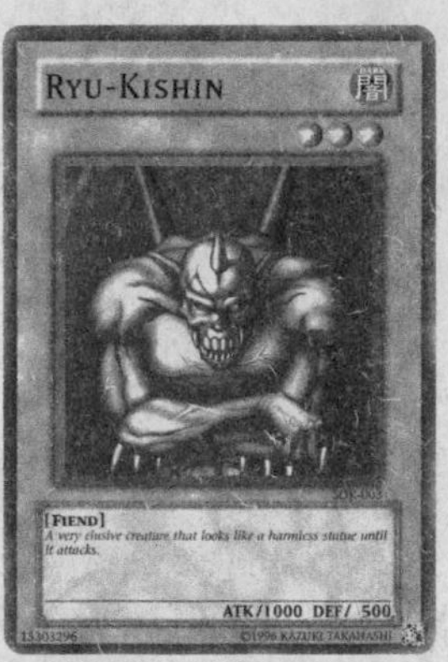
RYU-KISHIN
[FIEND]
A very elusive creature that looks like a harmless statue until it attacks.
ATK/1000 DEF/ 500

3. Ryu-Kishin
Known as "Gargoyle" in the original Japanese.

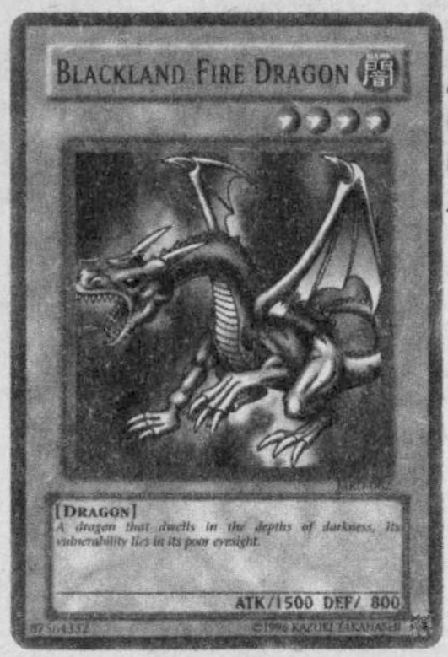
BLACKLAND FIRE DRAGON
[DRAGON]
A dragon that dwells in the depths of darkness. Its vulnerability lies in its poor eyesight.
ATK/1500 DEF/ 800

4. Blackland Fire Dragon
Known as "Dragon of Darkness" in the original Japanese.

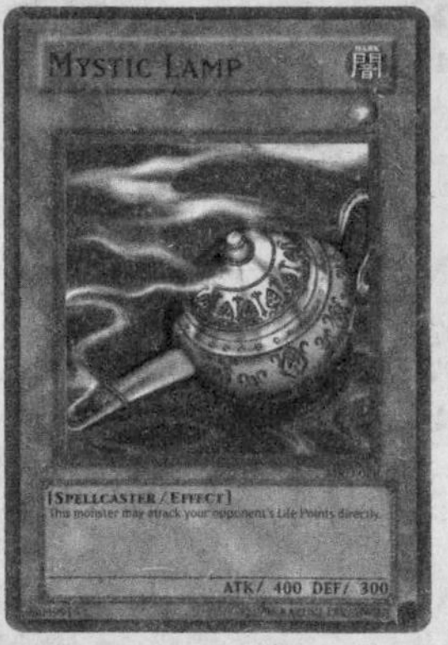
MYSTIC LAMP
[SPELLCASTER/EFFECT]
This monster may attack your opponent's Life Points directly.
ATK/ 400 DEF/ 300

5. Mystic Lamp
Not actually played in the manga, this card doesn't have the same special powers that it does in the real-life game.

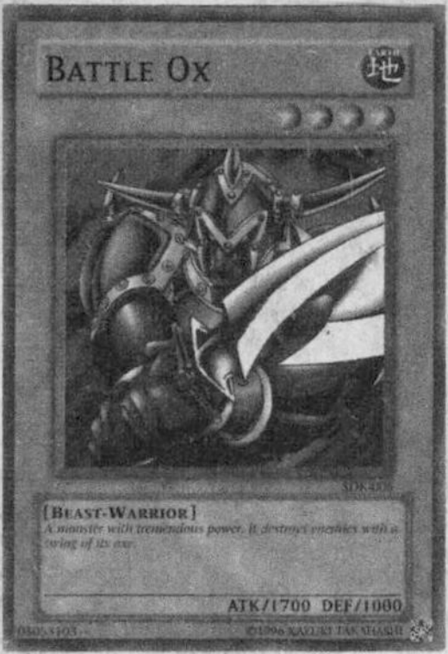

BATTLE OX
[BEAST-WARRIOR]
ATK/1700 DEF/1000

6. Battle Ox
Known as "Minotaurus" in the original Japanese. "Minotaurus" is the usual Japanese spelling of "Minotaur," the bull-headed monster from Greek myth.

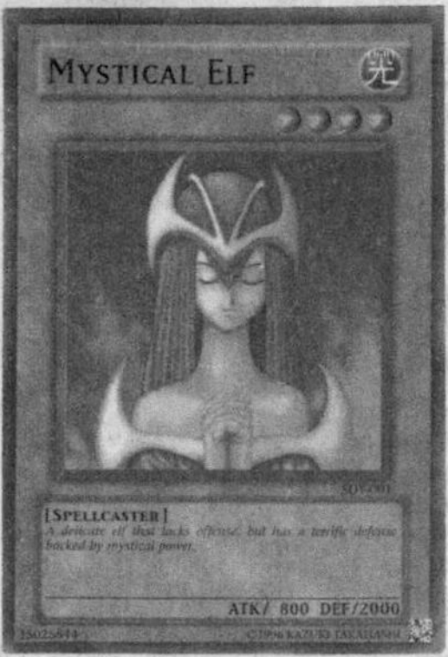

MYSTICAL ELF
[SPELLCASTER]
ATK/ 800 DEF/2000

7. Mystical Elf
Known as "Holy Elf" in the original Japanese.

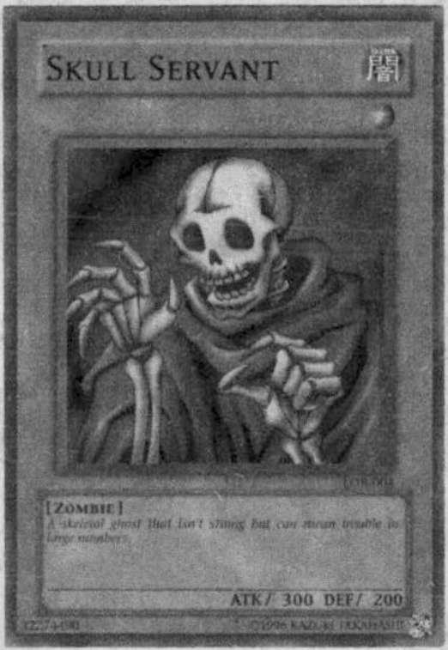

SKULL SERVANT
[ZOMBIE]
ATK/ 300 DEF/ 200

8. Skull Servant
Known as "Wight" in the original Japanese. A "wight" is an old English word for a ghost or a living corpse.

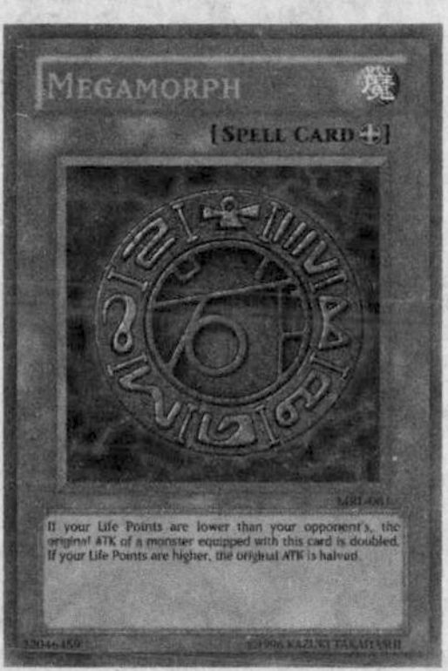

MEGAMORPH
[SPELL CARD]

9. Megamorph
In the real-life game, this card has different powers than it does in the manga, maybe so you don't have to do so much math to figure out 20% of your card's values. Because the manga and real-life cards have different powers, we translated the manga card's name as "Giant's Might" ("Become Giant" in the original Japanese).

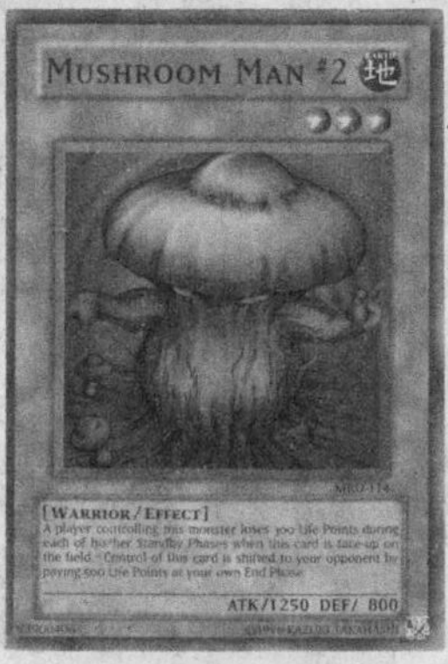

MUSHROOM MAN #2
[WARRIOR / EFFECT]
ATK/1250 DEF/ 800

10. Mushroom Man #2
This card only shows up briefly in the manga, and it has lower attack and defense values.

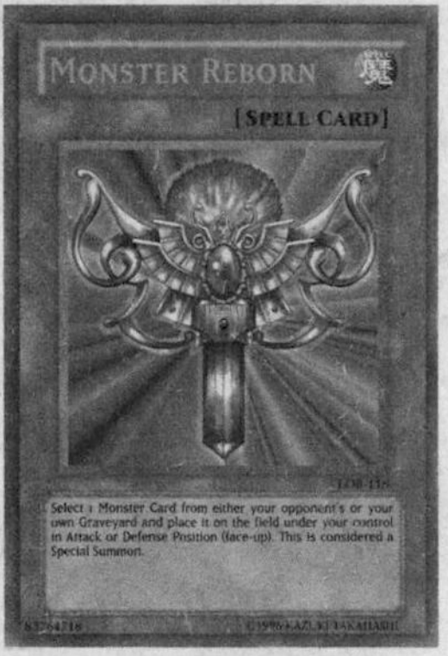

MONSTER REBORN
[SPELL CARD]

11. Monster Reborn
In the manga and the Japanese card game, the art for this card is an ankh—the Egyptian symbol of life and rebirth.

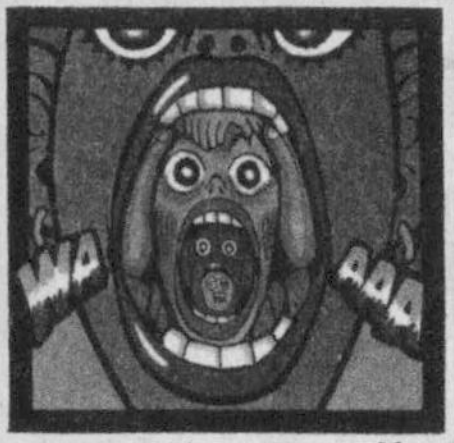
WA
AAA

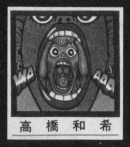

高 橋 和 希

MAN, IT REALLY IS HARD WORKING ON A WEEKLY DEADLINE! I'M SO BUSY, I CAN'T PLAY THE GAMES I LIKE. I WANNA SIT BACK AND GET SOME GAMING TIME IN, AND THE GAME I WANT TO PLAY MOST RIGHT NOW IS... *TABLETOP ROLEPLAYING GAMES (RPGS)!* IN THE PAST, ME AND MY FRIENDS WOULD GET TOGETHER AND HAVE A GOOD OL' TIME DOING THIS. WE'D STAY UP ALL NIGHT AND HAVE TONS OF FUN. I DEFINITELY RECOMMEND TABLETOP RPGS TO ANYONE. RECENTLY, I HAVEN'T BEEN ABLE TO HOOK UP WITH MY FRIENDS, BUT SOON WE GOTTA GET TOGETHER AND FIRE IT UP AGAIN!

—KAZUKI TAKAHASHI, 1997

SHONEN JUMP MANGA

Vol. 3
CAPSULE MONSTER CHESS

STORY AND ART BY
KAZUKI TAKAHASHI

THE STORY SO FAR...

When an Egyptian museum exhibit came to Tokyo, an unwelcome visitor came along with it: Shadi, the keeper of the Millennium Items, who sought to kill the archaeologist and museum owner who had desecrated the tomb. But Shadi was startled to discover that the Millennium Puzzle had been solved for the first time in 3,000 years—by Yugi Mutou! Using the Millennium Key to go inside Yugi's soul, Shadi fought the "other" Yugi—and was defeated. Determined to have a rematch, Shadi turned the archaeologist into a mindless zombie, to terrorize Yugi's "other self" into coming out!

DARK YUGI

武藤遊戯

YUGI MUTOU

The main character. When he solved the ancient Egyptian Millennium Puzzle, he developed an alter ego, "Dark Yugi," which emerges in times of stress. Afterwards, the regular Yugi doesn't remember what happened.

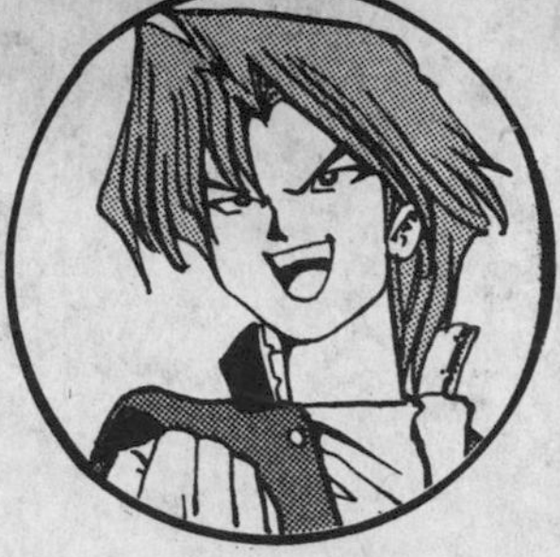

城之内克也

KATSUYA JONOUCHI

Yugi's classmate, a tough guy who gets in lots of fights. He used to think Yugi was a wimp, but now they are good friends. In the English anime he's known as "Joey Wheeler."

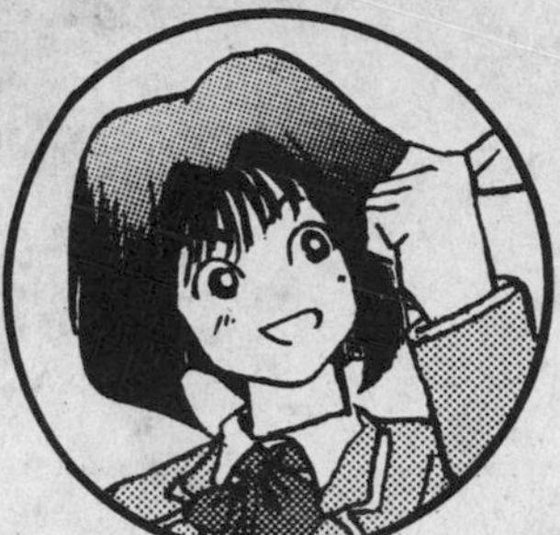

真崎杏子

ANZU MAZAKI

Yugi's classmate and childhood friend. She fell in love with the charismatic voice of Yugi's alter ego, but doesn't know that they're the same person. Her first name means "Apricot." In the English anime she's known as "Téa Gardner."

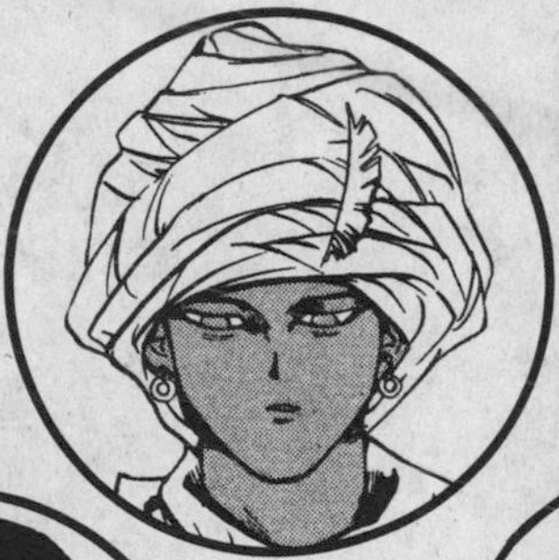

SHADI

A mysterious mystic whose bloodline has guarded the tombs of Egypt for 3000 years. He owns the Millennium Scales, which can weigh a person's sins, and the Millennium Key, which he can use to look inside people's souls and control them.

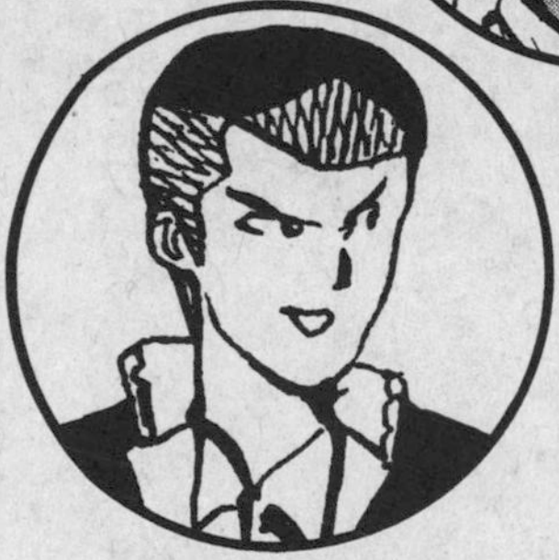

本田ヒロト

HIROTO HONDA

Yugi's classmate, a friend of Jonouchi. In the English anime he's known as "Tristan Taylor."

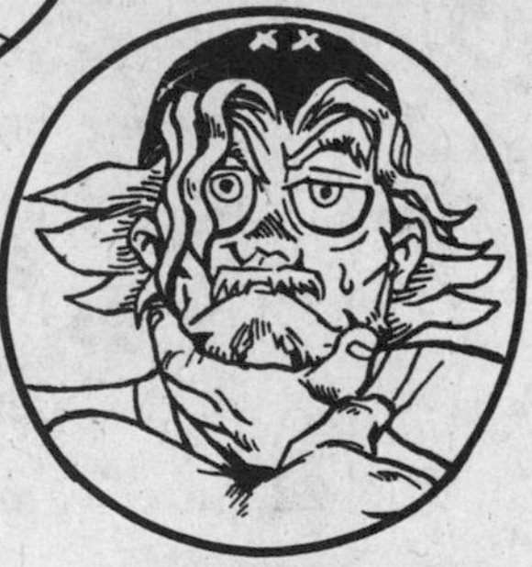

武藤双六

SUGOROKU MUTOU

Yugi's grandfather, the owner of the Kame ("Turtle") game store, and a friend of the archaeologist Professor Yoshimori.

Yu-Gi-Oh!

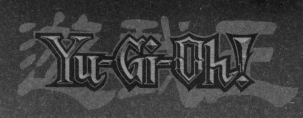

Vol. 3

CONTENTS

Duel 16: Shadi's Challenge

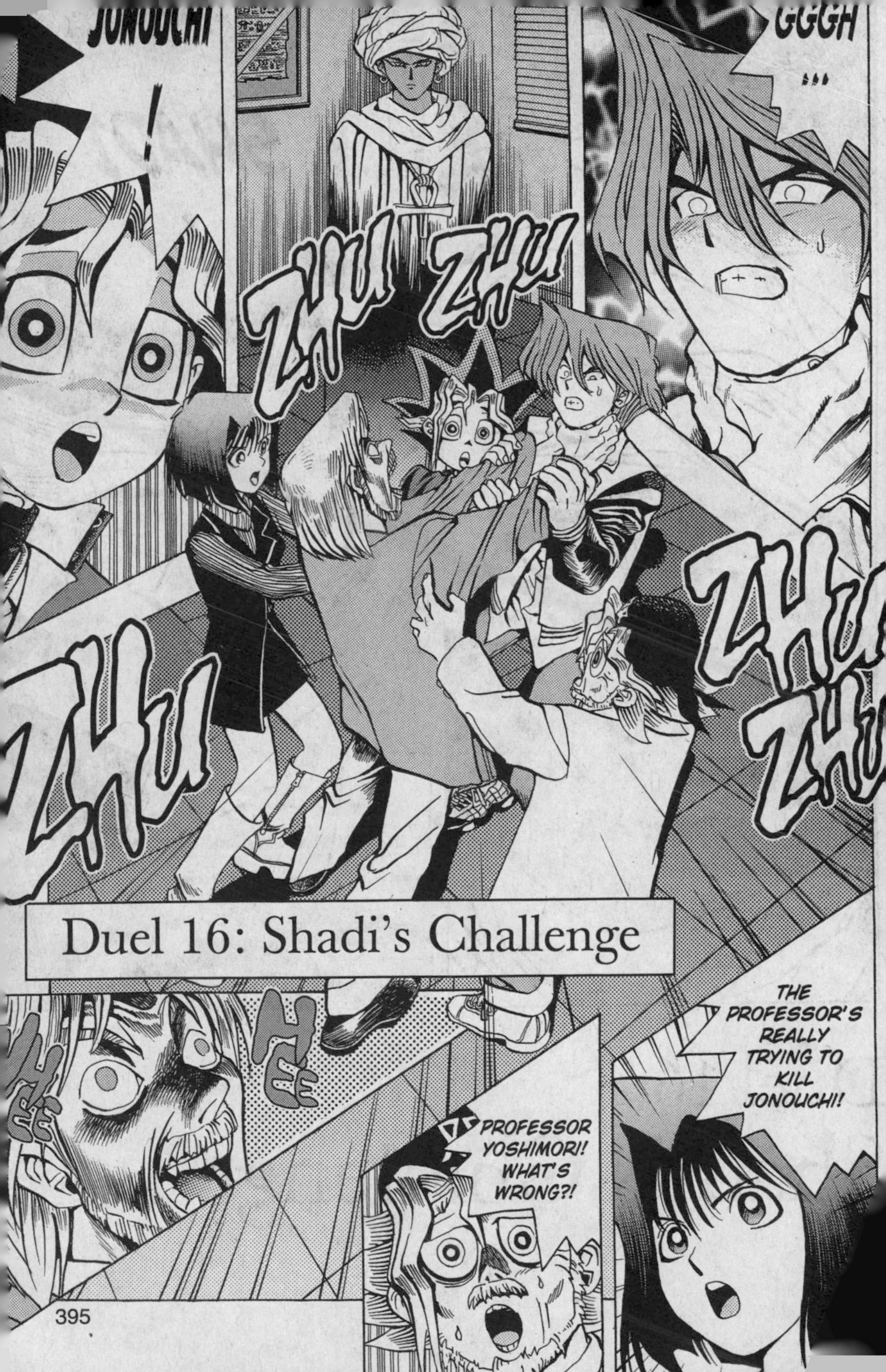
GGGH...
ZHU ZHU
JONOUCHI!
ZHU ZHU
ZHU
THE PROFESSOR'S REALLY TRYING TO KILL JONOUCHI!
PROFESSOR YOSHIMORI! WHAT'S WRONG?!
HE HE

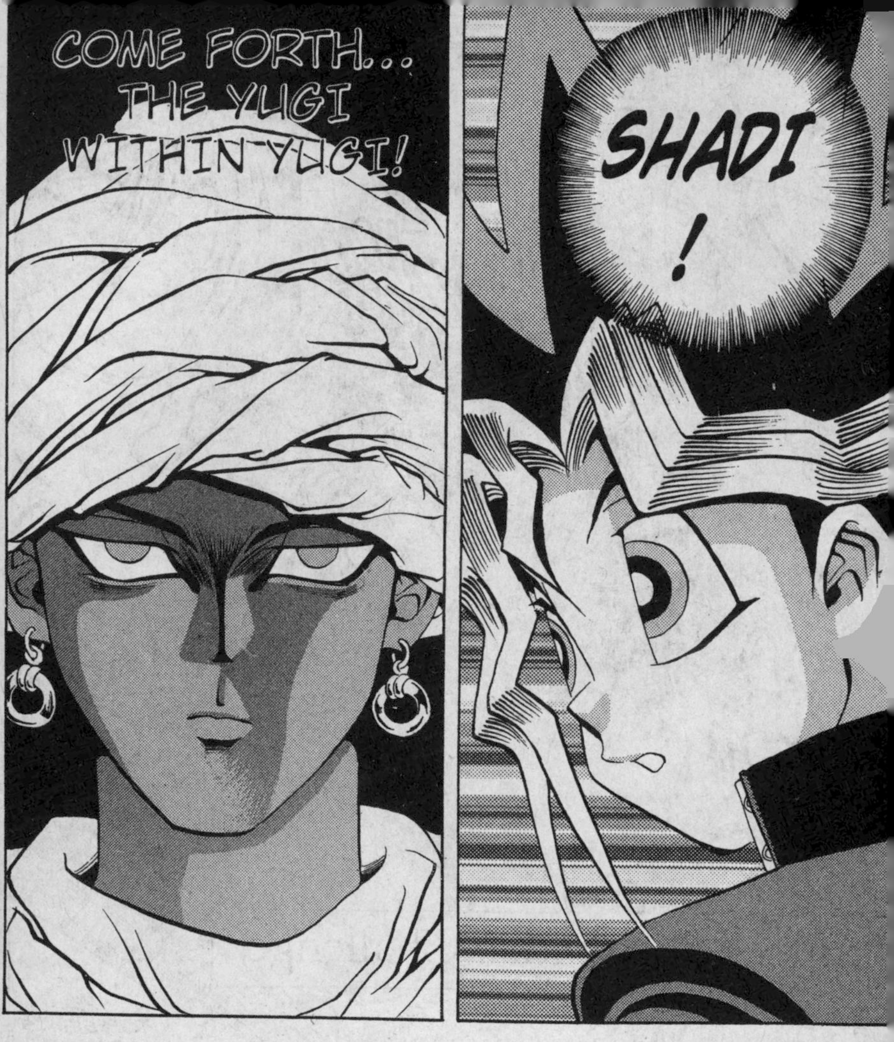
SHADI!
COME FORTH... THE YUGI WITHIN YUGI!

Duel 16: Shadi's Challenge

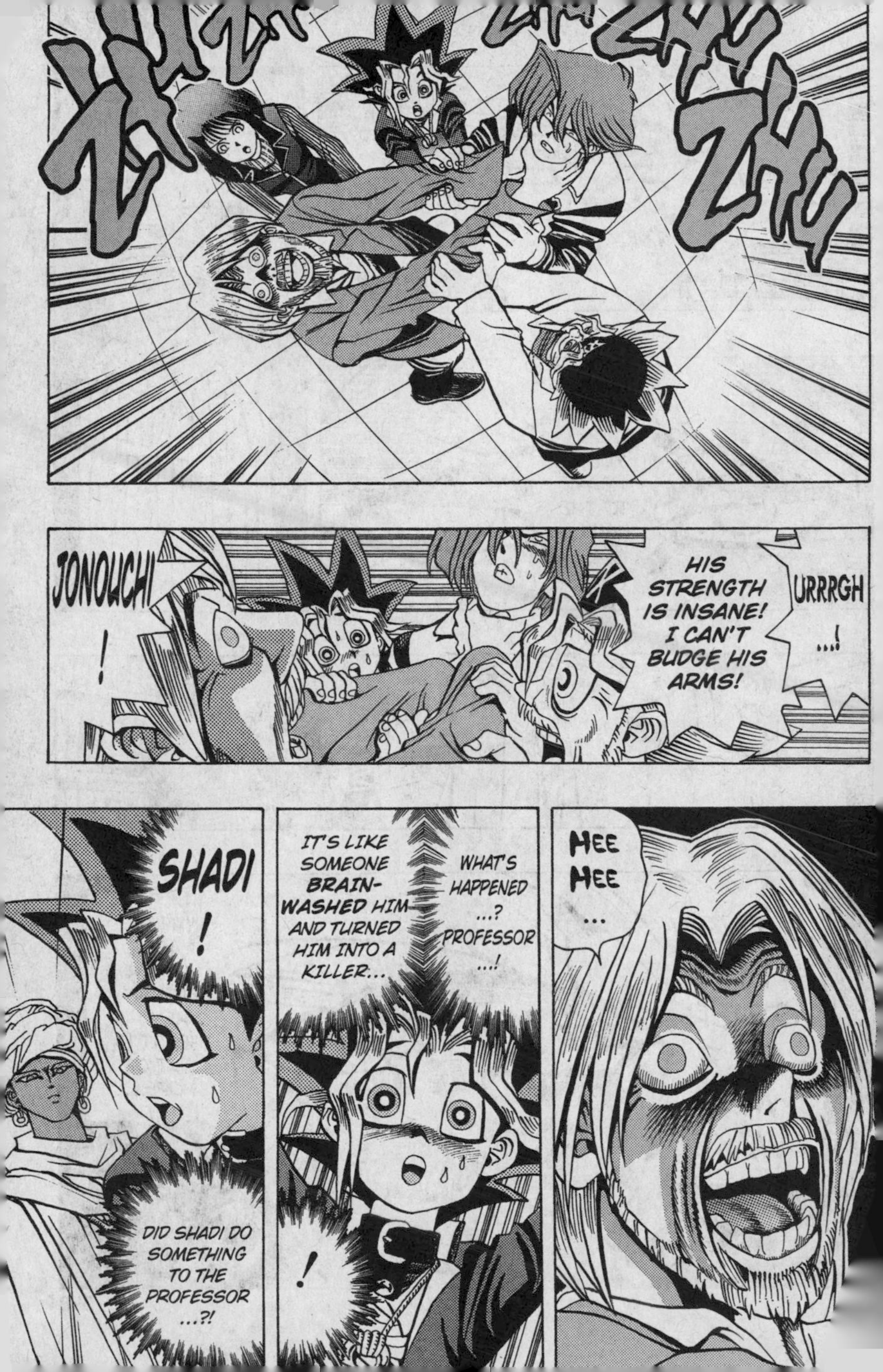
ZHU
URRRGH ...!
HIS STRENGTH IS INSANE! I CAN'T BUDGE HIS ARMS!
JONOUCHI !
HEE HEE ...
WHAT'S HAPPENED ...? PROFESSOR ...!
IT'S LIKE SOMEONE BRAIN-WASHED HIM AND TURNED HIM INTO A KILLER...
!
SHADI !
DID SHADI DO SOMETHING TO THE PROFESSOR ...?!

READ THIS WAY

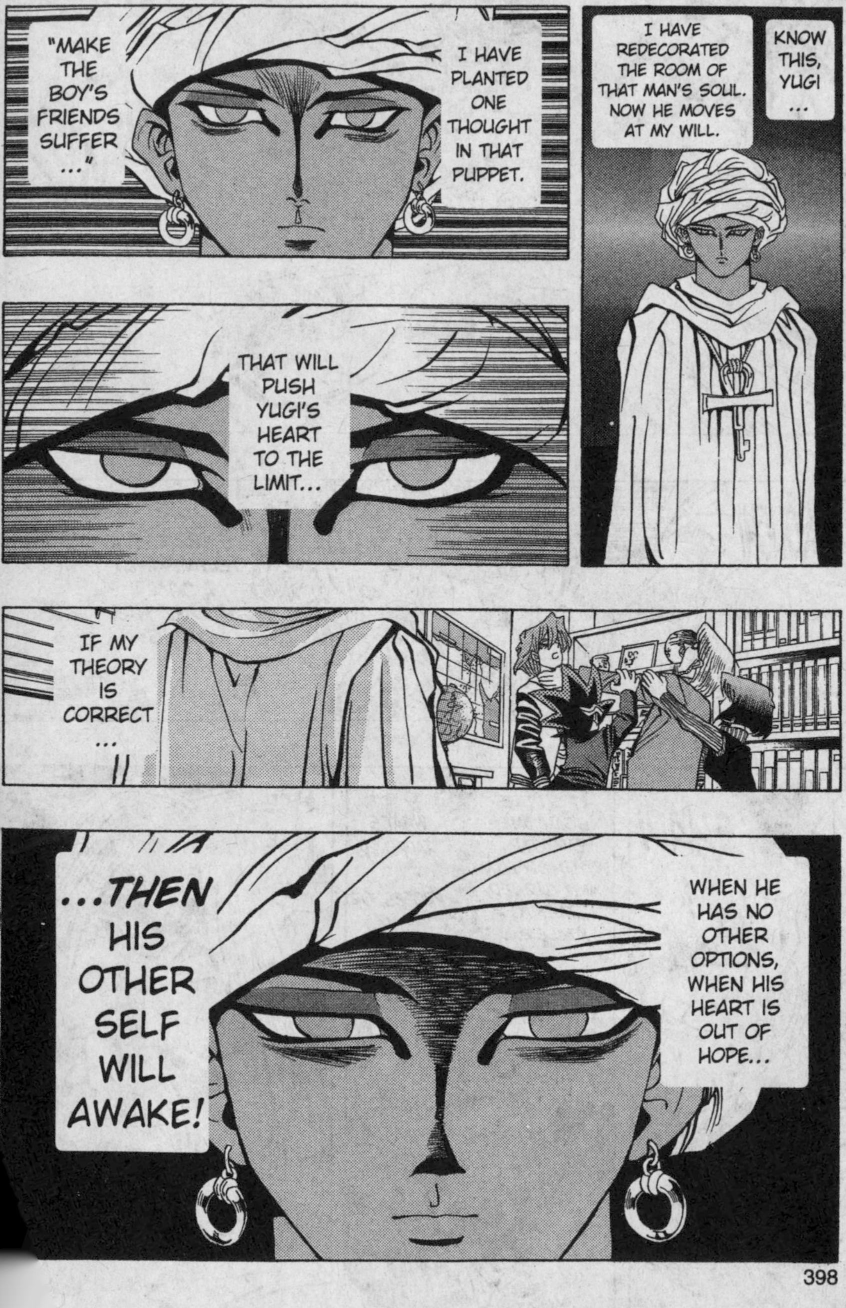
KNOW THIS, YUGI ...
I HAVE REDECORATED THE ROOM OF THAT MAN'S SOUL. NOW HE MOVES AT MY WILL.
I HAVE PLANTED ONE THOUGHT IN THAT PUPPET.
"MAKE THE BOY'S FRIENDS SUFFER ..."
THAT WILL PUSH YUGI'S HEART TO THE LIMIT...
IF MY THEORY IS CORRECT ...
WHEN HE HAS NO OTHER OPTIONS, WHEN HIS HEART IS OUT OF HOPE...
...THEN HIS OTHER SELF WILL AWAKE!

READ THIS WAY

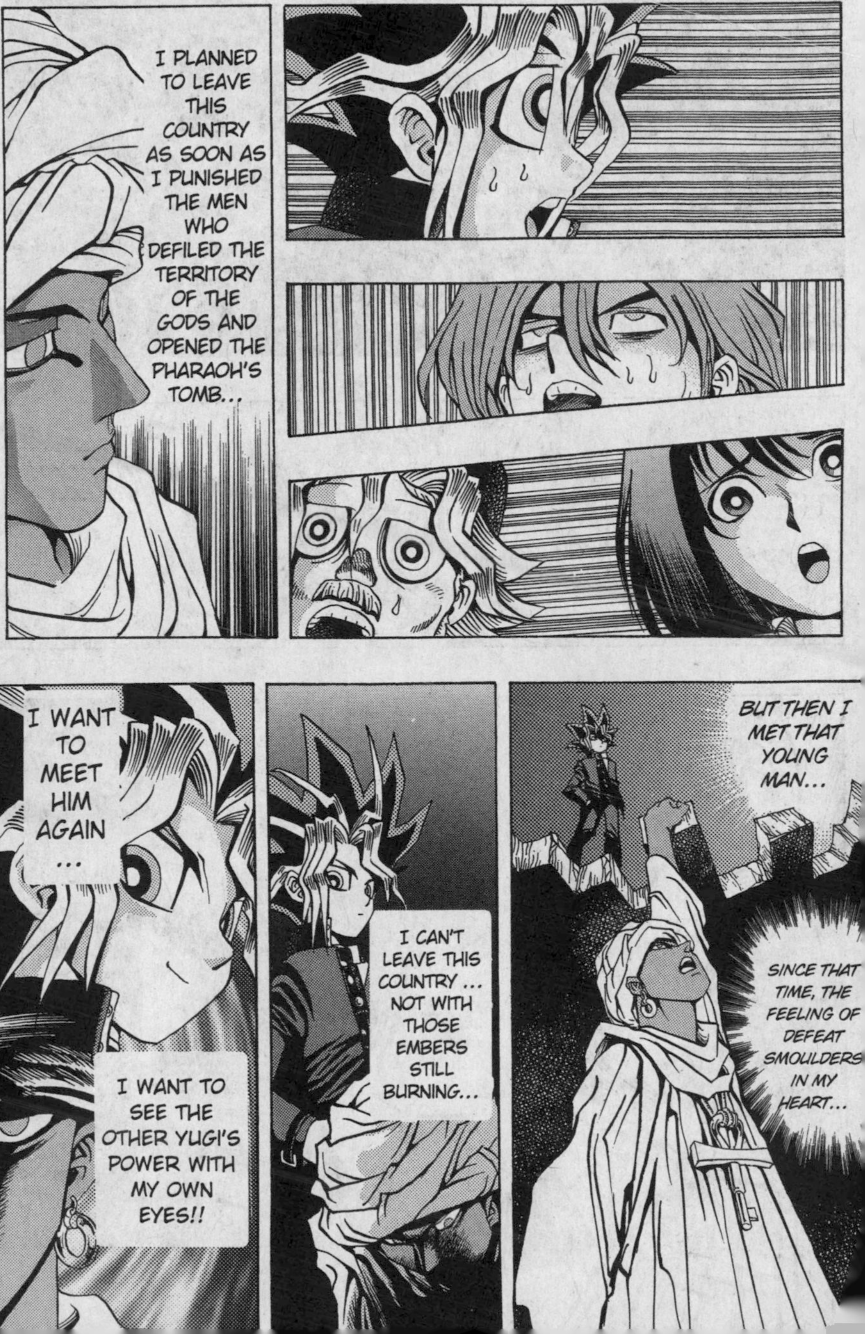
I PLANNED TO LEAVE THIS COUNTRY AS SOON AS I PUNISHED THE MEN WHO DEFILED THE TERRITORY OF THE GODS AND OPENED THE PHARAOH'S TOMB...
BUT THEN I MET THAT YOUNG MAN...
SINCE THAT TIME, THE FEELING OF DEFEAT SMOULDERS IN MY HEART...
I CAN'T LEAVE THIS COUNTRY ... NOT WITH THOSE EMBERS STILL BURNING...
I WANT TO MEET HIM AGAIN ...
I WANT TO SEE THE OTHER YUGI'S POWER WITH MY OWN EYES!!

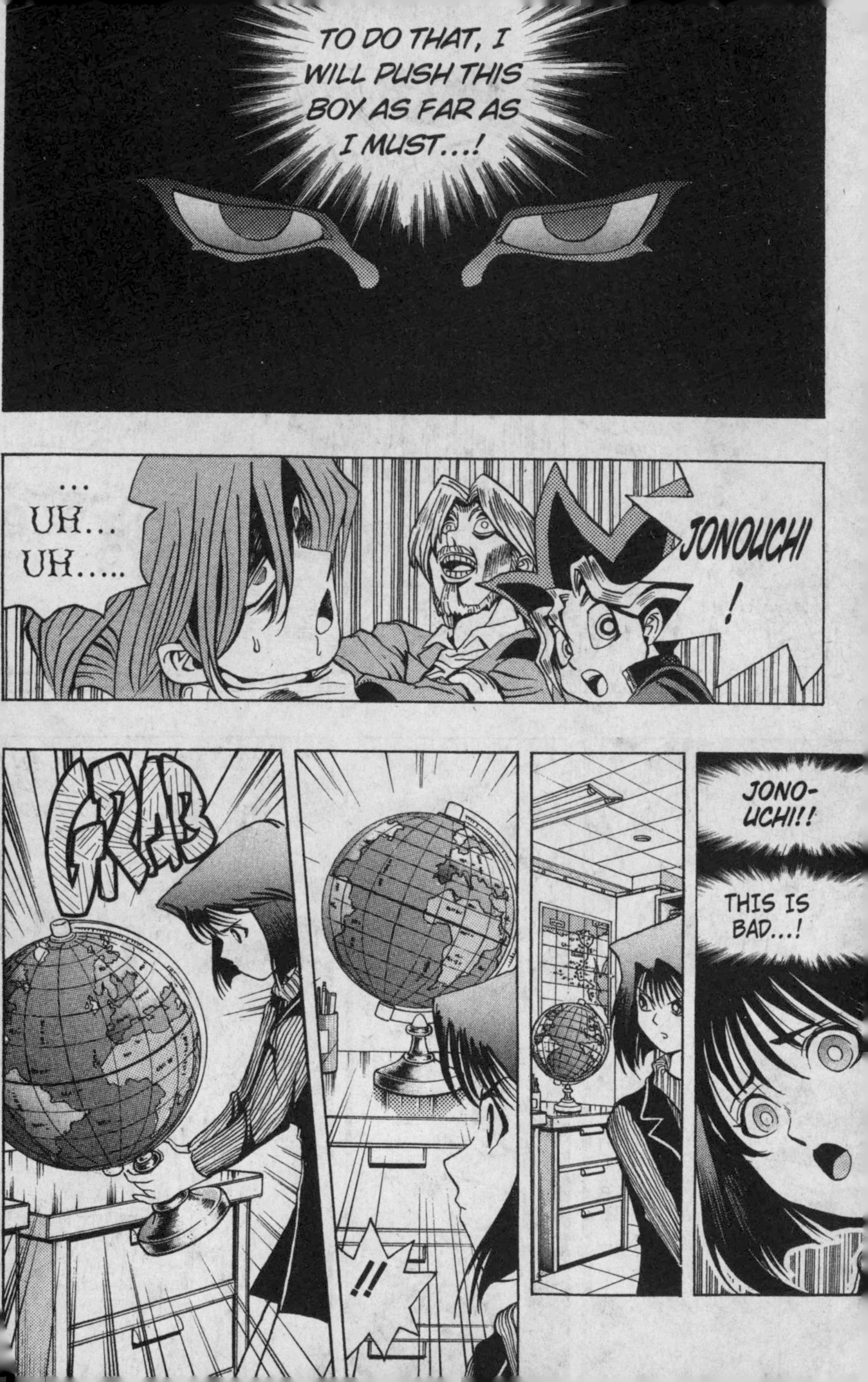
TO DO THAT, I WILL PUSH THIS BOY AS FAR AS I MUST...!
JONOUCHI !
... UH... UH.....
JONO-UCHI!!
THIS IS BAD...!
!!
GRAB

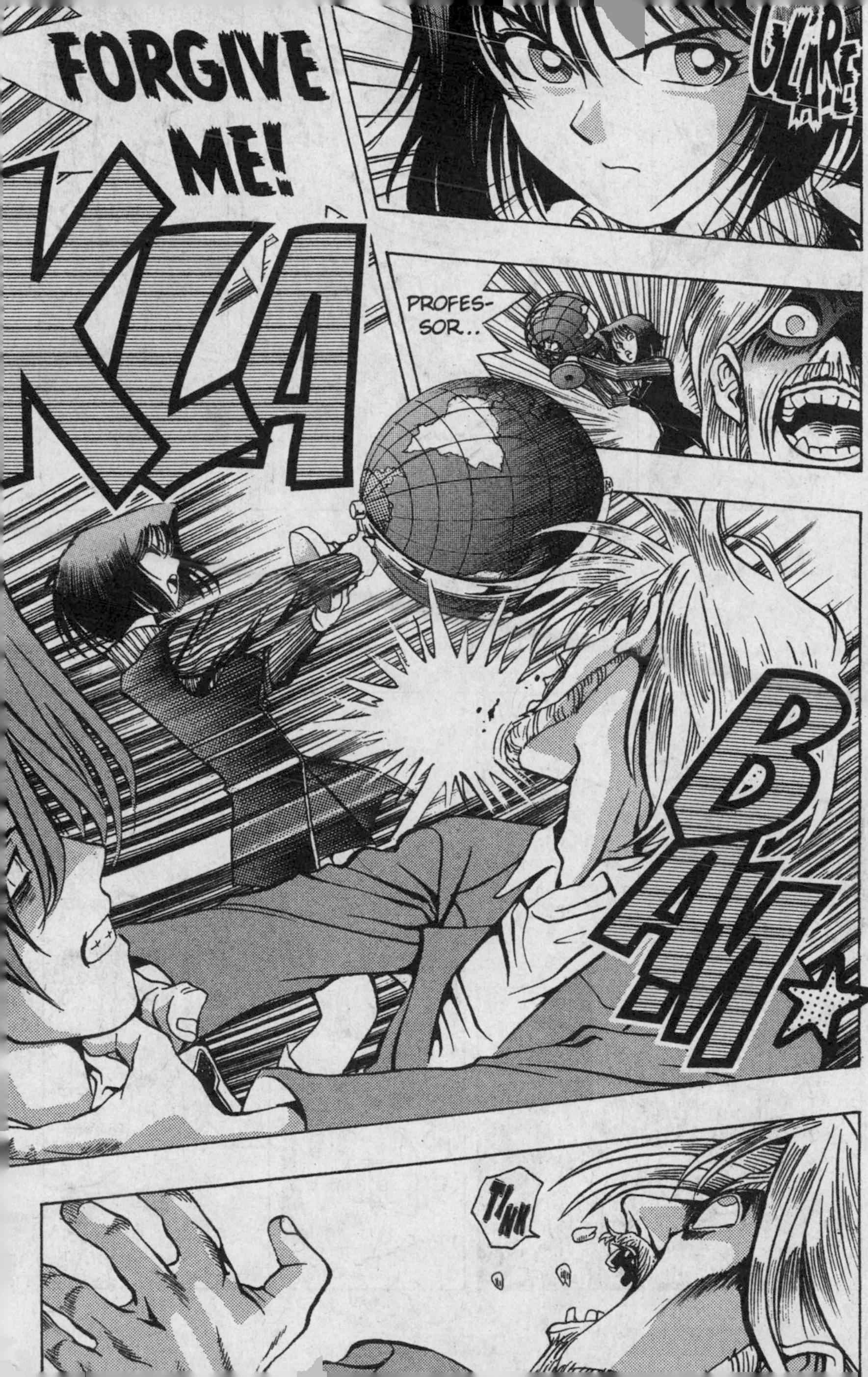
GLARE
FORGIVE ME!
KA
PROFES-SOR...
BAM
TINK

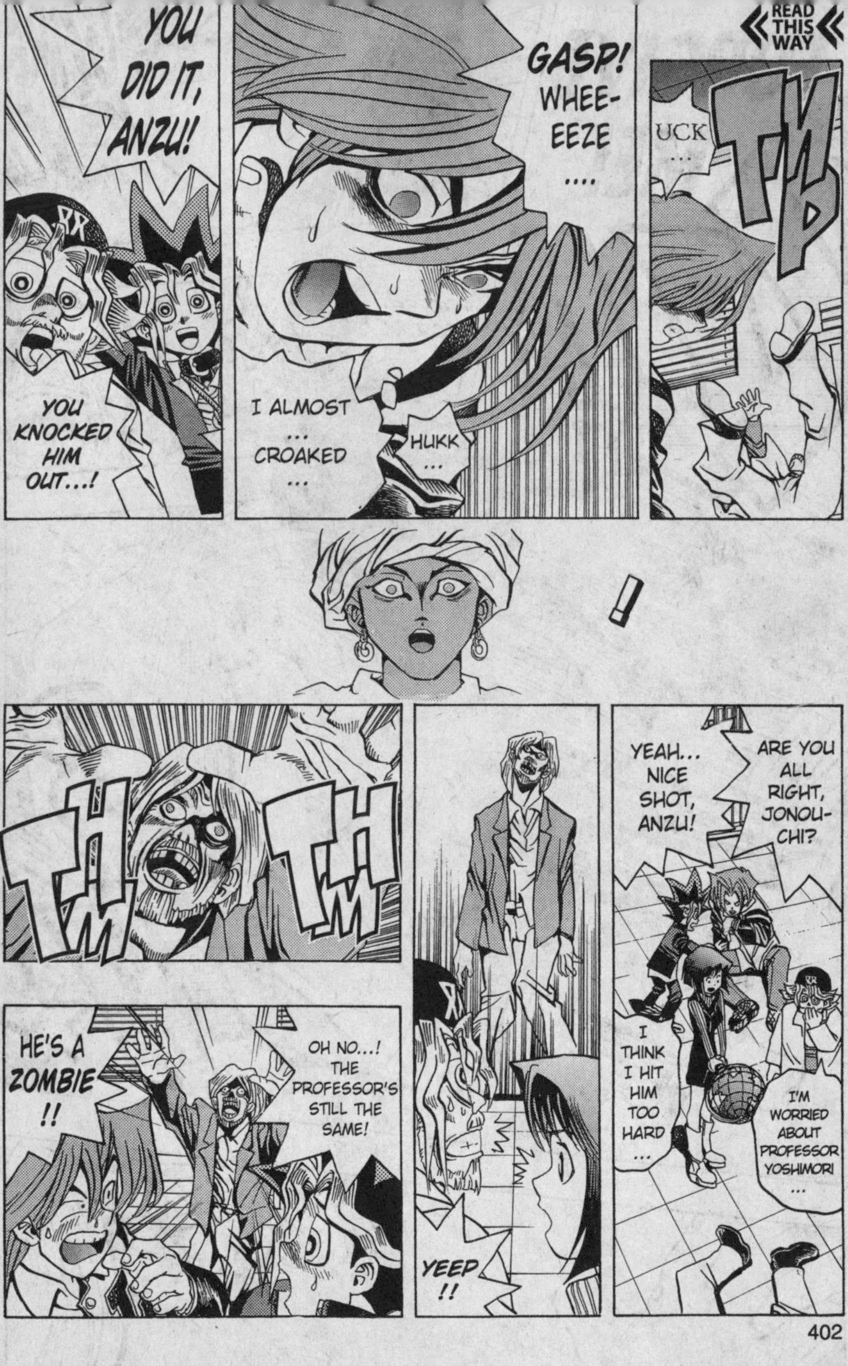
READ THIS WAY
UCK ...
GASP! WHEEE-EEZE ....
I ALMOST ... CROAKED ...
HUKK ...
YOU DID IT, ANZU!
YOU KNOCKED HIM OUT...!
!
ARE YOU ALL RIGHT, JONOUCHI?
YEAH... NICE SHOT, ANZU!
I'M WORRIED ABOUT PROFESSOR YOSHIMORI ...
I THINK I HIT HIM TOO HARD ...
YEEP !!
THM
THM
OH NO...! THE PROFESSOR'S STILL THE SAME!
HE'S A ZOMBIE !!

READ THIS WAY

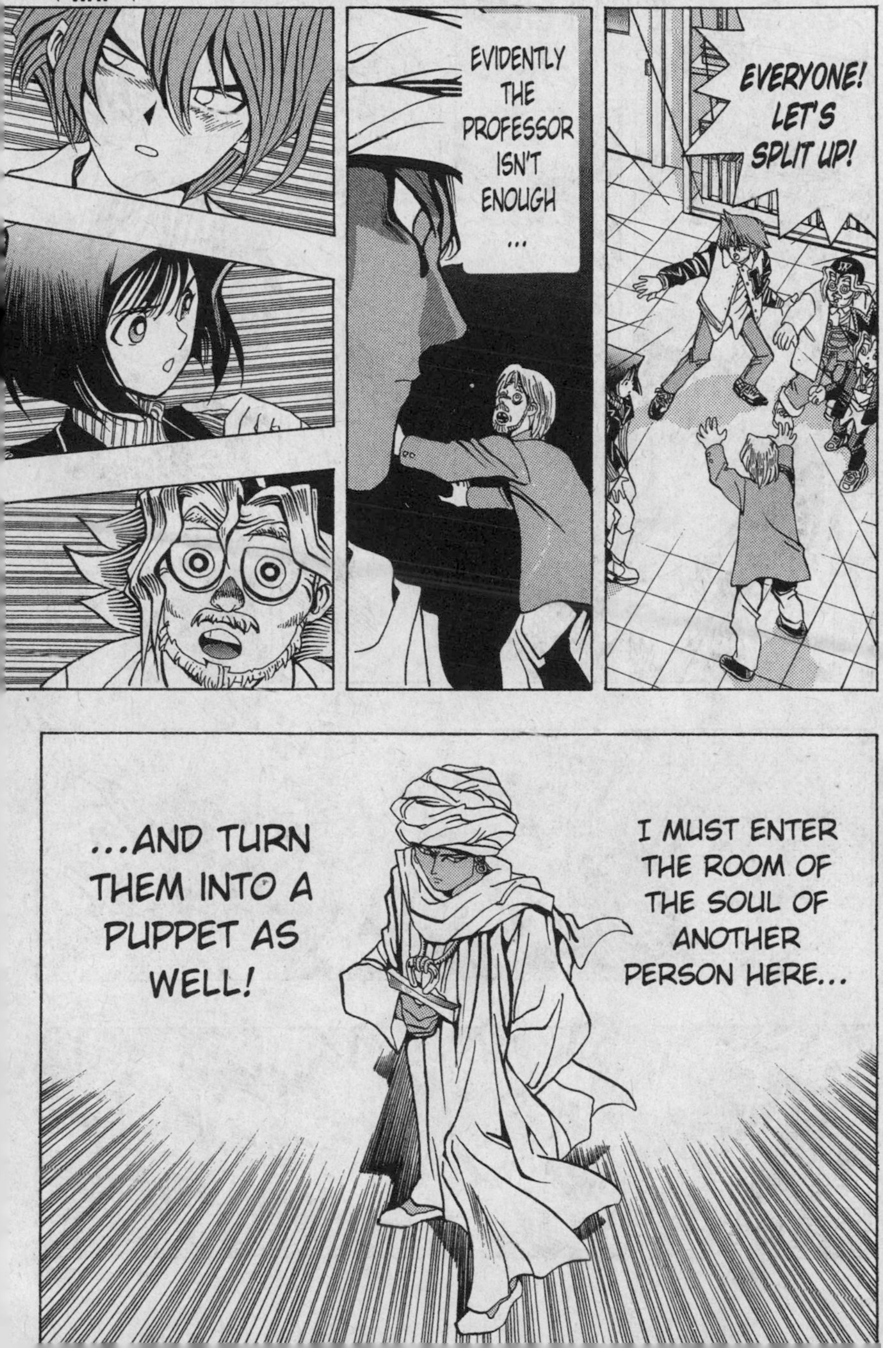
EVERYONE! LET'S SPLIT UP!
EVIDENTLY THE PROFESSOR ISN'T ENOUGH ...
I MUST ENTER THE ROOM OF THE SOUL OF ANOTHER PERSON HERE...
...AND TURN THEM INTO A PUPPET AS WELL!

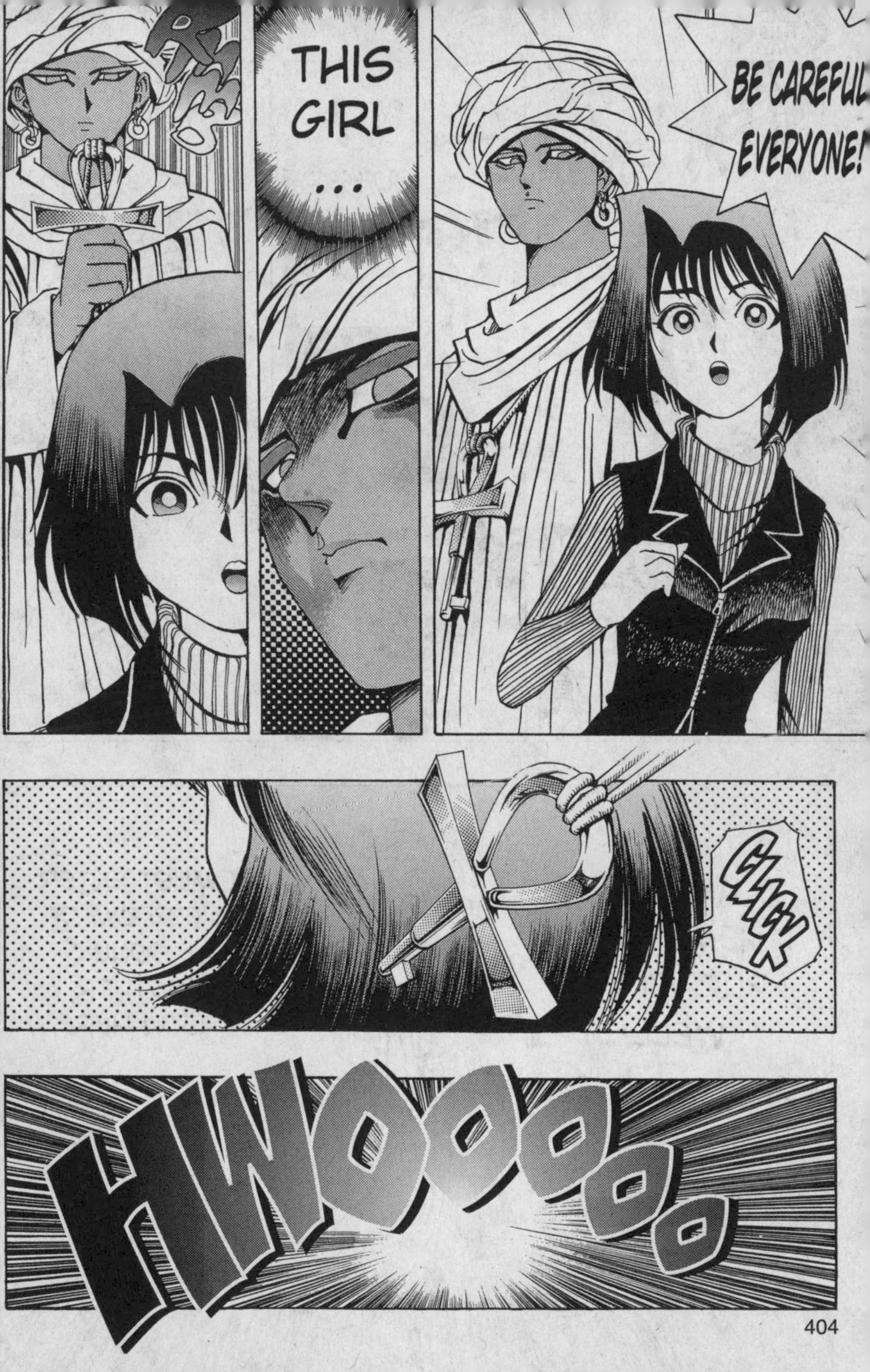
BE CAREFUL EVERYONE!
THIS GIRL ...
CLICK
HWOOOOO

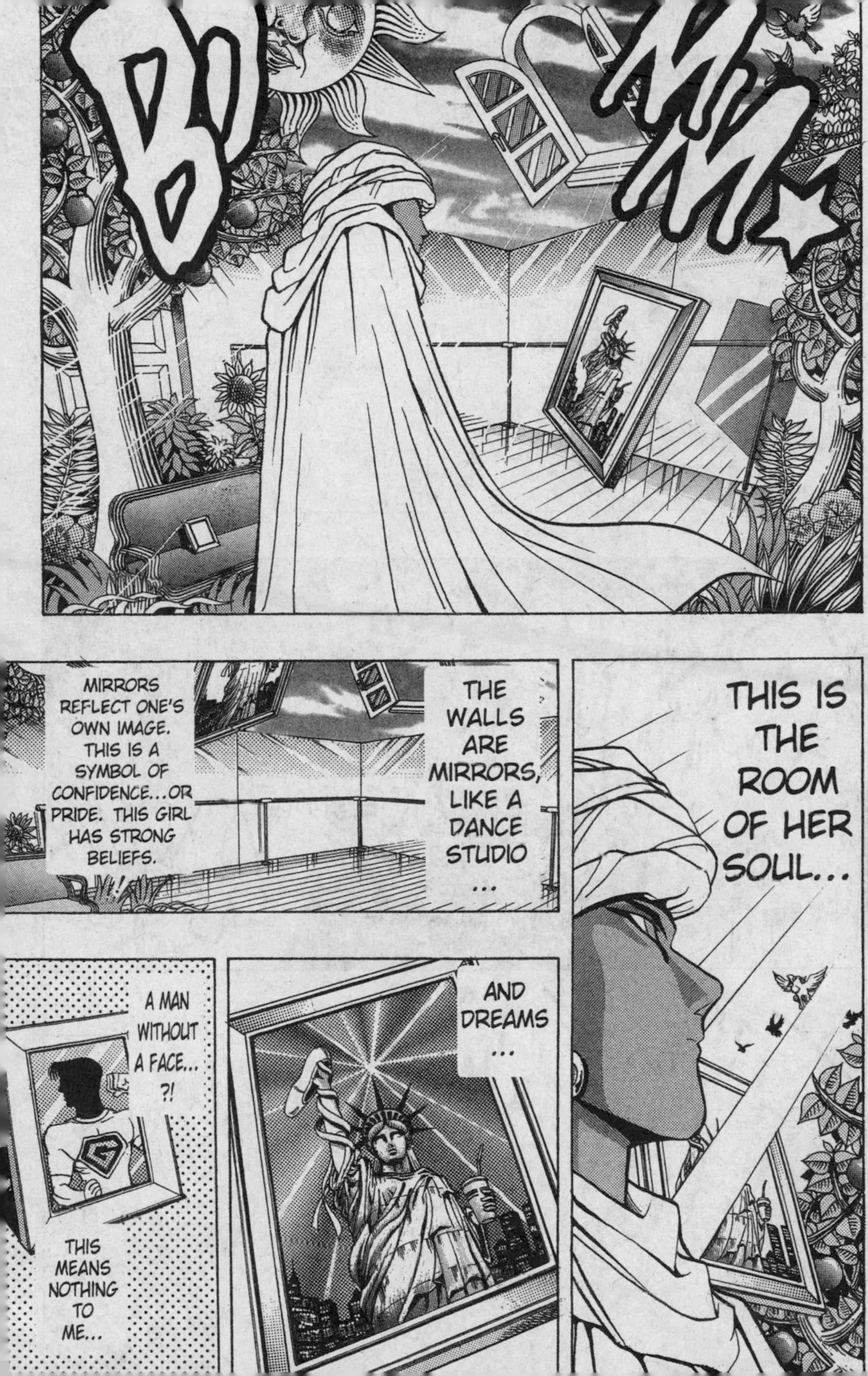
THIS IS THE ROOM OF HER SOUL...
THE WALLS ARE MIRRORS, LIKE A DANCE STUDIO ...
MIRRORS REFLECT ONE'S OWN IMAGE. THIS IS A SYMBOL OF CONFIDENCE...OR PRIDE. THIS GIRL HAS STRONG BELIEFS.
AND DREAMS ...
A MAN WITHOUT A FACE... ?!
THIS MEANS NOTHING TO ME...

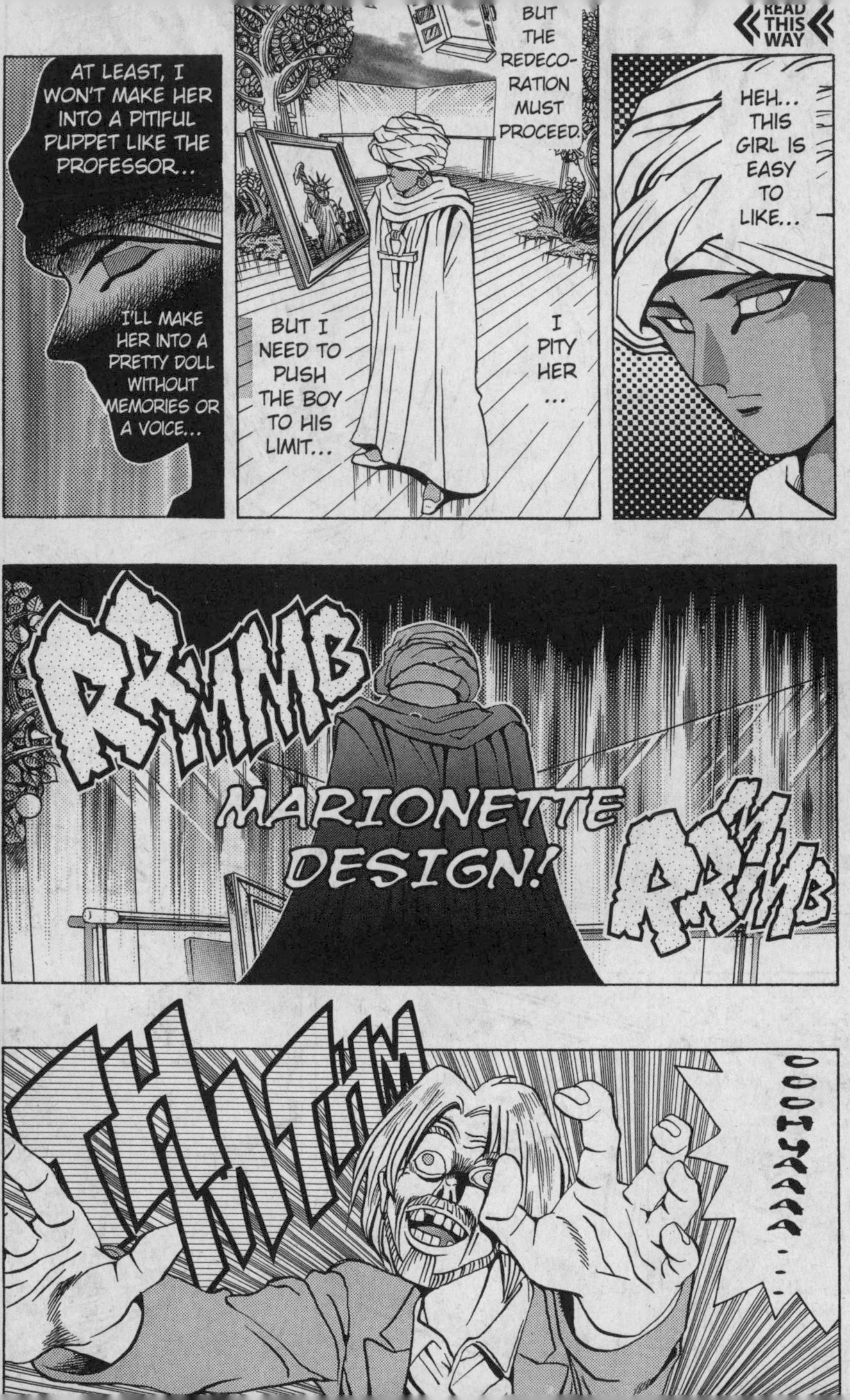
READ THIS WAY
HEH... THIS GIRL IS EASY TO LIKE...
BUT THE REDECO-RATION MUST PROCEED.
I PITY HER...
BUT I NEED TO PUSH THE BOY TO HIS LIMIT...
AT LEAST, I WON'T MAKE HER INTO A PITIFUL PUPPET LIKE THE PROFESSOR...
I'LL MAKE HER INTO A PRETTY DOLL WITHOUT MEMORIES OR A VOICE...
RRMMB
MARIONETTE DESIGN!
RRMB
OOOHYAAAA...
THMTHM

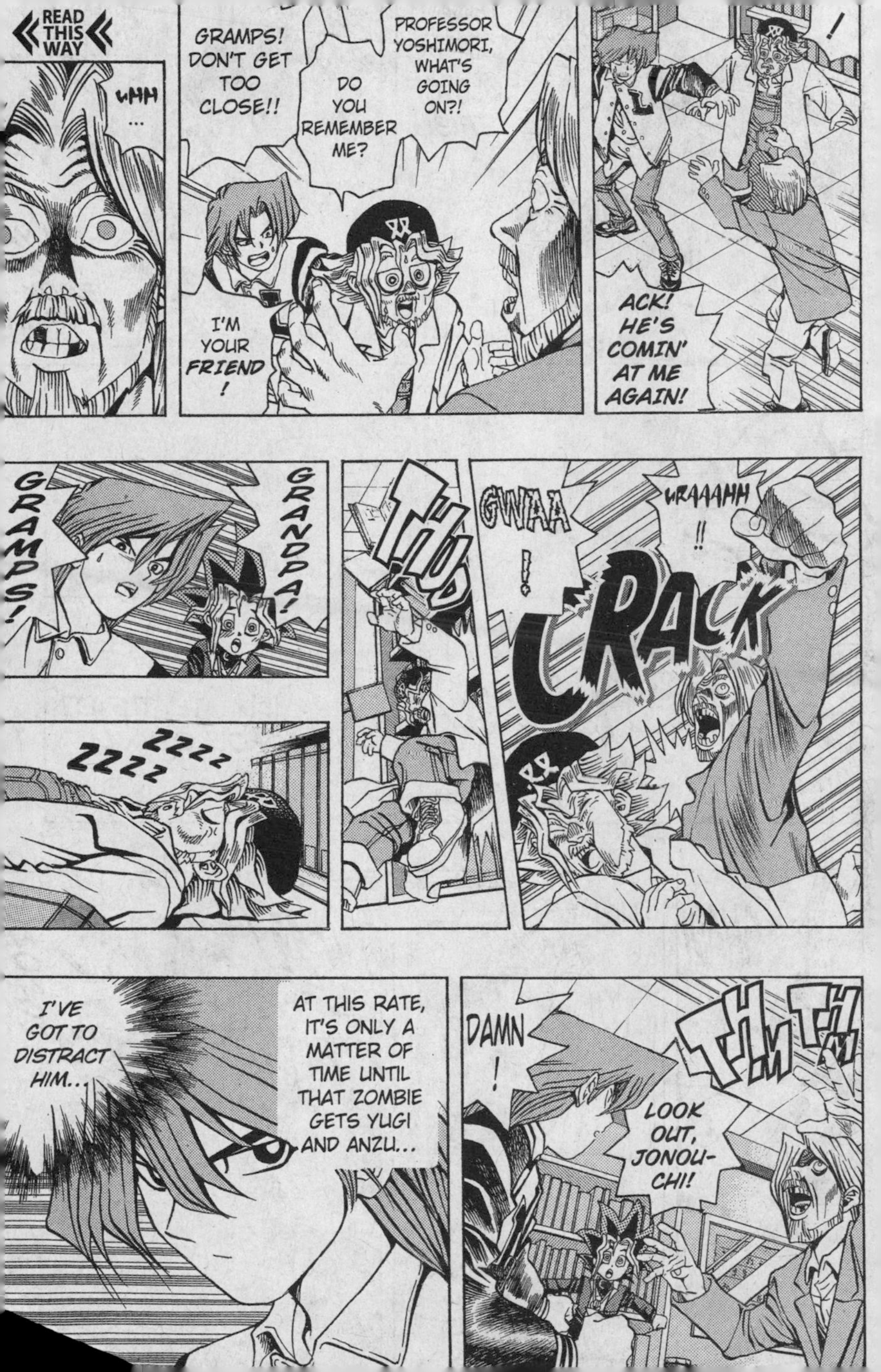
READ THIS WAY
!
ACK! HE'S COMIN' AT ME AGAIN!
PROFESSOR YOSHIMORI, WHAT'S GOING ON?!
DO YOU REMEMBER ME?
GRAMPS! DON'T GET TOO CLOSE!!
I'M YOUR FRIEND!
UMM ...
URAAAHH!!
GWAA!
CRACK
THUD
GRANDPA!
GRAMPS!
ZZZZ ZZZZ
TH TH
DAMN!
LOOK OUT, JONOUCHI!
AT THIS RATE, IT'S ONLY A MATTER OF TIME UNTIL THAT ZOMBIE GETS YUGI AND ANZU...
I'VE GOT TO DISTRACT HIM...

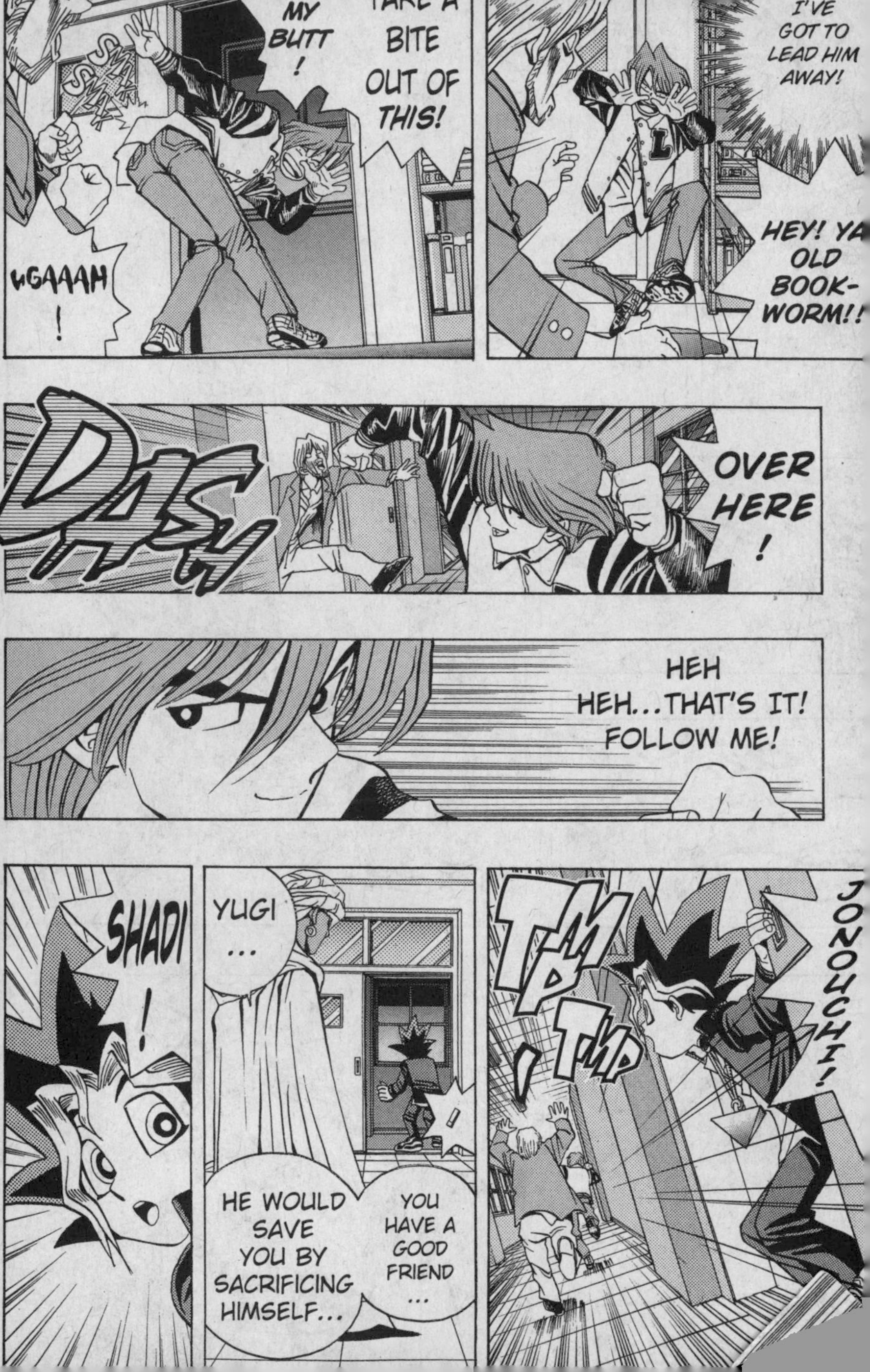
I'VE GOT TO LEAD HIM AWAY!
HEY! YA OLD BOOK-WORM!!
BITE OUT OF THIS!
MY BUTT!
UGAAAH!
DASH
OVER HERE!
HEH HEH...THAT'S IT! FOLLOW ME!
JONOUCHI!
YUGI...
YOU HAVE A GOOD FRIEND...
HE WOULD SAVE YOU BY SACRIFICING HIMSELF...
SHADI!

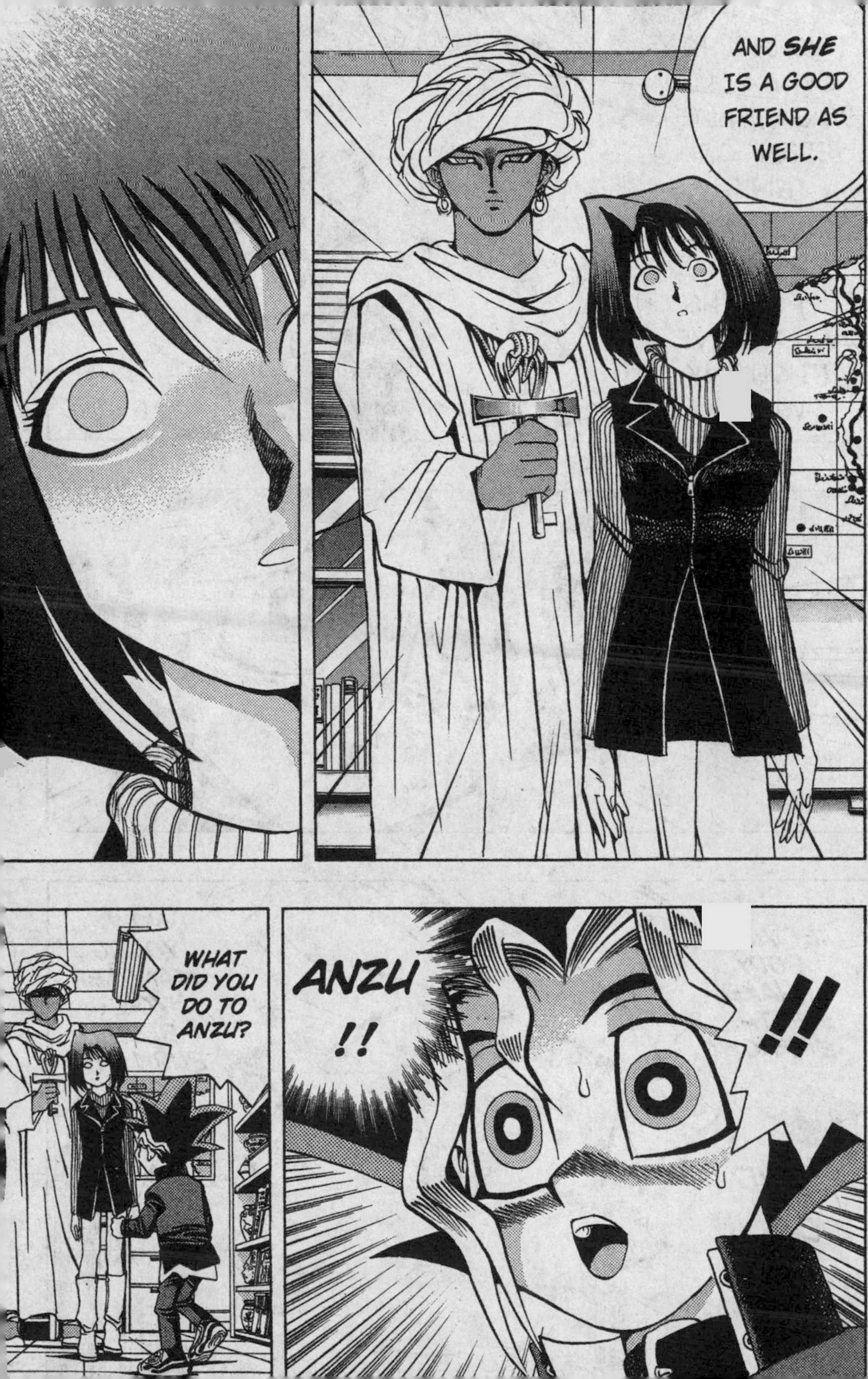
AND SHE IS A GOOD FRIEND AS WELL.
ANZU !!
!!
WHAT DID YOU DO TO ANZU?

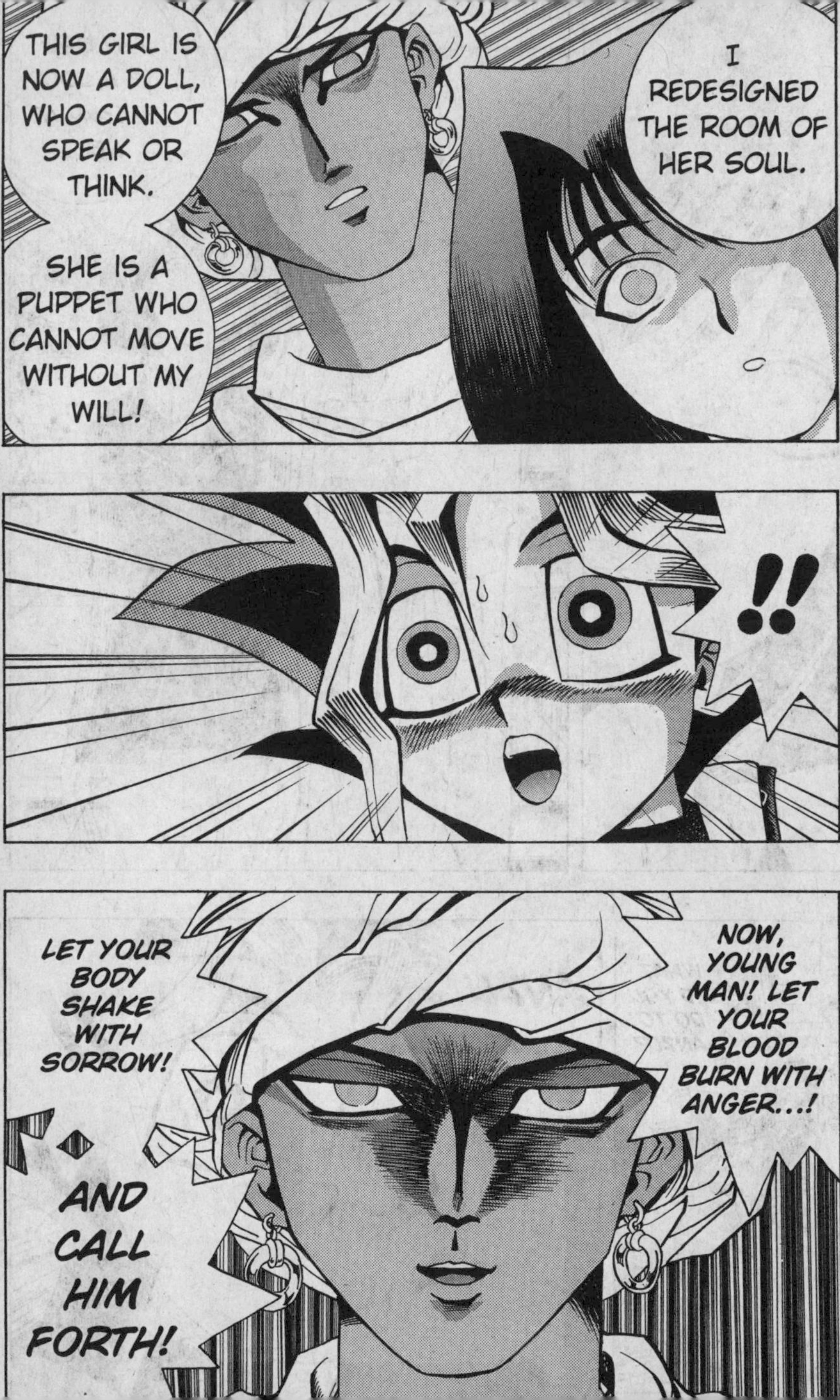
I REDESIGNED THE ROOM OF HER SOUL.
THIS GIRL IS NOW A DOLL, WHO CANNOT SPEAK OR THINK.
SHE IS A PUPPET WHO CANNOT MOVE WITHOUT MY WILL!
!!
NOW, YOUNG MAN! LET YOUR BLOOD BURN WITH ANGER...!
LET YOUR BODY SHAKE WITH SORROW!
AND CALL HIM FORTH!

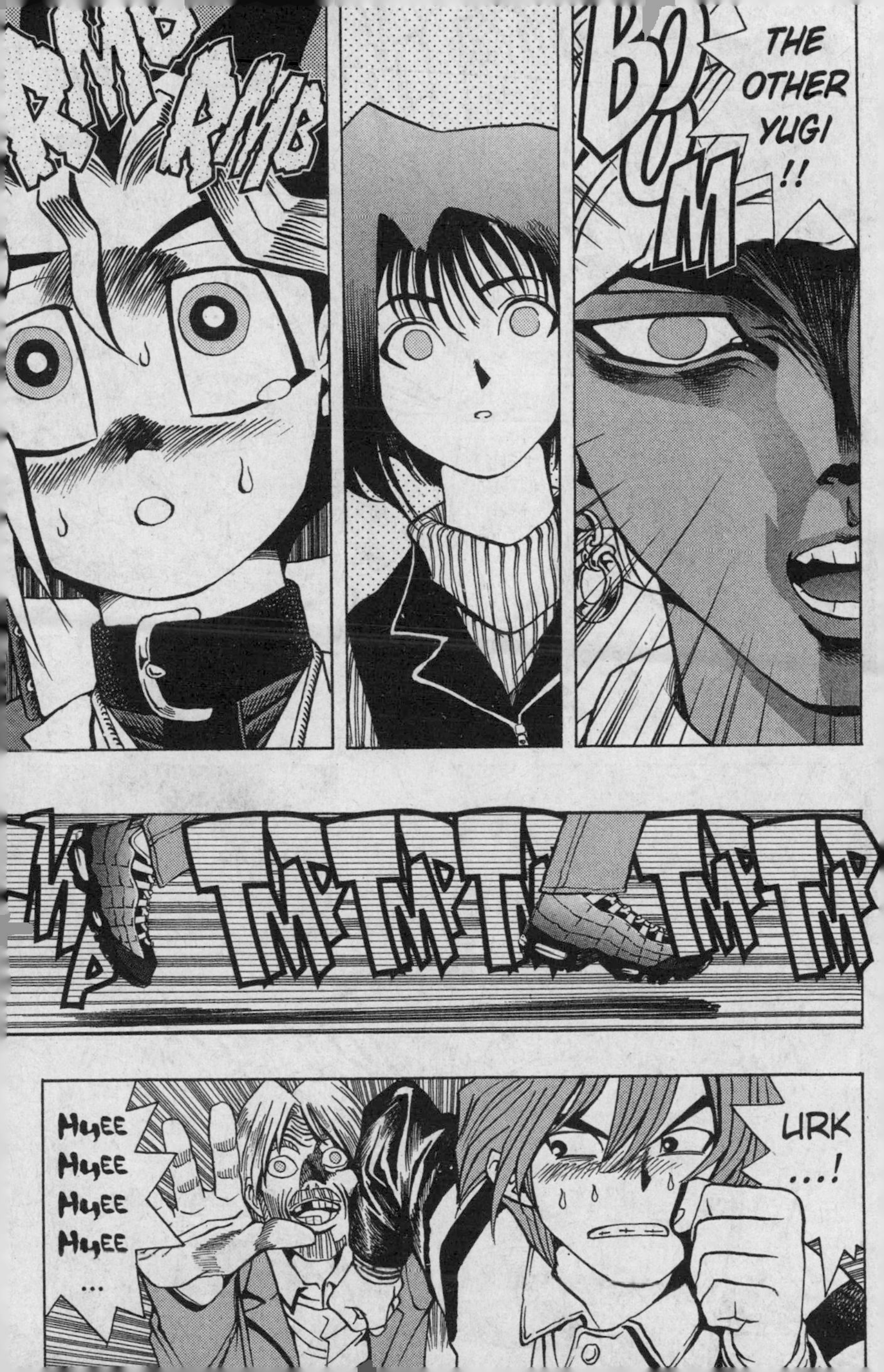
BOOM
THE OTHER YUGI !!
BAMB BAMB
TMP TMP TMP TMP TMP TMP
URK ...!
HYEE HYEE HYEE HYEE ...

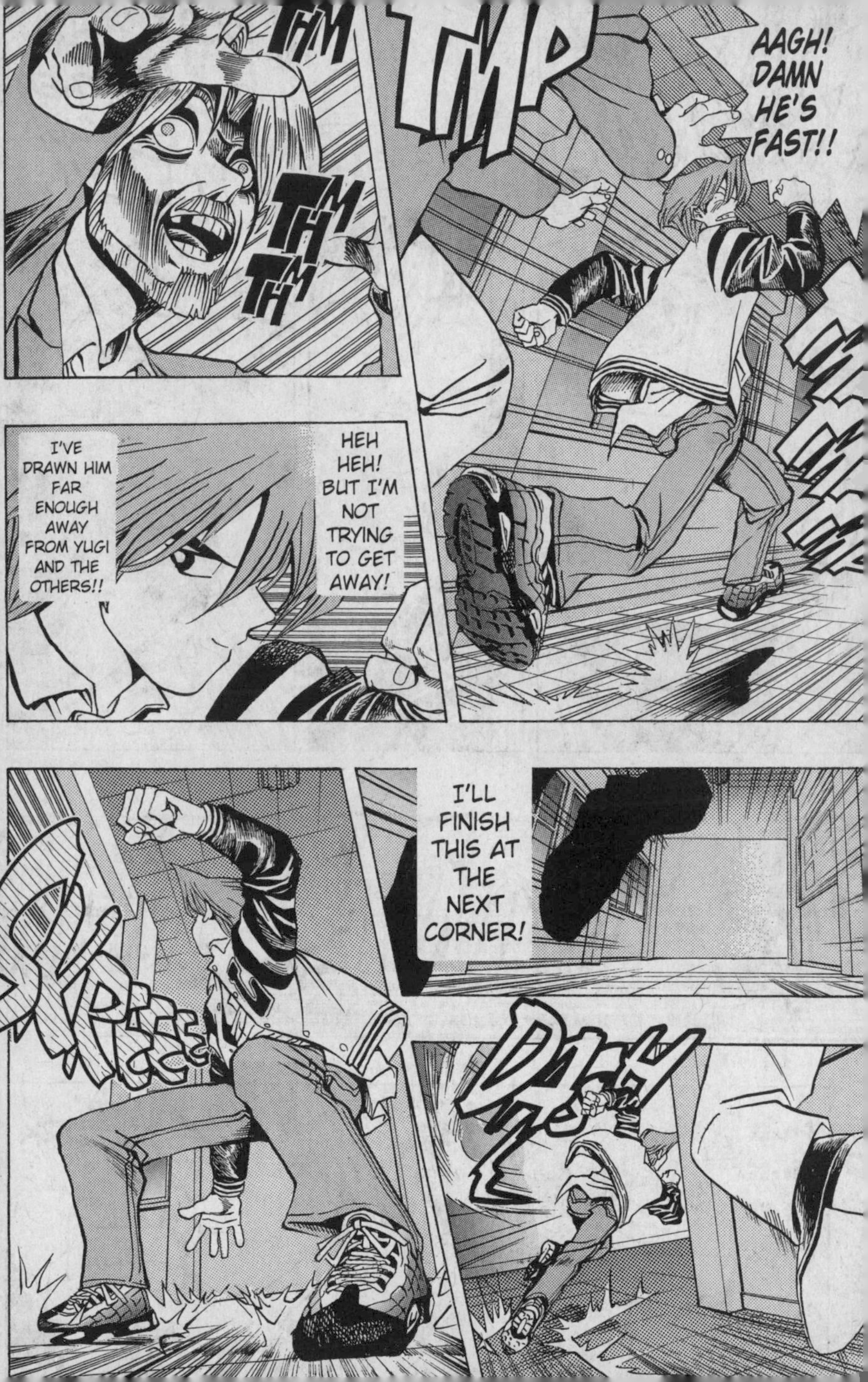
TMP
AAGH! DAMN HE'S FAST!!
THM
TH TH TH
I'VE DRAWN HIM FAR ENOUGH AWAY FROM YUGI AND THE OTHERS!!
HEH HEH! BUT I'M NOT TRYING TO GET AWAY!
I'LL FINISH THIS AT THE NEXT CORNER!
DASH
SKREEE

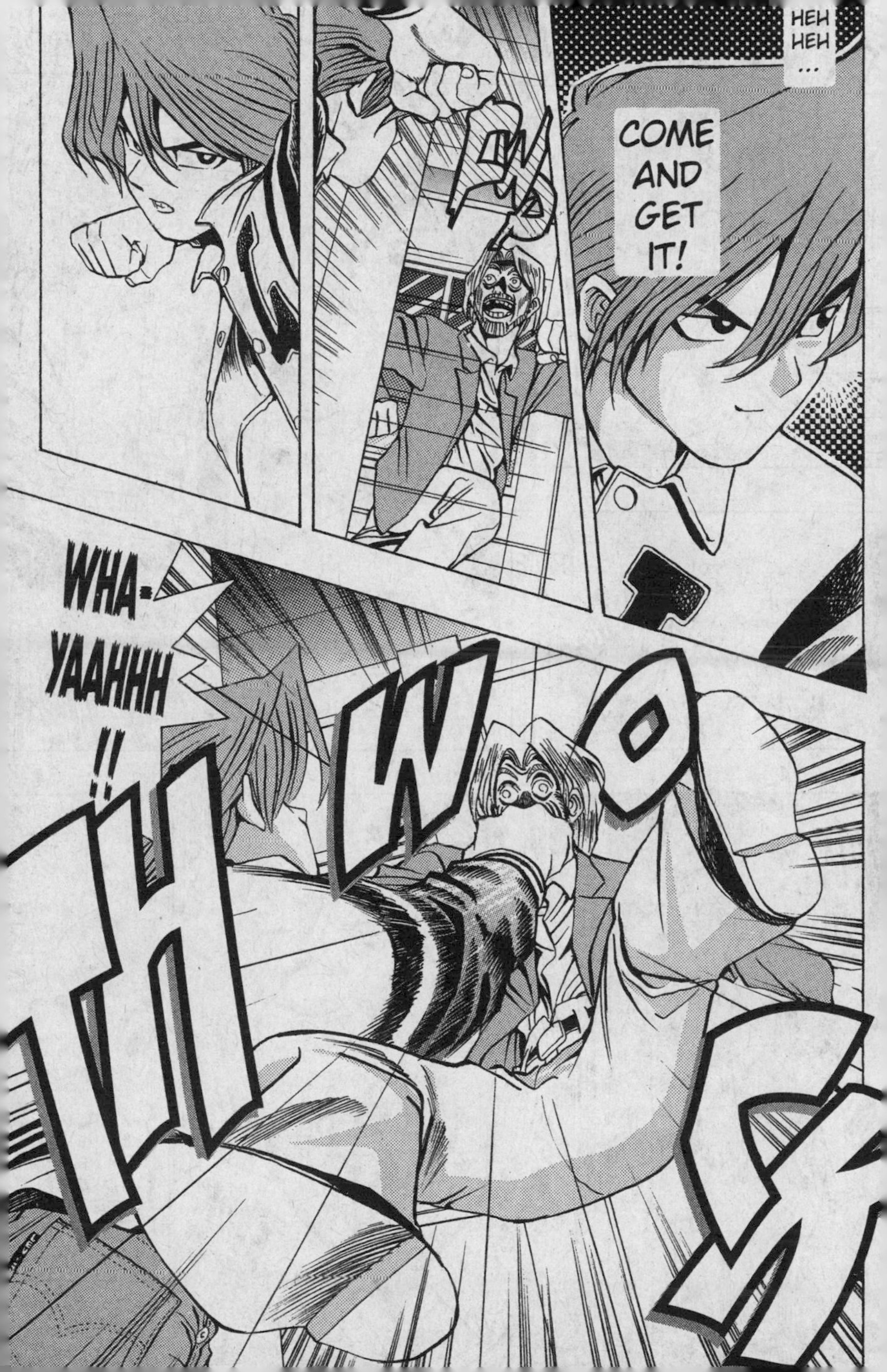
HEH HEH ...
COME AND GET IT!
WHA-YAAHHH !!
THWOCK

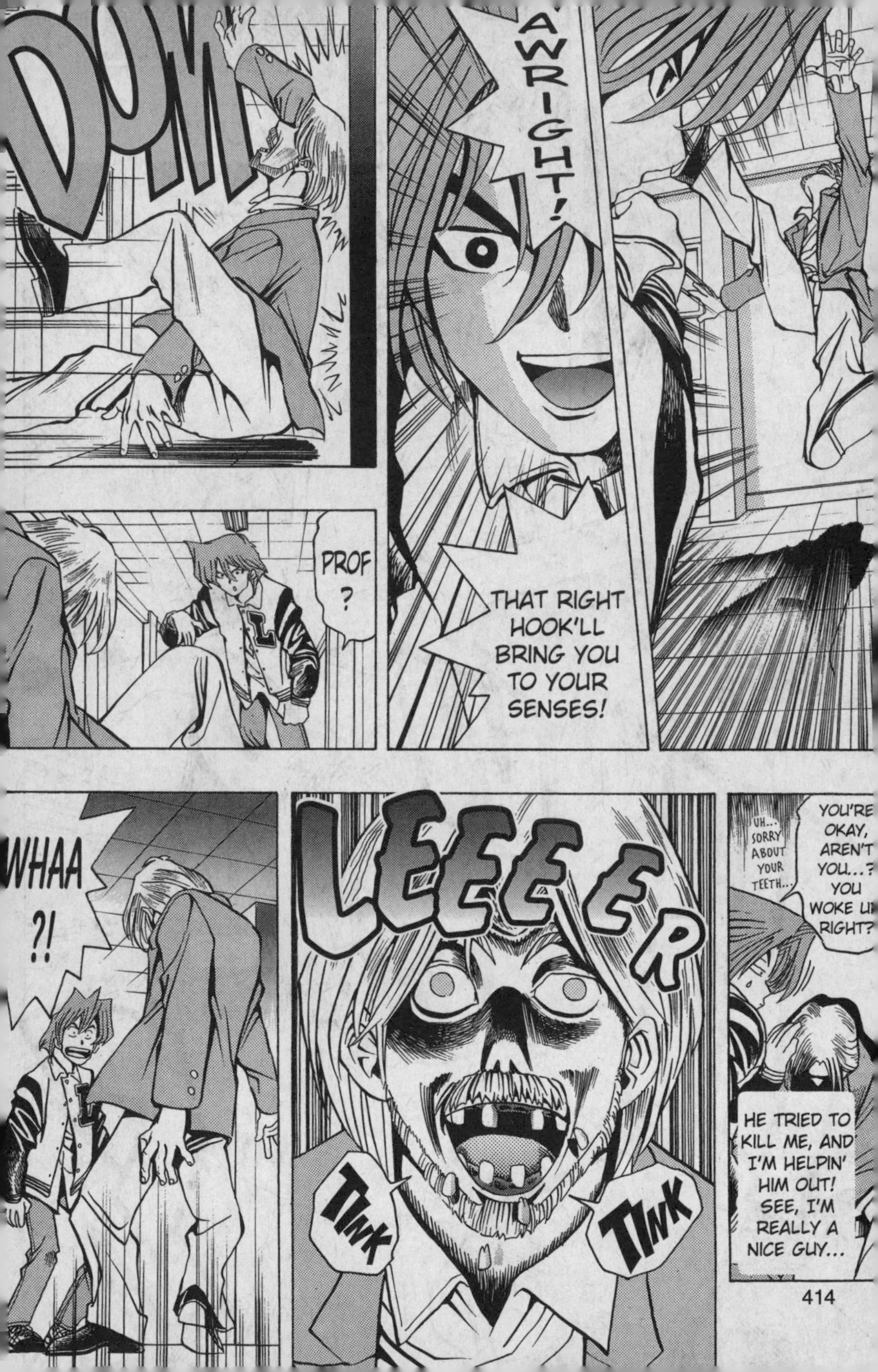
AWRIGHT!
THAT RIGHT HOOK'LL BRING YOU TO YOUR SENSES!
DOM
PROF ?
YOU'RE OKAY, AREN'T YOU...? YOU WOKE U RIGHT?
UH... SORRY ABOUT YOUR TEETH...
HE TRIED TO KILL ME, AND I'M HELPIN' HIM OUT! SEE, I'M REALLY A NICE GUY...
LEEEER
TINK
TINK
WHAA ?!

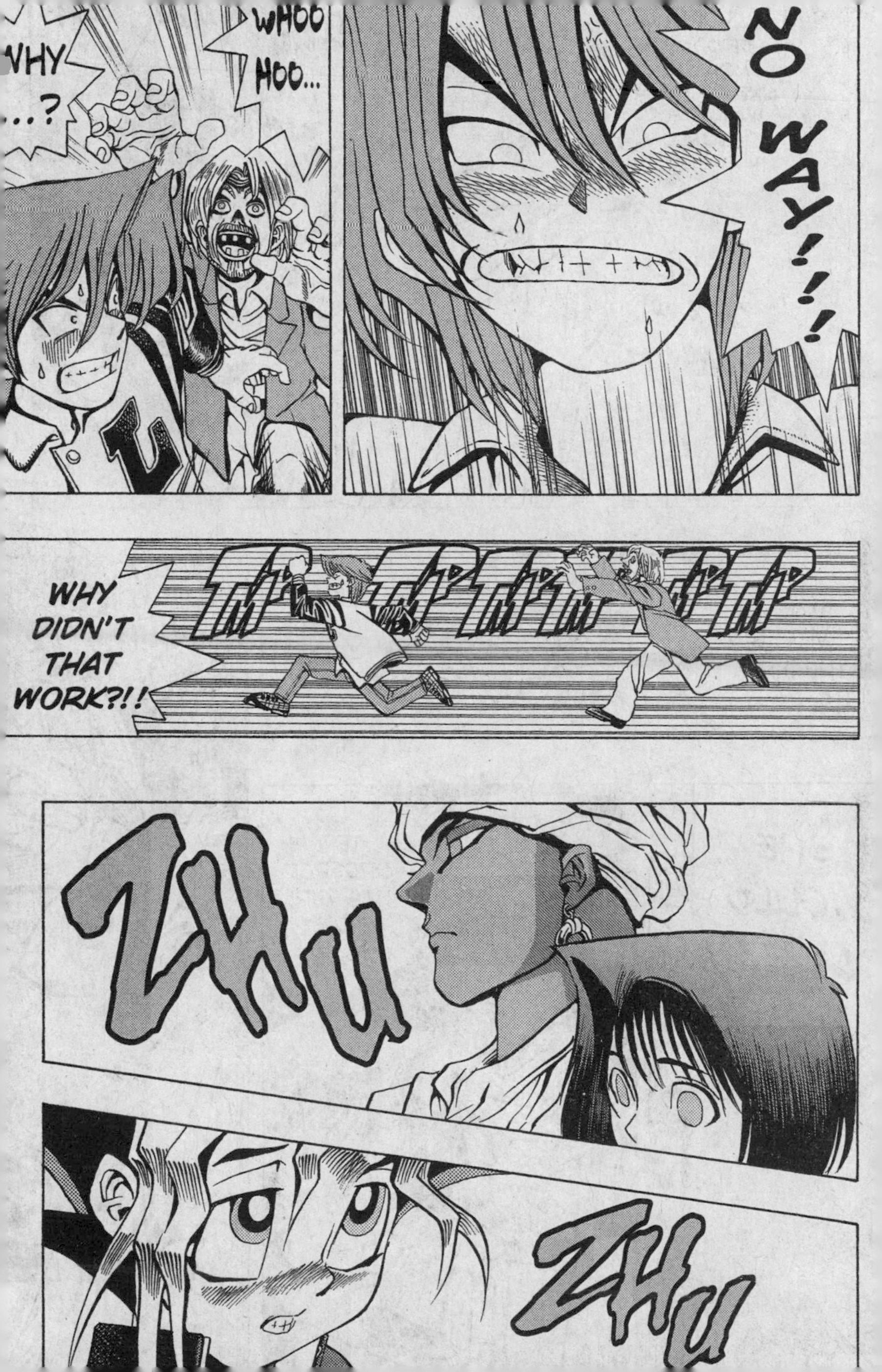
NO WAY!!!
WHOO HOO...
WHY ...?
WHY DIDN'T THAT WORK?!!
ZHU
ZHU

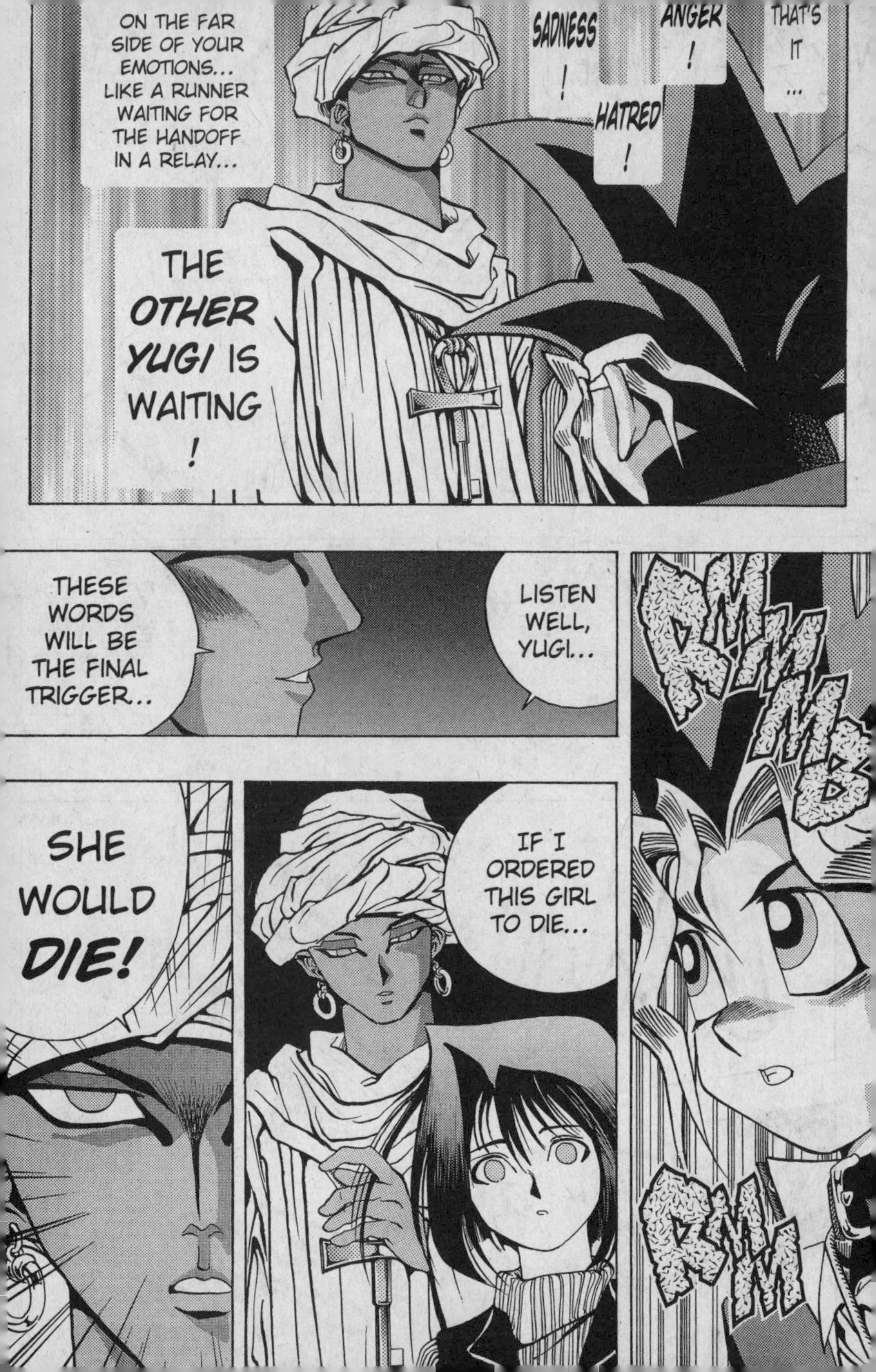
THAT'S IT ...
ANGER !
SADNESS !
HATRED !
ON THE FAR SIDE OF YOUR EMOTIONS... LIKE A RUNNER WAITING FOR THE HANDOFF IN A RELAY...
THE *OTHER YUGI* IS WAITING !
RMMB
RMM
LISTEN WELL, YUGI...
THESE WORDS WILL BE THE FINAL TRIGGER...
IF I ORDERED THIS GIRL TO DIE...
SHE WOULD *DIE!*

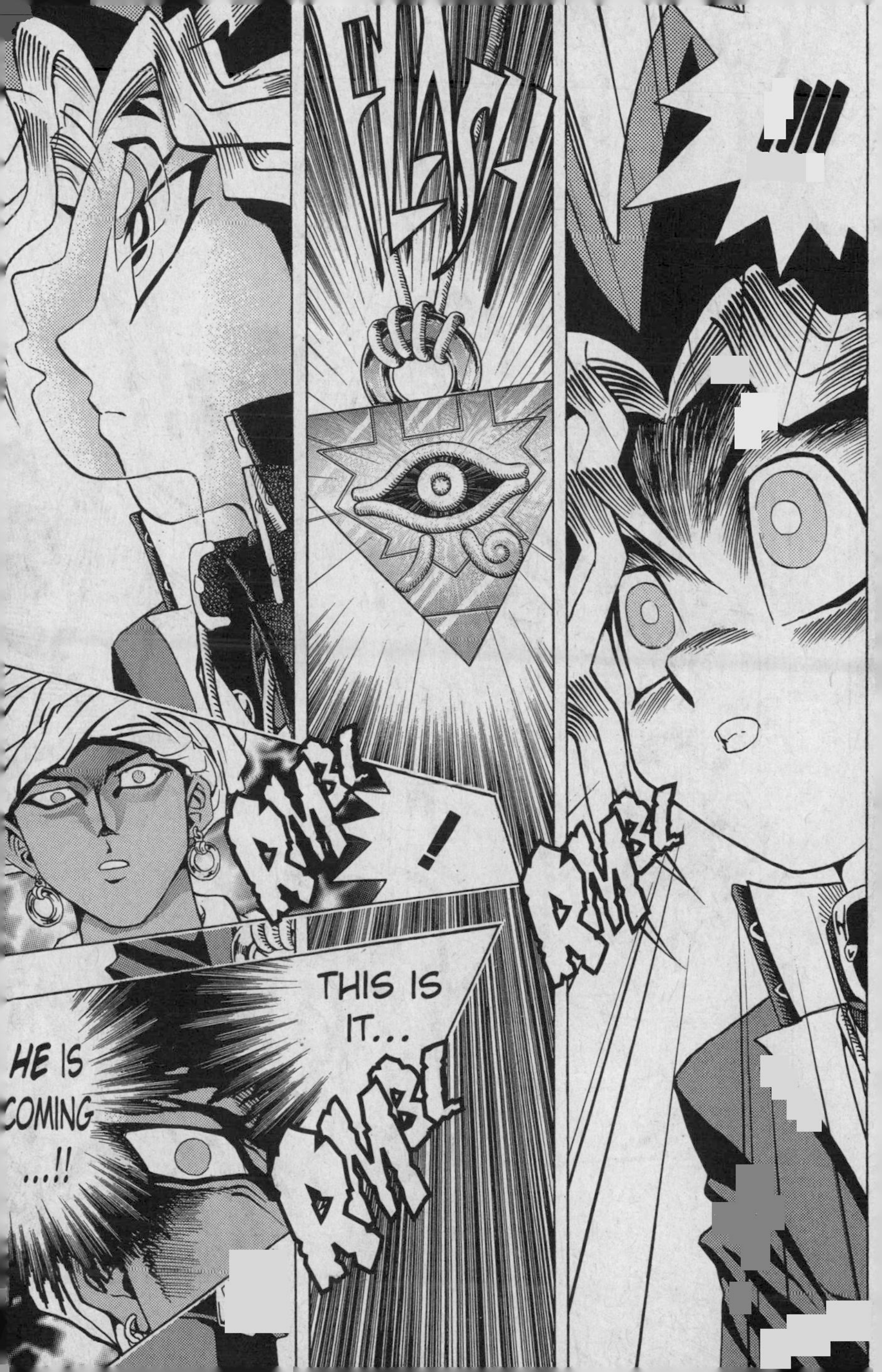

RMBL
FLASH
!
RMBL
THIS IS IT...
RMBL
HE IS COMING ...!!

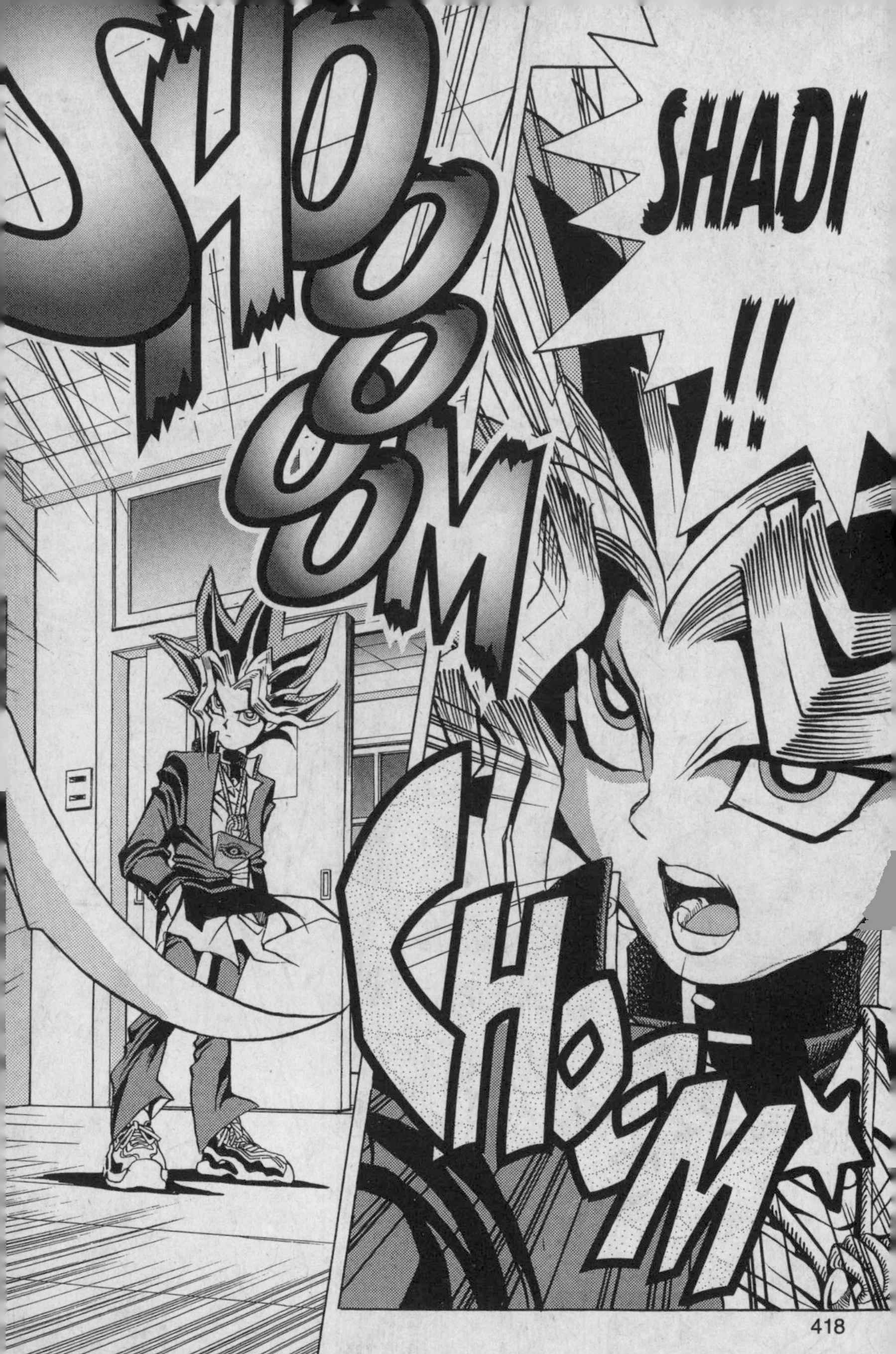
SHADI!!
SHOOOOM
SHOM

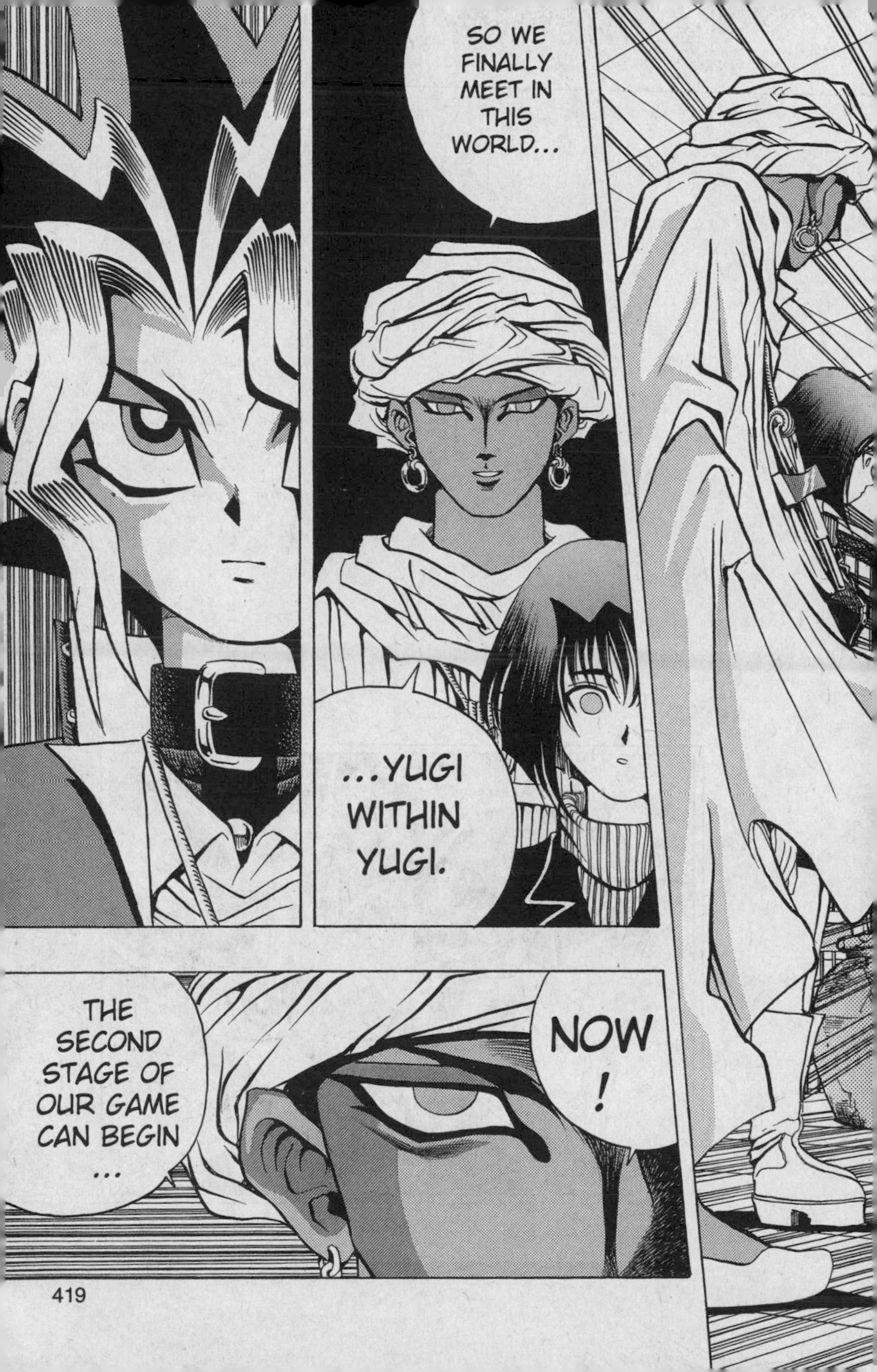
SO WE FINALLY MEET IN THIS WORLD...
...YUGI WITHIN YUGI.
NOW!
THE SECOND STAGE OF OUR GAME CAN BEGIN ...

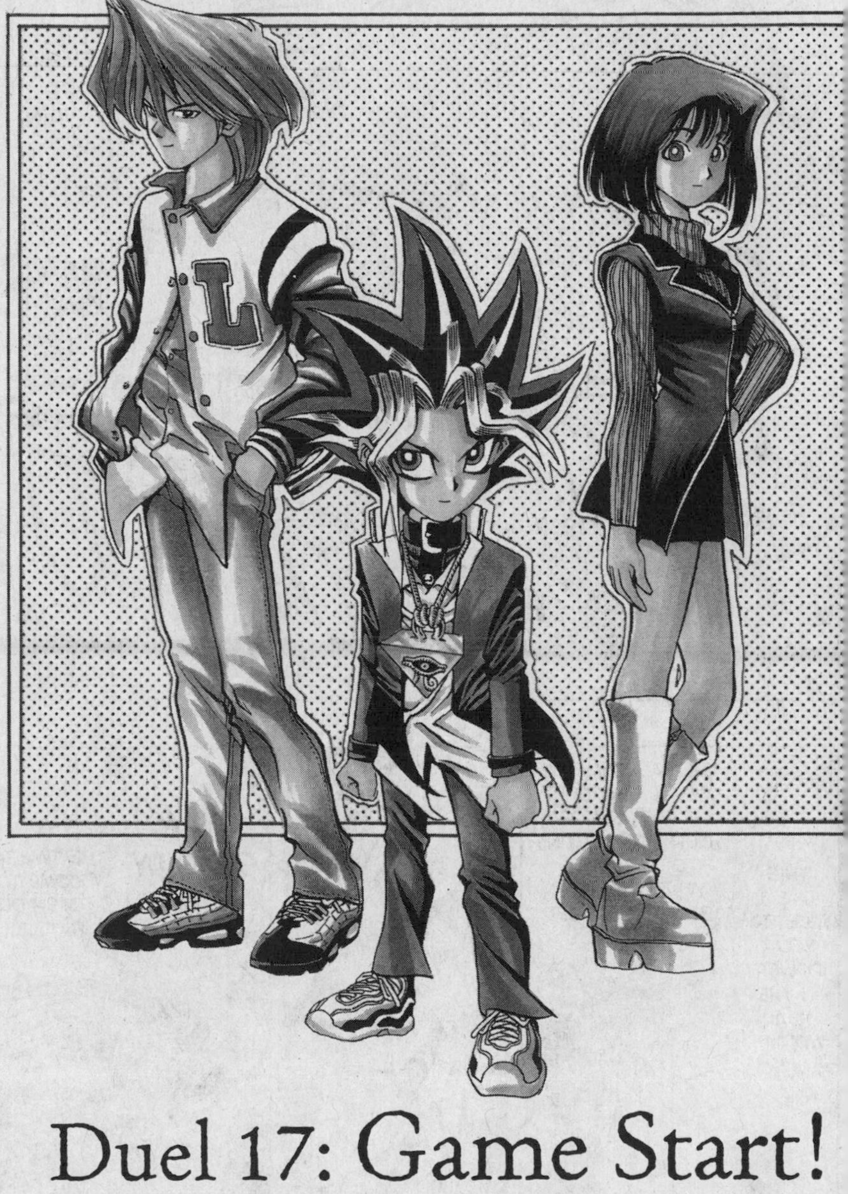

Duel 17: Game Start!

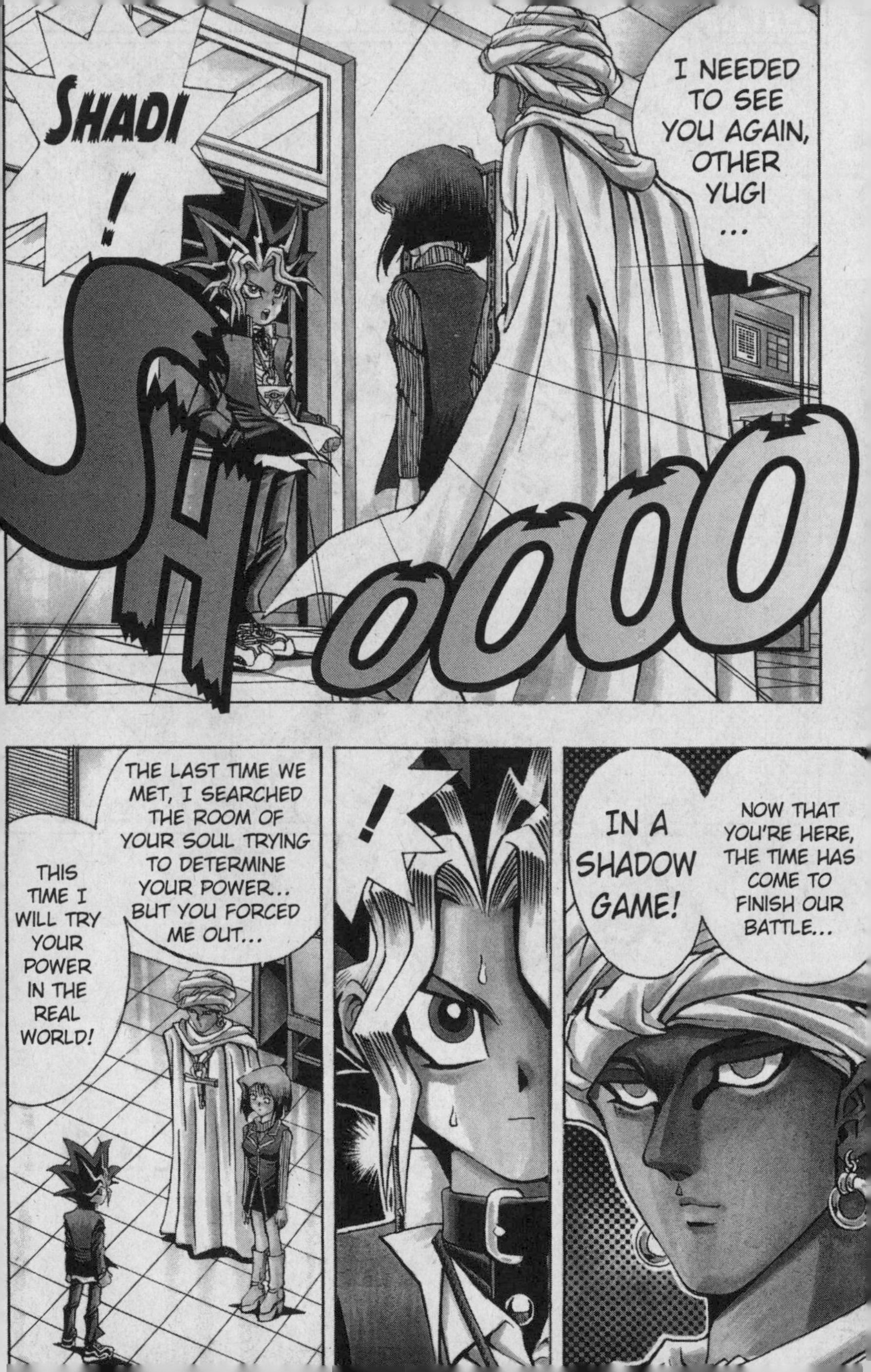
I NEEDED TO SEE YOU AGAIN, OTHER YUGI...
SHADI!
SHOOOO
NOW THAT YOU'RE HERE, THE TIME HAS COME TO FINISH OUR BATTLE...
IN A SHADOW GAME!
!
THE LAST TIME WE MET, I SEARCHED THE ROOM OF YOUR SOUL TRYING TO DETERMINE YOUR POWER... BUT YOU FORCED ME OUT...
THIS TIME I WILL TRY YOUR POWER IN THE REAL WORLD!

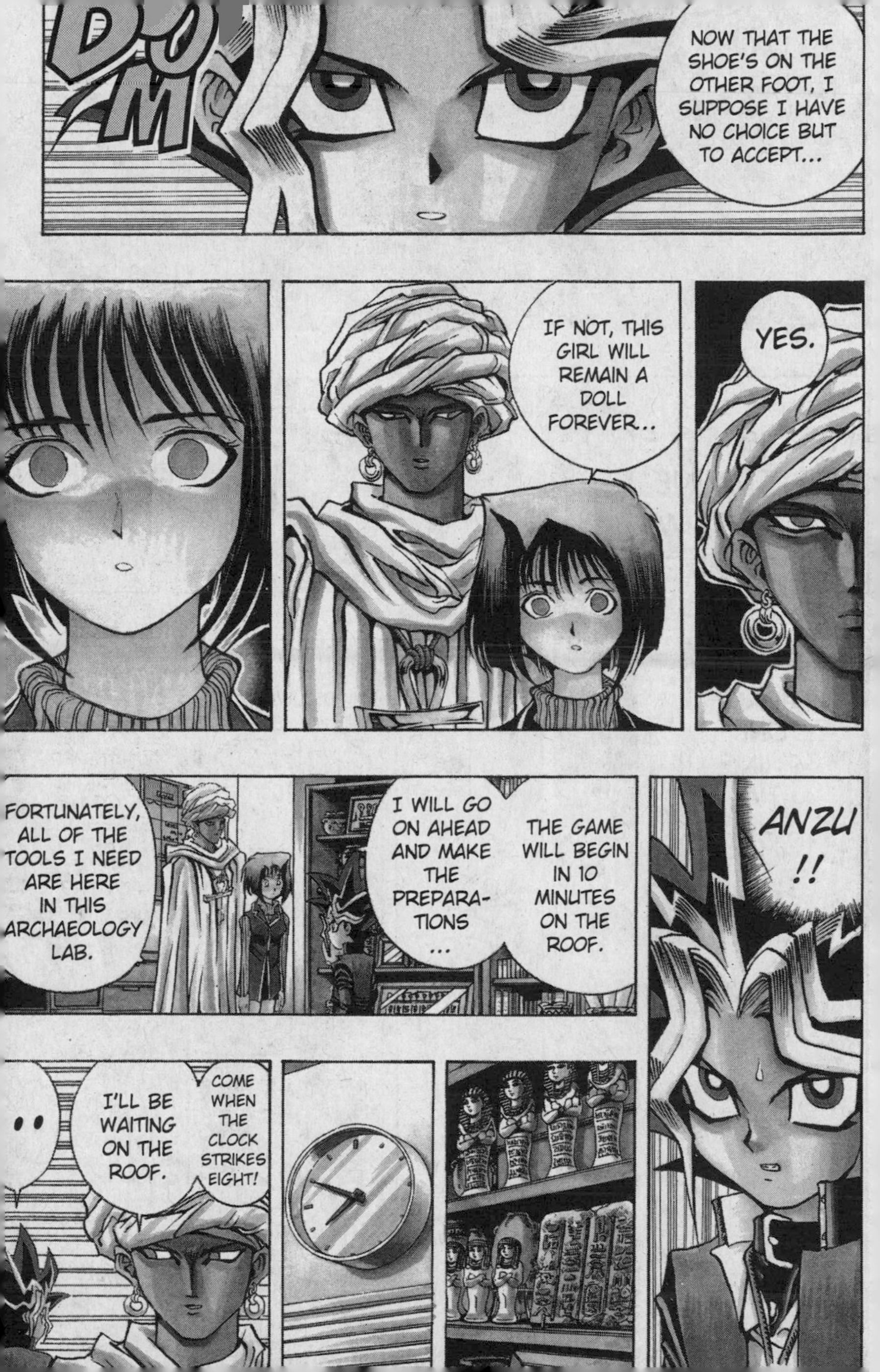
NOW THAT THE SHOE'S ON THE OTHER FOOT, I SUPPOSE I HAVE NO CHOICE BUT TO ACCEPT...
YES.
IF NOT, THIS GIRL WILL REMAIN A DOLL FOREVER...
THE GAME WILL BEGIN IN 10 MINUTES ON THE ROOF.
I WILL GO ON AHEAD AND MAKE THE PREPARATIONS...
FORTUNATELY, ALL OF THE TOOLS I NEED ARE HERE IN THIS ARCHAEOLOGY LAB.
COME WHEN THE CLOCK STRIKES EIGHT!
I'LL BE WAITING ON THE ROOF.
..
ANZU!!

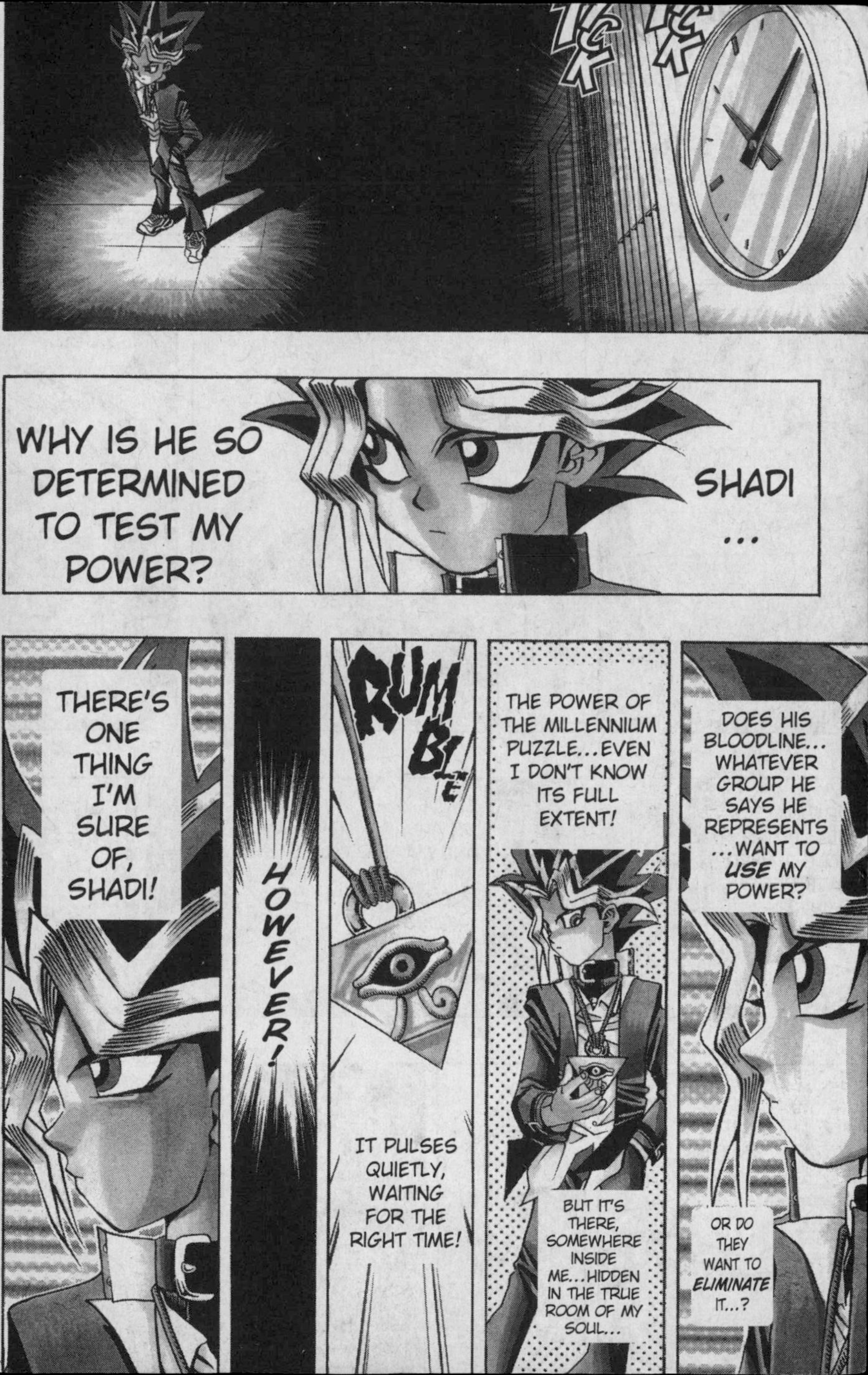

TICK
TICK
SHADI ...
WHY IS HE SO DETERMINED TO TEST MY POWER?
DOES HIS BLOODLINE... WHATEVER GROUP HE SAYS HE REPRESENTS ...WANT TO *USE* MY POWER?
OR DO THEY WANT TO *ELIMINATE* IT...?
THE POWER OF THE MILLENNIUM PUZZLE...EVEN I DON'T KNOW ITS FULL EXTENT!
BUT IT'S THERE, SOMEWHERE INSIDE ME...HIDDEN IN THE TRUE ROOM OF MY SOUL...
RUMBLE
IT PULSES QUIETLY, WAITING FOR THE RIGHT TIME!
HOWEVER!
THERE'S ONE THING I'M SURE OF, SHADI!

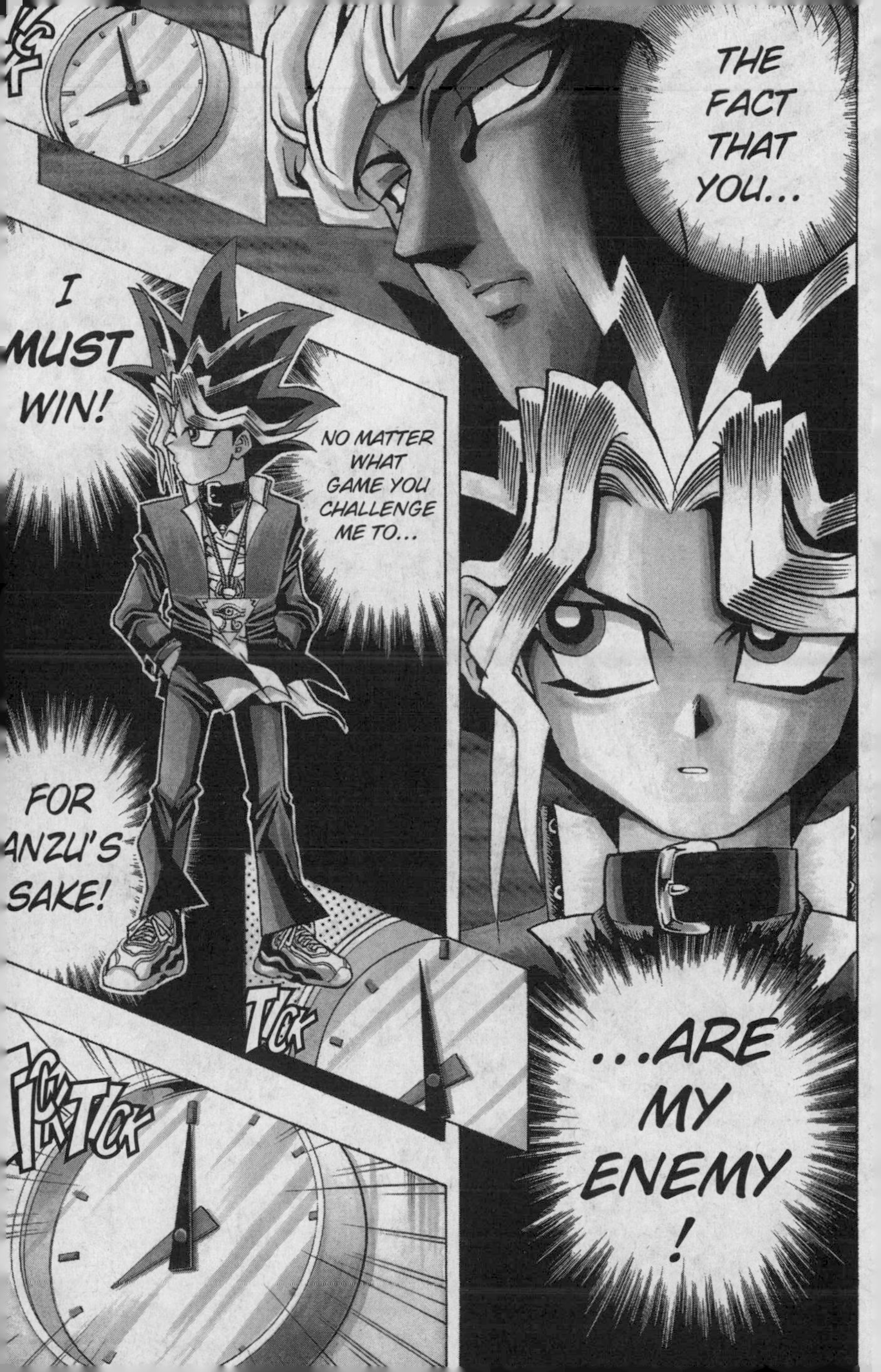
THE FACT THAT YOU...
I MUST WIN!
NO MATTER WHAT GAME YOU CHALLENGE ME TO...
FOR ANZU'S SAKE!
...ARE MY ENEMY!
TICK

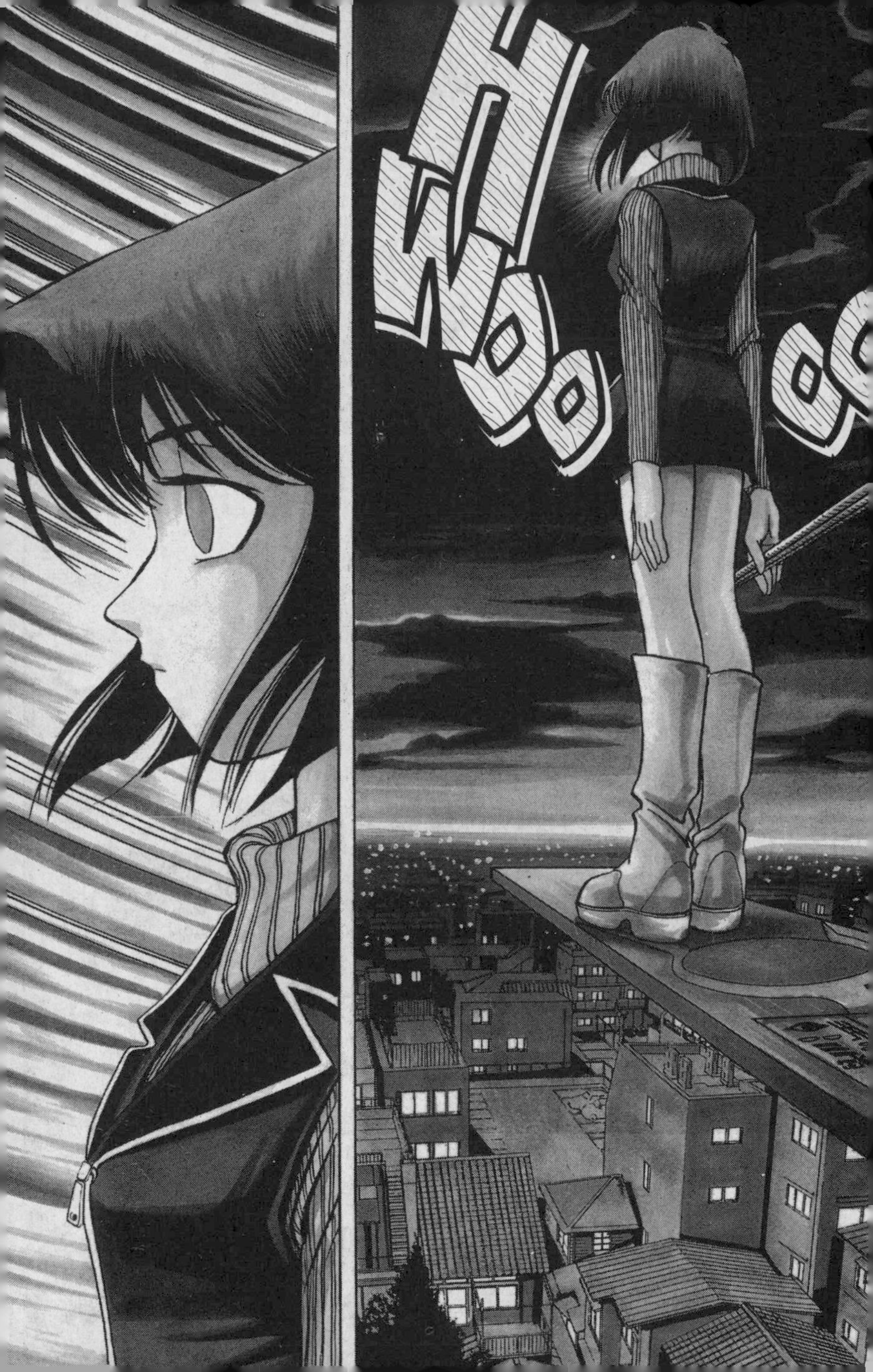
WHOOOO

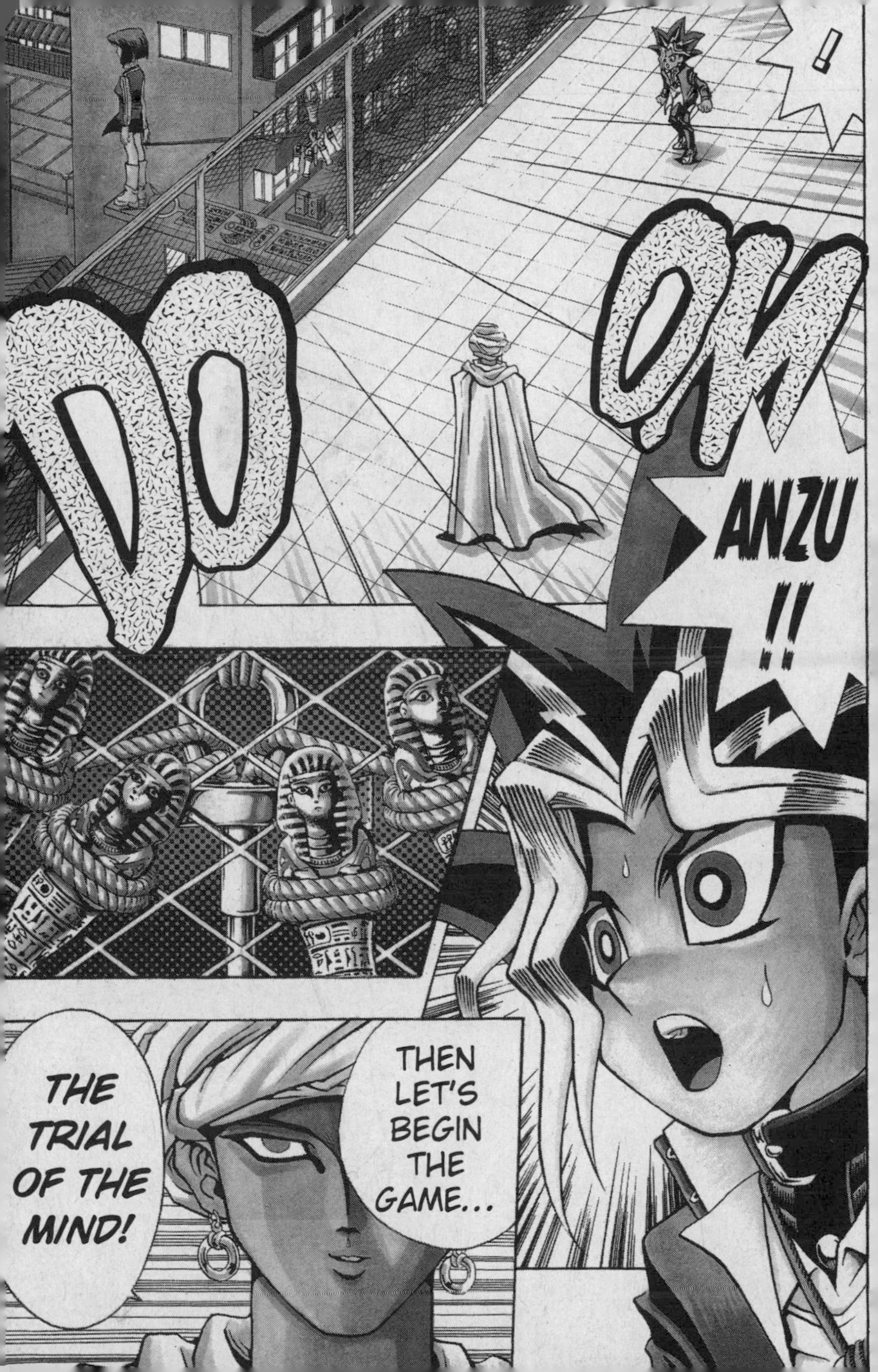
!
DO
OM
ANZU!!
THEN LET'S BEGIN THE GAME...
THE TRIAL OF THE MIND!

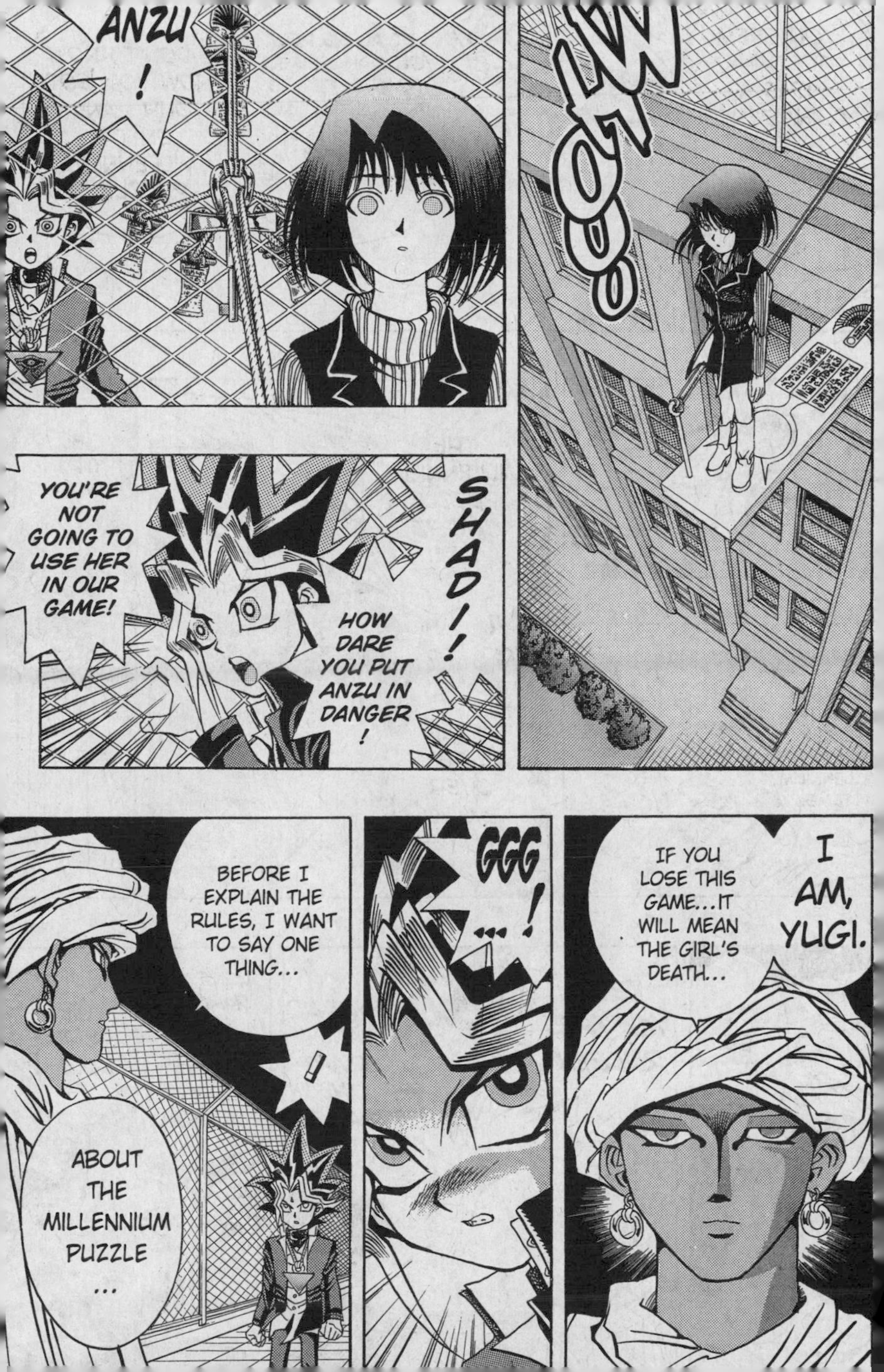
WOOOOO
ANZU!
SHAD!!
HOW DARE YOU PUT ANZU IN DANGER!
YOU'RE NOT GOING TO USE HER IN OUR GAME!
I AM, YUGI.
IF YOU LOSE THIS GAME...IT WILL MEAN THE GIRL'S DEATH...
GGG!
...!
BEFORE I EXPLAIN THE RULES, I WANT TO SAY ONE THING...
!
ABOUT THE MILLENNIUM PUZZLE...

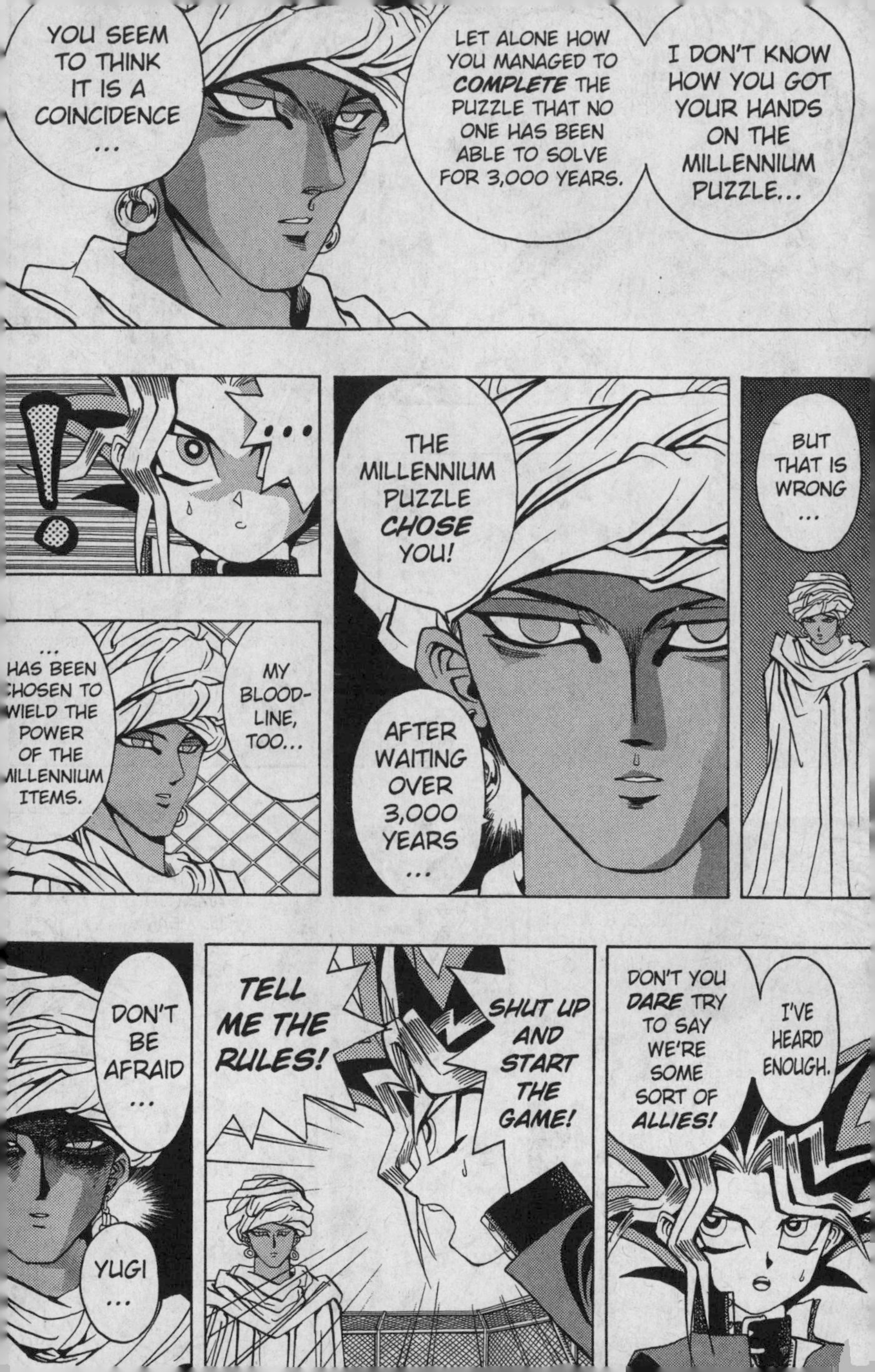
I DON'T KNOW HOW YOU GOT YOUR HANDS ON THE MILLENNIUM PUZZLE...
LET ALONE HOW YOU MANAGED TO *COMPLETE* THE PUZZLE THAT NO ONE HAS BEEN ABLE TO SOLVE FOR 3,000 YEARS.
YOU SEEM TO THINK IT IS A COINCIDENCE ...
BUT THAT IS WRONG ...
THE MILLENNIUM PUZZLE *CHOSE* YOU!
AFTER WAITING OVER 3,000 YEARS ...
!
...
MY BLOOD-LINE, TOO...
... HAS BEEN CHOSEN TO WIELD THE POWER OF THE MILLENNIUM ITEMS.
I'VE HEARD ENOUGH.
DON'T YOU *DARE* TRY TO SAY WE'RE SOME SORT OF *ALLIES!*
SHUT UP AND START THE GAME!
TELL ME THE RULES!
DON'T BE AFRAID ...
YUGI ...

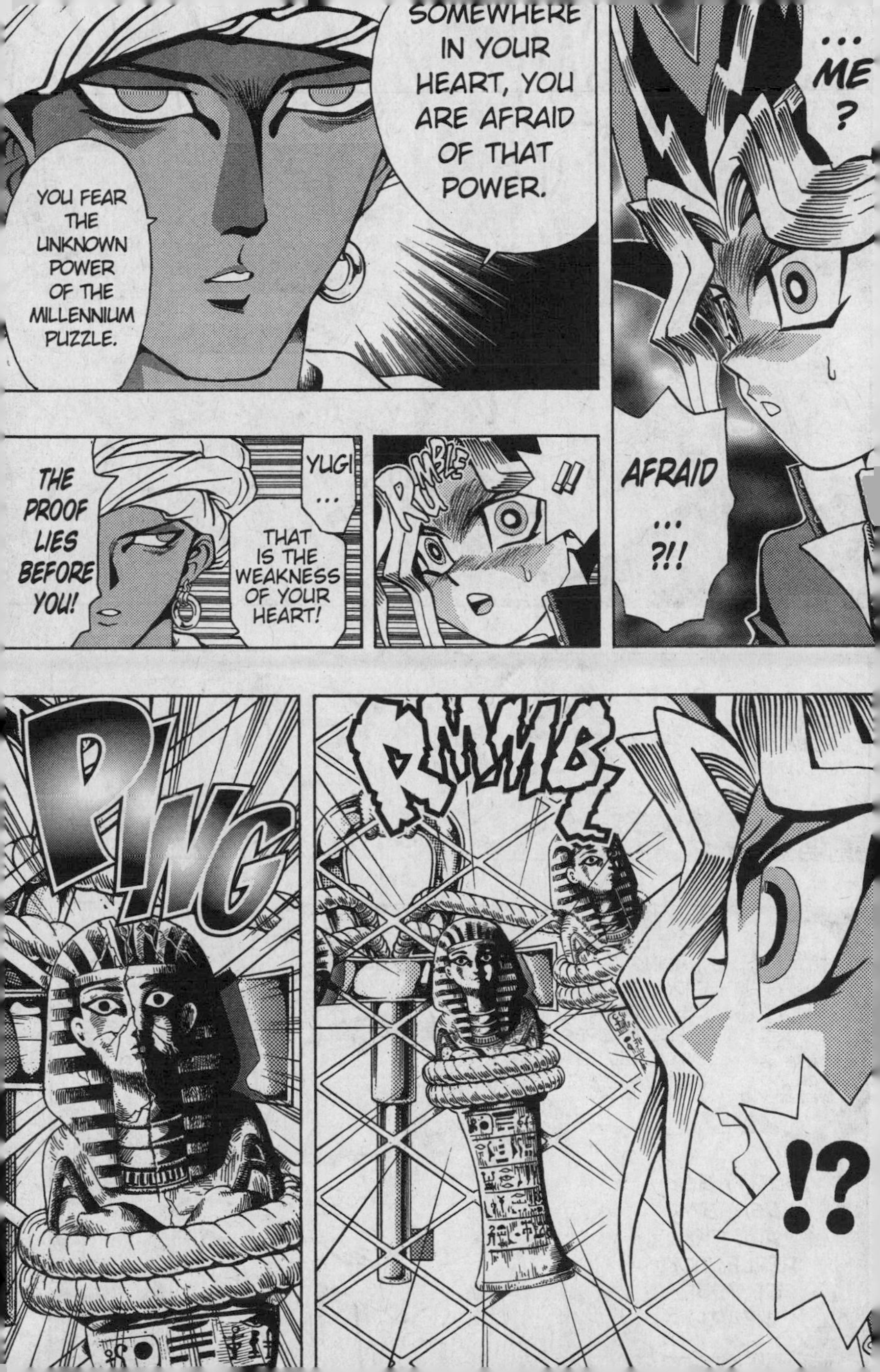
YOU FEAR THE UNKNOWN POWER OF THE MILLENNIUM PUZZLE.
SOMEWHERE IN YOUR HEART, YOU ARE AFRAID OF THAT POWER.
... ME ?
AFRAID ... ?!!
RUMBLE
!!
YUGI ...
THAT IS THE WEAKNESS OF YOUR HEART!
THE PROOF LIES BEFORE YOU!
!?
RUMB
PING

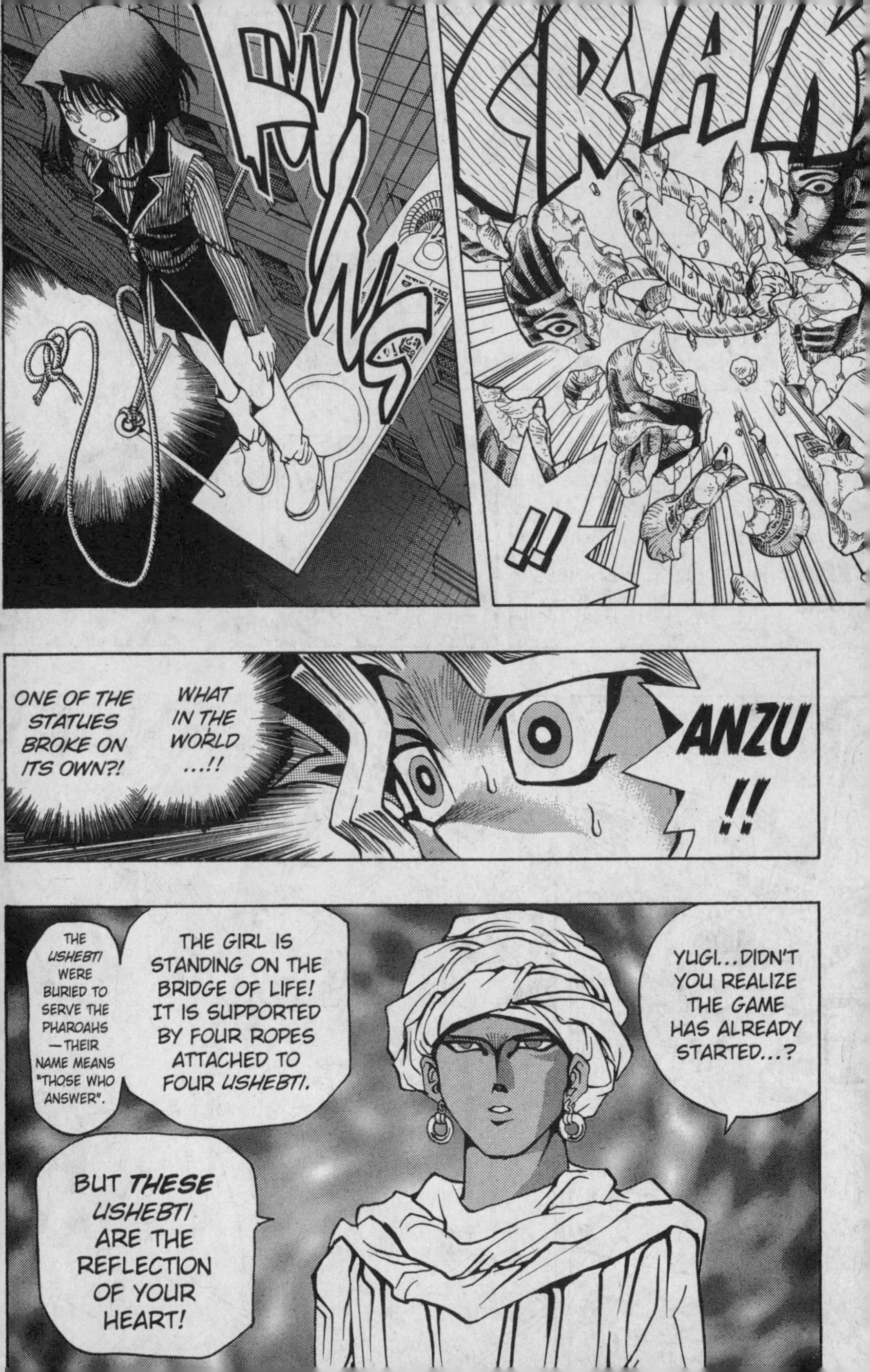
!!
ANZU !!
WHAT IN THE WORLD ...!!
ONE OF THE STATUES BROKE ON ITS OWN?!
YUGI...DIDN'T YOU REALIZE THE GAME HAS ALREADY STARTED...?
THE GIRL IS STANDING ON THE BRIDGE OF LIFE! IT IS SUPPORTED BY FOUR ROPES ATTACHED TO FOUR USHEBTI.
THE USHEBTI WERE BURIED TO SERVE THE PHAROAHS —THEIR NAME MEANS "THOSE WHO ANSWER".
BUT THESE USHEBTI ARE THE REFLECTION OF YOUR HEART!

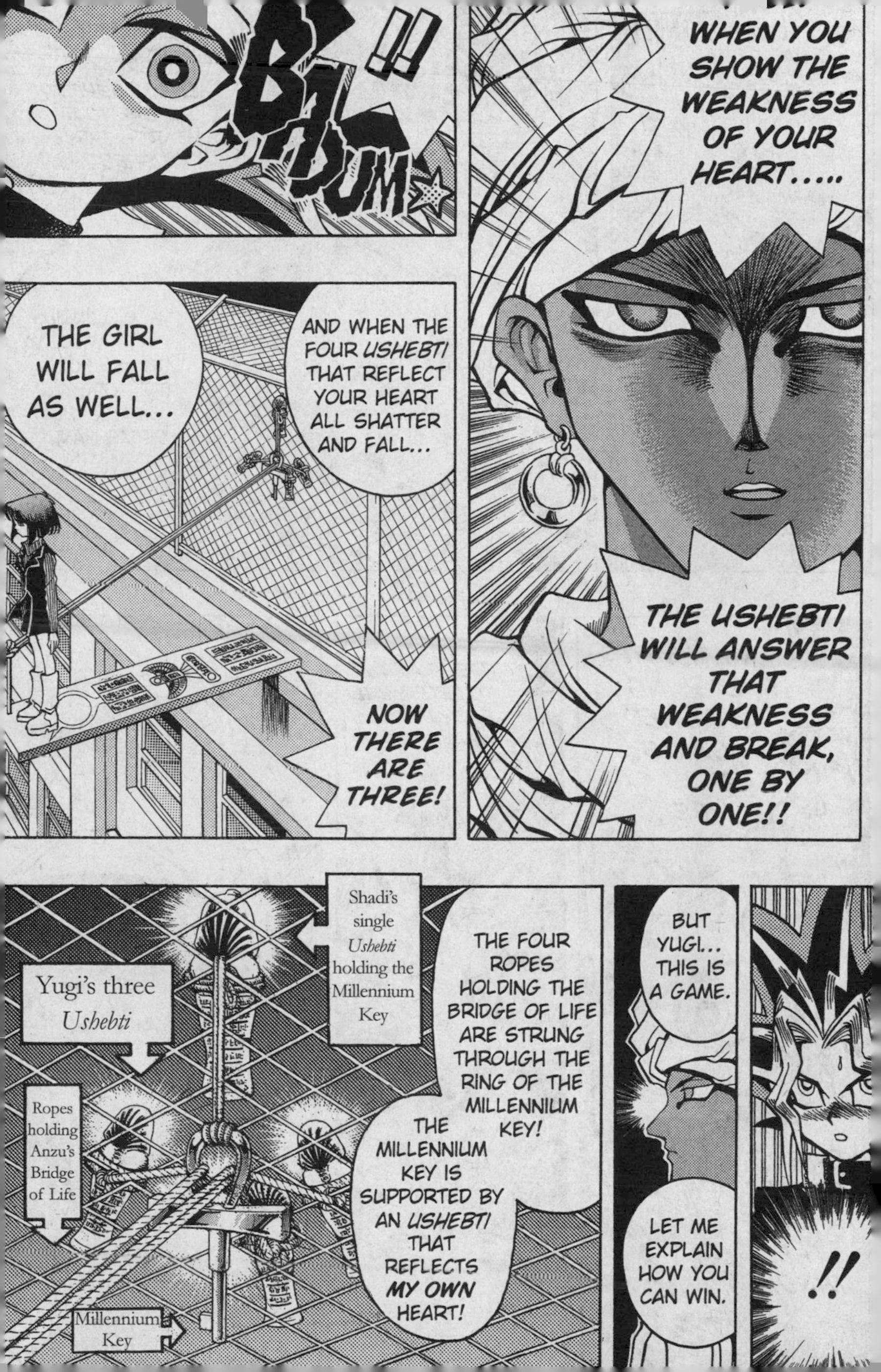
WHEN YOU SHOW THE WEAKNESS OF YOUR HEART.....
THE USHEBTI WILL ANSWER THAT WEAKNESS AND BREAK, ONE BY ONE!!
!!
BA DUM
AND WHEN THE FOUR *USHEBTI* THAT REFLECT YOUR HEART ALL SHATTER AND FALL...
THE GIRL WILL FALL AS WELL...
NOW THERE ARE THREE!
!!
BUT YUGI... THIS IS A GAME.
LET ME EXPLAIN HOW YOU CAN WIN.
THE FOUR ROPES HOLDING THE BRIDGE OF LIFE ARE STRUNG THROUGH THE RING OF THE MILLENNIUM KEY!
THE MILLENNIUM KEY IS SUPPORTED BY AN *USHEBTI* THAT REFLECTS *MY OWN* HEART!
Shadi's single *Ushebti* holding the Millennium Key
Yugi's three *Ushebti*
Ropes holding Anzu's Bridge of Life
Millennium Key

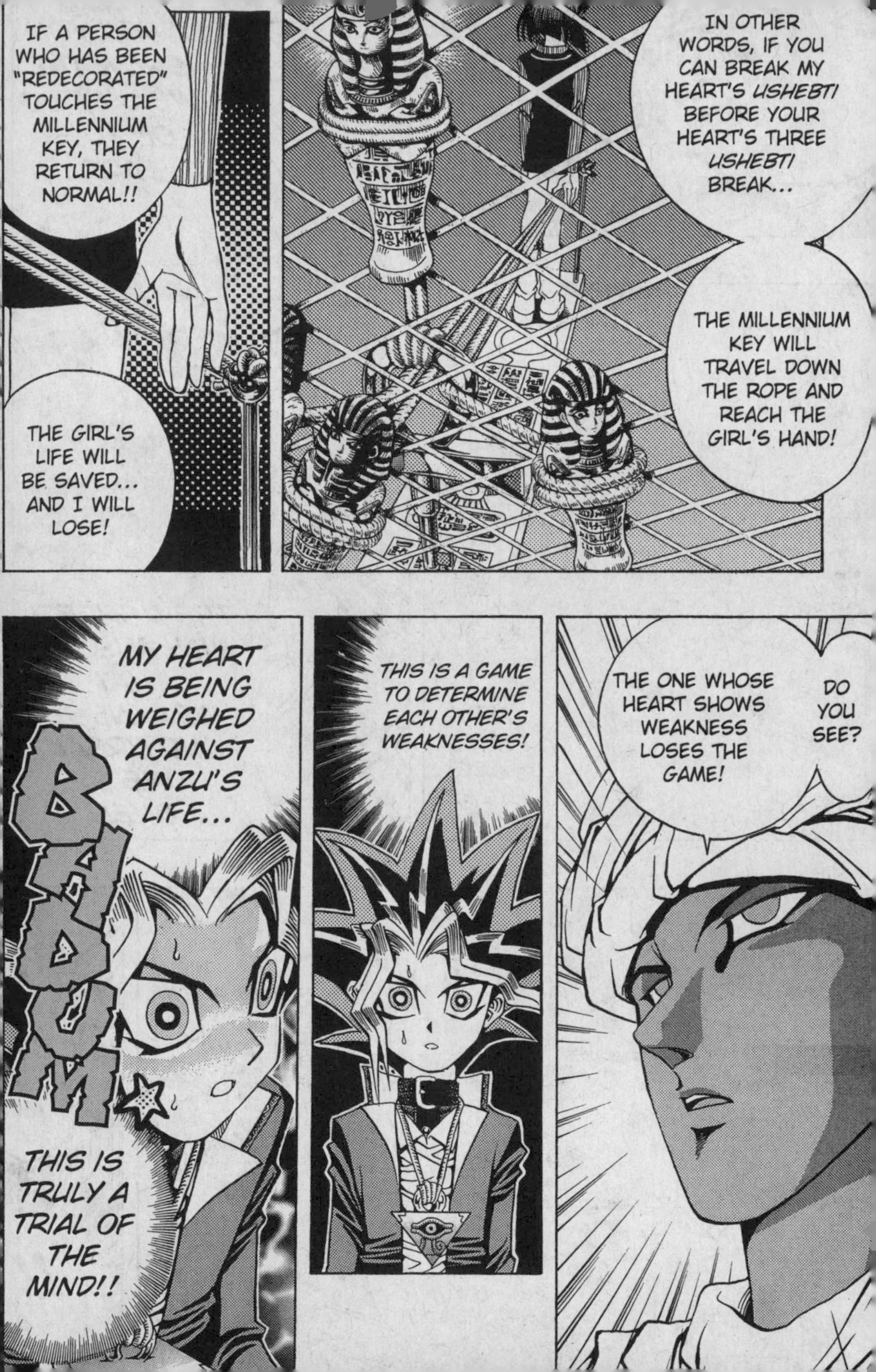
IN OTHER WORDS, IF YOU CAN BREAK MY HEART'S *USHEBTI* BEFORE YOUR HEART'S THREE *USHEBTI* BREAK...
THE MILLENNIUM KEY WILL TRAVEL DOWN THE ROPE AND REACH THE GIRL'S HAND!
IF A PERSON WHO HAS BEEN "REDECORATED" TOUCHES THE MILLENNIUM KEY, THEY RETURN TO NORMAL!!
THE GIRL'S LIFE WILL BE SAVED... AND I WILL LOSE!
DO YOU SEE?
THE ONE WHOSE HEART SHOWS WEAKNESS LOSES THE GAME!
THIS IS A GAME TO DETERMINE EACH OTHER'S WEAKNESSES!
MY HEART IS BEING WEIGHED AGAINST ANZU'S LIFE...
THIS IS TRULY A TRIAL OF THE MIND!!

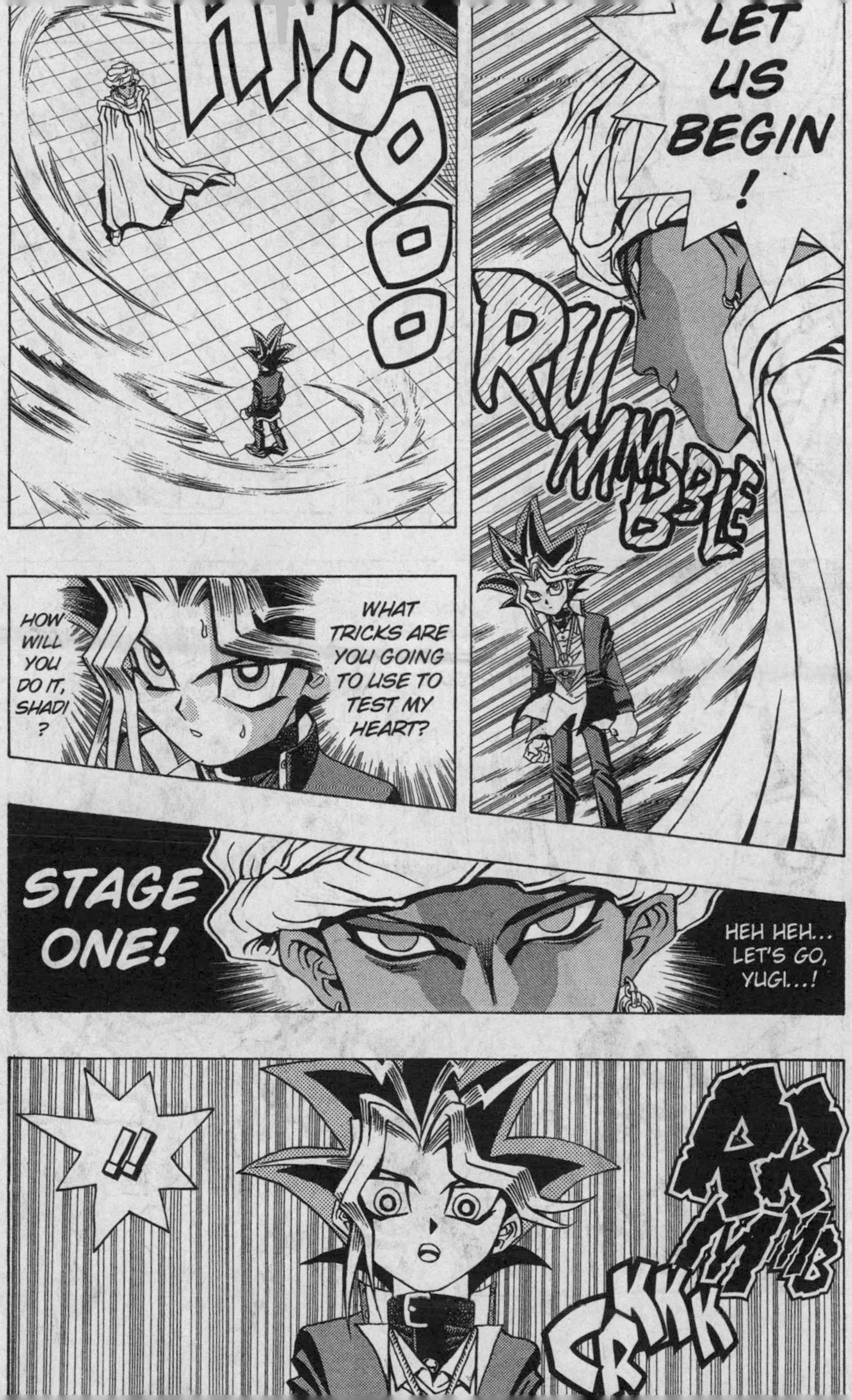
LET US BEGIN!
RUMMBLE
HOW WILL YOU DO IT, SHADI?
WHAT TRICKS ARE YOU GOING TO USE TO TEST MY HEART?
HEH HEH... LET'S GO, YUGI...!
STAGE ONE!
!!

THIS WAY

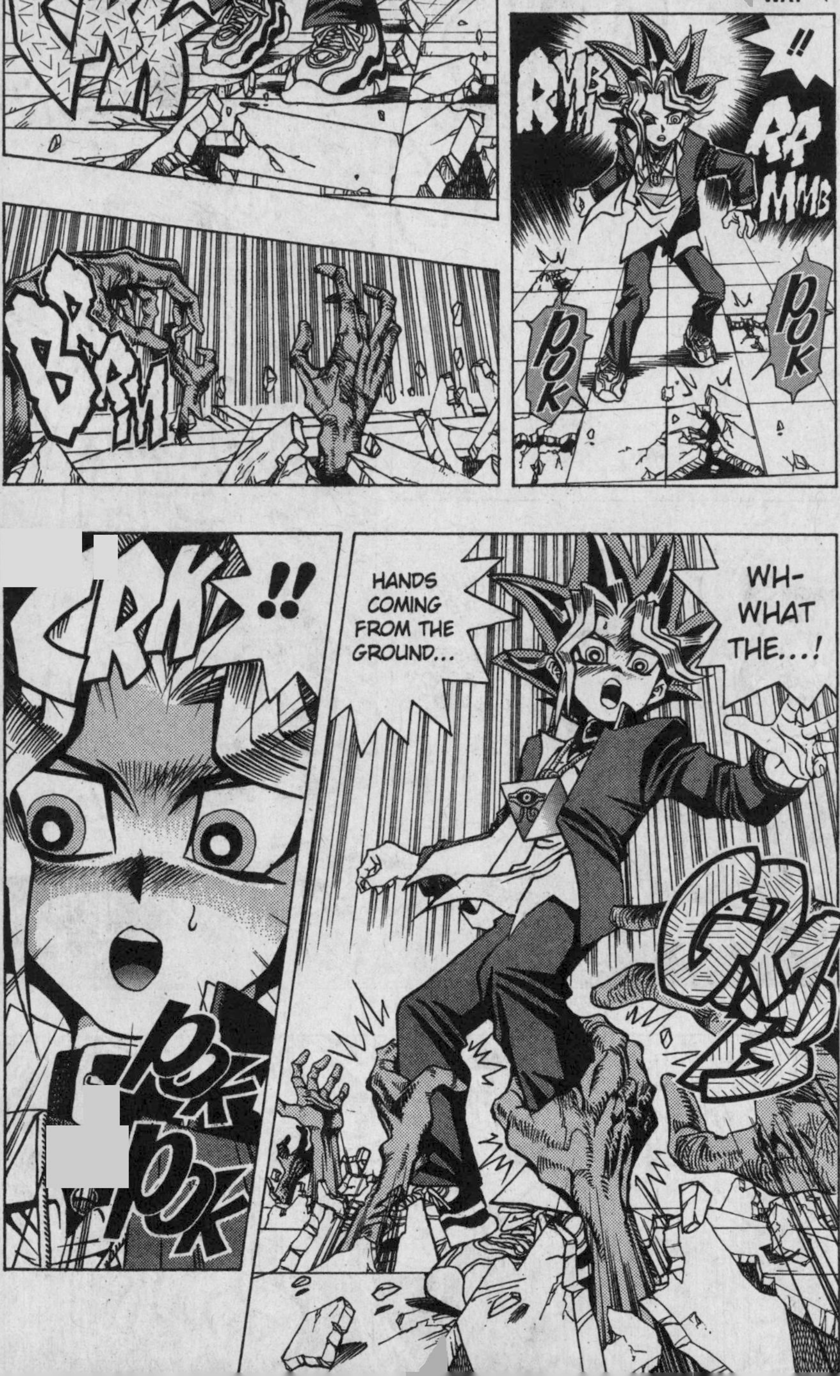
RMB
!!
RR MMB
POK
POK
BRM
HANDS COMING FROM THE GROUND...
WH- WHAT THE...!
CRK!!
POK
POOK

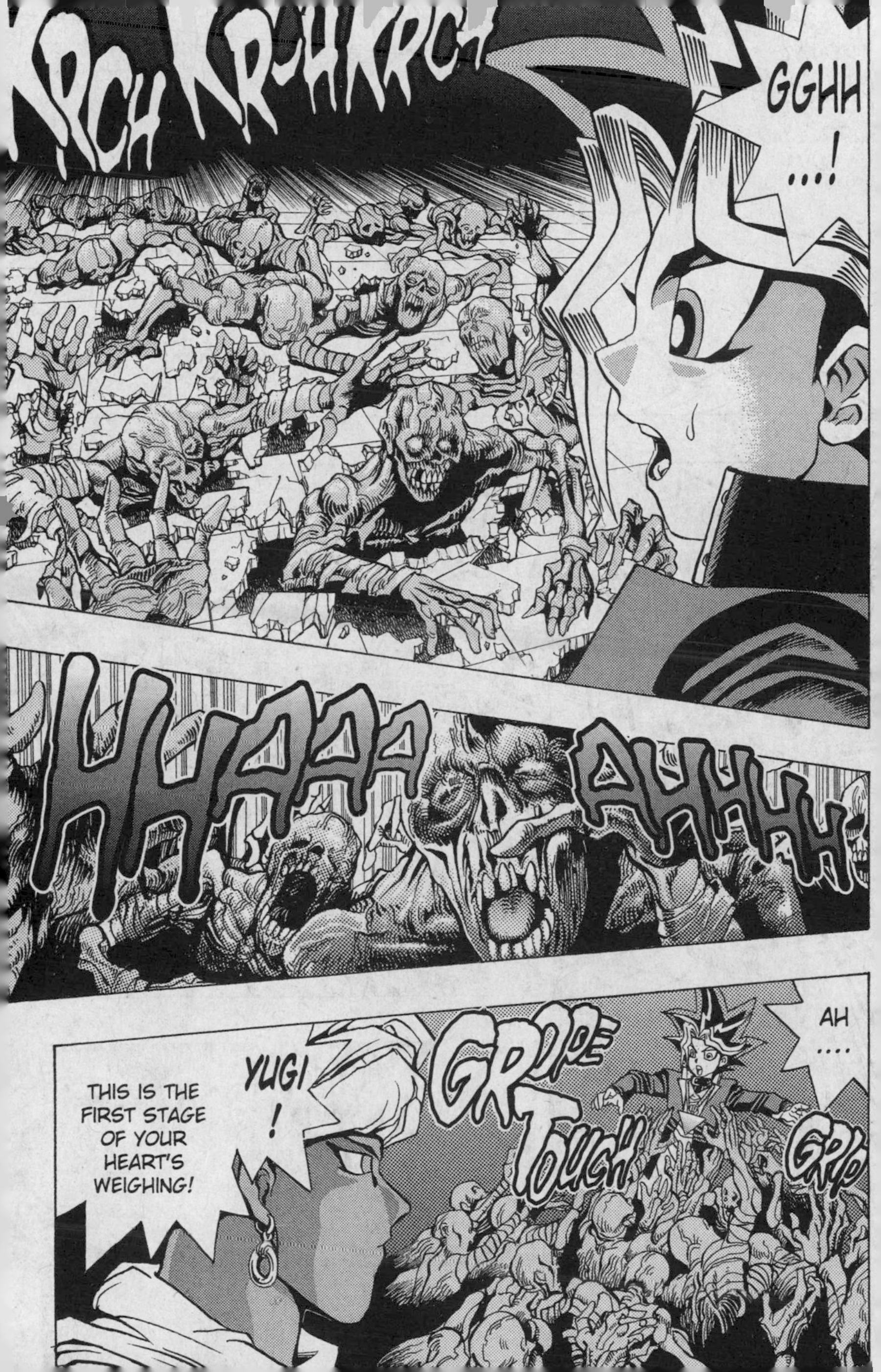
KRCH KRCH KRCH
GGHH ....!
HHAAA AHHHH
AH ....
GROPE
TOUCH
GROPE
YUGI!
THIS IS THE FIRST STAGE OF YOUR HEART'S WEIGHING!

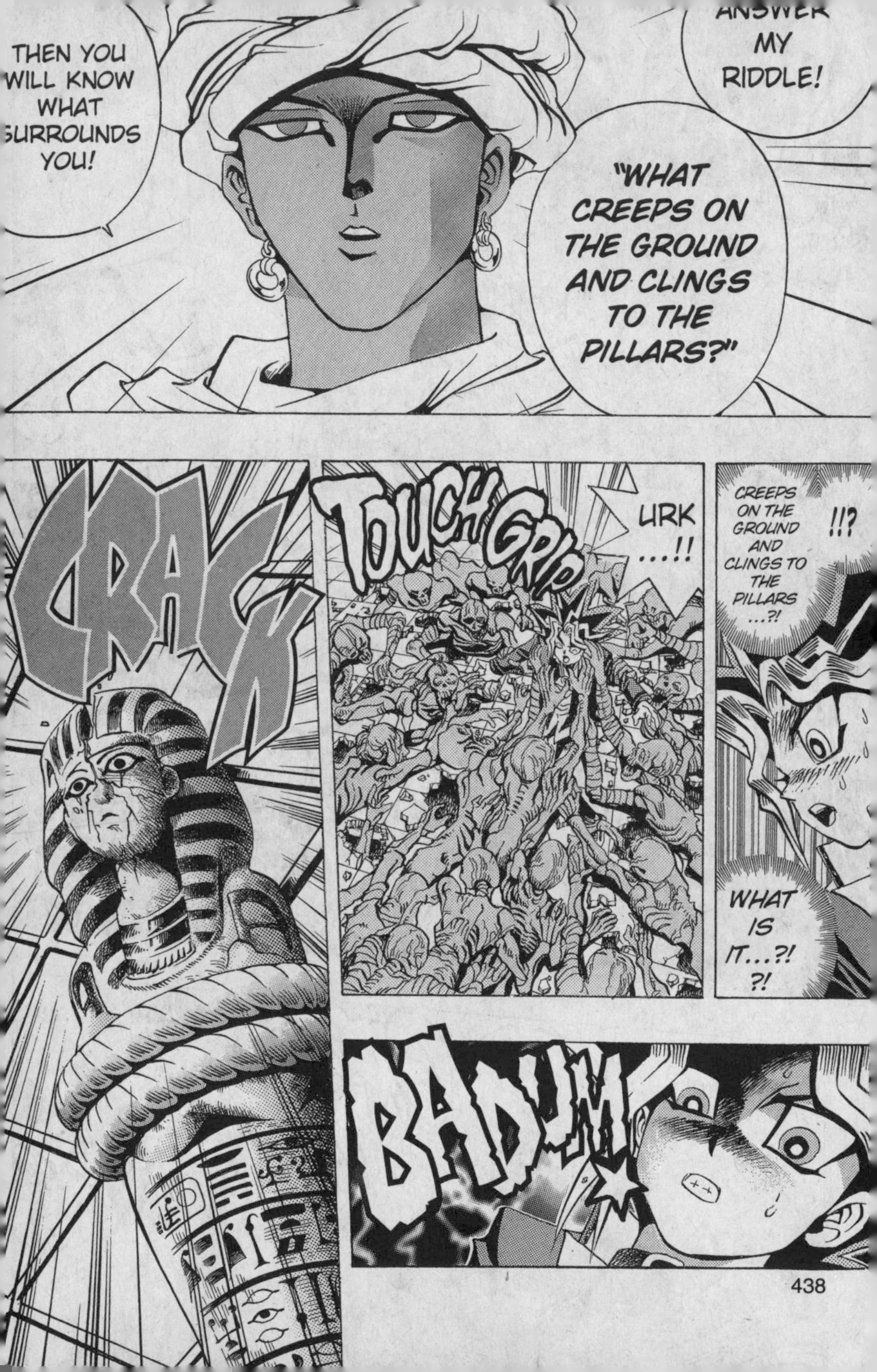
ANSWER MY RIDDLE!
"WHAT CREEPS ON THE GROUND AND CLINGS TO THE PILLARS?"
THEN YOU WILL KNOW WHAT SURROUNDS YOU!
CREEPS ON THE GROUND AND CLINGS TO THE PILLARS ...?!
!!?
WHAT IS IT...?! ?!
TOUCH
GRIP
URK ...!!
BADUM
CRACK

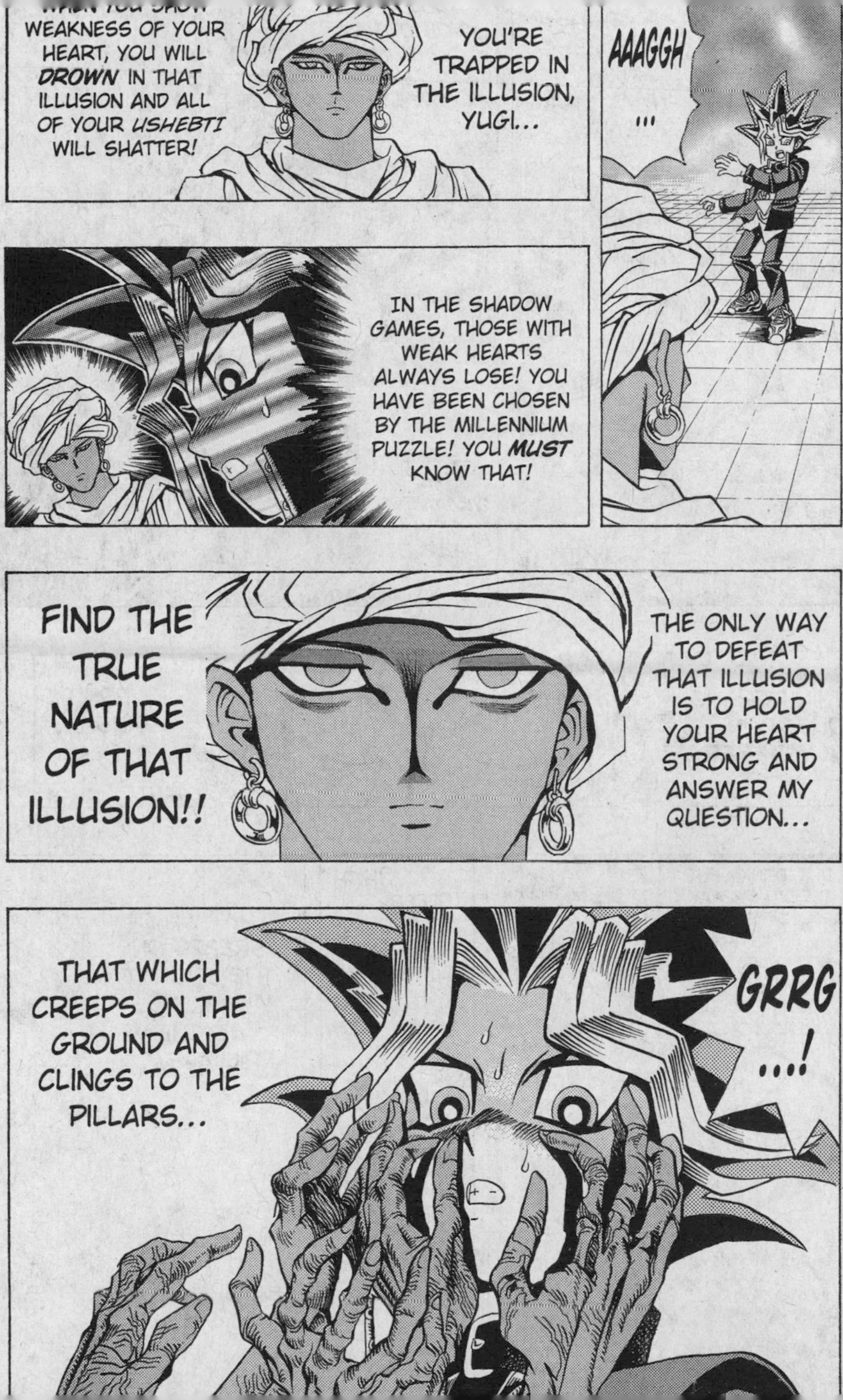
AAAGGH
...
YOU'RE TRAPPED IN THE ILLUSION, YUGI...
WEAKNESS OF YOUR HEART, YOU WILL DROWN IN THAT ILLUSION AND ALL OF YOUR USHEBTI WILL SHATTER!
IN THE SHADOW GAMES, THOSE WITH WEAK HEARTS ALWAYS LOSE! YOU HAVE BEEN CHOSEN BY THE MILLENNIUM PUZZLE! YOU MUST KNOW THAT!
THE ONLY WAY TO DEFEAT THAT ILLUSION IS TO HOLD YOUR HEART STRONG AND ANSWER MY QUESTION...
FIND THE TRUE NATURE OF THAT ILLUSION!!
GRRG
...!
THAT WHICH CREEPS ON THE GROUND AND CLINGS TO THE PILLARS...

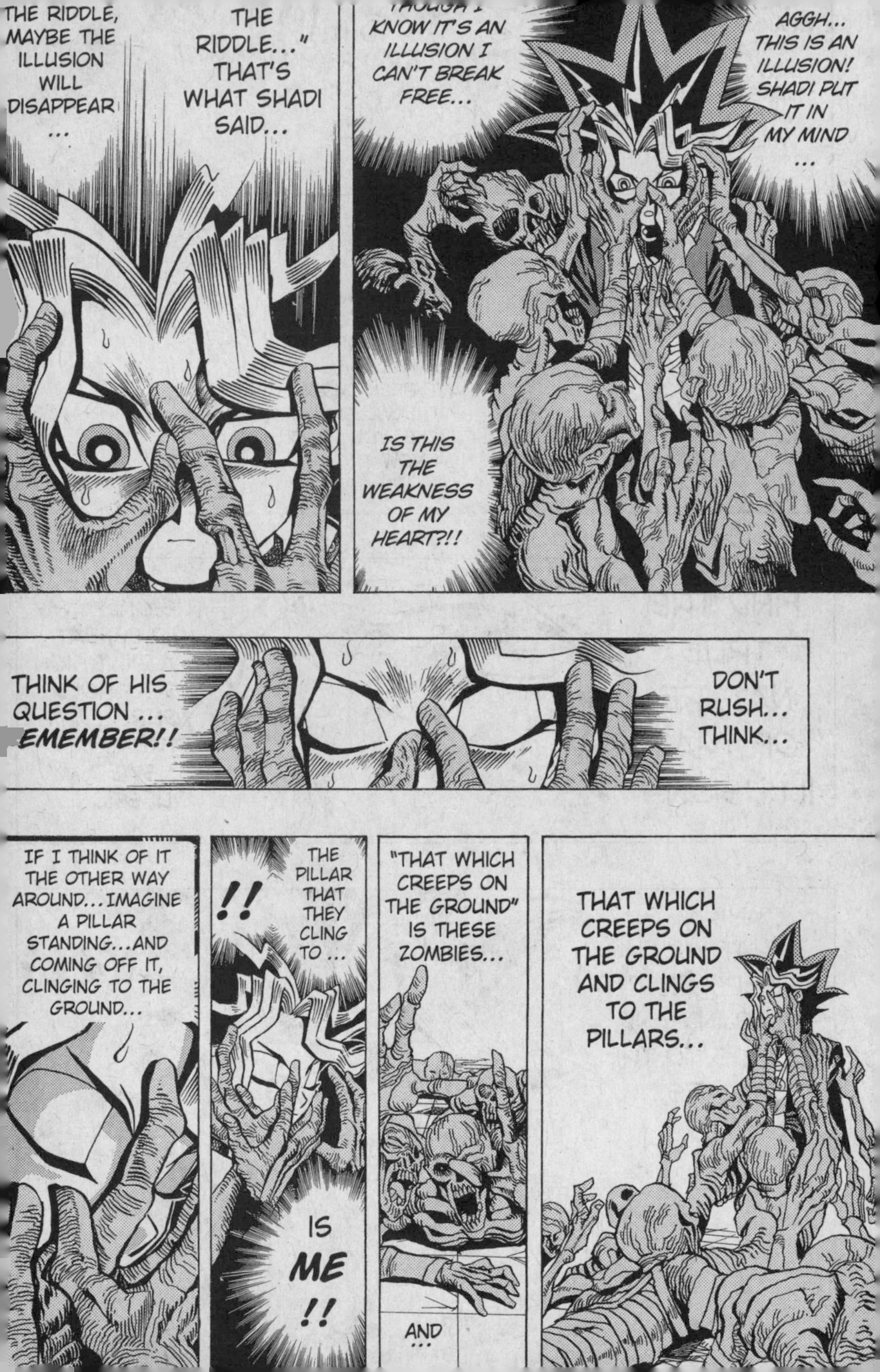
AGGH... THIS IS AN ILLUSION! SHADI PUT IT IN MY MIND ...
KNOW IT'S AN ILLUSION I CAN'T BREAK FREE...
IS THIS THE WEAKNESS OF MY HEART?!!
THE RIDDLE..." THAT'S WHAT SHADI SAID...
THE RIDDLE, MAYBE THE ILLUSION WILL DISAPPEAR ...
DON'T RUSH... THINK...
THINK OF HIS QUESTION ... EMEMBER!!
THAT WHICH CREEPS ON THE GROUND AND CLINGS TO THE PILLARS...
"THAT WHICH CREEPS ON THE GROUND" IS THESE ZOMBIES...
AND ...
THE PILLAR THAT THEY CLING TO ...
!!
IS ME !!
IF I THINK OF IT THE OTHER WAY AROUND...IMAGINE A PILLAR STANDING...AND COMING OFF IT, CLINGING TO THE GROUND...

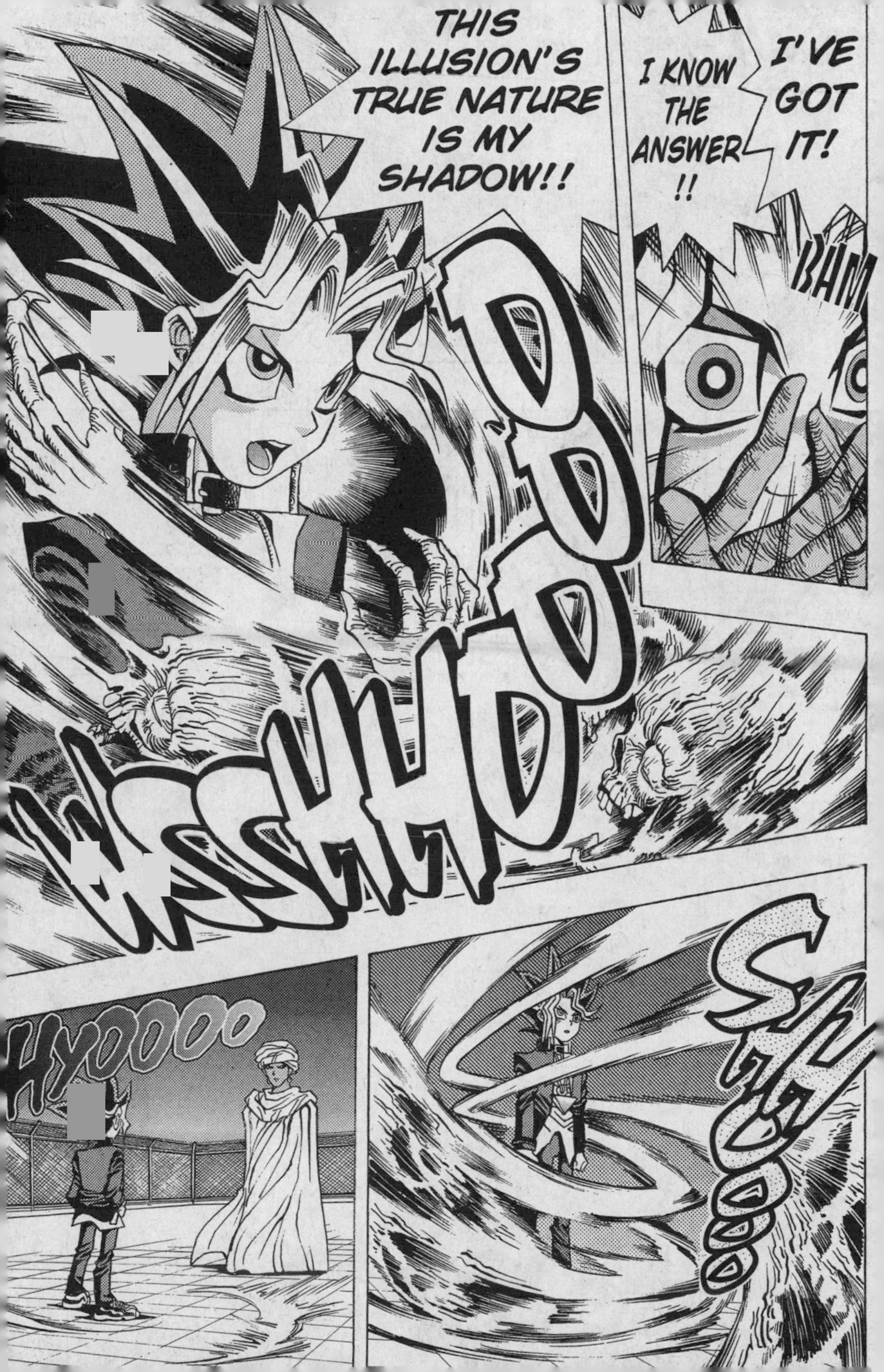
I'VE GOT IT!
I KNOW THE ANSWER!!
BAM
THIS ILLUSION'S TRUE NATURE IS MY SHADOW!!
HYOOOO

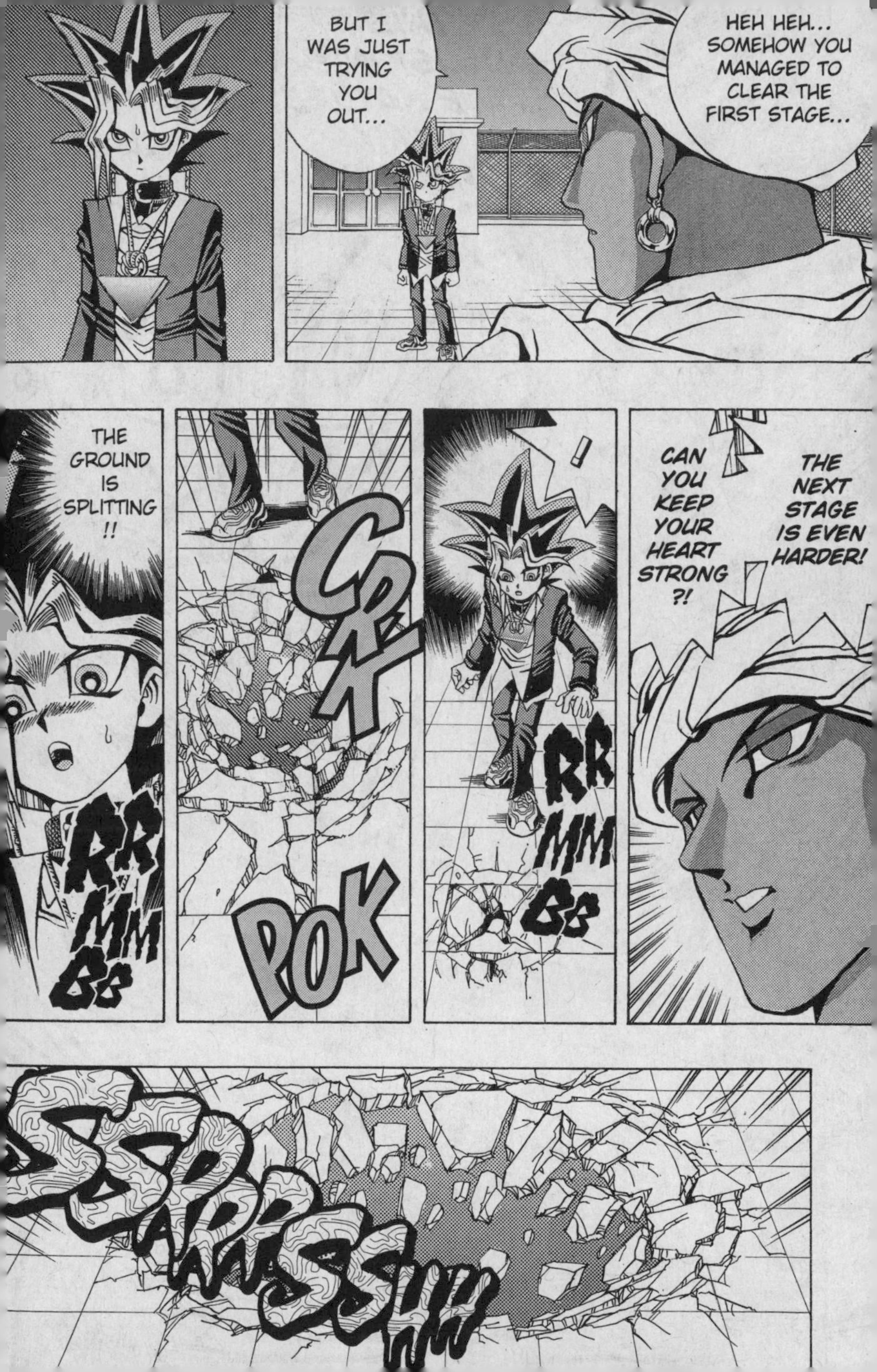
HEH HEH... SOMEHOW YOU MANAGED TO CLEAR THE FIRST STAGE...
BUT I WAS JUST TRYING YOU OUT...
THE NEXT STAGE IS EVEN HARDER!
CAN YOU KEEP YOUR HEART STRONG?!
!
RRMMBB
CRK
POK
THE GROUND IS SPLITTING!!
RRMMBB

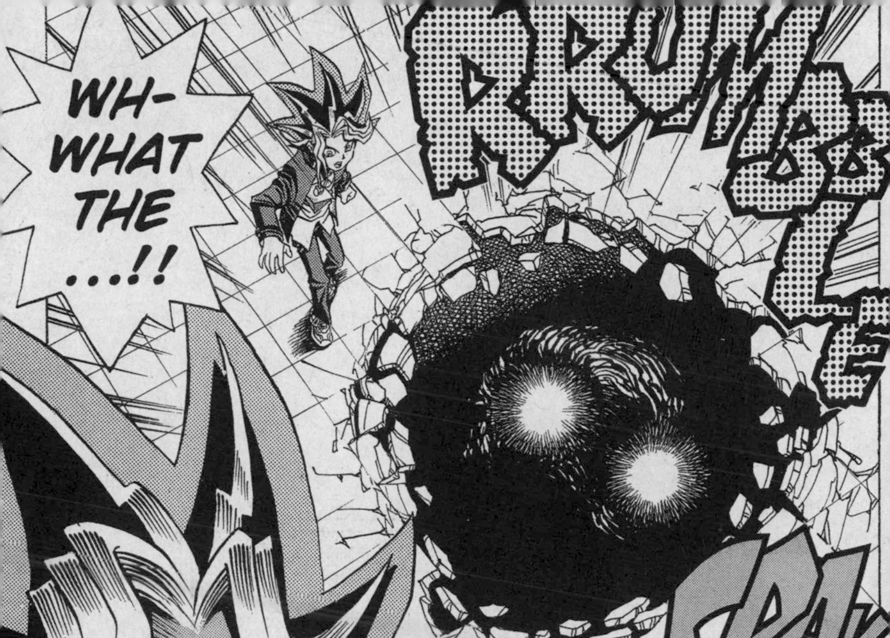
RUMBLE
WH- WHAT THE ...!!
CRAK
CRUNCH
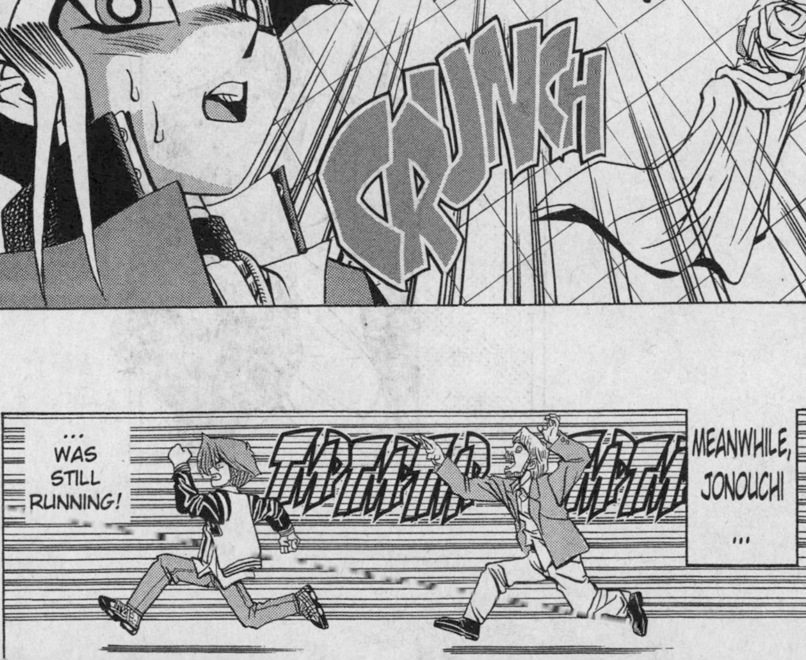
MEANWHILE, JONOUCHI ...
... WAS STILL RUNNING!

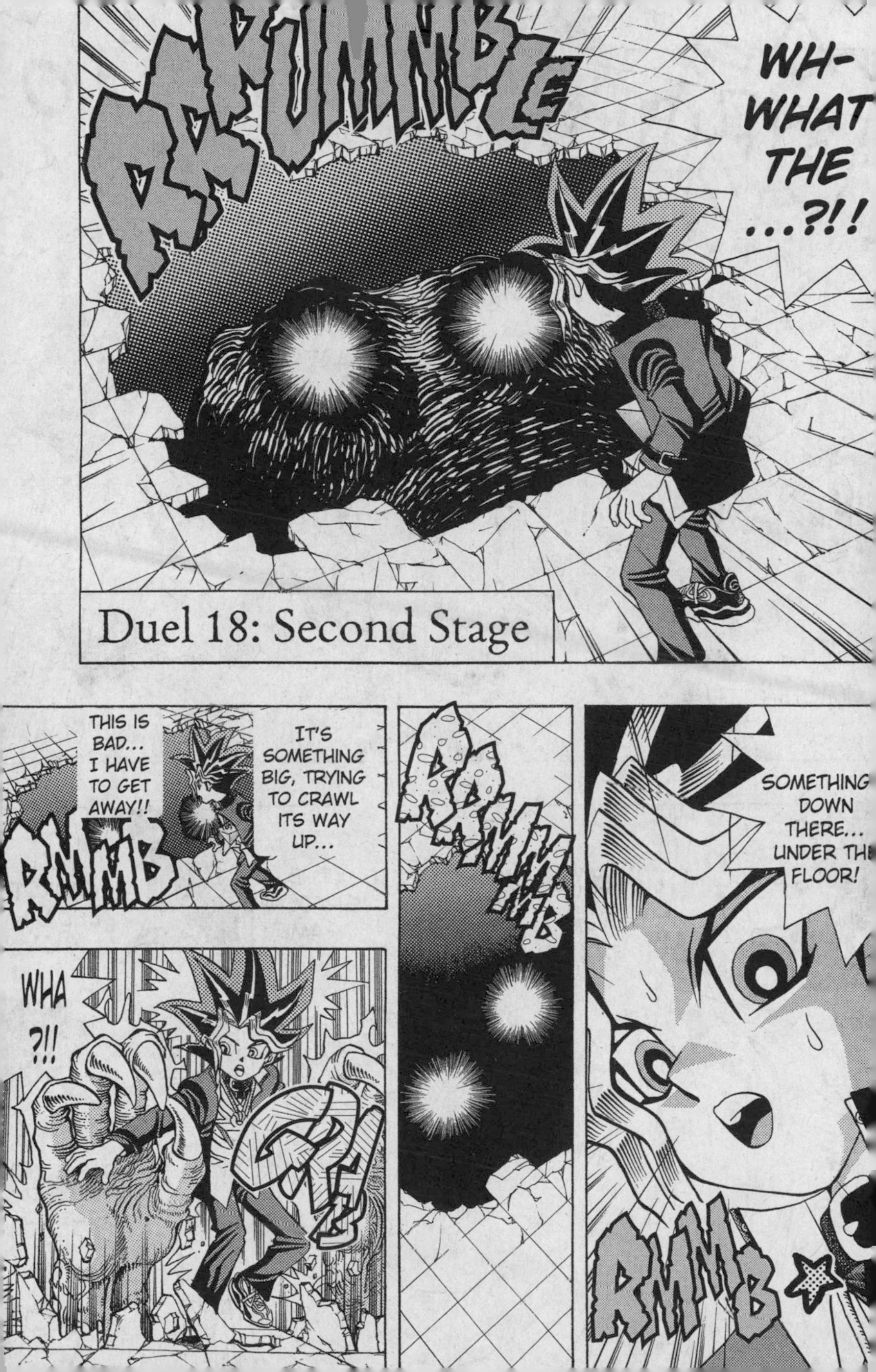
WH- WHAT THE ...?!!
Duel 18: Second Stage
SOMETHING DOWN THERE... UNDER THE FLOOR!
RMMB
IT'S SOMETHING BIG, TRYING TO CRAWL ITS WAY UP...
THIS IS BAD... I HAVE TO GET AWAY!!
RMMB
WHA ?!!

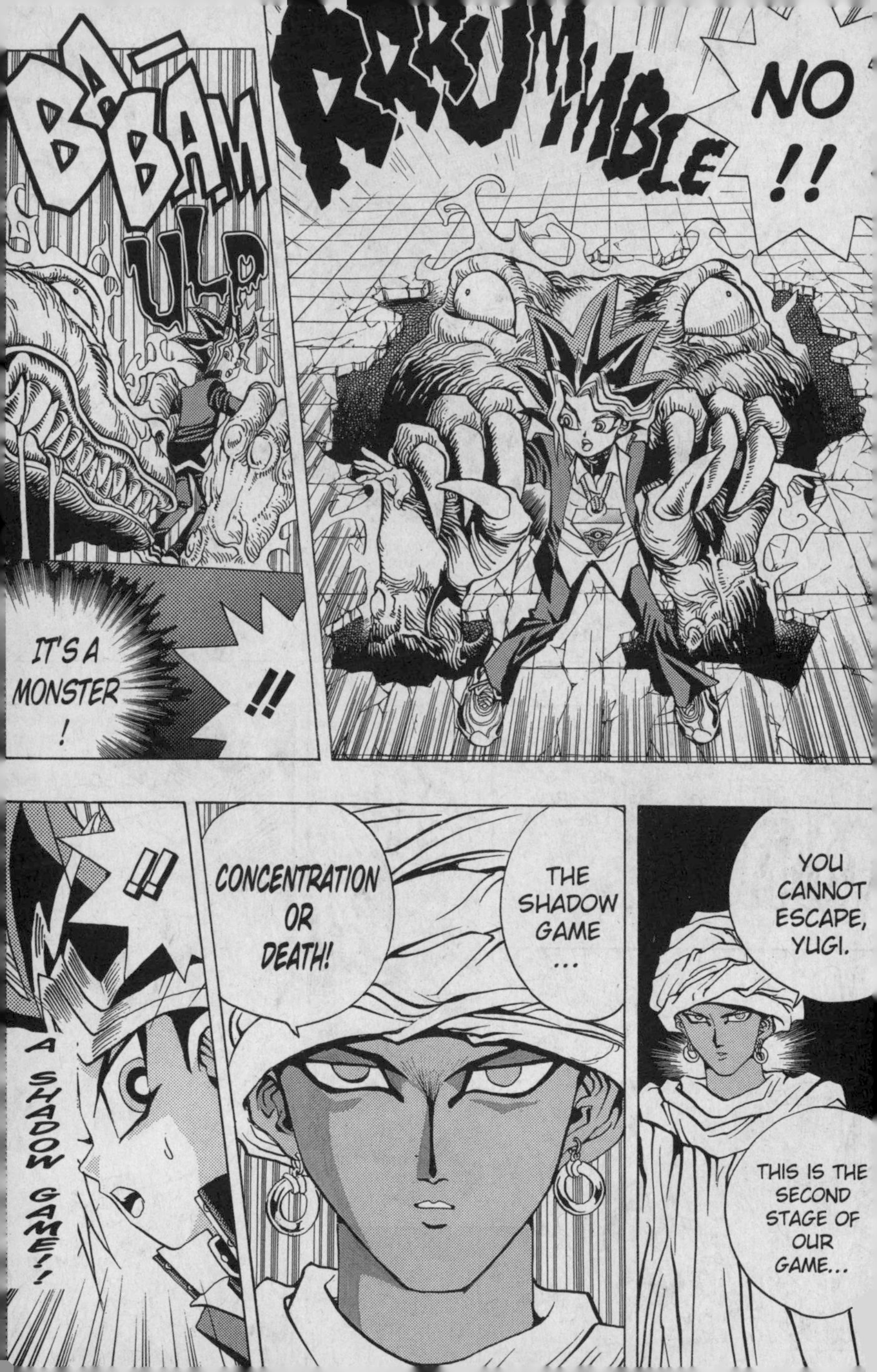
RRRUMMBLE
NO!!
BA-BAM
ULP
IT'S A MONSTER!
!!
YOU CANNOT ESCAPE, YUGI.
THIS IS THE SECOND STAGE OF OUR GAME...
THE SHADOW GAME...
CONCENTRATION OR DEATH!
!!
A SHADOW GAME!!

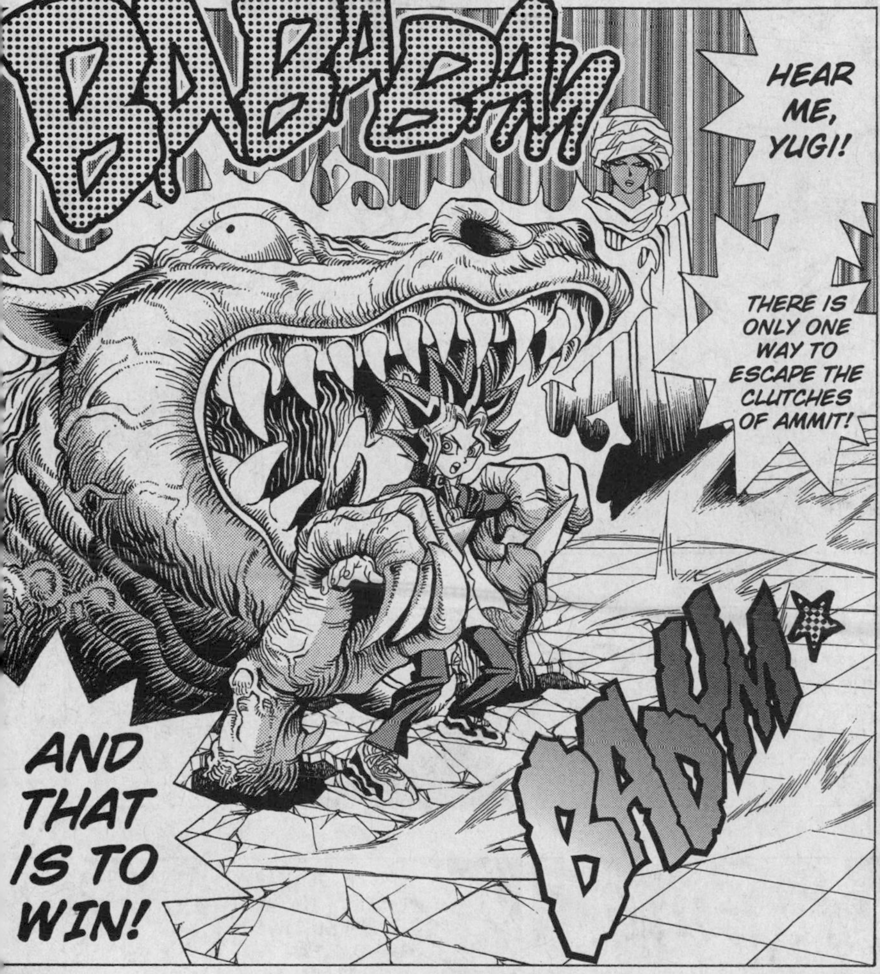
BABABAM
HEAR ME, YUGI!
THERE IS ONLY ONE WAY TO ESCAPE THE CLUTCHES OF AMMIT!
AND THAT IS TO WIN!
BADUM

Duel 18:
Second Stage

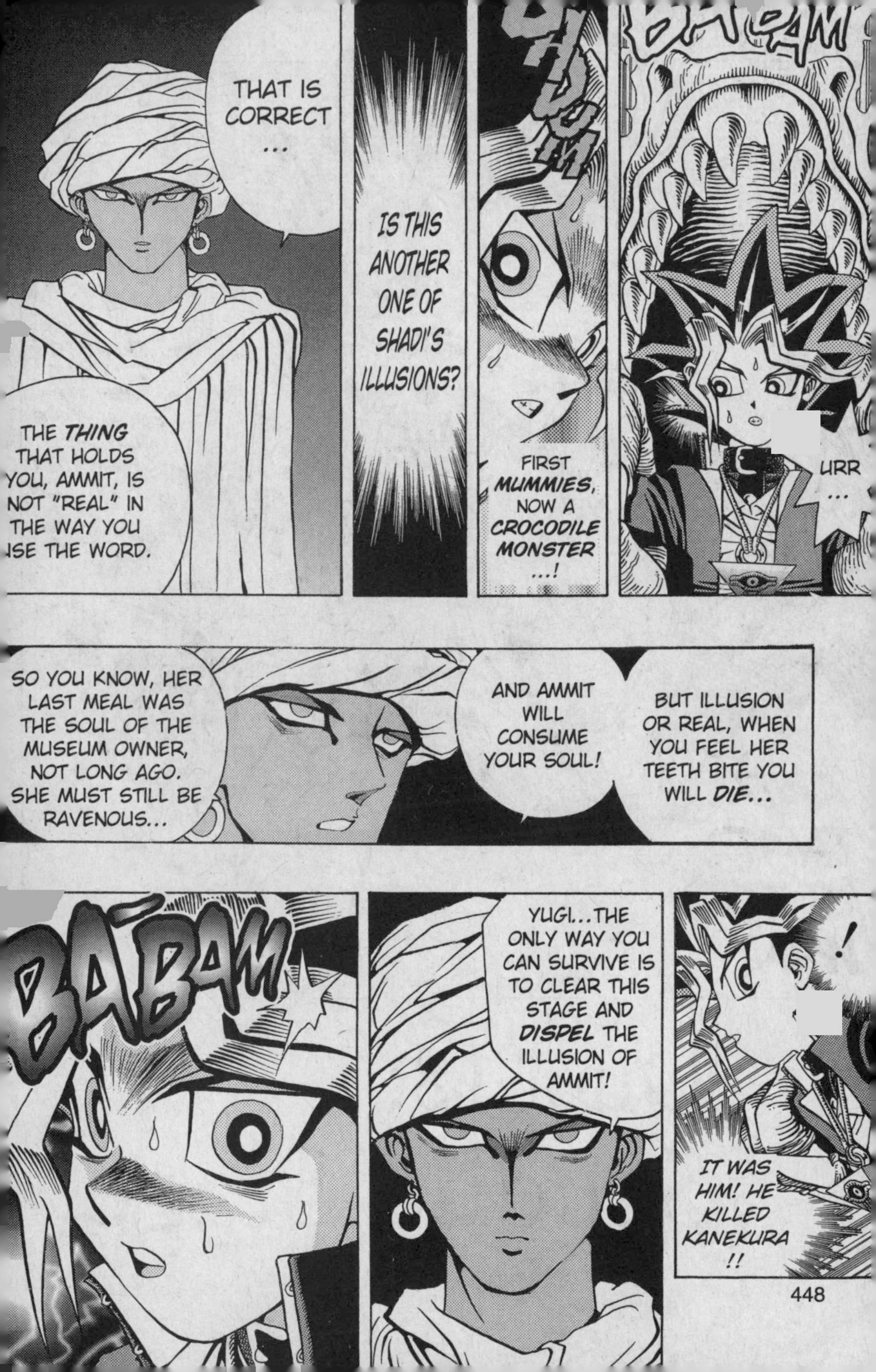
BADAM
URR...
BADUM
FIRST MUMMIES, NOW A CROCODILE MONSTER...!
IS THIS ANOTHER ONE OF SHADI'S ILLUSIONS?
THAT IS CORRECT...
THE THING THAT HOLDS YOU, AMMIT, IS NOT "REAL" IN THE WAY YOU USE THE WORD.
BUT ILLUSION OR REAL, WHEN YOU FEEL HER TEETH BITE YOU WILL DIE...
AND AMMIT WILL CONSUME YOUR SOUL!
SO YOU KNOW, HER LAST MEAL WAS THE SOUL OF THE MUSEUM OWNER, NOT LONG AGO. SHE MUST STILL BE RAVENOUS...
!
IT WAS HIM! HE KILLED KANEKURA!!
YUGI...THE ONLY WAY YOU CAN SURVIVE IS TO CLEAR THIS STAGE AND DISPEL THE ILLUSION OF AMMIT!
BABAM

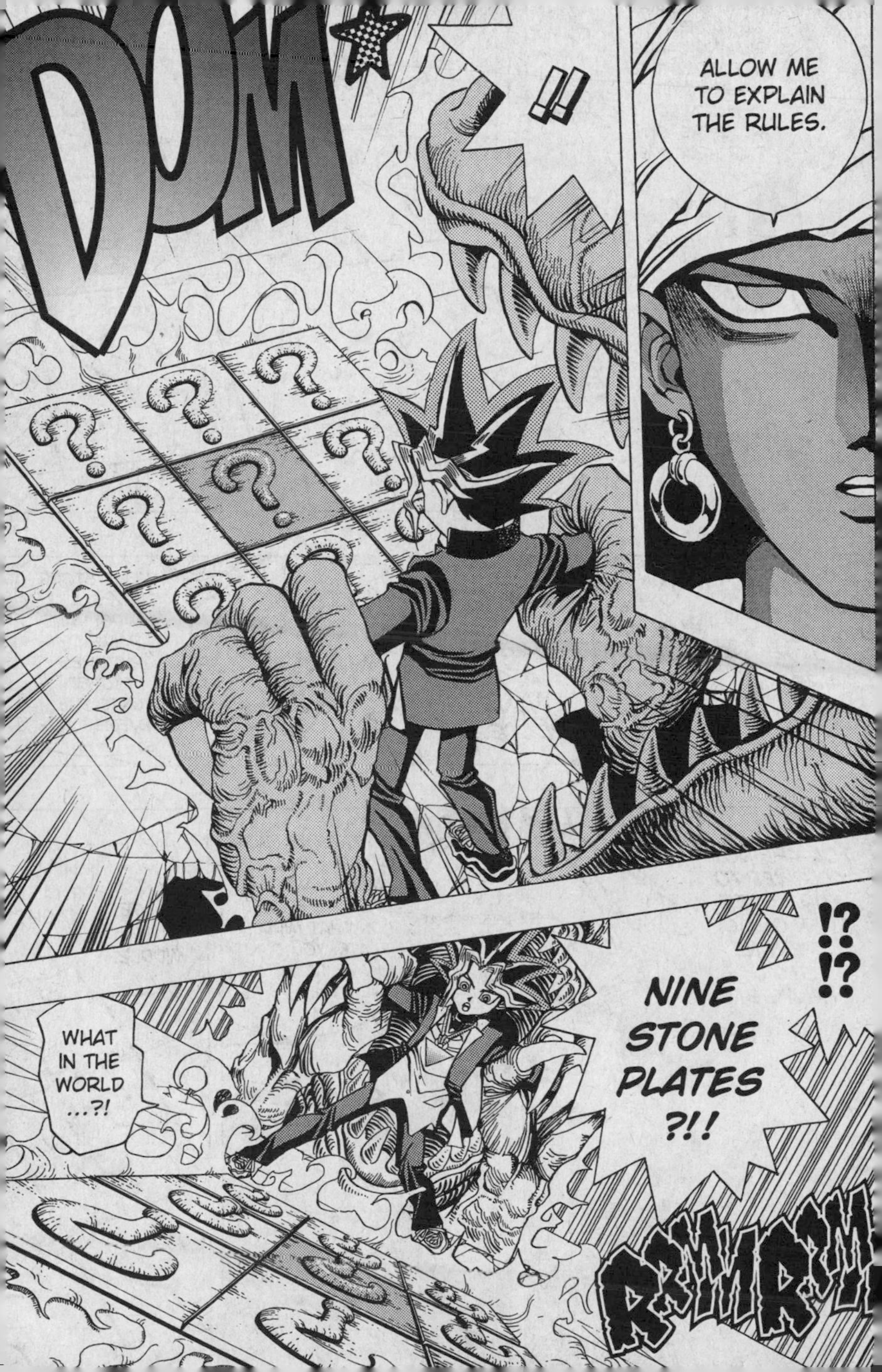
ALLOW ME TO EXPLAIN THE RULES.
DOM
!!
!? !?
NINE STONE PLATES ?!!
WHAT IN THE WORLD ...?!

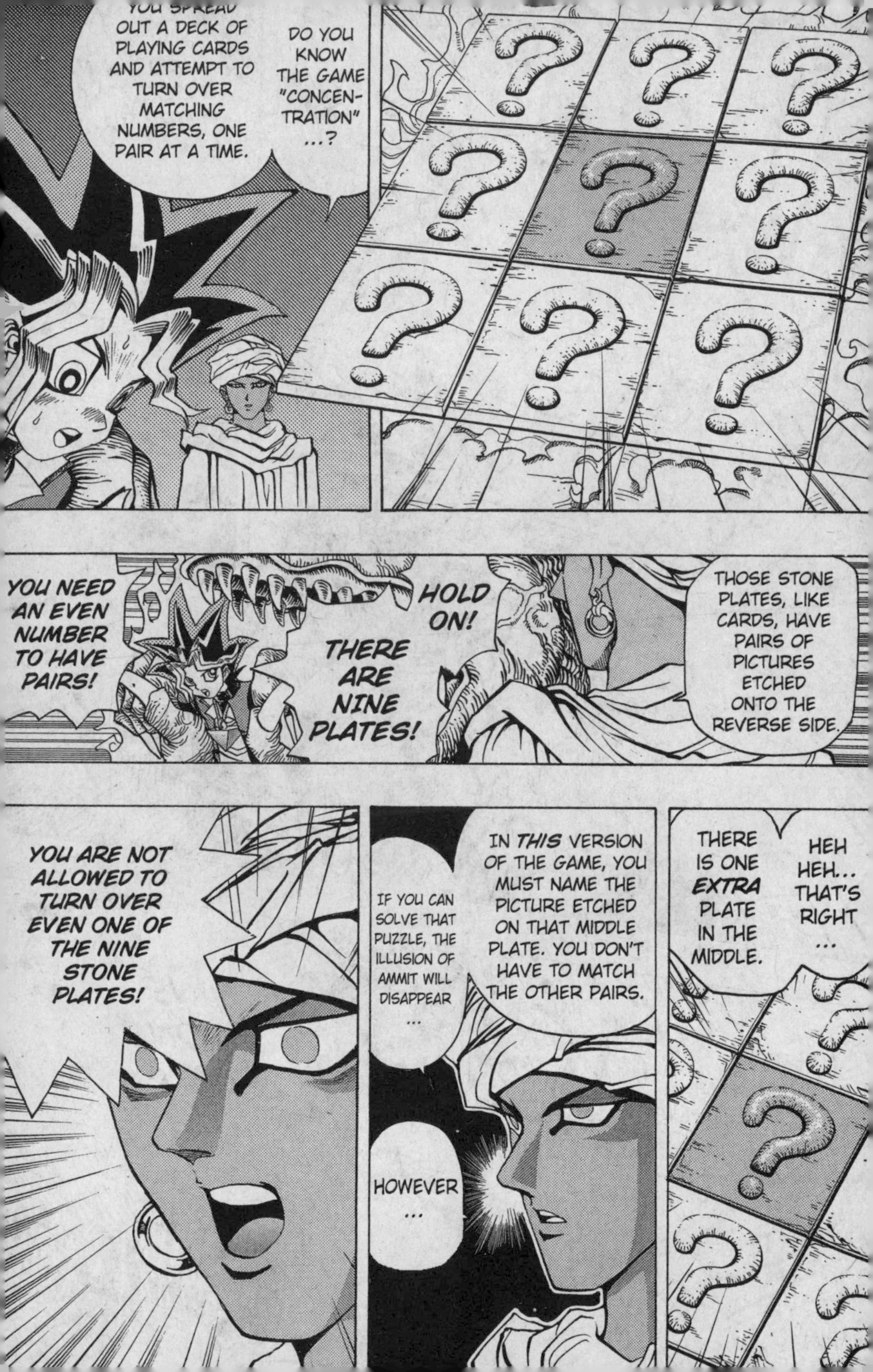
DO YOU KNOW THE GAME "CONCENTRATION" ...?
YOU SPREAD OUT A DECK OF PLAYING CARDS AND ATTEMPT TO TURN OVER MATCHING NUMBERS, ONE PAIR AT A TIME.
THOSE STONE PLATES, LIKE CARDS, HAVE PAIRS OF PICTURES ETCHED ONTO THE REVERSE SIDE.
HOLD ON!
THERE ARE NINE PLATES!
YOU NEED AN EVEN NUMBER TO HAVE PAIRS!
THERE IS ONE *EXTRA* PLATE IN THE MIDDLE.
HEH HEH... THAT'S RIGHT ...
IN *THIS* VERSION OF THE GAME, YOU MUST NAME THE PICTURE ETCHED ON THAT MIDDLE PLATE. YOU DON'T HAVE TO MATCH THE OTHER PAIRS.
IF YOU CAN SOLVE THAT PUZZLE, THE ILLUSION OF AMMIT WILL DISAPPEAR ...
HOWEVER ...
YOU ARE NOT ALLOWED TO TURN OVER EVEN ONE OF THE NINE STONE PLATES!

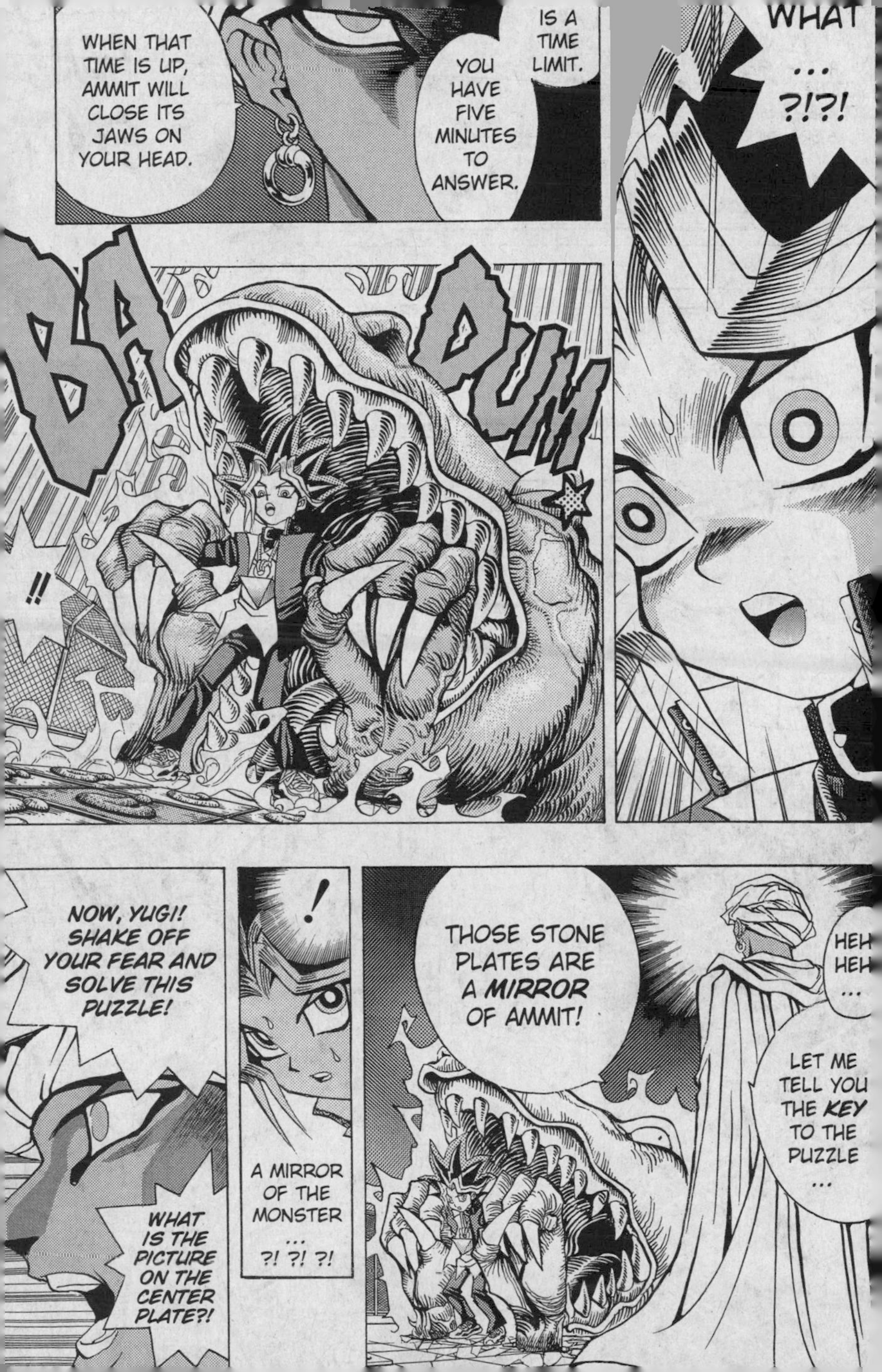
IS A TIME LIMIT.
YOU HAVE FIVE MINUTES TO ANSWER.
WHEN THAT TIME IS UP, AMMIT WILL CLOSE ITS JAWS ON YOUR HEAD.
BA
DUM
!!
WHAT ... ?!?!
HEH HEH ...
LET ME TELL YOU THE *KEY* TO THE PUZZLE ...
THOSE STONE PLATES ARE A *MIRROR* OF AMMIT!
!
A MIRROR OF THE MONSTER ... ?! ?! ?!
NOW, YUGI! SHAKE OFF YOUR FEAR AND SOLVE THIS PUZZLE!
WHAT IS THE PICTURE ON THE CENTER PLATE?!

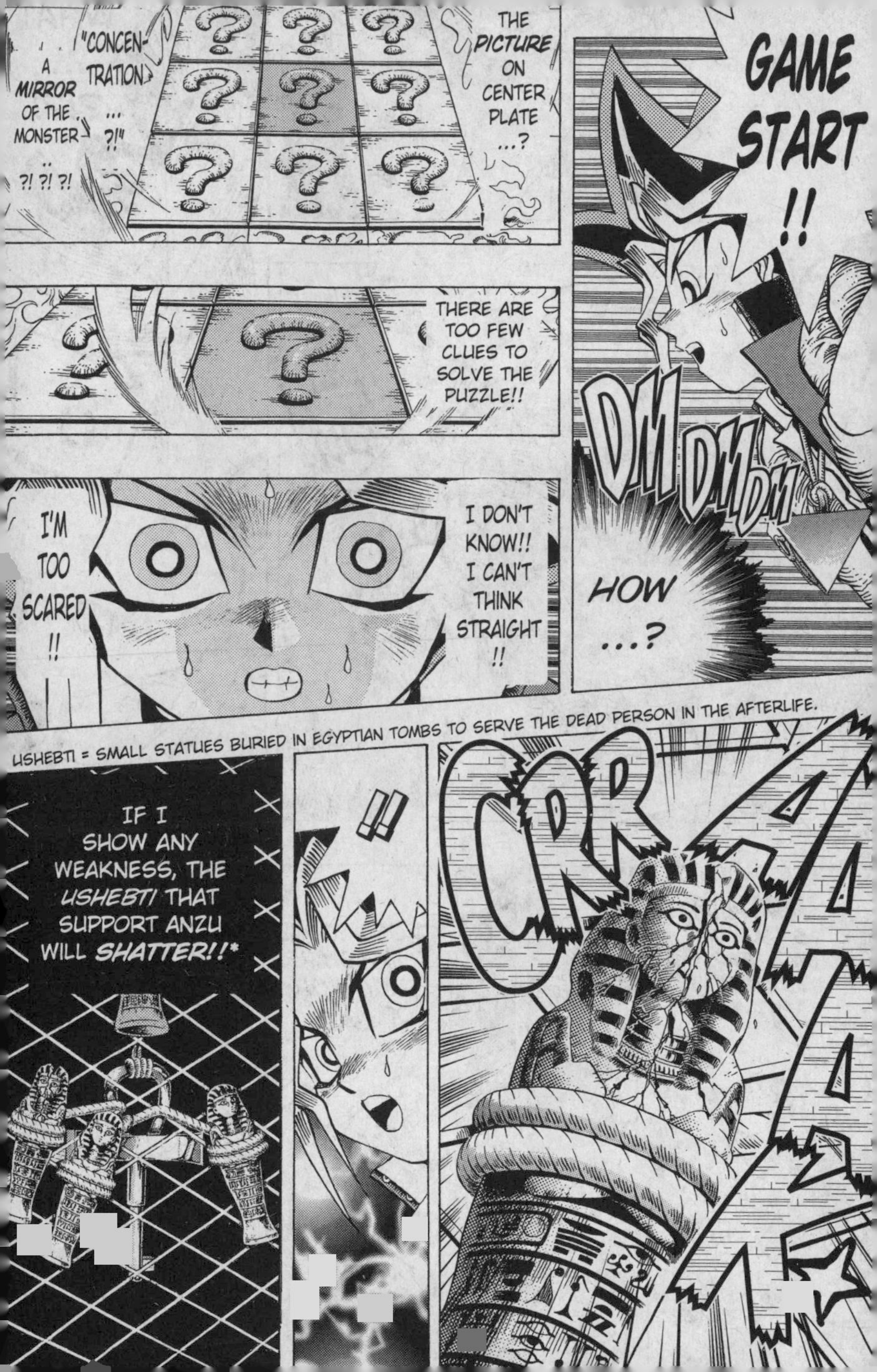
GAME START!!
DM DM DMDMDM
HOW ...?
THE PICTURE ON CENTER PLATE ...?
"CONCENTRATION" ... ?!"
A MIRROR OF THE MONSTER .. ?! ?! ?!
THERE ARE TOO FEW CLUES TO SOLVE THE PUZZLE!!
I DON'T KNOW!! I CAN'T THINK STRAIGHT!!
I'M TOO SCARED!!
USHEBTI = SMALL STATUES BURIED IN EGYPTIAN TOMBS TO SERVE THE DEAD PERSON IN THE AFTERLIFE.
CRR
!!
IF I SHOW ANY WEAKNESS, THE USHEBTI THAT SUPPORT ANZU WILL SHATTER!!*

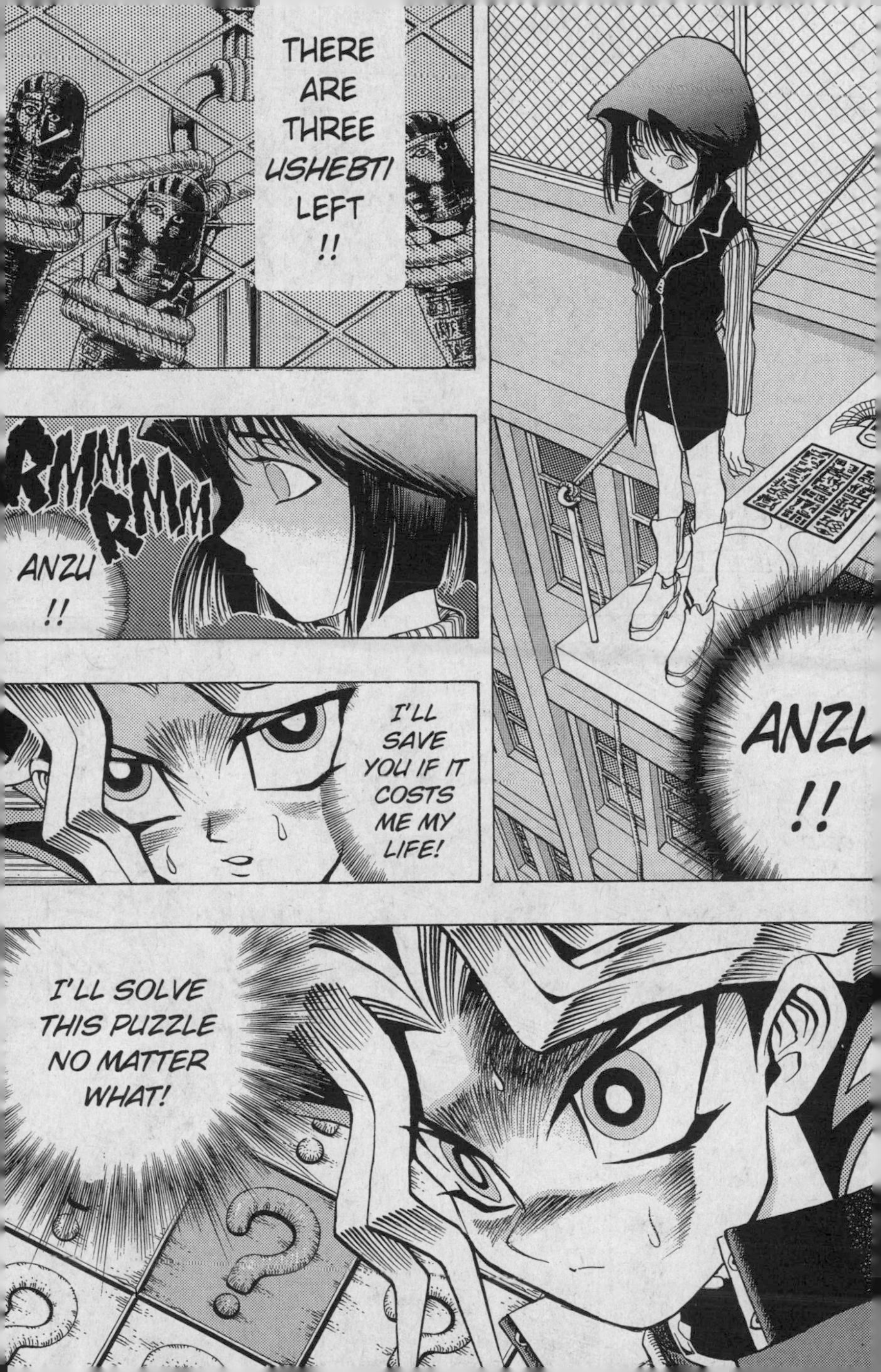
ANZU !!
THERE ARE THREE USHEBTI LEFT !!
RMM RMM
ANZU !!
I'LL SAVE YOU IF IT COSTS ME MY LIFE!
I'LL SOLVE THIS PUZZLE NO MATTER WHAT!

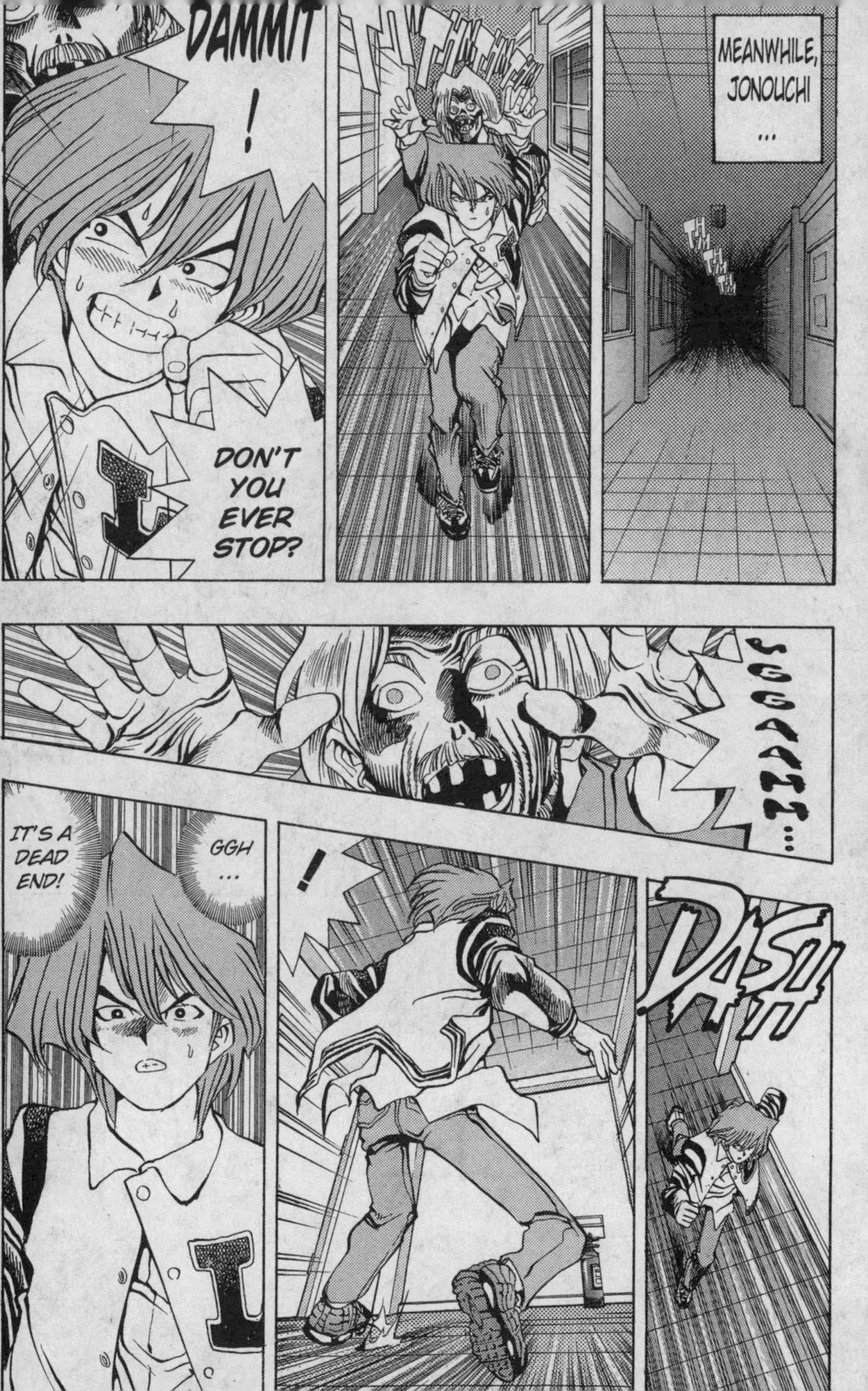
MEANWHILE, JONOUCHI ...
DAMMIT !
DON'T YOU EVER STOP?
SGGAAHH...
DASH
!
GGH ...
IT'S A DEAD END!

READ THIS WAY

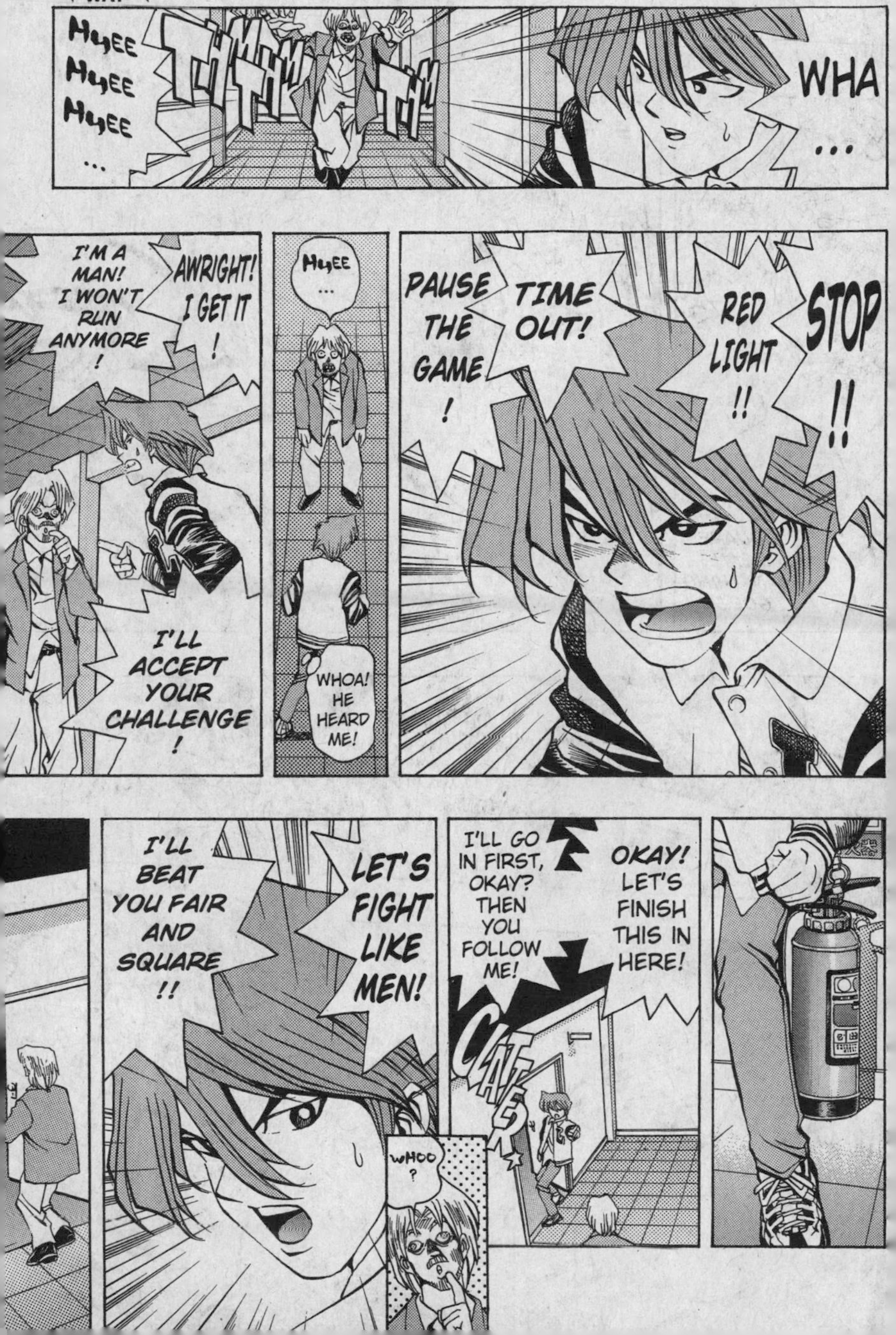
WHA ...
Hyee Hyee Hyee ...
STOP!!
RED LIGHT!!
TIME OUT!
PAUSE THE GAME!
Hyee ...
WHOA! HE HEARD ME!
AWRIGHT! I GET IT!
I'M A MAN! I WON'T RUN ANYMORE!
I'LL ACCEPT YOUR CHALLENGE!
OKAY! LET'S FINISH THIS IN HERE!
I'LL GO IN FIRST, OKAY? THEN YOU FOLLOW ME!
CLATTER
LET'S FIGHT LIKE MEN!
I'LL BEAT YOU FAIR AND SQUARE!!
WHOO?

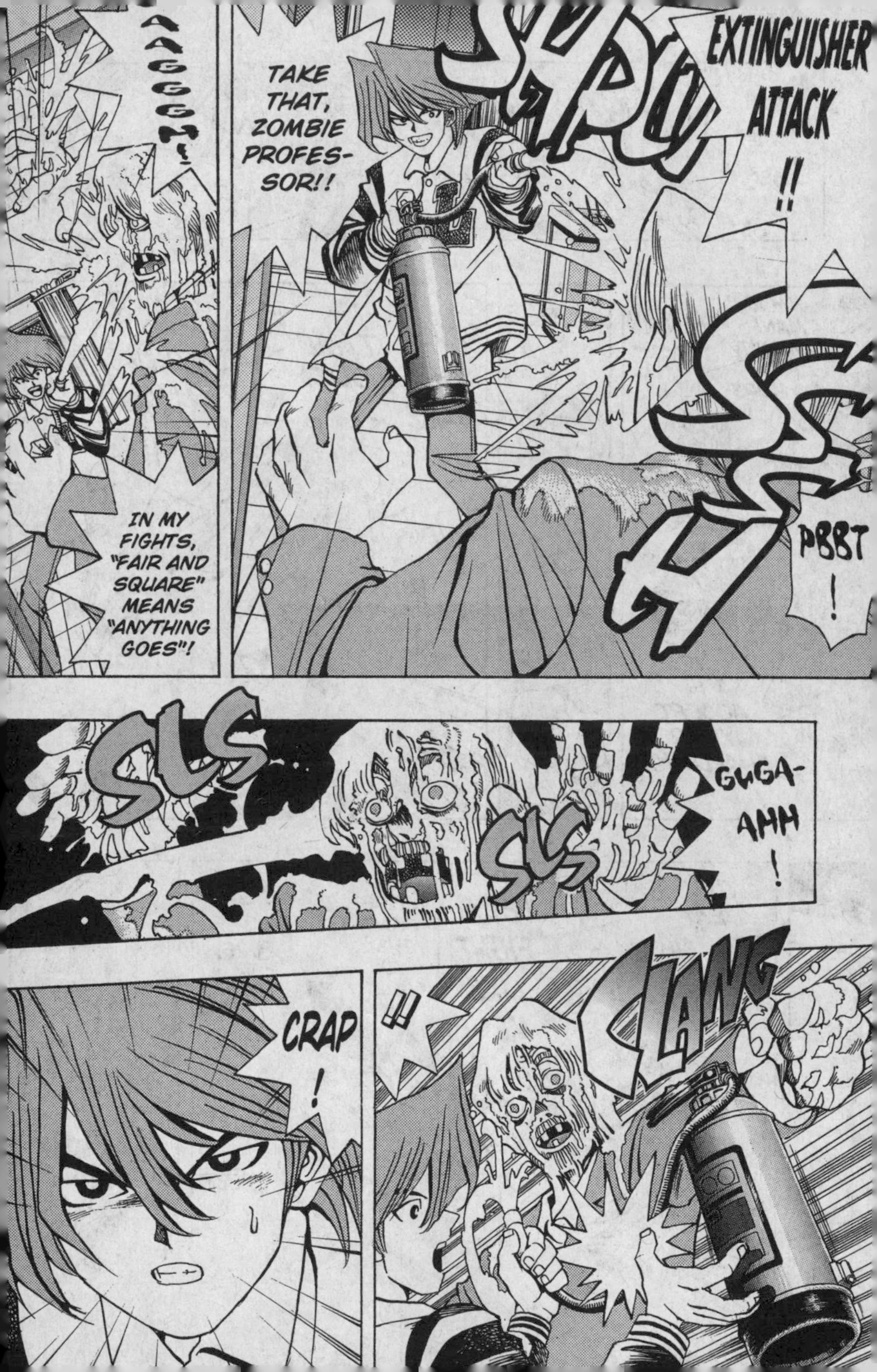
EXTINGUISHER ATTACK!!
TAKE THAT, ZOMBIE PROFESSOR!!
PBBT!
AAGGGH!
IN MY FIGHTS, "FAIR AND SQUARE" MEANS "ANYTHING GOES"!
GUGA-AHH!
SLS
SLS
!!
CLANG
CRAP!

READ THIS WAY

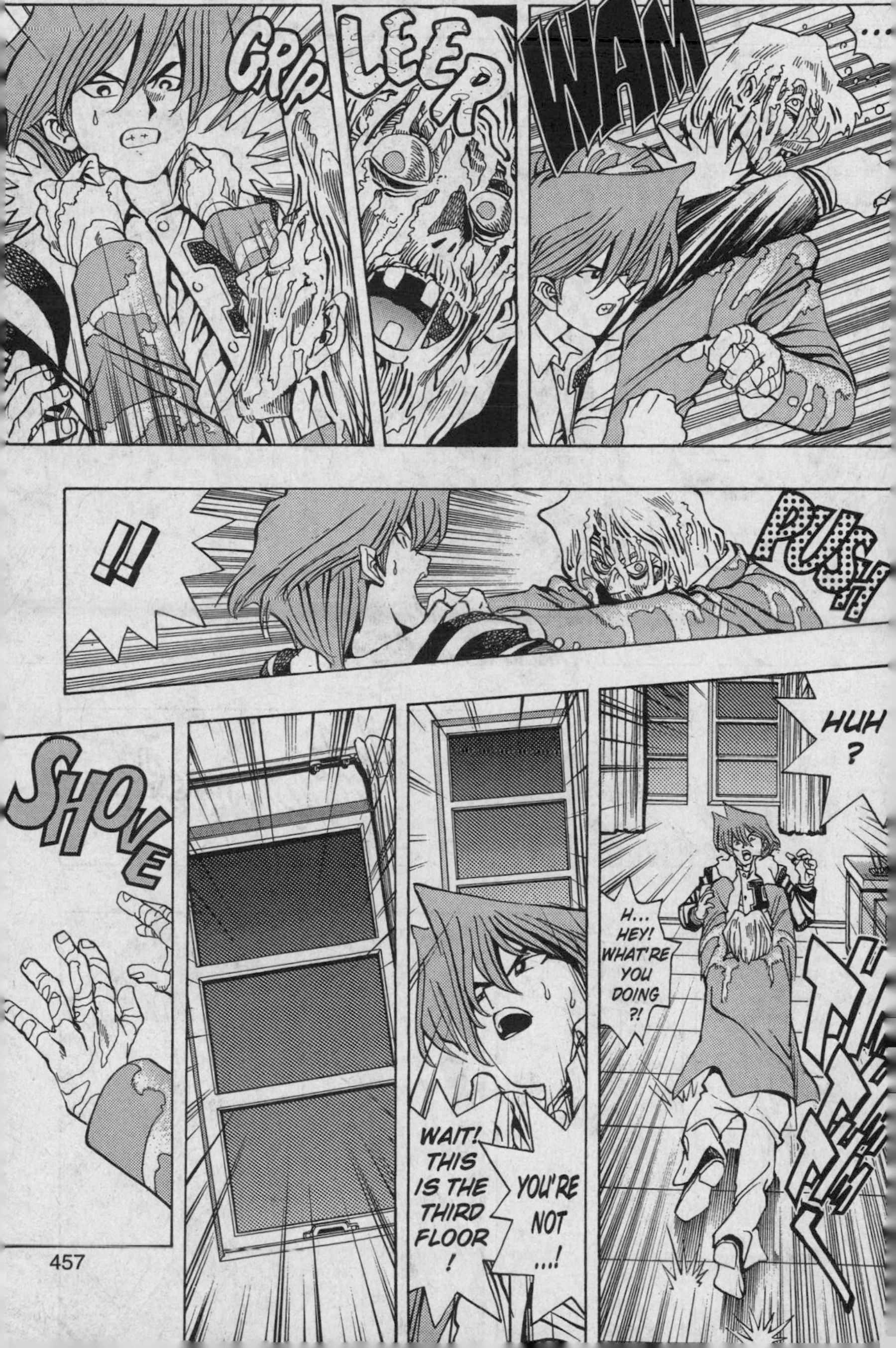
....
WAM
LEEP
GRIP
PUSH
!!
HUH?
H... HEY! WHAT'RE YOU DOING?!
WAIT! THIS IS THE THIRD FLOOR!
YOU'RE NOT ...!
SHOVE

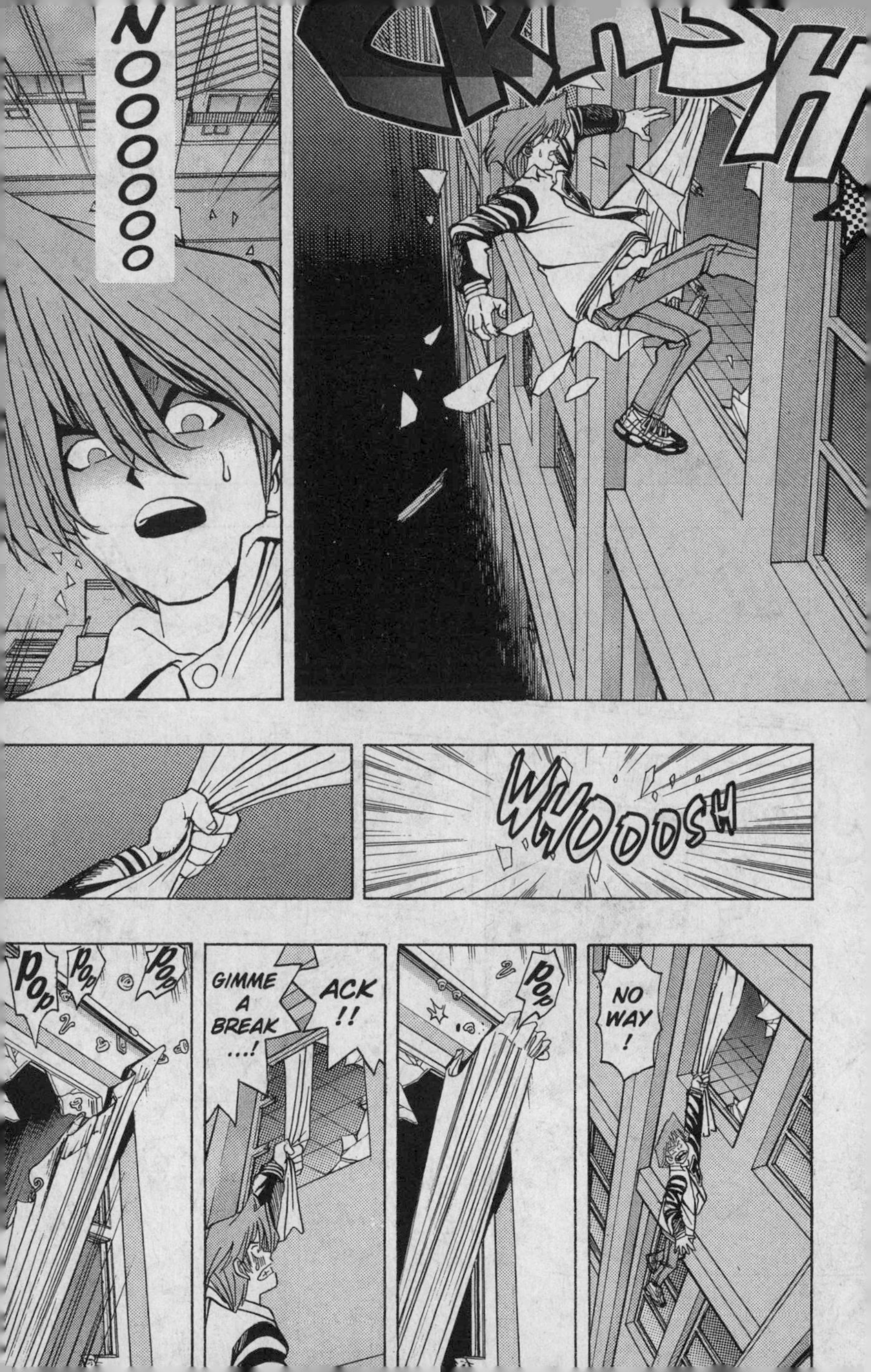
CRASH
NOOOOOOO
WHOOOSH
NO WAY!
POP
ACK!!
GIMME A BREAK...!
POP
POP
POP

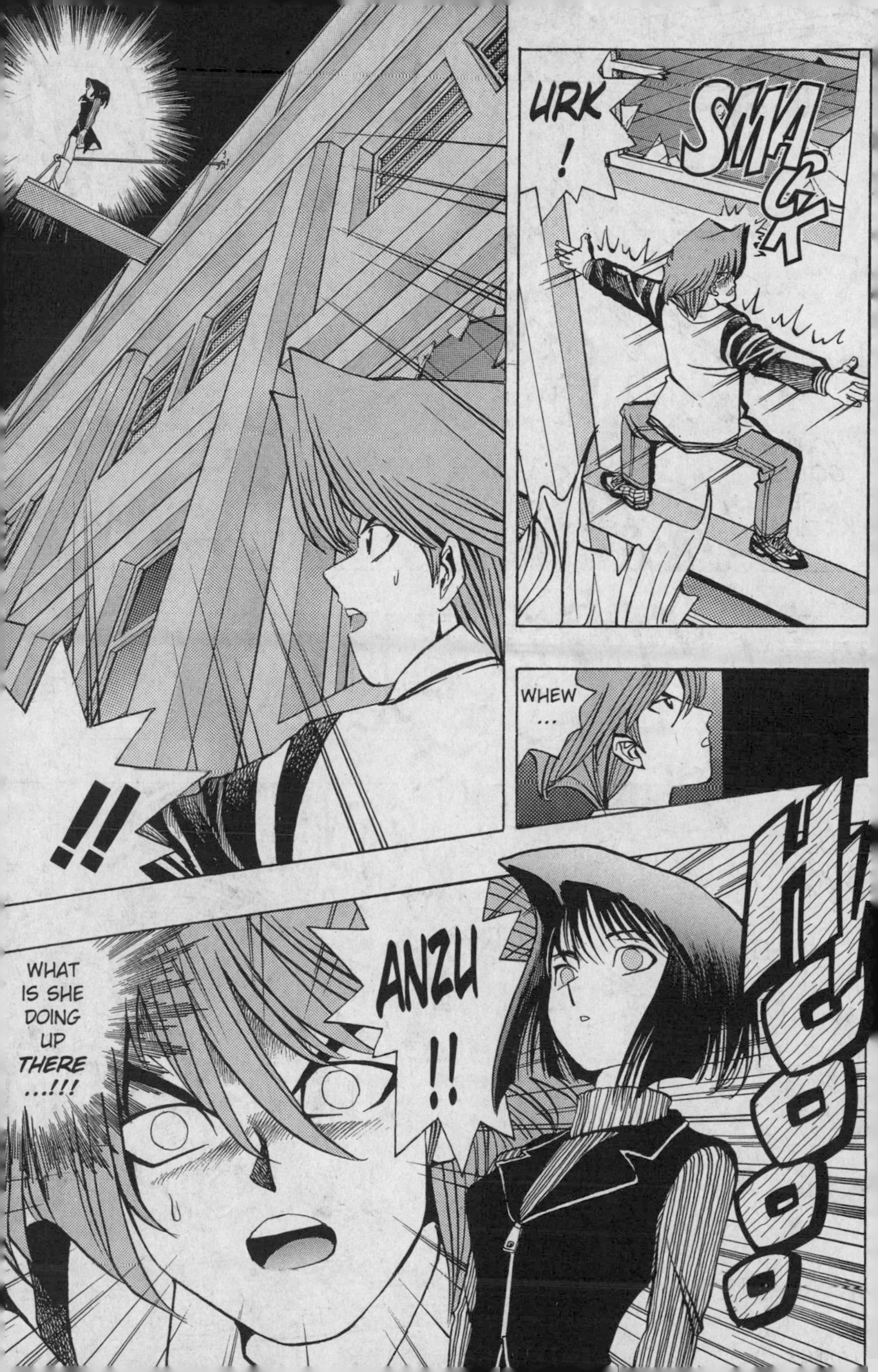
SMACK
URK!
WHEW...
!!
ANZU!!
WHAT IS SHE DOING UP THERE...!!!

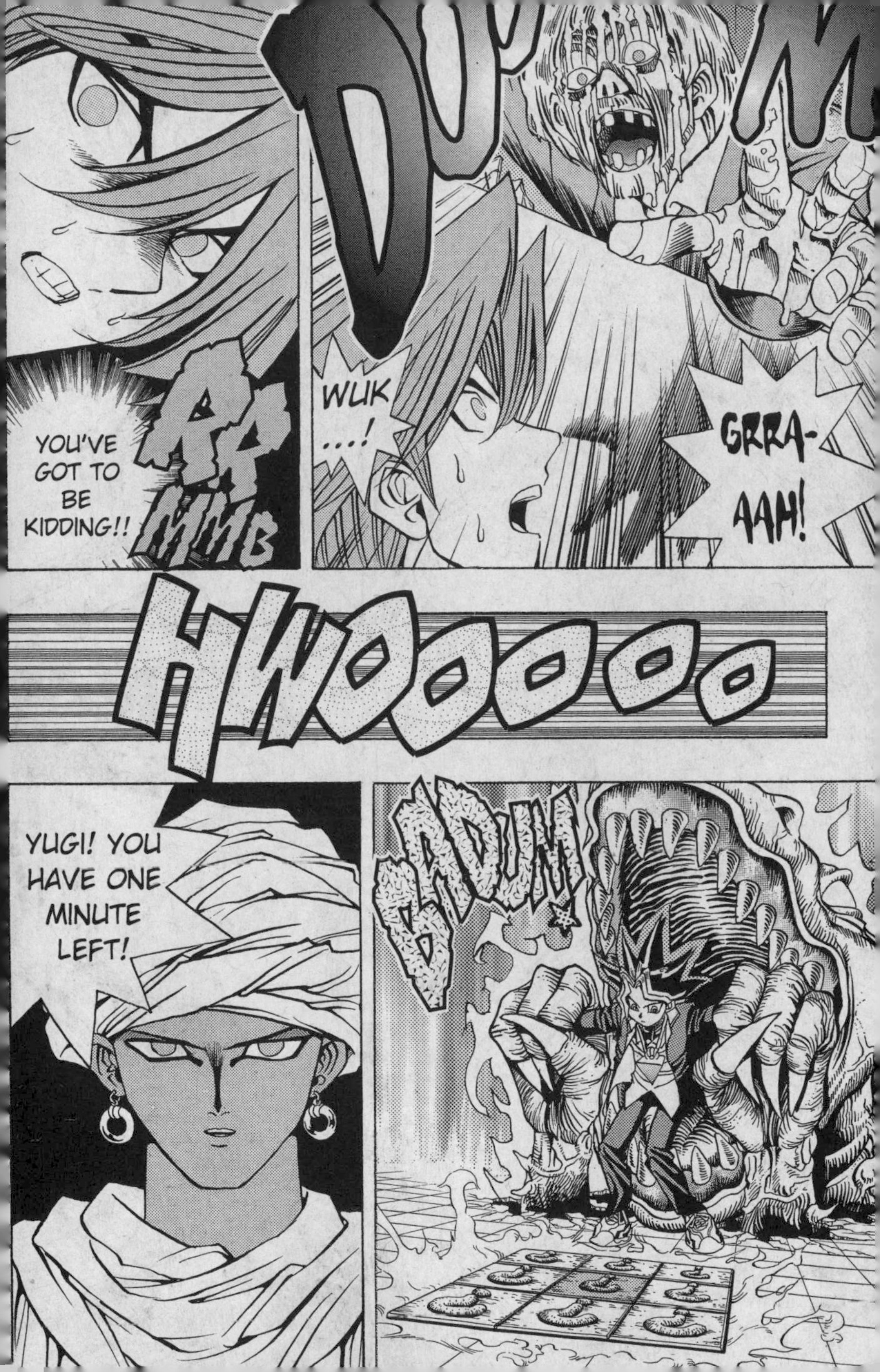
GRRA-AAH!
WUK ...!
RAMMB
YOU'VE GOT TO BE KIDDING!!
HWOOOOOO
BDUM
YUGI! YOU HAVE ONE MINUTE LEFT!

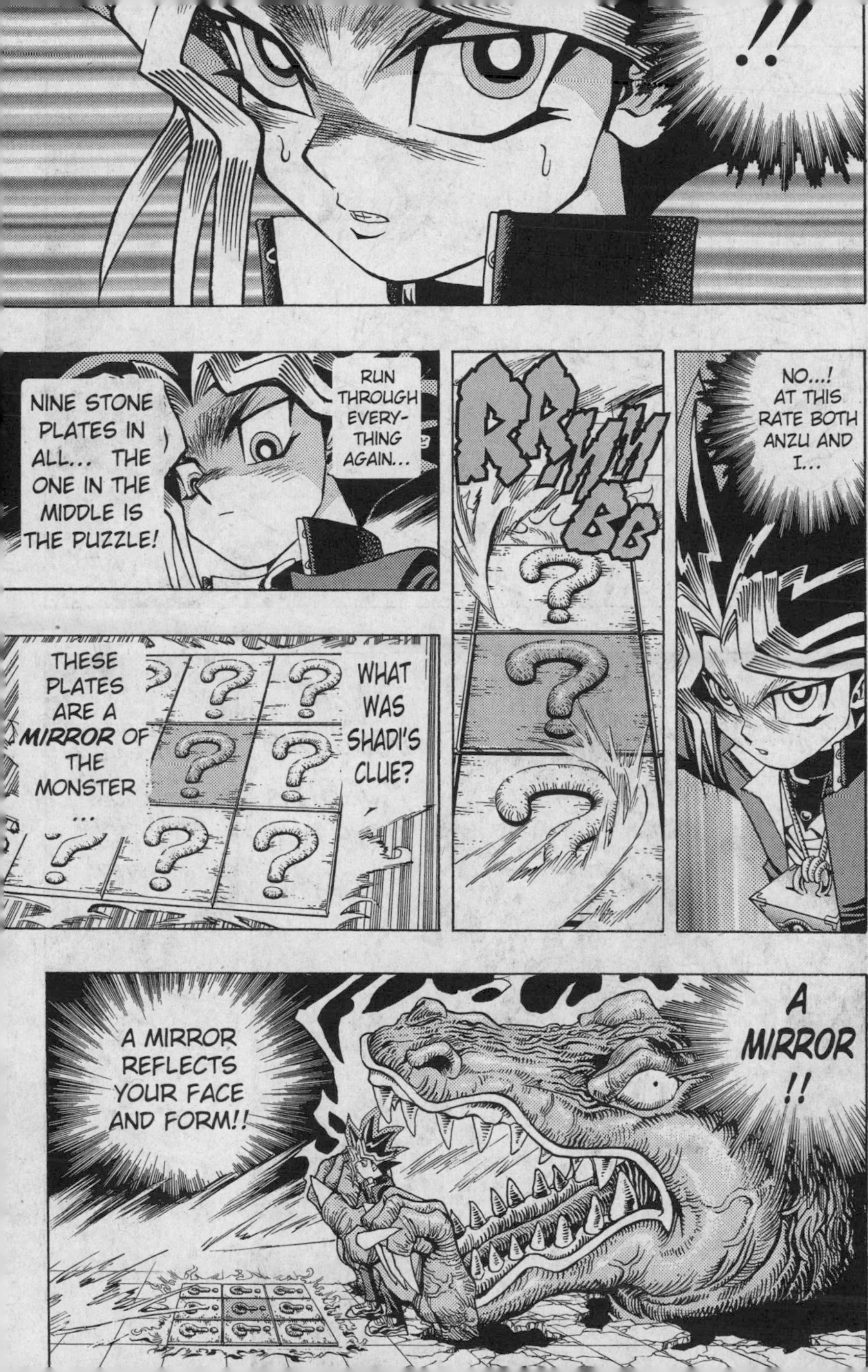
!!
NO...! AT THIS RATE BOTH ANZU AND I...
RRMMBB
RUN THROUGH EVERYTHING AGAIN...
NINE STONE PLATES IN ALL... THE ONE IN THE MIDDLE IS THE PUZZLE!
WHAT WAS SHADI'S CLUE?
THESE PLATES ARE A *MIRROR* OF THE MONSTER...
A MIRROR!!
A MIRROR REFLECTS YOUR FACE AND FORM!!

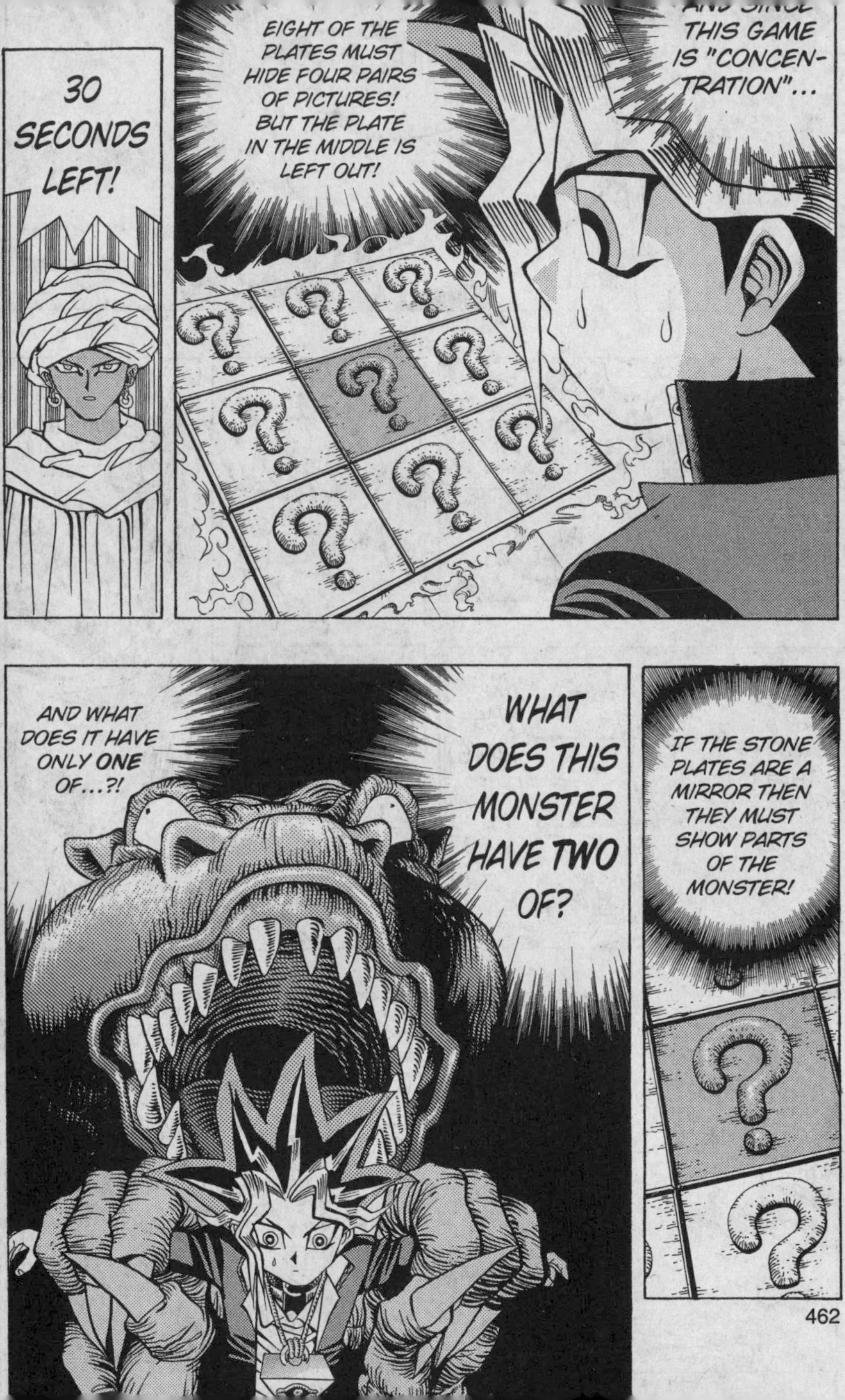

THIS GAME IS "CONCEN- TRATION"...
EIGHT OF THE PLATES MUST HIDE FOUR PAIRS OF PICTURES! BUT THE PLATE IN THE MIDDLE IS LEFT OUT!
30 SECONDS LEFT!
IF THE STONE PLATES ARE A MIRROR THEN THEY MUST SHOW PARTS OF THE MONSTER!
WHAT DOES THIS MONSTER HAVE TWO OF?
AND WHAT DOES IT HAVE ONLY ONE OF...?!

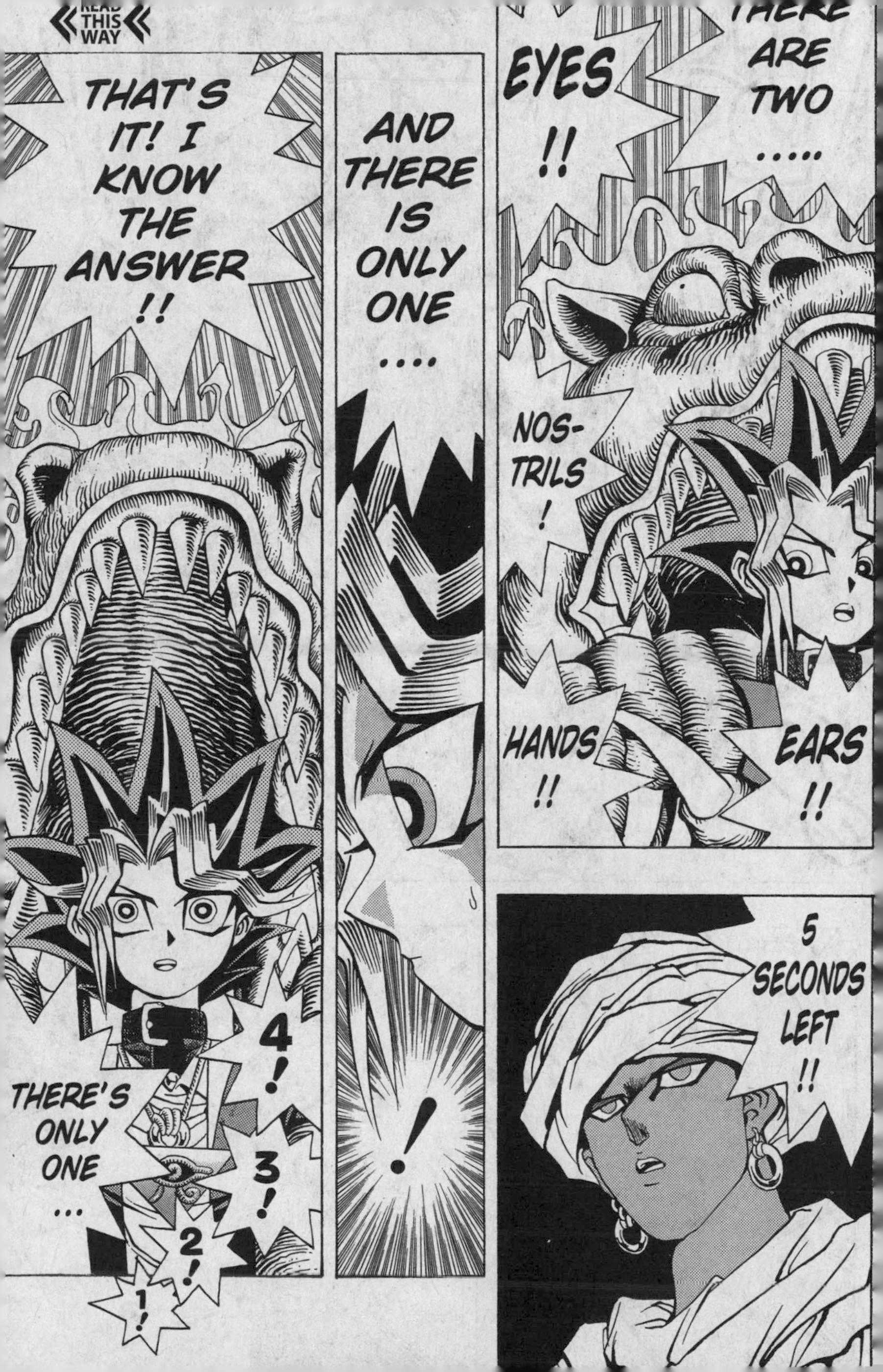
READ THIS WAY
THERE ARE TWO .....
EYES !!
NOS-TRILS !
EARS !!
HANDS !!
5 SECONDS LEFT !!
AND THERE IS ONLY ONE ....
!
THAT'S IT! I KNOW THE ANSWER !!
4!
3!
THERE'S ONLY ONE ...
2!
1!

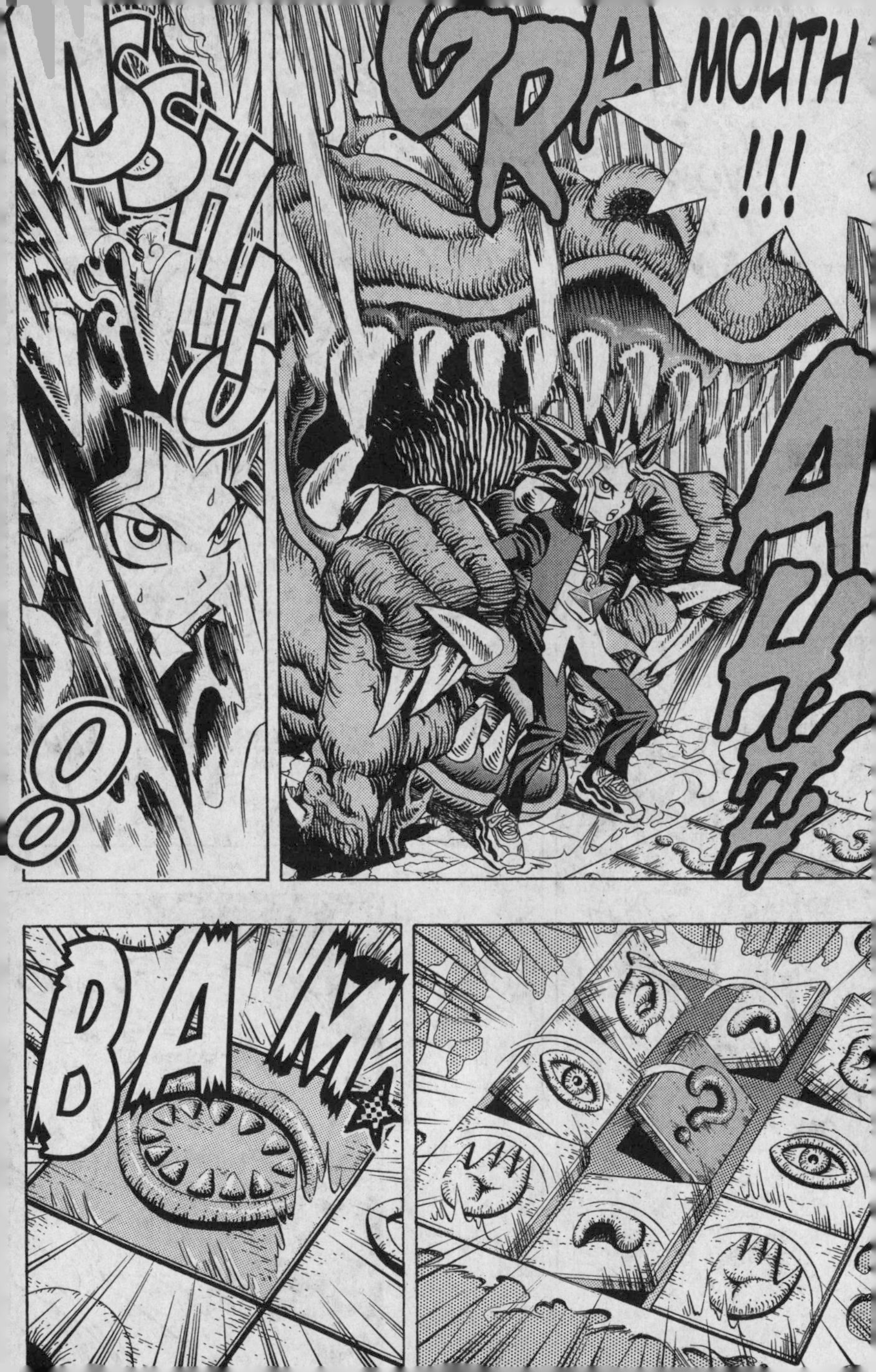
MOUTH !!!
BAM

READ THIS WAY

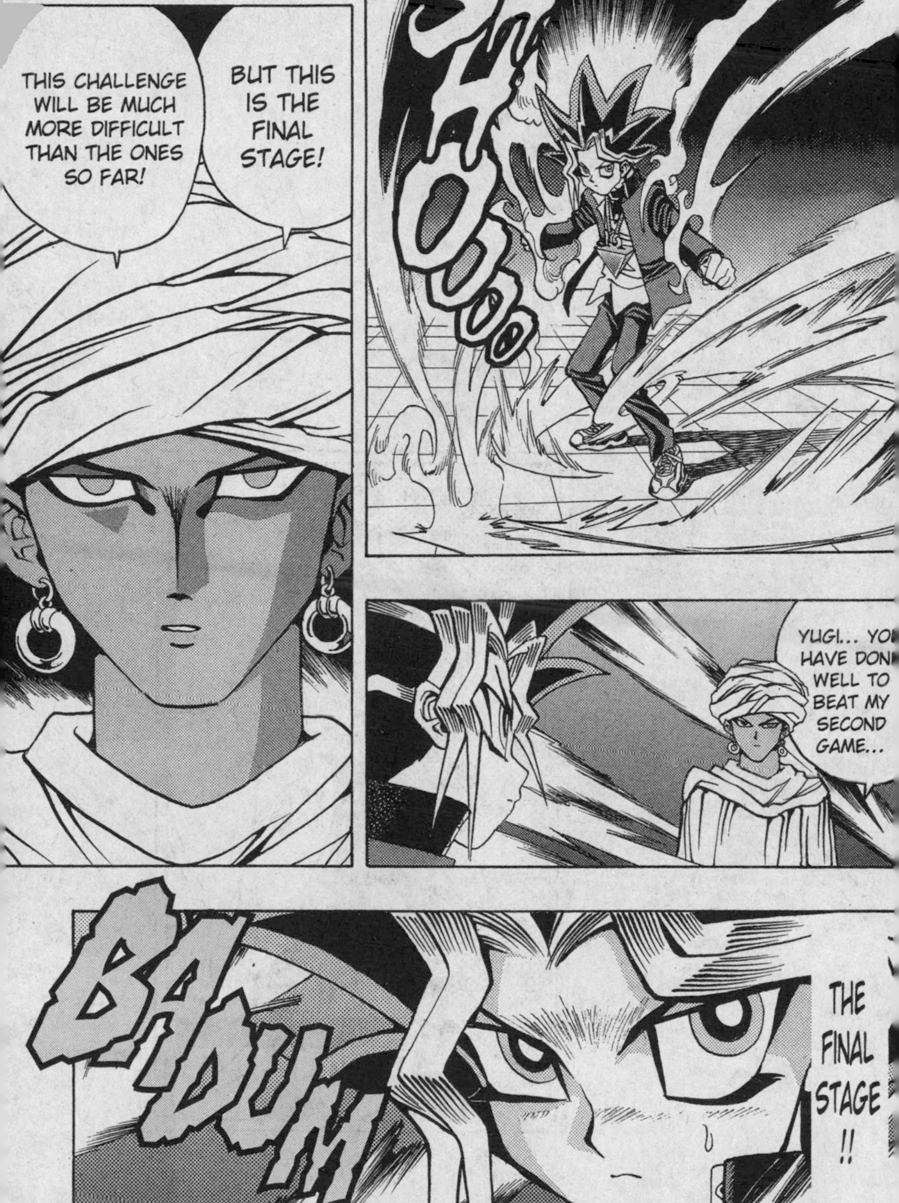
YUGI... YO HAVE DON WELL TO BEAT MY SECOND GAME...
BUT THIS IS THE FINAL STAGE!
THIS CHALLENGE WILL BE MUCH MORE DIFFICULT THAN THE ONES SO FAR!
THE FINAL STAGE !!
BA DUM

Duel 19: Final Stage

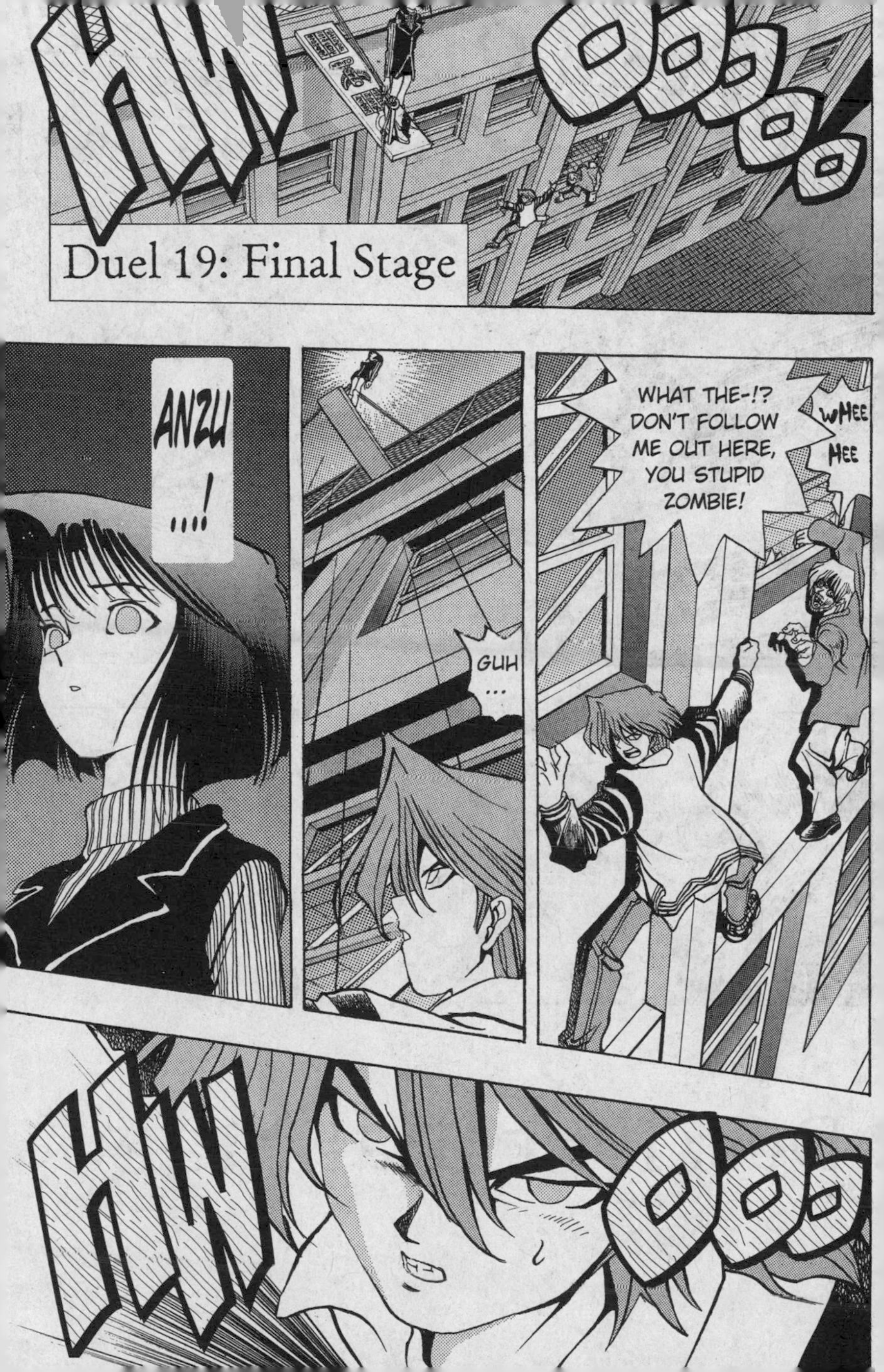
HIIN
OOOooo
WHAT THE-!? DON'T FOLLOW ME OUT HERE, YOU STUPID ZOMBIE!
WHEE HEE
GUH ...
ANZU ...!
HIIN
OOO

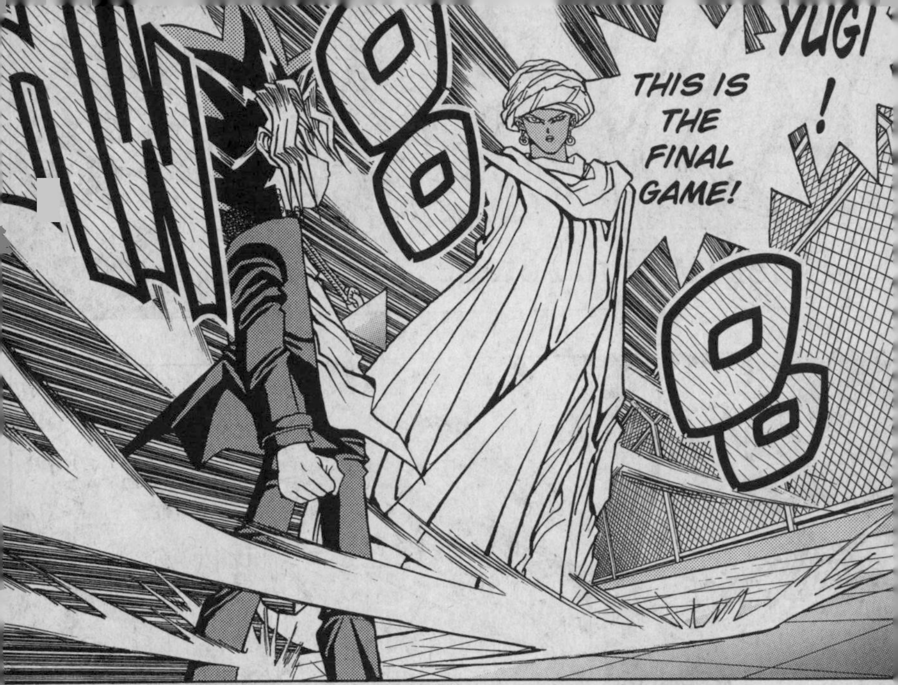
YUGI!
THIS IS THE FINAL GAME!

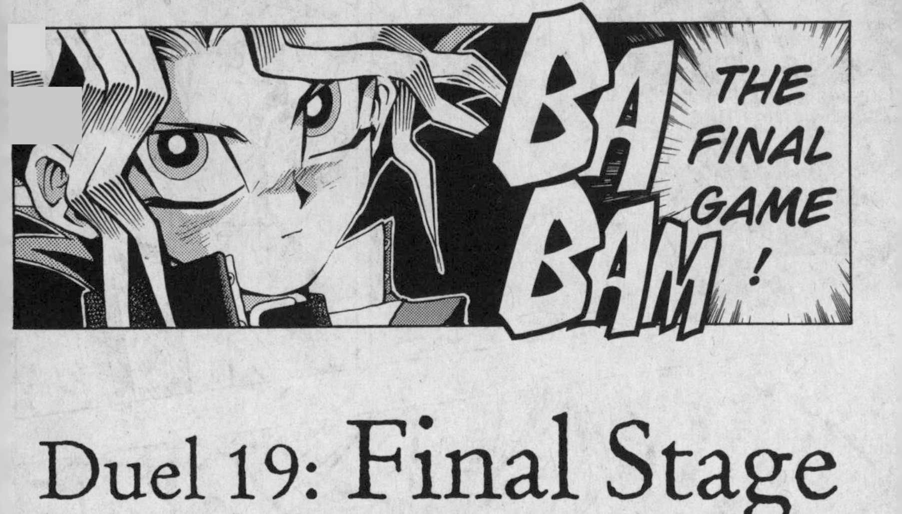
THE FINAL GAME!
BA BAM

Duel 19: Final Stage

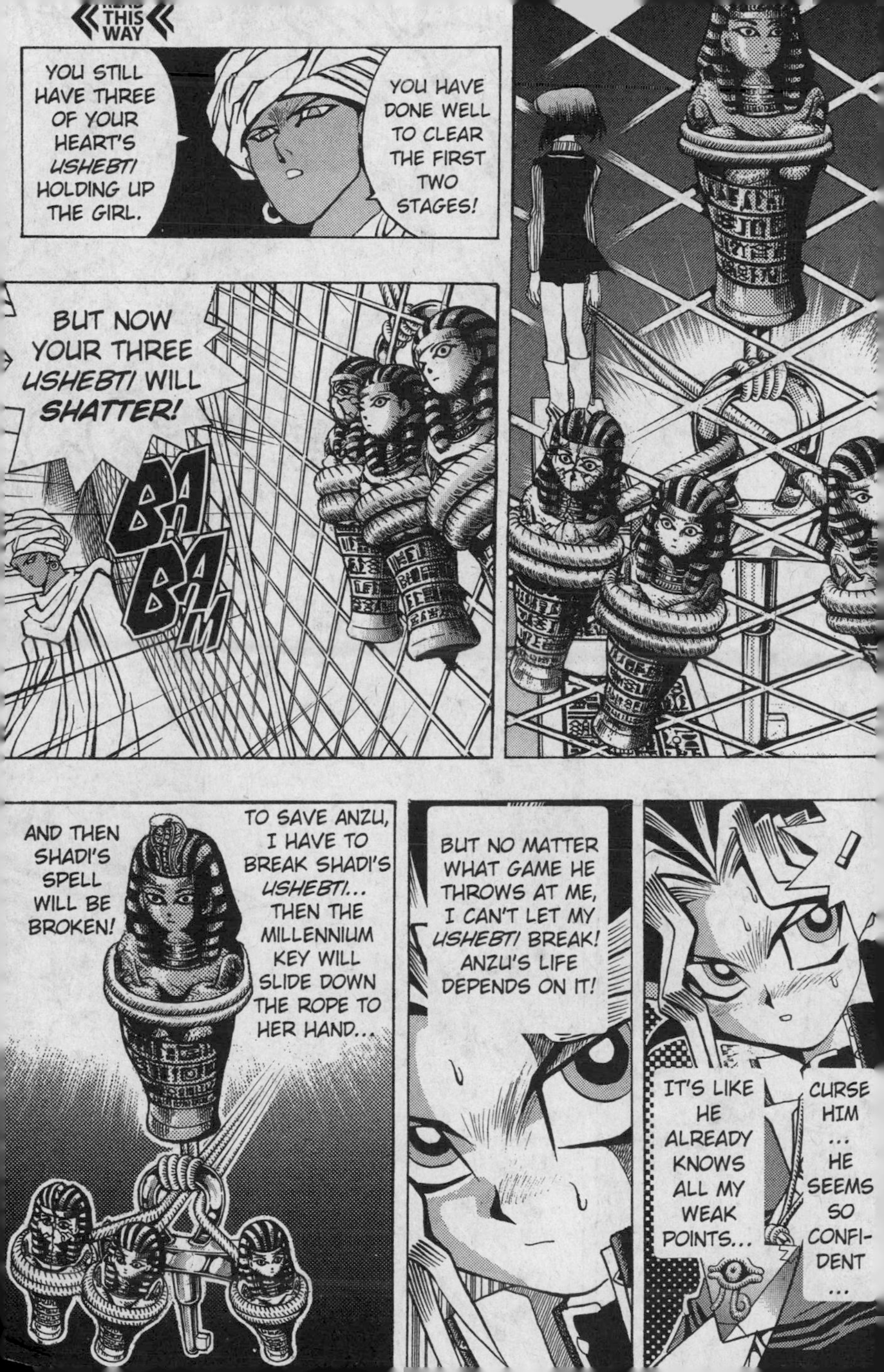
THIS WAY
YOU HAVE DONE WELL TO CLEAR THE FIRST TWO STAGES!
YOU STILL HAVE THREE OF YOUR HEART'S *USHEBTI* HOLDING UP THE GIRL.
BUT NOW YOUR THREE *USHEBTI* WILL ***SHATTER!***
BA BA BAM
CURSE HIM ... HE SEEMS SO CONFIDENT ...
IT'S LIKE HE ALREADY KNOWS ALL MY WEAK POINTS...
BUT NO MATTER WHAT GAME HE THROWS AT ME, I CAN'T LET MY *USHEBTI* BREAK! ANZU'S LIFE DEPENDS ON IT!
TO SAVE ANZU, I HAVE TO BREAK SHADI'S *USHEBTI*... THEN THE MILLENNIUM KEY WILL SLIDE DOWN THE ROPE TO HER HAND...
AND THEN SHADI'S SPELL WILL BE BROKEN!

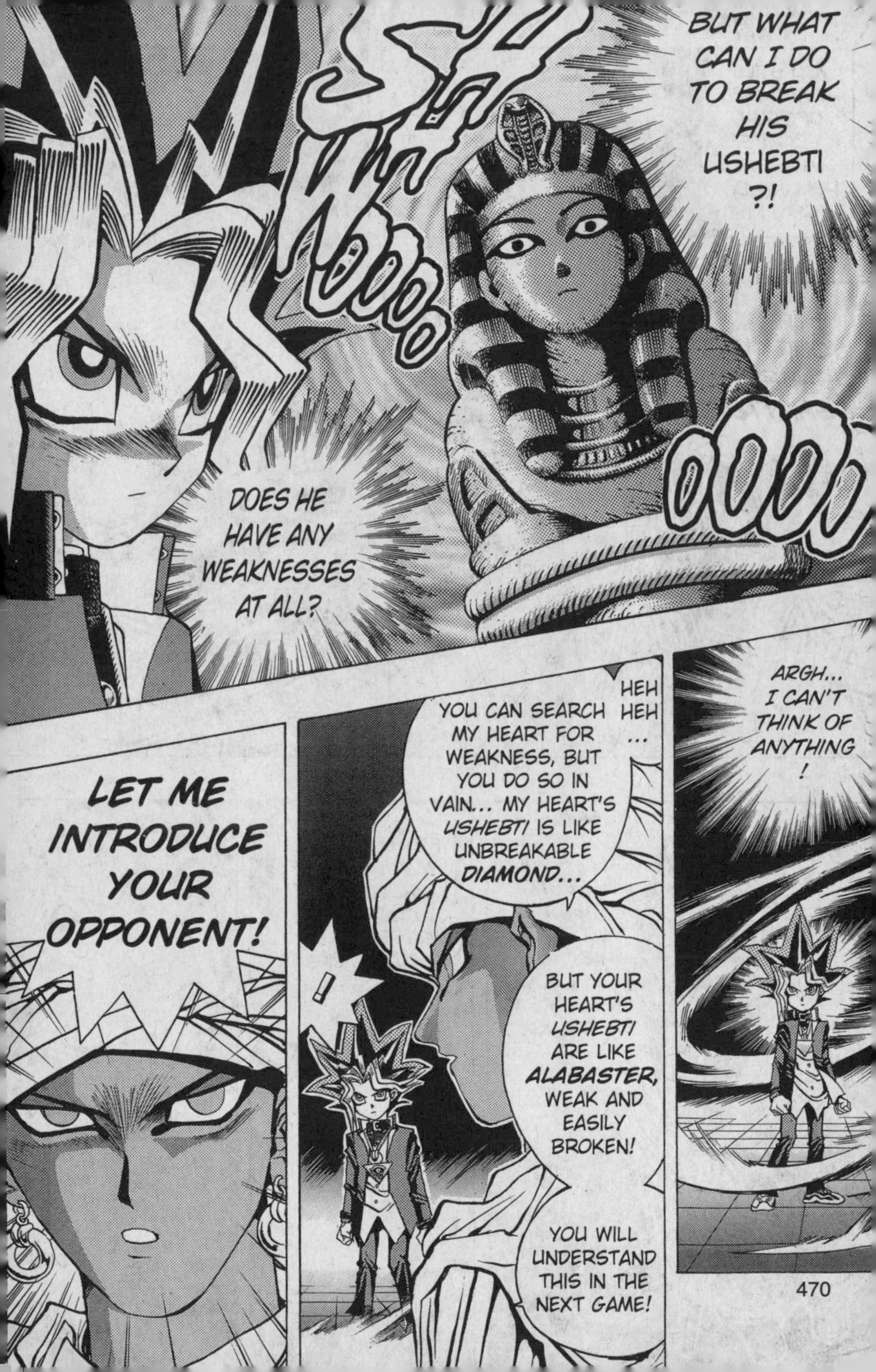
BUT WHAT CAN I DO TO BREAK HIS USHEBTI ?!
DOES HE HAVE ANY WEAKNESSES AT ALL?
ARGH... I CAN'T THINK OF ANYTHING!
HEH HEH...
YOU CAN SEARCH MY HEART FOR WEAKNESS, BUT YOU DO SO IN VAIN... MY HEART'S *USHEBTI* IS LIKE UNBREAKABLE **DIAMOND...**
!
BUT YOUR HEART'S *USHEBTI* ARE LIKE **ALABASTER,** WEAK AND EASILY BROKEN!
YOU WILL UNDERSTAND THIS IN THE NEXT GAME!
LET ME INTRODUCE YOUR OPPONENT!

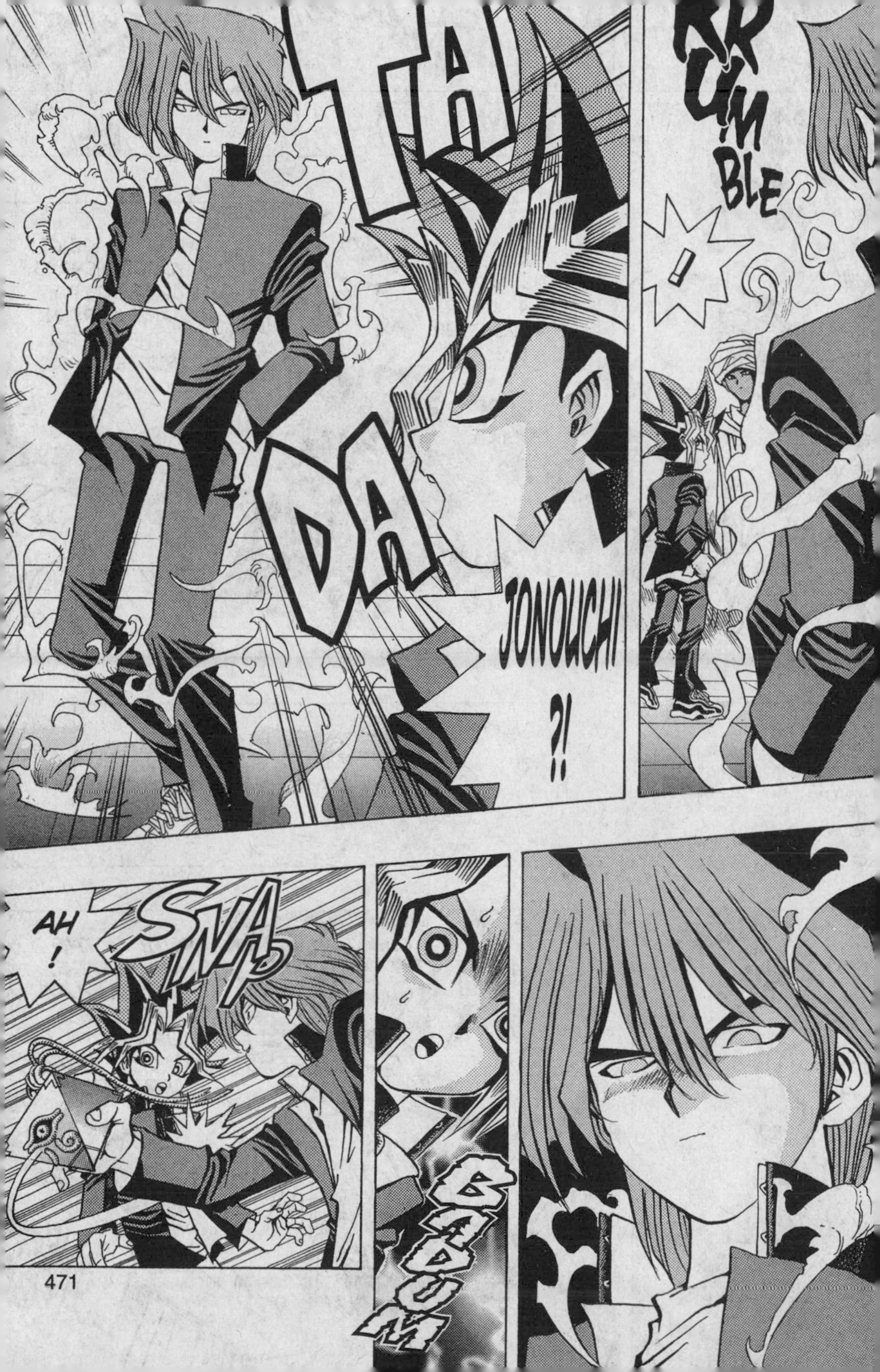
RUMBLE
!
JONOUCHI ?!
DA
TA
BADUM
SNA
AH !

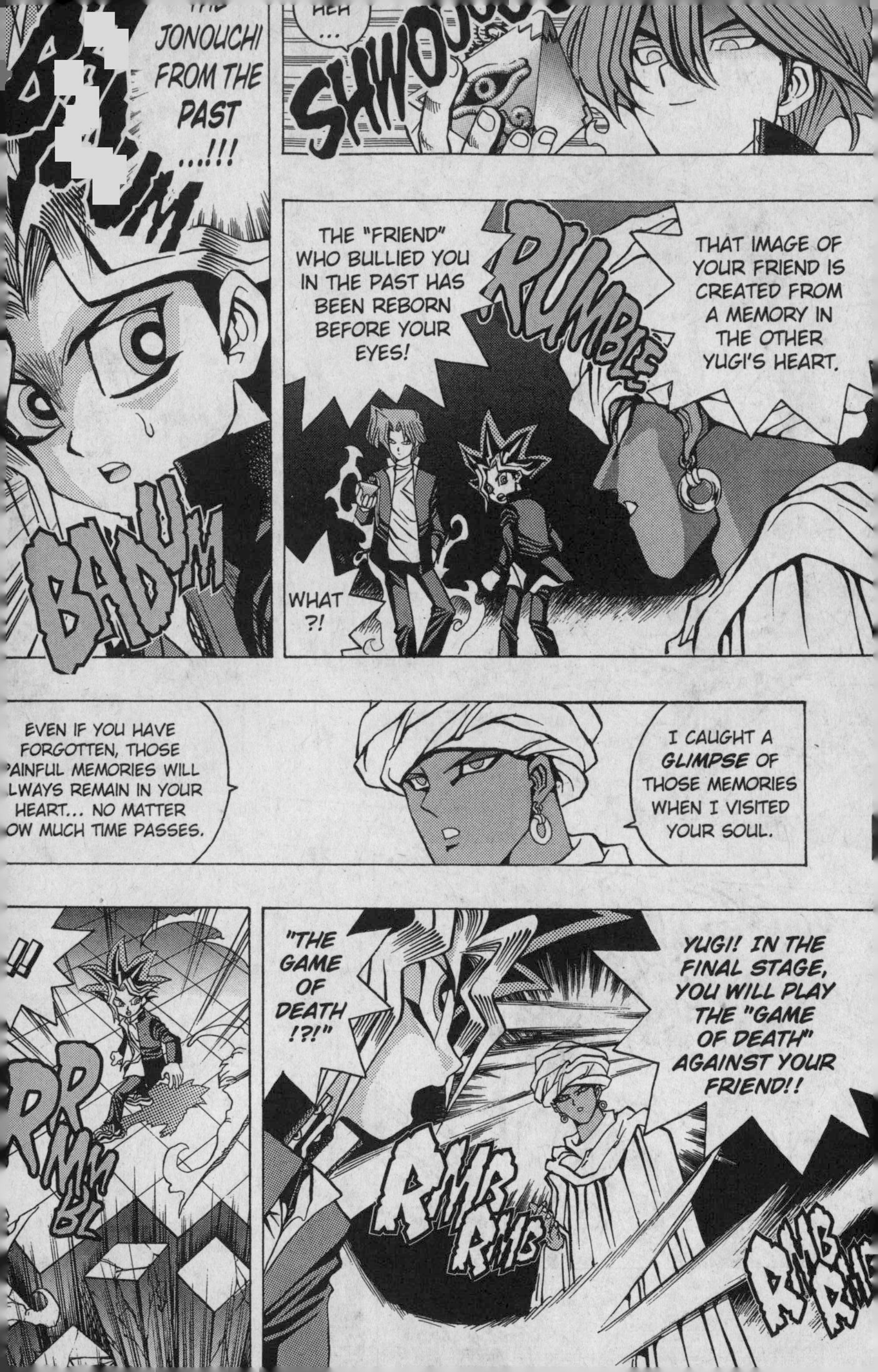

HEH ...
SHWOO
JONOUCHI FROM THE PAST ...!!!
BADUM
THAT IMAGE OF YOUR FRIEND IS CREATED FROM A MEMORY IN THE OTHER YUGI'S HEART.
RUMBLE
THE "FRIEND" WHO BULLIED YOU IN THE PAST HAS BEEN REBORN BEFORE YOUR EYES!
WHAT ?!
BADUM
I CAUGHT A *GLIMPSE* OF THOSE MEMORIES WHEN I VISITED YOUR SOUL.
EVEN IF YOU HAVE FORGOTTEN, THOSE PAINFUL MEMORIES WILL ALWAYS REMAIN IN YOUR HEART... NO MATTER HOW MUCH TIME PASSES.
YUGI! IN THE FINAL STAGE, YOU WILL PLAY THE "GAME OF DEATH" AGAINST YOUR FRIEND!!
"THE GAME OF DEATH !?!"
RMB RMB
RMB
!!

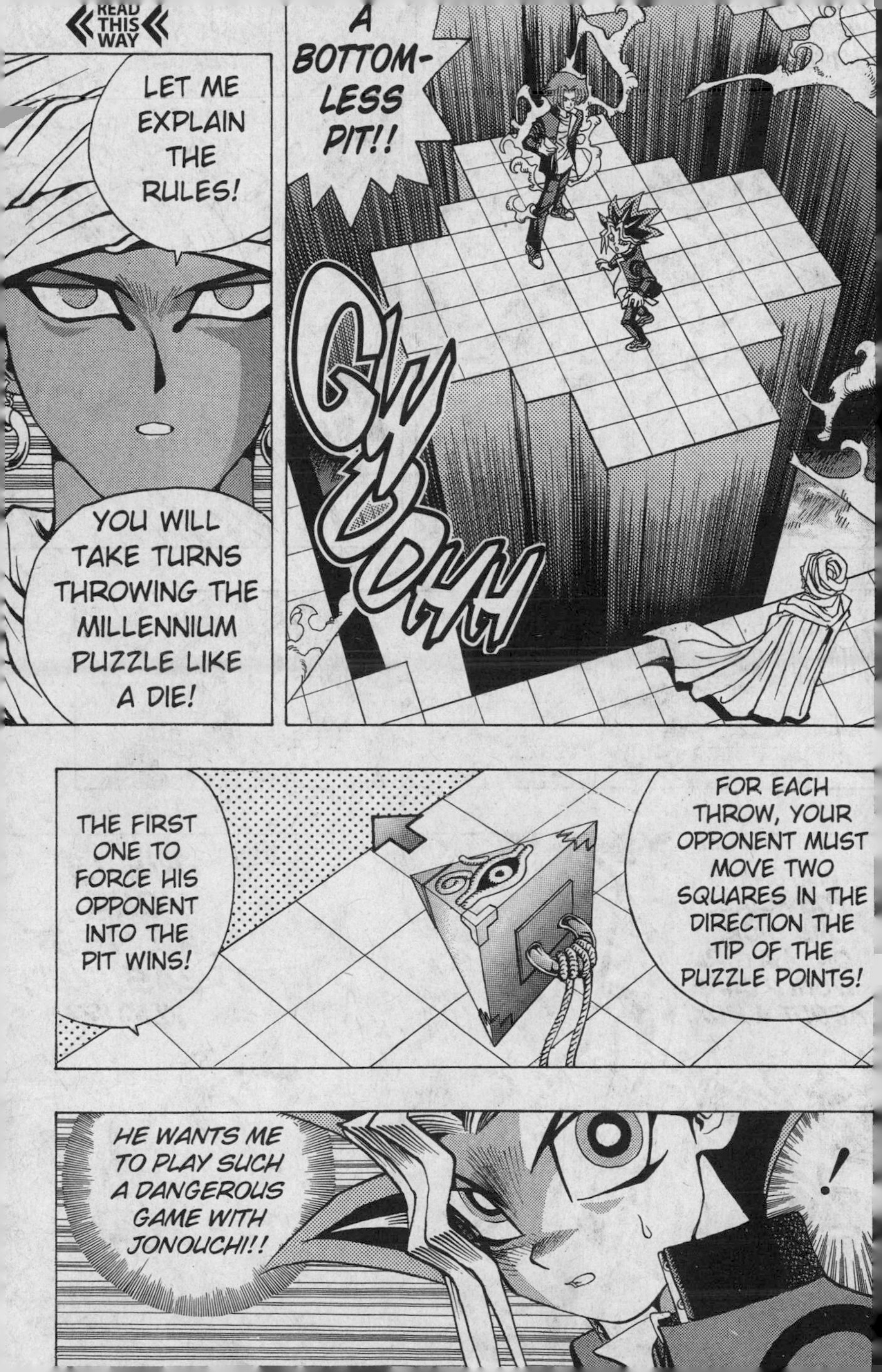
READ THIS WAY
A BOTTOMLESS PIT!!
GWOOHH
LET ME EXPLAIN THE RULES!
YOU WILL TAKE TURNS THROWING THE MILLENNIUM PUZZLE LIKE A DIE!
FOR EACH THROW, YOUR OPPONENT MUST MOVE TWO SQUARES IN THE DIRECTION THE TIP OF THE PUZZLE POINTS!
THE FIRST ONE TO FORCE HIS OPPONENT INTO THE PIT WINS!
!
HE WANTS ME TO PLAY SUCH A DANGEROUS GAME WITH JONOUCHI!!

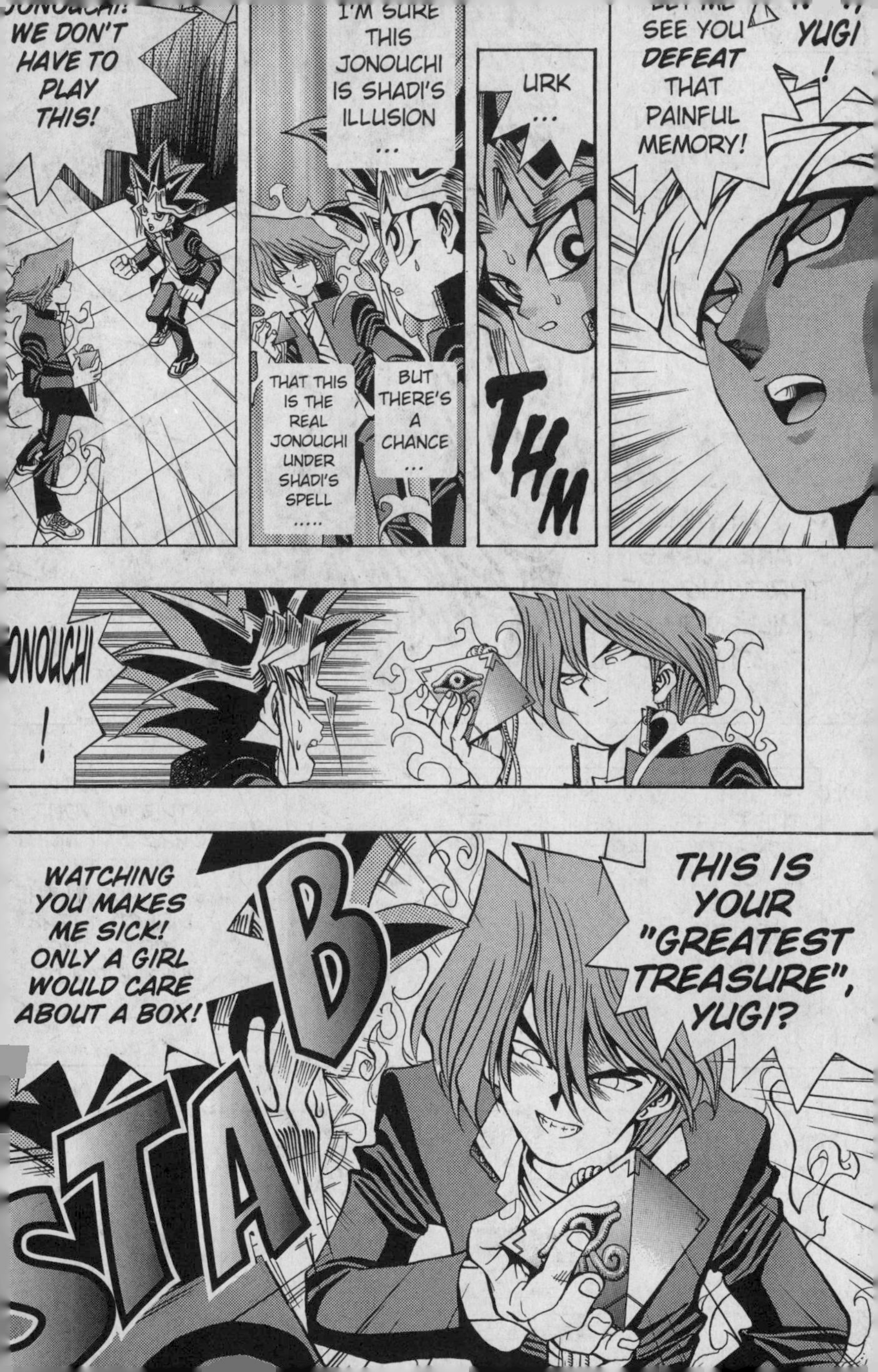
SEE YOU DEFEAT THAT PAINFUL MEMORY!
YUGI!
URK ...
THM
I'M SURE THIS JONOUCHI IS SHADI'S ILLUSION ...
BUT THERE'S A CHANCE ...
THAT THIS IS THE REAL JONOUCHI UNDER SHADI'S SPELL .....
WE DON'T HAVE TO PLAY THIS!
ONOUCHI !
THIS IS YOUR "GREATEST TREASURE", YUGI?
WATCHING YOU MAKES ME SICK! ONLY A GIRL WOULD CARE ABOUT A BOX!
TAB

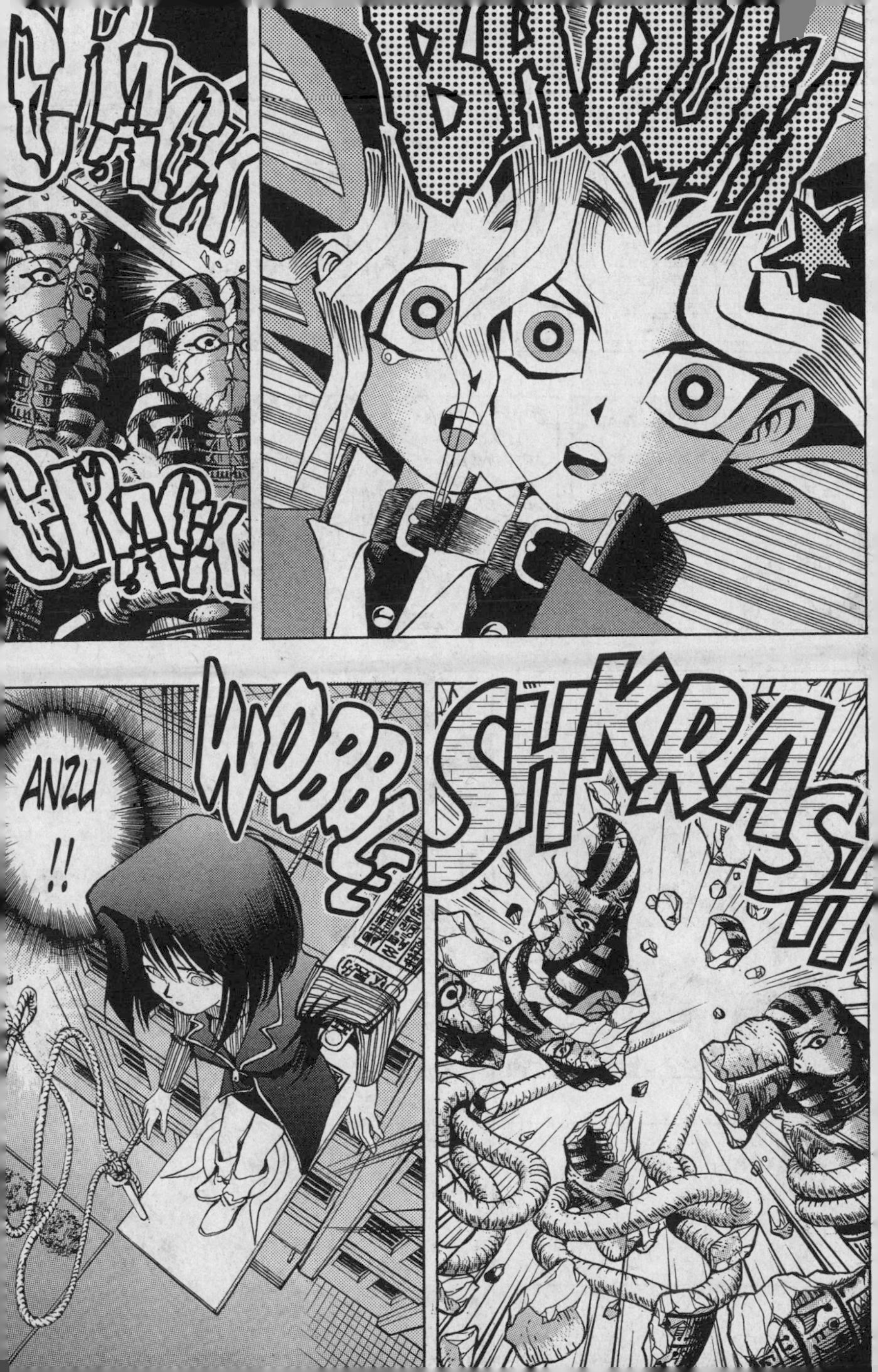
BADUM
CRACK
CRACK
SHKRASH
WOBBL
ANZU !!

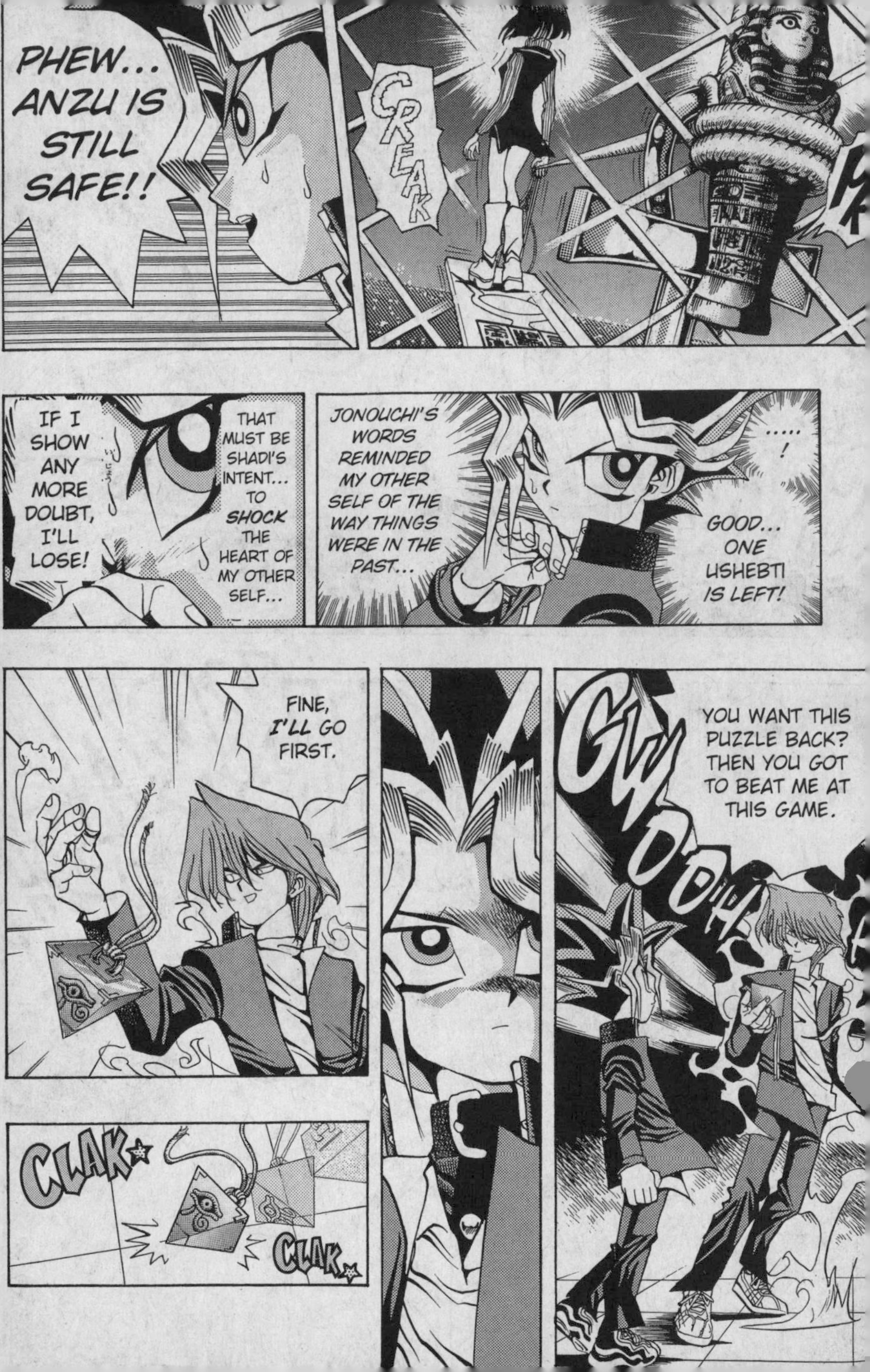
CREAK
PHEW... ANZU IS STILL SAFE!!
JONOUCHI'S WORDS REMINDED MY OTHER SELF OF THE WAY THINGS WERE IN THE PAST...
.....!
GOOD... ONE USHEBTI IS LEFT!
THAT MUST BE SHADI'S INTENT... TO SHOCK THE HEART OF MY OTHER SELF...
IF I SHOW ANY MORE DOUBT, I'LL LOSE!
GWOOOH
YOU WANT THIS PUZZLE BACK? THEN YOU GOT TO BEAT ME AT THIS GAME.
FINE, I'LL GO FIRST.
CLAK
CLAK

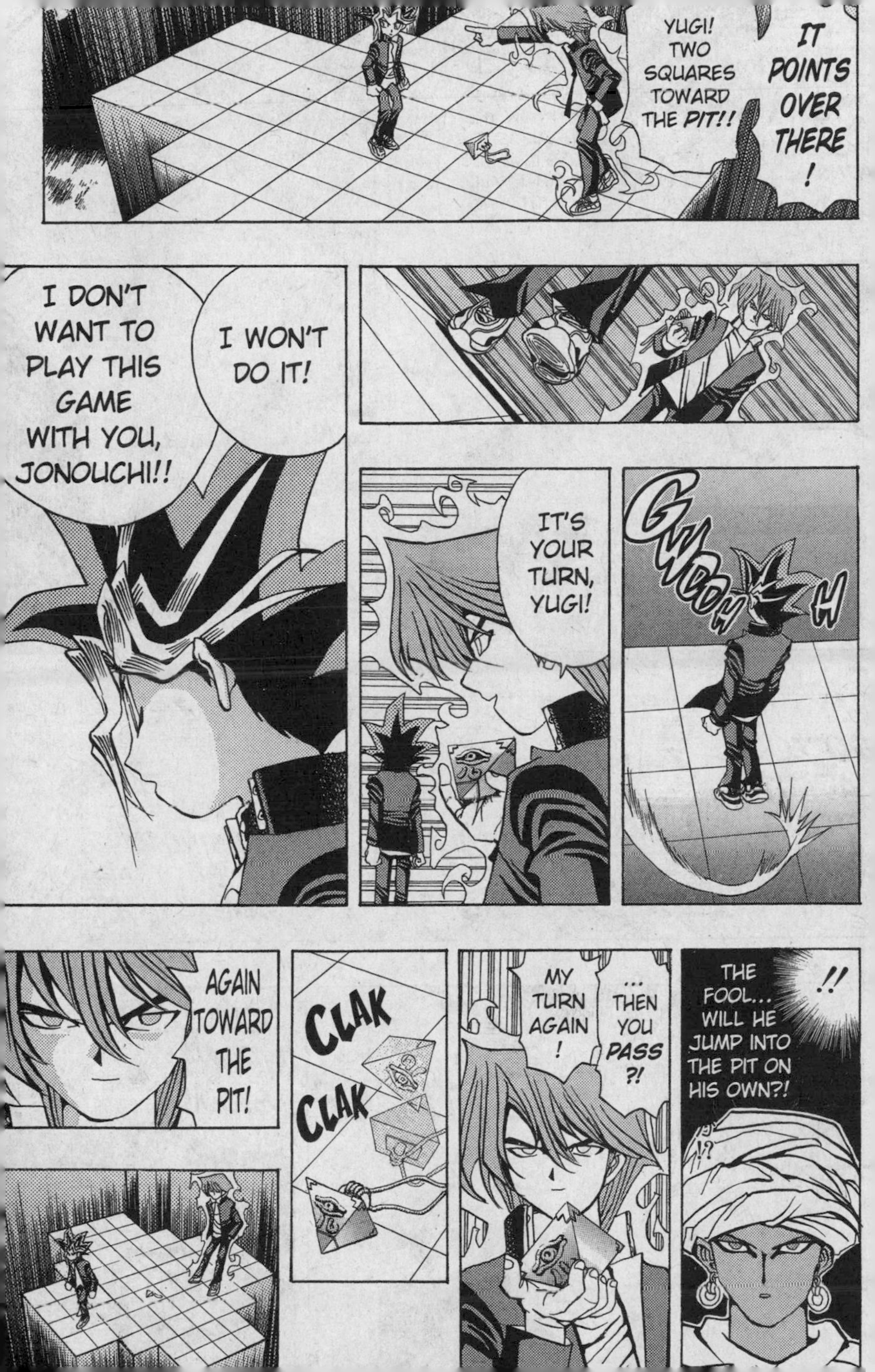
IT POINTS OVER THERE!
YUGI! TWO SQUARES TOWARD THE PIT!!
GWOOOHH
IT'S YOUR TURN, YUGI!
I WON'T DO IT!
I DON'T WANT TO PLAY THIS GAME WITH YOU, JONOUCHI!!
!!
THE FOOL... WILL HE JUMP INTO THE PIT ON HIS OWN?!
!?
... THEN YOU PASS?!
MY TURN AGAIN!
CLAK
CLAK
AGAIN TOWARD THE PIT!

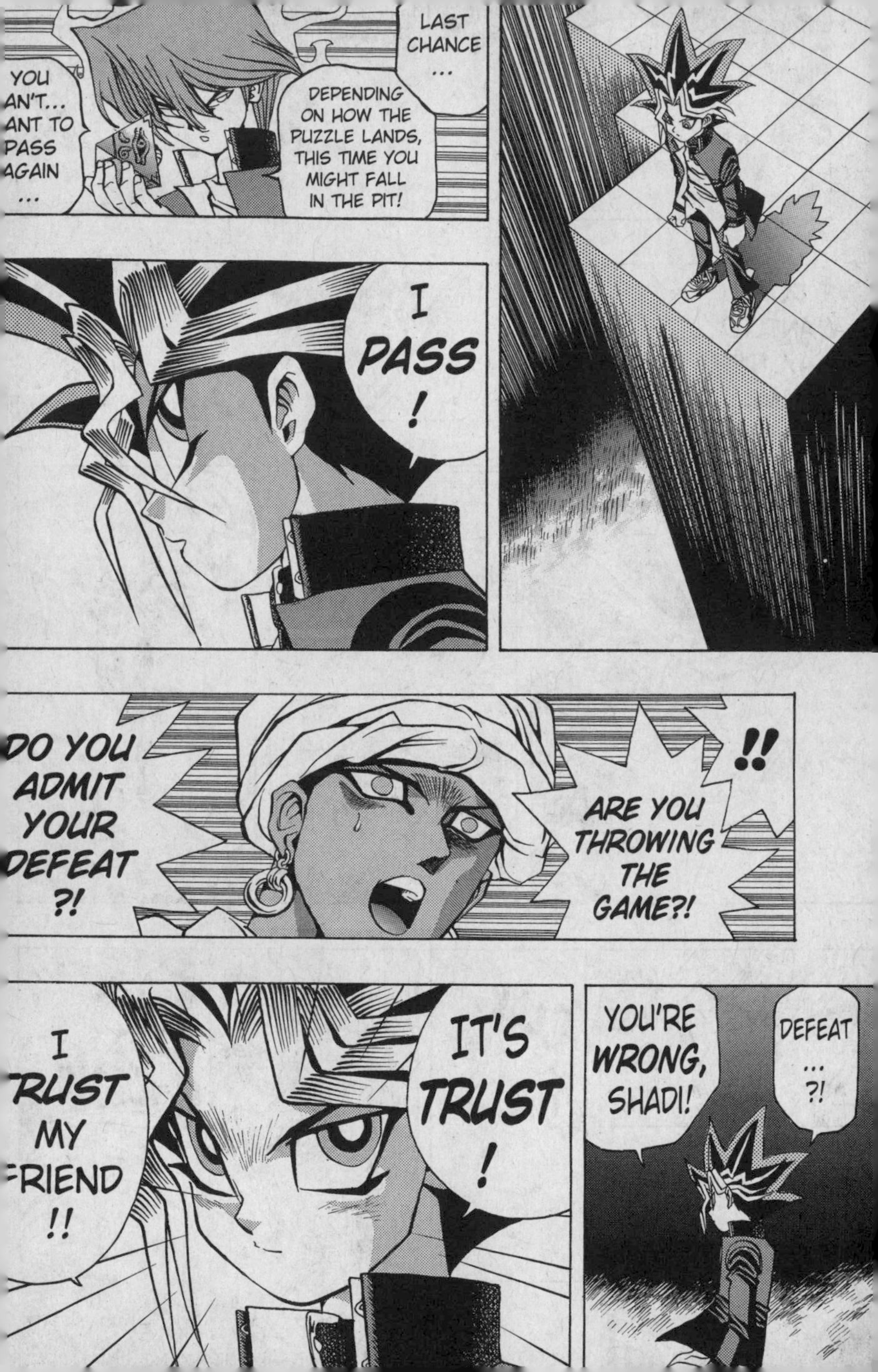
LAST CHANCE ...
DEPENDING ON HOW THE PUZZLE LANDS, THIS TIME YOU MIGHT FALL IN THE PIT!
YOU AN'T... ANT TO PASS AGAIN ...
I PASS!
!!
ARE YOU THROWING THE GAME?!
DO YOU ADMIT YOUR DEFEAT?!
DEFEAT ...?!
YOU'RE WRONG, SHADI!
IT'S TRUST!
I TRUST MY FRIEND!!

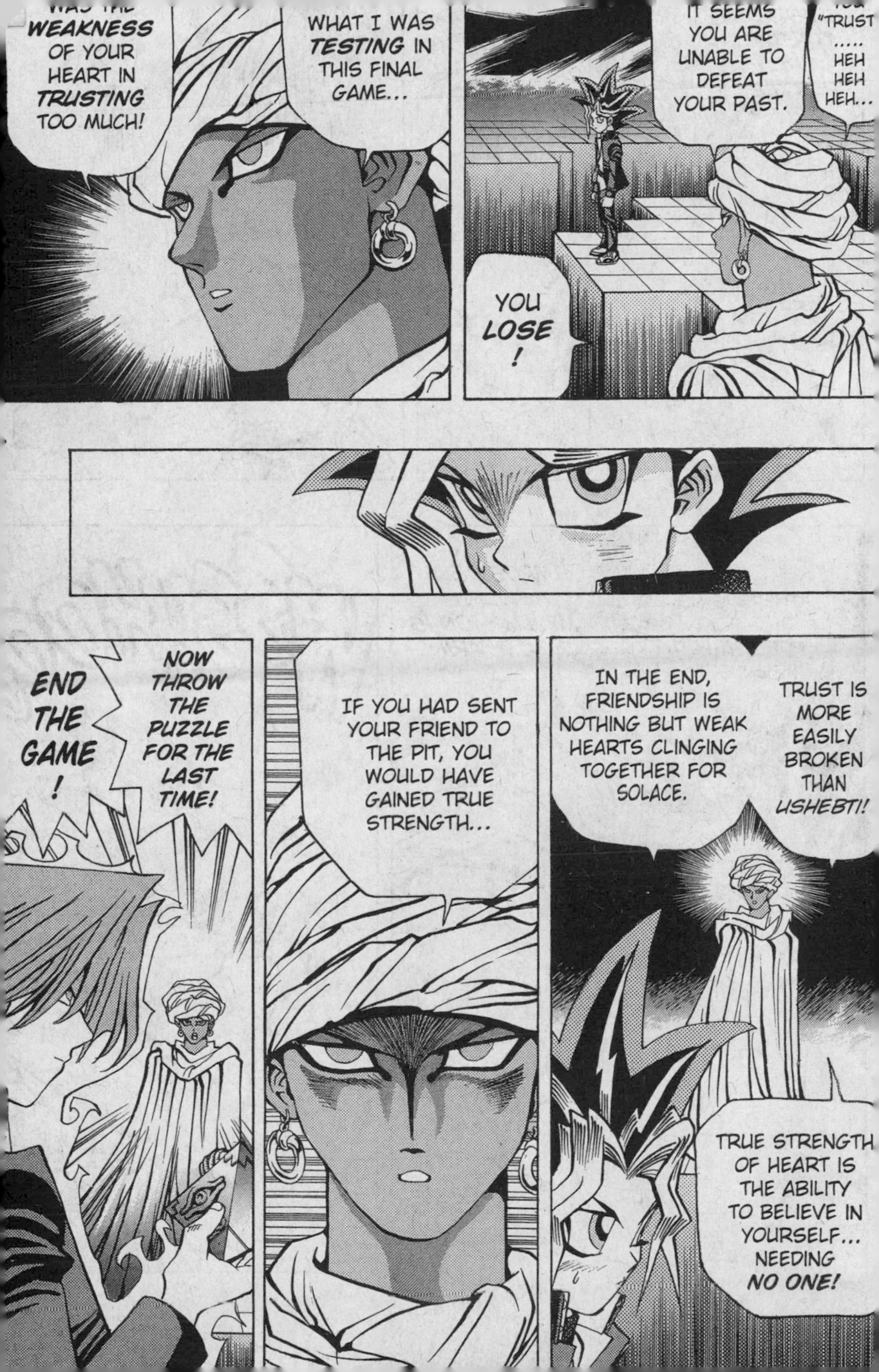
"TRUST" ..... HEH HEH HEH...
IT SEEMS YOU ARE UNABLE TO DEFEAT YOUR PAST.
YOU LOSE!
WHAT I WAS TESTING IN THIS FINAL GAME...
WEAKNESS OF YOUR HEART IN TRUSTING TOO MUCH!
TRUST IS MORE EASILY BROKEN THAN USHEBTI!
IN THE END, FRIENDSHIP IS NOTHING BUT WEAK HEARTS CLINGING TOGETHER FOR SOLACE.
TRUE STRENGTH OF HEART IS THE ABILITY TO BELIEVE IN YOURSELF... NEEDING NO ONE!
IF YOU HAD SENT YOUR FRIEND TO THE PIT, YOU WOULD HAVE GAINED TRUE STRENGTH...
NOW THROW THE PUZZLE FOR THE LAST TIME!
END THE GAME!

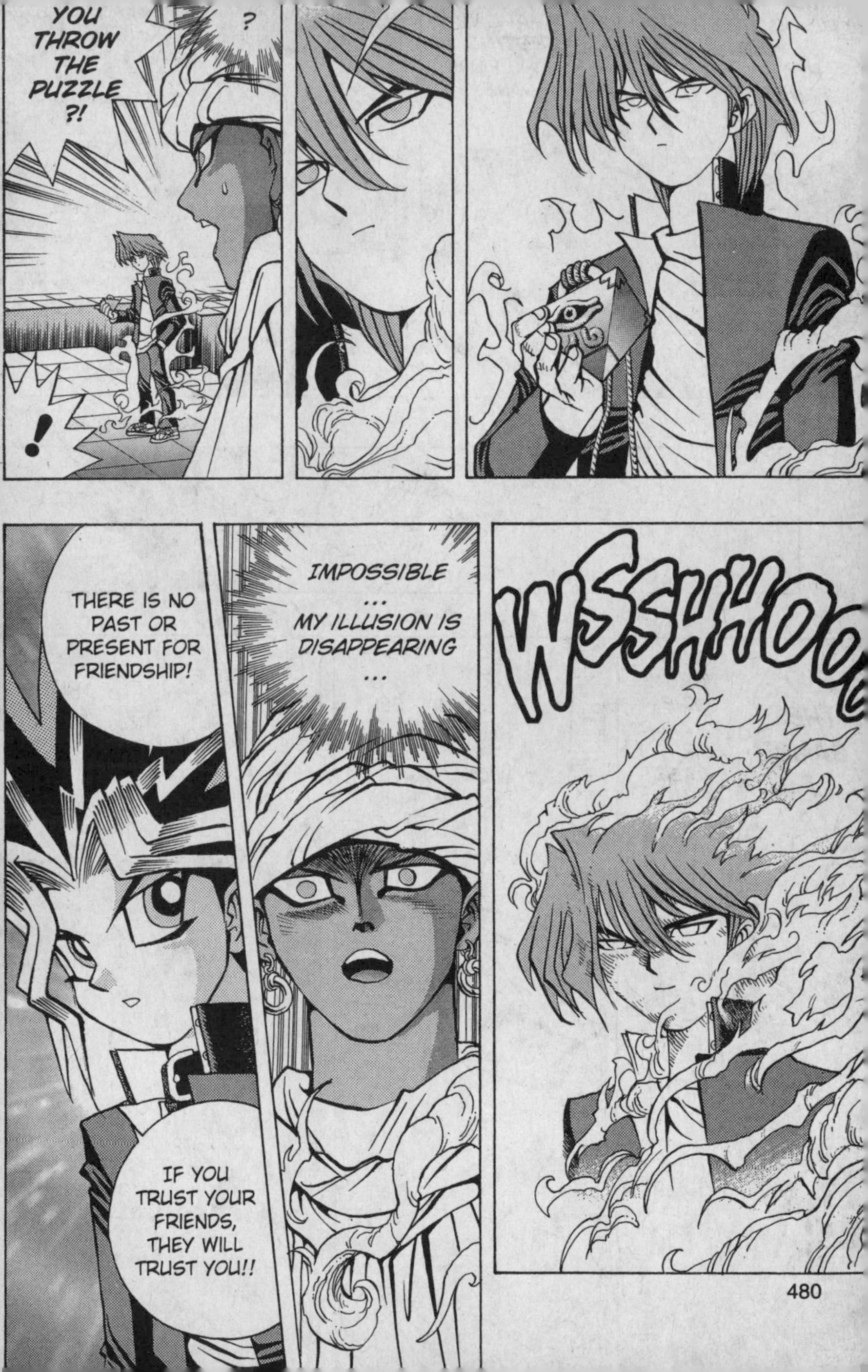
?
YOU THROW THE PUZZLE ?!
!
WSSHHOO
IMPOSSIBLE ... MY ILLUSION IS DISAPPEARING ...
THERE IS NO PAST OR PRESENT FOR FRIENDSHIP!
IF YOU TRUST YOUR FRIENDS, THEY WILL TRUST YOU!!

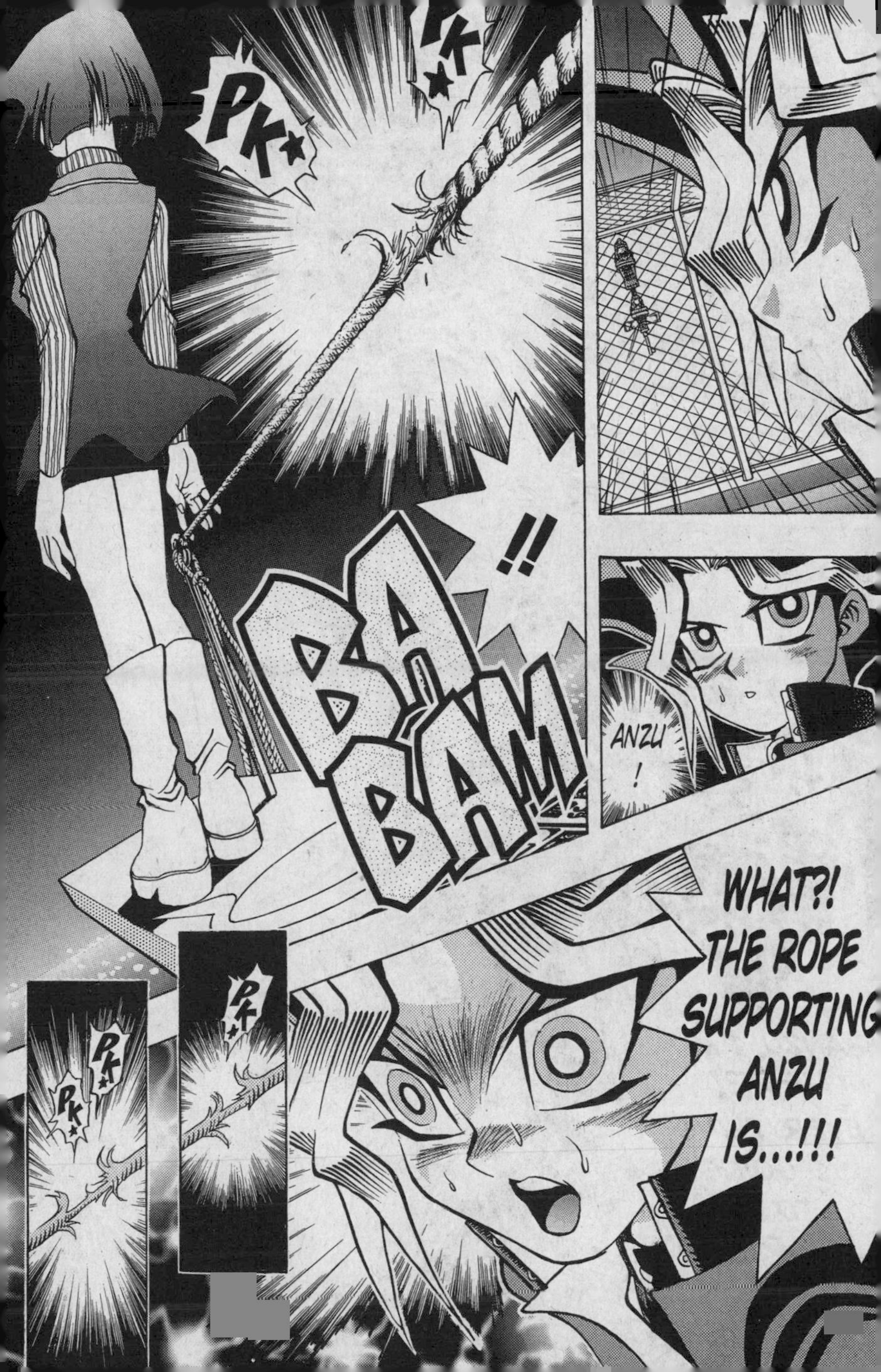

PK★
PK★
BA BAM
!!
ANZU !
WHAT?! THE ROPE SUPPORTING ANZU IS...!!!
PK★
PK★
PK★

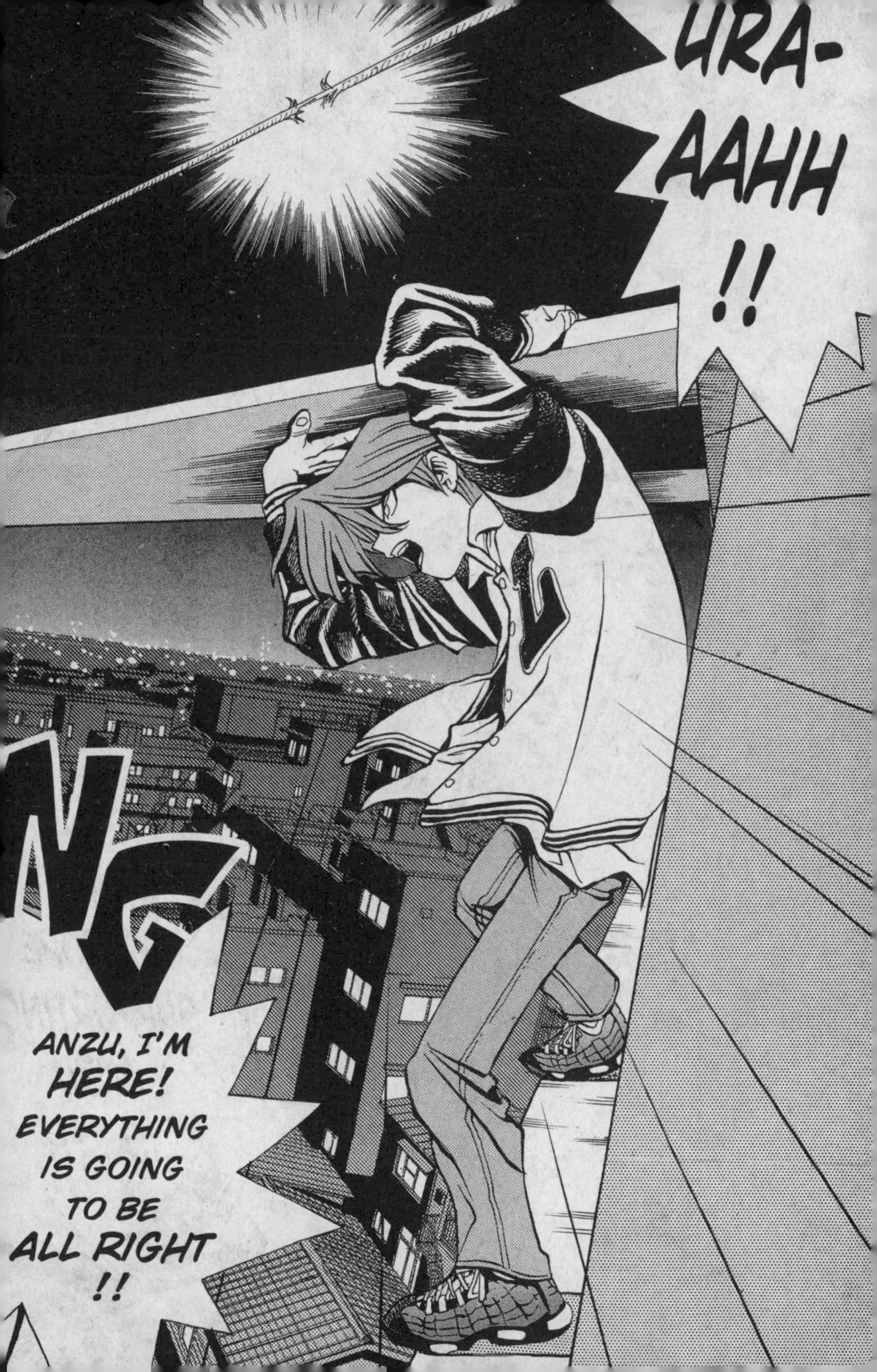
URA-
AAHH
!!
NG
ANZU, I'M
HERE!
EVERYTHING
IS GOING
TO BE
ALL RIGHT
!!

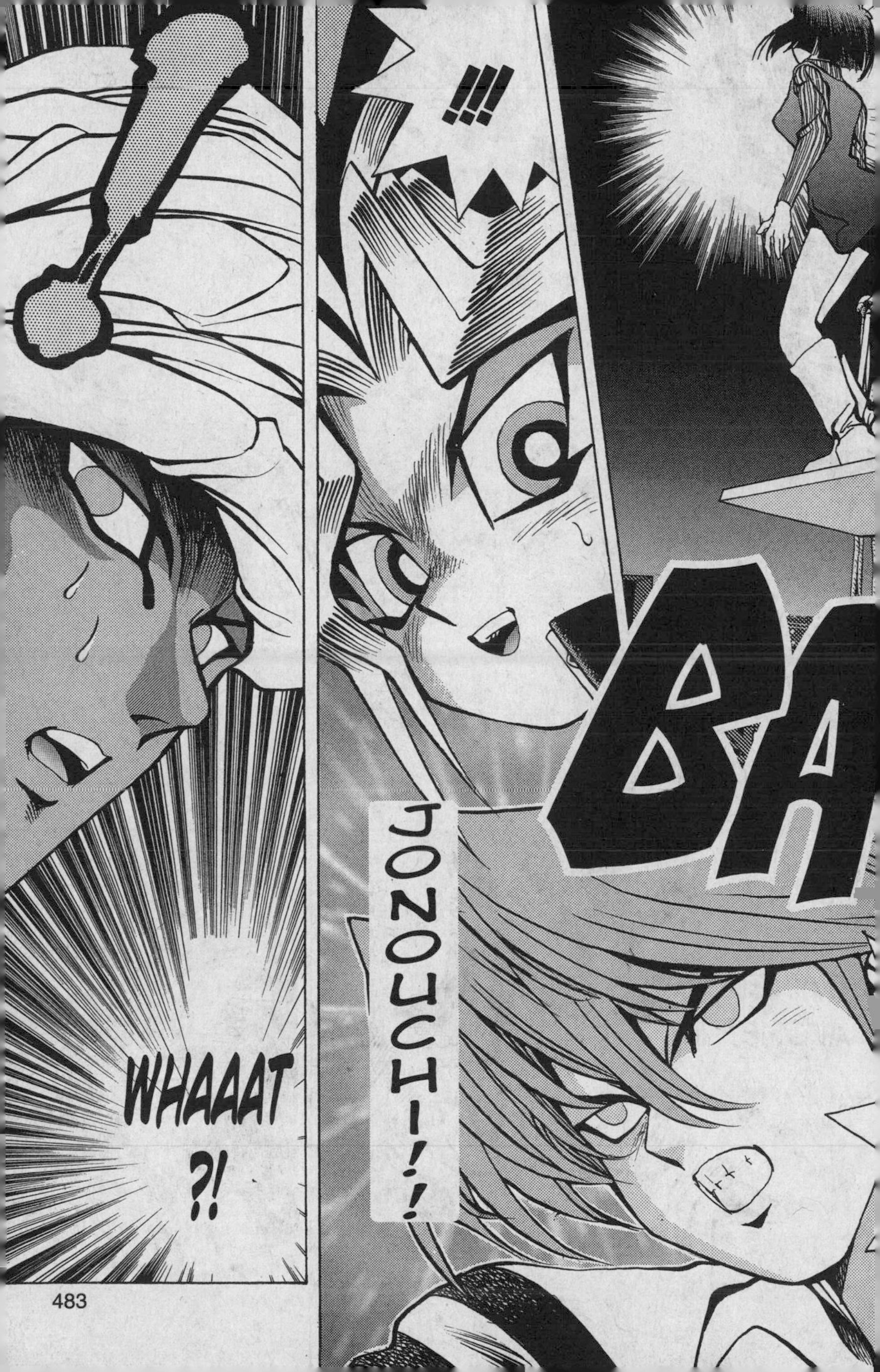
!!!
BA
JONOUCHI!!
!
WHAAAT ?!

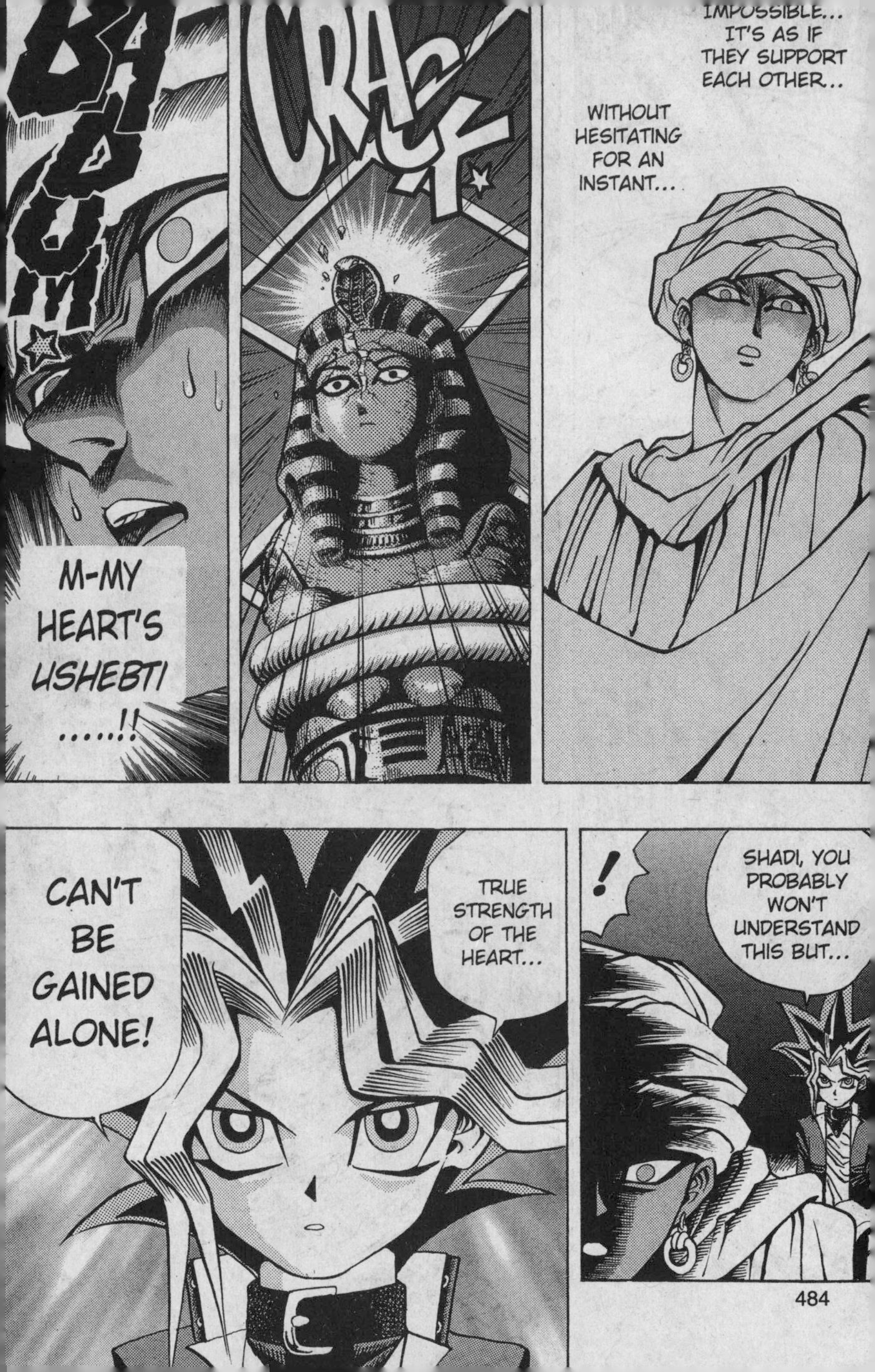
IMPOSSIBLE... IT'S AS IF THEY SUPPORT EACH OTHER...
WITHOUT HESITATING FOR AN INSTANT...
CRACK
M-MY HEART'S USHEBTI .....!!
!
SHADI, YOU PROBABLY WON'T UNDERSTAND THIS BUT...
TRUE STRENGTH OF THE HEART...
CAN'T BE GAINED ALONE!

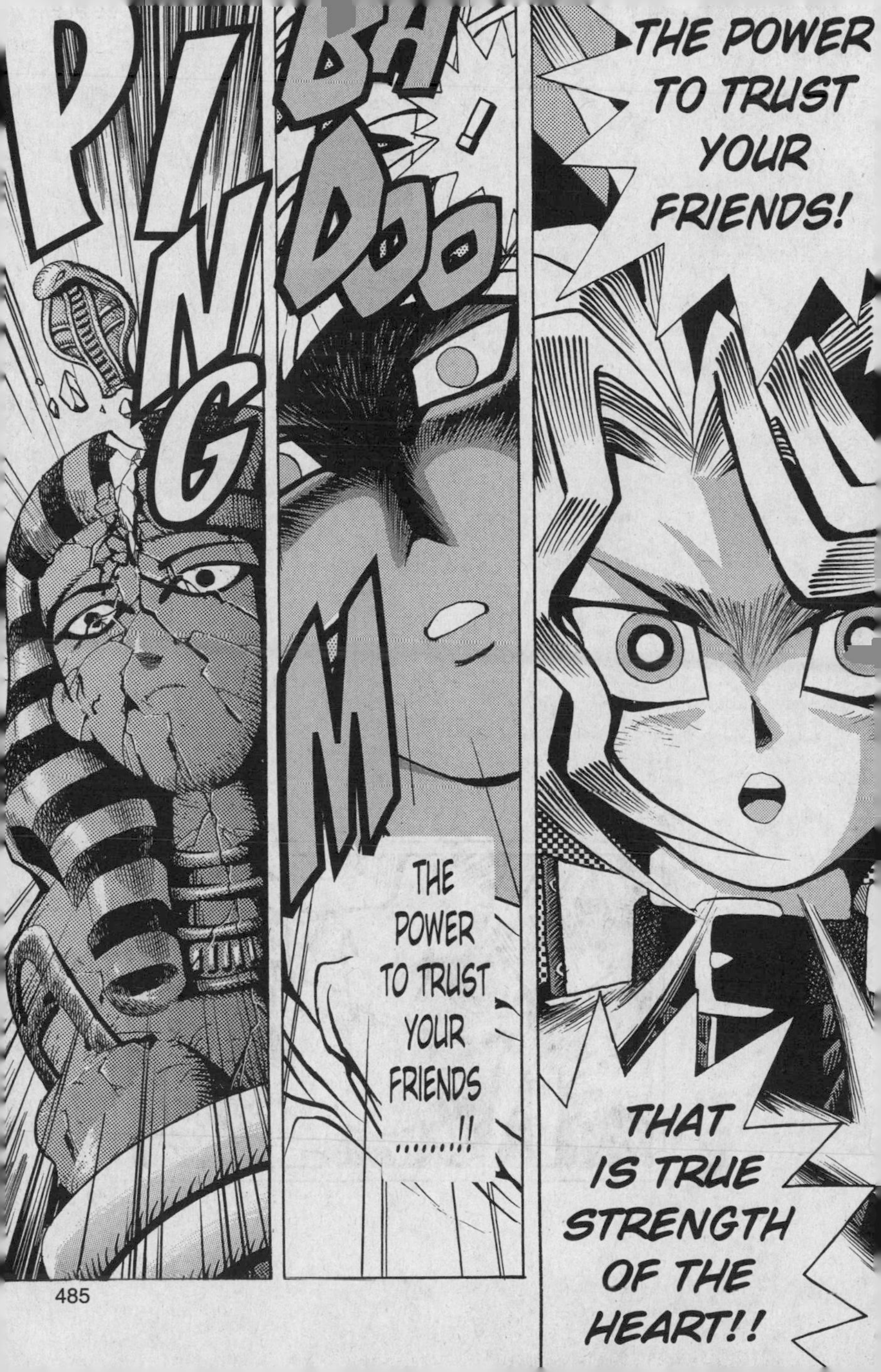
THE POWER TO TRUST YOUR FRIENDS!
THAT IS TRUE STRENGTH OF THE HEART!!
BADOOM!
THE POWER TO TRUST YOUR FRIENDS ......!!
PING

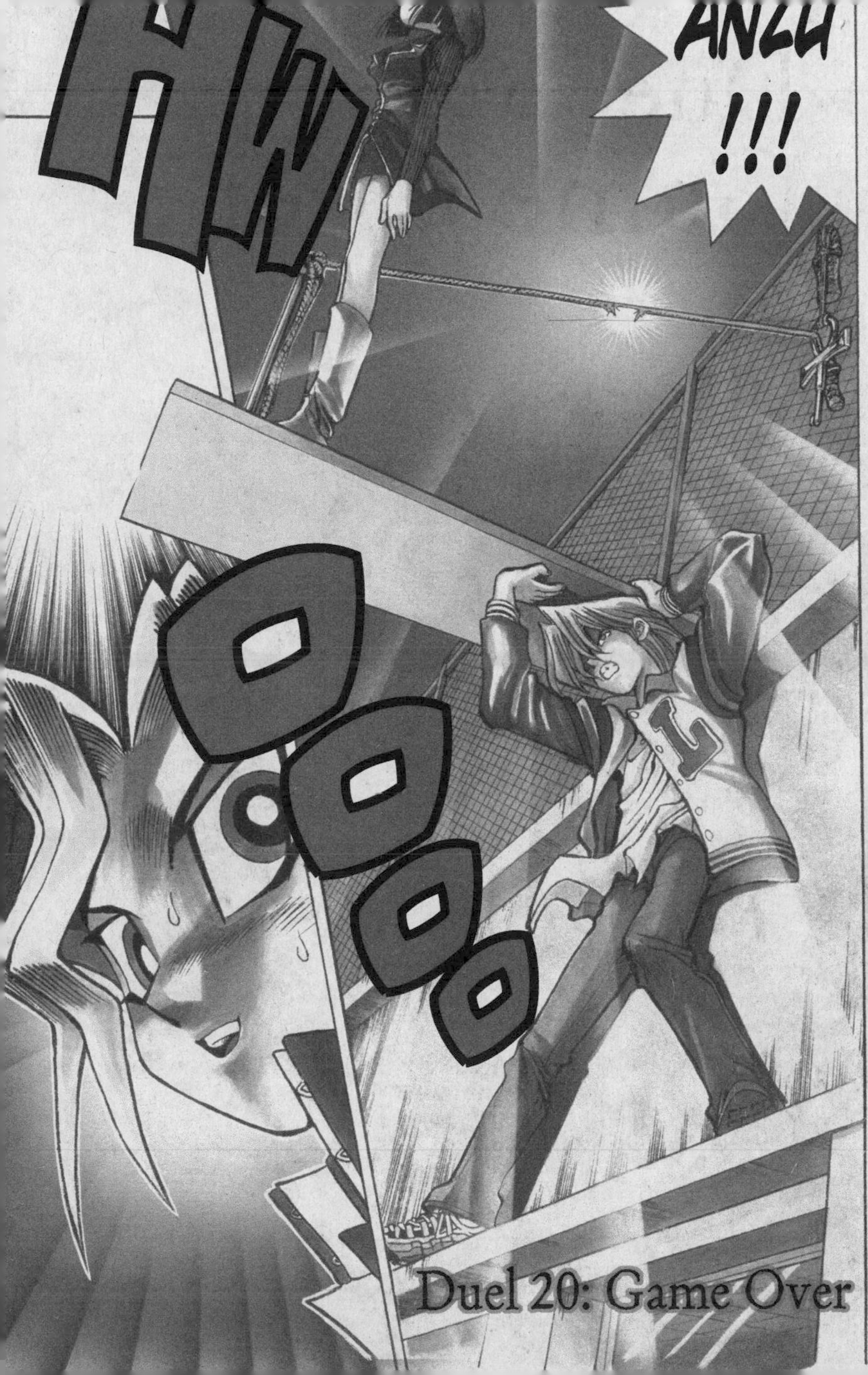
ANZU
!!!

Duel 20: Game Over

Duel 20: Game Over

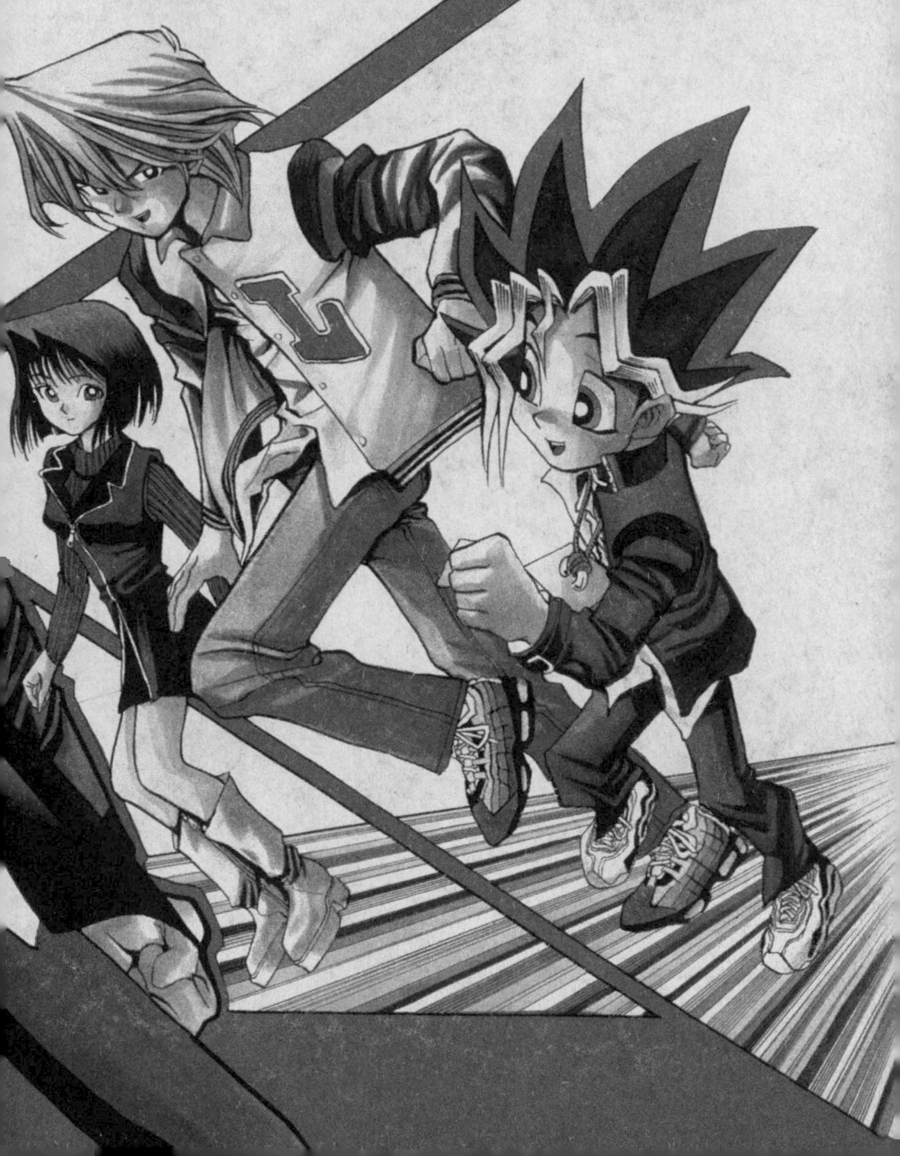

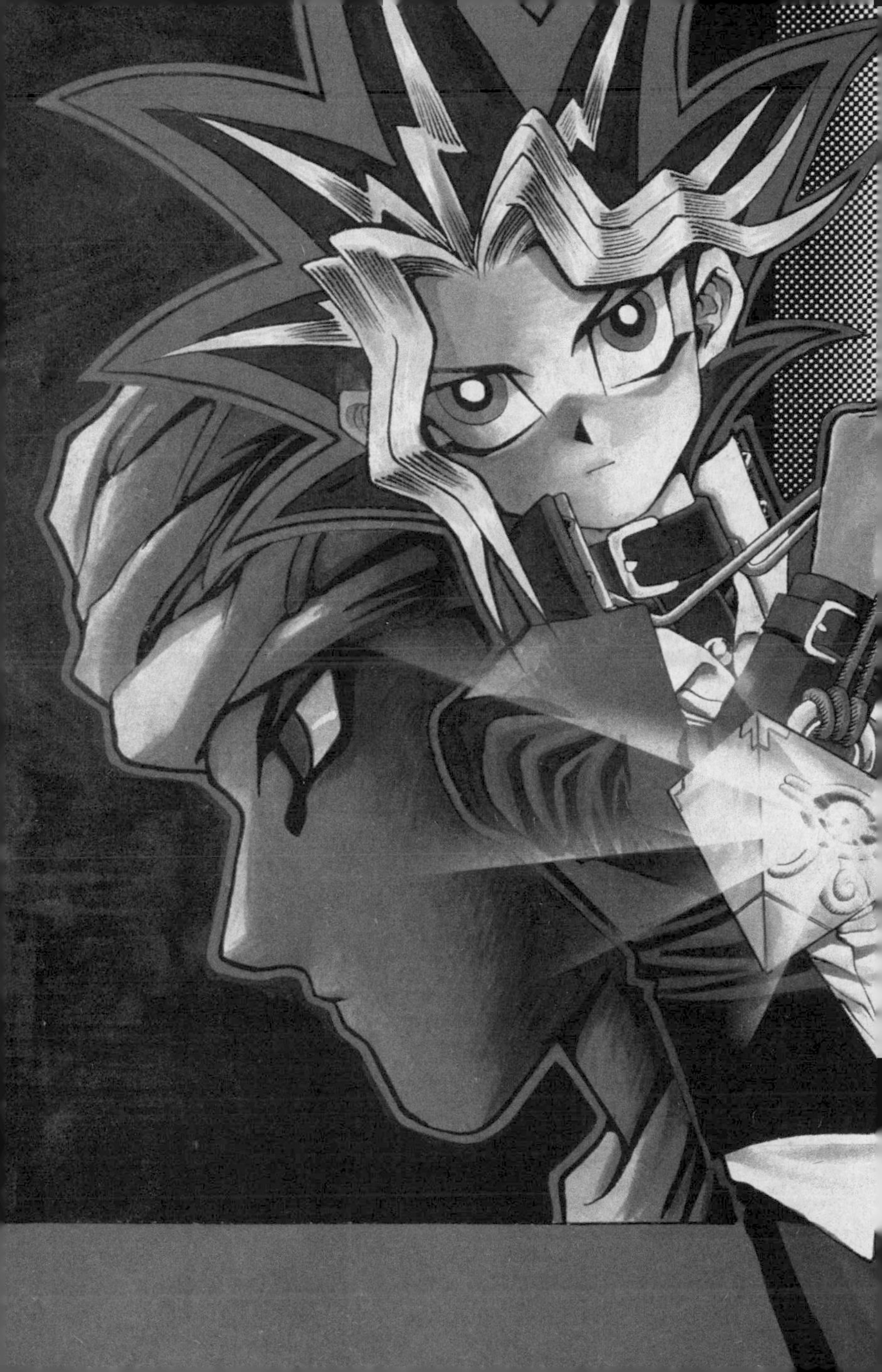

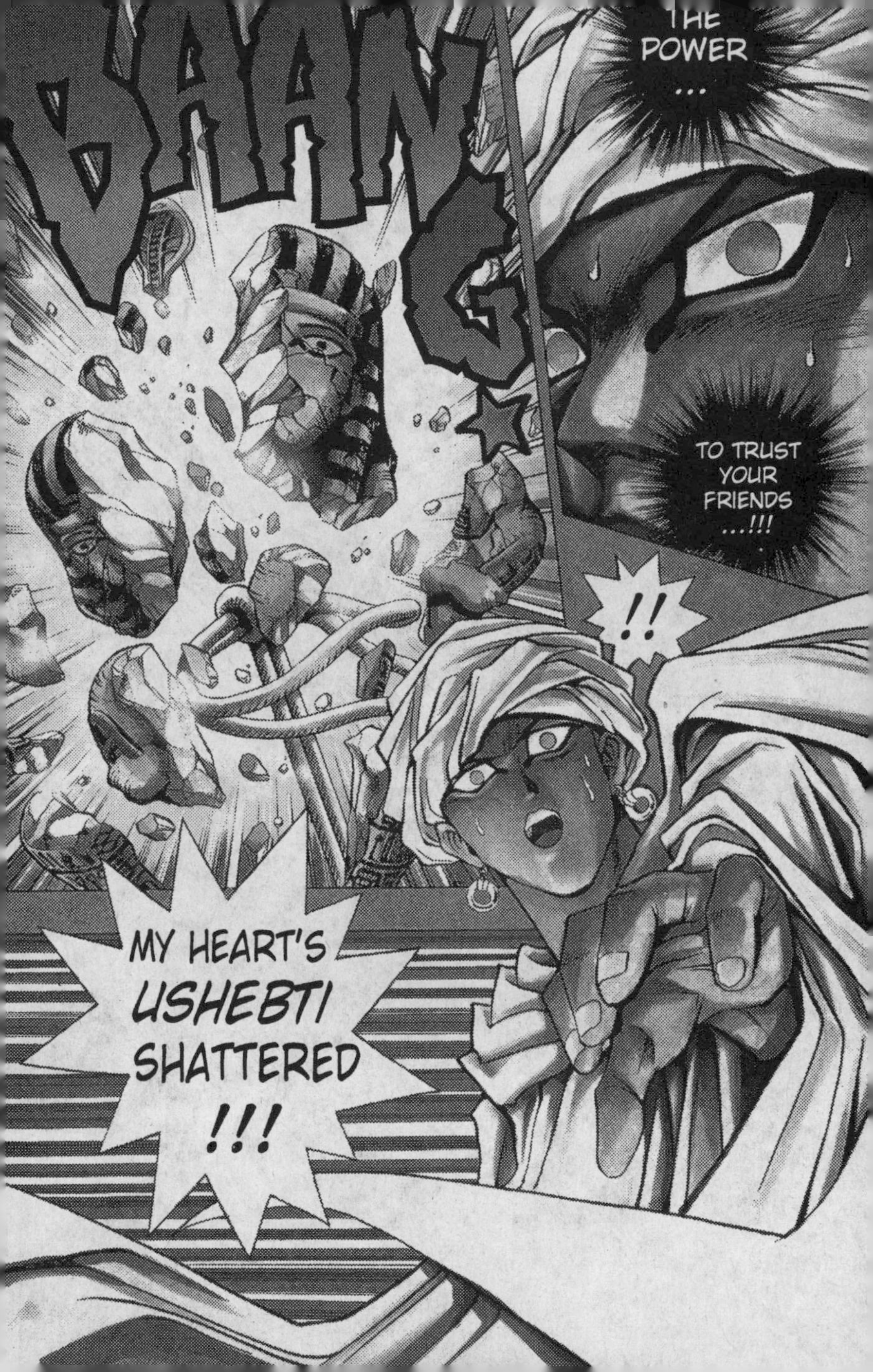
THE POWER ...
TO TRUST YOUR FRIENDS ...!!!
!!
MY HEART'S USHEBTI SHATTERED !!!

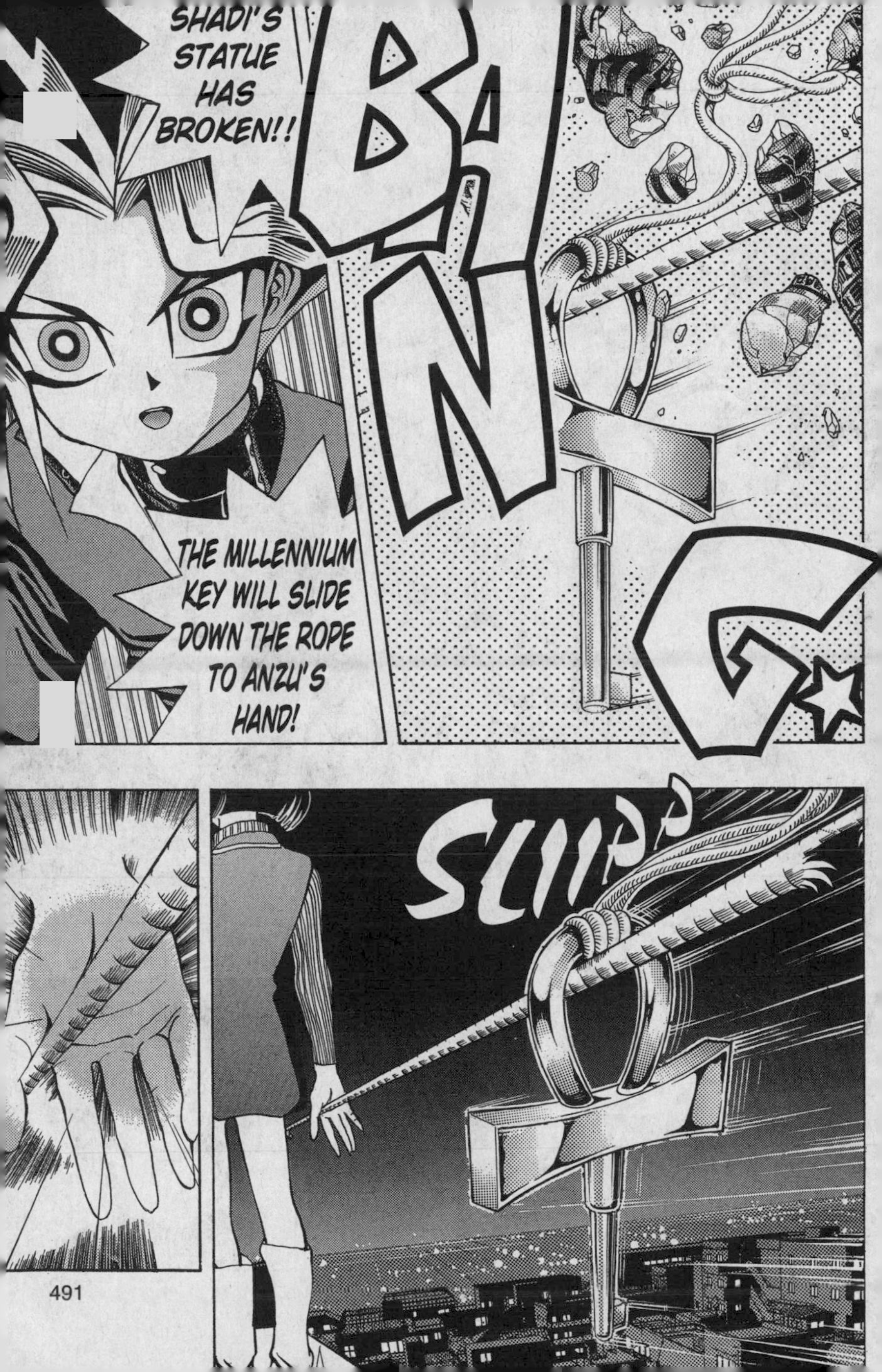
BANG☆
SHADI'S STATUE HAS BROKEN!!
THE MILLENNIUM KEY WILL SLIDE DOWN THE ROPE TO ANZU'S HAND!
SLIP

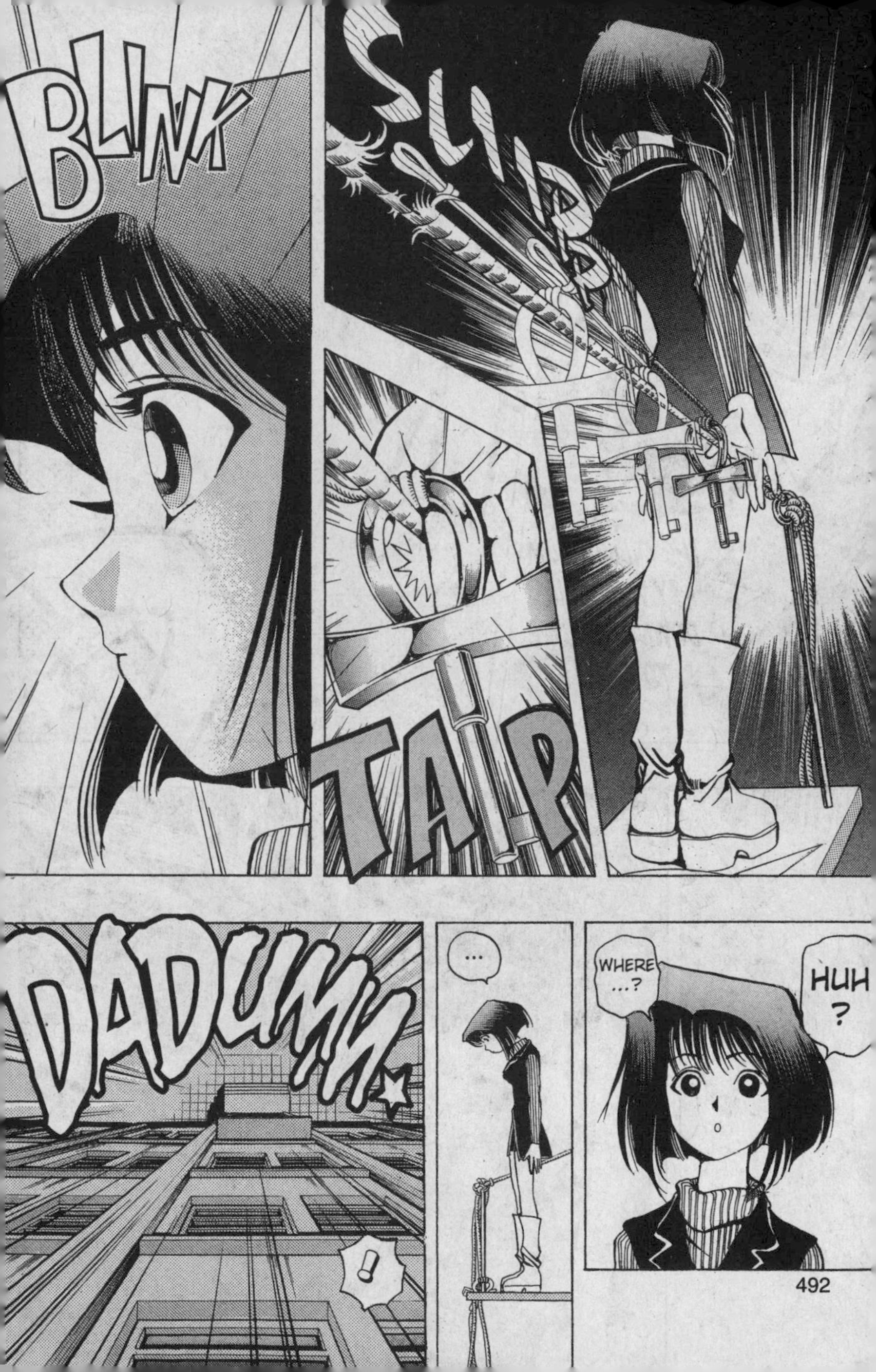
SLIP
SLIP
SLIP
TAP
BLINK
HUH?
WHERE ...?
...
DADUMM
!

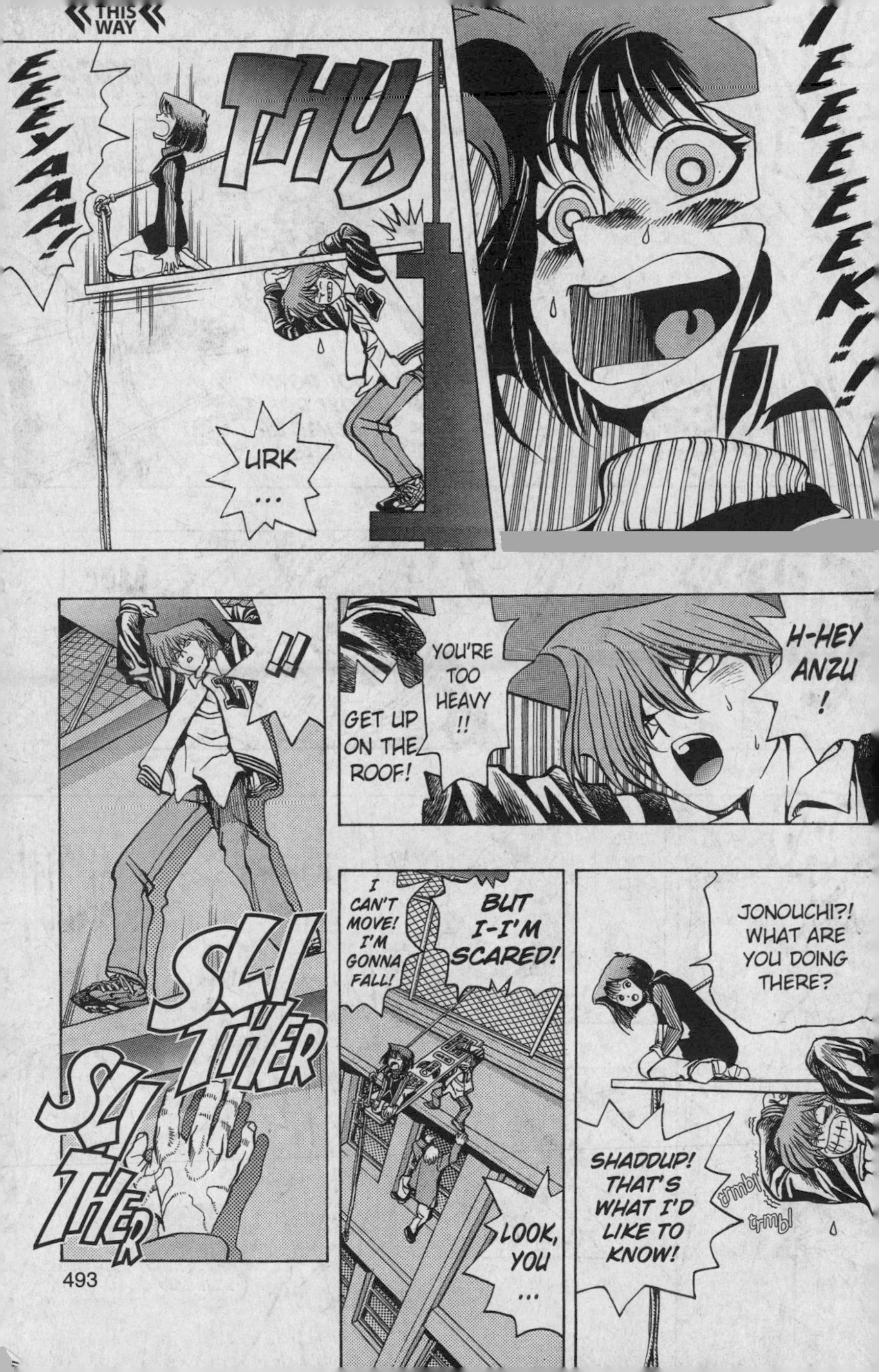
THIS WAY
IEEEEEK!!!
EEEYAAA!
THUD
URK ...
H-HEY ANZU!
YOU'RE TOO HEAVY!!
GET UP ON THE ROOF!
JONOUCHI?! WHAT ARE YOU DOING THERE?
SHADDUP! THAT'S WHAT I'D LIKE TO KNOW!
trmbl
trmbl
BUT I-I'M SCARED!
I CAN'T MOVE! I'M GONNA FALL!
LOOK, YOU ...
!!
SLITHER
SLITHER

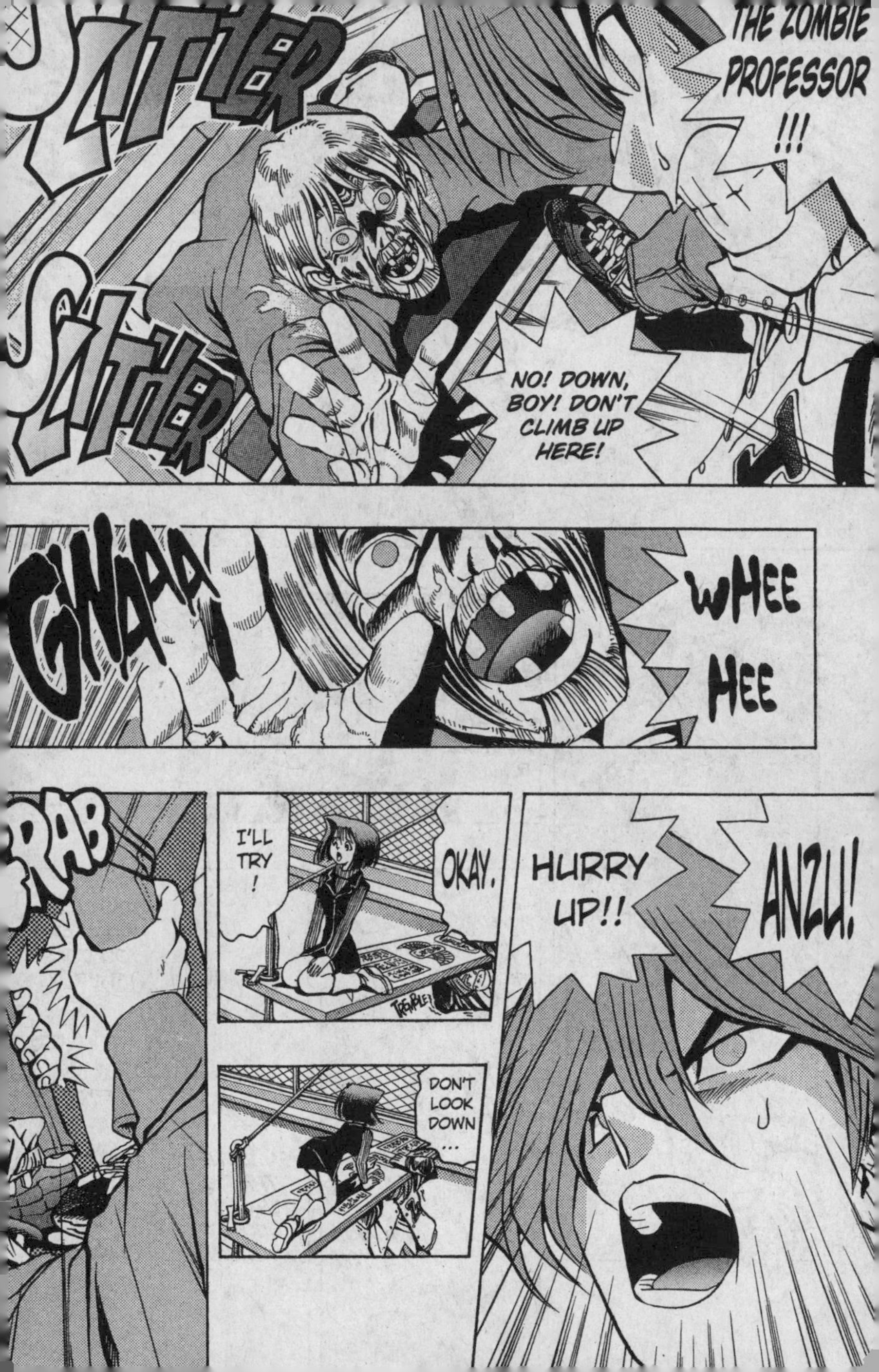
THE ZOMBIE PROFESSOR !!!
SLITHER
SLITHER
NO! DOWN, BOY! DON'T CLIMB UP HERE!
WHEE HEE
GNAA
ANZU!
HURRY UP!!
OKAY.
I'LL TRY!
DON'T LOOK DOWN ...
RAB

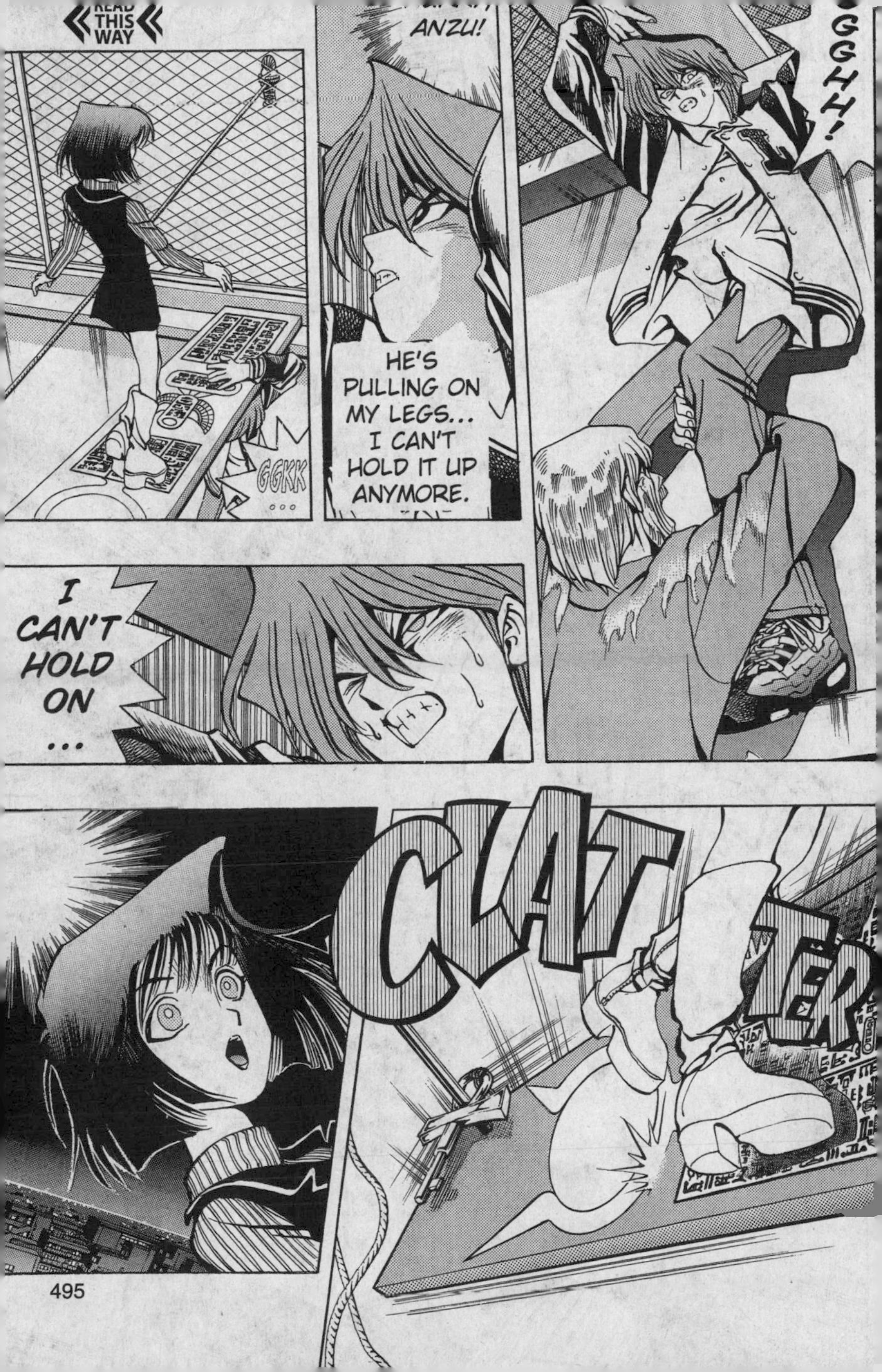
GGHH!
ANZU!
HE'S PULLING ON MY LEGS... I CAN'T HOLD IT UP ANYMORE.
GGKK...
I CAN'T HOLD ON...
CLATTER

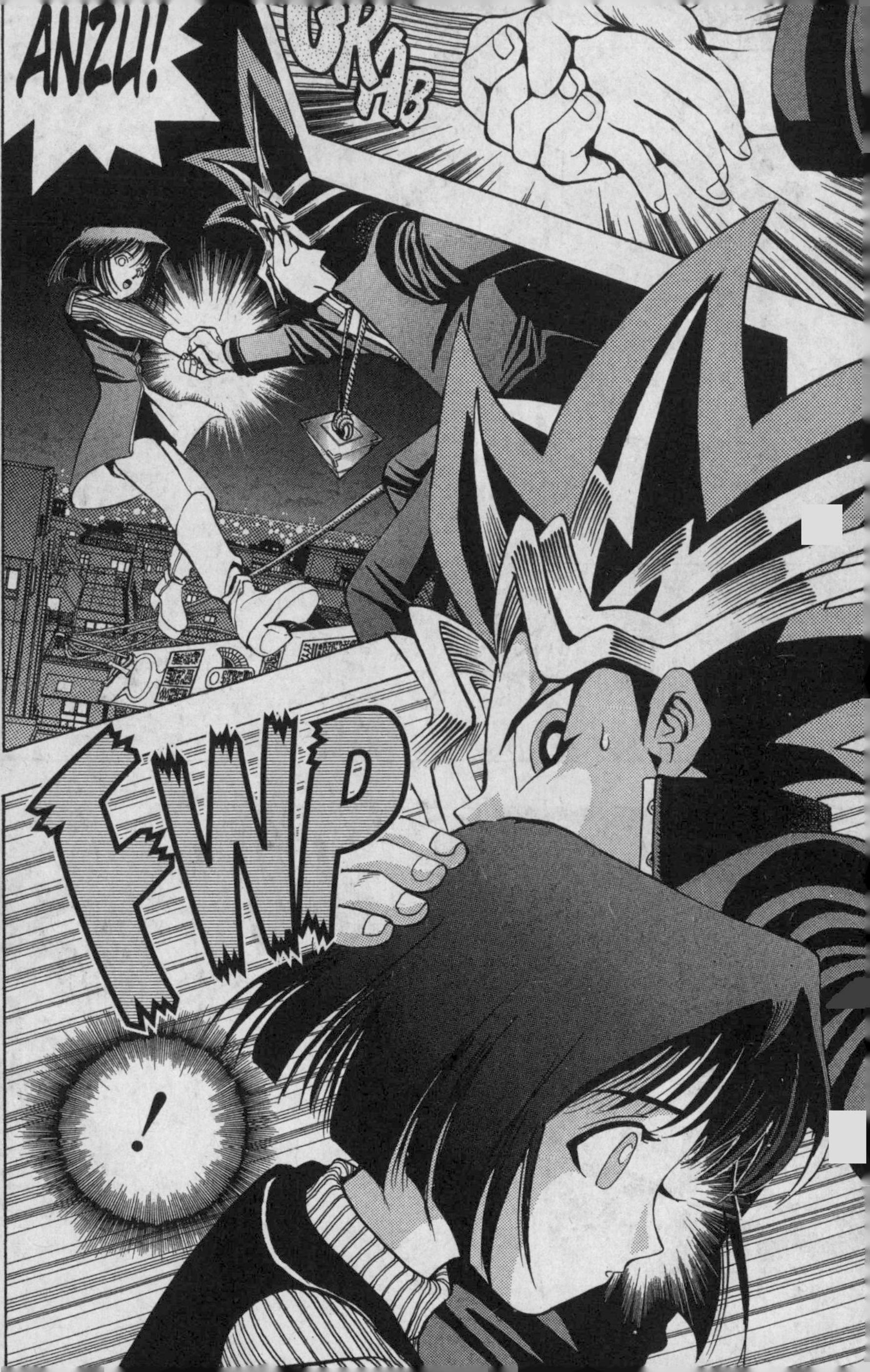
GRAB
ANZU!
FWP
!

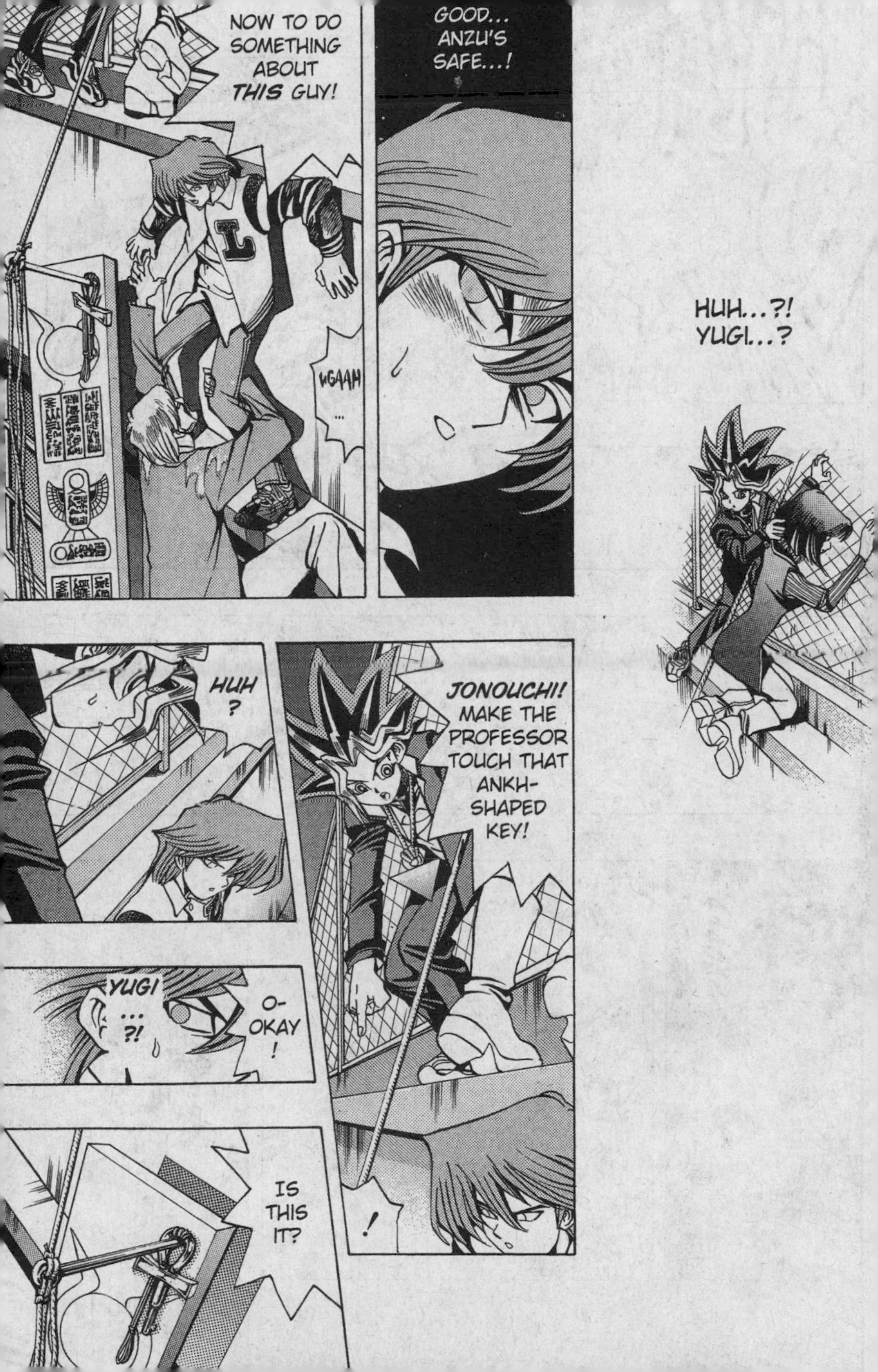
GOOD... ANZU'S SAFE...!
HUH...?! YUGI...?
NOW TO DO SOMETHING ABOUT THIS GUY!
UGAAH...
JONOUCHI! MAKE THE PROFESSOR TOUCH THAT ANKH-SHAPED KEY!
HUH?
YUGI...?!
O-OKAY!
!
IS THIS IT?

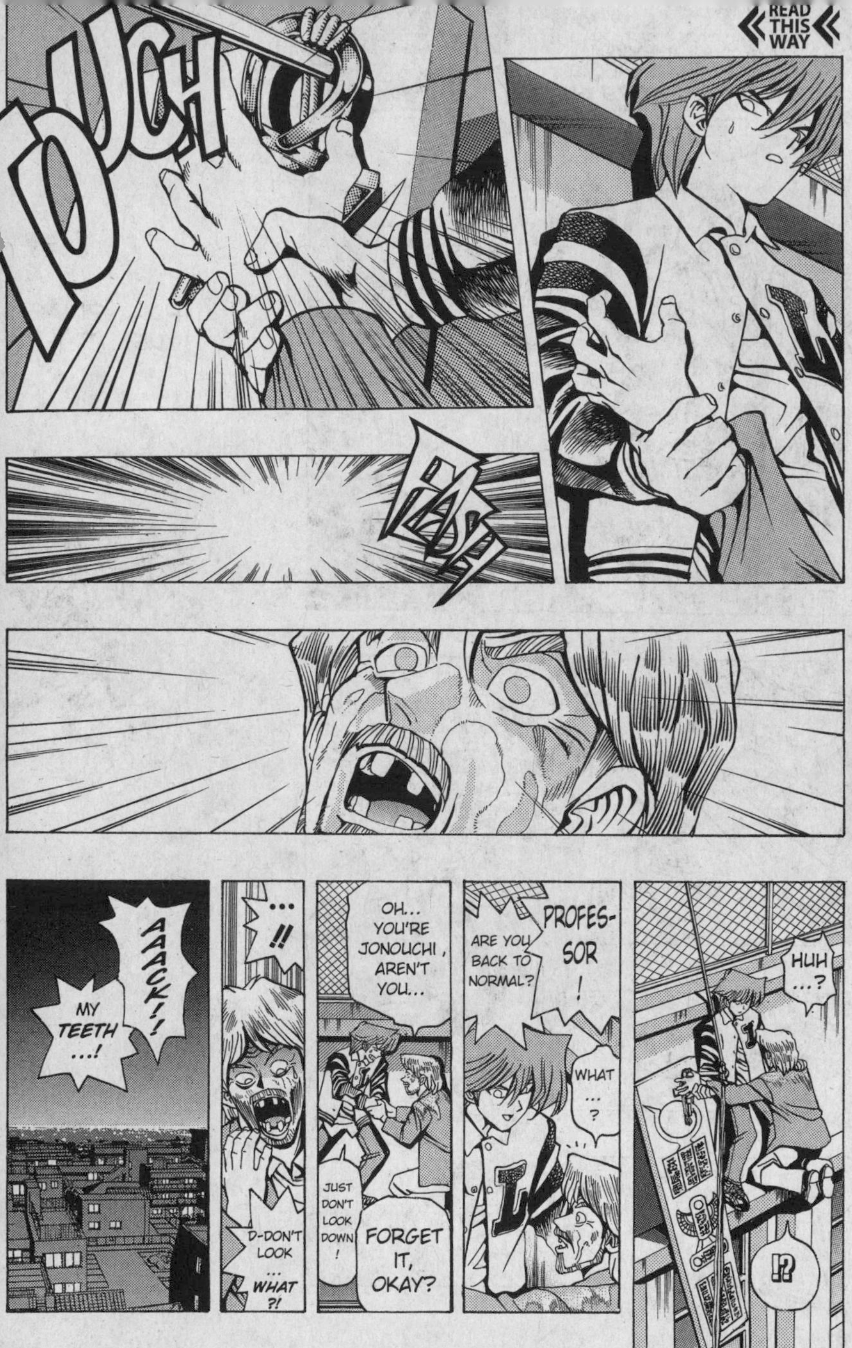
READ THIS WAY
OUCH
FLASH
HUH...?
!?
PROFES-SOR!
ARE YOU BACK TO NORMAL?
WHAT...?
OH... YOU'RE JONOUCHI, AREN'T YOU...
JUST DON'T LOOK DOWN!
FORGET IT, OKAY?
...!!
D-DON'T LOOK... WHAT?!
AAAACK!!
MY TEETH...!

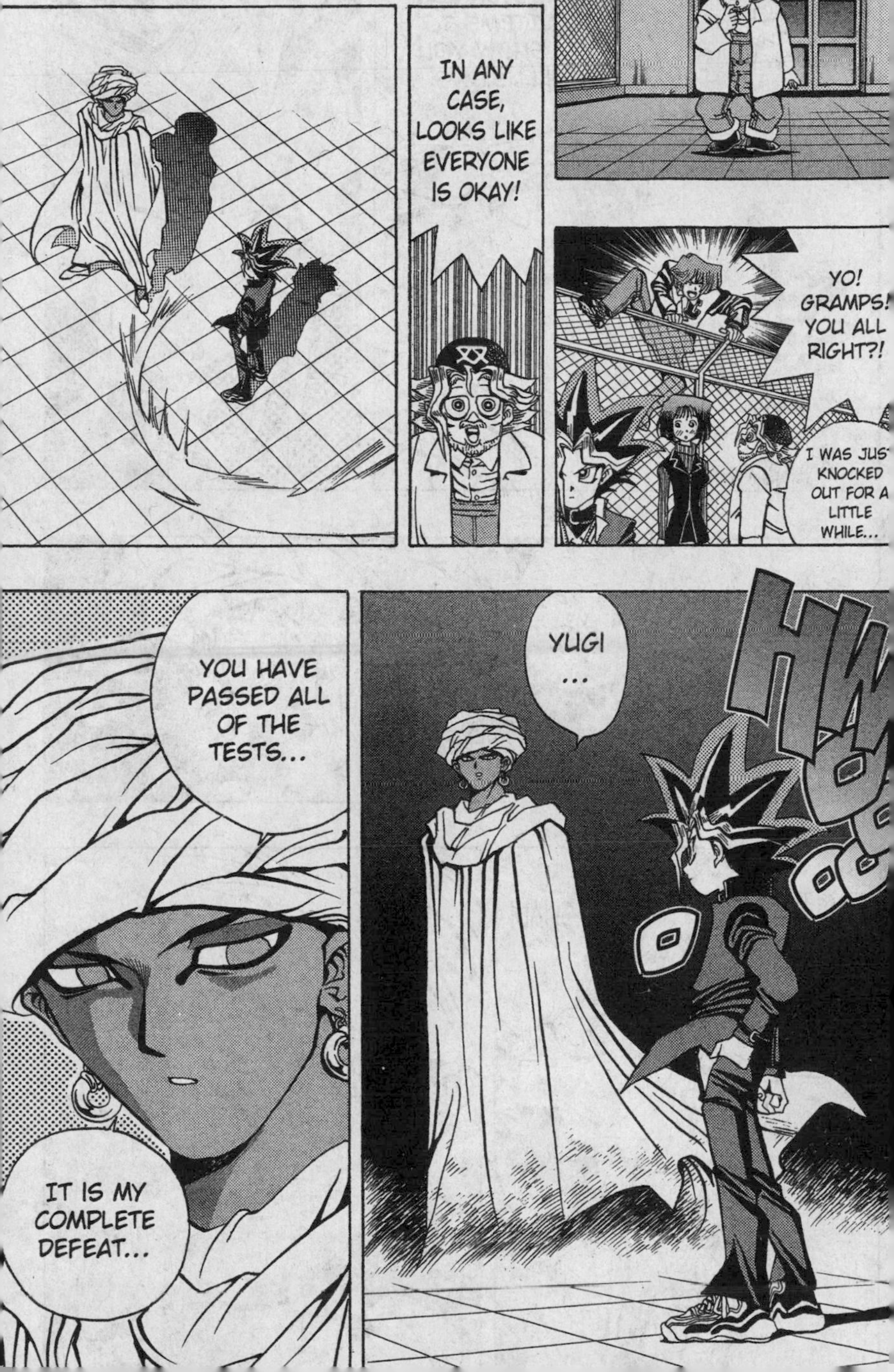
YO! GRAMPS! YOU ALL RIGHT?!
I WAS JUST KNOCKED OUT FOR A LITTLE WHILE...
IN ANY CASE, LOOKS LIKE EVERYONE IS OKAY!
YUGI ...
YOU HAVE PASSED ALL OF THE TESTS...
IT IS MY COMPLETE DEFEAT...

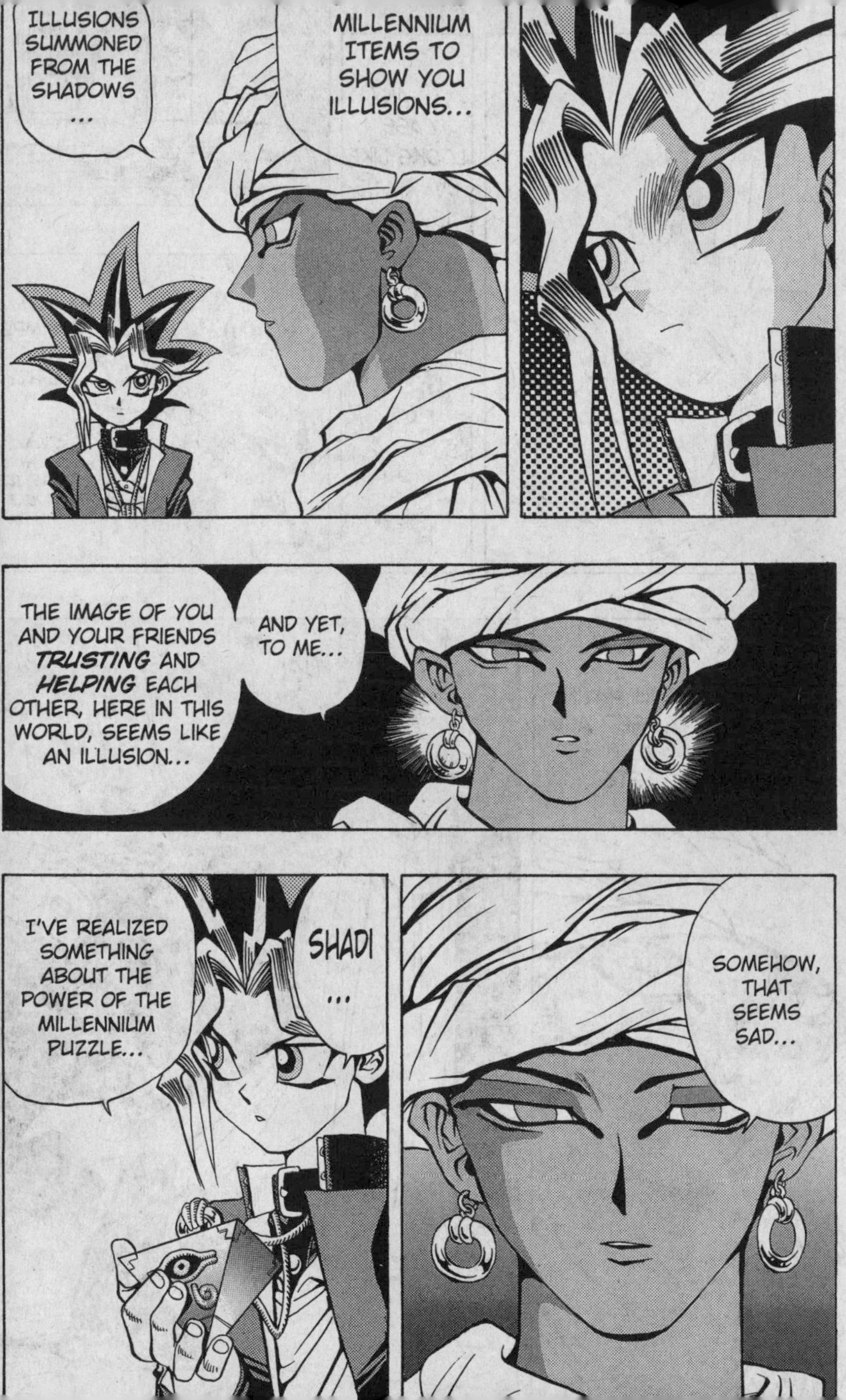
MILLENNIUM ITEMS TO SHOW YOU ILLUSIONS...
ILLUSIONS SUMMONED FROM THE SHADOWS ...
AND YET, TO ME...
THE IMAGE OF YOU AND YOUR FRIENDS TRUSTING AND HELPING EACH OTHER, HERE IN THIS WORLD, SEEMS LIKE AN ILLUSION...
SOMEHOW, THAT SEEMS SAD...
SHADI ...
I'VE REALIZED SOMETHING ABOUT THE POWER OF THE MILLENNIUM PUZZLE...

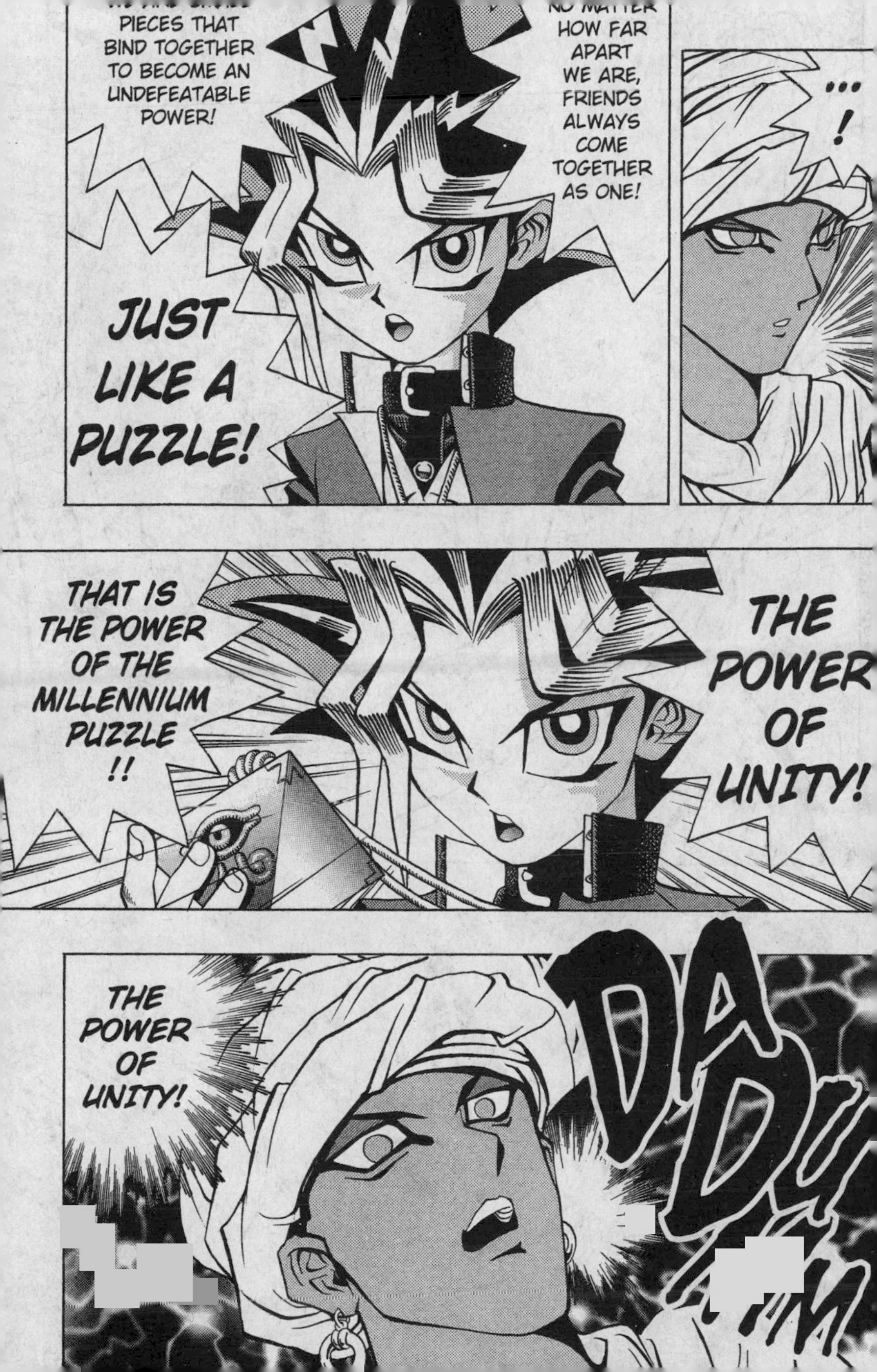
...!
HOW FAR APART WE ARE, FRIENDS ALWAYS COME TOGETHER AS ONE!
PIECES THAT BIND TOGETHER TO BECOME AN UNDEFEATABLE POWER!
JUST LIKE A PUZZLE!
THE POWER OF UNITY!
THAT IS THE POWER OF THE MILLENNIUM PUZZLE !!
DA
THE POWER OF UNITY!

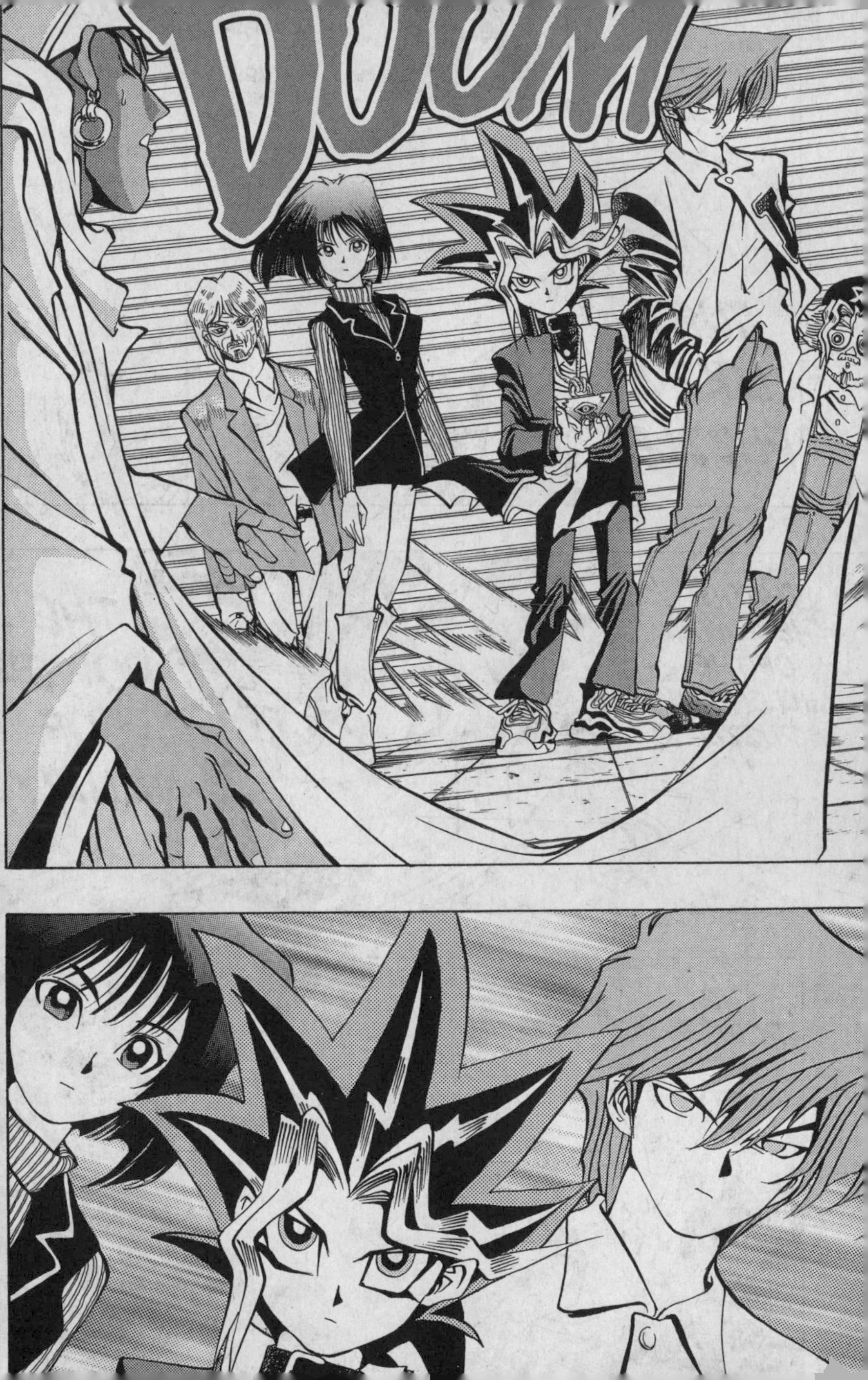
DOOM

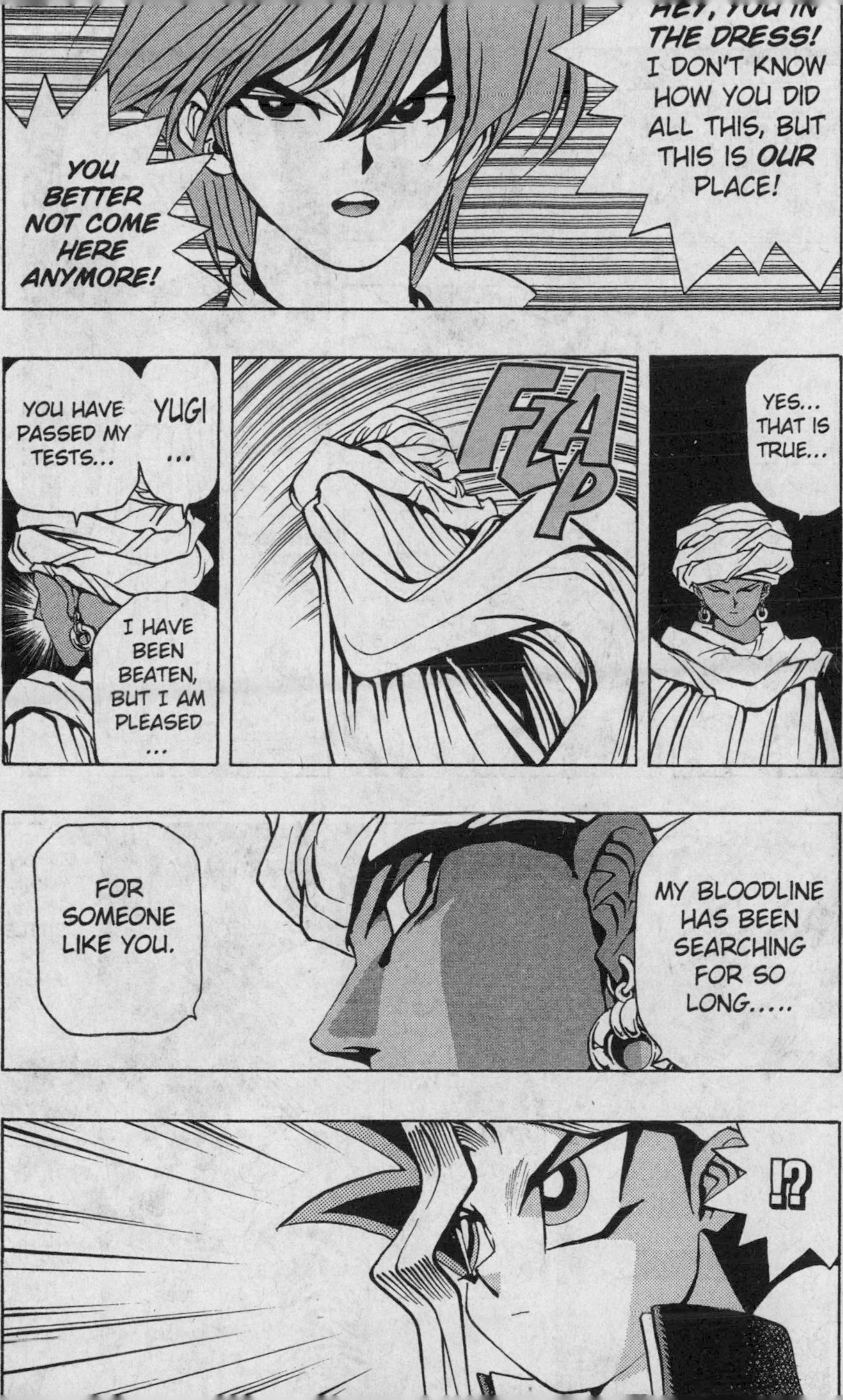
HEY, YOU IN THE DRESS! I DON'T KNOW HOW YOU DID ALL THIS, BUT THIS IS OUR PLACE!
YOU BETTER NOT COME HERE ANYMORE!
YES... THAT IS TRUE...
FLAP
YUGI ...
YOU HAVE PASSED MY TESTS...
I HAVE BEEN BEATEN, BUT I AM PLEASED ...
MY BLOODLINE HAS BEEN SEARCHING FOR SO LONG.....
FOR SOMEONE LIKE YOU.
!?

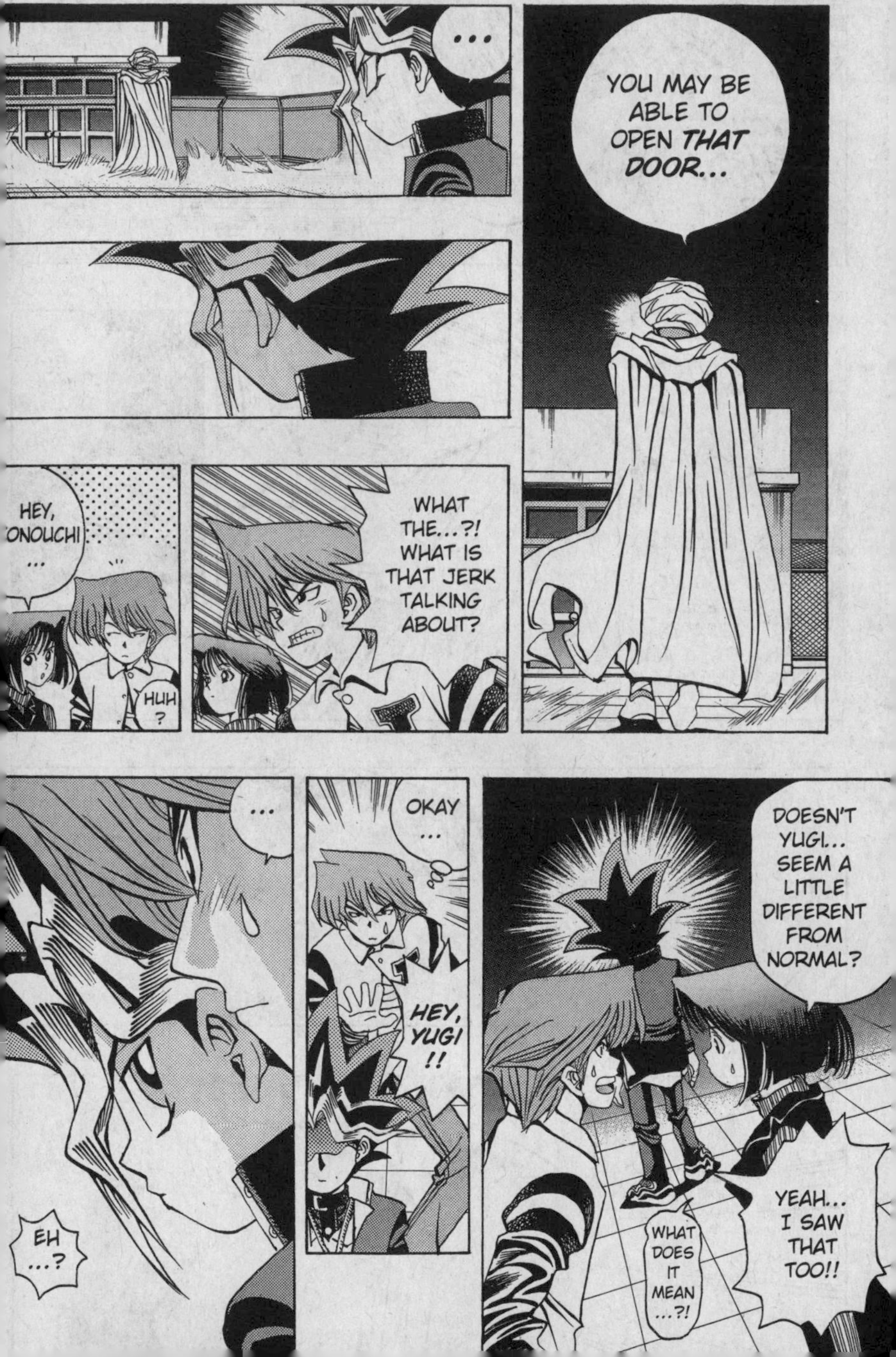
YOU MAY BE ABLE TO OPEN *THAT DOOR...*
...
WHAT THE...?! WHAT IS THAT JERK TALKING ABOUT?
HEY, ONOUCHI ...
HUH?
DOESN'T YUGI... SEEM A LITTLE DIFFERENT FROM NORMAL?
YEAH... I SAW THAT TOO!!
WHAT DOES IT MEAN ...?!
OKAY ...
HEY, YUGI!!
...
EH ...?

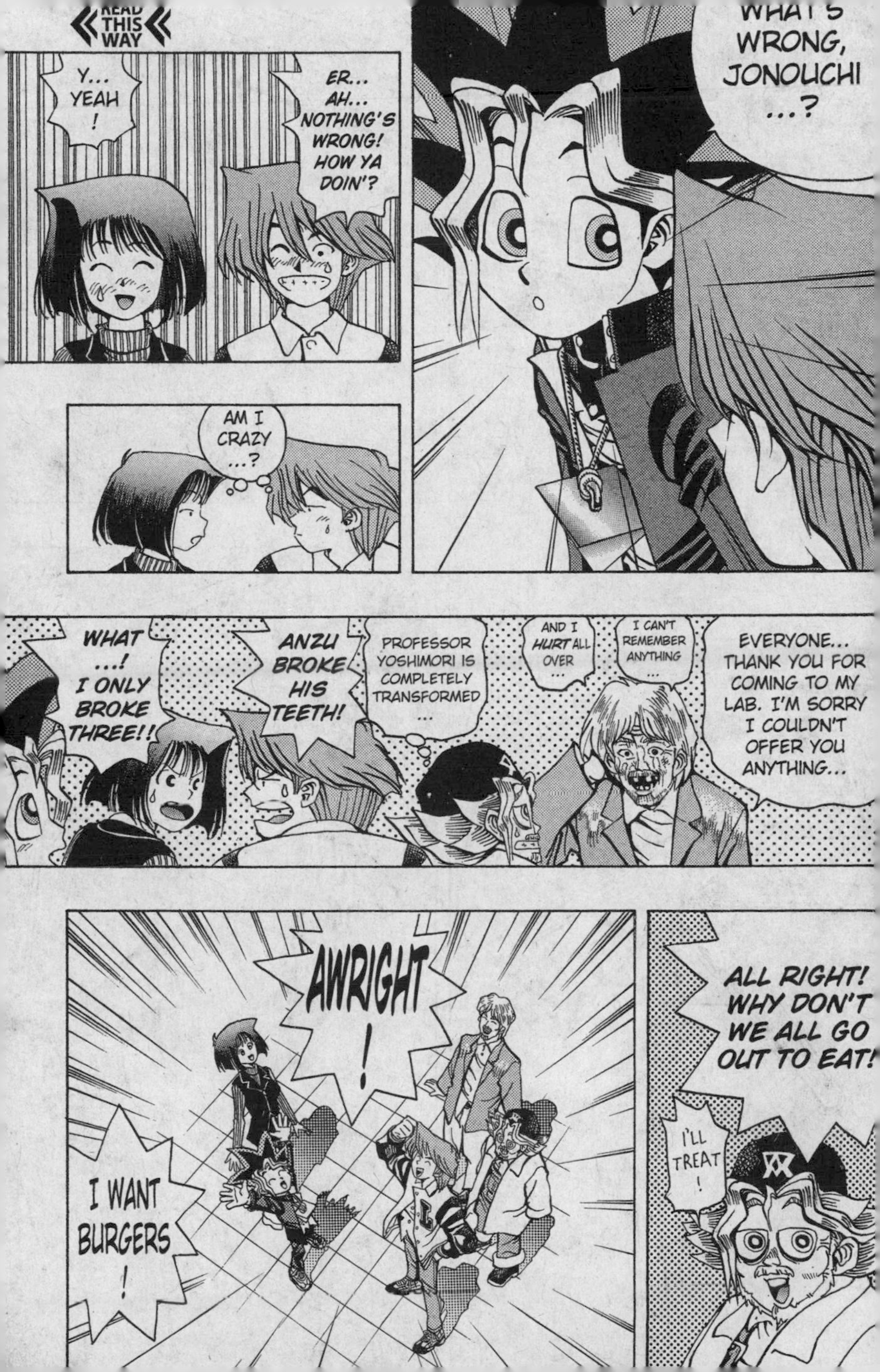
READ THIS WAY
WHAT'S WRONG, JONOUCHI ...?
ER... AH... NOTHING'S WRONG! HOW YA DOIN'?
Y... YEAH!
AM I CRAZY ...?
EVERYONE... THANK YOU FOR COMING TO MY LAB. I'M SORRY I COULDN'T OFFER YOU ANYTHING...
I CAN'T REMEMBER ANYTHING ...
AND I HURT ALL OVER ...
PROFESSOR YOSHIMORI IS COMPLETELY TRANSFORMED ...
ANZU BROKE HIS TEETH!
WHAT ...! I ONLY BROKE THREE!!
ALL RIGHT! WHY DON'T WE ALL GO OUT TO EAT!
I'LL TREAT!
AWRIGHT!
I WANT BURGERS!

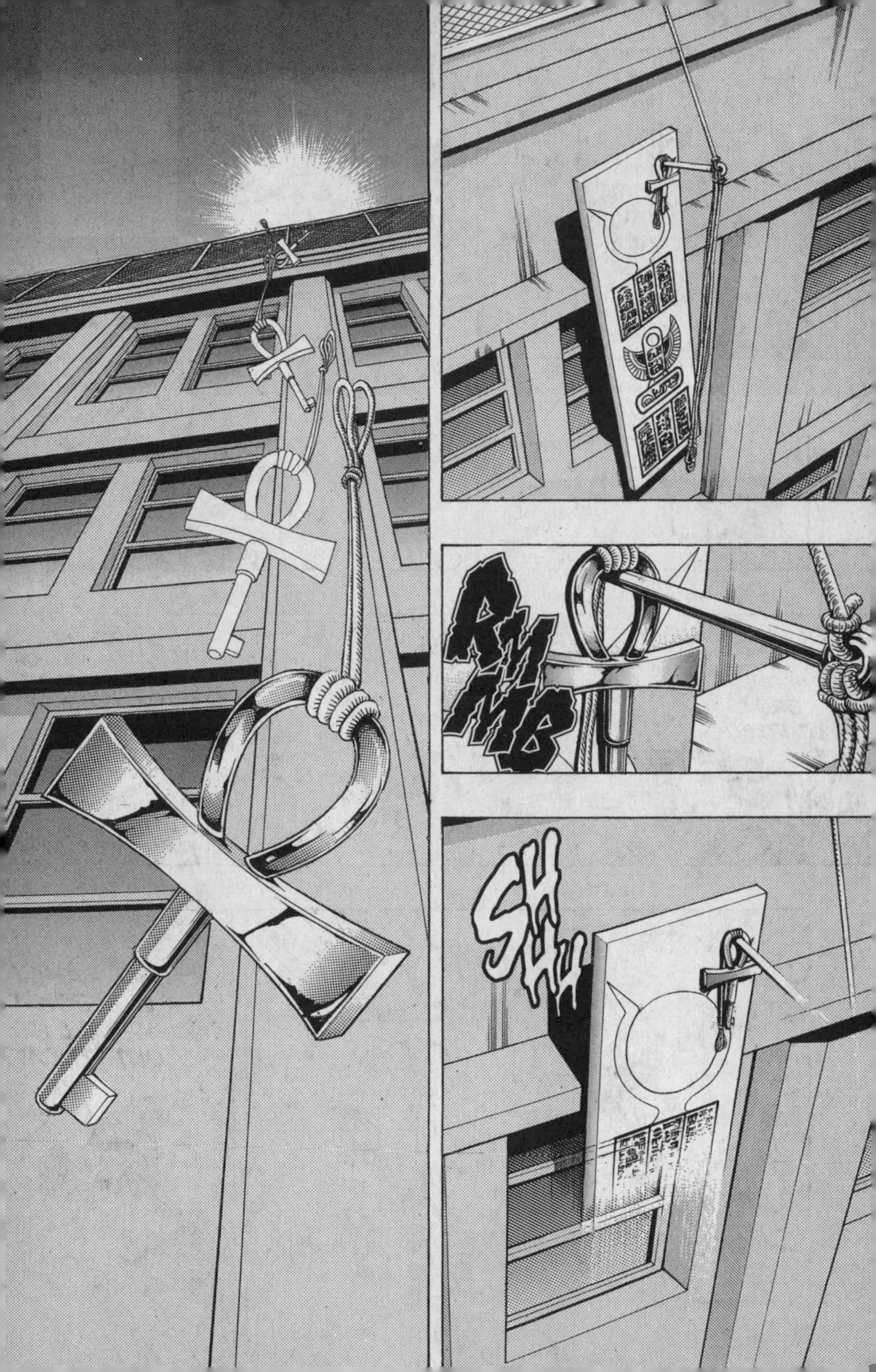
RUMB
SHUU

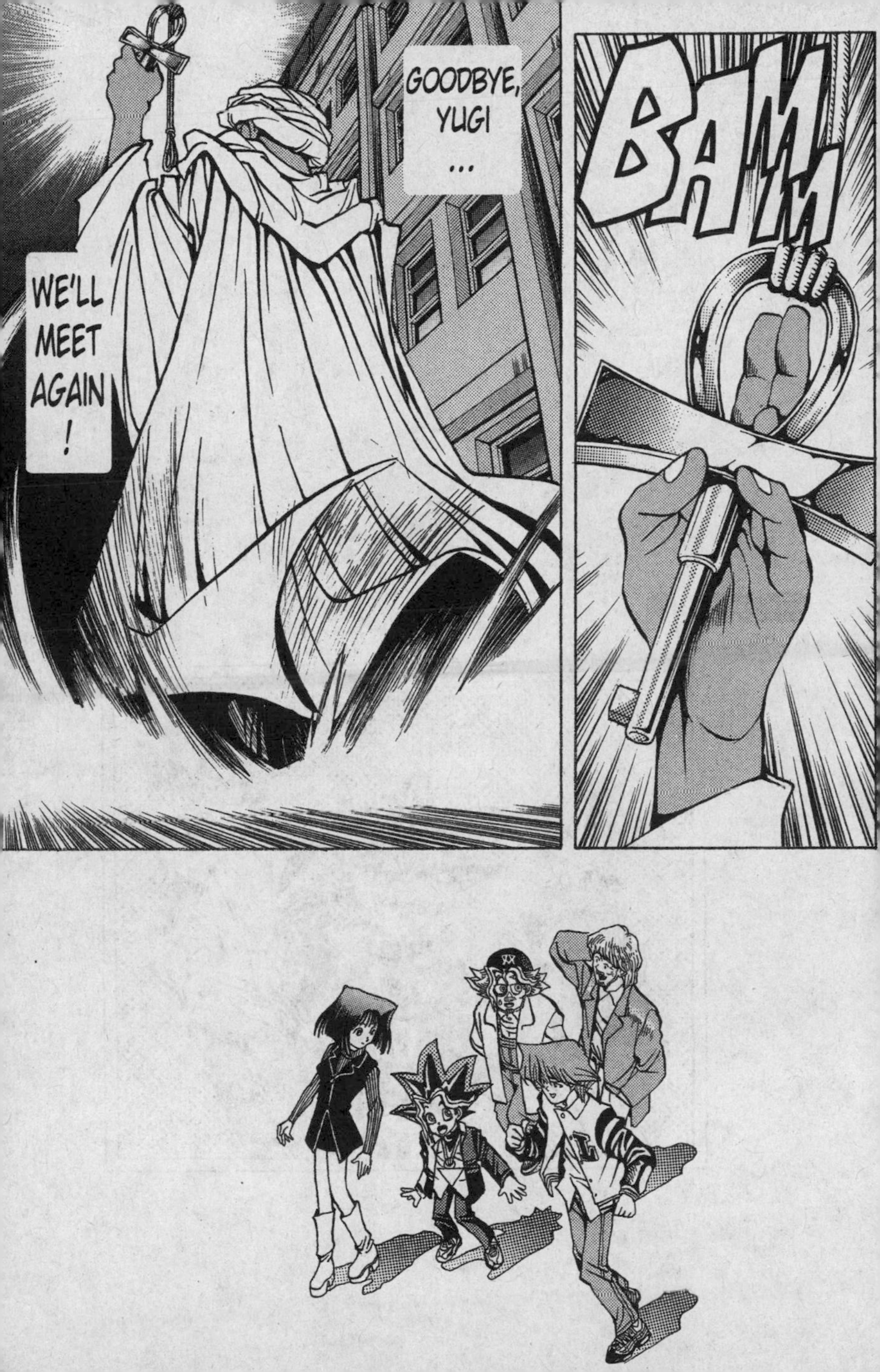
BAM
GOODBYE, YUGI ...
WE'LL MEET AGAIN !

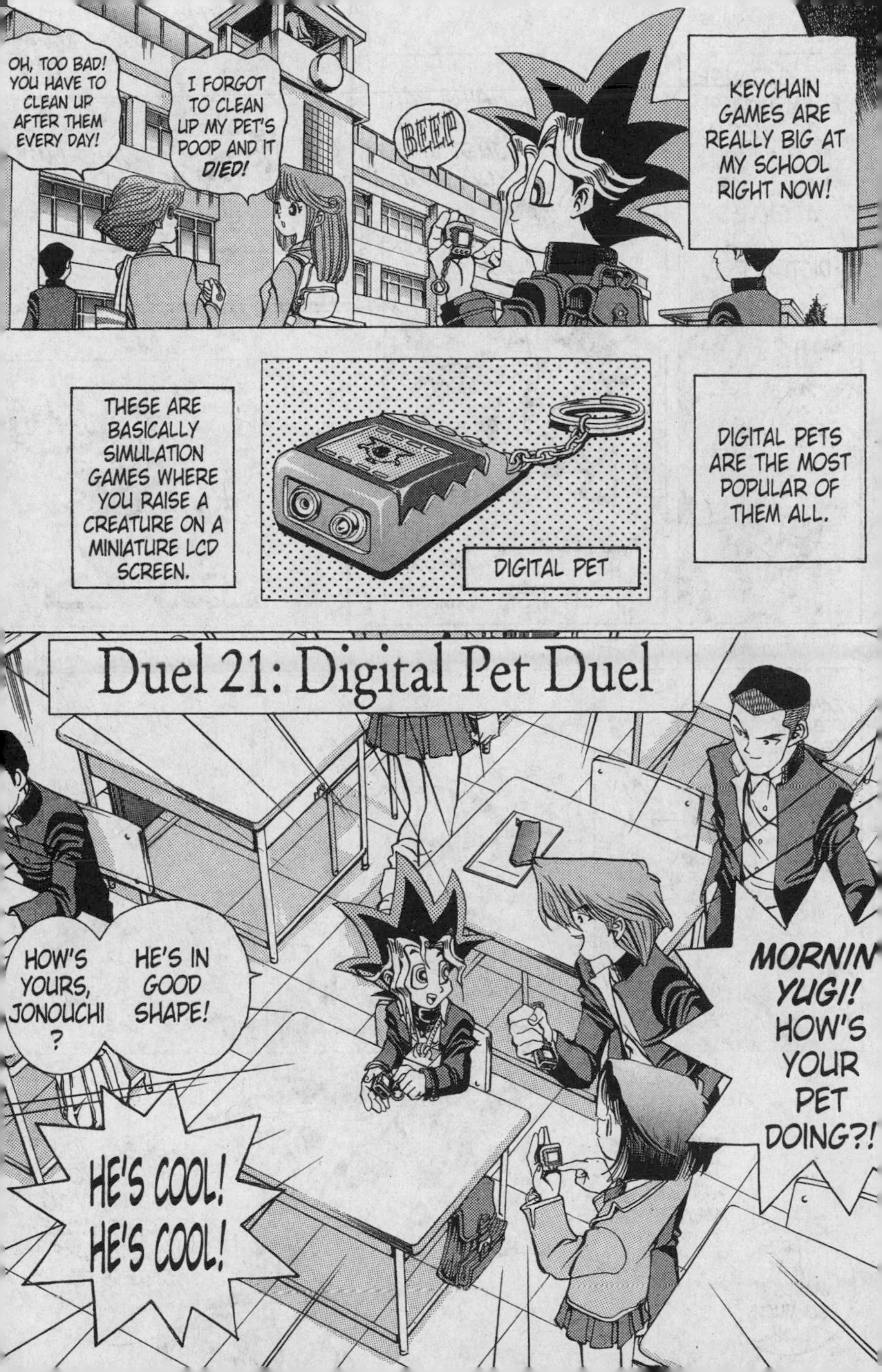
KEYCHAIN GAMES ARE REALLY BIG AT MY SCHOOL RIGHT NOW!
BEEP
I FORGOT TO CLEAN UP MY PET'S POOP AND IT DIED!
OH, TOO BAD! YOU HAVE TO CLEAN UP AFTER THEM EVERY DAY!
DIGITAL PETS ARE THE MOST POPULAR OF THEM ALL.
DIGITAL PET
THESE ARE BASICALLY SIMULATION GAMES WHERE YOU RAISE A CREATURE ON A MINIATURE LCD SCREEN.
Duel 21: Digital Pet Duel
MORNIN YUGI! HOW'S YOUR PET DOING?!
HE'S COOL! HE'S COOL!
HOW'S YOURS, JONOUCHI?
HE'S IN GOOD SHAPE!

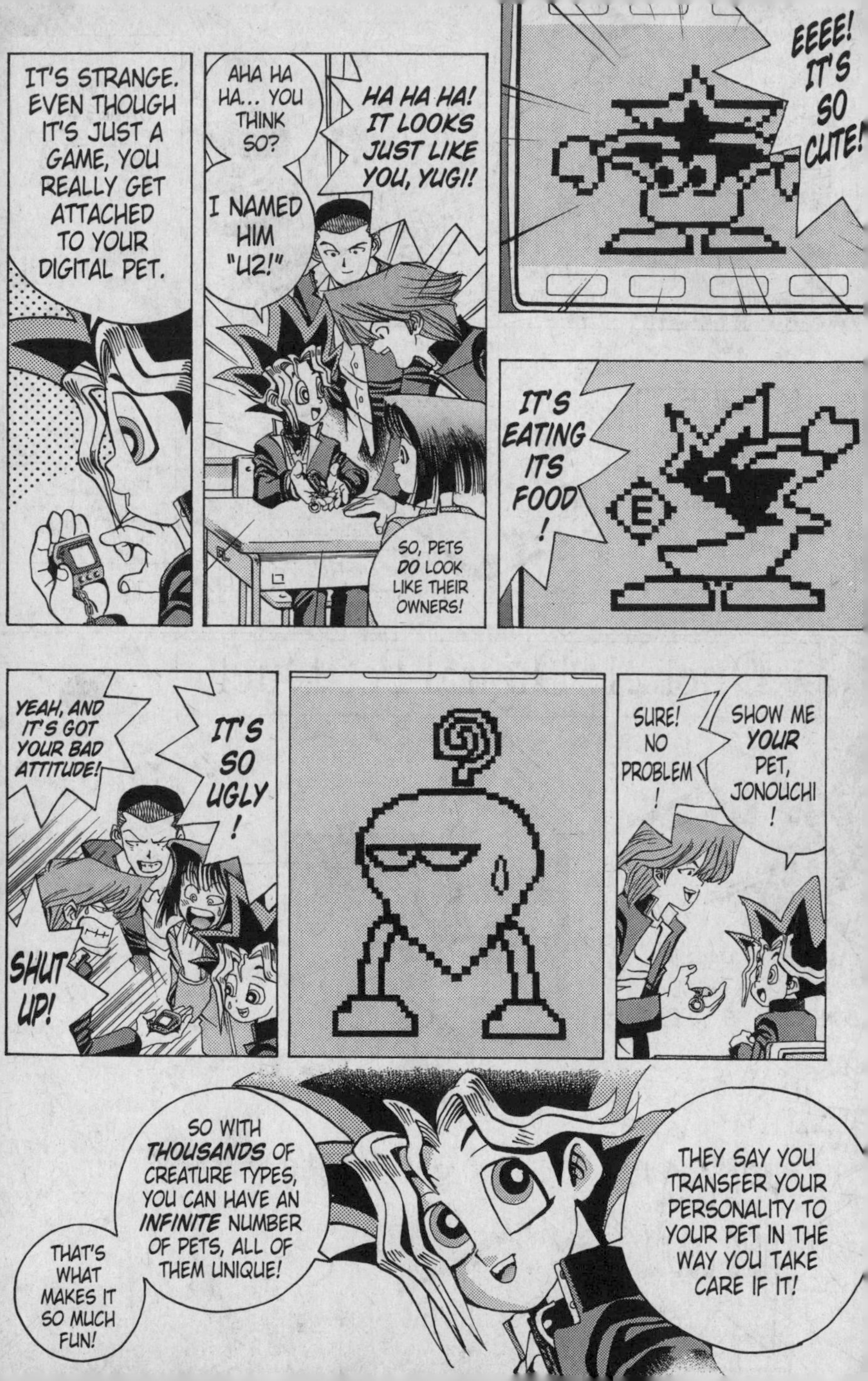
EEEE! IT'S SO CUTE!
IT'S EATING ITS FOOD!
HA HA HA! IT LOOKS JUST LIKE YOU, YUGI!
AHA HA HA... YOU THINK SO?
I NAMED HIM "U2!"
SO, PETS DO LOOK LIKE THEIR OWNERS!
IT'S STRANGE. EVEN THOUGH IT'S JUST A GAME, YOU REALLY GET ATTACHED TO YOUR DIGITAL PET.
SHOW ME YOUR PET, JONOUCHI!
SURE! NO PROBLEM!
IT'S SO UGLY!
YEAH, AND IT'S GOT YOUR BAD ATTITUDE!
SHUT UP!
THEY SAY YOU TRANSFER YOUR PERSONALITY TO YOUR PET IN THE WAY YOU TAKE CARE IF IT!
SO WITH THOUSANDS OF CREATURE TYPES, YOU CAN HAVE AN INFINITE NUMBER OF PETS, ALL OF THEM UNIQUE!
THAT'S WHAT MAKES IT SO MUCH FUN!

READ THIS WAY

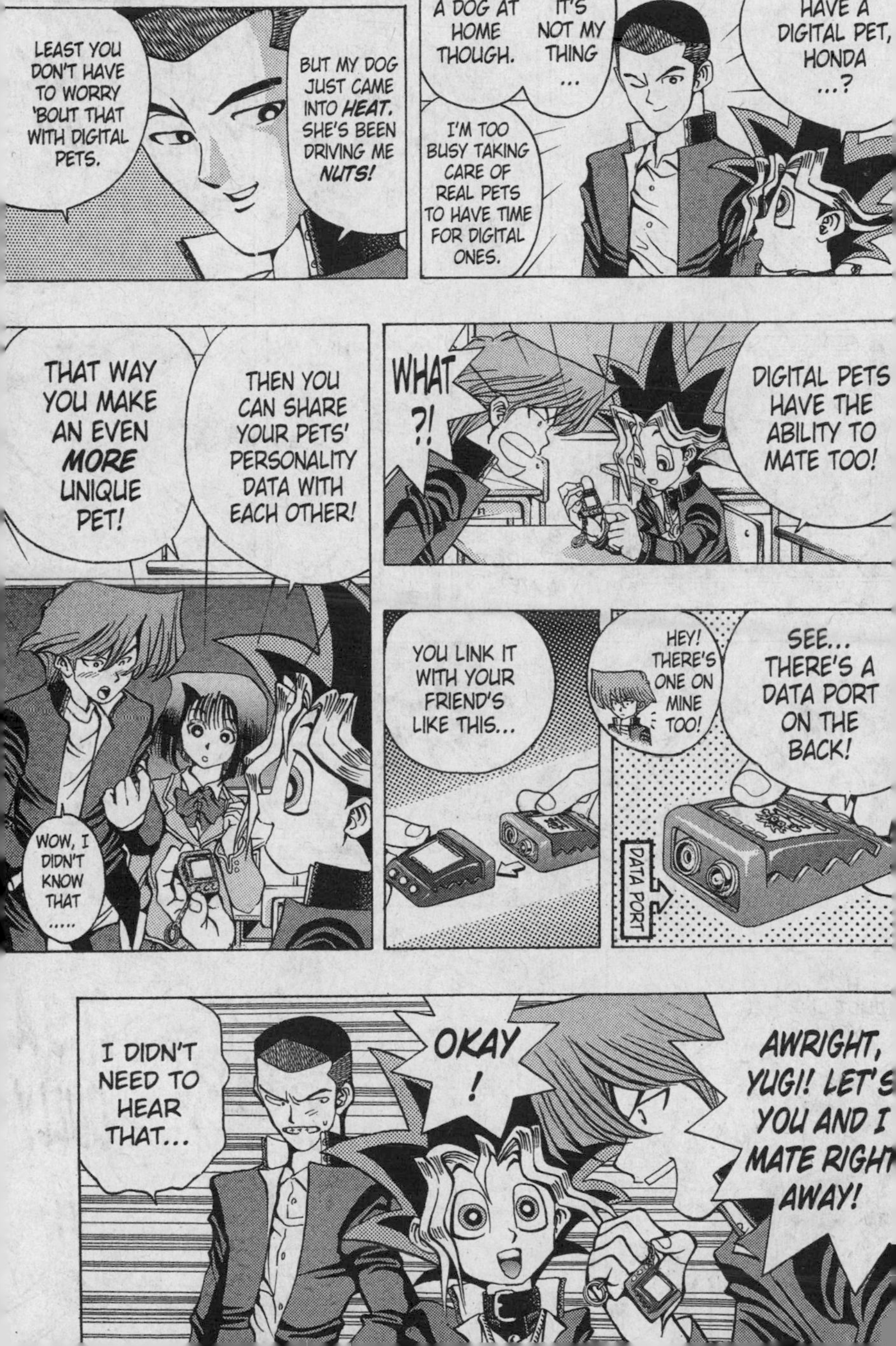
DO YOU HAVE A DIGITAL PET, HONDA ...?
NAW, IT'S NOT MY THING ...
I'VE GOT A DOG AT HOME THOUGH.
I'M TOO BUSY TAKING CARE OF REAL PETS TO HAVE TIME FOR DIGITAL ONES.
BUT MY DOG JUST CAME INTO HEAT. SHE'S BEEN DRIVING ME NUTS!
LEAST YOU DON'T HAVE TO WORRY 'BOUT THAT WITH DIGITAL PETS.
DIGITAL PETS HAVE THE ABILITY TO MATE TOO!
WHAT ?!
SEE... THERE'S A DATA PORT ON THE BACK!
HEY! THERE'S ONE ON MINE TOO!
DATA PORT
YOU LINK IT WITH YOUR FRIEND'S LIKE THIS...
THEN YOU CAN SHARE YOUR PETS' PERSONALITY DATA WITH EACH OTHER!
THAT WAY YOU MAKE AN EVEN MORE UNIQUE PET!
WOW, I DIDN'T KNOW THAT .....
AWRIGHT, YUGI! LET'S YOU AND I MATE RIGHT AWAY!
OKAY !
I DIDN'T NEED TO HEAR THAT...

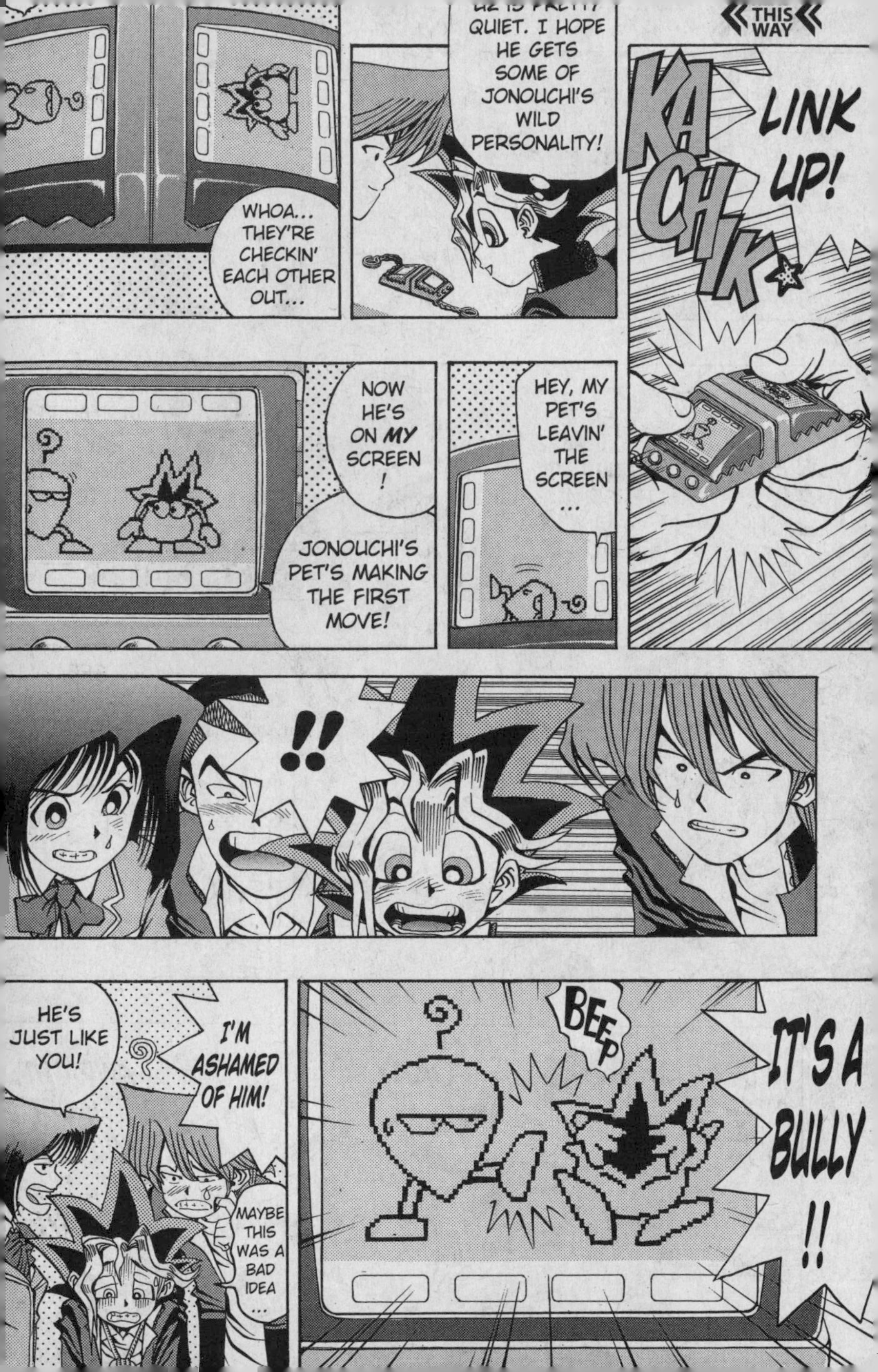
THIS WAY
KA CHIK
LINK UP!
QUIET. I HOPE HE GETS SOME OF JONOUCHI'S WILD PERSONALITY!
WHOA... THEY'RE CHECKIN' EACH OTHER OUT...
HEY, MY PET'S LEAVIN' THE SCREEN ...
NOW HE'S ON *MY* SCREEN !
JONOUCHI'S PET'S MAKING THE FIRST MOVE!
!!
BEEP
IT'S A BULLY !!
HE'S JUST LIKE YOU!
I'M ASHAMED OF HIM!
MAYBE THIS WAS A BAD IDEA ...

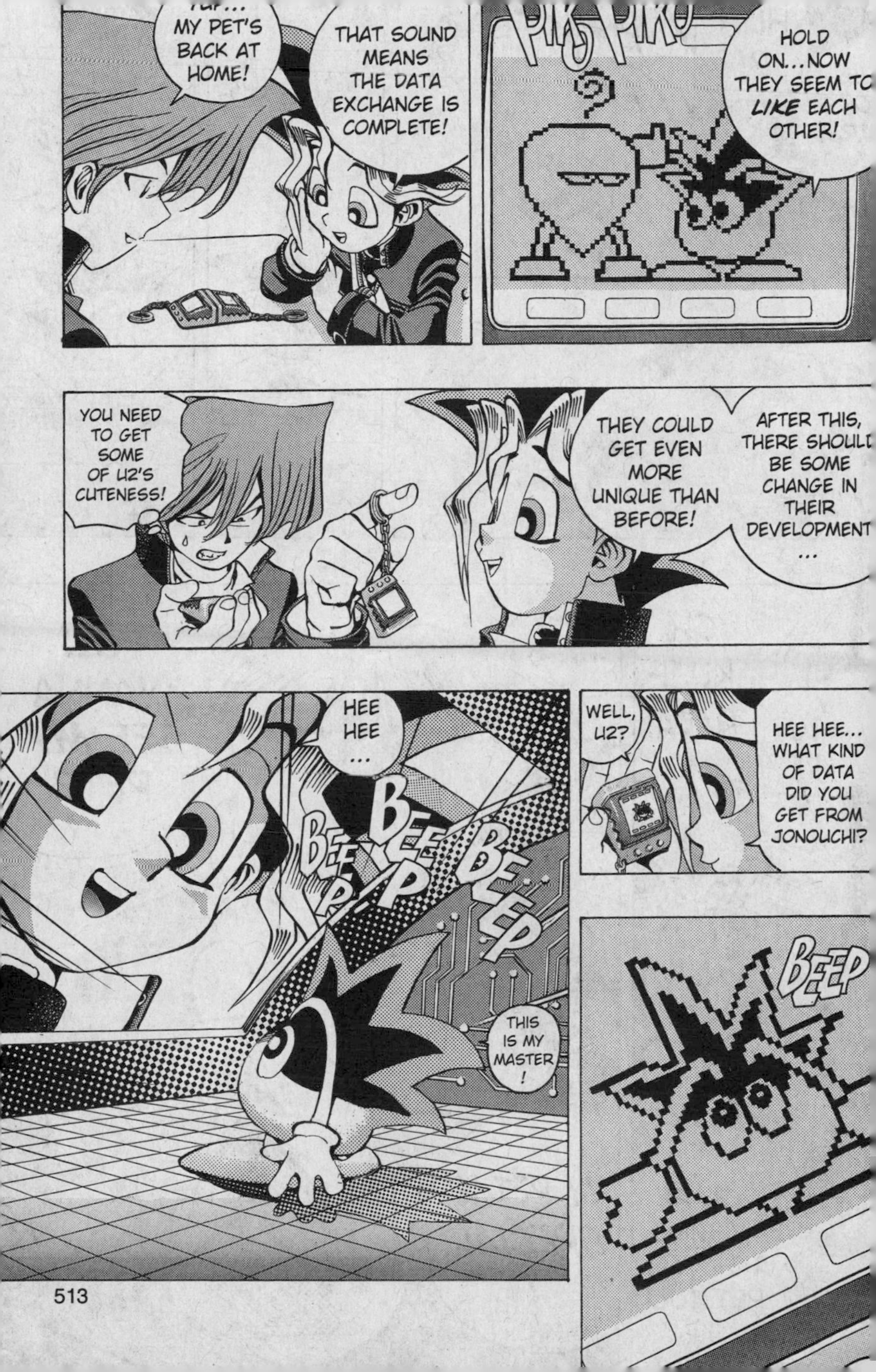
PIKO PIKO
HOLD ON...NOW THEY SEEM TO *LIKE* EACH OTHER!
THAT SOUND MEANS THE DATA EXCHANGE IS COMPLETE!
MY PET'S BACK AT HOME!
AFTER THIS, THERE SHOULD BE SOME CHANGE IN THEIR DEVELOPMENT ...
THEY COULD GET EVEN MORE UNIQUE THAN BEFORE!
YOU NEED TO GET SOME OF U2'S CUTENESS!
WELL, U2?
HEE HEE... WHAT KIND OF DATA DID YOU GET FROM JONOUCHI?
BEEP
HEE HEE ...
BEEP BEEP BEEP
THIS IS MY MASTER !

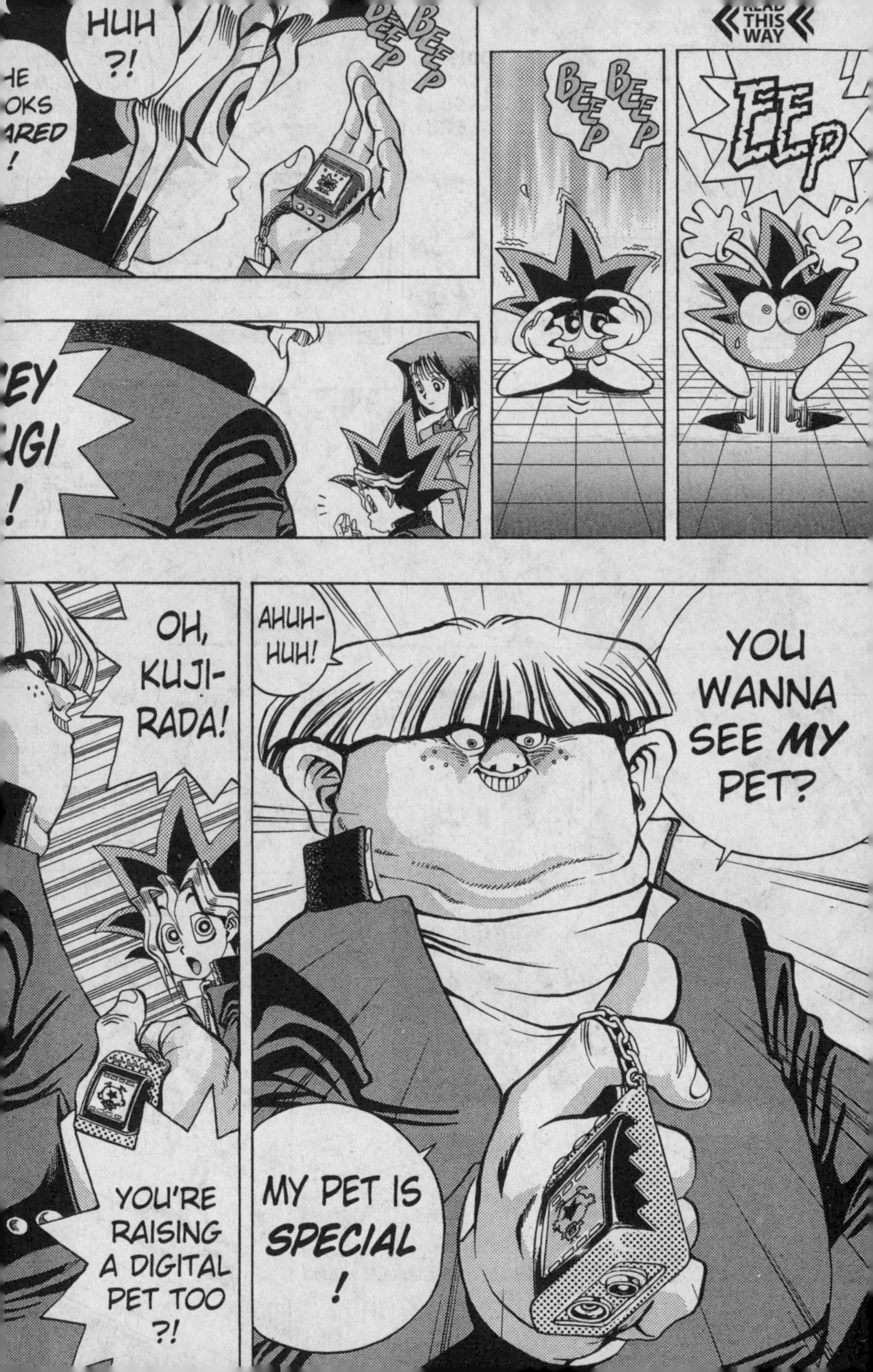
READ THIS WAY
EEP
BEEP BEEP
BEEP BEEP
HUH ?!
YOU WANNA SEE MY PET?
AHUH-HUH!
MY PET IS SPECIAL !
OH, KUJI-RADA!
YOU'RE RAISING A DIGITAL PET TOO ?!

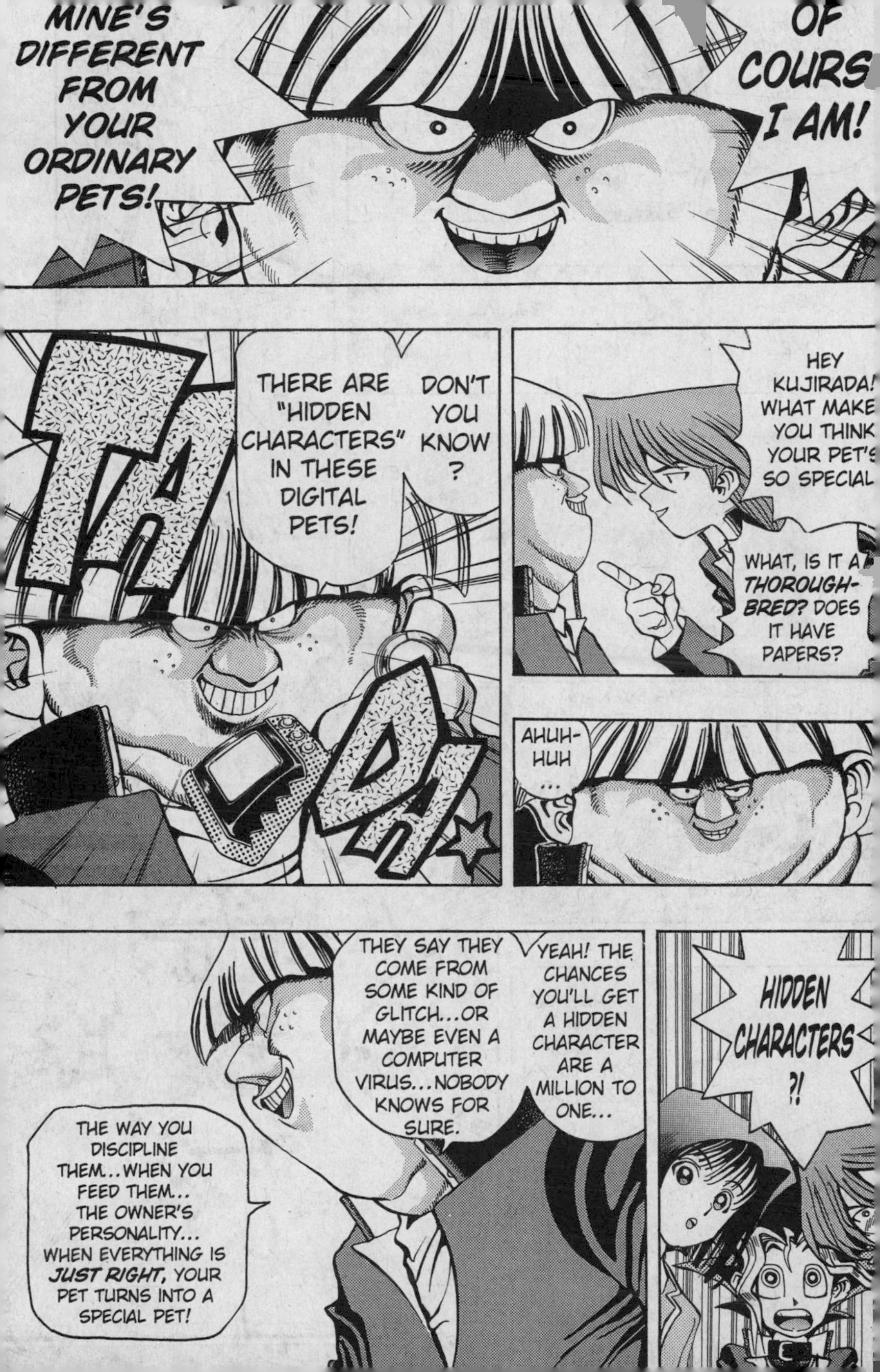
OF COURS I AM!
MINE'S DIFFERENT FROM YOUR ORDINARY PETS!
HEY KUJIRADA! WHAT MAKE YOU THINK YOUR PET'S SO SPECIAL
WHAT, IS IT A *THOROUGHBRED?* DOES IT HAVE PAPERS?
AHUH-HUH...
DON'T YOU KNOW?
THERE ARE "HIDDEN CHARACTERS" IN THESE DIGITAL PETS!
TA
DA
HIDDEN CHARACTERS?!
YEAH! THE CHANCES YOU'LL GET A HIDDEN CHARACTER ARE A MILLION TO ONE...
THEY SAY THEY COME FROM SOME KIND OF GLITCH...OR MAYBE EVEN A COMPUTER VIRUS...NOBODY KNOWS FOR SURE.
THE WAY YOU DISCIPLINE THEM...WHEN YOU FEED THEM... THE OWNER'S PERSONALITY... WHEN EVERYTHING IS *JUST RIGHT*, YOUR PET TURNS INTO A SPECIAL PET!

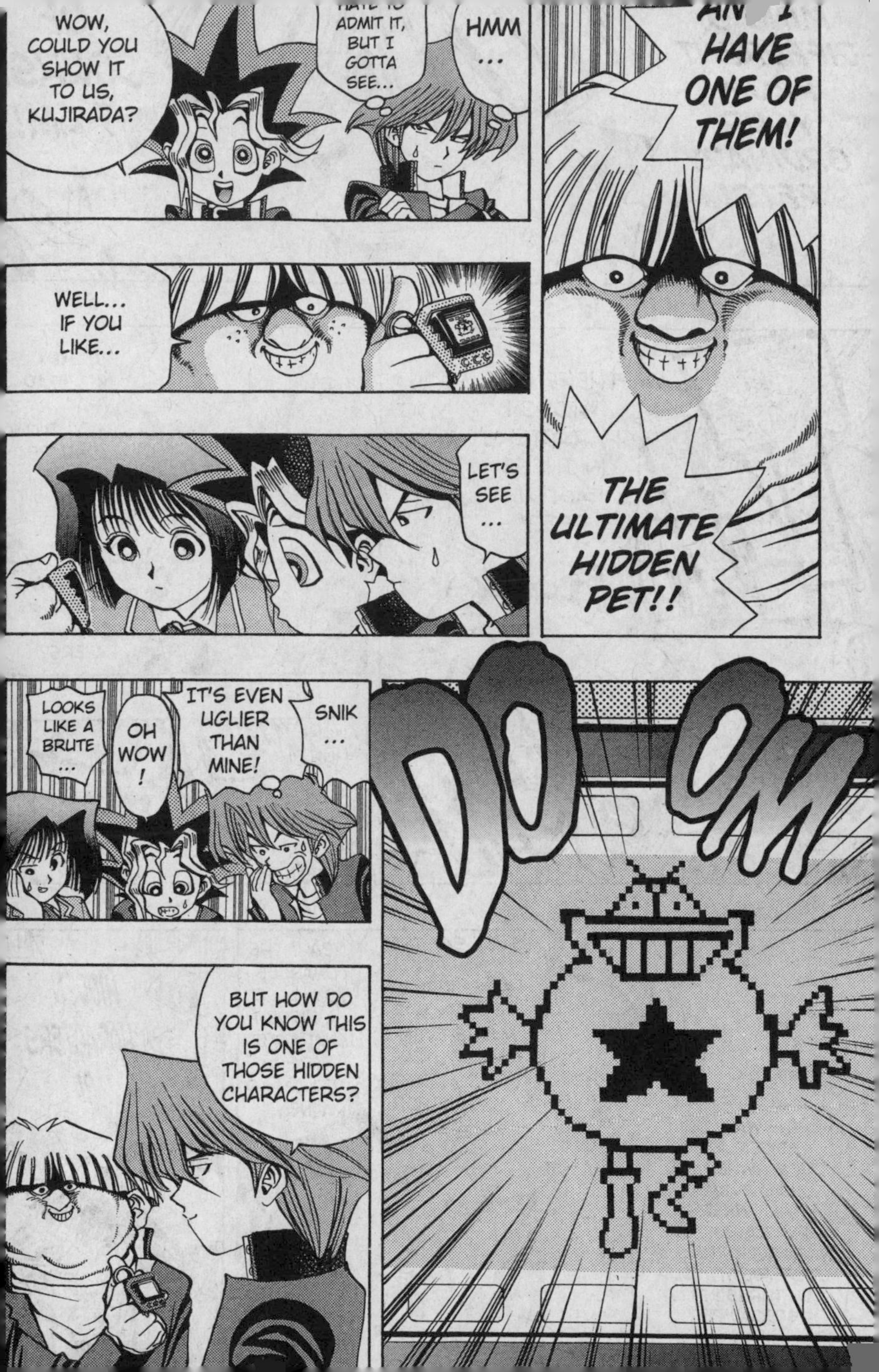
HAVE ONE OF THEM!
THE ULTIMATE HIDDEN PET!!
HMM...
ADMIT IT, BUT I GOTTA SEE...
WOW, COULD YOU SHOW IT TO US, KUJIRADA?
WELL... IF YOU LIKE...
LET'S SEE...
DOOM
SNIK...
IT'S EVEN UGLIER THAN MINE!
OH WOW!
LOOKS LIKE A BRUTE...
BUT HOW DO YOU KNOW THIS IS ONE OF THOSE HIDDEN CHARACTERS?

READ THIS WAY

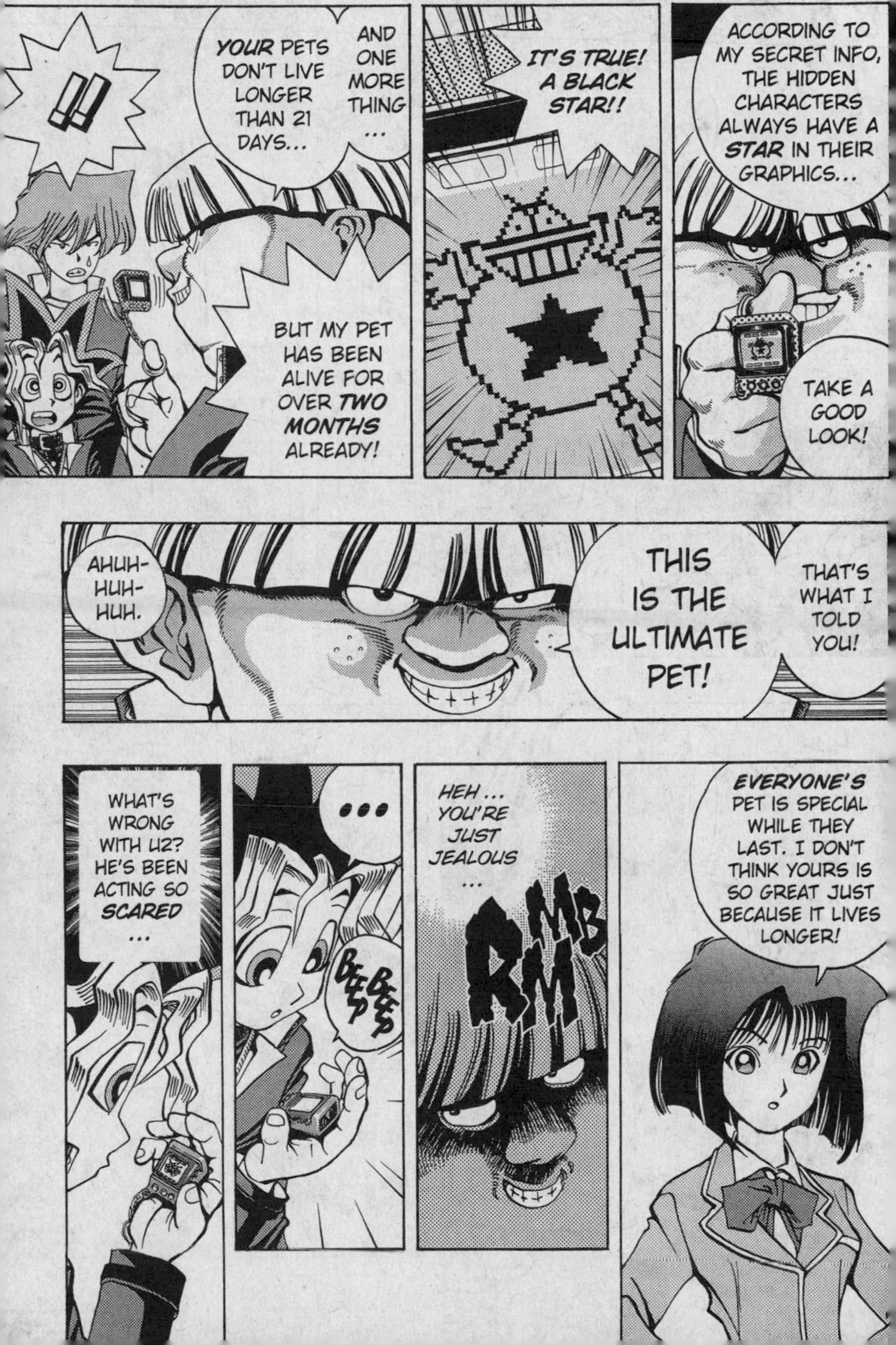

ACCORDING TO MY SECRET INFO, THE HIDDEN CHARACTERS ALWAYS HAVE A STAR IN THEIR GRAPHICS...
TAKE A GOOD LOOK!
IT'S TRUE! A BLACK STAR!!
AND ONE MORE THING...
YOUR PETS DON'T LIVE LONGER THAN 21 DAYS...
BUT MY PET HAS BEEN ALIVE FOR OVER TWO MONTHS ALREADY!
!!
THAT'S WHAT I TOLD YOU!
THIS IS THE ULTIMATE PET!
AHUH-HUH-HUH.
EVERYONE'S PET IS SPECIAL WHILE THEY LAST. I DON'T THINK YOURS IS SO GREAT JUST BECAUSE IT LIVES LONGER!
HEH... YOU'RE JUST JEALOUS...
...
BEEP BEEP
WHAT'S WRONG WITH U2? HE'S BEEN ACTING SO SCARED...

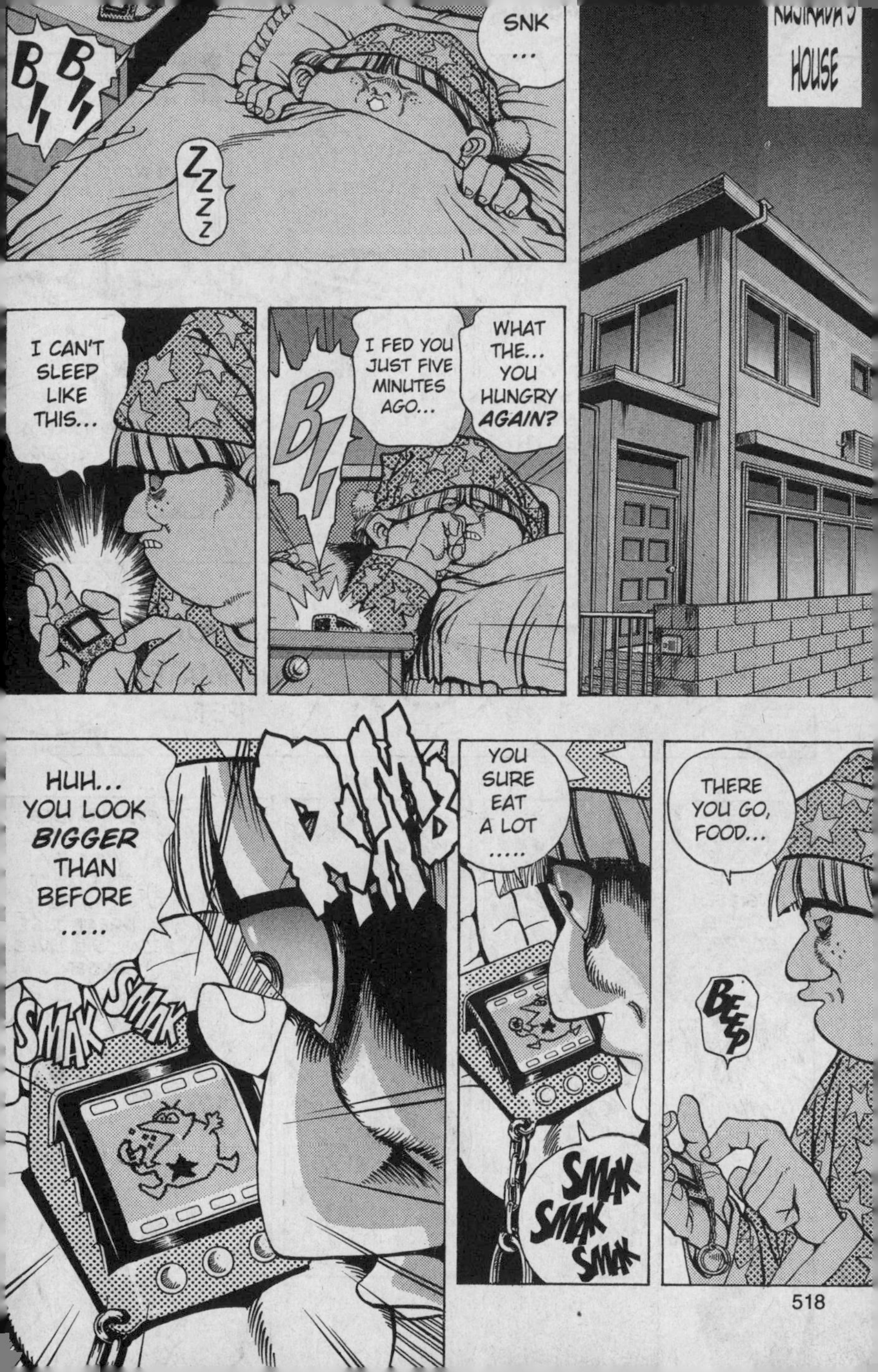
HOUSE
BI BI
SNK ...
ZZZZ
WHAT THE... YOU HUNGRY AGAIN?
I FED YOU JUST FIVE MINUTES AGO...
BI
I CAN'T SLEEP LIKE THIS...
THERE YOU GO, FOOD...
BEEP
YOU SURE EAT A LOT .....
SMAK SMAK SMAK
BAM
HUH... YOU LOOK BIGGER THAN BEFORE .....
SMAK SMAK

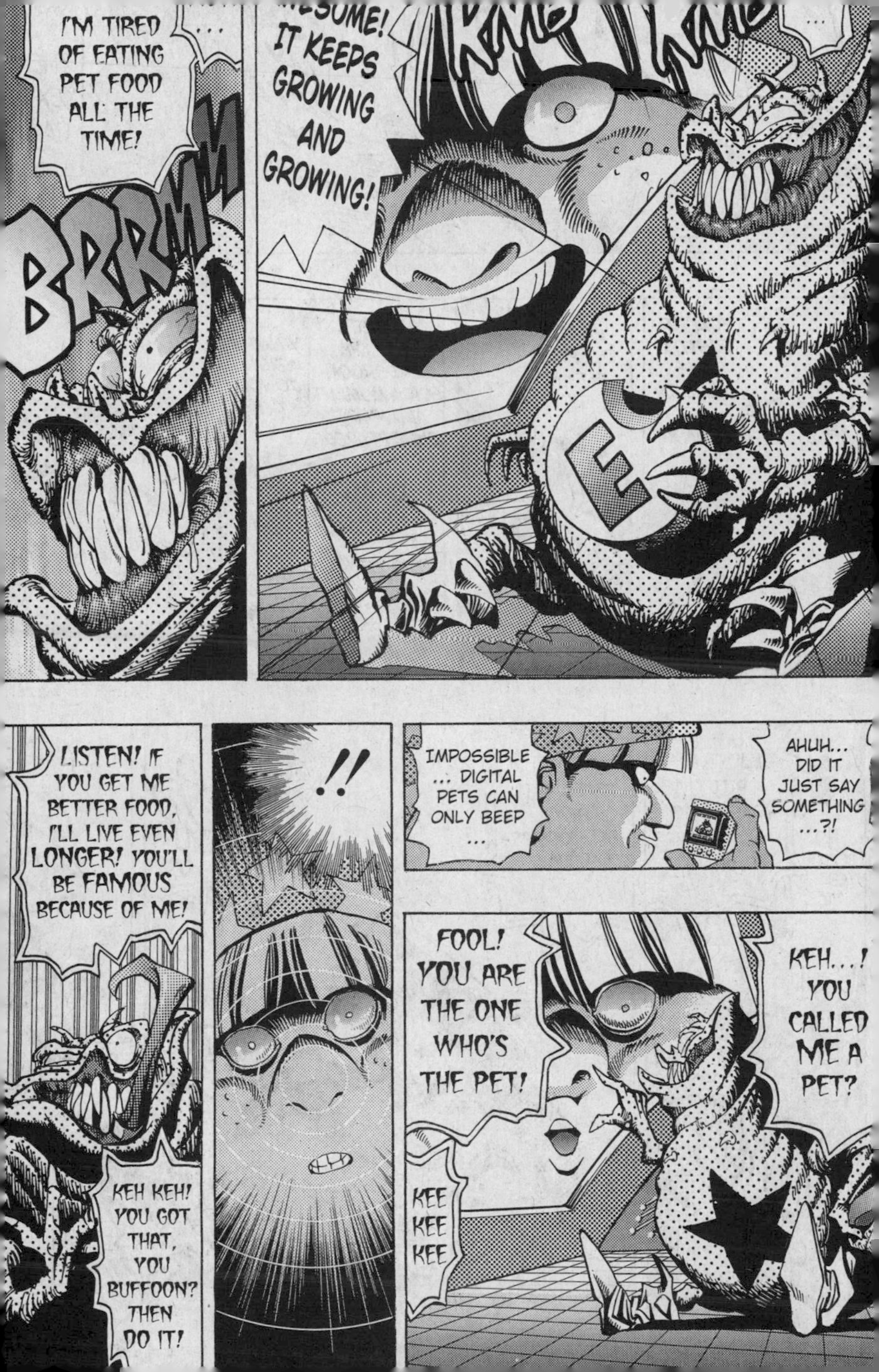
...
SOME! IT KEEPS GROWING AND GROWING!
...
I'M TIRED OF EATING PET FOOD ALL THE TIME!
BRRMM
AHUH... DID IT JUST SAY SOMETHING ...?!
IMPOSSIBLE ... DIGITAL PETS CAN ONLY BEEP ...
KEH...! YOU CALLED ME A PET?
FOOL! YOU ARE THE ONE WHO'S THE PET!
KEE KEE KEE
!!
LISTEN! IF YOU GET ME BETTER FOOD, I'LL LIVE EVEN LONGER! YOU'LL BE FAMOUS BECAUSE OF ME!
KEH KEH! YOU GOT THAT, YOU BUFFOON? THEN DO IT!

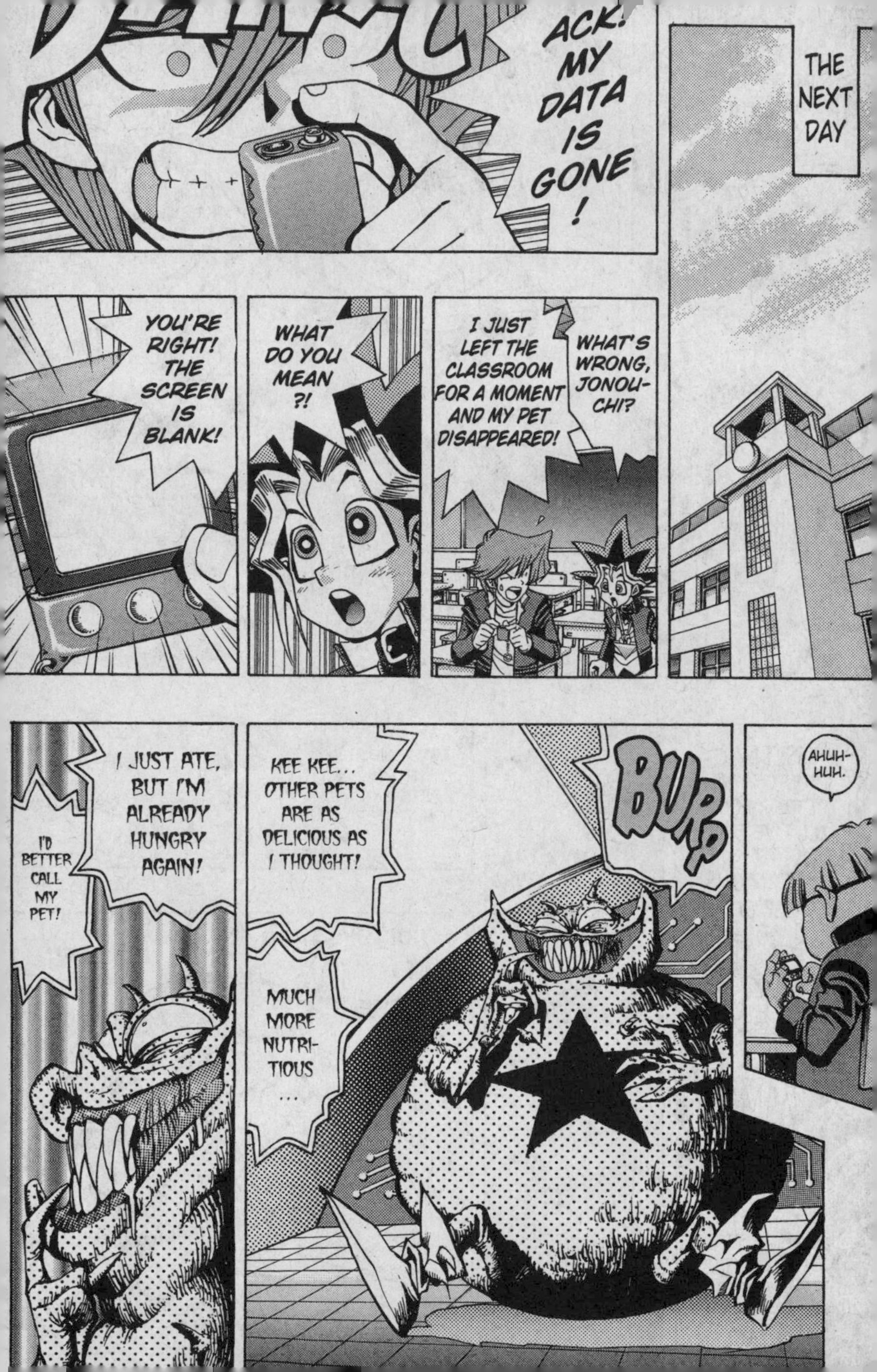
ACK! MY DATA IS GONE!
THE NEXT DAY
WHAT'S WRONG, JONOUCHI?
I JUST LEFT THE CLASSROOM FOR A MOMENT AND MY PET DISAPPEARED!
WHAT DO YOU MEAN?!
YOU'RE RIGHT! THE SCREEN IS BLANK!
AHUH-HUH.
BURP
KEE KEE... OTHER PETS ARE AS DELICIOUS AS I THOUGHT!
MUCH MORE NUTRITIOUS...
I JUST ATE, BUT I'M ALREADY HUNGRY AGAIN!
I'D BETTER CALL MY PET!

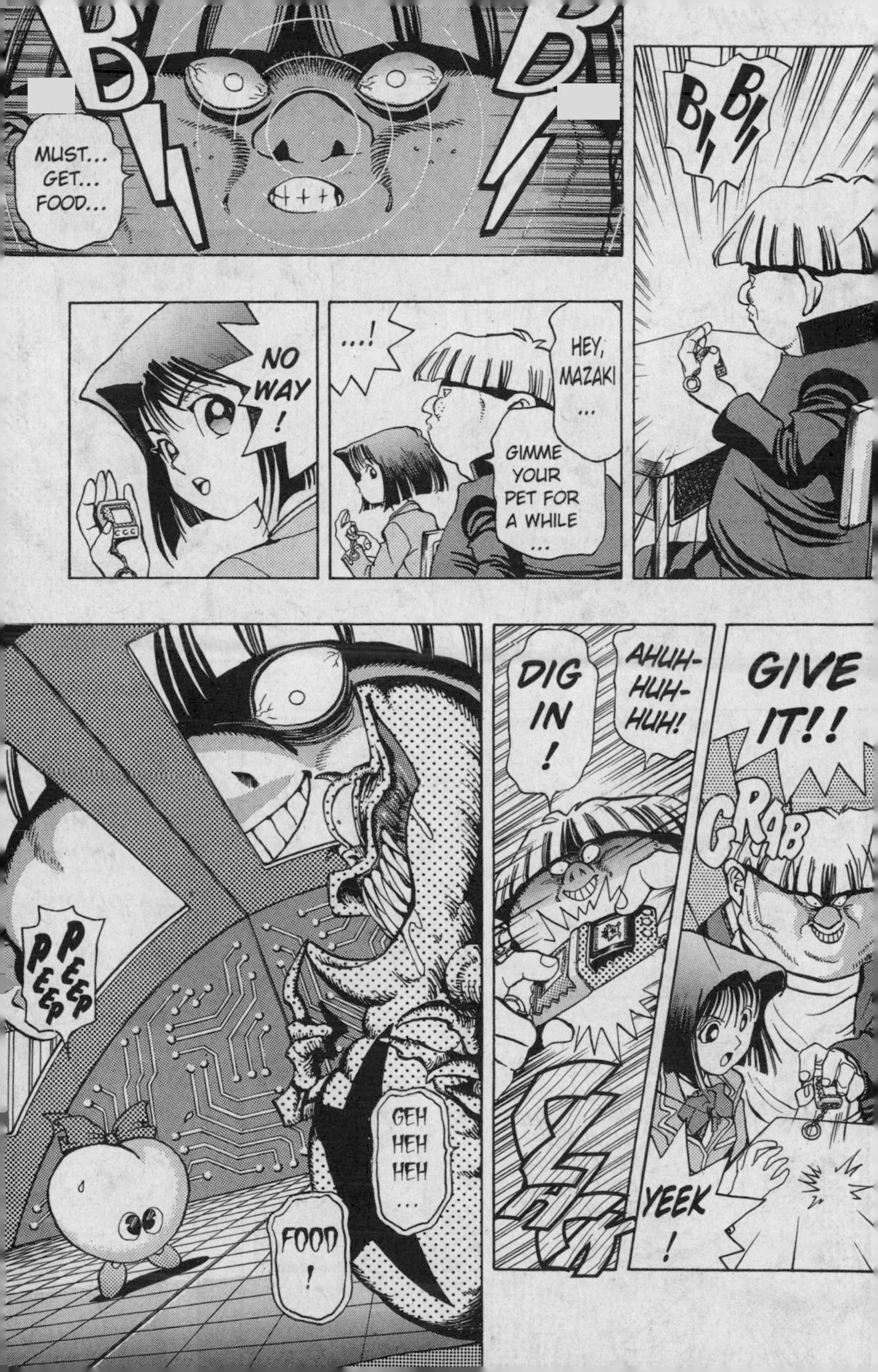

BI
BI
MUST... GET... FOOD...
BI BI
HEY, MAZAKI ...
GIMME YOUR PET FOR A WHILE ...
...!
NO WAY!
GIVE IT!!
GRAB
YEEK!
AHUH-HUH-HUH!
DIG IN!
GEH HEH HEH ...
FOOD!
PEEP PEEP

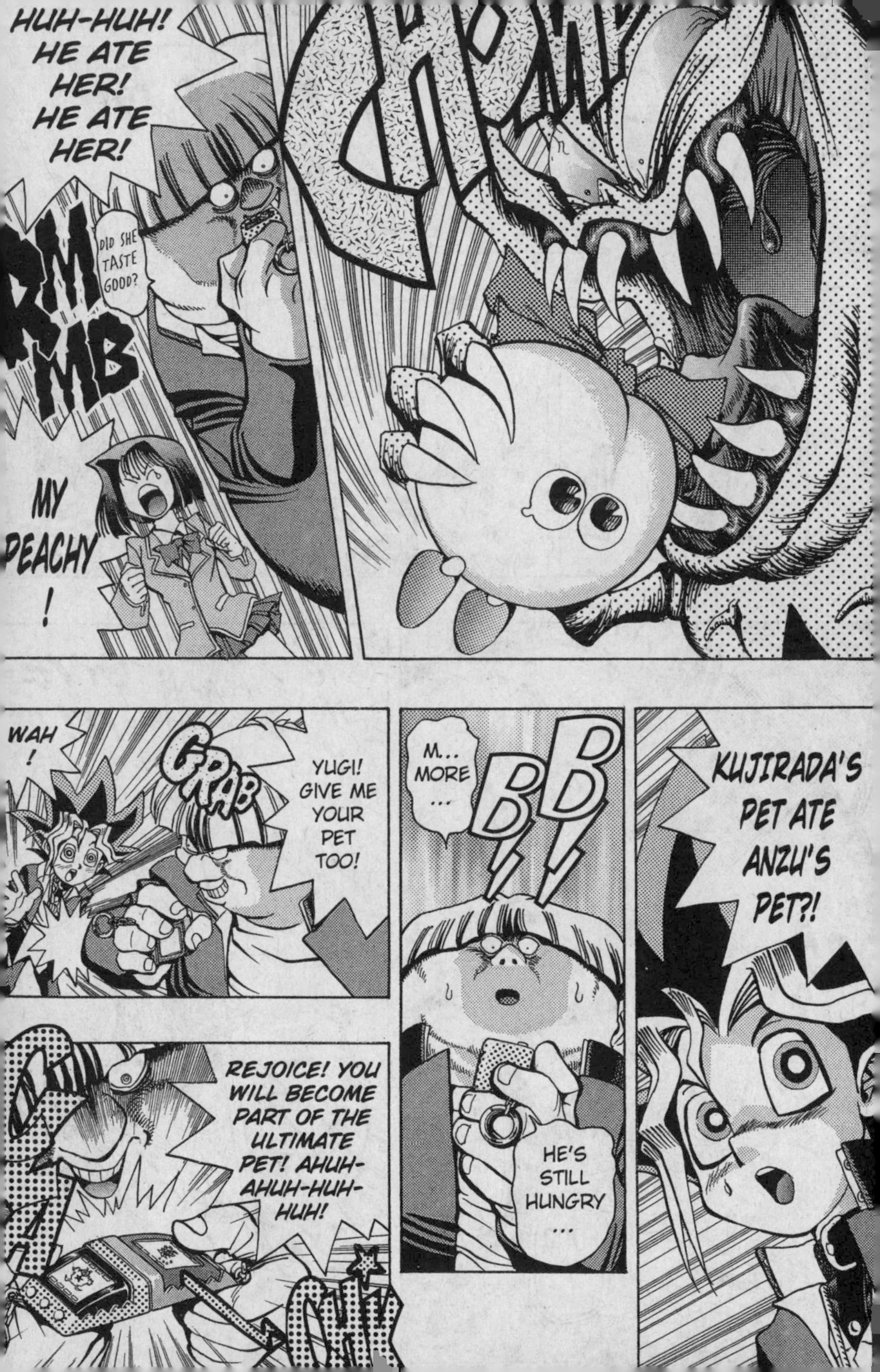
HUH-HUH! HE ATE HER! HE ATE HER!
DID SHE TASTE GOOD?
MY PEACHY!
KUJIRADA'S PET ATE ANZU'S PET?!
M... MORE...
HE'S STILL HUNGRY...
WAH!
GRAB
YUGI! GIVE ME YOUR PET TOO!
REJOICE! YOU WILL BECOME PART OF THE ULTIMATE PET! AHUH-AHUH-HUH-HUH!

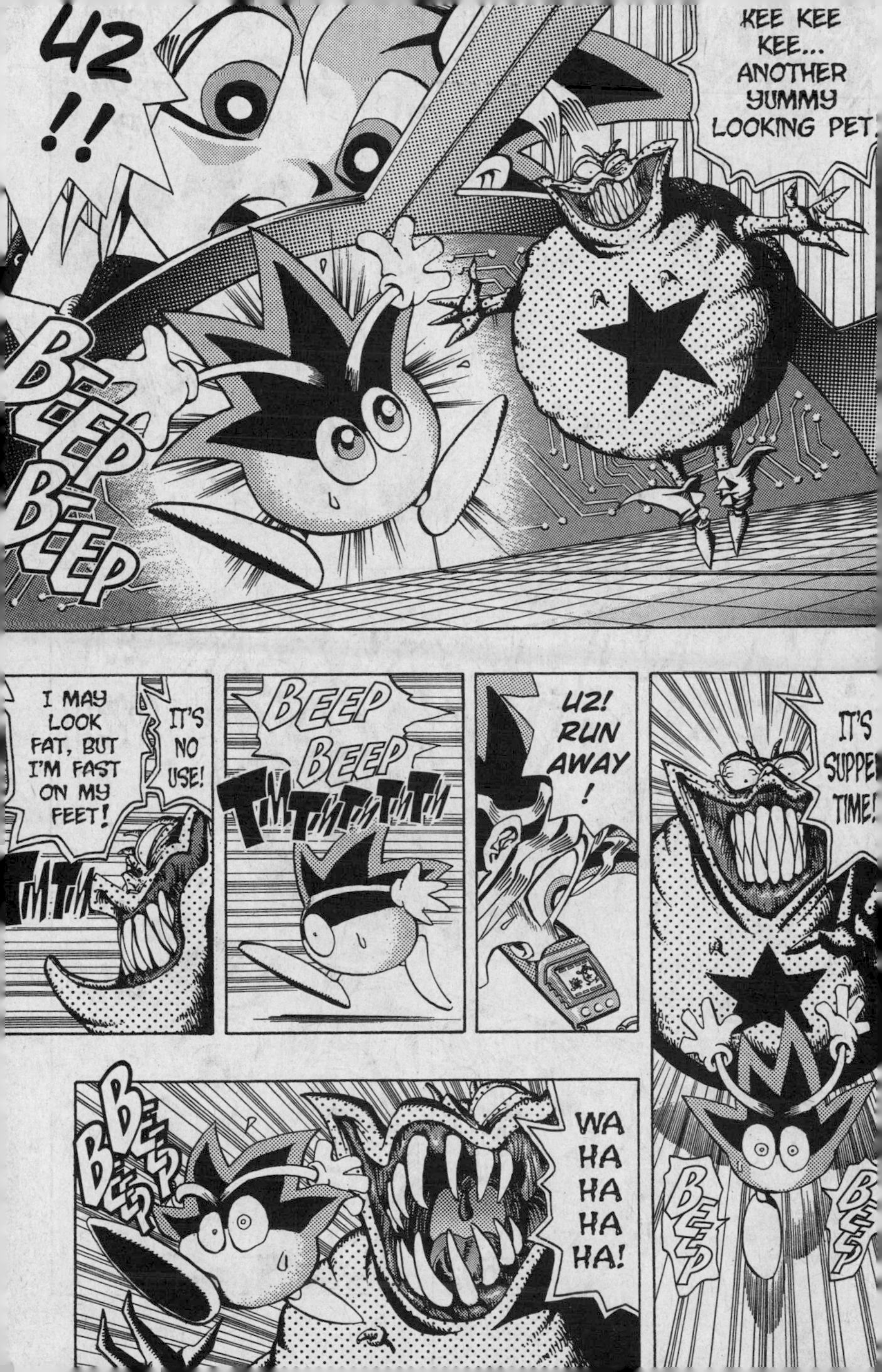
KEE KEE KEE... ANOTHER YUMMY LOOKING PET.
U2!!
BEEP BEEP BEEP
IT'S SUPPE TIME!
BEEP
BEEP
U2! RUN AWAY!
BEEP BEEP
TNTNTNTNTNTN
IT'S NO USE!
I MAY LOOK FAT, BUT I'M FAST ON MY FEET!
TNTN
WA HA HA HA HA!
BEEP BEEP

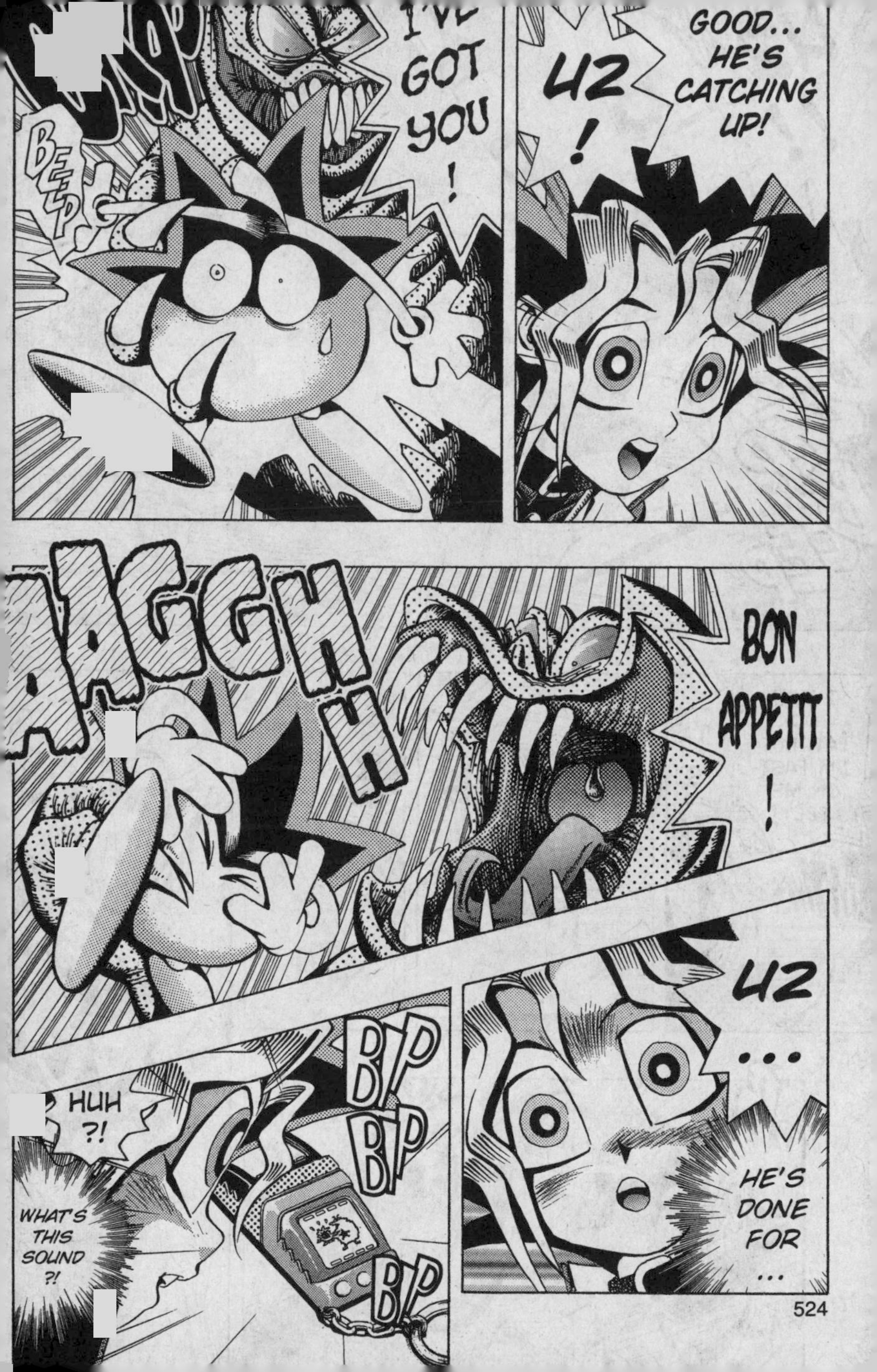
UZ
!
GOOD... HE'S CATCHING UP!
I'VE GOT YOU
!
BEEP
AGGHH
BON APPETIT
!
UZ
...
HE'S DONE FOR
...
BDP
BDP
BDP
HUH
?!
WHAT'S THIS SOUND ?!

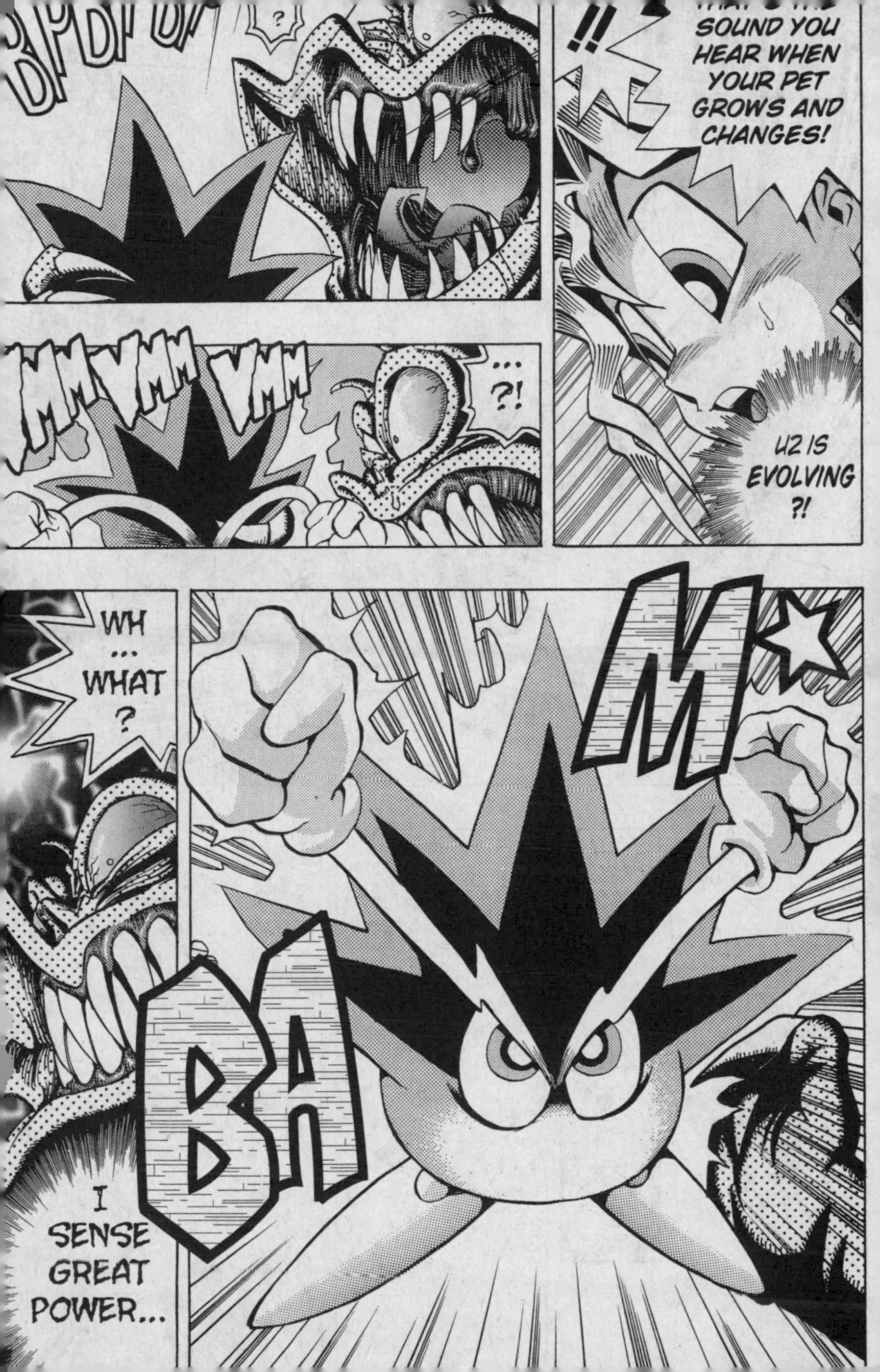
SOUND YOU HEAR WHEN YOUR PET GROWS AND CHANGES!
!!
U2 IS EVOLVING ?!
?
MMVMM VMM
...?!
BAM
WH ... WHAT ?
I SENSE GREAT POWER...

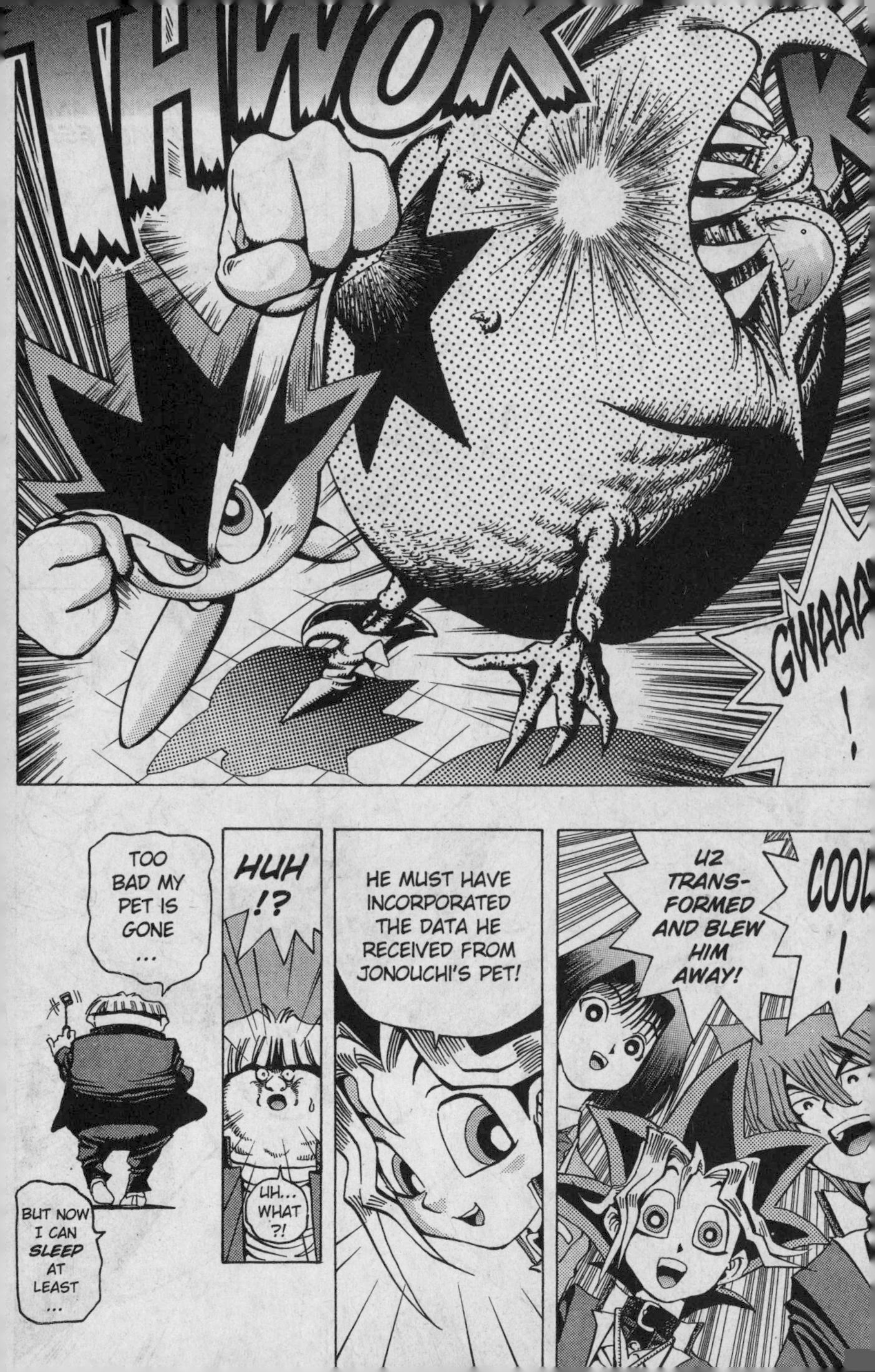
THWOK
GWAAA !
COOL !
U2 TRANS-FORMED AND BLEW HIM AWAY!
HE MUST HAVE INCORPORATED THE DATA HE RECEIVED FROM JONOUCHI'S PET!
HUH !?
UH... WHAT ?!
TOO BAD MY PET IS GONE ...
BUT NOW I CAN *SLEEP* AT LEAST ...

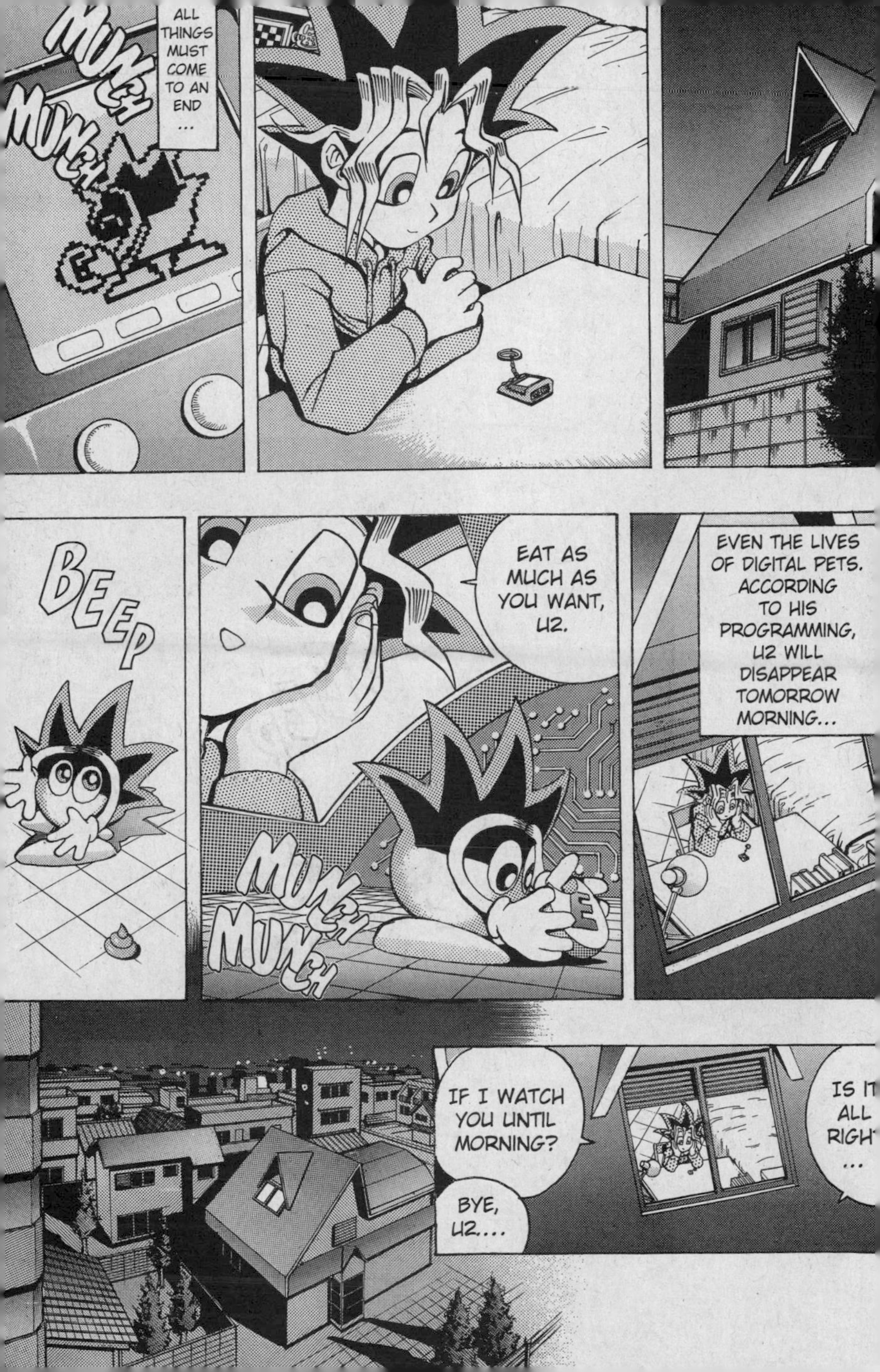

ALL THINGS MUST COME TO AN END...
MUNCH MUNCH
EVEN THE LIVES OF DIGITAL PETS. ACCORDING TO HIS PROGRAMMING, U2 WILL DISAPPEAR TOMORROW MORNING...
EAT AS MUCH AS YOU WANT, U2.
MUNCH MUNCH
BEEP
IS IT ALL RIGH...
IF I WATCH YOU UNTIL MORNING?
BYE, U2....

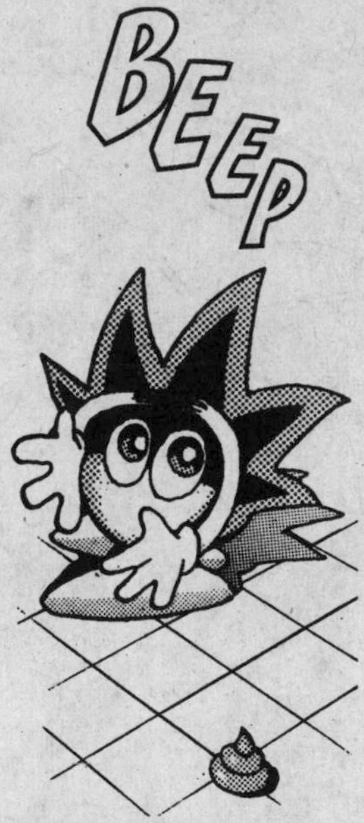
BEEP

Duel 22: American Hero (Part 1)

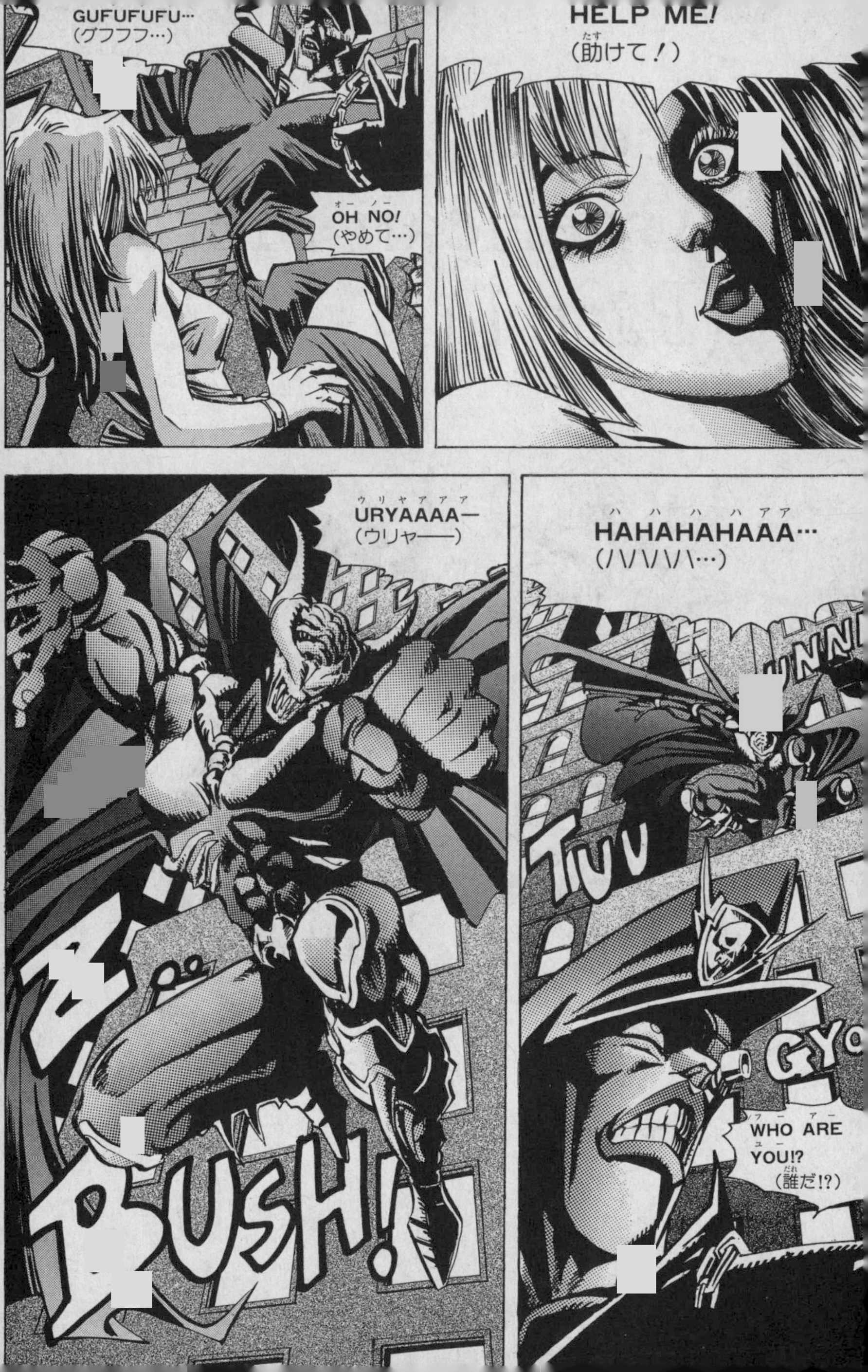
HELP ME! (助けて!)
GUFUFUFU… (グフフフ…)
OH NO! (やめて…)
HAHAHAHAAA… (ハハハハ…)
WHO ARE YOU!? (誰だ!?)
URYAAAA— (ウリャ——)

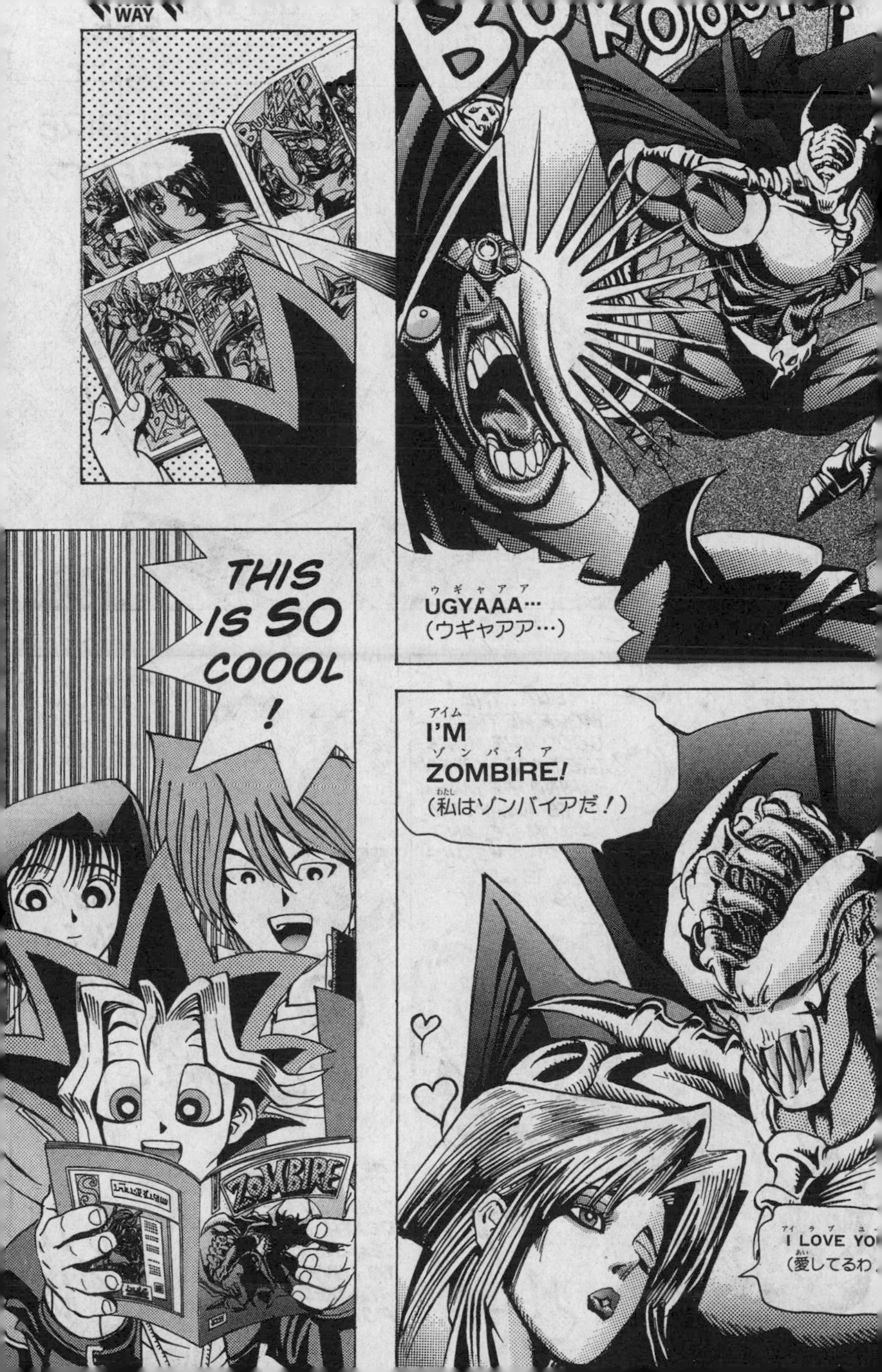
UGYAAA… (ウギャアア…)
WAY
I'M ZOMBIRE! (私はソンバイアだ!)
I LOVE YO (愛してるわ
THIS IS SO COOOL!
ZOMBIRE

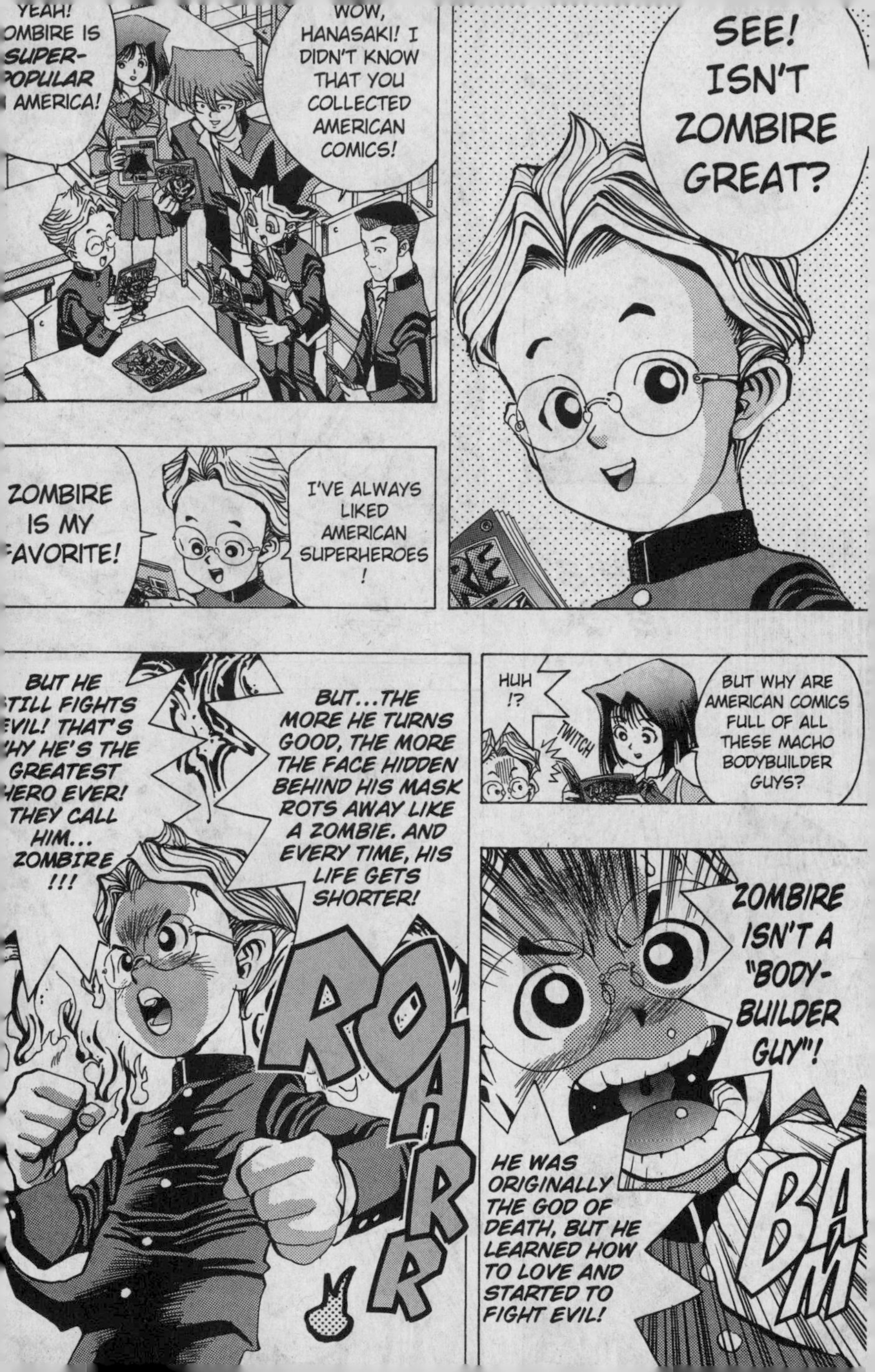
SEE! ISN'T ZOMBIRE GREAT?
WOW, HANASAKI! I DIDN'T KNOW THAT YOU COLLECTED AMERICAN COMICS!
YEAH! OMBIRE IS SUPER-POPULAR AMERICA!
I'VE ALWAYS LIKED AMERICAN SUPERHEROES!
ZOMBIRE IS MY AVORITE!
BUT WHY ARE AMERICAN COMICS FULL OF ALL THESE MACHO BODYBUILDER GUYS?
HUH !?
TWITCH
ZOMBIRE ISN'T A "BODY-BUILDER GUY"!
HE WAS ORIGINALLY THE GOD OF DEATH, BUT HE LEARNED HOW TO LOVE AND STARTED TO FIGHT EVIL!
BAM
BUT...THE MORE HE TURNS GOOD, THE MORE THE FACE HIDDEN BEHIND HIS MASK ROTS AWAY LIKE A ZOMBIE. AND EVERY TIME, HIS LIFE GETS SHORTER!
BUT HE TILL FIGHTS VIL! THAT'S HY HE'S THE GREATEST HERO EVER! THEY CALL HIM... ZOMBIRE !!!
ROAR

THIS WAY

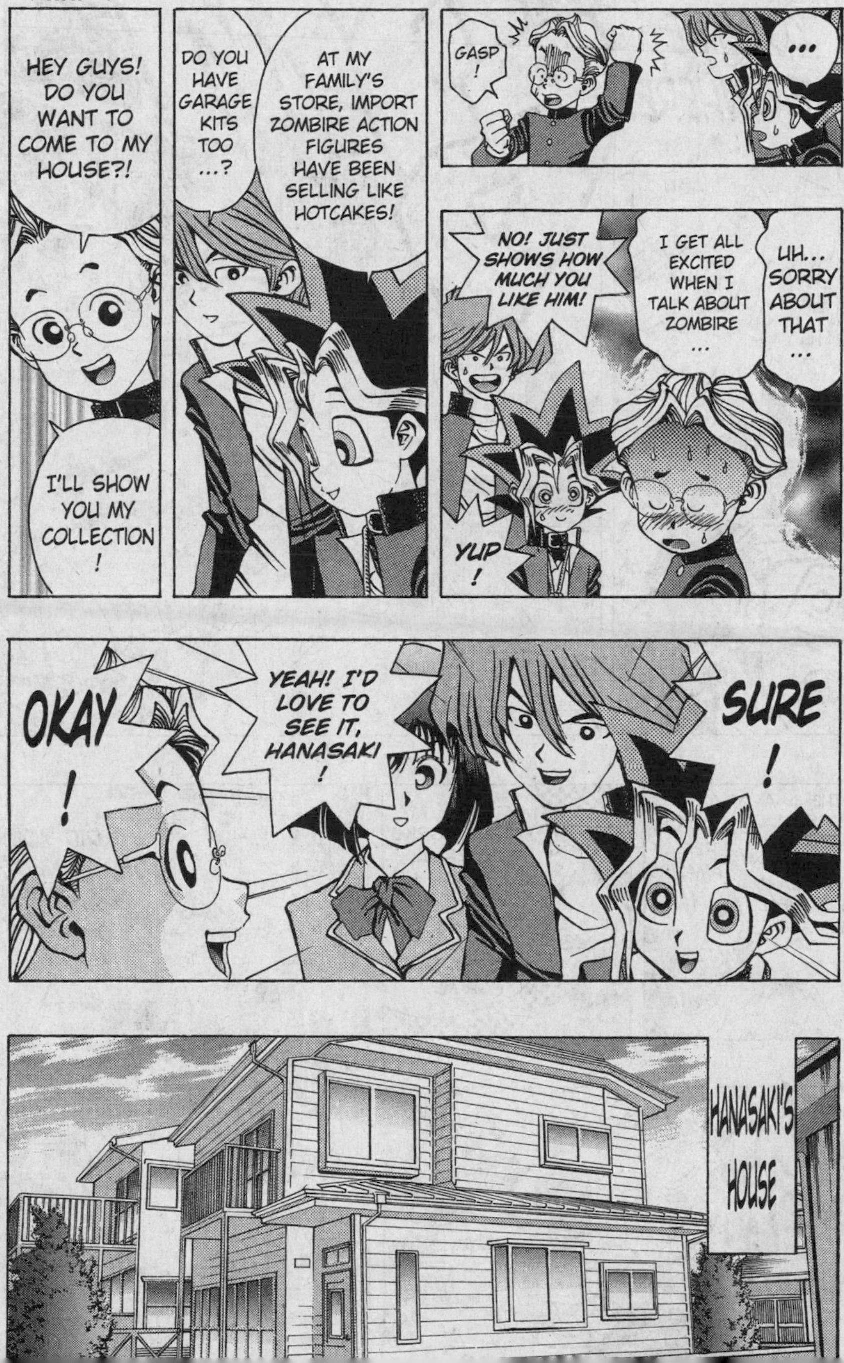
...
GASP!
UH... SORRY ABOUT THAT ...
I GET ALL EXCITED WHEN I TALK ABOUT ZOMBIRE ...
NO! JUST SHOWS HOW MUCH YOU LIKE HIM!
YUP!
AT MY FAMILY'S STORE, IMPORT ZOMBIRE ACTION FIGURES HAVE BEEN SELLING LIKE HOTCAKES!
DO YOU HAVE GARAGE KITS TOO ...?
HEY GUYS! DO YOU WANT TO COME TO MY HOUSE?!
I'LL SHOW YOU MY COLLECTION!
SURE!
YEAH! I'D LOVE TO SEE IT, HANASAKI!
OKAY!
HANASAKI'S HOUSE

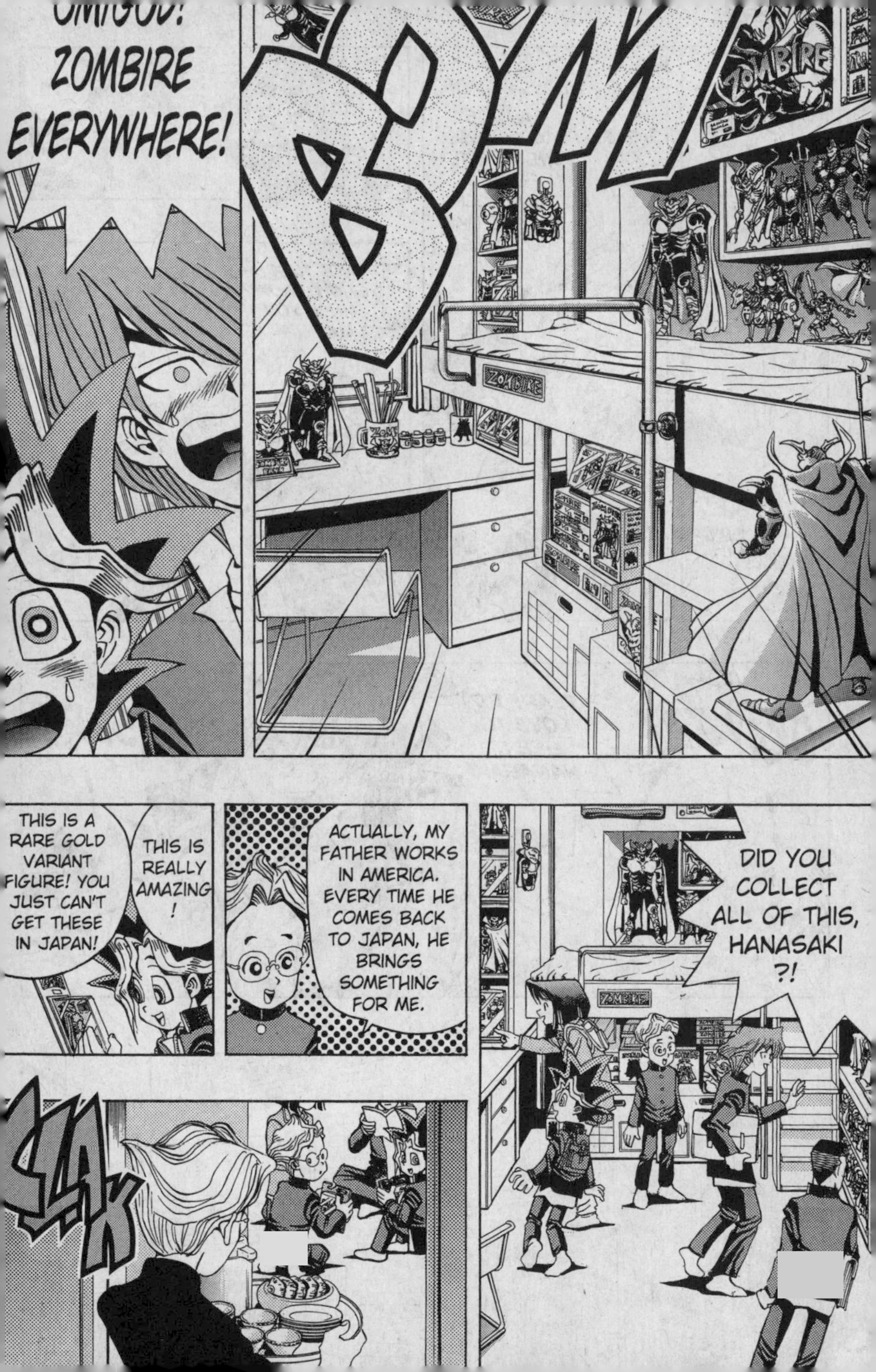
ZOMBIRE EVERYWHERE!
DID YOU COLLECT ALL OF THIS, HANASAKI ?!
ACTUALLY, MY FATHER WORKS IN AMERICA. EVERY TIME HE COMES BACK TO JAPAN, HE BRINGS SOMETHING FOR ME.
THIS IS REALLY AMAZING!
THIS IS A RARE GOLD VARIANT FIGURE! YOU JUST CAN'T GET THESE IN JAPAN!

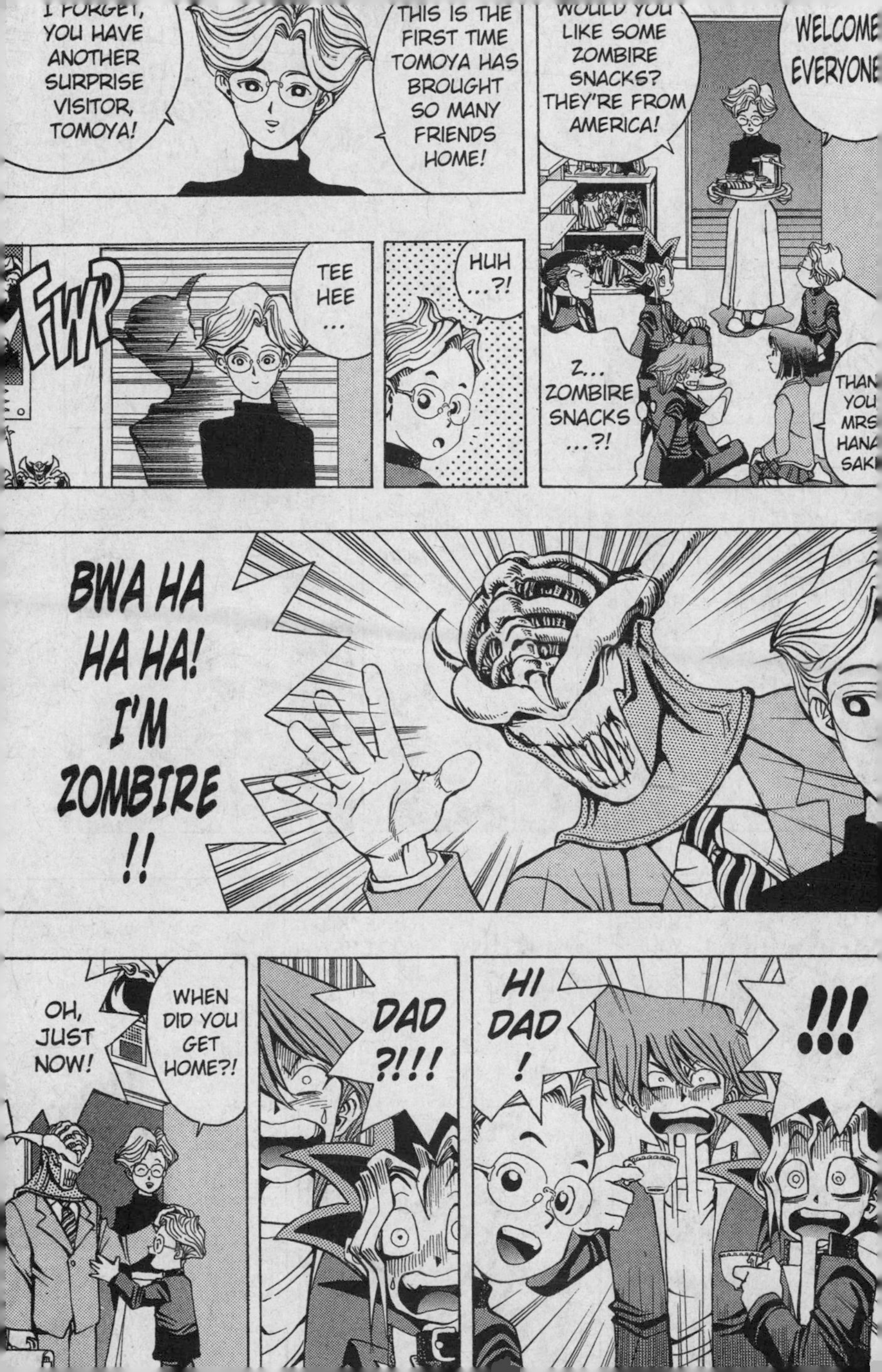
WELCOME EVERYONE
WOULD YOU LIKE SOME ZOMBIRE SNACKS? THEY'RE FROM AMERICA!
THAN YOU MRS HANASAK
Z... ZOMBIRE SNACKS ...?!
THIS IS THE FIRST TIME TOMOYA HAS BROUGHT SO MANY FRIENDS HOME!
I FORGET, YOU HAVE ANOTHER SURPRISE VISITOR, TOMOYA!
HUH ...?!
TEE HEE ...
FWP
BWA HA HA HA! I'M ZOMBIRE !!
!!!
HI DAD !
DAD ?!!!
WHEN DID YOU GET HOME?!
OH, JUST NOW!

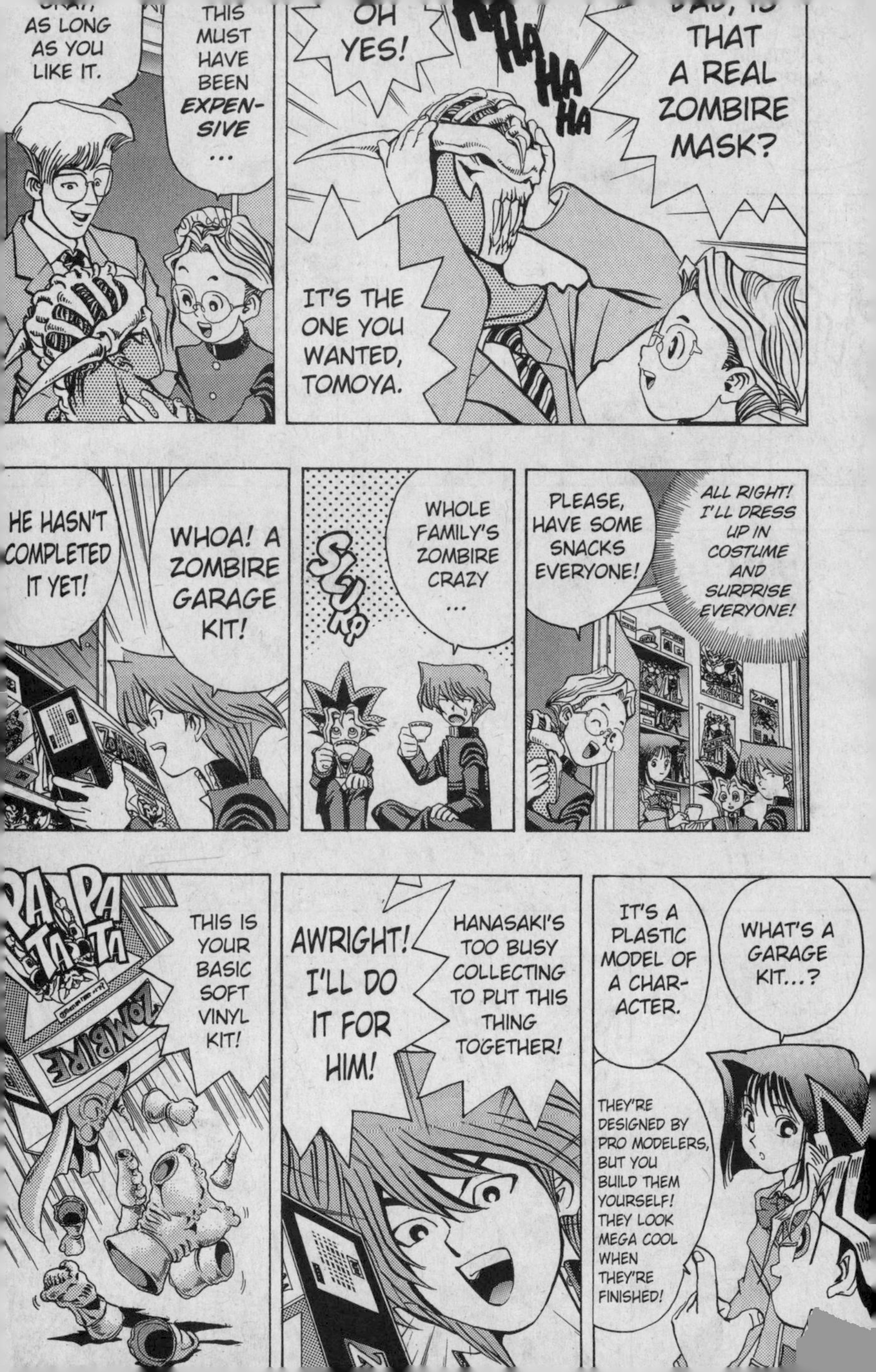
THAT A REAL ZOMBIRE MASK?
HA HA HA HA
OH YES!
IT'S THE ONE YOU WANTED, TOMOYA.
THIS MUST HAVE BEEN EXPENSIVE...
AS LONG AS YOU LIKE IT.
ALL RIGHT! I'LL DRESS UP IN COSTUME AND SURPRISE EVERYONE!
PLEASE, HAVE SOME SNACKS EVERYONE!
WHOLE FAMILY'S ZOMBIRE CRAZY...
SLURP
WHOA! A ZOMBIRE GARAGE KIT!
HE HASN'T COMPLETED IT YET!
WHAT'S A GARAGE KIT...?
IT'S A PLASTIC MODEL OF A CHARACTER.
THEY'RE DESIGNED BY PRO MODELERS, BUT YOU BUILD THEM YOURSELF! THEY LOOK MEGA COOL WHEN THEY'RE FINISHED!
HANASAKI'S TOO BUSY COLLECTING TO PUT THIS THING TOGETHER!
AWRIGHT! I'LL DO IT FOR HIM!
PA PA TA TA
THIS IS YOUR BASIC SOFT VINYL KIT!
ZOMBIRE

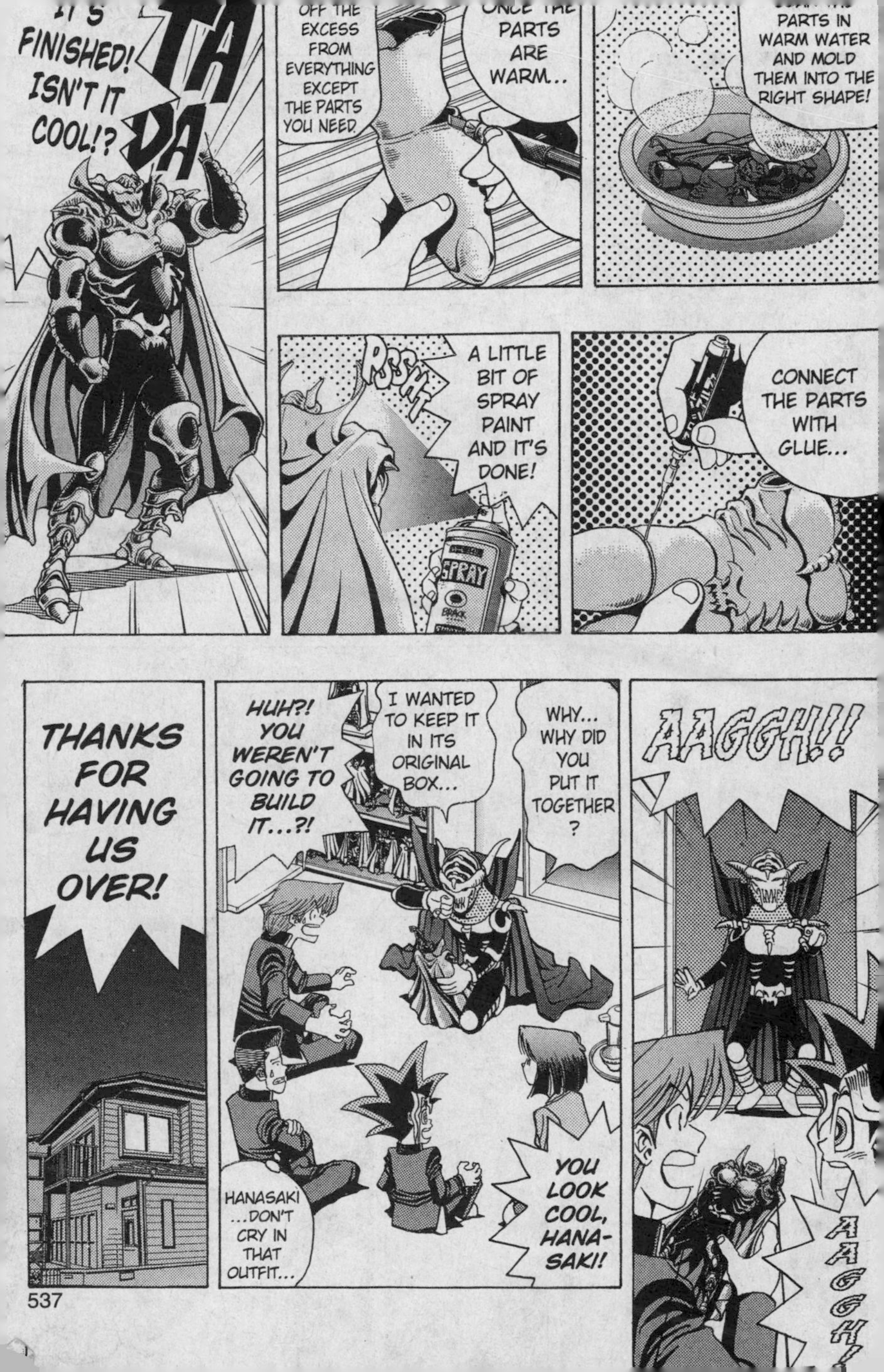
PARTS IN WARM WATER AND MOLD THEM INTO THE RIGHT SHAPE!
PARTS ARE WARM...
OFF THE EXCESS FROM EVERYTHING EXCEPT THE PARTS YOU NEED.
CONNECT THE PARTS WITH GLUE...
PSSHT
A LITTLE BIT OF SPRAY PAINT AND IT'S DONE!
SPRAY
TA DA
FINISHED! ISN'T IT COOL!?
AAGGH!!
AAGGH!!
WHY... WHY DID YOU PUT IT TOGETHER?
I WANTED TO KEEP IT IN ITS ORIGINAL BOX...
HUH?! YOU WEREN'T GOING TO BUILD IT...?!
YOU LOOK COOL, HANA-SAKI!
HANASAKI ...DON'T CRY IN THAT OUTFIT...
THANKS FOR HAVING US OVER!

READ THIS WAY

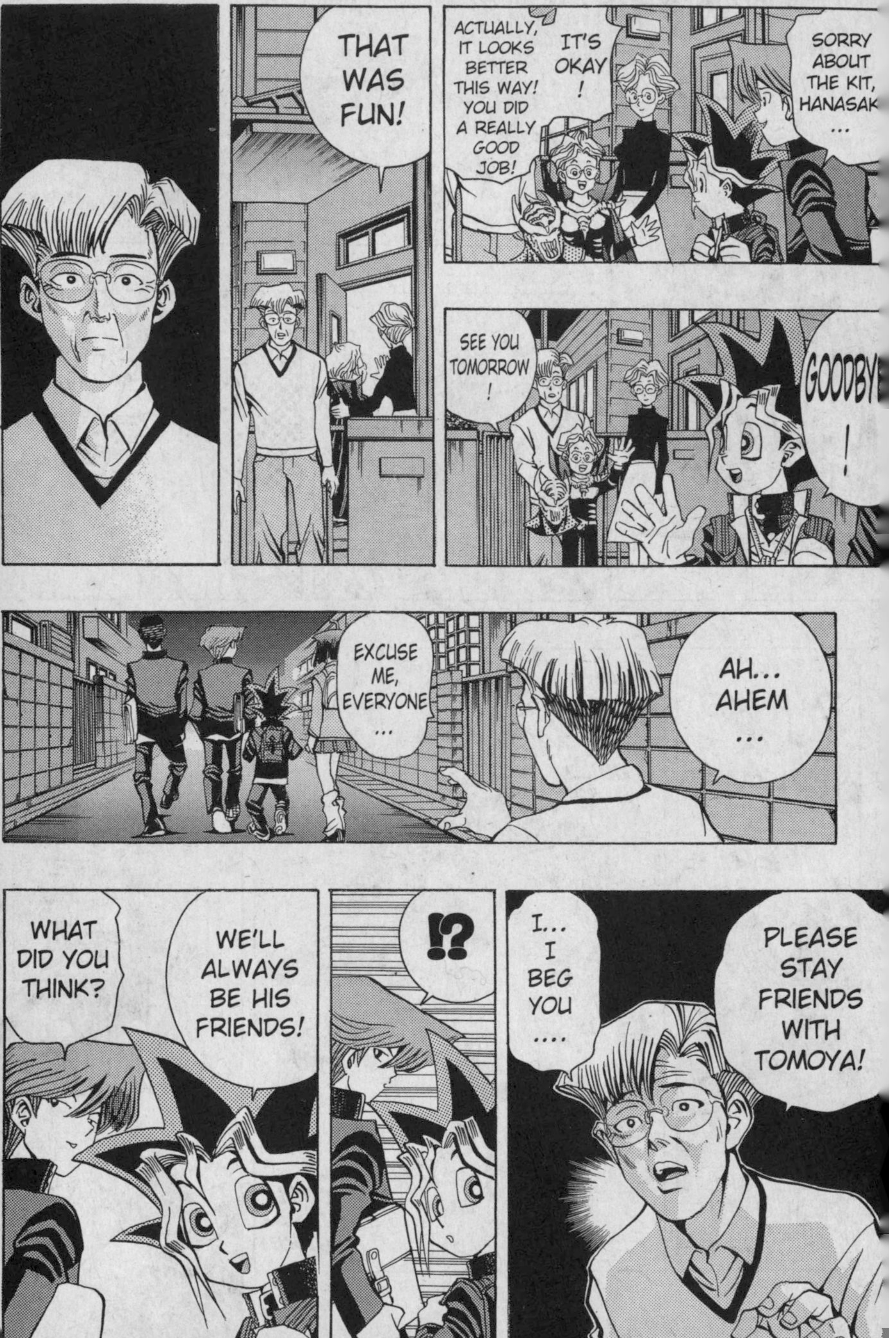
SORRY ABOUT THE KIT, HANASAK ...
IT'S OKAY!
ACTUALLY, IT LOOKS BETTER THIS WAY! YOU DID A REALLY GOOD JOB!
GOODBY !
SEE YOU TOMORROW!
THAT WAS FUN!
AH... AHEM ...
EXCUSE ME, EVERYONE ...
PLEASE STAY FRIENDS WITH TOMOYA!
I... I BEG YOU ....
!?
WE'LL ALWAYS BE HIS FRIENDS!
WHAT DID YOU THINK?

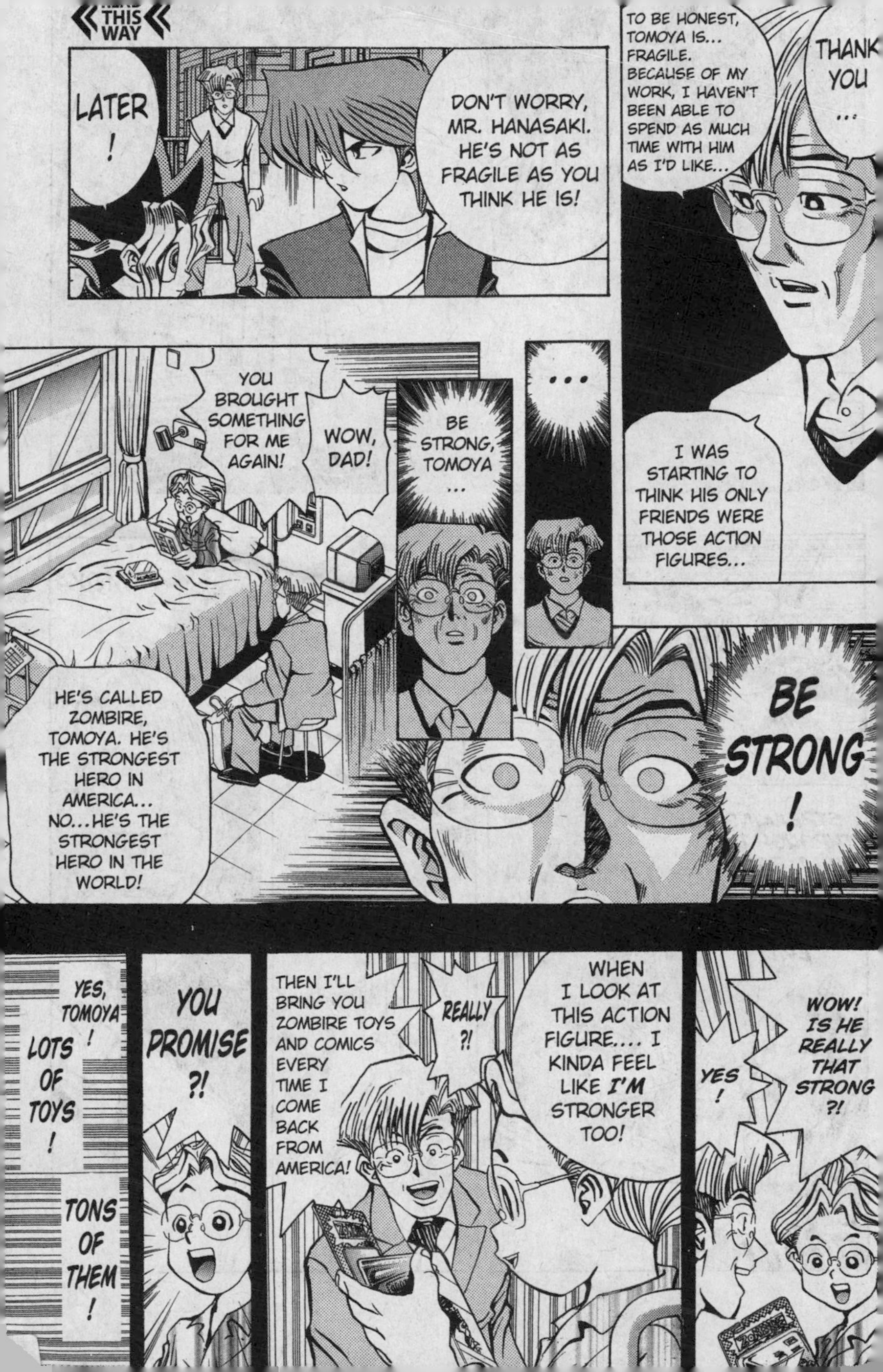
READ THIS WAY
THANK YOU...
TO BE HONEST, TOMOYA IS... FRAGILE. BECAUSE OF MY WORK, I HAVEN'T BEEN ABLE TO SPEND AS MUCH TIME WITH HIM AS I'D LIKE...
I WAS STARTING TO THINK HIS ONLY FRIENDS WERE THOSE ACTION FIGURES...
DON'T WORRY, MR. HANASAKI. HE'S NOT AS FRAGILE AS YOU THINK HE IS!
LATER!
...
BE STRONG, TOMOYA...
WOW, DAD!
YOU BROUGHT SOMETHING FOR ME AGAIN!
HE'S CALLED ZOMBIRE, TOMOYA. HE'S THE STRONGEST HERO IN AMERICA... NO...HE'S THE STRONGEST HERO IN THE WORLD!
BE STRONG!
WOW! IS HE REALLY THAT STRONG?!
YES!
WHEN I LOOK AT THIS ACTION FIGURE.... I KINDA FEEL LIKE *I'M* STRONGER TOO!
REALLY?!
THEN I'LL BRING YOU ZOMBIRE TOYS AND COMICS EVERY TIME I COME BACK FROM AMERICA!
YOU PROMISE?!
YES, TOMOYA!
LOTS OF TOYS!
TONS OF THEM!

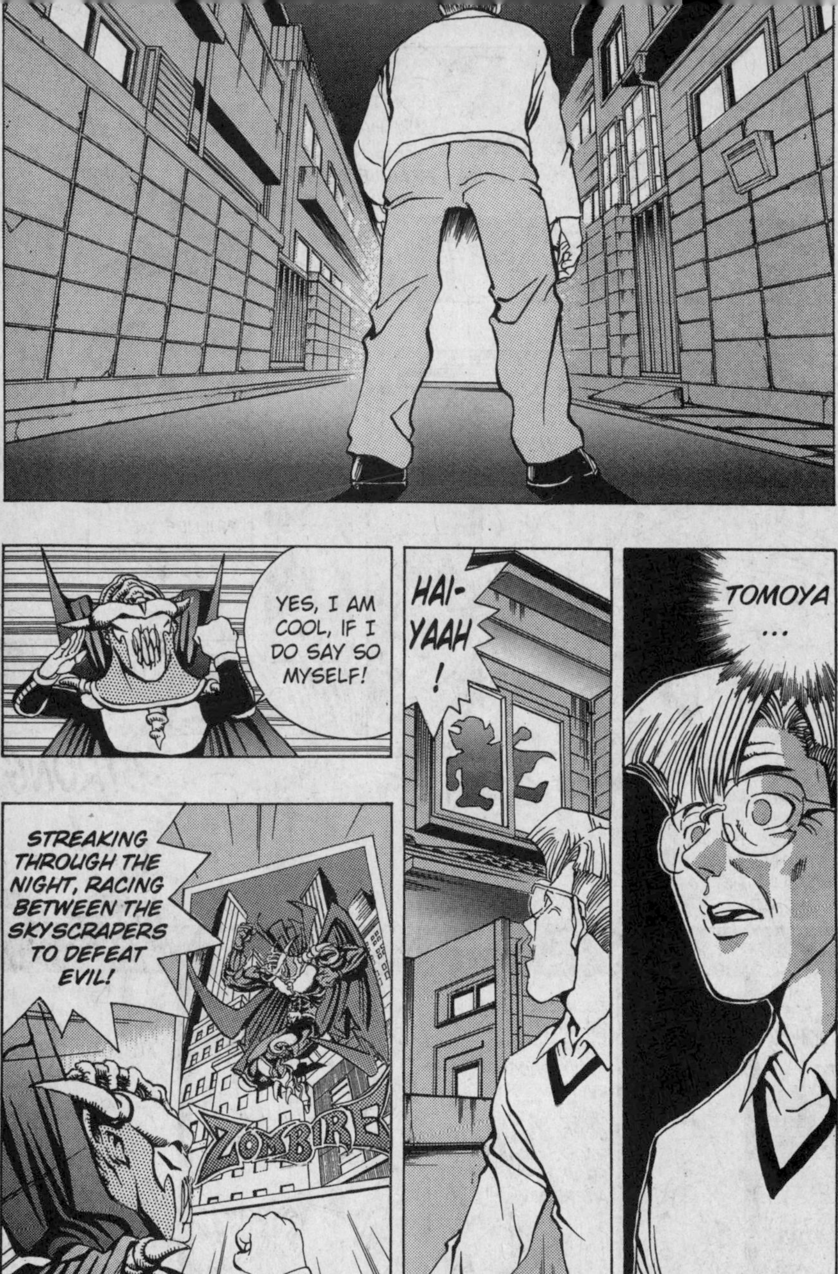

TOMOYA ...
HAI-YAAH!
YES, I AM COOL, IF I DO SAY SO MYSELF!
STREAKING THROUGH THE NIGHT, RACING BETWEEN THE SKYSCRAPERS TO DEFEAT EVIL!
ZOMBIRE

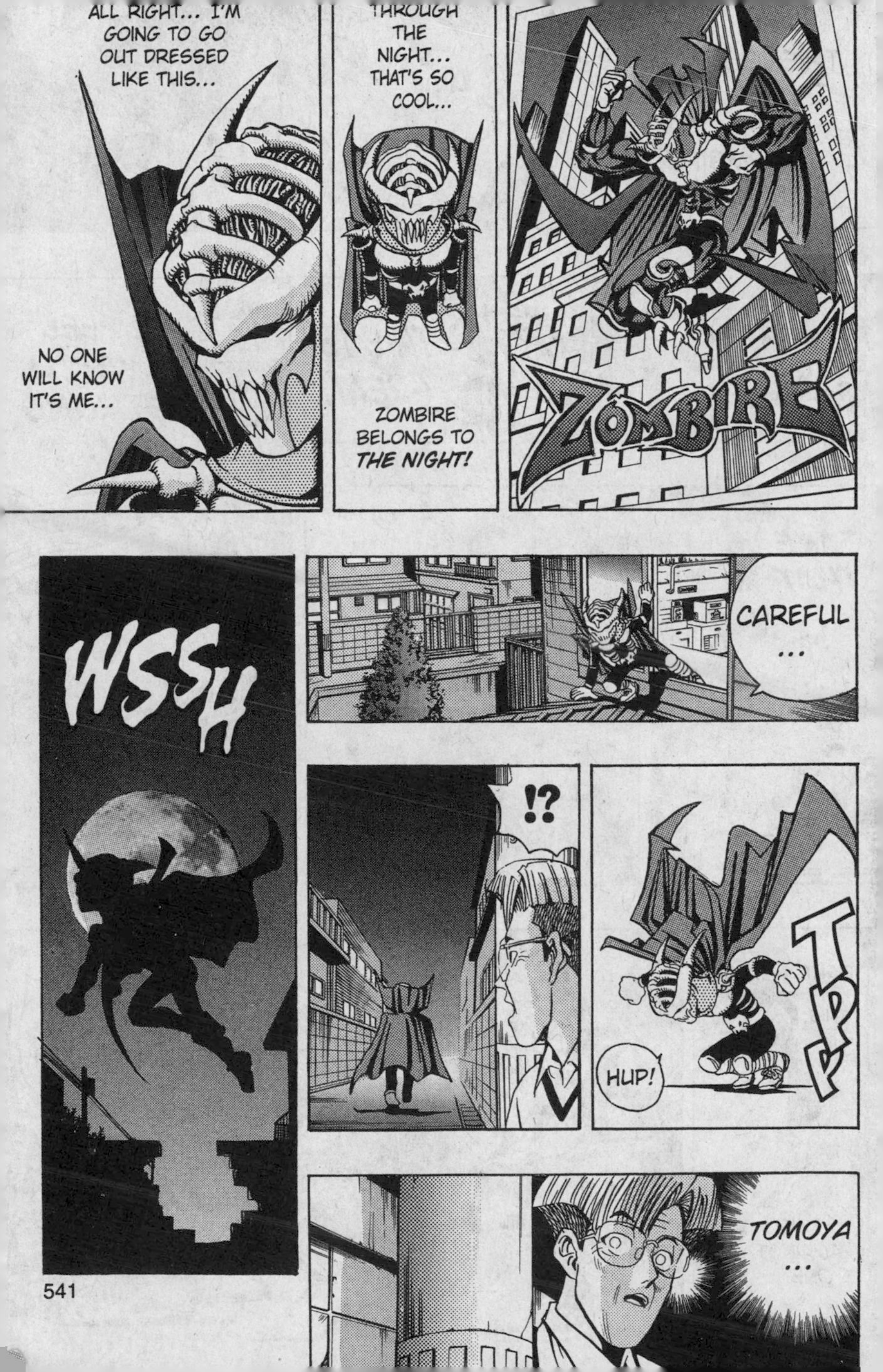
ALL RIGHT... I'M GOING TO GO OUT DRESSED LIKE THIS...
NO ONE WILL KNOW IT'S ME...
THROUGH THE NIGHT... THAT'S SO COOL...
ZOMBIRE BELONGS TO *THE NIGHT!*
ZOMBIRE
WSSH
CAREFUL ...
!?
HUP!
TP
TOMOYA ...

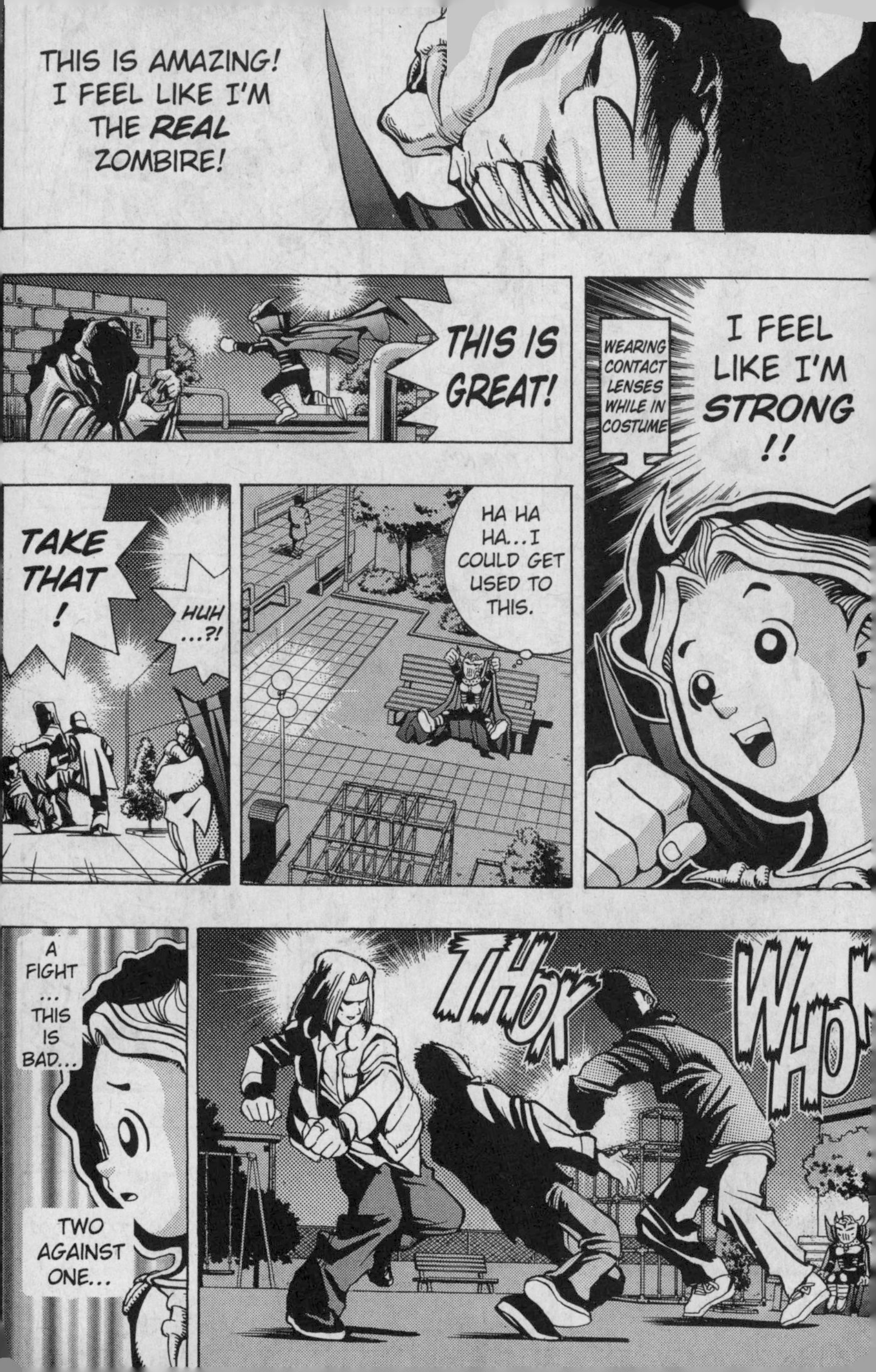
THIS IS AMAZING! I FEEL LIKE I'M THE *REAL* ZOMBIRE!
I FEEL LIKE I'M *STRONG*!!
WEARING CONTACT LENSES WHILE IN COSTUME
THIS IS GREAT!
HA HA HA...I COULD GET USED TO THIS.
HUH...?!
TAKE THAT!
THOK
A FIGHT... THIS IS BAD...
TWO AGAINST ONE...

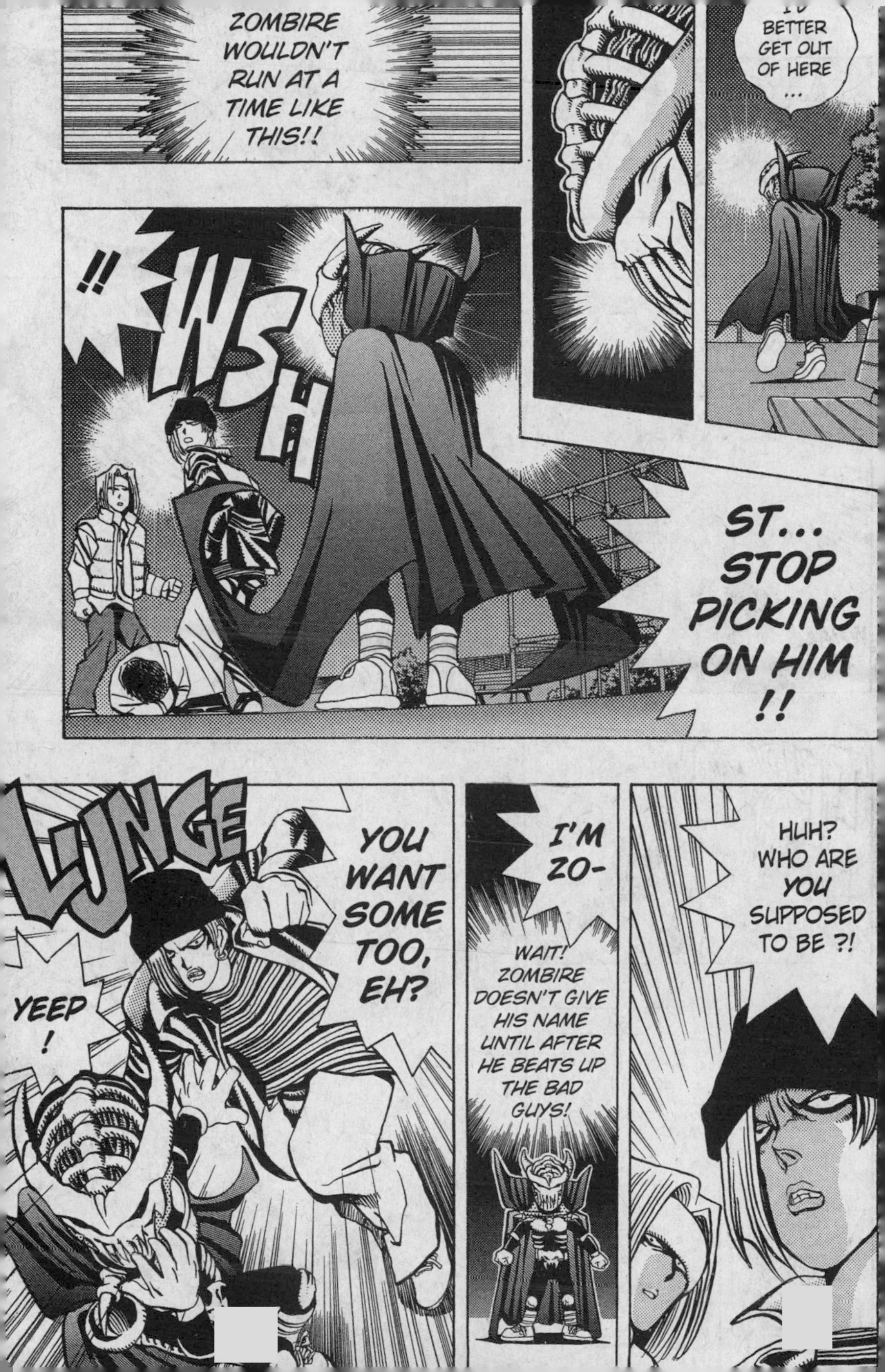
BETTER GET OUT OF HERE ...
ZOMBIRE WOULDN'T RUN AT A TIME LIKE THIS!!
!!
WSH
ST... STOP PICKING ON HIM !!
HUH? WHO ARE YOU SUPPOSED TO BE ?!
I'M ZO-
WAIT! ZOMBIRE DOESN'T GIVE HIS NAME UNTIL AFTER HE BEATS UP THE BAD GUYS!
LUNGE
YOU WANT SOME TOO, EH?
YEEP !

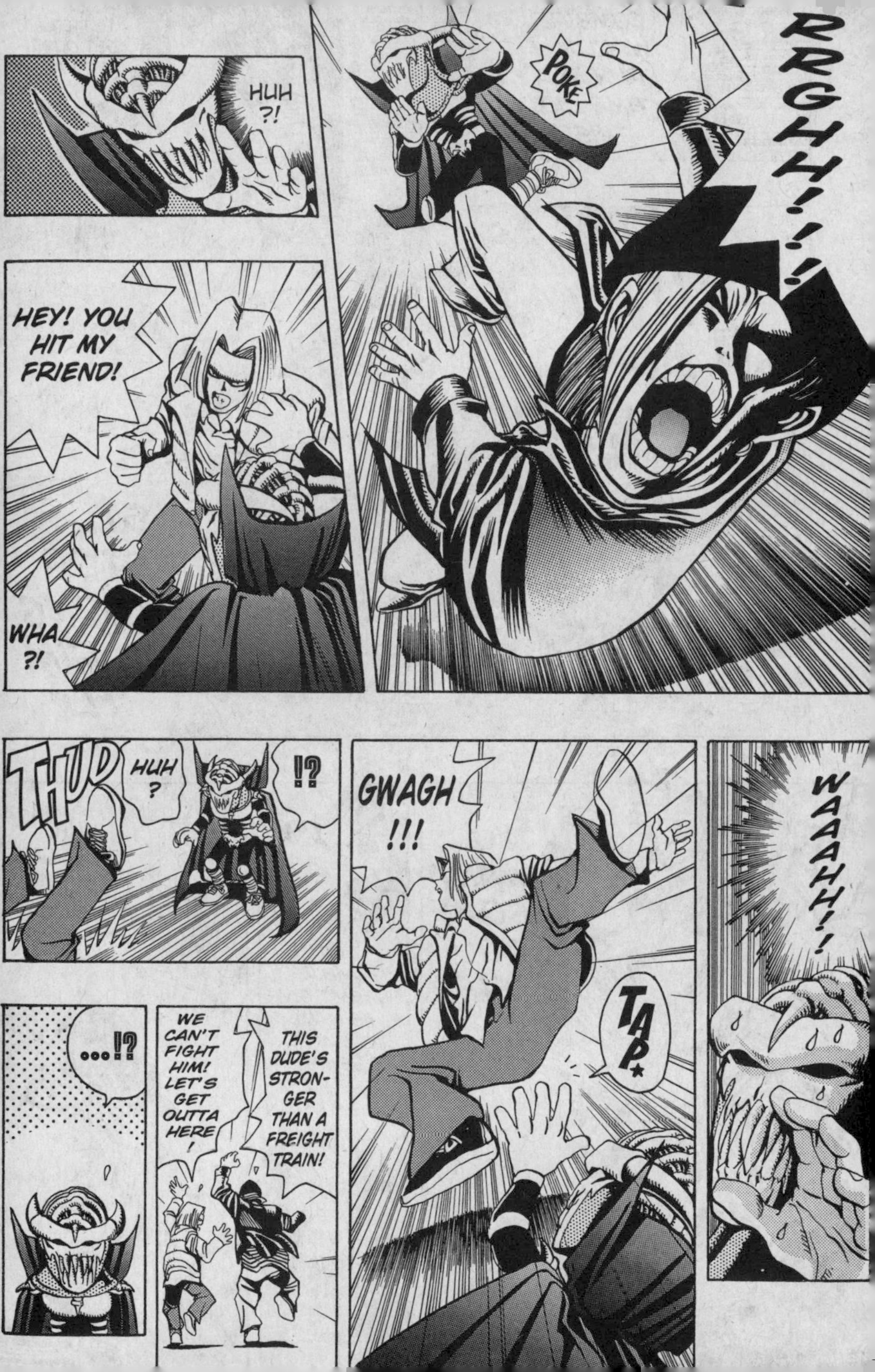
POKE
RRGHH!!!
HUH ?!
HEY! YOU HIT MY FRIEND!
WHA ?!
WAAAHH!!
GWAGH !!!
TAP
!?
HUH ?
THUD
THIS DUDE'S STRONGER THAN A FREIGHT TRAIN!
WE CAN'T FIGHT HIM! LET'S GET OUTTA HERE!
...!?

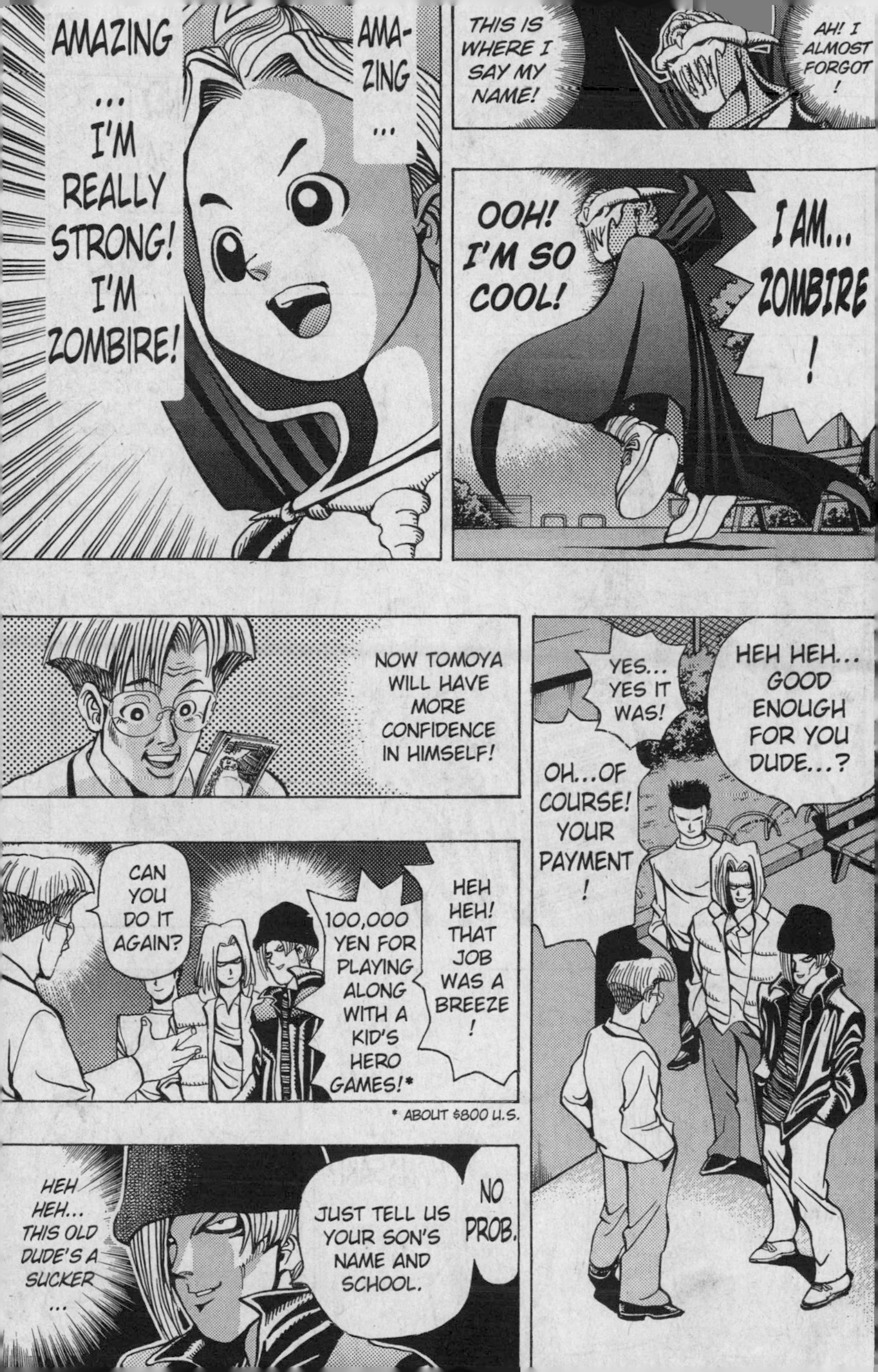
AH! I ALMOST FORGOT!
THIS IS WHERE I SAY MY NAME!
I AM... ZOMBIRE!
OOH! I'M SO COOL!
AMA-ZING...
AMAZING... I'M REALLY STRONG! I'M ZOMBIRE!
HEH HEH... GOOD ENOUGH FOR YOU DUDE...?
YES... YES IT WAS!
OH...OF COURSE! YOUR PAYMENT!
NOW TOMOYA WILL HAVE MORE CONFIDENCE IN HIMSELF!
HEH HEH! THAT JOB WAS A BREEZE!
100,000 YEN FOR PLAYING ALONG WITH A KID'S HERO GAMES!*
CAN YOU DO IT AGAIN?
* ABOUT $800 U.S.
NO PROB.
JUST TELL US YOUR SON'S NAME AND SCHOOL.
HEH HEH... THIS OLD DUDE'S A SUCKER...

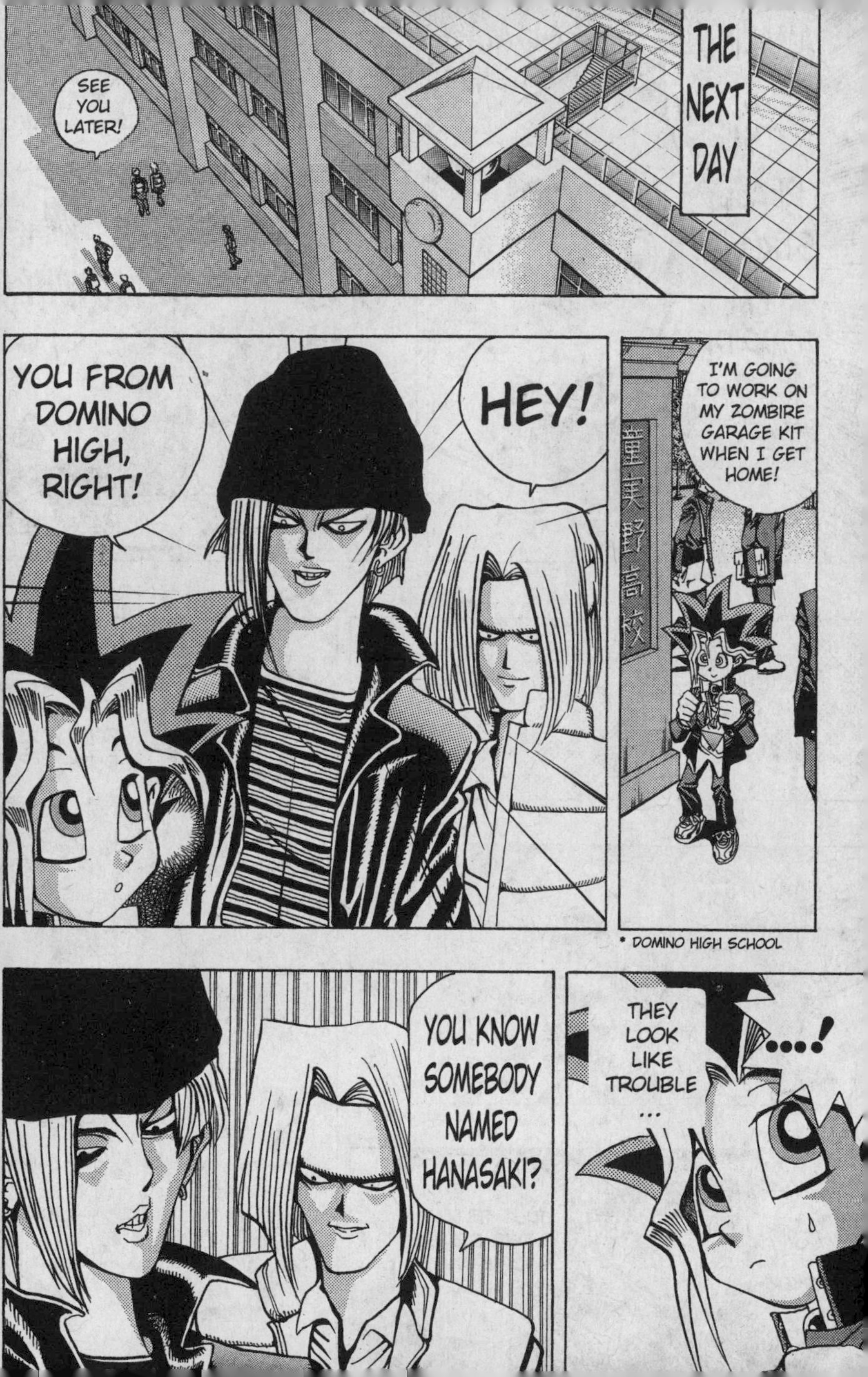
THE NEXT DAY
SEE YOU LATER!
童実野高校
I'M GOING TO WORK ON MY ZOMBIRE GARAGE KIT WHEN I GET HOME!
HEY!
YOU FROM DOMINO HIGH, RIGHT!
...!
THEY LOOK LIKE TROUBLE ...
YOU KNOW SOMEBODY NAMED HANASAKI?
* DOMINO HIGH SCHOOL

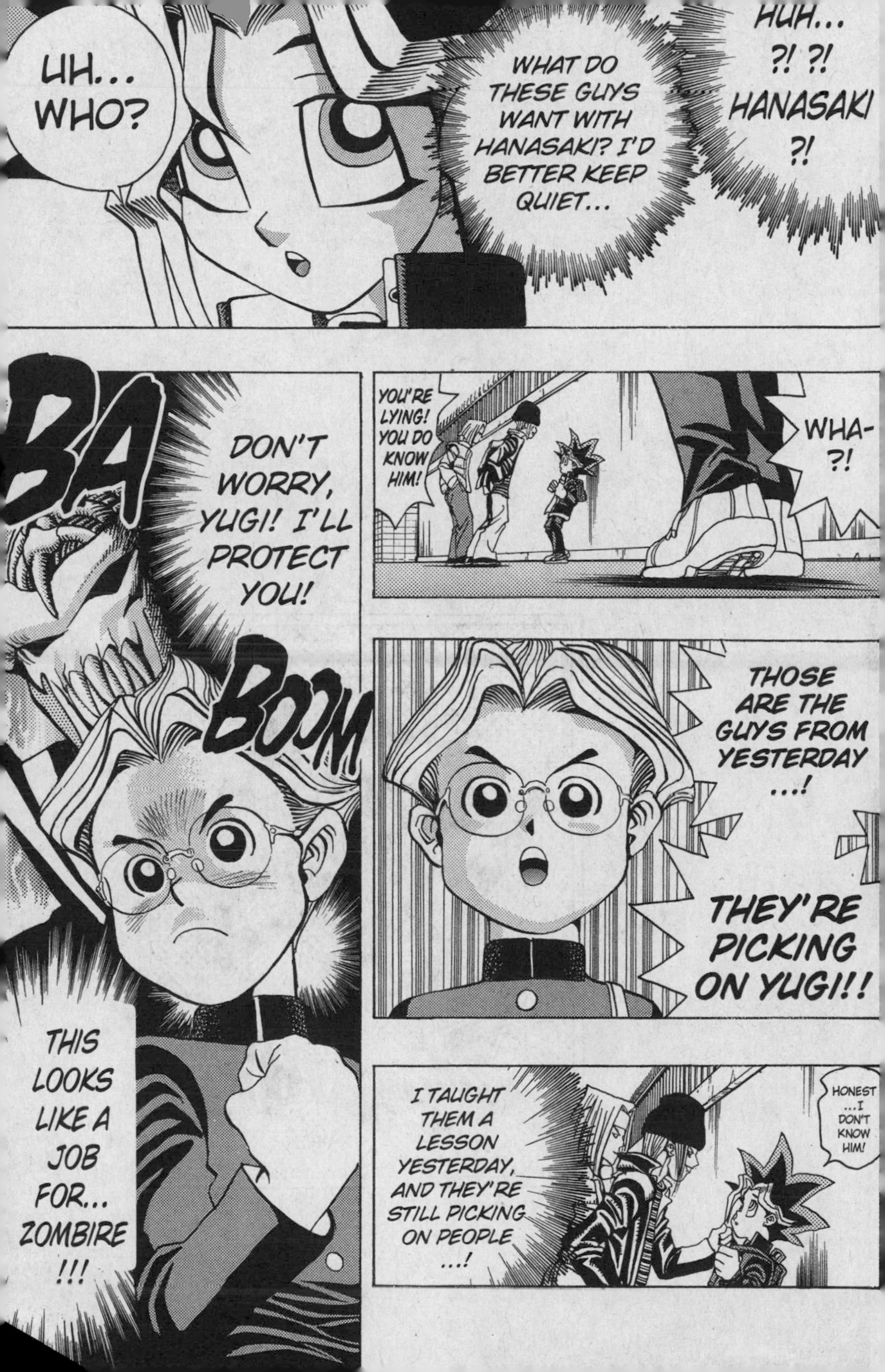
HUH... ?! ?! HANASAKI ?!
WHAT DO THESE GUYS WANT WITH HANASAKI? I'D BETTER KEEP QUIET...
UH... WHO?
WHA- ?!
YOU'RE LYING! YOU DO KNOW HIM!
THOSE ARE THE GUYS FROM YESTERDAY ...!
THEY'RE PICKING ON YUGI!!
HONEST ...I DON'T KNOW HIM!
I TAUGHT THEM A LESSON YESTERDAY, AND THEY'RE STILL PICKING ON PEOPLE ...!
BA
DON'T WORRY, YUGI! I'LL PROTECT YOU!
BOOM
THIS LOOKS LIKE A JOB FOR... ZOMBIRE !!!

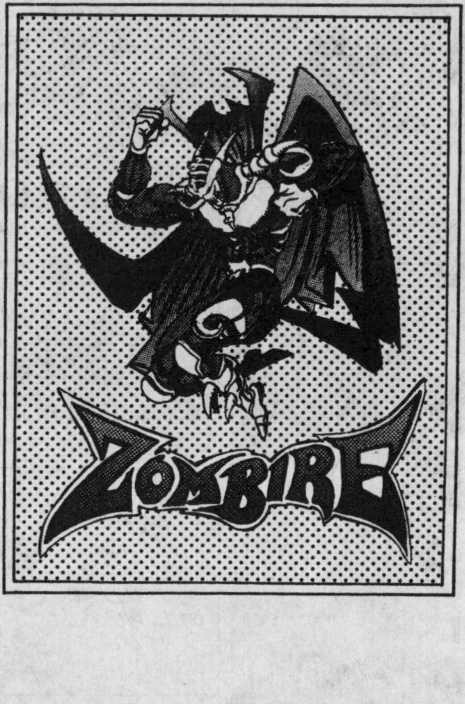
ZOMBIRE

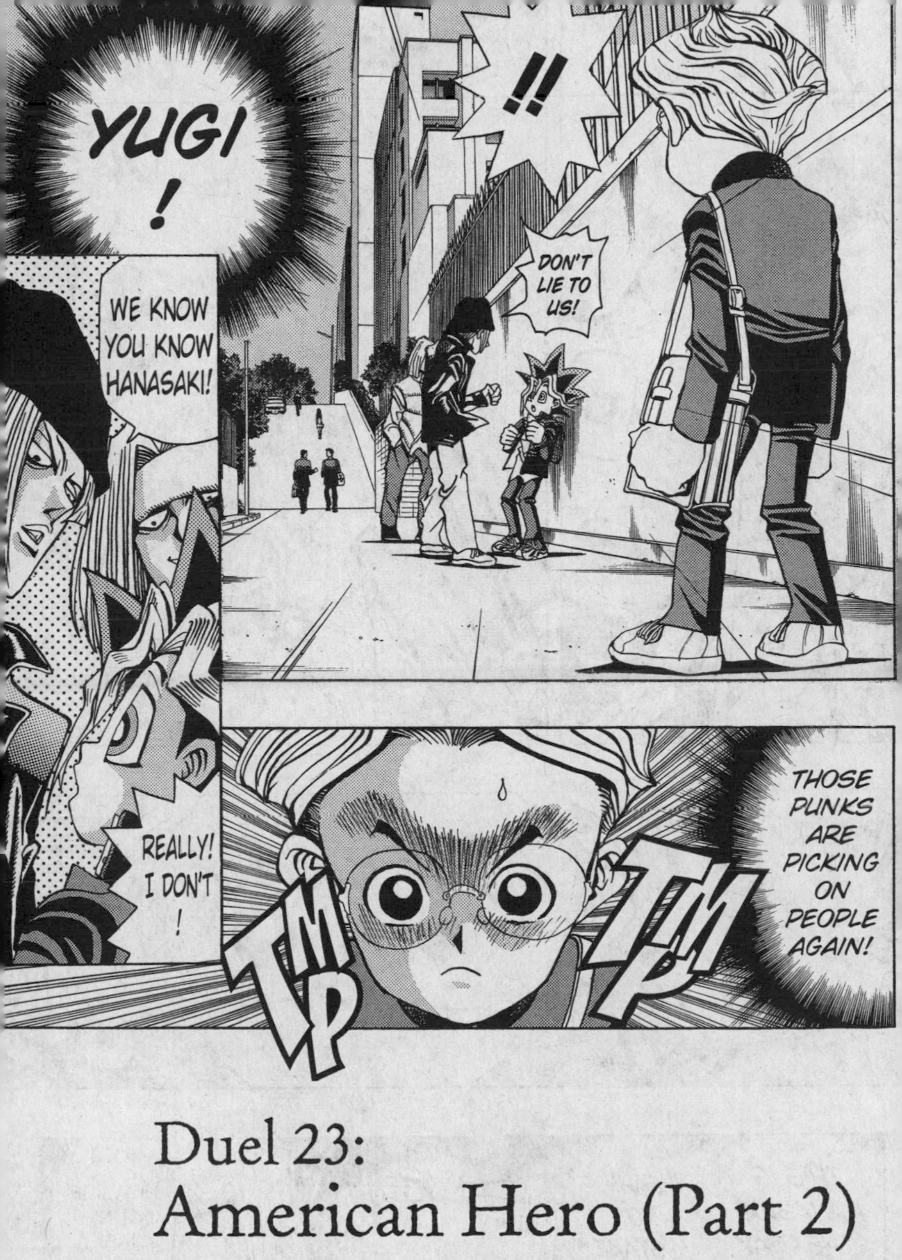
YUGI!
!!
DON'T LIE TO US!
WE KNOW YOU KNOW HANASAKI!
REALLY! I DON'T!
THOSE PUNKS ARE PICKING ON PEOPLE AGAIN!
TMP
TMP

Duel 23: American Hero (Part 2)

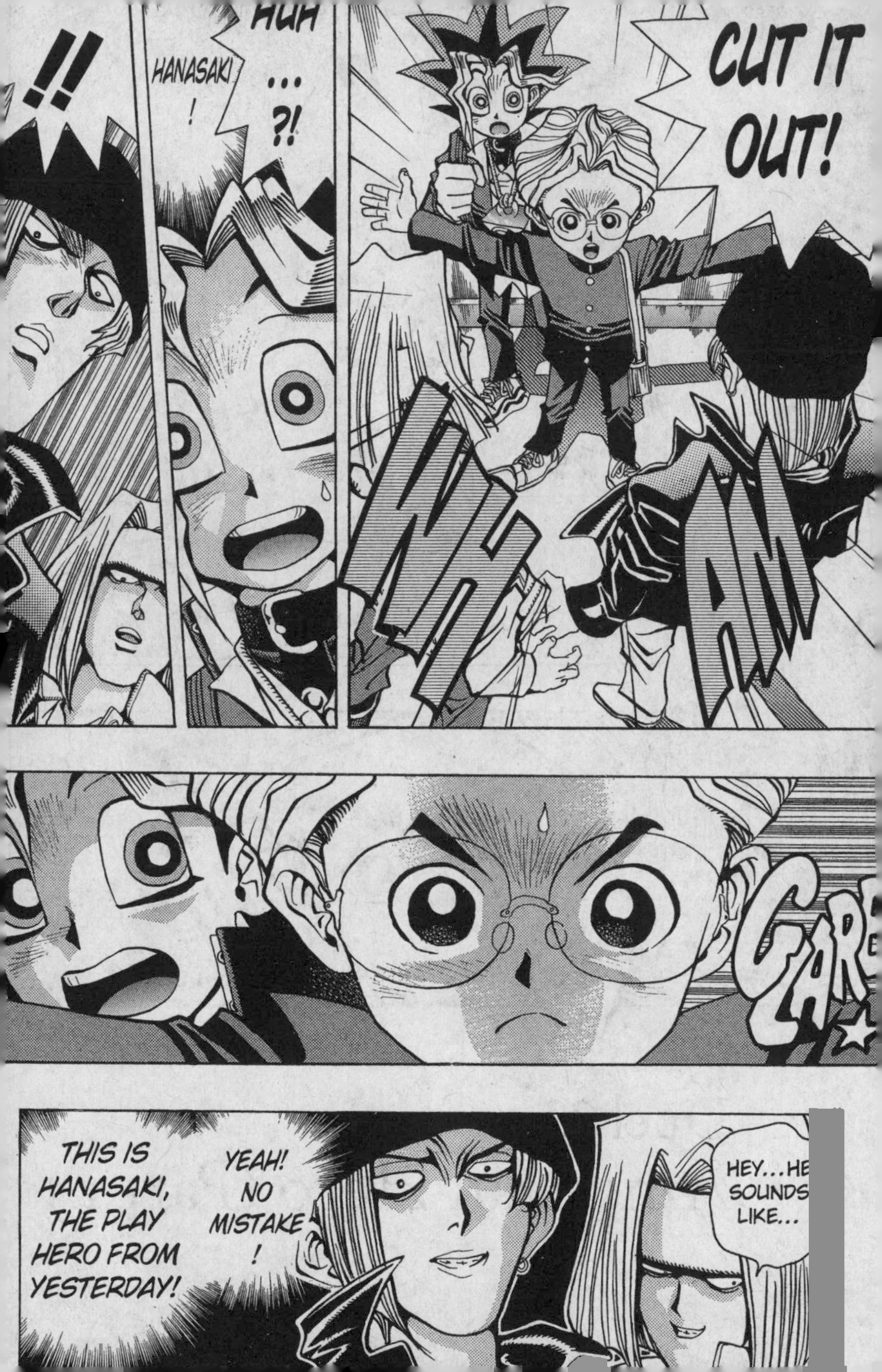

CUT IT OUT!
WHAM
HUH
...?!
HANASAKI!
!!
HEY...HE SOUNDS LIKE...
YEAH! NO MISTAKE!
THIS IS HANASAKI, THE PLAY HERO FROM YESTERDAY!

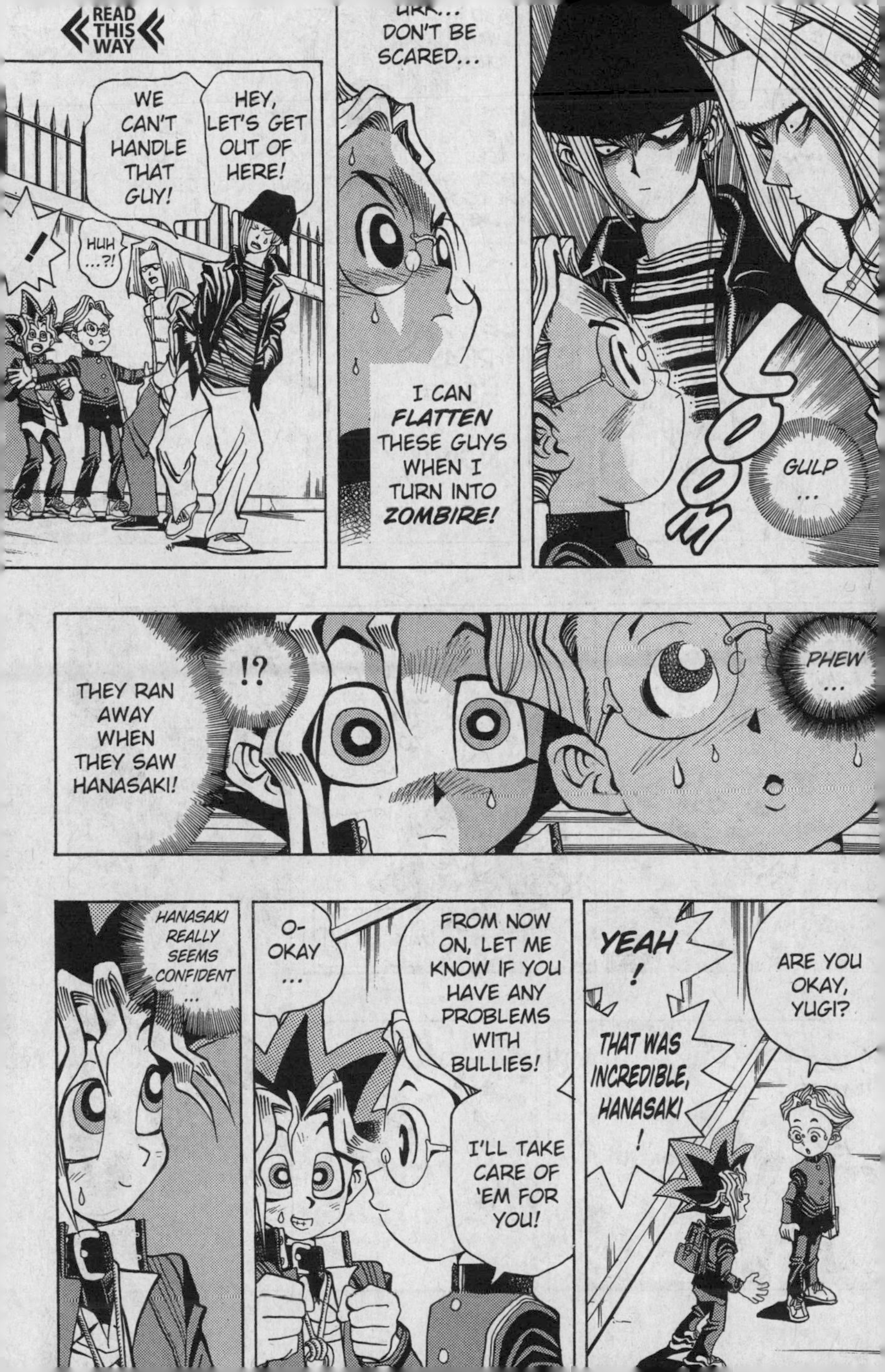
READ THIS WAY
DOOOM
GULP ...
DON'T BE SCARED...
I CAN *FLATTEN* THESE GUYS WHEN I TURN INTO *ZOMBIRE!*
HEY, LET'S GET OUT OF HERE!
WE CAN'T HANDLE THAT GUY!
HUH ...?!
!
PHEW ...
!?
THEY RAN AWAY WHEN THEY SAW HANASAKI!
ARE YOU OKAY, YUGI?
YEAH !
THAT WAS INCREDIBLE, HANASAKI !
FROM NOW ON, LET ME KNOW IF YOU HAVE ANY PROBLEMS WITH BULLIES!
I'LL TAKE CARE OF 'EM FOR YOU!
O-OKAY ...
HANASAKI REALLY SEEMS CONFIDENT ...

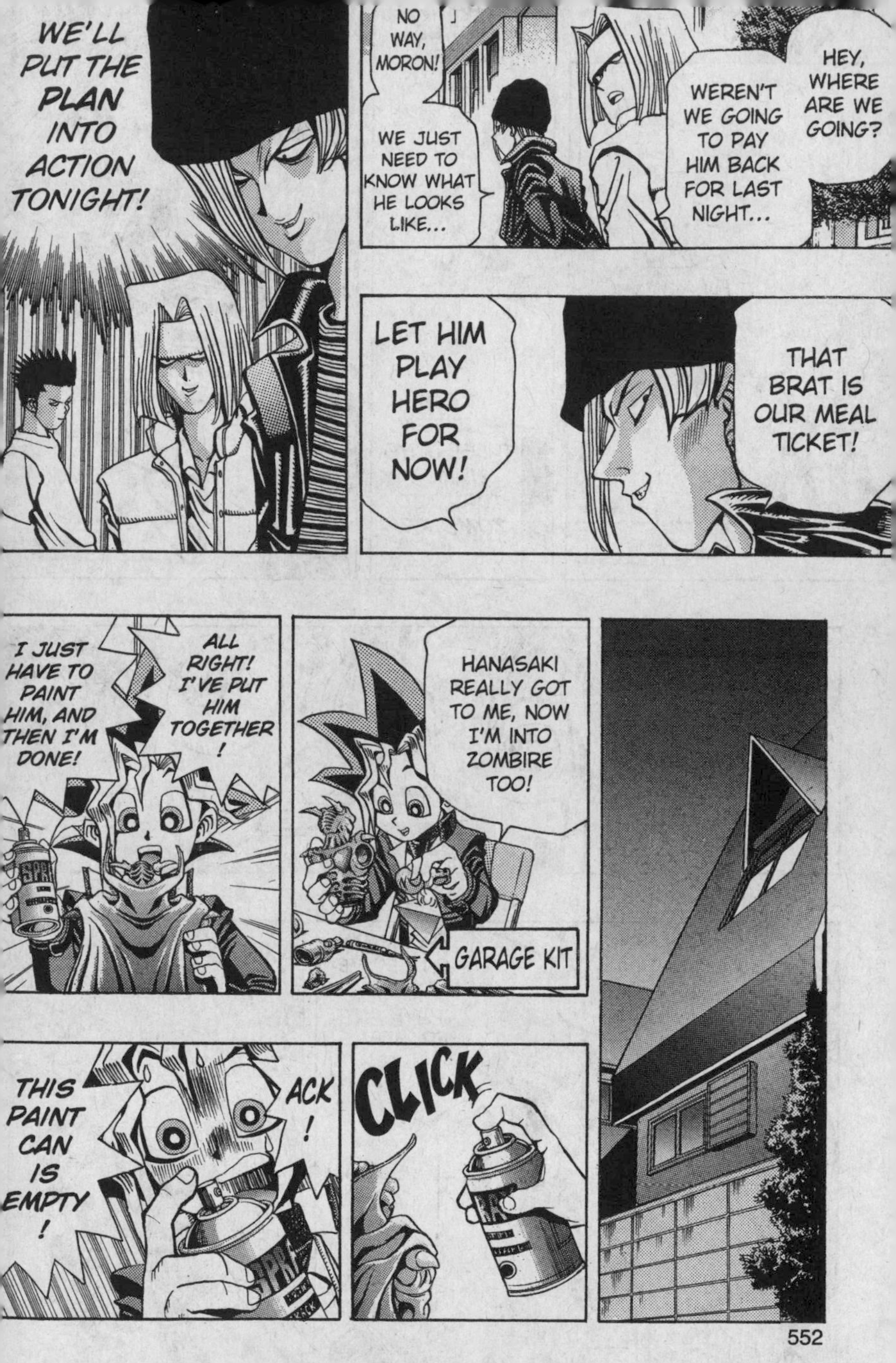
HEY, WHERE ARE WE GOING?
WEREN'T WE GOING TO PAY HIM BACK FOR LAST NIGHT...
NO WAY, MORON!
WE JUST NEED TO KNOW WHAT HE LOOKS LIKE...
THAT BRAT IS OUR MEAL TICKET!
LET HIM PLAY HERO FOR NOW!
WE'LL PUT THE PLAN INTO ACTION TONIGHT!
HANASAKI REALLY GOT TO ME, NOW I'M INTO ZOMBIRE TOO!
GARAGE KIT
ALL RIGHT! I'VE PUT HIM TOGETHER!
I JUST HAVE TO PAINT HIM, AND THEN I'M DONE!
CLICK
ACK!
THIS PAINT CAN IS EMPTY!

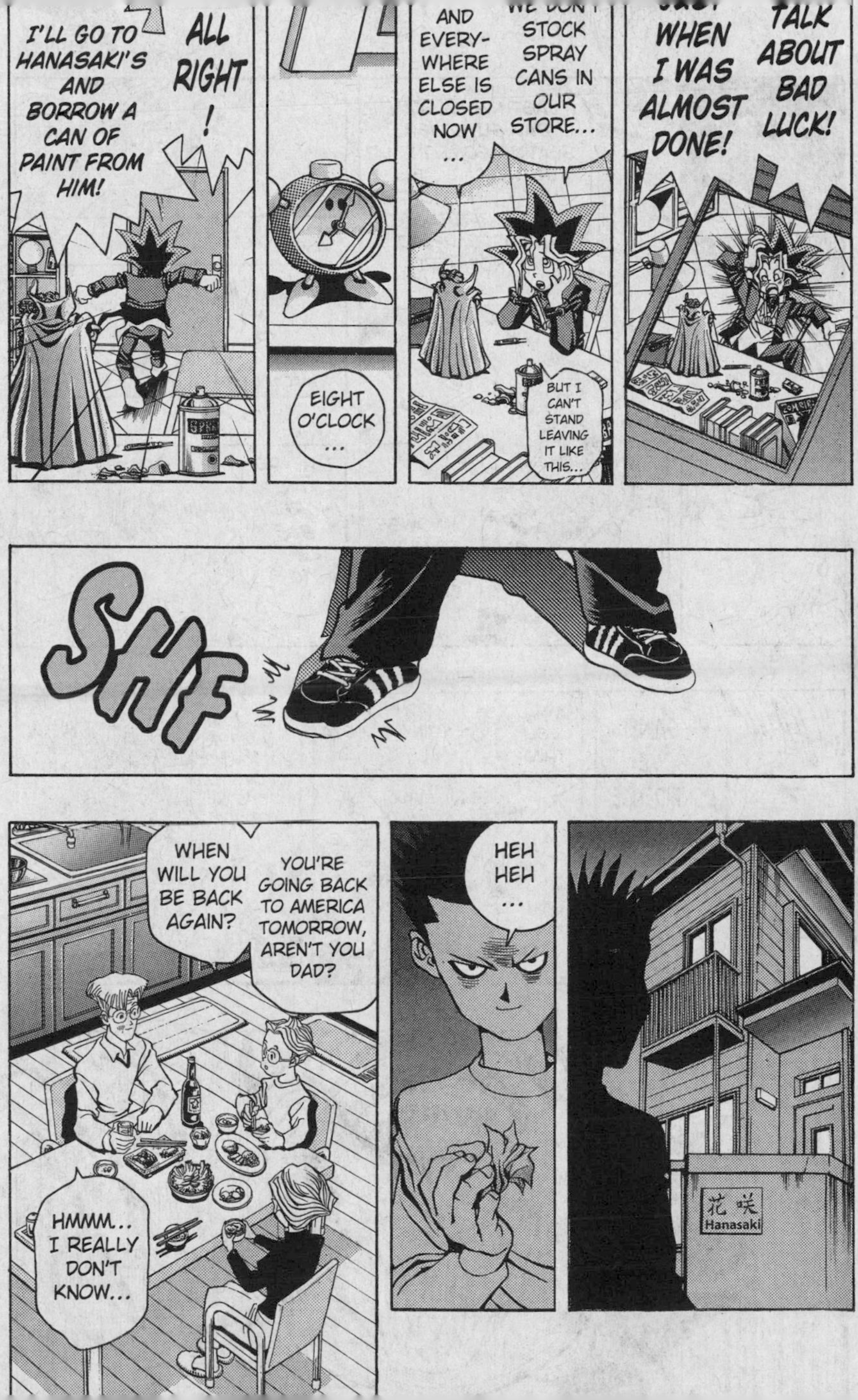
TALK ABOUT BAD LUCK!
WHEN I WAS ALMOST DONE!
STOCK SPRAY CANS IN OUR STORE...
AND EVERY-WHERE ELSE IS CLOSED NOW ...
BUT I CAN'T STAND LEAVING IT LIKE THIS...
EIGHT O'CLOCK ...
ALL RIGHT !
I'LL GO TO HANASAKI'S AND BORROW A CAN OF PAINT FROM HIM!
SHF
花咲
Hanasaki
HEH HEH ...
YOU'RE GOING BACK TO AMERICA TOMORROW, AREN'T YOU DAD?
WHEN WILL YOU BE BACK AGAIN?
HMMM.. I REALLY DON'T KNOW...

READ THIS WAY

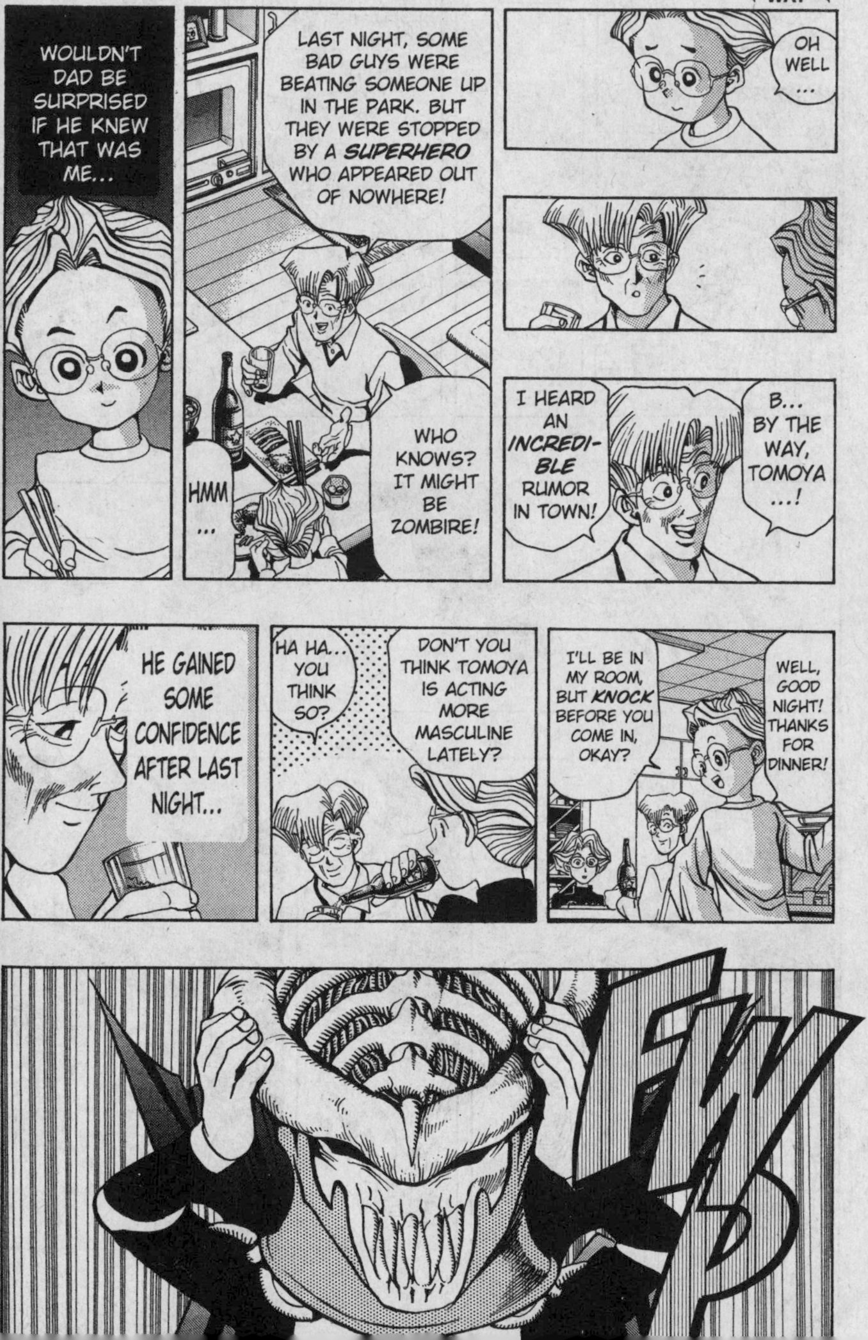
OH WELL ...
B... BY THE WAY, TOMOYA ...!
I HEARD AN INCREDIBLE RUMOR IN TOWN!
LAST NIGHT, SOME BAD GUYS WERE BEATING SOMEONE UP IN THE PARK. BUT THEY WERE STOPPED BY A SUPERHERO WHO APPEARED OUT OF NOWHERE!
WHO KNOWS? IT MIGHT BE ZOMBIRE!
HMM ...
WOULDN'T DAD BE SURPRISED IF HE KNEW THAT WAS ME...
WELL, GOOD NIGHT! THANKS FOR DINNER!
I'LL BE IN MY ROOM, BUT KNOCK BEFORE YOU COME IN, OKAY?
DON'T YOU THINK TOMOYA IS ACTING MORE MASCULINE LATELY?
HA HA... YOU THINK SO?
HE GAINED SOME CONFIDENCE AFTER LAST NIGHT...

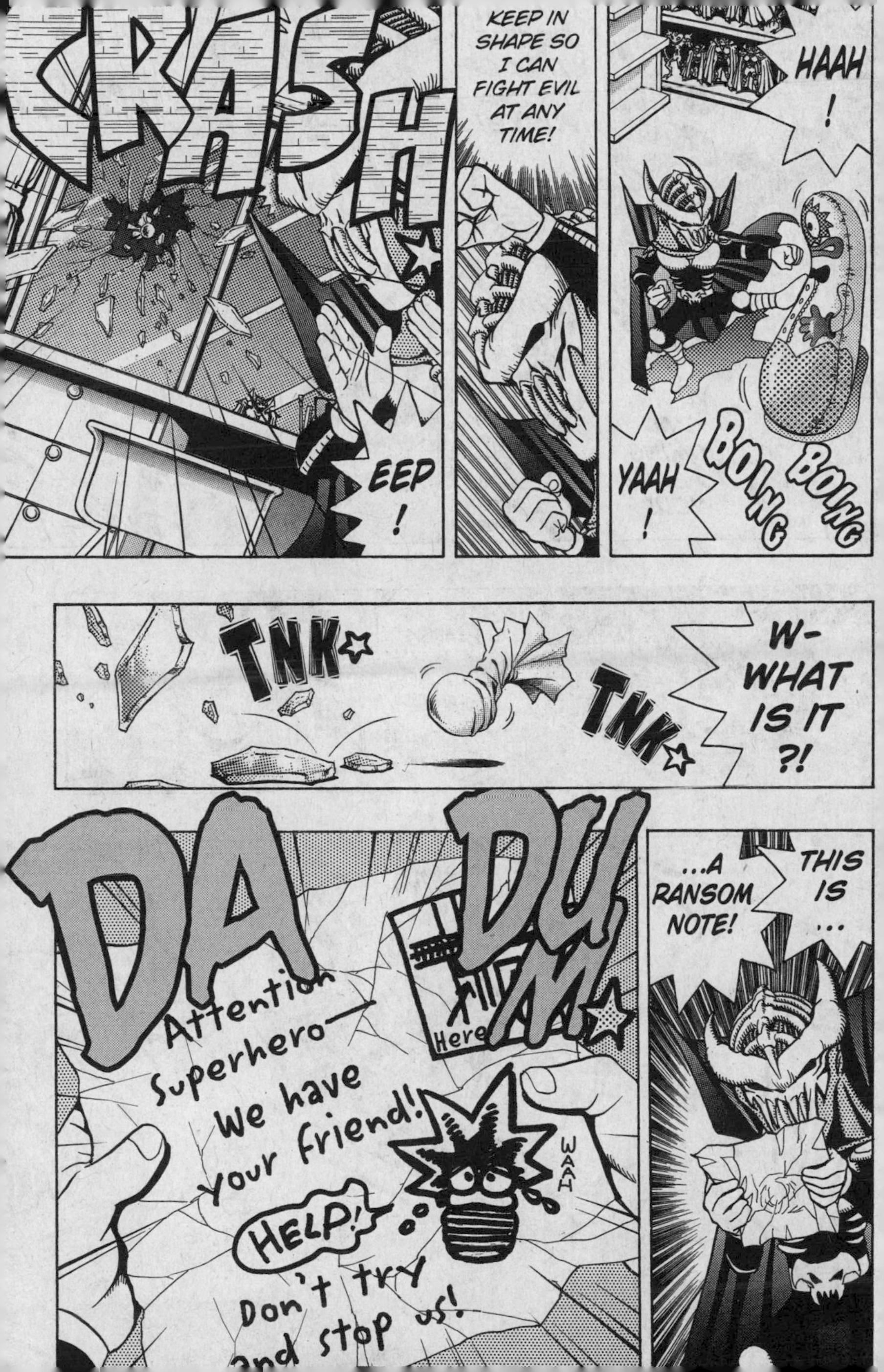
HAAH!
YAAH!
BOING
BOING
KEEP IN SHAPE SO I CAN FIGHT EVIL AT ANY TIME!
KASH
EEP!
W- WHAT IS IT ?!
TNK
TNK
THIS IS ...
...A RANSOM NOTE!
DA DUM
Attention Superhero—
We have your friend!
Here
WAAH
HELP!
Don't try and stop us!

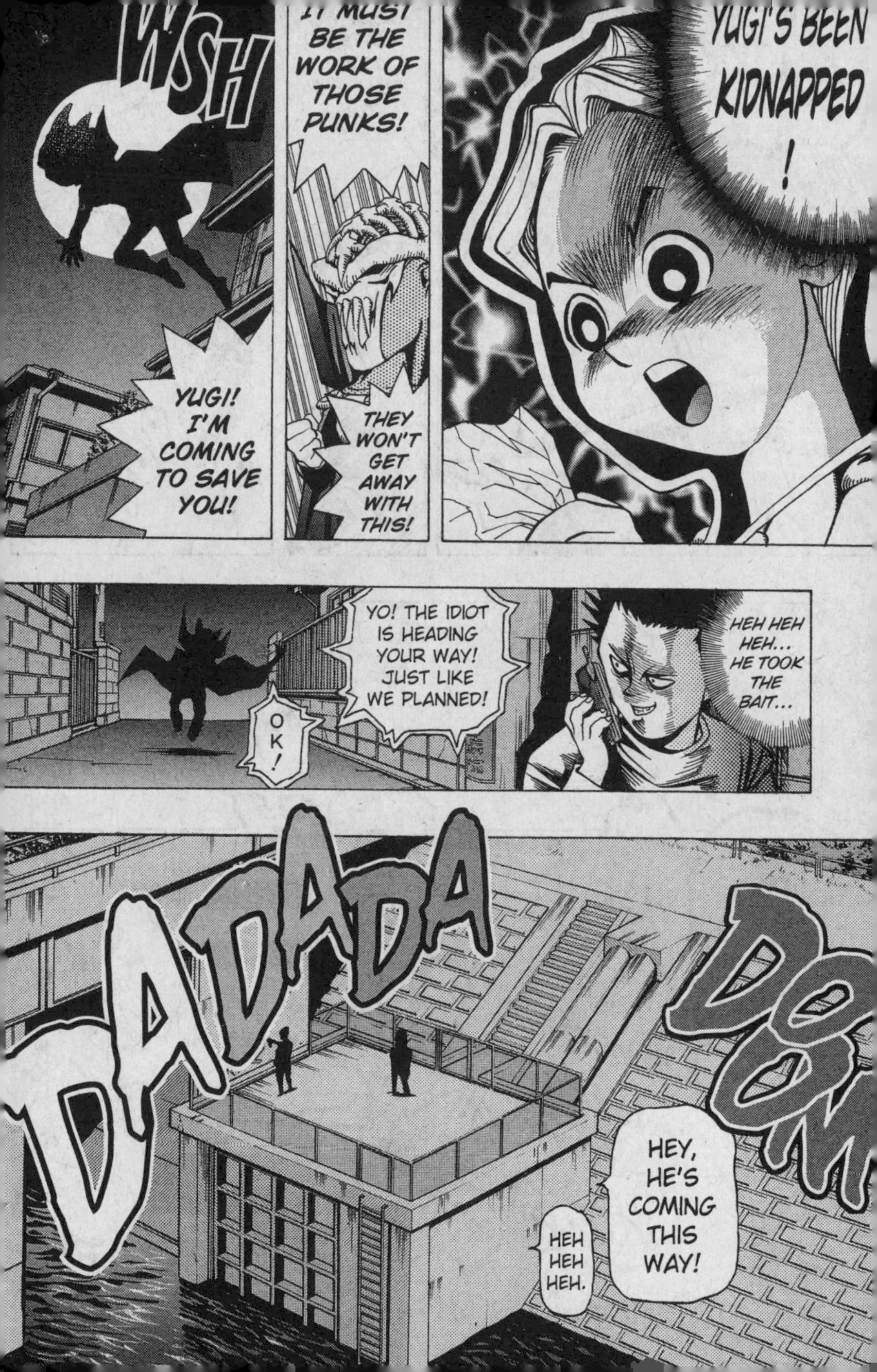
YUGI'S BEEN KIDNAPPED !
IT MUST BE THE WORK OF THOSE PUNKS!
THEY WON'T GET AWAY WITH THIS!
WSH
YUGI! I'M COMING TO SAVE YOU!
HEH HEH HEH... HE TOOK THE BAIT...
YO! THE IDIOT IS HEADING YOUR WAY! JUST LIKE WE PLANNED!
OK!
DADADA
HEY, HE'S COMING THIS WAY!
HEH HEH HEH.

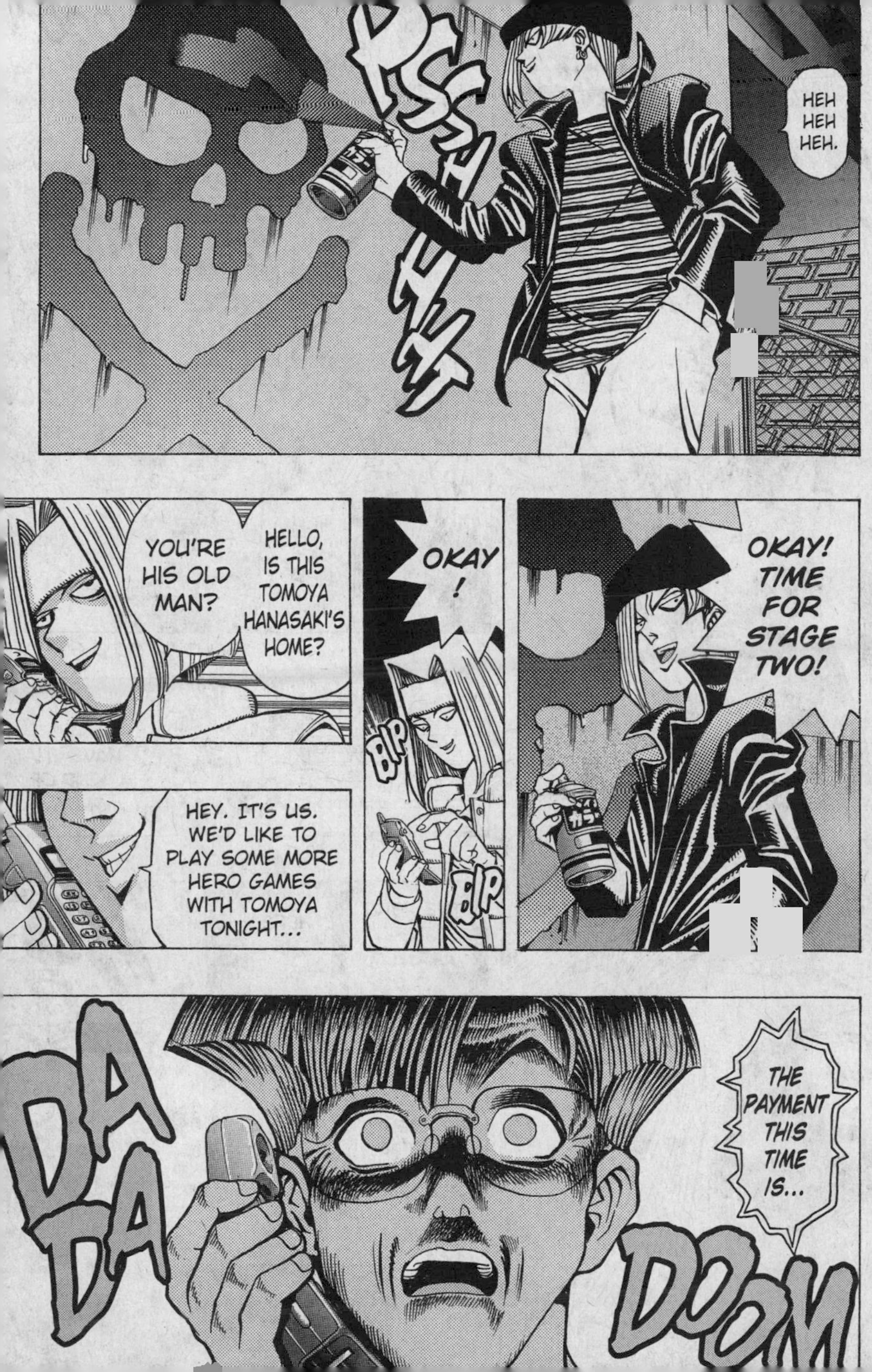
HEH HEH HEH.
OKAY! TIME FOR STAGE TWO!
OKAY!
BIP
BIP
HELLO, IS THIS TOMOYA HANASAKI'S HOME?
YOU'RE HIS OLD MAN?
HEY. IT'S US. WE'D LIKE TO PLAY SOME MORE HERO GAMES WITH TOMOYA TONIGHT...
THE PAYMENT THIS TIME IS...
DA DA
DOOM

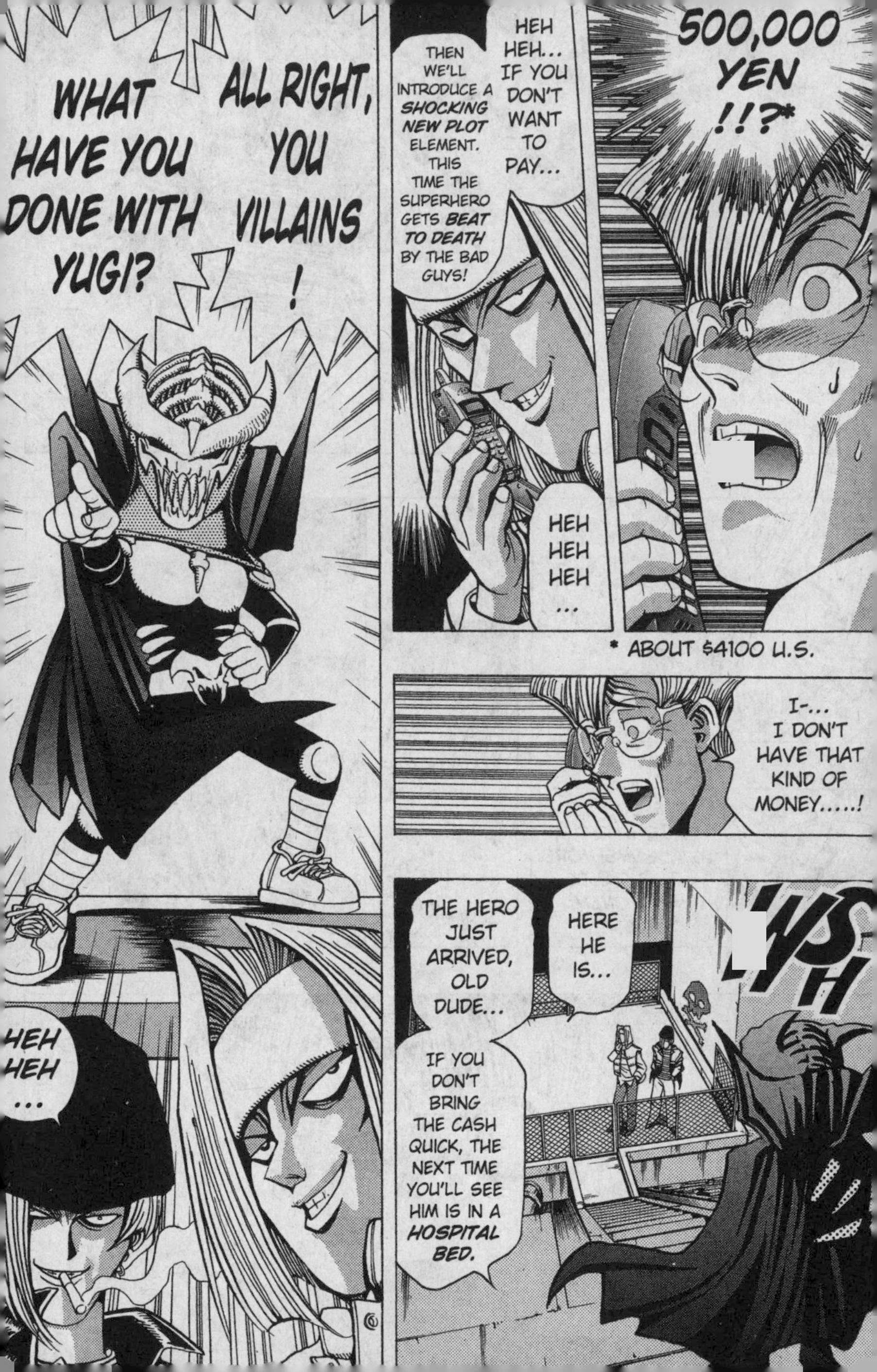
500,000 YEN!!?*
HEH HEH... IF YOU DON'T WANT TO PAY...
THEN WE'LL INTRODUCE A SHOCKING NEW PLOT ELEMENT. THIS TIME THE SUPERHERO GETS BEAT TO DEATH BY THE BAD GUYS!
HEH HEH HEH ...
* ABOUT $4100 U.S.
I-... I DON'T HAVE THAT KIND OF MONEY.....!
WSH
HERE HE IS...
THE HERO JUST ARRIVED, OLD DUDE...
IF YOU DON'T BRING THE CASH QUICK, THE NEXT TIME YOU'LL SEE HIM IS IN A HOSPITAL BED.
ALL RIGHT, YOU VILLAINS!
WHAT HAVE YOU DONE WITH YUGI?
HEH HEH ...

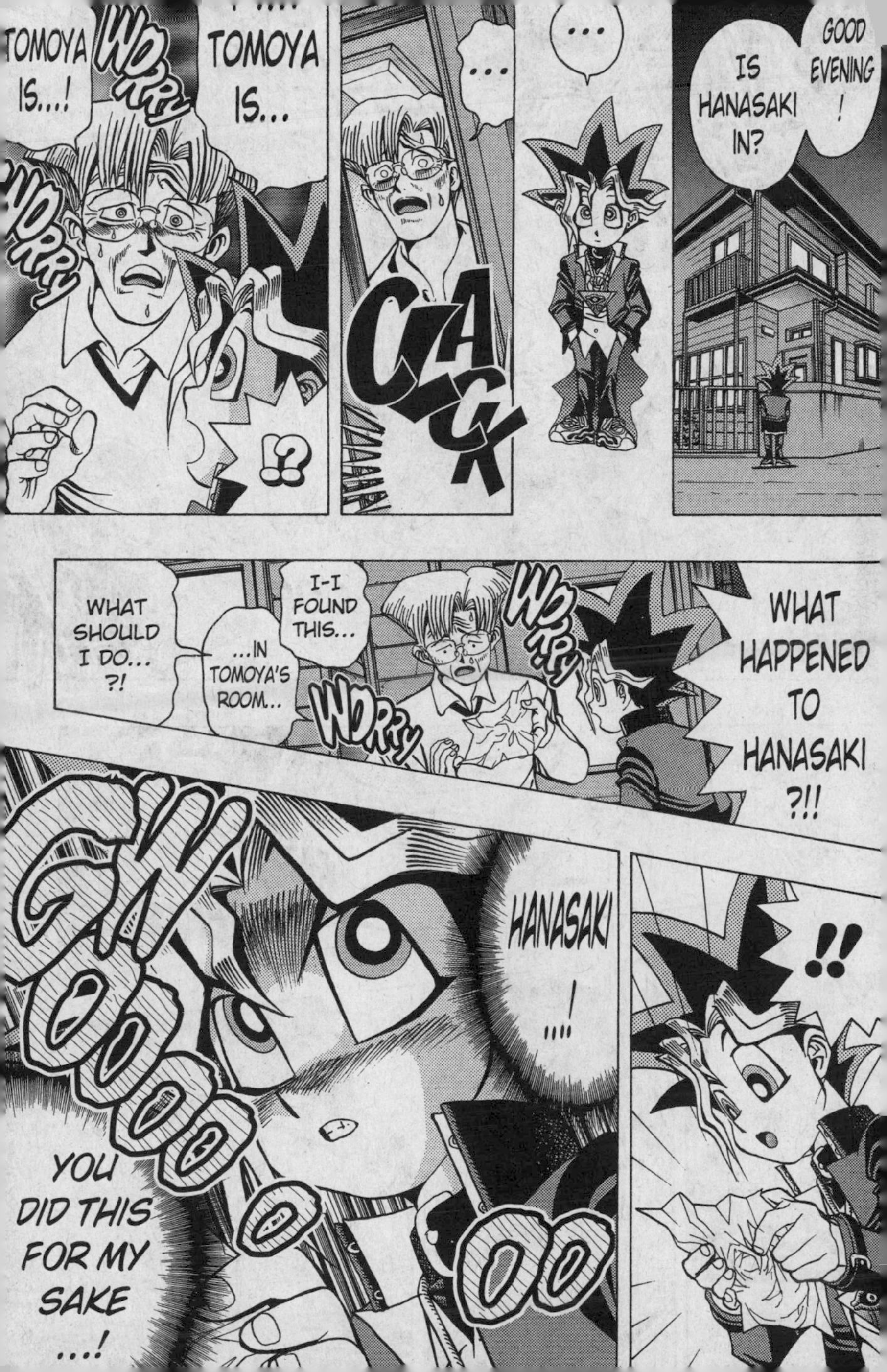
GOOD EVENING!
IS HANASAKI IN?
...
...
CLACK
TOMOYA IS...
TOMOYA IS...!
WORRY
WORRY
!?
WHAT HAPPENED TO HANASAKI?!!
I-I FOUND THIS...
...IN TOMOYA'S ROOM...
WHAT SHOULD I DO...?!
WORRY
WORRY
!!
HANASAKI...!
YOU DID THIS FOR MY SAKE...!

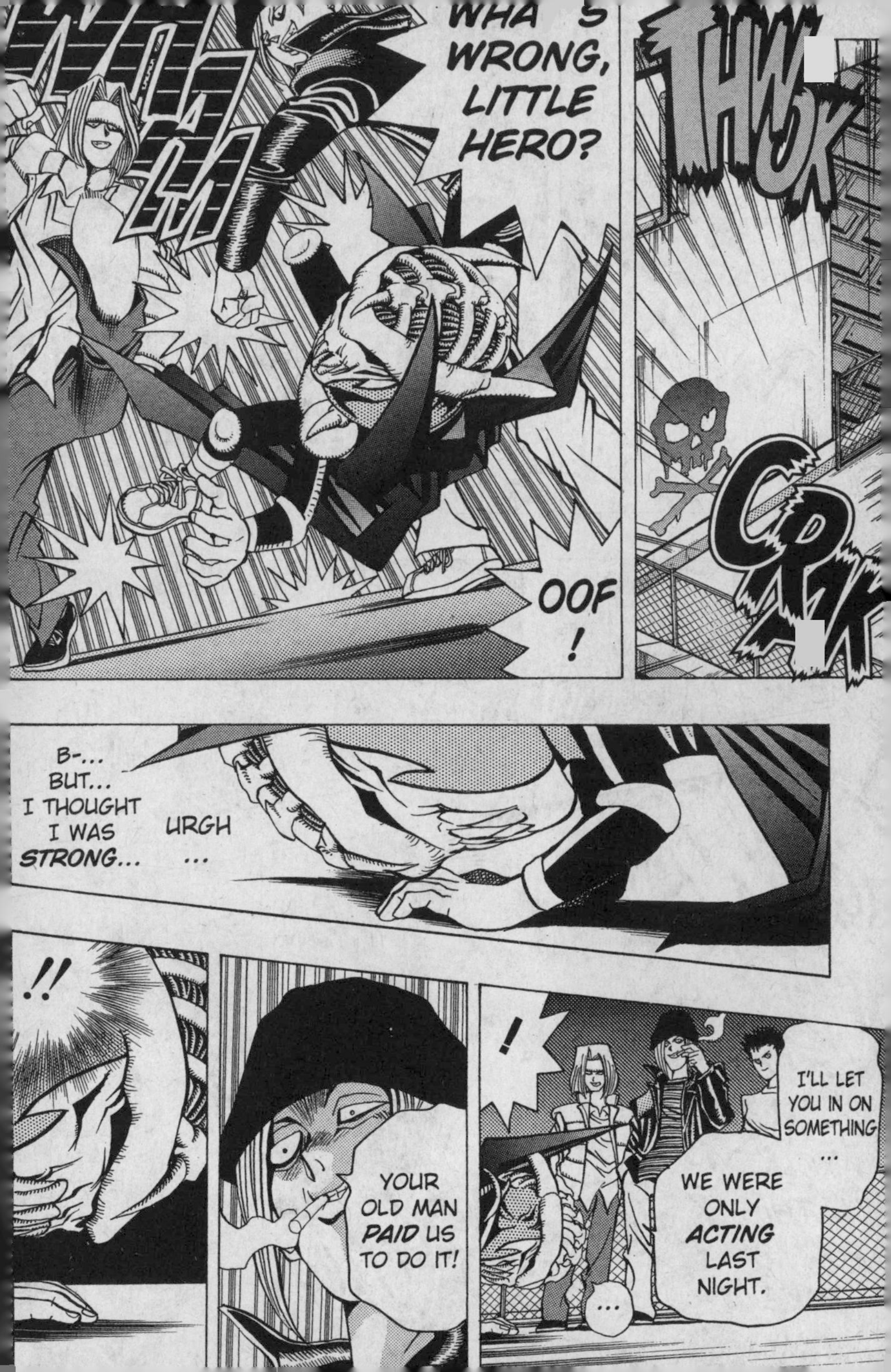
THWOK
CRAK
WHA S WRONG, LITTLE HERO?
OOF!
B-... BUT... I THOUGHT I WAS **STRONG**...
URGH ...
!
I'LL LET YOU IN ON SOMETHING ...
WE WERE ONLY **ACTING** LAST NIGHT.
...
YOUR OLD MAN **PAID** US TO DO IT!
!!

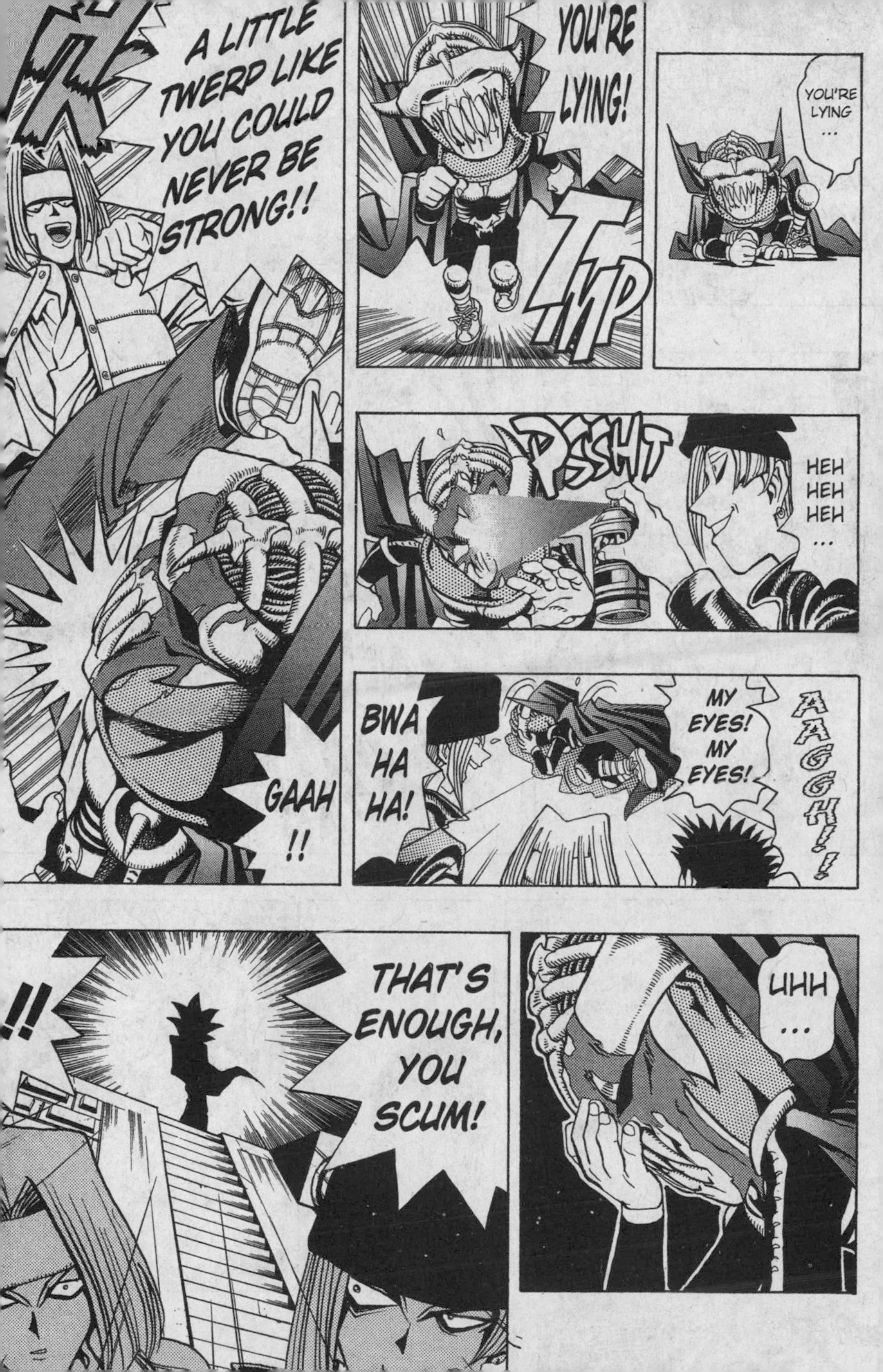
YOU'RE LYING ...
YOU'RE LYING!
TMP
PSSHT
HEH HEH HEH ...
AAGGH!!
MY EYES! MY EYES!
BWA HA HA!
A LITTLE TWERP LIKE YOU COULD NEVER BE STRONG!!
GAAH!!
UHH ...
THAT'S ENOUGH, YOU SCUM!
!!

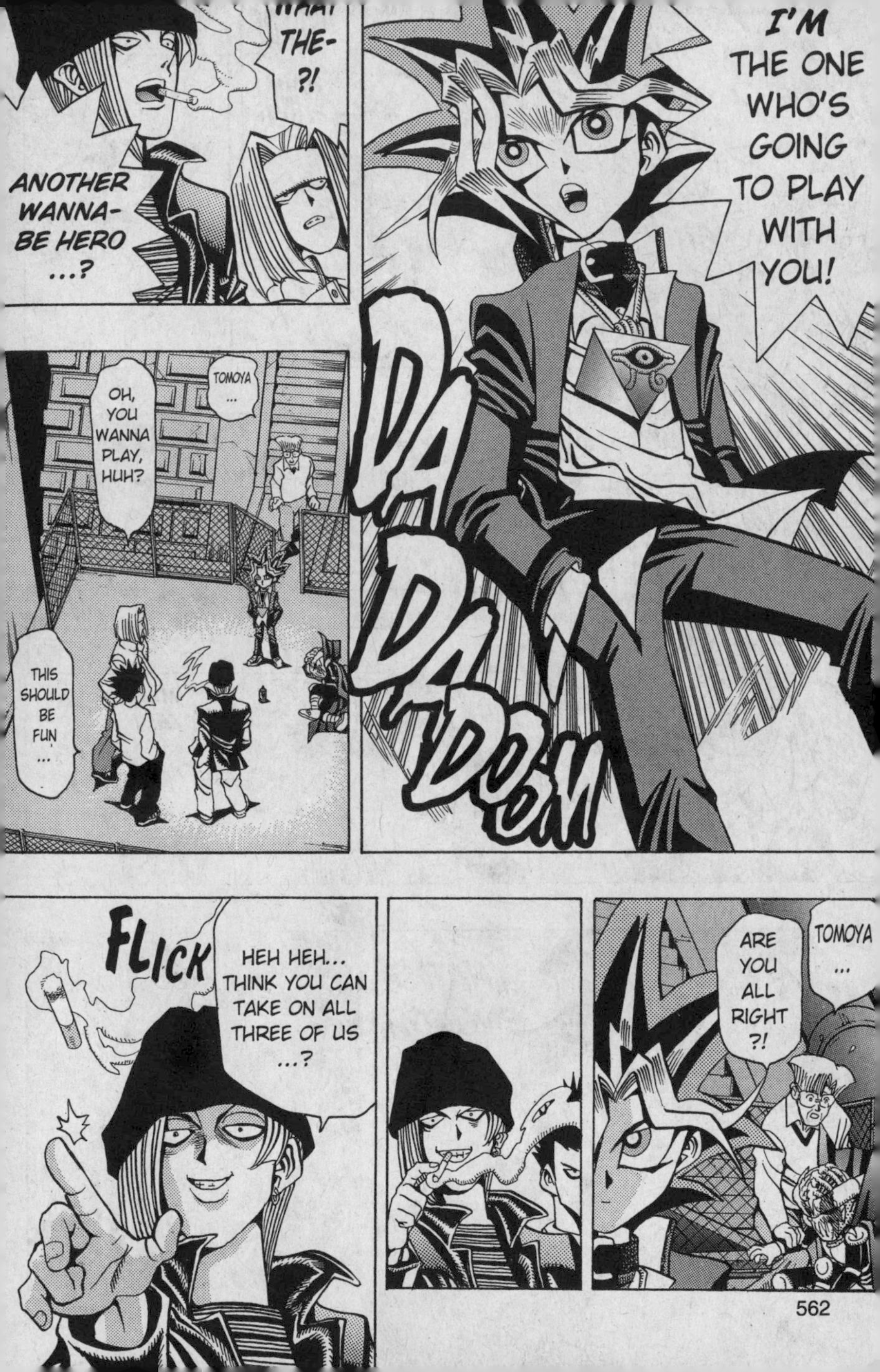
I'M THE ONE WHO'S GOING TO PLAY WITH YOU!
DA DA DOM
THE-?!
ANOTHER WANNA-BE HERO ...?
TOMOYA ...
OH, YOU WANNA PLAY, HUH?
THIS SHOULD BE FUN ...
TOMOYA ...
ARE YOU ALL RIGHT?!
FLICK
HEH HEH... THINK YOU CAN TAKE ON ALL THREE OF US ...?

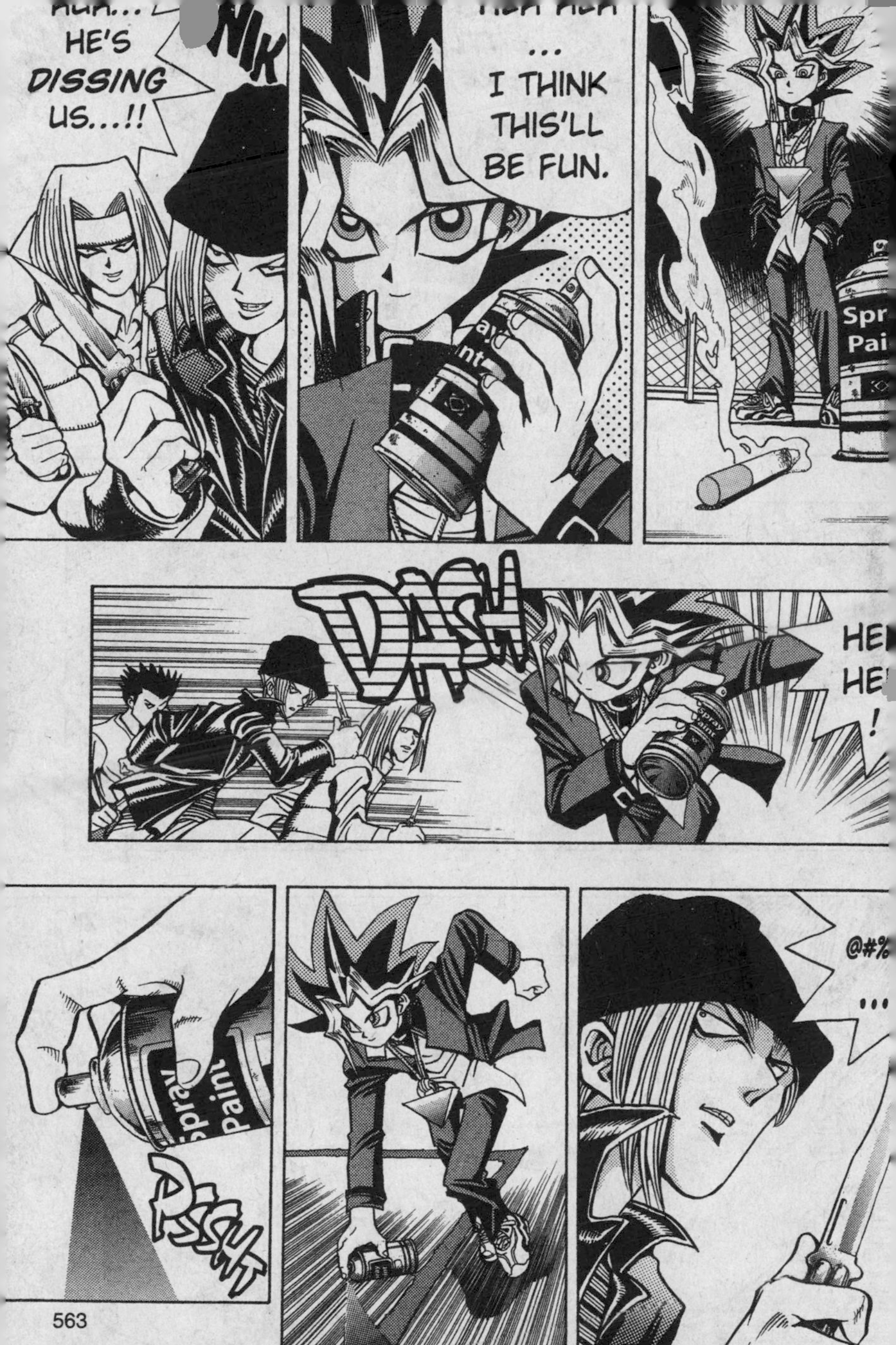
... I THINK THIS'LL BE FUN.
SNIK
HE'S DISSING US...!!
DASH
Spray Paint
@#%
...

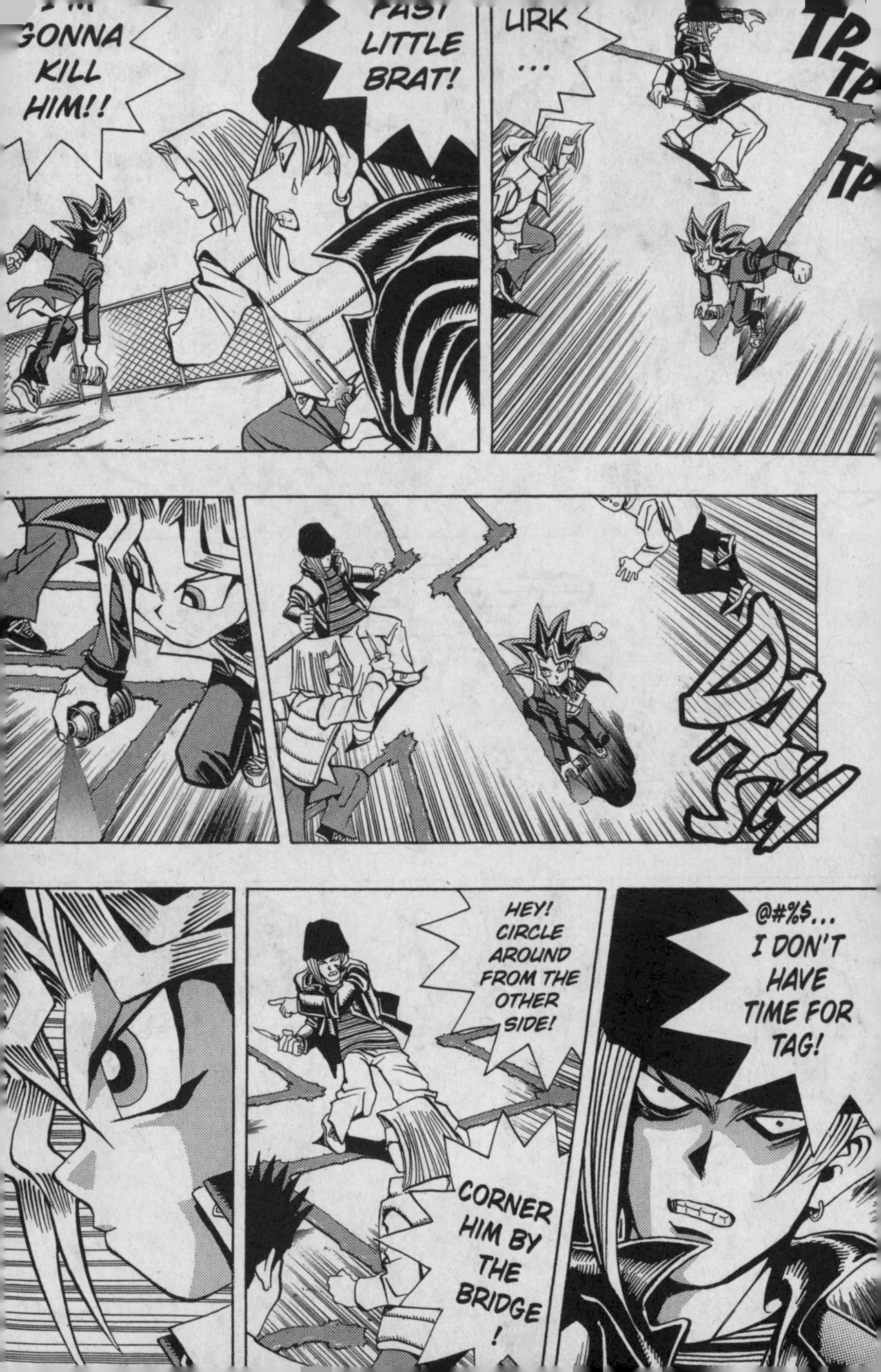

URK ...
TP TP TP
LITTLE BRAT!
GONNA KILL HIM!!
DASH
@#%$... I DON'T HAVE TIME FOR TAG!
HEY! CIRCLE AROUND FROM THE OTHER SIDE!
CORNER HIM BY THE BRIDGE!

READ THIS WAY

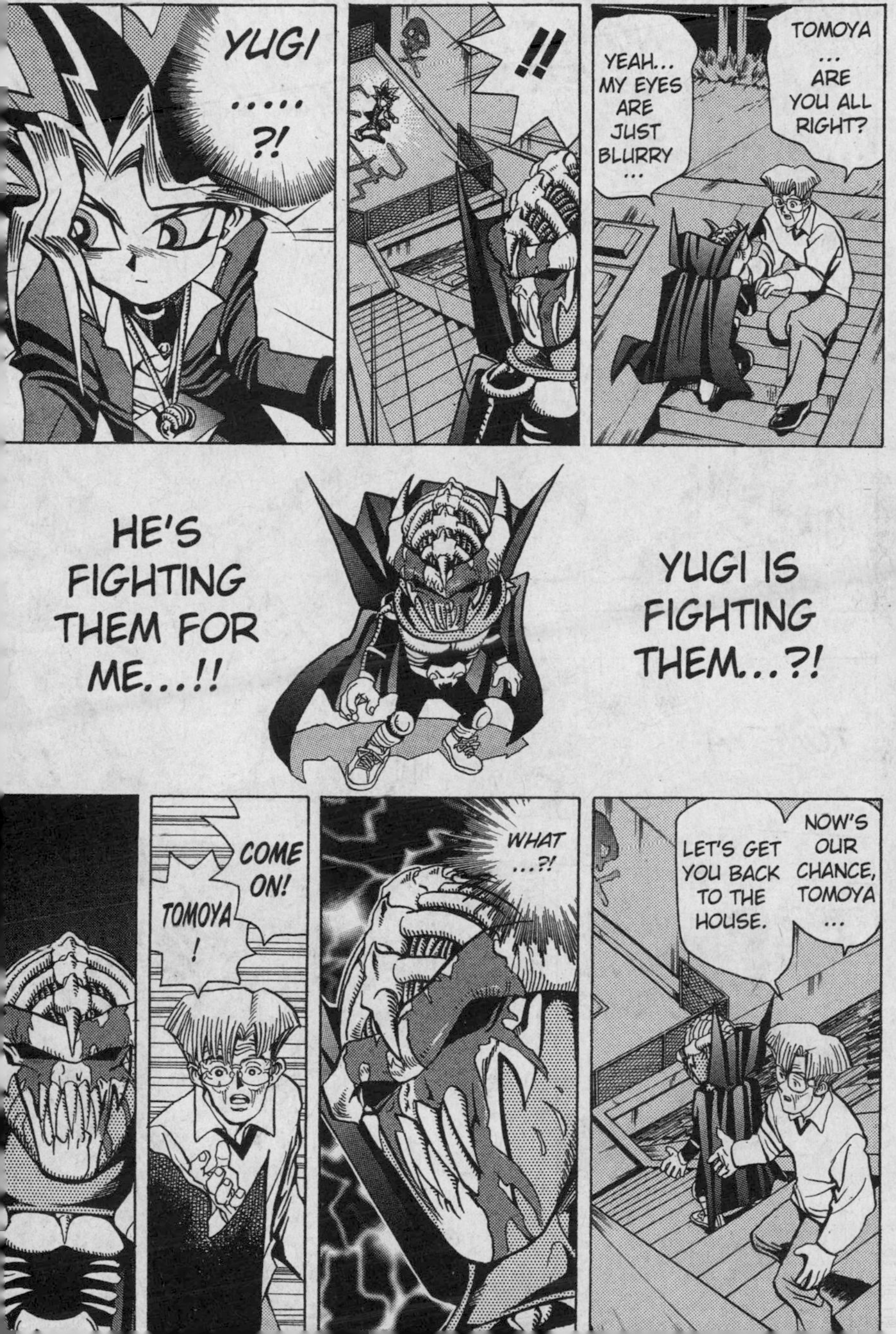

TOMOYA ... ARE YOU ALL RIGHT?
YEAH... MY EYES ARE JUST BLURRY ...
!!
YUGI ..... ?!
YUGI IS FIGHTING THEM...?!
HE'S FIGHTING THEM FOR ME...!!
NOW'S OUR CHANCE, TOMOYA ...
LET'S GET YOU BACK TO THE HOUSE.
WHAT ...?!
COME ON!
TOMOYA !

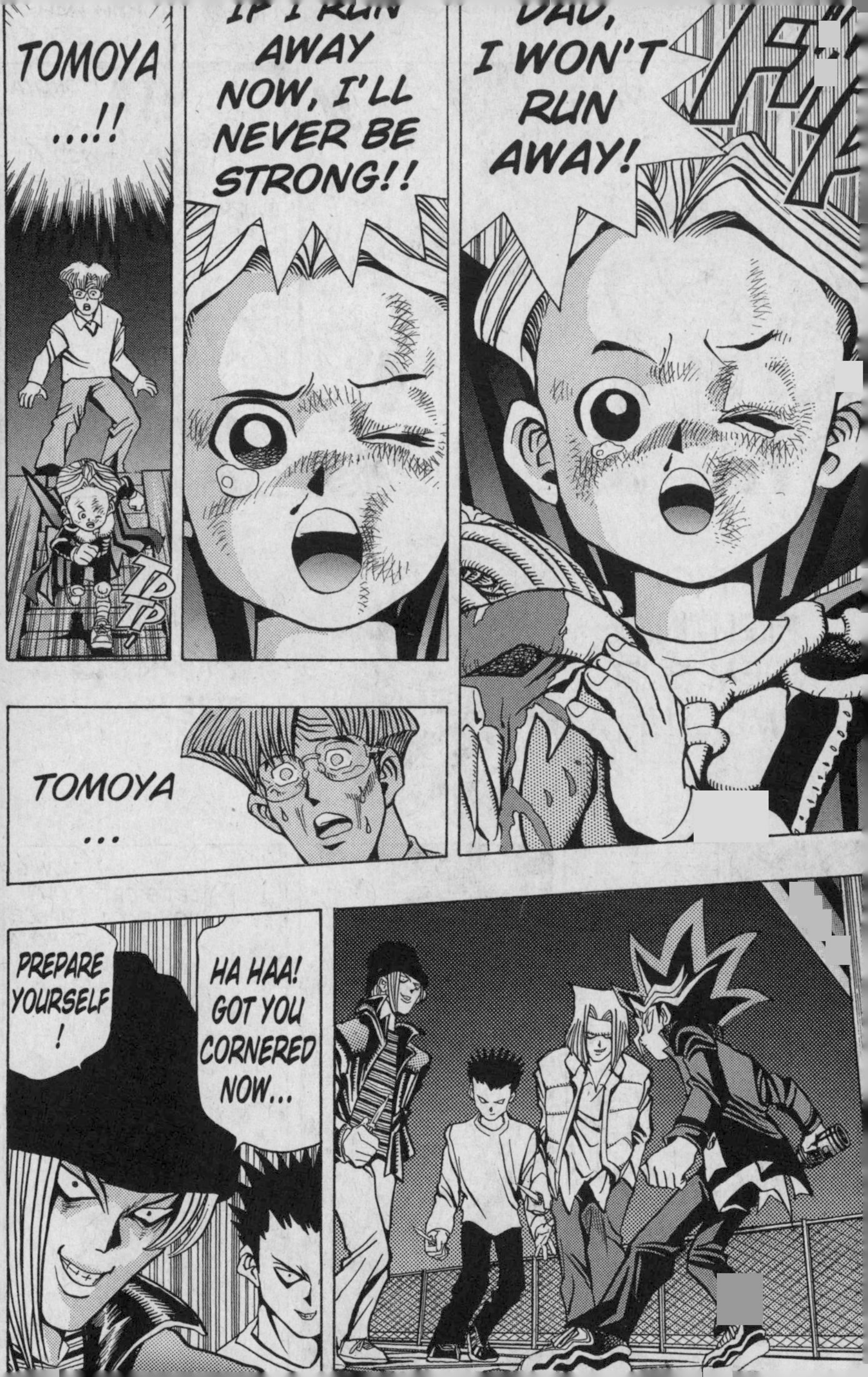
DAD, I WON'T RUN AWAY!
IF I RUN AWAY NOW, I'LL NEVER BE STRONG!!
TOMOYA ...!!
TP TP
TOMOYA ...
HA HAA! GOT YOU CORNERED NOW...
PREPARE YOURSELF!

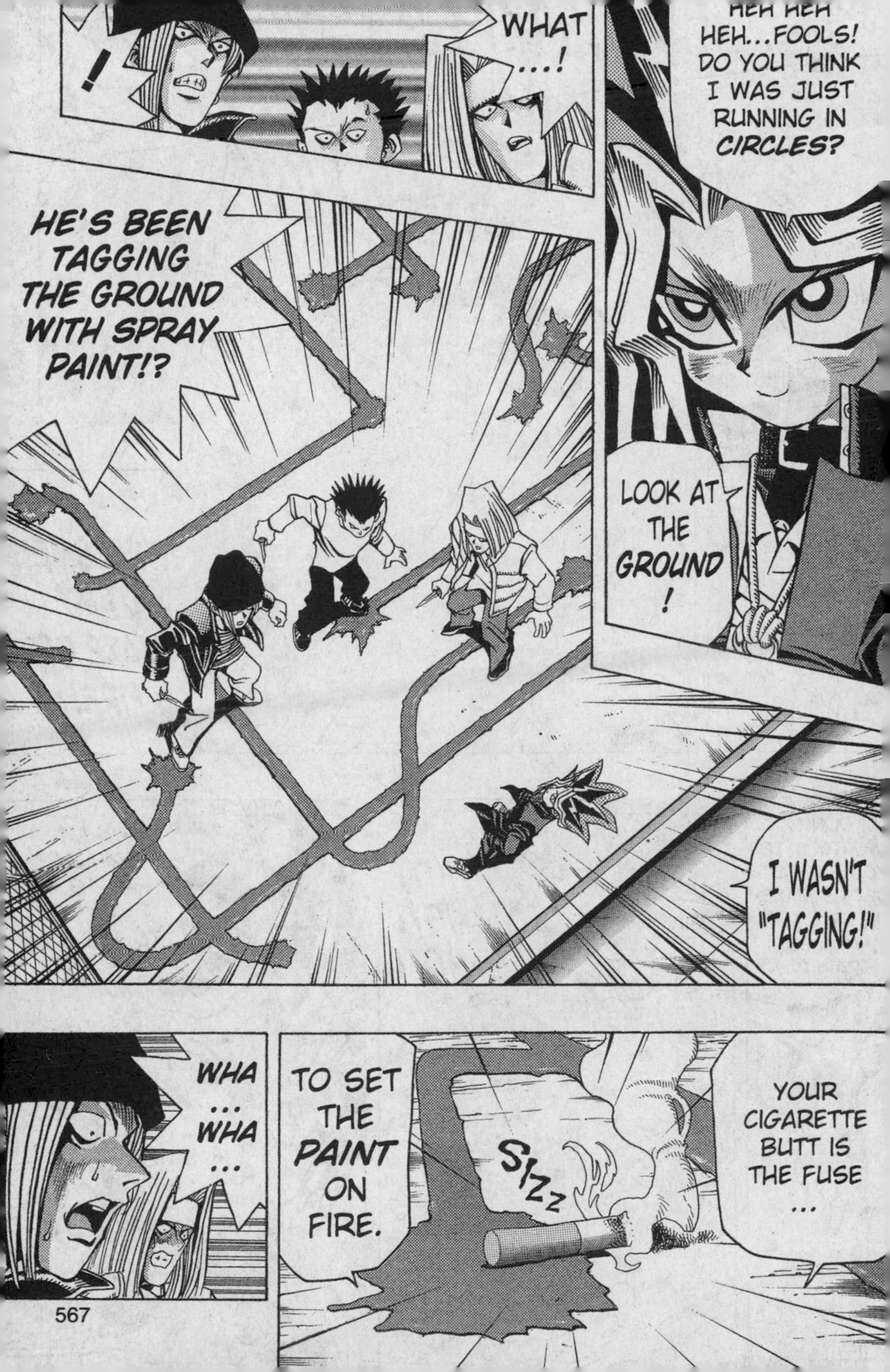
HEH HEH HEH...FOOLS! DO YOU THINK I WAS JUST RUNNING IN CIRCLES?
LOOK AT THE GROUND!
!
WHAT...!
HE'S BEEN TAGGING THE GROUND WITH SPRAY PAINT!?
I WASN'T "TAGGING!"
YOUR CIGARETTE BUTT IS THE FUSE...
SIZZ
TO SET THE PAINT ON FIRE.
WHA...WHA...

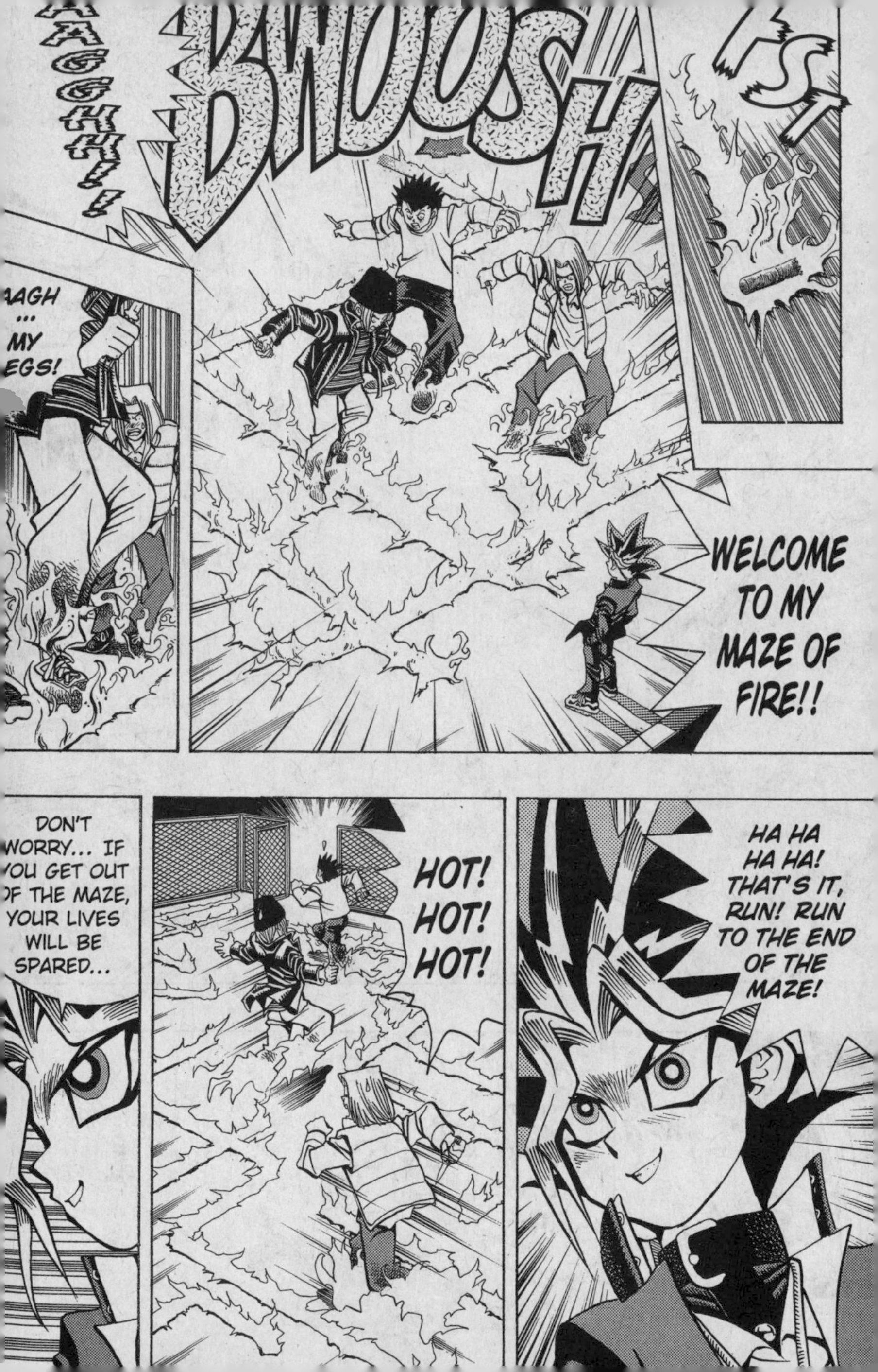
BWOOSH
WELCOME TO MY MAZE OF FIRE!!
AGGHH!!
AAGH ... MY EGS!
HA HA HA HA! THAT'S IT, RUN! RUN TO THE END OF THE MAZE!
HOT! HOT! HOT!
DON'T WORRY... IF OU GET OUT F THE MAZE, YOUR LIVES WILL BE SPARED...

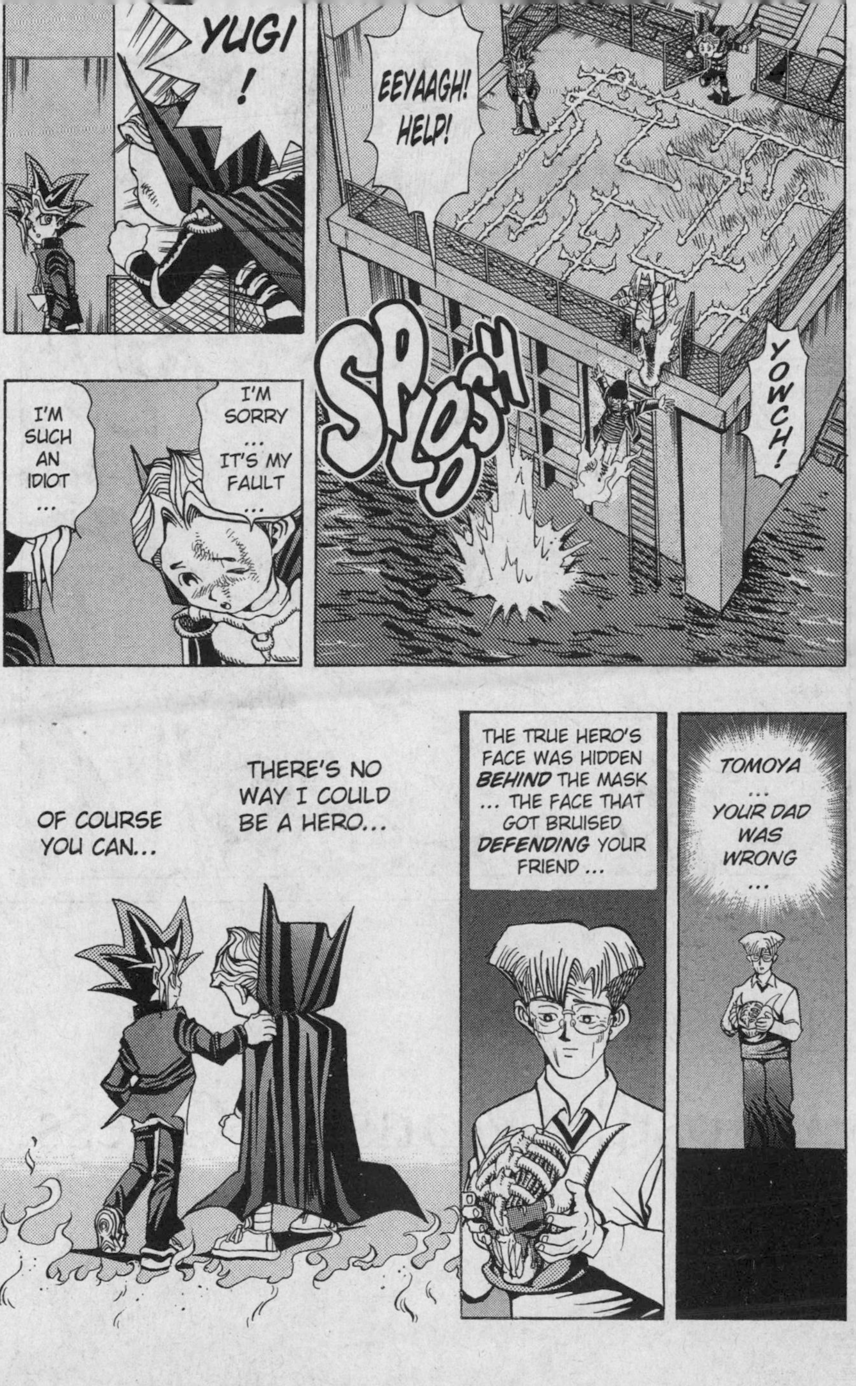
EEYAAGH! HELP!
YOWCH!
SPLOSH
YUGI !
I'M SORRY ... IT'S MY FAULT ...
I'M SUCH AN IDIOT ...
TOMOYA ... YOUR DAD WAS WRONG ...
THE TRUE HERO'S FACE WAS HIDDEN BEHIND THE MASK ... THE FACE THAT GOT BRUISED DEFENDING YOUR FRIEND ...
THERE'S NO WAY I COULD BE A HERO...
OF COURSE YOU CAN...

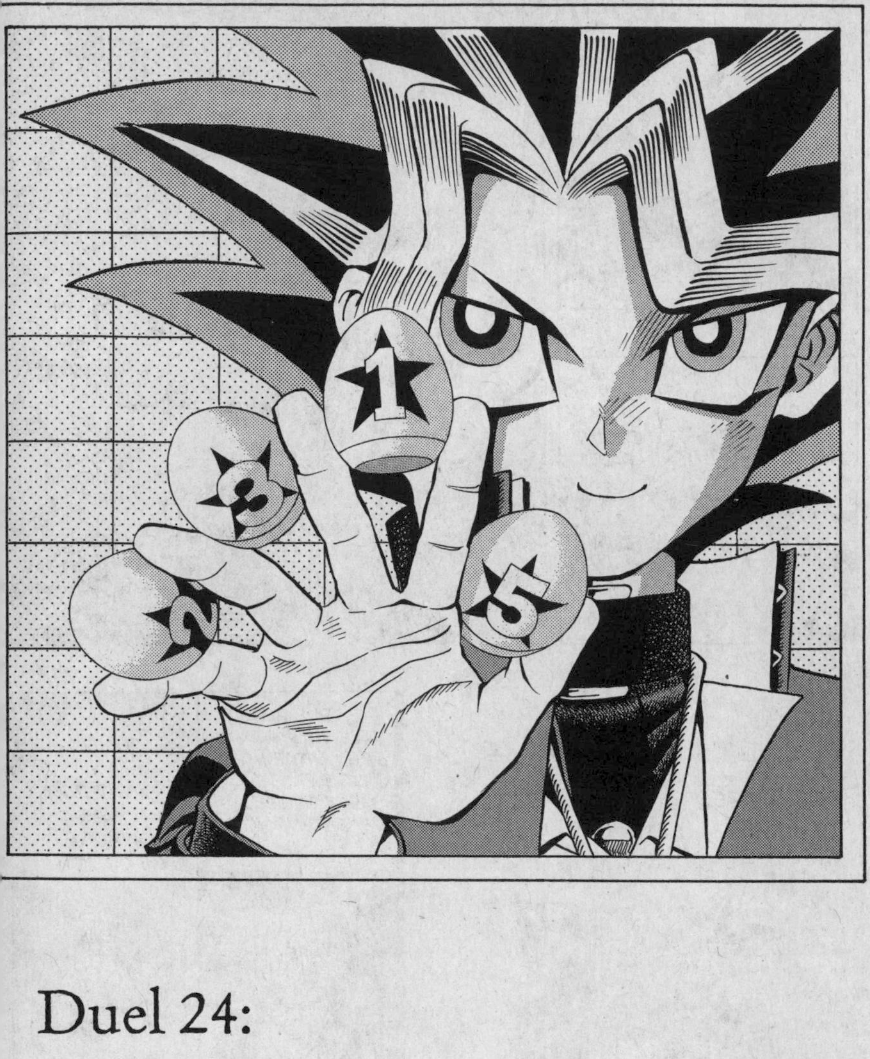
1
3
2
5

Duel 24:
Capsule Monster Chess

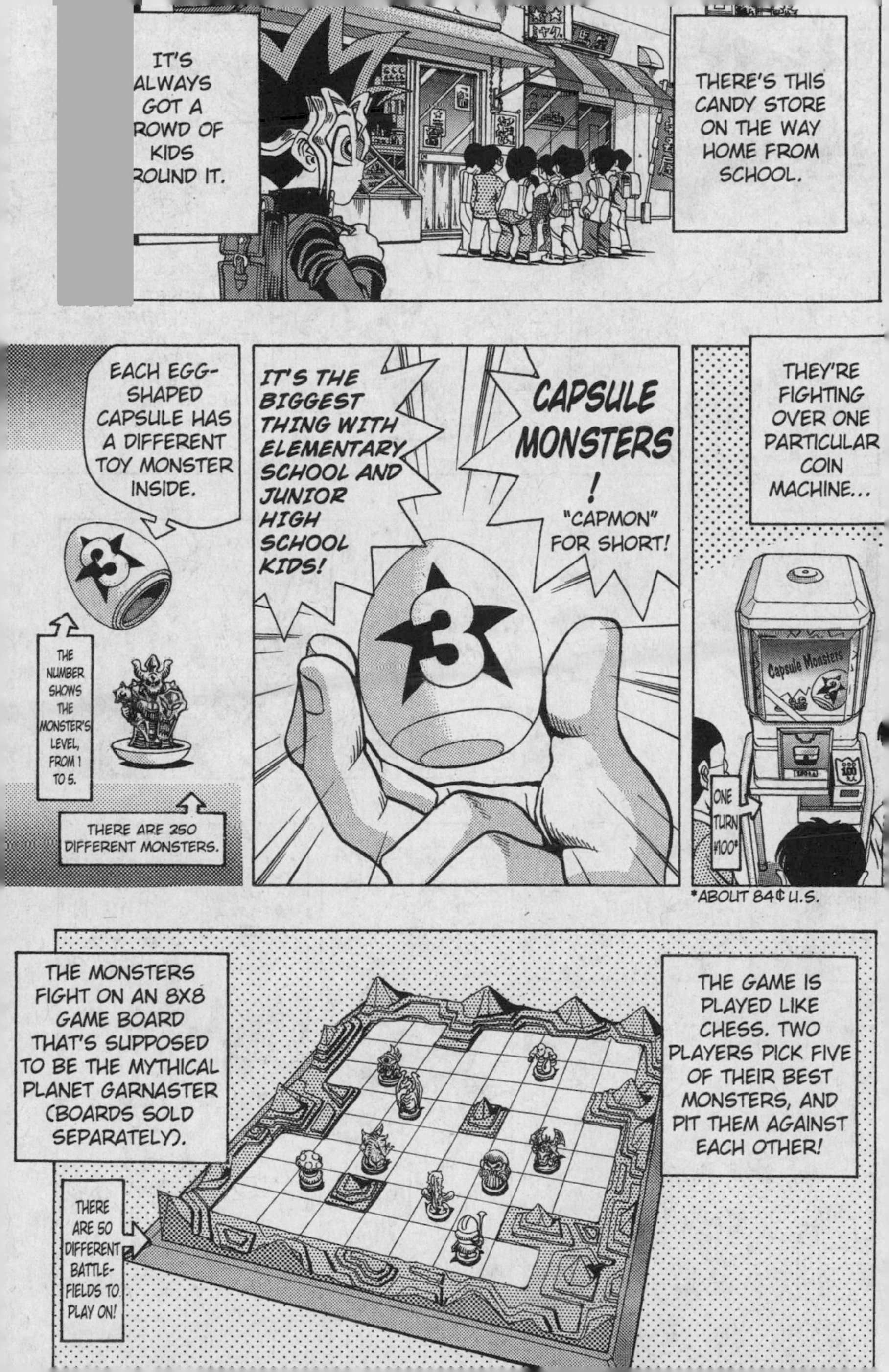
THERE'S THIS CANDY STORE ON THE WAY HOME FROM SCHOOL.
IT'S ALWAYS GOT A ROWD OF KIDS ROUND IT.
THEY'RE FIGHTING OVER ONE PARTICULAR COIN MACHINE...
Capsule Monsters
ONE TURN ¥100*
CAPSULE MONSTERS!
"CAPMON" FOR SHORT!
IT'S THE BIGGEST THING WITH ELEMENTARY SCHOOL AND JUNIOR HIGH SCHOOL KIDS!
EACH EGG-SHAPED CAPSULE HAS A DIFFERENT TOY MONSTER INSIDE.
THE NUMBER SHOWS THE MONSTER'S LEVEL, FROM 1 TO 5.
THERE ARE 250 DIFFERENT MONSTERS.
*ABOUT 84¢ U.S.
THE GAME IS PLAYED LIKE CHESS. TWO PLAYERS PICK FIVE OF THEIR BEST MONSTERS, AND PIT THEM AGAINST EACH OTHER!
THE MONSTERS FIGHT ON AN 8X8 GAME BOARD THAT'S SUPPOSED TO BE THE MYTHICAL PLANET GARNASTER (BOARDS SOLD SEPARATELY).
THERE ARE 50 DIFFERENT BATTLE-FIELDS TO PLAY ON!

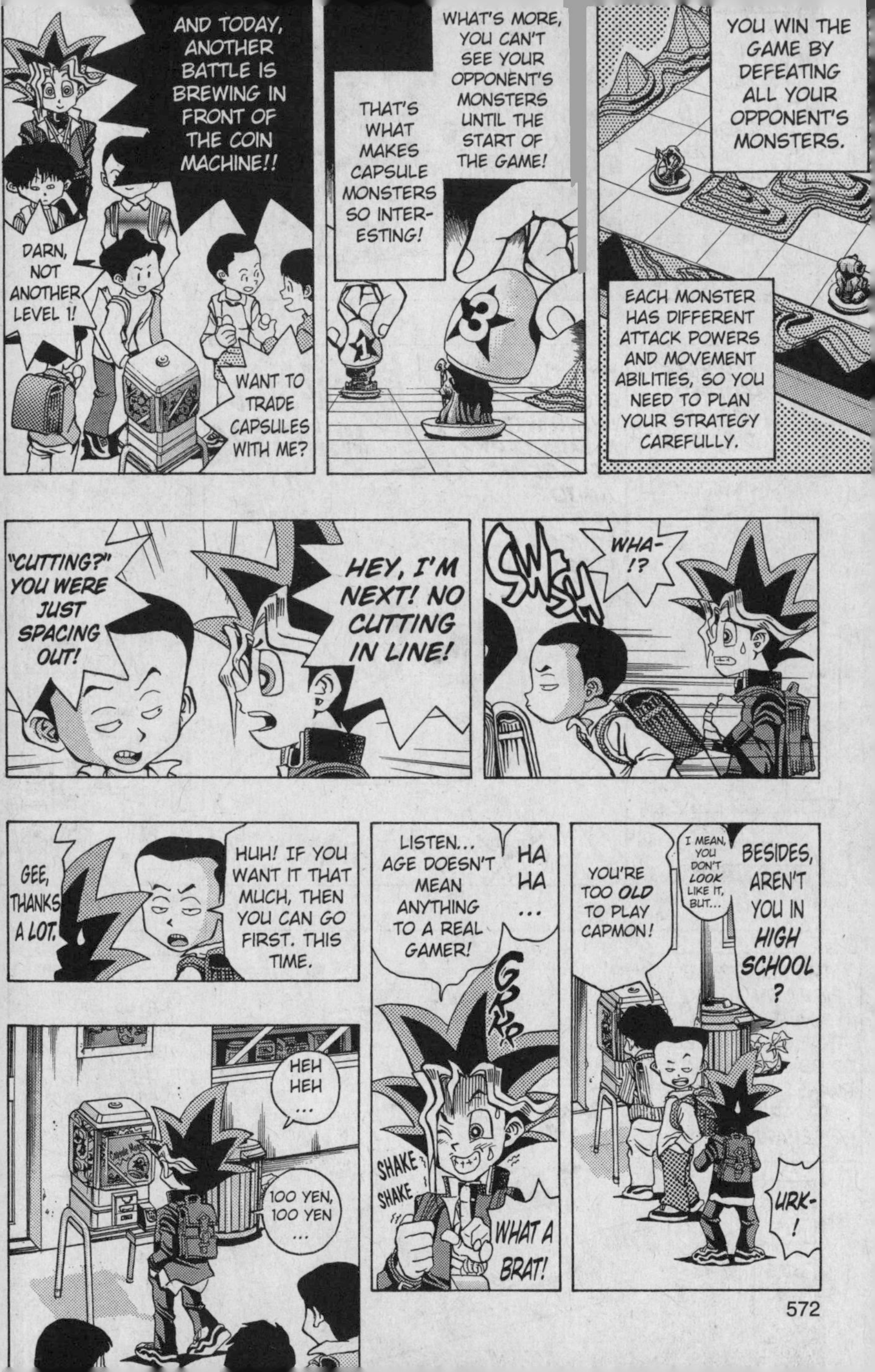
YOU WIN THE GAME BY DEFEATING ALL YOUR OPPONENT'S MONSTERS.
EACH MONSTER HAS DIFFERENT ATTACK POWERS AND MOVEMENT ABILITIES, SO YOU NEED TO PLAN YOUR STRATEGY CAREFULLY.
WHAT'S MORE, YOU CAN'T SEE YOUR OPPONENT'S MONSTERS UNTIL THE START OF THE GAME!
THAT'S WHAT MAKES CAPSULE MONSTERS SO INTERESTING!
AND TODAY, ANOTHER BATTLE IS BREWING IN FRONT OF THE COIN MACHINE!!
DARN, NOT ANOTHER LEVEL 1!
WANT TO TRADE CAPSULES WITH ME?
WHA-!?
HEY, I'M NEXT! NO CUTTING IN LINE!
"CUTTING?" YOU WERE JUST SPACING OUT!
BESIDES, AREN'T YOU IN HIGH SCHOOL?
I MEAN, YOU DON'T LOOK LIKE IT, BUT...
YOU'RE TOO OLD TO PLAY CAPMON!
URK-!
LISTEN... AGE DOESN'T MEAN ANYTHING TO A REAL GAMER!
HA HA ...
SHAKE SHAKE
WHAT A BRAT!
HUH! IF YOU WANT IT THAT MUCH, THEN YOU CAN GO FIRST. THIS TIME.
GEE, THANKS A LOT.
HEH HEH ...
100 YEN, 100 YEN ...

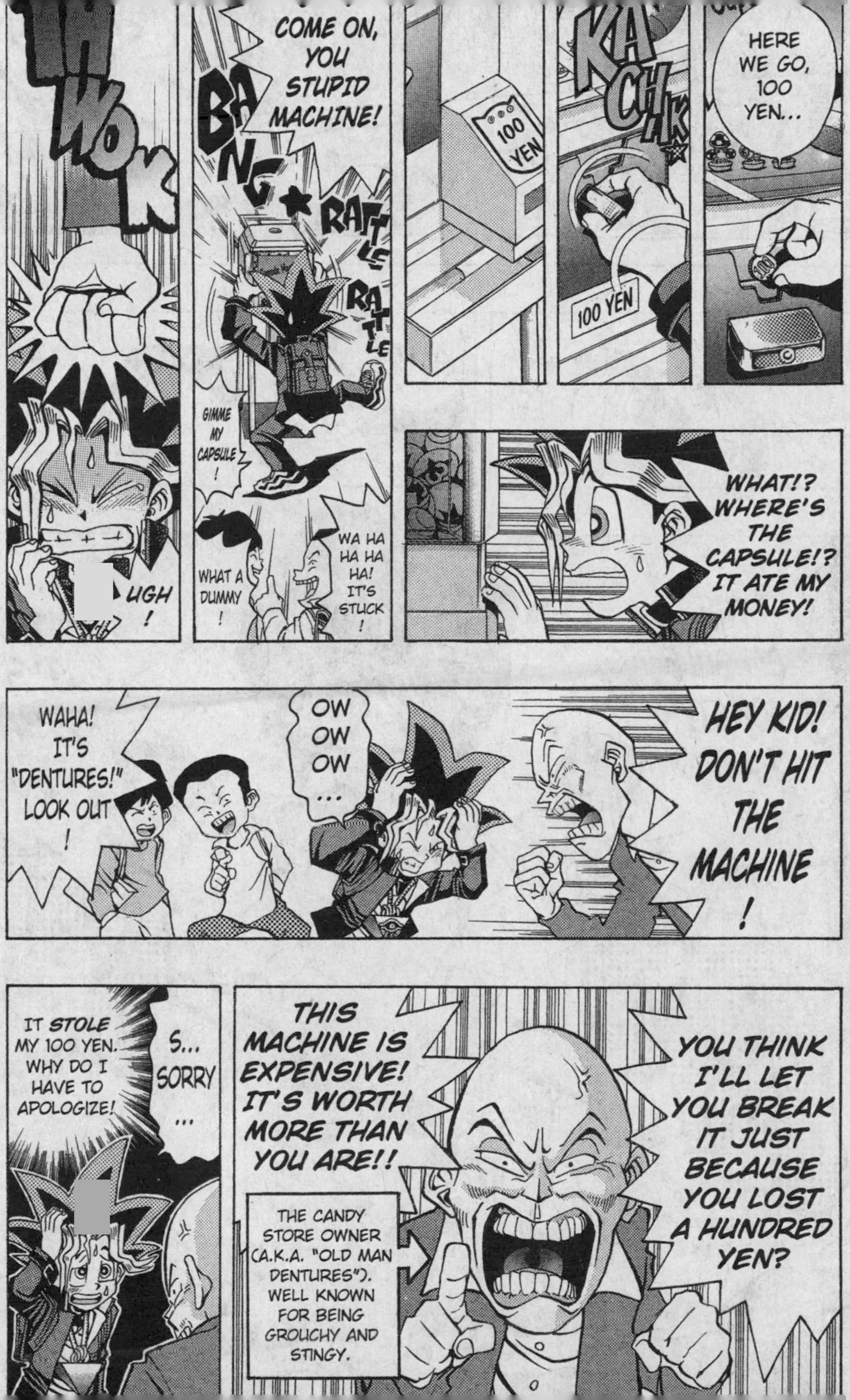
HERE WE GO, 100 YEN...
KA CHIK
100 YEN
100 YEN
WHAT!? WHERE'S THE CAPSULE!? IT ATE MY MONEY!
COME ON, YOU STUPID MACHINE!
BANG
RATTLE
RATTLE
GIMME MY CAPSULE!
WA HA HA HA HA! IT'S STUCK!
WHAT A DUMMY!
WHOK
UGH!
HEY KID! DON'T HIT THE MACHINE!
OW OW OW...
WAHA! IT'S "DENTURES!" LOOK OUT!
YOU THINK I'LL LET YOU BREAK IT JUST BECAUSE YOU LOST A HUNDRED YEN?
THIS MACHINE IS EXPENSIVE! IT'S WORTH MORE THAN YOU ARE!!
THE CANDY STORE OWNER (A.K.A. "OLD MAN DENTURES"). WELL KNOWN FOR BEING GROUCHY AND STINGY.
S... SORRY...
IT STOLE MY 100 YEN. WHY DO I HAVE TO APOLOGIZE!

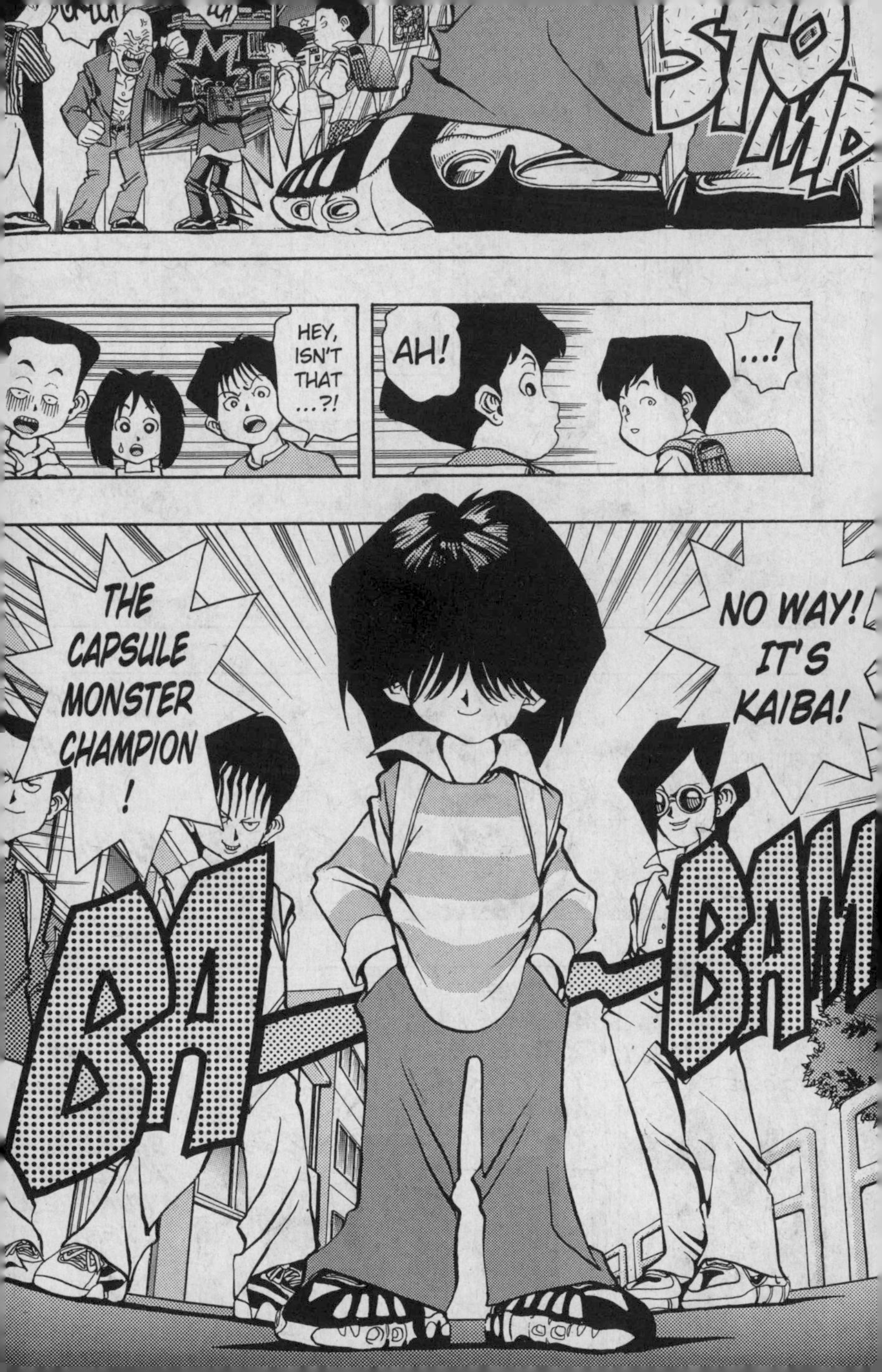
STOMP
HEY, ISN'T THAT ...?!
AH!
...!
NO WAY! IT'S KAIBA!
THE CAPSULE MONSTER CHAMPION!
BAM
BAM

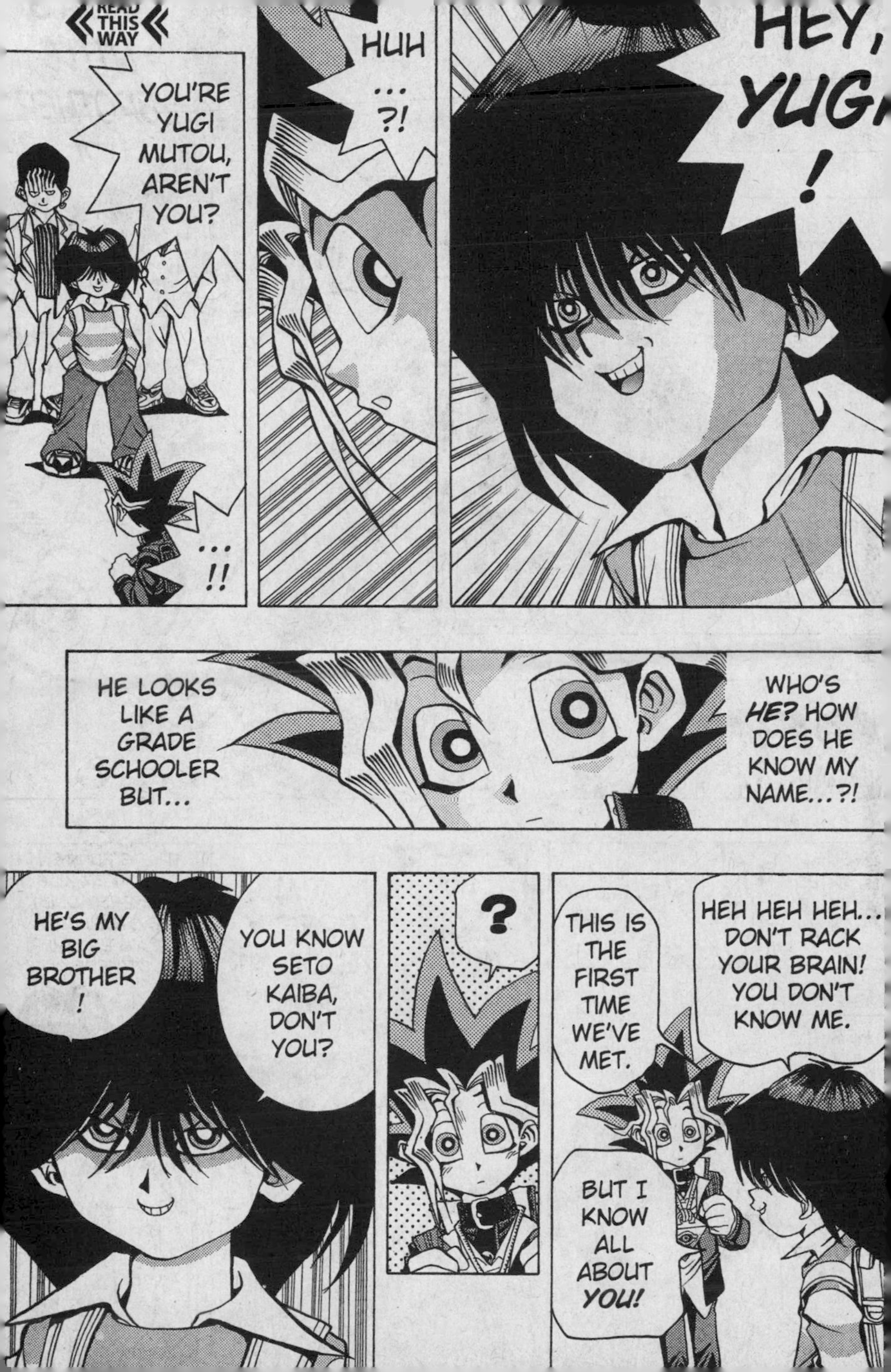
READ THIS WAY
HEY, YUGI!
HUH...?!
YOU'RE YUGI MUTOU, AREN'T YOU?
...!!
WHO'S *HE?* HOW DOES HE KNOW MY NAME...?!
HE LOOKS LIKE A GRADE SCHOOLER BUT...
HEH HEH HEH... DON'T RACK YOUR BRAIN! YOU DON'T KNOW ME.
THIS IS THE FIRST TIME WE'VE MET.
BUT I KNOW ALL ABOUT *YOU!*
?
YOU KNOW SETO KAIBA, DON'T YOU?
HE'S MY BIG BROTHER!

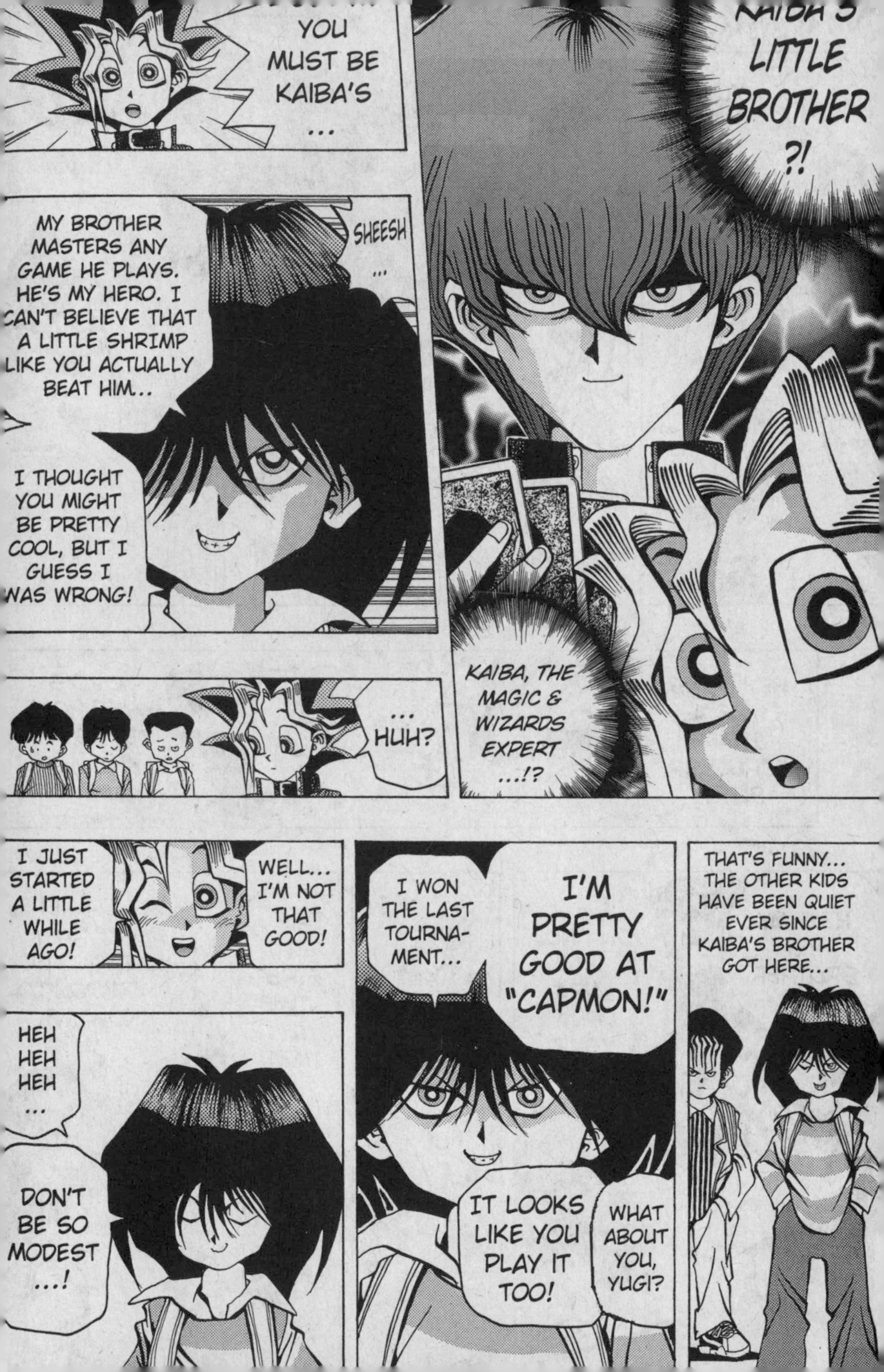
YOU MUST BE KAIBA'S ...
KAIBA'S LITTLE BROTHER ?!
MY BROTHER MASTERS ANY GAME HE PLAYS. HE'S MY HERO. I CAN'T BELIEVE THAT A LITTLE SHRIMP LIKE YOU ACTUALLY BEAT HIM...
SHEESH ...
I THOUGHT YOU MIGHT BE PRETTY COOL, BUT I GUESS I WAS WRONG!
... HUH?
KAIBA, THE MAGIC & WIZARDS EXPERT ...!?
I JUST STARTED A LITTLE WHILE AGO!
WELL... I'M NOT THAT GOOD!
HEH HEH HEH ...
DON'T BE SO MODEST ...!
I WON THE LAST TOURNAMENT...
I'M PRETTY GOOD AT "CAPMON!"
IT LOOKS LIKE YOU PLAY IT TOO!
WHAT ABOUT YOU, YUGI?
THAT'S FUNNY... THE OTHER KIDS HAVE BEEN QUIET EVER SINCE KAIBA'S BROTHER GOT HERE...

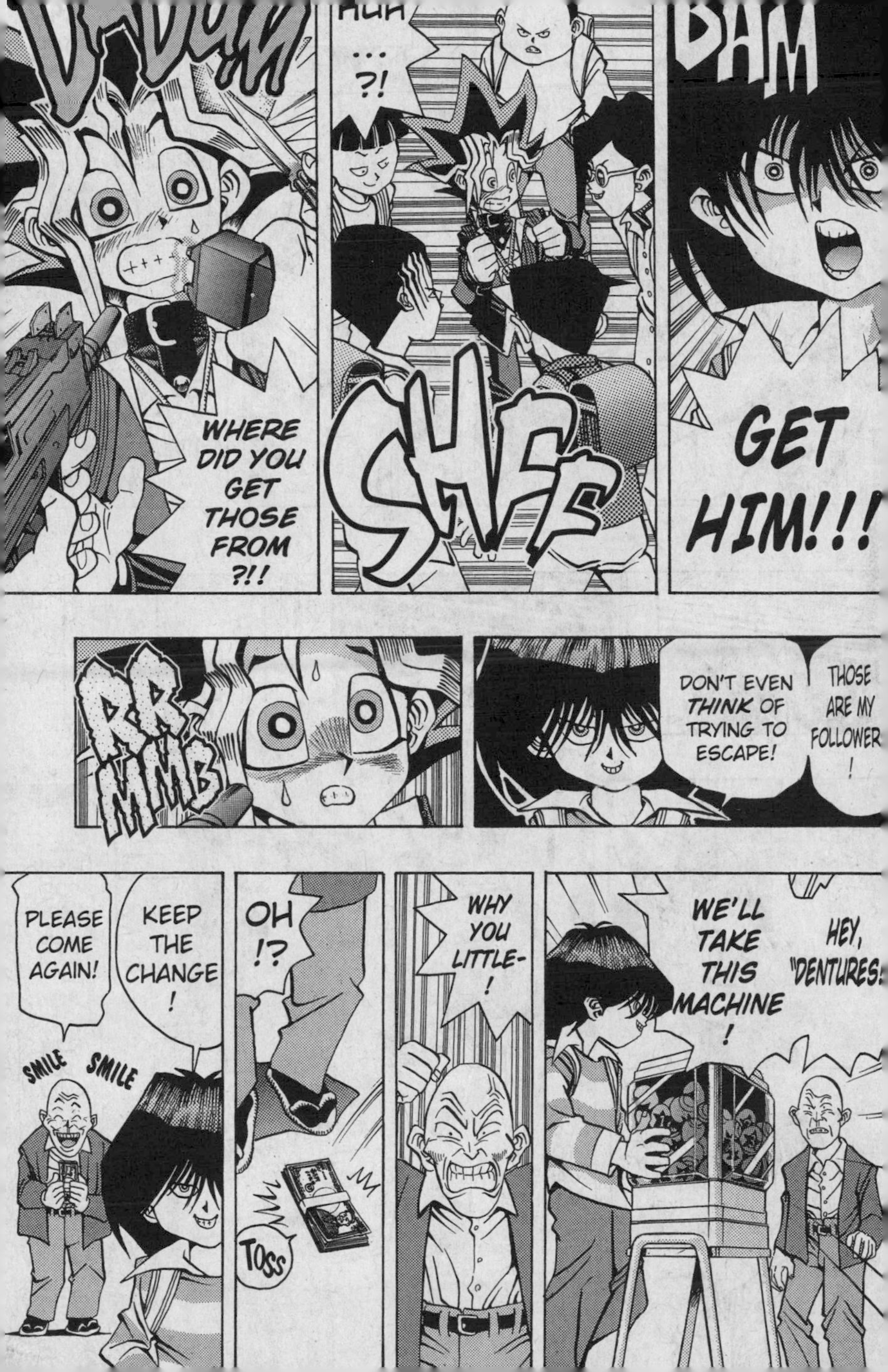
BAM
GET HIM!!!
HUH ...?!
SHFF
WHERE DID YOU GET THOSE FROM ?!!
THOSE ARE MY FOLLOWER !
DON'T EVEN THINK OF TRYING TO ESCAPE!
RRMMB
HEY, "DENTURES
WE'LL TAKE THIS MACHINE !
WHY YOU LITTLE- !
OH !?
TOSS
KEEP THE CHANGE !
PLEASE COME AGAIN!
SMILE SMILE

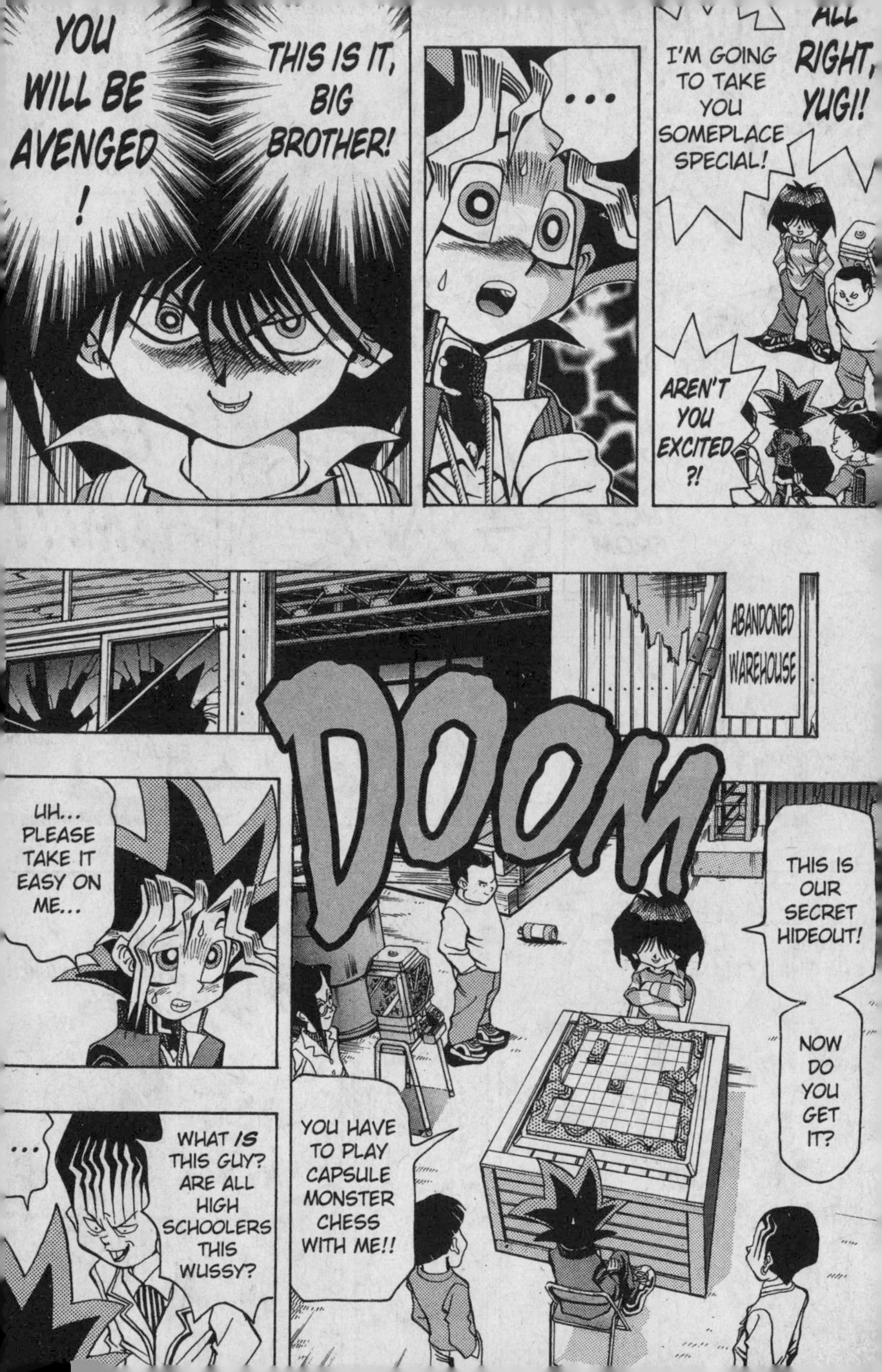
ALL RIGHT, YUGI!
I'M GOING TO TAKE YOU SOMEPLACE SPECIAL!
AREN'T YOU EXCITED?!
...
THIS IS IT, BIG BROTHER!
YOU WILL BE AVENGED!
ABANDONED WAREHOUSE
DOOM
THIS IS OUR SECRET HIDEOUT!
NOW DO YOU GET IT?
YOU HAVE TO PLAY CAPSULE MONSTER CHESS WITH ME!!
UH... PLEASE TAKE IT EASY ON ME...
WHAT *IS* THIS GUY? ARE ALL HIGH SCHOOLERS THIS WUSSY?
...

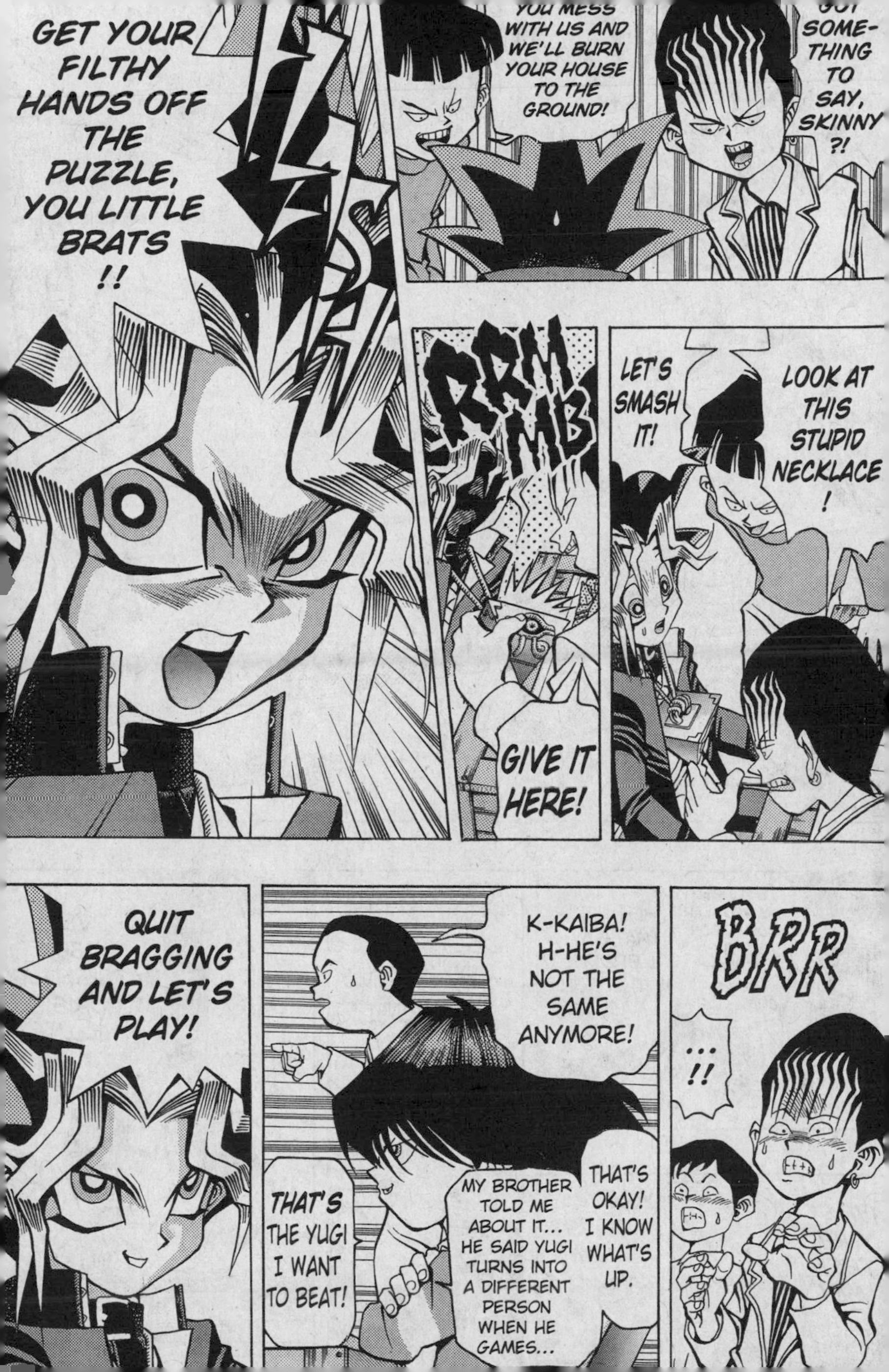
SOME-THING TO SAY, SKINNY ?!
YOU MESS WITH US AND WE'LL BURN YOUR HOUSE TO THE GROUND!
LOOK AT THIS STUPID NECKLACE !
LET'S SMASH IT!
GIVE IT HERE!
RRMMB
GET YOUR FILTHY HANDS OFF THE PUZZLE, YOU LITTLE BRATS !!
BRR
...!!
K-KAIBA! H-HE'S NOT THE SAME ANYMORE!
THAT'S OKAY! I KNOW WHAT'S UP.
MY BROTHER TOLD ME ABOUT IT... HE SAID YUGI TURNS INTO A DIFFERENT PERSON WHEN HE GAMES...
THAT'S THE YUGI I WANT TO BEAT!
QUIT BRAGGING AND LET'S PLAY!

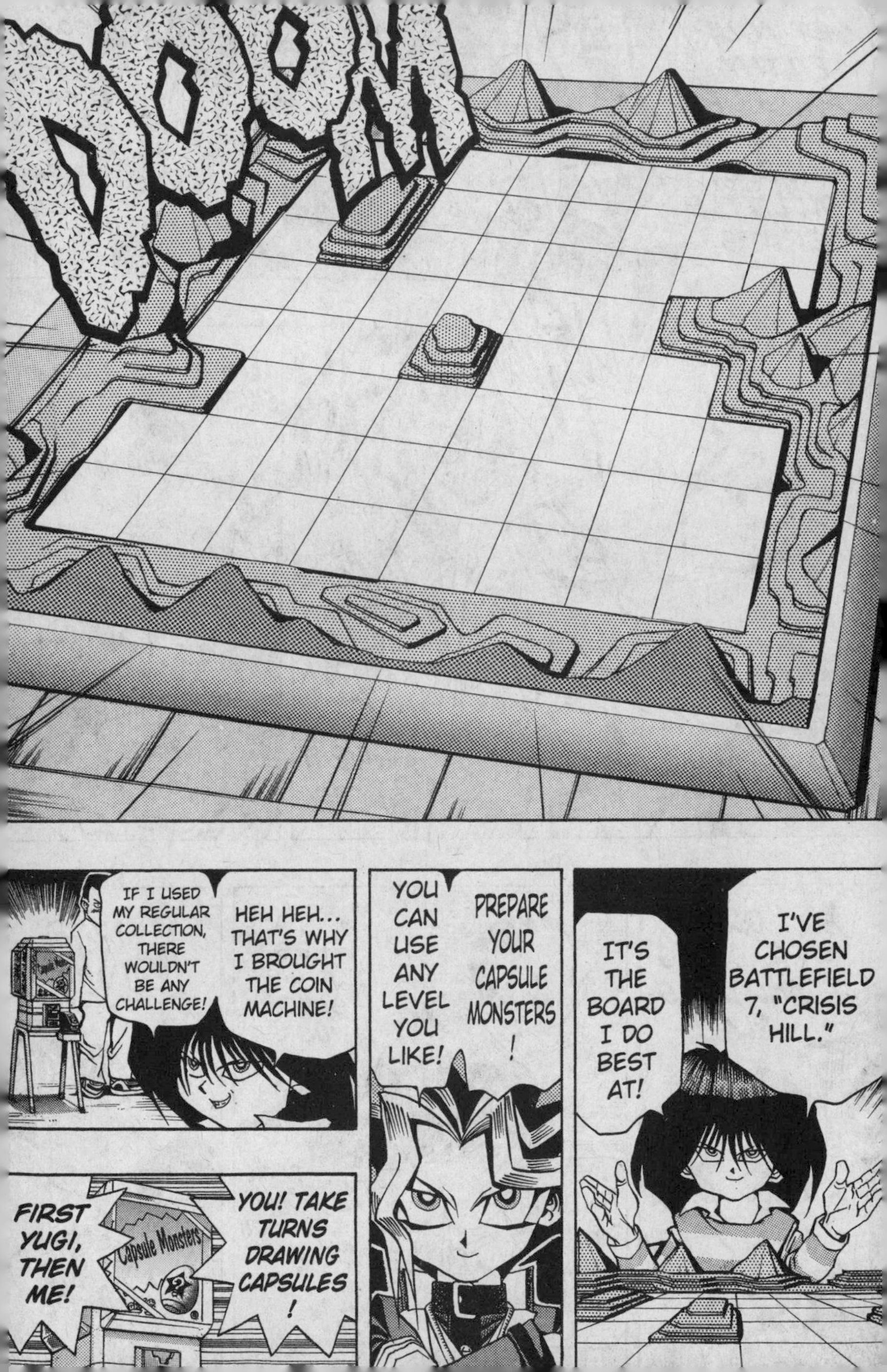
DOOM
I'VE CHOSEN BATTLEFIELD 7, "CRISIS HILL."
IT'S THE BOARD I DO BEST AT!
PREPARE YOUR CAPSULE MONSTERS!
YOU CAN USE ANY LEVEL YOU LIKE!
HEH HEH... THAT'S WHY I BROUGHT THE COIN MACHINE!
IF I USED MY REGULAR COLLECTION, THERE WOULDN'T BE ANY CHALLENGE!
YOU! TAKE TURNS DRAWING CAPSULES!
Capsule Monsters
FIRST YUGI, THEN ME!

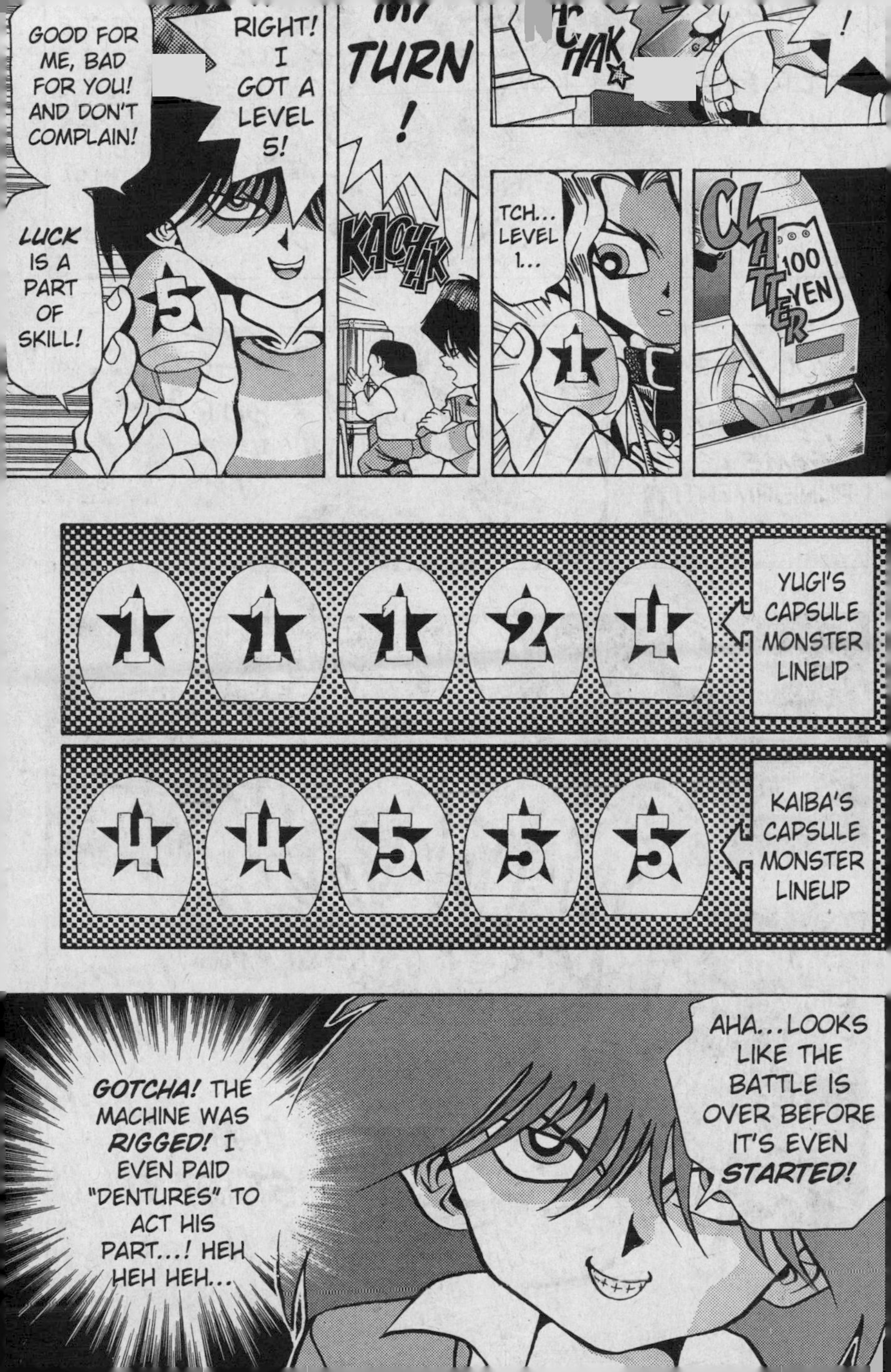

CHAK
!
CLATTER
100 YEN
TCH... LEVEL 1...
TURN !
KACHAK
RIGHT! I GOT A LEVEL 5!
GOOD FOR ME, BAD FOR YOU! AND DON'T COMPLAIN!
LUCK IS A PART OF SKILL!
YUGI'S CAPSULE MONSTER LINEUP
1 1 1 2 4
KAIBA'S CAPSULE MONSTER LINEUP
4 4 5 5 5
AHA...LOOKS LIKE THE BATTLE IS OVER BEFORE IT'S EVEN STARTED!
GOTCHA! THE MACHINE WAS RIGGED! I EVEN PAID "DENTURES" TO ACT HIS PART...! HEH HEH HEH...

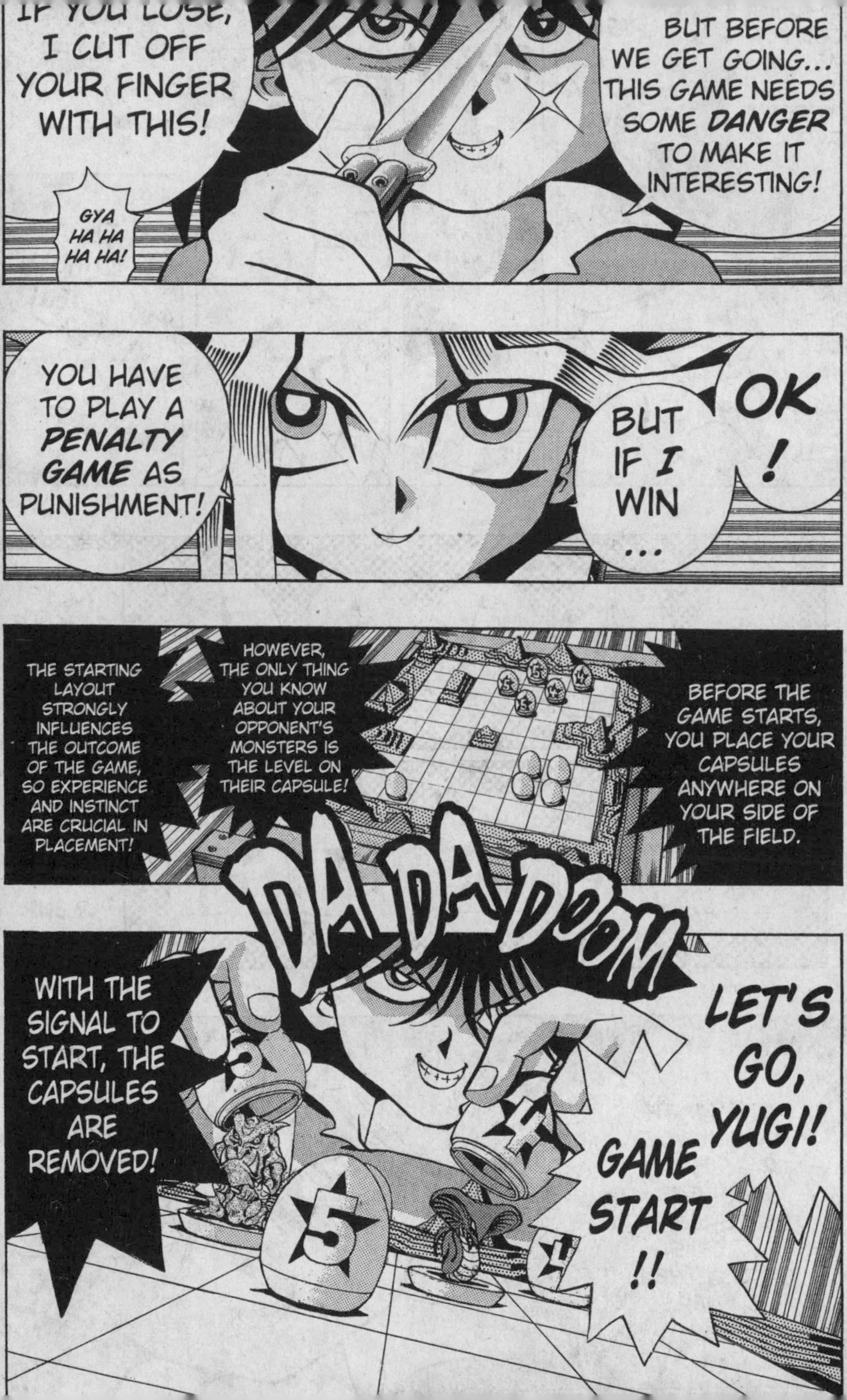

BUT BEFORE WE GET GOING... THIS GAME NEEDS SOME DANGER TO MAKE IT INTERESTING!
IF YOU LOSE, I CUT OFF YOUR FINGER WITH THIS!
GYA HA HA HA HA!
OK!
BUT IF I WIN...
YOU HAVE TO PLAY A PENALTY GAME AS PUNISHMENT!
BEFORE THE GAME STARTS, YOU PLACE YOUR CAPSULES ANYWHERE ON YOUR SIDE OF THE FIELD.
HOWEVER, THE ONLY THING YOU KNOW ABOUT YOUR OPPONENT'S MONSTERS IS THE LEVEL ON THEIR CAPSULE!
THE STARTING LAYOUT STRONGLY INFLUENCES THE OUTCOME OF THE GAME, SO EXPERIENCE AND INSTINCT ARE CRUCIAL IN PLACEMENT!
DA DA DOOM
LET'S GO, YUGI!
GAME START!!
WITH THE SIGNAL TO START, THE CAPSULES ARE REMOVED!

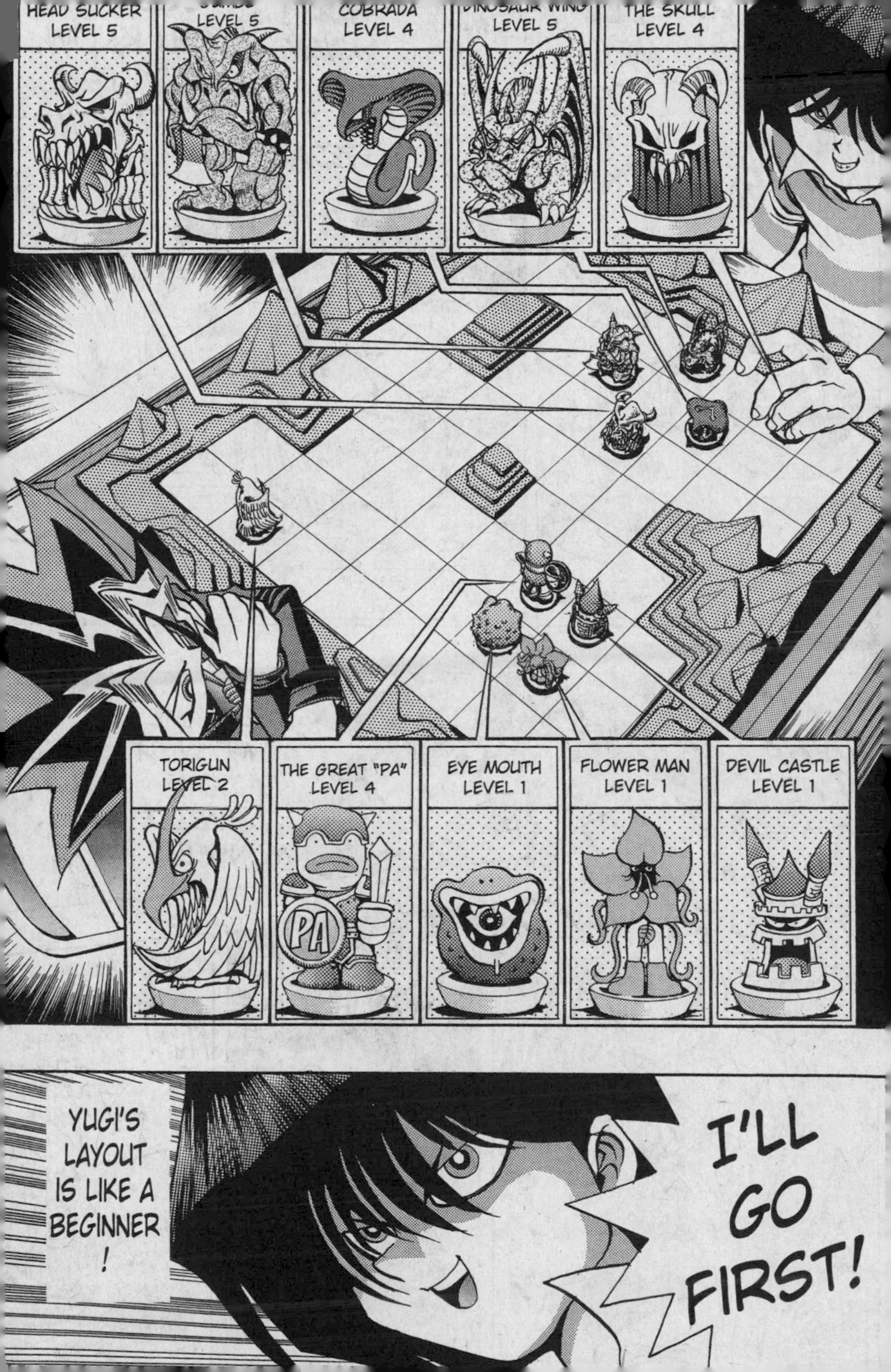
HEAD SUCKER LEVEL 5
LEVEL 5
COBRADA LEVEL 4
DINOSAUR WING LEVEL 5
THE SKULL LEVEL 4
TORIGUN LEVEL 2
THE GREAT "PA" LEVEL 4
EYE MOUTH LEVEL 1
FLOWER MAN LEVEL 1
DEVIL CASTLE LEVEL 1
I'LL GO FIRST!
YUGI'S LAYOUT IS LIKE A BEGINNER!

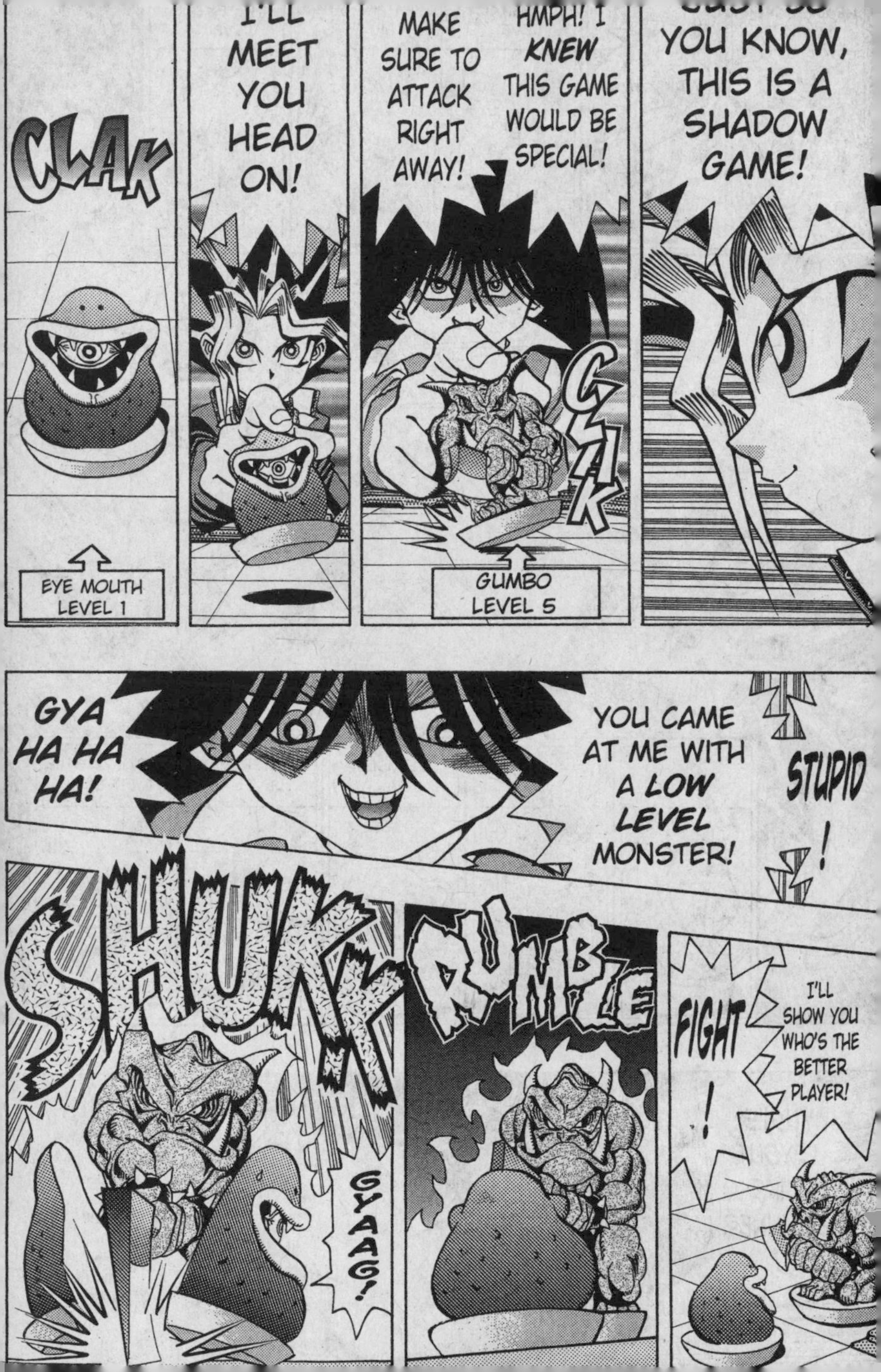
JUST SO YOU KNOW, THIS IS A SHADOW GAME!
HMPH! I KNEW THIS GAME WOULD BE SPECIAL!
CLAK
GUMBO LEVEL 5
MAKE SURE TO ATTACK RIGHT AWAY!
I'LL MEET YOU HEAD ON!
CLAK
EYE MOUTH LEVEL 1
STUPID!
YOU CAME AT ME WITH A LOW LEVEL MONSTER!
GYA HA HA HA!
FIGHT!
I'LL SHOW YOU WHO'S THE BETTER PLAYER!
RUMBLE
SHUK
GYAAAG!

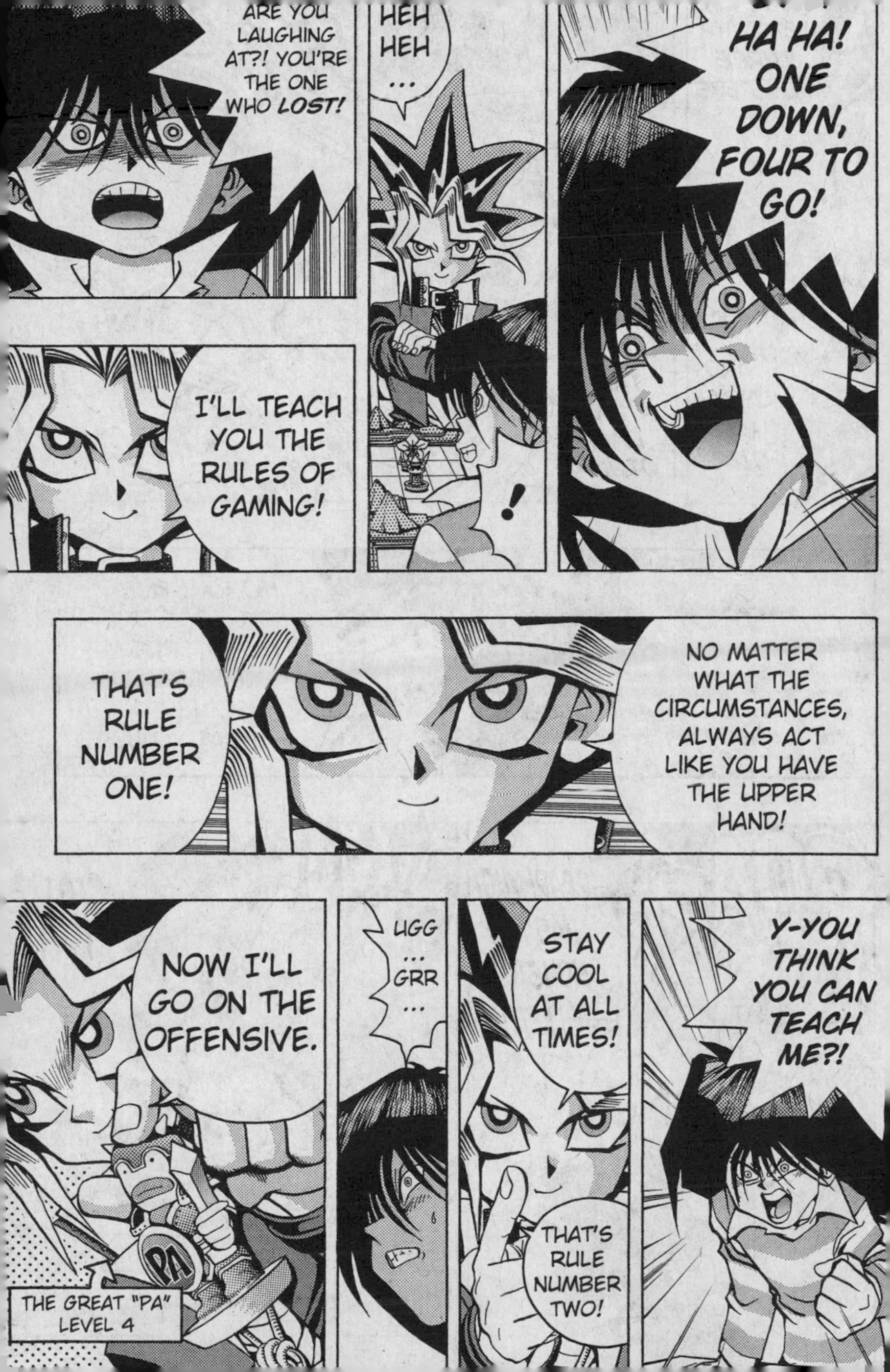
HA HA! ONE DOWN, FOUR TO GO!
HEH HEH ...
ARE YOU LAUGHING AT?! YOU'RE THE ONE WHO LOST!
!
I'LL TEACH YOU THE RULES OF GAMING!
NO MATTER WHAT THE CIRCUMSTANCES, ALWAYS ACT LIKE YOU HAVE THE UPPER HAND!
THAT'S RULE NUMBER ONE!
Y-YOU THINK YOU CAN TEACH ME?!
STAY COOL AT ALL TIMES!
THAT'S RULE NUMBER TWO!
UGG ... GRR ...
NOW I'LL GO ON THE OFFENSIVE.
PA
THE GREAT "PA" LEVEL 4

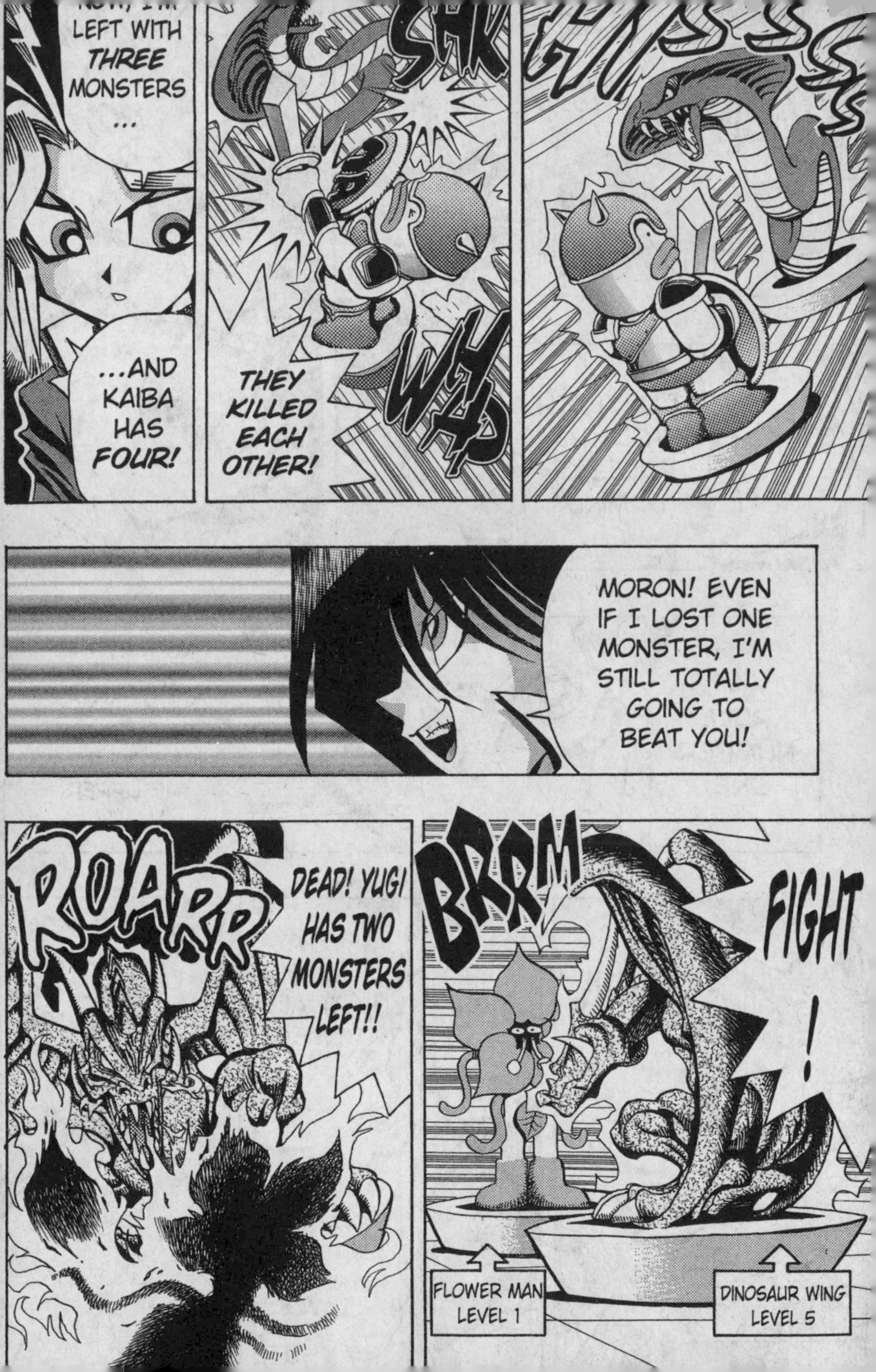
SHK
THEY KILLED EACH OTHER!
LEFT WITH THREE MONSTERS …
…AND KAIBA HAS FOUR!
MORON! EVEN IF I LOST ONE MONSTER, I'M STILL TOTALLY GOING TO BEAT YOU!
BRRM
FIGHT !
FLOWER MAN LEVEL 1
DINOSAUR WING LEVEL 5
ROARR
DEAD! YUGI HAS TWO MONSTERS LEFT!!

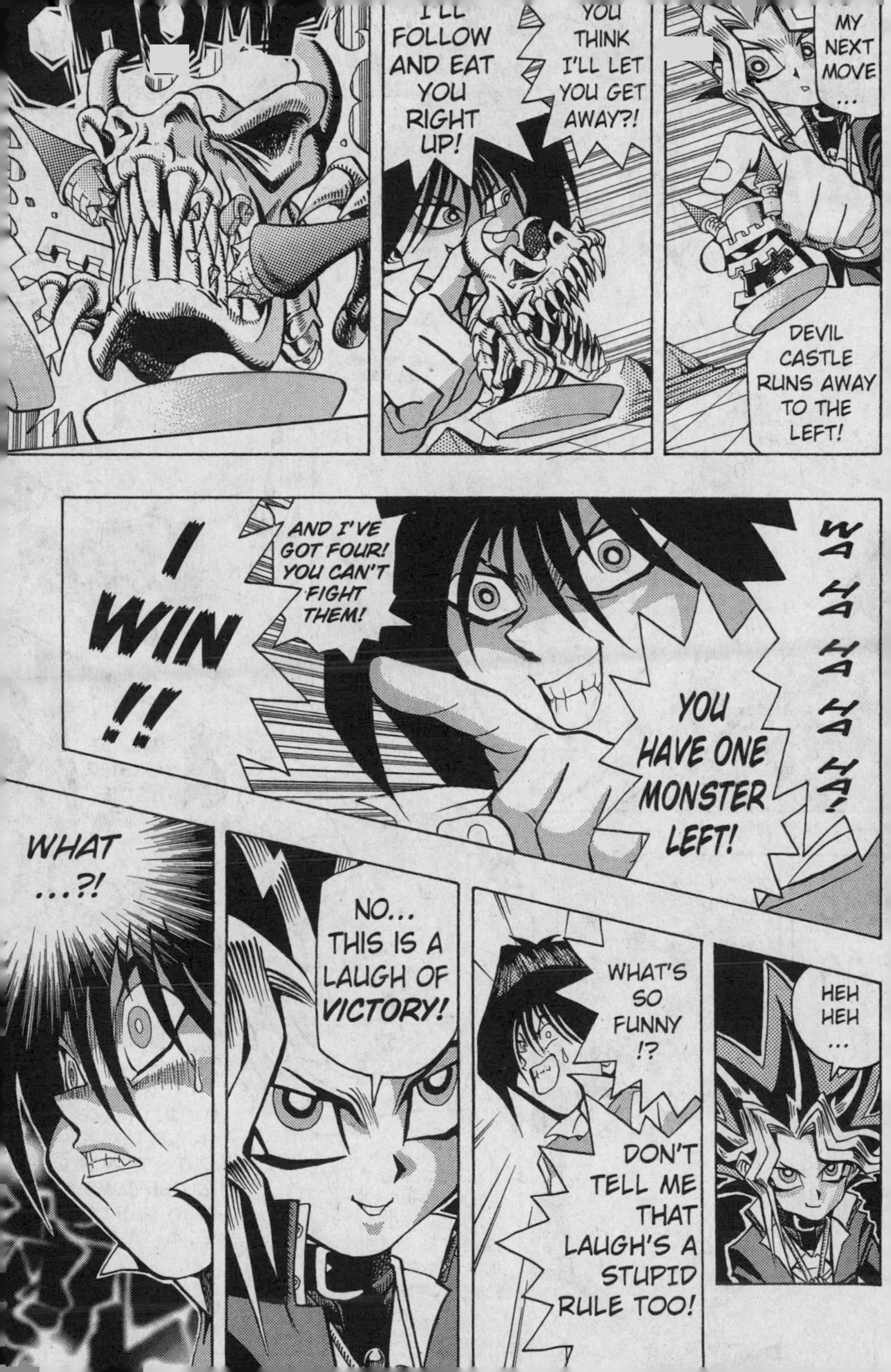
MY NEXT MOVE ...
DEVIL CASTLE RUNS AWAY TO THE LEFT!
YOU THINK I'LL LET YOU GET AWAY?!
I'LL FOLLOW AND EAT YOU RIGHT UP!
WA HA HA HA HA HA!
YOU HAVE ONE MONSTER LEFT!
AND I'VE GOT FOUR! YOU CAN'T FIGHT THEM!
I WIN!!
HEH HEH ...
WHAT'S SO FUNNY!?
DON'T TELL ME THAT LAUGH'S A STUPID RULE TOO!
NO... THIS IS A LAUGH OF VICTORY!
WHAT ...?!

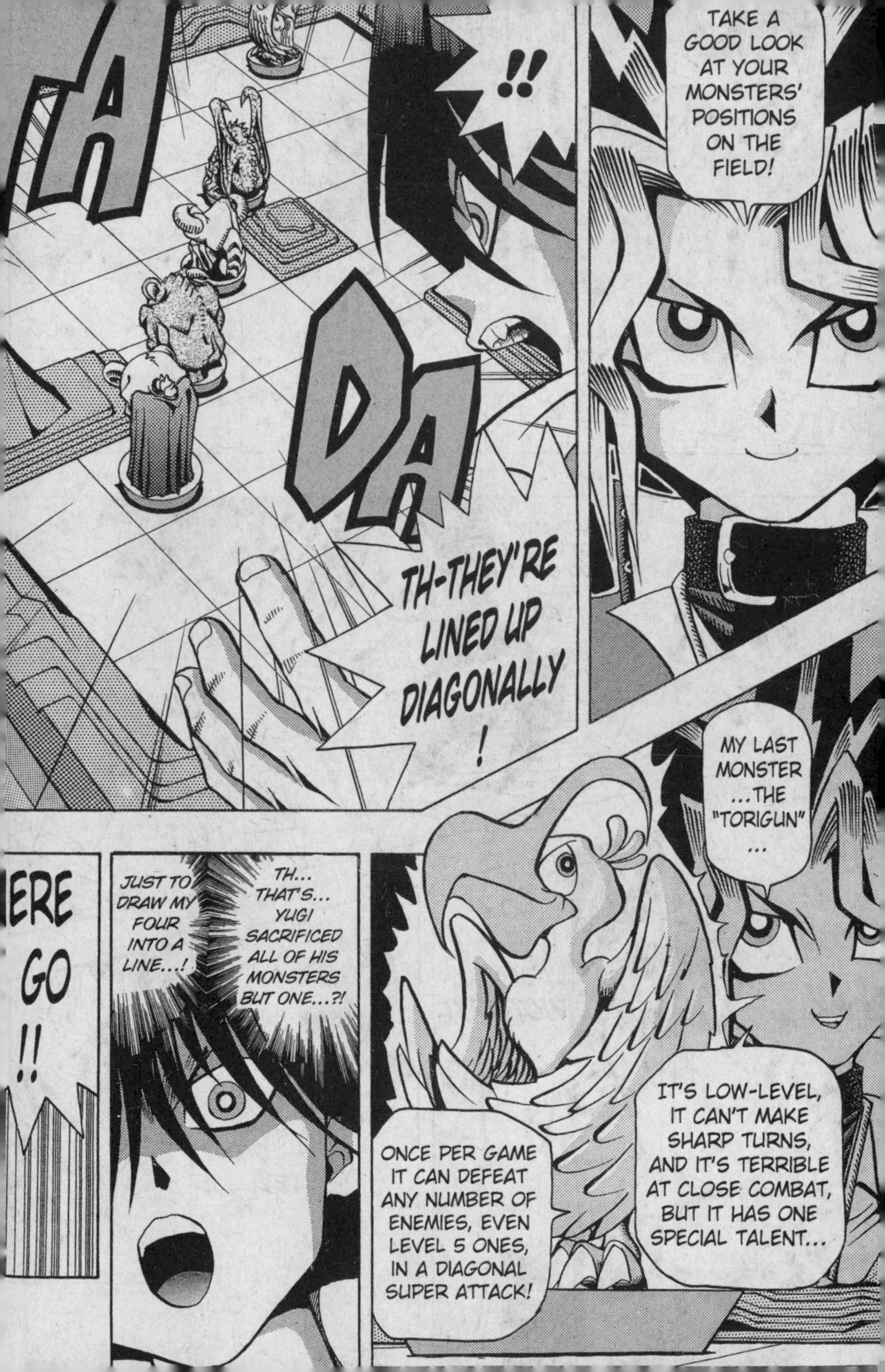
TAKE A GOOD LOOK AT YOUR MONSTERS' POSITIONS ON THE FIELD!
!!
A
DA
TH-THEY'RE LINED UP DIAGONALLY!
MY LAST MONSTER ...THE "TORIGUN" ...
IT'S LOW-LEVEL, IT CAN'T MAKE SHARP TURNS, AND IT'S TERRIBLE AT CLOSE COMBAT, BUT IT HAS ONE SPECIAL TALENT...
ONCE PER GAME IT CAN DEFEAT ANY NUMBER OF ENEMIES, EVEN LEVEL 5 ONES, IN A DIAGONAL SUPER ATTACK!
TH... THAT'S... YUGI SACRIFICED ALL OF HIS MONSTERS BUT ONE...?!
JUST TO DRAW MY FOUR INTO A LINE...!
ERE GO !!

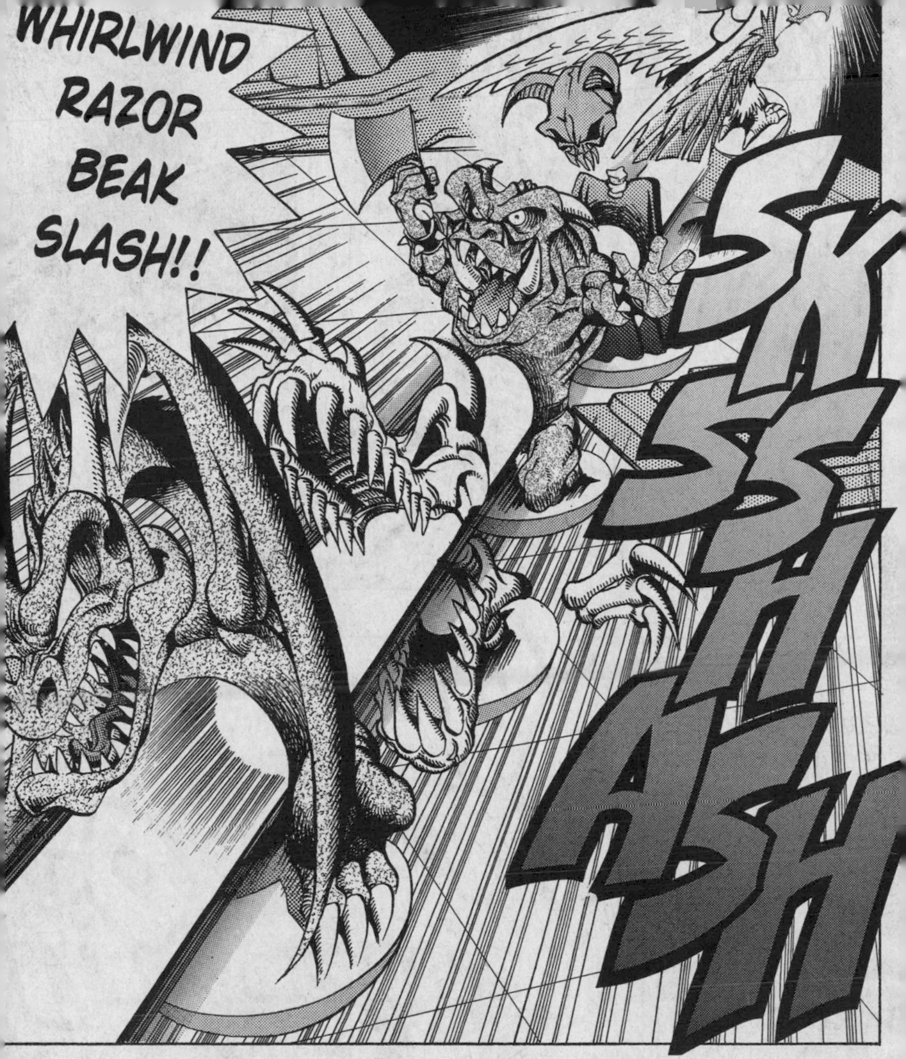
WHIRLWIND RAZOR BEAK SLASH!!
SHASH

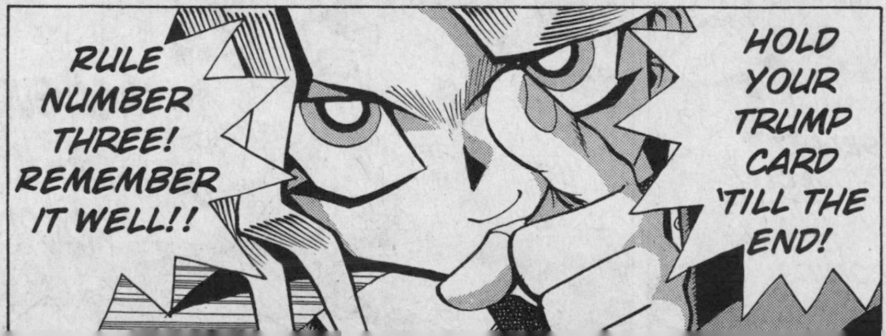
HOLD YOUR TRUMP CARD 'TILL THE END!
RULE NUMBER THREE! REMEMBER IT WELL!!

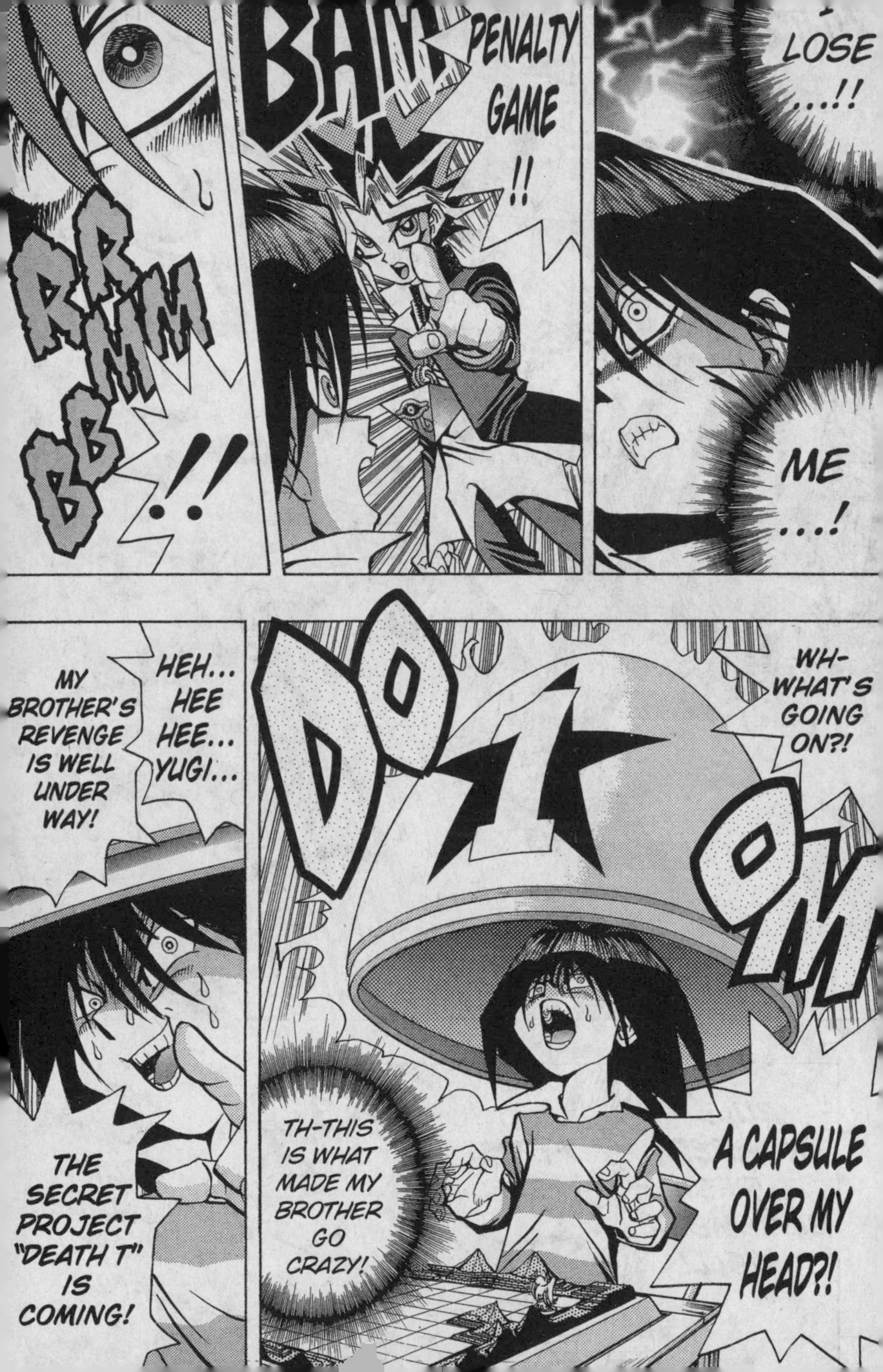
LOSE ...!!
ME ...!
BAM
PENALTY GAME !!
RRMMBB!!
WH-WHAT'S GOING ON?!
DOOM
A CAPSULE OVER MY HEAD?!
TH-THIS IS WHAT MADE MY BROTHER GO CRAZY!
HEH... HEE HEE... YUGI...
MY BROTHER'S REVENGE IS WELL UNDER WAY!
THE SECRET PROJECT "DEATH T" IS COMING!

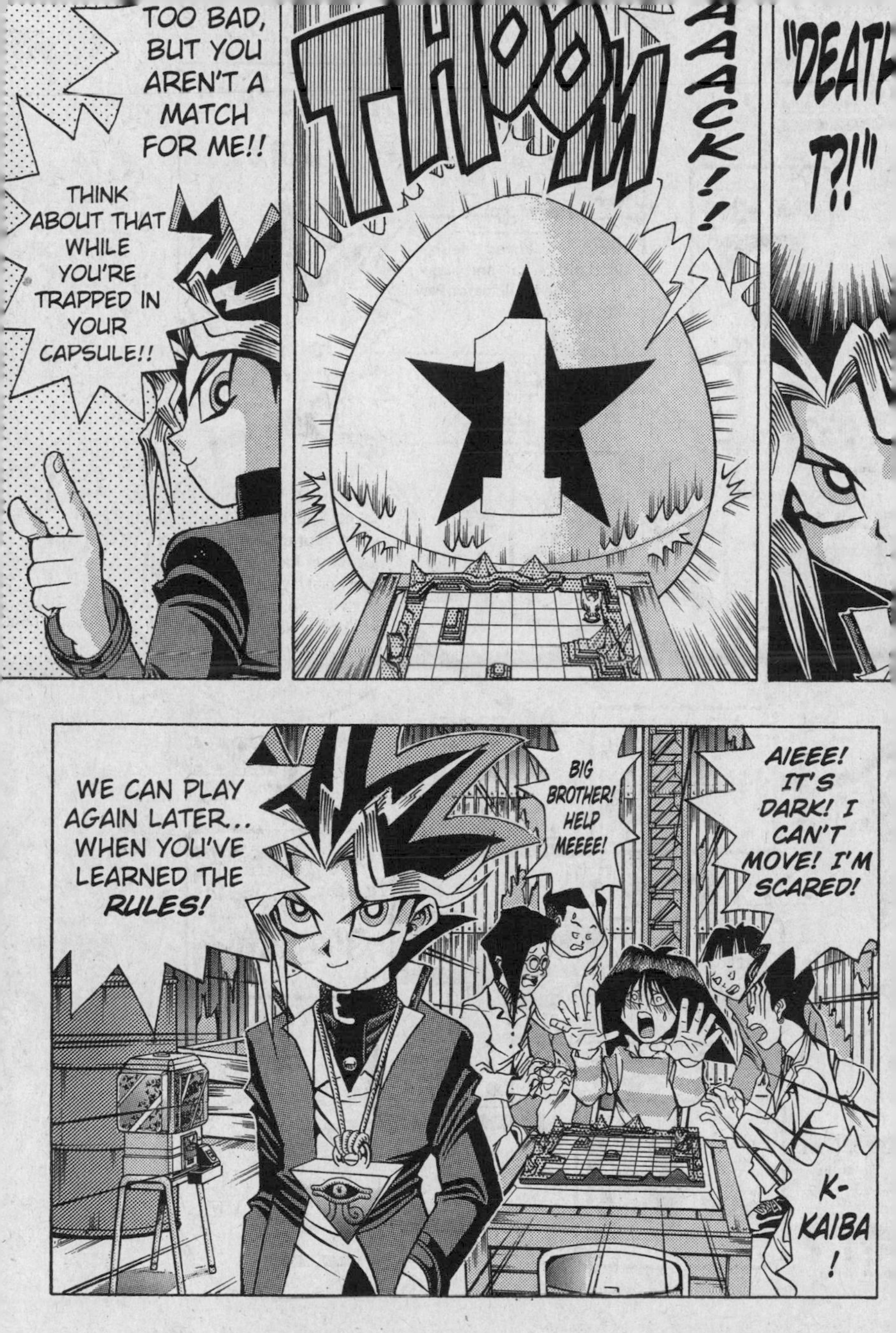
"DEATH T?!"
THOOM
AAACK!!
TOO BAD, BUT YOU AREN'T A MATCH FOR ME!!
THINK ABOUT THAT WHILE YOU'RE TRAPPED IN YOUR CAPSULE!!
AIEEE! IT'S DARK! I CAN'T MOVE! I'M SCARED!
BIG BROTHER! HELP MEEEE!
K-KAIBA!
WE CAN PLAY AGAIN LATER... WHEN YOU'VE LEARNED THE *RULES!*

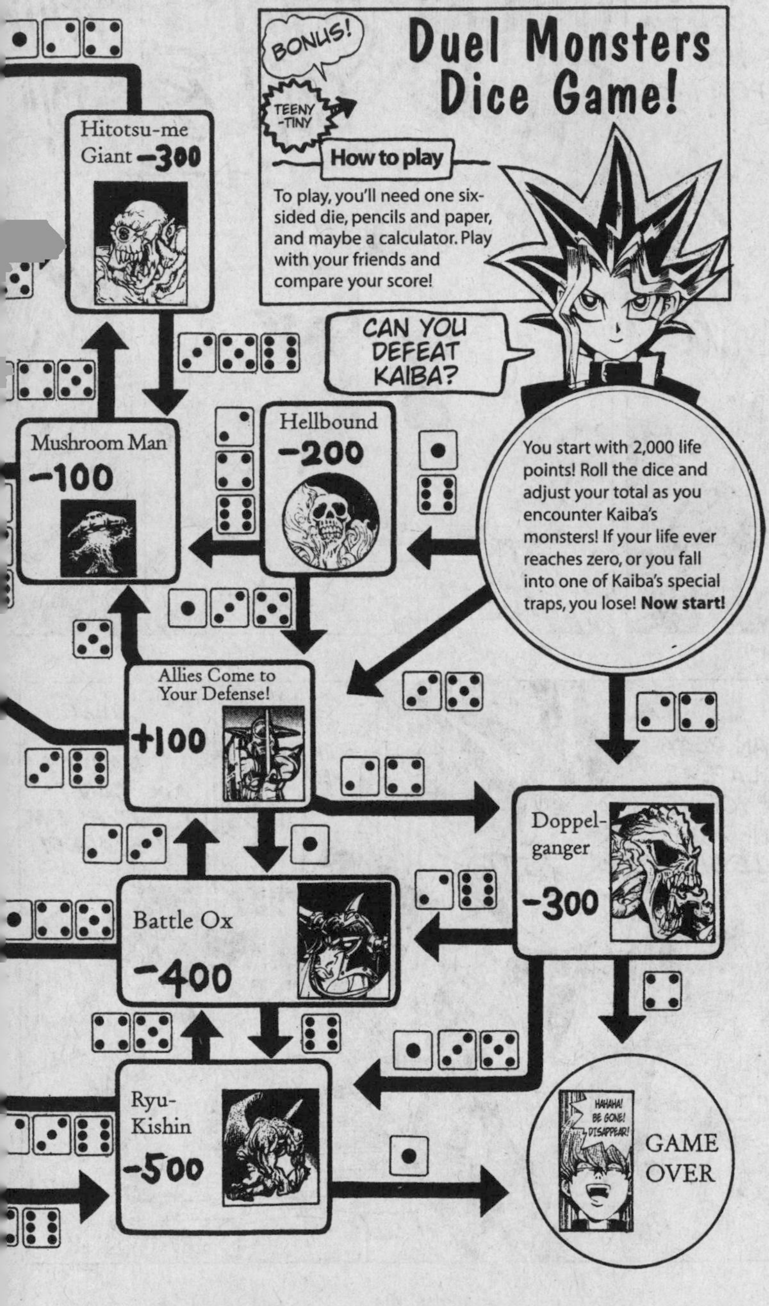
BONUS!
TEENY -TINY
Duel Monsters Dice Game!
How to play
To play, you'll need one six-sided die, pencils and paper, and maybe a calculator. Play with your friends and compare your score!
CAN YOU DEFEAT KAIBA?
You start with 2,000 life points! Roll the dice and adjust your total as you encounter Kaiba's monsters! If your life ever reaches zero, or you fall into one of Kaiba's special traps, you lose! Now start!
Hitotsu-me Giant -300
Mushroom Man -100
Hellbound -200
Allies Come to Your Defense! +100
Doppel-ganger -300
Battle Ox -400
Ryu-Kishin -500
HAHAHA! BE GONE! DISAPPEAR!
GAME OVER

STAGE 1

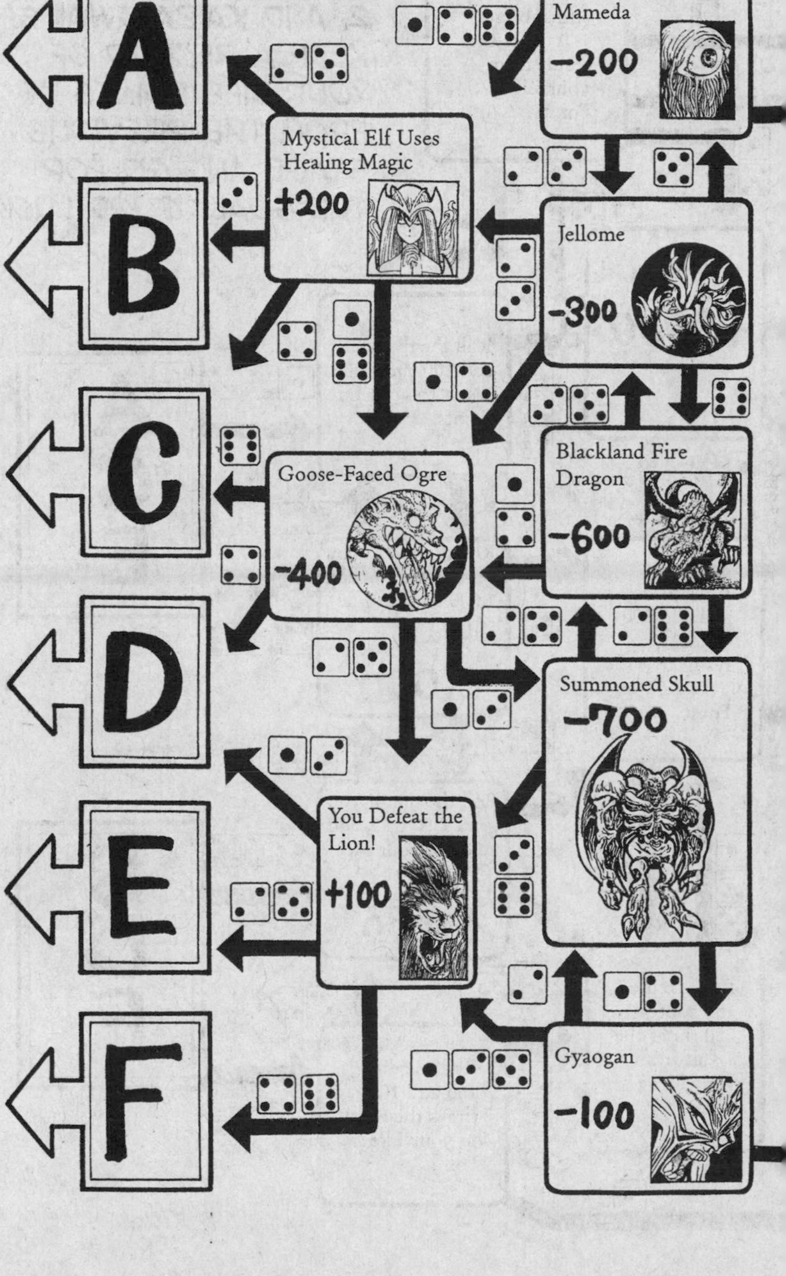
A
B
C
D
E
F
Mameda
-200
Mystical Elf Uses Healing Magic
+200
Jellome
-300
Goose-Faced Ogre
-400
Blackland Fire Dragon
-600
Summoned Skull
-700
You Defeat the Lion!
+100
Gyaogan
-100

LET'S GO! IT'S STAGE 2, AND KAIBA AWAITS! KEEP A RECORD OF YOUR LIFE POINTS FROM THE PREVIOUS STAGE AND GO FOR THE GOAL. GOOD LUCK!

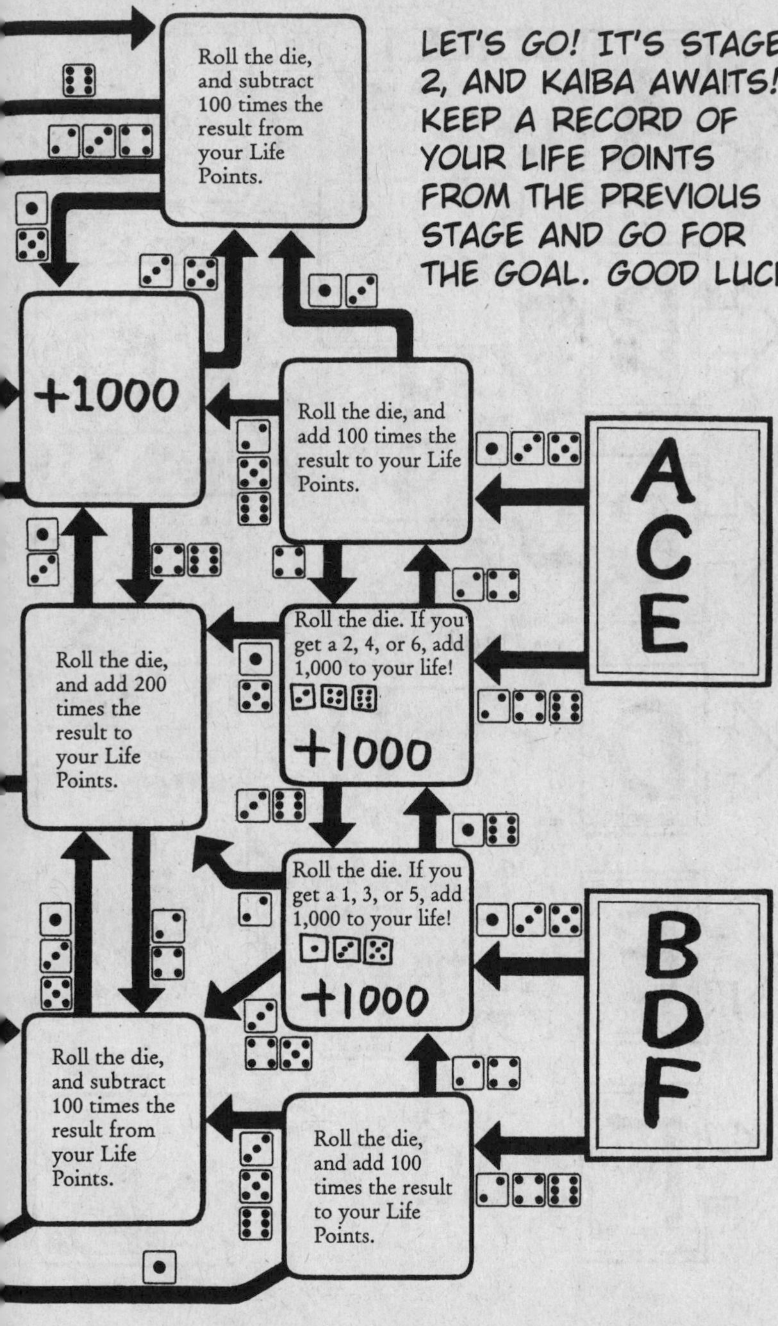
Roll the die, and subtract 100 times the result from your Life Points.
+1000
Roll the die, and add 100 times the result to your Life Points.
ACE
Roll the die, and add 200 times the result to your Life Points.
Roll the die. If you get a 2, 4, or 6, add 1,000 to your life!
+1000
Roll the die. If you get a 1, 3, or 5, add 1,000 to your life!
+1000
BDF
Roll the die, and subtract 100 times the result from your Life Points.
Roll the die, and add 100 times the result to your Life Points.

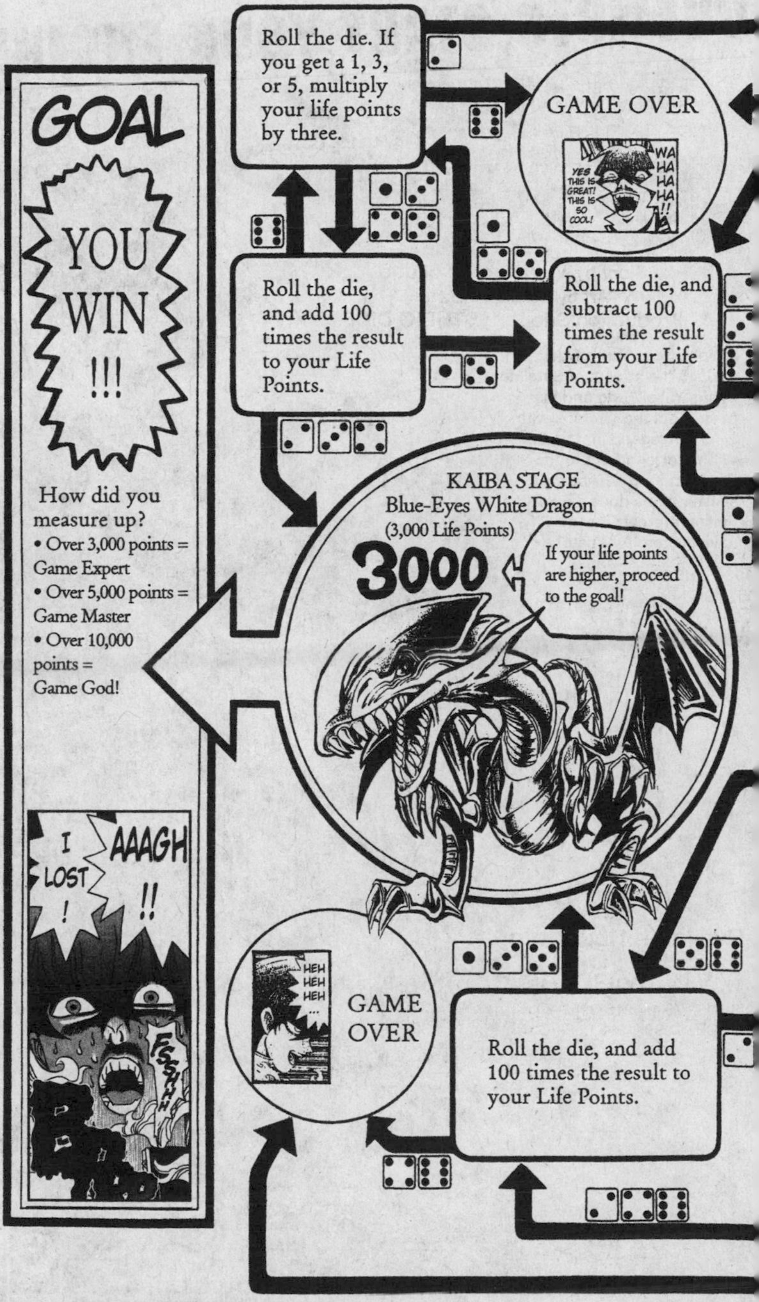
GOAL
YOU WIN !!!
How did you measure up?
• Over 3,000 points = Game Expert
• Over 5,000 points = Game Master
• Over 10,000 points = Game God!
I LOST !
AAAGH !!
FSSSHHH
Roll the die. If you get a 1, 3, or 5, multiply your life points by three.
GAME OVER
YES THIS IS GREAT! THIS IS SO COOL!
WA HA HA HA !!
Roll the die, and add 100 times the result to your Life Points.
Roll the die, and subtract 100 times the result from your Life Points.
KAIBA STAGE
Blue-Eyes White Dragon
(3,000 Life Points)
3000
If your life points are higher, proceed to the goal!
HEH HEH HEH ...
GAME OVER
Roll the die, and add 100 times the result to your Life Points.

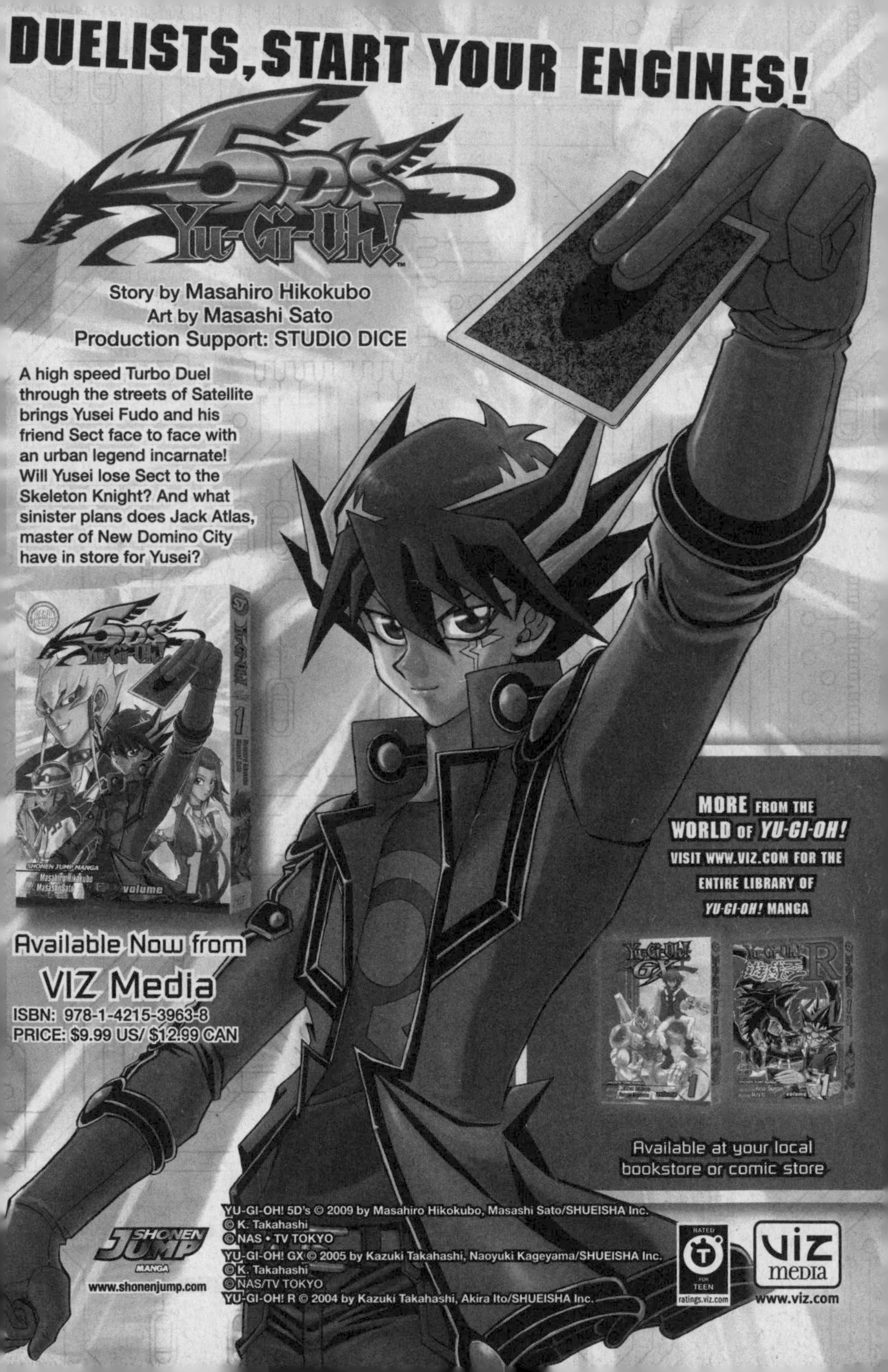
DUELISTS, START YOUR ENGINES!
5D's YU-GI-OH!
Story by Masahiro Hikokubo
Art by Masashi Sato
Production Support: STUDIO DICE
A high speed Turbo Duel through the streets of Satellite brings Yusei Fudo and his friend Sect face to face with an urban legend incarnate! Will Yusei lose Sect to the Skeleton Knight? And what sinister plans does Jack Atlas, master of New Domino City have in store for Yusei?
Available Now from
VIZ Media
ISBN: 978-1-4215-3963-8
PRICE: $9.99 US/ $12.99 CAN
MORE FROM THE WORLD OF YU-GI-OH!
VISIT WWW.VIZ.COM FOR THE ENTIRE LIBRARY OF YU-GI-OH! MANGA
Available at your local bookstore or comic store
SHONEN JUMP MANGA
www.shonenjump.com
YU-GI-OH! 5D's © 2009 by Masahiro Hikokubo, Masashi Sato/SHUEISHA Inc.
© K. Takahashi
© NAS • TV TOKYO
YU-GI-OH! GX © 2005 by Kazuki Takahashi, Naoyuki Kageyama/SHUEISHA Inc.
© K. Takahashi
© NAS/TV TOKYO
YU-GI-OH! R © 2004 by Kazuki Takahashi, Akira Ito/SHUEISHA Inc.
RATED T FOR TEEN
ratings.viz.com
viz media
www.viz.com

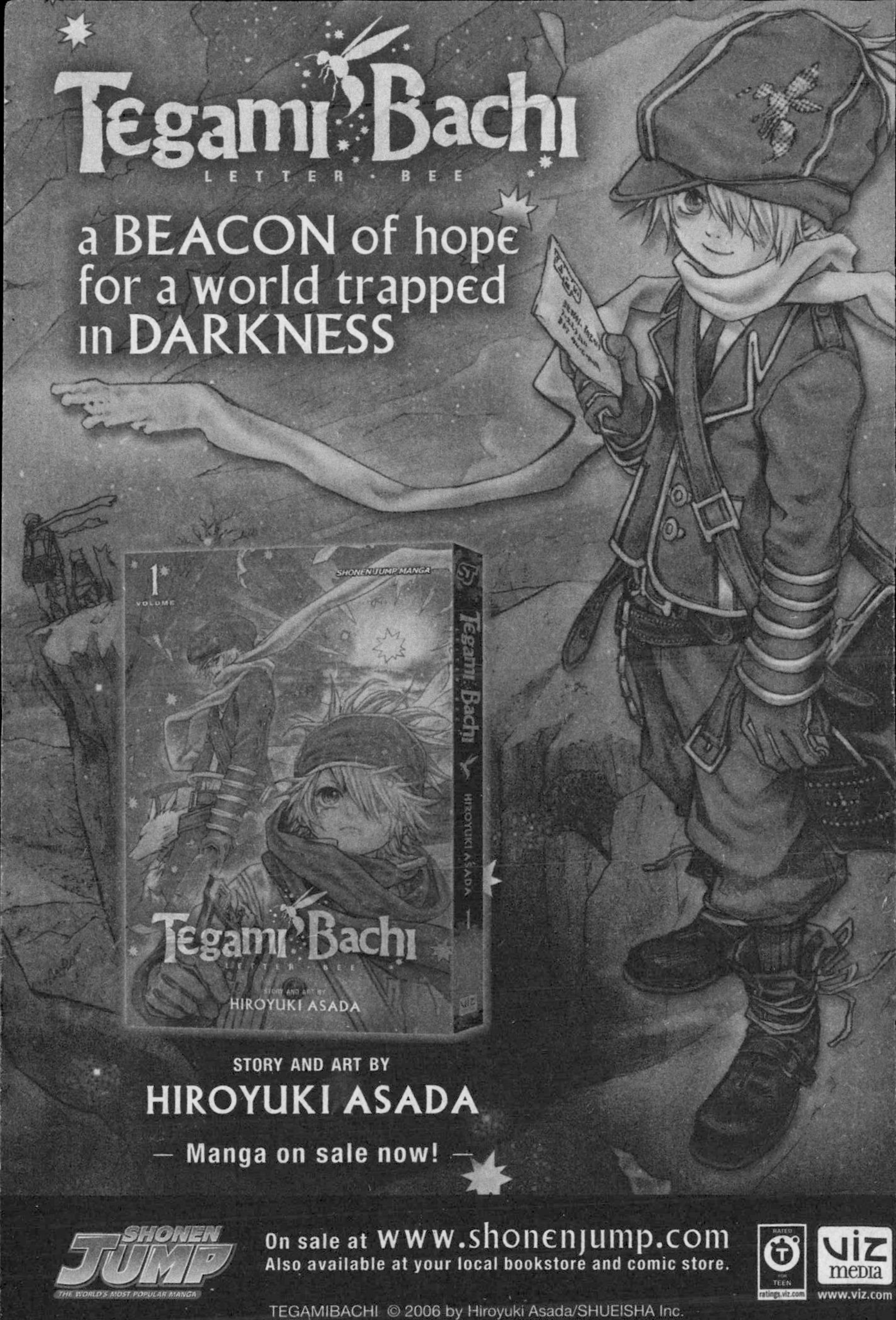

Tegami Bachi
LETTER · BEE
a BEACON of hope for a world trapped in DARKNESS
STORY AND ART BY
HIROYUKI ASADA
— Manga on sale now! —
SHONEN JUMP
THE WORLD'S MOST POPULAR MANGA
On sale at www.shonenjump.com
Also available at your local bookstore and comic store.
RATED T FOR TEEN
ratings.viz.com
VIZ media
www.viz.com
TEGAMIBACHI © 2006 by Hiroyuki Asada/SHUEISHA Inc.

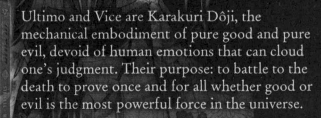

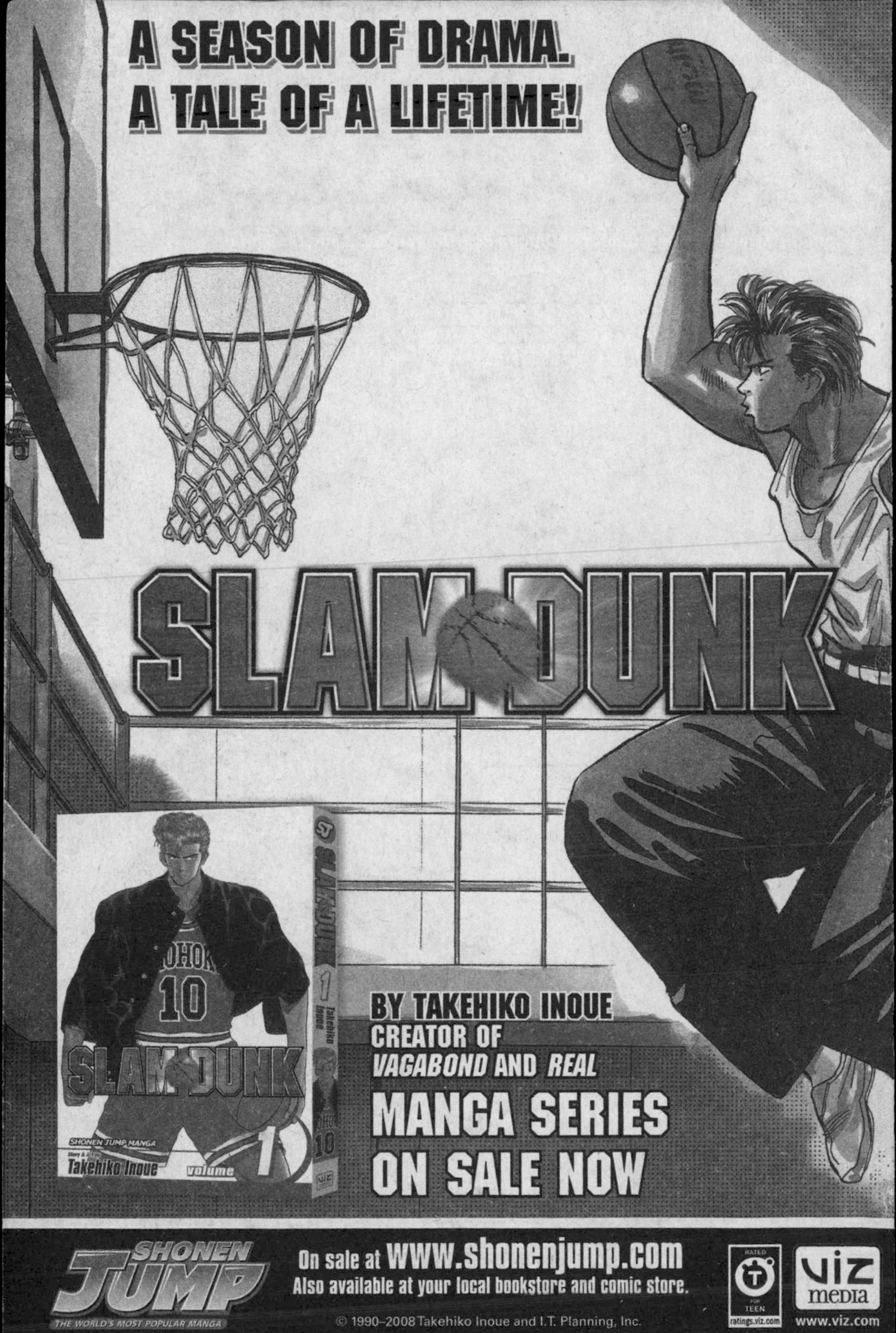
A SEASON OF DRAMA.
A TALE OF A LIFETIME!
SLAM DUNK
SHOHOKU
10
SLAM DUNK
SHONEN JUMP MANGA
Takehiko Inoue
volume 1
SLAM DUNK 1 Takehiko Inoue
BY TAKEHIKO INOUE
CREATOR OF
VAGABOND AND REAL
MANGA SERIES
ON SALE NOW
SHONEN JUMP
THE WORLD'S MOST POPULAR MANGA
On sale at www.shonenjump.com
Also available at your local bookstore and comic store.
RATED T FOR TEEN
ratings.viz.com
VIZ media
www.viz.com
© 1990–2008 Takehiko Inoue and I.T. Planning, Inc.

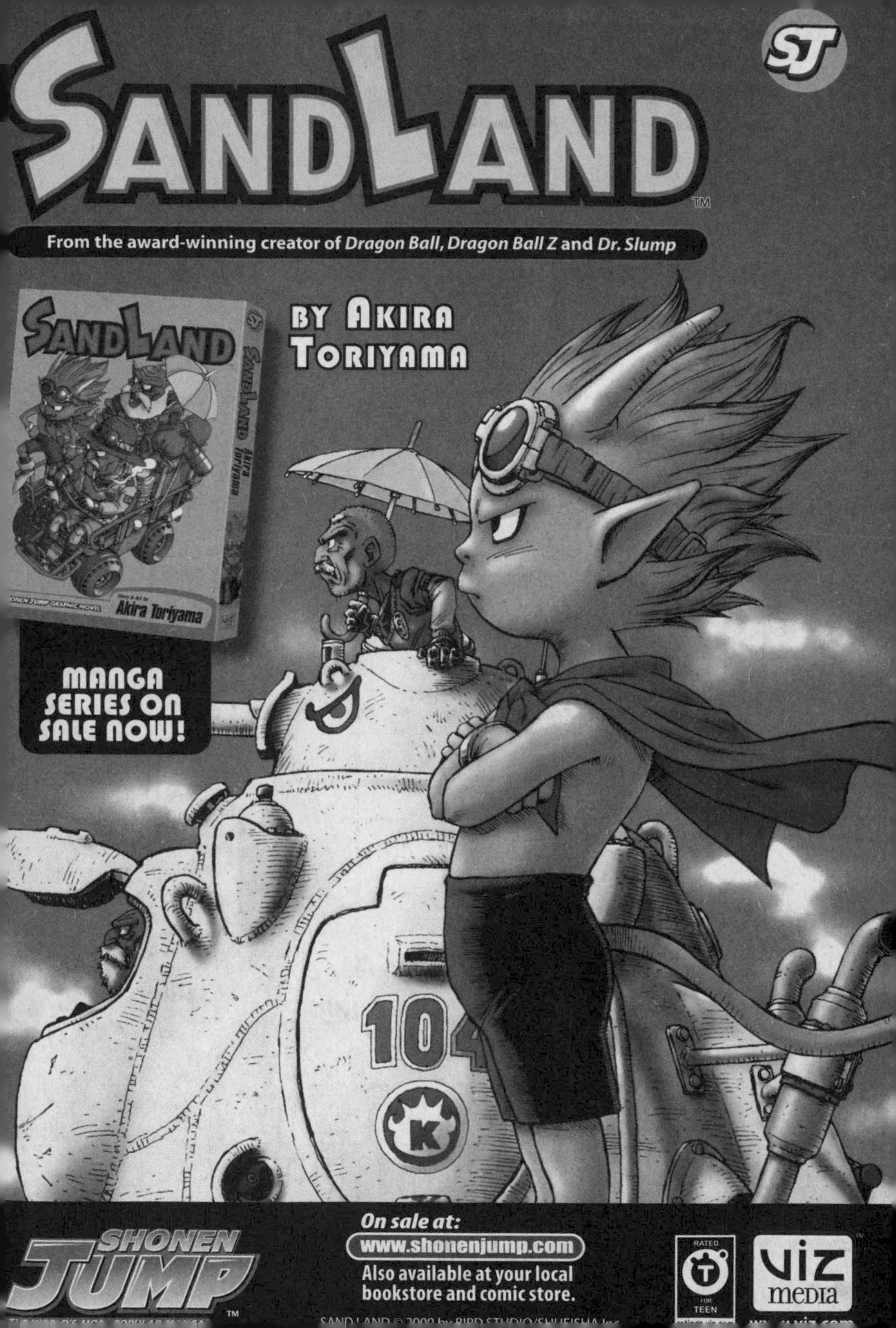

SJ
SANDLAND™
From the award-winning creator of Dragon Ball, Dragon Ball Z and Dr. Slump
BY AKIRA TORIYAMA
SANDLAND
Akira Toriyama
SHONEN JUMP GRAPHIC NOVEL
Story & Art by Akira Toriyama
MANGA SERIES ON SALE NOW!
104
K
SHONEN JUMP™
On sale at:
www.shonenjump.com
Also available at your local bookstore and comic store.
RATED T FOR TEEN
VIZ media

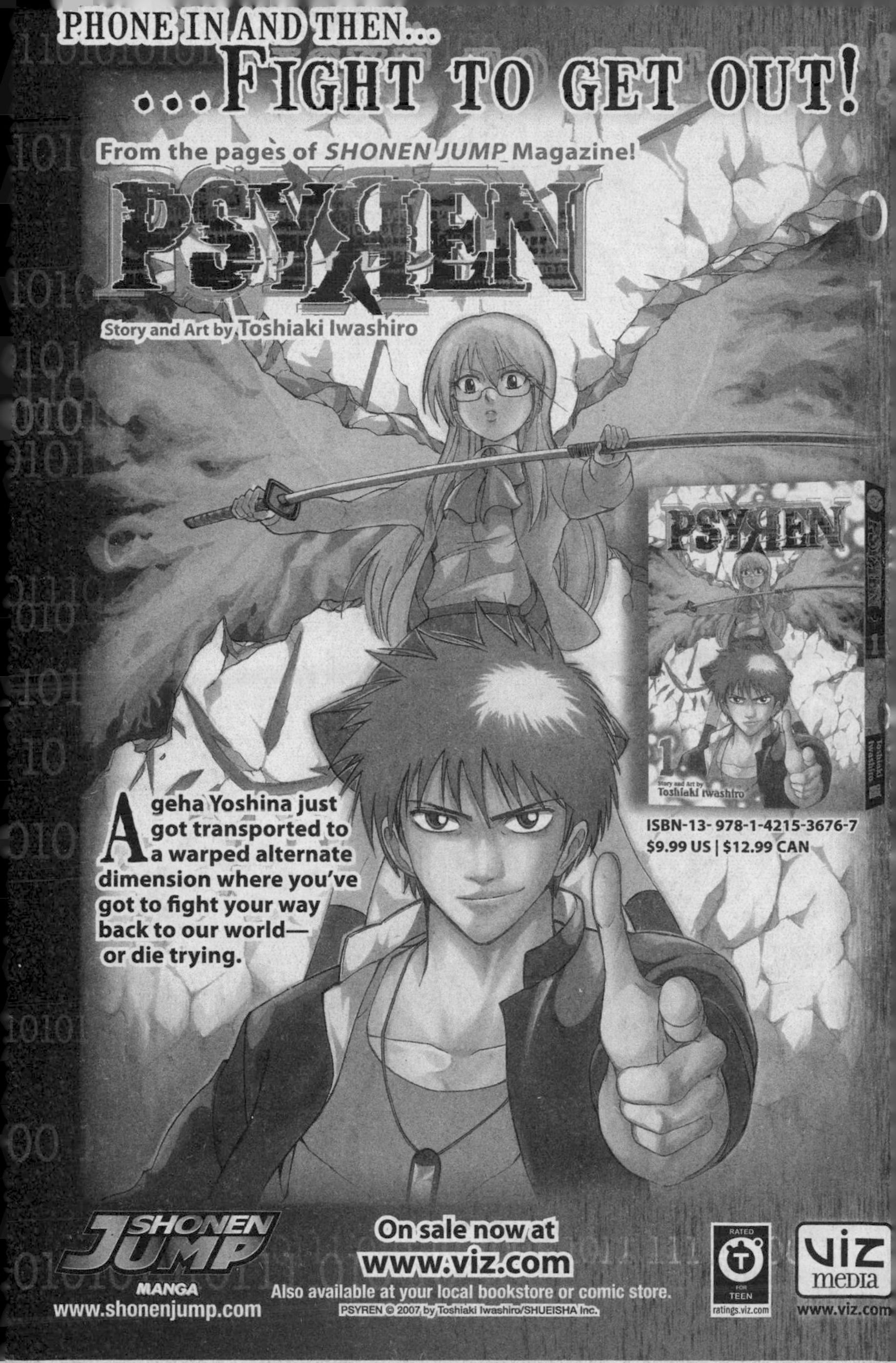
PHONE IN AND THEN...
...FIGHT TO GET OUT!
From the pages of SHONEN JUMP Magazine!
PSYREN
Story and Art by Toshiaki Iwashiro
Ageha Yoshina just got transported to a warped alternate dimension where you've got to fight your way back to our world—or die trying.
PSYREN
1
Story and Art by Toshiaki Iwashiro
ISBN-13- 978-1-4215-3676-7
$9.99 US | $12.99 CAN
SHONEN JUMP MANGA
www.shonenjump.com
On sale now at
www.viz.com
Also available at your local bookstore or comic store.
PSYREN © 2007 by Toshiaki Iwashiro/SHUEISHA Inc.
RATED T FOR TEEN
ratings.viz.com
VIZ media
www.viz.com

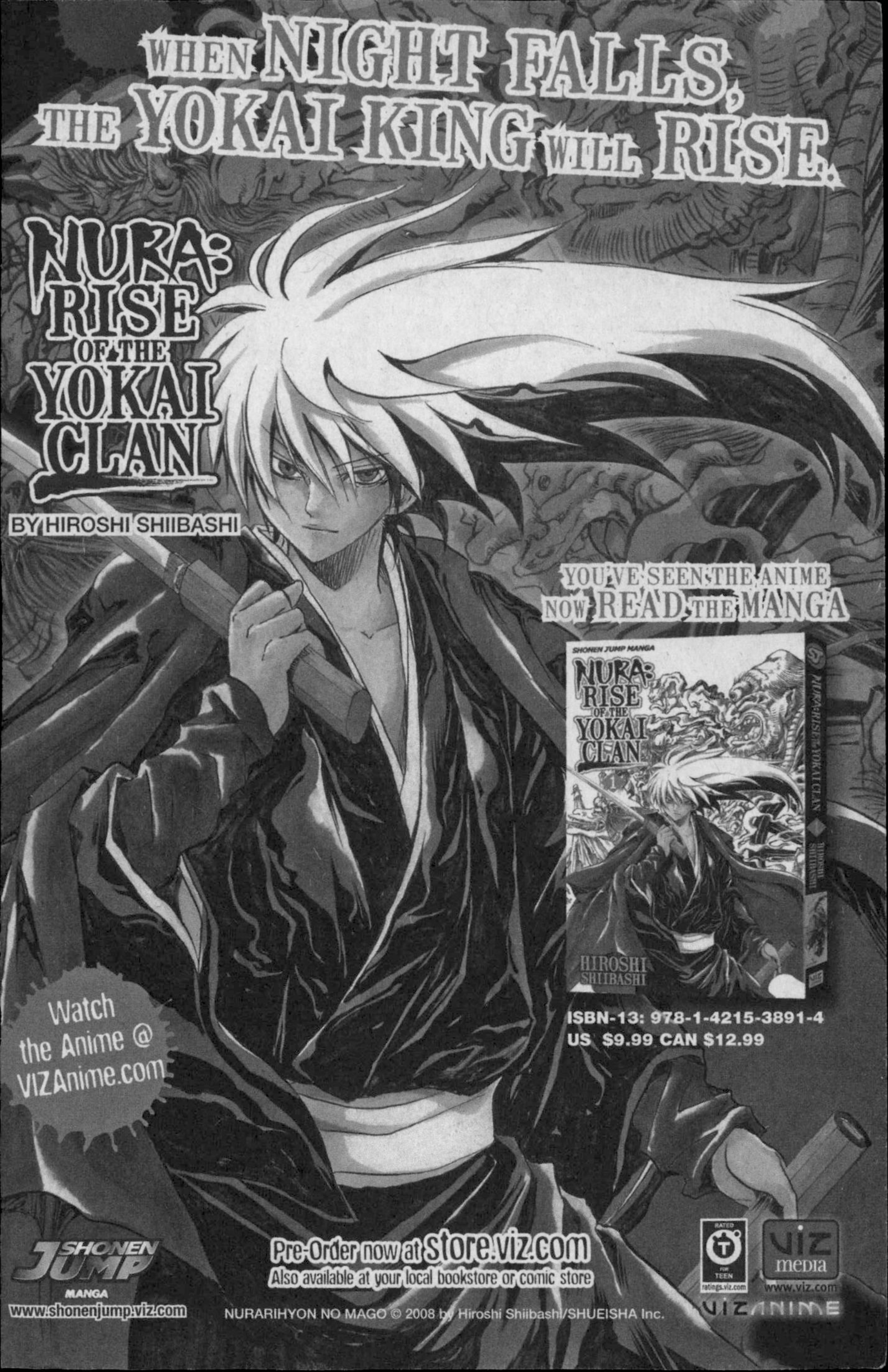
WHEN NIGHT FALLS, THE YOKAI KING WILL RISE.
NURA: RISE OF THE YOKAI CLAN
BY HIROSHI SHIIBASHI
YOU'VE SEEN THE ANIME NOW READ THE MANGA
SHONEN JUMP MANGA
NURA: RISE OF THE YOKAI CLAN
HIROSHI SHIIBASHI
ISBN-13: 978-1-4215-3891-4
US $9.99 CAN $12.99
Watch the Anime @ VIZAnime.com
SHONEN JUMP MANGA
www.shonenjump.viz.com
Pre-Order now at store.viz.com
Also available at your local bookstore or comic store
RATED T FOR TEEN
ratings.viz.com
viz media
www.viz.com
VIZANIME
NURARIHYON NO MAGO © 2008 by Hiroshi Shiibashi/SHUEISHA Inc.

BAKUMAN。

STORY BY TSUGUMI OHBA
ART BY TAKESHI OBATA

From the creators of *Death Note*

The mystery behind manga making REVEALED!

Average student Moritaka Mashiro enjoys drawing for fun. When his classmate and aspiring writer Akito Takagi discovers his talent, he begs to team up. But what exactly does it take to make it in the manga-publishing world?

Bakuman。, Vol. 1
ISBN: 978-1-4215-3513-5
$9.99 US / $12.99 CAN *

Manga on sale at store.viz.com
Also available at your local bookstore or comic store

COWA!

WHO'S GOT THE CURE FOR THE MONSTER FLU?

From AKIRA TORIYAMA, creator of *Dragon Ball*, *Dr. Slump*, and *Sand Land*

STORY & ART BY AKIRA TORIYAMA

MANGA SERIES ON SALE NOW

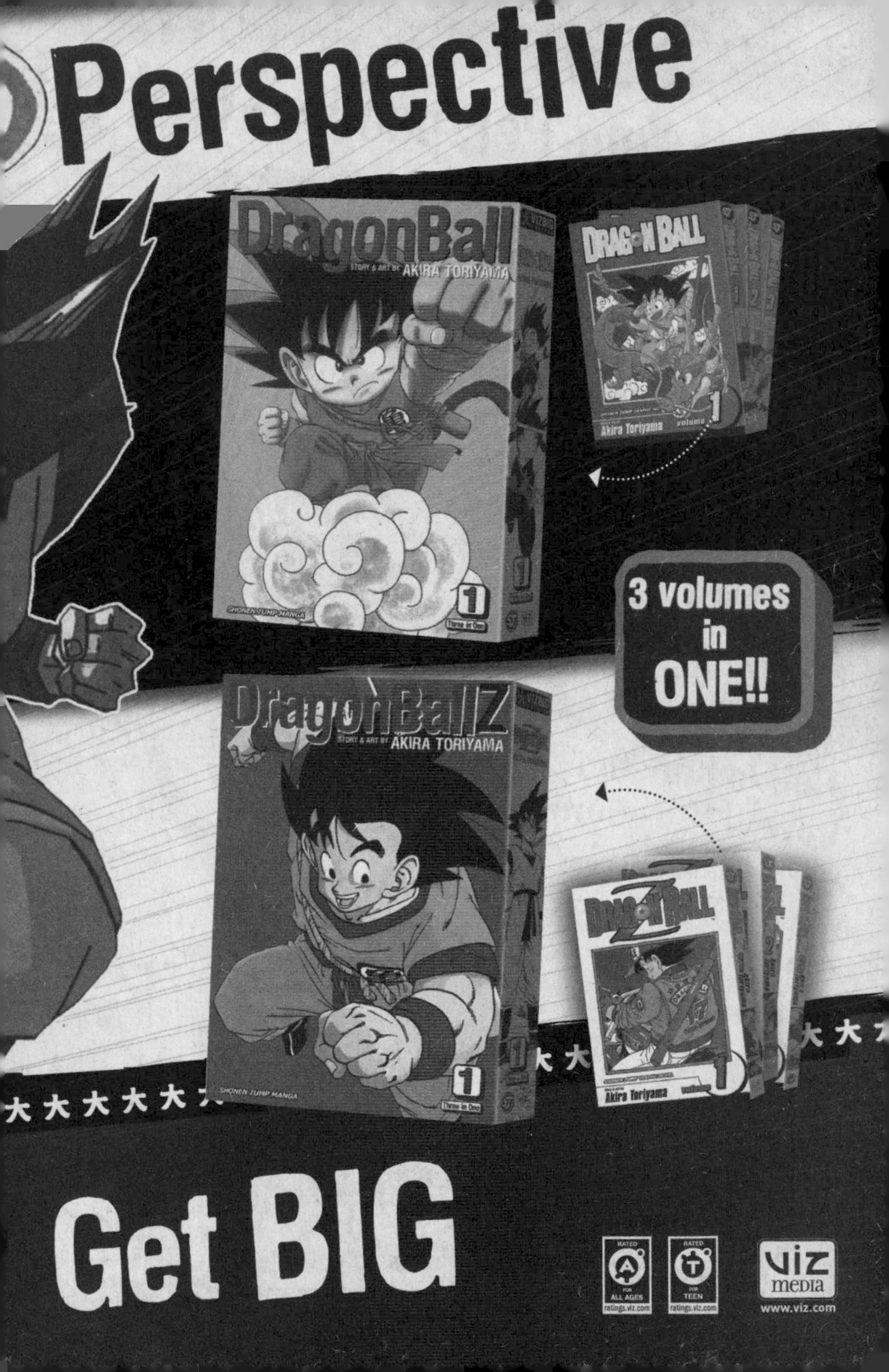
Perspective
DragonBall
STORY & ART BY AKIRA TORIYAMA
DragonBall Z
STORY & ART BY AKIRA TORIYAMA
3 volumes in ONE!!
Get BIG
RATED A FOR ALL AGES ratings.viz.com
RATED T FOR TEEN ratings.viz.com
VIZ media
www.viz.com